MCGRAW-HILL

ONLINE RESOURCES

IMPORTANT:

HERE IS YOUR REGISTRATION CODE TO ACCESS

YOUR PREMIUM McGRAW-HILL ONLINE RESOURCES.

For key premium online resources you need THIS CODE to gain access. Once the code is entered, you will be able to use the Web resources for the length of your course.

If your course is using **WebCT** or **Blackboard**, you'll be able to use this code to access the McGraw-Hill content within your instructor's online course.

Access is provided if you have purchased a new book. If the registration code is missing from this book, the registration screen on our Website, and within your WebCT or Blackboard course, will tell you how to obtain your new code.

Registering for McGraw-Hill Online Resources

TO gain access to your McGraw-Hill web resources simply follow the steps below:

1. USE YOUR WEB BROWSER TO GO TO: **www.mhhe.com/santedu3e**

2. CLICK ON **FIRST TIME USER**.

3. ENTER THE REGISTRATION CODE* PRINTED ON THE TEAR-OFF BOOKMARK ON THE RIGHT.

4. AFTER YOU HAVE ENTERED YOUR REGISTRATION CODE, CLICK **REGISTER**.

5. FOLLOW THE INSTRUCTIONS TO SET-UP YOUR PERSONAL UserID AND PASSWORD.

6. WRITE YOUR UserID AND PASSWORD DOWN FOR FUTURE REFERENCE. KEEP IT IN A SAFE PLACE.

TO GAIN ACCESS to the McGraw-Hill content in your instructor's **WebCT** or **Blackboard** course simply log in to the course with the UserID and Password provided by your instructor. Enter the registration code exactly as it appears in the box to the right when prompted by the system. You will only need to use the code the first time you click on McGraw-Hill content.

Thank you, and welcome to your McGraw-Hill Online Resources!

0-07-298150-4 T/A SANTROCK: EDUCATIONAL PSYCHOLOGY, 2/E

REGISTRATION CODE

XA7P-NKAO-3ZVN-IM6Z-6CE2

Educational Psychology

Classroom Update: Preparing for PRAXIS™ and Practice

John W. Santrock
University of Texas at Dallas

Boston   Burr Ridge, IL   Dubuque, IA   Madison, WI   New York   San Francisco   St. Louis
Bangkok   Bogotá   Caracas   Kuala Lumpur   Lisbon   London   Madrid   Mexico City
Milan   Montreal   New Delhi   Santiago   Seoul   Singapore   Sydney   Taipei   Toronto

McGraw-Hill Higher Education

A Division of The McGraw-Hill Companies

EDUCATIONAL PSYCHOLOGY: CLASSROOM UPDATE: PREPARING FOR
PRAXIS™ AND PRACTICE

ISBN 0-07-298142-3

Vice president and editor-in-chief: *Emily Barrosse*
Executive and sponsoring editor: *David S. Patterson*
Senior developmental editor: *Cara Harvey Labell*
Executive marketing manager: *Pamela S. Cooper*
Media producer: *Shannon Gattens*
Project manager: *Rick Hecker*
Senior production supervisor: *Carol A. Bielski*
Senior designer: *Kim Menning*
Media project manager: *Michele Borrelli*
Senior print supplement producer: *Louis Swaim*
Photo research coordinator: *Alexandra Ambrose*
Art editor: *Katherine McNab*
Freelance photo researcher: *LouAnn Wilson*
Art director: *Jeanne Schreiber*
Permissions editor: *Marty Granahan*
Cover design: *Caroline McGowan*
Interior design: *Ellen Pettengell Design/Glenda King*
Typeface: *10.5/12 Minion*
Compositor: *Cenveo*
Printer: *Quebecor World Dubuque, IA*

The credits section for this book begins on page C–1 and is considered an extension of the copyright page.

Library of Congress Cataloging-in-Publication Data

Santrock, John W.
    Educational psychology : update : preparing for PRAXIS™ and practice /
John W. Santrock.—[2nd ed. update]
        p. cm.
    Includes bibliographical references and index.
        ISBN 0-07-298142-3 (softcover : alk. paper)
    1. Educational psychology. 2. Learning, Psychology of. 3. Motivation in education. I.
Title.

LB1051.S262 2006
370.15—dc22

2004058797

www.mhhe.com

About the Author

John W. Santrock

John Santrock received his Ph.D. from the College of Education and Human Development at the University of Minnesota. He taught at the University of Charleston and the University of Georgia before joining the faculty at the University of Texas at Dallas. He has worked as a school psychologist and currently teaches educational psychology at both the undergraduate and graduate levels. John's grandmother taught all grades in a one-room school for many years and his father was superintendent of a large school district. John's research has included publications in the *Journal of Educational Psychology* that focus on the contextual aspects of affectively toned cognition and children's self-regulatory behavior as well as teachers' perceptions of children from divorced families. He has been a member of the editorial boards of *Child Development* and *Developmental Psychology*. His publications include these leading McGraw-Hill texts: *Child Development* (10th ed.), *Adolescence* (10th ed.), *Life-Span Development* (9th ed.), and *Psychology* (7th ed.).

John Santrock, teaching in his undergraduate educational psychology class, in which he makes good use of small-group discussion.

To Alan Venable:
Once Again, For Caring So Much About
This Book and Improving
Children's Education

Brief Contents

Contents

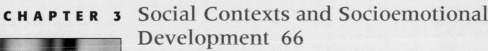

CHAPTER 11 · Learning and Cognition in the Content Areas 338

CHAPTER 12 · Planning, Instruction, and Technology 374

CHAPTER 13 Motivation, Teaching, and Learning 412

CHAPTER 14 Managing the Classroom 446

CHAPTER 15   Standardized Tests and Teaching   486

List of Features

SELF-ASSESSMENTS

TECHNOLOGY AND EDUCATION

CRACK THE CASE

Preface

It is very gratifying that the first edition of *Educational Psychology* was so well received. This is reflected in the book being given McGraw-Hill's award as the best first edition of a textbook published in 2001 and the extremely positive comments of instructors and students.

What do instructors really want in an educational psychology textbook? In preparation for the second edition and this updated second edition of the book, McGraw-Hill obtained extensive feedback from a large number of instructors about what their ideal educational psychology textbook would be like. In response to instructors' comments, much has stayed the same, and much has changed in the updated second edition.

What has stayed the same is *the commitment to present educational psychology as a critical foundation for becoming a competent teacher and to do so in an engaging way.* I want students to feel when they have finished reading and studying this book that the information will help them become outstanding teachers who can open minds to the excitement of learning.

My goal was to write a book that students say this about:

"I love this book!"
"I am using many of the ideas from my educational psychology text in my teaching and they are working great!"
"I teach in the inner city and my educational psychology text is a great resource for me. The focus on diversity and technology have been extremely useful. I am enriched by the book."

These comments come from Jennifer Holliman-McCarthy, Richard Harvell, and Greg Hill, who used the first edition of *Educational Psychology* and are now public school teachers. In addition, here are some very positive comments from instructors about the first edition of the text:

"I have only received very positive evaluations about [John Santrock's] text from students. Indeed, many students have told me that they keep the book after they have finished the course and continue to refer to it when they have become full-fledged teachers."

—LENA ERICKSEN *Western Washington University*

"This book seems more concrete, direct, and useful to preservice teachers than many of its competitors."

—DAVID DALTON *Kent State University*

"I wasn't prepared to like this text. In general, ed psych texts are all too predictable. While people claim to be innovative, in the end they are not. In contrast, John Santrock's text is a big WOW! His book is different. It is written for the prospective teacher and not the future educational psychologist."

—RANDY LENNON *University of Northern Colorado*

"Those who are not using Santrock have not seen it. Please communicate my sincere enjoyment of this quality text to John Santrock."

—ROBERT G. BROWN *Florida Atlantic University–Boca Raton*

"John Santrock has done an admirable job of writing an engaging text. His experience and reputation for writing quality material for students certainly shows in this book."

—CAROLYN EVERTSON *Vanderbilt University*

"I found John Santrock's text to be a very engaging and readable work with some wonderful pedagogical features that give it life. Obviously, this book was carefully conceived and developed."

—EVA ESSA *University of Nevada–Reno*

NEW IN THE CLASSROOM UPDATE: PREPARING FOR PRAXIS™ AND PRACTICE

The Classroom Update of the second edition of *Educational Psychology* provides readers with more resources to prepare them for their practice as teachers and for the PRAXIS II™ *Principles of Learning and Teaching (PLT)* exam. Integrated into the text and its media program are resources to help readers learn and apply theories and key content. As the majority of states now require the PRAXIS II™ PLT exam, *The Educational Psychology Guide to Preparing for the PRAXIS II™ Exam* has been created to allow students to confirm their understanding of PRAXIS-tested topics in *Educational Psychology.*

New Media Resources to Prepare Students for Practice

Expert Advice: Chapters are introduced by a video clip, referenced in the text and located on the Student Toolbox CD-ROM, of an expert in the field discussing his or her area of expertise and giving advice to new teachers.

Teaching Experience: Chapters now conclude with video clips, referenced in the text and located on the Student Toolbox CD-ROM, of in-service teachers talking about the relevance of the chapter's topics to their classrooms.

 Strategies in Practice: To expand the *Teaching Strategies* feature, Strategies in Practice, referenced in the text and located on the Student Toolbox CD-ROM, lists specific strategies offered by in-service teachers.

 **Video Lecture:** Formally called Video Observation Activities, these video clips, referenced in the text and located on the Student Toolbox CD-ROM, expand topics introduced in the textbook.

 **Video Observations:** Referenced in the text and located on the Student Toolbox CD-ROM, these clips feature K–12 classrooms, students, and teachers to show what the topics being discussed in the textbook could look like in action.

 Theory into Practice: Professors who teach the Educational Psychology course have told us that one of their main goals is to teach students the key theories of educational psychology and prepare them to apply them in their future classrooms. The Theory into Practice activity, referenced in the text and located on the Student Toolbox CD-ROM, allows students to do just that. The modules include resources to review the theory and then exercises to practice its application.

 Enter the Debate: There are two sides to many questions in the field of educational psychology. This feature, referenced in the text and located on the Online Learning Center, asks these questions and provides resources for their exploration and debate.

 The text continues to be extended through study (such as quizzes) and application (such as additional Crack the Case studies) resources on the Student Toolbox CD-ROM and the Online Learning Center at **www.mhhe.com/santedu2e**. For a listing of the resources on the Student Toolbox CD-ROM and the Online Learning Center, go to page xxxv.

New PRAXIS Study Resources for the PRAXIS II™ Exam

To help those students who are required to take the PRAXIS II™ *Principles of Learning and Teaching (PLT)* exam, *Educational Psychology* is now available with a study guide to help them practice with the PRAXIS™ topics covered in the text. The study guide includes objective quizzes to confirm understanding of topics and a practice test based on the PRAXIS II™ exam.

The study guide is located on the Student Toolbox CD-ROM in an interactive format and as a print guide (0-07-298151-2), which can be ordered as a free package item by instructors or purchased separately by students.

Coverage of Developments in the Educational Psychology Field

The highlights of the Classroom Update are the new media and PRAXIS™ resources for students and instructors. However, *Educational Psychology* has also been updated to reflect changes in the field since the second edition was published.

Updated Research

More than 300 references to 2004 and 2005 research have been added to the Classroom Update, maintaining the text's hallmark currency.

Chapter 1

- New discussion of accountability and No Child Left Behind
- New Through the Eyes of Teachers box: Paul August, "Finding Individuality in Diversity"
- Update of percentage of children in low-income families with computers in their homes

Chapter 2

- Update and expansion of what language is and developmental changes in language
- New coverage of recent research and thinking on changes in the adolescent brain

Chapter 3

- New section on curriculum controversy in early childhood education
- Expanded coverage of authoritative parenting and parenting styles, including the concept of training in Asian American families

Chapter 4

- New discussion of stereotype threat as a factor in cultural bias in intelligence tests

Chapter 5

- New coverage of a recent research review of links between poverty and adversity in children's lives
- New material on gender differences in prosocial behavior
- Updated material on gender and national reading scores

Chapter 6

- New figure 6.2, on the three highest percentages of students with a disability served by a federal program in 2000–2001 as a percentage of total school enrollment

- Updated and revised discussion of the use of stimulant drugs with children who have ADHD

- Updated material on inclusion and recent change in special education

- New coverage of Joseph Renzulli's Schoolwide Enrichment Model for improving outcomes in children who are gifted and children who are not gifted

Chapter 7

- Updated statistics on percentage of total classroom teachers in relation to gender and ethnicity

Chapter 8

- Expanded material on strategies

- New discussion of Patricia Alexander's acclimation stage of expertise

Chapter 9

- New material on the importance of presenting controversial topics and issues to students to encourage critical thinking

- Expanded coverage of creativity, including recent research on creative thinking at the individual and group levels (brainstorming), domain aspects of creativity, and school/classroom design

Chapter 10

- New Through the Eyes of Teachers box on the concept of transfer of learning: Chris Laster, "Bringing Science Alive"

- New Through the Eyes of Teachers box: Fraser Randolph, "Creating Learning Opportunities That Are Social but Structured"

- Coverage of recent research of the PALS peer tutoring program

Chapter 11

- Coverage of recent research that involved videotapes of math instruction in different countries and the implications of this study for U.S. math teachers

Chapter 12

- New section: "The Future of Technology in Education"

- New Through the Eyes of Students box that involves students' comments about technology in their lives and schools and their predictions of what technology in learning and education will be like in the future

Chapter 13

- New figure 13.2, on Maslow's characteristics of self-actualized individuals

Chapter 14

- Expanded and updated coverage of the increasing problem of bullying in schools; includes description of two effective bully prevention programs and where to obtain information about them

- New discussion of two programs that have been effective in improving students' positive behaviors toward others and conflict management skills: Lesson One and Skills for Life

Chapter 15

- New section on No Child Left Behind and the educational issues involved

- Updated data from the National Assessment of Educational Progress on U.S. students' reading and math scores

Chapter 16

- New section on web-based assessment, including information about three increasingly used web-based assessments that teachers can use

Please continue reading to learn about the revisions that were made to the second edition.

NEW IN THE SECOND EDITION

Educational psychology instructors were virtually unanimous in telling me to expand the material on learning and cognition. Instructors said that they also want a book that is very up-to-date. Further, they very much liked the emphasis on pedagogy in the first edition but challenged me to make it even better.

"This book is fabulous."
—PATRICIA WILLEMS *Florida Atlantic University–Davie*

Two New Chapters on Learning and Cognition The first edition had 14 chapters; the second edition has 16. The 2 new chapters are on learning and cognition. In the first edition, the chapter on information-processing approaches was very long and included many topics. Instructors said that they wanted a separate chapter on basic cognitive processes, such as memory, and complex cognitive processes, such as problem solving and thinking. The second edition of the book splits the information-processing chapter into 2 chapters and expands the discussion of cognitive processes: chapter 8 (The Information-Processing Approach) and chapter 9 (Complex Cognitive Processes).

Instructors also strongly urged me to expand the coverage of learning and cognition in the content areas and create a stand-alone chapter on this topic. Chapter 11 in the second edition is now devoted exclusively to this topic. Developing this separate chapter also allowed me to expand the coverage of social constructivist approaches and have a separate chapter (10) on this topic.

> *"I think the new organization provides a logical progression of topics with increasing emphasis given to cognition. I also like that cognition in content areas is a separate chapter."*
>
> —KIM LOOMIS *Kennesaw State University*

Contemporary Research Instructors told me that they wanted a book that is very up-to-date and includes the latest contemporary research. The following is what I did to make the book very contemporary.

More Than 600 Twenty-First-Century References The second edition of *Educational Psychology* has more than 600 citations from the twenty-first century, with more than 300 of these from 2001 through 2003.

> *"The wealth of up-to-date theory and research for each topic is wonderful!"*
>
> —REAGAN CURTIS *Northwestern State University*

> *"This text is well researched and up-to-date in its use of research and theory."*
>
> —PATRICIA WILLEMS *Florida Atlantic University–Davie*

Expert Research Consultants No single author can possibly be an expert in all areas of educational psychology. This is especially true today with the substantial expansion of research in the field. In the first edition, a number of leading experts in educational psychology research served as consultants. This tradition was continued in the second edition with many new experts contributing valuable feedback about cutting-edge research and ideas in their area of expertise. The expert consultants for this book are literally a Who's Who in the field of educational psychology. They each gave me very detailed feedback about one to three chapters that focus on their areas of expertise or about a main theme in the book (such as diversity). The information provided by these expert research consultants for *Educational Psychology,* second edition, significantly improved the book's content:

James McMillan *Virginia Commonwealth University*

Chapters 1 (Educational Psychology: A Tool for Effective Teaching), 15 (Standardized Tests and Teaching), and 16 (Classroom Assessment)

Eva Essa *University of Nevada–Reno*

Early childhood education coverage throughout the book

Kenji Hakuta *Stanford University*

Chapters 2 (Cognitive and Language Development), 5 (Sociocultural Diversity), and 11 (Learning and Cognition in the Content Areas)

Nathan Brody *Wesleyan University*

Chapter 4 (Individual Variations)

Valerie Pang *San Diego State University*

Chapter 5 (Sociocultural Diversity) and diversity coverage throughout the book

Carlos Diaz *Florida Atlantic University*

Chapter 5 (Sociocultural Diversity) and diversity coverage throughout the book

Daniel Hallahan *University of Virginia*

Chapter 6 (Learners Who Are Exceptional)

Dale Schunk *University of North Carolina–Greensboro*

Chapters 7 (Behavioral and Social Cognitive Approaches) and 13 (Motivation, Teaching, and Learning)

Albert Bandura *Stanford University*

Chapters 7 (Behavioral and Social Cognitive Approaches) and 13 (Motivation, Teaching, and Learning)

Michael Pressley *University of Notre Dame*

Chapters 8 (The Information-Processing Approach) and 9 (Complex Cognitive Processes)

Robert Siegler *Carnegie Mellon University*

Chapters 8 (The Information-Processing Approach) and 9 (Complex Cognitive Processes)

Gary Bitter *Arizona State University*

Chapter 12 (Planning, Instruction, and Technology) and technology coverage throughout the book

Carolyn Evertson *Vanderbilt University*

Chapter 14 (Managing the Classroom)

The biographies and photographs of the expert research consultants appear later in the Preface.

"The text is of very high quality. It covers a lot of important material at an interesting and accessible level."

—ROBERT SIEGLER *Carnegie Mellon University*

Research Content With the input from the expert research consultants, as well as an extensive number of instructors who teach educational psychology and my own examination of the research literature, I carefully modified and updated the content of each chapter where appropriate. The result is a number of improvements in content, which will be detailed shortly on a chapter-by-chapter basis.

"I am very impressed with this text. I certainly would recommend it for adoption. It is thorough but not overwhelming. It is clearly written in a style that undergraduates will appreciate. Educational psychology is a course that many students have difficulty with and do not appreciate why they are enrolled in it. They often complain that there is too much material and that the content is not well linked to practice. The typical student—an undergraduate teacher education major—is most concerned about how the content can be applied to teaching. It is evident that John Santrock knows his audience well, and he is to be congratulated for crafting a text that should deflect these criticisms."

—DALE SCHUNK *University of North Carolina–Greensboro*

Improved Text Pedagogy Now more than ever, students struggle to find the main ideas in their courses. To help them achieve the best possible outcome in educational psychology, I have created a new comprehensive Learning Goals system, which is integrated throughout each chapter. New Teaching Strategies interludes, Self-Assessments, and Diversity and Education interludes have been added and others fine-tuned. A new case study feature called Crack the Case has been written for each chapter, a new section called Portfolio Activities has been created, and new chapter-ending Internet activities have been developed.

"What distinguishes this text is the clarity of writing, the multiple pedagogical aspects found in each chapter, and the conscious effort to integrate theory and practice. This text is the quintessential effort to merge ideas with meaningful activities."

—ROBERT RICE *Western Oregon University*

"I loved the book (2nd edition)! The writing is clear and concise and the examples used are related to education."

—DOT MILES *Saint Louis University*

"What distinguishes this text is the very practical approach—all the examples and the Teaching Strategies interludes. As I read each chapter, I was aware that the focus was on learning about educational psychology to be able to be a good teacher. Theories were always discussed in terms of their practical applications in the classroom."

—BARBARA POWELL *Eastern Illinois University*

The Learning Goals System Built around the main text headings and each chapter's learning goals, the new learning system featured in this second edition keeps the key ideas in front of the reader from the beginning to the end of the chapter. Each chapter has no more than six main headings and corresponding Learning Goals (most have three or four), which are presented side-by-side on the chapter-opening spread. At the end of each main section of the chapter, the learning goal is repeated in a new feature called Review and Reflect, which prompts students to review the key topics in the section and poses bulleted questions to encourage them to think critically about what they have read. At the end of the chapter, under the heading Reach Your Learning Goals, the learning goals guide students through the bulleted chapter review, which essentially answers the bulleted questions in each of the chapter's review sections.

"The chapter Learning Goals/Reach Your Learning Goals is a terrific organizational tool for students."

—LINDA VERONIE *Slippery Rock University*

"Having a small number of learning goals for each chapter and then having each goal broken down in the Review and Reflect section made everything in the chapter tie together."

—BARBARA POWELL *Eastern Illinois University*

Teaching Strategies Interludes A critical aspect of an educational psychology text is the extent to which it provides excellent and practical strategies that students can use when they become teachers. Teaching Strategies appear a number of times in each chapter. The format of this feature has been changed to better integrate it with the text material. This feature has been noted to be one of the text's key strengths.

"The Teaching Strategies are remarkable and I think students will love them. Many instructors have a hard time translating theory and/or research into practice. John Santrock has done an excellent job and should be a model to other authors."

—RANDY LENNON *University of Northern Colorado*

"John Santrock does an extraordinary job of making the material meaningful to students through numerous, and well-developed, teaching strategies. He goes beyond the obvious by providing teaching strategies that generalize and appropriately transfer."

—CAROLINE GOULD *Eastern Michigan University*

Diversity and Education Diversity continues to be an important theme in the second edition. An entire chapter (5) is devoted to sociocultural diversity and each chapter has a Diversity and Education interlude, which is integrated with the text material, following immediately after material relevant to the diversity topic is presented. A number of the Diversity and Education interludes are new in this edition.

"You never feel like the diversity material is a politically correct 'add on' but rather the reflection of a personal philosophy and vision."

—CONNIE MOSS *Duquesne University*

"I think the coverage of diversity and multicultural issues in this text compared to others is outstanding."

—JULIA MATUGA *Bowling Green State University*

"I found issues of culture, ethnicity, and gender to be appropriately and naturally integrated into other chapters and not simply segregated in chapter 5 on sociocultural diversity."

—CARLOS DIAZ *Florida Atlantic University–Boca Raton*

Self-Assessment The Self-Assessment feature in the first edition was positively received by instructors and students. The Self-Assessments encourage students to examine their characteristics and skills related to the content of a chapter. New Self-Assessments have been added in the second edition, others have been deleted, and yet others have been fine-tuned. In addition, students can now fill these out online on the text's website and e-mail their responses to their instructors.

"The Self-Assessments are a great idea. I was tempted to complete some of them myself. Students will enjoy completing these."

—GABY VAN DER GIESSEN *Fairmont State College*

Technology and Education Each chapter has one Technology and Education box related to the content of the chapter. A number of new Technology and Education boxes were created for the second edition of the book.

"The coverage of technology is better than any text I've seen."

—WALTER HAPKIEWICZ *Michigan State University*

Case Studies A new, full-page case study feature entitled Crack the Case was written for each chapter by Dr. Nancy DeFrates-Densch of Northern Illinois University. These high-interest case studies appear at the end of each chapter and are closely tied to the content in the chapter. Critical thinking questions follow each case study.

"An excellent feature! Each of the case studies is a well-written, 'real-world' example of a realistic education situation."

—LYNNE HAMMANN *University of Akron*

"The Crack the Case feature is a great addition to the text. I would utilize these."

—BARBARA RADIGAN *Community College of Allegheny County*

Portfolio Activities At the end of each chapter, four Portfolio Activities related to the chapter content are presented.

They are organized into three categories for instructors' ease of use: Independent Reflection, Collaborative Work, and Research/Field Experience. In addition, downloadable portfolio templates are available on the text's website so that students can include these activities in their final teaching portfolios. Each Portfolio Activity is also coded to a specific INTASC standard.

"I find these particularly unique! They could be great class activities to really add meaning to course material. In some instances, they could be developed into alternative types of assessment for an instructor wishing to balance out assessment techniques."

—ALYSSA GONZALEZ *Florida Atlantic University–Jupiter*

Taking It to the Net An extensive effort was made to create Internet activities that will provide a meaningful learning experience for students. The Taking It to the Net exercises, authored by Veronica Rowland of University of California at Irvine, appear at the end of each chapter. Answers are coordinated with the book's website.

"I think these activities are great! They allow students to become involved with technology and to use outside resources to help them understand subject matter. I use them in my classes and have received excellent feedback from students on them."

—PATRICIA WILLEMS *Florida Atlantic University–Davie*

Study, Practice, and Succeed At the end of each chapter, the Study, Practice, and Succeed feature reminds students of the rich learning tools that can be found on the accompanying Student Toolbox CD-ROM (shrinkwrapped with every new book) and the book's Online Learning Center at **www.mhhe.com/santedu2e**. These tools will allow students to master each chapter's content.

Chapter-by-Chapter Changes Following are the highlights of the changes in each chapter of *Educational Psychology,* second edition.

CHAPTER 1:
Educational Psychology: A Tool for Effective Teaching

- More streamlined presentation in the first part of the chapter, with deletion of the section on the complex, fast-paced nature of teaching and the section on good and bad teachers at the request of instructors. Some of this material was moved later in the chapter under effective teaching.
- New section on diversity and early educational psychology

- New section on further historical developments that focuses on Skinner's behaviorism in the mid-twentieth century and the cognitive revolution that had taken hold by the 1980s
- New introduction to diversity section, highlighting characteristics of the new immigrant population of children in the United States (Suarez-Orozco, 2002)
- New Diversity and Education interlude: "The Cultural School" (Pang, 2001)
- Updated National Educational Technology Standards (2001)
- Deleted section on professional growth at the request of instructors
- Reorganization of research methods section into new subsections: descriptive, correlational, and experimental
- New section on ethnographic studies
- Moved discussion of participant methods to descriptive methods
- New examples of naturalistic observation research, including new figure (1.3) (Crowley & others, 2001; Tennenbaum & others, 2002)
- New figure (1.5) comparing correlational and experimental research methods

> *"The changes made to the research section are wonderful. This introduction to research gives them the overall big picture on research methods that will help them in interpreting educational research. . . . As far as introductory chapters go, this is one of the better ones."*
> —**Alyssa Gonzalez** *Florida Atlantic University–Jupiter*

CHAPTER 2:
Cognitive and Language Development

- All of the material on reading was deleted from this chapter and moved to new chapter 11, Learning and Cognition in the Content Areas, at the request of reviewers
- Also at the request of reviewers, the discussion of physical development was deleted from the chapter to allow for a more focused examination of cognitive and language development
- The introductory material on the nature of development was shortened and the coverage of the nature and nurture issue moved to the discussion of intelligence in chapter 4, Individual Variations
- New chapter-opening teaching story on Donene Polson that is linked to Vygotsky's cognitive sociocultural approach
- Important new, very contemporary section on the brain, focusing on cells and regions, lateralization, and the brain and children's education

- Expanded teaching strategies section in the coverage of Vygotsky
- New Technology and Education box, "Technology and Children's Vocabulary Development," focusing on computers, audiobooks, and educational television
- New Self-Assessment, "Applying Piaget and Vygotsky Theories in My Classroom"
- New discussion of concepts of organization and equilibration in the Piaget section

> *"Theory is translated into practice well. I have used a number of books for my course and John Santrock's seems to have better examples, and they are presented in a useable fashion."*
> —**Douglas Beed** *University of Montana–Missoula*

CHAPTER 3:
Social Contexts and Socioemotional Development

- New chapter-opening teaching story on Mr. Z and how he ties service learning to a unit on ecosystems in his fourth-grade class
- New Diversity and Education interlude: "Are America's Schools Leaving Latinas Behind?"
- Updated coverage of Joyce Epstein's (2001; Epstein & Sanders, 2002; Epstein & others, 2002) views on school-family linkages, including new examples of effective programs
- Coverage of a recent national survey (2000) on cheating in schools
- Included recent research (2001) on peer relations and problems
- New discussion of strategies for helping children from divorced families
- New section on high schools, including their problems and a number of recommendations for improving U.S. high schools (2001)
- Deleted section on emotional intelligence and moved to chapter 4, Individual Variations, at the request of reviewers
- Deleted section on adolescent problems to give the chapter a more manageable size and a smaller number of topics
- New discussion of high school dropouts, including trends from the 1940s through 2000 and new figure (3.5) (National Center for Education Statistics, 2001)
- New discussion of very recent data on developmental changes in self-esteem, especially for girls, and new figure (3.6) (Robins & others, 2002)
- New Self-Assessment: "Where Are You Now? Exploring Your Identity"
- Added examples of each type of identity status at the request of reviewers

"The amazing journey from social context to self to moral development and then the return to social context is a work of art. When I read the preview sections, I thought 'How can he ever link these very different areas?' But he did and very cogently."

—JEAN NEWMAN CLARK *University of South Alabama*

"The strongest asset of this chapter is the practical wisdom it conveys in light of research findings. The chapter helps to equip college students with ideas that will really matter to them in terms of their own success as future teachers."

—SUSAN ROGERS *Columbus State Community College*

CHAPTER 4:
Individual Variations

- New chapter-opening teaching story on Shiffy Landa, who uses the multiple-intelligences approach in her first-grade classroom
- New section added—"Do People Have a General Intelligence?—based on expert Nathan Brody's recommendation
- New Technology and Education box: "Technology and Multiple Intelligences"
- New coverage of links between intelligence and schooling
- Deleted section on creativity and moved to new chapter 9, Complex Cognitive Processes, at the request of reviewers
- Added Gardner's view of misuses of his multiple-intelligences concept
- Deleted section on systems of learning and thinking styles at the request of reviewers
- Added recent research on genes and intelligence
- Modified definition of intelligence
- Discussion of emotional intelligence now covered in this chapter in the multiple-intelligences section
- Added research on environmental influences in link between ethnicity and intelligence
- New section on evaluating learning and thinking styles

"John Santrock's text provides particularly strong coverage on the topics covered in chapter 4, Individual Variations. The topic of intelligence receives especially thorough coverage."

—JOHN T. BINFET *California State University–San Bernardino*

- New section on culturally relevant teaching
- New section on issues-centered education
- New discussion of strengths and courage of children and their families living in impoverished conditions
- Expanded teaching strategies for working with children from low-income backgrounds
- Added Joseph LeDoux's (2002) ideas on the emotional brain in females and males
- Extensively revised and updated discussion of gender bias and classrooms with new coverage of the situations in which gender bias occurs against males and the situations in which it occurs against females
- New section on gender differences in school attainment
- Revised, expanded, updated description of gender similarities and differences in math, science, reading, and writing
- Inclusion of recent study showing link between poverty and lower math and reading achievement scores in 12- to 14-year-olds (Eamon, 2002)
- New figure (5.1) comparing children's vocabulary development in welfare and professional homes and the language input children experience in these contexts
- New figure (5.2) on grammar proficiency and age at arrival in the United States
- New discussion of recent research on the gender difference in relational aggression (Ostrov, Keating, & Ostrov, 2004; Underwood, 2003, 2004)
- Added recent data from the National Assessment of Educational Progress (2001) on gender and reading achievement and gender and science achievement, including two new figures (5.3 and 5.4) illustrating these gender differences

"Overall evaluation: A++. It is exactly what I would plan for if writing an educational psychology text. John Santrock makes a potentially daunting task of comprehensively covering sociocultural issues in a sensitive manner seem effortless. . . . The real gems are the Teaching Strategies, and the section on gender bias has more expanded coverage than most ed psych texts."

—ALYSSA GONZALEZ *Florida Atlantic University–Jupiter*

"This chapter has some great ideas on how to provide classroom activities as they pertain to culturally relevant teaching."

—ROBERT RICE *Western Oregon University*

CHAPTER 5:
Sociocultural Diversity

- Addition of Kenji Hakuta's (2000) recent research on how long it takes language minority students to learn English

CHAPTER 6:
Learners Who Are Exceptional

- Reorganization of chapter with "Children Who Are Gifted" now a main heading and the last section in the chapter

- New Diversity and Education interlude on the disproportionate representation of minority students in special education
- New Through the Eyes of Teachers insert: "Discovery Centers"
- Updating of special education statistics for the twenty-first century
- New discussion of discrepancy issue in identification of learning disabilities
- Added recent major study (MTA) on treating ADHD (Swanson & others, 2001)
- Added comments about the cochlear implant controversy
- Updated coverage of issues involved in defining learning disabilities
- Added comments about structure and teacher-direction in working with children with ADHD
- New coverage of positive behavioral support and functional behavioral assessment, recommended by expert consultant Daniel Hallahan
- Description of recent study showing how inclusion benefits students with a learning disability (Rea, McLaughlin, & Walther-Thomas, 2002)

> *"I think this chapter is very well done. It is thorough but concise. It provides just the right amount of depth on this topic for an ed psych text."*
> —**DANIEL HALLAHAN** *University of Virginia*

> *"This is a great chapter that is very well organized. . . . It did not surprise me when I learned that John Santrock was a former school psychologist. His expertise in this area was evident."*
> —**KATHY BROWN** *University of Central Oklahoma*

CHAPTER 7:
Behavioral and Social Cognitive Approaches

- Revised definition of learning, as recommended by expert consultant Albert Bandura
- Revised, updated coverage of observational learning based on Bandura's recommendations
- Added comments about social cognitive theory evolving out of behavioral theories but strongly emphasizing cognition
- Added criticisms of the behavioral theories based on expert consultant Dale Schunk's recommendations
- Improved figure (7.2) on how classical conditioning works
- New discussion and figure (7.6) on cross-cultural attitudes toward corporal punishment (Curran & others, 2001)
- Description of recent study showing that the use of spanking by parents to discipline children is linked to an increase in problem behavior over time (McLoyd & Smith, 2002)

> *"The major theories and principles are covered well. The explanation of forms of reinforcement and punishment is very well done. . . . I am especially glad to see self-regulation included. . . . This chapter includes many applications and they accurately reflect the principles. The chapter achieves a successful balance between theory and applications."*
> —**DALE SCHUNK** *University of North Carolina–Greensboro*

CHAPTER 8:
The Information-Processing Approach

- Extensively reorganized chapter, with material on thinking, problem solving, and transfer moved to new chapter 9, resulting in a much more focused chapter on the information-processing approach
- Completely new section on expertise, including discussions of expertise and learning, acquiring expertise, and expertise and teaching
- New high-interest introduction to encoding and attention, including new figure (8.3) on the faces of famous individuals to illustrate the importance of attention
- New Technology and Education box: "Experts and Technology"
- New Diversity and Education interlude: "Culture, Gender, and Memory"
- Reorganized and updated coverage of working memory
- New discussion of recent research on the influence of expressive writing on working memory and its application to anxiety about math (Gray, 2001; Klein & Boals, 2001)
- Expanded and improved Self-Assessment: "How Effective Are My Memory and Study Strategies?"
- New discussion of developmental changes in the role of elaboration in memory, including new figure (8.3) of research data on this topic
- New discussion of developmental changes in the role of imagery in memory, including new figure (8.4) of data from a research study on this topic
- Expanded emphasis on the reconstructive nature of schema theory, including new figure (8.9) on the "War of the Ghosts"

> *"I think that the chapter's coverage of cognitive development in general, and the information-processing approach in particular, is quite successful. . . . The writing style, level of presentation, and interest level are all excellent."*
> —**ROBERT SIEGLER** *Carnegie Mellon University*

> *"The overall organization and coverage is extremely comprehensive. . . . An excellent presentation of complex concepts and their relationships. The Teaching Strategies for Getting Students to Pay Attention is excellent. The section on metacognition is also a strength. References and research are current and selective."*
> —**LYNNE HAMMANN** *University of Akron*

CHAPTER 9:
Complex Cognitive Processes

- Material from former chapter 8 in the first edition—concepts, thinking, and problem solving—now in a new, stand-alone chapter
- New section on creativity now in this chapter (this topic was in chapter 4, Individual Variations, in the first edition)
- New section on decision making with extensive coverage of the biases and flaws that can interfere with good decision making
- New discussion of the role of emotions in problem solving
- Revised and expanded material on inductive and deductive reasoning, including new figure (9.4)
- Revised and improved coverage of algorithms
- New Diversity and Education interlude: "Transfer and Cultural Practices"
- New chapter-opening teaching story on Marilyn Whirry, a twelfth-grade English teacher, who emphasizes depth of thinking
- Revised and separated Teaching Strategies for Improving Children's Thinking and Improving Students' Problem Solving to make them more focused and less cumbersome
- New research on the effectiveness of using the *Jasper* Series in fifth-grade math classrooms (Hickey, Moore, & Pellegrino, 2001)

> "This new chapter beautifully weaves together material on concept formation, thinking, reasoning, decision making, problem solving and transfer by leading the reader to a greater understanding of all the key concepts."
> —CAROLINE GOULD *Eastern Michigan University*

> "This chapter was very good. The section on concepts was one of the best I have read in an educational psychology text. . . . The sections on problem solving and transfer were also very good."
> —MARLA REESE-WEBER *Illinois State University*

CHAPTER 10:
Social Constructivist Approaches

- New chapter focused exclusively on social constructivist approaches (in the first edition, this material was in the same chapter as cognition in the content areas)
- New section added, "A Collaborative School," based on an innovative social constructivist program
- New Self-Assessment: "Evaluating My Social Constructivist Experiences"

- New recent research on schooling as a cultural process that focuses on comparison of students in a traditional school and a collaborative school (Matusov, Bell, & Rogoff, 2001)
- New section on Johnson and Johnson's (2002) emphasis on creating a cooperative community
- New recent research on achievement goals and collaboration with a peer (Gabriele & Montecinos, 2001)
- Added coverage of Mary Gauvain's (2001) view on why social constructivist approaches are important for understanding how children learn and think
- Expanded discussion of Reading Recovery
- New discussion of PALS (Peer-Assisted Learning Strategies), including recent research on the effectiveness of PALS reading and PALS math (Fuchs, Fuchs, & Burish, 2000)
- Addition of new research on the effectiveness of scaffolding (Pressley & others, 2001) and cognitive apprenticeship (Englert, Berry, & Dunsmore, 2001)

> "This chapter is excellent. It is well organized with learning, structuring groups, and social constructivist programs. Great reading!"
> —GABY VAN DER GIESSEN *Fairmont State College*

> "This is a great chapter! Currency: Very timely!"
> —DAVID DALTON *Kent State University*

CHAPTER 11:
Learning and Cognition in the Content Areas

- New, stand-alone chapter on learning and cognition in the content areas
- New section on pedagogical content knowledge
- Completely new section on social sciences, including material on themes of social studies teaching and learning, as well as constructivist approaches in teaching social studies
- New chapter-opening teaching story on Betty Teufel, a reading teacher
- Some of the reading material was in chapter 2 in the first edition; all of the book's discussion of reading is now in this chapter
- Updated, recent coverage of research on reading (National Reading Panel, 2000) with more detailed information about what works in teaching children to read; also new introduction to section on reading with Steve Stahl's (2002) ideas on the three main goals of reading instruction
- Updated, revised ideas on teaching science (Cocking, Mestre, & Brown, 2000)
- New material on interactive demonstration strategy in helping students overcome misconceptions in science

- Discussion of important contemporary issue of whether elementary school students should use calculators to learn math, including recent national study and figure of data from the study
- New themes of planning and reviewing highlighted in the discussion of writing
- Expanded coverage of problem solving in writing
- New recent study by Pressley and others (2001) documenting that effective reading instruction not only involves a balanced reading approach but also effective classroom management and encouragement of student self-regulation
- New figure (11.5), A Plan Think-Sheet, to help students with planning their compositions
- New Diversity and Education interlude: "UN Peacekeeping: A Constructivist Approach"
- New Through the Eyes of Teachers inserts
- Extensively revised and updated coverage of math education based on recent recommendations by the National Council of Teachers of Mathematics
- Recent research by Constance Flanagan (Flanagan & Faison, 2001) showing how teachers can effectively instill a sense of democracy in students
- Considerably expanded teaching strategies for incorporating writing into the curriculum
- New research and figure (11.2) based on the research that links working memory capacity and reading

> *"This is an excellent chapter. . . . The chapter is rich in content and provides engaging multi-grade examples."*
>
> —CAROLINE GOULD *Eastern Michigan University*

> *"A separate chapter for the five main content areas is a great idea! This chapter is well organized with attention to important content areas— excellent to support students in their ability to connect educational psychology concepts with their 'how to' courses and understanding the cognition aspect."*
>
> LYNNE HAMMANN *University of Akron*

- Updated search engines to include Google and others
- New discussion of an outstanding teacher who uses essential questions to direct what her students study
- Inclusion of recent research on parental involvement in homework (Hoover-Dempsey & others, 2001)
- New discussion of revision of Bloom's taxonomy to focus more on knowledge and cognitive processes (Anderson & Krathwohl, 2001)
- Coverage of recent large-scale study on students' perceptions of teachers and how these perceptions are linked to the students' motivation and achievement (McCombs, 2001; McCombs & Quiat, 2001)
- New section on ubiquitous computing and how students might benefit from it
- New Through the Eyes of Teachers inserts, one on Luis Recalde's efforts to foster learning and civic unity and one on Mary Lynn Peacher's strategies for guiding students to discover
- Revised, updated Self-Assessment: "Evaluating My Technology Skills and Attitudes"
- New figure (12.4) showing difference between Asian and U.S. parents' views on why children achieve in math
- New figure (12.7) based on recent research showing the relation of students' use of the Internet at home and science achievement
- Deleted section on integrating the curriculum to make the chapter more cohesive and briefer

> *"This chapter is better handled than any other educational psychology text I've seen."*
>
> —JAN HAYES *Middle Tennessee State University*

> *"In this chapter, students receive an excellent introduction to planning, instruction, and technology."*
>
> —REVEREND JOSEPH DI MAURO *DeSales University*

CHAPTER 12:

Planning, Instruction, and Cognitive Technology

- Extensive reorganization of technology section, including deletion of computer-supported approaches to learning as recommended by reviewers
- New chapter-opening teaching story on using laptop computers in the classroom
- New section on ISTE technology standards (2000) for different grade levels, including many new examples of effective technology activities

CHAPTER 13:

Motivation, Teaching, and Learning

- New discussion of Lance Armstrong's battle with cancer and motivation to win the Tour de France as an example of motivation for students
- Changing of wording in a number of places to underscore the point that motivation comes from students and that teachers can provide effective strategies to help students become motivated
- Revised definition of motivation based on expert consultant Dale Schunk's recommendation
- New section on social motivation

- Deleted section on general motivational strategies toward the end of the chapter and focused more on hard-to-reach, unmotivated students
- New study by Strobel (2001) on the achievement motivation of minority students from low-income families
- New summary paragraph about rewards, competence, and interest based on expert consultant Dale Schunk's recommendation
- Important point made in the discussion of rewards and achievement that it is not the reward itself that causes the effect when the reward is about mastery but, rather, the expectation of the reward, as recommended by Schunk
- New coverage of Nel Noddings' (1992, 2001) caring curriculum
- Expanded, updated material on teachers' supporting and caring behaviors, including new figure (13.5) on Wenzel's study of the qualities of caring teachers
- Revised definitions of intrinsic and extrinsic motivation, as recommended by Schunk

"This chapter presents a nice balance between theory, research, and applications. Well done! . . . Very clear writing is used to explain some complex processes."

—**Dale Schunk** *University of North Carolina–Greensboro*

"I completed both a master's thesis and doctoral dissertation on achievement goal theory in motivation. . . . I thought this chapter did an excellent job of taking the various cognitive theories of motivation and translating them into specific strategies for creating a positive motivational environment. . . . My overall evaluation of the chapter: Excellent."

—**Barbara Powell** *Eastern Illinois University*

CHAPTER 14:
Managing the Classroom

- Revision of headings/topics in designing the physical environment of the classroom
- New section on distinguishing rules and procedures, as recommended by expert consultant Carolyn Evertson
- New section on teaching rules and procedures
- Reversed order of major sections on being a good communicator and dealing with problem behaviors based on the recommendations of reviewers. Being a good communicator now comes first because these strategies are intended to meet the needs of a wide range of students. However, sometimes these general strategies are not enough, so then teachers have to deal with problem behaviors if they arise
- Extensive reorganization of section on being a good communicator based on reviewer recommendations;

now has three main parts (speaking skills, listening skills, and nonverbal communication)
- New section on speaking with your class and students at the request of reviewers
- Expanded and updated coverage of bullying, including a recent large-scale national study and figure of the data in the study and a recent longitudinal study
- New Through the Eyes of Teachers insert: "Great Teachers Have Few Discipline Problems"

"John Santrock does a good job with a complex topic. This chapter captures the key features that all teachers need to be aware of without overwhelming them with detail or secondary issues. . . . The research is quite current and the writing style flows and is easy to read."

—**Carolyn Evertson** *Vanderbilt University*

"This is an excellent chapter and my suggestions are for polishing a gem. The section on being an effective communicator is a huge selling point for this chapter. The section on dealing with conflict capitalizes brilliantly on the notion of assertive perspectives and helps students see the connections to student learning and safety—a must for today's classrooms and schools."

—**Connie Moss** *Duquesne University*

CHAPTER 15:
Standardized Tests and Teaching

- New section on fairness in standardized testing based on the recommendation of expert consultant James McMillan
- Much expanded, revised, and updated coverage of high-stakes state-mandated tests
- New section on using standardized test scores to plan and improve instruction
- Replaced concept of minimum-competency concept with standard-based tests
- Discussion of validity moved before reliability because most assessment experts consider validity to be more important—based on McMillan's recommendation
- Revised definition and coverage of validity to emphasize the importance of inferences about the accuracy of test scores—also based on McMillan's recommendation
- New discussion of what teachers should not do in preparing students to take standardized tests
- Added comment about percentile rank in standardized testing being determined by comparison with group norm distribution
- Updated and revised discussion of issue focused on alternative assessments versus standardized tests to tie in with high-stakes state-mandated testing
- New Through the Eyes of Children insert: Tania Garcia's view of standardized tests

- New discussion of the failure of high-stakes testing to provide information for improving instruction and strengths and weaknesses of students, including new figure (15.4)
- New commentary about multiple roles of standardized scores
- Recent data showing national trends in reading, math, and science, including new figure on math trends

> *"This chapter provides great coverage of contemporary issues concerning the use of standardized (and nonstandardized) testing at the regional, national, and international levels."*
> —SANDRA NAGEL RANDALL *Saginaw Valley State University*

> *"This is another fine chapter covering current issues and traditional concepts. . . . I am delighted at the completeness of terms, concepts, and examples.*
> —ROBERT G. BROWN *Florida Atlantic University–Boca Raton*

CHAPTER 16:
Classroom Assessment

- New chapter title, Classroom Assessment, replacing one in first edition, Assessing Students' Learning, based on the recommendation of expert consultant James McMillan because chapter 15 also focuses on assessing students' learning

- New figure 16.1, on decision making in assessment linked to pre-instruction assessment, assessment during instruction, and post-instruction assessment
- Revision of definition of reliability and its discussion to emphasize scores rather than the measure, as well as new examples of reliability and validity, based on McMillan's recommendations
- New section on the strengths and weaknesses of matching items
- New coverage of offensiveness and unfair penalization in fairness of assessment
- New example of self-assessment in performance-based assessment
- Much expanded coverage of scoring rubrics, including new figures (16.8 and 16.9)
- New Teaching Strategies for using scoring rubrics
- New discussion of standards-based grading

> *"Overall, this is an excellent chapter and again my suggestions are for polishing a gem! The topics are extremely current and well written and work together to produce another stellar chapter."*
> —CONNIE MOSS *Duquesne University*

> *"This is one of the best chapters on student assessment I've seen in an educational psychology textbook."*
> —DAVID E. TANNER *California State University–Fresno*

Expert Research Consultants

Albert Bandura

Albert Bandura, currently David Starr Jordan Professor of Social Science at Stanford University, is one of the world's leading theorists and researchers in learning and cognition. Over the past five decades, Dr. Bandura has been one of America's most influential psychologists and is a former president of the American Psychological Association. In 1999, he received the Thorndike Award for Distinguished Contributions of Psychology to Education from the American Psychological Association. In 2001, he received the Lifetime Achievement Award from the Association for the Advancement of Behavior Therapy. His theory and research pioneered the interest in the concept of observational learning. Today, his social cognitive theory is widely recognized as one of the most effective conceptual views of how children learn and has spawned thousands of research studies. One of his main current interests focuses on how children regulate their own motivation, thinking, and affect through self-efficacy.

Gary Bitter

Gary Bitter, Professor of Educational Technology and Executive Director of Technology Based Learning & Research at Arizona State University, is a leading expert on educational technology. He has been the Principal Investigator for numerous educational technology grants, is a past president of the International Society for Technology in Education, (ISTE) and served on the NCATE Technology Task Force releasing the report "Technology and the New Professional Teacher: Preparing for the 21st Century Classroom." Dr. Bitter has also served as Co-Principal Investigator for the National Educational Technology Standards (NETS) Project. He is presently on the leadership team for the ISTE Preparing Tomorrow's Teachers to Use Technology Grant as well as Principal Investigator of a FIPSE Learning Anytime Anywhere Grant.

Carlos F. Diaz

Carlos F. Diaz is a Professor of Education at Florida Atlantic University, Boca Raton, Florida, where he received his Ed.D., Ed.S., and M.Ed. in curriculum and instruction. He was formerly an Associate Professor of Education in the Department of Educational Foundations and Technology, and currently he is Project Director for the Master of Education in Cultural Foundations with E.S.O.L. Endorsement program. He has also been a Visiting Professor at the Center for Multicultural Education, University of Washington, Seattle. Dr. Diaz has authored several books, chapters, and articles, such as *Multicultural Education in the 21st Century* and *Global Perspectives for Educators.* He has received numerous honors and awards, such as the Teaching Incentive Program Award (1996), the University Award for Excellence in Undergraduate Teaching (1996), Professor of the Year (1993), the 2000 Notable American Men award (1992), and recognition in *Who's Who Among Hispanic Americans, Rising Young Americans,* and *American Education.*

Eva L. Essa

Eva L. Essa is a Professor of Human Development and Family Studies at the University of Nevada, Reno, where she has taught for over 30 years. Recently she was instrumental in starting an interdisciplinary undergraduate program in early childhood education at the university with the College of Education. For 16 years, Dr. Essa also served as the Director of the Child and Family Research Center, the campus early childhood program. She has published several widely used early childhood education texts and numerous articles. Her research is focused on ways of improving the quality of early childhood education programs.

R. Carolyn M. Evertson

R. Carolyn M. Evertson is one of the world's leading experts on classroom management and is Professor of Education at Vanderbilt University, where she is Director of COMP: Creating Conditions for Learning, a nationally disseminated program for helping teachers with classroom management. She received her Ph.D. in educational psychology from the University of Texas, Austin. Dr. Evertson has published numerous articles and chapters on the social context of classrooms and supporting students' social and academic learning in school environments. She is the coauthor of two textbooks on classroom management for preservice teachers and is a Fellow of the American Psychological Association.

Kenji Hakuta

Kenji Hakuta, the Vida Jacks Professor of Education at Stanford University, is one of the world's leading authorities and researchers in the area of bilingual education. He is especially interested in how we can improve the education of language minority students, how long it takes immigrant children to learn English, and whether there is a critical period for second-language acquisition.

Daniel P. Hallahan

Daniel P. Hallahan is one of the world's leading experts on children who are exceptional learners. He received his Ph.D. in education and psychology from the University of Michigan and has been a member of the faculty of the Curry School of Education at the University of Virginia since 1971. He was appointed Chair of the Department of Curriculum, Instruction, and Special Education in 1997. Dr. Hallahan received the University of Virginia Outstanding Teaching Award in 1998 and currently holds the university's Cavaliers' Distinguished Teaching Professorship. He was the Inaugural Editor of *Exceptionality* from 1990 to 1992 and currently serves on the editorial boards of *Learning Disabilities Research and Practice,* *Learning Disability Quarterly, The Journal of Special Education,* and *Exceptionality.* Hallahan is a Past President of the Division for Learning Disabilities of the Council for Exceptional Children (CEC), and in 2000 he received the CEC Research Award. Dr. Hallahan's primary research interests are in the areas of learning disabilities, attention deficit hyperactivity disorder, and the history of special education. Many of his most recent publications have focused on educational placement issues in special education. He is coauthor of several books, including the widely used *Exceptional Learners: Introduction to Special Education,* ninth edition (2003, with James Kauffman), and *Introduction to Learning Disabilities,* third edition (2005, with John Lloyd, James Kauffman, and others).

James H. McMillan

James H. McMillan is Professor of Educational Studies at Virginia Commonwealth University in Richmond and Director of the Metropolitan Educational Research Consortium. He is author of *Classroom Assessment: Principles and Practice for Effective Instruction,* second edition, and *Essential Assessment Concepts for Teachers and Administrators,* and he has written books in educational psychology and educational research. Some of his publications include articles in *Educational Measurement: Issues and Practice, Educational Horizons, Educational and Psychological Measurement,* the *Journal of Educational Psychology,* and the *American Educational Research Journal.* Dr. McMillan currently is investigating the relationship between classroom assessment and grading practices and teacher decision making about assessment. For the past several years he has been active in Virginia's new state testing and accountability program. Dr. McMillan also directs the Metropolitan Educational Research Consortium, a university/public school partnership that conducts and disseminates action research.

Valerie Pang

Valerie Pang is a Professor in the School of Teacher Education at San Diego State University and was formerly a first- and second-grade teacher in rural and urban schools. She recently authored *Multicultural Education: A Caring-Centered, Reflective Approach,* second edition (2005). Dr. Pang has published a number of articles on multicultural education in such journals as *Harvard Educational Review, Phi Delta Kappan,* and *Equity and Excellence.* She was given the 1997 Distinguished Scholar Award from the AERA Committee on Minorities in Education and has received the Outstanding Teaching Award from San Diego State University.

Michael Pressley

Michael Pressley is a leading educational psychologist who has conducted ground-breaking research and theorizing on children's memory, cognitive monitoring, and effective reading instruction. He is currently a faculty member at the University of Notre Dame, where he is the Notre Dame Professor in Catholic Education and Professor of Psychology. Dr. Pressley is also the current editor of the *Journal of Educational Psychology* and has published over 250 articles, chapters, and books. His book *Reading Instruction That Works: The Case for Balanced Teaching* has received considerable critical acclaim. Dr. Pressley is recognized as a leading expert in primary-level literacy education.

Dale Schunk

Dale Schunk, Dean of the School of Education and Professor of Curriculum and Instruction at the University of North Carolina at Greensboro, is a leading expert on children's learning and motivation in educational settings. He received his Ph.D. in educational psychology from Stanford University. Previously he was a faculty member at the University of Houston and the University of North Carolina at Chapel Hill, and he was head of the Department of Educational Studies at Purdue University. Dr. Schunk has published over 70 articles and chapters, is author of *Learning Theories: An Educational Perspective* and (with Paul Pintrich) *Motivation in Education: Theories, Research, and Applications,* and has edited several books on self-regulation and motivation. His awards include the Distinguished Service Award from the Purdue University School of Education, the Early Contributions Award in Educational Psychology from the American Psychological Association, and the Albert J. Harris Research Award from the International Reading Association.

Robert Siegler

Robert Siegler is one of the world's leading experts on children's information processing and is Teresa Heinz Professor of Cognitive Psychology at Carnegie Mellon University. He has been at Carnegie Mellon since receiving his Ph.D. in 1974 from SUNY at Stony Brook. In the ensuing years, he has written 5 books, edited 3 others, and authored more than 150 articles and book chapters. The books and articles have focused on children's reasoning and problem solving, particularly in scientific and mathematical domains. Among the books he has written are *How Children Discover New Strategies* (1989, with Eric Jenkins) and *Children's Thinking,* fourth edition (2005, with Martha Alibali). His book *Emerging Minds* was chosen one of the "Best Psychology Books of 1996" by the Association of American Publishers. Siegler also has served as Associate Editor of the journal *Developmental Psychology* and coedited the 1998 *Handbook of Child Psychology: Cognition, Perception, and Language.*

ACKNOWLEDGMENTS

I am deeply indebted to many people who helped me to create the Classroom Update of this text. I sincerely appreciate the support of this book provided by Steve Debow, president, and Thalia Dorwick, vice-president and editor-in-chief. My editors, David Patterson and Cara Harvey, provided invaluable support, resources, and coordination of this extensive project. Alan Venable, a remarkable developmental editor, significantly shaped the content and voice of the book. Rick Hecker, project manager, did a great job coordinating the production of the book.

On pages xxx–xxxii of the Preface, the numerous expert research consultants for the book are profiled. As stated earlier, their feedback clearly helped to make the book's content far superior to what I could have accomplished alone.

Peer Reviewers for the Classroom Update: Preparing for Practice and PRAXIS™ Edition In planning the Classroom Update Edition, we asked educational psychology instructors what resources they would like to help their students learn and them to teach. The suggestions I received were incredibly helpful in developing this special edition. A special thanks goes to

Jeffrey Baker, *Rochester Institute of Technology*
Richard Benedict, *Madonna University*
Melva M. Burke, *East Carolina University*
Russell N. Carney, *Southwest Missouri State University*
Sheryl Feinstein, *Augusta College*
Aubrey Fine, *California Polytechnic University*
Ericka Fisher, *College of the Holy Cross*
Charles R. Grah, *Austin Peay State University*
William E. Herman, *State University of New York, Potsdam*
John H. Hummel, *Valdosta State University*
Mona Ibrahim, *Concordia College*
Emilie Johnson, *Lindenwood University*
Robert L. Kohn, *University of Kansas*
Barbara F. Maestas, *Towson University*
Julia M. Matuga, *Bowling Green State University*
John K. Meis, *Flager College*
Dorothy D. Miles, *Saint Louis University*
Ronald Mulson, *Hudson Valley Community College*
Joeseph D. Nichols, *Indiana-Purdue University*
Jim Persinger, *Emporia State University*
Lynda Robinson, *University of the Ozarks*
Ala Samarapungavan, *Purdue University*
Marvin Seperson, *Nova Southeastern University*
David E. Tanner, *California State University, Fresno*
Karen Thierry, *Rutgers University*
Jina Yoon, *Wayne State University*

Peer Reviewers for the Second Edition An extensive number of educational psychology instructors gave me very detailed, helpful information about what they wanted in an ideal textbook for their course. Their ideas significantly influenced the content, organization, and pedagogy of the second edition of the book. The second edition of this text is much improved over the first edition because of the efforts of these instructors:

Eric Anderman, *University of Kentucky*
James M. Applefield, *University of North Carolina–Wilmington*
Dorothy A. Battle, *Georgia Southern University*
Douglas Beed, *University of Montana–Missoula*
John T. Binfet, *California State University–San Bernadino*
Joseph W. Braun, *California State University–Dominguez Hills*
Kathy Brown, *University of Central Oklahoma*
Robert G. Brown, *Florida Atlantic University*
Alison Bryant, *University of Missouri–Columbia*
Chuck Catania, *Miami University of Ohio*
Jean Newman Clark, *University of South Alabama*
Ellen Contopidis, *Keuka College*
Dorothy Valcarcel Craig, *Middle Tennessee State University*
Rhoda Cummings, *University of Nevada–Reno*
Reagan Curtis, *Northwestern State University*
David Dalton, *Kent State University*
Nancy DeFrates-Densch, *Northern Illinois University*
Gypsy Denzine, *Northern Arizona University*
Jesse Diaz, *Central Washington University*
Ronna Dillon, *Southern Illinois University–Carbondale*
Joseph DiMauro, *DeSales University*
Ruth Doyle, *Casper College*
Kenneth Durgans, *Xavier University*
Howard Epstein, *Miami University of Ohio*
Lena Ericksen, *Western Washington University*
Tsila Evers, *Miami University–Oxford*
Sheryl Feinstein, *Augustana College*
Aubrey Fine, *California State University–Pomona*
Diane L. Finley, *Prince George's Community College*
William R. Fisk, *Clemson University*
M. Arthur Garmon, *Western Michigan University*
Alyssa Gonzalez, *Florida Atlanta University*
Caroline Gould, *Eastern Michigan University*
Kim Grilliot, *Bowling Green State University*
Lynne A. Hammann, *University of Akron*
Andrew Hanson, *California State University–Chico*
Walter Hapkiewicz, *Michigan State University*
Gregory Harper, *State University of New York–Fredonia*
Diane J. Harris, *San Francisco State University*
Jan Hayes, *Middle Tennessee State University*
David Holliway, *Marshall University*
Sherri Horner, *University of Memphis*
Mara Huber, *State University of New York–Fredonia*
Judith Hughey, *Kansas State University*
Steven Kaatz, *Bethel College*
Deborah Kalkman, *Northern Illinois University*
Susan Kelley, *Lycoming College*
Lee Kem, *Murray State University*
Elizabeth W. Kirk, *Miami University of Ohio*

Elaine Kisisel, *Calumet College of Saint Joseph*
Becky K. Ladd, *Illinois State University*
Marvin Lee, *Shenandoah University*
Randy Lennon, *University of Northern Colorado*
Bernie Les, *Wayne State University*
Dov Liberman, *University of Houston*
Kim Loomis, *Kennesaw State University*
Catherine McCartney, *Bemidji State University*
John R. McClure, *Northern Arizona University*
P. Y. Mantzicopoulos, *Purdue University*
Julia Matuga, *Bowling Green State University*
Lisa Mehlig, *Northern Illinois University*
Dot Miles, *Saint Louis University*
Barbara Milligan, *Middle Tennessee State University*
Connie M. Moss, *Duquesne University*
Beverly Moore, *Auburn University*
Peter Myerson, *University of Wisconsin–Oshkosh*
Ernest Owen, *Western Kentucky University*
Nita A. Paris, *Kennesaw State University*
Barbara M. Powell, *Eastern Illinois University*
Barbara L. Radigan, *Community College of Allegheny County*
Sandra Nagel Randall, *Saginaw Valley State University*
Marla Reese-Weber, *Illinois State University*
Robert Rice, *Western Oregon University*
Susan Rogers, *Columbus State Community College*
Lawrence R. Rogien, *Boise State University*
Pearl Rosenberg, *Muhlenberg College*
Debbie Salih, *University of Northern Iowa*
Jill Salisbury-Glennon, *Auburn University*
Ala Samarapungavan, *Purdue University*
Charles Jeff Sandoz, *University of Louisiana*
Rolando A. Santos, *California State University–Los Angeles*
Gayle Schou, *Grand Canyon University*
Lisa Sethre-Hofstad, *Concordia College*
Patricia Slocum, *College of DuPage*
Brian G. Smith, *Moorhead State University*
Michael Smith, *Weber State University*
Daniel W. Stuempfig, *California State University–Chico*
Gabriele Sweidel, *Kutztown University of Pennsylvania*
David E. Tanner, *California State University–Fresno*
Sara Tannert, *Miami University of Ohio*
Yuma I. Tomes, *Virginia Commonwealth University*
Donna Townsend, *Southwestern Assemblies of God University*
Julie Turner, *University of Notre Dame*
Atilano Valencia, *California State University–Fresno*
Eva G. Vandergiessen, *Fairmont State College*
David Vawter, *Winthrop University*
Linda Veronie, *Slippery Rock University*
Libby Vesilind, *Bucknell University*
Penny Warner, *Winona State University*
Linda Weeks, *Lamar University*
Earl F. Wellborn, Jr., *Missouri Valley College*
David Wendler, *Martin Luther College*
Glenda Wilkes, *University of Arizona*

Patricia Willems, *Florida Atlantic University*
Victor Willson, *Texas A&M University*
Steven R. Wininger, *Western Kentucky University*
Betsy Wisner, *State University of New York–Cortland*
Patricia Whang, *California State University–Monterey Bay*
Michael Young, *University of Connecticut*

Reviewers of the First Edition I am also indebted to the many reviewers of the first edition of the text who did an outstanding job in helping me to create the foundation for the book. These instructors and expert research consultants provided this feedback:

Dr. Frank Adams, *Wayne State College*
Dr. Robert R. Ayres, *Western Oregon University*
Dr. James Applefield, *University of North Carolina–Wilmington*
Dr. Elizabeth C. Arch, *Pacific University*
Professor Roger Briscoe, *Indiana University of Pennsylvania*
Randy Brown, *University of Central Oklahoma*
Professor Kay Bull, *Oklahoma State University*
Dr. Mary D. Burbank, *University of Utah*
Dr. Sheryl Needle Cohn, *University of Central Florida*
Dr. Rayne Sperling Dennison, *Penn State*
Dr. Carlos F. Diaz, *Florida Atlantic University*
Professor Ronna Dillon, *Southern Illinois University*
Dr. Peter Doolittle, *Virginia Polytechnic University*
Dr. David Dungan, *Emporia State University*
Gordon Eisenmann, *Augusta State University*
Vicky Farrow, *Lamar University*
Dr. William L. Franzen, *University of Missouri–St. Louis*
Dr. Susan Goldman, *Vanderbilt University*
Dr. Algea Harrison, *Oakland University*
Dr. Jan Hayes, *Middle Tennessee State University*
Dr. Alice S. Honig, *Syracuse University*
Dr. Kathryn W. Linden, emeritus, *Purdue University*
Dr. Richard E. Mayer, *University of California–Santa Barbara*
Rita McKenzie, *Northern Arizona University*
Dr. James H. McMillan, *Virginia Commonwealth University*
Professor Sharon McNeely, *Northeastern Illinois University*
Ann Pace, *University of Missouri*
Dr. Karen Menke Paciorek, *Eastern Michigan University*
Dr. Peggy Perkins, *University of Nevada–Las Vegas*
Dr. Nan Bernstein Ratner, *University of Maryland–College Park*
Dr. Gilbert Sax, *University of Washington*
Dr. Dale Schunk, *University of North Carolina–Greensboro*
Judith Stechly, *West Liberty State University*
Dr. O. Suthern Sims, Jr., *Mercer University*
Dr. David Wendler, *Martin Luther College*
Dr. Allan Wigfield, *University of Maryland–College Park*

Dr. Tony L. Williams, *Marshall University*
Professor Ann K. Wilson, *Buena Vista University*
Dr. Peter Young, *Southern Oregon University*
Dr. Steven Yussen, *University of Minnesota*

Panel of Early Childhood, Elementary, Middle, and High School Teachers A large panel of individuals who teach at the early childhood, elementary, middle, and high school levels provided me with material about special teaching moments that they have experienced for both the first and the second editions of the book. These are outstanding teachers, many of whom have received local, regional, or national teaching awards. I owe these teachers a great deal of thanks for sharing the real world of their teaching experiences:

Karen Abra, *School of the Sacred Heart,* San Francisco, CA
Mrs. Lou Aronson, *Devils Lake High School,* Devils Lake, ND
Daniel Arnoux, *Lauderhill Middle Community School,* Broward, FL
Lynn Ayres, *East Middle School,* Ypsilanti, MI
Fay Bartley, *Bright Horizon Children Center,* Bronx, NY
Barbara M. Berry, *Ypsilanti High School,* Ypsilanti, MI
Kristin Blackenship, *Salem Church Elementary,* Midlothian, VA
Stella Cohen, *Hackley School,* Tarrytown, NY
Andrea Fenton, *Cortez High School,* Glendale Union, AZ
Mark Fodness, *Bemidji Middle School,* Bemidji, MN
Kathy Fuchser, *St. Francis High School,* Humphrey, NE
Lawren Giles, *Baechtel Grove Middle School,* Willits, CA
Jerri Hall, *Miller Magnet Middle School,* Bibb County, GA
Anita Marie Hitchcock, *Holley Navarre Primary,* Santa Rosa Schools, FL
Laura Johnson-Brickford, *Nordhoff High School,* Ojai, CA
Heidi Kaufman, *Associate Executive Director of Childcare, MetroWest YMCA,* Framingham, MA
Juanita Kerton, *Gramercy School/New York League for Early Learning,* New York, NY
Robynne Kirkpatrick, *Northwest Middle School,* Salt Lake City, UT
Chaille Lazar, *Hedgcoxe Elementary,* Plano, TX
Margaret Longworth, *St. Lucie West Middle School,* St. Lucie, FL
Adriane Lonzarich, *Heartwood,* San Mateo, CA
Dennis Peterson, *Deer River High School,* Bemidji, MN
Chuck Rawls, *Appling Middle School,* Bibb County, GA
Verna Brown Rollins, *West Middle School,* Ypsilanti, MI
Donna L. Shelhorse, *Short Pump Middle School,* Henrico County, VA
Michele Siegal, *Brockton High School,* Brockton, MA
Jason Stanley, *Syracuse Dunbar Avoca,* Syracuse, NE
Vicky Stone, *Cammack Middle School,* Huntington, WV
Tamela Varney, *Central City Elementary,* Cabell County, WV
Marlene Wendler, *St. Paul's Lutheran School,* New Ulm, MN
William Willford, *Perry Middle School,* Perry, GA

Yvonne Wilson, *North Elementary School,* Deer River, MN
Susan Youngblood, *Weaver Middle School,* Bibb County, GA

Special Features and Ancillaries Authors I also benefited enormously from the efforts of this outstanding group of educational psychology instructors who wrote material for special features in the text and the ancillaries. The excellence of the Classroom Update edition is a direct result of all their hard work:

- **Nancy DeFrates-Densch,** *Northern Illinois University,* author of Crack the Case, all case studies on the Student Toolbox CD-ROM, *The Educational Psychology Guide to Preparing for the PRAXIS II™ Exam,* the Theory into Practice module, and the Enter the Debate feature and Content Consultant for the *Educational Psychology* video
- **Alyssa Gonzalez** and **Patricia Willems** of *Florida Atlantic University,* authors of the second edition student study guide and the test bank
- **Deborah Kalkman,** *Northern Illinois University,* our Advising Editor for the entire supplements package and author of the instructor's manual and the PowerPoint and overhead package, and a contributer to the video program
- **Veronica Rowland,** *University of California–Irvine,* author of Taking It to the Net, the Student OLC, and *The Educational Psychology Guide to Preparing for the PRAXIS II™ Exam,* as well as revising author of the student study guide and test bank

ANCILLARIES

 Student Toolbox CD-ROM by Allysa Gonzalez, Patricia Willems, Nancy Defrates-Densch, Veronica Rowland, and Deborah Kalkman The Student Toolbox CD-ROM includes a study guide, application activities, and general resources for students. The study guide contains study resources, including multiple-choice, true/false, matching, short-answer, and essay quizzes. The application activities include a wealth of video clips (Video Lectures, Video Observations, and Expert Advice and Teaching Experience video clips), additional Crack the Case studies, self-assessment exercises, and observation activities. General resources on the CD-ROM include *The Educational Psychology Guide to Preparing for the PRAXIS II™ Exam,* the *Bibliomaker,* and a lesson planning tool.

 Online Learning Center by Veronica Rowland, Allysa Gonzalez, Patricia Willems, Nancy Defrates-Densch, and Deborah Kalkman The *Educational Psychology* Online Learning Center at **www.mhhe.com/santedu2e** contains the student study guide, a Web-linked version of each chapter's Crack the Case study, Enter the Debate questions and resources, links to the websites referenced in the text, links to online teaching strategies, application resources, and PowerWeb.

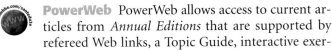 **PowerWeb** PowerWeb allows access to current articles from *Annual Editions* that are supported by refereed Web links, a Topic Guide, interactive exercises, and an instructor's resource guide. It also has Weekly Updates posted every Tuesday, a daily News Feed posting complete articles from worldwide sources, research tools, student study tools, and much more. Students use the registration code bound into their new texts to access the site through the Online Learning Center. The topics are aligned with the chapters, providing instructors and students with an easy way to expand on key material.

The Educational Psychology Guide to Preparing for the PRAXIS II™ Principles of Learning and Teaching Exam Guide by Nancy Defrates-Densch and Veronica Rowland

By request of instructors who teach students required to take the PRAXIS II™ *Principles of Learning and Teaching* exam, this study guide is designed to help students use *Educational Psychology* to prepare for the exam. The study guide includes objective quizzes to confirm understanding of topics and a practice test based on the PRAXIS II™ exam.

The guide is located on the Student Toolbox CD-ROM in an interactive format and as a print guide that can be ordered as a free package item by instructors or purchased separately by students (0-07-298151-2).

Instructor's Resource CD-ROM by Deborah Kalkman, Alyssa Gonzalez, Patricia Willems, and Veronica Rowland

The Instructor's Resource CD-ROM includes an instructor's manual, a test bank, a computerized test bank, PowerPoint slides, video clips, INTASC alignment information, and other resources for the instructor.

The **instructor's manual** is a flexible planner with teaching suggestions, learning objectives, extended chapter outlines, lecture/discussion suggestions, video and film recommendations, classroom activity tips, and handout forms. It also includes lecture and activity ideas on technology and diversity issues, as well as Controversies sections, which highlight provocative perspectives.

The **test bank** includes almost 1,000 questions, specifically related to the main text, consisting of multiple-choice questions, stem questions, short-answer questions, critical thinking questions, essay questions, and applied assessments. It is available in Word format and as a computerized test bank (accessible on both Macintosh and Windows platforms).

The **PowerPoint** presentation as been recreated to contain interactive content, such as through using video, slides.

Overhead Transparencies by Deborah Kalkman

Hundreds of full-color acetates packaged in a three-ring binder serve as a wonderful teaching tool.

Instructor's Video Program

Teaching Stories: A Video Collection contains 16 segments of teachers, students, and classrooms in action. Each segment was created specifically to depict the chapter topics of *Educational Psychology* in action. The video program is available in VHS and DVD formats.

To the Student

This visual student preface provides you with an overview of the features that will help you to learn the material in each chapter. The Student Toolbox CD-ROM and Online Learning Center icons indicate that the feature content is located on that resource.

BEGINNING OF CHAPTER

Chapter Outline and Learning Goals

The chapter outline shows the organization of topics by heading levels. The learning goals, which are linked to the chapter's main headings, give you an idea of the main information you need to learn in the chapter.

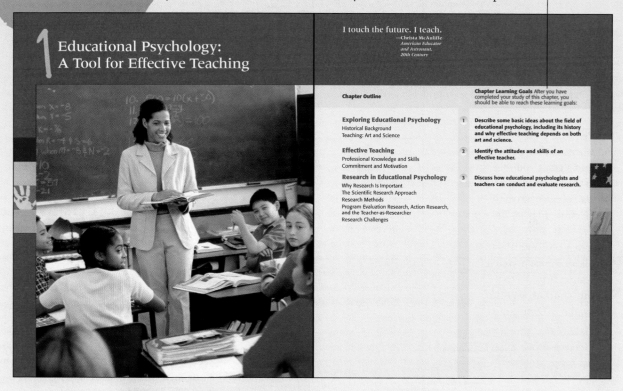

Teaching Stories

This features compelling, high-interest descriptions of outstanding teachers and how they teach related to the content of the chapter.

Expert Advice

Chapters are introduced by a video clip of an expert in the field discussing his or her area of expertise and giving advice to future teachers.

WITHIN CHAPTER

Self-Assessment

This box appears one or more times in each chapter and is closely related to the content of the chapter. It is a powerful tool that helps you to evaluate and understand yourself in your effort to become an outstanding teacher.

Chapter Web Links

A website icon appearing in the margin signals you that you can go to the Santrock *Educational Psychology* website to use connecting Internet links that provide you with additional information about the topic. The label for each Web icon corresponds to the same label on the Santrock website (www.mhhe.com/santedu2e).

Key Terms

Key terms are boldfaced in the text and their definitions are provided in the margin next to where they are introduced in the text.

Through the Eyes of Teachers

These inserts present motivating, revealing comments on relevant topics from classroom teachers, many of whom have won awards for their outstanding teaching.

Diversity and Education

This interlude appears once in each chapter, immediately following a related discussion of sociocultural diversity in the text. It focuses on important cultural, ethnic, and gender issues related to education.

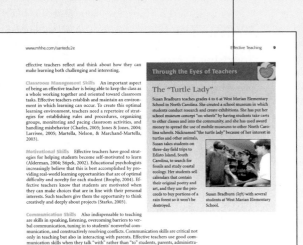

instruction is often inadequate to explain the effects of instruction on learning." The cognitive revolution in psychology began to take hold by the 1980s and ushered in a great deal of enthusiasm for applying the concepts of cognitive psychology—memory, thinking, reasoning, and so on—to helping students learn. Thus, toward the latter part of the twentieth century, many educational psychologists returned to an emphasis on the cognitive aspects of learning advocated by James and Dewey at the beginning of the century.

Both cognitive and behavioral approaches continue to be a part of educational psychology today. We will have much more to say about these approaches in chapters 7 through 11.

In the last several decades of the twentieth century, educational psychologists also increasingly focused on the socioemotional aspects of students' lives. For example, they analyzed the school as a social context and examined the role of culture in education. We will explore the socioemotional aspects of teaching and learning in many chapters of the book.

Teaching: Art and Science

How scientific can a teacher be in his or her approach to teaching? Both science and the art of skillful, experienced practice play important roles in a teacher's success (Arends, 2004; Freiberg & Driscoll, 2005; Johnson & others, 2002).

The field of educational psychology draws much of its knowledge from broader theory and research in psychology. For example, the theories of Jean Piaget and Lev Vygotsky were not created in an effort to inform teachers about ways to educate children, yet in chapter 2, "Cognitive and Language Development," you will see that both of these theories have many applications that can guide your teaching. The field also draws from theory and research more directly created and conducted by educational psychologists, and from the practical experiences of teachers. For example, in chapter 13, "Motivation, Teaching, and Learning," you will read about Dale Schunk's (2004; Schunk & Ertmer, 2000) classroom-oriented research on self-efficacy (the belief that one can master a situation and produce positive outcomes). Educational psychologists also recognize that teaching sometimes must depart from scientific recipes, requiring improvisation and spontaneity (Gage, 1978).

As a science, educational psychology's aim is to provide you with research knowledge that you can effectively apply to teaching situations. But your teaching will still remain an art. In addition to what you can learn from research, you will also continually make important judgments in the classroom based on your personal skills and experiences, as well as the accumulated wisdom of other teachers.

Through the Eyes of Students

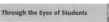

A Good Teacher

Mike, Grade 2:

A good teacher is a teacher that does stuff that catches your interest. Sometimes you start learning and you don't even realize it. A good teacher is a teacher that does stuff that makes you think. (Nikola-Lisa & Burnaford, 1994)

American Psychological Association (APA)
American Educational Research Association (AERA)

Review and Reflect

1 Describe some basic ideas about the field of educational psychology, including its history and why effective teaching depends on both art and science.

Review
- How is educational psychology defined? Who were some key thinkers in the history of educational psychology and what were their ideas?
- How would you describe the roles of art and science in the practice of teaching?

Reflect
- John Dewey argued that children should not sit quietly in their seats and learn in a rote manner. Do you agree with Dewey? Why or why not?

Through the Eyes of Students

This feature provides stimulating comments from students about their attitudes and feelings related to the chapter's content.

Review and Reflect

This important new feature, which appears at the end of each major section of a chapter, is linked to the learning goals stated at the beginning of the chapter. The learning goal for the section is restated and then questions stimulate you to review the main ideas of the section that you have just read. Then you are asked to use your critical thinking skills to reflect on a topic related to the section.

Video Lecture: Cognitive Variations

tests are useful and fair. They also argue about whether such tests should be used to place students in special classes or tracks. Educational psychologists debate whether we have a general mental capacity or a number of specific mental capacities. Also, if we have various mental capacities, what are they? How many do we have?

Twentieth-century English novelist Aldous Huxley said that children are remarkable for their curiosity and intelligence. What did Huxley mean when he used the word *intelligence*? Intelligence is one of our most prized possessions, yet even the most intelligent people have not been able to agree on what intelligence is. Unlike height, weight, and age, intelligence cannot be directly measured. You can't peer into a student's head and observe the intelligence going on inside. We only can evaluate a student's intelligence indirectly by studying the student's intelligent acts. For the most part, we have relied on written intelligence tests to provide an estimate of a student's intelligence.

Some experts describe intelligence as problem-solving skills. Others describe it as the ability to adapt to and learn from life's everyday experiences. Combining these ideas we can arrive at a fairly traditional definition of **intelligence**: problem-solving skills and the ability to adapt to and learn from life's everyday experiences. But even this broad definition doesn't satisfy everyone. As you will see shortly, some theorists propose that musical skills should be considered part of intelligence. Also, a definition of intelligence based on a theory such as Vygotsky's would have to include the ability to use the tools of the culture with help from more-skilled individuals. Page 51. Because intelligence is such

intelligence Problem-solving skills and the ability to adapt to and learn from life's everyday experiences.

106

Cross-Linkage

This is a system that refers you back to the main discussion of key concepts each time that they are introduced later in the text, which provides you with a more integrated learning experience across chapters and serves as an excellent study aid.

Technology and Education

This box occurs once in each chapter and highlights important issues involving how technology can be used to improve education.

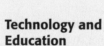

Technology and Education

Technology and Children's Vocabulary Development

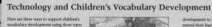

Here are three ways to support children's vocabulary development using three types of technology (Miller, 2001).

Computers
CD-ROMs of stories, such as *Living Books*, can promote children's vocabulary development, especially when there is an online option for students to find the meaning of unfamiliar words. Using the computer for listening to and watching stories can be part of a student's reading center rotations, reading assignment, or an option during choice time. Learning new words can be enhanced if teachers plan a way for students to keep track of new words. For example, students can record new words in a portfolio for future reference.

A recent analysis of software products for children's vocabulary development offered the following guidelines (Wood, 2001):

1. *Relate the new to the known.* New vocabulary words are presented in a way that builds on students' previously acquired word knowledge; students are encouraged to map new word meanings onto their own experiences.
2. *Promote active, in-depth processing.* Students are motivated to construct the meanings of words rather than being taught through rote memorization of word meanings. This involves introducing a synonym for the new word or showing how it relates to a particular context; helping students apply their understanding of the word to a particular context; and challenging children to use the new word in a novel way to illustrate their understanding of its meaning.
3. *Encourage reading.* Reading promotes vocabulary development. It is important for software that promotes vocabulary

development to motivate students to extend their learning through reading.

Audiobooks
Teachers can create listening centers to support vocabulary development. Listening centers should include tape recorders, headphones, audiobooks, and corresponding literature. Audiobooks can be used to supplement printed materials, listen to dramatization of stories, and pique student interest. Audiobooks may especially benefit students with special needs (Casbergue & Harris, 1996). For example, students whose primary language is not English can use tapes to improve vocabulary development, reading, and pronunciation. Weak readers can use the tapes to contribute to literature discussions in class even though they may be reading less-complex materials.

Educational Television
Educational television can be used to help children learn the alphabet, to see people using vocabulary in different contexts, and to hear stories that will motivate children to read these stories later (Lesser, 1989). One such program is *Reading Rainbow*. In one study, it was found that this program increases children's vocabulary and literacy (Wood & Duke, 1997). The show helps children to expand their vocabularies by introducing many potentially unfamiliar words per episode, linking the words by theme, creating rich contexts when using the words, clearly and directly explaining the meanings of new words, and linking new words in playful ways.

In a classic experiment that was designed to study children's understanding of morphological rules, Jean Berko (1958) presented preschool children and first-grade children with cards such as the one shown in figure 2.14. Children were asked to look at the card while the experimenter read aloud the words on the card. Then the children were asked to supply the missing word. This might sound easy, but Berko was interested not just in the children's ability to recall the right word but also in their ability to say it "correctly" (with the ending that was dictated by the morphological rules). "Wugs" would be the correct response for the card in figure 2.14.

Although the children's answers were not perfect, they were much better than chance. Moreover, the children demonstrated their knowledge of morphological rules, not only with plural forms of nouns ("There are two wugs") but with possessive forms of nouns and the third-person singular and past-tense forms of verbs. What makes Berko's study impressive is that most of the words were made up for the experiment. Thus, the children could not base their responses on remembering past instances of hearing the words. Instead, they were forced to rely on *rules*.

Young children also learn to manipulate syntax. They can generate questions, passives, clauses, and all the major syntactical structure of their language.

60

END OF CHAPTER

Crack the Case The Curriculum Decision

Mrs. Jefferson felt frustrated when teaching the social studies curriculum that her school district had used for the past eight years. The manner in which the material was presented bothered her. The books were not very exciting and didn't hold the students' interest. The print was small; there were few pictures, charts, maps, or graphs. The material itself bothered her also. It was ethnocentric and said little about the accomplishments of women. In addition, the teacher's guide didn't offer much besides worksheets and test items. The district had a policy of replacing curriculum materials every ten years. "This is the year to start looking," she thought. "I really want some input into this decision."

She talked to her principal, who told her that a committee of five teachers and one administrator was being established to look into various social studies curricula that would cover the entire grade span of the school. Mrs. Jefferson asked to be a part of the committee. "That's great," replied the principal. "Now we'll have a representative from each grade level and special education. I know you'll be a valuable part of the committee."

At the first committee meeting, Mrs. Jefferson was a bit overwhelmed by what some of the other teachers were saying. One saw no point in buying a new curriculum "because, after all, history doesn't change and we can always supplement with current events material." Another teacher wanted a curriculum that had no actual textbooks but had guidelines to several projects students could complete. He had read an article in a popular magazine touting this type of curriculum. Yet another teacher wanted to purchase a new version of the very same curriculum they had been using because if they bought something entirely different she would have to revamp her teaching, which would be "an incredible task." The administrator told the rest of the committee that they had one year to make their decision. "That way all the materials can be ordered and each teacher will have some time to become familiar with the material before implementing it," she said.

The committee called various publishers of social studies curricular materials and asked for preview copies of their materials. They were sent a veritable cornucopia of textbooks and ancillary materials, including reading lists, workbooks, instructor's guides, test banks, and CD-ROMs. Wading through all the materials to make a decision that would impact students for a decade seemed like a monumental task. However, Mrs. Jefferson and her colleagues were determined to choose the right curriculum for their students. In order to do this, they decided that they would need to engage in considerable research. "It's a good thing we have a year to do this in," thought Mrs. Jefferson.

- How would you go about engaging in the research necessary to make a good decision regarding what curriculum to purchase?
- What issues would need to be considered? Why?
- What type(s) of research would be appropriate? Why?
- What design would you use? Why?
- If you decided to use an experimental design, identify the independent and dependent variables.
- Considering the design that you chose, could you infer cause and effect? Why/why not?

Crack the Case

A new feature in this edition, Crack the Case presents a full-page case study related to the chapter's content after the last Review and Reflect section and before the chapter's summary. The case study gives you a chance to apply what you have learned in the chapter to a real-world teaching issue or problem in the classroom. At the end of each case study, you are asked a series of questions to reflect on and think critically about related to the case.

Reach Your Learning Goals

At the end of the chapter, you will find each learning goal restated. Then under each learning goal, a summary is presented of the main ideas related to each of the questions that you were asked in the Review sections earlier in the chapter.

Key Terms

All of the chapter's key terms are listed in the order in which they appear in the chapter, along with the page numbers where they appeared. The key terms also are listed alphabetically, defined, and page-referenced in the Glossary at the end of the book.

Portfolio Activities

A new feature in this edition of the book, four activities related to the chapter's content were created. Depending on your instructor's requirements, you may be asked to write about these educational circumstances in a portfolio and/or discuss them with other students.

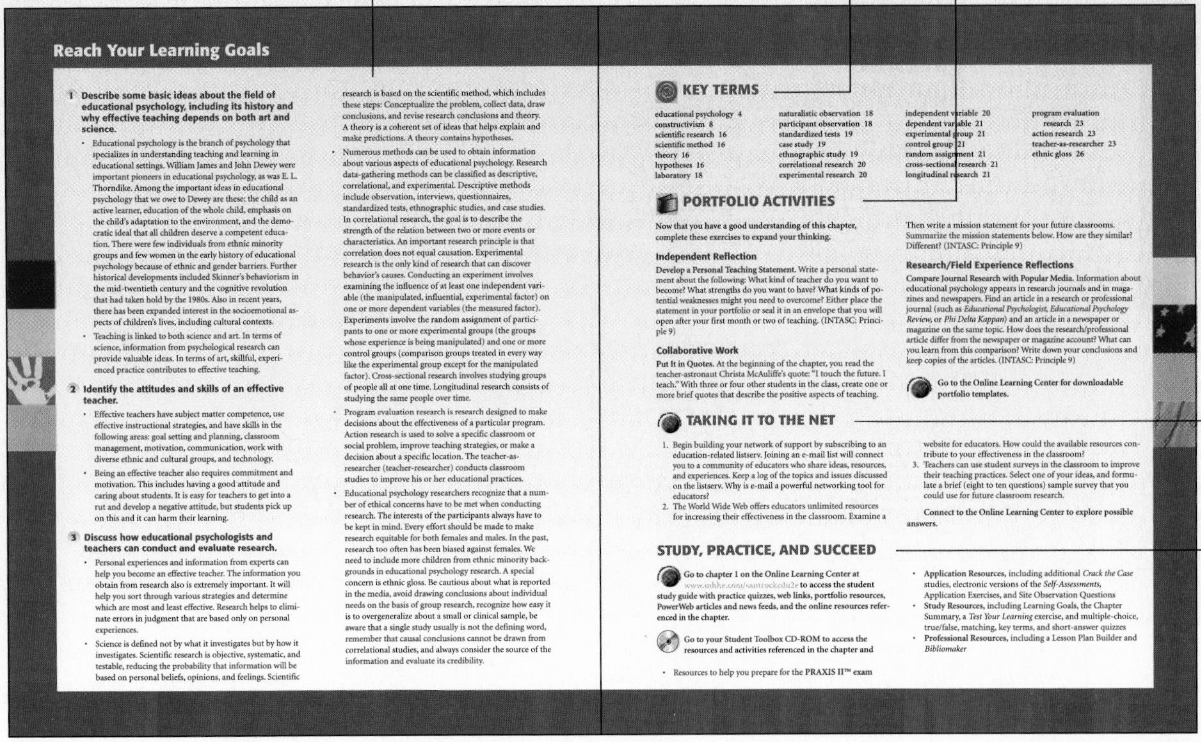

Reach Your Learning Goals

1 Describe some basic ideas about the field of educational psychology, including its history and why effective teaching depends on both art and science.

- Educational psychology is the branch of psychology that specializes in understanding teaching and learning in educational settings. William James and John Dewey were important pioneers in educational psychology, as was E. L. Thorndike. Among the important ideas in educational psychology that we owe to Dewey are these: the child as an active learner, education of the whole child, emphasis on the child's adaptation to the environment, and the democratic ideal that all children deserve a competent education. There were few individuals from ethnic minority groups and few women in the early history of educational psychology because of ethnic and gender barriers. Further historical developments included Skinner's behaviorism in the mid-twentieth century and the cognitive revolution that had taken hold by the 1980s. Also in recent years, there has been expanded interest in the socioemotional aspects of children's lives, including cultural contexts.
- Teaching is linked to both science and art. In terms of science, information from psychological research can provide valuable ideas. In terms of art, skillful, experienced practice contributes to effective teaching.

2 Identify the attitudes and skills of an effective teacher.

- Effective teachers have subject matter competence, use effective instructional strategies, and have skills in the following areas: goal setting and planning, classroom management, motivation, communication, work with diverse ethnic and cultural groups, and technology.
- Being an effective teacher also requires commitment and motivation. This includes having a good attitude and caring about students. It is easy for teachers to get into a rut and develop a negative attitude, but students pick up on this and it can harm their learning.

3 Discuss how educational psychologists and teachers can conduct and evaluate research.

- Personal experiences and information from experts can help you become an effective teacher. The information you obtain from research also is extremely important. It will help you sort through various strategies and determine which are most and least effective. Research helps to eliminate errors in judgment that are based only on personal experiences.
- Science is defined not by what it investigates but by how it investigates. Scientific research is objective, systematic, and testable, reducing the probability that information will be based on personal beliefs, opinions, and feelings. Scientific research is based on the scientific method, which includes these steps: Conceptualize the problem, collect data, draw conclusions, and revise research conclusions and theory. A theory is a coherent set of ideas that helps explain and make predictions. A theory contains hypotheses.
- Numerous methods can be used to obtain information about various aspects of educational psychology. Research data-gathering methods can be classified as descriptive, correlational, and experimental. Descriptive methods include observation, interviews, questionnaires, standardized tests, ethnographic studies, and case studies. In correlational research, the goal is to describe the strength of the relation between two or more events or characteristics. An important research principle is that correlation does not equal causation. Experimental research is the only kind of research that can discover behavior's causes. Conducting an experiment involves examining the influence of at least one independent variable (the manipulated, influential, experimental factor) on one or more dependent variables (the measured factor). Experiments involve the random assignment of participants to one or more experimental groups (the groups whose experience is being manipulated) and one or more control groups (comparison groups treated in every way like the experimental group except for the manipulated factor). Cross-sectional research involves studying groups of people all at one time. Longitudinal research consists of studying the same people over time.
- Program evaluation research is research designed to make decisions about the effectiveness of a particular program. Action research is used to solve a specific classroom or social problem, improve teaching strategies, or make a decision about a specific location. The teacher-as-researcher (teacher-researcher) conducts classroom studies to improve his or her educational practices.
- Educational psychology researchers recognize that a number of ethical concerns have to be met when conducting research. The interests of the participants always have to be kept in mind. Every effort should be made to make research equitable for both females and males. In the past, research too often has been biased against females. We need to include more children from ethnic minority backgrounds in educational psychology research. A special concern is ethnic gloss. Be cautious about what is reported in the media, avoid drawing conclusions about individual needs on the basis of group research, recognize how easy it is to overgeneralize about a small or clinical sample, be aware that a single study usually is not the defining word, remember that causal conclusions cannot be drawn from correlational studies, and always consider the source of the information and evaluate its credibility.

KEY TERMS

educational psychology 4	naturalistic observation 18	independent variable 20	program evaluation research 23
constructivism 8	participant observation 18	dependent variable 21	action research 23
scientific research 16	standardized tests 19	experimental group 21	teacher-as-researcher 23
scientific method 16	case study 19	control group 21	ethnic gloss 26
theory 16	ethnographic study 19	random assignment 21	
hypotheses 16	correlational research 20	cross-sectional research 21	
laboratory 18	experimental research 20	longitudinal research 21	

PORTFOLIO ACTIVITIES

Now that you have a good understanding of this chapter, complete these exercises to expand your thinking.

Independent Reflection

Develop a Personal Teaching Statement. Write a personal statement about the following: What kind of teacher do you want to become? What strengths do you want to have? What kinds of potential weaknesses might you need to overcome? Either place the statement in your portfolio or seal it in an envelope that you will open after your first month or two of teaching. (INTASC: Principle 9)

Collaborative Work

Put It in Quotes. At the beginning of the chapter, you read the teacher-astronaut Christa McAuliffe's quote: "I touch the future. I teach." With three or four other students in the class, create one or more brief quotes that describe the positive aspects of teaching. Then write a mission statement for your future classrooms. Summarize the mission statements below. How are they similar? Different? (INTASC: Principle 9)

Research/Field Experience Reflections

Compare Journal Research with Popular Media. Information about educational psychology appears in research journals and in magazines and newspapers. Find an article in a research or professional journal (such as *Educational Psychologist, Educational Psychology Review,* or *Phi Delta Kappan*) and an article in a newspaper or magazine on the same topic. How does the research/professional article differ from the newspaper or magazine account? What can you learn from this comparison? Write down your conclusions and keep copies of the articles. (INTASC: Principle 9)

Go to the Online Learning Center for downloadable portfolio templates.

TAKING IT TO THE NET

1. Begin building your network of support by subscribing to an education-related listserv. Joining an e-mail list will connect you to a community of educators who share ideas, resources, and experiences. Keep a log of the topics and issues discussed on the listserv. Why is e-mail a powerful networking tool for educators?
2. The World Wide Web offers educators unlimited resources for increasing their effectiveness in the classroom. Examine a website for educators. How could the available resources contribute to your effectiveness in the classroom?
3. Teachers can use student surveys in the classroom to improve their teaching practices. Select one of your ideas, and formulate a brief (eight to ten questions) sample survey that you could use for future classroom research.

Connect to the Online Learning Center to explore possible answers.

STUDY, PRACTICE, AND SUCCEED

Go to chapter 1 on the Online Learning Center at www.mhhe.com/santrockedu2e **to access the student study guide with practice quizzes, web links, portfolio resources, PowerWeb articles and news feeds, and the online resources referenced in the chapter.**

Go to your Student Toolbox CD-ROM to access the resources and activities referenced in the chapter and

- Resources to help you prepare for the **PRAXIS II™ exam**
- **Application Resources,** including additional *Crack the Case* studies, electronic versions of the *Self-Assessments,* Application Exercises, and Site Observation Questions
- **Study Resources,** including Learning Goals, the Chapter Summary, a *Test Your Learning* exercise, and multiple-choice, true/false, matching, key terms, and short-answer quizzes
- **Professional Resources,** including a Lesson Plan Builder and *Bibliomaker*

Taking It to the Net

You are presented with questions related to the chapter that you can explore on the Internet. You will find links to the websites listed in the activities under Taking It to the Net on the Santrock *Educational Psychology* website. These links will help you to think more deeply about the questions posed.

Study, Practice, and Succeed

This feature describes the various supplemental tools that you can use to master each chapter's content.

OVERVIEW OF THE LEARNING GOALS SYSTEM

As you have just seen, the Learning Goals system is integrated throughout the chapter. At the beginning of the chapter, you will see an outline with the three to six main learning goals aligned with the main headings of the chapter. After each of the main sections of the chapter, you will come across a Review and Reflect feature, which restates the main learning goal for the section and asks you a series of questions in bulleted form to encourage you to review the main ideas in the section you have just read. You also will be asked to think critically about an issue or a topic in the Reflect section. At the end of the chapter, Reach Your Learning Goals provides a summary of the main ideas in the chapter tied to the learning goals stated at the beginning of the chapter and in the Review and Reflect sections. The summary information appears in bulleted form under each learning goal and essentially answers the bulleted questions in each of the chapter's Review sections. The illustrations shown here are actual pages from the book to give you an idea of what the learning system looks like.

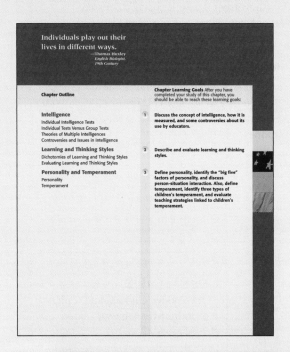

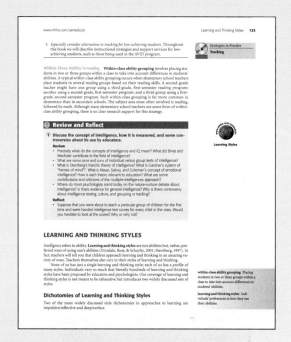

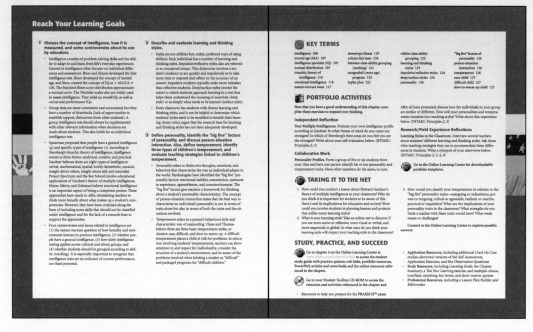

TEACHING STRATEGIES

This practical feature provides specific, research-based strategies for the classroom to prepare you to apply the theories and information covered in the chapter.

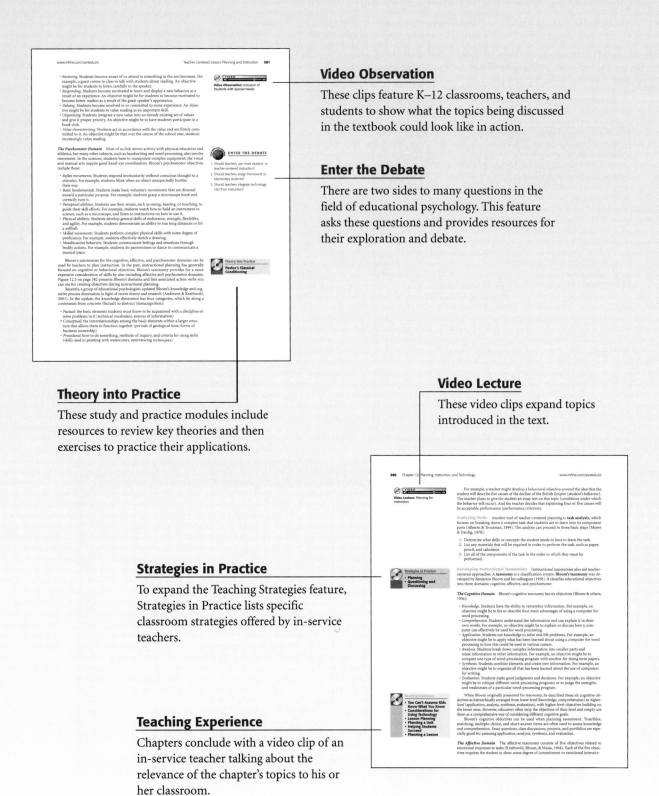

Video Observation

These clips feature K–12 classrooms, teachers, and students to show what the topics being discussed in the textbook could look like in action.

Enter the Debate

There are two sides to many questions in the field of educational psychology. This feature asks these questions and provides resources for their exploration and debate.

Theory into Practice

These study and practice modules include resources to review key theories and then exercises to practice their applications.

Video Lecture

These video clips expand topics introduced in the text.

Strategies in Practice

To expand the Teaching Strategies feature, Strategies in Practice lists specific classroom strategies offered by in-service teachers.

Teaching Experience

Chapters conclude with a video clip of an in-service teacher talking about the relevance of the chapter's topics to his or her classroom.

Educational Psychology

1 Educational Psychology: A Tool for Effective Teaching

> I touch the future. I teach.
>
> —Christa McAuliffe
> *American Educator
> and Astronaut,
> 20th Century*

Chapter Learning Goals After you have completed your study of this chapter, you should be able to reach these learning goals:

1 Describe some basic ideas about the field of educational psychology, including its history and why effective teaching depends on both art and science.

2 Identify the attitudes and skills of an effective teacher.

3 Discuss how educational psychologists and teachers can conduct and evaluate research.

Teaching Stories Margaret Metzger

Margaret Metzger has been an English teacher at Brookline (Massachusetts) High School for more than 25 years. Following is some advice she gave to a student teacher she was supervising:

Emphasize *how* to learn, rather than *what* to learn. Students may never know a particular fact, but they always will need to know how to learn. Teach students how to read with a genuine comprehension, how to shape an idea, how to master difficult material, how to use writing to clarify thinking. A former student, Anastasia Korniaris, wrote to me, "Your class was like a hardware store. All the tools were there. Years later I'm still using that hardware store that's in my head. . . ."

Include students in the process of teaching and learning. Every day ask such basic questions as, "What did you think of this homework? Did it help you learn the material? Was the assignment too long or too short? How can we make the next assignment more interesting? What should the criteria for assessment be?" Remember that we want students to take ownership of their learning. . . .

Useful research has been conducted lately on learning styles and frames of intelligence. Read that research. The basic idea to keep in mind is that students should think for themselves. Your job is to teach them how to think and to give them the necessary tools. Your students will be endlessly amazed at how intelligent they are. You don't need to show them how intelligent you are. . . .

In the early years of teaching you must expect to put in hours and hours of time. You would invest similarly long hours if you were an intern in medical school or an associate in a law firm. Like other professionals, teachers work much longer hours than outsiders know. . . .

Here are four final bits of advice. I've failed at all four of them for years—except the last one, which has kept me sane. When I follow my own advice, my teaching life feels happier:

1. Sign up for season tickets to cultural events. Schedule regular social events with friends.
2. Hunt for a place to work. Try to get your own classroom. Moving all your belongings every 50 minutes will drive you crazy.
3. Try to stay out of petty politics. There is more squabbling in schools than you can imagine.
4. Find a friend with a sense of humor. . . .

You have the potential to be an excellent teacher. My only concern is that you not exhaust yourself before you begin. Naturally, you will want to work very hard as you learn the craft.

(Source: Metzger, 1996, pp. 346–351).

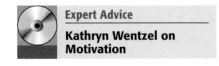

Expert Advice

Kathryn Wentzel on Motivation

In the quotation that opens this chapter, twentieth-century teacher and astronaut Christa McAuliffe commented that when she touched the future, she taught. As a teacher, you will touch the future because children are the future of any society. In this chapter, we will explore what the field of educational psychology is all about and how it can help you positively contribute to children's futures.

EXPLORING EDUCATIONAL PSYCHOLOGY

Psychology is the scientific study of behavior and mental processes. **Educational psychology** is the branch of psychology that specializes in understanding teaching and learning in educational settings. Educational psychology is a vast landscape that will take us an entire book to describe.

Historical Background

The field of educational psychology was founded by several pioneers in psychology just before the start of the twentieth century. Three pioneers stand out in the early history of educational psychology.

William James   Soon after launching the first psychology textbook, *Principles of Psychology* (1890), William James (1842–1910) gave a series of lectures called "Talks to Teachers" (James, 1899/1993) in which he discussed the applications of psychology to educating children. James argued that laboratory psychology experiments often can't tell us how to effectively teach children. He emphasized the importance of observing teaching and learning in classrooms for improving education. One of his recommendations was to start lessons at a point just beyond the child's level of knowledge and understanding, in order to stretch the child's mind.

educational psychology The branch of psychology that specializes in understanding teaching and learning in educational settings.

John Dewey A second major figure in shaping the field of educational psychology was John Dewey (1859–1952), who became a driving force in the practical application of psychology. Dewey established the first major educational psychology laboratory in the United States, at the University of Chicago in 1894. Later, at Columbia University, he continued his innovative work. We owe many important ideas to John Dewey (Glassman, 2001). First, we owe to him the view of the child as an active learner. Before Dewey it was believed that children should sit quietly in their seats and passively learn in a rote manner. In contrast, Dewey believed that children learn best by doing. Second, we owe to Dewey the idea that education should focus on the whole child and emphasize the child's adaptation to the environment. Dewey believed that children should not be just narrowly educated in academic topics but should learn how to think and adapt to a world outside school. He especially thought that children should learn how to be reflective problem solvers. Third, we owe to Dewey the belief that all children deserve to have a competent education. This democratic ideal was not in place at the beginning of Dewey's career in the latter part of the nineteenth century, when quality education was reserved for a small portion of children, especially boys from wealthy families. Dewey was one of the influential psychologists—educators who pushed for a competent education for all children—girls and boys, as well as children from different socioeconomic and ethnic groups.

E. L. Thorndike A third pioneer was E. L. Thorndike (1874–1949), who initiated an emphasis on assessment and measurement and promoted the scientific underpinnings of learning. Thorndike argued that one of schooling's most important tasks is to hone children's reasoning skills, and he excelled at doing exacting scientific studies of teaching and learning (Beatty, 1998). Thorndike especially promoted the idea that educational psychology must have a scientific base and that it should focus strongly on measurement (O'Donnell & Levin, 2001).

Diversity and Early Educational Psychology The most prominent figures in the early history of educational psychology, as in most disciplines, were mainly White males, such as James, Dewey, and Thorndike. Prior to changes in civil rights laws and policies in

William James
John Dewey

William James   *John Dewey*   *E. L. Thorndike*

James, Dewey, and Thorndike created and shaped the field of educational psychology. *What were their ideas about educational psychology?*

George Sanchez   *Mamie and Kenneth Clark*   *Leta Hollingworth*

Like other disciplines, educational psychology had few ethnic minority individuals and women involved in its early history. These individuals were among the few people from such backgrounds to overcome barriers and contribute to the field.

Video Lecture: Educational
Psychology and Learning

the 1960s, only a few dedicated non-White individuals managed to obtain the necessary degrees and break through the barriers of racial exclusion to take up research in the field (Banks, 1998).

Two pioneering African American psychologists were Mamie and Kenneth Clark, who conducted research on African American children's self-conceptions and identity (Clark & Clark, 1939). In 1971, Kenneth Clark became the first African American president of the American Psychological Association. In 1932, Latino psychologist George Sanchez conducted research showing that intelligence tests were culturally biased against ethnic minority children.

Like ethnic minorities, women also faced barriers in higher education and so have only gradually become prominent contributors to psychological research. One often overlooked person in the history of educational psychology is Leta Hollingworth. She was the first individual to use the term *gifted* to describe children who scored exceptionally high on intelligence tests (Hollingworth, 1916).

Further Historical Developments   Thorndike's approach to the study of learning guided educational psychology through the first half of the twentieth century. In American psychology, B. F. Skinner's (1938) view, which built on Thorndike's ideas, strongly influenced educational psychology in the middle of the century. Skinner's behavioral approach, which will be described in detail in chapter 7, involved attempts to precisely determine the best conditions for learning. Skinner argued that the mental processes proposed by psychologists such as James and Dewey were not observable and therefore could not be appropriate subject matter for a scientific study of psychology, which he defined as the science of observable behavior and its controlling conditions. In the 1950s, Skinner (1954) developed the concept of *programmed learning*, which involved reinforcing the student after each of a series of steps until the student reached a learning goal. In an early technological effort, he created a teaching machine to serve as a tutor and reinforce students for correct answers (Skinner, 1958).

However, the objectives that were so clearly spelled out in the behavioral approach to learning did not address many of the actual goals and needs of classroom educators (Hilgard, 1996). In reaction, as early as the 1950s, Benjamin Bloom created a taxonomy of cognitive skills that included remembering, comprehending, synthesizing, and evaluating, which he believed teachers should help students use and develop (Bloom & Krathwohl, 1956). A review chapter in the *Annual Review of Psychology* (Wittrock & Lumsdaine, 1977) stated, "A cognitive perspective implies that a behavioral analysis of instruction is often inadequate to explain the effects of instruction on learning." The cognitive revolution in psychology began to take hold by the 1980s and ushered in a great deal of enthusiasm for applying the concepts of cognitive psychology—memory, thinking, reasoning, and so on—to helping students learn. Thus, toward the latter part of the twentieth century, many educational psychologists returned to an emphasis on the cognitive aspects of learning advocated by James and Dewey at the beginning of the century.

Both cognitive and behavioral approaches continue to be a part of educational psychology today. We will have much more to say about these approaches in chapters 7 through 11.

In the last several decades of the twentieth century, educational psychologists also increasingly focused on the socioemotional aspects of students' lives. For example, they analyzed the school as a social context and examined the role of culture in education. We will explore the socioemotional aspects of teaching and learning in many chapters of the book.

Through the Eyes of Students

A Good Teacher

Mike, Grade 2:

> A good teacher is a teacher that does stuff that catches your interest. Sometimes you start learning and you don't even realize it. A good teacher is a teacher that does stuff that makes you think. (Nikola-Lisa & Burnaford, 1994)

Teaching: Art and Science

How scientific can a teacher be in his or her approach to teaching? Both science and the art of skillful, experienced practice play important roles in a teacher's success (Arends, 2004; Freiberg & Driscoll, 2005; Johnson & others, 2002).

The field of educational psychology draws much of its knowledge from broader theory and research in psychology. For example, the theories of Jean Piaget and Lev Vygotsky were not created in an effort to inform teachers about ways to educate children, yet in chapter 2, "Cognitive and Language Development," you will see that both of these theories have many applications that can guide your teaching. The field also draws from theory and research more directly created and conducted by educational psychologists, and from the practical experiences of teachers. For example, in chapter 13, "Motivation, Teaching, and Learning," you will read about Dale Schunk's (2004; Schunk & Ertmer, 2000) classroom-oriented research on self-efficacy (the belief that one can master a situation and produce positive outcomes). Educational psychologists also recognize that teaching sometimes must depart from scientific recipes, requiring improvisation and spontaneity (Gage, 1978).

As a science, educational psychology's aim is to provide you with research knowledge that you can effectively apply to teaching situations. But your teaching will still remain an art. In addition to what you can learn from research, you will also continually make important judgments in the classroom based on your personal skills and experiences, as well as the accumulated wisdom of other teachers.

www.mhhe.com/santedu2e

American Psychological Association (APA)

American Educational Research Association (AERA)

! Review and Reflect

1 Describe some basic ideas about the field of educational psychology, including its history and why effective teaching depends on both art and science.

Review
- How is educational psychology defined? Who were some key thinkers in the history of educational psychology and what were their ideas?
- How would you describe the roles of art and science in the practice of teaching?

Reflect
- John Dewey argued that children should not sit quietly in their seats and learn in a rote manner. Do you agree with Dewey? Why or why not?

EFFECTIVE TEACHING

Because of the complexity of teaching and individual variation among students, effective teaching is not like the "one-size-fits-all" sock (Diaz, 1997). Teachers must master a variety of perspectives and strategies and be flexible in their application. This requires two key ingredients: (1) professional knowledge and skills and (2) commitment and motivation.

Professional Knowledge and Skills

Effective teachers have good command of their subject matter and a solid core of teaching skills. They have excellent instructional strategies supported by methods of goal setting, instructional planning, and classroom management. They know how to motivate, communicate, and work effectively with students from culturally diverse backgrounds. They also understand how to use appropriate levels of technology in the classroom.

Subject Matter Competence   In the last decade, in their wish lists of teacher characteristics, secondary school students have increasingly mentioned "teacher knowledge of their subjects" (NASSP, 1997). Having a thoughtful, flexible, conceptual understanding of subject matter is indispensable for being an effective teacher. Of course, knowledge of subject matter includes much more than just facts, terms, and general concepts. It also includes knowledge about organizing ideas, connections among ideas, ways of thinking and arguing, patterns of change within a discipline, beliefs about a discipline, and the ability to carry ideas from one discipline to another.

Instructional Strategies   The principle of constructivism was at the center of William James' and John Dewey's philosophies of education. **Constructivism** emphasizes that individuals actively construct knowledge and understanding. In the constructivist view, teachers should not attempt to simply pour information into children's minds. Rather, children should be encouraged to explore their world, discover knowledge, reflect, and think critically (Ambrose, 2004; Brooks & Brooks, 2001; Magolda, 2004). Increasingly, the trend in educational reform is to teach from a constructivist perspective (Hickey, Moore, & Pellegrino, 2001). The constructivist belief is that for too long in American education children have been required to sit still, be passive learners, and rotely memorize irrelevant as well as relevant information (Henson, 2004).

Today, constructivism may include an emphasis on collaboration—children working with each other in their efforts to know and understand (Gauvain, 2001; Pontecorvo, 2004). A teacher with a constructivist instructional philosophy would not have children memorize information rotely but would give them opportunities to meaningfully construct the knowledge and understand the material (Ornstein, Lasley, & Mindes, 2005).

However, not everyone embraces the constructivist view. Some traditional educators believe that the teacher should direct and control children's learning more than the constructivist view implies. They also believe that constructivists often don't focus enough on basic academic tasks or have sufficiently high expectations for children's achievement. Some experts in educational psychology believe that whether you follow the current trend in educational reform and teach more from a constructivist perspective or adopt a more traditional direct-instruction approach, you can be an effective teacher. As you will see in the rest of our journey through evaluating what makes a teacher effective, many other domains and issues are involved.

Goal-Setting and Instructional Planning Skills   Whether constructivist or more traditional, effective teachers don't just "wing it" in the classroom. They set high goals for their teaching and organize plans for reaching those goals (Pintrich & Schunk, 2002). They also develop specific criteria for success. They spend considerable time in instructional planning, organizing their lessons to maximize students' learning. As they plan,

**Educator's Reference
Desk: Teaching**

National Library of Education

**National Center for
Research on Teacher Learning**

**Constructivist Teaching
and Learning**

Constructivism

Schools for Thought

constructivism An approach to learning which emphasizes that individuals actively construct knowledge and understanding.

effective teachers reflect and think about how they can make learning both challenging and interesting.

Classroom Management Skills An important aspect of being an effective teacher is being able to keep the class as a whole working together and oriented toward classroom tasks. Effective teachers establish and maintain an environment in which learning can occur. To create this optimal learning environment, teachers need a repertoire of strategies for establishing rules and procedures, organizing groups, monitoring and pacing classroom activities, and handling misbehavior (Charles, 2005; Jones & Jones, 2004; Larrivee, 2005; Martella, Nelson, & Marchand-Martella, 2003).

Motivational Skills Effective teachers have good strategies for helping students become self-motivated to learn (Alderman, 2004; Stipek, 2002). Educational psychologists increasingly believe that this is best accomplished by providing real-world learning opportunities that are of optimal difficulty and novelty for each student (Brophy, 2004). Effective teachers know that students are motivated when they can make choices that are in line with their personal interests. Such teachers give them the opportunity to think creatively and deeply about projects (Starko, 2005).

Communication Skills Also indispensable to teaching are skills in speaking, listening, overcoming barriers to verbal communication, tuning in to students' nonverbal communication, and constructively resolving conflicts. Communication skills are critical not only in teaching but also in interacting with parents. Effective teachers use good communication skills when they talk "with" rather than "to" students, parents, administrators, and others; keep criticism at a minimum; and have an assertive rather than aggressive, manipulative, or passive communication style (Alberti & Emmons, 1995; Evertson, Emmer, & Worsham, 2003). Effective teachers work to improve students' communication skills as well (Powell & Caseau, 2004). This is especially important because communication skills have been rated as the skills most sought after by today's employers (Collins, 1996).

Working Effectively with Students from Culturally Diverse Backgrounds Today, one of every five children in the United States is from an immigrant family and by 2040 one of every three U.S. children is projected to fit this description (Suarez-Orozco, 2002). Nearly 80 percent of the new immigrants are "people of color," arriving from Latin America, Asia, and the Caribbean. Approximately 75 percent of the new immigrants are of Spanish-speaking origin, although children speaking more than 100 different languages are entering U.S. schools (OBLEMA, 2000).

In today's world of increasing intercultural contact, effective teachers are knowledgeable about people from different cultural backgrounds and are sensitive to their needs (Cushner, 2003; Spring, 2004, 2005; Tozer, Senese, & Violas, 2005). Effective teachers encourage students to have positive personal contact with diverse students and think of ways to create such settings. They guide students in thinking critically about cultural and ethnic issues, and they forestall or reduce bias, cultivate acceptance, and serve as cultural mediators (Banks, 2001, 2002; Sheets, 2005). An effective teacher also needs to be a broker, or middle person, between the culture of the school and the culture of certain students, especially those who are unsuccessful academically (Diaz, 1997).

Through the Eyes of Teachers

The "Turtle Lady"

Susan Bradburn teaches grades 4 to 6 at West Marian Elementary School in North Carolina. She created a school museum in which students conduct research and create exhibitions. She has put her school museum concept "on wheels" by having students take carts to other classes and into the community, and she has used award money to spread the use of mobile museums to other North Carolina schools. Nicknamed "the turtle lady" because of her interest in turtles and other animals, Susan takes students on three-day field trips to Edisto Island, South Carolina, to search for fossils and study coastal ecology. Her students sell calendars that contain their original poetry and art, and they use the proceeds to buy portions of a rain forest so it won't be destroyed.

Susan Bradburn *(left)* with several students at West Marian Elementary School.

"My mom told me to tell you that I am the educational challenge you were told about in college."
Reprinted by permission of Heiser Zedonek.

What are some important aspects of professional knowledge and skills that make up effective teaching?

Cultural questions that competent teachers are sensitive to include (Pang, 2005):

• Do I recognize the power and complexity of cultural influences on students?
• Are my expectations for my students culturally based or biased?
• Am I doing a good job of seeing life from the perspective of my students who come from different cultures than mine?
• Am I teaching the skills students may need to talk in class if their culture is one in which they have little opportunity to practice "public" talking?

The Diversity and Education interlude further explores the cultural aspects of schools.

Diversity and Education
The Cultural School

Valerie Pang is a professor in the School of Teacher Education of San Diego State University and formerly an elementary school teacher. Valerie believes it is important for teachers to create a caring classroom that affirms all students.

Valerie Pang (2005), an expert on cultural issues in schools, believes that many teachers don't adequately take into account the cultural context of the school and cultural backgrounds that students bring to the classroom. They may not share the same cultural experiences as many of the students in their classes because the teachers live in neighborhoods far from the school in which they teach. The teachers and students also may have grown up in very different cultures. Pang (2005) says that it is important for teachers to become more familiar with the neighborhood in which the school is located if they live outside of it. They might shop at neighborhood stores, get to know the community leaders in the school area, and read community newspapers. In this way, teachers can become more in tune with the rhythm and culture of their students. Pang also recommends that teachers bring examples from the children's lives into their teaching. Though textbook teacher editions can be good sources for information about learning objectives and content that need to be taught, only the teacher can bring local, cultural meaning to such objectives and content.

An example of bringing local, cultural meaning into the classroom involves a high school social studies classroom in San Diego in which the teacher invited Dr. Dorothy Smith, an African American, to speak to her class. Dr. Smith is a college professor and community leader (she was formerly chair of the San Diego School Board) in the area where the school is located. Dr. Smith was asked to talk about issues that the students and parents are dealing with as citizens. She brought up many issues: What does it mean to be an African American? How important is it to go to college? How can I make a contribution to my neighborhood?

In preparation, the students developed interview questions to ask Dr. Smith. Also, one group of students videotaped her discussion so that the interview could be shown to other classes. Another group took notes and wrote an article about her talk for the student newspaper.

When students are given the opportunity to meet people like Dr. Smith, they are provided not only with important cultural role models but also with connections to the culture of the neighborhood they know.

Through the Eyes of Teachers

Paul August, Finding Individuality in Diversity

Paul August taught for six years in an integrated school but says that expereince did not adequately prepare him, a non-Latino White, for teaching in an all African American school. Initially, he perceived the African American students as looking alike. However, at the end of the school year, he realized how ridiculous this was and individuality had bloomed in his classroom both on his part and his students. He no longer was seen by his students as a White guy but as a teacher.

Later, when Paul was transferred to teach in a predominately Asian American school, he says that he regressed into the "they all look alike" stereotype. Once again, though, over time individuality trumped nationality and he "could see the differences in faces, names, and cultures of Chinese, Vietnamese, Cambodians, Laotians, Japanese, and Mien" (August, 2002, p. A29).

Technological Skills   Technology itself does not necessarily improve students' ability to learn. Other conditions are also necessary to create learning environments that support students' learning (Bitter & Pierson, 2005; Sharp, 2005; Ullman, 2005). These conditions include vision and support from educational leaders; teachers skilled in using technology for learning; content standards and curriculum resources; assessment of effectiveness of technology for learning; and an emphasis on the child as an active, constructive learner (International Society for Technology in Education, 2001).

Effective teachers develop their technological skills and integrate computers appropriately into classroom learning (Lockard & Abrams, 2004; Male, 2003). This integration should match up with students' learning needs, including the need to prepare for tomorrow's jobs, many of which will require technological expertise and computer-based skills.

Effective teachers know how to use computers and how to teach students to use computers for discovery and writing, can evaluate the effectiveness of instructional games and computer simulations, know how to use and teach students to use computer-mediated communication resources such as the Internet, and are knowledgeable about various assistive devices to support the learning of students with disabilities.

National Educational Technology Standards (NETS) are being established by the International Society for Technology in Education (ISTE) (2000, 2001). These NETS are currently under development:

- Technology foundation standards for students, which describe what students should know about technology and be able to do with technology
- Standards for using technology in learning and teaching, which describe how technology should be used throughout the curriculum for teaching, learning, and instructional management
- Educational technology support standards, which describe systems, access, staff development, and support services that are needed to provide effective use of technology
- Standards for student assessment and evaluation of technology use, which describe various means of assessing student progress and evaluating the use of technology in learning and teaching

Technology can be effective in teaching. For example, students in a Chicago elementary school are exploring the history of Ice Age animals in Illinois. Using the Internet, they "travel" to the Illinois State Museum (200 miles away) and to the Brookfield Zoo (10 miles away) to gather information and talk with experts via two-way video. Then

Technology Standards in Education

Technology in Education

Schools and Communities

Not only is technology helping children learn more effectively in school, but it also is increasingly opening up schools to communities (Dick, Carey, & Carey, 2005). In many districts, students and parents can communicate with teachers and administrators through e-mail. Teachers can post students' work on Web pages. Some schools provide students with take-home laptop computers.

Better communication between parents and teachers is one goal of a state-funded Indiana program called the Buddy System. In this program, computers and modems are placed in the homes of 7,000 elementary school students, most of them in grades 4 and 5, for one or two years. The students' parents, many of whom had never been to their children's schools before, had to go to the schools to pick up the computer equipment and get training on how to use the computers. Many of the parents and teachers report that the computer connection has resulted in increased communication with each other.

A special concern is to enable students from low-income backgrounds to have adequate access to computers. The Foshay Learning Center, a K–12 public school in Los Angeles, has created eight satellite learning centers in low-income apartment complexes. Without leaving their buildings, students in this school can use the computers to get help with homework, learn about technology, and participate in active learning experiences. Such programs are especially important because, according to one survey, in 2001 only 31 percent of U.S. students from families with an income of $20,000 or less had a computer at home, compared with 89 percent of those whose family income was $75,000 or more (*National Center for Education Statistics*, 2003).

IBM recently created a Team Tech Volunteer program that will provide technology services to more than 2,500 health and human service agencies. The Team Tech program gives students opportunities to become volunteers in their community and provide technological services that can improve the education and learning of students. Do a thorough assessment of the businesses in your community. Like IBM, some might be willing to provide technological services and expertise for your classroom.

Through the Eyes of Students

"You Are the Coolest"

I just want to thank you for all the extra time you took to help me. You didn't have to do that but you did and I want to thank you for it. Thanks also for being straight up with me and not beating around the bush and for that you are the coolest. I'm sorry for the hard times I gave you. You take so much junk but through all that you stay calm and you are a great teacher.

Jessica, Seventh-Grade Student
Macon, Georgia
Letter to Chuck Rawls, Her Teacher, at the End of the School Year

they construct an electronic database and organize and analyze their findings. They share their findings in multimedia reports posted on a website called "Mastadons in Our Own Back Yard." To think further about schools, communities, and technology, see the Technology and Education box.

Commitment and Motivation

Being an effective teacher also requires commitment and motivation. This includes having a good attitude and caring about students.

Beginning teachers often report that the investment of time and effort needed to be an effective teacher is huge. Some teachers, even experienced ones, report that they have "no life" from September to June. Even putting in hours on evenings and weekends, in addition to all of the hours spent in the classroom, might still not be enough to get things done.

In the face of these demands, it is easy to become frustrated. Commitment and motivation help get effective teachers through the tough and frustrating moments of teaching. Effective teachers also have confidence in their own self-efficacy and don't let negative emotions diminish their motivation.

In any job it is easy to get into a rut and develop a negative attitude. Initial enthusiasm can turn into boredom. Each day, effective teachers bring a positive attitude and enthusiasm to the classroom. These qualities are contagious and help make the classroom a place where students want to be.

What is likely to nurture your own positive attitudes and continued enthusiasm for teaching? As in all fields, success breeds success. It's important to become aware of times when you've made a difference in an individual student's life. Perhaps you know from personal experience that teachers do, indeed, make a difference. Or consider the words of one of the expert consultants for this book, Carlos Diaz (1997), now a professor of education at Florida Atlantic University, about Mrs. Oppel, his high school English teacher:

To this day, whenever I see certain words *(dearth, slake)* I recognize them fondly as some of Mrs. Oppel's vocabulary words. As a teacher, she was very calm and focused. She also was passionate about the power of language and the beauty of literature. I credit her, at least partially, for my determination to try to master the English language and become a professor and writer. I wish I could bottle these characteristics and implant them in all of my students.

The better teacher you become, the more rewarding your work will be. And the more respect and success you achieve in the eyes of your students, the better you will feel about your commitment to teaching.

With that in mind, stop for a moment and think about the images you have of your own former teachers. Some of your teachers likely were outstanding and left you with a very positive image. In a national survey of almost a thousand students 13 to 17 years of age, having a good sense of humor, making the class interesting, and having knowledge of the subject matter were the characteristics students listed as the most important for teachers to have (NASSP, 1997). The characteristics that secondary school students most frequently attributed to their worst teachers were having a boring class, not explaining things clearly, and showing favoritism. These characteristics and others that reflect students' images of their best and worst teachers are shown in figure 1.1.

Used by permission of the estate of Glen Dines

FIGURE 1.1 **Students' Images of Their Best and Worst Teachers**

CHARACTERISTICS OF BEST TEACHERS	
Characteristics	**% Total**
1. Have a sense of humor	79.2
2. Make the class interesting	73.7
3. Have knowledge of their subjects	70.1
4. Explain things clearly	66.2
5. Spend time to help students	65.8
6. Are fair to their students	61.8
7. Treat students like adults	54.4
8. Relate well to students	54.2
9. Are considerate of students' feelings	51.9
10. Don't show favoritism toward students	46.6

CHARACTERISTICS OF WORST TEACHERS	
Characteristics	**% Total**
1. Are dull/have a boring class	79.6
2. Don't explain things clearly	63.2
3. Show favoritism toward students	52.7
4. Have a poor attitude	49.8
5. Expect too much from students	49.1
6. Don't relate to students	46.2
7. Give too much homework	44.2
8. Are too strict	40.6
9. Don't give help/individual attention	40.5
10. Lack control	39.9

The Best and Worst Characteristics of My Teachers

When you studied figure 1.1, were you surprised by any of the characteristics listed by students to describe their best and worst teachers? Which of the top five characteristics students listed for the best teachers surprised you the most? Which of the top five characteristics of the worst teachers surprised you the most?

Now think about the top five characteristics of the best teachers you have had. Then think about the main five characteristics of the worst teachers you have had. In generating your lists, don't be constrained by the characteristics described in figure 1.1. Also, after you have listed each characteristic, write down one or more examples of situations that reflected the characteristic.

FIVE CHARACTERISTICS OF THE BEST TEACHERS I HAVE HAD

Characteristics   **Examples of Situations That Reflected the Characteristic**

1. _____   _____

2. _____   _____

3. _____   _____

4. _____   _____

5. _____   _____

FIVE CHARACTERISTICS OF THE WORST TEACHERS I HAVE HAD

Characteristics   **Examples of Situations That Reflected the Characteristic**

1. _____   _____

2. _____   _____

3. _____   _____

4. _____   _____

5. _____   _____

 Go to your Student Toolbox CD-ROM for an electronic version of this form.

Think about the roles that a good sense of humor and your own genuine enthusiasm are likely to play in your long-term commitment as a teacher. Also, notice other characteristics in figure 1.1 that relate to the caring nature of outstanding teachers. Effective teachers care for their students, often referring to them as "my students." They really want to be with the students and are dedicated to helping them learn. At the same time, they keep their role as a teacher distinct from student roles. Beyond their own caring, effective teachers also look for ways to help their students consider others' feelings and care about each other.

To think about the best and worst characteristics of the teachers you have had, complete Self-Assessment 1.1. Use the self-assessment to further explore the attitudes behind your commitment.

Strategies in Practice
- **Physical Fitness**
- **You Have to Like Your Job**
- **Daily Stress**
- **The Life Preserver**
- **Becoming an Effective Teacher**
- **Invaluable Strategies**

Teaching Strategies
For Becoming an Effective Teacher

1. *Effective teaching requires teachers to wear many different hats.* It's easy to fall into the trap of thinking that if you have good subject matter knowledge, excellent teaching will follow. Being an effective teacher requires many diverse skills.

2. *Engage often in perspective taking.* You want to be the very best teacher you can possibly be. Put yourself in your students' shoes and think about how they perceive you. Think about what they need from you to improve their academic and life skills. Put your heart and mind into helping them construct these skills.

3. *Keep the list of characteristics of effective teachers we have discussed in this chapter with you through your teaching career.* Looking at the list and thinking about the different areas of effective teaching can benefit you as you go through your student teaching; your days, weeks, and months as a beginning teacher; and even your years as an experienced teacher. By consulting it from time to time, you might realize that you have let one or two areas slip and need to spend time improving yourself in those areas.

Video Observation: Effective Teaching

 Review and Reflect

2 **Identify the attitudes and skills of an effective teacher.**

Review
- What professional knowledge and skills are required to be an effective teacher?
- Why is it important for teachers to be committed and motivated?

Reflect
- What is most likely to make teaching rewarding for you in the long run?

RESEARCH IN EDUCATIONAL PSYCHOLOGY

Research can be a valuable source of information about teaching. We will explore why research is important and how it is done, including how you can be a teacher-researcher.

Why Research Is Important

It sometimes is said that experience is the most important teacher. Your own experiences and those experiences that other teachers, administrators, and experts share with you will make you a better teacher. However, by providing you with valid information about the best ways to teach children, research also might make you a better teacher (Fraenkel & Wallen, 2005).

Video Lecture: Teacher as Researcher

We all get a great deal of knowledge from personal experience. We generalize from what we observe and frequently turn memorable encounters into lifetime "truths." But how valid are these conclusions? Sometimes we err in making these personal observations or misinterpret what we see and hear. Chances are, you can think of many situations in which you thought other people read you the wrong way, just as they might have felt that you misread them. When we base information only on personal experiences, we also aren't always totally objective because we sometimes make judgments that protect our ego and self-esteem (McMillan, 2000; McMillan & Wergin, 2002).

We get information not only from personal experiences but also from authorities or experts. In your teaching career, you will hear many authorities and experts spell out a "best way" to educate students. However, the authorities and experts don't always agree, do they? You might hear one expert one week tell you about a reading method that is absolutely the best yet the next week hear another expert tout a different method. One experienced teacher might tell you to do one thing with your students, while another experienced teacher tells you to do the opposite. How can you tell which one to believe? One way to clarify the situation is to look closely at research that has been conducted on the topic.

The Scientific Research Approach

Some people have difficulty thinking of educational psychology as being a science in the same way that physics or biology is a science. Can a discipline that studies the best way to help children learn or the ways poverty affects their behavior in the classroom be equated with disciplines that examine how gravity works or how blood flows through the body?

Science is defined not by *what* it investigates but by *how* it investigates. Whether you investigate photosynthesis, butterflies, Saturn's moons, or why some students think creatively and others don't, it is the way you investigate that makes an approach scientific or not.

Educational psychologists take a skeptical, scientific attitude toward knowledge. When they hear a claim that a particular method is effective in helping students learn, they want to know if the claim is based on good research. The science part of educational psychology seeks to sort fact from fancy by using particular strategies for obtaining information (Best & Kahn, 2003; Johnson & Christensen, 2000).

Scientific research is objective, systematic, and testable. It reduces the likelihood that information will be based on personal beliefs, opinions, and feelings. Scientific research is based on the **scientific method,** an approach that can be used to discover accurate information. It includes these steps: Conceptualize the problem, collect data, draw conclusions, and revise research conclusions and theory.

Conceptualizing a problem involves identifying the problem, theorizing, and developing one or more hypotheses. For example, a team of researchers decides that it wants to study ways to improve the achievement of students from impoverished backgrounds. The researchers have identified a problem, which at a general level might not seem like a difficult task. However, as part of the first step, they also must go beyond the general description of the problem by isolating, analyzing, narrowing, and focusing more specifically on what aspect of it they hope to study. Perhaps the researchers decide to discover whether mentoring that involves sustained support, guidance, and concrete assistance to students from impoverished backgrounds can improve their academic performance. At this point, even more narrowing and focusing need to take place. What specific strategies do they want the mentors to use? How often will the mentors see the students? How long will the mentoring program last? What aspects of the students' achievement do the researchers want to assess?

As researchers formulate a problem to study, they often draw on theories and develop hypotheses. A **theory** is an interrelated, coherent set of ideas that helps to explain and make predictions. A theory allows a scientist to form **hypotheses,** which are specific assumptions and predictions that can be tested to determine whether the theory holds up. For example, a theory about mentoring might attempt to explain and predict why sustained support, guidance, and concrete experience should make a difference in the lives of children from impoverished backgrounds. The theory might focus on children's opportunities to model the behavior and strategies of mentors, or it might focus on the effects of nurturing, which might be missing in the children's own lives.

The next step is to collect information (data). In the study of mentoring, the researchers might decide to conduct the mentoring program for six months. Their data might consist of classroom observations, teachers' ratings, and achievement tests given to the mentored students before the mentoring began and at the end of six months of mentoring.

Once data have been collected, educational psychologists use statistical procedures to understand the meaning of their quantitative data. Then they try to draw conclusions. In the study of mentoring, statistics would help the researchers determine whether their observations are due to chance. After data have been collected, educational psychologists compare their findings with what others have discovered about the same issue.

The final step in the scientific method is revising research conclusions and theory. Educational psychologists have generated a number of theories about the best ways for children to learn. Over time, some theories have been discarded and others have been

Generating Research Issues

scientific research Objective, systematic, and testable research that aims at reducing conclusions based on personal beliefs, opinions, and feelings.

scientific method A method for discovering accurate information that includes these steps: Conceptualize the problem, collect data, draw conclusions, and revise research conclusions and theory.

theory An interrelated, coherent set of ideas that helps to explain and make predictions that can be tested to determine their accuracy.

hypotheses Assumptions that can be tested to determine their accuracy; theories produce hypotheses.

Step 1
Conceptualize the Problem

A researcher identifies this problem: Many children from impoverished backgrounds have lower achievement than children from higher socioeconomic backgrounds. The researcher develops the hypothesis that mentoring will improve the achievement of children from impoverished backgrounds.

Step 2
Collect Information (Data)

The researcher conducts the mentoring program for 6 months and collects data before the program begins and after its conclusion, using classroom observations, teachers' ratings of children's achievement, and achievement test scores. If the research involves an experiment, the researcher also would collect data on children who are not receiving mentoring.

Step 3
Draw Conclusions

The researcher statistically analyzes the data and finds that, for the children being mentored, achievement improved over the 6 months of the study. The researcher concludes that mentoring is likely an important reason for the increase in the children's achievement.

Step 4
Revise Research Conclusions and Theory

This research on mentoring, along with other research that obtains similar results, increases the likelihood that mentoring will be considered as an important component of theorizing about how to improve the achievement of children from low-income backgrounds.

FIGURE 1.2 **The Scientific Method Applied to a Study of Mentoring**

revised. This text presents a number of useful theories, along with their support and implications. Figure 1.2 illustrates the steps in the scientific method applied to our study of mentoring.

Research Methods

As you have seen, collecting research information (or data) is an important step in the scientific method. The collection of data is the fundamental means of testing hypotheses. When educational psychology researchers want to find out, for example, whether

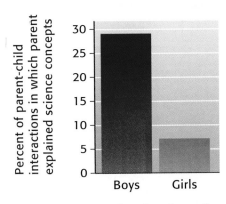

FIGURE 1.3 Parents' Explanations of Science to Sons and Daughters at a Science Museum
In a naturalistic observation study at a children's science museum, parents were three times more likely to explain science to boys than girls (Crowley & others, 2001). The gender difference occurred regardless of whether the father, the mother, or both parents were with the child, although the gender difference was greatest for fathers' science explanations to sons and daughters.

watching a lot of MTV detracts from student learning, eating a nutritional breakfast improves alertness in class, or getting more recess decreases absenteeism, they can choose from many methods of gathering research information.

There are three basic methods used to gather information in educational psychology: descriptive, correlational, and experimental.

Descriptive Research   Descriptive research has the purpose of observing and recording behavior. For example, an educational psychologist might observe the extent to which children are aggressive in a classroom or interview teachers about their attitudes toward a particular type of teaching strategy. By itself, descriptive research cannot prove what causes some phenomenon, but it can reveal important information about people's behavior and attitudes (Lammers & Badia, 2005; Leary, 2004).

Observation   We look at things all the time. However, casually watching two students interacting is not the same as the type of observation used in scientific studies. Scientific observation is highly systematic. It requires knowing what you are looking for, conducting observations in an unbiased manner, accurately recording and categorizing what you see, and effectively communicating your observations (Leary, 2005).

A common way to record observations is to write them down, often using shorthand or symbols. In addition, tape recorders, video cameras, special coding sheets, one-way mirrors, and computers increasingly are being used to make observation more accurate, reliable, and efficient.

Observations can be made in laboratories or in naturalistic settings. A **laboratory** is a controlled setting from which many of the complex factors of the real world have been removed. Some educational psychologists conduct research in laboratories at the colleges or universities where they work and teach. Although laboratories often help researchers gain more control in their studies, they have been criticized as being artificial.

In **naturalistic observation,** behavior is observed out in the real world. Educational psychologists conduct naturalistic observations of children in classrooms, at museums, on playgrounds, in homes, in neighborhoods, and in other settings. Naturalistic observation was used in one study that focused on conversations in a children's science museum (Crowley & others, 2001). Parents were three times as likely to engage boys as girls in explanatory talk while visiting different exhibits at the science museum (see figure 1.3). In another study, Mexican American parents who had completed high school used more explanations with their children as they were observed at a science museum than Mexican American parents who had not completed high school (Tennebaum & others, 2002).

Participant observation occurs when the observer-researcher is actively involved as a participant in the activity or setting (McMillan, 2004). The participant observer will often participate in a context and observe for a while, then take notes on what he or she has viewed. The observer usually makes these observations and writes down notes over a period of days, weeks, or months and looks for patterns in the observations. For example, to study a student who is doing poorly in the class without apparent reason, the teacher might develop a plan to observe the student from time to time and record observations of the student's behavior and what is going on in the classroom at the time.

laboratory A controlled setting from which many of the complex factors of the real world have been removed.

naturalistic observation Observation outside of a laboratory in the real world.

participant observation Observation conducted at the same time the teacher-researcher is actively involved as a participant in the activity or setting.

Interviews and Questionnaires   Sometimes the quickest and best way to get information about students and teachers is to ask them for it. Educational psychologists use interviews and questionnaires (surveys) to find out about children's and teachers' experiences, beliefs, and feelings. Most interviews take place face-to-face, although they can be done in other ways, such as over the phone or the Internet. Questionnaires are usually given to individuals in written form. They, too, can be transmitted in many ways, such as directly by hand, by mail, or via the Internet.

Good interviews and surveys involve concrete, specific, and unambiguous questions and some means of checking the authenticity of the respondents' replies (Rosnow & Rosenthal, 2005). However, interviews and surveys are not without problems. One crucial limitation is that many individuals give socially desirable answers, responding in a way they think is most socially acceptable and desirable rather than how they truly think or feel. For example, some teachers, when interviewed or asked to fill out a questionnaire about their teaching practices, hesitate to admit honestly how frequently they chide or criticize their students. Skilled interviewing techniques and questions that increase forth-right responses are crucial to obtaining accurate information. Another problem with interviews and surveys is that the respondents sometimes simply lie.

Standardized Tests **Standardized tests** have uniform procedures for administration and scoring. They assess students' aptitudes or skills in different domains. Many standardized tests allow a student's performance to be compared with the performance of other students at the same age or grade level, in many cases on a national basis (Aiken, 2003). Students might take a number of standardized tests, including tests that assess their intelligence, achievement, personality, career interests, and other skills. These tests are for a variety of purposes, including providing outcome measures for research studies, information that helps psychologists and educators make decisions about an individual student, and comparisons of students' performance across schools, states, and countries. Standardized tests play an important role in a major contemporary educational psychology issue—*accountability,* which involves holding teachers and students responsible for student performance (Phelps, 2005; Sadker & Sadker, 2005). Both students and teachers are increasingly being given standardized tests in the accountability effort. Many schools are being required to develop specific goals, such as minimum achievement on standardized tests, and are being held responsible for attaining these goals. The U.S. government's No Child Left Behind Act is at the centerpiece of accountability; it mandates that in 2005 every state has to give standardized tests to students in grades 3 through 8 in language arts and math, with testing for science achievement slated in 2007.

Case Studies A **case study** is an in-depth look at an individual. Case studies often are used when unique circumstances in a person's life cannot be duplicated, for either practical or ethical reasons. For example, consider the case study of Brandi Binder (Nash, 1997). She developed such severe epilepsy that surgeons had to remove the right side of her brain's cerebral cortex when she was six years old. Brandi lost virtually all control over muscles on the left side of her body, the side controlled by the right side of her brain. At age seventeen, however, after years of therapy ranging from leg lifts to mathematics and music training, Brandi is an *A* student. She loves music and art, which usually are associated with the right side of the brain. Her recuperation is not 100 percent—for example, she has not regained the use of her left arm—but her case study shows that if there is a way to compensate, the human brain will find it. Brandi's remarkable recovery also provides evidence against the stereotype that the left side (hemisphere) of the brain is solely the source of logical thinking and the right hemisphere exclusively the source of creativity. Brains are not that neatly split in terms of most functioning, as Brandi's case illustrates.

Although case studies provide dramatic, in-depth portrayals of people's lives, we need to exercise caution when interpreting them (Gall, Borg, & Gall, 2003). The subject of a case study is unique, with a genetic makeup and set of experiences that no one else shares. For these reasons, the findings often do not lend themselves to statistical analysis and may not generalize to other people.

Ethnographic Studies An **ethnographic study** consists of in-depth description and interpretation of behavior in an ethnic or a cultural group that includes direct involvement with the participants (McMillan & Wergin, 2002). This type of study might include observations in naturalistic settings as well as interviews. Many ethnographic studies are long-term projects.

In one ethnographic study, the purpose was to examine the extent to which schools were enacting educational reforms for language minority students (U.S. Office of Education, 1998). In-depth observations and interviews were conducted in a number of schools to determine if they were establishing high standards and restructuring the way

Brandi Binder is evidence of the brain's hemispheric flexibility and resilience. Despite having the right side of her cortex removed because of a severe case of epilepsy, Brandi engages in many activities often portrayed as only "right-brain" activities. She loves music and art and is shown here working on one of her paintings.

standardized tests Tests with uniform procedures for administration and scoring. They assess students' performance in different domains and allow a student's performance to be compared with the performance of other students at the same age or grade level on a national basis.

case study An in-depth look at an individual.

ethnographic study In-depth description and interpretation of behavior in an ethnic or a cultural group that includes direct involvement with the participants.

FIGURE 1.4 Possible Explanations of Correlational Data
An observed correlation between two events does not justify the conclusion that the first event caused the second event. Other possibilities are that the second event caused the first event or that a third, undetermined event causes the correlation between the first two events.

Observed correlation	Possible explanations for this correlation

As permissive teaching increases, children's self-control decreases

Permissive teaching — causes → Children's lack of self-control

Children's lack of self-control — causes → Permissive teaching

Other factors, such as genetic tendencies, poverty, or sociohistorical circumstances — cause both → Permissive teaching and Children's lack of self-control

education was being delivered. Several schools were selected for intensive evaluation, including Las Palmas Elementary School in San Clemente, California. The study concluded that this school, at least, was making the necessary reforms for improving the education of language minority students.

Correlational Research In **correlational research,** the goal is to describe the strength of the relation between two or more events or characteristics. Correlational research is useful because the more strongly two events are correlated (related or associated), the more effectively we can predict one from the other. For example, if researchers find that low-involved, permissive teaching is correlated with a student's lack of self-control, it suggests that low-involved, permissive teaching might be one source of the lack of self-control.

However, a caution is in order. Correlation by itself does not equal causation. The correlational finding just mentioned does not mean that permissive teaching necessarily causes low student self-control. It could mean that, but it also could mean that the student's lack of self-control caused the teachers to throw up their arms in despair and give up trying to control the out-of-control class. It also could be that other factors, such as heredity, poverty, or inadequate parenting, caused the correlation between permissive teaching and low student self-control. Figure 1.4 illustrates these possible interpretations of correlational data.

Experimental Research **Experimental research** allows educational psychologists to determine the causes of behavior. Educational psychologists accomplish this task by performing an experiment, a carefully regulated procedure in which one or more of the factors believed to influence the behavior being studied is manipulated and all other factors are held constant. If the behavior under study changes when a factor is manipulated, we say that the manipulated factor causes the behavior to change. *Cause* is the event that is being manipulated. *Effect* is the behavior that changes because of the manipulation. Experimental research is the only truly reliable method of establishing cause and effect. Because correlational research does not involve manipulation of factors, it is not a dependable way to isolate cause (Elmes, Kantowitz, & Roediger, 2003).

Experiments involve at least one independent variable and one dependent variable. The **independent variable** is the manipulated, influential, experimental factor. The label *independent* indicates that this variable can be changed independently of any other

Correlational Research

Experimental Research

correlational research Research that describes the strength of the relation between two or more events or characteristics.

experimental research Research that allows the determination of the causes of behavior; involves conducting an experiment, which is a carefully regulated procedure in which one or more of the factors believed to influence the behavior being studied is manipulated and all others are held constant.

independent variable The manipulated, influential, experimental factor in an experiment.

factors. For example, suppose we want to design an experiment to study the effects of peer tutoring on student achievement. In this example, the amount and type of peer tutoring could be an independent variable.

The **dependent variable** is the factor that is measured in an experiment. It can change as the independent variable is manipulated. The label *dependent* is used because the values of this variable depend on what happens to the participants in the experiment as the independent variable is manipulated. In the peer tutoring study, achievement is the dependent variable. This might be assessed in a number of ways. Let's say in this study it is measured by scores on a nationally standardized achievement test.

In experiments, the independent variable consists of differing experiences that are given to one or more experimental groups and one or more control groups. An **experimental group** is a group whose experience is manipulated. A **control group** is a comparison group that is treated in every way like the experimental group except for the manipulated factor. The control group serves as the baseline against which the effects of the manipulated condition can be compared. In the peer tutoring study, we need to have one group of students who get peer tutoring (experimental group) and one group of students who don't (control group).

Another important principle of experimental research is **random assignment:** Researchers assign participants to experimental and control groups by chance. This practice reduces the likelihood that the experiment's results will be due to any preexisting differences between the groups. In our study of peer tutoring, random assignment greatly reduces the probability that the two groups will differ on such factors as age, family status, initial achievement, intelligence, personality, health, and alertness.

To summarize the experimental study of peer tutoring and student achievement, each student is randomly assigned to one of two groups. One group (the experimental group) is given peer tutoring; the other (the control group) is not. The independent variable consists of the differing experiences (tutoring or no tutoring) that the experimental and control groups receive. After the peer tutoring is completed, the students are given a nationally standardized achievement test (dependent variable). Figure 1.5 on page 22 summarizes the distinction between correlational and experimental research methods applied to peer tutoring and homework.

Time Span of Research   In addition to choosing whether to gather descriptive, correlational, or experimental data, another research decision involves the time span of the research. We have several options—we can study groups of individuals all at one time or study the same individuals over time.

Cross-sectional research involves studying groups of people all at one time. For example, a researcher might be interested in studying the self-esteem of students in grades 4, 6, and 8. In a cross-sectional study, the students' self-esteem would be assessed at one time, using groups of children in grades 4, 6, and 8. The cross-sectional study's main advantage is that the researcher does not have to wait for the students to grow older. However, this approach provides no information about the stability of individual students' self-esteem, or how it might change over time.

Longitudinal research involves studying the same individuals over a period of time, usually several years or more. In a longitudinal research study of self-esteem, the researcher might examine the self-esteem of a group of fourth-grade students, then assess the same students' self-esteem again in sixth grade, and then again in eighth grade. One of the great values of longitudinal research is that we can evaluate how individual children change as they get older. However, because longitudinal research is time consuming and costly, most research is cross-sectional.

Program Evaluation Research, Action Research, and the Teacher-as-Researcher

In discussing research methods so far, we have referred mainly to methods that are used to improve our knowledge and understanding of general educational practices. The same methods also can be applied to research whose aim is more specific, such as determining

dependent variable The factor that is measured in an experiment.

experimental group The group whose experience is manipulated in an experiment.

control group In an experiment, a group whose experience is treated in every way like the experimental group except for the manipulated factor.

random assignment In experimental research, the assignment of participants to experimental and control groups by chance.

cross-sectional research Research in which the data are collected all at one time.

longitudinal research Research in which the same individuals are studied over a period of time, usually several years or more.

	Correlation	Example	Experiment	Example
Goal	Determine whether two (or more) factors are correlated (associated) with each other.	Question: Is parental tutoring associated with better homework?	Determine whether there is some causal relationship between two factors.	Question: Does parental tutoring cause children's homework to improve?
Method of gathering data	Record the occurrence of two different factors in a certain group of participants.	Find out whether each set of parents does or does not tutor its child. Examine the quality of each child's homework.	Divide students into two groups: experimental group and control group. Give the experimental group some type of treatment. Withhold treatment from the control group.	Randomly divide the class into two groups. Record the quality of the children's homework before the experiment begins. Then require the parents of the experimental group to tutor their children while forbidding the parents of the control group to tutor. Record the quality of homework in each group after the tutoring has been given.
Analysis	Statistically analyze whether the factors tend to correlate (occur together spatially or temporally) in some regular pattern.	Determine whether tutoring was (or was not) correlated with better homework.	Statistically analyze whether the experimental group is different than the control group after undergoing the treatment.	Analyze whether parental tutoring was (or was not) often followed by improvements in a child's homework.
Interpretation		Conclude that tutoring and homework are (or are not) associated. An association might suggest cause and effect, but it does not prove it.		Conclude that tutoring did or did not cause students' homework to improve in the experimental group.

FIGURE 1.5 Comparison of Correlational and Experimental Research Methods

how well a particular educational strategy or program is working (Gall, Gall, & Burg, 2005; Graziano & Raulin, 2000). This more narrowly targeted work often includes program evaluation research, action research, and the teacher-as-researcher.

Program Evaluation Research   **Program evaluation research** is research that is designed to make decisions about the effectiveness of a particular program (Fitzpatrick, Sanders & Worthen, 2004; McMillan, 2004). Program evaluation research often focuses on a specific location or type of program. Because it often is directed at answering a question about a specific school or school system, the results of program evaluation research are not intended to be generalized to other settings (Mertler & Charles, 2005). A program evaluation researcher might ask questions like these:

• Has a gifted program that was started two years ago had positive effects on students' creative thinking and academic achievement?
• Has a technology program that has been in place for one year improved students' attitudes toward school?
• Which of two reading programs being used in this school system has improved students' reading skills the most?

Action Research   **Action research** is used to solve a specific classroom or school problem, improve teaching and other educational strategies, or make a decision at a specific location (Arhar, Holly, & Kasten, 2001; Wiersma & Jurs, 2005). The goal of action research is to improve educational practices immediately in one or two classrooms, at one school, or at several schools. Action research is carried out by teachers and administrators rather than educational psychology researchers. However, the practitioners might follow many of the guidelines of scientific research that we described earlier, such as trying to make the research and observations as systematic as possible to avoid bias and misinterpretation. Action research can be carried out schoolwide or in more limited settings by a smaller group of teachers and administrators; it can even be accomplished in a single classroom by an individual teacher (Johnson, 2005).

Teacher-as-Researcher   The concept of **teacher-as-researcher** (also called "teacher-researcher") is the idea that classroom teachers can conduct their own studies to improve their teaching practices (Creswell, 2005). This is an important outgrowth of action research. Some educational experts believe that the increasing emphasis on the teacher-as-researcher reinvents the teacher's role, fuels school renewal, and improves teaching and

What methods can a teacher-as-researcher use to obtain information about students?

program evaluation research Research that is designed to make decisions about the effectiveness of a particular program.

action research Research that is used to solve a specific classroom or school problem, improve teaching and other educational strategies, or make a decision at a specific level.

teacher-as-researcher Also called teacher-researcher, this concept involves classroom teachers conducting their own studies to improve their teaching practice.

student learning (Cochran-Smith & Lytle, 1990; Flake & others, 1995; Gill, 1997). It is increasingly thought that the most effective teachers routinely ask questions and monitor problems to be solved, then collect data, interpret them, and share their conclusions with other teachers (Cochran-Smith, 1995).

To obtain information, the teacher-researcher uses methods such as participant observation, interviews, and case studies. One good, widely used technique is the clinical interview, in which the teacher makes the student feel comfortable, shares beliefs and expectations, and asks questions in a nonthreatening manner. Before conducting a clinical interview with a student, the teacher usually will put together a targeted set of questions to ask. Clinical interviews not only can help you obtain information about a particular issue or problem but also can provide you with a sense of how children think and feel.

In addition to participant observation, the teacher might conduct several clinical interviews with a student, discuss the student's situation with the child's parents, and consult with a school psychologist about the student's behavior. Based on this work as teacher-researcher, the teacher may be able to create an intervention strategy that improves the student's behavior.

Thus, learning about educational research methods not only can help you understand the research that educational psychologists conduct but also has another practical benefit. The more knowledge you have about research in educational psychology, the more effective you will be in the increasingly popular teacher-researcher role (Gay & Airasian, 2000; Thomas, 2005).

Teaching Strategies
For Becoming an Effective
Teacher-Researcher

1. *As you plan each week's lessons, think about your students and which ones might benefit from your role as a teacher-researcher.* As you reflect on the past week's classes, you might notice that one student seemed to be sliding further downhill in her performance and that another student seemed to be especially depressed. As you think about such students, you might consider using your observer participation and/or clinical interview skills in the following week in an effort to find out why they are having problems.
2. *Take a course in educational research methods.* This can improve your understanding of how research is conducted.
3. *Use the library or Internet resources to learn more about teacher-researcher skills.* This might include locating information about how to be a skilled clinical interviewer and a systematic, unbiased observer. A good book on improving your observation skills is *A Guide to Observation and Participation in the Classroom* (Reed, Bergemann, & Olson, 2001).
4. *Ask someone else (such as another teacher) to observe your class and help you develop some strategies for the particular research problem that you want to solve.*

Research Challenges

Research in educational psychology poses a number of challenges. Some of the challenges involve the pursuit of knowledge itself. Others involve the effects of research on participants. Still others relate to better understanding of the information derived from research studies.

Ethics Educational psychologists must exercise considerable caution to ensure the well-being of children participating in a research study. Most colleges and school systems have review boards that evaluate whether the research is ethical. Before research is conducted in a school system, an administrator or administrative committee evaluates the research plan and decides whether the research can potentially benefit the system.

Ethical Principles

The code of ethics adopted by the American Psychological Association (APA) instructs researchers to protect participants from mental and physical harm. The best interests of the participants must always be kept foremost in the researcher's mind (Hoyle & Judd, 2002; Kimmel, 1996). All participants who are old enough to do so must give their informed consent to participate. If they are not old enough, parental or guardian consent must be obtained. When children and adolescents are studied, parental or guardian informed consent is almost always obtained. Informed consent means that the participants (and/or their parents or legal guardians) have been told what their participation will entail and any risks that might be involved. For example, if researchers want to study the effects of conflict in divorced families on learning and achievement, the participants should be informed that in some instances discussion of a family's experiences might improve family relationships but in other cases might raise unwanted family stress. After informed consent is given, participants retain the right to withdraw at any time (Bersoff, 1999).

Because children are vulnerable and usually lack power and control when facing adults, educators always should strive to make their research encounters positive and supportive experiences for each child (Gall, Borg, & Gall, 2003). Even if the family gives permission for a child to participate in a research study, if the child doesn't want to participate, that desire should be respected.

Gender Traditionally, science has been presented as nonbiased and value free. However, many experts on gender believe that much educational and other research has been gender-biased (Worell, 2001). Educational researchers argue that for too long the female experience was subsumed under the male experience (Tetreault, 1997). For example, conclusions about females have been routinely drawn based on research done only with males. Similarly, with regard to socioeconomic bias, conclusions have been drawn about all males and all females from studies that do not include participants from all income backgrounds.

Here are three broad questions that female scholars have raised regarding gender bias in educational research (Tetreault, 1997):

- How might gender be a bias that influences the choice of theory, questions, hypotheses, participants, and research design? For example, the most widely known theory of moral development (Kohlberg's) was proposed by a male in a male-dominant society, and for many years males were the main participants in research conducted to support the theory (Gilligan, 1982, 1998; Kohlberg, 1976). Thus, generalizations about moral development were made on the basis of information collected from males and may have been less applicable to females.
- How might research on topics of primary interest to females, such as relationships, feelings, and empathy, challenge existing theory and research? For example, in studies of moral development, it has often been said that the highest level of moral development involves this question, which reflects common male preoccupations: "What is justice for the individual?" (Kohlberg, 1976). However, more recent theorizing has shifted away from the typically male emphasis on the individual and autonomy to incorporate a more commonly female "care" perspective, which focuses on relationships and connections with others (Gilligan, 1982, 1998). We will explore these aspects of moral development further in chapter 3, "Social Contexts and Socioemotional Development."
- How has research that has heretofore exaggerated gender differences between females and males influenced the way teachers think about and teach female and male students? For example, gender differences in mathematics often have been exaggerated and fueled by societal bias. Such exaggerations and bias can produce negative expectations about how well female students will do in math.

In chapter 5, "Sociocultural Diversity," we will explore many aspects of gender and education.

One research challenge involves ensuring that educational research does not involve gender bias. *What are some of the questions female scholars have raised about gender bias in educational research?*

Another research challenge focuses on children from ethnic minority backgrounds. *What are some of the ways research has been characterized by ethnic bias? How can this bias be reduced or eliminated?*

Ethnicity and Culture We need to include more children from ethnic minority backgrounds in our research on educational psychology (Graham, 1992; Lee, 1992). Historically, ethnic minority children essentially have been ignored in research or simply viewed as variations from the norm or average. Their developmental and educational problems have been viewed as "confounds," or "noise," in data, and researchers have deliberately excluded these children from the samples they have selected to study (Ryan-Finn, Cauce, & Grove, 1995). Because ethnic minority children have been excluded from research for so long, there likely is more variation in children's real lives than research studies have indicated in the past.

Researchers also have tended to practice **ethnic gloss** when they select and describe ethnic minority groups (Trimble, 1989). Practicing ethnic gloss means using an ethnic label such as African American, Latino, Asian American, or Native American in a superficial way that makes an ethnic group seem more homogeneous than it really is. For example, a researcher might describe a sample as "20 African Americans, 20 Latinos, and 20 Anglo-Americans" when a more precise description of the Latino group would need to specify: "The 20 Latino participants were Mexican Americans from low-income neighborhoods in the southwestern area of Los Angeles. Twelve were from homes in which Spanish is the dominant spoken language, 8 from homes in which English is the main spoken language. Ten were born in the United States, 10 in Mexico. Ten described themselves as Mexican American, 5 as Mexican, 3 as American, 2 as Chicano, and 1 as Latino." Ethnic gloss can cause researchers to obtain samples of ethnic groups that either are not representative or conceal the group's diversity, which can lead to overgeneralization and stereotyping.

Also, historically, when researchers have studied individuals from ethnic minority groups, they have focused on their problems. It is important to study problems such as poverty that ethnic minority groups may face, but it also is important to examine possible strengths, such as pride, self-esteem, problem-solving skills, and extended-family support systems. Fortunately, now, as a more pluralistic view of our society is emerging, researchers are increasingly studying the positive dimensions of ethnic minority groups (Swanson, 1997).

Being a Wise Consumer of Information About Educational Psychology We live in a society that generates a vast amount of information about children's education in various media, ranging from research journals to newspapers and television. The information varies greatly in quality. How can you evaluate the credibility of this information?

ethnic gloss The use of an ethnic label in a superficial way that stereotypes the ethnic group.

Be Cautious About What Is Reported in the Popular Media   Children's education is increasingly talked about in the news. Television, radio, newspapers, and magazines all frequently report on educational research. Many professional educators and researchers regularly supply the media with information. In some cases, this research has been published in professional journals or presented at national meetings and then picked up by the popular media. Most major colleges and universities also have a media relations department, which contacts the press about current faculty research.

However, not all information about education that appears in the media comes from professionals with excellent credentials and reputations. Most journalists, television reporters, and other media personnel are not scientifically trained and do not have the skills to sort through the avalanche of material they receive and make sound decisions about which information to report.

Unfortunately, the media focus on sensational, dramatic findings (Stanovich, 2001). They want you to stay tuned or buy their publication. When the information they gather from educational journals is not sensational, they might embellish it and sensationalize it, going beyond what the researcher intended.

Another problem with media reports about research is that the media often do not go into depth about a study. They often only devote a few lines or seconds to summarize complex findings. Too often this means that what is reported is overgeneralized and stereotyped.

Know How to Avoid Drawing Conclusions About Individual Needs on the Basis of Group Research   Most educational psychology research is conducted at the level of the group. Individual variations in how students respond is not a common focus. For example, if researchers are interested in the effects of divorce on children's school achievement, they might conduct a study with 50 children from divorced families and 50 children from intact, never divorced families. They might find that the children from divorced families, as a group, had lower achievement in school than did the children from intact families. That is a group finding that applies to children of divorce as a whole. And that is what is commonly reported in the media and in research journals. In this particular study, it likely was the case that some of the children from divorced families had higher school achievement than children from intact families—not as many, but some. Indeed, it is entirely possible that, of the 100 children in the study, the 2 or 3 children who had the highest school achievement were from divorced families—and that this fact was never reported in the popular media.

Group research can give teachers good information about the characteristics of a group of children, revealing strengths and weaknesses of the group. However, in many instances, teachers, as well as the child's parents, want to know about how to help one particular child cope and learn more effectively. Unfortunately, although group research can point up problems for certain groups of children, it does not always hold for an individual child.

Recognize How Easy It Is to Overgeneralize About a Small or Clinical Sample   There often isn't space or time in media presentations to go into details about the nature of the sample of children on which the study is based. In many cases, samples are too small to let us generalize readily to a larger population. For example, if a study of children from divorced families is based on only ten to twenty children, what is found in the study cannot be generalized to all children from divorced families. Perhaps the sample was drawn from families who have substantial economic resources, are Anglo-American, live in a small southern town, and are undergoing therapy. From this study, we clearly would be making unwarranted generalizations if we thought the findings also characterize children who are from low- to moderate-income families, are from other ethnic backgrounds, live in a different geographical location, and are not undergoing therapy.

Be Aware That a Single Study Usually Is Not the Defining Word   The media might identify an interesting research study and claim that it is something phenomenal with far-reaching implications. As a competent consumer of information, be aware that it is extremely rare for a single study to have earth-shattering, conclusive answers that apply to all students and teachers. In fact, where there are large numbers of studies that focus on a particular issue, it is not unusual to find conflicting results from one study to the next. Reliable answers about teaching and learning usually emerge only after many researchers have conducted similar studies and drawn similar conclusions. In our example of divorce, if one study reports that a school counseling program for students from divorced families improved their school achievement, we cannot conclude that the counseling will work as effectively with all students from divorced families until many more studies are conducted.

Remember That Causal Conclusions Cannot Be Drawn from Correlational Studies
Drawing causal conclusions from correlational studies is one of the most common mistakes made by the media. In nonexperimental studies (remember that in an experiment, participants are randomly assigned to treatments or experiences), two variables or factors might be related to each other. However, causal interpretations cannot be made when two or more factors simply are correlated. We cannot say that one causes the other. In the case of divorce, the headline might read "Divorce causes students to have problems in school." We read the story and find out that the information is based on the results of a research study. Because we obviously cannot, for ethical and practical reasons, randomly assign students to families that will become divorced or remain intact, this headline is based on a correlational study, and the causal statements are unproved. It could well be, for example, that some other factor, such as family conflict or economic problems, is responsible for both the children's poor school performance and the parents' divorce.

Always Consider the Source of the Information and Evaluate Its Credibility   Studies are not automatically accepted by the research community. Researchers usually must submit their findings to a research journal, where it is reviewed by their colleagues, who make a decision about whether or not to publish the paper. Although the quality of research in journals is far from uniform, in most cases the research has undergone far more scrutiny and careful consideration of the work's quality than is the case for research or any other information that has not gone through the journal process. Within the media, we can distinguish between what is presented in respected newspapers—such as the *New York Times* and *Washington Post,* as well as credible magazines, such as *Time* and *Newsweek*—and what is presented in the tabloids, such as the *National Enquirer* and *Star.*

ENTER THE DEBATE

Should teachers conduct research using their students as subjects?

Teaching Experience

- **A Passion for Teaching**
- **Helping Students Become Life-Long Learners**
- **A New "Education Theory"**
- **Why Teachers Need to Know About Educational Psychology**
- **Educational Psychology**
- **The Importance of Educational Psychology**
- **Advice to Teachers**

Review and Reflect

3 Discuss how educational psychologists and teachers can conduct and evaluate research.

Review

- Why is it important to go beyond knowledge based on personal experience?
- What concepts are most central to science and research?
- What are some types of research? What is the difference between correlational and experimental research and between cross-sectional and longitudinal research?
- What are some kinds of research that relate very directly to effective classroom practices? What tools might a teacher use to do classroom research?
- What are some challenges in conducting research in educational psychology?

Reflect

- In your own K–12 education, can you remember a time when one of your teachers might have benefited from conducting action research regarding the effectiveness of his or her own teaching methods? What action research questions and methods might have been useful to the teacher?

Mrs. Jefferson felt frustrated when teaching the social studies curriculum that her school district had used for the past eight years. The manner in which the material was presented bothered her. The books were not very exciting and didn't hold the students' interest. The print was small; there were few pictures, charts, maps, or graphs. The material itself bothered her also. It was ethnocentric and said little about the accomplishments of women. In addition, the teacher's guide didn't offer much besides worksheets and test items. The district had a policy of replacing curriculum materials every ten years. "This is the year to start looking," she thought. "I really want some input into this decision."

She talked to her principal, who told her that a committee of five teachers and one administrator was being established to look into various social studies curricula that would cover the entire grade span of the school. Mrs. Jefferson asked to be a part of the committee. "That's great," replied the principal. "Now we'll have a representative from each grade level and special education. I know you'll be a valuable part of the committee."

At the first committee meeting, Mrs. Jefferson was a bit overwhelmed by what some of the other teachers were saying. One saw no point in buying a new curriculum "because, after all, history doesn't change and we can always supplement with current events material." Another teacher wanted a curriculum that had no actual textbooks but had guidelines to several projects students could complete. He had read an article in a popular magazine touting this type of curriculum. Yet another teacher wanted to purchase a new version of the very same curriculum they had been using

because if they bought something entirely different she would have to revamp her teaching, which would be "an incredible task." The administrator told the rest of the committee that they had one year to make their decision. "That way all the materials can be ordered and each teacher will have some time to become familiar with the material before implementing it," she said.

The committee called various publishers of social studies curricular materials and asked for preview copies of their materials. They were sent a veritable cornucopia of textbooks and ancillary materials, including reading lists, workbooks, instructor's guides, test banks, and CD-ROMs. Wading through all the materials to make a decision that would impact students for a decade seemed like a monumental task. However, Mrs. Jefferson and her colleagues were determined to choose the right curriculum for their students. In order to do this, they decided that they would need to engage in considerable research. "It's a good thing we have a year to do this in," thought Mrs. Jefferson.

- How would you go about engaging in the research necessary to make a good decision regarding what curriculum to purchase?
- What issues would need to be considered? Why?
- What type(s) of research would be appropriate? Why?
- What design would you use? Why?
- If you decided to use an experimental design, identify the independent and dependent variables.
- Considering the design that you chose, could you infer cause and effect? Why/why not?

Reach Your Learning Goals

1 **Describe some basic ideas about the field of educational psychology, including its history and why effective teaching depends on both art and science.**

- Educational psychology is the branch of psychology that specializes in understanding teaching and learning in educational settings. William James and John Dewey were important pioneers in educational psychology, as was E. L. Thorndike. Among the important ideas in educational psychology that we owe to Dewey are these: the child as an active learner, education of the whole child, emphasis on the child's adaptation to the environment, and the democratic ideal that all children deserve a competent education. There were few individuals from ethnic minority groups and few women in the early history of educational psychology because of ethnic and gender barriers. Further historical developments included Skinner's behaviorism in the mid-twentieth century and the cognitive revolution that had taken hold by the 1980s. Also in recent years, there has been expanded interest in the socioemotional aspects of children's lives, including cultural contexts.

- Teaching is linked to both science and art. In terms of science, information from psychological research can provide valuable ideas. In terms of art, skillful, experienced practice contributes to effective teaching.

2 **Identify the attitudes and skills of an effective teacher.**

- Effective teachers have subject matter competence, use effective instructional strategies, and have skills in the following areas: goal setting and planning, classroom management, motivation, communication, work with diverse ethnic and cultural groups, and technology.

- Being an effective teacher also requires commitment and motivation. This includes having a good attitude and caring about students. It is easy for teachers to get into a rut and develop a negative attitude, but students pick up on this and it can harm their learning.

3 **Discuss how educational psychologists and teachers can conduct and evaluate research.**

- Personal experiences and information from experts can help you become an effective teacher. The information you obtain from research also is extremely important. It will help you sort through various strategies and determine which are most and least effective. Research helps to eliminate errors in judgment that are based only on personal experiences.

- Science is defined not by what it investigates but by how it investigates. Scientific research is objective, systematic, and testable, reducing the probability that information will be based on personal beliefs, opinions, and feelings. Scientific research is based on the scientific method, which includes these steps: Conceptualize the problem, collect data, draw conclusions, and revise research conclusions and theory. A theory is a coherent set of ideas that helps explain and make predictions. A theory contains hypotheses.

- Numerous methods can be used to obtain information about various aspects of educational psychology. Research data-gathering methods can be classified as descriptive, correlational, and experimental. Descriptive methods include observation, interviews, questionnaires, standardized tests, ethnographic studies, and case studies. In correlational research, the goal is to describe the strength of the relation between two or more events or characteristics. An important research principle is that correlation does not equal causation. Experimental research is the only kind of research that can discover behavior's causes. Conducting an experiment involves examining the influence of at least one independent variable (the manipulated, influential, experimental factor) on one or more dependent variables (the measured factor). Experiments involve the random assignment of participants to one or more experimental groups (the groups whose experience is being manipulated) and one or more control groups (comparison groups treated in every way like the experimental group except for the manipulated factor). Cross-sectional research involves studying groups of people all at one time. Longitudinal research consists of studying the same people over time.

- Program evaluation research is research designed to make decisions about the effectiveness of a particular program. Action research is used to solve a specific classroom or social problem, improve teaching strategies, or make a decision about a specific location. The teacher-as-researcher (teacher-researcher) conducts classroom studies to improve his or her educational practices.

- Educational psychology researchers recognize that a number of ethical concerns have to be met when conducting research. The interests of the participants always have to be kept in mind. Every effort should be made to make research equitable for both females and males. In the past, research too often has been biased against females. We need to include more children from ethnic minority backgrounds in educational psychology research. A special concern is ethnic gloss. Be cautious about what is reported in the media, avoid drawing conclusions about individual needs on the basis of group research, recognize how easy it is to overgeneralize about a small or clinical sample, be aware that a single study usually is not the defining word, remember that causal conclusions cannot be drawn from correlational studies, and always consider the source of the information and evaluate its credibility.

KEY TERMS

educational psychology 4
constructivism 8
scientific research 16
scientific method 16
theory 16
hypotheses 16
laboratory 18

naturalistic observation 18
participant observation 18
standardized tests 19
case study 19
ethnographic study 19
correlational research 20
experimental research 20

independent variable 20
dependent variable 21
experimental group 21
control group 21
random assignment 21
cross-sectional research 21
longitudinal research 21

program evaluation
    research 23
action research 23
teacher-as-researcher 23
ethnic gloss 26

 PORTFOLIO ACTIVITIES

Now that you have a good understanding of this chapter, complete these exercises to expand your thinking.

Independent Reflection

Develop a Personal Teaching Statement. Write a personal statement about the following: What kind of teacher do you want to become? What strengths do you want to have? What kinds of potential weaknesses might you need to overcome? Either place the statement in your portfolio or seal it in an envelope that you will open after your first month or two of teaching. (INTASC: Principle 9)

Collaborative Work

Put It in Quotes. At the beginning of the chapter, you read the teacher-astronaut Christa McAuliffe's quote: "I touch the future. I teach." With three or four other students in the class, create one or more brief quotes that describe the positive aspects of teaching.

Then write a mission statement for your future classrooms. Summarize the mission statements below. How are they similar? Different? (INTASC: Principle 9)

Research/Field Experience Reflections

Compare Journal Research with Popular Media. Information about educational psychology appears in research journals and in magazines and newspapers. Find an article in a research or professional journal (such as *Educational Psychologist, Educational Psychology Review,* or *Phi Delta Kappan*) and an article in a newspaper or magazine on the same topic. How does the research/professional article differ from the newspaper or magazine account? What can you learn from this comparison? Write down your conclusions and keep copies of the articles. (INTASC: Principle 9)

 Go to the Online Learning Center for downloadable portfolio templates.

 TAKING IT TO THE NET

1. Begin building your network of support by subscribing to an education-related listserv. Joining an e-mail list will connect you to a community of educators who share ideas, resources, and experiences. Keep a log of the topics and issues discussed on the listserv. Why is e-mail a powerful networking tool for educators?
2. The World Wide Web offers educators unlimited resources for increasing their effectiveness in the classroom. Examine a

website for educators. How could the available resources contribute to your effectiveness in the classroom?
3. Teachers can use student surveys in the classroom to improve their teaching practices. Select one of your ideas, and formulate a brief (eight to ten questions) sample survey that you could use for future classroom research.

Connect to the Online Learning Center to explore possible answers.

STUDY, PRACTICE, AND SUCCEED

 Go to chapter 1 on the Online Learning Center at www.mhhe.com/santrockedu2e **to access the student** study guide with practice quizzes, web links, portfolio resources, PowerWeb articles and news feeds, and the online resources referenced in the chapter.

 Go to your Student Toolbox CD-ROM to access the resources and activities referenced in the chapter and

• Resources to help you prepare for the **PRAXIS II™ exam**

• **Application Resources,** including additional *Crack the Case* studies, electronic versions of the *Self-Assessments,* Application Exercises, and Site Observation Questions
• **Study Resources,** including Learning Goals, the Chapter Summary, a *Test Your Learning* exercise, and multiple-choice, true/false, matching, key terms, and short-answer quizzes
• **Professional Resources,** including a Lesson Plan Builder and *Bibliomaker*

2 Cognitive and Language Development

Ah! What would the world be to us
If the children were no more?
We should dread the desert behind us
Worse than the dark before.
—Henry Wadsworth Longfellow
American Poet, 19th Century

Chapter Outline

Chapter Learning Goals After you have completed your study of this chapter, you should be able to reach these learning goals:

1 Explain the value of studying children's development, as well as the general processes and periods of development.

2 Discuss the development of the brain and compare the cognitive developmental theories of Jean Piaget and Lev Vygotsky.

3 Identify the key features of language, biological and environmental influences on language, and the typical growth of the child's language.

Teaching Stories Donene Polson

Donene Polson teaches at Washington Elementary School in Salt Lake City. Washington is an innovative school that emphasizes the importance of people learning together as a community of learners (Rogoff, Turkanis, & Bartlett, 2001). Children as well as adults plan learning activities. Throughout the day at school, students work in small groups.

Donene says that she loves working in a school in which students, teachers, and parents all work together as a community to help children learn (Polson, 2001). Before the school year begins, Donene meets with parents at the family's home to prepare for the upcoming year, getting acquainted and establishing schedules to determine when parents can contribute to classroom instruction. At monthly teacher-parent meetings, Donene and the parents plan the curriculum and discuss how children's learning is progressing. They brainstorm about resources in the community that can be used effectively to promote children's learning.

Classroom unity is built over the school year through a sharing circle. Each Monday morning, students share their experiences with other students. Sometimes Donene selects themes for a week's sharing topic.

Many of Donene's students come back to tell Donene that their experiences in her classroom made important contributions to their development and learning. For example, Luisa Magarian reflected on how her experience in Donene's classroom helped her in coordinating and planning with others in high school:

> From having responsibility in groups, kids learn how to deal with problems and listen to each other or try to understand different points of view. They learn how to help a group work smoothly and how to keep people interested in what they are doing. . . . As coeditor of the student news magazine at my high school, I have to balance my eagerness to get things done with patience to work with other students (Rogoff, Turkanis, & Bartlett, 2001, pp. 84–85).

Expert Advice

Kenji Hakuta on English Language Learners

Later in the chapter, you will study Lev Vygotsky's sociocultural cognitive theory of development. Donene Polson's classroom reflects Vygotsky's emphasis on the importance of collaboration among a community of learners.

Examining the shape of children's development allows us to understand it better. This chapter—the first of two on development—focuses on children's cognitive and language development.

AN OVERVIEW OF CHILD DEVELOPMENT

Twentieth-century Spanish-born American philosopher George Santayana once reflected, "Children are on a different plane. They belong to a generation and way of feeling properly their own." Let's explore what that plane is like.

Why Studying Development Is Important

Why study children's development? As a teacher, you will be responsible for a new wave of children each year in your classroom. The more you learn about children's development, the more you can understand at what level it is appropriate to teach them.

Childhood has become such a distinct phase of the human life span that it is hard to imagine that it was not always thought of in that way. However, in medieval times, laws generally did not distinguish between child and adult offenses and children were often treated like miniature adults.

Today we view children quite differently than they were viewed in medieval times. We conceive of childhood as a highly eventful and unique time of life that lays an important foundation for the adult years and is highly differentiated from them. We identify distinct periods within childhood in which children master special skills and confront new life tasks. We value childhood as a special time of growth and change, and we invest great resources in caring for and educating our children. We protect them from the excesses of adult work through tough child labor laws, treat their most serious transgressions under a special system of juvenile justice, and have government provisions for helping children when ordinary family support systems fail or when a family seriously threatens a child's well-being.

Each child develops partly like all other children, partly like some other children, and partly like no other children. We often direct our attention to a child's uniqueness.

Children's Issues
Prevention Programs

But psychologists who study development often are drawn to children's shared characteristics—as are teachers who must manage and educate groups of same- or similar-age children. As humans, every person travels some common paths—Leonardo da Vinci; Joan of Arc; Martin Luther King, Jr.; Madonna; and most likely you—all walked at about one year, engaged in fantasy play as a child, developed an expanded vocabulary in the elementary school years, and became more independent as a youth.

Just what do psychologists mean when they speak of a person's "development"? Development is the pattern of biological, cognitive, and socioemotional changes that begins at conception and continues through the life span. Most development involves growth, although it also eventually involves decay (dying).

Education should be developmentally appropriate. That is, teaching should take place at a level that is neither too difficult and stressful nor too easy and boring for the age of the child. As we discuss development in this chapter and the next, keep in mind how the developmental changes we describe can help you understand the optimal level for teaching and learning. For example, it is not a good strategy to try to push children to read before they are developmentally ready; but when they are ready, reading materials should be presented at the appropriate level.

Processes and Periods

The pattern of child development is complex because it is the product of several processes: biological, cognitive, and socioemotional. Development also can be described in terms of periods.

Biological, Cognitive, and Socioemotional Processes   *Biological processes* involve changes in the child's body. Genetic inheritance plays a large part. Biological processes underlie the development of the brain, gains in height and weight, changes in motor skills, and puberty's hormonal changes.

Cognitive processes involve changes in the child's thinking, intelligence, and language. Cognitive developmental processes enable a growing child to memorize a poem, imagine how to solve a math problem, come up with a creative strategy, or speak meaningfully connected sentences.

Socioemotional processes involve changes in the child's relationships with other people, changes in emotion, and changes in personality. Parents' nurturance toward their child, a boy's aggressive attack on a peer, a girl's development of assertiveness, and an adolescent's feelings of joy after getting good grades all reflect socioemotional processes in development.

Periods of Development   For the purposes of organization and understanding, we commonly describe development in terms of periods. In the most widely used system of classification, the developmental periods are infancy, early childhood, middle and late childhood, adolescence, early adulthood, middle adulthood, and late adulthood.

Infancy extends from birth to eighteen to twenty-four months. It is a time of extreme dependence on adults. Many activities, such as language development, symbolic thought, sensorimotor coordination, and social learning, are just beginning.

Early childhood (sometimes called the "preschool years") extends from the end of infancy to about five or six years. During this period, children become more self-sufficient, develop school readiness skills (such as learning to follow instructions and identify letters), and spend many hours with peers. First grade typically marks the end of early childhood.

Middle and late childhood (sometimes called the "elementary school years") extends from about six to eleven years of age. Children master the fundamental skills of reading, writing, and math at this time. Achievement becomes a more central theme of children's lives and they increase their self-control. In this period, they interact more with the wider social world beyond their family.

Trends in the Well-Being of Children and Youth

Children Now

Social Policy

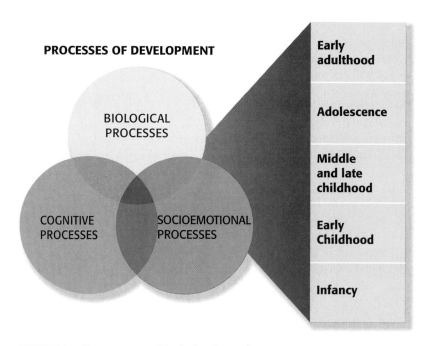

PROCESSES OF DEVELOPMENT

BIOLOGICAL PROCESSES

COGNITIVE PROCESSES

SOCIOEMOTIONAL PROCESSES

Early adulthood

Adolescence

Middle and late childhood

Early Childhood

Infancy

FIGURE 2.1 Processes and Periods of Development
Biological, cognitive, and socioemotional processes interact to produce the periods of development.

Adolescence involves the transition from childhood to adulthood. It begins around ages ten to twelve and ends around eighteen to twenty-two. Adolescence starts with rapid physical changes, including gains in height and weight and the development of sexual functions. In adolescence, individuals more intensely pursue independence and seek their own identity. Their thought becomes more abstract, logical, and idealistic.

Early adulthood begins in the late teens or early twenties and stretches into the thirties. It is a time when work and love become main themes in life. Individuals make important career decisions and usually seek to have an intimate relationship through marriage or a relationship with a significant other (Santrock, 2002). Other developmental periods have been described for older adults, but we will confine our discussion to the periods most relevant for children's education.

The periods of human development are shown in figure 2.1 along with the processes of development (biological, cognitive, and socioemotional). The interplay of these processes produces the periods of human development.

Review and Reflect

1 Explain the value of studying children's development, as well as the general processes and periods of development.

Review
- What implications does the concept of development have for the notion of "appropriate" learning?
- What three broad processes interact in a child's development? What general periods do children go through between birth and the end of adolescence?

Reflect
- Give an example of how a cognitive process could influence a socioemotional process in the age of children you plan to teach. Then give an example of how a socioemotional process could influence a cognitive process in this age group.

Now that we have discussed some basic ideas about the nature of development, we will examine cognitive development in greater length. In examining different processes of development—biological, cognitive, and socioemotional—we indicated that these processes interact. In keeping with this theme, in our exploration of cognitive development, we will describe the physical development of the brain.

COGNITIVE DEVELOPMENT

Twentieth-century American poet Marianne Moore said that the mind is "an enchanting thing." How this enchanting thing called the mind develops has intrigued many psychologists. First, we will explore the development of the brain and then turn to two major cognitive theories of development—Piaget's and Vygotsky's.

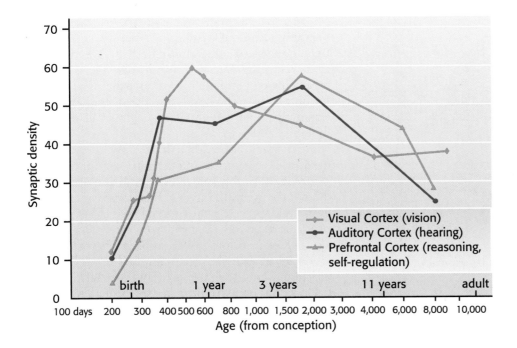

FIGURE 2.2 **Synaptic Density in the Human Brain from Infancy to Adulthood**
The graph shows the dramatic increase and then pruning in synaptic density for three regions of the brain: visual cortex, auditory cortex, and prefrontal cortex. Synaptic density is believed to be an important indication of the extent of connectivity between neurons.

The Brain

Until recently, little was known for certain about how the brain changes as children age and grow. Considerable progress is being made in charting developmental changes in the brain, although much is still unknown, and connections to children's education are difficult to make (Blair, 2002).

Brain Cells and Regions   The number and size of the brain's nerve endings continue to grow at least until adolescence. Some of the brain's increase in size also is due to *myelination,* a process in which many cells of the brain and nervous system are covered with an insulating layer of fat cells. This increases the speed at which information travels through the nervous system. Myelination in the areas of the brain related to hand-eye coordination is not complete until about four years of age. Myelination in brain areas that are important in focusing attention is not complete until the end of the elementary school years (Tanner, 1978). The implications for teaching are that children will have more difficulty focusing their attention and maintaining it for very long in early childhood but their attention will improve as they move through the elementary school years. Even in elementary school and later, many educators believe occasional short breaks sustain children's energy and motivation to learn.

Another important aspect of the brain's development at the cellular level is the dramatic increase in connections between neurons (nerve cells) (Ramey & Ramey, 2000). *Synapses* are tiny gaps between neurons where connections between neurons are made. Researchers have discovered an interesting aspect of synaptic connections. Nearly twice as many of these connections are made than ever will be used (Huttenlocher & Dabholkar, 1997; Huttenlocher & others, 1991). The connections that are used become strengthened and will survive, while the unused ones will be replaced by other pathways or disappear. That is, in the language of neuroscience, these connections will be "pruned." Figure 2.2 vividly shows the dramatic growth and later pruning of synapses in the visual, auditory, and prefrontal cortex areas of the brain. These areas are critical for higher-order cognitive functioning such as learning, memory, and reasoning. Notice that in the prefrontal cortex (where higher-level thinking and self-regulation take place) the peak of overproduction occurs at about one year of age. Notice also that it is not until middle to late adolescence that the adult density of the synapses is achieved.

Neural Processes

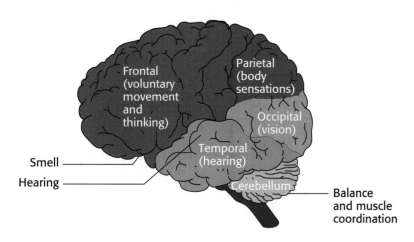

FIGURE 2.3 The Brain's Four Lobes
Shown here are the locations of the brain's four lobes: frontal, occipital, temporal, and parietal.

In a recent study that used sophisticated brain-scanning techniques, children's brains were shown to undergo substantial anatomical changes between the ages of three and fifteen (Thompson & others, 2000). By repeatedly obtaining brain scans of the same children for up to four years, it was found that children's brains experience rapid, distinct spurts of growth. The amount of brain material in some areas can nearly double within a year, followed by a drastic loss of tissue as un-needed cells are purged and the brain continues to reorganize itself. In this study, the overall size of the brain did not change from three to fifteen years of age. However, rapid growth in the frontal lobes, especially areas related to attention, occurred from three to six years of age. Figure 2.3 shows the location of the brain's four lobes. Rapid growth in the temporal lobes (language processing, long-term memory) and parietal lobes (spatial location) occurred from age six through puberty.

One of the most fascinating recent discoveries about the adolescent's brain focuses on developmental changes in the areas of the brain that involve emotion and higher-level cognitive functioning. The *amygdala* is a region of the brain that handles the processing of information about emotion; the prefrontal cortex is especially important in higher-level cognitive functioning (LeDoux, 2002). Researchers are finding that the very last part of the brain to mature is the prefrontal cortex, where planning, setting priorities, suppressing impulses, and weighing the consequences of one's actions take place (Rubia & others, 2000). This means that the brain region for putting the brakes on risky, impulsive behavior and thinking before acting is still under construction during adolescence (Casey, Giedd, & Thomas, 2000; Giedd & others 1999; Sowell & Jernigan, 1998). However, more research is needed to clarify these findings on possible developmental changes in brain activity and their links to adolescent thinking and behavior (Keating, 2004).

Lateralization   The cerebral cortex (the highest level of the brain) is divided into two halves, or hemispheres (see figure 2.4). **Lateralization** is the specialization of functions in each hemisphere of the brain.

In individuals with an intact brain, there is a specialization of function in some areas (Gazzaniga, Ivry, & Mangun, 2001):

1. *Verbal processing.* The most extensive research on the brain's two hemispheres involves language. In most individuals, speech and grammar are localized to the left hemisphere. However, this does not mean that all language processing is carried out in the brain's left hemisphere. For example, understanding such aspects of language as appropriate use of language in different contexts, evaluation of the emotional expressiveness of language, metaphor, and much of humor involves the right hemisphere (Gegeshidze & Tsaqareli, 2004).
2. *Nonverbal processing.* The right hemisphere is usually more dominant in processing nonverbal information, such as spatial perception, visual recognition, and emotion (Floel & others, 2004). For example, for most individuals, the right hemisphere is mainly at work when they process information about people's faces (O'Toole, 2001). The right hemisphere also may be more involved when people express emotions, or recognize others' emotions.

Because of the differences in functioning of the brain's two hemispheres, people commonly use the phrases "left-brained" and "right-brained" to say which hemisphere is dominant. Unfortunately, much of this talk is seriously exaggerated. For example, laypeople and the media commonly exaggerate hemispheric specialization by claiming that the left brain is logical and the right brain is creative. However, most complex functioning—such as logical and creative thinking—in normal people involves communication

lateralization The specialization of functions in each hemisphere of the brain.

between both sides of the brain. Scientists who study the brain are typically very cautious with terms such as *left-brained* and *right-brained* because the brain is more complex than those terms suggest (Knect & others, 2001).

The Brain and Children's Education   There have been numerous claims made about how children's education should be brain-based. Some journalists have asserted that educators should look to neuroscience for answers as to how best to teach children based on the brain's growth and development.

Unfortunately, too often bold statements have been made about the implications of brain science for children's education that are speculative at best and often far removed from what neuroscientists know about the brain (Breur, 1999). We don't have to look any further than the hype about "left-brained" individuals being more logical and "right-brained" individuals being more creative to see where links between neuroscience and brain education are incorrectly made (Sousa, 1995).

Another commonly promoted link between neuroscience and brain education is that there is a critical or sensitive period—a biological window of opportunity—when learning is easy, effective, and easily retained. However, there is no neuroscientific evidence to support this belief (Breur, 1999). One leading neuroscientist even told educators that although children's brains acquire a great deal of information during the early years, most learning likely takes place after synaptic formation stabilizes, which is after the age of ten (Goldman-Rakic, 1996).

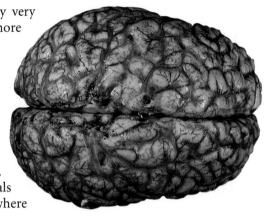

FIGURE 2.4 **The Human Brain's Hemispheres**
The two halves (hemispheres) of the human brain are clearly seen in this photograph.

Piaget's Theory

Poet Noah Perry once asked, "Who knows the thoughts of a child?" More than anyone, the famous Swiss psychologist Jean Piaget (1896–1980) knew.

Cognitive Processes   In actively constructing their world, children use schemas. A **schema** is a concept or framework that exists in an individual's mind to organize and interpret information. Schemas can range from the simple (such as a schema of a car) to complex (such as a schema for what constitutes the universe). A six-year-old who recognizes that five small toy cars can be stored in an equal number of small boxes is exercising a schema for number. Piaget's interest in schemas focused on how children organize and make sense out of their current experiences.

Piaget (1952) said that two processes are responsible for how children use and adapt their schemas: assimilation and accommodation. **Assimilation** occurs when a child incorporates new knowledge into existing knowledge. That is, in assimilation children assimilate the environment into a schema. **Accommodation** occurs when a child adjusts to new information. That is, children adjust their schemas to the environment.

Consider an eight-year-old girl who is given a hammer and nail to hang a picture on the wall. She has never used a hammer, but from observing others do this she realizes that a hammer is an object to be held, that it is swung by the handle to hit the nail, and that it usually is swung a number of times. Recognizing each of these things, she fits her behavior into this schema she already has (assimilation). But the hammer is heavy, so she holds it near the top. She swings too hard and the nail bends, so she adjusts the pressure of her strikes. These adjustments reflect her ability to slightly alter her conception of the world (accommodation). Just as both assimilation and accommodation are required in this example, so are they required in many of the child's thinking challenges (see figure 2.5 on page 40).

Piaget also emphasized that to make sense out of their world, children cognitively organize their experiences. **Organization** is Piaget's concept of grouping isolated behaviors into a higher-order, more smoothly functioning cognitive system. Every level of thought is organized. Continual refinement of this organization is an inherent part of development. Children who have only a vague idea about how to use a hammer might also have a vague idea about how to use other tools. After learning how to use each one,

The Jean Piaget Society
Piaget's Stages

schema A concept or framework that exists in a person's mind to organize and interpret information.

assimilation A mental process that occurs when a child incorporates new knowledge into existing knowledge.

accommodation A mental process that occurs when a child adjusts to new information.

organization Piaget's concept of grouping isolated behaviors into a higher-order, more smoothly functioning cognitive system; the grouping or arranging of items into categories. The use of organization improves long-term memory.

Assimilation occurs when people incorporate new information into their existing schematic knowledge. *How might this eight-year-old girl first attempt to use the hammer and nail, based on her preexisting schematic knowledge about these objects?*

Accommodation occurs when people adjust their knowledge schemas to new information. *How might the girl adjust her schemas regarding hammers and nails during her successful effort to hang the picture?*

FIGURE 2.5 Assimilation and Accommodation

children must interrelate these uses, or organize their knowledge, if they are to become skilled in using tools. In the same way, children continually integrate and coordinate the many other branches of knowledge that often develop independently. Organization occurs within stages of development as well as across them.

Equilibration is a mechanism that Piaget proposed to explain how children shift from one stage of thought to the next. The shift occurs as children experience cognitive conflict, or a disequilibrium, in trying to understand the world. Eventually, the child resolves the conflict and reaches a balance, or equilibrium, of thought. Piaget believed there is considerable movement between states of cognitive equilibrium and disequilibrium as assimilation and accommodation work in concert to produce cognitive change. For example, if children believe that an amount of liquid changes simply because it is poured into a container with a different shape (from a container that is short and wide into a container that is tall and narrow), they might be puzzled by such issues as where the "extra" liquid came from and whether there is actually more liquid to drink. The child will eventually resolve these puzzles as her thought becomes more advanced. In the everyday world, the child is constantly faced with such counterexamples and inconsistencies.

Piagetian Stages   Through his observations, Piaget also came to believe that cognitive development unfolds in a sequence of four stages. Each of the stages is age-related and consists of distinctive ways of thinking. It is the different way of thinking that makes one stage discontinuous from and more advanced than another. According to Piaget, knowing more information does not make the child's thinking more advanced. The advance is qualitatively different. Piaget's stages are called sensorimotor, preoperational, concrete operational, and formal operational (see figure 2.6).

The Sensorimotor Stage   The **sensorimotor stage,** which lasts from birth to about two years of age, is the first Piagetian stage. In this stage, infants construct an understanding of the world by coordinating their sensory experiences (such as seeing and hearing) with their motor actions (reaching, touching)—hence the term *sensorimotor*. At the beginning of this stage, infants show little more than reflexive patterns to adapt to the world. By the end of the stage, they display far more complex sensorimotor patterns.

Piaget believed that an especially important cognitive accomplishment in infancy is object permanence. This involves understanding that objects and events continue to exist even when they cannot be seen, heard, or touched. A second accomplishment is the gradual realization that there is a difference or boundary between oneself and the surrounding environment. Imagine what your thought would be like if you could not distinguish between yourself and your world. Your thought would be chaotic, disorganized, and unpredictable. This is what the mental life of a newborn is like, according to Piaget. The young infant does not differentiate between self and world and has no sense of object permanence. By the end of the sensorimotor period, the child does differentiate between the self and the world and is aware that objects continue to exist over time.

The Preoperational Stage   The **preoperational stage** is the second Piagetian stage. Lasting approximately from two to seven years of age, it is more symbolic than sensorimotor thought but does not involve operational thought. However, it is egocentric and intuitive rather than logical.

equilibration A mechanism that Piaget proposed to explain how children shift from one stage of thought to the next. The shift occurs as children experience cognitive conflict, or disequilibrium, in trying to understand the world. Eventually, they resolve the conflict and reach equilibrium of thought.

sensorimotor stage The first Piagetian stage, lasting from birth to about two years of age, in which infants construct an understanding of the world by coordinating sensory experiences with motor actions.

preoperational stage The second Piagetian stage, lasting from about two to seven years of age; symbolic thought increases but operational thought is not yet present.

SENSORIMOTOR STAGE	PREOPERATIONAL STAGE	CONCRETE OPERATIONAL STAGE	FORMAL OPERATIONAL STAGE
The infant constructs an understanding of the world by coordinating sensory experiences with physical actions. An infant progresses from reflexive, instinctual action at birth to the beginning of symbolic thought toward the end of the stage.	The child begins to represent the world with words and images. These words and images reflect increased symbolic thinking and go beyond the connection of sensory information and physical action.	The child can now reason logically about concrete events and classify objects into different sets.	The adolescent reasons in more abstract, idealistic, and logical ways.
Birth to 2 Years of Age	**2 to 7 Years of Age**	**7 to 11 Years of Age**	**11 Years of Age Through Adulthood**

FIGURE 2.6 **Piaget's Four Stages of Cognitive Development**

Preoperational thought can be subdivided into two substages: symbolic function and intuitive thought. The **symbolic function substage** occurs roughly between two and four years of age. In this substage, the young child gains the ability to represent mentally an object that is not present. This stretches the child's mental world to new dimensions. Expanded use of language and the emergence of pretend play are other examples of an increase in symbolic thought during this early childhood substage. Young children begin to use scribbled designs to represent people, houses, cars, clouds, and many other aspects of the world. Possibly because young children are not very concerned about reality, their drawings are fanciful and inventive. Suns are blue, skies are green, and cars float on clouds in their imaginative world. The symbolism is simple but strong, not unlike abstractions found in some modern art. As the famous twentieth-century Spanish artist Pablo Picasso once remarked, "I used to draw like Raphael but it has taken me a lifetime to draw like young children." One 3½-year-old looked at the scribble he had just drawn and described it as a pelican kissing a seal (see figure 2.7a on page 42). In the elementary school years, children's drawings become more realistic, neat, and precise (see figure 2.7b on page 42). Suns are yellow, skies are blue, and cars travel on roads.

Even though young children make distinctive progress in this substage, their pre-operational thought still has two important limitations: egocentrism and animism. *Egocentrism* is the inability to distinguish between one's own perspective and someone else's perspective. The following telephone interaction between four-year-old Mary, who is at home, and her father, who is at work, typifies egocentric thought:

Father: Mary, is Mommy there?

Mary: (Silently nods)

Father: Mary, can I speak to Mommy?

Mary: (Nods again silently)

Mary's response is egocentric in that she fails to consider her father's perspective; she does not realize that he cannot see her nod.

Piaget and Barbel Inhelder (1969) initially studied young children's egocentrism by devising the three mountains task (see figure 2.8 on page 42). The child walks around the model of the mountains and becomes familiar with what the mountains look like from different perspectives. The child also can see that there are different objects on the mountains. The child then is seated on one side of the table on which the mountains are placed. The experimenter moves a doll to different locations around the table. At each

Symbolic Thinking

symbolic function substage The first substage of preoperational thought, occurring between about two to four years of age; the ability to represent an object not present develops and symbolic thinking increases; egocentrism and animism occur.

(*a*) A 3½-year-old's symbolic drawing. Halfway into this drawing, the 3½-year-old said it was "a pelican kissing a seal."

(*b*) This 11-year-old's drawing is neater and more realistic but also less inventive.

FIGURE 2.7 Developmental Changes in Children's Drawings

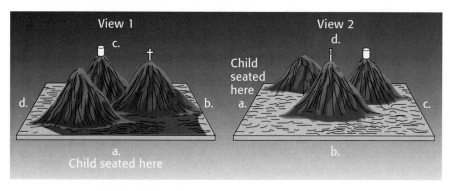

FIGURE 2.8 The Three Mountains Task

View 1 shows the child's perspective from where he or she is sitting. View 2 is an example of the photograph the child would be shown, mixed in with others from different perspectives. To correctly identify this view, the child has to take the perspective of a person sitting at spot *b*. Invariably, a preschool child who thinks in a preoperational way cannot perform this task. When asked what a view of the mountains looks like from position *b*, the child selects a photograph taken from location *a*, the child's view at the time.

intuitive thought substage The second substage of preoperational thought, lasting from about four to seven years of age. Children begin to use primitive reasoning and want to know the answer to all sorts of questions. They seem so sure about their knowledge in this substage but are unaware of how they know what they know.

location the child is asked to select from a series of photos the one that most accurately reflects the view the doll is seeing. Children in the preoperational stage often pick the view that reflects where they are sitting rather than the doll's view.

Animism also characterizes preoperational thought. It is the belief that inanimate objects have "lifelike" qualities and are capable of action. A young child might show animism by saying, "That tree pushed the leaf off and it fell down" or "The sidewalk made me mad. It made me fall down."

What further cognitive changes take place in the preoperational stage? The **intuitive thought substage** is the second substage of preoperational thought, starting at about four years of age and lasting until about seven years of age. At this substage, children begin to use primitive reasoning and want to know the answers to all sorts of questions. Piaget called this substage "intuitive" because the children seem so sure about their

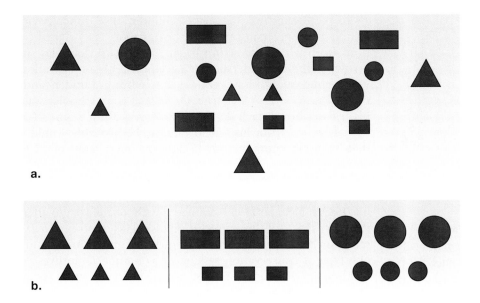

FIGURE 2.9 Arrays

(a) A random array of objects. *(b)* An ordered array of objects.

knowledge and understanding yet are unaware of how they know what they know. That is, they say they know something but know it without the use of rational thinking.

An example of young children's limitation in reasoning ability is the difficulty they have putting things into correct categories. Look at the collection of objects in figure 2.9a. You would probably respond to the direction "Put the things together that you believe belong together" by grouping the objects by size and shape. Your sorting might look something like that shown in figure 2.9b. Faced with a similar collection of objects that can be sorted on the basis of two or more properties, preoperational children seldom are capable of using these properties consistently to sort the objects into appropriate groupings. In the social realm, if a four-year-old girl is given the task of dividing her peers into groups according to whether they are friends and whether they are boys or girls, she is unlikely to arrive at a classification of friendly boys, friendly girls, unfriendly boys, unfriendly girls.

Many of these preoperational examples show a characteristic of thought called **centration,** which involves focusing (or centering) attention on one characteristic to the exclusion of all others. Centration is most clearly present in preoperational children's lack of **conservation,** the idea that some characteristic of an object stays the same even though the object might change in appearance. For example, to adults it is obvious that a certain amount of liquid stays the same regardless of a container's shape. But this is not obvious at all to young children. Rather, they are struck by the height of the liquid in the container. In this type of conservation task (Piaget's most famous), a child is presented with two identical beakers, each filled to the same level with liquid (see figure 2.10 on page 44). The child is asked if the beakers have the same amount of liquid. The child usually says yes. Then the liquid from one beaker is poured into a third beaker, which is taller and thinner. The child now is asked if the amount of liquid in the tall, thin beaker is equal to the liquid that remains in the second original beaker. Children younger than seven or eight usually say no. They justify their answer by referring to the differing height or width of the beakers. Older children usually answer yes. They justify their answers appropriately: If you poured the liquid back, the amount would still be the same.

In Piaget's view, failing the conservation of liquid task indicates that the child is at the preoperational stage of thinking. Passing the test suggests the child is at the concrete operational stage of thinking.

According to Piaget, preoperational children also cannot perform what he called *operations.* In Piaget's theory, operations are mental representations that are reversible.

centration Focusing, or centering, attention on one characteristic to the exclusion of all others; characteristic of preoperational thinking.

conservation The idea that some characteristic of an object stays the same even though the object might change in appearance; a cognitive ability that develops in the concrete operational stage, according to Piaget.

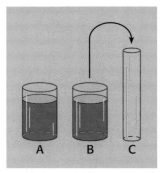
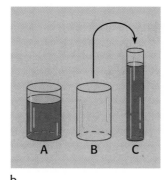

FIGURE 2.10 Piaget's Conservation Task

The beaker test is a well-known Piagetian test to determine whether a child can think operationally—that is, can mentally reverse actions and show conservation of the substance. *(a)* Two identical beakers are presented to the child. Then, the liquid is poured from B into C, which is taller and thinner than A or B. *(b)* The child is asked if these beakers (A and C) have the same amount of liquid. The preoperational child says no. When asked to point to the beaker that has more liquid, the preoperational child points to the tall, thin beaker.

"I still don't have all the answers, but I'm beginning to ask the right questions."
©The New Yorker Collection 1989 Lee Lorenz from cartoonbank.com. All Rights Reserved.

As in the beaker task, preschool children have difficulty understanding that reversing an action brings about the original conditions from which the action began. These two examples should further help you understand Piaget's concepts of operations. A young child might know that $4 + 2 = 6$ but not understand that the reverse, $6 - 2 = 4$, is true. Or let's say a preschooler walks to his friend's house each day but always gets a ride home. If asked to walk home from his friend's house, he probably would reply that he didn't know the way because he never had walked home before.

Some developmentalists do not believe Piaget was entirely correct in his estimate of when conservation skills emerge. For example, Rochel Gelman (1969) trained preschool children to attend to relevant aspects of the conservation task. This improved their conservation skills. Gelman also has shown that attentional training on one type of conservation task, such as number, improves young children's performance on another type of conservation task, such as mass. She believes that young children develop conservation skills earlier than Piaget envisioned and that such skills can be improved with attentional training.

Yet another characteristic of preoperational children is that they ask a lot of questions. The barrage begins around age three. By about five, they have just about exhausted the adults around them with "Why?" "Why" questions signal the emergence of the child's interest in figuring out why things are the way they are. Following is a sampling of four- to six-year-olds' questions (Elkind, 1976):

"What makes you grow up?"
"What makes you stop growing?"
"Who was the mother when everybody was a baby?"
"Why do leaves fall?"
"Why does the sun shine?"

Teaching Strategies
For Working with
Preoperational Thinkers

1. *Have children manipulate groups of objects.*
2. *To reduce egocentrism, involve children in social interactions.*
3. *Ask children to make comparisons.* These might involve such concepts as bigger, taller, wider, heavier, and longer.
4. *Give children experience in ordering operations.* For example, have children line up in rows from tall to short and vice versa. Bring in various examples of animal and plant life cycles, such as several photographs of butterfly development or the sprouting of beans or kernels of corn. Examples of these natural stages help children's ordering ability.
5. *Have children draw scenes with perspective.* Encourage them to make the objects in their drawings appear to be at the same location as in the scene they are viewing. For example, if they see a horse at the end of a field, they should place the horse in the same location in the drawing.
6. *Construct an inclined plane or a hill.* Let children roll marbles of various sizes down the plane. Ask them to compare how quickly the different-size marbles reach the bottom. This should help them understand the concept of speed.
7. *Ask children to justify their answers when they draw conclusions.* For example, when they say that pouring a liquid from a short, wide container into a tall, thin

container makes the liquid change in volume, ask, "Why do you think so?" or "How could you prove this to one of your friends?"

The Concrete Operational Stage   The **concrete operational stage,** the third Piagetian stage of cognitive development, lasts from about seven to about eleven years of age. Concrete operational thought involves using operations. Logical reasoning replaces intuitive reasoning, but only in concrete situations. Classification skills are present, but abstract problems go unsolved.

A concrete operation is a reversible mental action pertaining to real, concrete objects. Concrete operations allow the child to coordinate several characteristics rather than focus on a single property of an object. At the concrete operational level, children can do mentally what they previously could do only physically, and they can reverse concrete operations. For example, to test conservation of matter, the child is presented with two identical balls of clay. The experimenter rolls one ball into a long, thin shape. The child is asked if there is more clay in the ball or in the long, thin piece of clay. By the time children are seven or eight years old, most answer that the amount of clay is the same. To answer this problem correctly, children have to imagine that the clay ball can be rolled out into a long, thin strip and then returned to its original round shape. In this example, the preoperational child would have focused either on height or length. The concrete operational child coordinates information about both dimensions.

An important concrete operation is classifying or dividing things into different sets or subsets and considering their interrelationships. Reasoning about a family tree of four generations reveals a child's concrete operational skills (Furth & Wachs, 1975). The family tree shown in figure 2.11 suggests that the grandfather (A) has three children (B, C, and D), each of whom has two children (E through J), and one of these children (J) has three children (K, L, and M). Concrete operational thinkers understand the classification. For example, they can reason that person J can at the same time be father, brother, and grandson. A preoperational thinker cannot.

Some Piagetian tasks require children to reason about relations between classes. One such task is **seriation,** the concrete operation that involves ordering stimuli along some quantitative dimension (such as length). To see if students can serialize, a teacher might place eight sticks of different lengths in a haphazard way on a table. The teacher then asks the student to order the sticks by length. Many young children end up with two or three small groups of "big" sticks or "little" sticks rather than a correct ordering of all eight sticks. Another mistaken strategy they use is to evenly line up the tops of the sticks but ignore the bottoms. The concrete operational thinker simultaneously understands that each stick must be longer than the one that precedes it and shorter than the one that follows it.

Another aspect of reasoning about the relations between classes is **transitivity.** This involves the ability to logically combine relations to understand certain conclusions. In this case, consider three sticks (A, B, and C) of differing lengths. A is the longest, B is intermediate in length, and C is the shortest. Does the child understand that if $A > B$, and $B > C$, then $A > C$? In Piaget's theory, concrete operational thinkers do; preoperational thinkers do not.

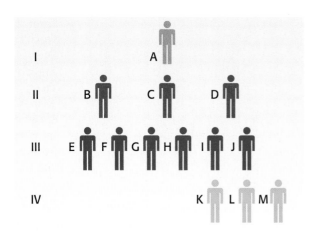

FIGURE 2.11 **Classification**

Classification is an important ability in concrete operational thought. When shown a family tree of four generations (I to IV), the preoperational child has trouble classifying the members of the four generations; the concrete operational child can classify the members vertically, horizontally, and obliquely (up and down and across).

concrete operational stage Piaget's third cognitive developmental stage, occurring between about seven to eleven years of age. At this stage the child thinks operationally and logical reasoning replaces intuitive thought but only in concrete situations; classification skills are present but abstract problems present difficulties.

seriation A concrete operation that involves ordering stimuli along some quantitative dimension.

transitivity The ability to logically combine relations to understand certain conclusions; develops in the concrete operational stage.

Teaching Strategies
For Working with Concrete
Operational Thinkers

1. *Encourage students to discover concepts and principles.* Ask relevant questions about what is being studied to help them focus on some aspect of their learning. Refrain

from telling students the answers to their questions outright. Try to get them to reach the answers through their own thinking.

2. *Involve children in operational tasks.* These include adding, subtracting, multiplying, dividing, ordering, seriating, and reversing. Use concrete materials for these tasks, possibly introducing math symbols later.

3. *Plan activities in which students practice the concept of ascending and descending classification hierarchies.* Have students list the following in order of size (such as largest to smallest): city of Atlanta, state of Georgia, country of United States, Western Hemisphere, and planet Earth.

4. *Include activities that require conservation of area, weight, and displaced volume.*

5. *Create activities in which children order and reverse order.* Many third-graders have difficulty in reversing order, such as going from tall to short rather than short to tall. They also have trouble, after listing the cities they will pass through in taking a trip, reversing the order for coming home.

6. *Continue to ask students to justify their answers when they solve problems.* Help them to check the validity and accuracy of their conclusions.

7. *Encourage children to work in groups and exchange thoughts with each other.* For example, ask a group of children to create a play, sharing their viewpoints with each other.

8. *Make sure that the materials in the classroom are rich enough to stimulate students' questions.* A versatile insect for classroom discussion is a mealworm. Have students observe it and describe it. An overnight appearance of a more mature mealworm may take place, which can surprise students and encourage them to think about why this occurred.

9. *When trying to teach anything complex, create props and visual aids.* For example, in teaching a social science lesson on what a democracy is, show a video that illustrates the concept.

10. *Encourage students to manipulate and experiment in science, use concrete materials in mathematics, create and act out in language arts, and discuss their perspectives with each other and take field trips in social studies.*

Video Lecture: The Concrete and Formal Operational Stages

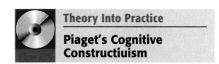

Theory Into Practice

Piaget's Cognitive Constructiuism

formal operational stage Piaget's fourth cognitive developmental stage, which emerges between about eleven and fifteen years of age; thought is more abstract, idealistic, and logical in this stage.

hypothetical-deductive reasoning Piaget's formal operational concept that adolescents can develop hypotheses to solve problems and systematically reach (deduce) a conclusion.

The Formal Operational Stage The **formal operational stage,** which emerges at about eleven to fifteen years of age, is Piaget's fourth and final cognitive stage. At this stage, individuals move beyond reasoning only about concrete experiences and think in more abstract, idealistic, and logical ways.

The abstract quality of formal operational thinking is evident in verbal problem solving. The concrete operational thinker needs to see the concrete elements A, B, and C to make the logical inference that if A = B and B = C, then A = C. In contrast, the formal operational thinker can solve this problem when it is verbally presented.

Accompanying the abstract nature of formal operational thought are the abilities to idealize and imagine possibilities. At this stage, adolescents engage in extended speculation about the ideal qualities they desire in themselves and others. These idealistic thoughts can merge into fantasy. Many adolescents become impatient with their newfound ideals and the problems of how to live them out.

At the same time as adolescents are thinking more abstractly and idealistically, they also are beginning to think more logically. As formal operational thinkers, they think more like scientists. They devise plans to solve problems and systematically test solutions. Piaget's term **hypothetical-deductive reasoning** embodies the concept that adolescents can develop hypotheses (best hunches) about ways to solve problems and systematically reach a conclusion.

One example of hypothetical-deductive reasoning involves a modification of the familiar game "Twenty Questions." Individuals are shown a set of 42 color pictures displayed in a rectangular array (six rows of seven pictures each) and asked to determine which picture the experimenter has in mind (that is, which is "correct"). The

What kind of cognitive changes take place in adolescence, according to Piaget?

subjects are only allowed to ask questions to which the experimenter can answer yes or no. The object of the game is to select the correct picture by asking as few questions as possible.

Adolescents who are deductive hypothesis testers formulate a plan and test a series of hypotheses, which considerably narrows the field of choices. The most effective plan is a "halving" strategy (*Q:* Is the picture in the right half of the array? *A:* No. *Q:* OK. Is it in the top half? And so on). A correct halving strategy guarantees the answer in seven questions or less. In contrast, the concrete operational thinker might persist with questions that continue to test some of the same possibilities that previous questions could have eliminated. For example, they might ask whether the correct picture is in row 1 and are told that it is not. Later, they ask whether the picture is *X,* which is in row 1.

Thus, formal operational thinkers test their hypotheses with judiciously chosen questions and tests. In contrast, concrete operational thinkers often fail to understand the relation between a hypothesis and a well-chosen test of it, stubbornly clinging to ideas that already have been discounted.

A form of egocentrism also emerges in adolescence (Elkind, 1978). *Adolescent egocentrism* is the heightened self-consciousness that is reflected in adolescents' beliefs that others are as interested in them as they themselves are. Adolescent egocentrism also includes a sense of personal uniqueness. It involves the desire to be noticed, visible, and "on stage." Consider twelve-year-old Tracy, who says, "Oh my gosh! I can't believe it. Help! I can't stand it!" Her mother asks, "What is the matter?" Tracy responds, "Everyone in here is looking at me." The mother queries, "Why?" Tracy says, "This one hair won't stay in place," as she rushes to the rest room to plaster it with hairspray. Perceived uniqueness also is evident in sixteen-year-old Margaret's feelings after her boyfriend has broken up with her. She tells her mother, "You have no idea how I feel. You have never experienced this kind of pain."

Egocentrism is a normal adolescent occurrence, more common in the middle school than in high school years. However, for some individuals, adolescent egocentrism can contribute to reckless behavior, including suicidal thoughts, drug use, and failure to use contraceptives during sexual intercourse. Egocentricity leads some adolescents to think that they are invulnerable.

Teaching Strategies
For Working with Formal
Operational Thinkers

Strategies in Practice

Piaget

1. *Realize that many adolescents are not full-fledged formal operational thinkers.* Although Piaget believed formal operational thought emerges between eleven and fifteen years of age, many students in this age range actually are concrete operational thinkers or are just beginning to use formal operational thought. Thus, many of the teaching strategies discussed earlier regarding the education of concrete operational thinkers still apply to many young adolescents. A curriculum that is too formal and too abstract will go over their heads.

2. *Propose a problem and invite students to form hypotheses about how to solve it.* For example, a teacher might say, "Imagine that a girl has no friends. What should she do?"

3. *Present a problem and suggest several ways it might be approached.* Then ask questions that stimulate students to evaluate the approaches. For example, describe several ways to investigate a robbery and ask students to evaluate which is best.

4. *Select a particular problem that is familiar to the class and ask questions related to it.* For example, the teacher asks, "What factors should be considered if we are going to be able to get the economy back on track?"

5. *Ask students to discuss their prior conclusions.* For example, ask, "What steps did you go through in solving this problem?"

6. *Develop projects and investigations for students to carry out.* Periodically ask them how they are going about collecting and interpreting the data.

7. *Encourage students to create hierarchical outlines when you ask them to write papers.* Make sure they understand how to organize their writing in terms of general and specific points. The abstractness of formal operational thinking also means that teachers with students at this level can encourage them to use metaphors.

8. *Recognize that adolescents are more likely to use formal operational thinking in the areas in which they have the most expertise and experience.* For example, a student who loves English and reads and writes a lot might use formal operational thinking in that area. However, the same student might not like math and might show concrete operational thinking in that area.

Piaget is shown here with his family. Piaget's careful observations of his three children—Lucienne, Laurent, and Jacqueline—contributed to the development of his cognitive theory.

Evaluating Piaget's Theory   What were Piaget's main contributions? Has his theory withstood the test of time?

Contributions   Piaget is a giant in the field of developmental psychology. We owe to him the present field of children's cognitive development. We owe to him a long list of masterful concepts of enduring power and fascination, including the concepts of assimilation, accommodation, object permanence, egocentrism, conservation, and hypothetical-deductive reasoning. Along with William James and John Dewey, we also owe to him the current vision of children as active, constructive thinkers.

Piaget also was a genius when it came to observing children. His careful observations showed us inventive ways to discover how children act on and adapt to their world (Vidal, 2000). Piaget showed us some important things to look for in cognitive development, such as the shift from preoperational to concrete operational thinking. He also showed us how children need to make their experiences fit their schemas (cognitive frameworks) yet simultaneously adapt their schemas to experience. Piaget also revealed how cognitive growth is likely to occur if the context is structured to allow gradual movement to the next higher level. And we owe to him the current belief that concepts do not emerge all of a sudden, full-blown, but instead emerge through a series of partial accomplishments that lead to increasingly comprehensive understanding (Haith & Benson, 1998).

Criticisms   Piaget's theory has not gone unchallenged. Questions have been raised about these areas: estimates of children's competence at different developmental levels; stages; the training of children to reason at higher levels; and culture and education.

- *Estimates of children's competence.* Some cognitive abilities emerge earlier than Piaget thought. For example, as just noted, some aspects of object permanence emerge earlier than he believed. Even two-year-olds are non-egocentric in some contexts. When they realize that another person will not see an object, they investigate whether the person is blindfolded or looking in a different direction. Conservation of number has been demonstrated as early as age three, although Piaget did not think it emerged until seven. Young children are not as uniformly "pre-" this and "pre-" that (precausal, preoperational) as Piaget thought.

  Other cognitive abilities can emerge later than Piaget thought. Many adolescents still think in concrete operational ways or are just beginning to master formal operations. Even many adults are not formal operational thinkers. In sum, recent theoretical revisions highlight more cognitive competencies of infants and young children and more cognitive shortcomings of adolescents and adults (Baillargeon, 2004; Keating, 2004; Meltzoff, 2004).
- *Stages.* Piaget conceived of stages as unitary structures of thought. Thus, his theory assumes developmental synchrony—that is, various aspects of a stage should emerge at the same time. However, some concrete operational concepts do not appear in synchrony. For example, children do not learn to conserve at the same time as they learn to cross-classify. Thus, most contemporary developmentalists agree that children's cognitive development is not as stagelike as Piaget thought (Garton, 2004; Siegler & Alibali, 2005).
- *Training of children to reason at a higher level.* Some children who are at one cognitive stage (such as preoperational) can be trained to reason at a higher cognitive stage (such as concrete operational). This poses a problem for Piaget. He argued that such training is only superficial and ineffective, unless the child is at a maturational transition point between the stages (Gelman & Opfer, 2004; Gelman & Williams, 1998).
- *Culture and education.* Culture and education exert stronger influences on children's development than Piaget believed (Gelman & Brennerman, 1994; Greenfield, 2000). The age at which children acquire conservation skills is related to the extent to which their culture provides relevant practice (Cole, 1999). An outstanding teacher and educator in the logic of math and science can promote concrete and formal operational thought.

Still, some developmental psychologists believe we should not throw out Piaget altogether (Smith, 2004). These **neo-Piagetians** argue that Piaget got some things right but that his theory needs considerable revision. In their revision of Piaget, more emphasis is given to how children process information through attention, memory, and strategies (Case, 2000). They especially believe that a more accurate vision of children's thinking requires more knowledge of strategies, how fast and how automatically children process information, the particular cognitive task involved, and the division of cognitive problems into smaller, more precise steps.

Through the Eyes of Teachers

Piaget as a Guide

I use Piaget's developmental theory as a guide in helping children learn mathematics. I know that in the sixth, seventh, and eighth grades, children are in the process of moving from the concrete to the abstract stage in their cognitive processes; therefore, when I teach a lesson, I try to use different methods in order to aid my students in understanding a concept. For example, I use fraction circles to help students understand how to add, subtract, multiply and divide fractions, and the students are allowed to use these until they become proficient with the algorithms. With every concept that I teach, I try to incorporate hands-on experiences in which the students discover the rules themselves, rather than just teaching the methods and having the students practice them with drill. It is extremely important for students to understand the why behind a mathematical rule in order for them to have a better understanding of the concept.

Jerri Hall
Mathematics Teacher
Miller Magnet Middle School
Bibb County, Georgia

Piaget and Education
Challenges to Piaget

neo-Piagetians Developmental psychologists who believe that Piaget got some things right but that his theory needs considerable revision; emphasize how to process information through attention, memory, and strategies.

Despite such criticisms, Piaget's theory is a very important one, and as we already have seen, information about his stages of development can be applied to teaching children. Here are some more ideas for applying Piaget's theory to children's education.

Piaget and Constructivism

Teaching Strategies
For Applying Piaget's Theory
to Children's Education

1. *Take a constructivist approach.* In a constructivist vein, Piaget emphasized that children learn best when they are active and seek solutions for themselves. Piaget opposed teaching methods that treat children as passive receptacles. The educational implication of Piaget's view is that in all subjects students learn best by making discoveries, reflecting on them, and discussing them, rather than blindly imitating the teacher or doing things by rote.

2. *Facilitate rather than direct learning.* Effective teachers design situations that allow students to learn by doing. These situations promote students' thinking and discovery. Teachers listen, watch, and question students to help them gain better understanding. Ask relevant questions to stimulate their thinking and ask them to explain their answers.

3. *Consider the child's knowledge and level of thinking.* Students do not come to class with empty heads. They have many ideas about the physical and natural world. They have concepts of space, time, quantity, and causality. These ideas differ from the ideas of adults. Teachers need to interpret what a student is saying and respond in a mode of discourse that is not too far from the student's level.

4. *Use ongoing assessment.* Individually constructed meanings cannot be measured by standardized tests. Math and language portfolios (which contain work in progress as well as finished products), individual conferences in which students discuss their thinking strategies, and written and verbal explanations by students of their reasoning can be used to evaluate progress.

5. *Promote the student's intellectual health.* When Piaget came to lecture in the United States, he was asked, "What can I do to get my child to a higher cognitive stage sooner?" He was asked this question so often here compared with other countries that he called it the American question. For Piaget, children's learning should occur naturally. Children should not be pushed and pressured into achieving too much too early in their development, before they are maturationally ready. Some parents spend long hours every day holding up large flash cards with words on them to improve their baby's vocabulary. In the Piagetian view, this is not the best way for infants to learn. It places too much emphasis on speeding up intellectual development, involves passive learning, and will not work.

6. *Turn the classroom into a setting of exploration and discovery.* What do actual classrooms look like when the teachers adopt Piaget's views? Several first- and second-grade math classrooms provide some good examples (Kamii, 1985, 1989). The teachers emphasize students' own exploration and discovery. The classrooms are less structured than what we think of as a typical classroom. Workbooks and predetermined assignments are not used. Rather, the teachers observe the students' interests and natural participation in activities to determine what the course of learning will be. For example, a math lesson might be constructed around counting the day's lunch money or dividing supplies among students. Often games are prominently used in the classroom to stimulate mathematical thinking. For example, a version of dominoes teaches children about even-numbered combinations. A variation on tic-tac-toe involves replacing *Xs* and *Os* with numbers. Teachers encourage peer interaction during the lessons and games because students' different viewpoints can contribute to advances in thinking.

Piaget's is not the only theory of children's cognitive development. Another that has received increased attention in recent years was proposed by Lev Vygotsky.

Vygotsky's Theory

Like Piaget, the Russian Lev Vygotsky (1896–1934) also believed that children actively construct their knowledge. Vygotsky was born in Russia in the same year as Piaget was born, but he died much younger than Piaget did, at the age of thirty-seven. Both Piaget's and Vygotsky's ideas remained virtually unknown to American scholars for many years, being introduced to American audiences through English translations in the 1960s. In the last several decades, American psychologists and educators have shown increased interest in Vygotsky's (1962) views.

Video Lecture: Vygotsky

Vygotsky's Assumptions   Three claims capture the heart of Vygotsky's view (Tappan, 1998): (1) The child's cognitive skills can be understood only when they are developmentally analyzed and interpreted; (2) cognitive skills are mediated by words, language, and forms of discourse, which serve as psychological tools for facilitating and transforming mental activity; and (3) cognitive skills have their origins in social relations and are embedded in a sociocultural backdrop.

For Vygotsky, taking a developmental approach means understanding the child's cognitive functioning by examining its origins and transformations from earlier to later forms. Thus, a particular mental act such as using inner speech (see p. 52) cannot be viewed accurately in isolation but should be evaluated as a step in a gradual developmental process.

Vygotsky's second claim, that to understand cognitive functioning it is necessary to examine the tools that mediate and shape it, led him to believe that language is the most important of these tools (Robbins, 2001). Vygotsky argued that in early childhood, language begins to be used as a tool that helps the child plan activities and solve problems.

Vygotsky's third claim was that cognitive skills originate in social relations and culture. Vygotsky portrayed the child's development as inseparable from social and cultural activities (Holland & others, 2001; Rowe & Wertsch, 2004). He believed that the development of memory, attention, and reasoning involves learning to use the inventions of society, such as language, mathematical systems, and memory strategies. In one culture this could consist of learning to count with the help of a computer; in another it could consist of counting on one's fingers or using beads.

Vygotsky's theory has stimulated considerable interest in the view that knowledge is situated and collaborative (Roqoff, 2003; Tudge & Scrimsher, 2003). That is, knowledge is distributed among people and environments, which include objects, artifacts, tools, books, and the communities in which people live. This suggests that knowing can best be advanced through interaction with others in cooperative activities.

Within these basic claims, Vygotsky articulated unique and influential ideas about the relation between learning and development. These ideas especially reflect his view that cognitive functioning has social origins. One of Vygotsky's unique ideas was his concept of the zone of proximal development.

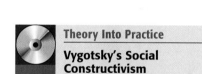

Theory Into Practice

Vygotsky's Social Constructivism

The Zone of Proximal Development   **Zone of proximal development (ZPD)** is Vygotsky's term for the range of tasks that are too difficult for children to master alone but that can be learned with guidance and assistance from adults or more-skilled children. Thus, the lower limit of the ZPD is the level of problem solving reached by the child working independently. The upper limit is the level of additional responsibility the child can accept with the assistance of an able instructor (see figure 2.12 on page 52). Vygotsky's emphasis on the ZPD underscores his belief in the importance of social influences, especially instruction, on children's cognitive development (Hasse, 2001).

Vygotsky (1987) gave this example of how to assess a child's ZPD: Suppose that, by an intelligence test, the mental age of two children is determined to be eight years. With Vygotsky in mind, we can't stop there. To go on, we seek to determine how each of these

zone of proximal development (ZPD) Vygotsky's term for the range of tasks that are too difficult for children to master alone but that can be mastered with guidance and assistance from adults or more-skilled children.

Upper limit — Level of additional responsibility child can accept with assistance of an able instructor

Zone of proximal development (ZPD)

Lower limit — Level of problem solving reached on these tasks by child working alone

FIGURE 2.12 Vygotsky's Zone of Proximal Development
Vygotsky's zone of proximal development has a lower limit and an upper limit. Tasks in the ZPD are too difficult for the child to perform alone. They require assistance from an adult or a more-skilled child. As children experience the verbal instruction or demonstration, they organize the information in their existing mental structures, so they can eventually perform the skill or task alone.

www.mhhe.com/santedu2e

Scaffolding

Cognitive Apprenticeship

Vygotsky on Language and Thought

scaffolding A technique that involves changing the level of support for learning. A teacher or more-advanced peer adjusts the amount of guidance to fit the student's current performance.

children will attempt to solve problems meant for older children. We assist each child by demonstrating, asking leading questions, and introducing the initial elements of the solution. With this help or collaboration with the adult, one of these children solves problems at the level of a twelve-year-old child and the other solves problems at the level of a nine-year-old child. This difference between the children's mental ages and the level of performance they achieve in collaboration with an adult defines the zone of proximal development. Thus, the ZPD involves the child's cognitive skills that are in the process of maturing and his or her performance level with the assistance of a more-skilled person (Panofsky, 1999). Vygotsky (1978) called these the "buds" or "flowers" of development, to distinguish them from the "fruits" of development, which the child already can accomplish independently. An application of Vygotsky's concept of the zone of proximal development is the one-on-one tutoring provided by New Zealand teachers in the Reading Recovery program. Tutoring begins with familiar work, gradually introducing unfamiliar aspects of reading strategies, and then passing increasing control of the activity to the child (Clay & Cazden, 1990).

Scaffolding Closely linked to the idea of zone of proximal development is the concept of **scaffolding,** a technique of changing the level of support. Over the course of a teaching session, a more-skilled person (teacher or more-advanced peer of the child) adjusts the amount of guidance to fit the student's current performance level. When the task the student is learning is new, the more-skilled person might use direct instruction. As the student's competence increases, less guidance is given.

Dialogue is an important tool of scaffolding in the zone of proximal development (John-Steiner & Mahn, 1996; Tappan, 1998). Vygotsky viewed children as having rich but unsystematic, disorganized, and spontaneous concepts. These meet with the skilled helper's more systematic, logical, and rational concepts. As a result of the meeting and dialogue between the child and the skilled helper, the child's concepts become more systematic, logical, and rational. We will have much more to say about scaffolding and other social interactive aspects of learning in chapter 10, "Social Constructivist Approaches."

Language and Thought Vygotsky (1962) believed that young children use language not only for social communication but also to plan, guide, and monitor their behavior in a self-regulatory fashion. The use of language for self-regulation is called inner speech or private speech. For Piaget, private speech was egocentric and immature, but for Vygotsky it was an important tool of thought during the early childhood years.

Vygotsky believed that language and thought initially develop independently of each other and then merge. He said that all mental functions have external or social origins. Children must use language to communicate with others before they can focus inward on their own thoughts. Children also must communicate externally and use language for a long period of time before the transition from external to internal speech takes place. This transition period occurs between the ages of three and seven and involves talking to oneself. After a while, the self-talk becomes second nature to children and they can act without verbalizing. When this occurs, children have internalized their egocentric speech in the form of inner speech, which becomes their thoughts. Vygotsky believed that children who use a lot of private speech are more socially competent than those who don't. He argued that private speech represents an early transition in becoming more socially communicative (Shamier & Tzuriel, 2004).

Vygotsky's view challenged Piaget's ideas on language and thought. Vygotsky said that language, even in its earliest forms, is socially based, whereas Piaget emphasized young children's egocentric and nonsocial speech. For Vygotsky, when young children talk to themselves they are using language to govern their behavior and guide themselves, whereas Piaget believed that such self-talk reflects immaturity. Researchers have found support for Vygotsky's view of the positive role of private speech in children's development (Winsler, Diaz, & Montero, 1997).

Video Observation: Scaffolded Instruction

Teaching Strategies
For Applying Vygotsky's Theory to Children's Education

1. *Use the zone of proximal development.* Teaching should begin toward the zone's upper limit, where the student is able to reach the goal only through close collaboration with the instructor. With adequate continuing instruction and practice, the student organizes and masters the behavioral sequences required to perform the target skill. As the instruction continues, the performance transfers from the teacher to the student. The teacher gradually reduces the explanations, hints, and demonstrations until the student is able to perform the skill alone. Once the goal is achieved, it can become the foundation for the development of a new ZPD.

2. *Use scaffolding.* Look for opportunities to use scaffolding when students need help with self-initiated learning activities (Elicker, 1996). Also use scaffolding to help students move to a higher level of skill and knowledge. Offer just enough assistance. You might ask, "What can I do to help you?" Or simply observe the student's intentions and attempts, smoothly providing support when needed. When the student hesitates, offer encouragement. Encourage the student to practice the skill. You may watch and appreciate the student's practice or offer support when the student forgets what to do.

3. *Use more-skilled peers as teachers.* Remember that it is not just adults that Vygotsky believed are important in helping students learn important skills. Students also benefit from the support and guidance of more-skilled students. We will say more about the role of peers in teaching in chapter 10, "Social Constructivist Approaches," including peers as tutors.

4. *Encourage collaborative learning and recognize that learning involves a community of learners.* Both children and adults engage in learning activities in a collaborative way. Peers, teachers, parents, and other adults work together in a community of learners rather than the child learning as an isolated individual (Rogoff, Turkanis, & Bartlett, 2001).

5. *Consider the cultural context of learning.* An important function of education is to guide children in learning the skills that are important in the culture in which they live.

6. *Monitor and encourage children's use of private speech.* Be aware of the developmental change from externally talking to oneself when solving a problem during the preschool years to privately talking to oneself in the early elementary school years. In the elementary school years, encourage students to internalize and self-regulate their talk to themselves.

7. *Assess the ZPD, not IQ.* Like Piaget, Vygotsky did not believe that formal, standardized tests are the best way to assess children's learning or their readiness to learn. Rather, Vygotsky argued that assessment should focus on determining the student's zone of proximal development. The skilled helper presents the child with tasks of varying difficulty to determine the best level at which to begin instruction. The ZPD is a measure of learning potential. IQ, also a measure of learning potential, emphasizes that intelligence is a property of the child. By contrast, ZPD

Applying Piaget and Vygotsky in My Classroom

The grade level at which I plan to teach is _____

PIAGET

The Piagetian stage of the majority of children in my classroom will likely be

_____

The Piagetian concepts that I believe will help me the most in understanding and teaching children at this grade level are

Concept   **Example**

_____ _____

_____ _____

_____ _____

VYGOTSKY

The concepts in Vygotsky's theory that I believe will help me the most in understanding and teaching children at this grade level are

Concept   **Example**

_____ _____

_____ _____

_____ _____

 Go to your Student Toolbox CD-ROM for an electronic version of this form.

emphasizes that learning is interpersonal. It is inappropriate to say that the child "has" a ZPD in the same sense that the child might "have" an IQ.

We have discussed a number of ideas about both Piaget's and Vygotsky's theories and how the theories can be applied to the education of children. To evaluate how you might apply their theories to your own classroom, complete Self-Assessment 2.1.

Evaluating and Comparing Vygotsky's and Piaget's Theories Awareness of Vygotsky's theory came later than for Piaget's theory, so Vygotsky's theory has not yet been evaluated as thoroughly. However, it already has been embraced by many teachers and successfully applied to education (Doolittle, 1997). Vygotsky's view of the importance of sociocultural influences on children's development fits with the current belief that it is important to evaluate the contextual factors in learning. However, criticisms of his theory also have emerged. For example, some critics say he overemphasizes the role of language in thinking.

We already have mentioned several comparisons of Vygotsky's and Piaget's theories, such as Vygotsky's emphasis on the importance of inner speech in development and Piaget's view that such speech is immature. We also said earlier that both Vygotsky's and Piaget's theories are constructivist, emphasizing that children actively construct knowledge and understanding rather than being passive receptacles.

Although both theories are constructivist, Vygotsky's is a **social constructivist approach,** which emphasizes the social contexts of learning and that knowledge is mutually built and constructed. Piaget's theory does not have this strong social emphasis (Hogan & Tudge, 1999). Moving from Piaget to Vygotsky, the conceptual shift is from the individual to collaboration, social interaction, and sociocultural activity (Rogoff, 1998). For Piaget, children construct knowledge by transforming, organizing, and reorganizing previous knowledge. For Vygotsky, children construct knowledge through social interac-

Piaget's Theory
Vygotsky's Theory

social constructivist approach
Emphasizes the social contexts of learning and that knowledge is mutually built and constructed; Vygotsky's theory exemplifies this approach.

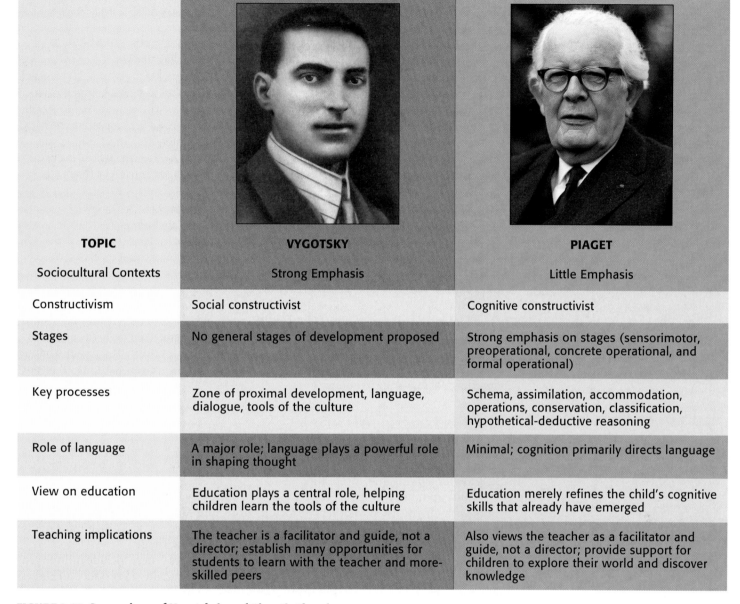

TOPIC	VYGOTSKY	PIAGET
Sociocultural Contexts	Strong Emphasis	Little Emphasis
Constructivism	Social constructivist	Cognitive constructivist
Stages	No general stages of development proposed	Strong emphasis on stages (sensorimotor, preoperational, concrete operational, and formal operational)
Key processes	Zone of proximal development, language, dialogue, tools of the culture	Schema, assimilation, accommodation, operations, conservation, classification, hypothetical-deductive reasoning
Role of language	A major role; language plays a powerful role in shaping thought	Minimal; cognition primarily directs language
View on education	Education plays a central role, helping children learn the tools of the culture	Education merely refines the child's cognitive skills that already have emerged
Teaching implications	The teacher is a facilitator and guide, not a director; establish many opportunities for students to learn with the teacher and more-skilled peers	Also views the teacher as a facilitator and guide, not a director; provide support for children to explore their world and discover knowledge

FIGURE 2.13 Comparison of Vygotsky's and Piaget's Theories

tion with others. The implications of Piaget's theory provide support for teaching strategies that encourage children to explore their world and discover knowledge. The main implication of Vygotsky's theory for teaching is that we should establish many opportunities for students to learn with the teacher and more-skilled peers. In both Piaget's and Vygotsky's theories, teachers serve as facilitators and guides rather than directors and molders of learning. Figure 2.13 compares Vygotsky's and Piaget's theories.

In our coverage of cognitive development, we have focused on the views of two giants in the field: Piaget and Vygotsky. However, information processing also has emerged as an important perspective in understanding children's cognitive development. It emphasizes how information enters the mind, how it is stored and transformed, and how it is retrieved to perform mental activities such as problem solving and reasoning. It also focuses on how automatically and quickly children process information. Because information processing will be covered extensively in chapters 8 and 9, we have only mentioned it briefly here.

! Review and Reflect

2 **Discuss the development of the brain and compare the cognitive developmental theories of Jean Piaget and Lev Vygotsky.**

Review

- How does the brain develop and what implications does this development have for children's education?
- What three main ideas did Piaget use to describe cognitive processes? What stages did he identify in children's cognitive development?
- What were Vygotsky's three main assumptions? How are his concepts of zone of proximal development, scaffolding, and the role of language useful in teaching?

Reflect

- Do you consider yourself to be a formal operational thinker? Do you still sometimes feel like a concrete operational thinker? Give examples.

LANGUAGE DEVELOPMENT

As you learned earlier, in Vygotsky's view, language plays a key role in children's cognitive development. In this section we will explore what language is, biological and environmental influences on language, and how language develops. In a later chapter (Chapter 11: Learning and Cognition in the Content Areas), we will examine an important aspect of language: reading.

What Is Language?

Language is a form of communication—whether spoken, written, or signed—that is based on a system of symbols. Language consists of the words used by a community and the rules for varying and combining them.

Think about how important language is in our everyday lives. We need language to speak with others, listen to others, read, and write. Our language enables us to describe past events in detail and to plan for the future. Language lets us pass down information from one generation to the next and create a rich cultural heritage.

All human languages have some common characteristics. These include infinite generativity and organizational rules. *Infinite generativity* is the ability to produce an endless number of meaningful sentences using a finite set of words and rules. Let's further explore what these rules involve.

Language is highly ordered and organized. The organization involves five systems of rules; phonology, morphology, syntax, semantics, and pragmatics. When we say "rules," we mean that language is orderly and the rules describe the way language works.

Every language is made up of basic sounds, or phonemes. **Phonology** is the sound system of the language, including the sounds that are used and how they may be combined. For example, English has the initial consonant cluster *spr*, as in *spring*, but no words begin with the cluster *rsp*. Phonology provides a basis for constructing a large and expandable set of words out of two or three dozen phonemes. The basic unit of sound in a language is a *phoneme*; it is the smallest unit of sound that affects meaning. A good example of phonemes in English is /k/, the sound represented by the letter *k* in the word *ski* and the letter *c* in the word *cat*. The /k/ sound is slightly different in the two words. However, this variation is not distinguished in English, and the /k/ sound is therefore a single phoneme. In some languages, such as Arabic, this variation represents separate phonemes.

Morphology refers to the units of meaning involved in word formation. A *morpheme* is a minimal unit of meaning; it is a word or a part of a word that cannot be broken into smaller meaningful parts. Every word in the English language is made up of one or more morphemes. Some words consist of a single morpheme (for example, *help*), whereas others are made up of more than one morpheme (for example, *helper*, which has

language A form of communication, whether spoken, written, or signed, that is based on a system of symbols.

phonology A language's sound system.

morphology The units of meaning involved in word formation.

FRANK & ERNEST reprinted by permission of Newspaper Enterprise Association, Inc.

two morphemes, *help + er*, with the morpheme *-er* meaning "one who"—in this case, "one who helps"). Thus, not all morphemes are words by themselves (for example, *-pre, -tion*, and *-ing*).

Just as the rules that govern phonology describe the sound sequences that can occur in a language, the rules of morphology describe the way meaningful units (morphemes) can be combined in words (Ravid, Levi, & Ben-Zvi, 2004). Morphemes have many jobs in grammar, such as marking tense (for example, "she walks" versus "she walked") and number ("she walks" versus "they walk").

Syntax involves the way words are combined to form acceptable phrases and sentences. If someone says to you, "Bob slugged Tom" or "Bob was slugged by Tom," you know who did the slugging and who was slugged in each case because you have a syntactic understanding of these sentence structures. You also understand that the sentence "You didn't stay, did you?" is a grammatical sentence but that "You didn't stay, didn't you?" is unacceptable and ambiguous. If you learn another language, English syntax will not get you very far. For example, in English an adjective usually precedes a noun (as in *blue sky*), whereas in Spanish the adjective usually follows the noun *(cielo azul)*. Despite the differences in their syntactic structures, however, the world's languages have much in common. For example, consider the following short sentenes: *The cat killed the mouse. The mouse ate the cheese. The farmer chased the cat.* In many languages it is possible to combine these sentences into more complex sentences—for example, *The farmer chased the cat that killed the mouse. The mouse the cat killed ate the cheese.* However, no known language permits sentences like the following one: *The mouse the cat the farmer chased killed ate the cheese.* Can you make sense of this sentence? If you can, you probably can do it only after wrestling with it for several minutes. You likely could not understand it at all if someone uttered it during a conversation. It appears that language users cannot process subjects and objects arranged in too complex a fashion in a sentence. That is good news for language learners, because it means that all syntactic systems adhere to a common ground. Such findings are also considered important by researchers who are interested in the universal properties of syntax (de Jong, 2004).

Semantics refers to the meaning of words and sentences. Every word has a set of semantic features, or required attributes related to meaning (Stahl & Nagy, 2005). *Girl* and *woman,* for example, share many semantic features but differ semantically in regard to age. Words have semantic restrictions on how they can be used in sentences. The sentence *The bicycle talked the boy into buying a candy bar* is syntactically correct but semantically incorrect. The sentence violates our semantic knowledge that bicycles don't talk!

A final set of language rules involves **pragmatics,** the appropriate use of language in different contexts (Lee, 2005). The domain of language is broad. When you take turns speaking in a discussion or use a question to convey a command ("Why is it so noisy in here?" "What is this, Grand Central Station?"), you are demonstrating a knowledge of pragmatics. You also apply the pragmatics of English when you use polite language in appropriate situations (for example, when talking to one's teacher) or tell stories that are interesting, jokes that are funny, and lies that convince.

syntax The ways that words must be combined to form acceptable phrases and sentences.

semantics The meaning of words and sentences.

pragmatics The appropriate use of language in different contexts.

The Development of Language and Parenting

Biological and Environmental Influences

Famous linguist Noam Chomsky (1957) argued that humans are prewired to learn language at a certain time and in a certain way. Some language scholars view the remarkable similarities in how children acquire language all over the world, despite the vast variation in language input they receive, as strong evidence that language has a biological basis.

Children also vary in their acquisition of language in ways that cannot be explained by environmental input alone (Hoff, 2001; Lachlan & Feldman, 2003). For example, pioneering language researcher Roger Brown (1973) searched for evidence that parents reinforce their children for speaking grammatically. He found that they sometimes smiled and praised their children for grammatical sentences but they also reinforced sentences that were ungrammatical. From these observations, Brown concluded that processes operating within the child were overriding the environmental input of reinforcement.

However, children clearly do not learn language in a social vacuum (Nelson, Aksu-Koc, & Johnson, 2001; Snow & Beals, 2001). Enough variation occurs in language development when children's caregivers differ substantially in input styles to know that the environment plays a significant role in language development, especially in the acquisition of vocabulary (Nagy, 2005; Tamis-LeMonda, Bornstein, & Baumwell, 2001). For example, in one recent study, by the time they were three years old, children living in poverty conditions showed vocabulary deficits, compared with their counterparts in middle-income families, and the deficits continued to be present when they entered school at six years of age (Farkas, 2001).

In sum, children are neither exclusively biological linguists nor exclusively social architects of language (Berko Gleason, 2000; Dick & others, 2004; Tomasello & Slobin, 2004). No matter how long you converse with a dog, it won't learn to talk, because it doesn't have the human child's biological capacity for language. Unfortunately, though, some children fail to develop good language skills even in the presence of very good role models and interaction. An interactionist view emphasizes the contributions of both biology and experience in language development. That is, children are biologically prepared to learn language as they and their caregivers interact.

In or out of school, encouragement of language development, not drill and practice, is the key (Hiebert, 2005; Oates & Grayson, 2004). Language development is not simply a matter of being rewarded for saying things correctly and imitating a speaker. Children benefit when their parents and teachers actively engage them in conversation, ask them questions, and emphasize interactive rather than directive language. You can read about how urban poverty conditions can restrict the language development of African American children in the Diversity and Education interlude.

Diversity and Education
African American Language Traditions and Poverty

Shirley Heath (1989) examined the language traditions of African Americans from low-income backgrounds. She traced some aspects of African American English to the time of slavery. Heath also examined how those speech patterns have carried over into African American English today. She found that agricultural areas in the southern United States have an especially rich oral tradition.

Specifically she found that adults do not simplify or edit their talk for children, in essence challenging the children to be highly active listeners. Also, adults ask only "real questions" of children—that is, questions for which the adult does not already know the answer. Adults also engage in a type of teasing with children, encouraging them to use their wits in communication. For example, a grandmother might pretend that she wants to take a child's hat and then starts a lively exchange in which the child must understand many subtleties of argument, mood, and humor: Does Grandma really want my hat? Is she mad at me? Is she making a joke? Can I persuade her to give it back to me? Finally, there is an appreciation of wit and flexibility in how language is used, as well as an acknowledgment of individual differences—one person might be respected for recounting stories, another for negotiating and peacemaking skills.

Heath argues that the language tradition she describes is richly varied, cognitively demanding, and well suited to many real-life situations. She says that the oral and literary traditions among poor African Americans in the cities are well suited for many job situations. Years ago many inner-city jobs required only that a person follow directions in order to perform repetitive tasks. Today many positions require continuous interactions involving considerable flexibility in language, such as the ability to persuade coworkers or to express dissatisfaction, in a subtle way, for example.

Despite its utility in many job situations, the rich language tradition possessed by low-income African Americans does not meet with the educational priorities of our nation's schools. Too often schools stress rote memorization, minimizing group interaction and discouraging individual variations in communicative style. Also, the language tradition of African American culture is rapidly dying in the face of current life among poor African Americans, where the structure of low-income, frequently single-parent families often provides little verbal stimulation for children.

One mother agreed to let researcher Heath tape-record her interactions with her children over a two-year period and to write notes about her activities with them. Within 500 hours of tape and more than a thousand lines of notes, the mother initiated talk with her three preschool children on only eighteen occasions (other than giving them a brief directive or asking a quick question). Few of the mother's conversations involved either planning or executing actions with or for her children.

Heath (1989) points out that the lack of family and community supports is widespread among urban housing projects, especially among African Americans. The deteriorating, impoverished conditions of these inner-city areas severely impede the ability of young children to develop the language skills they need to function competently.

How Language Develops

Language acquisition advances past a number of milestones (Edwards, 2004; McGregor, 2004). Babbling begins at about three to six months. Infants usually utter their first word at about ten to thirteen months. By eighteen to twenty-four months, infants usually have begun to string two words together. In this two-word stage, they quickly grasp the importance of language in communication, creating phrases such as "Book there," "My candy," "Mama walk," and "Give Papa."

As children go through the early childhood years, their grasp of the rule systems that govern language increase. These rule systems include phonology (the sound system), morphology (the rules for combining minimal units of meaning), syntax (rules for making sentences), semantics (the meaning system), and pragmatics (the rules for use in different contexts).

Children become increasingly capable of producing all the sounds of their language. They can even produce complex consonant clusters.

By the time children move beyond two-word utterances, they demonstrate a knowledge of morphology rules. Children begin using the plural and possessive forms of nouns (such as *dogs* and *dog's*). They put appropriate endings on verbs (such as *-s* when the subject is third-person singular and *-ed* for the past tense). They use prepositions (such as *in* and *on*), articles (such as *a* and *the*), and various forms of the verb *to be* (such as "I *was* going to the store"). Some of the best evidence for changes in children's use of morphological rules occurs in their overgeneralization of the rules. Have you ever heard a preschool child say "foots" instead of "feet," or "goed" instead of "went"? If you do not remember hearing such usage, talk to parents who have young children or to the young children themselves. You will hear some interesting morphological errors.

Language Learning

Language and Literacy Development

Language Development: 4 to 6 Years

Technology and Children's Vocabulary Development

Here are three ways to support children's vocabulary development using three types of technology (Miller, 2001).

Computers

CD-ROMs of stories, such as *Living Books*, can promote children's vocabulary development, especially when there is an online option for students to find the meaning of unfamiliar words. Using the computer for listening to and watching stories can be part of a student's reading center rotations, reading assignment, or an option during choice time. Learning new words can be enhanced if teachers plan a way for students to keep track of new words. For example, students can record new words in a portfolio for future reference.

A recent analysis of software products for children's vocabulary development offered the following guidelines (Wood, 2001):

1. *Relate the new to the known.* New vocabulary words are presented in a way that builds on students' previously acquired word knowledge; students are encouraged to map new word meanings onto their own experiences.
2. *Promote active, in-depth processing.* Students are motivated to construct the meanings of words rather than being taught through rote memorization of word meanings. This involves introducing a synonym for the new word or showing how it relates to a particular context; helping students apply their understanding of the word to a particular context; and challenging children to use the new word in a novel way to illustrate their understanding of its meaning.
3. *Encourage reading.* Reading promotes vocabulary development. It is important for software that promotes vocabulary

development to motivate students to extend their learning through reading.

Audiobooks

Teachers can create listening centers to support vocabulary development. Listening centers should include tape recorders, headphones, audiobooks, and corresponding literature. Audiobooks can be used to supplement printed materials, listen to dramatization of stories, and pique student interest. Audiobooks may especially benefit students with special needs (Casbergue & Harris, 1996). For example, students whose primary language is not English can use tapes to improve vocabulary development, reading, and pronunciation. Weak readers can use the tapes to contribute to literature discussions in class even though they may be reading less-complex materials.

Educational Television

Educational television can be used to help children learn the alphabet, to see people using vocabulary in different contexts, and to hear stories that will motivate children to read these stories later (Lesser, 1989). One such program is *Reading Rainbow.* In one study, it was found that this program increases children's vocabulary and literacy (Wood & Duke, 1997). The show helps children to expand their vocabularies by introducing many potentially unfamiliar words per episode, linking the words by theme, creating rich contexts when using the words, clearly and directly explaining the meanings of new words, and linking new words in playful ways.

In a classic experiment that was designed to study children's understanding of morphological rules, Jean Berko (1958) presented preschool children and first-grade children with cards such as the one shown in figure 2.14. Children were asked to look at the card while the experimenter read aloud the words on the card. Then the children were asked to supply the missing word. This might sound easy, but Berko was interested not just in the children's ability to recall the right word but also in their ability to say it "correctly" (with the ending that was dictated by the morphological rules). "Wugs" would be the correct response for the card in figure 2.14.

Although the children's answers were not perfect, they were much better than chance. Moreover, the children demonstrated their knowledge of morphological rules, not only with plural forms of nouns ("There are two wugs") but with possessive forms of nouns and the third-person singular and past-tense forms of verbs. What makes Berko's study impressive is that most of the words were made up for the experiment. Thus, the children could not base their responses on remembering past instances of hearing the words. Instead, they were forced to rely on *rules*.

Young children also learn to manipulate syntax. They can generate questions, passives, clauses, and all the major syntactical structure of their language.

As children move beyond the two-word stage, their knowledge of semantics or meanings also rapidly advances (Hiebert & Kamil, 2005). The speaking vocabulary of a 6-year-old child ranges from 8,000 to 14,000 words. Assuming that word learning began when the child was 12 months old, this translates into a rate of 5 to 8 new word meanings a day between the ages of 1 and 6. After 5 years of word learning, the 6-year-old child does not slow down (Biemiller, 2005). According to some estimates, the average child of this age is moving along at the aweinspiring rate of 22 words a day! How would you fare if you were given the task of learning 22 new words every day? It is truly miraculous how quickly children learn language. To read about strategies for using technology to support children's vocabulary, see the Technology and Education box.

Although there are many differences between a 2-year-old's language and a 6-year-old's language, the most dramatic differences pertain to pragmatics. A 6-year-old is simply a much better conversationalist than a 2-year-old. What are some of the changes in pragmatics that are made in the preschool years? At about 3 years of age, children improve in their ability to talk about things that are not physically present. That is, they improve their command of the characteristic of language known as "displacement." Children become increasingly removed from the "here and now" and are able to talk about things that are not physically present, as well as things that happened in the past, or may happen in the future. Preschoolers can tell you what they want for lunch tomorrow, something that would not have been possible at the two-word stage in infancy. Preschool children also become increasingly able to talk in different ways to different people.

The advances in language that take place in early childhood lay the foundation for later development in the elementary school years. Children gain new skills as they enter school that make it possible to learn to read and write: These include increasingly using language in a displaced way, learning what a word is, and learning how to recognize and talk about sounds (Berko Gleason, 2002). They have to learn the alphabetic principle, that the alphabet letters represent sounds of the language. As children develop during middle and late childhood, changes in their vocabulary and grammar also take place.

During middle and late childhood, a change occurs in the way children select words. When asked to say the first word that comes to mind when they hear a word, young children typically provide a word that often follows the word in a sentence. For example, when asked to respond to "dog" the young child may say "barks," or to the word "eat" say "lunch." At about seven years of age, children begin to respond with a word that is the same part of speech as the stimulus word. For example, a child may now respond to the word "dog" with "cat" or "horse." To "eat," they now might say "drink." This is evidence that children now have begun to categorize their vocabulary by parts of speech (Berko Gleason, 2002). The process of categorizing becomes easier as children increase their vocabulary. Likewise, a larger vocabulary facilitates learning to read. Children who begin elementary school with a small vocabulary are at risk when it comes to learning to read (Berko Gleason, 2002). We will have much more to say about reading in Chapter 11.

Children also make advances in grammar. The elementary school child's improvement in logical reasoning and analytical skills helps in the understanding of such constructions as the appropriate use of comparatives (shorter, deeper) and subjectives ("If you were president, . . ."). During the elementary school years, children become increasingly able to understand and use complex grammar, such as the following sentence: The boy who kissed his mother wore a hat. They also learn to use language in a more connected way, producing connected discourse (Bloome & others, 2005). They become able to relate sentences to one another to produce descriptions, definitions, and narratives that make sense. Children must be able to do these things orally before they can be expected to deal with them in written assignments.

In adolescence, vocabulary increases with the addition of more abstract words. More complex grammar forms are better understood, as is the function a word plays in a sentence. Adolescents also show an increased understanding of metaphor and satire. In late adolescence, individuals can better appreciate adult literary works. Figure 2.15 summarizes some of the main milestones in language.

This is a wug.

Now there is another one. There are two of them. There are two _____.

FIGURE 2.14 **Stimuli in Berko's Study of Young Children's Understanding of Morphological Rules**
In Jean Berko's (1958) study, young children were presented cards such as this one with a "wug" on it. Then the children were asked to supply the missing word and say it correctly. "Wugs" is the correct response here.

Children's Vocabulary Development and Software

Age Period	Child's Development/Behavior
0 to 6 months	Cooing Discrimination of vowels Babbling present by end of period
6 to 12 months	Babbling expands to include sounds of spoken language Gestures used to communicate about objects
12 to 18 months	First words spoken Understand vocabulary 50+ words on the average
18 to 24 months	Vocabulary increases to an average of 200 words Two-word combinations
2 years	Vocabulary rapidly increases Correct use of plurals Use of past tense Use of some prepositions
3 to 4 years	Mean length of utterances increases to 3 to 4 morphemes a sentence Use of "yes"/"no" questions, *wh-* questions Use of negatives and imperatives Increased awareness of pragmatics
5 to 6 years	Vocabulary reaches an average of about 10,000 words Coordination of simple sentences
6 to 8 years	Vocabulary continues to increase rapidly More skilled use of syntactical rules Conversational skills improve
9 to 11 years	Word definitions include synonyms Conversational strategies continue to improve
11 to 14 years	Vocabulary increases with addition of more abstract words Understanding of complex grammar forms Increased understanding of function a word plays in a sentence Understanding of metaphor and satire
15 to 20 years	Can understand adult literary works

Note: This list is meant not to be exhaustive but, rather, to highlight some of the main language milestones. Also keep in mind that there is a great deal of variation in the ages at which children can reach these milestones and still be considered within the normal range of language development.

FIGURE 2.15 Language Milestones

ENTER THE DEBATE

1. Should teachers allow P-1 students to play for the bulk of their school day?

2. Should we teach algebra to students before high school?

Teaching Experience
- **The Work of Piaget**
- **Piaget's Learning Theory**
- **Vygotsky's Social Constructivist Theory in Practice**

Review and Reflect

3 Identify the key features of language, biological and environmental influences on language, and the typical growth of the child's language.

Review
- What is language? Describe these five features of spoken language: phonology, morphology, syntax, semantics, and pragmatics.
- What evidence supports the idea that humans are "prewired" for learning language? What evidence supports the importance of environmental factors?
- What milestones does a child go through in the course of learning language?
- What are the typical ages of these milestones?

Reflect
- How have teachers encouraged or discouraged your own mastery of language? What experiences have done the most to expand your language skills?

Mr. Johnson assigned his high school senior American government students to read two books during the semester that had "something, anything, to do with government or political systems" and to write a brief report about each of their chosen books.

One student in the class, Cindy, chose to read *1984* and *Animal Farm,* both by George Orwell. *1984* is a book about what could happen in "the future" year of 1984, given certain political decisions earlier on. In essence, the world turns into a terrible place in which "Big Brother" monitors all of one's actions via two-way television-like screens. Infractions of minor rules are punished severely. *Animal Farm* is a brief novel about political systems in which the characters are portrayed as various farm animals such as pigs and dogs. Cindy enjoyed both books and finished them both before mid-term. Her reports were insightful, reflecting on the symbolism contained in the novels and the implications for present-day government.

Cindy's friend, Lucy, had put off reading her first book until the last minute. She knew Cindy enjoyed reading about government and had finished her reports. Lucy asked Cindy if she knew of a "skinny book" she could read to fulfill the assignment. Cindy gladly shared her copy of *Animal Farm,* with her friend. Lucy accepted the book, very pleased that it was so short. However, as she began reading the book she wondered why Cindy had given her this book. It didn't seem to fit the requirements of the assignment at all.

The day before the first reports were due Mr. Johnson overheard the girls talking.

Lucy complained to Cindy, "I don't get it. It's a story about pigs and dogs."

Cindy responded, "They aren't really supposed to be farm animals. It's a story about the promises of communism and what happened in the Soviet Union once the communists took over. It's a great story! Don't you see? The pigs represent the communist regime that overthrew the czars during the Russian Revolution. They made all kinds of promises about equality for everyone. The people went along with them because they were sick and tired of the rich and powerful running everything while they starved. Once the czars had been gotten rid of, the communists set up a new government. They didn't keep any of their promises. They just sort of took the place of the czars. They controlled everything. Remember in the book when the pigs moved into the house and started walking on two legs? That's supposed to be like when the communist leaders began acting just like the czars. They even began a secret police force—that'd be the dogs in the story. Remember how they bullied the other animals? Just like the secret police in the Soviet Union. Remember?"

"I still don't get it. How can a pig or a dog be a communist or a cop? They're just animals."

Cindy looked at her friend, dumbfounded. How could she NOT understand this book? It was so obvious.

1. Using Piaget's theory, explain why Cindy understood the book.
2. Using Piaget's theory, explain why Lucy didn't understand the book.
3. What could Mr. Johnson do to help Lucy understand?
4. How could Mr. Johnson have presented this assignment differently, so that Lucy did not need to rush through a book?

Reach Your Learning Goals

1 Explain the value of studying children's development, as well as the general processes and periods of development.

- The more you learn about children's development, the better you will understand the level at which to appropriately teach them. Childhood provides a foundation for the adult years.

- Development is the product of biological, cognitive, and socioemotional processes, which often are intertwined. Periods of development include infancy, early childhood, middle and late childhood, adolescence, and early adulthood.

2 Discuss the development of the brain and compare the cognitive developmental theories of Jean Piaget and Lev Vygotsky.

- An especially important part of growth is the development of the brain and nervous system. Myelination involving hand-eye coordination is not complete until about four years of age, and myelination involving focusing attention is not finished until about ten. Substantial synaptic pruning of the brain connections takes place, and the adult level of density of synaptic connections is not reached until some point in adolescence. Different regions of the brain grow at different rates. Lateralization in some verbal and nonverbal functions occurs, but in many instances functioning is linked to both hemispheres. Little is known about links between neuroscience and education, and often the effects of such links have been overstated.

- Jean Piaget proposed a major theory of children's cognitive development that involves these important processes: schema, assimilation, accommodation, organization, and equilibration. In his theory, cognitive development unfolds in a sequence of four stages: sensorimotor (birth to age two), preoperational (ages three to seven), concrete operational (ages seven to eleven), and formal operational (ages eleven to fifteen). Each stage is a qualitative advance. In the sensorimotor stage, infants construct an understanding of the world by coordinating sensory experiences with motor actions and accomplish object permanence. Thought is more symbolic at the preoperational stage, although the child has not yet mastered some important mental operations. Preoperational thought includes symbolic function and intuitive thought substages. Egocentrism, animism, and centration are constraints. At the concrete operational stage, children can perform operations, and logical thought replaces intuitive thought when reasoning can be applied to specific or concrete examples. Classification, seriation, and transitivity are important concrete operational skills. At the formal operational stage, thinking is more abstract, idealistic, and logical. Hypothetical-deductive reasoning becomes important. Adolescent egocentrism characterizes many young

adolescents. We owe to Piaget a long list of masterful concepts as well as the current vision of the child as an active, constructivist thinker. Criticisms of his view focus on estimates of children's competence, stages, the training of children to reason at a higher cognitive level, and the neo-Piagetian criticism of not being precise enough about how children learn.

- Lev Vygotsky proposed another major theory of cognitive development. Vygotsky's view emphasizes that cognitive skills need to be interpreted developmentally, are mediated by language, and have their origins in social relations and culture. *Zone of proximal development (ZPD)* is Vygotsky's term for the range of tasks that are too difficult for children to master alone but that can be learned with the guidance and assistance of adults and more-skilled children. Scaffolding and dialogue are important concepts in Vygotsky's theory. He also believed that language plays a key role in guiding cognition. Comparisons of Vygotsky's and Piaget's theories involve constructivism, metaphors for learning, stages, key processes, role of language, views on education, and teaching implications.

3 Identify the key features of language, biological and environmental influences on language, and the typical growth of the child's language.

- Language is a form of communication, whether spoken, written, or signed, that is based on a system of symbols. Human languages are infinitely generative. All human languages also have organizational rules of phonology, morphology, syntax, semantics, and pragmatics.

- Children are biologically prepared to learn language as they and their caregivers interact. The strongest evidence for the biological basis of language is that children all over the world reach language milestones at about the same age despite vast differences in their environmental experiences. However, children do not learn language in a social vacuum. Children benefit when parents and teachers actively engage them in conversation, ask them questions, and talk with, not just to, them. In sum, biology and experience interact to produce language development.

- Language acquisition advances through stages. Babbling occurs at about three to six months, the first word at ten to thirteen months, and two-word utterances at eighteen to twenty-four months. As children move beyond two-word utterances, they can demonstrate that they know some morphological rules, as documented in Berko Gleason's study. Children also make advances in phonology, syntax, semantics, and pragmatics. By the end of elementary school, most children can apply appropriate rules of grammar. In adolescence, vocabulary increases with the addition of more abstract words. In late adolescence, individuals can better appreciate adult literary works.

KEY TERMS

lateralization 38
schema 39
assimilation 39
accommodation 39
organization 39
equilibration 40
sensorimotor stage 40
preoperational stage 40

symbolic function substage 41
intuitive thought substage 42
centration 43
conservation 43
concrete operational stage 45
seriation 45
transitivity 45
formal operational stage 46

hypothetical-deductive
reasoning 46
neo-Piagetians 49
zone of proximal development
(ZPD) 51
scaffolding 52
social constructivist
approach 54

language 56
phonology 56
morphology 56
syntax 57
semantics 57
pragmatics 57

 PORTFOLIO ACTIVITIES

Now that you have a good understanding of this chapter, complete these exercises to expand your thinking.

Independent Reflection

Supporting Language Development. Write a brief overview of the language development of children living in poverty conditions. What can teachers and schools do to help support language development in impoverished students? What impact can language development have on the future success of children? (INTASC: Principles 2, 3, 6)

Collaborative Work

Comparing Cognitive Differences Among Children. Select the general age of the child you expect to teach one day. Make a list of that child's characteristic ways of thinking, according to Piaget's

theory of cognitive development. With three or four other students in the class, compare your lists. In what important cognitive ways do the children represented in your lists differ? How will these differences impact the teaching methods you use in the classroom? (INTASC: Principles 2, 3)

Research/Field Experience Reflections

The Brain and Children's Education. Find an education article in a magazine or on the Internet that promotes "left-brained" and "right-brained" activities for learning. Write a critical review of the article based on what you read in this chapter about neuroscience and brain education. (INTASC: Principles 3, 7, 9)

 Go to the Online Learning Center for downloadable portfolio templates.

 TAKING IT TO THE NET

1. Piaget and Vygotsky are often portrayed as theorists with opposite ideas—Piaget believed in the child's personal discovery of ideas. Vygotsky believed in the child's social discovery of ideas. What do you believe? Is learning more social or more individual? Why?
2. Health and physical development highly impact students' academic achievement. Describe high-risk health factors that inhibit students' success. How can school health education and services improve academic performance?

3. Giving students frequent opportunities for reading, writing, oral presentations, and/or collaborative group work can reinforce language skills. Locate a language arts Web resource and assess its value for developing children's language skills. How could you use the resource to engage and challenge students of all English language abilities?

Connect to the Online Learning Center to explore possible answers.

STUDY, PRACTICE, AND SUCCEED

 Go to chapter 2 on the Online Learning Center at www.mhhe.com/santrockedu2e to access the student study guide with practice quizzes, web links, portfolio resources, PowerWeb articles and news feeds, and the online resources referenced in the chapter.

 Go to your Student Toolbox CD-ROM to access the resources and activities referenced in the chapter and

• Resources to help you prepare for the PRAXIS II™ exam

• **Application Resources,** including additional *Crack the Case* studies, electronic versions of the *Self-Assessments,* Application Exercises, and Site Observation Questions
• **Study Resources,** including Learning Goals, the Chapter Summary, a *Test Your Learning* exercise, and multiple-choice, true/false, matching, key terms, and short-answer quizzes
• **Professional Resources,** including a Lesson Plan Builder and *Bibliomaker*

3 Social Contexts and Socioemotional Development

> In the end, the power behind development is life.
>
> —Erik Erikson
> *European-Born American*
> *Psychotherapist, 20th Century*

Chapter Outline

Contemporary Theories

Bronfenbrenner's Ecological Theory

Erikson's Life-Span Development Theory

Social Contexts of Development

Families

Peers

Schools

Socioemotional Development

The Self

Moral Development

Chapter Learning Goals After you have completed your study of this chapter, you should be able to reach these learning goals:

1 Describe two contemporary perspectives on socioemotional development: Bronfenbrenner's ecological theory and Erikson's life-span development theory.

2 Discuss how the social contexts of families, peers, and schools are linked with socioemotional development.

3 Explain these aspects of children's socioemotional development: self-esteem, identity, and moral concepts.

Teaching Stories Mike Zimmerman

Mike Zimmerman's fourth-grade students were worried that wildlife near their Montgomery County, Maryland, school was going to die. Mr. Z, as the kids call him, had shown them pools of bright green liquid by a gas station near their school.

After discussing what it could be, the students decided the gas station was dumping antifreeze. Their computer search uncovered that antifreeze could kill animals, so they called local environmental groups to ask what could be done. Told dumping antifreeze was illegal, the kids decided the station's owner simply didn't know, so they wrote to him. To their relief, the liquid was a harmless cement cleaner.

This is how Mr. Z begins his science unit on ecosystems. His students worked on their research, writing, and critical thinking skills. Most importantly, they learned how their actions could affect the environment and how to be active participants in their community (Sanders, 2000, p. 25A). Had Mr. Z simply told the students that he thought the gas station was dumping what looked like antifreeze and that he had told the owner that it needed to be cleaned up, his student would have missed some valuable learning opportunities.

Expert Advice

Joyce Epstein on School, Family, and Community Partnerships

Later in the chapter we will examine the topic of moral development, including the concept of service learning and providing students opportunities to participate in activities that promote social responsibility and service to the community, just as Mr. Z did. In addition to moral development, we will explore how parents cradle children's lives as well as how children's development is influenced by successive waves of peers, friends, and teachers. Children's small world widens as they become students and develop relationships with many new people. In this second chapter on development, we will study these social worlds and examine children's socioemotional development.

CONTEMPORARY THEORIES

A number of theories address children's socioemotional development. In this chapter we will focus on two main theories: Bronfenbrenner's ecological theory and Erikson's life-span development theory. These two theories were chosen for their comprehensiveness in addressing the social contexts in which children develop (Bronfenbrenner) and major changes in children's socioemotional development (Erikson). In chapter 7, we will discuss other theories (behavioral and social cognitive) that also are relevant to socioemotional development.

Bronfenbrenner's Ecological Theory

The ecological theory developed by Urie Bronfenbrenner (1917–) primarily focuses on the social contexts in which children live and the people who influence their development.

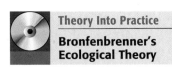

Theory Into Practice

Bronfenbrenner's Ecological Theory

Five Environmental Systems Bronfenbrenner's **ecological theory** consists of five environmental systems that range from close interpersonal interactions to broad-based influences of culture. Bronfenbrenner (1995, 2000, 2004; Bronfenbrenner & Morris, 1998) calls the five systems the microsystem, mesosystem, exosystem, macrosystem, and chronosystem (see figure 3.1).

A *microsystem* is a setting in which the individual spends considerable time. Some of these contexts are the student's family, peers, school, and neighborhood. Within these microsystems, the individual has direct interactions with parents, teachers, peers, and others. For Bronfenbrenner, the student is not a passive recipient of experiences in these settings but is someone who reciprocally interacts with others and helps to construct the settings.

The *mesosystem* involves linkages between microsystems. Examples are the connections between family experiences and school experiences and between family and peers. For example, consider one important mesosystem, the connection between schools and

ecological theory Bronfenbrenner's theory that consists of five environmental systems: microsystem, mesosystem, exosystem, macrosystem, and chronosystem.

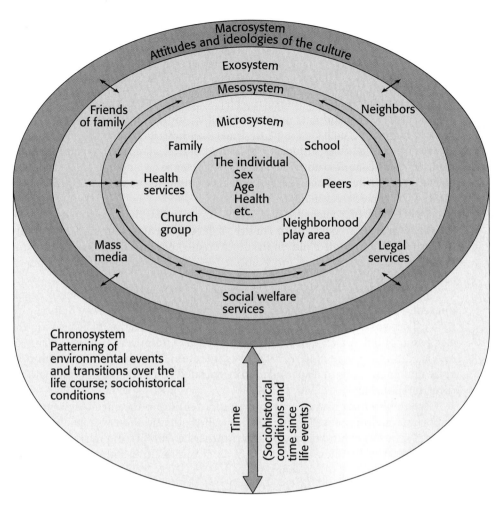

FIGURE 3.1 Bronfenbrenner's Ecological Theory of Development
Bronfenbrenner's ecological theory consists of five environmental systems: microsystem, ·
mesosystem, exosystem, macrosystem, and chronosystem.

families. In one study of a thousand eighth-graders, the joint impact of family and class-room experiences on students' attitudes and achievement was examined as the students made the transition from the last year of middle school to the first year of high school (Epstein, 1983). Students who were given greater opportunities for communication and decision making, whether at home or in the classroom, showed more initiative and earned better grades.

In another mesosystem study, middle school and high school students participated in a program that was designed to connect their families, peers, schools, and parents' work (Cooper, 1995). This outreach program (administered by a university) targeted Latino and African American students in low-income areas. The students commented that the outreach program helped them to bridge the gaps across their different social worlds. Many of the students saw their schools and neighborhoods as contexts in which people expected them to fail, become pregnant and leave school, or behave delinquently. The outreach program provided students with expectations and moral goals to do "something good for your people," such as working in the community and encouraging siblings to go to college. We will have more to say about family-school connections later in the chapter.

The *exosystem* is at work when experiences in another setting (in which the student does not have an active role) influence what students and teachers experience in the im-mediate context. For example, consider the school and park supervisory boards in a

Urie Bronfenbrenner developed ecological theory, a perspective that is receiving increased attention. This theory emphasizes the importance of both micro and macro dimensions of the environment in which the child lives.

Bronfenbrenner's Theory

Bronfenbrenner and a Multicultural Framework

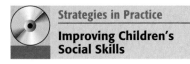

Strategies in Practice

Improving Children's Social Skills

community. They have strong roles in determining the quality of schools, parks, recreation facilities, and libraries. Their decisions can help or hinder a child's development.

The *macrosystem* involves the broader culture. *Culture* is a very broad term that includes the roles of ethnicity and socioeconomic factors in children's development. It's the broadest context in which students and teachers live, including the society's values and customs. For example, some cultures (such as those of Islamic countries, such as Egypt or Iran) emphasize traditional gender roles. Other cultures (such as found in the United States) accept more varied gender roles. In most Islamic countries, educational systems promote male dominance. In the United States, schools increasingly have endorsed the value of equal opportunities for females and males.

One aspect of socioeconomic status for some students is growing up in poverty. Poverty can overwhelm children's development and impair their ability to learn, although some children in impoverished circumstances are remarkably resilient. We will say much more about poverty and education in chapter 5, "Sociocultural Diversity."

The *chronosystem* includes the sociohistorical conditions of students' development. For example, students today are living a childhood of many firsts (Louv, 1990). They are the first day-care generation, the first generation to grow up in the electronic bubble of an environment defined by computers and new forms of media, the first post-sexual-revolution generation, and the first generation to grow up in new kinds of dispersed, deconcentrated cities that are not quite urban, rural, or suburban.

Bronfenbrenner has increasingly given attention to the chronosystem as an important environmental system. He has called attention to two alarming problems: (1) the large number of children in America who live in poverty, especially in single-parent families; and (2) a decline in values (Bronfenbrenner & others, 1996).

Evaluating Bronfenbrenner's Theory Bronfenbrenner's theory has gained popularity in recent years. It provides one of the few theoretical frameworks for systematically examining social contexts on both micro and macro levels, bridging the gap between behavioral theories that focus on small settings and anthropological theories that analyze larger settings. His theory has been instrumental in calling attention to the importance of looking at children's lives in more than one setting. As we just saw, teachers often need to consider not just what goes on in the classroom but also what happens in students' families, neighborhoods, and peer groups.

Critics of Bronfenbrenner's theory say that it gives too little attention to biological and cognitive factors in children's development. They also point out that the theory does not address the step-by-step developmental changes that are the focus of theories such as Piaget's and Erikson's.

Teaching Strategies
For Educating Children Based on Bronfenbrenner's Theory

1. *Think about the child as embedded in a number of environmental systems and influences.* These include schools and teachers, parents and siblings, the community and neighborhood, peers and friends, the media, religion, and culture.
2. *Pay attention to the connection between schools and families.* Build these connections through formal and informal outreach.
3. *Recognize the importance of the community, socioeconomic status, and culture in the child's development.* These broader social contexts can have powerful influences on the child's development (Valsiner, 2000).

Erikson's Life-Span Development Theory

Complementing Bronfenbrenner's analysis of the social contexts in which children develop and the people who are important in their lives, the theory of Erik Erikson (1902–1994) presents a developmental view of people's lives in stages. Let's take Erikson's journey through the human life span.

Eight Stages of Human Development   In Erikson's (1968) theory, eight stages of development unfold as people go through the human life span (see figure 3.2). Each stage consists of a developmental task that confronts individuals with a crisis. For Erikson, each crisis is not catastrophic but a turning point of increased vulnerability and enhanced potential. The more successfully an individual resolves each crisis, the more psychologically healthy the individual will be. Each stage has both positive and negative sides.

Trust versus mistrust is Erikson's first psychosocial stage. It occurs in the first year of life. The development of trust requires warm, nurturant caregiving. The positive outcome is a feeling of comfort and minimal fear. Mistrust develops when infants are treated too negatively or are ignored.

Autonomy versus shame and doubt is Erikson's second psychosocial stage. It occurs in late infancy and the toddler years. After gaining trust in their caregivers, infants begin to discover that their behavior is their own. They assert their independence and realize their will. If infants are restrained too much or punished too harshly, they develop a sense of shame and doubt.

Initiative versus guilt is Erikson's third psychosocial stage. It corresponds to early childhood, about three to five years of age. As young children experience a widening social world, they are challenged more than they were as infants. To cope with these challenges, they need to engage in active, purposeful behavior. In this stage, adults expect children to become more responsible and require them to assume some responsibilities for taking care of their bodies and belongings. Developing a sense of responsibility increases initiative. Children develop uncomfortable guilt feelings if they are irresponsible or are made to feel too anxious.

Industry versus inferiority is Erikson's fourth psychosocial stage. It corresponds approximately with the elementary school years, from six years of age until puberty or early adolescence. Children's initiative brings them into contact with a wealth of new experiences. As they move into the elementary school years, they direct their energy toward mastering knowledge and intellectual skills. At no time are children more enthusiastic about learning than at the end of early childhood, when their imagination is expansive. The danger in the elementary school years is developing a sense of inferiority, unproductiveness, and incompetence.

Identity versus identity confusion is Erikson's fifth psychosocial stage. It corresponds to the adolescent years. Adolescents try to find out who they are, what they are all about, and where they are going in life. They are confronted with many new roles and adult statuses (such as vocational and romantic). Adolescents need to be allowed to explore different paths to attain a healthy identity. If adolescents do not adequately explore different roles and don't carve out a positive future path, they can remain confused about their identity.

Intimacy versus isolation is Erikson's sixth psychosocial stage. It corresponds to the early adult years, the twenties and thirties. The developmental task is to form positive close relationships with others. Erikson describes intimacy as finding oneself but losing oneself in another person. The hazard of this stage is that one will fail to form an intimate relationship with a romantic partner or friend and become socially isolated. For such individuals, loneliness can become a dark cloud over their lives.

Generativity versus stagnation is Erikson's seventh psychosocial stage. It corresponds to the middle adulthood years, the forties and fifties. Generativity means transmitting something positive to the next generation. This can involve such roles as parenting and teaching, through which adults assist the next generation in developing useful lives. Erikson described stagnation as the feeling of having done nothing to help the next generation.

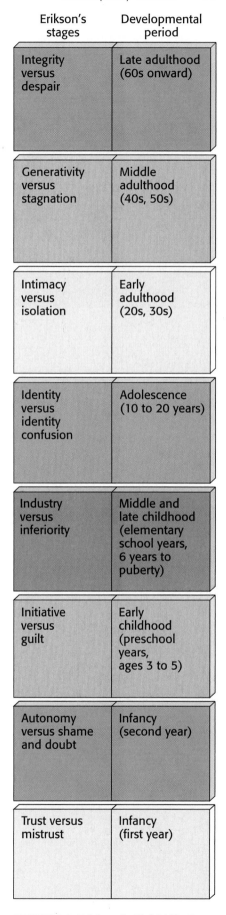

FIGURE 3.2 Erikson's Eight Life-Span Stages

Erik Erikson with his wife, Joan, who is an artist. Erikson generated one of the most important developmental theories of the twentieth century.

Integrity versus despair is Erikson's eighth and final psychosocial stage. It corresponds to the late adulthood years, the sixties until death. Older adults review their lives, reflecting on what they have done. If the retrospective evaluations are positive, they develop a sense of integrity. That is, they view their life as positively integrated and worth living. In contrast, older adults become despairing if their backward glances are mainly negative.

Evaluating Erikson's Theory   Erikson's theory captures some of life's key socioemotional tasks and places them in a developmental framework. His concept of identity is especially helpful in understanding older adolescents and college students. His overall theory was a critical force in forging our current view of human development as lifelong rather than being restricted only to childhood.

Erikson's theory is not without criticism. Some experts believe that his stages are too rigid. Bernice Neugarten (1988) says that identity, intimacy, independence, and many other aspects of socioemotional development are not like beads on a string that appear in neatly packaged age intervals. Rather, they are important issues throughout most of our lives. Although much research has been done on some of Erikson's stages (such as identity), the overall scope of his theory (such as whether the eight stages always occur in the order he proposed) has not been scientifically documented. For example, for some individuals (especially females), intimacy concerns precede identity or develop simultaneously.

Teaching Strategies
For Educating Children Based on Erikson's Theory

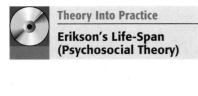

Theory Into Practice

Erikson's Life-Span (Psychosocial Theory)

www.mhhe.com/santedu2e

Erikson's Theory

1. *Encourage initiative in young children.* Children in preschool and early childhood education programs should be given a great deal of freedom to explore their world. They should be allowed to choose some of the activities they engage in. If their requests for doing certain activities are reasonable, the requests should be honored. Provide exciting materials that will stimulate their imagination. Children at this stage love to play. It not only benefits their socioemotional development but also is an important medium for their cognitive growth. Especially encourage social play with peers and fantasy play. Help children assume responsibility for putting toys and materials back in place after they have used them. Children can be given a plant or flower to care for and be assisted in caring for it. Criticism should be kept to a minimum so that children will not develop high levels of guilt and anxiety. Young children are going to make lots of mistakes and have lots of spills. They need good models far more than harsh critics. Structure their activities and environment for successes rather than failures by giving them developmentally appropriate tasks. For example, don't frustrate young children by having them sit for long periods of time doing academic paper-and-pencil tasks.

2. *Promote industry in elementary school children.* Teachers have a special responsibility for children's development of industry. It was Erikson's hope that teachers could provide an atmosphere in which children become passionate about learning. In Erikson's words, teachers should mildly but firmly coerce children into the adventure of finding out that they can learn to accomplish things that they themselves would never have thought they could do. In elementary school, children thirst to know. Most arrive at elementary school steeped in curiosity and a motivation to master tasks. In Erikson's view, it is important for teachers to nourish this motivation for mastery and curiosity. Challenge students, but don't overwhelm them. Be firm in requiring students to be productive, but don't be overly critical. Especially be tolerant of honest mistakes and make sure that every student has opportunities for many successes.

3. *Stimulate identity exploration in adolescence.* Recognize that the student's identity is multidimensional. Aspects include vocational goals; intellectual achievement; and interests in hobbies, sports, music, and other areas. Ask adolescents to write essays about such dimensions, exploring who they are and what they want to do with their lives. Encourage adolescents to think independently and to freely express their views. This stimulates self-exploration. Also encourage adolescents to listen to debates on religious, political, and ideological issues. This will stimulate them to examine different perspectives.

   Recognize that some of the roles adolescents adopt are not permanent. They try on many different faces as they search for a face of their own. Also recognize that a successful identity is attained in bits and pieces over many years. Many adolescents in middle schools are just beginning to explore their identity, but even at this time exposing them to various careers and life options can benefit their identity development. Encourage adolescents to talk with a school counselor about career options as well as other aspects of their identity. Have people from different careers come and talk with your students about their work regardless of the grade you teach.

4. *Examine your life as a teacher through the lens of Erikson's eight stages.* (Gratz & Bouton, 1996). For example, you might be at the age at which Erikson says the most important issue is identity versus identity confusion or intimacy versus isolation. Erikson believed that one of identity's most important dimensions is vocational. Your successful career as a teacher could be key in your overall identity. Another important aspect of development for young adults is to have positive, close relationships with others. Your identity will benefit from having a positive relationship with a partner and with one or more friends. Many teachers develop strong camaraderie with other teachers or their mentors, which can be very rewarding.

5. *Benefit from the characteristics of some of Erikson's other stages.* Competent teachers trust, show initiative, are industrious and model a sense of mastery, and are motivated to contribute something meaningful to the next generation. In your role as a teacher, you will actively meet the criteria for Erikson's concept of generativity.

❗ Review and Reflect

1 **Describe two contemporary perspectives on socioemotional development: Bronfenbrenner's ecological theory and Erikson's life-span development theory.**

Review
- What are Bronfenbrenner's five environmental systems and how are they useful in thinking about children's development?
- What Eriksonian stages does a person pass through between birth and the end of adolescence? What are the possibilities for each stage?

Reflect
- How well do you think your own socioemotional development can be described using Erikson's theory?

SOCIAL CONTEXTS OF DEVELOPMENT

In Bronfenbrenner's theory, the social contexts in which children live are important influences on their development. Let's explore three of the contexts in which children spend much of their time: families, peers, and schools.

Families

Children grow up in diverse families. Some parents nurture and support their children. Others treat them harshly or ignore them. Some children have experienced their parents' divorce. Others live their entire childhood in a never-divorced family. Others live in a stepfamily. Some children's mothers and fathers work full-time and place them in after-school programs. Other children's mothers or fathers are present when they come home from school. Some children grow up in an ethnically uniform neighborhood, others in a neighborhood that is more mixed. Some children's families live in poverty; others are economically advantaged. Some children have siblings; others don't. These varying circumstances affect children's development and influence students in and beyond the classroom (Garbarino, Bradshaw, & Kostelny, 2005; Luster & Okagaki, 2005).

Parenting Styles   There can be times when you as a teacher will be asked to give parents advice. There also might be times when it is helpful for you to understand how parents are rearing their children and the effects this has on the children.

   Is there a best way to parent? Diana Baumrind (1971, 1996), a leading authority on parenting, thinks so. She believes that parents should be neither punitive nor aloof. Rather, they should develop rules for children while at the same time being supportive and nurturant. Hundreds of research studies, including her own, support her view (Bornstein, 1995; Grotevant, 1998). Baumrind says that parenting styles come in four main forms:

Parenting Styles

- **Authoritarian parenting** is restrictive and punitive. Authoritarian parents exhort children to follow their directions and respect them. They place firm limits and controls on their children and allow little verbal exchange. For example, an authoritarian parent might say, "Do it my way or else. There will be no discussion!" Children of authoritarian parents often behave in socially incompetent ways. They tend to be anxious about social comparison, fail to initiate activity, and have poor communication skills.
- **Authoritative parenting** encourages children to be independent but still places limits and controls on their actions. Extensive verbal give-and-take is allowed and parents are nurturant and supportive. An authoritative parent might put his or her arm on the child's shoulder in a comforting way and say, "You know you should not have done that. Let's talk about how you can handle the situation differently the next time." Children whose parents are authoritative often behave in socially competent ways. They tend to be self-reliant, delay gratification, get along with their peers, and show high self-esteem. Because of these positive outcomes, Baumrind strongly endorses authoritative parenting.
- **Neglectful parenting** is a parenting style in which parents are uninvolved in their children's lives. When their offspring are adolescents or perhaps even young children, these parents cannot answer the question "It is 10 P.M. Do you know where your child is?" Children of neglectful parents develop the sense that other aspects of their parents' lives are more important than they are. Children of neglectful parents often behave in socially incompetent ways. They tend to have poor self-control, don't handle independence well, and aren't achievement motivated.
- **Indulgent parenting** is a parenting style in which parents are highly involved with their children but place few limits or restrictions on their behaviors. These parents often let their children do what they want and get their way because they believe the combination of nurturant support and lack of restraints will produce a creative, confident child. The result is that these children usually don't learn to control their own behavior. These parents do not take into account the development of the whole child.

Do the benefits of authoritative parenting transcend the boundaries of ethnicity, socioeconomic status, and household composition? Although exceptions to patterns have been found, the evidence linking authoritative parenting with competence on the part of

authoritarian parenting A restrictive and punitive parenting style in which there is little verbal exchange between parents and children; associated with children's social incompetence.

authoritative parenting A positive parenting style that encourages children to be independent but still places limits and controls on their actions; extensive verbal give-and-take is allowed; associated with children's social competence.

neglectful parenting A parenting style of uninvolvement in which parents spend little time with their children; associated with children's social incompetence.

indulgent parenting A parenting style of involvement but few limits or restrictions on children's behavior; linked with children's social incompetence.

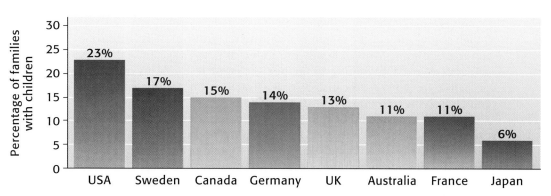

FIGURE 3.3 **Single-Parent Families in Various Countries**

Note: Children are under 18 years of age.

the child has been found in research across a wide range of ethnic groups, social strata, cultures, and family stuctures (Steinberg & Silk, 2002).

Nonetheless, researchers have found that in some ethnic groups, aspects of the authoritarian style may be associated with more positive child outcomes than Baumrind predicts. Aspects of traditional Asian child-rearing practices are often continued by Asian American families. In some cases, these practices have been described as authoritarian. However, Ruth Chao (2001; Chao & Tseng, 2002) argues that the style of parenting used by many Asian American parents is best conceptualized as a type of training in which parents are concerned and involved in their children's lives rather than reflecting strict or authoritarian control. Thus, the parenting style Chao describes, *training,* is based on a type of parental control that is distinct from the more "domineering" control reflected in the authoritarian parenting style. The positive outcomes of the training parenting style in Asian American families occur in the high academic achievement of Asian American children (Stevenson & Zusho, 2002; Tseng, 2004).

The Changing Family in a Changing Society   Increasing numbers of children are being raised in divorced families, stepparent families, and families in which the mother works outside the home. As divorce has become epidemic, a staggering number of children have been growing up in single-parent families. The United States has a higher percentage of single-parent families than virtually any other industrialized country (see figure 3.3). Today, about one in every four children in the United States have lived a portion of their lives in a stepfamily by the time they are eighteen. Also, more than two of every three mothers with a child from six to seventeen years of age are in the labor force.

Children of Divorce   The effects of divorce on children are complex, depending on such factors as the age of the child, strengths and weaknesses of the child at the time of the divorce, the type of custody involved, socioeconomic status, and postdivorce family functioning (Amato, 2004; Clingempeel & Brand-Clingempeel, 2004; Palmer 2004; Wallerstein & Johnson-Reitz, 2004). The use of support systems (relatives, friends, housekeepers), an ongoing positive relationship between the custodial parent and the exspouse, the ability to meet financial needs, and quality schooling help children adjust to the stressful circumstances of divorce (Cox & Harter, 2001).

E. Mavis Hetherington's (1995, 2000; Hetherington & Kelly, 2002; Hetherington & Stanley-Hagan, 2002) research documents the importance of schools when children grow up in a divorced family. Throughout elementary school, children in divorced families had the highest achievement and fewest problems when both the parenting environment and the school environment were authoritative (according to Baumrind's categorization). In the divorced families, when only one parent was authoritative, an authoritative school improved the child's adjustment. The most negative parenting environment occurred when neither parent was authoritative. The most negative school environment was chaotic and neglecting.

Children and Divorce

In response to the high divorce rate, the state of Florida passed a law requiring that all high school students be taught marital and relationship skills (Peterson, 1998). Many schools teach some form of family life course, but marriage and family experts believe such courses need upgrading to include the latest research on communication skills, the factors most likely to cause divorce, strategies for conflict resolution, and family problem-solving techniques (Gottman, 1996).

Let's look at a child in the midst of a family situation in which parents are getting divorced (Brodkin & Coleman, 1995). Maggie is a ten-year-old fifth-grader who had been a cheerful child and had done well in school, but all of that changed when her parents separated about one month ago. Her father moved out and Maggie's mother became depressed. Maggie began to not show up for school. Now, although she is at school regularly, she has trouble concentrating on her schoolwork.

How might you as a teacher help Maggie? Some strategies include

1. *Reach out to the parents.* Call Maggie's mother instead of waiting to see if things get better on their own.
2. *Suggest professional guidance.* Mention to the parent(s) that many people going through a divorce—including parents and children—benefit from professional counseling. In some school districts, there are regular meetings for children of divorce or divorced parents, led by a mental health professional or a teacher with special training.
3. *Support the child.* The day-to-day caring you give children like Maggie can make a difference in their ability to cope with the divorce and concentrate on their schoolwork.
4. *Recommend a good book related to divorce.* Here are three excellent books on divorce (Norcross & others, 2000):
   - For children three to about eight years old: Brown & Brown (1988), *Dinosaurs Divorce*
   - For older children and adolescents: Gardner (1985), *The Boys and Girls Book About Divorce*
   - For parents: Kalter (1990), *Growing Up with Divorce*

Ethnic and Socioeconomic Variations in Families   Families in different ethnic groups vary in their size, structure, and composition; their reliance on kinship networks; and their levels of income and education (Coll & Pachter, 2002; Diggs & Socha, 2004; Leyendecker & others, 2005; Parke, 2004; Parke & others, 2005). Large and extended families are more common among some minority groups than among the general population (McAdoo, 2002). For example, 19 percent of Latino families have three or more children, compared with 14 percent of African American and 10 percent of non-Latino White families. African American and Latino children interact more with grandparents, aunts, uncles, cousins, and more-distant relatives than do non-Latino White children (Gonzales & others, 2004).

Single-parent families are more common among African Americans and Latinos than among non-Latino White Americans. Single parents often have less time, money, and energy than do two-parent households. Ethnic minority parents are less educated and more likely to be low-income than their White counterparts (Harwood & others, 2002). Still, many impoverished ethnic minority families manage to find ways to raise competent children (Harrison-Hale, McLoyd, & Smedley, 2004; Tucher, Subramanian, & James, 2004).

Some aspects of home life can help to protect ethnic minority children from injustice. The community and the family can filter out destructive racist messages, and parents can present alternative frames of reference to counter negative messages. The extended family also can serve as an important buffer to stress (Wakschlag, Chase-Lansdale, & Brooks-Gunn, 1996). It is especially important for teachers to guard against having biased expectations about parents based on their ethnicity. We will say more about ethnicity and children's schooling in chapter 5, "Sociocultural Diversity."

In the United States and most other Western cultures, child-rearing practices have been found to differ among different socioeconomic status (SES) groups (*SES* refers to a grouping of people with similar occupational, educational, and economic characteristics). Low-income parents often place a high value on external characteristics such as obedience and neatness. In contrast, middle-SES families frequently place a high value on internal characteristics, such as self-control and delay of gratification. Middle-SES parents are more likely to explain, praise, accompany their discipline with reasoning, and ask their children questions. Low-income parents are more likely to use physical punishment and criticize their children (Hoff-Ginsberg & Tardif, 1995).

There also are socioeconomic differences in the way that parents think about education (Hoff, Laursen, & Tardif, 2002; Lareau, 1996). Middle-SES parents more often think of education as something that should be mutually encouraged by parents and teachers. Low-income parents are more likely to view education as the teacher's job.

In the Diversity and Education interlude, we will explore educational concerns about America's fastest-growing female minority population—Latinas.

Diversity and Education
Are America's Schools Leaving Latinas Behind?

The high school graduation rate of Latinas is lower than for girls in any other ethnic group, and they are the least likely to go to college (National Center for Education Statistics, 2001). Findings like these prompted a recent report by the American Association of University Women, which concluded that U.S. schools are not meeting the educational needs of Latinas (Ginorio & Huston, 2000). The report found that although Latinas bring many strengths and personal resources to the schools they attend, for them to be successful it is important for schools to view bilingualism and other values as assets rather than liabilities.

In spite of the importance of education to the Latino community, family needs and peer pressure often clash with Latinas' school expectations. For example, many Latinas face pressure about going to college from boyfriends and fiancés who expect their girlfriends or future wives to not be "too educated."

Contrary to stereotypes about Latino communities, most Latino parents hope that their children will excel in school. However, many Latino families face economic and social problems that defer the realization of those dreams for their children.

Latino girls and boys face similar educational challenges and experience stereotyping and other obstacles that discourage their success in schools. Some obstacles, though, are different for Latinas than Latinos. Latinas are three times as likely to fear for their personal safety in schools as other girls, and too often Latinos are assumed to be gang members by teachers and counselors simply because they speak Spanish (Ginorio & Huston, 2000).

Recommendations for improving the education of Latinas and Latinos include

- *All adults need to encourage academic success.* It is important for Latinas and Latinos to hear from all the adults in their lives that college and professional careers are rewarding options and ones that they can achieve.
- *Involve the whole family in the process of college preparation.* Teachers and counselors need to work with Latino families to demystify college requirements and the long-term benefits of college.
- *Deal meaningfully with stereotypes and challenges such as adolescent pregnancy that impact school performance.* This includes offering child care and alternative scheduling and recognizing that being a young mother and completing one's education are not incompatible.

Source: American Association of University Women (2003), pp. 1–2.

School-Family Linkages

School-Family Linkages   In Bronfenbrenner's theory, linkages between the family and the school are an important mesosystem. Also, in Hetherington's study, which we just discussed, an authoritative school environment benefited children from divorced families.

Experienced teachers know the importance of getting parents involved in children's education. In one survey, teachers listed parental involvement as the number one priority in improving education (Chira, 1993). However, schools often don't set goals or implement effective programs to make that involvement occur (Epstein, 2001).

What else stands in the way of parental involvement? For one thing, education expert Joyce Epstein (1997, 2001; Epstein & Sanders, 2002; Epstein & others, 2002) says, most parents know so little about their children's education that they can't even ask questions about it. That is why so many conversations begin with a parent asking, "How was school today?" and end with the child responding, "Fine." This low level of parental involvement concerns educators because it is linked with students' low achievement (Eccles & Harold, 1996). By contrast, in a study of more than 16,000 students, the students were more likely to get *A*s and less likely to repeat a grade or be expelled if both parents were highly involved in their schooling (National Center for Education Statistics, 1997). In this study, high involvement was defined as the parent participating in three or four of the following: school meetings, a teacher conference, a class meeting, or volunteering. A goal of family inclusion and community involvement was made part of the Goals 2000: Educate America Act. This was a welcome official endorsement of the critical role that families play in children's education. Students of all ages report that they want their parents to be more involved in their education (Connors & Epstein, 1995).

One problem that can interfere with building partnerships between school and family is negative perceptions of families (Workman & Gage, 1997). Some children come to school poorly clothed, on drugs, with knives or guns, and without their homework. They might not be motivated to learn and might show little respect for the teacher. In such circumstances, it can be hard to get past blaming parents for the problems that children present to the teacher. However, to get parents more positively involved in their children's education, you have to get past the blaming. Think of parents as having potential strengths that, if tapped, can help you educate the child more effectively (Hiatt-Michael, 2001).

Consider several examples of successful partnerships between schools and families. In Lima, Ohio, the goal is for each school to establish a personal relationship with every parent. At an initial parent-teacher conference, parents are given a packet that discusses how they can participate in the child's learning activities at home. Conferences, regular phone calls, and home visits strengthen the school-family connection. These make other kinds of communication (such as progress reports, report cards, activity calendars, or discussion of problems that arise during the year) more welcome and successful. For more about effective communication with parents, see the Technology and Education box.

In a joint effort of the New York City School System and the Children's Aid Society, community organizations have been invited to provide school-based programs for

Through the Eyes of Teachers

Parents and the Community

Parents are a primary ingredient of the classroom team at Gramercy School. Many parents of preschool children who are developmentally delayed have no idea as to how or if their child will develop. It becomes the job of the educators and other professionals to assist that parent in the development of their child. We then become partners. There are ongoing parent training groups, support groups, and time can be spent in school with a therapist at any time that the parent wishes. Gramercy School has an open-door policy. Teachers have access to telephones throughout the building and daily communication books and notes are sent home. There are times when some families face a very challenging situation. At these times, I might meet with this parent or I might call in the psychologist to assist with specific issues. We have on occasion asked parents to assist other parents or to be a resource for others. This is powerful and gives support from family to family.

Use of the community is very important. New York City is full of opportunities. I have been able to work closely with the Disabled Library in the neighborhood. They have been great at supplying the school with audio books for the children and lending special equipment for their use. The local fire department has been used for numerous trips. The firemen have been especially attentive to the students because of their various disabilities. The fire department has also come to visit the school, which was very exciting for the children. It was amazing to see how patient they were with the students. I am also encouraged to see that many of the area colleges and universities send interns and student teachers to visit the school. Donations from Hasbro toy company during the holidays make a big difference in the way some students and families get to spend their holiday vacation. Our students are very visible in the New York City community, where we are located. This helps our neighbors to get to know the staff and children and creates a safer environment.

Juanita Kirton
Assistant Principal
YAI/NYL Gramercy School
New York City

Communicating with Parents About Television and Children's Development

Many children spend more time in front of the television set than they do with their parents. In the 1990s, children averaged 26 hours a week watching television. Watching lots of television is related to poor physical fitness in children. It also can diminish the amount of time children spend doing homework and in school-related activities. Amazingly, the 20,000 hours of television, on the average, that children watch by the time they graduate from high school represents more hours than they have spent in the classroom!

Here are some recommendations that you can communicate to parents about reducing TV's negative impact and increasing its positive impact on their children's development (Singer & Singer, 1987):

- Help children develop good viewing habits early in life.
- Monitor your children's viewing habits and plan what they will watch, instead of letting them view TV randomly. Be active with young children between planned programs.
- Look for children's programs that feature children in the child's age group.
- Make sure that television is not a substitute for other activities.
- Develop discussions about sensitive television themes with children. Give them the opportunity to ask questions about the programs.
- Balance reading and television activities. Children can "follow up" on interesting television programs by checking out the library books from which some programs have been adapted and by pursuing additional stories by the authors of those books.
- Help children develop a balanced viewing schedule of education, action, comedy, fine arts, fantasy, sports, and so on. Make sure that children are not primarily watching television shows filled with sex and violence.
- Point out positive examples that show how various ethnic and cultural groups contribute to a better society.
- Point out positive examples of females performing competently both in professions and at home.

1,200 adolescents and their families since 1992 (Carnegie Council on Adolescent Development, 1995). The participating school's family resource center is open from 8:30 A.M. to 8:30 P.M. Staffed by social workers, parents, and other volunteers, the center houses adult education, drug-abuse prevention, and other activities. Because many of the families who send adolescents to the school are of Dominican origin, the school offers English-as-a-second-language classes for parents, 400 of whom are currently enrolled.

 ## Teaching Strategies
For Forging Family-School Linkages

This mother is working with her son at a Saturday math workshop in Oakland, California, sponsored by Family Math.

Joyce Epstein (1996, 2001; Epstein & Sanders, 2002; Epstein & others, 2002) described six areas in which school-family linkages can be forged:

1. *Provide assistance to families.* Schools can provide parents with information about child-rearing skills, the importance of family support, child and adolescent development, and home contexts that enhance learning at each grade level. Teachers are an important contact point between schools and families. Teachers can become aware of whether the family is meeting the basic physical and health needs of the child.
2. *Communicate effectively with families about school programs and their child's progress.* This involves both school-to-home and home-to-school communication. Encourage parents to attend parent-teacher conferences and other school functions. Their attendance conveys to their children that they are interested in their children's school performance. Set up times for parent meetings that are convenient for them to attend. Most parents cannot come to meetings during the school day because of other obligations. One option is "work nights" for parents and children to come to school and work on various projects to improve the school's physical appearance, mount artwork, and so on. Teachers can monitor the

percentage of parents who come to functions. If the turnout is low, brainstorm with parents, other teachers, and administrators to come up with strategies that will increase participation. Also, work on developing activities in which parents can get to know each other, not just know the teacher.

Here are some specific strategies for improving communication (Rosenthal & Sawyers, 1997):

- Invite parents to meet you before the school year begins at an orientation, or invite parents to a potluck dinner.
- Send home children's work each week accompanied by a note or a letter. The letter might review the week's activities and include suggestions for helping children with their homework. Send the letter in the parents' primary language.
- In schools with computerized telephone systems, record messages about study units and homework assignments so that parents can call at their convenience. In McAllen, Texas, the school district has developed a community partnership with local radio stations. The district sponsors "Discusiones Escolares," a weekly program in Spanish that encourages parents to become more involved in their children's education. Parents can check out copies of the script or a cassette tape of each program from the parent coordinators at their schools.
- Encourage principals to set up lunch meetings with parents to find out their concerns and ask for suggestions.
- Use PTA/PTO meetings effectively. Sometimes the parent-teacher conference is the only contact teachers have with parents. Schedule the first conference in the first two weeks of school so that parents can raise concerns, ask questions, and make suggestions. This can avoid potential problems from the outset. At this first meeting, try to find out about the family's structure (intact, divorced, stepfamily), rules, roles, and learning style. Practice active listening skills and say something positive about their child to establish yourself as someone who can be approached.
- Another way of making a school family-friendly is to create a parent room or parent center at the school (Johnson, 1994). Here parents can help each other, help the school, and receive information or assistance from the school or community.

3. *Encourage parents to be volunteers.* Improve training, work, and schedules to involve parents as volunteers at school and to increase attendance at school meetings. Try to match the skills of volunteers to classroom needs. Remember from the opening story in chapter 2 that in some schools parents are extensively involved in educational planning and assisting teachers.

4. *Involve families with their children in learning activities at home.* This includes homework and other curriculum-linked activities and decisions. Parents are the most effective when they learn good tutoring strategies and support the work of schools. Epstein (1998; Epstein, Salinas, & Jackson, 1995) coined the term *interactive homework* and designed a program that encourages students to go to their parents for help. In one elementary school that uses Epstein's approach, a weekly teacher's letter informs parents about the objective of each assignment, gives directions, and asks for comments. One interactive homework assignment had parents accompany their children to neighbors' houses to discuss the local citrus industry. Epstein and her colleagues (1995) have developed manuals for teachers that provide hundreds of examples of interactive homework exercises in elementary schools. These can be obtained from the Center on Families, Communities, Schools, and Children's Learning at Johns Hopkins University in Baltimore.

5. *Include families as participants in school decisions.* Parents can be invited to be on PTA/PTO boards, various committees, councils, and other parent organizations. At Antwa Elementary School in a rural area of Wisconsin, potluck supper parent-teacher organization meetings involve discussions with parents about school and district educational goals, age-appropriate learning, child discipline, and testing performance.

6. *Coordinate community collaboration.* Help interconnect the work and resources of community businesses, agencies, colleges and universities, and other groups to strengthen school programs, family practices, and student learning. Schools can alert families to community programs and services that will benefit them.

    An example of coordinating community collaboration is First Thursdays at the Baltimore Museum of Art and Locerman-Bunday Elementary School in Baltimore. On one First Thursday, the school provided a hot dog dinner for 247 students and their families before boarding buses to the museum for an evening that focused on "Portraits in Paris."

Peers

In addition to families and teachers, peers also play powerful roles in children's development. Just what are peers?

    In the context of child development, peers are children of about the same age or maturity level. Same-age peer interaction plays a unique role. Age grading would occur even if schools were not age graded and children were left alone to determine the composition of their own societies. One of the most important functions of the peer group is to provide a source of information and comparison about the world outside of the family.

    Good peer relations might be necessary for normal development (Howes & Tonyan, 2000; Rubin, 2000). Social isolation, or the inability to "plug in" to a social network, is linked with many problems and disorders, ranging from delinquency and problem drinking to depression (Kupersmidt & Coie, 1990). In one study, poor peer relations in childhood were associated with dropping out of school and delinquent behavior in adolescence (Roff, Sells, & Golden, 1972). In another study, harmonious peer relations in adolescence were related to positive mental health at midlife (Hightower, 1990).

    Peer relations may influence whether adolescents develop problems. In one recent study of more than 3,000 eleventh-grade students, peer pressure was strongly linked to alcohol use (Borden, Donnermeyer, & Scheer, 2001). In another study, associating with certain crowds in the tenth grade ("jocks" and "criminals") was linked with being in a substance-abuse program in the early twenties (Barber, Eccles, & Stone, 2001).

Peer Statuses Developmentalists have pinpointed five types of peer status: popular children, average children, neglected children, rejected children, and controversial children (Rubin, Bukowski, & Parker, 1998; Wentzel & Asher, 1995; Wentzel & Battle, 2001).

    Many children worry about whether or not they are popular. *Popular children* are frequently nominated as a best friend and are rarely disliked by their peers. Popular children give out reinforcements, listen carefully, maintain open lines of communication with peers, are happy, act like themselves, show enthusiasm and concern for others, and are self-confident without being conceited (Hartup, 1983). *Average children* receive an average number of both positive and negative nominations from their peers. *Neglected children* are infrequently nominated as a best friend but are not disliked by their peers. *Rejected children* are infrequently nominated as someone's best friend and are often actively disliked by their peers. *Controversial children* are frequently nominated both as someone's best friend and as being disliked.

    Rejected children often have more serious adjustment problems than do neglected children (Buhs & Ladd, 2001; Goie, 2004). In one study, more than a hundred fifth-grade boys were evaluated over a period of seven years until the end of high school (Kupersmidt & Coie, 1990). The most important factor in predicting whether rejected children would engage in delinquent behavior or drop out of secondary school was aggression toward peers in elementary school. Aggression, impulsiveness, and disruptiveness characterize the majority of rejected children, although 10 to 20 percent of rejected children are actually shy.

    Not all rejected children are aggressive (Haselager & others, 2002; Hymel, McDougall, & Renshaw, 2004; Sandstrom & Zakriski, 2004). Although aggression and its

Through the Eyes of Students

We Defined Each Other with Adjectives

"I was funky. Dana was sophisticated. Liz was crazy. We walked to school together, went for bike rides, cut school, got stoned, talked on the phone, smoked cigarettes, slept over, discussed boys and sex, went to church together, and got angry at each other. We defined each other with adjectives and each other's presence. As high school friends, we simultaneously resisted and anticipated adulthood and womanhood.

What was possible when I was fifteen and sixteen? We still had to tell our parents where we were going! We wanted to do excitedly forbidden activities like going out to dance clubs and drinking whiskey sours. Liz, Dana, and I wanted to do these forbidden things in order to feel: to have intense emotional and sensual experiences that removed us from the suburban sameness we shared with each other and everyone else we knew. We were tired of the repetitive experiences that our town, our siblings, our parents, and our school offered to us. . . .

The friendship between Dana, Liz, and myself was born out of another emotional need: the need for trust. The three of us had reached a point in our lives when we realized how unstable relationships can be, and we all craved safety and acceptance. Friendships all around us were often uncertain. We wanted and needed to be able to like and trust each other." (Garrod & others, 1992, pp. 199–200)

Children spend considerable time with peers and friends. *What peer statuses can children have? How do peer relations change developmentally?*

related characteristics of impulsiveness and disruptiveness underlie rejection abouth half the time, approximately 10 to 20 percent of rejected children are shy.

How can neglected children and rejected children be trained to intereact more effectively with their peers? The goal of many training programs for neglected children is to help them attract attention from their peers in positive ways and to hold their attention by asking questions, by listening in a warm and friendly way, and by saying things about themselves that relate to the peers' interests. They also are taught to enter groups more effectively. Rejected children may be taught to more accurately assess whether the intentions of their peers are negative (Bierman, 2004). Rejected children also may be asked to engage in role-playing or to discuss hypothetical situations involving negative encounters with peers, such as when a peer cuts into line ahead of them. In some programs, children are shown videotapes of appropriate peer interaction; then they are asked to comment on them and to draw lessons from what they have seen (Ladd, Buhs, & Troop, 2004).

A special peer relations problem involves bullying. We will discuss bullying in chapter 14, "Managing the Classroom," where we will provide strategies for dealing with bullies.

Friendship   Friendships contribute to peer status and provide other benefits:

- *Companionship.* Friendship gives children a familiar partner, someone who is willing to spend time with them and join in collaborative activities.
- *Physical support.* Friendship provides resources and assistance in times of need.
- *Ego support.* Friendship helps children feel they are competent, worthy individuals. Especially important in this regard is social approval from friends.
- *Intimacy/affection.* Friendship provides children with a warm, trusting, close relationship with others. In this relationship, children often feel comfortable about disclosing private, personal information.

Having friends can be a developmental advantage, but friendships are not all alike (Gest, Graham-Bermann, & Hartup, 2001; Hartup, 2000). There are developmental advantages for children in having friends who are socially skilled and supportive. However, it is not developmentally advantageous to have coercive and conflict-ridden friendships. And it sometimes is disadvantageous to a child or an adolescent to be friends with someone who is several years older. Students with older friends engage in more deviant behaviors than their counterparts who have same-age friends (Berndt, 1999). Early-maturing adolescents are especially vulnerable in this regard (Magnusson, 1988).

Developmental Changes in Peer Relations   During the elementary school years, children's peer groups increasingly consist of same-sex peers (Maccoby, 1995). After extensive observations of elementary school playgrounds, two researchers characterized the settings as "gender school" (Luria & Herzog, 1985). They said that boys teach one another the required masculine behavior and strictly reinforce it, and girls often pass on the female culture and mainly congregate with each other.

In early adolescence, participation in coed groups increases (Dunphy, 1963). Also in adolescence, many students become members of cliques, and allegiance to the clique can exert a powerful influence over their lives. Group identity with the clique can override the adolescent's personal identity. In any secondary school there will be three to six well-formed cliques. Some typical cliques are jocks, populars, brains, druggies, and toughs. Although many adolescents want to be in a clique, some are fiercely independent and have no desire to be in one.

Friendship likely plays a more important developmental role in secondary school than in elementary school (Sullivan, 1953). Adolescents disclose more personal information to their friends than younger children do (Buhrmester & Furman, 1987). And adolescents say that they depend more on their friends than on their parents to satisfy their needs for companionship, reassurance of worth, and intimacy (Furman & Buhrmester, 1992).

Teaching Strategies
For Improving Children's Social Skills

In every class you teach, some children will likely have weak social skills. One or two might be rejected children. Several others might be neglected. Are there things you can do to help these children improve their social skills? As you think about this, keep in mind that improving social skills is easier when children are ten years of age or younger (Malik & Furman, 1993). In adolescence, peer reputations become more fixed as cliques and peer groups take on more importance. Here are some good strategies for improving children's social skills:

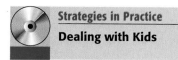
Strategies in Practice
Dealing with Kids

1. *Help rejected children learn to listen to peers and "hear what they say" instead of trying to dominate peers.* In one study, socially rejected young adolescents were coached on the importance of showing behaviors (such as having better empathy, listening carefully, and improving communication skills) that would improve their chance of being liked by others (Murphy & Schneider, 1994). The intervention helped the rejected youth develop better friendships.
2. *Help neglected children attract attention from peers in positive ways and hold their attention.* They can do this by asking questions, listening in a warm and friendly way, and saying things about themselves that relate to the peers' interests. Also work with neglected children on entering groups more effectively.
3. *Provide children low in social skills with knowledge about how to improve these skills.* In one study of sixth- and seventh-graders, knowledge of both appropriate and inappropriate strategies for making friends was related positively to peer acceptance (Wentzel & Erdley, 1993). Knowledge of appropriate strategies included knowing
   • How to initiate interaction, such as asking someone about his or her favorite activities and asking the other child to do things together
   • That it is important to be nice, kind, and considerate
   • That it is necessary to show respect for others by being courteous and listening to what others have to say
   • That providing social support helps a friendship, that you need to show that you care, and that it is a good idea to compliment others
   Knowledge of inappropriate strategies included knowing
   • That it is not a good idea to be aggressive, show disrespect, be inconsiderate, hurt others' feelings, gossip, spread rumors, embarrass others, or criticize others

- Not to present yourself negatively, be self-centered, care only about yourself, or be jealous, grouchy, or angry all the time
- Not to engage in antisocial behavior, such as fighting, yelling at others, picking on others, making fun of others, being dishonest, breaking school rules, or taking drugs

4. *Read and discuss appropriate books on peer relations with students and devise supportive games and activities.* Include these as thematic units in your curriculum for young children. Make books on peer relations and friendship available to older children and adolescents.

Schools

In school, children spend many years as members of a small society that exerts a tremendous influence on their socioemotional development. How does this social world change as children develop?

Schools' Changing Social Developmental Contexts Social contexts vary through the early childhood, elementary school, and adolescent years (Minuchin & Shapiro, 1983). The early childhood setting is a protected environment whose boundary is the classroom. In this limited social setting, young children interact with one or two teachers, usually female, who are powerful figures in their lives. Young children also interact with peers in dyads or small groups.

The classroom still is the main context in elementary school, although it is more likely to be experienced as a social unit than is the early childhood classroom. The teacher symbolizes authority, which establishes the climate of the classroom, the conditions of social interaction, and the nature of group functioning. Peer groups are more important now and students have an increased interest in friendship.

As children move into middle and junior high school, the school environment increases in scope and complexity (Anfara, 2001). The social field is now the whole school rather than the classroom. Adolescents interact with teachers and peers from a broader range of cultural backgrounds on a broader range of interests. More of the teachers are male. Adolescents' social behavior becomes weighted more strongly toward peers, extracurricular activities, clubs, and the community. Secondary school students are more aware of the school as a social system and might be motivated to conform to it or challenge it.

Early Childhood Education There are many variations in how young children are educated. However, an increasing number of education experts advocate that this education be developmentally appropriate (Slentz & Krogh, 2001).

Developmentally Appropriate Education **Developmentally appropriate education** is based on knowledge of the typical development of children within an age span (age appropriateness) as well as the uniqueness of the child (individual appropriateness). Developmentally appropriate education contrasts with developmentally inappropriate practice, which ignores concrete, hands-on methods in the teaching of young children. Direct teaching, largely through abstract paper-and-pencil tasks presented to large groups of young children, is believed to be developmentally inappropriate. Although we are discussing developmentally appropriate education in this chapter on socioemotional development, the concept applies to children's physical and cognitive development as well.

Here are some of the themes of developmentally appropriate education (Bredekamp & Copple, 1997; National Association for the Education of Young Children [NAEYC], 1996):

- *Domains of children's development—physical, cognitive, and socioemotional—are closely linked and development in one domain can influence and be influenced by*

developmentally appropriate education Education based on knowledge of the typical development of children within an age span (age appropriateness) as well as the uniqueness of the child (individual appropriateness).

development in other domains. Recognition of the connections across domains can be used to plan children's learning experiences.

- *Development occurs in a relatively orderly sequence with later abilities, skills, and knowledge building on those already acquired.* Knowledge of typical development within the age range served by the program provides a general framework to guide teachers in preparing the learning environment.
- *Individual variation characterizes children's development.* Each child is a unique individual and all children have their own strengths, needs, and interests. Recognizing this individual variation is a key aspect of being a competent teacher.
- *Development is influenced by multiple social and cultural contexts.* Early childhood teachers need to understand how sociocultural contexts—such as poverty and ethnicity—affect children's development. Teachers should learn about the culture of the majority of the children they serve if the culture differs from their own.
- *Children are active learners and should be encouraged to construct an understanding of the world around them.* Children contribute to their own learning as they strive to make meaning out of their daily experiences.
- *Development advances when children have opportunities to practice newly acquired skills as well as when they experience a challenge just beyond their present level of mastery.* In tasks that are just beyond the child's independent reach, the adult and more competent peers can provide scaffolding that allows the child to learn.
- *Children develop best in the context of a community where they are safe and valued, their physical needs are met, and they feel psychologically secure.* Children benefit from having caring teachers who genuinely want to help them learn and develop in positive ways.

Do developmentally appropriate educational practices improve young children's development? Yes. Young children in developmentally appropriate classrooms are likely to have less stress, be more motivated, be more skilled socially, have better work habits, be more creative, have better language skills, and demonstrate better math skills than children in developmentally inappropriate classrooms (Hart & others, 1996, 2003; Sherman & Mueller, 1996; Stipek & others, 1995).

How common are programs that use developmentally appropriate practice? As few as one-third to one-fifth of early childhood programs follow this educational strategy. Even fewer elementary schools do. Child-initiated activities and small-group instruction are the exception rather than the rule (Dunn & Kontos, 1997).

An increasingly popular approach to young children's education in the United States is the developmentally appropriate education practiced in Reggio Emilia, a small town in northern Italy (Stegelini, 2003). There children are encouraged to learn by investigating and exploring topics that interest them. A wide range of stimulating media and materials are available for children to use as they learn. Children often explore topics in a group. Two co-teachers serve as guides. The Reggio Emilia teachers view a project as an adventure. The project might start from a teacher's suggestion, a child's idea, or an event such as a snowfall or something else unexpected. Children are given ample time to think about and plan the project. Cooperation is a major theme in the Reggio Emilia approach (Firlik, 1996). Reggio Emilia reflects the constructivist approach to education that initially was described in chapters 1 and 2 and will be explored in greater depth in later chapters, especially chapter 10, "Social Constructivist Approaches."

Curriculum Controversy in Early Childhood Education   Currently, there is controversy about what the curriculum for U.S. early childhood education should be (Brewer, 2004; Hill, Stremmel, & Fu, 2005). On one side are those who advocate a child-centered, constructivist approach much like that emphasized by the National Association for the Education of Young Children along the lines of developmentally appropriate practice. On the other side are those who advocate an academic, instructivist approach. From the academic, instructivist perspective, the child is viewed as dependent on adults' instruction in the academic knowledge and skills that can serve as a foundation for later

Early Childhood Education
NAEYC
Reggio Emilia

What is the nature of the current curriculum controversy in early childhood education?

academic achievement. The academic approach involves teachers directly instructing young children to learn basic academic skills, especially in reading and math.

Early childhood education expert Lilian Katz (1999) argues that both sides in this argument may be overlooking and undervaluing a third option—curriculum and teaching methods that emphasize children's *intellectual development*. Both academic and constructivist approaches endorse early childhood programs that promote young children's intellectual development. Katz' observations of large numbers of early childhood programs indicate that many of these include both academic and constructivist approaches in their effort to develop young children's intellectual competence. What many experts, such as Katz, do not advocate are academic early childhood programs that pressure young children to achieve; do not provide them with opportunities to actively construct their learning, at least in part of the curriculum; and do not emphasize the development of socioemotional skills.

The National Association for the Education of Young Children (2002) recently addressed the dramatic increase in the use of standards regarding desired results, outcomes, or learning expectations for U.S. children. NAEYC states that these standards can be a valuable part of early education but only if early learning standards (1) emphasize signaficant, developmentally appropriate content and outcomes; (2) are developed through inclusive, informed processes (in all instances, experts in early childhood education should be involved in creating the standards); (3) use implementation and assessment strategies that are ethical and appropriate for young children (assessment and accountability should be used to improve practices and services and should not be used to rank, sort, or penalize young children); and (4) are accompanied by strong supports for early childhood programs, professionals, and families.

Early Childhood Education for Children from Low-Income Families   For many years, many children from low-income families did not receive any education before they entered first grade. In the 1960s, an effort was made to break the cycle of poverty and inadequate education for young children in the United States. *Project Head Start* was designed to provide young children from low-income families opportunities to acquire the skills and experiences that are important for success in school. Funded by the federal government, Project Head Start began in 1965 and continues to serve disadvantaged children today.

In high-quality Head Start programs, parents and communities are involved in positive ways (Thurgood, 2001). The teachers are knowledgeable about children's development and use developmentally appropriate practices. Researchers have found that when young children from low-income families experience a quality Head Start program, there are substantial long-term benefits. These include being less likely to drop out of school, to be in a special education class, or to be on welfare than their low-income counterparts who did not attend a Head Start program (Lazar & others, 1982; Schweinhart, 1999). However, Head Start programs are not all created equal (McCarty, Abbott-Shim, & Lambert, 2001). One estimate is that 40 percent of the 1,400 Head Start programs are inadequate (Zigler & Finn-Stevenson, 1999). More attention needs to be given to developing high-quality Head Start programs (Raver & Zigler, 1997; Zigler & Styco, 2004).

The Transition to Elementary School   As children make the transition to elementary school, they interact and develop relationships with new and significant others. School provides them with a rich source of ideas to shape their sense of self.

A special concern about early elementary school classrooms is that they not proceed primarily on the basis of negative feedback. I (your author) vividly remember my first-grade teacher. Unfortunately, she never smiled; she ran the classroom in a dictatorial manner, and learning (or lack of learning) progressed more on the basis of fear than of enjoyment and passion. Fortunately, I experienced some warmer, more student-friendly teachers later on.

Children's self-esteem is higher when they begin elementary school than when they complete it (Blumenfeld & others, 1981). Is that because they experienced so much negative feedback and were criticized so much along the way? We will say more about the roles of reinforcement and punishment in children's learning in chapter 7 and about managing the classroom in chapter 14.

For now, though, consider the following two elementary school classrooms and what effect they might have on children's learning and self-esteem (Katz & Chard, 1989). In one, students spend the entire morning making identical pictures of traffic lights as they sit glued to their chairs. The teacher seems uninterested in their work, except when she occasionally comes around and informs them of their mistakes. The teacher makes no attempt to get the students to relate the pictures to anything else the class is doing.

In the other class, students are investigating a school bus. They write to the district's school superintendent and ask if they can have a bus parked at their school for a few days. They study the bus, discover how it functions, and discuss traffic rules. Then, in the classroom, they build their own bus out of cardboard. The students are having fun, but they also are practicing writing, reading, and even some arithmetic. When the class has parents' night, the teacher is ready to report on how each child is doing. But the main thing the parents want to do is to see the bus, because their children have been coming home and talking about the bus for weeks. Which class would you say reflects developmentally appropriate education?

The Schooling of Adolescents   Three special concerns about adolescent schooling are (1) the transition to middle or junior high school, (2) effective schooling for young adolescents, and (3) the quality of high schools. How might the transition to middle or junior high school be difficult for many students?

The Transition to Middle or Junior High School   This transition can be stressful because it coincides with many other developmental changes (Conti, 2001; Eccles, 2000; Seidman, 2000). Students are beginning puberty and have increased concerns about their body image. The hormonal changes of puberty stimulate increased interest in sexual matters. Students are becoming more independent from their parents and want to spend more time with peers. They are changing from learning in a small, more personalized classroom to learning in a larger, more impersonal school. Achievement becomes more serious business and getting good grades becomes more competitive.

As students move from elementary to middle or junior high school, they experience the *top-dog phenomenon.* This refers to moving from the top position (in elementary school, being the oldest, biggest, and most powerful students in the school) to the lowest

Elementary Education

Through the Eyes of Teachers

Reflections of a Middle School Teacher

I believe that a good teacher should passionately be on the side of her students. That does not mean I support them in everything they do. It means I demand the best of them and am willing to help them be their best selves. It means I listen, explain, support, and allow without judgment, sarcasm, or the need to impose the truth from the outside in. The passage from childhood to adulthood we call adolescence is a very vulnerable journey. It is often a difficult time for students and for their families. It is an adolescent's "job" to rebel at times and to question the family environment that was such a comfortable cocoon during childhood. No matter how wonderful the parents, how loving the family, each adolescent needs to have other adults in whom to confide. . . .

Sarah Lawrence Lightfoot, a professor of education at Harvard, says that we teachers need to see ourselves reflected in our students—we need to see them as our destiny, and the students need to see themselves in us. The faces of my students have changed since my mother's generation. The immigrants now are more likely to come from the Philippines, Hong Kong, Guatemala, Mexico, or El Salvador than from Italy, Germany, Norway, or France. But the journey is similar, the experiences echo each other, and the welcome need be just as tender. When I look at them I see my past, and I hope that they are able to see in me something of their future.

Judy Logan
Middle School Teacher
San Francisco

Middle School Education

Middle School Teachers and Students

Middle School Resources

position (in middle or junior high school, being the youngest, smallest, and least powerful students in the school). Schools that provide more support, less anonymity, more stability, and less complexity improve student adjustment during this transition (Fenzel, Blyth, & Simmons, 1991). Also, one study found that when parents were attuned to their young adolescents' developmental needs and supported their autonomy in decision making, the students were better adjusted during the school transition (Eccles, Lord, & Buchanan, 1996).

Effective Schools for Young Adolescents   When Joan Lipsitz (1984) was director of the Center for Early Adolescence at the University of North Carolina, she searched for the nation's best middle schools. Based on the recommendations of education experts and observations in schools across the nation, four middle schools were chosen for their excellence. Three main themes characterized these truly outstanding schools:

1. *Adapt school practices to individual variations in students' physical, cognitive, and socioemotional development.* One competent middle school created an advisory system in which each student interacted on a daily basis with an adult whose goal was to carefully listen to students' needs, challenge students to succeed, and guide them in the right direction.
2. *Focus on the developmental aspects of early adolescence.* Too many middle schools are simply downward extensions of high schools yet younger adolescents and older adolescents differ in many ways. For example, the dramatic changes of puberty occur almost exclusively in early adolescence. Taking into account the needs of young adolescents, one successful middle school kept a number of mini-courses on Friday so that students could spend more time with friends and engage in personal interests.
3. *Emphasis on both socioemotional and cognitive development.* Young adolescents are often emotionally fragile as they widen their social worlds and shoulder more responsibility. In our achievement-oriented society, it is easy to lose sight of just how important students' socioemotional needs are. These effective middle schools did not.

Recognizing that the vast majority of middle schools do not approach the excellence of the schools described by Lipsitz, in 1989 the Carnegie Council on Adolescent Development issued a very negative evaluation of America's middle schools. The report, *Turning Points: Preparing Youth for the 21st Century,* concluded that most young adolescents attend massive, impersonal schools; learn irrelevant curricula; trust few adults in school; and lack access to health care and counseling. To improve middle schools, the Carnegie report recommended

- Developing smaller "communities" or "houses" to lessen the impersonal nature of large middle schools
- Lowering the student-to-counselor ratios from several hundred-to-1 to 10-to-1
- Involving parents and community leaders in schools
- Developing curricula that produce students who are literate, understand the sciences, and have a sense of health, ethics, and citizenship

- Having teachers team-teach in more flexibly designed curriculum blocks that integrate several disciplines, rather than presenting students with disconnected, rigidly separated 50-minute segments
- Boosting students' health and fitness with more in-school programs and helping students who need health care to get it

Improving America's High Schools   Just as there are concerns about U.S. middle school education, so are there concerns about U.S. high school education (Kaufman, 2001). Many students graduate from high school with inadequate reading, writing, and mathematical skills, including many who go on to college and have to enroll in remediation classes there. Other students drop out of high school and do not have skills that will allow them to advance in the work world (Christensen & Thurlow, 2004; Lehr & others, 2003).

In the last half of the twentieth century, high school dropout rates declined overall (National Center for Education Statistics, 2001). For example, in the 1940s, more than half of U.S. fifteen- to twenty-four-year-olds dropped out of school, but in 2000 this figure decreased to about 11 percent. Figure 3.4 shows the trends in high school dropout rates from 1972 through 2000. Notice that the dropout rate of Latino adolescents remains precariously high (27.8 percent of fifteen- to twenty-four-year-old Latino adolescents dropped out of school in 2000). The highest dropout rate in the United States, though, occurs for Native American youth—only about 10 percent finish their high school education. In one recent study, students were less likely to drop out of school when they had positive relationships with teachers (Lee & Burkham, 2001).

Many high school graduates not only are poorly prepared for college, but they also are poorly prepared for the demands of the modern, high-performance workplace. In a review of hiring practices at major companies, it was concluded that many companies now have sets of basic skills they want the individuals they hire to have. These include the ability to read at relatively high levels, do at least elementary algebra, use personal computers for straightforward tasks such as word processing, solve semistructured problems in which hypotheses must be formed and tested, communicate effectively (orally and in writing), and work effectively in groups with persons of various backgrounds (Murnane & Levy, 1996).

An increasing number of educators believe that the nation's high schools need a new mission for the twenty-first century, one which addresses these problems (National Commission on the High School Senior Year, 2001):

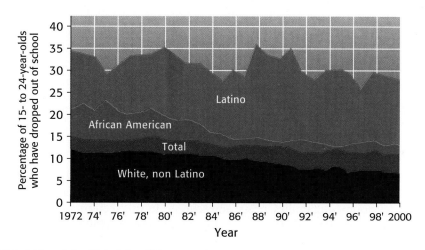

FIGURE 3.4 Trends in High School Dropout Rates
From 1972 through 2000, the school dropout rate for Latinos remained very high (27.8 percent of 15- to 24-year-olds in 2000). The African American dropout rate was still higher (13.1 percent) than the White non-Latino rate (6.9 percent) in 2000. The overall dropout rate declined considerably from the 1940s through the 1960s but has declined only slightly since 1972.

1. More support is needed to enable all students to graduate from high school with the knowledge and skills needed to succeed in postsecondary education and careers. Many parents and students, especially those in low-income and minority communities, are unaware of the knowledge and level of skills required to succeed in postsecondary education.

2. High schools need to have higher expectations for student achievement. A special concern is the senior year of high school, which has become too much of a party-time rather than a time to prepare for one of life's most important transitions. Some students who have been accepted to college routinely ignore the academic demands of their senior year. Low academic expectations harm students from all backgrounds.

3. U.S. high school students spend too much time working in low-level service jobs. Researchers have found that when tenth-graders work more than fourteen hours a week their grades drop, and when eleventh-graders work twenty or more hours a week their grades decline (Greenberger & Steinberg,1986). At the same time, shorter, higher-quality work experiences, including community service and internships, have been shown to benefit high school students.

4. There has been too little coordination and communication across the different levels of K–12 schools, as well as between K–12 schools and institutions of higher education.

5. At the middle and secondary school levels, every student needs strong, positive connections with adults, preferably many of them, as they explore options for school, postsecondary education, and work.

⚠ Review and Reflect

2 **Discuss how the social contexts of families, peers, and schools are linked with socioemotional development.**

Review

- In most instances, which is likely to be the most effective parenting style? Why? Also, how do aspects of families such as divorce and ethnicity/socioeconomic status affect children's development and education?
- What differences can positive or negative peer relations make in a child's and an adolescent's development and education? What risks are attached to certain peer statuses? How do friendships matter?
- What is meant by developmentally appropriate education? What transitional problems do students face as they move through different levels of schooling? In what ways do middle schools and high schools need to be improved?

Reflect

- What parenting style(s) have you witnessed and experienced? What effects did they have?

SOCIOEMOTIONAL DEVELOPMENT

So far we have discussed three important social contexts that influence students' socioemotional development: families, peers, and schools. In this section, we will focus more on the individual students themselves, as we explore the development of the self and morality.

The Self

According to twentieth-century Italian playwright Ugo Betti, when children say "I," they mean something unique, not to be confused with any other. Psychologists often refer to that "I" as the self. Two important aspects of the self are self-esteem and identity.

Self-Esteem   **Self-esteem** refers to an individual's overall view of himself or herself. Self-esteem also is referred to as self-worth or self-image. For example, a child with high self-esteem might perceive that she is not just a person but a *good* person.

Interest in self-esteem arose from the work of psychotherapist Carl Rogers (1961). Rogers said that the main reason individuals have low self-esteem is that they have not been given adequate emotional support and social approval. He especially thought that as children grow up, they get told, "You didn't do that right," "Don't do that," "You should have done that better," or "How could you be so dumb?"

For many students, periods of low self-esteem come and go. But for some students, persistent low self-esteem translates into other, more serious problems. Persistent low self-esteem is linked with low achievement, depression, eating disorders, and delinquency (Harter, 1999). The seriousness of the problem depends not only on the nature of the student's low self-esteem but on other conditions as well. When low self-esteem is compounded by difficult school transitions (such as the transition to middle school) or family problems (such as divorce), the student's problems can intensify.

Researchers have found that self-esteem changes as children develop. In one recent study, both boys and girls had high self-esteem in childhood but their self-esteem dropped considerably in early adolescence (Robins & others, 2002). The self-esteem of girls dropped about twice as much as that of boys during adolescence (see figure 3.5). Other researchers have found that the self-esteem of girls drops more than that of boys during adolescence (Kling & others, 1999; Major & others, 1999). Among the reasons given for the self-esteem decline in both boys and girls are the upheaval in physical changes of puberty, increased achievement demands and expectations, and inadequate support from schools and parents. Among the reasons given for the gender disparity in the decline of self-esteem are the high expectations for physical attractiveness in girls, which becomes more pronounced with pubertal change, and motivation for social relationships that is not rewarded by society (Crawford & Unger, 2000).

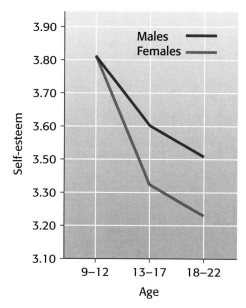

FIGURE 3.5 The Decline of Self-Esteem in Adolescence

In one study, the self-esteem of both boys and girls declined during adolescence, but it declined considerably more for girls than boys (Robins & others, 2002). The self-esteem scores represent the mean self-esteem scores on a 5-point scale, with higher scores reflecting higher self-esteem.

Teaching Strategies
For Improving Children's Self-Esteem

Research suggests four keys to improving students' self-esteem (Bednar, Wells, & Peterson, 1995; Harter, 1999):

1. *Identify the causes of low self-esteem and the areas of competence important to the self.* This is critical. Is the child's low self-esteem due to poor school achievement? family conflict? weak social skills? Students have the highest self-esteem when they perform competently in areas that they themselves feel are important. Thus, find out from students with low self-esteem what areas of competence they value. In Susan Harter's (1990, 1996, 1999) research, physical appearance and social approval from classmates were especially important contributors to self-esteem. Social approval from classmates was more important to young adolescents' self-esteem than approval from teachers. Nonetheless, teacher approval was still important by playing a role in the self-esteem of young adolescents whose parents showed them little approval.

2. *Provide emotional support and social approval.* Virtually every class has children who have gotten too many negative evaluations. These children might come from an abusive and demeaning family that constantly puts them down, or they might have been in prior classrooms that delivered too much negative feedback. Your emotional support and social approval can make a big difference in helping them value themselves more. A school counselor also likely will benefit these children.

self-esteem   Also called self-image and self-worth, the individual's overall conception of himself or herself.

For children in single-parent families, a Big Brother or Big Sister program can provide another significant adult who can give the child emotional support and social approval. Keep in mind that peer approval becomes especially important in the secondary school years. In one study, both parental and peer support were related to adolescents' general feelings of self-worth (Robinson, 1995). Thus, the recommendations made earlier in the chapter for improving children's social skills might improve adolescents' self-esteem as well.

3. *Help children achieve.* Achieving can improve children's self-esteem. Straightforward teaching of real academic skills often improves children's achievement, and subsequently their self-esteem. Often it is not enough to tell children they can achieve something; you also have to help them develop their academic skills.

Henry Gaskins is a volunteer who began an after-school tutorial program for students in Washington, DC. For four hours a night and all day Saturday, 80 students receive one-on-one assistance from Gaskins, his wife, two adult volunteers, and academically talented peers. In addition to being tutored in specific subjects, students set personal goals and develop a plan to reach these goals. Many of the parents of these students are high school dropouts and either can't or aren't motivated to provide academic support for their children. Gaskins improves children's self-esteem by improving their academic skills.

4. *Develop children's coping skills.* When children face a problem and cope with it rather than avoid it, their self-esteem often improves. Students who cope rather than avoid are likely to face problems realistically, honestly, and nondefensively. This produces in them favorable thoughts about themselves that raise their self-esteem. On the other hand, for students with low self-esteem, their unfavorable self-evaluations trigger denial, deception, and avoidance. This type of self-generated disapproval makes a student feel personally inadequate. Much more about improving students' coping skills appears later in this chapter.

Identity Development

Video Lecture: Teaching Strategies to Encourage Socioemotional Development

identity diffusion The identity status in which individuals have neither explored meaningful alternatives nor made a commitment.

identity foreclosure The identity status in which individuals have made a commitment but have not explored meaningful alternatives.

identity moratorium The identity status in which individuals are in the midst of exploring alternatives but have not yet made a commitment.

Identity Development   Another important aspect of the self is identity. Earlier in the chapter we indicated that Erik Erikson (1968) believed that the most important issue in adolescence involves identity development—searching for answers to questions like these: Who am I? What am I all about? What am I going to do with my life? Not usually considered during childhood, these questions become nearly universal concerns during the high school and college years (Phinney & others, 2001).

Canadian researcher James Marcia (1980, 1998) analyzed Erikson's concept of identity and concluded that it is important to distinguish between exploration and commitment. *Exploration* involves examining meaningful alternative identities. *Commitment* means showing a personal investment in an identity and staying with whatever that identity implies.

The extent of an individual's exploration and commitment is used to classify him or her according to one of four identity statuses (see figure 3.6).

- **Identity diffusion** occurs when individuals have not yet experienced a crisis (that is, they have not yet explored meaningful alternatives) or made any commitments. Not only are they undecided about occupational and ideological choices, but they are also likely to show little interest in such matters.
- **Identity foreclosure** occurs when individuals have made a commitment but have not yet experienced a crisis. This occurs most often when parents hand down commitments to their adolescents, more often than not in an authoritarian manner. In these circumstances, adolescents have not had adequate opportunities to explore different approaches, ideologies, and vocations on their own.
- **Identity moratorium** occurs when individuals are in the midst of a crisis but their commitments are either absent or only vaguely defined.

		Has the person made a commitment?	
		Yes	**No**
Has the person explored meaningful alternatives regarding some identity question?	**Yes**	Identity Achievement	Identity Moratorium
	No	Identity Foreclosure	Identity Diffusion

FIGURE 3.6 Marcia's Four Statuses of Identity

• **Identity achievement** occurs when individuals have undergone a crisis and have made a commitment.

Let's explore some examples of Marcia's identity statuses. A thirteen-year-old adolescent has neither begun to explore her identity in any meaningful way nor made an identity commitment, so she is *identity diffused*. An eighteen-year-old boy's parents want him to be a medical doctor, so he is planning on majoring in premedicine in college and really has not adequately explored any other options; he is *identity foreclosed*. Nineteen-year-old Sasha is not quite sure what life paths she wants to follow, but she recently went to the counseling center at her college to find out about different careers, so she is in *identity moratorium* status. Twenty-one-year-old Marcelo extensively explored a number of different career options in college, eventually getting his degree in science education, and is looking forward to his first year of teaching high school students, so he is *identity achieved*. Our examples of identity statuses have focused on the career dimension, but remember that other dimensions are also important. Adolescents can be exploring alternative identities in numerous areas, such as vocational, religious, intellectual, political, sexual, gender, ethnic, and interests. An adolescent can be farther along the path to identity in some of these areas than in others. While many high school students are exploring different areas of their identity, some will be identity diffused and others will be foreclosed because of the authoritarian ways of their parents.

To further consider identity, complete Self-Assessment 3.1 on page 94. There you will be able to apply Marcia's identity statuses to a number of different areas of identity in your own life.

"While we're at supper, Billy, you'd make Daddy and Mommy very happy if you'd remove your hat, your sunglasses, and your earring."

Moral Development

Few people are neutral about moral development. Many parents worry that their children are growing up without traditional values. Teachers complain that their students don't consider others' feelings. There also is evidence that many U.S. high school students cheat on tests. In one recent survey of 8,600 U.S. high school students, 70 percent admitted that they had cheated on at least one school exam in the current school year, up from 60 percent in 1990 (*Upfront*, 2000). In this survey, almost 80 percent said they had lied to a teacher at least once.

Domains of Moral Development   **Moral development** concerns rules and conventions about just interactions between people. These rules can be studied in three domains: cognitive, behavioral, and emotional.

identity achievement The identity status in which individuals have explored meaningful alternatives and made a commitment.

moral development Development with respect to the rules and conventions of just interactions between people.

Where Are You Now? Exploring Your Identity

Your identity is made up of many different parts, and so too will your students' identities be comprised of many different dimensions. By completing this checklist, you should gain a better sense of your own identity and the different aspects of your future students' identities. For each component, check your identity status as diffused, foreclosed, in a moratorium, or achieved.

| | | Identity Status | | |
Identity Component	Diffused	Foreclosed	Moratorium	Achieved
Vocational identity				
Religious identity				
Achievement/intellectual identity				
Political identity				
Sexual identity				
Gender identity				
Relationship identity				
Lifestyle identity				
Ethnic and cultural identity				
Personality characteristics				
Interests				

If you checked "Diffused" or "Foreclosed" for any areas, take some time to think about what you need to do to move into a "Moratorium" identity status in those areas and write about this in your portfolio.

 Go to your Student Toolbox CD-ROM for an electronic version of this form.

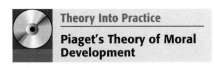

Theory Into Practice

Piaget's Theory of Moral Development

In the cognitive domain, the key issue is how students reason or think about rules for ethical conduct. In the behavioral domain, the focus is on how students actually behave rather than on the morality of their thinking. In the emotional domain, the emphasis is on how students morally feel. For instance, do they associate strong enough guilt feelings with an immoral action to resist performing that action? Do they show empathy toward others (Damon, 2000)?

Piaget's Theory   Piaget (1932) stimulated interest in how students think about moral issues. He extensively observed and interviewed four- to twelve-year-old children. He watched them play marbles, seeking to learn how they used and thought about the game's rules. He also asked children about ethical rules, quizzing them about theft, lies, punishment, and justice. From this he derived a stage theory of moral development.

Heteronomous morality is Piaget's first stage of moral development. It lasts from approximately four to seven years of age. At this stage, justice and rules are conceived of as unchangeable properties of the world, removed from the control of people. **Autonomous morality** is Piaget's second stage of moral development, reached at about ten years of age or older. At this point, the child becomes aware that rules and laws are created by people and that, in judging an action, the actor's intentions as well as the consequences should be considered. Children seven to ten years of age are in a transition between the two stages, showing some features of both.

The heteronomous thinker also believes in immanent justice, the concept that if a rule is broken, punishment will be meted out immediately. Young children believe that a violation is in some way automatically connected to punishment. They often look around in a worried fashion after committing a transgression, expecting inevitable punishment. Older children, being moral autonomists, recognize that punishment is socially mediated and occurs only if a relevant person witnesses the wrongdoing and that, even then, punishment is not inevitable.

Piaget said that moral development is mainly advanced through the mutual give-and-take of peer relations. In the peer group, where all members have similar power and status, rules are negotiated and disagreements reasoned about and eventually settled. In Piaget's view, parents play a less important role in children's moral development because they have so much more power than children and hand down rules in an authoritarian way.

Kohlberg's Theory   Lawrence Kohlberg (1976, 1986), like Piaget, stressed that moral development primarily involves moral reasoning and occurs in stages. Kohlberg arrived at his theory after interviewing children, adolescents, and adults (primarily males) about their views on a series of moral dilemmas. Here is an example of the type of dilemma he presented:

> A woman is near death and is suffering from a special kind of cancer. There is only one drug that doctors think might save her. It was recently discovered by a druggist living in the same town as the woman. The drug was expensive to make, but the druggist is charging 10 times what the drug cost him to make. The sick woman's husband, Heinz, tries to borrow the money to buy the drug from every place he can think of but he can't raise enough money. He tells the druggist that his wife is dying and asks him to sell it to him cheaper or let him pay later. But the druggist says, "No, I discovered it and I deserve to make money from it." Later, Heinz gets desperate, breaks into the druggist's store, and steals the drug for his wife.

After reading the story (or, in the case of young children, hearing it read to them), individuals are asked a series of questions, such as these: Was Heinz right to steal the drug? Is it a husband's duty to steal the drug? Would a good husband steal? Did the druggist have the right to charge so much for the drug? Why or why not?

Kohlberg's Levels and Stages of Moral Development   Based on the reasons individuals gave in response to the dilemma just discussed and ten others like it, Kohlberg constructed a theory of moral development that has three main levels with two stages at each of the levels. A key concept in understanding Kohlberg's theory is *internalization,* which refers to the developmental change from behavior that is externally controlled to behavior that is internally controlled.

Preconventional reasoning is the lowest level of moral development in Kohlberg's theory. At this level, the child shows no internalization of moral values. Moral reasoning is controlled by external rewards and punishment.

Conventional reasoning is the second, or intermediate, level in Kohlberg's theory. At this level, the child's internalization is intermediate. The child abides internally by certain standards, but they are essentially the standards imposed by other people, such as parents, or by society's laws.

Lawrence Kohlberg, the architect of a provocative cognitive developmental theory of moral development.

heteronomous morality In Piaget's theory, the first stage of moral development (about four to seven years of age), in which justice and rules are conceived of as unchangeable properties of the world, beyond the control of people.

autonomous morality In Piaget's theory, the second stage of moral development (entered at about ten years of age), in which children become aware that rules and laws are created by people and that in judging action, the actor's intentions as well as consequences need to be considered.

preconventional reasoning In Kohlberg's theory, the lowest level of moral development; at this level, the child shows no internalization of moral values and moral reasoning is controlled by external rewards and punishments.

conventional reasoning In Kohlberg's theory, the middle level of moral development; at this level, internalization is intermediate in the sense that individuals abide by certain standards (internal) but these essentially are the standards of others (external).

LEVEL 1 **Preconventional Level No Internalization**		LEVEL 2 **Conventional Level Intermediate Internalization**		LEVEL 3 **Postconventional Level Full Internalization**	
Stage 1 Heteronomous Morality	**Stage 2 Individualism, Purpose, and Exchange**	**Stage 3 Mutual Interpersonal Expectations, Relationships, and Interpersonal Conformity**	**Stage 4 Social System Morality**	**Stage 5 Social Contract or Utility and Individual Rights**	**Stage 6 Universal Ethical Principles**
Children obey because adults tell them to obey. People base their moral decisions on fear of punishment.	Individuals pursue their own interests but let others do the same. What is right involves equal exchange.	Individuals value trust, caring, and loyalty to others as a basis for moral judgments.	Moral judgments are based on understanding and the social order, law, justice, and duty.	Individuals reason that values, rights, and principles undergird or transcend the law.	The person has developed moral judgments that are based on universal human rights. When faced with a dilemma between law and conscience, a personal, individualized conscience is followed.

FIGURE 3.7 Kohlberg's Levels and Stages of Moral Development

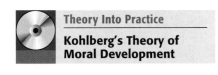

Theory Into Practice

Kohlberg's Theory of Moral Development

Theory Into Practice

Gilligan's Theory of Moral Development

postconventional reasoning In Kohlberg's theory, the highest level of moral development; at this level, moral development is internalized and moral reasoning is self-generated.

justice perspective A moral perspective that focuses on the rights of the individual; Kohlberg's theory is a justice perspective.

Postconventional reasoning is the highest level in Kohlberg's theory. At this level, morality is completely internalized and not based on external standards. The student recognizes alternative moral courses, explores options, and then decides on the moral code that is best for him or her. A summary of Kohlberg's three levels and six stages, along with examples of each of the stages, is presented in figure 3.7.

In studies of Kohlberg's theory, longitudinal data show a relation of the stages to age, although the two highest stages, especially stage 6, rarely appear (Colby & others, 1983). Before age nine, most children reason about moral dilemmas at a preconventional level. By early adolescence, they are more likely to reason at the conventional level.

Kohlberg believed that underlying changes in cognitive development promote more advanced moral thinking. He also said that children construct their moral thoughts as they pass through the stages—that they do not just passively accept a cultural norm for morality. Kohlberg argued that a child's moral thinking can be advanced through discussions with others who reason at the next higher stage. Like Piaget, Kohlberg thought that the mutual give-and-take of peer relations promotes more advanced moral thinking because of the role-taking opportunities they provide children.

Kohlberg's Critics   Kohlberg's provocative theory has not gone unchallenged (Gibbs, 2003; Nucci, 2004). One powerful criticism centers on the idea that moral thoughts don't always predict moral behavior. The criticism is that Kohlberg's theory places too much emphasis on moral thinking and not enough on moral behavior. Moral reasons sometimes can be a shelter for immoral behavior. Bank embezzlers and U.S. presidents endorse the loftiest of moral virtues, but their own behavior can prove to be immoral. No one wants a nation of stage-6 Kohlberg thinkers who know what is right yet do what is wrong.

Another line of criticism is that Kohlberg's theory is too individualistic. Carol Gilligan (1982, 1998) distinguishes between the justice perspective and the care perspective. Kohlberg's is a **justice perspective** that focuses on the rights of the individual, who stands alone and makes moral decisions. The **care perspective** views people in terms of their connectedness. Emphasis is placed on relationships and concern for others. According to Gilligan, Kohlberg greatly underplayed the care perspective—possibly because he was a male, most of his research was on males, and he lived in a male-dominant society.

In extensive interviews with girls from six to eighteen years of age, Gilligan found that they consistently interpret moral dilemmas in terms of human relationships, not in terms of individual rights. Gilligan (1996) also recently argued that girls reach a critical juncture in their development in early adolescence. At about eleven or twelve years of age, they become aware of how much they prize relationships, yet they also come to realize that this interest is not shared by the male-dominant society. The solution, says Gilligan, is to give relationships and concern for others a higher priority in our society. Gilligan does not recommend totally throwing out Kohlberg's theory. She believes the highest level of moral development occurs when individuals combine the care and justice perspectives in positive ways.

Moral Education   Moral education is hotly debated in educational circles. We will study one of the earliest analyses of moral education, then turn to some contemporary views.

The Hidden Curriculum   Recall from chapter 1 that John Dewey was one of educational psychology's pioneers. Dewey (1933) recognized that even when schools do not have specific programs in moral education, they provide moral education through a "hidden curriculum." The **hidden curriculum** is conveyed by the moral atmosphere that is a part of every school. The moral atmosphere is created by school and classroom rules, the moral orientation of teachers and school administrators, and text materials. Teachers serve as models of ethical or unethical behavior. Classroom rules and peer relations at school transmit attitudes about cheating, lying, stealing, and consideration for others. Through its rules and regulations, the school administration infuses the school with a value system.

Character Education   **Character education** is a direct approach to moral education that involves teaching students basic moral literacy to prevent them from engaging in immoral behavior and doing harm to themselves or others. The argument is that behaviors such as lying, stealing, and cheating are wrong and that students should be taught this throughout their education (Nucci, 2001). According to the character education approach, every school should have an explicit moral code that is clearly communicated to students. Any violations of the code should be met with sanctions (Bennett, 1993). Instruction in moral concepts with respect to specific behaviors, such as cheating, can take the form of example and definition, class discussions and role-playing, or rewards to students for proper behavior.

Some character education movements are the Character Education Partnership, the Character Education Network, the Aspen Declaration on Character Education, and the publicity campaign "Character Counts." Among the books that promote character education are William Bennett's (1993) *The Book of Virtues* and William Damon's (1995) *Greater Expectations*.

Values Clarification   **Values clarification** means helping people to clarify what their lives are for and what is worth working for. In this approach, students are encouraged to define their own values and to understand the values of others. Values clarification differs from character education in not telling students what their values should be.

In this values clarification example, students are asked to select, from among ten people, the six who will be admitted to a safe shelter because a third world war has broken out (Johnson, 1990):

Carol Gilligan believes that girls experience life differently than boys do; in Gilligan's words, girls have a "different voice." She believes that relationships are central to every aspect of a female's life.

care perspective A moral perspective that focuses on connectedness and relationships among people; Gilligan's approach reflects a care perspective.

hidden curriculum Dewey's concept that every school has a pervasive moral atmosphere even if it does not have a program of moral education.

character education A direct approach to moral education that involves teaching students basic moral literacy to prevent them from engaging in immoral behavior and doing harm to themselves or others.

values clarification An approach to moral education that emphasizes helping people clarify what their lives are for and what is worth working for; students are encouraged to define their own values and understand the values of others.

Video Lecture: Social Development of Adolescents

Video Observation: Moral Reasoning and Cheating

Moral Education

Character Education

Moral Development and Education

Service Learning

You work for a government agency in Washington and your group has to decide which six of the following ten people will be admitted to a small fallout shelter. Your group has only 20 minutes to make the decision. These are your choices:

- A 30-year-old male bookkeeper
- The bookkeeper's wife, who is six months pregnant
- A second-year African American male medical student who is a political activist
- A forty-two-year-old male who is a famous historian-author
- A Hollywood actress who is a singer and dancer
- A female biochemist
- A fifty-four-year-old male Rabbi
- A male Olympic athlete who is good in all sports
- A female college student
- A policeman with a gun

In this type of values clarification exercise, there are no right or wrong answers. The clarification of values is left up to the individual student. Advocates of values clarification say it is value free. However, critics argue that its controversial content offends community standards. They also say that because of its relativistic nature, values clarification undermines accepted values and fails to stress right behavior.

Cognitive Moral Education   **Cognitive moral education** is an approach based on the belief that students should learn to value things such as democracy and justice as their moral reasoning develops. Kohlberg's theory has been the basis for a number of cognitive moral education programs. In a typical program, high school students meet in a semester-long course to discuss a number of moral issues. The instructor acts as a facilitator rather than as a director of the class. The hope is that students will develop more advanced notions of such concepts as cooperation, trust, responsibility, and community. Toward the end of his career, Kohlberg (1986) recognized that the moral atmosphere of the school is more important than he initially envisioned. For example, in one study, a semester-long moral education class based on Kohlberg's theory was successful in advancing moral thinking in three democratic schools but not in three authoritarian schools (Higgins, Power, & Kohlberg, 1983).

Service Learning   **Service learning** is a form of education that promotes social responsibility and service to the community. In service learning, students might engage in tutoring, help the elderly, work in a hospital, assist at a day-care center, or clean up a vacant lot to make a play area. An important goal of service learning is for students to become less self-centered and more motivated to help others (Flanagan, 2004; Furco & Billing, 2001; Waterman, 1997; Youniss & others, 2003).

Service learning takes education out into the community (Levesque & Prosser, 1996). One eleventh-grade student worked as a reading tutor for students from low-income homes with reading skills well below their grade levels. She commented that until she did the tutoring she didn't realize how many students had not experienced the same opportunities that she had had when she was growing up. An especially rewarding moment was when one young girl told her, "I want to learn to read like you do so I can go to college when I grow up." Thus, service learning can benefit not only students but also the recipients of their help.

Researchers have found that service learning benefits students in a number of ways:

- Their grades improve, they become more motivated, and they set more goals (Johnson & others, 1998; Serow, Ciechalski, & Daye, 1990).
- Their self-esteem improves (Hamburg, 1997).
- They become less alienated (Calabrese & Schumer, 1986).
- They increasingly reflect on society's political organization and moral order (Yates, 1995).

cognitive moral education   An approach to moral education based on the belief that students should value things such as democracy and justice as their moral reasoning develops; Kohlberg's theory has served as the foundation for many cognitive moral education efforts.

service learning   A form of education that promotes social responsibility and service to the community.

Required community service has increased in high schools. In one survey, 15 percent of the nation's largest school districts had such a requirement (National Community Service Coalition, 1995). Even though required community service has increased in high schools, in another survey of 40,000 adolescents, two-thirds said they had never done any volunteer work to help other people (Benson, 1993). The benefits of service learning, for both the volunteer and the recipient, suggest that more adolescents should be required to participate in such programs.

Teaching Strategies
For Improving Children's Prosocial Behavior

This adolescent volunteered to work in the National Helpers Network, which gives students an opportunity to participate in service learning. Among the services provided are helping with environmental concerns, improving neighborhoods, and tutoring. Students also participate in weekly seminars that encourage them to reflect on their active involvement in the community. For more information about the National Helpers Network, call 212-679-7461.

Prosocial behavior involves the positive side of moral development (in contrast to antisocial behavior such as cheating, lying, and stealing). Prosocial behavior is behavior that is regarded as being altruistic, fair, sharing, or generally empathetic (Eisenberg & Fabes, 1998). Here are some strategies that teachers can adopt to improve students' prosocial behavior (Wittmer & Honig, 1994, pp. 5–10):

1. "*Value and emphasize consideration of others' needs.*" This encourages students to engage in more helping activities. Nel Noddings (1992a) explains the morality of caring as one of teaching students to feel for others, which leads to empathy and concern.
2. "*Model prosocial behaviors.*" Students imitate what teachers do. For example, a teacher who comforts a student in times of stress is likely to observe students imitating her comforting behavior. When teachers yell at students, they likely will observe more incidents of students yelling at others, too.
3. "*Label and identify prosocial and antisocial behaviors.*" Often go beyond just saying, "That's good" or "That's nice" to a student. Be specific in identifying prosocial behaviors. Say, "You are being helpful" or "You gave him a tissue; he really needed it to wipe his nose." Or regarding antisocial behavior, to a young child you might say something like "That's not being nice. How would you feel if he messed up your papers like that?"
4. "*Attribute positive social behaviors to each child.*" Attribute positive intentions to a positive act, such as "You shared because you like to help others."
5. "*Notice and positively encourage prosocial behaviors, but do not overuse external rewards.*" Commenting on positive behaviors and attributing positive characteristics to students rather than using external rewards helps students to internalize prosocial attitudes.
6. "*Facilitate perspective taking and understanding others' feelings.*" Helping students notice and respond to others' feelings can increase their consideration of others.
7. *Use positive discipline strategies.* Reason with students when they do something wrong. If a student is too aggressive and harms another student, point out the consequences of the student's behavior for the victim. Avoid harsh, punitive behavior with students. We will explore discipline strategies more extensively in chapter 14, "Managing the Classroom."
8. *Lead discussions on prosocial interactions.* Set up discussion sessions and let children evaluate how goods and benefits are distributed justly among people with varying needs, temperaments, talents, and troubles.

Through the Eyes of Students

Amos Bear Gets Hurt

Amos is a large, squishy plush bear that resides in a kindergarten class. Each weekend he travels home with a different child, returning on Monday morning to relate his "adventures." He often is the first object children head to when they are tired, ill, or upset.

The teacher noticed that the children recently had been using Amos as a punching bag, so she arrived early the next day and bandaged Amos' arm with surgical gauze. When the children arrived, they wanted to know what was wrong with Amos. The teacher replied that he must have gotten hurt last night.

The children's response in caring for Amos was intense. One child wanted "to fetch drugs, another to make coffee; still another went in search for money to use to pay the doctor's bill." Amos got shots, was rebandaged, and was given medicine. Once he survived this ordeal, the children's consensus was that Amos needed a rest and some food. This led Amanda to remark, "Could we give him a diet cola? I think he is a vegetarian. He has no pulse."

Throughout the ordeal, the children treated Amos in a caring, tender way. He was cradled in someone's arms most of the time, was not allowed to bump into anything, and was passed from one child to the next with great delicacy.

Amos' situation stimulated the children's empathy. The Amos Bear situation took place at the Helen Turner School in Hayword, California, where Laurie Read taught until her death in 1992.

(Source: Read, 1995, pp. 19–23).

Amos Bear getting assistance from his young caregivers.

ENTER THE DEBATE

1. Should teachers help young adolescents explore their identities?

2. Should teachers teach students values and morality?

Teaching Experience
- **Self-Esteem**
- **Adolescent Identity**

9. *Develop class and school projects that foster altruism.* Let children come up with examples of projects they can engage in that will help others. These projects might include cleaning up the schoolyard, writing as pen pals to children in troubled lands, collecting toys or food for individuals in need, and making friends with older adults during visits to a nursing home.

! Review and Reflect

3 **Explain these aspects of children's socioemotional development: self-esteem, identity, and moral concepts.**

Review
- What is self-esteem and what are some risks of low-esteem? What is the nature of identity development and what are the four statuses of identity?
- What stages of moral development were described by Piaget and Kohlberg? Contrast the justice and care perspectives. What are some forms of moral education?

Reflect
- What is the level of moral development likely to be among the children you intend to teach? How might this affect your approach to how you manage students' relations with others in class?

In chapters 2 and 3 we have examined how students develop, focusing mainly on the general pattern. In chapter 4, we will explore how individual students vary with regard to intelligence and other personal characteristics.

Many schools, including the one in which Miss Mahoney teaches, are placing considerable emphasis on character education as a means of violence prevention. The basic idea is to promote empathy among children and to disallow behaviors such as teasing, name-calling, and threats of any kind. Miss Mahoney has included character education in the curriculum of her fifth-grade class. Many of her students, particularly the boys, continue to exhibit the very behaviors she is trying to eliminate.

John and Luke are on the same club soccer team and often get into verbal conflicts with each other, though they appreciate each other's talents on the field. Tuesday night at practice, in violation of the team's rules, John told Luke that he "sucks." Luke decided to let it go. He did not want John to suffer a one-game suspension, as he recognized John's value to the team and they were facing a tough opponent that weekend.

Thursday in class, John accused Luke of stealing the cards he was using to organize a project. John was very angry. Luke also became angry and claimed he did not steal them. He then found them on the floor and handed them to John. "Here's your dumb cards, John," he said. "See, I didn't steal them."

In anger, John said, "Fine. Then how come they're all crinkled? You know, I could beat you up and maybe I just will."

"Yeah, right. You and who else?" asked Luke with a sneer.

Two other boys working nearby overheard the altercation and began contributing their perspectives.

"Yeah, John, Luke would kick your butt," said Grant.

"I think John would win," said Peter.

"Meet me at the park tomorrow after school and let's just see!" demanded John.

"No problem," retorted Luke.

Thursday evening they were both at soccer practice. Nothing was said about the fight that was to take place the next day after school.

Friday morning John's mother called Miss Mahoney to tell her that John was afraid to come to school because Luke had threatened to beat him up. Obviously, Miss Mahoney was concerned and realized she must address the situation. John's mother also talked to the principal about the situation. However, all John's mother told either of them is that Luke had threatened to beat up her son. She didn't know why and did not think the reason mattered in the least. She wanted her son protected and the other boy punished.

That morning Luke's mother was in the school for another purpose. The principal stopped her to talk about the situation, telling her that John had told his mother he was afraid to come to school because Luke was going to beat him up. Luke's mother asked for more information. Upon hearing John's side of the story, which was simply that Luke had threatened him, she told the principal that this didn't sound right—that Luke is impulsive enough that if he'd wanted to beat up John, he probably would have just hit him, not planned a fight for a later date. She wanted to talk to Luke before she jumped to any conclusions and asked that Miss Mahoney and the principal talk to both of the boys and any other children involved.

Both Miss Mahoney and the principal did as Luke's mother asked. The story that came out is the one you read. They decided that Luke should serve an in-school suspension the following day and miss recess all week "because it is the third 'incident' we've had with him this year." John received no punishment and walked away from the meeting, grinning.

- What are the issues in this case?
- At what stage of moral development would you expect these boys to be, based on the information you have? What predictions can you make regarding each boy's sense of self and emotional development?
- What can you say about the boys' mothers?
- What do you think about the punishment that Luke received? And John? How would you have handled this situation?
- What impact do you think this will have on the boys' future relationship? What impact on their attitudes toward school?

Reach Your Learning Goals

1 Describe two contemporary perspectives on socioemotional development: Bronfenbrenner's ecological theory and Erikson's life-span development theory.

- Bronfenbrenner's ecological theory seeks to explain how environmental systems influence children's development. Bronfenbrenner described five environmental systems that include both micro and macro inputs: microsystem, mesosystem, exosystem, macrosystem, and chronosystem. Bronfenbrenner's theory is one of the few systematic analyses that includes both micro and macro environments. Critics say the theory lacks attention to biological and cognitive factors. They also point out that it does not address step-by-step developmental changes.

- Erikson's life-span development theory proposes eight stages, each centering on a particular type of challenge or dilemma: trust versus mistrust, autonomy versus shame and doubt, initiative versus guilt, industry versus inferiority, identity versus identity confusion, intimacy versus isolation, generativity versus stagnation, and integrity versus despair. Erikson's theory has made important contributions to understanding socioemotional development, although some critics say the stages are too rigid and that their sequencing lacks research support.

2 Discuss how the social contexts of families, peers, and schools are linked with socioemotional development.

- Baumrind proposed four parenting styles: authoritarian, authoritative, neglectful, and indulgent. Authoritative parenting is associated with children's social competence. Greater numbers of children are growing up in diverse family structures than at any other point in history. A special concern is the number of children of divorce. Other special concerns are ethnic and socioeconomic variations in families. Middle-income families are more likely to use discipline that encourages internalization; low-income families are more likely to use discipline that focuses on external characteristics. Fostering school-family partnerships involves providing assistance to families, communicating effectively with families about school programs and student progress, encouraging parents to be volunteers, involving families with their children in learning activities at home, including families in school decisions, and coordinating community collaboration.

- Peers are children of about the same age or maturity level. Social isolation, or the inability to "plug in" to a social network, is linked with many problems. Children can have one of five peer statuses: popular, average, rejected, neglected, or controversial. Rejected children often have more serious adjustment problems than neglected children. Friendship is an important aspect of students' social relations. Peer relations begin to consume more of children's time in elementary and secondary schools. Same-sex peer groups predominate in elementary school. In early adolescence, participation in coed groups increases.

- Schools involve changing social developmental contexts from preschool through high school. The early childhood setting is a protected environment with one or two teachers, usually female. Peer groups are more important in elementary school. In middle school, the social field enlarges to include the whole school, and the social system becomes more complex. Controversy characterizes early childhood education curricula. On the one side are the developmentally appropriate, child-centered, constructivist advocates; on the other are those who advocate an instructivist, academic approach. Head Start has provided early childhood education for children from low-income families. High-quality Head Start programs are effective educational interventions, but up to 40 percent of these programs may be ineffective. A special concern is that many early elementary school classrooms rely mainly on negative feedback. The transition to middle or junior high is stressful for many students because it coincides with so many physical, cognitive, and socioemotional changes. It involves going from the top-dog position to the lowest position in a school hierarchy. Effective schools for young adolescents adapt to individual variations in students, take seriously what is known about the development of young adolescents, and give as much emphasis to socioemotional as to cognitive development. An increasing number of educational experts also believe that substantial changes need to be made in U.S. high school education.

3 Explain these aspects of children's socioemotional development: self-esteem, identity, and moral concepts.

- Self-esteem, also referred to as self-worth or self-image, is the individual's overall conception of himself or herself. Four keys to increasing students' self-esteem are to (1) identify the causes of low self-esteem and the domains of competence important to the student, (2) provide emotional support and social approval, (3) help students achieve, and (4) develop students' coping skills. Marcia proposed that adolescents have one of four identity statuses (based on the extent to which they have explored or are exploring alternative paths and whether they have made a commitment): identity diffusion, identity foreclosure, identity moratorium, identity achievement.

- Moral development concerns rules and conventions about just interactions between people. These rules can be studied in three domains: cognitive, behavioral, and emotional. Piaget proposed two stages of moral thought: heteronomous morality (ages four to seven years) and autonomous morality (ten years and older). Piaget believed that the mutual give-and-take of peer relations advances moral development. Kohlberg, like Piaget, stressed that the key to understanding moral development is moral reasoning and that it unfolds in stages. Kohlberg identified three levels of moral development (preconventional, conventional, and postconventional), with two stages at each level. As individuals go through the three levels, their moral thinking becomes more internalized. Two main criticisms of Kohlberg's theory are (1) Kohlberg did not give enough attention to moral behavior, and (2) Kohlberg's theory gave too much power to the individual and not enough to relationships with others. In this regard, Gilligan argued that Kohlberg's theory is a male-oriented justice perspective. She believes that what is needed in moral development is a female-oriented care perspective. The hidden curriculum is the moral atmosphere that every school has. Three types of moral education are character education, values clarification, and cognitive moral education. Service learning is becoming increasingly important in schools.

KEY TERMS

ecological theory 68
authoritarian parenting 74
authoritative parenting 74
neglectful parenting 74
indulgent parenting 74
developmentally appropriate
   education 84

self-esteem 91
identity diffusion 92
identity foreclosure 92
identity moratorium 92
identity achievement 93
moral development 93
heteronomous morality 95

autonomous morality 95
preconventional reasoning 95
conventional reasoning 96
postconventional reasoning 96
justice perspective 96
care perspective 97
hidden curriculum 97

character education 97
values clarification 97
cognitive moral education 98
service learning 98

PORTFOLIO ACTIVITIES

Now that you have a good understanding of this chapter, complete these exercises to expand your thinking.

Independent Reflection

Meeting the Socioemotional Needs of Students. Think about the age of students you intend to teach. Which of Erikson's stages is likely to be central for them? What, if anything, does Bronfenbrenner's theory suggest about important resources for students at that age? Does his system suggest particular challenges to students or ways that you as a teacher might facilitate their success? Discuss your ideas. (INTASC: Principles *2, 3, 5, 7*)

Collaborative Work

The Role of Moral Education in Schools. Which approach to moral education (character education, values clarification, or cog-nitive moral education) do you like the best? Why? Should schools be in the business of having specific moral education programs? Get together with several other students in this class and discuss your perspectives. Then write a brief statement that reflects your own perspective on moral education. (INTASC: Principles *2, 4, 9*)

Research/Field Experience Reflections

Fostering Family-School Linkages. Interview several teachers from local schools about how they foster family-school linkages. Try to talk with a kindergarten teacher, an elementary teacher, a middle school teacher, and a high school teacher. Summarize your discoveries. (INTASC: Principles *9, 10*)

 Go to the Online Learning Center for downloadable portfolio templates.

TAKING IT TO THE NET

1. How can teachers help children and youth successfully resolve the challenges of the different stages of psychosocial development? Describe a teaching strategy that could be used to foster independence, confidence, and risk-taking in students.
2. Research shows that family involvement greatly influences student attitudes, attendance, and academic achievement. Develop an action plan for involving families in your classroom in a variety of ways. What are some of the challenges to involving families, and how do you plan to overcome these?

3. Do you believe that helping students develop good character is just as important as teaching reading, writing, and math? Or should families solely be in control of character and moral instruction? Why? In what ways do teachers inherently impact students' character development through their daily interactions?

Connect to the Online Learning Center to explore possible answers.

STUDY, PRACTICE, AND SUCCEED

 Go to chapter 3 on the Online Learning Center at www.mhhe.com/santrockedu2e to access the student study guide with practice quizzes, web links, portfolio resources, PowerWeb articles and news feeds, and the online resources referenced in the chapter.

 Go to your Student Toolbox CD-ROM to access the resources and activities referenced in the chapter and

- Resources to help you prepare for the **PRAXIS II™** exam

- **Application Resources,** including additional *Crack the Case* studies, electronic versions of the *Self-Assessments*, Application Exercises, and Site Observation Questions
- **Study Resources,** including Learning Goals, the Chapter Summary, a *Test Your Learning* exercise, and multiple-choice, true/false, matching, key terms, and short-answer quizzes
- **Professional Resources,** including a Lesson Plan Builder and *Bibliomaker*

4 Individual Variations

> # Individuals play out their lives in different ways.
> —Thomas Huxley
> *English Biologist,*
> *19th Century*

Chapter Learning Goals After you have completed your study of this chapter, you should be able to reach these learning goals:

1 **Discuss the concept of intelligence, how it is measured, and some controversies about its use by educators.**

2 **Describe and evaluate learning and thinking styles.**

3 **Define personality, identify the "big five" factors of personality, and discuss person-situation interaction. Also, define temperament, identify three types of children's temperament, and evaluate teaching strategies linked to children's temperament.**

Teaching Stories Shiffy Landa

Shiffy Landa, a first-grade teacher at H. F. Epstein Hebrew Academy in St. Louis, Missouri, uses the multiple-intelligences approach of Howard Gardner (1983, 1993) in her classroom. Gardner argues that there is not just one general type of intelligence but at least eight specific types.

Landa (2000, pp. 6–8) believes that the multiple-intelligences approach is the best way to reach children because they have many different kinds of abilities. In Landa's words, "My role as a teacher is quite different from the way it was just a few years ago. No longer do I stand in front of the room and lecture to my students. I consider my role to be one of a facilitator rather than a frontal teacher. The desks in my room are not all neatly lined up in straight rows. . . . students are busily working in centers in cooperative learning groups, which gives them the opportunity to develop their interpersonal intelligences."

Students use their "body-kinesthetic intelligence to form the shapes of the letters as they learn to write . . . They also use this in-

telligence to move the sounds of the vowels that they are learning, blending them together with letters, as they begin to read."

Landa believes that "intrapersonal intelligence is an intelligence that often is neglected in the traditional classroom." In her classroom, students "complete their own evaluation sheets after they have concluded their work at the centers. They evaluate their work and create their own portfolios," in which they keep their work so they can see their progress.

As she was implementing the multiple-intelligences approach in her classroom, Landa recognized that she needed to educate parents about it. She created "a parent education class called The Parent-Teacher Connection," which meets periodically to view videos, talk about multiple-intelligences, and discuss how they are being introduced in the classroom. She also sends a weekly newsletter to parents, informing them about the week's multiple-intelligences activities and students' progress.

In this introduction to Gardner's multiple intelligences, we described three of the intelligences he has proposed: interpersonal, bodily-kinesthetic, and intrapersonal. Later in the chapter, we will explore Gardner's theory in greater depth, including the five other types of intelligences he believes exist. You will see that there is spirited debate about whether people have a general intelligence or a number of specific intelligences. Intelligence is but one of several main topics in this chapter. We also will examine learning and thinking styles, as well as personality and temperament. For each of these topics, an important theme is students' individual variations and the best strategies for teachers to use related to these variations.

INTELLIGENCE

The concept of intelligence generates controversy and heated debate, often in reaction to the idea that each person has a general mental capacity that can be measured and quantified in a number. Educational panels and school boards debate whether intelligence tests are useful and fair. They also argue about whether such tests should be used to place students in special classes or tracks. Educational psychologists debate whether we have a general mental capacity or a number of specific mental capacities. Also, if we have various mental capacities, what are they? How many do we have?

Video Lecture: Cognitive Variations

Twentieth-century English novelist Aldous Huxley said that children are remarkable for their curiosity and intelligence. What did Huxley mean when he used the word *intelligence?* Intelligence is one of our most prized possessions, yet even the most intelligent people have not been able to agree on what intelligence is. Unlike height, weight, and age, intelligence cannot be directly measured. You can't peer into a student's head and observe the intelligence going on inside. We only can evaluate a student's intelligence indirectly by studying the student's intelligent acts. For the most part, we have relied on written intelligence tests to provide an estimate of a student's intelligence.

intelligence Problem-solving skills and the ability to adapt to and learn from life's everyday experiences.

Some experts describe intelligence as problem-solving skills. Others describe it as the ability to adapt to and learn from life's everyday experiences. Combining these ideas we can arrive at a fairly traditional definition of **intelligence**: problem-solving skills and the ability to adapt to and learn from life's everyday experiences. But even this broad definition doesn't satisfy everyone. As you will see shortly, some theorists propose that musical skills should be considered part of intelligence. Also, a definition of intelligence based on a theory such as Vygotsky's would have to include the ability to use the tools of the culture with help from more-skilled individuals. ◀ Page 51. Because intelligence is such an abstract, broad concept, it is not surprising that there are so many different possible definitions of it.

Interest in intelligence has often focused on individual differences and assessment (Kaufman & Lictenberger, 2002; Lubinski, 2000; Molfese & Martin, 2001). Individual differences are the stable, consistent ways in which people are different from one another. We can talk about individual differences in personality and other domains, but it is intelligence that has been given the most attention and about which the most conclusions have been drawn about the different abilities of students.

Individual Intelligence Tests

Robert J. Sternberg recalls being terrified of taking IQ tests as a child. He says that he literally froze when the time came to take such tests. Even as an adult, Sternberg feels stung by humiliation when he recalls being in sixth grade and taking an IQ test with fifth-graders. Sternberg eventually overcame his anxieties about IQ tests. Not only did he begin to perform better on them, but at age thirteen he devised his own IQ test and began using it to assess classmates—until the school principal found out and scolded him. Sternberg became so fascinated by intelligence that he made its study one of his lifelong pursuits. Later in the chapter we will discuss his theory of intelligence. To begin, though, let's go back in time to examine the first valid intelligence test.

The Binet Tests   In 1904 the French Ministry of Education asked psychologist Alfred Binet to devise a method of identifying children who were unable to learn in school. School officials wanted to reduce crowding by placing in special schools students who did not benefit from regular classroom teaching. Binet and his student Theophile Simon developed an intelligence test to meet this request. The test is called the 1905 Scale. It consisted of 30 questions, ranging from the ability to touch one's ear to the abilities to draw designs from memory and define abstract concepts.

Binet developed the concept of **mental age (MA),** an individual's level of mental development relative to others. Not much later, in 1912, William Stern created the concept of **intelligence quotient (IQ),** which refers to a person's mental age divided by chronological age (CA), multiplied by 100. That is, $IQ = MA/CA \times 100$.

If mental age is the same as chronological age, then the person's IQ is 100. If mental age is above chronological age, then IQ is more than 100. For example, a six-year-old with a mental age of eight would have an IQ of 133. If mental age is below chronological age, then IQ is less than 100. For example, a six-year-old with a mental age of five would have an IQ of 83.

The Binet test has been revised many times to incorporate advances in the understanding of intelligence and intelligence testing. These revisions are called the Stanford-Binet tests (because the revisions were made at Stanford University). By administering the test to large numbers of people of different ages from different backgrounds, researchers have found that scores on a Stanford-Binet test approximate a normal distribution (see figure 4.1 on page 108). As described more fully in chapter 15, "Standardized Tests and Teaching," a **normal distribution** is symmetrical, with a majority of the scores falling in the middle of the possible range of scores and few scores appearing toward the extremes of the range.

The current Stanford-Binet is administered individually to people aged two through adult. It includes a variety of items, some of which require verbal responses, others nonverbal responses. For example, items that reflect a typical six-year-old's level of performance on the test include the verbal ability to define at least six words, such as *orange* and *envelope,* as well as the nonverbal ability to trace a path through a maze. Items that reflect an average adult's level of performance include defining such words as *disproportionate* and *regard,* explaining a proverb, and comparing idleness and laziness.

The fourth edition of the Stanford-Binet was published in 1985. One important addition to this version was the analysis of the individual's responses in terms of four functions: verbal reasoning, quantitative reasoning, abstract visual reasoning, and short-term

Theories of Intelligence/Intelligence Tests
Mental Measurements Yearbook
Alfred Binet

mental age (MA) An individual's level of mental development relative to others.

intelligence quotient (IQ) A person's mental age (MA) divided by chronological age (CA), multiplied by 100.

normal distribution A symmetrical distribution, with a majority of scores falling in the middle of the possible range of scores and few scores appearing toward the extremes of the range.

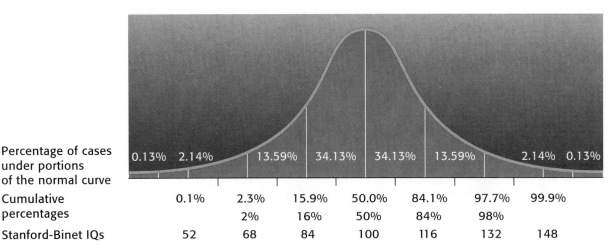

Percentage of cases under portions of the normal curve	0.13%	2.14%		13.59%	34.13%	34.13%	13.59%		2.14%	0.13%
Cumulative percentages		0.1%	2.3%	15.9%	50.0%	84.1%	97.7%	99.9%		
			2%	16%	50%	84%	98%			
Stanford-Binet IQs		52	68	84	100	116	132	148		

FIGURE 4.1 The Normal Curve and Stanford-Binet IQ Scores
The distribution of IQ scores approximates a normal curve. Most of the population falls in the middle range of scores. Notice that extremely high and extremely low scores are very rare. Slightly more than two-thirds of the scores fall between 84 and 116. Only about 1 in 50 individuals has an IQ of more than 132, and only about 1 in 50 individuals has an IQ of less than 68.

memory. A general composite score is still obtained to reflect overall intelligence. The Stanford-Binet continues to be one of the most widely used tests to assess students' intelligence (Aiken, 2003; Walsh & Betz, 2001).

The Wechsler Scales   Another set of tests widely used to assess students' intelligence is called the Wechsler scales, developed by David Wechsler. They include the Wechsler Preschool and Primary Scale of Intelligence–Revised (WPPSI-R) to test children 4 to 6½ years of age; the Wechsler Intelligence Scale for Children–Revised (WISC-R) for children and adolescents 6 to 16 years of age; and the Wechsler Adult Intelligence Scale–Revised (WAIS-R).

In addition to an overall IQ, the Wechsler scales also yield verbal and performance IQs. Verbal IQ is based on six verbal subscales, performance IQ on five performance subscales. This allows the examiner to quickly see patterns of strengths and weaknesses in different areas of the student's intelligence (Woolger, 2001). Examples of Wechsler subscales are shown in figure 4.2.

Individual Tests Versus Group Tests

Intelligence tests such as the Stanford-Binet and Wechsler are given on an individual basis. A psychologist approaches an individual assessment of intelligence as a structured interaction between the examiner and the student. This provides the psychologist with an opportunity to sample the student's behavior. During the testing, the examiner observes the ease with which rapport is established, the student's enthusiasm and interest, whether anxiety interferes with the student's performance, and the student's degree of tolerance for frustration.

David Wechsler

Students also often are given an intelligence test in a group all at the same time (Drummond, 2000). Group intelligence tests include the Lorge-Thorndike Intelligence Tests, the Kuhlman-Anderson Intelligence Tests, and the Otis-Lennon School Mental Abilities Tests. Group intelligence tests are more convenient and economical than individual tests, but they do have their drawbacks. When a test is given to a large group, the examiner cannot establish rapport, determine the student's level of anxiety, and so on. In a large-group testing situation, students might not understand the instructions or might be distracted by other students.

Verbal Subscales
Similarities A child must think logically and abstractly to answer a number of questions about how things might be similar. For example, "In what ways are a saw and a hammer alike?"

Example of a Performance Subscale
Block design An individual must assemble a set of multicolored blocks to match designs that the examiner shows. Visual-motor coordination, perceptual organization, and the ability to visualize spatially are assessed. For example, "Use the four blocks on the left to make the pattern at the right."

Remember that the Wechsler includes 11 subscales, 6 verbal and 5 nonverbal.

FIGURE 4.2 Sample Subscales of the Wechsler Adult Intelligence Scale for Children–Revised

Simulated items similar to those in the Wechsler Intelligence Scales for Children: Third Edition. Copyright © 1949, 1974, 1981, 1991 by The Psychological Corporation. Reproduced by permission. All rights reserved.

Because of such limitations, when important decisions are made about students, a group intelligence test should always be supplemented with other information about the student's abilities. For that matter, the same strategy holds for an individual intelligence test, although it usually is wise to have less confidence in the accuracy of group intelligence test scores. Many students take tests in large groups at school, but a decision to place a student in a class for students who have mental retardation, a special education class, or a class for students who are gifted should not be based on a group test alone. In such instances, an extensive amount of relevant information about the student's abilities should be obtained outside the testing situation (Domino, 2000).

Teaching Strategies
For Interpreting Intelligence Test Scores

Psychological tests are tools. Like all tools, their effectiveness depends on the knowledge, skill, and integrity of the user. A hammer can be used to build a beautiful kitchen cabinet and a hammer can be used as a weapon of assault. Similarly, psychological tests can be well used or badly abused. Here are some cautions about IQ that can help teachers avoid using information about a student's intelligence in negative ways:

1. *Avoid unwarranted stereotypes and negative expectations about students based on IQ scores.* Too often, sweeping generalizations are made on the basis of an IQ score. Imagine that you are in the teachers' lounge on the second day of school in the fall. You mention one of your students, and another teacher remarks that she had him in her class last year. She says that he was a real dunce and that he scored 83 on an IQ test. How hard is it to ignore this information as you go about teaching your class? Probably difficult. But it is important that you not develop the expectation that because Johnny scored low on an IQ test it is useless to spend much time teaching him. An IQ test should always be considered a measure of current

Robert J. Sternberg, who developed the triarchic theory of intelligence.

performance. It is not a measure of fixed potential. Maturational changes and enriched environmental experiences can advance a student's intelligence.

2. *Don't use IQ tests as the main or sole characteristic of competence.* A high IQ is not the ultimate human value. As we will see in this chapter, it is important for teachers to consider not only students' intellectual competence in areas such as verbal skills but also their creative and practical skills.

3. *Especially be cautious in interpreting the meaningfulness of an overall IQ score.* It is wiser to think of intelligence as consisting of a number of domains. Keep in mind that many educational psychologists believe that it is important to consider the strengths and weaknesses of students in different areas of intelligence. Intelligence tests such as the Wechsler scales can provide information about those strengths and weaknesses.

Theories of Multiple Intelligences

Is it more appropriate to think of a student's intelligence as a general ability or as a number of specific abilities?

Sternberg's Theory
Robert J. Sternberg

Early Views Binet and Stern both focused on a concept of general intelligence, which Stern called IQ. Wechsler believed it is possible and important to describe both a person's general intelligence and more specific verbal and performance intelligences. He was building on the ideas of Charles Spearman (1927), who said that people have both a general intelligence, which he called *g*, and specific types of intelligence, which he called *s*. Whether such a thing as *g* really exists is an ongoing controversy that we will explore in greater depth later in the chapter.

As early as the 1930s, L. L. Thurstone (1938) said people have seven specific intellectual abilities, which he called primary abilities: verbal comprehension, number ability word fluency, spatial visualization, associative memory, reasoning, and perceptual speed. More recently, the search for specific types of intelligence has heated up (Gregory, 2000).

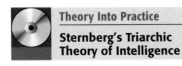

Theory Into Practice
Sternberg's Triarchic Theory of Intelligence

Sternberg's Triarchic Theory According to Robert J. Sternberg's (1986, 2000) **triarchic theory of intelligence,** intelligence comes in three forms: analytical, creative, and practical. Analytical intelligence involves the ability to analyze, judge, evaluate, compare, and contrast. Creative intelligence consists of the ability to create, design, invent, originate, and imagine. Practical intelligence focuses on the ability to use, apply, implement, and put into practice. Consider these three students:

- Ann scores high on traditional intelligence tests, such as the Stanford-Binet, and is a star analytical thinker.
- Todd does not have the best test scores but has an insightful and creative mind.
- Art is street-smart and has learned to deal in practical ways with his world, although his scores on traditional intelligence tests are low.

Some students are equally high in all three areas; others do well in one or two.

Sternberg (2000; Sternberg, Torff, & Grigorenko, 1998) says that students with different triarchic patterns "look different" in school. Students with high analytic ability tend to be favored in conventional schooling. They often do well in direct-instruction classes in which the teacher lectures and students are given objective tests. They often are considered to be "smart" students who get good grades, show up in high-level tracks, do well on traditional tests of intelligence and the SAT, and later get admitted to competitive colleges.

Students who are high in creative intelligence often are not on the top rung of their class. Sternberg says that creatively intelligent students might not conform to teachers' expectations about how assignments should be done. Instead of giving conformist answers, they give unique answers, for which they sometimes get reprimanded or

triarchic theory of intelligence
Sternberg's view that intelligence comes in three main forms: analytical, creative, and practical.

marked down. No good teacher wants to discourage creativity, but Sternberg believes that too often a teacher's desire to improve students' knowledge suppresses creative thinking.

Like students high in creative intelligence, students with high practical intelligence often do not relate well to the demands of school. However, these students often do well outside the classroom. They might have excellent social skills and good common sense. As adults, they sometimes become successful managers, entrepreneurs, or politicians, despite undistinguished school records.

Sternberg believes that few tasks are purely analytical, creative, or practical. Most require some combination of these skills. For example, when students write a book report, they might (1) analyze the book's main themes, (2) generate new ideas about how the book might have been written better, and (3) think about how the book's themes can be applied to people's lives.

Sternberg believes it is important in teaching to balance instruction related to the three types of intelligence. That is, students should be given opportunities to learn through analytical, creative, and practical thinking, in addition to conventional strategies that focus on simply "learning" and remembering a body of information. You might be wondering whether there is a Sternberg triarchic intelligence test available. As yet, there isn't.

"You're wise, but you lack tree smarts."
© The New Yorker Collection 1988 Donald Reilly from cartoonbank.com. All Rights Reserved.

Gardner's Eight Frames of Mind   As we indicated in the Teaching Stories introduction to this chapter, Howard Gardner (1983, 1993, 2002) believes there are many specific types of intelligence, or frames of mind. They are described here along with examples of the occupations in which they are reflected as strengths (Campbell, Campbell, & Dickinson, 2004):

Multiple-Intelligences Links

- *Verbal skills:* the ability to think in words and to use language to express meaning (authors, journalists, speakers)
- *Mathematical skills:* the ability to carry out mathematical operations (scientists, engineers, accountants)
- *Spatial skills:* the ability to think three-dimensionally (architects, artists, sailors)
- *Bodily-kinesthetic skills:* the ability to manipulate objects and be physically adept (surgeons, craftspeople, dancers, athletes)
- *Musical skills:* a sensitivity to pitch, melody, rhythm, and tone (composers, musicians, and sensitive listeners)
- *Intrapersonal skills:* the ability to understand oneself and effectively direct one's life (theologians, psychologists)
- *Interpersonal skills:* the ability to understand and effectively interact with others (successful teachers, mental health professionals)
- *Naturalist skills:* the ability to observe patterns in nature and understand natural and human-made systems (farmers, botanists, ecologists, landscapers)

Gardner believes that each form of intelligence can be destroyed by a different pattern of brain damage, that each involves unique cognitive skills, and that each shows up in unique ways in both the gifted and idiot savants (individuals who have mental retardation but have an exceptional talent in a particular domain, such as drawing, music, or numerical computation).

Although Gardner has endorsed the application of his model to education, as we will describe here, he has also witnessed some misuses of the approach. Here are some cautions he gives about using it (Gardner, 1998):

- There is no reason to assume that every subject can be effectively taught in eight different ways to correspond to the eight intelligences and attempting to do this is a waste of effort.

Howard Gardner, here working with a young child, developed the view that intelligence comes in the forms of these eight kinds of skills: verbal, mathematical, spatial, bodily-kinesthetic, musical, intrapersonal, interpersonal, and naturalist.

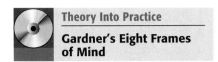

Theory Into Practice

Gardner's Eight Frames of Mind

VIDEO

Video Lecture: Introduction to Multiple Intelligences

VIDEO

Video Observation: Multiple Intelligences in the Classroom

• Don't assume that it is enough just to apply a certain type of intelligence. For example, in terms of bodily-kinesthetic skills, random muscle movements have nothing to do with cultivating cognitive skills.

• There is no reason to believe that it is helpful to use one type of intelligence as a background activity while children are working on an activity related to a different type of intelligence. For example, Gardner believes that playing music in the background while students solve math problems is a misapplication of his theory.

Project Spectrum Project Spectrum is an innovative attempt by Gardner (1993; Gardner, Feldman, & Krechevsky, 1998) to examine the proposed eight intelligences in young children. Project Spectrum begins with the basic idea that every student has the potential to develop strengths in one or more areas. It provides a context in which to see more clearly the strengths and weaknesses of individual children.

What is a Spectrum classroom like? The classroom has rich and engaging materials that can stimulate the range of intelligences. However, teachers do not try to evoke an intelligence directly by homogeneously grouping activity materials that are labeled "spatial," "verbal," and so on. Rather, they use materials that relate to a combination of intelligence domains. For example, a naturalist corner houses biological specimens that students can explore and compare, eliciting not only students' sensory capacities but also their logical analytical skills. In a story-telling area, students create imaginative tales with stimulating props and design their own storyboards, thus encouraging students to use their linguistic, dramatic, and imaginative skills. In a building corner, students can construct a model of their classroom and arrange small-scale photographs of the students and teachers in their class. This area stimulates the use of both spatial and personal skills. In all, the Spectrum classroom has twelve such areas, which are designed to elicit and improve students' multiple intelligences.

The Spectrum classroom can identify skills that are typically missed in a regular classroom. In one first-grade Spectrum classroom was a boy who was the product of a highly conflicted home and had been at risk for school failure. When Project Spectrum was introduced, the boy was identified as being the best student in the class at taking apart and putting together common objects, such as a food grinder or a doorknob. His teacher became encouraged when she found that he possessed this skill, and his overall school performance began to improve.

In addition to identifying unexpected strengths in students, Project Spectrum also can locate undetected weaknesses. Gregory was doing very well in first grade, especially in skills in math computation and conceptual knowledge. However, he performed poorly in a number of other Spectrum areas. He did well only in the areas in which he needed to give the correct answer and a person in authority gave it to him. As a result of the Spectrum program, Gregory's teacher began to search for ways to encourage him to take risks on more open-ended tasks, to try things out in innovative ways, and to realize that it's okay to make mistakes.

Project Spectrum has developed theme-related kits that tap the range of intelligences. Two such themes are "Night and Day" and "About Me." Students experience the basics of reading, writing, and calculating in the context of themes and materials with which they are motivated to work.

The Key School The Key School, a K–6 elementary school in Indianapolis, immerses students in activities that involve a range of skills that closely correlate with Gardner's eight frames of mind (Goleman, Kaufman, & Ray, 1993). Each day every student is exposed to materials that are designed to stimulate a whole range of human abilities. These include art, music, language skills, math skills, and physical games. In addition, attention is given to understanding oneself and others.

These children attend the Key School, which has "pods" where they can pursue activities of special interest to them. Every day, each child can choose from activities that draw on Gardner's eight frames of mind. The school's pods include gardening, architecture, gliding, and dancing.

Technology and Multiple Intelligences

Technology can be used to facilitate learning in each area of intelligence:

Verbal Skills. Computers encourage students to revise and rewrite compositions; this should help them to produce more competent papers. "Learning keyboarding is as important today as learning to write with a pencil, and learning to use a word processor is as important as learning to type."

Logical/Mathematical Skills. "Students of every ability can learn effectively through interesting software programs that provide immediate feedback and go far beyond drill-and-practice exercises." These programs challenge students to use their thinking skills to solve math problems.

Spatial Skills. Computers allow students to see and manipulate material. They can create many different forms before they make final copies of a written project. Virtual-reality technology can provide students with opportunities to exercise their visual-spatial skills.

Bodily-Kinesthetic Skills. "Computers rely mostly on eye-hand coordination for their operation—keyboarding and the use of a mouse or touch-screen. This kinesthetic activity . . . makes the student an active participant in the learning." Programs such as Lego Logo allow students to invent numerous kinds of machines that they can operate on the computer.

Musical Skills. "The development of musical intelligence can be enhanced by technology in the same way that verbal fluency is enhanced by word processors . . . The Musical Instrument Digital Interface (MIDI) makes it possible to compose for and orchestrate many different instruments through the computer."

Interpersonal Skills. "When students use computers in pairs or small groups, their comprehension and learning are facilitated and accelerated. Positive learning experiences can result as students share discoveries, support each other in solving problems, and work collaboratively on projects."

Intrapersonal Skills. "Technology offers the means to explore a line of thought in great depth" and to have extensive access to a range of personal interests. "The opportunity for students to make such choices is at the heart of giving them control over their own learning and intellectual development."

Naturalist Skills. Electronic technologies can "facilitate scientific investigation, exploration, and other naturalist activities. Telecommunications technologies help students to understand the world beyond their own environments." For example, National Geographic Online allows students to go on expeditions with famed explorers and photographers.

(Source: Dickinson, 1998, 1–3).

Like other public schools, the Key School is open to any child in Indianapolis, but it is so popular that its students have to be chosen by lottery. The teachers are selected with an eye toward special abilities in certain domains. For example, one teacher is competent at signing for the deaf, a skill in both linguistic and kinesthetic domains.

The Key School's goal is to allow students to discover where they have natural curiosity and talent, then let them explore these domains. Gardner believes that if teachers give students the opportunities to use their bodies, imaginations, and different senses, almost every student finds that he or she is good at something. Even students who are not outstanding in a any single area will still find that they have relative strengths.

Every nine weeks, the school emphasizes different themes, such as the Renaissance in sixteenth-century Italy and "Renaissance Now" in Indianapolis. Students develop projects related to the theme. The projects are not graded. Instead, students present them to their classmates, explain them, and answer questions. Collaboration and teamwork are emphasized in the theme projects and in all areas of learning.

The Technology and Education box describes how technology can be used in Gardner's eight types of intelligence.

Teaching Strategies
For Each of Gardner's Eight Frames of Mind

Following are some further strategies that teachers can use that are related to Gardner's eight types of intelligence (Berger & Pollman, 1996; Campbell, Campbell, & Dickinson, 2004):

1. *Verbal Skills*
   - Read to children and let them read to you.
   - Discuss authors of books with children.

Strategies in Practice
- **Portfolios**
- **Gardner's Multiple Intelligences**
- **Teaching with Gardner's Eight Types of Intelligences**
- **A Project Using Gardner's Eight Types of Intelligences**
- **Social Studies and Multiple Intelligences**

- Visit libraries and bookstores with children.
- Have children keep journals of significant events.
- Have children summarize and retell a story they have read.

2. *Mathematical Skills*
   - Play games of logic with children.
   - Be on the lookout for situations that can inspire children to think about and construct an understanding of numbers.
   - Take children on field trips to computer labs, science museums, and electronics exhibits.
   - Do math activities with children, such as counting objects and experimenting with numbers.

3. *Spatial Skills*
   - Have a variety of creative materials for children to use.
   - Have children navigate mazes and create charts.
   - Take children to art museums and hands-on children's museums.
   - Go on walks with children. When they get back, ask them to visualize where they have been and then draw a map of their experiences.

4. *Bodily-Kinesthetic Skills*
   - Provide children with opportunities for physical activity and encourage them to participate.
   - Provide areas where children can play indoors and outdoors. If this is not possible, take them to a park.
   - Take children to sporting events and the ballet.
   - Encourage children to participate in dance activities.

5. *Musical Skills*
   - Provide children with a tape recorder or record player they can use.
   - Give children an opportunity to play musical instruments.
   - Create opportunities for children to make music and rhythms together using voices and simple instruments.
   - Take children to concerts.
   - Encourage children to make up their own songs.

6. *Intrapersonal Skills*
   - Encourage children to have hobbies and interests.
   - Listen to children's feelings and give them sensitive feedback.
   - Encourage children to use their imagination.
   - Have children keep a journal or scrapbook of their ideas and experiences.

7. *Interpersonal Skills*
   - Encourage children to work in groups.
   - Help children to develop communication skills.
   - Provide group games for children to play.
   - Encourage children to join clubs.

8. *Naturalist Skills*
   - Take children to natural science museums.
   - Create a naturalist learning center in the classroom.
   - Engage children in outdoor naturalist activities, such as taking a nature walk or adopting a tree.
   - Have children make collections of flora or fauna and classify them.

We have discussed a number of ideas about Gardner's eight types of intelligence. To evaluate your strengths and weaknesses in these areas, complete Self-Assessment 4.1.

Emotional Intelligence   Both Gardner's and Sternberg's theories include one or more categories of social intelligence. In Gardner's theory, the categories are interpersonal intelligence and intrapersonal intelligence. In Sternberg's theory, the category is practical intelligence. Another theory that captures the importance of the interpersonal,

Evaluating Myself on Gardner's Eight Types of Intelligence

Read these items and rate yourself on a 4-point scale. Each rating corresponds to how well a statement describes you: 1 = not like me at all, 2 = somewhat unlike me, 3 = somewhat like me, and 4 = a lot like me.

	1	2	3	4

Verbal Thinking
1. I do well on verbal tests, such as the verbal part of the SAT.
2. I am a skilled reader and read prolifically.
3. I love the challenge of solving verbal problems.

Logical/Mathematical Thinking
4. I am a very logical thinker.
5. I like to think like a scientist.
6. Math is one of my favorite subjects.

Spatial Skills
7. I am good at visualizing objects and layouts from different angles.
8. I have the ability to create maps of spaces and locations in my mind.
9. If I had wanted to be, I think I could have been an architect.

Bodily-Kinesthetic Skills
10. I have great hand-eye coordination.
11. I excel at sports.
12. I am good at using my body to carry out an expression, as in dance.

Musical Skills
13. I play one or more musical instruments well.
14. I have a good "ear" for music.
15. I am good at making up songs.

Insightful Skills for Self-Understanding
16. I know myself well and have a positive view of myself.
17. I am in tune with my thoughts and feelings.
18. I have good coping skills.

Insightful Skills for Analyzing Others
19. I am very good at "reading" people.
20. I am good at collaborating with other people.
21. I am a good listener.

Naturalist Skills
22. I am good at observing patterns in nature.
23. I excel at identifying and classifying objects in the natural environment.
24. I understand natural and human-made systems.

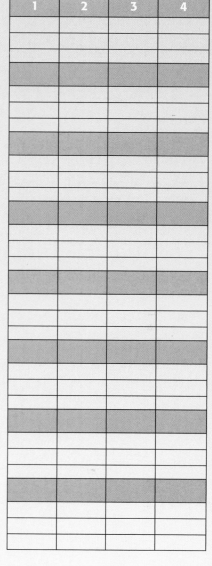

Scoring and Interpretation

Total your scores for each of the eight types of intelligence and place the totals in the blank that follows the label for each kind of intelligence. Which areas of intelligence are your strengths? In which are you the least proficient? It is highly unlikely that you will be strong in all eight areas or weak in all eight areas. By being aware of your strengths and weaknesses in different areas of intelligence, you can get a sense of which areas of teaching students will be the easiest and most difficult for you. If I (your author) had to teach musical skills, I would be in big trouble because I just don't have the talent. However, I do have reasonably good movement skills and spent part of my younger life playing and coaching tennis. If you are not proficient in some of Gardner's areas and you have to teach students in those areas, consider getting volunteers from the community to help you. For example, Gardner says that schools need to do a better job of calling on retired people, most of whom likely would be delighted to help students improve their skills in the domain or domains in which they are competent. This strategy also helps to link communities and schools with a sort of "intergenerational glue."

 Go to your Student Toolbox CD-ROM for an electronic version of this form.

Gardner	Sternberg	Mayer/Salovy/Goleman
Verbal	Analytical	
Mathematical		
Spatial		
Movement		
Musical		
Intrapersonal	Practical	Emotional
Interpersonal		
Naturalistic		
	Creative	

FIGURE 4.3 **Comparing Gardner's, Sternberg's, and Mayer/Salovy/Goleman's Approaches**

intrapersonal, and practical aspects of intelligence has generated a great deal of interest recently. It is called **emotional intelligence,** defined by Peter Salovy and John Mayer (1990) as the ability to monitor one's own and others' feelings and emotions, to discriminate among them, and to use this information to guide one's thinking and action.

The concept of emotional intelligence has been popularized by Daniel Goleman (1995). Goleman believes that when it comes to predicting a person's competence, IQ as measured by traditional intelligence tests matters less than emotional intelligence. In Goleman's view, emotional intelligence involves these four areas:

- *Developing emotional awareness*—such as the ability to separate feelings from actions
- *Managing emotions*—such as being able to control anger
- *Reading emotions*—such as taking the perspective of others
- *Handling relationships*—such as the ability to solve relationship problems

Evaluating the Multiple-Intelligences Approaches The multiple-intelligence theories have much to offer (Beachner & Pickett, 2001; Kornhaber, Fierros, & Veenema, 2004; Lopes, Cote, & Salovey, 2005). They have stimulated us to think more broadly about what makes up people's intelligence and competence. And they have motivated educators to develop programs that instruct students in different domains.

Figure 4.3 provides a comparison of Gardner's, Sternberg's, and Mayer/Salovy/Goleman's views. Notice that Gardner includes a number of types of intelligence that are not addressed by the other views and that Sternberg is unique in emphasizing creative intelligence.

Some critics say that Gardner's classification of such domains as musical skills as a type of intelligence is off base. They ask whether there might not be other skills domains that Gardner has left out. For example, there are outstanding chess players, prizefighters, writers, politicians, physicians, lawyers, ministers, and poets, yet we don't refer to chess intelligence, prizefighter intelligence, and so on. Other critics say that the research base has not yet been developed to support the eight intelligences of Gardner, the three intelligences of Sternberg, and the emotional intelligence of Mayer/Salovy/Goleman as the best way to characterize intelligence (Brody, 2000).

Gardner (1998)—the ultimate multiple-intelligences advocate—has himself even criticized the emotional intelligence advocates as going too far in including emotions in the concept of intelligence. He also believes that creativity should not be included in the

emotional intelligence The ability to monitor one's own and others' emotions and feelings, to discriminate among them, and to use this information to guide one's thinking and action.

concept of intelligence. Although he believes that understanding emotions and being creative are important aspects of human competence and functioning, Gardner says he thinks that emotional understanding and creativity are different from intelligence.

Controversies and Issues in Intelligence

The topic of intelligence is surrounded by controversy. Controversies include whether nature or nurture is more important in determining intelligence, whether individuals have a general intelligence and the extent to which intelligence tests predict success in school and occupations, how much intelligence tests are culturally biased, and whether IQ tests should be used to place children in particular schooling tracks.

Nature and Nurture   The **nature-nurture issue** involves the debate about whether development is primarily influenced by nature or by nurture. *Nature* refers to a child's biological inheritance, *nurture* to environmental experiences. "Nature" promoters claim that the most important influence on the child's development is biological inheritance. "Nurture" proponents claim that environmental experiences are the most important influence.

Some scientists proclaim that intelligence is primarily inherited and that environmental experiences play only a minimal role in its manifestation (Detterman, 2000; Herrnstein & Murray, 1994; Jensen, 1969). The emerging view of the nature-nurture issue is that many complicated qualities, such as intelligence, probably have some genetic loading that gives them a propensity for a particular developmental trajectory, such as low, average, or high intelligence. However, the actual development of intelligence requires more than just heredity.

Most experts today agree that the environment also plays an important role (Ceci & others, 1997; Okagaki, 2000; Sternberg & Grigorenko, 2001; Williams & Sternberg, 2002). This means that improving children's environments can raise their intelligence. It also means that enriching children's environments can improve their school achievement and the acquisition of skills needed for employment. Craig Ramey and his associates (1988) found that high-quality early educational day care (through five years of age) significantly raised the tested intelligence of young children from impoverished backgrounds. Positive effects of this early intervention were still evident in the intelligence and achievement of these students when they were thirteen and twenty-one years of age (Campbell & Ramey, 1994; Campbell & others, 2001; Ramey, Ramey, & Lanzi, 2001).

Another argument for the importance of environment in intelligence involves the increasing scores on IQ tests around the world. Scores on these tests have been increasing so fast that a high percentage of people regarded as having average intelligence in the early 1900s would be considered below average in intelligence today (Howard, 2001)(see figure 4.4 on page 118). If a representative sample of today's children took the Stanford-Binet test used in 1932, about one-fourth would be defined as very superior, a label usually accorded to fewer than 3 percent of the population (Horton, 2001). Because the increase has taken place in a relatively short period of time, it can't be due to heredity but, rather, might be due to such environmental factors as the explosion in information people are exposed to and the much higher percentage of the population receiving education.

Studies of schooling also reveal effects on intelligence (Ceci & Gilstrap, 2000; Christian, Bachnan, & Morrison, 2001). The biggest effects have been found when large groups of children have been deprived of formal education for an extended period of time, resulting in lower intelligence. In one study, the intellectual functioning of ethnic Indian children in South Africa, whose schooling was delayed by four years because of the unavailability of teachers, was investigated (Ramphal, 1962). Compared with children in nearby villages who had teachers, the Indian children whose entry into school was delayed by four years experienced a drop of five IQ points for each year of delay.

In one analysis of studies on schooling and intelligence, it was concluded that schooling and intelligence influence each other (Ceci & Williams, 1997). For example,

The Bell-Curve Controversy

nature-nurture issue *Nature* refers to an organism's biological inheritance, *nurture* to environmental influences. The "nature" proponents claim biological inheritance is the most important influence on development; the "nurture" proponents claim that environmental experiences are the most important.

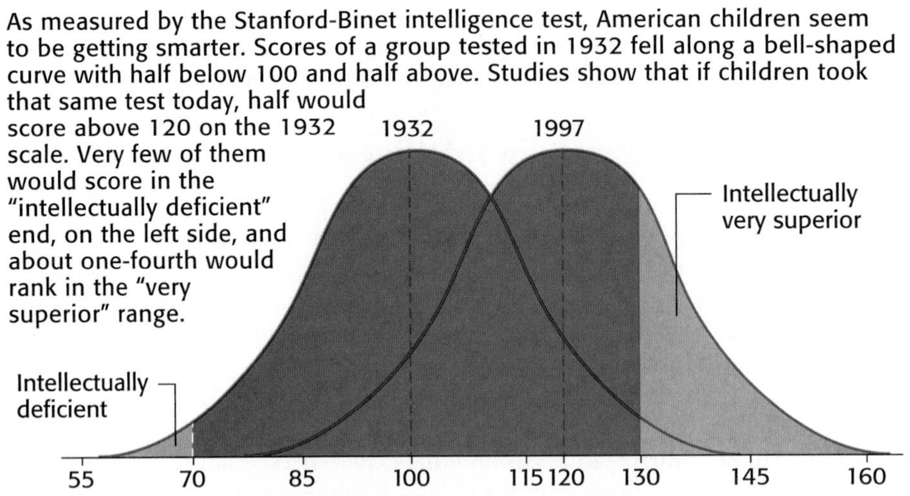

As measured by the Stanford-Binet intelligence test, American children seem to be getting smarter. Scores of a group tested in 1932 fell along a bell-shaped curve with half below 100 and half above. Studies show that if children took that same test today, half would score above 120 on the 1932 scale. Very few of them would score in the "intellectually deficient" end, on the left side, and about one-fourth would rank in the "very superior" range.

1932   1997

Intellectually very superior

Intellectually deficient

55   70   85   100   115 120   130   145   160

FIGURE 4.4 **Increasing IQ Scores from 1932 to 1997**

individuals who finish high school are more intelligent than those who drop out of school. This might be because brighter individuals stay in school longer because of genetically inherited higher intelligence, or it might be because the environmental influence of schooling contributes to their intelligence.

Further, intelligence test scores tend to rise during the school year and decline during the summer months (Ceci & Gilstrap, 2000). Also, children whose birthdays just make the cutoff point for school entrance temporarily have higher intelligence scores than those born just slightly later, who are a year behind them in school (Ceci & Gilstrap, 2000). Discontinuing schooling also produces lower intelligence (Harnqvist, 1968).

As the foregoing discussion has implied, the interactive effects of heredity and environment on intelligence are complex and dynamic, so much so that psychologist William Greenough (1997, 2000) says that to ask what's more important, nature or nurture, is like asking what's more important to a rectangle, its length or its width. We still do not know what, if any, specific genes actually promote or restrict a general level of intelligence. If such genes exist, they certainly are found both in children whose families and environments appear to promote the development of children's abilities and in children whose families and environments do not appear to be as supportive. Regardless of one's genetic background, growing up "with all the advantages" does not guarantee high intelligence or success, especially if those advantages are taken for granted. Nor does the absence of such advantages guarantee low intelligence or failure, especially if the family and child can make the most of whatever opportunities are accessible to them.

Do People Have a General Intelligence?   Recall the mention of a general intelligence factor called g from the start of our discussion of general intelligence. With all of the interest in multiple intelligences, it might seem that it is unwise to think about children having a general intelligence. However, a number of experts argue that not only do individuals have a general intelligence but it has real-world applications as a predictor of school and job success (Bouchard, 2004; Brody, 2000). For example, scores on what are claimed to be tests of general intelligence are substantially correlated with academic achievement and moderately correlated with work performance (Lubinski, 2000). Individuals with higher scores on tests designed to measure general intelligence tend to get higher-paying, more prestigious jobs (Wagner, 1997).

However, general IQ tests predict only about one-fourth of the variation in job success, with most variation being attributable to other factors such as motivation and education (Wagner & Sternberg, 1986). Further, the correlations between IQ and achievement decrease the longer people work at a job, presumably because as they gain more job experience they perform better (Hunt, 1995).

Experts on general intelligence agree that it includes abstract reasoning or thinking, the capacity to acquire knowledge, and problem-solving ability (Brody, 2000; Carroll, 1993). And, as we noted earlier, some experts who argue for the importance of general intelligence believe that individuals also have specific intellectual abilities (Brody, 2000). In one study, John Carroll (1993) conducted an extensive examination of intellectual abilities and concluded that while all intellectual abilities are related to each other, which supports the concept of general intelligence, there are many specialized abilities as well. Some of these specialized abilities, such as spatial abilities and mechanical abilities, are not adequately reflected in the curriculum of most schools.

Ethnicity and Culture   Are there ethnic differences in intelligence? Are conventional tests of intelligence biased, and if so, can we develop culture-fair tests?

Ethnic Comparisons   On average in the United States, children from African American and Latino families score below children from non-Latino White families on standardized intelligence tests. Most comparisons have focused on African Americans and Whites. African American schoolchildren score 10 to 15 points lower than White American schoolchildren (Neisser & others, 1996). Keep in mind that this is an average difference. Many African American children score higher than many White children. Estimates are that 15 to 25 percent of African American schoolchildren score higher than half of all White schoolchildren.

Are these differences based on heredity or environment? The consensus answer is environment (Brooks-Gunn, Klebanov, & Duncan, 1996; Ogbu & Stern, 2001; Onwuegbuzie & Daley, 2001). One reason to think so is that in recent decades, as African Americans have experienced improved social, economic, and educational opportunities, the gap between White and African American children on conventional intelligence tests has declined (Jones, 1984). Between 1977 and 1996, as educational opportunities for African Americans increased, the gap between their SAT scores and those of their White counterparts also shrank 23 percent (College Board, 1996). The gap especially narrows in college, where African American and White students often experience more similar educational environments than in the elementary and high school years (Myerson & others, 1998). Also, when children from disadvantaged African American families are adopted by more-advantaged middle-income families, their scores on intelligence tests are closer to the national average for middle-income children than to the national average for children from low-income families (Scarr & Weinberg, 1983).

Cultural Bias and Culture-Fair Tests   Many of the early tests of intelligence were culturally biased, favoring urban children over rural children, children from middle-income families over children from low-income families, and White children over minority children (Miller-Jones, 1989). The standards for the early tests were almost exclusively based on White, middle-socioeconomic-status children. Also, some of the items were obviously culturally biased. For example, one item on an early test asked what you should do if you find a three-year-old in the street. The "correct" answer was "Call the police." However, children from impoverished inner-city families might not choose this answer if they have had bad experiences with the police, and children living in rural areas might not have police nearby. The contemporary versions of intelligence tests attempt to reduce such cultural bias.

Another problem is that even if the content of test items is appropriate, the language in which they appear might not be (Serpell, 2000). Some children from ethnic minority groups will have trouble understanding the written language of the test. Yet another potential influence on intelligence test performance is **stereotype threat,** the anxiety that one's behavior might confirm a negative stereotype about one's group. For example, when African Americans take an intelligence test, they may experience anxiety about confirming the old stereotype that they are "intellectually inferior." Some studies have confirmed the existence of stereotype threat. African American students do more poorly on standardized tests if they believe they are being evaluated. If they believe the test

stereotype threat The anxiety that one's behavior might confirm a negative stereotype about one's group.

doesn't count, they perform as well as White students (Aronson, 2002; Aronson, Fried, & Good, 2002; Aronson & others, 1999; Steele & Aronson, 2004). However, some critics believe that the extent to which stereotype threat explains the testing gap has been exaggerated (Sackett, 2003; Sackett, Hardison, & Cullen, 2004.) The Diversity and Education interlude further explores possible IQ test bias.

Diversity and Education
Larry P. and the Controversy over Cultural Bias in IQ Tests

Larry P. is African American and poor. When he was six years old, he was placed in a class for the "educable mentally retarded" (EMR), which is supposed to mean that Larry learns much more slowly than average students. The primary reason Larry was placed in the EMR class was his very low score of 64 on an intelligence test.

Is there a possibility that the intelligence test Larry took was culturally biased? This question continues to be debated. The controversy has been the target of various lawsuits that challenge the use of standardized IQ tests to place African American students in EMR classes. The initial lawsuit, filed on Larry P.'s behalf in California, claimed that the IQ test underestimated his true learning ability. His lawyers argued that IQ tests place too much emphasis on verbal skills and fail to account for the backgrounds of African American students from low-income families and that Larry P. was incorrectly labeled as mentally retarded and might be burdened with that stigma forever.

As part of the lengthy court battle involving Larry P., six African American EMR students were independently retested by psychologists. The psychologists made sure that they established good rapport with the students and made special efforts to overcome the students' defeatism and distraction. For example, items were reworded in terms more consistent with the students' social background and recognition was given to nonstandard answers that showed a logical, intelligent approach to problems. This modified testing approach produced scores of 79 to 104—17 to 38 points higher than the students received when initially tested. In every case, the scores were above the ceiling for placement in an EMR class.

In Larry's case, the judge ruled that IQ tests are culturally biased and should not be used in decisions about placing students in EMR classes. However, in subsequent rulings, such as *Pase* v. *Hannon* in Illinois, judges have ruled that IQ tests are not culturally biased. Also, a task force established by the American Psychological Association concluded that IQ tests are not culturally biased (Neisser & others, 1996). The controversy continues.

Cultural Bias and Tests

Culture-fair tests are tests of intelligence that are intended to be free of cultural bias. Two types of culture-fair tests have been devised. The first includes items that are believed to be familiar to children from all socioeconomic and ethnic backgrounds or items that at least are familiar to the children taking the test. For example, a child might be asked how a bird and a dog are different, on the assumption that all children have been exposed to birds and dogs. The second type of culture-fair test has all of the verbal items removed. Figure 4.5 shows a sample from the Raven Progressive Matrices Test, which exemplifies this approach. Even though such tests are designed to be culture-fair, students with more education score higher on them than their less-educated counterparts.

These attempts to produce culture-fair tests remind us that conventional intelligence tests probably are culturally biased, yet the effort to create a truly culture-fair test has not yet succeeded. It is important to consider also that what is viewed as intelligent in one culture might not be thought of as intelligent in another culture (Lonner, 1990). In most Western cultures, students are considered intelligent if they are both smart (have considerable knowledge and can solve verbal problems) and fast (can process information

culture-fair tests Tests of intelligence that are intended to be free of cultural bias.

A 5

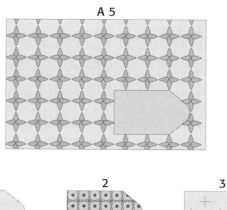

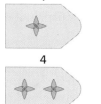
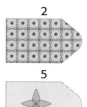
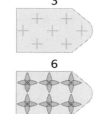

FIGURE 4.5 Sample Item from the Raven Progressive Matrices Test
Individuals are presented with a matrix arrangement of symbols, such as the one at the top of this figure, and must then complete the matrix by selecting the appropriate missing symbol from a group of symbols.

"You can't build a hut, you don't know how to find edible roots and you know nothing about predicting the weather. In other words, you do terribly on our I.Q. test."
© 2002 by Sydney Harris. Reprinted with permission.

quickly). In contrast, in the Buganda culture in Uganda, students who are wise, are slow in thought, and say the socially correct thing are considered intelligent. And in the widely dispersed Caroline Islands, one of the most important dimensions of intelligence is the ability to navigate by the stars.

Ability Grouping and Tracking   Another controversial issue is whether it is beneficial to use students' scores on an intelligence test to place them in ability groups. Two types of ability grouping have been used in education: between-class and within-class.

Between-Class Ability Grouping (Tracking)   **Between-class ability grouping (tracking)** consists of grouping students based on their ability or achievement. Tracking has long been used in schools as a way to organize students, especially at the secondary level (Slavin, 1990, 1995a). The positive view of tracking is that it narrows the range of skill in a group of students, making it easier to teach them. Tracking is said to prevent less-able students from "holding back" more talented students.

A typical between-class grouping in schools involves dividing students into a college preparatory track and a general track. Within the two tracks, further ability groupings might be made, such as two levels of math instruction for college preparatory students. Another form of tracking takes place when a student's abilities in different subject areas are taken into account. For example, the same student might be in a high-track math class and a middle-track English class.

Critics of tracking argue that it stigmatizes students who are consigned to low-track classes (Smith-Maddox & Wheelock, 1995). For example, students can get labeled as "low-track" or "the dummy group." Critics also say that low-track classrooms often have less-experienced teachers, fewer resources, and lower expectations (Wheelock, 1992). Further, critics stress that tracking is used to segregate students according to ethnicity and socioeconomic status because higher tracks have fewer students from ethnic minority and impoverished backgrounds. In this way, tracking can actually replay segregation

Tracking

between-class ability grouping (tracking) Grouping students based on their ability or achievement.

within schools. The detractors also argue that average and above-average students do not get substantial benefits from being grouped together.

Does research support the critics' contention that tracking is harmful to students? Researchers have found that tracking harms the achievement of low-track students (Brewer, Rees, & Argys, 1995; Slavin, 1990). However, tracking seems to benefit high-track students (such as those in a gifted program).

One variation of between-class ability grouping is the **nongraded (cross-age) program,** in which students are grouped by their ability in particular subjects regardless of their age or grade level (Fogarty, 1993). This type of program is used far more in elementary than in secondary schools, especially in the first three grades. For example, a math class might be composed of first-, second-, and third-graders grouped together because of their similar math ability. The **Joplin plan** is a standard nongraded program for instruction in reading. In the Joplin plan, students from second, third, and fourth grade might be placed together because of their similar reading level.

We mentioned that tracking has negative effects on low-track students. When tracks are present, it is especially important to give low-achieving students an opportunity to improve their academic performance and thus change tracks. In the San Diego County Public Schools, the Achieving Via Individual Determination (AVID) program provides support for underachieving students. Instead of being placed in a low track, they are enrolled in rigorous courses but are not left to achieve on their own. A comprehensive system of support services helps them succeed. For example, a critical aspect of the program is a series of workshops that teach students note-taking skills, question-asking skills, thinking skills, and communication skills. The students also are clustered into study groups and urged to help each other clarify questions about assignments. College students, many of them AVID graduates, serve as role models, coaches, and motivators for the students. At each AVID school, a lead teacher oversees a team of school counselors and teachers from every academic discipline. In the summer, these teams attend a week-long professional development institute at which experienced AVID teachers give workshops on effective teaching strategies. In recent years, the dropout rate in AVID schools has declined by more than one-third, and an amazing 99 percent of the AVID graduates have enrolled in college.

In sum, tracking is a controversial issue especially because of the restrictions it places on low-track students. Too often, scores on a single group IQ test are used to place students in a particular track. Researchers have found that group IQ tests are not good predictors of how well students will do in a particular subject area (Garmon & others, 1995).

In chapter 6, "Learners Who Are Exceptional," we will discuss issues that are closely related to ability grouping in our coverage of children with various disabilities and gifted children.

Teaching Strategies
For the Use of Tracking

1. *Use other measures of student knowledge and potential in particular subject areas to place students in ability groups rather than a group-administered IQ test.*
2. *Avoid labeling groups as "low," "middle," and "high."* Also avoid comparisons of groups.
3. *Don't form more than two or three ability groups.* You won't be able to give a larger number of groups adequate attention and instruction.
4. *Consider the students' placements in various ability groups as subject to review and change.* Carefully monitor students' performance, and if a low-track student progresses adequately, move the student to a higher group. If a high-track student is doing poorly, evaluate whether the high track is the right one for the student and decide what supports the student might need to improve performance.

nongraded (cross-age) program A variation of between-class ability grouping in which students are grouped by their ability in particular subjects, regardless of their age or grade level.

Joplin plan A standard nongraded program for instruction in reading.

5. *Especially consider alternatives to tracking for low-achieving students.* Throughout this book we will describe instructional strategies and support services for low-achieving students, such as those being used in the AVID program.

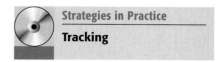

Strategies in Practice
Tracking

Within-Class Ability Grouping   **Within-class ability grouping** involves placing students in two or three groups within a class to take into account differences in students' abilities. A typical within-class ability grouping occurs when elementary school teachers place students in several reading groups based on their reading skills. A second-grade teacher might have one group using a third-grade, first-semester reading program; another using a second-grade, first-semester program; and a third group using a first-grade, second-semester program. Such within-class grouping is far more common in elementary than in secondary schools. The subject area most often involved is reading, followed by math. Although many elementary school teachers use some form of within-class ability grouping, there is no clear research support for this strategy.

❗ Review and Reflect

1 **Discuss the concept of intelligence, how it is measured, and some controversies about its use by educators.**

Review

- Precisely what do the concepts of intelligence and IQ mean? What did Binet and Wechsler contribute to the field of intelligence?
- What are some pros and cons of individual versus group tests of intelligence?
- What is Sternberg's triarchic theory of intelligence? What is Gardner's system of "frames of mind"? What is Mayer, Salovy, and Goleman's concept of emotional intelligence? How is each theory relevant to education? What are some contributions and criticisms of the multiple-intelligences approach?
- Where do most psychologists stand today on the nature-nurture debate about intelligence? Is there evidence for general intelligence? Why is there controversy about intelligence testing, culture, and grouping or tracking?

Reflect

- Suppose that you were about to teach a particular group of children for the first time and were handed intelligence test scores for every child in the class. Would you hesitate to look at the scores? Why or why not?

Learning Styles

LEARNING AND THINKING STYLES

Intelligence refers to ability. **Learning and thinking styles** are not abilities but, rather, preferred ways of using one's abilities (Drysdale, Ross, & Schuyltz, 2001; Sternberg, 1997). In fact, teachers will tell you that children approach learning and thinking in an amazing variety of ways. Teachers themselves also vary in their styles of learning and thinking.

None of us has just a single learning and thinking style; each of us has a profile of many styles. Individuals vary so much that literally hundreds of learning and thinking styles have been proposed by educators and psychologists. Our coverage of learning and thinking styles is not meant to be exhaustive but introduces two widely discussed sets of styles.

Dichotomies of Learning and Thinking Styles

Two of the most widely discussed style dichotomies in approaches to learning are impulsive/reflective and deep/surface.

within-class ability grouping Placing students in two or three groups within a class to take into account differences in students' abilities.

learning and thinking styles Individuals' preferences in how they use their abilities.

Through the Eyes of Teachers

Learning Styles and Different Forms of Reading

In teaching, I have long been aware of learning styles and realized that children learn in various ways. What is right for one may not be right for another. Sometimes a student will need to read a passage aloud to grasp and retain its meaning while the student next to her may need to have someone else read it. Still another student may need to block out all sound and read it silently several times, allowing the sight of the words to push the knowledge into her memory. Then there are those who may need to read it or have it read to them after which they must make something or draw something. For this reason, I try to provide a variety of activities for students to choose so several methods of learning will be covered.

Verna Rollins
Language Arts Teacher
West Middle School
Ypsilanti, Michigan

Impulsive/Reflective Styles **Impulsive/reflective styles,** also referred to as conceptual tempo, involve a student's tendency either to act quickly and impulsively or to take more time to respond and reflect on the accuracy of an answer (Kagan, 1965). Impulsive students often make more mistakes than reflective students.

Research on impulsivity/reflection has implications for education (Jonassen & Grabowski, 1993). Reflective students are more likely than impulsive students to do well at these tasks:

- Remembering structured information
- Reading comprehension and text interpretation
- Problem solving and decision making

Reflective students also are more likely than impulsive students to set their own learning goals and concentrate on relevant information. Reflective students usually have higher standards for performance. The evidence is strong that reflective students learn more effectively and do better in school than impulsive students.

In thinking about impulsive and reflective styles, keep in mind that although most children learn better when they are reflective rather than impulsive, some children are simply fast, accurate learners and decision makers. Reacting quickly is a bad strategy only if you come up with wrong answers. Also, some reflective children might ruminate forever about a problem and have difficulty getting closure. Teachers can encourage these children to retain their reflective orientation but arrive at more timely solutions. In chapter 7, "Behavioral and Social Cognitive Approaches," we will discuss a number of other strategies for helping students self-regulate their behavior.

Teaching Strategies
For Working with Impulsive Children

1. *Monitor students in the class to determine which ones are impulsive.*
2. *Talk with them about taking their time to think through an answer before they respond.*
3. *Encourage them to label new information as they work with it.*
4. *Model the reflective style as a teacher.*
5. *Help students set high standards for their performance.*
6. *Recognize when impulsive students start to take more time to reflect.* Compliment them on their improvement.
7. *Guide students in creating their own plan to reduce impulsivity.*

impulsive/reflective styles Also referred to as conceptual tempo, they involve a student's tendency either to act quickly and impulsively or to take more time to respond and reflect on the accuracy of the answer.

deep/surface styles Involve the extent to which students approach learning materials in a way that helps them understand the meaning of the materials (deep style) or as simply what needs to be learned (surface style).

Deep/Surface Styles **Deep/surface styles** involve the extent to which students approach learning materials in a way that helps them understand the meaning of the materials (deep style) or as simply what needs to be learned (surface style) (Marton, Hounsell, & Entwistle, 1984). Students who approach learning with a surface style fail to tie what they are learning into a larger conceptual framework. They tend to learn in a passive way, often rotely memorizing information. Deep learners are more likely to actively construct what they learn and give meaning to what they need to remember. Thus, deep learners take a constructivist approach to learning. Deep learners also are more likely to be self-motivated to learn, whereas surface learners are more likely to be motivated to learn because of external rewards, such as grades and positive feedback from the teacher (Snow, Corno, & Jackson, 1996).

Teaching Strategies
For Helping Surface Learners Think More Deeply

1. *Monitor students to determine which ones are surface learners.*
2. *Discuss with students the importance of not just rotely memorizing material.* Encourage them to connect what they are learning now with what they have learned in the past.
3. *Ask questions and give assignments that require students to fit information into a larger framework.* For example, instead of just asking students to name the capital of a particular state, ask them if they have visited the capital and what their experiences were, what other cities are located in that section of the United States, or how large or small the city is.
4. *Be a model who processes information deeply rather than just scratching the surface.* Explore topics in depth and talk about how the information you are discussing fits within a larger network of ideas.
5. *Avoid using questions that require pat answers.* Instead, ask questions that require students to deeply process information. Connect lessons more effectively with children's existing interests.

Evaluating Learning and Thinking Styles

Your classroom will have students with diverse learning and thinking styles. Remember not to confuse these styles with abilities, such as intelligence. Styles involve how students use their abilities.

It can be helpful to determine which students are impulsive thinkers and surface learners. Think of ways that you can help them to become more reflective and examine material in greater depth.

Learning and thinking styles may vary with the context and across schools, grades, and subjects. Howard Gardner (1993) said that a student may have an impulsive style in the musical realm but a reflective style when working on a jigsaw puzzle.

We chose to describe only two sets of learning and thinking styles, selecting those that appear to have the most direct, logical application to classroom learning and the best research base. Some critics argue that the research base for many learning and thinking styles has not been adequately developed (Brody, 2001).

 Review and Reflect

2 **Describe and evaluate learning and thinking styles.**

Review
- What is meant by *learning and thinking styles?* Describe impulsive/reflective and deep/surface styles. Is one style better than another? How?
- How can learning and thinking styles be evaluated?

Reflect
- Describe yourself or someone else you know well in terms of the learning and thinking styles presented in this section.

PERSONALITY AND TEMPERAMENT

We have seen that it is important to be aware of individual variations in children's cognition. It also is important to understand individual variations in their personality and temperament.

Personality

We make statements about personality all the time and prefer to be around people with certain types of personality. Let's examine just what the term *personality* means.

Personality refers to distinctive thoughts, emotions, and behaviors that characterize the way an individual adapts to the world. Think about yourself for a moment. What is your personality like? Are you outgoing or shy? considerate or caring? friendly or hostile? These are some of the characteristics involved in personality. As we see next, one view stresses that there are five main factors that make up personality.

The "Big Five" Personality Factors   As with intelligence, psychologists are interested in identifying the main dimensions of personality (Feist & Feist, 2002). Some personality researchers believe they have identified the **"big five" factors of personality,** the "supertraits" that are thought to describe the main dimensions of personality: openness, conscientiousness, extraversion, agreeableness, and neuroticism (emotional stability) (see figure 4.6). (Notice that if you create an acronym from these trait names, you get the word *OCEAN.*) A number of research studies point toward these factors as important dimensions of personality (Costa, 2000; Costa & McRae, 1998; McRae, 2001).

Thinking about personality in terms of the "big five" factors can give you a framework for thinking about the personalities of your students. Your students will differ in their emotional stability, how extraverted or introverted they are, how open to experience they are, how agreeable they are, and how conscientious they are. However, some experts believe that the "big five" factors do not capture all of personality. They argue that the range of personality also should include such factors as how positive (joyous, happy) or negative (angry, sad) students are, as well as how self-assertive they are.

Person-Situation Interaction   In discussing learning and thinking styles, we indicated that a student's style can vary according to the subject matter the student is learning or thinking about. The same is true for personality characteristics. According to the concept of **person-situation interaction,** the best way to characterize an individual's personality is not in terms of personal traits or characteristics alone but also in terms of the situation involved. Researchers have found that students choose to be in some situations and avoid others (Ickes, Snyder, & Garcia, 1997).

Suppose you have an extravert and an introvert in your class. According to the theory of person-situation interaction, you can't predict which one will show the best adaptation unless you consider the situation they are in. The theory of person-situation interaction predicts that the extravert will adapt best when he is asked to collaborate with others and that the introvert will adapt best when she is asked to carry out tasks independently. Similarly, the extravert likely will be happier when socializing with lots of people at a party, the introvert when in a more private setting alone or with a friend.

In sum, don't think of personality traits as always dooming a student to behave in a particular way across all situations. The context or situation matters (Burger, 2000; Derlega, Winstead, & Jones, 1999). Monitor situations in which students with varying personality characteristics seem to feel most comfortable and provide them with opportunities to learn in those situations. If a particular personality trait is detrimental to the student's school performance (perhaps one student is so introverted that he or she fears working in a group), think of ways you can support the student's efforts to change.

Temperament

Temperament is closely related to personality and to learning and thinking styles. **Temperament** is a person's behavioral style and characteristic ways of responding. Some

The "Big Five" Factors

personality Distinctive thoughts, emotions, and behaviors that characterize the way an individual adapts to the world.

"big five" factors of personality Emotional stability, extraversion, openness to experience, agreeableness, and conscientiousness.

person-situation interaction The view that the best way to conceptualize personality is not in terms of personal traits or characteristics alone but also in terms of the situation involved.

temperament A person's behavioral style and characteristic ways of responding.

Openness	**C**onscientiousness	**E**xtraversion	**A**greeableness	**N**euroticism (emotional stability)
• Imaginative or practical • Interested in variety or routine • Independent or conforming	• Organized or disorganized • Careful or careless • Disciplined or impulsive	• Sociable or retiring • Fun-loving or somber • Affectionate or reserved	• Softhearted or ruthless • Trusting or suspicious • Helpful or uncooperative	• Calm or anxious • Secure or insecure • Self-satisfied or self-pitying

FIGURE 4.6 **The "Big Five" Factors of Personality**
Each column represents a broad "supertrait" that encompasses more narrow traits and characteristics. Using the acronym OCEAN can help you to remember the big five personality factors (Openness, Conscientiousness, and so on).

students are active; others are calm. Some respond warmly to people; others fuss and fret. Such descriptions involve variations in temperaments.

Scientists who study temperament seek to find the best ways to classify temperaments. The most well-known classification was proposed by Alexander Chess and Stella Thomas (Chess & Thomas, 1977; Thomas & Chess, 1991). They believe that there are three basic styles, or clusters, of temperament:

- An **easy child** is generally in a positive mood, quickly establishes regular routines, and easily adapts to new experiences.
- A **difficult child** tends to react negatively, has aggressive tendencies, lacks self-control, and is slow to accept new experiences.
- A **slow-to-warm-up child** has a low activity level, is somewhat negative, shows low adaptability, and displays a low intensity of mood.

A difficult temperament or a temperament that reflects a lack of control can place a student at risk for problems. In one study, adolescents with a difficult temperament had unusually high incidences of drug abuse and stressful events (Tubman & Windle, 1995). In another study, a temperament factor labeled "out of control" (being irritable and distractible) assessed when children were three to five years of age was related to acting out and behavioral problems at thirteen to fifteen years of age (Caspi & others, 1995). Across the same age span, a temperament factor labeled "approach" (friendliness, eagerness to explore new situations) was associated with a low incidence of anxiety and depression.

New classifications of temperament continue to be forged. In a recent review of temperament, Mary Rothbart and John Bates (1998) concluded that, based on current research, the best framework for classifying temperament involves a revision of Chess and Thomas' categories (easy, difficult, and slow-to-warm-up). The classification of temperament now focuses more on (1) positive affect and approach, (2) negative affect, and (3) effortful control (self-regulation). There also is increased interest in examining how contexts, such as schools and classrooms, moderate the expression of temperament (Goldsmith & others, 2001; Sanson & Rothbart, 2002; Wachs & Kohnstamm, 2001).

Temperament

 Teaching Strategies
Linked to Children's Temperament

These are some teaching strategies related to students' temperaments (Sanson & Rothbart, 1995):

1. *Show attention to and respect for individuality.* Teachers need to be sensitive to the student's signals and needs. The goal of good teaching might be accomplished in

easy child A temperament style in which the child is generally in a positive mood, quickly establishes regular routines, and easily adapts to new experiences.

difficult child A temperament style in which the child tends to react negatively, has aggressive tendencies, lacks self-control, and is slow to accept new experiences.

slow-to-warm-up child A temperament style in which the child has a low activity level, is somewhat negative, shows low adaptability, and displays a low intensity of mood.

ENTER THE DEBATE

Should schools use intelligence tests for placement purposes?

one way with one student, in another way with another student, depending on the students' temperaments. Some temperament characteristics pose more teaching challenges than others. For example, a student's proneness to distress, as exhibited by frequent irritability, might contribute to avoidant or coercive interchanges with teachers.

2. *Consider the structure of the students' environment.* Crowded, noisy classrooms often pose greater problems for a "difficult" child than for an "easy" child. Fearful, withdrawn students often benefit from slower entry into new contexts.

3. *Be aware of problems that can emerge by labeling a child "difficult" and packaged programs for "difficult children."* Some books and programs for parents and teachers focus specifically on the child's temperament (Cameron, Hansen, & Rosen, 1989; Turecki & Tonner, 1989). Most of these focus on the difficult child. Acknowledging that some children are harder to teach than others is often helpful. Advice on how to handle a particular temperament also can be useful. However, whether a particular characteristic is truly "difficult" depends on its fit with the environment, so the problem does not necessarily rest with the child. As with labeling a child as more or less intelligent, labeling the child as "difficult" has the danger of becoming a self-fulfilling prophecy. Also keep in mind that temperament can be modified to some degree (Sanson & Rothbart, 2002).

Teaching Experience

- **Differentiating Instruction**
- **Learning About Individual Students**
- **Working with Students with Diverse Needs**
- **Differentiating Instruction**
- **Meeting Individual Needs**

Review and Reflect

3 **Define personality, identify the "big five" factors of personality, and discuss person-situation interaction. Also, define temperament, identify three types of children's temperament, and evaluate teaching strategies linked to children's temperament.**

Review

- What is meant by the concept of personality? What are the "big five" factors of personality? What does the idea of person-situation interaction suggest about personality?

- How is temperament different from personality? Describe an "easy child," a "difficult child," and a "slow-to-warm-up" child. What are some good teaching strategies related to children's temperament?

Reflect

- Describe yourself in terms of the "big five" personality factors. In your K–12 education, how aware do you think your teachers were of your personality strengths and weaknesses? Might things have been different if they had known you better?

This chapter has been about individual variations. Because individual variations are so important in effectively teaching children, we will address them throughout the book. For example, in chapter 6 we will focus on teaching exceptional students, including those with a learning disability and those who are gifted. Also, in chapter 5 we will explore individual variations in students' culture, ethnicity, socioeconomic status, and gender.

Mr. Washington and his colleague Ms. Kaufman had just attended a workshop on adapting instruction to children's multiple intelligences. Ms. Jacobson and her colleague Mr. Adams had just attended a workshop on adapting instruction to cover Gardner's eight intelligences, or frames of mind. The four met in the teachers' workroom and were discussing what they had learned.

"Well," said Mr. Washington, "this certainly explains why some students seem to want to sit and listen to me talk, while others like to be more actively involved. Joe's obviously an executive type. He likes lectures. Martha, on the other hand, must be legislative. She just loves to work on projects and can't stand it when I tell her how to do things."

"No, I don't think so," Ms. Jacobson replied. "I think Joe's high in verbal intelligence. That's why he can make sense out of your lectures. He writes well, too. Martha likes to do things with her hands. She's higher in spatial and bodily-kinesthetic intelligence."

Mr. Washington responded, "No, no, no. Learning styles explain their differences much better. Here, look at this."

At that point, Mr. Washington showed Ms. Jacobson the handouts from the workshop he and Ms. Kaufman had attended. Mr. Adams got out the handouts from the workshop he and Ms. Jacobson had attended as well. They began comparing notes. All four of them recognized students in each of the schemes in the handouts. In fact, they could recognize the same student in both sets of handouts.

Just then Mrs. Peterson and Mrs. Darby walked into the room. They were very excited about a graduate class they were taking at a nearby university.

Mrs. Peterson said, "You know, I never thought about personality when considering teaching methods. It's no wonder Martha doesn't behave terribly well in my class. She's just too impulsive for the kind of structure I have."

Ms. Jacobson was dismayed. "You mean they're telling you we have to adapt our classrooms to the students' personalities now, too?!" she asked.

Mr. Adams also was upset. "Gosh," he said, "just when I thought I had it all figured out. Used to be we just had to consider IQ. Now all this. We have 25 kids in our classes. How can we possibly adapt to all these differences? What are we supposed to do, have 25 different lesson plans? Maybe we should do some kind of profile on them and then group them by profile. What do you think, guys?"

- What are the issues in this case?
- To what extent should teachers adapt their instruction to the strengths, learning styles, and personalities of their students? Why?
- What will you do in your classroom to accommodate individual differences such as students' intellectual strengths, learning styles, and personalities?
- What other individual differences do you think you might have to accommodate? How will you do this?

Reach Your Learning Goals

1 Discuss the concept of intelligence, how it is measured, and some controversies about its use by educators.

- Intelligence consists of problem-solving skills and the ability to adapt to and learn from life's everyday experiences. Interest in intelligence often focuses on individual differences and assessment. Binet and Simon developed the first intelligence test. Binet developed the concept of mental age, and Stern created the concept of IQ as = MA/CA × 100. The Stanford-Binet score distribution approximates a normal curve. The Wechsler scales also are widely used to assess intelligence. They yield an overall IQ, as well as verbal and performance IQs.

- Group tests are more convenient and economical, but they have a number of drawbacks (lack of opportunities to establish rapport, distraction from other students). A group intelligence test should always be supplemented with other relevant information when decisions are made about students. This also holds for an individual intelligence test.

- Spearman proposed that people have a general intelligence (g) and specific types of intelligence (s). According to Sternberg's triarchic theory of intelligence, intelligence comes in three forms: analytical, creative, and practical. Gardner believes there are eight types of intelligence: verbal, mathematical, spatial, bodily-kinesthetic, musical, insight about others, insight about self, and naturalist. Project Spectrum and the Key School involve educational applications of Gardner's theory of multiple intelligences. Mayer, Salovy, and Goleman believe emotional intelligence is an important aspect of being a competent person. These approaches have much to offer, stimulating teachers to think more broadly about what makes up a student's competencies. However, they have been criticized along the lines of including some skills that should not be classified under intelligence and for the lack of a research base to support the approaches.

- Four controversies and issues related to intelligence are (1) the nature-nurture question of how heredity and environment interact to produce intelligence, (2) whether people have a general intelligence, (3) how fairly intelligence testing applies across cultural and ethnic groups, and (4) whether students should be grouped according to ability (tracking). It is especially important to recognize that intelligence tests are an indicator of current performance, not fixed potential.

2 Describe and evaluate learning and thinking styles.

- Styles are not abilities but, rather, preferred ways of using abilities. Each individual has a number of learning and thinking styles. Impulsive/reflective styles also are referred to as conceptual tempo. This dichotomy involves a student's tendency to act quickly and impulsively or to take more time to respond and reflect on the accuracy of an answer. Impulsive students typically make more mistakes than reflective students. Deep/surface styles involve the extent to which students approach learning in a way that helps them understand the meaning of materials (deep style) or as simply what needs to be learned (surface style).

- Every classroom has students with diverse learning and thinking styles, and it can be helpful to determine which students' styles need to be modified to benefit their learning. Some critics argue that the research base for learning and thinking styles has not been adequately developed.

3 Define personality, identify the "big five" factors of personality, and discuss person-situation interaction. Also, define temperament, identify three types of children's temperament, and evaluate teaching strategies linked to children's temperament.

- *Personality* refers to distinctive thoughts, emotions, and behaviors that characterize the way an individual adapts to the world. Psychologists have identified the "big five" personality factors: emotional stability, extraversion, openness to experience, agreeableness, and conscientiousness. The "big five" factors give teachers a framework for thinking about a student's personality characteristics. The concept of person-situation interaction states that the best way to characterize an individual's personality is not in terms of traits alone but also in terms of both the traits and the situations involved.

- *Temperament* refers to a person's behavioral style and characteristic way of responding. Chess and Thomas believe there are three basic temperament styles, or clusters: easy, difficult, and slow-to-warm-up. A difficult temperament places a child at risk for problems. In education involving students' temperaments, teachers can show attention to and respect for individuality, consider the structure of a student's environment, and be aware of the problems involved when labeling a student as "difficult" and packaged programs for "difficult children."

KEY TERMS

 PORTFOLIO ACTIVITIES

Now that you have a good understanding of this chapter, complete these exercises to expand your thinking.

Independent Reflection

Your Multiple Intelligences. Evaluate your own intelligence profile according to Gardner. In what frames of mind do you come out strongest? In which of Sternberg's three areas do you feel you are the strongest? Write about your self-evaluation below. (INTASC: Principles *2, 3*)

Collaborative Work

Personality Profiles. Form a group of five or six students from your class and have one person identify his or her personality and temperament traits. Have other members do the same, in turn.

After all have presented, discuss how the individuals in your group are similar or different. How will your personalities and temperaments translate into teaching styles? Write about this experience below. (INTASC: Principles *2, 3*)

Research/Field Experience Reflections

Learning Styles in the Classroom. Interview several teachers about students' different learning and thinking styles. Ask them what teaching strategies they use to accommodate these differences in students. Write a synopsis of your interviews below. (INTASC: Principles *2, 3, 4, 9*)

 Go to the Online Learning Center for downloadable portfolio templates.

 TAKING IT TO THE NET

1. How could you conduct a lesson about Howard Gardner's theory of multiple intelligences in your classroom? Why do you think it is important for students to be aware of this theory and its implications for education and society? How could you involve students in planning lessons and projects that utilize many learning styles?

2. What is your learning style? Take an online test to discover if you are more active or reflective, more visual or verbal, and more sequential or global. In what ways do you think your learning style will impact your teaching style in the classroom?

3. How would you classify your temperament in relation to the "big five" personality traits—easygoing or industrious, private or outgoing, critical or agreeable, resilient or reactive, practical or inquisitive? What are the implications of your personality traits in the classroom? What strengths do you think a teacher with these traits would have? What weaknesses or challenges?

    Connect to the Online Learning Center to explore possible answers.

STUDY, PRACTICE, AND SUCCEED

 Go to chapter 4 on the Online Learning Center at www.mhhe.com/santrockedu2e to access the student study guide with practice quizzes, web links, portfolio resources, PowerWeb articles and news feeds, and the online resources referenced in the chapter.

 Go to your Student Toolbox CD-ROM to access the resources and activities referenced in the chapter and

• Resources to help you prepare for the **PRAXIS II™** exam

• **Application Resources,** including additional *Crack the Case* studies, electronic versions of the *Self-Assessments,* Application Exercises, and Site Observation Questions
• **Study Resources,** including Learning Goals, the Chapter Summary, a *Test Your Learning* exercise, and multiple-choice, true/false, matching, key terms, and short-answer quizzes
• **Professional Resources,** including a Lesson Plan Builder and *Bibliomaker*

5 Sociocultural Diversity

> We need every human gift and cannot afford to neglect any gift because of artificial barriers of sex or race or class or national origin.

—Margaret Mead
American Anthropologist,
20th Century

Chapter Outline

Culture and Ethnicity

Culture
Socioeconomic Status
Ethnicity
Language Issues

Multicultural Education

Empowering Students
Culturally Relevant Teaching
Issues-Centered Education
Improving Relationships Among Children from Different Ethnic Groups
The Issue of Whether a Core of "White" Values Should Be Taught

Gender

Views on Gender Development
Gender Stereotyping, Similarities, and Differences
Gender-Role Classification
Gender in Context
Eliminating Gender Bias

Chapter Learning Goals After you have completed your study of this chapter, you should be able to reach these learning goals:

1 **Discuss how variations in culture, socioeconomic status, and ethnic background might raise special classroom needs.**

2 **Describe some ways to promote multicultural education.**

3 **Explain the various facets of gender, including similarities and differences in boys and girls; discuss gender issues in teaching.**

Teaching Stories Margaret Longworth

Margaret Longworth taught high school for a number of years and was a teacher of the year. She recently moved to the middle school level and currently teaches language arts at West Middle School in St. Lucie, Florida. When considering the sociocultural diversity of students, she believes it is important for teachers to make schools "user friendly" for parents. In her words,

> Many parents—especially ethnic minority parents of color—are very intimidated by schools. They think teachers know everything. Principals know everything. And God forbid that they ever would need to approach the school board. To combat this intimidation, I became "user friendly." Many students and parents center their lives around the church in my community. So, to break the barriers between school and home, my Haitian paraprofessional began setting up meetings for me at the Haitian churches. The churches gave me their Sunday evening services. After they completed their preliminaries, they turned the service over to me. Through the assistance of an interpreter, I presented opportunities to help them develop academic and life skills through education. I talked with them about special education classes, gifted classes, language programs, and scholarships, and encouraged them to keep their children in school. In turn, they felt confident enough to ask me about different happenings at school. Because of the parent school church connections that I was able to build up, I rarely had a discipline problem. If I did have to call

parents, they would leave work or whatever they were doing and show up in my classroom. Many of these parents developed a relationship with the principal and guidance counselor and felt free to talk with school officials.

Margaret Longworth believes that in the classroom the key to improving children's interethnic relations is understanding. She comments:

> Understanding other persons' points of view requires spending time with them and getting to know them—how they think and feel. As students talk with each other and begin to appreciate each other, they soon learn that in many ways they aren't that different after all.

An indication of Margaret Longworth's success as teacher is the note Marie Belvillius, a Haitian American high school student, recently sent to her:

> When I looked out the window I'd see darkness. When I looked at the sky I would see shadows of sadness. All the crazy things in this world make me wonder about the madness. Since you came into our lives you have given us happiness. You showed us how to turn our back on sadness and madness. A lot of us have done some stupid or crazy things. But you didn't give up on us. You showed us what we are capable of. You never let us down. I'd like to say: THANK YOU.

Ours is a multicultural world of diverse backgrounds, customs, and values. Questions about how best to educate boys and girls from diverse ethnic and socioeconomic backgrounds are of considerable interest today.

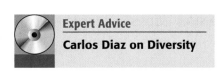

Expert Advice

Carlos Diaz on Diversity

Video Observation: Understanding Diversity

CULTURE AND ETHNICITY

The students in the schools of Fairfax County, Virginia, near Washington, DC, come from 182 countries and speak more than a hundred languages. Although the Fairfax County schools are a somewhat extreme example, they are harbingers of what is coming to America's schools. We can predict that by the year 2025, 50 percent of all public school students will be from backgrounds that are currently classified as "minority." This challenges current definitions of the term. It also points to an important educational goal of helping students develop respect for people from different cultural and ethnic backgrounds (Banks, 2003; Koppelman & Goodhart, 2005; Nieto, 2004; Sheets, 2005).

In this section, we will explore diversity in terms of cultures, socioeconomic status, and ethnicity. We'll also examine language issues, including the debate about bilingual education.

Culture

culture The behavior patterns, beliefs, and all other products of a particular group of people that are passed on from generation to generation.

Culture refers to the behavior patterns, beliefs, and all other products of a particular group of people that are passed on from generation to generation. These products result from the interactions among groups of people and their environments over many years (Chun, Organista, & Marin, 2002; Thomas, 2000). A cultural group can be as large as the United States or as small as an isolated Amazon tribe. Whatever its size, the group's culture influences the behavior of its members (Berry, 2000; Matsumoto, 2004).

Psychologist Donald Campbell and his colleagues (Brewer & Campbell, 1976; Campbell & LeVine, 1968) found that people in all cultures tend to

- believe that what happens in their culture is "natural" and "correct" and what happens in other cultures is "unnatural" and "incorrect,"
- perceive their cultural customs as universally valid,
- behave in ways that favor their cultural group,
- feel proud of their cultural group, and
- feel hostile toward other cultural groups.

Psychologists and educators who study culture are often interested in comparing what happens in one culture with what happens in one or more other cultures. **Cross-cultural studies** involve such comparisons, providing information about the degree to which people are similar and to what degree certain behaviors are specific to certain cultures.

Comparisons of American students with Chinese, Japanese, and Taiwanese students revealed that American students tend to go about their work more independently, whereas Asian students are more likely to work in groups (Stevenson, 1995). These differences in cultures have been described with two terms: *individualism* and *collectivism* (Triandis, 2000, 2001). **Individualism** refers to a set of values that give priority to personal goals rather than to group goals. Individualist values include feeling good, personal distinction, and independence. **Collectivism** consists of a set of values that support the group. Personal goals are subordinated to preserve group integrity, interdependence of the group's members, and harmonious relationships. Many Western cultures such as those of the United States, Canada, Great Britain, and the Netherlands are described as individualistic. Many Eastern cultures such as those of China, Japan, India, and Thailand are labeled collectivistic. Mexican culture also has stronger collectivistic characteristics than U.S. culture. However, the United States has many collectivistic subcultures, such as Chinese American and Mexican American.

Many of psychology's basic concepts have developed in individualistic cultures such as found in the United States. Consider the flurry of *self*-terms in psychology that have an individualistic focus: self-actualization, self-esteem, self-concept, self-efficacy, self-reinforcement, self-criticism, self-serving bias, self-doubt, and so on. These self-terms all were created by American psychologists, leading some critics to argue that American psychology is strongly tilted toward individualistic rather than collectivist values (Lonner, 1990).

Humans always have lived in groups, whether large or small. They always have needed one another for survival. Critics argue that the Western emphasis on individualism undermines the human species' need for relatedness (Kagiticibasi, 1996). Some social scientists believe that many problems in Western cultures have intensified because of the cultural emphasis on individualism. Compared with collectivistic cultures, individualistic cultures tend to have higher rates of suicide, drug abuse, crime, adolescent pregnancy, divorce, child abuse, and mental disorders (Triandis, 1994, 2000). However, regardless of their cultural background, people need a positive sense of self and connectedness to others to develop fully as human beings (Brown & Kysilka, 2002).

Teaching Strategies
For Working with Students from Individualistic and Collectivistic Backgrounds

You yourself come from a cultural background that has individualistic or collectivistic leanings, or in some cases possibly both. As a teacher, you will need to interact effectively with students, parents, teachers, and school personnel who come from individualistic and collectivistic backgrounds.

cross-cultural studies Studies that compare what happens in one culture with what happens in one or more other cultures; they provide information about the degree to which people are similar and to what degree behaviors are specific to certain cultures.

individualism A set of values that give priority to personal rather than to group goals.

collectivism A set of values that support the group.

If you are an individualist, these strategies will help you interact more effectively with students, parents, and school personnel from collectivistic cultures (Triandis, Brislin, & Hui, 1988):

1. *Pay more attention to group memberships.*
2. *Place more emphasis on cooperation than on competition.*
3. *If you have to criticize, do so carefully and only in private.* Criticizing people from a collectivistic culture in public places causes them to "lose face."
4. *Cultivate long-term relationships.* Be patient. People in collectivistic cultures like dealing with "old friends."

If you are a collectivist, these strategies will help you interact more effectively with students, parents, and school personnel from individualistic cultures (Triandis, Brislin, & Hui, 1988):

1. *Compliment the person more than you are used to doing in your culture.*
2. *Avoid feeling threatened if the individualist acts competitively.*
3. *It is okay to talk about your accomplishments and be less modest than you are used to being, but don't boast.*
4. *Recognize that individualists don't value allegiance to the group as much as you do.*

Socioeconomic Status

Most countries have many subcultures. One of the most common ways of categorizing subcultures involves socioeconomic status. **Socioeconomic status (SES)** refers to the categorization of people according to their economic, educational, and occupational characteristics. In the United States, the most attention is paid to differences between low and middle SES and the persistence of poverty. Socioeconomic status carries certain inequities. Low-SES individuals often have less education, less power to influence a community's institutions (such as schools), and fewer economic resources.

The Extent of Poverty in America   In a report on the state of America's children, the Children's Defense Fund (1992) described what life is like for all too many children. When sixth-graders in a poverty-stricken area of St. Louis were asked to describe a perfect day, one boy said that he would erase the world, then sit and think. Asked if he wouldn't rather go outside and play, the boy responded, "Are you kidding, out there?"

In 2000, 16 percent of U.S. children lived in poverty (Children's Defense Fund, 2000). In 1998, the poverty line for a family of four was an income of $16,450. The poverty rate for U.S. children is almost twice as high as in other industrialized nations. For example, Canada has a child poverty rate of 9 percent; Sweden, 2 percent. The U.S. child poverty rate is especially high for female-headed families—just short of 50 percent. More than 40 percent of African American and almost 40 percent of Latino children currently live below the poverty line. Compared with non-Latino White children, children of color are more likely to experience persistent poverty over many years. Nonetheless, in terms of actual numbers, there are more non-Latino White children (almost 9 million) living below the poverty line than African American children (almost 4 million) or Latino children (also almost 4 million) living in poverty, because there are far more non-Latino White children overall in the United States.

Educating Students from Low-SES Backgrounds   Children in poverty often face problems at home and at school that compromise their learning (Blumenfeld & others, 2005; Books, 2004; Cooper & others, 2005; Leventhal & Brooks-Gunn, 2004; Magnuson & Duncan, 2002; McLoyd, 2005). A recent review of the environment of childhood poverty concluded that compared with their economically more-advantaged counterparts, poor children experience these adversities (Evans, 2004, p. 77):

Children's Defense Fund

Poverty and Learning

Urban Education and Children in Poverty

socioeconomic status (SES) The categorization of people according to their economic, educational, and occupational characteristics.

- Exposure "to more family turmoil, violence, separation from their families, instability, and chaotic households" (Emery & Laumann-Billings, 1998).
- "Less social support, and their parents are less responsive and more authoritarian" (Bo, 1994; Cochran & others, 1990).
- "Read to relatively infrequently, watch more TV, and have less access to books and computers" (Bradley & others, 2001; Hart & Risley, 1995).
- Schools and child care facilities that are inferior and parents who "are less involved in their children's school activities" (Benveniste, Carnoy, & Rothstein, 2003; U.S. Department of Health and Human Services, 1999).
- Air and water that are more polluted and homes that "are more crowded, more noisy, and of lower quality" (Myers, Baer, & Choi, 1996).
- More dangerous and physically deteriorating neighborhoods with less adequate municipal services (Brody & others, 2001; Sampson, Raudenbush, & Earls, 1997).

These two studies illustrate how poverty can negatively impact learning and development:

- One study compared the home language environments of three-year-old children from professional and welfare families (Hart & Risley, 1995). All of the children developed normally in terms of learning to talk and acquiring all of the forms of English and basic vocabulary. However, there were enormous differences in the sheer amount of language to which the children were exposed and the level of language development the children eventually attained. As can be seen in figure 5.1 on page 138, professional parents talked much more to their young children than welfare parents talked to their young children, and this difference was linked with the vocabulary development of the children.
- Another study of more than 1,200 adolescents twelve to fourteen years of age examined the role of poverty in math and reading achievement (Eamon, 2002). Poverty was related to lower math and reading scores through its association with less cognitively stimulating and supportive home environments. The study also found that poverty was related to behavior problems at school.

Through the Eyes of Students

Lafayette and Pharoah

Ten-year-old Lafayette lives in an impoverished housing project in Chicago. His father has a drug habit and has trouble holding down a job. Lafayette lives with his mother.

The housing project where Lafayette lives is not safe. Lafayette told his friend, "You grow up 'round it. There are a lot of people in the projects who say they're not gonna do drugs, that they're not gonna drop out of school, that they won't be on the streets. But they're doing it now. Never say never. But I say never. My older brother didn't set a good example for me, but I'll set a good example for my younger brother."

A few days later, the police came to get his seventeen-year-old brother, Terrence, because he had been identified as a robbery suspect. The police came into the apartment and handcuffed Terrence in front of Lafayette and his younger brother, seven-year-old Pharoah, who told his mother, "I'm just too young to understand how life really is."

Several months later, their mother herded Lafayette and Pharoah into the hallway, where they crouched against the walls to avoid stray bullets. Lafayette told his mother, "If we don't get away, someone's gonna end up dead. I feel it." Shortly thereafter, a nine-year-old friend of the boys was shot in the back of the head as he was walking into the building where he lived. The bullet was meant for someone else (Kotlowitz, 1991).

Clearly, Lafayette and Pharoah face a lot of hurdles in being able to make the transition from childhood to adulthood competently. They live in a violent, decaying neighborhood, have older siblings who already have dropped out of school and who are engaging in delinquency, don't have a quiet place to do homework or have anyone in their family who can help them with it, and are growing up in a family in which education has not had a high priority. If you were a teacher in the inner-city school they attend, what would you do to help Lafayette and Pharoah overcome such challenging obstacles to their educational success?

The schools that children from impoverished backgrounds attend often have fewer resources than schools in higher-income neighborhoods (Shade, Kelly, & Oberg, 1997). Schools in low-income areas are more likely to have more students with lower achievement test scores, lower graduation rates, and lower percentages of students going to college. School buildings and classrooms are often old, crumbling, and poorly maintained. They are also more likely to be staffed by young teachers with less experience than schools in higher-income neighborhoods, although federal aid has helped improve learning in some schools located in low-income areas. Schools in low-income areas also are more likely to encourage rote learning, whereas schools in higher-income areas are more likely to work with children to improve their thinking skills (Spring, 2002). In sum, far too many schools in low-income neighborhoods provide students with environments that are not conducive to effective learning.

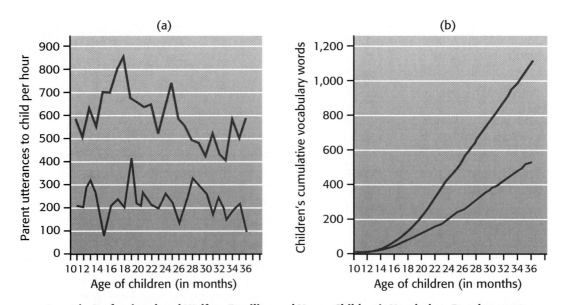

FIGURE 5.1 Language Input in Professional and Welfare Families and Young Children's Vocabulary Development
(*a*) Parents from professional families talked with their young children more than parents from welfare families. (*b*) Children from professional families developed vocabularies that were twice as large as those from welfare families. Thus, by the time children went to preschool, they already had experienced considerable differences in language input in their families and had developed different levels of vocabulary depending on the socioeconomic context in which they had lived.

In *Savage Inequalities*, Jonathan Kozol (1991) vividly described some of the problems that children of poverty face in their neighborhood and at school. Here are some of Kozol's observations in one inner-city area. East St. Louis, Illinois, which is 98 percent African American, has no obstetric services, no regular trash collection, and few jobs. Nearly one-third of the families live on less than $7,500 a year, and 75 percent of its population lives on welfare of some form. Blocks upon blocks of housing consist of dilapidated, skeletal buildings. Residents breathe the chemical pollution of nearby Monsanto Chemical Company. Raw sewage repeatedly backs up into homes. Lead from nearby smelters poisons the soil. Child malnutrition is common. Fear of violence is real. The problems of the streets spill over into the schools, where sewage also backs up from time to time. Classrooms and hallways are old and unattractive, athletic facilities inadequate. Teachers run out of chalk and paper, the science labs are 30 to 50 years out of date, and one school's heating system has never worked right. A history teacher has 110 students but only 26 books. Kozol says that anyone who visits places like East St. Louis, even for a brief time, comes away profoundly shaken. After all, these are innocent children who have done nothing to deserve such terrible conditions.

Kozol's interest was in describing what life is like in the nation's inner-city neighborhoods and schools, which are predominantly African American and Latino. Kozol argues that many inner-city schools are still segregated, are grossly underfunded, and do not provide anywhere near adequate opportunities for children to learn effectively. However, as we indicated earlier, there are many non-Latino White children who live in poverty, many in suburban or rural areas.

Another message from Kozol's observations is that although children in low-income neighborhoods and schools often experience many inequities, these children and their families also have many strengths, including courage. Parents in such impoverished circumstances may intensely pursue ways to get more effective teachers and better opportunities for their children.

One recent trend in antipoverty programs is two-generational intervention (McLoyd, 1998, 2000). This involves providing both services for children (such as educational day care or preschool education) and services for parents (such as adult education, literacy training, and job skills training). Recent evaluations of the two-generation programs suggest that they have more positive effects on parents than they do on children (St. Pierre,

In his book *Savage Inequalities,* Jonathan Kozol vividly portrayed the problems that children of poverty face in their neighborhood and at school. *What are some of these problems?*

Layzer, & Barnes, 1996). Also discouraging for the education of these children is that when the two-generational programs show benefits, they are more likely to be health benefits than cognitive gains. To learn about one effective program for intervening in the lives of children living in poverty, read the Diversity and Education interlude.

Jonathan Kozol

Diversity and Education
The Quantum Opportunities Program

A downward trajectory is not inevitable for students living in poverty. One potential path for these students is to become involved with a caring mentor. The Quantum Opportunities Program, funded by the Ford Foundation, was a four-year, year-round mentoring effort (Carnegie Council on Adolescent Development, 1995). The ninth-grade students in the program were from ethnic minority, poverty backgrounds. Each day for four years, mentors provided sustained support, guidance, and concrete assistance to the students.

The Quantum program required students to participate in these kinds of activities:

• Academic-related activities outside school hours, including reading, writing, math, science, social studies, peer tutoring, and computer skills training
• Community service projects, including tutoring elementary school students, cleaning up the neighborhood, and volunteering in hospitals, nursing homes, and libraries
• Cultural enrichment and personal development activities, including life skills training and planning for college or a job

In exchange for their commitment to the program, students were offered financial incentives that encouraged their participation, completion, and long-range planning. A stipend of $1.33 was given to students for each hour they participated in these activities. For every 100 hours of education, service, or development activities completed, a student received a $100 bonus. The average cost per participant was $10,600 for all four years, which was one-half the cost of only one year in prison.

An evaluation of the Quantum project compared the mentored students with a nonmentored control group. Follow-up studies found that 63 percent of the mentored students graduated from high school but only 42 percent of the control group did; 42 percent of the mentored students were enrolled in college, but only 16 percent of the control group were; and compared with the mentored group, the control group students were twice as likely to receive food stamps or welfare and had more arrests.

Teaching Strategies
For Working with Children in Poverty

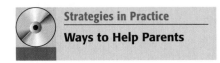

Strategies in Practice
Ways to Help Parents

1. *Improve thinking skills.* If you teach in a school in a low-income neighborhood, adopt the goal of helping children improve their thinking skills.
2. *Don't overdiscipline.* Where poverty and other factors make it difficult to maintain safety and discipline, recognize the right, workable tradeoff between discipline and children's freedom. We will say more about classroom discipline in chapter 14, "Managing the Classroom."
3. *Make student motivation a high priority.* Because many children from low-income backgrounds might come to your class not having experienced high parental standards for achievement and thus might lack the motivation to learn, pay special attention to motivating these children to learn. We will address this topic further in chapter 13, "Motivation, Teaching, and Learning."
4. *Think about ways to help parents.* Recognize that many parents in poor areas are not able to provide much academic supervision or assistance to their children. Look for ways to support the parents who can be trained and helped to do so. Find ways that parents can contribute to their children's education even if they can't read themselves, can't afford to donate money, or have trouble making it to a PTA meeting because the bus is unsafe.
5. *Look for ways to involve talented people from impoverished communities.* Recognize that parents in poor areas can be quite talented, caring, responsive people in ways that teachers might not expect. Most impoverished communities have people whose wisdom and experience defy stereotypes. Find these people and ask them to volunteer their services to help support children's learning in your classroom, accompany children on field trips, and make the school more attractive.
6. *Avoid creating tension between poorer and richer children.* When these children share the same classroom or school, don't favor the products or performances of children who have greater opportunities, such as dance lessons, acting classes, and money for special projects.
7. *Use mentoring.* Many children from low-income backgrounds benefit from having a mentor, a positive role model who agrees to be responsible for spending time with the child and helping to improve the child's learning and coping. Look around the community for possible mentors whose contributions you believe would benefit low-income students. We will have much more to say about mentoring in chapter 7, "Behavioral and Social Cognitive Approaches" and chapter 13, "Motivation, Teaching, and Learning."
8. *Observe the strengths of children from low-income backgrounds.* Many children from these circumstances come to school with considerable untapped knowledge and teachers can access such richness (Pang, 2001). For example, these children may have substantial knowledge about how to use mass transit, while richer children are simply transported in cars.

Ethnicity

The word *ethnic* comes from the Greek word that means "nation." **Ethnicity** refers to a shared pattern of characteristics such as cultural heritage, nationality, race, religion, and language. Everyone is a member of one or more ethnic groups and relations between people from different ethnic backgrounds, not just in the United States but in virtually every corner of the world, are often charged with bias and conflict.

How does ethnicity differ from race? The term *race,* now discredited as a biological concept, refers to the classification of people or other living things according to specific physiological characteristics. The term has never worked well in describing people in any scientific sense because humans are so diverse that they don't fit into neatly packaged racial categories. Thus, race no longer is recognized as an authentic scientific concept. Popularly, the word *race* has loosely been used to refer to everything from a person's mannerisms to religion to skin color. Social psychologist James Jones (1994, 1997) points out that thinking in racial terms has become embedded in most cultures. He says that people often stereotype other people because of their supposed race and inappropriately classify them as being more or less intelligent, competent, responsible, or socially acceptable on this basis. Although the term *race* is still embedded in the American vocabulary, we will mainly use the term *ethnicity* in this book.

Nowhere is the changing tapestry of American culture more apparent than in the changing ethnic balances among America's citizens (García Coll & Pachter, 2002; Goodkind, Hang, & Yang, 2004; Ishii-Kuntz, 2004). At the onset of the twenty-first century, one-third of all school-age children fell into the category now loosely referred to as "children of color" (principally African Americans, Latinos, Asian Americans, and Native Americans). By the year 2025 that portion will reach one-half. This changing demographic promises not only the richness that diversity produces but also difficult challenges in extending the American dream to individuals of all ethnic groups (Fulgini & Yoshikawa, 2004; Gonzales & others, 2004). Historically, people of color have found themselves at the bottom of the American economic and social order. They have been disproportionately represented among the poor and the inadequately educated (Edelman, 1997).

An important point about any ethnic group is that it is diverse (Martinez & Halgunseth, 2004; Pang, 2004; Tucker, Subramanian, & James, 2004). There are many ready examples: Mexican Americans and Cuban Americans are Latinos, but they had different reasons for migrating to the United States, come from varying socioeconomic backgrounds, and experience different rates and types of employment in the United States. Individuals born in Puerto Rico are distinguished from Latino individuals who have immigrated to the United States in that they are born U.S. citizens and are therefore not immigrants, regardless of where they live in the United States. The U.S. government currently recognizes 511 different Native American tribes, each having a unique ancestral background with differing values and characteristics. Asian Americans include individuals of Chinese, Japanese, Filipino, Korean, and Southeast Asian origin, each group having distinct ancestries and languages. The diversity of Asian Americans is reflected in their educational attainment. Some achieve a high level of education; many others have little education (Park, 2002). For example, 90 percent of Korean American males graduate from high school, but only 71 percent of Vietnamese males do.

Ethnicity and Schools   Educational segregation is still a reality for children of color in the United States (Buck, 2002; Simons, Finlay, & Yang, 1991). Almost one-third of African American and Latino students attend schools in which 90 percent or more of the students are from minority groups, typically their own minority group. The school experiences of students from different ethnic groups also depart in other ways (Reid & Zalk, 2001; Yeakey & Henderson, 2002). For example, African American and Latino students are much less likely than non-Latino White or Asian American students to be enrolled in academic, college preparatory programs and much more likely to be enrolled in remedial and special education programs. Asian American students are far more likely than students from other ethnic minority groups to take advanced math and science

ethnicity A shared pattern of characteristics such as cultural heritage, nationality, race, religion, and language.

Pride and Prejudice

Ypsilanti is a very interesting school district. It's about 50% Black and 50% White, now. When I came here, thirty-three years ago, we were having frequent racial incidents, riots, and demonstrations. I heard about my (future) school while I was still teaching in another state because it was on the national TV news as a result of racial protests. There was not a week that went by, my first few years of teaching in Ypsilanti, that I was not accused of being prejudiced against Blacks. I took it personally until I realized that the color of *every*one's skin was a daily issue in this town at that time. In the cafeteria and in the gym, when the kids were permitted to select their own seats, all the Black kids would be on one side and all the Whites would be on the other. There was one racially mixed kid that I had my third year of teaching, and I could always pick him out of any crowd because he'd be the darkest kid on the White side or the whitest kid on the Black side of the gym. Of course, I arrived in Ypsilanti a few months after Dr. King's assassination, so mine was not a unique experience for that era. What *was* unusual was the way Ypsilanti dealt with the problem.

The Ypsilanti School District is now a national model for race relations. Our Perry Pre-School and kindergarten program has been written up in national teaching textbooks. I'm always amazed at how much we take it for granted here in Ypsi. What our school district has done to change the racial climate in our school district is a source of tremendous pride to me.

What we did was really quite simple. We bussed all of our kindergarten kids to one school which we then made into an exemplary pre-school and kindergarten program. We then equally distributed our first through sixth graders among our other six elementary schools. Now, by the time I get our kids in seventh grade, whenever I tell my kids to select their own groups to do a project, they almost always self-select into male groups and female groups, but I almost never see a self-selected all Black or all White group.

These days, if the kids accuse me of being prejudiced, it's because they think I favor the girls over the boys. They have no idea how happy that accusation makes me.

Lynn Ayres
English and Drama Teacher
East Middle School
Ypsilanti, Michigan

courses in high school. African American students are twice as likely as Latinos, Native Americans, or Whites to be suspended from school. Ethnic minorities of color constitute the majority in 23 of the 25 largest school districts in the United States, a trend that is increasing (Banks, 1995). However, 90 percent of the teachers in America's schools are non-Latino White, and the percentage of minority teachers is projected to be even lower in coming years.

Prejudice, Discrimination, and Bias   **Prejudice** is an unjustified negative attitude toward an individual because of the individual's membership in a group. The group toward which the prejudice is directed might be defined by ethnicity, sex, age, or virtually any other detectable difference (Monteith, 2000). Our focus here is prejudice against ethnic groups of color.

People who oppose prejudice and discrimination often have contrasting views about it. On the one side are individuals who value and praise the strides made in civil rights in recent years. On the other side are individuals who criticize American schools and other institutions because they believe that many forms of discrimination and prejudice still exist there (Jackson, 1997; Murrell, 2000).

American anthropologist John Ogbu (1989; Ogbu & Stern, 2001) proposed the view that ethnic minority students are placed in a position of subordination and exploitation in the American educational system. He believes that students of color, especially African American and Latino students, have inferior educational opportunities, are exposed to teachers and school administrators who have low academic expectations for them, and encounter negative stereotypes of ethnic minority groups.

Like Ogbu, educational psychologist Margaret Beale Spencer (Spencer & Dornbusch, 1990) believes that a form of institutional racism permeates many American schools. That is, well-meaning teachers, acting out of misguided liberalism, fail to challenge children of color to achieve. Such teachers prematurely accept a low level of performance from these children, substituting warmth and affection for high standards of academic success.

Diversity and Differences   Historical, economic, and social experiences produce both prejudicial and legitimate differences among various ethnic groups ◀ p. 9. Individuals who live in a particular ethnic or cultural group adapt to the values, attitudes, and stresses of that culture. Their behavior might be different from one's own yet be functional for them. Recognizing and respecting these differences is an important aspect of getting along in a diverse, multicultural world (Spencer, 2000).

Unfortunately, the emphasis often placed on differences between ethnic minority groups and the White majority has been damaging to ethnic minority individuals. For too long, virtually all differences were thought of as deficits or inferior characteristics on the part of the ethnic minority group (Meece & Kurtz-Costes, 2001).

Another important dimension of every ethnic group is its diversity (Wong & Rowley, 2001) ◀ p. 26. Not only is U.S. culture diverse—so is every ethnic group within the U.S. culture, as we underscored earlier in the chapter.

prejudice An unjustified negative attitude toward an individual because of the individual's membership in a group.

Language Issues

In chapter 2, we described how children develop language. Here we will examine several issues related to learning a second language ← p. 56.

Bilingual Education   Octavio's parents moved to the United States a year before he was born. They do not speak English fluently and always have spoken to Octavio in Spanish. At age six, Octavio has just entered first grade in San Antonio. He speaks no English. What is the best way to teach Octavio?

As many as 10 million children in the United States come from homes in which English is not the primary language. Many, like Octavio, live in a community in which English is the main form of communication. To be successful, they have to master the English language.

Bilingual education aims to teach academic subjects to immigrant children in their native languages (most often Spanish), while gradually adding English instruction (Adamson, 2004; Diaz-Rico, 2004). Most bilingual programs are transitional programs developed to support students until they can understand English well enough to learn in the regular classroom (Minaya-Rowe, 2002). A typical program changes to English-only classes at the end of second or third grade, although some programs continue instruction in the child's primary language until sixth grade. In most programs, at least half of instruction will be in English from the beginning (Garcia & others, 2002).

Proponents of bilingual education argue that teaching immigrants in their native language shows respect for their family and community culture and increases the students' self-esteem, making their academic success more likely. Critics argue that bilingual education harms immigrant children by failing to adequately instruct them in English, which will leave them unprepared for the workplace. In rebuttal, supporters of bilingual education say that it aims to teach English. Some states have recently passed laws declaring English to be their official language, creating conditions in which schools are not obligated to teach minority children in languages other than English. In 1998, California voters repealed bilingual education altogether. Supporters of the repeal claimed that most Spanish-speaking voters opposed bilingual education, though polling after the election did not bear out this contention. Ironically, test scores released shortly after the election revealed that the scores of children in bilingual programs in several large school districts were higher, on average, than scores of native English-speaking children.

Diversity Resources
Prejudice

A first- and second-grade bilingual English-Cantonese teacher instructing students in Chinese in Oakland, California. *What is the nature of bilingual education?*

bilingual education Instruction on academic subjects for immigrant children in their native languages (most often Spanish), while gradually adding English instruction.

Bilingual Education

How long does it take language minority students to learn English? Kenji Hakuta and his colleagues (2000) collected data on children in four school districts to determine how long it takes students to develop oral and academic English proficiency, which refers to the ability to use language in academic contexts, such as reading a school text. Oral proficiency took three to five years to develop, and academic English proficiency took four to seven years. These results suggest that policies that assume rapid acquisition of English by language minority students, such as within one year, are unrealistic.

A common fear is that early exposure to English will lead to children's loss of their native language. However, researchers have found that bilingualism (the ability to speak two languages) is not detrimental to the child's performance in either language (Hakuta, 2000; Hakuta & García, 1989). In studies of Latino American children, there was no evidence of a loss in Spanish proficiency (productive language, receptive language, and language complexity) for children attending a bilingual preschool (Rodriguez & others, 1995). Children who attended bilingual preschool, compared with those who remained at home, showed significant and parallel gains in both English and Spanish.

Researchers have also found that bilingualism has a positive effect on children's cognitive development. Children who are fluent in two languages perform better than their single-language counterparts on tests of attentional control, concept formation, analytical reasoning, cognitive flexibility, and cognitive complexity (Bialystok, 1999, 2001). They also are more conscious of the structure of spoken and written language and better at noticing errors of grammar and meaning, skills that benefit their reading ability (Bialystok, 1993, 1997).

Other Second-Language Considerations The United States is one of the few countries in the world in which most students graduate from high school knowing only their own language. For example, in Russia, schools have ten grades, called forms, that roughly correspond to the twelve grades in American schools. Children begin school at age seven in Russia. Russian students begin learning English in the third form. Because of the emphasis on teaching English in Russian schools, most Russian citizens under the age of forty today are bilingual, able to speak at least some English in addition to their native language.

Is it better to learn a second language as a child or as an adult? Adults make faster initial progress but their eventual success in the second language is not as great as children's. For example, in one study, Chinese and Korean adults who immigrated to the United States at different ages were given a test of grammatical knowledge (Johnson & Newport, 1991). Those who began learning English from three to seven years of age scored as well as native speakers of English on the test, but those who came to the United States (and started learning English) in later childhood or adolescence had lower test scores (see figure 5.2). Children's ability to learn to pronounce a second language with the correct accent also decreases with age, with an especially sharp decline occurring after the age of about ten to twelve (Asher & García, 1969). Adolescents and adults can become competent in a second language but this is a more difficult task than learning it as a child. However, these findings do not mean that there is a critical period for learning a second language. Indeed, in a recent study, no evidence was found of a critical period in which, beyond a certain age, learning a second language was severely hampered (Hakuta,

Through the Eyes of Teachers

Helping a Romanian Student Develop Proficiency in English

Cristina, a twelve-year-old Romanian student, has been in America for about fifteen months and is developing proficiency in English. Knowing she needs to learn to speak, read, and write standard English to be a successful, contributing member of American society, I looked for strengths that she brought to our community. She was fortunate in being able to attend school in Romania and was able to read and write in her first language at an appropriate level for her age. I have altered many assignments I give to her to take into account the context of her language learning. Once, when the class was engaging in a writing exercise, I had to use gestures and my knowledge of other Romance languages to help her understand the writing task. I also had her accompany her writing with drawings that were unhampered by language deficiencies.

Verna Rollins
Language Arts Teacher
West Middle School
Ypsilanti, Michigan

Bialystok, & Wiley, in press). In this study, the more education individuals had experienced, the more readily they learned a second language.

Teaching Strategies
For Working with Linguistically and Culturally Diverse Children

Here are some classroom recommendations for working with linguistically and culturally diverse children:

1. "*Recognize that all children are cognitively, linguistically, and emotionally connected to the language and culture of their home.*"
2. "*Acknowledge that children can demonstrate their knowledge and capacity in many ways.* Whatever language children speak, they should be able to show their capabilities and feel appreciated and valued."
3. "*Understand that without comprehensible input, second-language learning can be difficult.* It takes time to be linguistically competent in any language." Although verbal proficiency in a second language can be accomplished in three to five years, the skills necessary to understand academic content through reading and writing can take four to seven years. Children who do not become proficient in their second language after these time frames usually are not academically proficient in their first language, either.
4. *Model appropriate use of English and provide the child with opportunities to use newly acquired vocabulary and language.* Learn at least a few words in the child's first language to demonstrate respect for the child's culture.
5. "*Actively involve parents and families in the early learning program and setting.*" Encourage and assist parents in becoming knowledgeable about the value for children of knowing more than one language. Provide parents with strategies to support and maintain home language learning.
6. "*Recognize that children can and will acquire the use of English even when their home language is used and respected.*"
7. *Collaborate with other teachers to learn more about working with linguistically and culturally diverse children.*

(Source: National Association Education of Young Children, 1996, pp. 7–11).

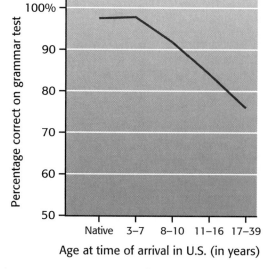

FIGURE 5.2 Grammar Proficiency and Age at Arrival in the United States

In one study, ten years after arriving in the United States, individuals from China and Korea took a grammar test (Johnson & Newport, 1991). People who arrived before the age of eight had a better grasp of grammar than those who arrived later.

⚠ Review and Reflect

1 Discuss how variations in culture, socioeconomic status, and ethnic background might raise special classroom needs.

Review

- What is culture? How do individualistic and collectivistic cultures differ, and how is this difference relevant to the classroom?
- What is socioeconomic status? In what ways are children from impoverished backgrounds likely to have difficulty in school? What kind of interventions might help them?
- How is ethnicity involved in children's schooling?
- What is bilingual education? What arguments are raised for and against it? What are some other second-language considerations?

Reflect

- In the context of education, are all ethnic differences negative? Come up with some differences that might be positive in U.S. classrooms.

MULTICULTURAL EDUCATION

In 1963, President John Kennedy said, "Peace is a daily, a weekly, a monthly process, of gradually changing opinions, slowly eroding old barriers, quietly building new structures." Cultural and ethnic tensions regularly threaten this fragile peace. The hope is that multicultural education can contribute to making our nation more like what the late civil rights leader Martin Luther King dreamed of: a nation where children will be judged not by the color of their skin but by the quality of their character.

Multicultural education is education that values diversity and includes the perspectives of a variety of cultural groups on a regular basis. Its enthusiasts believe that children of color should be empowered and that multicultural education benefits all students. An important goal of multicultural education is equal educational opportunity for all students. This includes closing the gap in academic achievement between mainstream students and students from underrepresented groups (Bennett, 2003; Pang, 2005; Schmidt & Mosenthal, 2001; Sheets, 2005).

Multicultural education grew out of the civil rights movement of the 1960s and the call for equality and social justice in society for women and people of color. As a field, multicultural education includes issues related to socioeconomic status, ethnicity, and gender. Because social justice is one of the foundational values of the field, prejudice reduction and equity pedagogy are core components (Banks, 2001). *Prejudice reduction* refers to the activities that teachers can implement in the classroom to eliminate negative and stereotypical views of others. *Equity pedagogy* refers to the modification of the teaching process to incorporate materials and learning strategies appropriate to both boys and girls and to various ethnic groups.

Empowering Students

The term **empowerment** refers to providing people with the intellectual and coping skills to succeed and make this a more just world. In the 1960s to 1980s, multicultural education was concerned with empowering students and better representing minority and cultural groups in curricula and textbooks. Empowerment continues to be an important theme of multicultural education today (Schmidt, 2001). In this view, schools should give students the opportunity to learn about the experiences, struggles, and visions of many different ethnic and cultural groups (Banks, 2001, 2002, 2003). The hope is that this will raise minority students' self-esteem, reduce prejudice, and provide more-equal educational opportunities. The hope also is that it will help White students become more tolerant toward minority groups and that both White students and students of color will develop multiple perspectives within their curricula.

Sonia Nieto (1992), a Puerto Rican who grew up in New York City, believes that her education made her feel that her cultural background was somehow deficient. She provides these recommendations:

- The school curriculum should be openly anti-racist and anti-discriminatory. Students should feel free to discuss issues of ethnicity and discrimination.
- Multicultural education should be a part of every student's education. This includes having all students become bilingual and study different cultural perspectives. Multicultural education should be reflected everywhere in the school, including bulletin boards, lunch rooms, and assemblies.
- Students should be trained to be more conscious of culture. This involves getting students to be more skillful at analyzing culture and more aware of the historical, political, and social factors that shape their views of culture and ethnicity. The hope is that such critical examination will motivate students to work for political and economic justice.

Exploring Multicultural Education

Multicultural Education Resources

multicultural education Education that values diversity and includes the perspectives of a variety of cultural groups on a regular basis.

empowerment Providing people with intellectual and coping skills to succeed and make this a more just world.

Culturally Relevant Teaching

Culturally relevant teaching is an important aspect of multicultural education (Farr, 2005; Gay, 2000; Irvine & Armento, 2001). It seeks to make connections with the learner's cultural background (Pang, 2005). Let's consider the subject of history and see how one teacher made the subject culturally relevant.

> Carol, a seventh-grader, asked her history teacher, "Why do I have to learn about this stuff? It's boring and it's past. It doesn't mean anything to me."
>
> The teacher knew that she could not just ignore the student's statement because she might lose this student as well as others who thought the same way but were not bold enough to say so, so the teacher asked, "Carol, where were you born? Did your family always live in Chicago?"
>
> Carol then began to tell how her family was originally from Arizona. Her grandfather was a member of the Pima nation, near Phoenix. When he was younger, his father wanted him to join the army to become more disciplined. But he did not want to leave the reservation because his friends and family were there. However, his father won, so Carol's grandfather enlisted in the army, and after his service he moved to Chicago and went to college, where he studied accounting and got a job as an accountant.
>
> Following Carol's family story, the teacher made the bridge to U.S. history by telling the class that Carol's family story is a part of our national family story, which is what our history is. Our national story tells about the people, their struggles, their values, the issues they were concerned about, and what they did.

Multicultural education experts believe that good teachers are aware of and integrate culturally relevant teaching into the curriculum because it makes teaching more effective (Diaz, 2001). Some researchers have found that students from some ethnic groups behave in ways that may make some educational tasks more difficult than others. For example Jackie Irvine (1990) and Janice Hale-Benson (1982) observed that African American students are often expressive and high in energy. They recommended that, when students behave in this way, giving them opportunities to make presentations rather than always being required to perform on a written exam might be a good strategy. Other researchers have found that many Asian American students prefer visual learning more than their European American peers (Litton, 1999; Park, 1997). Thus, with these students teachers might want to use more three-dimensional models, graphic organizers, photographs, charts, and writing on the board.

Issues-Centered Education

Issues-centered education also is an important aspect of multicultural education. In this approach, students are taught to systematically examine issues that involve equity

Through the Eyes of Teachers

She Slid Under Her Desk

After moving from Haiti to New York City in 1969, I graduated from Hunter College with a B.S. in accounting and worked in that field from 1974 to 1991. When I moved to Florida in that year I was immediately approached by some Haitian educators who asked me to join their field because of a dire need for Haitian educators there.

I told them I was not a teacher, but at their insistence I accepted work as a substitute teacher at an elementary school in Fort Lauderdale. As I was looking at the student roster in class, I noticed the last name Louis. I called out the child's name and asked her if she was Haitian, unaware at that time of the stigma attached to my nationality in South Florida. She became so embarrassed by my question that she literally slid under her desk and disappeared. Later she told me one-on-one, "You're not supposed to say that you are Haitian around here."

That is when I understood the immensity of the problem, and that is why I became a teacher. For the past seven years I have been teaching ESOL (English for Speakers of Other Languages) in addition to other middle school subjects. I believe that I've made a difference in the lives of my students by giving them a sense of pride in their heritage and by providing a learning environment in which they can grow.

I believe that to achieve equality, the educational system must recognize the ethnic background and gender of the student. The student's home culture isn't to be discarded, but used instead as a teaching tool. What works best in improving children's interethnic problems is to confront the problems head-on. I create actual lessons teaching empathy and tolerance toward others. I have used my free time to go to mainstreamed teachers' rooms to talk to American students about human rights and prejudice toward students of different nationalities and cultures, in particular the Haitian students who are continually harassed and sometimes beaten in school.

Try always to know your students as human beings, and they will surely open up to you and learn. Tell them that you believe in them. If you believe they can achieve, they will.

Daniel Arnoux
ESOL Teacher
Lauderhill Middle Community School
Broward, Florida

Through the Eyes of Teachers

Finding Parallels

The meatpacking industry of Nebraska has brought many Latinos to our area. I find my students have a definite negative attitude toward them, usually as a result of their parents' influence. My effort at helping them realize their prejudice is to teach David Guterson's *Snow Falling on Cedars* to senior-level students. Though the fictional novel takes place off Puget Sound and deals with Japanese immigrants during World War II, I take students through discussion questions that provide striking similarity to their prejudice against Latinos. I have no way to measure the degree of their prejudice, but I feel that education and awareness are key steps in decreasing the problem.

Kathy Fuchser
English and Journalism Teacher
St. Francis High School
Humphrey, Nebraska

and social justice. They not only clarify their values but also examine alternatives and consequences if they take a particular stance on an issue. Issues-centered education is closely related to moral education, which we discussed in chapter 3, "Social Contexts and Socioemotional Development" ← p. 97.

Consider the circumstance when some students were concerned with the lunch policy at a high school (Pang, 2001). The students who were on federally subsidized programs were forced to use a specific line in the cafeteria, which automatically labeled them. Many of these low-income students felt humiliated and embarrassed to the point that they went without lunch. The students alerted teachers to what had happened to them and discussions were held. Together, the students and teachers developed a plan of action to address this issue involving social justice. The plan was presented to the school district, which revised its lunch line policy at the ten high schools affected by it.

Improving Relations Among Children from Different Ethnic Groups

A number of strategies and programs are available to improve relationships among children from different ethnic groups. To begin, we will discuss one of the most powerful strategies.

The Jigsaw Classroom   When social psychologist Eliot Aronson was a professor at the University of Texas at Austin, the school system contacted him for ideas to reduce the increasing racial tension in classrooms. Aronson (1986) developed the concept of the **jigsaw classroom,** which involves having students from different cultural backgrounds cooperate by doing different parts of a project to reach a common goal. Aronson used the term *jigsaw* because he saw the technique as much like a group of students cooperating to put different pieces together to complete a jigsaw puzzle.

How might this work? Consider a class of students, some White, some African American, some Latino, some Native American, and some Asian American. The lesson concerns the life of Joseph Pulitzer. The class might be broken up into groups of six students each, with the groups being as equally mixed as possible in terms of ethnic composition and achievement level. The lesson about Pulitzer's life is divided into six parts, and one part is assigned to each member of each six-person group. The parts might be passages from Pulitzer's biography, such as how the Pulitzer family came to the United States, Pulitzer's childhood, his early work, and so on. All students in each group are given an allotted time to study their parts. Then the groups meet, and each member works to teach his or her part to the group. Learning depends on the students' interdependence and cooperation in reaching the same goal. We will say much more about cooperative learning in chapter 10.

Sometimes the jigsaw classroom strategy is described as creating a superordinate goal or common task for students. Team sports, drama productions, and music performances are additional examples of contexts in which students cooperatively and often very enthusiastically participate to reach a superordinate goal.

jigsaw classroom A classroom in which students from different cultural backgrounds cooperate by doing different parts of a project to reach a common goal.

Positive Personal Contact with Others from Different Cultural Backgrounds
Contact by itself does not do the job of improving relationships. For example, busing ethnic minority students to predominantly White schools, or vice versa, has not reduced prejudice or improved interethnic relations (Minuchin & Shapiro, 1983). What matters is what happens after students arrive at a school. In one comprehensive study of more than

5,000 fifth-graders and 4,000 tenth-graders, multiethnic curricula projects that focused on ethnic issues, mixed work groups, and supportive teachers and principals all helped improve students' interethnic relations (Forehand, Ragosta, & Rock, 1976).

Relations improve when students talk with each other about their personal worries, successes, failures, coping strategies, interests, and so on. When students reveal personal information about themselves, they are more likely to be perceived as individuals than simply as members of a group. Sharing personal information frequently produces this discovery: People from different backgrounds share many of the same hopes, worries, and feelings. Sharing personal information can help break down in-group/out-group and we/they barriers.

Positive personal contact that involves sharing doubts, hopes, ambitions, and much more is one way to improve interethnic relations.

Perspective Taking   Exercises and activities that help students see other people's perspectives can improve interethnic relations. In one exercise, students learn certain proper behaviors of two distinct cultural groups (Shirts, 1997). Subsequently, the two groups interact with each other in accordance with those behaviors. As a result, they experience feelings of anxiety and apprehension. The exercise is designed to help students understand the culture shock that comes from being in a cultural setting with people who behave in ways that are very different from what one is used to. Students also can be encouraged to write stories or act out plays that involve prejudice or discrimination. In this way, students "step into the shoes" of students who are culturally different from themselves and feel what it is like to not be treated as an equal (Cushner, McClelland, & Safford, 1996).

In language arts, students can study familiar stories and be asked to take the perspective of different characters. A retelling of the familiar story "Little Red Riding Hood" from the perspective of the wolf is *The Maligned Wolf* (Fearn, 1972). As students read the story, they become aware of biases against various groups, such as wolves, and the perspectives of different characters within the same story. Students also can be asked to rewrite the story from the perspectives of other characters, such as the grandmother. They also can be asked to retell other stories from different points of view, such as the story of "Cinderella" from the stepmother's view.

Studying people from different parts of the world also encourages students to understand different perspectives (Mazurek, Winzer, & Majorek, 2000). In social studies, students can be asked why people in certain cultures have customs different from their own. Teachers can also encourage students to read books on many different cultures. To read further about bringing the global community into American students' classrooms, see the Technology and Education box on page 150.

An increasing number of Internet websites allow students to communicate with students in other parts of the United States and around the world. Among these projects are the Global Lab Project (discussed in the Technology and Education box on page 150), the Global Schoolhouse Project, the Jason Project, and Global Show-n-Tell. You can access these student global communication projects by visiting the Santrock *Educational Psychology* website and clicking on the Global Internet Communication entry for chapter 5.

Critical Thinking and Emotional Intelligence   Students who learn to think deeply and critically about interethnic relations are likely to decrease their prejudice and

Through the Eyes of Teachers

Understanding Unfairness

I use literature to help students understand other people and how they have sometimes been treated unfairly. During January I focus on the southeastern United States in our social studies class and integrate language arts by having the whole class read *Meet Addy* and *Mississippi Bridge*. On Martin Luther King Day we read his biography.... We get a little overview of how the Jews were treated in World War II through *Number the Stars*. We also get interested in learning more about Anne Frank. When the children read how these minorities were treated, they understand more fully that all people are more similar to them than different.

Marlene Wendler
Fourth-Grade Teacher
St. Paul's Lutheran School
New Ulm, Minnesota

The Global Lab and Other Technology Connections with Students Around the World

Traditionally, students have learned within the walls of their classroom and interacted with their teacher and other students in the class. With advances in telecommunications, students can learn from and with teachers and students around the world. The teachers and students might be from schools in such diverse locations as Warsaw, Tokyo, Istanbul, and a small village in Israel.

The Global Laboratory Project is one example that has capitalized on advances in telecommunications (Schrum & Berenfeld, 1997). It consists of science investigations that involve monitoring the environment sharing data via telecommunication hookups, and placing local findings in a global context. In an initial telecommunications meeting, students introduced themselves and described their schools, communities, and study locations. The locations included Moscow, Russia; Warsaw, Poland; Kenosha, Wisconsin; San Antonio, Texas; Pueblo, Colorado; and Aiken, South Carolina. This initial phase was designed to help students develop a sense of community and become familiar with their collaborators from around the world. As their data collection and evaluation evolved, students continued to communicate with their peers worldwide and to learn more not only about science but also about the global community.

Classrooms or schools also can use fax machines to link students from around the country and world (Cushner, McClelland, & Safford, 1996). Fax machines transfer artwork, poetry, essays, and other materials to other students in locations as diverse as Europe, Asia, Africa, and South America. Students also can communicate the same day with pen pals through e-mail, when once it took weeks for a letter to reach someone in a faraway place. An increasing number of schools also use videotelephone technology in

foreign language instruction. Instead of simulating a French café in a typical French language class, American students might talk with French students who have placed a videotelephone in a café in France.

Such global technology projects can go a long way toward reducing American students' ethnocentric beliefs. The active building of connections around the world through telecommunications gives students the opportunity to experience others' perspectives, better understand other cultures, and reduce prejudice.

Global technology projects can help students become less ethnocentric.

stereotyping of others. Students who think in narrow ways are often prejudiced. However, when students learn to ask questions, think first about issues rather than respond automatically, and delay judgment until more complete information is available, they become less prejudiced.

Emotional intelligence benefits interethnic relations. Recall from chapter 4 that being emotionally intelligent means having emotional self-awareness, managing your emotions, reading emotions, and handling relationships ← p. 116. Consider how the following emotionally intelligent skills can help students to improve their relations with diverse others: understanding the causes of one's feelings, being good at managing one's own anger, being good at listening to what other people are saying, and being motivated to share and cooperate.

The Global Lab Project
Global Internet Communication

Reducing Bias Louise Derman-Sparks and the Anti-Bias Curriculum Task Force (1989) created a number of tools to help young children reduce, handle, or even eliminate their biases. The anti-bias curriculum argues that although differences are good, discriminating against someone is not. It encourages teachers to confront troublesome bias issues rather than covering them up.

These are some of the anti-bias strategies recommended for teachers:

• Create an anti-bias classroom environment by displaying images of children from various ethnic and cultural groups. The books you select for students also should reflect this diversity.

James Comer *(left)* is shown with some inner-city African American students who attend a school where Comer has implemented his community team approach.

- Select play materials, art materials, and classroom activities that encourage ethnic and cultural understanding. Use dramatic play to illustrate nonstereotypic roles and families from diverse backgrounds.
- Use the "persona" dolls with young children. The sixteen dolls represent diverse ethnic and cultural backgrounds. Each doll comes with a life story designed to reduce bias.
- Help students resist stereotyping and discriminating against others. Make it a firm rule that no aspect of a child's or an adult's identity is an acceptable target of teasing or exclusion.
- Participate in consciousness-raising activities to better understand your cultural views and deal with any stereotypes or biases you might have.
- Establish genuine parent/teacher dialogue that opens up discussion of each other's views; exchange information on how children develop prejudices; and inform parents about the anti-bias curriculum.

Increasing Tolerance   The "Teaching Tolerance Project" provides schools with resources and materials to improve intercultural understanding and relationships between White children and children of color (Heller & Hawkins, 1994). The biannual magazine *Teaching Tolerance* is distributed to every public and private school in the United States (you can obtain a free copy by contacting Teaching Tolerance, 400 Washington Ave., Birmingham, AL 36104). The magazine's purpose is to share views on and provide resources for teaching tolerance. For elementary school teachers, the "Different and Same" videos and materials can help children become more tolerant (they are available from Family Communications, 4802 Fifth Ave., Pittsburgh, PA 15213).

The School and Community as a Team   Yale psychiatrist James Comer (1988; Comer & others, 1996) believes that a community team approach is the best way to educate children. Three important aspects of the Comer Project for Change are (1) a governance and management team that develops a comprehensive school plan, assessment strategy, and staff development program; (2) a mental health or school support team; and (3) a parents' program (Goldberg, 1997b). The Comer program emphasizes no-fault (the focus should be on solving problems, not blaming), no decisions except by consensus, and no paralysis (that is, no naysayer can stand in the way of a strong majority decision). Comer believes the entire school community should have a cooperative rather than an adversarial attitude. The Comer program is currently operating in more than 600 schools in 82 school districts in 26 states.

One of the first schools to implement the Comer approach was the Martin Luther King, Jr., Elementary School in New Haven, Connecticut. When the Comer program began there, its students were an average of nineteen months below grade level in language arts and eighteen months below grade level in math. After ten years of the Comer program, the students' national achievement test scores were at grade level, and after fifteen years they were twelve months above grade level. Even though no socioeconomic changes had taken place in this predominantly African American, low-income, inner-city area over this period, school absenteeism dropped dramatically, serious behavior problems decreased, parent participation increased substantially, and staff turnover was almost nil.

The Issue of Whether a Core of "White" Values Should Be Taught

Some educators have opposed the emphasis on including information about diverse ethnic groups in the curriculum. They also have opposed ethnocentric education that emphasizes any particular non-White minority group. In one proposal, Arthur Schlesinger (1991) argued that all students should be taught a set of core values that, he claimed, are derived from the White Anglo-Protestant tradition. These core values include mutual respect, individual rights, and tolerance of differences. Critics of Schlesinger's view point out that these are not peculiarly White Anglo-Protestant values but values that most ethnic and religious groups in American endorse. Indeed, multicultural education includes the Western tradition.

In another proposal, E. D. Hirsch (1987) stressed that all students should be taught a common core of cultural knowledge to ensure that they become "culturally literate." He listed a number of names, phrases, dates, and concepts that he believes students at different grade levels should know. Hirsch claims that a program of cultural literacy based on his terms and concepts will help students from impoverished backgrounds and immigrants adapt to mainstream American culture. Although Hirsch's early presentation of his ideas did not address cultural differences or social injustice, he recently updated his work to make it more multicultural.

Thus, multicultural education has its critics who argue that all children should be taught a common core of cultural values, especially White Anglo-Protestant values. However, advocates of multicultural education don't oppose teaching a core of such values as long as it does not make up the entire curriculum.

The Comer School Development Program

McGraw-Hill Multicultural Supersite

Teaching Strategies
For Multicultural Education

We already have discussed many ideas that will benefit children's relations with people who are from ethnic and cultural backgrounds different from their own. Further guidelines for multicultural teaching include these recommendations from leading multicultural education expert James Banks (2001):

1. *Become more sensitive to racist content in materials and classroom interactions.* A good source for learning more about racism is Paul Kivel's (1995) book *Uprooting Racism.*

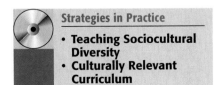

Strategies in Practice

- **Teaching Sociocultural Diversity**
- **Culturally Relevant Curriculum**

2. *Learn more about different ethnic groups.* Read at least one major book on the history and culture of American ethnic groups. One book that includes historical descriptions of these groups is Banks' (2003) *Teaching Strategies for Ethnic Studies.*

3. *Be sensitive to your students' ethnic attitudes and don't accept the belief that "kids do not see colors."* Respond to students' cultural views in sensitive ways.

4. *Use trade books, films, videotapes, and recordings to portray ethnic perspectives.* Banks' (2003) book *Teaching Strategies for Ethnic Studies* describes a number of these.

5. *Be sensitive to the developmental needs of your students when you select various cultural materials.* In early childhood and elementary school classrooms, make the learning experience specific and concrete. Banks believes that fiction and biographies are especially good choices for introducing cultural concepts to these students. Banks recommends that students at these levels can study such concepts as similarities, differences, prejudice, and discrimination but are not developmentally ready to study concepts such as racism and oppression.

6. *View students positively regardless of their ethnicity.* All students learn best when their teachers have high achievement expectations for them and support their learning efforts.

7. *Recognize that most parents, regardless of their ethnicity, are interested in their children's education and want them to succeed in school.* However, understand that many parents of color have mixed feelings about schools because of their own experiences with discrimination. Think of positive ways to get parents of color more involved in their children's education and view them as partners in their children's learning.

⚠ Review and Reflect

2 **Describe some ways to promote multicultural education.**

Review
- What is multicultural education? What is the aim of "empowering" students?
- In the eyes of students, how can teaching be made more "culturally relevant"?
- What is issues-centered education? Give an example of it.
- How can teachers improve relationships among children from different ethnic groups?
- Why do some teachers think we should still teach a core of "White Anglo-Protestant values"?

Reflect
- In terms of multicultural education, what do you hope to do differently as a teacher than what your former teachers did?

GENDER

A well-known nineteenth-century nursery rhyme by J. O. Halliwell goes like this:

> What are little boys made of?
>   Frogs and snails and puppy dogs' tails.
> What are little girls made of?
>   Sugar and spice and all that's nice.

What differences does the rhyme imply exist between boys and girls? Are any of them valid? Issues of real and perceived gender differences can be vital to effective teaching.

Gender refers to the sociocultural and psychological dimensions of being female or male. Gender is distinguished from *sex,* which involves the biological dimensions of

gender The sociocultural and psychological dimensions of being female or male.

being female or male. **Gender roles** are the social expectations that prescribe how males and females should think, act, and feel.

Views on Gender Development

There are various ways to view gender development. Some stress biological factors in the behavior of males and females; others emphasize social or cognitive factors (Lippa, 2002).

Biological Views   In humans the 23rd pair of chromosomes (the sex chromosomes) determine whether the fetus is a female (XX) or a male (XY). No one denies the presence of genetic, biochemical, and anatomical differences between the sexes. Even gender experts with a strong environmental orientation acknowledge that girls and boys are treated differently because of their physical differences and their different roles in reproduction. What is at issue is the directness or indirectness of biological and environmental influences. For example, androgen is the predominant sex hormone in males. If a high androgen level directly influences brain functioning, which in turn increases some behavior such as aggression or activity level, then the biological effect is direct. If a child's high androgen level produces strong muscle development, which in turn causes others to expect the child to be a good athlete and, in turn, leads the child to participate in sports, then the biological effect on behavior is more indirect.

Some biological approaches address differences in the brains of females and males (Eisenberg, Martin, & Fabes, 1996). One approach focuses on differences between females and males in the corpus callosum, the massive band of fibers that connects the brain's two hemispheres (LeDoux, 1996, 2002). The corpus collosum is larger in females than in males, and this may explain why females are more aware than are males of their own and others' emotions. This might occur because the right hemisphere is able to pass more information about emotions to the left hemisphere.

However, the brains of females and males are far more similar than they are different. We also know that the brain has considerable plasticity and that experiences can modify its growth. In sum, biology is not destiny when gender attitudes and behavior are at issue. Children's socialization experiences matter a great deal (Lippa, 2005).

Socialization Views   Both psychoanalytic and social cognitive theories describe social experiences that influence children's gender development. The **psychoanalytic theory of gender** stems from Sigmund Freud's view that the preschool child develops a sexual attraction to the opposite-sex parent. Then, by about five or six years of age, the child renounces this attraction because of anxious feelings. Subsequently the child identifies with the same-sex parent, unconsciously adopting the same-sex parent's characteristics. Today, most gender experts do not believe gender development proceeds in this way. Children become gender-typed much earlier than five or six years of age. Also, males typically become masculine and females feminine even when the same-sex parent is not around.

The **social cognitive theory of gender** emphasizes that children's gender development occurs through observation and imitation of gender behavior, as well as through reinforcement and punishment of gender behavior. Parents often use rewards and punishments to teach their offspring to be feminine ("Karen, you are being a good girl when you play gently with your doll") or masculine ("Keith, a big boy like you is not supposed to cry").

Many parents encourage boys and girls to engage in different types of play and activities (Lott & Maluso, 2001). Girls are more likely to be given dolls and, when old enough, are more likely to be assigned baby-sitting duties. Girls are encouraged to be more nurturant than boys. Fathers are more likely to engage in aggressive play with their sons than with their daughters. Parents allow their adolescent sons to have more freedom than their adolescent daughters.

Gender Resources

gender roles The social expectations that prescribe how males and females should think, act, and feel.

psychoanalytic theory of gender A theory that stems from Freud's view that the preschool child develops a sexual attraction to the opposite-sex parent, then by about five or six years of age renounces the attraction because of anxious feelings. Subsequently, the child identifies with the same-sex parent, unconsciously adopting the same-sex parent's characteristics.

social cognitive theory of gender A theory that children's gender development occurs through observation and imitation of gender behavior, as well as reinforcement and punishment of gender behavior.

As reflected in this tug-of-war battle between boys and girls, the playground in elementary school is like going to "gender school." Elementary school children show a clear preference for being with and liking same-sex peers. Eleanor Maccoby has studied children's gender development for many years. She believes peers play especially strong roles in socializing each other about gender roles.

Peers also extensively reward and punish gender-related behavior. After extensive observations of elementary school classrooms, two researchers characterized the play settings as "gender school" (Luria & Herzog, 1985). In elementary school, boys usually hang out with boys and girls with girls. It is easier for "tomboy" girls to join boys' groups than for "feminine" boys to join girls' groups, because of our society's greater sex-typing pressure on boys. Developmental psychologist Eleanor Maccoby (1998, 2002), who has studied gender for a number of decades, believes that peers play an especially important gender-socializing role, teaching each other what is acceptable and unacceptable gender behavior.

Television also has a gender-socializing role, portraying females and males in particular gender roles (Brown, Steele, & Walsh-Childers, 2001). Even with the onset of more diverse programming in recent years, researchers still find that television presents males as more competent than females (Pacheco & Hurtado, 2001). In one analysis of rap videos on TV, teenage girls were primarily shown as concerned with dating, shopping, and their appearance (Campbell, 1988). They were rarely depicted as interested in school or career plans. Attractive girls were mainly pictured as "airheads," unattractive girls as intelligent. Schools and teachers also have gender-socializing influences on boys and girls. We will discuss these influences later in the chapter.

Cognitive Views Two cognitive views on gender are (1) cognitive developmental theory and (2) gender schema theory. According to the **cognitive developmental theory of gender,** children's gender typing occurs after they have developed a concept of gender. Once they consistently conceive of themselves as female or male, children organize their world on the basis of gender. Initially developed by Lawrence Kohlberg (1966) (whose theory of moral development you read about in chapter 3), this theory argues that gender development proceeds this way: "I am a girl. I want to do girl things. Therefore, the opportunity to do girl things is rewarding." Kohlberg believes it is not until children reach Piaget's concrete operational stage of thinking at about seven years of age that they understand gender constancy—that a male is still a male regardless of whether he wears pants or a skirt or whether his hair is long or short (Tavris & Wade, 1984).

Fathers and Children

cognitive developmental theory of gender Kohlberg's theory that children adopt a gender after they have developed a concept of gender.

Gender schema theory states that an individual's attention and behavior are guided by an internal motivation to conform to gender-based sociocultural standards and stereotypes (Martin & Dinella, 2001). A gender schema is a cognitive structure, or network of associations, that organizes and guides an individual's perceptions along gender lines. Gender schema theory suggests that gender typing occurs when children are ready to encode and organize information along the lines of what is considered appropriate or typical for females and males in a society (Rodgers, 2000).

Gender Stereotyping, Similarities, and Differences

What are the real differences between boys and girls? Before attempting to answer that question, let's consider the problem of gender stereotypes.

Gender Stereotypes   **Gender stereotypes** are broad categories that reflect impressions and beliefs about what behavior is appropriate for females and males. All stereotypes, whether they relate to gender, ethnicity, or other categories, refer to an image of what the typical member of a category is like. Many stereotypes are so general that they become ambiguous. Consider the categories of "masculine" and "feminine." Diverse behaviors can be assigned to each category, such as scoring a touchdown or growing facial hair for "masculine," playing with dolls or wearing lipstick for "feminine." But the behaviors that make up a category can be modified by cultural change. At one point in history, muscular development might be thought of as masculine; at another time a more lithe, slender physique might be the ideal masculine body. Likewise, at some points in history, the "ideal" feminine body has been voluptuous and round. Today, it is thinner and athletic. Earlier in the twentieth century, being dependent was thought to be an important dimension of femininity, whereas today a much greater emphasis is placed on females' sensitivity to others in relationships. Which behaviors are popularly held to reflect a category also can fluctuate according to socioeconomic circumstances. For example, more low-income than middle-class individuals have a rough-and-tough image of masculinity.

Stereotyping students as "masculine" or "feminine" can have significant consequences (Kite, 2001). Labeling a male "feminine" or a female "masculine" can diminish his or her social status and acceptance in groups.

Gender stereotyping changes developmentally. Stereotypic gender beliefs begin to take root during the early childhood years, increase in the early elementary school years, and then decline somewhat in the middle and late elementary school years (Bigler, Liben, & Yekel, 1992). In early adolescence, gender stereotyping might increase again. As their bodies change dramatically during puberty, boys and girls are often confused and concerned about what is happening to them. The safe strategy for boys is to become the very best male possible (that is, "masculine"), and the safe strategy for girls is to become the very best female possible (that is, "feminine"). Thus, gender intensification created by pubertal change can produce greater stereotyping in young adolescents (Galambos & others, 1985).

Stereotypes are often negative and can be wrapped in prejudice and discrimination. **Sexism** is prejudice and discrimination against an individual because of the person's sex. A person who says that women cannot be competent engineers is expressing sexism. So is a person who says that men cannot be competent early childhood teachers. Later in this chapter, when we discuss gender in the schools, we will describe some strategies for creating a nonsexist classroom.

Gender Similarities and Differences in Academically Relevant Domains
Many aspects of students' lives can be examined to determine how similar or different girls and boys are (Crawford & Unger, 2000).

Physical Performance   Because physical education is an integral part of U.S. educational systems, it is important to address gender similarities and differences in physical

gender schema theory A theory that an individual's attention and behavior are guided by an internal motivation to conform to gender-based sociocultural standards and stereotypes.

gender stereotypes Broad categories that reflect impressions and beliefs about what behavior is appropriate for females and males.

sexism Prejudice and discrimination against an individual because of the person's sex.

performance (Eisenberg, Martin, & Fabes, 1996). In general, boys outperform girls in athletic skills such as running, throwing, and jumping. In the elementary school years the differences often are not large; they become more dramatic in the middle school years (Smoll & Schutz, 1990). The hormonal changes of puberty result in increased muscle mass for boys and increased body fat for girls. This leads to an advantage for boys in activities related to strength, size, and power. Nonetheless, environmental factors are involved in physical performance even after puberty. Girls are less likely to participate in activities that promote the motor skills necessary to do well in sports (Thomas & Thomas, 1988).

Activity level is another area of physical performance in which gender differences occur. From very early in life, boys are more active than girls are in terms of gross motor movements. In the classroom, this means that boys are more likely than girls to fidget and move around the room, and they are less likely to be paying attention. In physical education classes, boys expend more energy through movement than girls do.

Math and Science Skills   Mixed findings have been reported regarding math skills. In some analyses, boys perform better at math and this has long been a source of concern (Eisenberg, Martin, & Fabes, 1996). Overall, however, when they exist, gender differences in math skills tend to be small. Statements such as "Males outperform females in math" should not be read as a claim that all males outperform all females in math. Rather, such statements refer to averages (Hyde & Plant, 1995). Also, not all recent studies have shown differences. For example, in a national study, no differences in boys' and girls' math performance were found in the fourth, eighth, and twelfth grades (Coley, 2001).

In addition, when gender differences in math do appear, they are not uniform across contexts. Boys do better at math related to measurement, science, and sports; girls do better at math that involves such traditional female tasks as cooking and sewing (Linn & Hyde, 1989).

One area of math that has been examined for possible gender differences is visual-spatial skills, which include being able to rotate objects mentally and determine what they would look like when rotated. These types of skills are important in courses such as plane and solid geometry. Some experts argue that if there is a gender difference in visual-spatial skills, it is very small (Hyde & Mezulis, 2001).

What about science? Are there gender differences? In one recent national study of science achievement, boys did slightly better in science than girls in the fourth and eighth grades, but there were no gender differences in the twelfth grade (National Assessment of Educational Progress, 2001) (see figure 5.3 on page 158). In another study focused on eighth- and tenth-graders, boys scored higher than girls on science tests, especially among average- and high-ability students (Burkham, Lee, & Smerdon, 1997). In science

"So according to the stereotype, you can put two and two together, but I can read the handwriting on the wall."

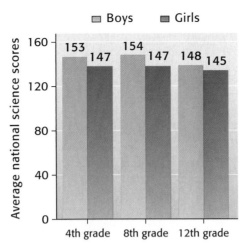

FIGURE 5.3 National Science Scores for Boys and Girls

In the National Assessment of Educational Progress (2001), data collected in 2000 indicated that boys had slightly higher scores than girls in the fourth and eighth grades, but there was no statistical gender difference in the twelfth grade. The science scores could range from 0 to 300.

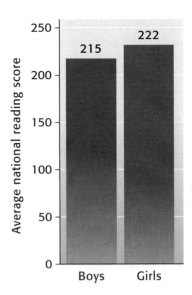

FIGURE 5.4 National Reading Scores for Boys and Girls

In the National Assessment of Educational Progress, data collected in 2003 indicated that girls did better in reading in the fourth and eighth grades (National Center for Education Statistics, 2004). The data for the fourth grade are shown above. An earlier assessment found that the gender difference in reading favoring girls also occurs in the twelfth grade (National Assessment of Educational Progress, 1998).

classes that emphasized "hands-on" lab activities, girls' science test scores improved considerably. This suggests the importance of active involvement of students in science classrooms, which may promote gender equity.

Many gender experts believe the gender differences in math and science that do exist are due to the experiences that boys and girls have. There are far more male than female math and science models in the culture. Boys take more math and science courses than girls do. For example, in one recent national survey males were overwhelmingly more likely to take computer science and physics courses (Coley, 2001). Also, parents have higher expectations for boys' math and science skills. In one study of 1,500 families, parents bought more math and science books and games for their sons than for their daughters, said that boys have more math talent than girls, and commented that boys are better suited to a career in math (Eccles & others, 1991).

Verbal Skills A major review of gender similarities and differences conducted in the 1970s concluded that girls have better verbal skills than boys do (Maccoby & Jacklin, 1974). However, more recent analyses suggest that in some instances there may be little or no differences in girls' and boys' verbal skills. For example, today males score as high as females on the verbal portion of the SAT test (Educational Testing Service, 2002).

However, during the elementary and secondary school years there is strong evidence that females outperform males in reading and writing. In recent national studies, females had higher reading achievement than males in grades 4, 8, and 12, with the gap widening as students progressed through school (Coley, 2001; National Assessment of Educational Progress, 1998, 2001). Figure 5.4 shows the gender gap in reading in a national assessment of reading in the fourth grade (National Assessment of Educational Progress, 2001). In the same studies, females also performed better than males in grades 4, 8, and 12 in writing skills.

Educational Attainment   Males are more likely to drop out of school than females, although the difference is small (15 percent versus 13 percent) (National Center for Education Statistics, 2001). Females (90 percent) are more likely than males (87 percent) to complete high school in the United States.

Recent evidence suggests that boys predominate in the academic bottom half of high school classes (DeZolt & Hull, 2001). That is, although many boys perform at the average or advanced level, the bottom 50 percent academically is made up mainly of boys.

The percentage of males in college during the 1950s was almost 60 percent. Today, the percentage of males enrolled in college classes has dropped to approximately 45 percent (DeZolt & Hull, 2001).

Piecing together the information about school dropouts the percentage of males in the bottom half of their high school classes, and the percentage of males in college classes, we can conclude that females show greater overall academic interest and achievement than males in the United States. Females are more likely to be engaged with academic material, be attentive in class, put forth more academic effort, and participate more in class than boys are (DeZolt & Hull, 2001).

Relationship Skills   Sociolinguist Deborah Tannen (1990) distinguishes between rapport talk and report talk. **Rapport talk** is the language of conversation and a way of establishing connections and negotiating relationships. **Report talk** is talk that gives information. Making a speech is an example of report talk. Males hold center stage through such verbal performances as storytelling, joking, and lecturing with information. Females enjoy private talk more and conversation that is relationship-oriented.

Tannen says that boys and girls grow up in different worlds of talk. Parents, siblings, peers, teachers, and others talk to girls and boys differently. The play of boys and girls is different. Boys tend to play in large groups that are hierarchically structured, and their groups usually have a leader who tells the others what to do and how to do it. Boys' games have winners and losers, and boys often argue about who won. Boys often boast of their skill and argue about who is best at what. In contrast, girls are more likely to play in small groups or pairs, and the center of a girl's world is often a best friend. In girls' friendships and peer groups, intimacy is pervasive. Turn-taking is more characteristic of girls' games than boys' games. Much of the time, girls simply like to sit and talk with each other, concerned more about being liked by others than jockeying for status in some obvious way.

Prosocial Behavior   Are there gender differences in prosocial behavior (positive moral behavior)? Females view themselves as more prosocial and empathetic, and they engage in more prosocial behavior than do males (Eisenberg & Morris, 2004). For example, a review of research found that across childhood and adolescence, females engaged in more prosocial behavior (Eisenberg & Fabes, 1998). The biggest gender difference occurred for kind and considerate behavior, with a smaller difference in sharing.

Aggression and Self-Regulation   One of the most consistent gender differences is that boys are more physically aggressive than girls. The difference is especially pronounced when children are provoked, and this difference occurs across all cultures and appears very early in children's development (Ostrov, Keating, & Ostrov, 2004). Both biological and environmental factors have been proposed to account for gender differences in physical aggression. Biological factors include heredity and hormones; environmental factors include cultural expectations, adult and peer models, and the rewarding of physical aggression in boys.

Although boys are consistently more physically aggressive than girls, might girls show as much or more verbal aggression, such as yelling, than boys? When verbal aggression is examined, gender differences typically either disappear or are sometimes even more pronounced in girls (Eagly & Steffen, 1986). Also, girls are far more likely to engage in what is called *relational aggression,* which involves such behaviors as trying to make others dislike a certain child by spreading malicious rumors about the child or ignoring another child when angry at him or her (Underwood, 2003, 2004).

Video Lecture: Gender Variations

rapport talk The language of conversation and a way of establishing connections and negotiating relationships; more characteristic of females than males.

report talk Talk that gives information; more characteristic of males than females.

An important skill is to be able to regulate and control one's emotions and behavior. Males usually show less self-regulation than females (Eisenberg, Martin, & Fabes, 1996). This low self-control can translate into behavior problems. In one study, children's low self-regulation was linked with greater aggression, teasing of others, overreaction to frustration, low cooperation, and inability to delay gratification (Block & Block, 1980).

Gender Controversy   The previous sections revealed some substantial differences in physical abilities, reading and writing skills, aggression and self-regulation, and relationship skills but small or nonexistent differences in many areas of math and science. Controversy swirls about such similarities and differences (Hyde, 2004; Hyde & Mezulis, 2001). Alice Eagly (1996, 2000, 2001) argues that the belief that gender differences are small or nonexistent is rooted in the feminist commitment to gender similarity and political equality. Many feminists fear that gender differences will be interpreted as deficiencies on the part of females and be seen as biologically based. They argue that such conclusions could revive traditional stereotypes that females are innately inferior to males (Crawford & Unger, 2000). Eagly responds that a large body of research on gender now exists and reveals stronger gender differences than feminists acknowledge. This controversy shows how difficult it can be to negotiate the science and politics of gender.

Gender-Role Classification

Gender-role classification involves evaluating boys and girls in terms of groups of personality traits. In the past, a well-adjusted boy was supposed to be independent, aggressive, and powerful. A well-adjusted female was supposed to be dependent, nurturant, and uninterested in power. At the same time, overall, masculine characteristics were considered to be healthy and good by society, while feminine characteristics were considered undesirable.

In the 1970s, as more females and males began to express open dissatisfaction with the burdens imposed by rigid gender expectations, alternatives to femininity and masculinity were proposed. Instead of restricting masculinity to male competency and femininity to female competency, it was proposed that individuals could have both "masculine" and "feminine" traits. This thinking led to the development of the concept of **androgyny,** which refers to the presence of desirable masculine and feminine characteristics in the same person (Bem, 1977; Spence & Helmreich, 1978). The androgynous boy might be assertive ("masculine") and nurturant ("feminine"). The androgynous girl might be powerful ("masculine") and sensitive to others' feelings ("feminine").

Measures have been developed to assess androgyny. One of the most widely used measures is the Bem Sex-Role Inventory. To see whether your gender-role classification is masculine, feminine, or androgynous, complete Self-Assessment 5.1.

Gender experts such as Sandra Bem argue that androgynous individuals are more flexible, competent, and mentally healthy than their masculine or feminine counterparts. To some degree, though, which gender-role classification is "best" depends on the context. For example, feminine orientations might be more desirable in close relationships because of the expressive nature of close relationships, and masculine orientations might be more desirable in traditional academic and work settings because of the achievement demands in these contexts.

Of special concern are adolescent boys who adopt a strong masculine role. Researchers have found that high-masculinity adolescent boys often engage in problem behaviors, such as delinquency, drug abuse, and unprotected sexual intercourse (Pleck, 1995). They present themselves as virile, macho, and aggressive and often do poorly in school. Too many adolescent males base their manhood on the caliber of gun they carry or the number of children they have fathered (Sullivan, 1991).

androgyny The presence of desirable masculine and feminine characteristics in the same individual.

Androgyny and Education   Can and should androgyny be taught to students? In general, it is easier to teach androgyny to girls than to boys, and it is easier to teach it before the middle school grades. For example, in one study a gender curriculum was put in

What Gender-Role Orientation Will I Present to My Students?

The items below are from the Bem Sex-Role Inventory. To find out whether your gender-role classification is masculine, feminine, or androgynous, rate yourself on each item from 1 (never or almost never true) to 7 (always or almost always true).

1. self-reliant	1	2	3	4	5	6	7	31. makes decisions easily	1	2	3	4	5	6	7
2. yielding	1	2	3	4	5	6	7	32. compassionate	1	2	3	4	5	6	7
3. helpful	1	2	3	4	5	6	7	33. sincere	1	2	3	4	5	6	7
4. defends own beliefs	1	2	3	4	5	6	7	34. self-sufficient	1	2	3	4	5	6	7
5. cheerful	1	2	3	4	5	6	7	35. eager to soothe hurt feelings	1	2	3	4	5	6	7
6. moody	1	2	3	4	5	6	7	36. conceited	1	2	3	4	5	6	7
7. independent	1	2	3	4	5	6	7	37. dominant	1	2	3	4	5	6	7
8. shy	1	2	3	4	5	6	7	38. soft spoken	1	2	3	4	5	6	7
9. conscientious	1	2	3	4	5	6	7	39. likable	1	2	3	4	5	6	7
10. athletic	1	2	3	4	5	6	7	40. masculine	1	2	3	4	5	6	7
11. affectionate	1	2	3	4	5	6	7	41. warm	1	2	3	4	5	6	7
12. theatrical	1	2	3	4	5	6	7	42. solemn	1	2	3	4	5	6	7
13. assertive	1	2	3	4	5	6	7	43. willing to take a stand	1	2	3	4	5	6	7
14. flatterable	1	2	3	4	5	6	7	44. tender	1	2	3	4	5	6	7
15. happy	1	2	3	4	5	6	7	45. friendly	1	2	3	4	5	6	7
16. strong personality	1	2	3	4	5	6	7	46. aggressive	1	2	3	4	5	6	7
17. loyal	1	2	3	4	5	6	7	47. gullible	1	2	3	4	5	6	7
18. unpredictable	1	2	3	4	5	6	7	48. inefficient	1	2	3	4	5	6	7
19. forceful	1	2	3	4	5	6	7	49. acts as a leader	1	2	3	4	5	6	7
20. feminine	1	2	3	4	5	6	7	50. childlike	1	2	3	4	5	6	7
21. reliable	1	2	3	4	5	6	7	51. adaptable	1	2	3	4	5	6	7
22. analytical	1	2	3	4	5	6	7	52. individualistic	1	2	3	4	5	6	7
23. sympathetic	1	2	3	4	5	6	7	53. does not use harsh language	1	2	3	4	5	6	7
24. jealous	1	2	3	4	5	6	7	54. unsystematic	1	2	3	4	5	6	7
25. has leadership abilities	1	2	3	4	5	6	7	55. competitive	1	2	3	4	5	6	7
26. sensitive to the needs of others	1	2	3	4	5	6	7	56. loves children	1	2	3	4	5	6	7
27. truthful	1	2	3	4	5	6	7	57. tactful	1	2	3	4	5	6	7
28. willing to take risks	1	2	3	4	5	6	7	58. ambitious	1	2	3	4	5	6	7
29. understanding	1	2	3	4	5	6	7	59. gentle	1	2	3	4	5	6	7
30. secretive	1	2	3	4	5	6	7	60. conventional	1	2	3	4	5	6	7

Scoring
Add up your ratings for items 1, 4, 7, 10, 13, 16, 19, 22, 25, 28, 31, 34, 37, 40, 43, 46, 49, 55, and 58. Divide the total by 20. That is your masculinity score.

Add up your ratings for items 2, 5, 8, 11, 14, 17, 20, 23, 26, 29, 32, 35, 38, 41, 44, 47, 50, 53, 56, and 59. Divide the total by 20. That is your femininity score.

Interpretation
If your masculinity score is above 4.9 (the approximate median for the masculinity scale) and your femininity score is above 4.9 (the approximate femininity median), then you would be classified as androgynous on Bem's scale.

 Go to your Student Toolbox CD-ROM for an electronic version of this form.

place for one year in the kindergarten, fifth, and ninth grades (Guttentag & Bray, 1976). It involved books, discussion materials, and classroom exercises with an androgynous bent. The program was most successful with the fifth-graders, least successful with the ninth-graders. The ninth-graders, especially the boys, showed a boomerang effect—more traditional gender-role attitudes after the year of androgynous instruction than before it.

Despite such mixed findings, the advocates of androgyny programs believe that traditional sex typing is harmful for all students and especially has prevented many girls from experiencing equal opportunity. The detractors argue that androgynous educational programs are too value-laden and ignore the diversity of gender roles in our society.

Gender-Role Transcendence Some critics of androgyny say that enough is enough and that there is too much talk about gender. They believe that androgyny is less of a panacea than originally envisioned (Paludi, 1998). An alternative is **gender-role transcendence,** the view that people's competence should be conceptualized in terms of them as persons rather than in terms of their masculinity, femininity, or androgyny (Pleck, 1983). That is, we should think about ourselves and our students as people, not as masculine, feminine, or androgynous.

Parents should rear their children to be competent individuals, not masculine, feminine, or androgynous, say the gender-role critics. They believe such gender-role classification leads to too much stereotyping.

Gender in Context

Earlier we said that the concept of gender-role classification involves categorizing people in terms of personality traits. However, recall from our discussion of personality in chapter 4, "Individual Variations," that it is beneficial to think of personality in terms of person-situation interaction rather than personality traits alone ◄ p. 126.

Helping Behavior and Emotion To see the importance of also considering gender in context, let's examine helping behavior and emotion. The stereotype is that females are better than males at helping. But it depends on the situation. Females are more likely than males to volunteer their time to help children with personal problems and engage in caregiving behavior. However, in situations where males feel a sense of competence or that involve danger, males are more likely to help (Eagly & Crowley, 1986). For example, a male is more likely than a female to stop and help a person stranded by the roadside with a flat tire.

She is emotional; he is not. That's the master emotional stereotype. However, like helping behavior, emotional differences in males and females depend on the particular emotion involved and the context in which it is displayed (Shields, 1991). Males are more likely to show anger toward strangers, especially male strangers, when they feel they have been challenged. Males also are more likely to turn their anger into aggressive action. Emotional differences between females and males often show up in contexts that highlight social roles and relationships. For example, females are more likely to discuss emotions in terms of relationships. They also are more likely to express fear and sadness.

Culture The importance of considering gender in context is most apparent when examining what is culturally prescribed behavior for females and males in different countries around the world (Best, 2001). In the United States there is now more acceptance of androgyny and similarities in male and female behavior, but in many other countries roles have remained gender-specific. For example, in many Middle Eastern countries the division of labor between males and females is dramatic. For example, in Iraq, males are socialized and schooled to work in the public sphere; females are socialized to remain in the private world of home and child rearing. The Islamic religion that predominates in Iraq dictates that the man's duty is to provide for his family and the woman's is to care for her family and household. Any deviations from this traditional masculine and feminine behavior is severely disapproved of. Likewise, in China, although women have made some strides, the male role is still dominant. Androgynous behavior and gender equity are not what most males in China want to see happen.

Eliminating Gender Bias

How gendered are social interactions between teachers and students? What can teachers do to reduce or eliminate gender bias in their classrooms ◄ p. 25?

gender-role transcendence The view that people's competence should be conceptualized in terms of them as persons rather than in terms of whether they are masculine, feminine, or androgynous.

What are some of the ways that teachers interact with students on the basis of gender?

Teacher-Student Interaction   What evidence is there that the classroom is biased against boys? Here are some factors to consider (DeZolt & Hull, 2001):

- Complying, following rules, and being neat and orderly are valued and reinforced in many classrooms. These are behaviors that are typically associated with girls rather than boys.
- A large majority of teachers are females, especially in the elementary school. This may make it more difficult for boys than girls to identify with their teachers and model their teachers' behavior.
- Boys are more likely than girls to be identified as having learning problems.
- Boys are more likely than girls to be criticized.
- School personnel tend to ignore that many boys are clearly having academic problems, especially in the language arts.
- School personnel tend to stereotype boys' behavior as problematic.

What evidence is there that the classroom is biased against girls? Consider that (Sadker & Sadker, 2000)

- In a typical classroom, girls are more compliant, boys more rambunctious. Boys demand more attention; girls are more likely to quietly wait their turn. Educators worry that girls' tendency to be compliant and quiet comes at a cost: diminished assertiveness.
- In many classrooms, teachers spend more time watching and interacting with boys, while girls work and play quietly on their own. Most teachers don't intentionally favor boys by spending more time with them, yet somehow the classroom frequently ends up with this type of gendered profile.
- Boys get more instruction than girls and more help when they have trouble with a question. Teachers often give boys more time to answer a question, more hints at the correct answer, and further tries if they give the wrong answer.
- Boys are more likely than girls to get lower grades and to be grade repeaters, yet girls are less likely to believe that they will be successful in college work.
- Girls and boys enter first grade with roughly equal levels of self-esteem, yet by the middle school years, girls' self-esteem is significantly lower than boys' (American Association of University Women, 1992).

Gender Equity
Male Issues

Through the Eyes of Teachers

Providing Girls with Positive Math Experiences

As a math teacher, I hope I do everything in my power to encourage girls to have more confidence in math. Of course, I want every girl *and* boy in my class to see that they can succeed in math. I do not allow boys to monopolize the answering of questions in my classroom. I call on girls and boys equally and I don't let any student get off the hook by saying "I don't know" or by shrugging their shoulders. I will guide students to a solution.

In one project I assign to my eighth-grade algebra students, they have to research a math concept and report about it to the class. I encourage as many students as possible, boys and girls, to research some of the famous female mathematicians. When the girls see how much women had to sacrifice in the name of mathematics years ago, it helps them to see how fortunate their opportunities are today.

Jeri Hall
Mathematics Teacher
Miller Magnet Middle School
Bibb County, Georgia

• When elementary school children are asked to list what they want to do when they grow up, boys describe more career options than girls do.

Thus, there is evidence of gender bias against both males and females in schools (DeZolt & Hull, 2001). Many school personnel are not aware of their gender-biased attitudes. These attitudes are deeply entrenched in and supported by the general culture. Increasing awareness of gender bias in schools is clearly an important strategy in reducing such bias.

Curriculum Content and Athletics Content   Schools have made considerable progress in reducing sexism and sex stereotyping in books and curriculum materials (Eisenberg, Martin, & Fabes, 1996)—largely in response to Title IX of the Educational Amendment Act of 1972, which states that schools are obligated to ensure equal treatment of females and males. As a result, textbooks and class materials are available that are free of gender bias. Also, schools now offer girls far more opportunities to take vocational educational courses and participate in athletics than was the case when their parents and grandparents went to school (Gill, 2001). In 1972, 7 percent of high school athletes were girls. Today, that figure has risen to nearly 40 percent. In addition, schools no longer can expel or eliminate services for pregnant adolescents.

Nonetheless, bias still remains at the curricular level. For example, school text adoptions occur infrequently, and therefore many students still are studying outdated, gender-biased books.

Sexual Harassment   Sexual harassment occurs in many schools (Bracey, 1997; Fitzgerald, Collinsworth, & Harned, 2001). In a study of eighth- to eleventh-graders by the American Association of University Women (1993), 83 percent of the girls and 60 percent of the boys said that they had been sexually harassed. Girls reported being more severely harassed than boys. Sixteen percent of the students said they had been sexually harassed by a teacher. Examples of harassment by students and teachers in this study included

• sexual comments, jokes, gestures, or looks
• sexual messages about a student on bathroom walls and other places or sexual rumors spread about the student
• spying on a student who was dressing or showering at school
• flashing or mooning
• comments that a student was gay or lesbian
• touching, grabbing, or pinching in a sexual manner
• intentionally brushing up against a student in a sexual way
• pulling a student's clothing off or down
• blocking or cornering a student in a sexual way
• being forced to kiss someone or do something sexual other than kissing

quid pro quo sexual harassment
Threats by a school employee to base an educational decision (such as a grade) on a student's submission to unwelcome sexual conduct.

The Office for Civil Rights of the U.S. Department of Education recently published a 40-page policy guide on sexual harassment. In this guide, a distinction is made between quid pro quo and hostile environment sexual harassment. **Quid pro quo sexual harassment** occurs when a school employee threatens to base an educational decision (such as a grade) on a student's submission to unwelcome sexual conduct. For example, a teacher gives a student an *A* for allowing the teacher's sexual advances, or the teacher gives the student an *F* for resisting the teacher's approaches. **Hostile environment sexual harassment** occurs when students are subjected to unwelcome sexual conduct that is so severe, persistent, or pervasive that it limits the students' ability to benefit from their education. Such a hostile environment is usually created by a series of incidents, such as repeated sexual overtures.

Sexual harassment is a form of power and dominance of one person over another, which can result in harmful consequences for the victim. Sexual harassment can be especially damaging when the perpetrators are teachers and other adults who have considerable power and authority over students (Lee & others, 1995). As a society, we need to be less tolerant of sexual harassment (Firpo-Triplett, 1997).

Teaching Strategies
For Reducing Gender Bias

Every student, female or male, deserves an education that is free of gender bias. Here are some strategies for attaining this desirable educational climate (Derman-Sparks & the Anti-Bias Curriculum Task Force, 1989; Sadker & Sadker, 1994):

1. *If you are given textbooks that are gender-biased, discuss this with your students.* By talking with your students about stereotyping and bias in the texts, you can help them think critically about such important social issues. If these textbooks are not gender-fair, supplement them with other materials that are. Many schools, libraries, and colleges have gender-fair materials that you can use.

2. *Make sure that school activities and exercises are not gender-biased.* Assign students projects in which they find articles about nonstereotypical males and females, such as a female engineer or a male early childhood education teacher. Have students create a display of photographs and pictures of women and men performing the same kind of tasks at home and at work. Use the display to talk with students about the tasks that adults do and what the students will be doing when they grow up. Invite people from the community who have nonstereotypical jobs (such as a male flight attendant or a female construction worker) to come to your class and talk with your students.

3. *Be a nonsexist role model as a teacher.* Help students learn new skills and share tasks in a nonsexist manner.

4. *Analyze the seating chart in your classroom and determine whether there are pockets of gender segregation.* When your students work in groups, monitor whether the groups are balanced by gender.

5. *Enlist someone to track your questioning and reinforcement patterns with boys and girls.* Do this on several occasions to ensure that you are giving equal attention and support to girls and boys.

6. *Use nonbiased language.* Don't use the pronoun *he* to refer to inanimate objects or unspecified persons. Replace words such as *fireman, policeman,* and *mailman* with words such as *firefighter, police officer,* and *letter carrier.* To improve your use of nonsexist language, consult *The Non-Sexist Word Finder: A Dictionary of Gender-Free Usage* (Maggio, 1987). Also ask students to suggest fair terminology (Wellhousen, 1996).

7. *Keep up-to-date on sex equity in education.* Read professional journals on this topic. Be aware of your own rights as a female or male and don't stand for sexual inequity and discrimination.

8. *Be aware of sexual harassment in schools and don't let it happen.*

Sexual Harassment

hostile environment sexual harassment Subjection of students to unwelcome sexual conduct that is so severe, persistent, or pervasive that it limits the students' ability to benefit from their education.

Through the Eyes of Teachers

The Inclusive Quilt

Judy Logan has taught language arts and social studies for many years in San Francisco. Following is her description of the inclusive quilt project.

In my 25 years of teaching middle school, one of my goals has been for my classroom to be a blend of some of the things I know and some of the things my students know. The quilt experience serves as an example. . . . My idea was to have the students feel connected not only to the women in the fields of science, politics, art, social reform, music, sports, literature, journalism, space, law, civil rights, education, humor, etc., but also to the women in their own families.

I put a big piece of butcher paper on the blackboard, with the word *Inclusive* at the top, and asked the students to develop a list of what was needed to make our quilt truly inclusive. Hands popped up, and students volunteered categories first. We should have women in medicine. Sports. Civil Rights. The list grew.

What else? How else can we make this quilt inclusive? What else do we know about diversity? Hands popped up again to create a second list. We should have Native American women. European American women. Latino women. Asian American women. Lesbian women. Again, our list grew. . . . We began to brainstorm a third list of individual women who were potential subjects for quilt squares. We created a long list of possibilities like Nancy Reagan, Jackie Kennedy, and Martha Washington, who did not end up on the final quilt itself, because the students decided they didn't want to have a lot of presidents' wives on the quilt. They ended up honoring Eleanor Roosevelt and Abigail Adams, who fit other categories on our list, such as social reform. . . .

Seventh- and eighth-graders, who are not officially part of this sixth-grade core assignment, began to hear about the quilt and volunteer to join us. They come in at lunch time. "Can we do a patch, too?" Yes . . . "Mrs. Logan, can I do you?" Yes, I would be honored. Frankie, an eighth-grader, asks if she can do herself as a Future Woman. What a good idea I reply, and give her a blank patch. . . .

I give some thought to whom I want to honor on my patch. I decide to honor Brenda Collins, who is also named Eagle Woman. She is a member of the Bird Clan of the Cherokee Nation. She is a medicine woman, the first woman of her clan to get a Ph.D. and a teacher at Santa Rosa Junior College. She is also a friend and mentor. I have heard her speak several times, and I remember her saying that to be an educated Indian women is like having a foot in each of two canoes, in rapid waters, always balancing two cultures. I decide to put two canoes and rapid water on her patch, with an eagle's wing by one canoe, and her doctoral degree by the other canoe. . . .

The finished quilt is colorful and diverse. No two patches are the same. I have provided the outline, the framework for the assignment, but each participant has created something uniquely their own. . . . A good curriculum is like a poem that follows a particular pattern, but that allows the audience to bring their own experiences to the construction of its meaning. It leaves a corner open for the reader to enter (Logan, 1997, pp. 1–23).

Judy Logan, in front of the inclusive quilt in her classroom.

⚠ **Review and Reflect**

③ Explain the various facets of gender, including similarities and differences in boys and girls; discuss gender issues in teaching.

Review

- What is gender and what are gender roles? How have psychologists attempted to explain gender from biological, socialization, and cognitive perspectives?
- What problems are created by gender stereotypes? How are boys and girls similar and different?
- How can gender roles be classified?
- How might looking at behaviors in context reduce gender stereotyping?
- What evidence is there of gender bias in the classroom? What progress have schools made in reducing bias?

Reflect

- From your own K–12 education, come up with at least one instance in which your school or teacher favored either boys or girls. As a teacher, how would you try to correct that gender bias?

 ENTER THE DEBATE

1. Should teachers treat boys and girls differently?
2. Should students whose first language is not English be taught in a bilingual program?

 Teaching Experience

- **Working with English Language Learners**
- **Using Student Culture to Help Motivate Learning**
- **Teaching a Puerto Rican Novel**

Crack the Case These Boys

Larry is a nine-year-old boy in the fourth-grade class in which you are student teaching. You have heard him and a number of other students complaining about gender bias on the part of their teacher, Mrs. Jones. One day you overhear Larry being reprimanded by Mrs. Jones for an altercation he had with Annie, a female classmate.

"It isn't fair, Mrs. Jones," Larry says. "Annie took my homework and ripped it, and I get in trouble for taking it back."

"Now, Larry," admonishes Mrs. Jones. "You know Annie would never do that. You go apologize to her. I'll see you after school."

Larry walks away with a very angry look on his face, muttering, "The girls *never* get in trouble. It's always the boys."

You have heard this from students of Mrs. Jones in the past but have never really believed it. Over the course of the next three weeks you pay much closer attention to Mrs. Jones' behavior with a special sensitivity to gender bias. You notice that girls receive higher grades than do boys, except in math. Boys are required to stay after school several times, girls not at all. When Mrs. Jones is on recess duty and there are altercations between boys and girls on the playground, the boys end up standing against the wall, while the girls walk away, smiling. In class, the girls are used as models of behaviors *much* more frequently than the boys. Their work receives more praise as well. You examine what students have been

reading over the course of the year. Their required reading thus far consists of *Little House on the Prairie, Charlotte's Web,* and *Little Women.*

The only thing you notice that appears to favor the boys is the amount of attention received. They seem to receive much more of Mrs. Jones' attention. Upon further examination, however, you see that much of the attention is disciplinary in nature.

At one point, you overhear Mrs. Jones as she is walking down the hall, saying to a colleague, "These boys, I just don't know what I am going to do with them."

- What are the issues in this case?
- Based on the ideas and information presented in your text to this point, discuss what you believe to be happening in this classroom and the possible influences on Mrs. Jones' ideas of gender. Cite research and theories of gender development.
- What influence do you believe Mrs. Jones' behavior will have on her students? Why?
- What should Mrs. Jones do at this point? Why? What sort of outside assistance might help her?
- If you were a student teacher in this classroom, what, if anything, would you do? Why?
- What will you do in your own classroom to minimize gender bias?

Reach Your Learning Goals

1. **Discuss how variations in culture, socioeconomic status, and ethnic background might raise special classroom needs.**

   - *Culture* refers to the behavior patterns, beliefs, and all other products of a particular group of people that are passed on from generation to generation. The products result from the interaction among groups of people and their environment over many years. Cross-cultural studies compare what happens in one culture with what happens in one or more other cultures, providing information about the degree to which people are similar and the degree to which certain behaviors are specific to certain cultures. Cultures have been classified as individualistic (having a set of values that give priority to personal goals rather than group goals) and collectivistic (having a set of values that support the group). Many Western cultures are individualistic, many Eastern cultures collectivistic.

   - Socioeconomic status (SES) is the categorization of people according to economic, educational, and occupational characteristics. The most emphasis is given to distinctions between individuals with low and middle socioeconomic status. Low-SES individuals usually have less education, less power to influence schools and other community institutions, and fewer economic resources than higher-SES individuals. Currently more than 20 percent of America's children live in poverty. Children in poverty face problems at home and at school that present barriers to their learning. Schools in low-income neighborhoods often have fewer resources and less-experienced teachers, and they are more likely to encourage rote learning rather than thinking skills.

   - The word *ethnic* comes from the Greek word meaning "nation." *Ethnicity* refers to a shared pattern of characteristics such as cultural heritage, nationality, race, religion, and language. Everyone is a member of one or more ethnic groups. The term *race* is now discredited as a biological term but unfortunately continues to be used in stereotyping people. The school population increasingly consists of children of color, predicted to reach 50 percent by 2025. School segregation is still a factor in the education of children of color. African American and Latino students are less likely than non-Latino White and Asian American students to be enrolled in college preparatory courses. Prejudice is an unjustified negative attitude toward an individual because of the individual's membership in a group. Ogbu believes there continues to be considerable prejudice against children of color in American education. Historical, economic, and social experiences produce legitimate differences among ethnic groups, and it is important to recognize these differences. However, too often the differences are viewed as deficits on the part of the minority group when compared with the mainstream non-Latino White group. It is important to recognize the extensive diversity that exists within each cultural group.

   - Bilingual education aims to teach academic subjects to immigrant children in their native languages (most often in Spanish) while gradually adding English instruction. Proponents of bilingual education argue that it helps immigrants to value their family and culture, as well as increase their self-esteem, thus making academic success more likely. Critics say it harms immigrant children by failing to adequately instruct them in English and leaving them unprepared for the workplace. However, researchers have found that bilingualism does not interfere with performance in either language. Other second-language considerations focus on the United States being one of the few countries in the world in which most students graduate from high school knowing only their own language and second-language learning being more successful in childhood than in adolescence.

2. **Describe some ways to promote multicultural education.**

   - Multicultural education is education that values diversity and includes the perspectives of a variety of cultural groups on a regular basis. Empowerment, which consists of providing people with the intellectual and coping skills to succeed and make this a more just world, is an important aspect of multicultural education today. It involves giving students the opportunity to learn about the experiences, struggles, and visions of many different ethnic and cultural groups. The hope is that empowerment will raise minority students' self esteem, reduce prejudice, and provide more-equal educational opportunities.

   - Culturally relevant teaching is an important aspect of multicultural education. It seeks to make connections with the learner's cultural background.

   - Issues-centered education also is an important aspect of multicultural education. In this approach, students are taught to systematically examine issues that involve equity and social justice.

   - Among the strategies/related ideas for improving relationships between children from different ethnic groups are these: the jigsaw classroom (having students from different cultural backgrounds cooperate by doing different parts of a project to reach a common goal), positive personal contact, perspective taking, critical thinking and emotional intelligence, reduced bias, increased tolerance, and development of the school and community as a team.

   - Proponents of teaching a core of White Anglo-Protestant values argue that such values as mutual respect, individual rights, and tolerance of differences should be taught to all children. Critics argue that these are not peculiarly White Anglo-Protestant values but simply Western tradition. Hirsch argues that students should be taught a common core of cultural knowledge to ensure that they become "culturally literate."

3 Explain the various facets of gender, including similarities and differences in boys and girls; discuss gender issues in teaching.

- *Gender* refers to the sociocultural dimension of being female or male, as distinguished from *sex,* which is the biological dimension of being female or male. Gender roles are expectations that prescribe how males and females should think, feel, and act. In terms of biological views on gender development, the 23rd pair of chromosomes (the sex chromosomes) determines whether a fetus is female (XX) or male (XY). At issue is the directness or indirectness of biological effects. The brains of females and males are far more similar than different. When students' gender behavior is at issue, biology is not destiny. Two social views of gender are psychoanalytic theory and social cognitive theory. Peers especially play a powerful role in rewarding gender-appropriate behavior and punishing gender-inappropriate behavior. Two cognitive views on gender are cognitive developmental theory and gender schema theory.

- Gender stereotypes are broad categories that reflect impressions and beliefs about what behavior is appropriate for females and males. All stereotypes involve an image of what the typical member of a category is like. Some gender stereotypes can be harmful for children, especially those that involve sexism (prejudice and discrimination against a person because of the person's sex).

- Psychologists have studied gender similarities and differences in physical performance, math and science skills, verbal skills, school attainment, relationship skills (rapport talk and report talk), and aggression/self-regulation. In some cases, gender differences are substantial (as in physical performance, reading and writing skills, school attainment, physical aggression, and relationship skills); in others they are small or nonexistent (as in many math skills). Today, controversy still swirls about how common or rare such differences really are.

- Gender-role classification focuses on how masculine, feminine, or androgynous an individual is. In the past, competent males were supposed to be masculine (powerful, for example), females feminine (nurturant, for example). The 1970s brought the concept of androgyny, the idea that the most competent individuals have both masculine and feminine positive characteristics. A special concern involves adolescents who adopt a strong masculine role. Programs that have tried to teach androgyny to students have had mixed results. Some experts believe too much attention is given to gender in our society and that we should instead pursue gender-role transcendence. Evaluation of gender-role categories and gender similarities and differences in areas such as helping behavior and emotion suggest that the best way to think about gender is not in terms of personality traits but instead in terms of person-situation interaction (gender in context). Although androgyny and multiple gender roles are often available for American children to choose from, many countries around the world still are male-dominant.

- There is gender bias in schools against boys and girls. Many school personnel are unaware of these biases. An important teaching strategy is to attempt to eliminate gender bias. Schools have made considerable progress in reducing sexism and sex stereotyping in books and curriculum materials, but some bias still exists. Sexual harassment is a special concern in schools and is more pervasive than once believed. Recently, a distinction has been made between quid pro quo and hostile environment sexual harassment.

 KEY TERMS

culture 134	bilingual education 143	social cognitive theory of gender 154	report talk 159
cross-cultural studies 135	multicultural education 146	cognitive developmental theory of gender 155	androgyny 160
individualism 135	empowerment 146		gender-role transcendence 162
collectivism 135	jigsaw classroom 148	gender schema theory 156	quid pro quo sexual harassment 164
socioeconomic status (SES) 136	gender 153	gender stereotypes 156	hostile environment sexual harassment 165
ethnicity 141	gender roles 154	sexism 156	
prejudice 142	psychoanalytic theory of gender 154	rapport talk 159	

PORTFOLIO ACTIVITIES

Now that you have a good understanding of this chapter, complete these exercises to expand your thinking.

Independent Reflection

Fostering Cultural Understanding in the Classroom. Imagine that you are teaching a social studies lesson about the westward movement in U.S. history and a student makes a racist, stereotyped statement about Native Americans, such as "The Indians were hot-tempered and showed their hostility toward the White settlers." How would you handle this situation? (Banks, 1997b). Describe the strategy you would adopt. (INTASC: Principles *1, 2, 4, 6, 7*)

Collaborative Work

Planning for Diversity. With three or four other students in the class, come up with a list of specific diversity goals for your future classrooms. Also brainstorm and come up with some innovative activities to help students gain positive diversity experiences, such as the inclusive quilt discussed in this chapter. Summarize the diversity goals and activities. (INTASC: Principles *3, 4, 5, 6*)

Research/Field Experience Reflections

Equity in Action. Observe lessons being taught in several classrooms that include boys and girls and students from different ethnic groups. Did the teachers interact with females and males differently? If so, how? Did the teachers interact with students from different ethnic groups in different ways? If so, how? Describe your observations. (INTASC: Principles *3, 6, 9*)

 Go to the Online Learning Center for downloadable portfolio templates.

TAKING IT TO THE NET

1. How does your state measure up in the area of children's socioeconomic status and school resources? Offer some evidence as to why you think your state ranks low/average/high, compared with other states. How can conditions be improved?
2. What is your position on the debate about multicultural education? Do you believe that multicultural perspectives should be integrated into academic subjects? Or do you think that multicultural education dilutes the rigor of a "regular" curriculum and that many subjects do not lend themselves well to this approach? Why?
3. Analyze a curriculum activity at the Teaching Tolerance website, such as "Critical Equations." Discuss how conducting this kind of lesson could help reduce gender, racial, or cultural bias in the classroom.

Connect to the Online Learning Center to explore possible answers.

STUDY, PRACTICE, AND SUCCEED

 Go to chapter 5 on the Online Learning Center at www.mhhe.com/santrockedu2e to access the student study guide with practice quizzes, web links, portfolio resources, PowerWeb articles and news feeds, and the online resources referenced in the chapter.

 Go to your Student Toolbox CD-ROM to access the resources and activities referenced in the chapter and

- Resources to help you prepare for the PRAXIS II™ exam

- **Application Resources,** including additional *Crack the Case* studies, electronic versions of the *Self-Assessments,* Application Exercises, and Site Observation Questions
- **Study Resources,** including Learning Goals, the Chapter Summary, a *Test Your Learning* exercise, and multiple-choice, true/false, matching, key terms, and short-answer quizzes
- **Professional Resources,** including a Lesson Plan Builder and *Bibliomaker*

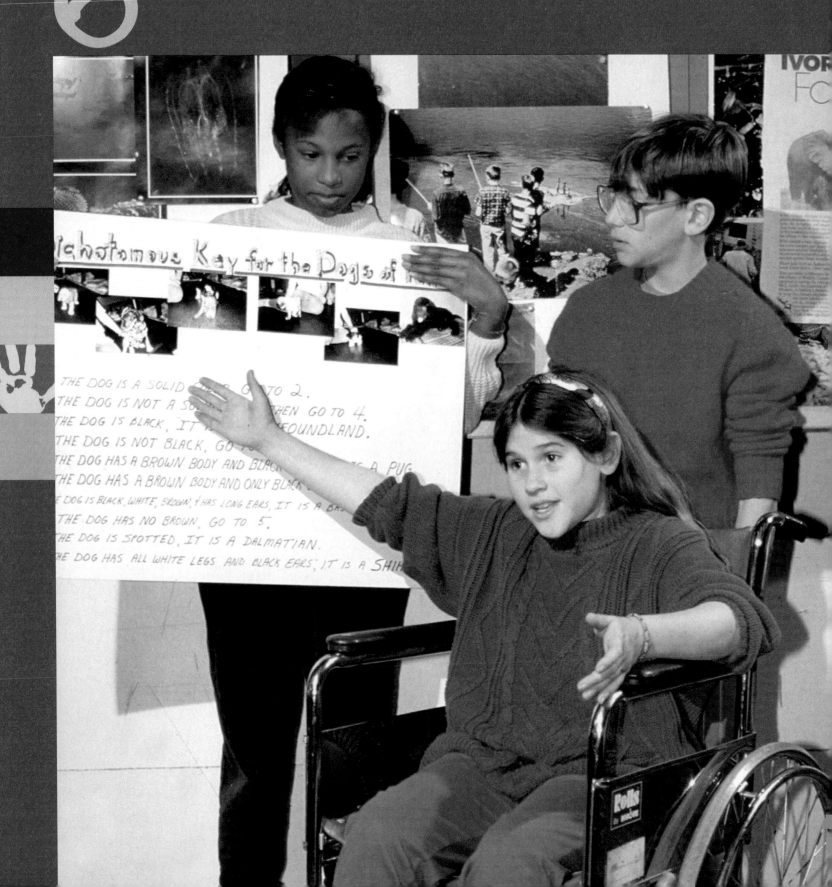

> Only the educated are free.
> —Epicurus
> *Greek Philosopher,*
> *4th Century* B.C.

Chapter Learning Goals After you have completed your study of this chapter, you should be able to reach these learning goals:

1 Describe the various types of disabilities and disorders.

2 Explain the legal framework, planning, placement, and provision of services for children with disabilities.

3 Define what gifted means and discuss some approaches to teaching children who are gifted.

Teaching Stories Verna Rollins

Verna Rollins teaches language arts at West Middle School in Ypsilanti, Michigan, and has developed a reputation for effectively dealing with so-called hard to teach or difficult students. She has found that the best strategy to use with these students is to find out what they need, decide how to provide it, provide it, and constantly evaluate whether it is working. She tells the story of one such student who was taught in her regular education classroom at the insistence of his mother but against the wishes of the special education staff. Here is Verna Rollins' description of how this went:

> Jack was in a special education classroom for children with physical disabilities. He has twisted legs, cerebral palsy, seizures, and some other brain damage from birth. He also has a comparatively short attention span. Since he drools, speaks in a loud monotone, stutters when he is excited, and has so little motor control that his penmanship is unreadable, people often think he is mentally retarded. He was not challenged to read or to write in his special classroom, essentially being made to think that he couldn't really do well at either one. Actually, he is quite bright.

> My strategies included making sure that he had all the equipment he needed to succeed. I gave him tissues for the drooling and mutually agreed-upon reminders to wipe his mouth. I found that he could speak softly and without stuttering if he calmed down. We developed a signaling plan in which I would clear my throat when he talked too loudly and I would prompt him with the phrase "slow speech" when he was too excited to speak in a smooth voice.

> He used a computer to take quizzes and needed a little more time to complete any task, but he was so excited about being "out in the real world" that his attention span improved, as did his self-worth. In fact, his mother wrote a letter to me expressing her gratitude for the "most positive influence you have been on him! You have reinstilled and greatly increased his love of reading and writing. You have given my child a wonderful gift."

For many years, public schools did little to educate children with disabilities. However, in the last several decades, federal legislation has mandated that children with disabilities receive a free, appropriate education. Increasingly, children with disabilities are being educated in the regular classroom.

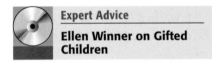

Expert Advice

Ellen Winner on Gifted Children

Learners who are exceptional include both children with some type of disability and children who are classified as gifted. We will discuss both types of exceptionalities but focus mainly on the former.

WHO ARE CHILDREN WITH DISABILITIES?

Approximately 11 percent of all children from six to seventeen years of age in the United States receive special education or related services. Figure 6.1 shows the approximate percentages of children with various disabilities who receive special education services (U.S. Department of Education, 2000). Within this group, a little more than half have a learning disability. Substantial percentages of students also have speech or language

The currently accepted description is "children with disabilities" rather than "disabled children" or "handicapped children." *Why the changes in terminology?*

Learning Disabilities	2,817,148	50.8%
Speech and Language Impairments	1,074,548	19.4
Mental Retardation	611,076	11.0
Emotional Disturbance	463,262	8.4
Multiple Disabilities	107,763	1.9
Hearing Impairments	70,883	1.3
Orthopedic Impairments	69,495	1.3
Other Health Impairments	220,831	4.0
Visual Impairments	26,132	0.5
Autism	53,576	1.0
Deaf-Blindness	1,609	>0.1
Traumatic Brain Injury	12,933	0.2
Developmental Delay	11,910	0.2
Total	5,541,166	

Note: The figures represent children with a disability who received special education services in the 1998–1999 school year. Children with multiple disabilities also have been counted under various single disabilities.

FIGURE 6.1 **The Diversity of Children Who Have a Disability**

impairments (19 percent of those with disabilities), mental retardation (11 percent), or serious emotional disturbance (8 percent). Figure 6.2 shows the three highest percentages of students with a disability who were served by federal programs in 2000–2001 (National Center for Education Statistics, 2002.)

At one time the terms *disability* and *handicap* were used interchangeably, but today a distinction is made between them. A **disability** involves a limitation on a person's functioning that restricts the individual's abilities. A **handicap** is a condition imposed on a person who has a disability. This condition could be imposed by society, the physical environment, or the person's own attitudes (Lewis, 2002).

Educators increasingly speak of "children with disabilities" rather than "disabled children" to emphasize the person, not the disability. Also, children with disabilities are no longer referred to as "handicapped," although the term *handicapping conditions* is still used to describe the impediments to the learning and functioning of individuals with a disability that have been imposed by society. For example, when children who use a wheelchair do not have adequate access to a bathroom, transportation, and so on, this is referred to as a handicapping condition.

Our discussion will group disabilities and disorders as follows: sensory disorders, physical disorders, mental retardation, speech and language disorders, learning disabilities, attention deficit hyperactivity disorder, and emotional and behavioral disorders.

Sensory Disorders

Sensory disorders include visual and hearing impairments.

Visual Impairments   Some students have mild vision problems that have not been corrected. If you notice students squinting a lot, holding books close to their faces to read

Disability	Percentage Served
Specific Learning Disabilities	6.02
Speech or Language Impairments	2.03
Mental Retardation	1.27

FIGURE 6.2 **The Three Highest Percentages of Students with a Disability Served by a Federal Program in 2000–2001 as a Percentage of Total School Enrollment**

disability A personal limitation that restricts an individual's functioning.

handicap A condition imposed on a person who has a disability.

Visual Impairments

Hearing Impairments

them, rubbing their eyes frequently, and complaining that things appear blurred or that words move about on the page, refer them to the appropriate school professionals to have their vision checked (Boyles & Contadino, 1997). Many will only need corrective lenses. However, a small portion of students (about 1 in every 1,000 students) have more serious visual problems and are classified as visually impaired. This includes students who have low vision and students who are blind.

Children with *low vision* have a visual acuity of between 20/70 and 20/200 (on the familiar Snellen scale, in which 20/20 vision is normal) with corrective lenses. Children with low vision can read large-print books or with the aid of a magnifying glass. Children who are *educationally blind* cannot use their vision in learning and must use their hearing and touch to learn. Approximately 1 in every 3,000 children is educationally blind. Almost one-half of these children were born blind, and another one-third lost their vision in the first year of life. Many children who are educationally blind have normal intelligence and function very well academically with appropriate supports and learning aids. However, multiple disabilities are not uncommon in educationally blind students. Students who have multiple disabilities often require a range of support services to meet their educational needs.

An important task in working with a child who has visual impairments is to determine the modality (such as touch or hearing) through which the child learns best. Seating in the front of the class often benefits the child with a visual impairment.

For half a century, recorded textbooks from Recording for the Blind & Dyslexic have contributed to the educational progress of students with visual, perceptual, or other disabilities. More than 90,000 volumes of these audio and computerized books are available at no charge (phone: 1-800-221-4792). One issue in the education of students who are blind involves the underusage of Braille and the low rates of Braille proficiency among teachers who instruct blind students (Hallahan & Kauffman, 2003).

Hearing Impairments   A hearing impairment can make learning very difficult for children. Children who are born deaf or experience a significant hearing loss in the first several years of life usually do not develop normal speech and language. You also might have some children in your class who have hearing impairments that have not yet been detected. If you have students who turn one ear toward a speaker, frequently ask to have something repeated, don't follow directions, or frequently complain of earaches, colds, and allergies, consider having the student's hearing evaluated by a specialist, such as an audiologist (Patterson & Wright, 1990).

Through the Eyes of Students

Eyes Closed

In kindergarten, children truly begin to appreciate, not fear or think strange, each other's differences. A few years ago a child in my kindergarten class was walking down the hall with his eyes closed and ran into the wall. When I asked him what he was doing, he said, "I was just trying to do like Darrick. How come he does it so much better?" Darrick is his classmate who is legally blind. He wanted to experience what it was like to be blind. In this case, imitation truly was the greatest form of flattery.

Anita Marie Hitchcock
Kindergarten Teacher
Holle Navarre Primary
Santa Rosa County, Florida

Many children with hearing impairments receive supplementary instruction beyond the regular classroom. Educational approaches to help students with hearing impairments learn fall into two categories: oral and manual. *Oral approaches* include using lip reading, speech reading (a reliance on visual cues to teach reading), and whatever hearing the student has. *Manual approaches* involve sign language and finger spelling. Sign language is a system of hand movements that symbolize words. Finger spelling consists of "spelling out" each word by signing each letter of a word. Oral and manual approaches are increasingly used together for students who are hearing-impaired (Hallahan & Kauffman, 2000).

A number of medical and technological advances, such as listed here, also have improved the learning of children with hearing impairments (Boyles & Contadino, 1997):

• Cochlear implants (a surgical procedure). This is controversial because many people in the deaf community are opposed to them, viewing them as intrusive and antagonistic to the deaf culture. Others argue that cochlear implants have substantially improved the lives of many children who are hearing-impaired (Hallahan & Kauffman, 2003).

- Tubes in the ears (a surgical procedure for middle-ear dysfunction). This is not a permanent procedure.
- Hearing aids and amplification systems
- Telecommunication devices, the teletypewriter-telephone, and RadioMail (using the Internet)

Teaching Strategies
For Working with Children Who Have a Hearing Impairment

1. *Be patient.*
2. *Speak normally (not too slowly or too fast).*
3. *Don't shout, because this doesn't help.* Speaking distinctly is more helpful.
4. *Reduce distractions and background noises.*
5. *Face the student to whom you are speaking, because the student needs to read your lips and see your gestures.*

Physical Disorders

Physical disorders in children include orthopedic impairments, such as cerebral palsy, and seizure disorders. Many children with physical disorders require special education and related services, such as transportation, physical therapy, school health services, and psychological services.

Orthopedic Impairments   **Orthopedic impairments** involve restricted movement or lack of control over movement due to muscle, bone, or joint problems. The severity of problems ranges widely. Orthopedic impairments can be caused by prenatal or perinatal problems, or they can be due to disease or accident during the childhood years. With the help of adaptive devices and medical technology, many children with orthopedic impairments function well in the classroom (Boyles & Contadino, 1997).

Cerebral palsy is a disorder that involves a lack of muscular coordination, shaking, or unclear speech. The most common cause of cerebral palsy is lack of oxygen at birth. In the most common type of cerebral palsy, which is called *spastic,* children's muscles are stiff and difficult to move. The rigid muscles often pull the limbs into contorted positions. In a less common type, *ataxia,* the child's muscles are rigid one moment and floppy the next moment, making movements clumsy and jerky.

Computers especially can help children with cerebral palsy to learn. If they have the coordination to use the keyboard, they can do their written work on the computer. A pen with a light can be added to a computer and used by the student as a pointer. Many children with cerebral palsy have unclear speech. For these children, speech and voice synthesizers, communication boards, talking notes, and page turners can improve their communication.

Seizure Disorders   The most common seizure disorder is **epilepsy,** a nervous disorder characterized by recurring sensorimotor attacks or movement convulsions. Epilepsy comes in different forms (Barr, 2000). In one common form called *absent seizures,* a child's seizures are brief in duration (often less than thirty seconds) and occur anywhere from several to a hundred times a day. Often they occur as brief staring spells, sometimes accompanied by motor movements such as twitching of the eyelids. In another common form of epilepsy labeled *tonic-clonic,* the child loses consciousness and

Cerebral Palsy

orthopedic impairments Restricted movements or lack of control of movements, due to muscle, bone, or joint problems.

cerebral palsy A disorder that involves a lack of muscle coordination, shaking, or unclear speech.

epilepsy A nervous disorder characterized by recurring sensorimotor attacks or movement convulsions.

Through the Eyes of Students

It's Okay to Be Different

Why me? I often ask myself, why did I have to be the one? Why did I get picked to be different? It took more than ten years for me to find answers and to realize that I'm not *more* different than anyone else. My twin sister was born with no birth defects but I was born with cerebral palsy.

People thought I was stupid because it was hard for me to write my own name. So when I was the only one in the class to use a typewriter, I began to feel I was different. It got worse when the third-graders moved on to the fourth grade and I had to stay behind. I got held back because the teachers thought I'd be unable to type fast enough to keep up. Kids told me that was a lie and the reason I got held back was because I was a retard. It really hurt to be teased by those I thought were my friends. . . .

I have learned that no one was to blame for my disability. I realize that I can do things and that I can do them very well. Some things I can't do, like taking my own notes in class or running in a race, but I will have to live with that. . . .

There are times when I wish I had not been born with cerebral palsy, but crying isn't going to do me any good. I can only live once, so I want to live the best I can. . . . Nobody else can be the Angela Marie Erickson who is writing this. I could never be, or ever want to be, anyone else.

Angie Erickson
Ninth-Grade Student
Wayzata, Minnesota

Epilepsy
Mental Retardation

mental retardation A condition with an onset before age eighteen that involves low intelligence (usually below 70 on a traditional individually administered intelligence test) and difficulty in adapting to everyday life.

becomes rigid, shakes, and moves jerkily. The most severe portion of a tonic-clonic seizure lasts for about three to four minutes. Children who experience seizures are usually treated with one or more anticonvulsant medications, which often are effective in reducing the seizures but do not always eliminate them. When they are not having a seizure, students with epilepsy show normal behavior. If you have a child in your class who has a seizure disorder, become well acquainted with the procedures for monitoring and helping the child during a seizure. Also, if a child seems to space out in your class, especially under stress, it might be worthwhile to explore whether the problem is boredom, drugs, or potentially a neurological condition. One individual was diagnosed with mild epilepsy late in high school after he had several accidents while learning to drive. The only prior indication was that he did poorly on some of his tests in school and said that he seemed to just space out on them. His teachers thought he was malingering, but the spacing out likely represented the beginning signs of mild epilepsy.

Mental Retardation

Increasingly, children with mental retardation are being taught in the regular classroom. The most distinctive feature of mental retardation is inadequate intellectual functioning (Zigler, 2002). Long before formal tests were developed to assess intelligence, individuals with mental retardation were identified by a lack of age-appropriate skills in learning and in caring for themselves. Once intelligence tests were created, numbers were assigned to indicate how mild or severe the retardation was p. 107. A child might be only mildly retarded and able to learn in the regular classroom or severely retarded and unable to learn in that setting.

In addition to low intelligence, deficits in adaptive behavior and developmental onset also are included in the definition of mental retardation. Adaptive skills include skills needed for self-care and social responsibility such as dressing, toileting, feeding, self-control, and peer interaction. By definition, **mental retardation** is a condition with an onset before age eighteen that involves low intelligence (usually below 70 on a traditional individually administered intelligence test) and difficulty in adapting to everyday life. The low IQ and low adaptiveness should be evident in childhood, not following a long period of normal functioning that is interrupted by an accident or other type of assault on the brain.

Classification and Types of Mental Retardation As indicated in figure 6.3, mental retardation is classified as mild, moderate, severe, or profound. Approximately 85 percent of students with mental retardation fall into the mild category (Shonkoff, 1996). By late adolescence, individuals with mild mental retardation can be expected to develop academic skills at approximately the sixth-grade level (Terman & others, 1996). In their adult years, many can hold jobs and live on their own with some supportive supervision or in group homes. Individuals with more severe mental retardation require more support.

If you have a student with mental retardation in your classroom, the degree of retardation is likely to be mild. Children with severe mental retardation are more likely to also show signs of other neurological complications, such as cerebral palsy, epilepsy, hearing impairment, visual impairment, or other metabolic birth defects that affect the central nervous system (Terman & others, 1996).

Most school systems still use the classifications mild, moderate, severe, and profound. However, because these categorizations based on IQ ranges aren't perfect predictors of functioning, the American Association on Mental Retardation (1992) developed a new classification system based on the degree of support required for the child with mental retardation to function at their highest level (Hallahan & Kauffman, 2000). As shown in figure 6.4, these are the new categories: intermittent, limited, extensive, and pervasive.

TYPE OF MENTAL RETARDATION	IQ RANGE	PERCENTAGE
Mild	55–70	89
Moderate	40–54	6
Severe	25–39	4
Profound	Below 25	1

FIGURE 6.3 **Classification of Mental Retardation Based on IQ**

Causes Mental retardation is caused by genetic factors and brain damage (Dykens, Hodapp, & Finucane, 2000). Let's explore genetic causes first.

Genetic Factors The most commonly identified form of mental retardation is **Down syndrome,** which is genetically transmitted. Children with Down syndrome have an extra (47th) chromosome. They have a round face, a flattened skull, an extra fold of skin over the eyelids, a protruding tongue, short limbs, and retardation of motor and mental abilities. It is not known why the extra chromosome is present, but the health of the male sperm or female ovum might be involved (MacLean, 2000; Nokelainen & Flint, 2002). Women between the ages of eighteen and thirty-eight are far less likely than younger or older women to give birth to a child with Down syndrome. Down syndrome appears in about 1 in every 700 live births. African American children are rarely born with Down syndrome.

With early intervention and extensive support from the child's family and professionals, many children with Down syndrome can grow into independent adults (Boyles & Contadino, 1997). Children with Down syndrome can fall into the mild to severe retardation categories (Terman & others, 1996).

Fragile X syndrome is the second most commonly identified form of mental retardation. It is genetically transmitted by an abnormality on the X chromosome, resulting in mild to severe mental retardation. In general, the level is more severe in males than in females. Characteristics of fragile X children include an elongated face, prominent jaws, elongated ears, a flattened bridge of the nose, and poor coordination. About 7 percent of mild mental retardation in females is a result of fragile X syndrome.

Intermittent	Supports are provided "as needed." The individual may need episodic or short-term support during life-span transitions (such as job loss or acute medical crisis). Intermittent supports may be low- or high-intensity when provided.
Limited	Supports are intense and relatively consistent over time. They are time-limited but not intermittent. They require fewer staff members and cost less than more-intense supports. These supports likely will be needed for adaptation to the changes involved in the school-to-adult period.
Extensive	Supports are characterized by regular involvement (e.g., daily) in at least some setting (such as home or work) and are not time-limited (for example, extended home-living support).
Pervasive	Supports are constant, are very intense, and are provided across settings. They may be of a life-sustaining nature. These supports typically involve more staff members and intrusiveness than the other support categories.

FIGURE 6.4 **Classification of Mental Retardation Based on Levels of Support**

Down syndrome A genetically transmitted form of mental retardation due to an extra (47th) chromosome.

fragile X syndrome A genetically transmitted form of mental retardation due to an abnormality on the X chromosome.

A child with Down syndrome. *What causes a child to develop Down syndrome?*

Brain Damage Brain damage can result from many different infections and environmental hazards (Das, 2000). Infections in the pregnant mother-to-be, such as rubella (German measles), syphilis, herpes, and AIDS, can cause retardation in the child. Meningitis and encephalitis are infections that can develop in childhood. They cause inflammation in the brain and can produce mental retardation.

Environmental hazards that can result in mental retardation include blows to the head, malnutrition, poisoning, birth injury, and alcoholism or heavy drinking on the part of the pregnant woman. **Fetal alcohol syndrome (FAS)** involves a cluster of abnormalities, including mental retardation and facial abnormalities, that appear in the offspring of mothers who drink alcohol heavily during pregnancy. FAS appears in approximately one-third of the offspring of pregnant alcoholic women.

Teaching Strategies
For Working with Children
Who Are Mentally Retarded

During the school years, the main goals often are to teach children with mental retardation basic educational skills such as reading and mathematics, as well as vocational skills (Boyles & Contadino, 1997). Here are some positive teaching strategies for interacting with children who have mental retardation:

1. *Help children who are mentally retarded to practice making personal choices and to engage in self-determination when possible* (Westling & Fox, 2000).
2. *Always keep in mind the child's level of mental functioning.* Children who have mental retardation will be at a considerably lower level of mental functioning than most other students in your class. If you start at one level of instruction, and the child is not responding effectively, move to a lower level.
3. *Individualize your instruction to meet the child's needs.*
4. *As with other children with a disability, make sure that you give concrete examples of concepts.* Make your instructions clear and simple.
5. *Give these children opportunities to practice what they have learned.* Have them repeat steps a number of times and overlearn a concept to retain it.
6. *Be sensitive to the child's self-esteem.* Especially avoid comparisons with children who do not have mental retardation.
7. *Have positive expectations for the child's learning.* It is easy to fall into the trap of thinking that the child with mental retardation cannot achieve academically. Set a goal to maximize his or her learning.
8. *Recognize that many children with mental retardation not only have academic needs but also require help in improving their self-maintenance and social skills.*
9. *Look for resource support.* Use teacher aides and recruit volunteers to help you educate children with mental retardation. Many well-educated, sensitive older adults who are retired might be especially interested in helping. They can assist you in increasing the amount of one-on-one instruction the child receives.
10. *Consider using applied behavior analysis strategies.* Some teachers report that these strategies improve children's self-maintenance, social, and academic skills. If you are interested in using these strategies, consult a resource such as *Applied Behavior Analysis for Teachers,* by Paul Alberto and Anne Troutman (1999). All children need to be positively reinforced. The precise steps involved in applied behavior analysis

fetal alcohol syndrome (FAS) A cluster of abnormalities, including mental retardation and facial abnormalities, that appear in the offspring of mothers who drink alcohol heavily during pregnancy.

can especially help you use positive reinforcement effectively with children who have mental retardation. We will examine applied behavior analysis extensively in chapter 7, "Behavioral and Social Cognitive Approaches."

11. *If you teach in a secondary school, evaluate the vocational skills students with mental retardation will need in order to obtain a job* (Rogan, Luecking, & Held, 2001).

12. *Involve parents as equal partners in the child's education.*

Speech and Language Disorders

Speech and language disorders include a number of speech problems (such as articulation disorders, voice disorders, and fluency disorders) and language problems (difficulties in receiving information and expressing language) (Reed, 2005). As you saw in figure 6.1, about one-fifth of all children who receive special education services have a speech or language impairment.

Articulation Disorders **Articulation disorders** are problems in pronouncing sounds correctly. A child's articulation at six or seven years is still not always error-free, but it should be by age eight. A child with an articulation problem might find communication with peers and the teacher difficult or embarrassing. As a result, the child might avoid asking questions, participating in discussions, or communicating with peers. Articulation problems can usually be improved or resolved with speech therapy, though it might take months or years (Spiel, Brunner, & Allmayer, 2001).

Speech and Language Disorders

Voice Disorders **Voice disorders** are reflected in speech that is hoarse, harsh, too loud, too high-pitched, or too low-pitched. Children with cleft palate often have a voice disorder that makes their speech difficult to understand. If a child speaks in a way that is consistently difficult to understand, refer the child to a speech therapist.

Fluency Disorders **Fluency disorders** often involve what is commonly called "stuttering." Stuttering occurs when a child's speech has a spasmodic hesitation, prolongation, or repetition. The anxiety many children feel because they stutter often just makes their stuttering worse. Speech therapy is recommended.

Language Disorders **Language disorders** include a significant impairment in a child's receptive or expressive language. Language disorders can result in significant learning problems (Bernstein & Tiegerman-Farber, 2002). Treatment by a language therapist generally produces improvement in the child with a language disorder, but the problem usually is not eradicated (Goldstein & Hockenberger, 1991). Language disorders include difficulties in these areas:

- Phrasing questions properly to get the desired information
- Understanding and following oral directions
- Following conversation, especially when it is rapid and complex

These difficulties involve both receptive and expressive language.

Receptive language involves the reception and understanding of language. Children with a receptive language disorder have a glitch in the way they receive information. Information comes in, but the child's brain has difficulty processing it effectively, which can cause the child to appear disinterested or aloof.

Once a message is received and interpreted, the brain needs to form a response. **Expressive language** involves the ability to use language to express one's thoughts and communicate with others. Some children can easily understand what is said to them, but they have difficulties when they try to form a response and express themselves. A problem in speaking is a common expressive language disorder. There are several observable characteristics of children who have an oral expressive language disorder (Boyles & Contadino, 1997, pp. 189–190):

speech and language disorders A number of speech problems (such as articulation disorders, voice disorders, and fluency disorders) and language problems (difficulties in receiving information and expressing language).

articulation disorders Problems in pronouncing sounds correctly.

voice disorders Disorders producing speech that is hoarse, harsh, too loud, too high-pitched, or too low-pitched.

fluency disorders Disorders that often involve what is commonly referred to as "stuttering."

language disorders Significant impairments in a child's receptive or expressive language.

receptive language The reception and understanding of language.

expressive language The ability to use language to express one's thoughts and communicate with others.

- They might appear "shy and withdrawn" and have problems "interacting socially."
- They might "give delayed responses to questions."
- They might have a problem "finding the correct words."
- Their thoughts might be "disorganized and disjointed," frustrating the listener.
- They might "omit integral parts of the sentence or information needed for understanding."

Teaching Strategies
For Working with Children with a Receptive or an Oral Expressive Language Disorder

Here are some strategies to support students with a receptive language disorder:

1. *Use a multisensory approach to learning rather than an oral approach alone.* Supplement oral information with written materials or directions.
2. *Monitor the speed with which you present information.* Slow down or go back and check with the children for understanding.
3. *Give them some time to respond, as much as ten to fifteen seconds.*
4. *Provide concrete, specific examples of abstract concepts.*

Here are some strategies to support a child with an oral expressive language disorder:

1. *Give the child plenty of time to respond.*
2. *Recognize that the child has trouble responding orally, so consider asking the child to do written work rather than an oral report.*
3. *Provide choices or give the child the initial sound in word-finding problems.*
4. *Let the child know ahead of time what question might be asked so that the child can prepare an answer and thus appear more competent among peers.*

Learning Disabilities
Exploring Learning Disabilities

Learning Disabilities

Paula doesn't like kindergarten and can't seem to remember the names of her teacher and classmates. Bobby's third-grade teacher complains that his spelling is awful. Eleven-year-old Tim says reading is really hard for him and many times the words don't make much sense. Each of these students could have a learning disability.

By definition, children with a **learning disability** (1) are of normal intelligence or above; (2) have difficulty in at least one academic area and usually several; and (3) have no other diagnosed problem or disorder, such as mental retardation, that is causing the difficulty. The global concept of learning disabilities includes problems in listening, concentrating, speaking, thinking, memory, reading, writing, spelling, and/or social skills (Kamphaus, 2000).

About 5 percent of the total population of all school-age children receive special education or related services because of a learning disability. The percentage of children classified as having a learning disability has increased substantially—from less than 30 percent of all children receiving special education and related services in 1977–1978 to a little more than 50 percent today. Some experts say that the dramatic increase in children classified as having a learning disability reflects poor diagnostic practices and overidentification. They believe that teachers sometimes are too quick to label children with the slightest learning problem as having a learning disability instead of recognizing that the problem might be ineffective teaching. Other experts say that much of the increase in children being classified as having a learning disability is justified (Hallahan & others, 2005).

Learning disabilities are difficult to diagnose (Bos & Vaughn, 2002). A learning disability often encompasses co-occurring conditions, which can include problems in

learning disability A disability in which children (1) are of normal intelligence or above; (2) have difficulty in at least one academic area and usually several; and (3) have no other diagnosed problem or disorder, such as mental retardation, that is causing the difficulty.

listening, concentrating, speaking, reading, writing, reasoning, math, or social interaction. Thus, individual children with a learning disability can have very different profiles (Henley, Ramsey, & Algozzine, 1999). Learning disabilities may appear in association with such medical conditions as fetal alcohol syndrome (American Psychiatric Association, 1994). Learning disabilities can also occur with other disabilities such as communication disorders and emotional behavioral disorders (Polloway & others, 1997).

About three times as many boys as girls are classified as having a learning disability (U.S. Department of Education, 1996). This gender difference has been given various explanations, such as greater biological vulnerability of boys and referral bias (boys are more likely to be referred by teachers because of their disruptive, hyperactive behavior).

Some of the most common academic areas in which children with a learning disability have problems are reading, written language, and math (Hallahan & others, 2005; Lerner, 2000). The most common area for children with a learning disability is reading, especially phonological skills, which involve being able to understand how sounds and letters match up to make words) (Pothos & Kirk, 2004; Spafford, Grosser, & Dautrich, 2005). **Dyslexia** is a severe impairment in the ability to read and spell.

Children with a learning disability often have difficulties in handwriting, spelling, or composition (Hammil, 2004; Vellutino & others, 2004). They might write extremely slowly, their writing might be virtually illegible, and they might make numerous spelling errors because of their inability to match up sounds and letters.

Early in the history of diagnosing learning disabilities, difficulties in math were given little attention. Increasingly, though, math is being recognized as an academic area in which learning disabilities can occur (Micallef & Prior, 2004). Students with a learning disability in math might make an abundance of computational errors or use inefficient strategies in solving math problems.

Current classification of learning disabilities involves an "either/or" determination: A child either has a learning disability or does not, yet in reality, learning disabilities vary in their intensity (Reschly, 1996; Terman & others, 1996). Severe learning disabilities, such as dyslexia, have been recognized for more than a century and are relatively easy to diagnose. However, most children with a learning disability have a milder form, which often makes them hard to distinguish from children without a learning disability (Bender, 2004). In the absence of nationally accepted criteria for classification, there continues to be considerable variability in the identification of students with a learning disability from one state to the next and even one teacher to the next (Lyon, 1996).

Through the Eyes of Teachers

Creating the Character Uey Long

Nancy Downing, a second-grade teacher at McDermott Elementary School in Little Rock, Arkansas, takes a multisensory approach to education, which she developed while working with her own child, who has learning difficulties. She created Downfeld Phonics using phonics, sign language, and lively jingles to make learning fun for students. She developed the character Uey Long (a uey is the sign over a short vowel) to demonstrate vowel rules. Nancy acts creatively and proactively beyond a teacher's usual classroom concerns, including looking after her students' physical and emotional welfare. For example, she makes sure that every child has a coat, even if she has to donate one, and gives each student a hug and a final compliment or piece of advice at the end of the school day.

Nancy Downing

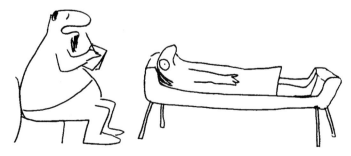

"Your feelings of insecurity seem to have started when Mary Lou Gumblatt said, 'Maybe I don't have a learning disability—maybe you have a teaching disability.'"
© 1975 Tony Saltzman, Phi Delta Kappan. Reprinted with permission.

dyslexia A severe impairment in the ability to read and spell.

Despite variations in degree, the impact of having a learning disability is real and persistent (Bender, 1998; Raymond, 2000; Wong & Donahue, 2002). Most learning disabilities are lifelong. Compared with children without a learning disability, children with a learning disability are more likely to show poor academic performance, high dropout rates, and poor employment and postsecondary education records (Wagner & Blackorby, 1996). Children with a learning disability who are taught in the regular classroom without extensive support rarely achieve the level of competence of even children who are low-achieving and do not have a disability (Hocutt, 1996). Still, despite the problems they encounter, many children with a learning disability grow up to lead normal lives and engage in productive work (Pueschel & others, 1995).

Improving outcomes for children with a learning disability is a challenging task and generally has required intensive intervention for even modest improvement in outcomes. No model program has proven to be effective for all children with learning disabilities (Terman & others, 1996).

Identification   As we said earlier, diagnosing a child with a learning disability, especially in a mild form, is very difficult. A child with a learning disability typically does not look disabled, can communicate verbally, and does not stand out in a crowd.

There currently is considerable debate about how to define learning disabilities and how to identify the condition in children (Hughes & McIntosh, 2002; Pierangelo & Giuliani, 2002). One identification procedure requires a significant discrepancy between actual achievement and expected achievement, the latter being estimated by an individually administered intelligence test. However, a number of people in education doubt the adequacy of this approach.

Initial identification of a possible learning disability is usually made by the classroom teacher. If a learning disability is suspected, the teacher calls on specialists. An interdisciplinary team of professionals is best suited to verify whether a student has a learning disability (Venn, 2000). Individual psychological evaluations (of intelligence) and educational assessments (such as current level of achievement) are required (Overton, 2000). In addition, tests of visual-motor skills, language, and memory may be used.

In the early childhood years, disabilities are often identified in receptive and expressive language. Input from parents and teachers is considered before making a final diagnosis. For many school systems, the trigger for assessing students with learning disabilities is a two-grade-level lag in reading (Purcell-Gates, 1997). This can be a major impediment to identifying disabilities at the age when help can be the most effective—during the first two years of elementary school. If the two-grade lag is rigidly interpreted, many children can't get help even if they are showing clear signs of a learning disability.

Through the Eyes of Teachers

Some Learning Disabilities Show Up Later

For some children, it's not until third or fourth grade that teachers become aware that children are having problems with reading. This may occur because the number of words that children are called upon to read expands at such a phenomenal rate. Children can't just learn them by sight anymore. Most children begin to infer the relationships between sounds and symbols by fourth grade or earlier; by fourth grade they have made those inferences even if they haven't explicitly been taught to them. By contrast, children with learning disabilities often don't figure out those links for themselves or during the course of normal classroom learning. Thus, they need to be explicitly taught about them to a greater degree than other students.

Later, students start having more trouble with the complex vocabulary that is being introduced to them and they may not be able to remember as many words. As the pace of learning accelerates in later grades, more and more information has to be gained through reading. In the earlier grades students get a lot of information orally; they are not expected to get all or even most of their information from reading. When the switch takes place from learning-to-read to reading-to-learn, children with learning disabilities may have trouble because they don't read competently. What also shows up in elementary school is that many children with learning disabilities have difficulty with spelling.

Gail Venable
Language Arts/Special Education
Teacher/Consultant, San Francisco

Intervention Strategies   Many interventions have focused on improving the student's reading ability (Lyon & Moats, 1997). For example, in one study, instruction in phonological awareness at the kindergarten level had positive effects on reading development when these children reached first grade (Blachman & others, 1994).

Unfortunately, not all children who have a learning disability that involves reading problems have the benefit of appropriate early intervention. Most children whose reading disability is not diagnosed until third grade or later and receive standard interventions fail to show noticeable improvement (Lyon, 1996). However, intensive instruction over a period of time by a competent teacher can remediate the deficient reading skills of many students. For example, in one study, 65 severely dyslexic students were given 65 hours of individual instruction in addition to group instruction in phonemic awareness and thinking skills (Alexander & others, 1991). This intensive intervention significantly improved the dyslexic children's reading skills.

Children with severe phonological deficits that lead to poor decoding and word recognition skills respond to intervention more slowly than children with mild to moderate reading problems (Torgesen, 1995). Also, the success of even the best-designed reading intervention depends on the training and skills of the teacher.

Disability in basic reading skills has been the most common target of intervention studies because it is the most common form of learning disability, is identifiable, and represents the area of learning disabilities about which we have the most knowledge (Coyne & others, 2004). Interventions for other types of learning disabilities have been created, but they have not been as extensively researched.

One analysis of intervention studies with children with learning disabilities found that a combined model of strategy instruction and direct instruction had the most positive effects (Swanson & Hoskyn, 1998). These types of instruction especially had positive effects on reading comprehension, vocabulary, and creativity. Among the instructional components that worked the best with children with learning disabilities were small interactive groups, technology, augmentation of teacher instruction (such as homework), directed questioning, and strategy cueing.

Through the Eyes of Teachers

Teaching Children with Learning Disabilities

Throughout the last several years, up to one-half of the 24 students in my third-grade class have been diagnosed with learning disabilities. The majority of these students have difficulties with reading; therefore, modifications are often made in the other subject areas where reading is involved. For example, in math, I often have my students pair up to work on word problems. They take turns reading the problems and thinking through the solutions together. Both students seem to benefit from each other in these situations.

In social studies and science, I often have teams work on discussing related problems, such as planning a fund-raiser as a part of an economics unit. Within the team, leaders and recorders are assigned to read the directions and write the answers for their team, which takes some pressure off of having to spell and read independently. Tests and quizzes are also read aloud in these subject areas. Another strategy that is helpful when teaching students with learning disabilities is to give directions in short pieces, often demonstrating what you want them to do.

These children especially seem to benefit from hands-on experiences as well as art activities. After making salt dough maps one year, my students developed an understanding of the landforms and three regions of Virginia. They may not have been able to grasp these concepts just from reading the textbook and listening to discussions. I have found that many of the strategies that are useful when teaching students with learning disabilities actually benefit the whole class.

Kristin Blankenship
Salem Church Elementary
Chesterfield County, Virginia

Teaching Strategies
For Working with Children Who Have Learning Disabilities

1. *Take the needs of the child with a learning disability into account during instructional time.* Clearly state the objective of each lesson. Present it visually on the board or with an overhead projector as well. Be sure directions are explicit. Explain them orally. Use concrete examples to illustrate abstract concepts.
2. *Provide accommodations for testing and assignments.* This refers to changing the academic environment so that these children can demonstrate what they know. An accommodation usually does not involve altering the amount of learning the child has to demonstrate. Common accommodations include reading instructions to children, highlighting important words (such as *underline*, or *answer two of the three questions*), using/giving untimed tests, and extra time on assignments.
3. *Make modifications.* This strategy changes the work itself, making it different from other children's work in an effort to encourage children's confidence and success. Asking a child with dyslexia to give an oral report while other children give written reports is an example of a modification.
4. *Improve organizational and study skills.* As we mentioned earlier, many children with a learning disability do not have good organizational skills. Teachers and

Strategies in Practice

Working with Children Who Have Learning Disabilities

parents can encourage them to keep long-term and short-term calendars and create "to-do" lists each day. Projects should be broken down into their elements, with steps and due dates for each part (Strichart & Mangrum, 2002).

5. *Work with reading and writing skills.* As we indicated earlier, the most common type of learning disability involves reading problems. Make sure that an expert diagnosis of the child's reading problems has been made, including the particular deficits in the reading skills involved. Children with a reading problem often read slowly, so they need more advance notice of outside reading assignments and more time for in-class reading. Many children with a learning disability that involves writing deficits find that a word processor helps them compose their writing projects more quickly and competently. Compensatory tools that can be used include handheld talking electronic dictionaries (such as the Franklin Language Master, which gives students alternate spellings for phonetic attempts—*nummonia* for *pneumonia*, for example—where spellcheckers might fail them, and provides definitions for easily confused words, such as *there* and *their*), talking word processors that give valuable auditory feedback, and taped books. Some agencies will record textbooks for students for a minimal fee.

Using such teaching strategies is not meant to give children with a learning disability an unfair advantage, just an equal chance to learn. Balancing the needs of children with learning disabilities and those of other children is a challenging task.

Attention Deficit Hyperactivity Disorder

Matthew has attention deficit hyperactivity disorder, and the outward signs are fairly typical. He has trouble attending to the teacher's instructions and is easily distracted. He can't sit still for more than a few minutes at a time, and his handwriting is messy. His mother describes him as very fidgety.

Attention deficit hyperactivity disorder (ADHD) is a disability in which children consistently show one or more of the following characteristics over a period of time: (1) inattention, (2) hyperactivity, and (3) impulsivity. Children who are inattentive have difficulty focusing on any one thing and might become bored with a task after only a few minutes. Children who are hyperactive show high levels of physical activity, almost always seeming to be in motion. Children who are impulsive have difficulty curbing their reactions and don't do a good job of thinking before they act. Depending on the characteristics children with ADHD display, they can be diagnosed as having (1) ADHD with predominantly inattention, (2) ADHD with predominantly hyperactivity/impulsivity, or (3) ADHD with both inattention and hyperactivity/impulsivity.

The number of children diagnosed and treated for ADHD has increased substantially, by some estimates doubling in the 1990s. Current estimates are that 3 to 5 percent of the school population are identified as having ADHD (Barkley, 1998; Hallahan & Kauffman, 2000). The disorder occurs as much as four to nine times more in boys than in girls. There is controversy about the increased diagnosis of ADHD (Terman & others, 1996). Some experts attribute the increase mainly to heightened awareness of the disorder. Others are concerned that many children are being misdiagnosed without undergoing extensive professional evaluation based on input from multiple sources.

Signs of ADHD can be present in the preschool years. Parents and preschool or kindergarten teachers might notice that the child has an extremely high activity level and limited attention span. They might say the child is "always on the go," "can't sit still even for a second," or "never seems to listen." Many children with ADHD are difficult to discipline, have little tolerance for frustration, and have problems in peer relations. Other common characteristics of children with ADHD include general immaturity and clumsiness.

Although signs of ADHD are often present in the preschool years, their classification often doesn't take place until the elementary school years (Guyer, 2000). The increased academic and social demands of formal schooling, as well as stricter standards for

ADHD
Exploring ADHD

attention deficit hyperactivity disorder (ADHD) A disability in which children consistently show one or more of the following characteristics over a period of time: (1) inattention, (2) hyperactivity, and (3) impulsivity.

Many children with ADHD show impulsive behavior, such as this child who is jumping out of his seat and throwing a paper airplane at other children. *How would you handle this situation if this were to happen in your classroom?*

behavioral control, often illuminate the problems of the child with ADHD (Whalen, 2000). Elementary school teachers typically report that this type of child has difficulty in working independently, completing seatwork, and organizing work. Restlessness and distractibility also are often noted. These problems are more likely to be observed in repetitive or taxing tasks, or tasks the child perceives to be boring (such as completing worksheets or doing homework).

It used to be thought that ADHD decreased in adolescence, but now it is believed that this often is not the case. Estimates suggest that ADHD decreases in only about one-third of adolescents. Increasingly it is recognized that these problems also can continue into adulthood (Samuelson, Lundberg, & Herkner, 2004; Sparks, Javorsky, & Phillips, 2004).

Definitive causes of ADHD have not been found. For example, scientists have not been able to identify causal sites in the brain. However, a number of causes have been proposed, such as low levels of certain neurotransmitters (chemical messengers in the brain), prenatal abnormalities, and postnatal abnormalities (Auerbach & others, 2001; Oades, 2002; Steger & others, 2001). Heredity might play a role, as 30 to 50 percent of children with ADHD have a sibling or parent who has the disorder (Woodrich, 1994).

About 85 to 90 percent of children with ADHD are taking medication, such as Ritalin or Adderal (which has fewer side effects than Ritalin), to control their behavior (Denny, 2001). Ritalin and Adderal are stimulants, and for most individuals, they speed up the nervous system and behavior. However, in many children with ADHD, the drug speeds up underactive areas of the prefrontal cortex, which controls attention, impulsivity, and planning. This enhanced ability to focus their attention results in what *appears* to be a "slowing down" of behavior in these children (Reeves & Schweitzer, 2004). Researchers have found that a combination of medication (such as Ritalin) and behavior management improves the behavior of children with ADHD better than medication alone or behavior management alone (Chronis & others, 2004; Swanson & others, 2001). Critics argue that many physicians are too quick to prescribe stimulants for children with milder forms of ADHD (Clay, 1997).

The teacher plays an important role in observing whether the medication is at too high a level, making the child dazed and lethargic. Sometimes, especially for elementary school students, teachers administer medication when a dosage is required during the school day. It is important for teachers and parents not to convey a message to children that medication is the answer to all of their academic difficulties (Hallahan & Kauffman, 2000). Children with ADHD should be encouraged to take responsibility for their behavior in addition to any help that medication may provide them.

Teaching Strategies
For Working with Children Who Have Attention Deficit Hyperactivity Disorder

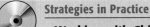

Strategies in Practice

- **Working with Children with ADHD or ADD**
- **A Seating Strategy for Students with ADHD**

1. *Monitor whether the child's stimulant medication is working effectively.*
2. *Repeat and simplify instructions about in-class and homework assignments.*
3. *Supplement verbal instructions with visual instructions.*
4. *Modify testing if necessary.*
5. *Involve a special education resource teacher.*
6. *State clear expectations and give the child immediate feedback.*
7. *Use behavior management strategies, especially providing positive feedback for progress.* We will discuss these approaches in considerable detail in chapter 7, "Behavioral and Social Cognitive Approaches."
8. *Provide structure and teacher-direction.* In many instances, a structured learning environment benefits children with ADHD.
9. *Connect learning to real-life experiences.*
10. *Use computer instruction, especially learning that involves a gamelike format.*
11. *Provide opportunities for students to get up and move around.*
12. *Break assignments into shorter segments.*

Emotional and Behavioral Disorders

Most children have emotional problems at sometime during their school years. A small percentage have problems that are so serious and persistent that they are classified as having an emotional or a behavioral disorder (Lane, Greshman, & O'Shaughnessy, 2002). **Emotional and behavioral disorders** consist of serious, persistent problems that involve relationships, aggression, depression, fears associated with personal or school matters, and other inappropriate socioemotional characteristics. Approximately 8 percent of children who have a disability and require an individualized education plan fall into this classification. Boys are three times as likely as girls to have the disorder (U.S. Department of Education, 2000).

Various terms have been used to describe emotional and behavioral disorders, including *emotional disturbances, behavior disorders,* and *maladjusted children* (Coleman & Webber, 2002). The term *serious emotional disturbance (SED)* recently has been used to describe children with these types of problems for whom it has been necessary to create individualized learning. However, critics argue that this category has not been clearly defined (Council for Exceptional Children, 1998).

emotional and behavioral disorders
Serious, persistent problems that involve relationships, aggression, depression, fears associated with personal or school matters, and other inappropriate socioemotional characteristics.

Aggressive, Out-of-Control Behaviors   Some children who are classified as having a serious emotional disturbance and engage in disruptive, aggressive, defiant, or dangerous behaviors are removed from the classroom (Terman & others, 1996). These children are much more likely to be boys than girls and more likely to come from low-income than from middle- or high-income families (Achenbach & others, 1991). Children with a serious emotional disturbance are more likely than any other children with a disability to initially be classified as having a disability-related problem during the secondary school years. However, the majority of these children began to show signs of their emotional problem in the elementary school years (Wagner, 1995).

Experts on behavioral and emotional disorders say that when these children are returned to the regular classroom, both the regular classroom teacher and a special education teacher or consultant must spend a great deal of time helping them adapt and learn effectively (Hocutt, 1996). This means devoting several hours per week for several weeks for one or two students to help them make an effective transition back into the classroom. The more severe the problem, the less likely it is that a return to the classroom will work (Wagner, 1995).

In chapter 3, we discussed rejected students and improving students' social skills ◀ p. 83. Many of the comments and recommendations we made there apply to children with a serious emotional disturbance. In chapter 7, "Behavioral and Social Cognitive Approaches," and chapter 14, "Managing the Classroom," we will discuss more strategies and plans for effectively dealing with children who show emotional and behavioral problems.

Behavioral Disorders
Conduct Disorders

Depression, Anxiety, and Fears   Some children turn their emotional problems inward. Their depression, anxiety, or fears become so intense and persistent that their ability to learn is significantly compromised. All children feel depressed from time to time, but most get over their despondent, down mood in a few hours or a few days. However, for some children the negative mood is more serious and longer-lasting. *Depression* is a type of mood disorder in which the individual feels worthless, believes that things are not likely to get better, and behaves lethargically for a prolonged period of time. When children show these signs for two weeks or longer, they likely are experiencing depression. Having a poor appetite and not being able to sleep well also can be associated with depression.

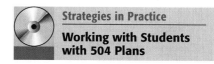

Strategies in Practice

Working with Students with 504 Plans

Depression is much more likely to appear in adolescence than in childhood and has a much higher incidence in girls than in boys (Culbertson, 1997). Experts on depression say that this gender difference is likely due to a number of factors. Females tend to ruminate on their depressed mood and amplify it, whereas males tend to distract themselves from the negative mood; girls' self-images are often more negative than those of boys during adolescence; and societal bias against female achievement might be involved (Nolen-Hoeksema, 2001).

Be vigilant in recognizing the signs of depression in children. Because it is turned inward, depression is far more likely to go unnoticed than aggressive, acting-out behaviors. If you think that a child has become depressed, have the child meet with the school counselor. Cognitive therapy has been especially effective in helping individuals become less depressed, as have some drug therapies (Beckham, 2000).

Anxiety involves a vague, highly unpleasant feeling of fear and apprehension (Kowalski, 2000). It is normal for children to be concerned or worried when they face life's challenges, but some children have such intense and prolonged anxiety that it substantially impairs their school performance. Some children also have personal or school-related fears that interfere with their learning. If a child shows marked or substantial fears that persist, have the child see the school counselor. Some behavioral therapies have been especially effective in reducing inappropriate anxiety and fear (Davidson & Neale, 2001). More information about anxiety appears in chapter 13, "Motivation, Teaching, and Learning."

At this point we have explored many different disabilities and disorders. To evaluate your experiences with people who have these disabilities and disorders, complete Self-Assessment 6.1 on page 190.

Evaluating My Experiences with People Who Have Various Disabilities and Disorders

Read each of these statements and place a checkmark next to the ones that apply to you.

1. SENSORY DISORDERS
_____ I know someone with a sensory disorder and have talked with him or her about the disability.
_____ I have observed students with sensory disorders in the classroom and talked with their teachers about their strategies for educating them.

2. PHYSICAL DISORDERS
_____ I know someone with a physical disorder and have talked with him or her about the disability.
_____ I have observed students with physical disorders in the classroom and talked with their teachers about strategies for educating them.

3. MENTAL RETARDATION
_____ I know someone who has mental retardation and have talked with his or her parents about their child's disability.
_____ I have observed in the classroom students with mental retardation and talked with their teachers about their strategies for educating them.

4. SPEECH AND LANGUAGE DISORDERS
_____ I know someone with a speech and language disorder and have talked with him or her about the disability.
_____ I have observed students with a speech and language disorder in the classroom and talked with their teacher about strategies for educating them.

5. LEARNING DISABILITIES
_____ I know someone who has a learning disability and have talked with him or her about the disability.
_____ I have observed students with learning disabilities in the classroom and talked with teachers about their strategies for educating them.

6. ATTENTION DEFICIT HYPERACTIVITY DISORDER
_____ I know someone with ADHD and have talked with him or her about the disability.
_____ I have observed students with ADHD in the classroom and talked with teachers about their strategies for educating them.

7. EMOTIONAL AND BEHAVIORAL DISORDERS
_____ I know someone with an emotional and behavioral disorder and have talked with him or her about the disorder.
_____ I have observed students with emotional and behavioral disorders and talked with their teachers about strategies for educating them.

For those disabilities that you did not place a checkmark beside, make it a point to get to know and talk with someone who has the disability and observe students with the disability in the classroom. Then talk with their teachers about their strategies for educating them.

 Go to your Student Toolbox CD-ROM for an electronic version of this form.

Review and Reflect

1 Describe the various types of disabilities and disorders.

Review
- How common are disabilities among children in school?
- What are some common visual and hearing sensory disorders in children?
- What types of physical disabilities in children are teachers likely to see?
- What is the nature of mental retardation?
- What are the differences among articulation, voice, fluency, and language disorders?
- What is the definition of a learning disability? What are some common learning disabilities? How are they identified? How are they best treated?

190

- What are some important aspects of attention deficit hyperactivity disorder for teachers to know?
- What are the main types of emotional and behavioral disorders?

Reflect

- Considering the age group of children and the subject that you plan to teach, which of the disabilities that we have discussed do you think will present the most difficulty for your teaching? Where should you focus your attention in learning more about this disability?

EDUCATIONAL ISSUES INVOLVING CHILDREN WITH DISABILITIES

The legal requirement that schools serve all children with a disability is fairly recent. We will explore the legal aspects of working with children who have a disability, profile the placements and services available to these children, and examine the roles of parents and technology in educating children with a disability.

Legal Aspects

Beginning in the mid 1960s to mid 1970s, legislatures, the federal courts, and the United States Congress laid down special educational rights for children with disabilities. Prior to that time, most children with a disability were either refused enrollment or inadequately served by schools. In 1975, Congress enacted **Public Law 94-142,** the Education for All Handicapped Children Act, which required that all students with disabilities be given a free, appropriate public education and which provided the funding to help implement this education.

Individuals with Disabilities Education Act (IDEA)   In 1990, Public Law 94-142 was recast as the **Individuals with Disabilities Education Act (IDEA).** The IDEA spells out broad mandates for services to all children with disabilities. These include evaluation and eligibility determination, appropriate education and an individualized education plan (IEP), and education in the least restrictive environment (LRE).

Children who are thought to have a disability are evaluated to determine their eligibility for services under the IDEA. Schools are prohibited from planning special education programs in advance and offering them on a space-available basis.

Children must be evaluated before a school can begin providing special services (Wolery, 2000). Parents must be invited to participate in the evaluation process. Reevaluation is required at least every three years (sometimes every year), when requested by parents, or when conditions suggest a reevaluation is needed. A parent who disagrees with the school's evaluation can obtain an independent evaluation, which the school is required to consider in providing special education services. If the evaluation finds that child has a disability and requires special services, the school must provide the child with appropriate services.

The IDEA requires that students with disabilities have an **individualized education plan (IEP).** The IEP is a written statement that spells out a program specifically tailored for the student with a disability. In general, the IEP should be (1) related to the child's learning capacity, (2) specially constructed to meet the child's individual needs and not merely copy what is offered to other children, and (3) designed to provide educational benefits.

The IDEA has many other specific provisions that relate to the parents of a child with a disability (Hardman, Drew, & Egan, 2002). These include requirements that schools send notices to parents of proposed actions, that parents be allowed to attend

Legal Aspects

Public Law 94-142 The Education for All Handicapped Children Act, which required that all students with disabilities be given a free, appropriate public education and which provided the funding to help implement this education.

Individuals with Disabilities Education Act (IDEA) This act spells out broad mandates for services to all children with disabilities, including evaluation and determination of eligibility, appropriate education and an individualized education plan (IEP), and education in the least restrictive environment (LRE).

individualized education plan (IEP) A written statement that spells out a program specifically tailored for the student with a disability.

meetings regarding the child's placement or individualized education plan, and the right to appeal school decisions to an impartial evaluator.

Amendments were made to the IDEA in 1997. Two of these involve positive behavioral support and functional behavioral assessment.

Positive behavioral support focuses on culturally appropriate application of positive behavioral interventions to attain important behavior changes in children. "Culturally appropriate" refers to considering the unique and individualized learning histories of children (social, community, historical, gender, and so on). Positive behavioral support especially emphasizes supporting desirable behaviors rather than punishing undesirable behaviors in working with children with a disability or disorder.

Functional behavioral assessment involves determining the consequences (what purpose the behavior serves), antecedents (what triggers the behavior), and setting events (in which contexts the behavior occurs). Functional behavioral assessment emphasizes understanding behavior in the context in which it is observed and guiding positive behavioral interventions that are relevant and effective (Hallahan & Kauffman, 2003).

Least Restrictive Environment (LRE)   Under the IDEA, the child with a disability must be educated in the **least restrictive environment (LRE).** This means a setting that is as similar as possible to the one in which children who do not have a disability are educated. This provision of the IDEA has given a legal basis to making an effort to educate children with a disability in the regular classroom. The education of children with a disability in the regular classroom used to be called *mainstreaming.* However, that term has been replaced by the term **inclusion,** which means educating a child with special educational needs full-time in the regular classroom (Haager & Klingner, 2005; Idol, 1997). One recent study found that the academic achievement of students with learning disabilities benefited from inclusion (Rea, McLaughlin, & Walther-Thomas, 2002).

Increasingly, children with disabilities are being taught in the regular classroom, as is this child with mild mental retardation.

least restrictive environment (LRE) A setting that is as similar as possible to the one in which children who do not have a disability are educated.

inclusion Educating children with special education needs full-time in the regular classroom.

Not long ago it was considered appropriate to educate children with disabilities outside the regular classroom. However, today schools must make every effort to provide inclusion for children with disabilities (Friend & Bursuck, 2002). These efforts can be very costly financially and very time consuming in terms of faculty effort.

The principle of "least restrictive environment" compels schools to examine possible modifications of the regular classroom before moving the child with a disability to a more restrictive placement. Also, regular classroom teachers often need specialized training to help some children with a disability, and state educational agencies are required to provide such training (Heward, 2000).

James Kauffman and his colleagues (Kauffman & Hallahan, 2005; Kauffman, McGee, & Brigham, 2004) recently argued that special education has been negatively influenced by the pursuit of full inclusion. They stress that the emphasis in special education has moved away from independence and competence and toward whatever special programs and accommodations can be used (Kauffman & others, 2004). They say the "goal seems to have become the *appearance* of normalization without the *expectation* of competence" (p. 614). They accept that students with disabilities have specific shortcomings and need the services of specially trained professionals to reach their potentials. They may need altered curricula or adaptations to make learning possible. However, it is important for teachers to challenge students with a disability to reach their full potentials.

Many legal changes regarding children with disabilities have been extremely positive. Compared with even several decades ago, far more children today are receiving competent, specialized services. For many children, inclusion in the regular classroom, with modifications or supplemental services, is appropriate. However, some experts believe that separate programs can be more effective and appropriate for other children with disabilities (Martin, Martin, & Terman, 1996).

Research on outcomes for inclusion suggest these conclusions (Hocutt, 1996):

- *Children's academic and social success.* These outcomes are affected more by the quality of the instruction given than by where the child is placed (such as regular classroom, resource room, or special education classroom). When inclusion is used, it works best when regular classroom teachers are given lengthy, often multiyear training, planning time, administrative support, and sometimes additional instructional staff.
- *Children with severe emotional disturbance.* Children with this disorder are more likely to succeed if they participate in vocational education and are integrated into the school through activities such as sports. However, children who have a long history of course failures are more likely to drop out of school if they are placed in the regular classroom.
- *Children with hearing impairments.* Children with these disorders gain some academic advantages but have lower self-esteem when they are in the regular classroom. The strength of the child's auditory and oral skills is crucial to success in the regular classroom.
- *Children with educable mental retardation (usually defined as having an IQ from 50 to 70 along with adaptive behavior problems in the same range).* A supportive teacher, competent instruction, and supportive classmates seem to have an even greater impact on these children than on children without disabilities.
- *Children who do not have a disability.* They do not appear to be negatively affected by the inclusion of children with a disability in the regular classroom as long as supportive services are provided (Cole, Waldron, & Majid, 2004). This research finding is especially important because many parents of students who are not disabled worry that teachers will not have adequate time to help their child learn because they will be spending so much time with children who have disabilities. When the inclusion program brings a lower overall teacher-child ratio, children who do not have a disability actually are likely to benefit academically from inclusion.

One concern about special education involves disproportionate representation of students from minority backgrounds in special education programs and classes (Hosp & Reschly, 2004). The Diversity and Education interlude addresses this issue.

The Council for Exceptional Children

Special Education Resources

Special Education Projects

Inclusion

Diversity and Education
Disproportionate Representation of Minority Students in Special Education

The U.S. Department of Education (2000) has three concerns about the overrepresentation of minority students in special education programs and classes:

1. Students may be unserved or receive services that do not meet their needs.
2. Students may be misclassified or inappropriately labeled.
3. Placement in special education classes may be a form of discrimination.

African American students account for 16 percent of the U.S. student population but they represent 32 percent of the students in programs for mild mental retardation, 29 percent in programs for moderate mental retardation, and 24 percent in programs for serious emotional disturbance.

However, it is not just a simple matter of overrepresentation of certain minority groups in special education. Latino children are underidentified in the categories of mental retardation and emotional disturbance (Hallahan & Kauffman, 2003).

More appropriate inclusion of minority students in special education is a complex problem and requires the creation of a successful school experience for all students. Recommendations for reducing disproportionate representation in special education include (Burnette, 1998)

1. Reviewing school practices to identify and address factors that might contribute to school difficulties
2. Forming policy-making groups that include community members and promote partnerships with service agencies and cultural organizations
3. Helping families get social, medical, mental health, and other support services
4. Training more teachers from minority backgrounds and providing all teachers with more extensive course work and training in educating children with disabilities and diversity issues

Placements and Services

Children with disabilities can be placed in a variety of settings, and a range of services can be used to improve their education (Kauffman & Hallahan, 2005).

Video Lecture: Inclusion

Placements   The following range of placements of children with disabilities is ordered from least restrictive to most restrictive (Deno, 1970):

• Regular classroom with supplementary instructional support provided in the regular classroom
• Part of time spent in a resource room
• Full-time placement in a special education class
• Special schools
• Homebound instruction
• Instruction in a hospital or another institution

As indicated in figure 6.5, of children receiving special education, slightly more than one-third receive it in the regular classroom; approximately the same percentage get

FIGURE 6.5 Percentage of Special Education Services Provided in Various Settings

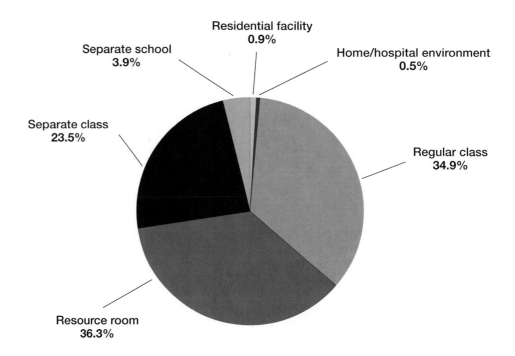

services in a resource room; and slightly less than 25 percent receive services in a separate class (U.S. Department of Education, 2000). About one-third of children who receive special education in a separate class spend 80 percent or more of their school day in the regular classroom. Another one-third spend 40 to 79 percent of their school day in the regular classroom, and the final one-third spend 0 to 39 percent there (Hocutt, 1996).

Services   Services for children can be provided by the regular classroom teacher, a resource teacher, a special education teacher, a collaborative consultant, other professionals, or an interactive team (Dettmer, Dyck, & Thurston, 2002).

The Regular Classroom Teacher   With the increase in inclusion, the regular classroom teacher is responsible for providing more of the education of children with disabilities than in the past (Smith & others, 2004; Vaughn, Bos, & Schumm, 2002). The Teaching Strategies interlude can help you provide a more effective education for these children.

Teaching Strategies
For Working with Children
with Disabilities as a Regular
Classroom Teacher

1. *Carry out each child's individualized education plan (IEP).*
2. *Encourage your school to provide increased support and training in how to teach children with disabilities.*
3. *Use the support that is available and seek other support.* Many well-educated, conscientious people in the community might be willing to volunteer some of their time to help you provide more individualized instruction for students with disabilities. This in turn provides a lower teacher-student ratio that benefits all of your students.
4. *Become more knowledgeable about the types of children with disabilities in your classroom.* Read education journals, such as *Exceptional Children, Teaching Exceptional Children,* and *Journal of Learning Disabilities,* to keep up-to-date on the latest information about these children. Look into taking a class at a college or university or a continuing education course on topics such as exceptional children, mental retardation, learning disabilities, and emotional and behavioral disorders.
5. *Be cautious about labeling children with a disability.* It is easy to fall into the trap of using the label as an explanation of the child's learning difficulties. For example, a teacher might say, "Well, Larry has trouble with reading because he has a learning disability," when, in fact, the teacher really knows only that for some unknown reason Larry is having trouble with reading. Also, labels have a way of remaining after the child has improved considerably. Remember that terms such as *mental retardation* and *learning disability* are descriptive labels for disorders. Always think of children with disabilities in terms of what the best conditions are for improving their learning and how they can be helped to make progress rather than in terms of unchanging labels.
6. *Remember that children with disabilities benefit from many of the same teaching strategies that benefit children without disabilities.* These include
   • Be caring, accepting, and patient.
   • Have positive expectations for learning.
   • Help children with their social and communication skills as well as academic skills.
   • Plan and organize the classroom effectively.
   • Be enthusiastic and help children become motivated to learn.
   • Monitor children's learning and provide effective feedback.

Video Observation: Inclusion of Students with Special Needs

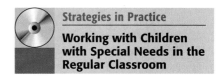

Strategies in Practice

Working with Children with Special Needs in the Regular Classroom

Through the Eyes of Teachers

Take Responsibility

It is really important for general education teachers to take responsibility for students with special needs. These children are part of their classroom. Teachers should not think of their classroom roster as twenty students plus the child in the wheelchair. Always make sure that children with special needs are not left behind. This happens more than you think. The class may go to the library with the teacher leading the line. The students follow in a single file, but no one thinks to push the child sitting in the wheelchair into the line. And special education teachers and assistants may not always be around to perform routine tasks; they service many children throughout the school.

Read and review the Individual Education Plan (IEP) for each child in your class and preferably your entire grade level to ensure that all goals and objectives as well as any classroom modifications are being met. Is the child supposed to be seated near the teacher? Is the student hearing impaired and should not sit near a fan or air conditioning unit? Is the student supposed to take tests in small groups, one-on-one, or read aloud? Don't presume the special education teacher will tell you everything in a child's IEP.

Chaille Lazar
Special Education Teacher
Hedgrove Elementary School
Plano, Texas

7. *Help children without a disability to understand and accept children with a disability.* Give children without a disability information about children with a disability and create opportunities for them to interact with each other in positive ways. Peer tutoring and cooperative learning activities can be used to encourage positive interaction between children without a disability and children with a disability (Fuchs & others, 1994; Slavin, 1995a). We will discuss these activities further in chapter 10, "Social Constructivist Approaches." In one study, peer-assisted learning strategies benefited the reading skills of children with disabilities (Fuchs, Fuchs, & Mathes, & Simmons, 1997).
8. *Keep up-to-date on the technology that is available for educating children with a disability.* We will discuss this topic shortly.

The Resource Teacher   A resource teacher can provide valuable services for many children who have a disability. Many children with disabilities spend most of their school day in a regular classroom and a small portion of their day in a resource room where a resource teacher works with them. In a typical arrangement, a child might spend one or two hours a day in the resource room and the remainder of time in the regular classroom. In many situations, resource teachers work with these children to improve their reading, writing, or mathematical skills.

It is important for the regular classroom teacher and the resource teacher to collaborate and coordinate their efforts. In some cases, the resource teacher will work with the child in the regular classroom setting rather than seeing the child in a resource room.

The Special Education Teacher   Some teachers have extensive training in special education and teach children with disabilities in a separate "special education classroom." Some children will spend time with the special education teacher part of the school day the rest of the day in the regular classroom, as happens with a resource teacher. However, the special education teacher typically assumes greater responsibility for the child's overall program than the resource teacher, who usually works in support of the regular classroom teacher. A child might learn reading, writing, mathematics, or science with the special education teacher and be in the regular classroom for physical education, art, or music. The most frequent area in which the special education teacher works with the child who has a disability is reading, and the most frequent classification of a special education teacher is as a teacher of children who have specific learning disabilities (U.S. Department of Education, 2000).

In some school systems, if more than a set percentage (say, 60 percent) of the child's time is spent with a special education teacher, the child's program is called *self-contained special education.* Self-contained special education also is in effect when children are educated in separate schools for children with disabilities.

Related Services   In addition to regular classroom teachers, resource teachers, and special education teachers, a number of other special education personnel provide services for children with disabilities (U.S. Department of Education, 2000). These include teacher aides, psychologists, counselors, school social workers, nurses, physicians, occupational therapists, and physical therapists, as well as speech and hearing specialists, such as audiologists (Lacey, 2001). In addition, transportation services also might be provided if needed by the children.

Teacher aides especially can help the regular classroom teacher provide individualized instruction for children with disabilities (Hardman, Drew, & Egan, 2005). Some teacher aides are certified to work with children who have disabilities. Psychologists might be involved in assessing whether a child has a disability and might be part of the team that creates the IEP. They and counselors might also work with some children who have a disability. My (your author's) first job was as a school psychologist assigned to a reading clinic to evaluate the cognitive and socioemotional skills of children with reading problems. School psychologists might make recommendations to teachers about ways that children with a disability can learn more effectively. School social workers often help to coordinate family and community services for children with a disability. Nurses and physicians might conduct medical assessments and/or prescribe medication for children with disabilities. Physical therapists and occupational therapists might be involved in helping children recover from remediable physical or cognitive impairments. Speech and hearing specialists may be included when their skills will help improve children's skills in their area of expertise.

Collaborative Consultation and Interactive Teaming   In the last two decades, experts on educating children with disabilities have increasingly advocated more collaborative consultation (Idol, 1997). In collaborative consultation, people with diverse expertise interact to provide services for children. Researchers have found that collaborative consultation often results in gains for children, as well as improved skills and attitudes for teachers (Idol, Nevin, & Paolucci-Whitcomb, 1994).

Ideally, collaborative consultation encourages shared responsibility in planning and decision making. It also enables educators with diverse expertise to construct effective alternatives to traditional educational approaches. When collaborative consultation is used, many children remain in the regular classroom and the regular classroom teacher is actively involved in planning the child's education (Bryant & Bryant, 1998).

Increasingly, the term *interactive teaming* is being used (Thomas, Correa, & Morsink, 1995). Interactive team members are professionals and parents who collaborate to provide direct or indirect services to children (Coben & others, 1997). They share knowledge and skills, teaching other members their expertise when appropriate. Actual team sizes vary, and teams change in composition depending on the complexity of the child's needs. Persons involved can include educational, medical, administrative, vocational, and allied health specialists; social services personnel; and parents.

Parents as Educational Partners

Educators and researchers increasingly recognize how important it is for teachers and parents to jointly guide the learning of children with disabilities (Friend, 2005; Hardman, Drew, & Egan, 2005; Williams & Cartledge, 1997). The Individuals with Disabilities Education Act (IDEA) mandates parent participation in developing educational programs for all children with disabilities.

Through the Eyes of Teachers

Discovery Centers

Larry Statler is a special education teacher at Santa Teresa Elementary School in San Jose, California. He developed a "hands on, minds-on" Discovery program to let children with severe disabilities learn along with children who do not have disabilities. Larry launched the Discovery program in 1989 and it is still going strong. The program consists of hundreds of Discovery centers that allow students to learn at their own pace, from a dinosaur figurine counting station to a stencil-stocked publishing station. Children who complete the tasks go to a trinket-stocked treasure chest for a reward. Many children who do not have a disability go to learn at his Discovery centers during their recess time. Larry believes that every child deserves a special education.

Larry Statler with one of the many manipulative learning devices he created for his Discovery centers.

Teaching Strategies
For Communicating with Parents of Children with Disabilities

1. *Let parents know that you understand and appreciate their child's individuality.* Make it a point to talk about their child's strengths rather than focusing only on their child's problems. Especially focus on positive aspects of their child at the beginning and the end of the conversation.

2. *Place yourself in the shoes of parents of a child with a disability.* It is important to realize the frustration that many parents with a child who has a disability often feel. They may be struggling with a new diagnosis of their child or be confronting the complexities of an education plan for their child for the first time. Relay a diagnosis with compassion and an appropriate degree of hope for the child.

3. *Provide parents with information about their child's disability.* Once a child has been diagnosed with a disability, teachers should engage parents in an ongoing conversation about what this diagnosis means for the child. It is important for teachers and parents to work cooperatively in establishing and meeting realistic learning goals for the child. Know what resources can be used to help the child and discuss these with parents.

4. *Talk with parents, not to them.* View each meeting with the child's parents as an opportunity to learn more about the child. It is easy to fall into the trap of acting like an authority and talking "to" rather than "with" parents. View parents as being an equal partner with you and other professionals in educating the child with a disability. Encourage parents to ask questions and express their emotions. If you don't know the answer to a parent's question, tell them that you will try to find out the information for them.

5. *Avoid stereotyping children.* Educate yourself about children's diversity and the range of backgrounds they come from. Avoid making stereotypical judgments about children and their parents based on their socioeconomic status, ethnicity, family structure, religion, or gender. Good relationships and effective communication are undermined by biased assumptions.

6. *Reach out to parents to establish and maintain effective communication with them.* Tell them how important they are in helping you and other school professionals to understand and educate their child. Be sure to support their attendance at individualized education plan (IEP) meetings.

7. *Talk with parents about how the media can provide erroneous portrayals of children with disabilities.* Popular magazines, newspapers, movies, television, and radio at times provide inaccurate information about children with disabilities. Caution parents about this and tell them that they are always welcome to discuss anything they read about or hear pertaining to their child's disability with you or other school personnel.

Technology

The Individuals with Disabilities Education Act (IDEA), including its 1997 amendments, requires that technology devices and services be provided to students with disabilities if they are necessary to ensure a free, appropriate education (Male, 2003; Ulman, 2005). Earlier in this chapter, we briefly mentioned technology devices that can be used to help students with disabilities (such as students with a visual impairment, a hearing impairment, or cerebral palsy). Here we will provide a more comprehensive look at using technology in the education of students with disabilities. In chapter 12, "Planning, Instruction, and Technology," we will explore technology and learning in more detail.

Exploring Instructive and Assistive Technologies

Instructive and assistive technologies include traditional applications, constructivist applications, word processing, and other assistive technologies (Roblyer, Edwards, & Havrileck, 1997).

Traditional Applications

Traditional applications involve the use of computer-based tutorials, drill and practice, and games. For example, these applications have been used to improve the decoding and vocabulary skills of children with a learning disability, especially those who have reading problems. Game-type software is often used to motivate children with a disability.

Constructivist Applications

An increasing trend is to use computer-based applications that are constructivist rather than based on tutorial or drill-and-practice methods. Constructivist applications focus on students' understanding and thinking skills. More and more computer-based learning programs include simulation of real-world problems (Cognition and Technology Group at Vanderbilt, 1997).

Among the constructivist technology applications that can be used effectively with children with disabilities are cognitive organizers such as *IdeaFisher* and *Inspiration*. Both can be used with children who have a learning disability. Word prediction software can be used to help children with physical disabilities write on a computer.

Word Processing

Word processing has helped many children with disabilities make progress in their written language skills (Hetzroni & Shrieber, 2004; Holzberg, 1995). Talking word processors such as *Write: Outloud, Intellitalk, KidsWorks 2,* and *The Amazing Writing Machine* can be especially helpful in the education of children with speech problems. On request, these programs read text aloud.

Other Assistive Technologies

Many children with physical disabilities (such as cerebral palsy) cannot use traditional devices such as a keyboard and a mouse. Touch screens, touch tablets, optical pointers, alternative keyboards, and voice-controlled devices are alternatives that allow them to use a computer.

Software or special hardware such as closed-circuit television can enlarge computer images and text for children with a visual impairment. Printers can produce large print or Braille. Tactile devices that scan a page and translate the text into vibrating, tactile displays also can be used with children who are visually impaired. Captioned video provides subtitles for television and other video presentations so that children who are hearing-impaired can read what others are saying.

Telecommunication technologies for the deaf allow children with hearing impairments to communicate with people over the phone. The Internet allows children with a disability who are homebound to access educational opportunities.

(a)

(b)

These special input devices can help students with physical disabilities use computers more effectively. *(a)* A student uses a special input device attached to the student's head to send signals to the computer. *(b)* Many students with physical disabilities such as cerebral palsy cannot use a conventional keyboard and mouse. Many can use alternative keyboards effectively.

Two types of technology that can be used to improve the education of students with disabilities are instructional technology and assistance technology (Blackhurst, 1997). *Instructional technology* includes various types of hardware and software, combined with innovative teaching methods, to accommodate students' learning needs in the classroom.

This technology includes videotapes, computer-assisted instruction, and complex hypermedia programs in which computers are used to control the display of audio and visual images stored on videodisc. The use of telecommunications systems, especially the Internet and its World Wide Web, holds considerable promise for improving the education of students with or without a disability.

Assistive technology consists of various services and devices to help students with disabilities function within their environment. Examples include communication aids, alternative computer keyboards, and adaptive switches. To locate such services, educators can use computer databases such as the Device Locator System (Academic Software, 1996).

Teams of educators and other professionals often combine these technologies to improve the learning of students with disabilities (Ulman, 2005). For example, students who are unable to use their hands to operate a computer keyboard might use a voice-operated computer (assistive technology) that provides instruction from a software program that was designed to provide spelling instruction (instructional technology). To read further about instructional and assistive technologies, see the Technology and Education box on page 199.

Technology Resources

Assistive Technology

> ## ❗ Review and Reflect
>
> **2 Explain the legal framework, planning, placement, and provision of services for children with disabilities.**
>
> **Review**
> - What is IDEA? How is it related to IEPs and LREs? What is the current thinking about inclusion?
> - What different types of placement and services are possible? Who carries them out?
> - How can teachers best communicate with parents as educational partners?
> - What is the difference between instructional and assistive technology?
>
> **Reflect**
> - What do you think will present the greatest challenges to you in teaching children with a disability?

CHILDREN WHO ARE GIFTED

The final type of exceptionality we will discuss is quite different from the disabilities and disorders that we have described so far. **Children who are gifted** have above-average intelligence (usually defined as an IQ of 130 or higher) and/or superior talent in some domain such as art, music, or mathematics. Programs for children who are gifted in schools typically base admission to the programs on intelligence and academic aptitude, although there is increasing call to widen the criteria to include such factors as creativity and commitment (Renzulli & Reis, 1997). Some critics argue that too many children in "gifted programs" aren't really gifted in a particular area but are just somewhat bright, usually cooperative, and, usually, non-Latino White (Castellano & Diaz, 2002). They believe the mantle of brilliance is cast on many children who are not that far from simply being "smart normal." Although general intelligence as defined by an overall IQ score still remains as a key criterion in many states' decision of whether a child should be placed in a gifted program, changing conceptions of intelligence increasingly include ideas such as Gardner's multiple intelligences, and placement criteria are likely to move away from an IQ criterion in the future (Davidson, 2000; Davis & Rimm, 2004).

children who are gifted Children with above-average intelligence (usually defined as an IQ of 130 or higher) and/or superior talent in some domain such as art, music, or mathematics.

Characteristics

Ellen Winner (1996), an expert on creativity and giftedness, recently described three criteria that characterize children who are gifted:

1. *Precocity.* Children who are gifted are precocious when given the opportunity to use their gift or talent. They begin to master an area earlier than their peers. Learning in their domain is more effortless for them than for children who are not gifted. In most instances, children who are gifted are precocious because they have an inborn high ability in a particular domain or domains, although this inborn precocity has to be identified and nourished.

2. *Marching to their own drummer.* Children who are gifted learn in a qualitatively different way than children who are not gifted. One way they march to a different drummer is that they require less support, or scaffolding (discussed in chapter 2), from adults to learn than their nongifted peers do. Often they resist explicit instruction. They also often make discoveries on their own and solve problems in unique ways within their area of giftedness. They can be normal or below normal in other areas.

3. *A passion to master.* Children who are gifted are driven to understand the domain in which they have high ability. They display an intense, obsessive interest and an ability to focus. They are not children who need to be pushed by their parents. They frequently have a high degree of internal motivation.

In addition to the three characteristics of gifted children that we have just mentioned (precocity, marching to a different drummer, and a passion to master), a fourth area in which they excel involves information-processing skills. Researchers have found that children who are gifted learn at a faster pace, process information more rapidly, are better at reasoning, use better strategies, and monitor their understanding better than their nongifted counterparts (Sternberg & Clinkenbeard, 1995).

The Classic Terman Studies

Lewis Terman (1925) followed the lives of approximately 1,500 children whose Stanford-Binet IQs averaged 150 into the adult years. Their developmental outcomes were impressive. For the 800 men, 78 obtained doctorates (they include two past presidents of the American Psychological Association), 48 earned M.D.s, and 85 earned law degrees. These figures are 10 to 30 times greater than the educational achievements of the 800 men of the same age chosen randomly as a comparison control group.

Of the 672 women studied, two-thirds graduated from college in the 1930s and one-fourth attended graduate school (Terman & Oden, 1959). Despite their impressive educational achievements for their time, when asked to order life's priorities they often placed family first, friendship second, and career third, even though 25 of the 30 most successful women did not have children. The gifted women in Terman's study represented a cohort whose childhood, and most of their adulthood, was lived prior to the women's movement and the prevalence of the dual-career couple and the single-parent family (Tomlinson-Keasey, 1993). Studies of gifted girls and women today suggest that they have a stronger confidence in their cognitive abilities than did their gifted counterparts in Terman's study (Tomlinson-Keasey, 1997).

As a group, Terman's gifted were intellectually precocious but they were not emotionally disordered or maladjusted. This finding also has appeared in a number of studies of children who are gifted—namely, that they are as well adjusted as, or are better adjusted than, children who are not gifted (Winner, 1996). However, children who are extremely precocious (such as those having an IQ of 180 or higher) often show more adjustment problems than children who are not gifted (Keogh & Macmillan, 1996).

Steven Ceci (1990) has argued that an analysis of the Terman group's development brings up an important point. It was not just their high IQs that gained them success. Many of Terman's gifted children came from upper-income families, and their parents

At two years of age, art prodigy Alexandra Nechita colored in coloring books for hours and took up pen and ink. She had no interest in dolls or friends. By age five she was using watercolors. Once she started school, she would start painting as soon as she got home. At the age of eight, in 1994, she saw the first public exhibit of her work. In succeeding years, working quickly and impulsively on canvases as large as 5 feet by 9 feet, she has completed hundreds of paintings, some of which sell for close to $100,000 apiece. As a teenager, she continues to paint—relentlessly and passionately. It is, she says, what she loves to do. *What are some characteristics of children who are gifted?*

Gifted Education

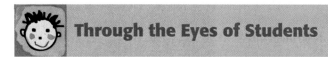
Through the Eyes of Students

Children Who Are Gifted Speak

James Delisle (1987) interviewed hundreds of elementary school children who are gifted. Here are some of their comments.
In response to: Describe Your Typical School Day

> Oh what a bore to sit and listen,
> To stuff we already know.
> Do everything we've done and done again,
> But we must still sit and listen.
> Over and over read one more page
> Oh bore, oh bore, oh bore.

Girl, Age 9, New York

> I sit there pretending to be reading along when I'm really six pages ahead. When I understand something and half the class doesn't, I have to sit there and listen.

Girl, Age 11, New York

In response to: Describe a Perfect Day

> If I learned to understand something new in most subjects.

Boy, Age 12, New York

In response to: What Activities and Methods Do Teachers Use That Make Learning Worthwhile?

> My fifth-grade teacher makes learning fun by doing an activity to help you learn. We have math sales and that helps us with money while it's also fun to learn. In studying the Constitution we made bills and voted on them.

Girl, Age 10, Connecticut

In response to: What Makes a Teacher a Gifted Teacher?

> She is capable of handling our problems and has a good imagination to help us learn.

Girl, Age 10, Louisiana

> Will challenge you and let the sky be your limit.

Boy, Age 11, Michigan

> Opens your mind to help you with your life.

Boy, Age 11, New Jersey

had high achievement expectations for them and played a guiding role in their success. However, a few of the most successful gifted individuals in Terman's study did come from low-income families. Thus, success in life for individuals who are gifted doesn't require being born into material wealth.

Educating Children Who Are Gifted

Underchallenged gifted children can become disruptive, skip classes, and lose interest in achieving. Sometimes these children just disappear into the woodwork, becoming passive and apathetic toward school (Rosselli, 1996).

Four program options for gifted children are these (Hertzog, 1998):

- *Special classes.* Historically, this has been the common way to educate children who are gifted. The special classes during the regular school day are called "pull-out" programs. Some special classes also are held after school, on Saturdays, or in the summer.
- *Acceleration and enrichment in the regular classroom setting*
- *Mentor and apprenticeship programs.* Some experts believe these are important, underutilized ways to motivate, challenge, and effectively educate children who are gifted (Pleiss & Feldhusen, 1995).
- *Work/study and/or community service programs*

Educational reform has brought into the regular classroom many strategies that once were the domain of separate gifted programs. These include an emphasis on problem-based learning, having children do projects, creating portfolios, and critical thinking. Combined with the increasing emphasis on educating all children in the regular classroom, many schools now try to challenge and motivate children who are gifted in the regular classroom (Hertzog, 1998). Some schools also include after-school or Saturday programs or develop mentor apprenticeship, work/study, or community service programs. Thus, an array of in-school and out-of-school opportunities is provided.

An ongoing debate focuses on whether children who are gifted should be placed in acceleration or enrichment programs (Feldhusen, 1997). An *acceleration program* moves children through the curriculum as quickly as they are able to progress. Acceleration programs include early entrance (to kindergarten, first grade, middle school, high school, or college), skipping grades, extra courses or honors courses, and advanced placement classes. Curriculum compacting is a variation of acceleration in which teachers skip over aspects of the curriculum that they believe children who are gifted do not need.

An *enrichment program* provides children with opportunities for learning that are usually not present in the curriculum. Enrichment opportunities can be made available in the regular classroom, through "pullout" to a special class; through a gifted education resource teacher who consults with the regular classroom teacher; through independent study, in after-school, Saturday, or summer sessions, and in apprenticeship and mentoring programs; and through work/study arrangements.

The Schoolwide Enrichment Model (SEM), developed by Joseph Renzulli (1998), is a program for educating children who are gifted that focuses on total school improvement. Renzulli says that when enrichment has a schoolwide emphasis, positive outcomes are likely to occur, not only for children who are gifted but also for nongifted children and for classroom and resource teachers. When schoolwide enrichment is emphasized, "us" versus "them" barriers often decrease and classroom teachers are more willing to use curriculum compacting with their most gifted children. Instead of feeling isolated, resource teachers begin to feel more like members of a team, especially when they work with regular classroom teachers on enriching the entire classroom. Thus, important goals of SEM are to improve outcomes for both students who are gifted and those who are not gifted and to improve the contributions and relationships of classroom and resource teachers.

Research evaluation of acceleration and enrichment programs has not revealed which approach is best (Winner, 1997). Some researchers have found support for acceleration programs (Kulik, 1992), although critics say a potential problem of grade skipping is that it places children with others who are physically more advanced and socioemotionally different. Other researchers have found support for enrichment programs (Renzulli & Reis, 1997).

Ellen Winner (1997) argues that too often children who are gifted are socially isolated and underchallenged in the classroom. It is not unusual for them to be ostracized and labeled "nerds" or "geeks" (Silverman, 1993). A gifted child who is the only such child in the room does not have the opportunity to learn with students of like ability. Many eminent adults report that school was a negative experience for them, that they were bored and sometimes knew more than their teachers (Bloom, 1985). Winner believes that American education will benefit when standards are raised for all children. When some children are still underchallenged, she recommends that they be allowed to attend advanced classes in their domain of exceptional ability. For example, some especially precocious middle school students are allowed to take college classes in their area of expertise.

This concludes our coverage of children who are exceptional learners. From time to time in this chapter, we described some behavioral strategies for changing children's behavior. For example, we indicated that children who are mentally retarded often benefit from the use of precise steps in using positive reinforcement to change their behavior. In chapter 7, we will explore many aspects of positive reinforcement and other learning strategies.

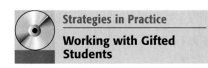

Strategies in Practice
Working with Gifted Students

ENTER THE DEBATE

1. Should gifted children have individual education plans just as students with disabilities typically do?

2. Should students with disabilities be taught in an inclusionary environment?

Teaching Experience

- **Working with Children with Special Needs**
- **Working with a Child with a Hearing Disability**
- **Working with a Child with a Pervasive Developmental Disorder**

! Review and Reflect

3 Define what gifted means and discuss some approaches to teaching children who are gifted.

Review
- What is the definition of being gifted? What characteristics does Winner ascribe to children who are gifted?
- What did the Terman studies discover about individuals who are gifted?
- What are some options for educating students who are gifted?

Reflect
- Suppose that you had several students in your class who were strikingly gifted. Might this lead to problems? Explain. What might you do to prevent such problems from developing?

Before the school year starts, Mrs. Peterson always holds a "get-acquainted meeting" with the parents of her incoming kindergartners. She does this so that she can explain what the children will be doing in kindergarten, what her educational philosophy is, what her expectations are, and what the procedure is for dropping students off at school the first day and, of course, to allow parents to ask any questions and share any concerns they might have. Inevitably, parents do have concerns and questions they would like addressed.

This is what she hears from the parents:

"Joey still naps in the afternoon. Is there any way we can have him changed to the morning class?"

"Ashley has severe asthma. She'll need to have her nebulizer close by in case she has an asthma attack. Do you know how to use one?"

"I just know that Steve won't be able to sit still for very long. Do you allow the children to move a lot?"

"I sure hope you give the kids a lot of time to be active. Bill won't be able to sit still for long, either."

"Alex is very advanced for his age. What can you do to challenge him?"

"Amanda is advanced, too."

"So is my Timmy."

"Well, Peter seems to be behind. I just don't know what to do with him. He doesn't speak very well."

Mrs. Peterson listens respectfully to each concern or question and assures the parents, "I'll do everything I can to ensure your children have a good year in my class. All children are different and learn at different rates, so I wouldn't be too worried about being a little bit behind or ahead. I think we'll all do fine together." As she is leaving for the evening, she chuckles at the number of parents who think their children are advanced. It's the same every year—about a third of the parents are convinced that their child is the next Einstein.

The school year begins uneventfully. The children seem to enjoy playing with each other and are adjusting to school nicely. Mrs. Peterson uses the children's free-play time to observe them. While there are obvious differences among the children, she doesn't notice that any of the children are exceptional, except perhaps for Bill and Steve. Their lack of attention and inability to sit still during story time is beginning to be a bit disruptive. Mrs. Peterson makes a note to herself to talk to their parents about the possibility that they have attention deficit hyperactivity disorder and recommend testing. A couple of other students might be candidates for this as well, including Alex. What bundles of energy they are. While Mrs. Peterson did learn how to use Ashley's nebulizer, she hasn't had a need to use it thus far, a fact for which she is very grateful.

Each day at the beginning of class, the students have calendar time. Mrs. Peterson marks off the day of the month on the calendar with a large X and discusses the weather. She then writes a statement on the blackboard describing the day's weather. On the tenth day of school she writes on the board, "Today is sunny and hot." She then reads the statement to the students so that they might begin to make word associations. "Today is sunny and warm." Alex shouts out, "That isn't what you wrote. You wrote today is sunny and hot." Mrs. Peterson is astounded.

Later, during free-play time she asks Alex to sit with her. Alex looks longingly at the puzzles but grudgingly complies. "Alex, will you read this book to me?"

"Sure," replies Alex, and he does so flawlessly.

"Do you have this book at home?"

"Yep. Lots of others, too."

"How about this one? Do you have it?"

"Nope."

"Well then, suppose you try to read this one to me."

"Okay, but then can I go play with the puzzles?"

"Certainly."

Alex reads the book to Mrs. Peterson, missing only a few words, and then rushes off to play with the puzzles, build towers of blocks and knock them down, and play with trucks.

The next day during calendar time Mrs. Peterson asks the class, "If today is the fifteenth day of the month and there are thirty days in the month, how could we find out how many days are left?"

The children call out, "We could count the days that don't have Xs on them."

"Very good," replies Mrs. Peterson.

Alex looks puzzled. "What's wrong, Alex?" asks Mrs. Peterson. "Why don't we just subtract?" he asks.

- What are the issues in this case?
- Why do you suppose Mrs. Peterson makes light of parents' perceptions of their children's strengths?
- How should Mrs. Peterson approach the parents of the students she believes might have ADHD?
- Is it appropriate for her to recommend testing of any of the children? Why or why not? Would it be appropriate for her to recommend a particular doctor for this testing? Why or why not?
- If Alex can already read and subtract, are there other skills he has likely mastered? If so, what might they be? How might this impact his experiences in kindergarten? How should Mrs. Peterson address this?

Reach Your Learning Goals

1 Describe the various types of disabilities and disorders.

- An estimated 10 percent of U.S. children with a disability receive special education services. Slightly more than 50 percent of these students are classified as having a learning disability (in the federal classification, this includes attention deficit hyperactivity disorder [ADHD]). Substantial percentages of children with a disability have mental retardation, speech and language disorders, or a serious emotional disturbance. The term *children with disabilities* is now used rather than *disabled children,* and children with disabilities are no longer referred to as *handicapped children.*

- Sensory disorders include visual and hearing impairments. Visual impairments include having low vision and being educationally blind. An important task is to determine which modality (such as touch or hearing) the student who is visually impaired learns best in. A number of technological devices help these students learn. Educational strategies for students with hearing impairments fall into two main categories: oral and manual. Increasingly, both approaches are used with the same student in a total-communication approach.

- Among the physical disorders that students might have are orthopedic impairments (such as cerebral palsy) and seizure disorders (such as epilepsy).

- Mental retardation is a condition with an onset before age eighteen that involves low intelligence (usually below 70 on an individually administered intelligence test) and difficulty in adapting to everyday life. Mental retardation has been classified in terms of four categories based mainly on IQ scores: mild, moderate, severe, and profound. More recently, a classification system based on degree of support required has been advocated. Causes of mental retardation include genetic factors (as in Down syndrome and fragile X syndrome), brain damage (which can result from many different infections, such as AIDS), and environmental hazards.

- Speech and language disorders include a number of speech problems (such as articulation disorders, voice disorders, and fluency disorders) and language problems (difficulties in receiving and expressing language). Articulation disorders are problems in pronouncing words correctly. Voice disorders are reflected in speech that is too hoarse, loud, high-pitched, or low-pitched. Children with cleft palate often have a voice disorder. Fluency disorders often involve what we commonly call "stuttering." Language disorders involve significant impairments in children's receptive or expressive language. Receptive language involves the reception and understanding of language. Expressive language involves using language for expressing one's thoughts and communicating with others.

- Children with a learning disability are of normal intelligence or above; they have difficulties in at least one academic area and usually several; and their difficulty is not attributable to some other diagnosed problem or disorder, such as mental retardation. Diagnosing whether a child has a learning disability is difficult. About three times as many boys as girls have a learning disability. The most common academic problem for children with a learning disability is reading. Dyslexia is a severe impairment in the ability to read and spell. Children with a learning disability often have difficulties in handwriting, spelling, or composition and increasingly are diagnosed with difficulties in math. Controversy surrounds the "learning disability" category; some critics believe it is overdiagnosed; others argue that it is not. Diagnosis is difficult, especially for mild forms. Initial identification of children with a possible learning disability often is made by the classroom teacher, who then asks specialists to evaluate the child. Many interventions targeted for learning disabilities focus on reading ability and include such strategies as improving decoding skills. The success of even the best-designed interventions depends on the training and skills of the teacher.

- Attention deficit hyperactivity disorder (ADHD) is a disability in which children consistently show problems in one or more of these areas: inattention, hyperactivity, and impulsivity. Although signs of ADHD may be present in early childhood, diagnosis of ADHD often doesn't occur until the elementary school years. Many experts recommend a combination of academic, behavioral, and medical interventions to help students with ADHD learn and adapt.

- Emotional and behavioral disorders consist of serious, persistent problems that involve relationships, aggression, depression, fears associated with personal or school matters, and other inappropriate socioemotional characteristics. The term *serious emotional disturbances* recently has been used to describe this category of disorders, although it is not without criticism. In severe instances of aggressive, out-of-control behaviors, students are removed from the classroom. The problems are far more characteristic of boys than of girls. Problems involving depression, anxiety, and fear, involving turning problems inward, are much more likely to appear in girls than in boys.

2 Explain the legal framework, planning, placement, and provision of services for children with disabilities.

- The educational rights for children with disabilities were laid down in the mid 1960s. In 1975, Congress enacted Public Law 94-142, the Education for All Handicapped Children Act, which mandated that all children be given a free, appropriate public education. Public Law 94-142 was recast as the Individuals with Disabilities Education

Act (IDEA), which spells out broad requirements for services to all children with disabilities. Children who are thought to have a disability are evaluated to determine their eligibility for services. The IDEA has many provisions that relate to the parents of children with disabilities.

- The IEP is a written plan of the program specifically tailored for the child with a disability. The plan should (1) relate to the child's learning capacity, (2) be individualized and not a copy of a plan that is offered to other children, and (3) be designed to provide educational benefits. The concept of least restrictive environment (LRE) is contained in the IDEA. It states that children with disabilities must be educated in a setting that is as similar as possible to the one in which children without disabilities are educated. This provision of IDEA has given a legal basis to making an effort to educate children with disabilities in the regular classroom. The term *inclusion* means educating children with disabilities full-time in the regular classroom. The trend is toward using inclusion more. Children's academic and social success is affected more by the quality of instruction they receive than by where they are placed.

- The range of placements include regular classroom with supplementary instructional support provided in the regular classroom; part of the time spent in a resource room; full-time placement in a special education class; special schools; homebound instruction; and instruction in a hospital or another institution. Services include those provided by the classroom teacher in the regular classroom, those provided by a resource teacher (either in a separate resource room or in the regular classroom), those provided by a special education teacher, and other services provided by teacher aides, psychologists, collaborative consultants, and interactive teams.

- Some good communication strategies include letting parents know that you understand and appreciate their child's individuality; placing yourself in the parents' shoes; providing them with information about their child's disability; talking with, not to, parents; avoiding stereotypes;

reaching out to establish and maintain contact with parents; and talking with parents about how the media sometimes erroneously portray children with disabilities.

- Instructional technology includes various types of hardware and software, combined with innovative teaching methods, to accommodate children's needs in the classroom. Assistive technology consists of various services and devices to help children with disabilities function within their environment.

3 Define what gifted means and discuss some approaches to teaching children who are gifted.

- Children who are gifted have above-average intelligence (usually defined as an IQ of 130 or higher) and/or superior talent in some domain, such as art, music, or mathematics. Some critics argue that gifted programs include too many children who are just somewhat bright, usually cooperative, and, usually, non-Latino White. Winner described children who are gifted as having three main characteristics: precocity, marching to the tune of a different drummer, and a passion to master.

- The Terman studies revealed the successful lives of many children who are gifted. Many of the Terman gifted not only had superior IQs but also came from high-income families in which their parents guided and monitored their achievement. Most children who are gifted do not have emotional disorders. Underchallenged gifted students can show school-related problems.

- Educational programs available for children who are gifted include special classes ("pullout" programs), acceleration, enrichment, mentor and apprenticeship programs, as well as work/study or community service programs. Debate focuses on whether acceleration or enrichment programs most benefit children who are gifted. Children who are gifted increasingly are being educated in the regular classroom. Some experts recommend that increasing the standards in the regular classroom will help children who are gifted, although programs such as mentoring and additional instruction might be needed for children who are still underchallenged.

◎ KEY TERMS

disability 175
handicap 175
orthopedic impairments 177
cerebral palsy 177
epilepsy 177
mental retardation 178
Down syndrome 179
fragile X syndrome 179

fetal alcohol syndrome (FAS) 180
speech and language disorders 181
articulation disorders 181
voice disorders 181
fluency disorders 181
language disorders 181
receptive language 181

expressive language 181
learning disability 182
dyslexia 183
attention deficit hyperactivity disorder (ADHD) 186
emotional and behavioral disorders 188
Public Law 94-142 191

Individuals with Disabilities Education Act (IDEA) 191
individualized education plan (IEP) 191
least restrictive environment (LRE) 192
inclusion 192
children who are gifted 200

PORTFOLIO ACTIVITIES

Now that you have a good understanding of this chapter, complete these exercises to expand your thinking.

Independent Reflection

Fostering Positive School-Home Linkages for Children with Disabilities. Place yourself in the role of a parent. Imagine that the school has just notified you that your child has a learning disability. Write down answers to these questions: 1) What feelings are you likely to be having as a parent? 2) As a parent, what questions do you want to ask the teacher? 3) Now put yourself in the role of the teacher. How would you respond to these questions? (INTASC: Principles 3, 10)

Collaborative Work

Technology Resources for Gifted Students. Together with 3 or 4 other students in your class, come up with a list and description of software programs that you think would benefit children who are gifted. One good source of information on such software is the *Journal of Electronic Learning*. Write down the list and descriptions below. (INTASC: Principles 3, 4, 9)

Research/Field Experience Reflections

Inclusion in Action. Interview elementary school, middle school, and high school teachers about their impressions of inclusion and other aspects of educating children with disabilities. Ask them what their most successful strategies are in working with children who have disabilities. Also ask what the biggest challenges are. Write a summary of the interviews below. (INTASC: Principle 9)

 Go to the Online Learning Center for downloadable portfolio templates.

TAKING IT TO THE NET

1. Teachers who work with special needs children typically develop an individual education plan (IEP) for each child. What is an IEP? Review sample IEPs online, and discuss how all students could benefit from receiving the type of feedback present in an IEP. How could you use an IEP as a model for tailoring your instruction to the special needs of all students?

2. You recommend that a student be assessed for possible entry into your school's gifted program, but the school psychologist informs you that the child is a *C* student. Is it possible to be a "gifted underachiever"? Explain.

3. Imagine that you have two students in your classroom who have been diagnosed with ADHD. What are some strategies for helping these children succeed in the classroom? Why is family support so important, and what specific actions will you take to maintain ongoing communication with them?

   Connect to the Online Learning Center to explore possible answers.

STUDY, PRACTICE, AND SUCCEED

 Go to chapter 6 on the Online Learning Center at www.mhhe.com/santrockedu2e to access the student study guide with practice quizzes, web links, portfolio resources, PowerWeb articles and news feeds, and the online resources referenced in the chapter.

Go to your Student Toolbox CD-ROM to access the resources and activities referenced in the chapter and

- Resources to help you prepare for the PRAXIS II™ exam

- **Application Resources,** including additional *Crack the Case* studies, electronic versions of the *Self-Assessments*, Application Exercises, and Site Observation Questions
- **Study Resources,** including Learning Goals, the Chapter Summary, a *Test Your Learning* exercise, and multiple-choice, true/false, matching, key terms, and short-answer quizzes
- **Professional Resources,** including a Lesson Plan Builder and *Bibliomaker*

7 Behavioral and Social Cognitive Approaches

To learn is a natural pleasure.
—Aristotle
Greek Philosopher,
4th Century B.C.

Teaching Stories Garnetta Chan

Garnetta Chan teaches third grade at McKinley School in the outskirts of New Brunswick, New Jersey, amid low-income housing projects and deteriorating factories. She has been teaching for more than twenty-five years. One of her main goals is for her students to enjoy learning. She also strives to provide them with a safe and secure environment. Class rules are clearly posted in her room. Garnetta believes that the children in her class have so much uncertainty in their lives that they need to know the classroom is a place where things are consistent. She says, "They have to have limits. There need to be consequences for their behaviors so that they will develop responsibility for their actions."

Along with limits, Garnetta provides praise for her students. She calms an angry child with a soft word and prevents disruption with a hand on a shoulder. She offers many of the relationship qualities they lack in their personal lives. It is not unusual for students to return to her classroom years after they have moved on, just to chat or to discuss a problem.

Garnetta's caring extends beyond the classroom walls. For example, one day a little boy appeared outside her classroom windows, his face pressed against the glass. He had been in Garnetta's class but a social service agency had removed him from his foster home and placed him with his father, which meant he had to go to another school. Although Garnetta was opposed to the move, she had not been able to convince the authorities that he was better off where he was. Garnetta invited him in. He found his old chair and the sweatshirt he had left behind. The children accepted him, and you could tell by the smile on his face that he felt at home. Garnetta had heard that the boy was not attending school regularly and was seen out late at night unsupervised. She immediately got on the phone and called his caseworker, recommending that he be allowed to return to her school. Garnetta even volunteered to pick him up at his new address and drive him each day to her school. Although his return to the school was not allowed, that day Garnetta gave him all the support she could and in a caring way tried to help him understand why he had to return to the other school.

Garnetta hopes that her efforts pay off and that potential high school dropouts will become high school graduates. She strives to be a positive model for her students, wanting them to see the pride she has in herself and her career. She says, "I want them to see that teaching is as great as being a doctor or a lawyer."

Virtually everyone agrees that helping students learn is an important function of schools. However, not everyone agrees on the best way to learn. In this chapter, we will explore the behavioral and social cognitive approaches to learning.

Expert Advice

Dale Schunk on Social Cognitive Learning and Bandura's Theory

WHAT IS LEARNING?

Learning is a central focus of educational psychology. When people are asked what schools are for, a common reply is "To help children learn."

What Learning Is and Is Not

When children learn how to use a computer, they might make some mistakes along the way, but at a certain point they will get the knack of the behaviors required to use the computer effectively. The children will change from being individuals who cannot operate a computer into being individuals who can. Once they have learned how to use a computer, they don't lose those skills. It's like learning to drive a car. Once you have learned how, you don't have to learn all over again. Thus, **learning** can be defined as a relatively permanent influence on behavior, knowledge, and thinking skills, which comes about through experience.

Not everything we know is learned. We inherit some capacities—they are inborn or innate, not learned. For example, we don't have to be taught to swallow, to flinch at loud noises, or to blink when an object comes too close to our eyes. However, most human behaviors do not involve heredity alone. When children use a computer in a new way, work harder at solving problems, ask better questions, explain an answer in a more logical way, or listen more attentively, the experience of learning is at work.

The scope of learning is broad (Domjan, 2000, 2002). It involves academic behaviors and nonacademic behaviors. It occurs in schools and everywhere else that children experience their world.

learning A relatively permanent influence on behavior, knowledge, and thinking skills, which comes about through experience.

Approaches to Learning

A number of approaches to learning have been proposed, including behavioral and cognitive approaches.

210

Behavioral   The learning approaches that we discuss in the first part of this chapter are called *behavioral*. **Behaviorism** is the view that behavior should be explained by observable experiences, not by mental processes. For the behaviorist, behavior is everything that we do that can be directly observed: a child creating a poster, a teacher smiling at a child, one student picking on another student, and so on. **Mental processes** are defined by psychologists as the thoughts, feelings, and motives that each of us experiences but that cannot be observed by others. Although we cannot directly see thoughts, feelings, and motives, they are no less real. Mental processes include children thinking about ways to create the best poster, a teacher feeling good about children's efforts, and children's inner motivation to control their behavior.

Behavioral Approaches

For the behaviorist, these thoughts, feelings, and motives are not appropriate subject matter for a science of behavior because they cannot be directly observed. Classical conditioning and operant conditioning, two behavioral views that we will discuss shortly, adopt this stance. Both of these views emphasize **associative learning,** which consists of learning that two events are connected (associated) (Pearce, 2001). For example, associative learning occurs when a student associates a pleasant event with learning something in school, such as the teacher smiling when the student asks a good question. The discussion of applied behavior analysis later in the chapter also reflects the behavioral view of focusing on observable behavior and associative learning.

Cognitive   Psychology became more cognitive in the last part of the twentieth century and the cognitive emphasis continues today. This cognitive emphasis has become the basis for numerous approaches to learning (Driscoll, 2000; Hunt, 2002; Roediger, 2000; Wells & Claxton, 2002). We discuss four main cognitive approaches to learning in this book: social cognitive; cognitive information-processing; cognitive constructivist; and social constructivist. The *social cognitive* approaches, which emphasize how behavior, environment, and person (cognitive) factors interact to influence learning, will be covered later in this chapter. The second set of approaches, *information-processing,* focuses on how children process information through attention, memory, thinking, and other cognitive processes. It will be explored in chapters 8 and 9. The third set of approaches, *cognitive constructivist,* emphasizes the child's cognitive construction of knowledge and understanding. It was introduced in the form of Piaget's theory in chapter 2 and will be further examined in chapters 8 and 9 ◀ p. 39. The fourth set of cognitive approaches, *social constructivist,* focuses on collaboration with others to produce knowledge and understanding. The social constructivist approaches initially were introduced in the form of Vygotsky's theory in chapter 2 and they will be further evaluated in chapter 10 ◀ p. 51.

Adding these four cognitive approaches to the behavioral approaches, we arrive at five main approaches to learning that we discuss in this book: behavioral, social cognitive, cognitive information-processing, cognitive constructivist, and social constructivist. All contribute to our understanding of how children learn. A summary of the five approaches is presented in figure 7.1 on page 212.

ⓘ Review and Reflect

① Define learning and describe five approaches to studying it.

Review
- Are there any behaviors that don't reflect learning? What is learning?
- What essentially is behaviorism? What are four main cognitive approaches to learning?

Reflect
- How do you learn? Think of a behavior you engage in and describe how you learned it.

behaviorism The view that behavior should be explained by observable experiences.

mental processes Thoughts, feelings, and motives that cannot be observed by others.

associative learning Learning that two events are connected (associated).

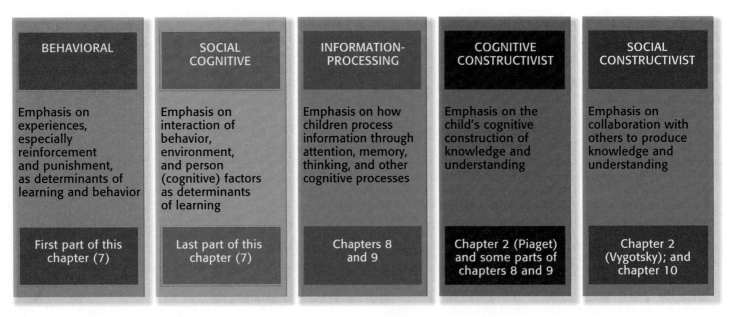

BEHAVIORAL	SOCIAL COGNITIVE	INFORMATION-PROCESSING	COGNITIVE CONSTRUCTIVIST	SOCIAL CONSTRUCTIVIST
Emphasis on experiences, especially reinforcement and punishment, as determinants of learning and behavior	Emphasis on interaction of behavior, environment, and person (cognitive) factors as determinants of learning	Emphasis on how children process information through attention, memory, thinking, and other cognitive processes	Emphasis on the child's cognitive construction of knowledge and understanding	Emphasis on collaboration with others to produce knowledge and understanding
First part of this chapter (7)	Last part of this chapter (7)	Chapters 8 and 9	Chapter 2 (Piaget) and some parts of chapters 8 and 9	Chapter 2 (Vygotsky); and chapter 10

FIGURE 7.1 Approaches to Learning

BEHAVIORAL APPROACHES TO LEARNING

The behavioral approaches emphasize the importance of children making connections between experiences and behavior. The first behavioral approach we will examine is classical conditioning.

Classical Conditioning

Ivan Pavlov (1849–1936), the Russian physiologist who developed the concept of classical conditioning.

classical conditioning A form of associative learning in which a neutral stimulus becomes associated with a meaningful stimulus and acquires the capacity to elicit a similar response.

In the early 1900s, Russian physiologist Ivan Pavlov was interested in the way the body digests food. In his experiments, he routinely placed meat powder in a dog's mouth, causing the dog to salivate. The dog salivated in response to a number of stimuli associated with the food, such as the sight of the food dish, the sight of the individual who brought the food into the room, and the sound of the door closing when the food arrived. Pavlov recognized that the dog's association of these sights and sounds with the food was an important type of learning, which came to be called *classical conditioning*.

Classical conditioning is a type of learning in which an organism learns to connect, or associate, stimuli. In classical conditioning, a neutral stimulus (such as the sight of a person) becomes associated with a meaningful stimulus (such as food) and acquires the capacity to elicit a similar response. To fully understand Pavlov's (1927) theory of classical conditioning we need to understand two types of stimuli and two types of responses: unconditioned stimulus (US), unconditioned response (UR), conditioned stimulus (CS), and conditioned response (CR).

Figure 7.2 summarizes the way classical conditioning works. An *unconditioned stimulus (US)* is a stimulus that automatically produces a response without any prior learning. Food was the US in Pavlov's experiments. An *unconditioned response (UR)* is an unlearned response that is automatically elicited by the US. In Pavlov's experiments, the dog's salivation in response to food was the UR. A *conditioned stimulus (CS)* is a previously neutral stimulus that eventually elicits a conditioned response after being associated with the US. Among the conditioned stimuli in Pavlov's experiments were various sights and sounds that occurred prior to the dog's actually eating the food, such as the sound of the door closing before the food was placed in the dog's dish. A *conditioned response (CR)* is a learned response to the conditioned stimulus that occurs after US-CS pairing.

Classical conditioning can be involved in both positive and negative experiences of children in the classroom. Among the things in the child's schooling that produce

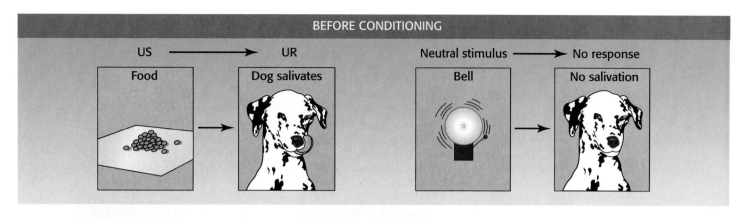

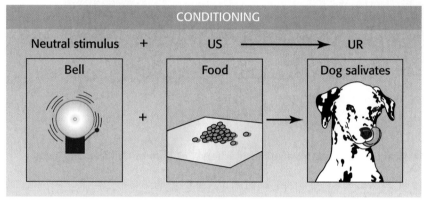

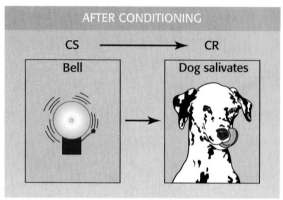

FIGURE 7.2 **Pavlov's Classical Conditioning**
In one experiment, Pavlov presented a neutral stimulus (bell) just before an unconditioned stimulus (food). The neutral stimulus became a conditioned stimulus by being paired with the unconditioned stimulus. Subsequently, the conditioned stimulus (bell) by itself was able to elicit the dog's salivation.

pleasure because they have become classically conditioned are a favorite song, feelings that the classroom is a safe and fun place to be, and a teacher's warmth and nurturing. For example, a song could be neutral for the child until the child joins in with other classmates to sing it with accompanying positive feelings.

Children can develop fear of the classroom if they associate the classroom with criticism, so the criticism becomes a CS for fear. Classical conditioning also can be involved in test anxiety. For example, a child fails and is criticized, which produces anxiety; thereafter, the child associates tests with anxiety, so they then can become a CS for anxiety (see figure 7.3 on page 214).

Some children's health problems also might involve classical conditioning. Certain physical complaints—asthma, headaches, ulcers, high blood pressure—might be partly due to classical conditioning. We usually say that such health problems are caused by stress. Often what happens, though, is that certain stimuli, such as a parent's or teacher's heavy criticism, are conditioned stimuli for physiological responses. Over time, the frequency of the physiological responses can produce a health problem. A teacher's persistent criticism of a student can cause the student to develop headaches, muscle tension, and so on. Anything associated with the teacher, such as classroom learning exercises and homework, might trigger the student's stress and subsequently be linked with ulcers or other physiological responses.

Classical Conditioning
Ivan Pavlov

Generalization, Discrimination, and Extinction   In studying a dog's responses to various stimuli, Pavlov rang a bell before giving meat powder to the dog. By being paired with the US (meat), the bell became a CS and elicited the dog's salivation. After a time, Pavlov found that the dog also responded to other sounds, such as a whistle. The more

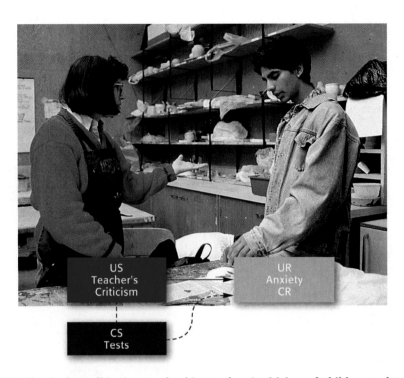

FIGURE 7.3 Classical Conditioning Involved in Teachers' Criticism of Children and Tests

bell-like the noise, the stronger the dog's response. *Generalization* in classical conditioning involves the tendency of a new stimulus similar to the original conditioned stimulus to produce a similar response (Jones, Kemenes, & Benjamin, 2001). Let's assume that the test on which the student was criticized was a biology test. When the student begins to prepare for a chemistry test, she also becomes very nervous because these two subjects are closely related in the sciences. Thus, the student's anxiety generalizes from taking a test in one subject to taking a test in another.

Discrimination in classical conditioning occurs when the organism responds to certain stimuli but not others (Murphy, Baker, & Fouguet, 2001). To produce discrimination, Pavlov gave food to the dog only after ringing the bell and not after any other sounds. Subsequently, the dog responded only to the bell. In the case of the student taking tests in different classes, she doesn't become nearly as nervous about taking an English test or a history test because they are very different subject areas.

Extinction in classical conditioning involves the weakening of the conditioned response (CR) in the absence of the unconditioned stimulus (US). In one session, Pavlov rang the bell repeatedly but did not give the dog any food. Eventually the dog quit salivating. Similarly, if the student who gets nervous while taking tests begins to do much better on tests, her anxiety will fade.

Systematic Desensitization   Sometimes the anxiety and stress associated with negative events can be eliminated by classical conditioning (Powell & Symbaluk, 2002). **Systematic desensitization** is a method based on classical conditioning that reduces anxiety by getting the individual to associate deep relaxation with successive visualizations of increasingly anxiety-producing situations. Imagine that you have a student in your class who is extremely nervous about talking in front of the class. The goal of systematic desensitization is to get the student to associate public speaking with relaxation rather than anxiety. Using successive visualizations, the student might practice systematic desensitization two weeks before the talk, then a week before, four days before, two days before, the day before, the morning of the talk, on entering the room where the talk is to be given, on the way to the podium, and during the talk.

systematic desensitization A method based on classical conditioning that reduces anxiety by getting the individual to associate deep relaxation with successive visualizations of increasingly anxiety-provoking situations.

Desensitization involves a type of counterconditioning (McNeil, 2000). The relaxing feelings that the student imagines (US) produce relaxation (UR). The student then associates anxiety-producing cues (CS) with the relaxing feelings. Such relaxation is incompatible with anxiety. By initially pairing a weak anxiety-producing cue with relaxation and gradually working up the hierarchy (from two weeks before the talk to walking up to the podium to give the talk), all of the anxiety-producing cues should generate relaxation (CR).

Chances are you will have students who fear speaking in front of the class or have other anxieties, and there may be circumstances in your own life where you might benefit from replacing anxiety with relaxation. For example, it is not unusual for some teachers to feel very comfortable when talking in front of their students but to get very nervous if asked to give a presentation at a teaching conference. Counselors and mental health professionals have been very successful at getting individuals to overcome their fear of public speaking using systematic desensitization. Should you be interested in adopting this strategy, do it with the help of a school psychologist rather than on your own.

Evaluating Classical Conditioning   Classical conditioning helps us understand some aspects of learning better than others. It excels in explaining how neutral stimuli become associated with unlearned, involuntary responses (LoLordo, 2000). It is especially helpful in understanding students' anxieties and fears. However, it is not as effective in explaining voluntary behaviors, such as why a student studies hard for a test or likes history better than geography. For these areas, operant conditioning is more relevant.

Video Lecture: Behaviorism

Operant Conditioning

Our examination of operant conditioning begins with a general definition, then turns to the views of Thorndike and Skinner.

Operant conditioning (also called *instrumental conditioning*) is a form of learning in which the consequences of behavior produce changes in the probability that the behavior will occur. Operant conditioning's main architect was B. F. Skinner, whose views built on the connectionist views of E. L. Thorndike.

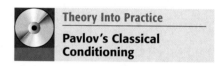

Theory Into Practice

Pavlov's Classical Conditioning

Thorndike's Law of Effect   At about the same time that Ivan Pavlov was conducting classical conditioning experiments with dogs, American psychologist E. L. Thorndike (1906) was studying cats in puzzle boxes ← p. 5. Thorndike placed a hungry cat inside a box and put a piece of fish outside. To escape from the box, the cat had to learn how to open the latch inside the box. At first the cat made a number of ineffective responses. It clawed or bit at the bars and thrust its paw through the openings. Eventually the cat accidentally stepped on the treadle that released the door bolt. When the cat was returned to the box, it went through the same random activity until it stepped on the treadle once more. On subsequent trials, the cat made fewer and fewer random movements, until it immediately clawed the treadle to open the door. Thorndike's **law of effect** states that behaviors followed by positive outcomes are strengthened and that behaviors followed by negative outcomes are weakened.

The key question for Thorndike was how the correct stimulus-response (S-R) bond strengthens and eventually dominates incorrect stimulus-response bonds. According to Thorndike, the correct S-R association strengthens, and the incorrect association weakens, because of the consequences of the organism's actions. Thorndike's view is called *S-R theory* because the organism's behavior is due to a connection between a stimulus and a response. As we see next, Skinner's approach significantly expanded on Thorndike's basic ideas.

Skinner's Operant Conditioning   Operant conditioning, in which the consequences of behavior lead to changes in the probability that the behavior will occur, is at the heart of B. F. Skinner's (1938) behaviorism ← p. 6. Consequences—rewards or punishments—are contingent on the organism's behavior. More needs to be said about reward and punishment.

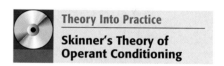

Theory Into Practice

Skinner's Theory of Operant Conditioning

Thorndike Connections

operant conditioning   Also called *instrumental conditioning*, this is a form of learning in which the consequences of behavior produce changes in the probability that the behavior will occur.

law of effect   The principle that behaviors followed by positive outcomes are strengthened and that behaviors followed by negative outcomes are weakened.

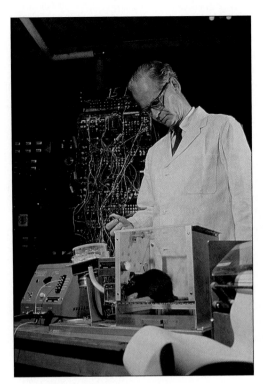

B. F. Skinner (1904–1990), an American psychologist who was the main architect of the concept of operant conditioning.

Skinner's Operant Conditioning

Positive Reinforcement

Stimulus Control of Operant Behavior

reinforcement (reward) A consequence that increases the probability that a behavior will occur.

punishment A consequence that decreases the probability that a behavior will occur.

positive reinforcement Reinforcement based on the principle that the frequency of a response increases because it is followed by a rewarding stimulus.

negative reinforcement Reinforcement based on the principle that the frequency of a response increases because an aversive (unpleasant) stimulus is removed.

Reinforcement and Punishment **Reinforcement (reward)** is a consequence that increases the probability that a behavior will occur. In contrast, **punishment** is a consequence that decreases the probability a behavior will occur. For example, you might tell one of your students, "Congratulations. I'm really proud of how good the story is that you wrote." If the student works harder and writes an even better story the next time, your positive comments are said to reinforce, or reward, the student's writing behavior. If you frown at a student for talking in class and the student's talking decreases, your frown is said to punish the student's talking.

Reinforcement can be complex. Reinforcement means to strengthen. In **positive reinforcement,** the frequency of a response increases because it is followed by a rewarding stimulus, as in the example in which the teacher's positive comments increased the student's writing behavior. Similarly, complimenting parents on being at a parent-teacher conference might encourage them to come back again.

Conversely, in **negative reinforcement,** the frequency of a response increases because it is followed by the removal of an aversive (unpleasant) stimulus (Frieman, 2002). For example, a father nags at his son to do his homework. He keeps nagging. Finally, the son gets tired of hearing the nagging and does his homework. The son's response (doing his homework) removed the unpleasant stimulus (nagging). Consider your own behavior after a stressful day of teaching. You have a headache, you take some aspirin, and the headache goes away. Taking aspirin is reinforced when this behavior is followed by a reduction of pain.

One way to remember the distinction between positive and negative reinforcement is that in positive reinforcement something is added or obtained. In negative reinforcement, something is subtracted or removed. It is easy to confuse negative reinforcement and punishment. To keep these terms straight, remember that negative reinforcement increases the probability a response will occur, while punishment decreases the probability it will occur. Figure 7.4 summarizes and presents examples of the concepts of positive reinforcement, negative reinforcement, and punishment.

Generalization, Discrimination, and Extinction In our coverage of classical conditioning, we discussed generalization, discrimination, and extinction. These processes also are important dimensions of operant conditioning (Hergenhan & Olson, 2001). Remember that in classical conditioning, generalization is the tendency of a stimulus similar to the conditioned stimulus to produce a response similar to the conditioned response. *Generalization* in operant conditioning means giving the same response to similar stimuli. Especially of interest is the extent to which behavior generalizes from one situation to another. For example, if a teacher's praise gets a student to work harder in class, will this generalize to the student working harder out of class on homework assignments? Or if the teacher praises the student for asking good questions related to English, will this generalize to harder work in history, math, and other subjects?

Remember that in classical conditioning, discrimination means responding to certain stimuli but not others. *Discrimination* in operant conditioning involves differentiating among stimuli or environmental events. For example, a student knows that the tray on the teacher's desk labeled "Math" is where she is supposed to place today's math work, while another tray labeled "English" is where today's English assignments are to be put. This might sound overly simple, but it is important because students' worlds are filled with such discriminative stimuli. Around school these discriminative stimuli might include signs that say "Stay Out," "Form a Line Here," and so on. We will have more to say about discriminative stimuli later in the section on applied behavior analysis.

In operant conditioning, *extinction* occurs when a previously reinforced response is no longer reinforced and the response decreases. In the classroom, the most common use of extinction is for the teacher to withdraw attention from a behavior that the attention is maintaining. For example, in some cases a teacher's attention inadvertently reinforces a student's disruptive behavior, as when a student pinches another student and the teacher immediately talks with the perpetrator. If this happens on a regular basis, the

POSITIVE REINFORCEMENT

BEHAVIOR	CONSEQUENCE	FUTURE BEHAVIOR
Student asks a good question	Teacher praises student	Student asks more good questions

NEGATIVE REINFORCEMENT

BEHAVIOR	CONSEQUENCE	FUTURE BEHAVIOR
Student turns homework in on time	Teacher stops criticizing student	Student increasingly turns homework in on time

PUNISHMENT

BEHAVIOR	CONSEQUENCE	FUTURE BEHAVIOR
Student interrupts teacher	Teacher verbally reprimands student	Student stops interrupting teacher

Remember that reinforcement comes in positive and negative forms. In both forms, the consequences increase behavior. In punishment, behavior is decreased.

FIGURE 7.4 Reinforcement and Punishment

Through the Eyes of Teachers

Positive Reinforcement Works

Early in my career, I was teaching first-year foreign language classes (French, Latin and Spanish) to ninth graders in a junior high school. Collaborating with a colleague, a guidance counselor, I experimented with positive verbal reinforcement as a way of focusing students on the task at hand and engaging them in learning. I consciously tried to offer positive reinforcement whenever possible and kept track of the number of times per class I did. I and the counselor observed the effects on the amount of participation and behavior of the students. Participation increased and behavior improved.

Barbara Berry
French and Humanities Teacher
Ypsilanti High School
Ypsilanti, Michigan

student might learn that pinching other students is a good way to get the teacher's attention. If the teacher withdraws his attention, the pinching might extinguish. We will have more to say about extinction in our discussion of applied behavior analysis.

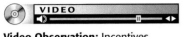

Video Observation: Incentives

! Review and Reflect

2 Compare classical conditioning and operant conditioning.

Review
- What is classical conditioning? Create your own example to illustrate the relationship among US, UR, CS, and CR. In the context of classical conditioning, what is generalization, discrimination, extinction, and desensitization?
- How is operant conditioning related to Thorndike's law of effect? Explain the different types of reinforcement and punishment. In the context of operant conditioning, what is generalization, discrimination, and extinction?

Reflect
- Do you think that your emotions are the result of classical conditioning, operant conditioning, or both? Explain.

APPLIED BEHAVIOR ANALYSIS IN EDUCATION

Many applications of operant conditioning have been made outside of research laboratories in the wider worlds of classrooms, homes, business settings, hospitals, and other real-world settings (Hill, 2002).

What Is Applied Behavior Analysis?

Behavior Analysis Resources

Applied behavior analysis involves applying the principles of operant conditioning to change human behavior. Three uses of applied behavior analysis are especially important in education: increasing desirable behavior, using prompts and shaping, and decreasing undesirable behavior (Alberto & Troutman, 1999). Applications of applied behavior analysis often use a series of steps (Hayes, 2000). These often begin with some general observations and then turn to determining the specific target behavior that needs to be changed, as well as observing its antecedent conditions. Behavioral goals are then set, particular reinforcers or punishers are selected, a behavior management program is carried out, and the success or failure of the program is evaluated.

Increasing Desirable Behaviors

Five operant conditioning strategies can be used to increase a child's desirable behaviors: choose effective reinforcers; make reinforcers contingent and timely; select the best schedule of reinforcement; consider contracting; negative reinforcement effectively; and use prompts and shaping.

Choose Effective Reinforcers   Not all reinforcers are the same for every child. Applied behavior analysts recommend that teachers find out what reinforcers work best with which children—that is, individualize the use of particular reinforcers. For one student it might be praise, for another it might be getting to spend more time participating in a favorite activity, for another it might involve being a hall monitor for a week, and for yet another it could be getting to surf the Internet. To find out the most effective reinforcers for a child, you can examine what has motivated the child in the past (reinforcement history), what the student wants but can't easily or frequently get, and the child's perception of the reinforcer's value. Some applied behavior analysts recommend asking

applied behavior analysis Application of the principles of operant conditioning to change human behavior.

children which reinforcers they like best (Raschke, 1981). Another recommendation is to consider novel reinforcers to reduce the child's boredom. Natural reinforcers such as praise and privileges are generally recommended over material rewards such as candy, stars, and money (Hall & Hall, 1998).

Activities are some of the most common reinforcers used by teachers. Named after psychologist David Premack, the **Premack principle** states that a high-probability activity can serve as a reinforcer for a low-probability activity. The Premack principle is at work when an elementary school teacher tells a child, "When you complete your writing assignment, you can play a game on the computer," or an early education teacher says to a child, "If you pick up the blocks, then you may help Mrs. Manson prepare the snacks." The use of the Premack principle is not restricted to a single child. It also can be used with the entire class. A teacher might tell the class, "If all of the class gets their homework done by Friday, we will take a field trip next week."

Make Reinforcers Contingent and Timely   For a reinforcer to be effective, the teacher must give it only after the child performs the particular behavior. Applied behavior analysts often recommend that teachers make "If . . . then" statements to children—for example, "Tony, if you finish ten math problems, then you can go out to play." This makes it clear to Tony what he has to do to get the reinforcer. Applied behavior analysts say that it is important to make the reinforcer contingent on the child's behavior. That is, the child has to perform the behavior to get the reward. If Tony does not complete ten math problems and the teacher still lets him go out to play, the contingency has not been established.

Reinforcers are more effective when they are given in a timely way, as soon as possible after the child performs the target behavior. This helps children see the contingency connection between the reward and their behavior. If the child completes the target behavior (such as doing ten math problems by midmorning) and the teacher doesn't give

Through the Eyes of Students

"Watch Her, Mom"

One year a third-grade teacher at Salem Church Elementary School in Chesterfield County, Virginia, had an especially loud, active group of third-graders. The teacher, Kristen Blankenship, used a combination of individual and group positive reinforcement as a management strategy.

Not having a cafeteria, students ate their lunches in the classroom. While joining her son, Daniel, for lunch one day, his mother pulled Kristen aside, smiled, and said that Daniel had just whispered to her, "Watch her, Mom. She never yells, but she sure knows how to keep them in line."

"Once it became clear to me that, by responding correctly to certain stimuli, I could get all the bananas I wanted, getting this job was a pushover."

Premack principle The principle that a high-probability activity can serve as a reinforcer for a low-probability activity.

the child playtime until late afternoon, the child might have trouble making the contingency connection.

Select the Best Schedule of Reinforcement   Most of the examples given so far assume continuous reinforcement; that is, the child is reinforced every time he or she makes a response. In continuous reinforcement, children learn very rapidly, but when the reinforcement stops (the teacher stops praising), extinction also occurs rapidly. In the classroom, continuous reinforcement is rare. A teacher with a classroom of twenty-five or thirty students can't praise a child every time the student makes an appropriate response.

Partial reinforcement involves reinforcing a response only part of the time. Skinner (1953) developed the concept of **schedules of reinforcement,** which are partial reinforcement timetables that determine when a response will be reinforced. The four main schedules of reinforcement are fixed-ratio, variable-ratio, fixed-interval, and variable-interval.

On a *fixed-ratio schedule,* a behavior is reinforced after a set number of responses. For example, a teacher might praise the child only after every fourth correct response, not after every response. On a *variable-ratio schedule,* a behavior is reinforced after an average number of times, but on an unpredictable basis. For example, a teacher's praise might average out to being given every fifth response but be given after the second correct response, after eight more correct responses, after the next seven correct responses, and after the next three correct responses.

Interval schedules are determined by the amount of time elapsed since the last behavior was reinforced. On a *fixed-interval schedule,* the first appropriate response after a fixed amount of time is reinforced. For example, a teacher might praise a child for the first good question the child asks after two minutes have elapsed or give a quiz every week. On a *variable-interval schedule,* a response is reinforced after a variable amount of time has elapsed. On this schedule, the teacher might praise the child's question-asking after three minutes have gone by, then after fifteen minutes have gone by, after seven minutes have gone by, and so on. Giving a pop quiz at uneven intervals also reflects a variable-interval schedule.

What is the effect of using these schedules of reinforcement with children?

- Initial learning is usually faster with continuous rather than partial reinforcement, which means that when a behavior is first being learned, continuous reinforcement works better. However, partial reinforcement produces greater persistence and greater resistance to extinction than continuous reinforcement does (Hackenberg, 2000). Thus, once a response is mastered, partial reinforcement works better than continuous reinforcement.

- Children on fixed schedules show less persistence and faster response extinction than children on variable schedules. The most persistence is shown by children on a variable-interval schedule. This schedule produces slow, steady responding because children don't know when the wait is going to be over. As we mentioned earlier, a pop quiz given at uneven intervals is a good example of the variable-interval schedule. If the teacher starts making the quizzes more predictable (for example, once a week on Fridays), children will begin to show the stop-start work pattern that characterizes the fixed-interval schedule. That is, they won't work hard for most of the week; then toward the end of the week they will start cramming for the quiz. Thus, if your goal as a teacher is to increase children's persistence after the behavior has been established, variable schedules work best, especially the variable-interval schedule (Lee & Belfiore, 1997). Figure 7.5 shows the different response patterns associated with the different schedules of reinforcement.

Consider Contracting   **Contracting** involves putting reinforcement contingencies in writing. If problems arise and children don't uphold their end of the bargain, the teacher can refer the children to the contract they agreed to. Applied behavior analysts suggest

Schedules of Reinforcement

schedules of reinforcement Partial reinforcement timetables that determine when a response will be reinforced.

contracting Putting reinforcement contingencies into writing.

that a classroom contract should be the result of input from both the teacher and the student. Classroom contracts have "If . . . then" statements and are signed by the teacher and child, then dated. A teacher and child might agree on a contract that states that the child agrees to be a good citizen by doing _____, _____, and _____. As part of the contract, the teacher agrees to _____ if the student behaves in this manner. In some instances, the teacher asks another child to sign the contract as a witness to the agreement.

Use Negative Reinforcement Effectively

Remember that in negative reinforcement, the frequency of response increases because the response removes an aversive (unpleasant) stimulus (Alberto & Troutman, 1999). A teacher who says, "Thomas, you have to stay in your seat and finish writing your story before you join the other students in making a poster," is using negative reinforcement. The negative condition of being left in his seat while the other children are doing something enjoyable will be removed if Thomas finishes the story he should have completed earlier. In another example of negative reinforcement, Maria stops her disruptive behavior in order to avoid being ridiculed by her peers.

Using negative reinforcement has some drawbacks. Sometimes when teachers try to use this behavioral strategy, children throw a tantrum, run out of the room, or destroy materials. These negative outcomes happen most often when children don't have the skills or capabilities to do what the teacher asks of them. We will discuss such self-regulatory skills later in this chapter.

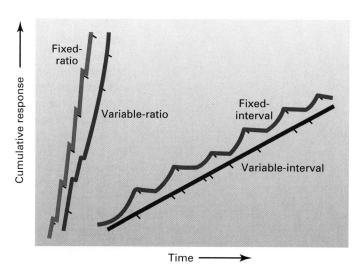

FIGURE 7.5 **Schedules of Reinforcement and Different Patterns of Responding**
In this figure, each hash mark indicates the delivery of reinforcement. Notice that ratio schedules (reinforcement is linked with number of responses) produce higher rates of responding than interval schedules (reinforcement is linked with the amount of time elapsed). The predictability of a reward also is important in that a predictable (fixed) schedule produces a higher response rate than an unpredictable (variable) schedule.

Use Prompts and Shaping

Earlier in our discussion of operant conditioning, we indicated that discrimination involves differentiating among stimuli or environmental events. Students can learn to discriminate among stimuli or events through differential reinforcement. Two differential reinforcement strategies available to teachers are prompts and shaping (Alberto & Troutman, 1999).

Prompts A **prompt** is an added stimulus or cue that is given just before a response and increases the likelihood that the response will occur. A reading teacher who holds up a card with the letters *w-e-r-e* and says, "Not was, but . . ." is using a verbal prompt. An art teacher who places the label *watercolors* on one group of paints and *oils* on another also is using prompts. Prompts help get behavior going. Once the students consistently show the correct responses, the prompts are no longer needed.

Instructions can be used as prompts. For example, as the art period is drawing to a close, the teacher says, "Let's get ready for reading." If the students keep doing art, the teacher adds the prompt, "Okay, put away your art materials and come with me over to the reading area." Some prompts come in the form of hints, as when the teacher tells students to line up "quietly." Bulletin boards are common locations for prompts, frequently displaying reminders of class rules, due dates for projects, the location of a meeting, and so on. Some prompts are presented visually, as when the teacher places her hand on her ear when a student is not speaking loudly enough.

prompt An added stimulus or cue that is given just before a response and increases the likelihood the response will occur.

shaping Teaching new behaviors by reinforcing successive approximations to a specified target behavior.

Shaping When teachers use prompts, they assume that students can perform the desired behaviors. But sometimes students do not have the ability to perform them. In this case, shaping is required. **Shaping** involves teaching new behaviors by reinforcing successive approximations to a specified target behavior. Initially, you reinforce any response that in some way resembles the target behavior. Subsequently, you reinforce a response that more closely resembles the target, and so on until the student performs the target behavior, and then you reinforce it (Chance, 2003).

Suppose you have a student who has never completed 50 percent or more of her math assignments. You set the target behavior at 100 percent, but you reinforce her for successive approximations to the target. You initially might provide a reinforcer (some type of privilege, for example) when she completes 60 percent, then the next time only when she completes 70 percent, then 80, then 90, and finally 100 percent.

Consider also a boy's shy behavior. The target behavior is to get him to approach a group of peers and talk with them. Initially you might need to reinforce him for simply smiling at a classmate. Next, you might reinforce him only if he says something to a classmate. Next, you might reinforce him only if he engages in a prolonged conversation with a classmate. And finally, you should reward him only if he engages in the target behavior, joining in with a group of peers and talking with them.

Shaping can be an important tool for the classroom teacher because most students need reinforcement along the way to reaching a learning goal. Shaping can be especially helpful for learning tasks that require time and persistence to complete. However, when using shaping, remember to implement it only if the other types of positive reinforcement and prompts are not working. Also remember to be patient. Shaping can require the reinforcement of a number of small steps en route to a target behavior, and these might take place only over an extended period of time.

Decreasing Undesirable Behaviors

When teachers want to decrease children's undesirable behaviors (such as teasing, hogging a class discussion, or smarting off to the teacher), what are their options? Applied behavior analysts Paul Alberto and Anne Troutman (1999) recommend that when teachers want to decrease a child's undesirable behavior, they should consider using these steps in this order:

1. Use differential reinforcement.
2. Terminate reinforcement (extinction).
3. Remove desirable stimuli.
4. Present aversive stimuli (punishment).

Thus, the teacher's first option should be differential reinforcement. Punishment should be used only as a last resort and always in conjunction with providing the child information about appropriate behavior.

Use Differential Reinforcement In differential reinforcement, the teacher reinforces behavior that is more appropriate or that is incompatible with what the child is doing. For example, the teacher might reinforce a child for doing learning activities on a computer rather than playing games with it, for being courteous rather than interrupting, for being seated rather than running around the classroom, or for doing homework on time rather than late.

Terminate Reinforcement (Extinction) The strategy of terminating reinforcement involves withdrawing positive reinforcement from a child's inappropriate behavior. Many inappropriate behaviors are inadvertently maintained by positive reinforcement, especially the teacher's attention. Applied behavior analysts point out that this can occur even when the teacher gives attention to an inappropriate behavior by criticizing, threatening, or yelling at the student. Many teachers find it difficult to determine whether they are giving too much attention to inappropriate behavior. A good strategy is to get someone to observe your classroom on several occasions and chart the patterns of reinforcement you use with your students. If you become aware that you are giving too much attention to a student's inappropriate behavior, ignore that behavior and give attention to the student's appropriate behavior. Always combine taking attention away from inappropriate behavior with giving attention to appropriate behavior. For instance, when a

This second-grade student has been placed in "time-out" for misbehaving. *What are some guidelines for using "time-out"?*

student stops monopolizing the conversation in a group discussion after you withdraw your attention, compliment the student on her improved behavior.

Remove Desirable Stimuli   Suppose you have tried the first two options, and they haven't worked. A third option is to remove desirable stimuli from the student. Two strategies for accomplishing this are "time-out" and "response cost."

Time-Out   The most widely used strategy that teachers use to remove desirable stimuli is **time-out.** In other words, take the student away from positive reinforcement.

 Teaching Strategies
For Using Time-Out

In using time-out, you have several options:

1. *Keep the student in the classroom, but deny the student access to positive reinforcement.* This strategy is most often used when a student does something minor. The teacher might ask the student to put his head down on the desk for a few minutes or might move the student to the periphery of an activity so the student can still observe other students experiencing positive reinforcement.
2. *For time-out to be effective, the setting from which the student is removed has to be positively reinforcing and the setting in which the student is placed has to not be positively reinforcing.* For example, if you seat a student in the hall outside your classroom and students from other classes come down the hall and talk with the student, the time-out is clearly not going to serve its intended purpose.
3. *If you use time-out, be sure to identify the student's behaviors that resulted in time-out.* For example, say to the student, "You tore up Corey's paper, so go to time-out right now for five minutes." Don't get into an argument with the student or accept lame excuses as to why the student should not get a time-out. If necessary, take the student to the time-out location. If the misbehavior occurs again, reidentify it and place the student in a time-out again. If the student starts yelling, knocking over

time-out Removing an individual from positive reinforcement.

COUNTRY	MEAN SCORE
Canada	3.14
United States	3.13
South Korea	3.00
Malaysia	2.90
Great Britain	2.68
Finland	2.34
Greece	2.26
Germany	2.13
Spain	2.05
Argentina	1.96
Sweden	1.35

FIGURE 7.6 Attitudes About Corporal Punishment in Different Countries
A 5-point scale was used to assess attitudes toward corporal punishment, with scores closer to 1 indicating an attitude against its use and scores closer to 5 suggesting an attitude for its use.

furniture, and so on when you assess time-out, add time to time-out. Be sure to let the student out of time-out when the designated time away from positive reinforcement is up. Don't comment on how well the student behaved during time-out; just return the student to the prior activity.

4. *Keep records of each time-out session, especially if a time-out room is used.* This will help you monitor effective and ethical use of time-outs.

Response Cost A second strategy for removing desirable stimuli involves **response cost,** which refers to taking a positive reinforcer away from a student, as when the student loses certain privileges. For example, after a student misbehaves, the teacher might take away ten minutes of recess time or the privilege of being a class monitor. Response cost typically involves some type of penalty or fine. As with the time-out, response cost should always be used in conjunction with strategies for increasing the student's positive behaviors.

Present Aversive Stimuli (Punishment)   Most people associate the presentation of aversive (unpleasant) stimuli with punishment, as when a teacher yells at a student or a parent spanks a child. However, in accordance with the definition of punishment given earlier in the chapter, the consequence has to decrease the undesirable behavior (Branch, 2000; Mazur, 2002). All too often, though, aversive stimuli are not effective punishments, in that they do not decrease the unwanted behavior and indeed sometimes increase the unwanted behavior over time. One recent study found that when parents used spanking to discipline children when they were four to five years of age, the spanking predicted an increase in problem behavior over time (McLoyd & Smith, 2002).

The most common types of aversive stimuli that teachers use are verbal reprimands. These are more effectively used when the teacher is near the student rather than across the room and when used together with a nonverbal reprimand such as a frown or eye contact (Van Houten & others, 1982). Reprimands are more effective when they are given immediately after unwanted behavior rather than later and when they are quick and to the point. Such reprimands do not have to involve yelling and shouting, which often just raise the noise level of the classroom and present the teacher as an uncontrolled model for students. Instead, a firmly stated "stop doing that" with eye contact is often sufficient to stop unwanted behavior. Another strategy is to take the student aside and reprimand the student in private rather than in front of the entire class.

Many countries, such as Sweden, have banned the physical punishment of schoolchildren (which usually involves school paddling) by principals and teachers. However, in America, 24 states still allow it (Hyman, 1994). One recent study of college students in 11 countries found that the United States and Canada have more favorable attitudes toward corporal punishment than many other countries (Curran & others, 2001; Hyman & others, 2001) (see figure 7.6).

In the United States, male minority students from low-income backgrounds are the most frequent recipients of physical punishment in schools. Most psychologists and educators argue that physical punishment of students should not be used in any circumstance. It can be abusive and magnifies all of the problems associated with punishment.

Physical or otherwise, numerous problems are associated with using aversive stimuli as intended punishment (Hyman, 1997; Hyman & Snook, 1999):

- Especially when you use intense punishment such as yelling or screaming, you are presenting students with an out-of-control model for handling stressful situations.
- Punishment can instill fear, rage, or avoidance in students. Skinner's biggest concern was this: What punishment teaches is how to avoid something. For example, a student who experiences a punitive teacher might show a dislike for the teacher and not want to come to school.
- When students are punished, they might become so aroused and anxious that they can't concentrate clearly on their work for a long time after the punishment has been given.

response cost Taking a positive reinforcer away from an individual.

- Punishment tells students what not to do rather than what to do. If you make a punishing statement, such as "No, that's not right," always accompany it with positive feedback, such as "but why don't you try this."
- What is intended as punishment can turn out to be reinforcing. A student might learn that misbehaving will not only get the teacher's attention but put the student in the limelight with classmates as well.

A final lesson in all of this is to spend a lot more class time monitoring what students do right rather than what they do wrong (Maag, 2001). Too often it is disruptive behavior, not competent behavior, that grabs a teacher's attention. Every day make it a point to scan your classroom for positive student behaviors that you ordinarily would not notice and give students attention for them.

Evaluating Operant Conditioning and Applied Behavior Analysis

Operant conditioning and applied behavior analysis have made contributions to teaching practice (Kazdin, 2001; Martin & Pear, 2002; Purdy & others, 2001). Reinforcing and punishing consequences are part of teachers' and students' lives. Teachers give grades, praise and reprimand, smile and frown. Learning about how such consequences affect students' behavior improves your capabilities as a teacher. Used effectively, behavioral techniques can help you manage your classroom. Reinforcing certain behaviors can improve some students' conduct and, used in conjunction with the time-out, can increase desired behaviors in some incorrigible students (Charles, 2002; Kauffman & others, 2002).

Critics of operant conditioning and applied behavior analysis argue that the whole approach places too much emphasis on external control of students' behavior. They say that a better strategy is to help students learn to control their own behavior and become internally motivated. Some critics argue that it is not the reward or punishment that changes behavior but, rather, the belief or expectation that certain actions will be rewarded or punished (Schunk, 2000). In other words, the behavioral theories do not give adequate attention to cognitive processes involved in learning. Critics also point to potential ethical problems when operant conditioning is used inappropriately, as when a teacher immediately resorts to punishing students instead of first considering reinforcement strategies, or punishes a student without also giving the student information about appropriate behavior. Another criticism is that when teachers spend a lot of time using applied behavior analysis, they might focus too much on student conduct and not enough on academic learning. We will have much more to say about student conduct in chapter 14, "Managing the Classroom."

! Review and Reflect

3 **Apply behavior analysis to education.**

Review

- What is applied behavior analysis?
- What are five ways to increase desirable behaviors?
- What are four ways to decrease undesirable behaviors?
- In what areas of learning are operant conditioning and applied behavior analysis most useful? What are some of their limitations?

Reflect

- Come up with your own example in an educational setting for each of the five ways to increase desirable behavior.

SOCIAL COGNITIVE APPROACHES TO LEARNING

Students' thoughts affect their behavior and learning. In this section, we will explore several variations on this theme, beginning with social cognitive theory. This theory evolved out of behavioral theories but has become increasingly more cognitive (Schunk, 2000).

Bandura's Social Cognitive Theory

Social cognitive theory states that social and cognitive factors, as well as behavior, play important roles in learning. Cognitive factors might involve the student's expectations for success; social factors might include students' observing their parents' achievement behavior.

Albert Bandura (1986, 1997, 2000, 2001, 2004) is one of the main architects of social cognitive theory. He says that when students learn, they can cognitively represent or transform their experiences. Recall that in operant conditioning, connections occur only between environmental experiences and behavior.

Bandura developed a *reciprocal determinism model* that consists of three main factors: behavior, person/cognitive, and environment. As shown in figure 7.7, these factors can interact to influence learning: Environmental factors influence behavior, behavior affects the environment, person (cognitive) factors influence behavior, and so on. Bandura uses the term *person,* but I have modified it to *person cognitive* because so many of the person factors he describes are cognitive. The person factors Bandura describes that do not have a cognitive bent are mainly personality traits and temperament. Recall from chapter 4, "Individual Variations," that such factors might include being introverted or extraverted, active or inactive, calm or anxious, and friendly or hostile. Cognitive factors include expectations, beliefs, attitudes, strategies, thinking, and intelligence.

Consider how Bandura's model might work in the case of the achievement behavior of a high school student we will call Sondra:

- *Cognition influences behavior.* Sondra develops cognitive strategies to think more deeply and logically about how to solve problems. The cognitive strategies improve her achievement behavior.
- *Behavior influences cognition.* Sondra's studying (behavior) has led her to achieve good grades, which in turn produce positive expectancies about her abilities and give her self-confidence (cognition).
- *Environment influences behavior.* The school Sondra attends recently developed a pilot study-skills program to help students learn how to take notes, manage their time, and take tests more effectively. The study-skills program improves Sondra's achievement behavior.
- *Behavior influences environment.* The study-skills program is successful in improving the achievement behavior of many students in Sondra's class. The students' improved achievement behavior stimulates the school to expand the program so that all students in the high school participate in it.
- *Cognition influences environment.* The expectations and planning of the school's principal and teachers made the study-skills program possible in the first place.
- *Environment influences cognition.* The school establishes a resource center where students and parents can go to check out books and materials on improving study skills. The resource center also makes study-skills tutoring services available to students. Sondra and her parents take advantage of the center's resources and tutoring. These resources and services improve Sondra's thinking skills.

In Bandura's learning model, person (cognitive) factors play important roles. The person (cognitive) factor that Bandura (1997, 2004) has emphasized the most in recent years is **self-efficacy,** the belief that one can master a situation and produce positive outcomes. Bandura says that self-efficacy has a powerful influence over behavior. For example, a student who has low self-efficacy might not even try to study for a test because he

Albert Bandura has been one of the leading architects of social cognitive theory.

Albert Bandura

Self-Efficacy

social cognitive theory Bandura's theory that social and cognitive factors, as well as behavior, play important roles in learning.

self-efficacy The belief that one can master a situation and produce positive outcomes.

doesn't believe it will do him any good. We will have much more to say about self-efficacy in chapter 13, "Motivation, Teaching, and Learning."

Next, we discuss an important learning process, the exploration of which is another of Bandura's main contributions. As you read about observational learning, note how person (cognitive) factors are involved.

Observational Learning

Observational learning, also called *imitation* or *modeling,* is learning that occurs when a person observes and imitates someone else's behavior. The capacity to learn behavior patterns by observation eliminates tedious trial-and-error learning. In many instances, observational learning takes less time than operant conditioning.

The Classic Bobo Doll Study   An experiment by Bandura (1965) illustrates how observational learning can occur even by watching a model who is not reinforced or punished. The experiment also illustrates a distinction between learning and performance.

Equal numbers of kindergarten children were randomly assigned to watch one of three films in which a person (the model) beat up an adult-size plastic toy called a Bobo doll (see figure 7.8). In the first film, the aggressor was rewarded with candy, soft drinks, and praise for aggressive behavior. In the second film, the aggressor was criticized and spanked for the aggressive behavior. And in the third film, there were no consequences for the aggressor's behavior.

Subsequently, each child was left alone in a room filled with toys, including a Bobo doll. The child's behavior was observed through a one-way mirror. Children who watched the films in which the aggressor's behavior either was reinforced or went unpunished imitated the aggressor's behavior more than did the children who saw the aggressor be punished. As you might expect, boys were more aggressive than girls. However, an important point in this study is that observational learning occurred just as extensively when modeled aggressive behavior was not reinforced as when it was reinforced.

A second important point in this study focuses on the distinction between learning and performance. Just because students don't perform a response doesn't mean they

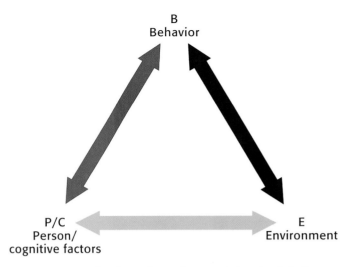

FIGURE 7.7 Bandura's Reciprocal Determinism Model of Learning

In Bandura's model, person/cognitive factors, environmental factors, and behavior reciprocally influence each other. What are some examples of person/cognitive factors in learning?

FIGURE 7.8 Bandura's Classic Bobo Doll Study: The Effects of Observational Learning on Children's Aggression

In the left frame, an adult model aggressively attacks the Bobo doll. In the right frame, a kindergarten-age girl who has observed the model's aggressive actions follows suit. In Bandura's experiment, under what conditions did the children reproduce the model's aggressive actions?

observational learning Also called *imitation* or *modeling,* the learning process in which a person observes and imitates someone else's behavior.

FIGURE 7.9 Bandura's Model of Observational Learning
In Bandura's model of observational learning, four processes need to be considered: attention, retention, production, and motivation. *How might these processes be involved in this classroom situation in which a teacher is demonstrating how to tell time?*

didn't learn it. In Bandura's study, when children were given an incentive (with stickers or fruit juice) to imitate the model, differences in the children's imitative behavior in the three conditions were eliminated. Bandura believes that when a child observes behavior but makes no observable response, the child may still have acquired the modeled response in cognitive form.

Bandura's Contemporary Model of Observational Learning   Since his early experiments, Bandura (1986) has focused on the specific processes that are involved in observational learning. These include attention, retention, production, and motivation (see figure 7.9):

- *Attention.* Before students can imitate a model's actions, they must attend to what the model is doing or saying. A student who is distracted by two other students who are talking might not hear what a teacher is saying. Attention to the model is influenced by a host of characteristics. For example, warm, powerful, atypical people command more attention than do cold, weak, typical people. Students are more likely to be attentive to high-status models than to low-status models. In most cases, teachers are high-status models for students.

- *Retention.* To reproduce a model's actions, students must code the information and keep it in memory so that it can be retrieved. A simple verbal description or a vivid image of what the model did assists students' retention. For example, the teacher might say, "I'm showing the correct way to do this. You have to do this step first, this step second, and this step third," as she models how to solve a math problem. A video with a colorful character demonstrating the importance of considering other students' feelings might be remembered better than if the teacher just tells the students to do this. Such colorful characters are at the heart of the popularity of *Sesame Street* with children. Students' retention will be improved when teachers give vivid, logical, and clear demonstrations. In chapter 8, we will further examine the role of memory in children's learning.

- *Production.* Children might attend to a model and code in memory what they have seen but, because of limitations in their motor ability, not be able to reproduce the model's behavior. A thirteen-year-old might watch basketball player David Robinson and golfer Nancy Lopez execute their athletic skills to perfection, or observe a famous pianist or artist perform their skills, but not be able to reproduce their motor actions. Teaching, coaching, and practice can help children improve their motor performances.

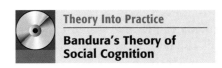

Theory Into Practice

Bandura's Theory of Social Cognition

- *Motivation.* Often children attend to what a model says or does, retain the information in memory, and possess the motor skills to perform the action but are not motivated to perform the modeled behavior. This was demonstrated in Bandura's classic Bobo doll study when children who saw the model being punished did not reproduce the punished model's aggressive actions. However, when they subsequently were given a reinforcement or incentive (stickers or fruit juice), they did imitate the model's behavior.

Bandura believes that reinforcement is not always necessary for observational learning to take place. But if the child does not reproduce the desired behaviors, three types of reinforcement can help do the trick: (1) reward the model, (2) reward the child, or (3) instruct the child to make self-reinforcing statements such as "Good, I did it!" or "Okay, I've done a good job of getting most of this right; now if I keep trying I will get the rest." We will have much more to say about such self-management strategies shortly.

As you can see, you will be an important model in students' lives and you have many options for providing students with an array of competent models. To evaluate the roles that models and mentors have played in your own life and can play in your students' lives, complete Self-Assessment 7.1 on page 230. To explore the lack of male and minority role models and mentors in children's education, read the Diversity and Education interlude.

Diversity and Education
Wanted: Male and Minority Role Models and Mentors in Children's Education

As students in U.S. schools have become more ethnically diverse in recent decades, their teachers are overwhelmingly non-Latino White females. In 2000, approximately 17 percent of U.S. public school students were African American, but less than 8 percent of their teachers were African American (National Center for Education Statistics, 2002). Only a small percentage of the African American teachers were males. In the same year, Latinos made up about 16 percent of U.S. public school students, but only 6 percent of their teachers were Latino. In 2000, 38 percent of U.S. public schools did not have a single ethnic minority teacher.

Men comprise about 10 percent of elementary school teachers but nearly half of middle and high school teachers (many of whom are lured by additional incentives for coaching athletic teams). The situation is likely to get worse. In a recent national survey of college students, only 1.5 percent of males said their probable career would be as an elementary school teacher or administrator and only 4.3 percent indicated that a similar career in secondary education was likely to be in their future (Sax & others, 2003).

The education program at Livingstone College in Salisbury, North Carolina, is trying to do something about the shortage of male teachers of color. They developed a special program to recruit men of color into the teaching profession. One of the program's graduates, Nakia Douglas, teaches kindergarten. He says he wants to eliminate negative stereotypes about African American males—that they are poor role models, aren't responsible, and shouldn't be teaching young children. Another graduate, Mistor Williams, teaches history to eighth-graders in a school with a large percentage of ethnic minority students. He says that he feels the responsibility to provide a role model and support for ethnic minority students.

If you are a White female, think about ways you can bring women and men of color into your classroom to talk with students and demonstrate their work skills. This is especially important when you have a number of students of color in your class.

Models and Mentors in My Life and My Students' Lives

Having positive role models and mentors can make an important difference in whether individuals develop optimally and reach their full potential. First, evaluate the role models and mentors who have played an important part in your life. Second, think about the type of role model you want to be for your students. Third, give some thought to how you will incorporate other models and mentors into your students' lives. Fourth, explore who your education mentor might be.

My Models and Mentors
List the most important role models and mentors in your life. Then describe what their positive modeling and mentoring have meant to your development.

Role Models and Mentors   **Their Contributions**

1. _____

2. _____

3. _____

4. _____

5. _____

The Type of Role Model I Want to Be for My Students
Describe which characteristics and behaviors you believe are the most important for you to model for your students.

1. _____

2. _____

3. _____

4. _____

5. _____

How I Will Incorporate Models and Mentors in My Classroom?
Describe a systematic plan for bringing models and mentors into your students' lives in one or more domain(s) you plan to teach, such as math, English, science, and music.

_____

_____

_____

_____

Who Will Be My Education Mentor? What Would My Ideal Education Mentor Be Like?
Do you have someone in mind who might serve as an education mentor when you become a teacher? If so, describe the person.

_____

_____

What would your ideal education mentor be like?

_____

_____

_____

_____

_____

 Go to your Student Toolbox CD-ROM for an electronic version of this form.

Regardless of your ethnic background, look around the community for possible mentors for students, especially students who come from low-income backgrounds and who lack positive role models. For example, the aim of the 3-to-1 mentoring program is to surround each ethnic minority male student with three positive ethnic minority role models. The program began when several African American men were challenged by a sermon delivered by Zach Holmes at the St. Luke's Methodist Church in Dallas. In the sermon, Reverend Holmes urged his congregation to become more involved with children, both their own and children in the community who don't have good role models. The 3-to-1 mentoring program has signed up more than 200 men and 100 boys (ages four to eighteen). That's far short of the goal of three mentors for each boy, but the men are working on increasing the number of mentors in the program. Some of the men in the mentoring program have their own children, like Dr. Leonard Berry, a physician, who has two sons and a daughter. He heeded the minister's challenge and regularly participates in the mentoring program, which involves academic tutoring as well as outings to activities such as sporting and cultural events. The mentors also take the students to visit the Johnson Space Center in Houston.

As a teacher you do not have to wait for someone in the community to bring mentors to your students. Look around the community in which you teach and evaluate who would be good candidates for mentoring your students or starting a mentoring program. Contact them and get the program started. Clearly, mentoring programs can benefit all students, male or female, of any ethnic background.

Dr. Leonard Berry is a mentor in the 3-to-1 program in Dallas. He is shown here with Brandon Scarbough, 13 *(front)*, and his own son, Leonard, 12 *(back)*. Brandon not only has benefited from Dr. Berry's mentoring but also has become friends with his son.

In the present educational climate that emphasizes reflection and critical thinking, it is easy to overlook the power of observational learning in educating children (Schunk, 2004), yet observational learning remains one of the most common and effective means of learning. The Teaching Strategies interlude can help you to use this powerful form of learning in your classroom.

Teaching Strategies
For Effectively Using
Observational Learning

1. *Think about what type of model you will present to students.* Every day, hour after hour, students will watch and listen to what you say and do. Just by being around you, students will absorb a great deal of information. They will pick up your good or bad habits, your expectations for their high or low achievement, your enthusiastic or bored attitude, your controlled or uncontrolled manner of dealing with stress, your learning style, your gender attitudes, and many other aspects of your behavior.

2. *Demonstrate and teach new behaviors.* Demonstrating means that you, the teacher, are a model for your students' observational learning. Demonstrating how to do something, such as solve a math problem, read, write, think, control anger, and perform physical skills, is a common teacher behavior in classrooms. For example, a teacher might model how to diagram a sentence, develop a strategy for solving algebraic equations, or shoot a basketball. When demonstrating how to do something, you need to call students' attention to the relevant details of the learning situation. Your demonstrations also should be clear and follow a logical sequence.

   Observational learning can especially be effective in teaching new behaviors. The first time students are required to learn how to multiply, to solve an algebraic equation, to write a paragraph with a topical sentence, or to give an effective talk, they benefit from watching and listening to a competent model.

3. *Think about ways to use peers as effective models.* The teacher is not the only model in the classroom. As with teachers, children can pick up their peers' good and bad

Strategies in Practice

- **Behavior and Social Cognitive Approaches**
- **Behavior Modification**

habits, high or low achievement orientations, and so on through observational learning. Remember that students are often motivated to imitate high-status models. Older peers usually have higher status than same-age peers. Thus, a good strategy is to have older peers from a higher grade model how to engage in the behaviors you want your students to perform. For students with low abilities or who are not performing well, a low-achieving student who struggles but puts considerable effort into learning and ultimately performs the behaviors can be a good model. More will be said in chapter 10, "Social Constructivist Approaches," about peer collaboration and peers as tutors.

4. *Think about ways that mentors can be used as models.* Students and teachers benefit from having a mentor—someone they look up to and respect, someone who serves as a competent model, someone who is willing to work with them and help them achieve their goals. As a teacher, a potential mentor for you is a more experienced teacher, possibly someone who teaches down the hall and has had a number of years of experience in dealing with some of the same problems and issues you will have to cope with.

    In the Quantum Opportunities program, students from low-income backgrounds significantly benefited from meeting with a mentor over a four-year-period (Carnegie Council on Adolescent Development, 1995). These mentors modeled appropriate behavior and strategies, gave sustained support, and provided guidance. Just spending a few hours a week with a mentor can make a difference in a student's life, especially if the student's parents have not been good role models.

5. *Evaluate which classroom guests will provide good models for students.* Who else would be beneficial models for your students? To change the pace of classroom life for you and your students, invite guests who have something meaningful to talk about or demonstrate. Recall what we said in chapter 4 about Gardner's theory of multiple intelligences: There likely are some domains (physical, musical, artistic, or other) in which you don't have the skills to serve as a competent model for your students ◀ p. 110. When you need to have such skills demonstrated to your students, spend some time locating competent models in the community. Invite them to come to your classroom to demonstrate and discuss their skills. If this can't be arranged, set up field trips in which you take students to see them where they are working or performing.

6. *Consider the models children observe on television, videos, and computers.* Students observe models when they watch television programs, videos, films, or computer screens in your classroom. The principles of observational learning we described earlier apply to these media. For example, the extent to which the students perceive the media models as high or low in status, intriguing or boring, and so on will influence the extent of their observational learning. And as we indicated in chapter 3, "Social Contexts and Socioemotional Development," it is important to monitor children's TV watching to ensure that they are not being exposed to too many negative models, especially violent ones.

To read about applications of observational learning in the popular children's television show *Sesame Street,* see the Technology and Education box.

Cognitive Behavior Approaches and Self-Regulation

Operant conditioning spawned applications and other real-world settings, and the interest in cognitive behavior approaches has also produced such applications.

cognitive behavior approaches
Changing behavior by getting people to monitor, manage, and regulate their own behavior rather than letting it be controlled by external factors.

Cognitive Behavior Approaches   In the **cognitive behavior approaches,** the emphasis is on getting students to monitor, manage, and regulate their own behavior rather than letting it be controlled by external factors. In some circles, this has been called *cognitive behavior modification.* Cognitive behavior approaches stem from both cognitive

Educational Lessons from *Sesame Street*

One of television's major programming attempts to educate young children is *Sesame Street,* which is designed to teach both cognitive and social skills (Cole, Richman, & Brown, 2001; Fisch, 2004; Fisch & Truglio, 2001). The program began in 1969 and is still going strong. A fundamental message of *Sesame Street* is that education and entertainment work well together (Lesser, 1972). On *Sesame Street,* learning is exciting and entertaining.

Sesame Street also illustrates the point that teaching can be done in both direct and indirect ways. Using the direct way, a teacher tells children exactly what they are going to be taught and then actually teaches it to them. This method is often used on *Sesame Street* to teach cognitive skills. But social skills usually are communicated in indirect ways on the show. Thus, rather than telling children "You should cooperate with people," a sequence of events is shown to help children figure out what it means to be cooperative and what the advantages are.

Should the world be shown to children as it is, or as it ought to be? The *Sesame Street* advisory board of educators and psychologists decided that the real world should be shown, but with an emphasis on what the world would be like if everyone treated each other with decency and kindness. To show the world as it really is, the program might show an adult doing something unjustifiably inconsiderate to another adult, with alternative ways of coping with this acted out. Finally, the program would portray the happy outcomes when people stop acting inconsiderately.

Some of the attentional techniques used on *Sesame Street* are worthwhile to consider in the classroom. These involve first *catching* the child's attention, then *directing* it, and finally *sustaining* it. Music and sound are very effective in eliciting children's attention. For example, in teaching children to discriminate sounds, an automobile horn might be sounded or a computer's keyboard repeatedly pressed. Music is especially useful because it leads children to become actively involved in what they are watching or listening. It is not unusual for children watching *Sesame Street* to get up out of their seats and start dancing and singing along with the jingles.

Once the child's attention has been captured, it should be directed to something. Surprise and novelty are especially helpful in this regard. They make children work hard to figure out what is going to happen. Their attention is directed because they begin to anticipate what is going to happen next.

Once attention is directed, it then needs to be maintained. *Sesame Street* especially uses humor to accomplish this. Humor is judiciously placed: Ernie outsmarts Bert; the Cookie Monster annoyingly interrupts a lecture given by Kermit the Frog. For young children, physical gags often are funnier than verbal ones, and much of the humor that is effective involves physical acts that are surprising and incongruous.

What educational lessons can be learned from Sesame Street?

---

psychology, with its emphasis on the effects of thoughts on behavior, and behaviorism, with its emphasis on techniques for changing behavior. Cognitive behavior approaches try to change students' misconceptions, strengthen their coping skills, increase their self-control, and encourage constructive self-reflection (Meichenbaum, 1993).

Self-instructional methods are cognitive behavior techniques aimed at teaching individuals to modify their own behavior. Self-instructional methods help people alter what they say to themselves.

Imagine a situation in which a high school student is extremely nervous about taking standardized tests, such as the SAT. The student can be encouraged to talk to himself in more positive ways. Following are some self-talk strategies that students and teachers can use to cope more effectively with such stressful situations (Meichenbaum, Turk, & Burstein, 1975):

- Prepare for anxiety or stress.
  "What do I have to do?"
  "I'm going to develop a plan to deal with it."
  "I'll just think about what I have to do."
  "I won't worry. Worry doesn't help anything."
  "I have a lot of different strategies I can use."
- Confront and handle the anxiety or stress.
  "I can meet the challenge."

self-instructional methods Cognitive behavior techniques aimed at teaching individuals to modify their own behavior.

"I'll keep on taking just one step at a time."

"I can handle it. I'll just relax, breathe deeply, and use one of the strategies."

"I won't think about my stress. I'll just think about what I have to do."

• Cope with feelings at critical moments.

"What is it I have to do?"

"I knew my anxiety might increase. I just have to keep myself in control."

"When the anxiety comes, I'll just pause and keep focusing on what I have to do."

• Use reinforcing self-statements.

"Good, I did it."

"I handled it well."

"I knew I could do it."

"Wait until I tell other people how I did it!"

In many instances, the strategy is to replace negative self-statements with positive ones. For example, a student might say to herself, "I'll never get this work done by tomorrow." This can be replaced with positive self-statements such as these: "This is going to be tough but I think I can do it." "I'm going to look at this as a challenge rather than a stressor." "If I work really hard, I might be able to get it done." Or in having to participate in a class discussion, a student might replace the negative thought "Everyone else knows more than I do, so what's the use of saying anything" with positive self-statements such as these: "I have as much to say as anyone else." "My ideas may be different, but they are still good." "It's okay to be a little nervous; I'll relax and start talking." Figure 7.10 shows posters that students in one fifth-grade class developed to help them remember how to talk to themselves while listening, planning, working, and checking.

Talking positively to oneself can help teachers and students reach their full potential. Uncountered negative thinking has a way of becoming a self-fulfilling prophecy. You think you can't do it, and so you don't. If negative self-talk is a problem for you, at random times during the day ask yourself, "What am I saying to myself right now?" Moments that you expect will be potentially stressful are excellent times to examine your self-talk. Also monitor your students' self-talk. If you hear students saying, "I can't do

POSTER 1
While Listening

1. Does this make sense?
2. Am I getting this?
3. I need to ask a question before I forget.
4. Pay attention.
5. Can I do what the teacher is saying to do?

POSTER 3
While Working

1. Am I working fast enough?
2. Stop staring at my girlfriend (boyfriend) and get back to work.
3. How much time is left?
4. Do I need to stop and start all over?
5. This is hard for me but I can manage it.

POSTER 2
While Planning

1. Do I have everything together?
2. Do I have my friends tuned out so I can get this done?
3. I need to get organized first.
4. What order can I do this in?
5. I know this stuff.

POSTER 4
While Checking

1. Did I finish everything?
2. What do I need to recheck?
3. Am I proud of this work?
4. Did I write all of the words?
5. I think I'm finished. I organized myself. Did I daydream too much, though?

FIGURE 7.10 Some Posters Developed by a Fifth-Grade Class to Help Them Remember How to Effectively Talk to Themselves

Self-Monitoring

Self-monitoring can benefit you as well as your students. Many successful learners regularly self-monitor their progress to see how they are doing in their effort to complete a project, develop a skill, or perform well on a test or other assessment. For the next month, self-monitor your study time for this course you are taking in educational psychology. To achieve high grades, most instructors recommend that students spend two or three hours out of class studying, doing homework, and working on projects for every hour they are in class in college (Santrock & Halonen, 2002). The experience of self-monitoring your own study time should give you a sense of how important such skills are for your students to develop. You might adapt this form for students' homework, for example. Remember from our discussion of Bandura's cognitive social learning theory that self-efficacy involves your belief that you can master a situation and produce positive outcomes. One way to evaluate self-efficacy is your expectancy for attaining a particular score on an upcoming quiz or test. Determine what score or grade you want to achieve on your next quiz or test. Then each day you study, rate your self-efficacy for achieving the score you desire on a 3-point scale: 1 = not very confident, 2 = moderately confident, and 3 = very confident.

FORM FOR SELF-MONITORING STUDY TIME

Date	Assignment	Time Started	Time Finished	STUDY CONTEXT			Self-Efficacy
				Where?	With Whom?	Distractions	

 Go to your Student Toolbox CD-ROM for an electronic version of this form.

this" or "I'm so slow I'll never get this done," spend some time getting them to replace their negative self-talk with positive self-talk.

Cognitive behaviorists recommend that students improve their performance by monitoring their own behavior. This can involve getting students to keep charts or records of their behavior. When I (your author) wrote this book, I had a chart on my wall with each of the chapters listed. I planned how long it would take me to do each of the chapters, and then as I completed each one I checked it off and wrote down the date of completion. Teachers can get students to do some similar monitoring of their own progress by getting them to keep records of how many assignments they have finished, how many books they have read, how many homework papers they have turned in on time, how many days in a row they have not interrupted the teacher, and so on. In some cases, teachers place these self-monitoring charts on the walls of the classroom. Alternatively, if the teacher thinks that negative social comparison with other students will be highly stressful for some students, then a better strategy might be to have students keep private records (in a notebook, for example) that are periodically checked by the teacher.

Self-monitoring is an excellent strategy for improving learning, and one that you can help students learn to do effectively. By completing Self-Assessment 7.2 on page 235, you should get a sense of the benefits of self-monitoring for your students.

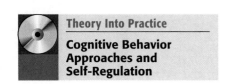

Theory Into Practice

Cognitive Behavior Approaches and Self-Regulation

Self-Regulatory Learning **Self-regulatory learning** consists of the self-generation and self-monitoring of thoughts, feelings, and behaviors in order to reach a goal. These goals might be academic (improving comprehension while reading, becoming a more organized writer, learning how to do multiplication, asking relevant questions) or they might be socioemotional (controlling one's anger, getting along better with peers). What are some of the characteristics of self-regulated learners? Self-regulatory learners (Winne, 1995, 1997, 2001)

- Set goals for extending their knowledge and sustaining their motivation
- Are aware of their emotional makeup and have strategies for managing their emotions
- Periodically monitor their progress toward a goal
- Fine-tune or revise their strategies based on the progress they are making
- Evaluate obstacles that may arise and make the necessary adaptations

Researchers have found that high-achieving students are often self-regulatory learners (Paris & Paris, 2001; Pintrich, 2000; Pintrich & Schunk, 2002; Schunk & Zimmerman, 2003; Zimmerman & Schunk, 2001, 2004). For example, compared with low-achieving students, high-achieving students set more specific learning goals, use more strategies to learn, self-monitor their learning more, and more systematically evaluate their progress toward a goal.

Teachers, tutors, mentors, counselors, and parents can help students become self-regulatory learners (Randi & Corno, 2000; Weinstein, Husman, & Dierking, 2000). Barry Zimmerman, Sebastian Bonner, and Robert Kovach (1996) developed a model for turning low-self-regulatory students into students who engage in these multistep strategies: (1) self-evaluation and monitoring, (2) goal setting and strategic planning, (3) putting a plan into action and monitoring it, and (4) monitoring outcomes and refining strategies (see figure 7.11).

Zimmerman and colleagues describe a seventh-grade student who is doing poorly in history and apply their self-regulatory model to her situation. In step 1, she self-evaluates her studying and test preparation by keeping a detailed record of them. The teacher gives her some guidelines for keeping these records. After several weeks, the student turns the records in and traces her poor test performance to low comprehension of difficult reading material.

In step 2, the student sets a goal, in this case of improving reading comprehension, and plans how to achieve the goal. The teacher assists her in breaking the goal into components, such as locating main ideas and setting specific goals for understanding a series

self-regulatory learning The self-generation and self-monitoring of thoughts, feelings, and behaviors in order to reach a goal.

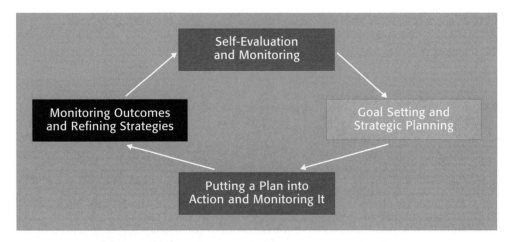

FIGURE 7.11 **A Model of Self-Regulatory Learning**

of paragraphs in her textbook. The teacher also provides the student with strategies, such as focusing initially on the first sentence of each paragraph and then scanning the others as a means of identifying main ideas. Another support the teacher might offer the student is adult or peer tutoring in reading comprehension if it is available.

In step 3, the student puts the plan into action and begins to monitor her progress. Initially, she may need help from the teacher or tutor in identifying main ideas in the reading. This feedback can help her monitor her reading comprehension more effectively on her own.

In step 4, the student monitors her improvement in reading comprehension by evaluating whether it has had any impact on her learning outcomes. Most importantly, has her improvement in reading comprehension led to better performance on history tests?

Self-evaluations reveal that the strategy of finding main ideas has only partly improved her comprehension, and only when the first sentence contained the paragraph's main idea, so the teacher recommends further strategies. Figure 7.12 on page 238 describes how teachers can apply the self-regulatory model to homework.

The development of self-regulation is influenced by many factors, among them modeling and self-efficacy (Pintrich & Schunk, 2002; Zimmerman & Schunk, 2001, 2004). Models are important sources for conveying self-regulatory skills. Among the self-regulatory skills that models can engage in are planning and managing time effectively, attending to and concentrating, organizing and coding information strategically, establishing a productive work environment, and using social resources. For example, students might observe a teacher engage in an effective time management strategy and verbalize appropriate principles. By observing such models, students can come to believe that they also can plan and manage time effectively, which creates a sense of self-efficacy for academic self-regulation and motivates students to engage in those activities.

Self-efficacy can influence a student's choice of tasks, effort expended, persistence, and achievement (Bandura, 1997, 2004; Bandura & Locke, 2003; Pintrich & Schunk, 2002; Zimmerman & Schunk, 2004). Compared with students who doubt their learning capabilities, those with high self-efficacy for acquiring a skill or performing a task participate more readily, work harder, persist longer in the face of difficulty, and achieve at a higher level. Self-efficacy can have a strong effect on achievement, but it is not the only influence. High self-efficacy will not result in competent performance when requisite knowledge and skills are lacking. We will further explore self-efficacy, goal setting, planning, and self-regulation in chapter 13, "Motivation, Teaching, and Learning."

Teachers who encourage students to be self-regulatory learners convey the message that students are responsible for their own behavior, for becoming educated, and for becoming contributing citizens to society. Another message conveyed by self-regulatory

Self-Regulatory Learning

1. Self-Evaluation and Monitoring

- The teacher distributes forms so that students can monitor specific aspects of their studying.
- The teacher gives students daily assignments to develop their self-monitoring skills and a weekly quiz to assess how well they have learned the methods.
- After several days, the teacher begins to have students exchange their homework with their peers. The peers are asked to evaluate the accuracy of the homework and how effectively the student engaged in self-monitoring. Then the teacher collects the homework for grading and reviews the peers' suggestions.

2. Goal Setting and Strategic Planning

- After a week of monitoring and the first graded exercise, the teacher asks students to give their perceptions of the strengths and weaknesses of their study strategies. The teacher emphasizes the link between learning strategies and learning outcomes.
- The teacher and peers recommend specific strategies that students might use to improve their learning. Students may use the recommendations or devise new ones. The teacher asks students to set specific goals at this point.

3. Putting a Plan into Action and Monitoring It

- The students monitor the extent to which they actually enact the new strategies.
- The teacher's role is to make sure that the new learning strategies are openly discussed.

4. Monitoring Outcomes and Refining Strategies

- The teacher continues to give students opportunities to gauge how effectively they are using their new strategies.
- The teacher helps students summarize their self-regulatory methods by reviewing each step of the self-regulatory learning cycle. She also discusses with students the hurdles the students had to overcome and the self-confidence they have achieved.

FIGURE 7.12 Applying the Self-Regulatory Model to Homework

learning is that learning is a personal experience that requires active and dedicated participation by the student (Zimmerman, Bonner, & Kovach, 1996).

Evaluating the Social Cognitive Approaches

Video Lecture: Social Cognitive Approaches

The social cognitive approaches have made important contributions to educating children. While keeping the behaviorists' scientific flavor and emphasis on careful observation, they significantly expanded the emphasis of learning to include social and cognitive factors. Considerable learning occurs through watching and listening to competent models and then imitating what they do. The emphasis in the cognitive behavior approach on self-instruction, self-talk, and self-regulatory learning provides an important shift from learning controlled by others to responsibility for one's own learning (Higgins, 2000; Pintrich & Schunk, 2002). These self-enacted strategies can significantly improve students' learning.

Critics of the social cognitive approaches come from several camps. Some cognitive theorists believe the approaches still focus too much on overt behavior and external factors and not enough on the details of how cognitive processes such as thinking, memory, and problem solving actually take place. Some developmentalists criticize them for being nondevelopmental, in the sense that they don't specify age-related, sequential changes in learning. And humanistic theorists fault them for not placing enough attention on self-esteem and caring, supportive relationships. All of these criticisms also can be, and have been, leveled at the behavioral approaches, such as Skinner's operant conditioning, discussed earlier in the chapter.

! Review and Reflect

4 **Summarize social cognitive approaches to learning.**

Review
- How does figure 7.7 help to summarize Bandura's social cognitive theory? What does he mean by self-efficacy?
- What did the Bobo doll study demonstrate? What is Bandura's model of observational learning?
- What is the focus of self-instructional methods? What does self-regulatory learning involve?

Reflect
- Give some examples of how you use self-instructional and self-regulatory methods in your personal life. How effective are these methods? Should you use them more than you do? Explain.

ENTER THE DEBATE

1. Should teachers use tangible reinforcers for good behavior? For academic performance?
2. Should teachers use corporal punishment with students?
3. Should teachers use students as examples for other students?

Crack the Case   Consequences

Adam, a student in Mr. Potter's fourth-grade class, is disruptive from time to time. He is also very bright.

One day during language arts, Adam began talking very loudly to the other students in his area. He was also laughing and telling jokes. Mr. Potter chose to ignore Adam's behavior in hopes that he would stop on his own. Adam didn't stop. Instead, his behavior became more raucous. Still Mr. Potter ignored it. Soon Adam was making enough noise that Mr. Potter was afraid that students in the neighboring classrooms would be disturbed. He verbally reprimanded Adam.

Adam was a bit quieter for the next few minutes. After that, however, he once again became loud and disruptive. Again Mr. Potter verbally reprimanded him. This time he also told Adam that if he continued with his disruptive behavior, he would have to go to the office. Adam's behavior became even more disruptive. Mr. Potter sent him to the office.

When Adam arrived at the office it was full of people—teachers getting their mail and making copies, volunteers signing in, students who were ill, students sent on errands, and other students who had been sent for disciplinary reasons. The school secretary told Adam to have a seat, which he did. He conversed with every person who entered the office as well as those who were there when he arrived. Half an hour after his arrival, he was sent back to class. He behaved quite well for the rest of the day, to Mr. Potter's relief.

The next day when students were assigned to write a paragraph, Adam once again became disruptive. He loudly told jokes to his classmates, laughed until tears were streaming down his face, and threw a paper airplane across the room. Mr. Potter reprimanded him and asked him to stop. When Adam didn't comply, Mr. Potter sent him to the office, which was once again bustling with activity.

Over the course of the next two weeks, Adam was sent to the office for disrupting class each day, always during a writing assignment. Mr. Potter was perplexed. Even more perplexing was that within three school days other children were becoming disruptive as well, requiring that they, too, be sent to the office.

- What are the issues in this case?

Answer these questions using principles of behavioral learning theories and correct terminology:

- Why did Adam continue to disrupt class despite the consequences?
- What has Adam learned?
- Why did the other students join Adam in his disruptive behavior?
- What should Mr. Potter do now?

Reach Your Learning Goals

1 Define learning and describe five approaches to studying it.

- Learning is a relatively permanent change in behavior, knowledge, and cognitive skills that occurs through experience. Experience is a great teacher. Learning is not involved in inborn, innate behaviors.

- The approaches discussed in the first part of this chapter are called behavioral. Behaviorism is the view that behavior should be explained by experiences that can be directly observed, not by mental processes. Classical conditioning and operant conditioning are behavioral views that emphasize associative learning. Psychology became more cognitive in the last part of the twentieth century and the cognitive emphasis continues today. This is reflected in four cognitive approaches to learning we discuss in this book. Social cognitive approaches emphasize the interaction of behavior, environment, and person (cognition) in explaining learning. Information-processing approaches focus on how children process information through attention, memory, thinking, and other cognitive processes. Cognitive constructivist approaches emphasize the child's construction of knowledge and understanding. Social constructivist approaches focus on collaboration with others to produce knowledge and understanding.

2 Compare classical conditioning and operant conditioning.

- In classical conditioning, the organism learns to connect, or associate, stimuli. A neutral stimulus (such as the sight of a person) becomes associated with a meaningful stimulus (such as food) and acquires the capacity to elicit a similar response. Classical conditioning involves these factors: unconditioned stimulus (US), conditioned stimulus (CS), unconditioned response (UR), and conditioned response (CR). Classical conditioning also involves generalization, discrimination, and extinction. Generalization is the tendency of a new stimulus similar to the original conditioned stimulus to produce a similar response. Discrimination occurs when the organism responds to certain stimuli and not to others. Extinction involves the weakening of the CR in the absence of the US. Systematic desensitization is a method based on classical conditioning that reduces anxiety by getting the individual to associate deep relaxation with successive visualizations of increasingly anxiety-producing situations. Classical conditioning is better at explaining involuntary behavior than voluntary behavior.

- In operant conditioning (also called instrumental conditioning), the consequences of behavior produce changes in the probability that the behavior will occur. Operant conditioning's main architect was B. F. Skinner, who built on

the connectionist view of E. L. Thorndike. Thorndike's law of effect states that behaviors followed by positive outcomes are strengthened; those followed by negative behaviors are weakened. His view was called S-R theory. Skinner greatly expanded on Thorndike's ideas. Reinforcement (reward) is a consequence (either positive or negative) that increases the probability that a behavior will occur; punishment is a consequence that decreases the probability that a behavior will occur. In positive reinforcement, a behavior increases because it is followed by a rewarding stimulus (such as praise). In negative reinforcement, a behavior increases because the response removes an aversive (unpleasant) stimulus. Generalization, discrimination, and extinction also are involved in operant conditioning. Generalization means giving the same response to similar stimuli. Discrimination is differentiating among stimuli or environmental events. Extinction occurs when a previously reinforced response is no longer reinforced and the response decreases.

3 Apply behavior analysis to education.

- Applied behavior analysis involves applying the principles of operant conditioning to change human behavior.

- Find out which reinforcers work best with which students. The Premack principle states that a high-probability activity can be used to reinforce a low-probability activity. "If . . . then" statements can be used to make it clear to students what they have to do to get a reward. Applied behavior analysts recommend that a reinforcement be contingent—that is, be given in a timely manner and only if the student performs the behavior. Skinner described a number of schedules of reinforcement. Most reinforcement in the classroom is partial. Skinner described four schedules of partial reinforcement: fixed-ratio, variable-ratio, fixed-interval, and variable-interval. Contracting involves putting reinforcement contingencies in writing. Although negative reinforcement can increase some students' desirable behavior, exercise caution with students who don't have good self-regulatory skills. A prompt is an added stimulus or cue that increases the likelihood that a discriminative stimulus will produce a desired response. Shaping involves teaching new behaviors by reinforcing successive approximations to a specified target behavior.

- Strategies for decreasing undesirable behaviors include using differential reinforcement, terminating reinforcement, removing desirable stimuli, and presenting aversive stimuli. In differential reinforcement, the teacher might reinforce behavior that is more appropriate or that is incompatible with what the student is doing. Terminating reinforcement (extinction) involves taking reinforcement away from a behavior. Many inappropriate behaviors are maintained by teacher attention, so taking away the attention can decrease the behavior. The most widely used strategy for removing desirable stimuli is time-out. A second strategy is response cost, which occurs when a positive reinforcer, such as a privilege, is taken away from the student. An aversive stimulus becomes a punisher only when it decreases behavior. The most common forms of punisher in the classroom are verbal reprimands. Punishment should be used only as the last option and in conjunction with reinforcement of desired responses. Physical punishment should not be used in the classroom.

- Used effectively, behavioral techniques can help you manage your classroom. Critics say that these approaches place too much emphasis on external control and not enough on internal control. They also argue that ignoring cognitive factors leaves out much of the richness of students' lives. Critics warn about potential ethical problems when operant conditioning is used inappropriately. And some critics say that teachers who focus too much on managing the classroom with operant techniques may place too much emphasis on conduct and not enough on academic learning.

4 **Summarize social cognitive approaches to learning.**

- Albert Bandura is the main architect of social cognitive theory. His reciprocal determinism model of learning includes three main factors: person/cognition, behavior, and environment. The person (cognitive) factor given the most emphasis by Bandura in recent years is self-efficacy, the belief that one can master a situation and produce positive outcomes.

- Also called imitation or modeling, observational learning is learning that occurs when a person observes and imitates someone else's behavior. In the Bobo doll experiment, Bandura illustrated how observational learning can occur even by watching a model who is not reinforced or punished. The experiment also demonstrates a distinction between learning and performance. Since his early experi-

ments, Bandura has focused on the specific processes that are involved in observational learning. These include attention, retention, production, and motivation.

- Cognitive behavior approaches emphasize getting students to monitor, manage, and regulate their own behavior rather than letting it be externally controlled. In some circles, this is called *cognitive behavior modification.* Cognitive behavior approaches try to change students' misconceptions, strengthen their coping skills, increase their self-control, and encourage their constructive self-reflection. Self-instructional methods are cognitive behavior techniques aimed at teaching individuals to modify their own behavior. In many cases, it is recommended that students replace negative self-statements with positive ones. Cognitive behaviorists believe that students can improve their performance by monitoring their behavior. Self-regulatory learning consists of the self-generation and self-monitoring of thoughts, feelings, and behaviors to reach a goal. High-achieving students are often self-regulatory learners. One model of self-regulatory learning involves these components: self-evaluation and monitoring, goal setting and strategic planning, putting a plan into action, and monitoring outcomes and refining strategies. Self-regulatory learning gives students responsibility for their learning.

- The social cognitive approaches have significantly expanded the scope of learning to include cognitive and social factors, in addition to behavior. The concept of observational learning is an important one, and a considerable amount of learning in classrooms takes place in this manner. The cognitive behavior emphasis on self-instruction, self-talk, and self-regulatory learning provides an important shift from learning controlled by others to self-management of learning. Critics of the cognitive and social learning approaches say that they still place too much emphasis on behavior and external factors and not enough on the details of cognitive processes. They also are criticized for being nondevelopmental and not giving enough attention to self-esteem and warmth.

KEY TERMS

PORTFOLIO ACTIVITIES

Now that you have a good understanding of this chapter, complete these exercises to expand your thinking.

Independent Reflection

Design a Self-Regulation Plan. Letitia is a high school student who doesn't have adequate self-regulatory skills and this is causing her to have serious academic problems. She doesn't plan or organize, has poor study strategies, and uses ineffective time management. Using Zimmerman's four-step strategy, design an effective self-regulation program for Letitia. (INTASC: Principle 5)

Collaborative Work

Decreasing Undesirable Behaviors. Together with 3 or 4 other students in your class, consider the following students' undesirable behaviors. You want to decrease the behaviors. What is the best strategy for each? Discuss and compare your strategies with the group. 1) Andrew, who likes to utter profanities every now and then; 2) Sandy, who tells you to quit bugging her when you ask her questions; 3) Matt, who likes to mess up other students' papers; 4) Rebecca, who frequently talks with other students around her while you are explaining or demonstrating something. (INTASC: Principles 2, 5)

Research/Field Experience Reflections

"Sesame Street" and Social Cognitive Learning. "Sesame Street" uses many effective techniques to increase children's attention and help them learn. Watch an episode. Analyze the show. How were these techniques used on the show you watched? Describe any additional techniques you observed that you might be able to use in your classroom. (INTASC: Principles 2, 7, 9)

 Go to the Online Learning Center for downloadable portfolio templates.

 TAKING IT TO THE NET

1. Imagine that you are observing a master teacher who facilitates a highly social and collaborative classroom environment. What implications does this have for teacher and student roles? Are these roles equivalent to how you have envisioned conducting your own classroom? Why or why not? Discuss possible challenges you could encounter when implementing social cognitive approaches in the classroom.
2. An important principle of Bandura's social cognitive theory is that exposure to positive role models can alter students' attitudes. How do you think a teacher's behavior and attitude in the classroom influences students' behaviors and attitudes? What kind of student behavior would you expect to find in a classroom with an authoritarian teacher? authoritative teacher? permissive teacher?
3. What is your position on the debate about extrinsic motivators and rewards in the classroom? Describe the connections between social conditioning and the use of classroom rewards/consequences. Does a rewards system ultimately achieve the goal of "learning" for students? Discuss the benefits or disadvantages of implementing such a system, and give evidence to support your arguments.

Connect to the Online Learning Center to explore possible answers.

STUDY, PRACTICE, AND SUCCEED

 Go to chapter 7 on the Online Learning Center at **www.mhhe.com/santrockedu2e to access the student** study guide with practice quizzes, web links, portfolio resources, PowerWeb articles and news feeds, and the online resources referenced in the chapter.

 Go to your Student Toolbox CD-ROM to access the resources and activities referenced in the chapter and

• Resources to help you prepare for the PRAXIS II™ exam

• **Application Resources,** including additional *Crack the Case* studies, electronic versions of the *Self-Assessments,* Application Exercises, and Site Observation Questions
• **Study Resources,** including Learning Goals, the Chapter Summary, a *Test Your Learning* exercise, and multiple-choice, true/false, matching, key terms, and short-answer quizzes
• **Professional Resources,** including a Lesson Plan Builder and *Bibliomaker*

8 The Information-Processing Approach

The mind is an enchanting thing.

—Marianne Moore,
*American Poet,
20th Century*

Chapter Learning Goals After you have completed your study of this chapter, you should be able to reach these learning goals:

1 Describe the information-processing approach.

2 Discuss memory in terms of encoding, storage, and retrieval.

3 Draw some lessons about learning from the way experts think.

4 Explain the concept of metacognition and identify some ways to improve children's metacognition.

Teaching Stories Laura Bickford

Laura Bickford chairs the English Department at Nordoff High School in Ojai, California. She recently spoke about how she encourages students to think:

I believe the call to teach is a call to teach students how to think. In encouraging critical thinking, literature itself does a good bit of work for us but we still have to be guides. We have to ask good questions. We have to show students the value in asking their own questions, in having discussions and conversations. In addition to reading and discussing literature, the best way to move students to think critically is to have them write. We write all the time in a variety of modes: journals, formal essays, letters, factual reports, news articles, speeches, or other formal oral presentations. We have to show students where they merely scratch the surface in their thinking and writing. I call these moments "hits and runs." When I see this "hit and run" effort, I draw a window on the paper. I tell them it is a "window of opportunity" to go deeper, elaborate, and clarify. Many students don't do this kind of thinking until they are prodded to do so.

I also use metacognitive strategies all the time—that is, helping students know about knowing. These include: asking students to comment on their learning after we have finished particular pieces of projects and asking them to discuss in advance what we might be seeking to learn as we begin a new project or activity. I also ask them to keep reading logs so they can observe their own thinking as it happens. For example, they might copy a passage from a reading selection and comment on it. Studying a passage from J. D. Salinger's *The Catcher in the Rye,* a student might write: "I've never thought about life the way that Holden Caulfield does. Maybe I see the world differently than he does. He always is so depressed. I'm not depressed. Salinger is good at showing us someone who is usually depressed. How does he manage to do that?" In addition, I ask students to comment on their own learning by way of grading themselves. This year a student gave me one of the most insightful lines about her growth as a reader that I have ever seen from a student. She wrote, "I no longer think in a monotone when I'm reading." I don't know if she grasps the magnitude of that thought or how it came to be that she made that change. It is magic when students see themselves growing like this.

In the opening story, teacher Laura Bickford tells how she uses metacognitive strategies. Laura Bickford's emphasis on children's metacognitive strategies is one of the important themes of this chapter. In addition to metacognition, we'll explore what it means to take an information-processing approach in teaching children and examine children's memory and expertise.

THE NATURE OF THE INFORMATION-PROCESSING APPROACH

How capable are children? Proponents of the information-processing approach to learning believe they are highly capable. Children attend to information being presented and tinker with it. They develop strategies for remembering. They form concepts. They reason and solve problems.

Information, Memory, and Thinking

The **information-processing approach** emphasizes that children manipulate information, monitor it, and strategize about it. Central to this approach are the processes of memory and thinking. According to the information-processing approach, children develop a gradually increasing capacity for processing information, which allows them to acquire increasingly complex knowledge and skills.

Some information-processing approaches have stronger constructivist leanings than others. Those that do have a constructivist bent see teachers as cognitive guides for academic tasks and children as learners who are trying to make sense of these tasks (Mayer, 2001, 2002). Like Piaget's cognitive developmental theory, which was discussed in chapter 2, some of the information-processing approaches described in this chapter exemplify the cognitive constructivist approach ◀ p. 211. Information-processing approaches that emphasize a more passive child who simply memorizes information provided by the environment are not constructivist.

Behaviorism and its associative model of learning was a dominant force in psychology until the 1950s and 1960s, when many psychologists began to acknowledge that they

information-processing approach A cognitive approach in which children manipulate information, monitor it, and strategize about it. Central to this approach are the cognitive processes of memory and thinking.

could not explain children's learning without referring to mental processes such as memory and thinking (Gardner, 1985). The term *cognitive psychology* became a label for approaches that sought to explain behavior by examining mental processes. Although a number of factors stimulated the growth of cognitive psychology, none was more important than the development of computers. The first modern computer, developed by John von Neumann in the late 1940s, showed that inanimate machines could perform logical operations. This suggested that some mental operations might be carried out by computers, possibly telling us something about the way human cognition works. Cognitive psychologists often draw analogies to computers to help explain the relation between cognition and the brain. The physical brain is compared to the computer's hardware, cognition to its software. Although computers and software aren't perfect analogies for brains and cognitive activities, nonetheless, the comparison contributed to our thinking about the child's mind as an active information-processing system.

Siegler's View

Robert Siegler (1998; Siegler & Alibali, 2005) described three main characteristics of the information-processing approach: thinking, change mechanisms, and self-modification.

Thinking   In Siegler's view, thinking is information processing (Siegler & Alibali, 2005). In this regard, Siegler provides a broad perspective on thinking. He says that when children perceive, encode, represent, and store information from the world, they are engaging in thinking. Siegler believes that thinking is highly flexible, which allows individuals to adapt and adjust to many changes in circumstances, task requirements, and goals. However, there are some limits on the human's remarkable thinking abilities. Individuals can pay attention to only a limited amount of information at any one moment, and there are limits on how fast we can process information. Later in the chapter we will explore children's powers of attention.

Change Mechanisms   Siegler argues that in information processing the main focus should be on the role of mechanisms of change in development. He believes that four main mechanisms work together to create changes in children's cognitive skills: encoding, automatization, strategy construction, and generalization (Siegler & Alibali, 2005).

Encoding is the process by which information gets into memory. Siegler states that a key aspect of solving problems is to encode the relevant information and ignore the irrelevant parts. Because it often takes time and effort to construct new strategies, children must practice them in order to eventually execute them automatically and maximize their effectiveness. The term **automaticity** refers to the ability to process information with little or no effort. With age and experience, information processing becomes increasingly automatic on many tasks, allowing children to detect new connections among ideas and events that they otherwise would miss (Kail, 2002).

The third change mechanism is **strategy construction,** which involves the discovery of new procedures for processing information. Siegler (2001) says that children need to encode key information about a problem and coordinate the information with relevant prior knowledge to solve the problem.

To fully benefit from a newly constructed strategy, *generalization* is needed. Children need to generalize, or apply the strategy to other problems. In chapter 9, we will discuss generalization under the topic of transfer of learning. *Transfer* occurs when the child applies previous experiences and knowledge to learning or problem solving in a new situation.

Self-Modification   The contemporary information-processing approach argues that, as in Piaget's theory of cognitive development, children play an active role in their development. They use knowledge and strategies that they have learned in previous circumstances to adapt their responses to a new learning situation. In this manner, children build newer and more sophisticated responses from prior knowledge and strategies. The

Strategies

Theory Into Practice

Siegler's Theory of Information Processing

encoding The process by which information gets into memory.

automaticity The ability to process information with little or no effort.

strategy construction The discovery of new procedures for processing information.

importance of self-modification in processing information is exemplified in **metacognition,** which means cognition about cognition, or "knowing about knowing" (Flavell, 1999; Flavell, Miller, & Miller, 2002). We will study metacognition in the final section of this chapter and especially will emphasize how students' self-awareness can enable them to adapt and manage their strategies during problem solving and thinking.

⚠ Review and Reflect

1 Describe the information-processing approach.

Review
- What view does the information-processing approach take of children as learners?
- What is Siegler's view of information processing?

Reflect
- In terms of your ability to learn, are there ways that you wish you were more like a computer? Or are you better than any computer in all aspects of processing information? Explain.

Now that we have studied some general properties of the information-processing approach, let's examine some of its main cognitive processes in greater detail. We will begin with memory.

MEMORY

Twentieth-century playwright Tennessee Williams once commented that life is all memory except for that one present moment that goes by so quickly that you can hardly catch it going. But just what is memory?

What Is Memory?

Memory is the retention of information over time. Educational psychologists study how information is initially placed or encoded into memory, how it is retained or stored after being encoded, and how it is found or retrieved for a certain purpose later. Memory anchors the self in continuity. Without memory you would not be able to connect what happened to you yesterday with what is going on in your life today. Today, educational psychologists emphasize that it is important not to view memory in terms of how children add something to it but, rather, to underscore how children actively construct their memory (Schacter, 2001).

The main body of our discussion of memory will focus on encoding, storage, and retrieval. Thinking about memory in terms of these processes should help you to understand it better (see figure 8.1). For memory to work, children have to take information in, store it or represent it, and then retrieve it for some purpose later.

As you learned earlier, *encoding* is the process by which information gets into memory. *Storage* is the retention of information over time. *Retrieval* means taking information out of storage. Let's now explore each of these three important memory activities in greater detail.

Encoding

In everyday language, encoding has much in common with attention and learning. When a student is listening to a teacher, watching a movie, listening to music, or talking with a friend, he or she is encoding information into memory. Six concepts related to

Memory Links

metacognition Cognition about cognition, or "knowing about knowing."

memory The retention of information over time, which involves encoding, storage, and retrieval.

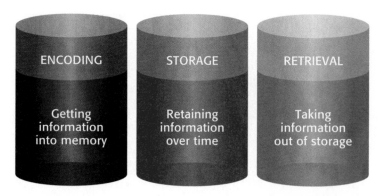

FIGURE 8.1 Processing Information in Memory
As you read about the many aspects of memory in this chapter, it should help you to think about the organization of memory in terms of these three main activities.

encoding are attention, rehearsal, deep processing, elaboration, constructing images, and organization.

Attention Look at the pictures of the three individuals in figure 8.2 for a few seconds. Then, before reading further, look away from them and state what you remember about the pictures.

These actually are faces of famous people—George Washington, Mona Lisa, and George Bush, Sr.—with Elvis Presley's hair grafted onto their images. You likely did not recognize these famous people because of the prominent hair. When we remember a face, we usually only attend to a few key features and ignore the others. In this case, you may have focused more on the hair than on the facial features of the famous individuals.

To begin the process of memory encoding, children have to attend to information. **Attention** involves concentrating and focusing mental resources. One critical skill in paying attention is being selective. Attention is selective by nature because the brain's resources are limited (Mangels, Piction, & Craik, 2001). As a teacher gives instructions for completing a task, students need to attend to what she is saying and not be distracted by other students who are talking. As students study for a test, they need to focus selectively on the book they are reading and tune out or eliminate other stimuli such as the sound of a television.

Being able to shift from one activity to another when appropriate is another challenge related to attention. For example, learning to write good stories requires shifting among the competing tasks of forming letters, composing grammar, structuring paragraphs, and conveying the story as a whole. Older children and adolescents are better than younger children at making appropriate shifts of attention.

attention Concentrating and focusing mental resources.

FIGURE 8.2 Encoding Memories
Look at these three pictures for a few seconds; then look away and state what you remember about them.

What are some good strategies teachers can use to get students' attention?

Another problem for many young children is that they focus too much on the attention-grabbing aspects of a task or situation rather than on what is important. They focus on salient aspects of a situation rather than on its relevant aspects. For example, when preschoolers watch a video in which a clown is giving directions for solving a problem, they often focus more on the clown's attention-grabbing appearance than on the instructions he is giving. By the middle of elementary school, children are better at focusing their attention on the relevant dimensions of a task (Paris & Lindauer, 1982). This change often signals greater reflection and less impulsiveness. Of course, there are individual differences in attention, and some elementary school children need help in attending to the relevant dimensions of a task rather than the salient dimensions.

One reason older children are better at deploying attention than younger children is that they are more likely to construct a plan of action to guide their attentional efforts when they are trying to solve a problem. However, younger children often can effectively use attention-focusing strategies when these are provided to them. Possibly school experiences help children become more aware of their own attentional capabilities, or perhaps as they develop, they come to understand that their mind works best when it is active and constructive (Lovett & Pillow, 1996). Attending to something relevant is an active, effortful process that draws on mental resources, rather than a passive process of receiving the available information.

Teaching Strategies
For Helping Students Pay Attention

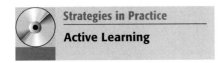

Strategies in Practice

Active Learning

1. *Encourage students to pay close attention and minimize distraction.* Talk with children about how important it is to pay attention when they need to remember something. Give them exercises in which they get opportunities to give their undivided attention to something.
2. *Use cues or gestures to signal that something is important.* This might involve raising your voice, repeating something with emphasis, and writing the concept on the board or on a transparency.

3. *Help students generate their own cue or catch phrase for when they need to pay attention.* Possibly vary this from month to month. Give them a menu of options to select from, such as "Alert," "Focus," or "Zero in." Get them to say their word or pet phrase quietly but firmly to themselves when they catch their minds wandering.

4. *Use instructional comments.* These might include "Okay, we are ready to start discussing . . . Now, pay attention" or "I'm going to ask you a question about this next topic on the test next week."

5. *Make learning interesting.* Boredom can set in quickly for students, and when it does their attention wanes. Relating ideas to students' interests increases their attention. So does infusing the classroom with novel, unusual, or surprising exercises. Just starting off a biology exercise on heredity and aging with a question such as "Can you live to be 100?" or "Might someone be able to live to be even 400 some day?" is sure to capture students' attention. Think of dramatic questions such as these to introduce various topics.

6. *Use media and technology effectively as part of your effort to vary the pace of the classroom.* Video and television programs have built-in attention-getting formats, such as zooming in on an image; flashing a vivid, colorful image on the screen; and switching from one setting to another. Look for relevant videos and television programs that can help you vary the classroom's pace and increase students' attention. Also, the next time you watch a video or a TV program, think about the way your attention is being captured and reflect on how you might use variations of this in your own classroom. Unfortunately, too many teachers show videos only to keep students quiet, which does not promote learning. Also, if the curriculum is dull, it doesn't matter what kinds of "tricks" or "splashes" the teacher uses—students will not learn effectively. Make sure that the media and technology you use captures students' attention in meaningful ways that promote effective learning (Goldman, 1998).

7. *Focus on active learning to make learning enjoyable.* Using media and technology effectively is not the only way to do this. A different exercise, a guest, a field trip, and many other activities can be used to make learning more enjoyable, reduce student boredom, and increase attention.

8. *Don't overload students with too much information.* We live in an information society where sometimes the tendency is to feel like you have to get students to learn everything. But students who are given too much information too fast might not attend to anything.

9. *Be aware of individual differences in students' attentional skills.* As we saw in chapter 6, "Learners Who Are Exceptional," some students have severe problems in paying attention. You will need to take this into account when presenting material. Before you begin an exercise, look around the room for potential distractions, such as an open window to a playground where students are being noisy. Close the window and draw the shade to eliminate the distraction.

Rehearsal   **Rehearsal** is the conscious repetition of information over time to increase the length of time information stays in memory. Rehearsal works best when individuals need to encode and remember a list of items for a brief period of time. When they must retain information over long periods of time, as when they are studying for a test they won't take until next week, other strategies usually work better than rehearsal. A main reason that rehearsal does not work well for retaining information over the long term is that rehearsal often involves just rotely repeating information without imparting any meaning to it. When students construct their memory in meaningful ways, they remember better. As we will see next, they also remember better when they process material deeply and elaborate it.

Deep Processing   Following the discovery that rehearsal is not an efficient way to encode information for long-term memory, Fergus Craik and Robert Lockhart (1972)

rehearsal The conscious repetition of information over time to increase the length of time information stays in memory.

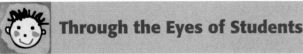

Through the Eyes of Students

The Cobwebs of Memory

I think the point of having memories is to share them, especially with close friends or family. If you don't share them, they are just sitting inside your brain getting cobwebs. If you have a great memory of Christmas and no one to share it with, what's the point of memories?

Seventh-Grade Student
West Middle School
Ypsilanti, Michigan

Levels of Processing

---

levels of processing theory The theory that processing of memory occurs on a continuum from shallow to deep, with deeper processing producing better memory.

elaboration The extensiveness of information processing involved in encoding.

---

proposed that we can process information at a variety of levels. Their theory, **levels of processing theory,** states that the processing of memory occurs on a continuum from shallow to deep, with deeper processing producing better memory. The sensory, or physical, features of stimuli are analyzed first at a shallow level. This might involve detecting the lines, angles, and contours of a printed word's letters or a spoken word's frequency, duration, and loudness. At an intermediate level of processing, the stimulus is recognized and given a label. For example, a four-legged, barking object is identified as a dog. Then, at the deepest level, information is processed semantically, in terms of its meaning. For example, if a child sees the word *boat,* at the shallow level she might notice the shapes of the letters, at the intermediate level she might think of the characteristics of the word (for instance, that it rhymes with *coat*), and at the deepest level she might think about the last time she went fishing with her dad on a boat and the kind of boat it was. Researchers have found that individuals remember information better when they process it at a deeper level (Otten, Henson, & Rugg, 2001).

Elaboration   Cognitive psychologists soon recognized, however, that there is more to good encoding than just depth of processing. They discovered that when individuals use elaboration in their encoding of information, their memory benefits (Terry, 2003). **Elaboration** is the extensiveness of information processing involved in encoding. Thus, when you present the concept of democracy to students, they likely will remember it better if they come up with good examples of it. Thinking of examples is a good way to elaborate information. For instance, self-reference is an effective way to elaborate information. If you are trying to get students to remember the concept of fairness, the more they can generate personal examples of inequities and equities they have personally experienced, the more likely it is that they will remember the concept. Likewise, students will likely remember the concept of a symphony if they associate it with the last time their parents or teacher took them to the symphony rather than just rehearse the words that define what a symphony is. Thinking about personal associations with information makes the information more meaningful and helps students remember it.

The use of elaboration changes developmentally (Schneider & Pressley, 1997). Adolescents are more likely to use elaboration spontaneously than children. Elementary school children can be taught to use elaboration strategies on a learning task but they are less likely than adolescents to use the strategies on other learning tasks in the future. Nonetheless, verbal elaboration can be an effective memory strategy even with young elementary school children. Elaboration in one study involved the experimenter telling second- and fifth-grade children to construct a meaningful sentence for a key word (such as "The postman carried a letter in his cart" for the keyword *cart*). As shown in figure 8.3, both second- and fifth-grade children remembered the keywords better when they constructed a meaningful sentence containing the word than when the keyword and its definition were told to the child (Pressley, Levin, & McCormick, 1980).

One reason elaboration works so well in encoding is that it adds to the distinctiveness of memory code (Ellis, 1987). To remember a piece of information, such as a name, an experience, or a fact about geography, students need to search for the code that contains this information among the mass of codes in their long-term memory. The search process is easier if the memory code is unique (Hunt & Kelly, 1996). The situation is not unlike searching for a friend at a crowded airport—if your friend is 6 feet 3 inches tall

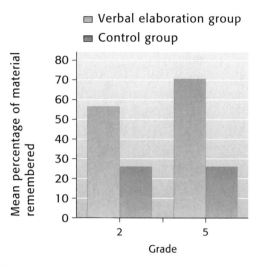

FIGURE 8.3 Verbal Elaboration and Memory
Both second- and fifth-grade children remembered words better when they constructed a meaningful sentence for the word (verbal elaboration group) than when they merely heard the word and its definition (control group). The verbal elaboration worked better for the fifth-graders than the second-graders.

and has flaming red hair, it will be easier to find him in the crowd than if he has more common features. Also, as a person elaborates information, more information is stored. And as more information is stored, it becomes easier to differentiate the memory from others. For example, if a student witnesses another student being hit by a car that speeds away, the student's memory of the car will be far better if she deliberately encodes her observations that the car is a red 1995 Pontiac with tinted windows and spinners on the wheels than if she observes only that it is a red car.

Constructing Images   When we construct an image of something, we are elaborating the information. For example, how many windows are there in the apartment or house where your family has lived for a substantial part of your life? Few of us ever memorize this information, but you probably can come up with a good answer, especially if you reconstruct a mental image of each room. Take a "mental walk" through the house, counting the windows as you go.

Allan Paivio (1971, 1986) believes that memories are stored in one of two ways: as a verbal code or as an image code. For example, you can remember a picture by a label (*The Last Supper*, a verbal code) or by a mental image. Paivio says that the more detailed and distinctive the image code, the better your memory of the information will be.

Researchers have found that encouraging children to use imagery to remember verbal information works better for older children than for younger children (Schneider, 2004). In one study, twenty sentences were presented to first- through sixth-grade children to remember (such as "The angry bird shouted at the white dog" and "The policeman painted the circus tent on a windy day") (Pressley & others, 1987). Children were randomly assigned to an imagery condition (make a picture in your head for each sentence) and a control condition (children were told just to try hard). Figure 8.4, on page 254, shows that the imagery instructions improved memory for the sentences in the older elementary school children (grades 4 through 6) but

Through the Eyes of Teachers

Imagination as a Form of Transportation

Second-grade teacher Beth Belcher transforms a lesson about transportation into the game of "Scattergories." After her students settle on a description of transportation as "a way of getting from one place to another," she divides them into teams and asks them to list as many types of transportation they can think of. Belcher says she wants students to engage in deep thinking. If more than one team comes up with the same answer, such as "car," "train," or "plant," they don't get any points. "Elevator" is a winner. And then a six-year-old girl says that "imagination" is a form of transportation, a way of getting from one place to another. Belcher says that moments like that are incredibly rewarding (Briggs, 1998).

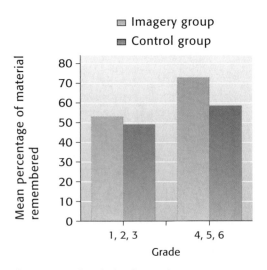

FIGURE 8.4 Imagery and Memory of Verbal Information
Imagery improved older elementary school children's memory for sentences more than younger elementary school children's memory for sentences.

not for the younger elementary school children (grades 1 through 3). Researchers have found that young elementary school children can use imagery to remember pictures better than they can verbal materials, such as sentences (Schneider & Pressley, 1997).

Organization   If students organize information when they are encoding it, their memory benefits. To understand the importance of organization in encoding, complete the following exercise: Recall the twelve months of the year as quickly as you can. How long did it take you? What was the order of your recall? Your answers are probably a few seconds and in natural order (January, February, March, and so on). Now try to remember the months in alphabetical order. Did you make any errors? How long did it take you? There is a clear distinction between recalling the months in natural order and recalling alphabetically. This exercise is a good one to use with your students to help them understand the importance of organizing their memories in meaningful ways.

The more you present information in an organized way, the easier your students will remember it. This is especially true if you organize information hierarchically or outline it. Also, if you simply encourage students to organize information, they often will remember it better than if you give them no instructions about organizing (Mandler, 1980).

Chunking is a beneficial organizational memory strategy that involves grouping, or "packing," information into "higher-order" units that can be remembered as single units. Chunking works by making large amounts of information more manageable and more

chunking Grouping, or "packing," information into "higher-order" units that can be remembered as single units.

Frank and Ernest

FRANK & ERNEST by Bob Thaves. Reprinted by permission of Newspaper Enterprise Association, Inc. 6-24-79.

"Can we hurry up and get to the test? My short-term memory is better than my long-term memory."
© 1985: reprinted courtesy of Bill Hoest and Parade Magazine.

meaningful. For example, consider this simple list of words: *hot, city, book, forget, tomorrow, smile.* Try to hold these in memory for a moment; then write them down. If you recalled all 7 words, you succeeded in holding 34 letters in your memory.

Storage

After children encode information, they need to retain, or store, the information. Among the most prominent aspects of memory storage are the three main stores, which correspond to three different time frames: sensory memory, working (or short-term) memory, and long-term memory.

Memory's Time Frames   Children remember some information for less than a second, some for about half a minute, and other information for minutes, hours, years, even a lifetime. The three types of memory that vary according to their time frames are *sensory memory* (which lasts a fraction of a second to several seconds); *short-term memory* (also called *working memory;* lasts about 30 seconds), and *long-term memory* (which lasts up to a lifetime).

Sensory Memory   **Sensory memory** holds information from the world in its original sensory form for only an instant, not much longer than the brief time a student is exposed to the visual, auditory, and other sensations.

Students have a sensory memory for sounds for up to several seconds, sort of like a brief echo. However, their sensory memory for visual images lasts only for about one-fourth of a second. Because sensory information lasts for only a fleeting moment, an important task for the student is to attend to the sensory information that is important for learning.

Short-Term Memory   **Short-term memory** is a limited-capacity memory system in which information is retained for as long as 30 seconds, unless the information is rehearsed or otherwise processed further, in which case it can be retained longer. Compared with sensory memory, short-term memory is limited in capacity but relatively longer in duration. Its limited capacity intrigued George Miller (1956), who described this in a paper with a catchy title: "The Magical Number Seven, Plus or Minus Two." Miller pointed out that on many tasks, students are limited in how much information they can keep track of without external aids. Usually the limit is in the range of 7 ± 2 items.

Short-Term Memory
Exploring Memory Models

sensory memory Memory that holds information from the world in its original form for only an instant.

short-term memory A limited-capacity memory system in which information is retained for as long as 30 seconds, unless the information is rehearsed, in which case it can be retained longer.

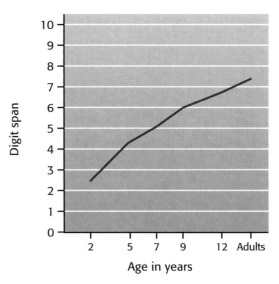

FIGURE 8.5 Developmental Changes in Memory Span
In one study, memory span increased about 3 digits from 2 years of age to 5 digits at 7 years of age (Dempster, 1981). By 12 years of age, memory span had increased on average another 1½ digits.

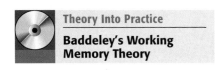

Theory Into Practice

Baddeley's Working Memory Theory

Baddeley's Research

Explore Working Memory

memory span The number of digits an individual can report back without error in a single presentation.

working memory A kind of "mental workbench" that lets individuals manipulate, assemble, and construct information when they make decisions, solve problems, and comprehend written and spoken language.

The most widely cited example of the 7 ± 2 phenomenon involves **memory span,** the number of digits an individual can report back without error from a single presentation. How many digits individuals can report back depends on how old they are. In one study, memory span increased from two digits in two-year-olds, to five digits in seven-year-olds, to six to seven digits in twelve-year-olds (Dempster, 1981) (see figure 8.5). Many college students can handle lists of eight or nine digits. Keep in mind that these are averages and individuals differ. For example, many seven-year-olds have a memory span of fewer than six or seven digits; others have a memory span of eight or more digits.

Related to short-term memory, British psychologist Alan Baddeley (1993, 1998, 2000, 2001) proposed that **working memory** is a three-part system that temporarily holds information as people perform tasks. Working memory is a kind of mental "workbench" where information is manipulated and assembled to help us make decisions, solve problems, and comprehend written and spoken language. Notice that working memory is not like a passive storehouse with shelves to store information until it moves to long-term memory. Rather, it is a very active memory system (Kane & others, 2004).

Figure 8.6 shows Baddeley's view of working memory and its three components: phonological loop, visual-spatial memory, and central executive. Think of them as an executive (central executive) with two assistants (phonological loop and visual-spatial working memory) to help do your work.

- The *phonological loop* is specialized to briefly store speech-based information about the sounds of language. The phonological loop contains two separate components: an acoustic code, which decays in a few seconds, and rehearsal, which allows individuals to repeat the words in the phonological store.
- *Visual-spatial working memory* stores visual and spatial information, including visual imagery. Like the phonological loop, visual-spatial working memory has a limited capacity. The phonological loop and visual-spatial working memory function independently. You could rehearse numbers in the phonological loop while making spatial arrangements of letters in visual-spatial working memory.
- The *central executive* integrates information not only from the phonological loop and visual-spatial working memory but also from long-term memory. In Baddeley's view, the central executive plays important roles in attention, planning, and organizing behavior. The central executive acts much like a supervisor who monitors which

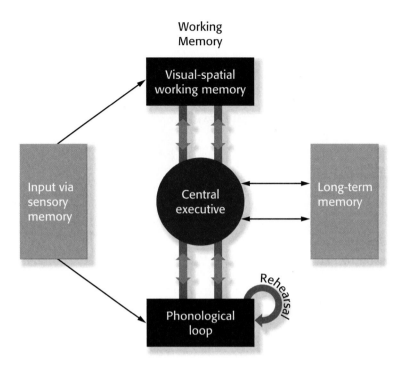

FIGURE 8.6 Working Memory
In Baddeley's working memory model, working memory is like a "mental workbench" where a great deal of information processing is carried out. Working memory consists of three main components. The phonological loop and visual-spatial working memory serve as assistants in helping the central executive do its work. Input from sensory memory goes to the phonological loop, where information about speech is stored and rehearsal takes place, and to visual-spatial working memory, where visual and spatial information, including imagery, are stored. Working memory is a limited-capacity system and information is stored there only for a brief time. Working memory interacts with long-term memory, using information from long-term memory in its work and transmitting information to long-term memory for longer storage.

information and issues deserve attention and which should be ignored. It also selects which strategies to use to process information and solve problems. As with the other two components of working memory—the phonological loop and visual-spatial working memory—the central executive has a limited capacity.

Let's examine an aspect of life in which working memory is involved. In one recent study, verbal working memory was impaired by negative emotion (Gray, 2001). In other words, when people are feeling bad about something, their working memory may become less efficient. In another recent study, college students who wrote about a negative emotional event showed sizeable improvement in working memory, compared with students who wrote about a positive emotional event and those in a control group who wrote about their daily schedule (Klein & Boals, 2001). The writing effect on working memory was associated with higher grade point averages. An important implication of this study is its demonstration that working memory is malleable and can be affected by an experience such as writing about one's emotional experiences (Miyake, 2001). For example, students with math anxiety often experience deficiencies in working memory when doing math problems because of intrusive thoughts and worries about math (Ashcraft & Kirk, 2001). Such students might benefit from writing about their math anxiety.

Long-Term Memory **Long-term memory** is a type of memory that holds enormous amounts of information for a long period of time in a relatively permanent fashion. A

long-term memory A type of memory that holds enormous amounts of information for a long period of time in a relatively permanent fashion.

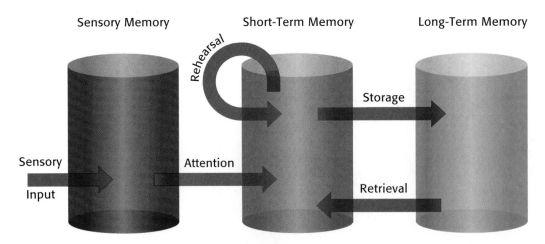

FIGURE 8.7 Atkinson and Shiffrin's Theory of Memory
In this model, sensory input goes into sensory memory. Through the process of attention, information moves into short-term memory, where it remains for 30 seconds or less, unless it is rehearsed. Then, the information goes into long-term memory storage; from here it can be retrieved for some purpose later.

typical human's long-term memory capacity is staggering. The distinguished computer scientist John von Neumann put the size at 2.8 × 10 (280 quintillion) bits, which in practical terms means that long-term memory storage is virtually unlimited. Even more impressive is the efficiency with which individuals can retrieve information. It often takes only a moment to search through this vast storehouse to find the information we want. Think about your own long-term memory. Who wrote the Gettysburg Address? Who was your first-grade teacher? When were you born? Where do you live? You can answer thousands of such questions instantly. Of course, not all information is retrieved so easily from long-term memory. Later in this chapter we will describe ways that students can retrieve hard-to-recall information.

A Model of the Three Memory Stores   This three-stage concept of memory we have been describing was developed by Richard Atkinson and Richard Shiffrin (1968). According to the **Atkinson-Shiffrin model,** memory involves a sequence of sensory memory, short-term memory, and long-term memory stages (see figure 8.7). As we have seen, much information makes it no further than the sensory memories of sounds and sights. This information is retained only for a brief instant. However, some information, especially that to which we pay attention, is transferred to short-term memory, where it can be retained for about 30 seconds (or longer with the aid of rehearsal). Atkinson and Shiffrin claimed that the longer information is retained in short-term memory through the use of rehearsal, the greater its chance is of getting into long-term memory. Notice in figure 8.7 that information in long-term memory also can be retrieved back into short-term memory.

Some contemporary experts on memory believe that the Atkinson-Shiffrin model is too simple (Bartlett, 2001). They argue that memory doesn't always work in a neatly packaged three-stage sequence, as Atkinson and Shiffrin proposed. For example, these contemporary experts stress that *working memory* uses long-term memory's contents in more flexible ways than simply retrieving information from it. Despite these problems, the model is useful in providing an overview of some components of memory.

Long-Term Memory's Contents   Just as different types of memory can be distinguished by how long they last, memory can be differentiated on the basis of its contents. For long-term memory, many contemporary psychologists accept the hierarchy of contents described in figure 8.8 (Bartlett, 2001; Squire, 1987). In this hierarchy, long-term

Atkinson-Shiffrin model A model of memory that involves a sequence of three stages: sensory memory, short-term memory, and long-term memory.

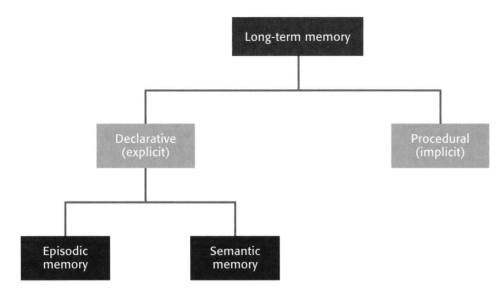

FIGURE 8.8 **Classification of Long-Term Memory's Contents**

memory is divided into the subtypes of declarative and procedural memory. Declarative memory is subdivided into episodic memory and semantic memory.

Declarative and Procedural Memory   **Declarative memory** is the conscious recollection of information, such as specific facts or events that can be verbally communicated. Declarative memory has been called "knowing that" and more recently has been labeled "explicit memory." Demonstrations of students' declarative memory could include recounting an event they have witnessed or describing a basic principle of math. However, students do not need to be talking to be using declarative memory. If students simply sit and reflect on an experience, their declarative memory is involved.

Procedural memory is nondeclarative knowledge in the form of skills and cognitive operations. Procedural memory cannot be consciously recollected, at least not in the form of specific events or facts. This makes procedural memory difficult, if not impossible, to communicate verbally. Procedural memory is sometimes called "knowing how," and recently it also has been described as "implicit memory" (Schacter, 2000). When students apply their abilities to perform a dance, ride a bicycle, or type on a computer keyboard, their procedural memory is at work. It also is at work when they speak grammatically correct sentences without having to think about how to do it.

Episodic and Semantic Memory   Cognitive psychologist Endel Tulving (1972, 2000) distinguishes between two subtypes of declarative memory: episodic and semantic. **Episodic memory** is the retention of information about the where and when of life's happenings. Students' memories of the first day of school, whom they had lunch with, or the guest who came to talk with their class last week are all episodic.

Semantic memory is a student's general knowledge about the world. It includes

- Knowledge of the sort learned in school (such as knowledge of geometry)
- Knowledge in different fields of expertise (such as knowledge of chess, for a skilled fifteen-year-old chess player)
- "Everyday" knowledge about meanings of words, famous people, important places, and common things (such as what the word *pertinacious* means or who Nelson Mandela or Alan Greenspan is)

Semantic memory is independent of the person's identity with the past. For example, students might access a fact—such as "Lima is the capital of Peru"—and not have the foggiest idea when and where they learned it.

declarative memory The conscious recollection of information, such as specific facts or events that can be verbally communicated.

procedural memory Knowledge in the form of skills and cognitive operations. Procedural memory cannot be consciously recollected, at least not in the form of specific events or facts.

episodic memory The retention of information about the where and when of life's happenings.

semantic memory A student's general knowledge about the world.

Representing Information in Memory   How do students represent information in their memory? Two main theories have addressed this question: network and schema.

Network Theories   **Network theories** describe how information in memory is organized and connected. They emphasize nodes in the memory network. The nodes stand for labels or concepts. Consider the concept "bird." One of the earliest network theories described memory representation as hierarchically arranged with more-concrete concepts ("canary," for example) nestled under more abstract concepts (such as "bird"). However, it soon was realized that such hierarchical networks are too neat to accurately portray how memory representation really works. For example, students take longer to answer the question "Is an ostrich a bird?" than to answer the question "Is a canary a bird?" Thus, today memory researchers envision the memory network as more irregular and distorted. A typical bird, such as a canary, is closer to the node, or center, of the category "bird" than is the atypical ostrich.

Schemas

Schema Theories   Long-term memory has been compared to a library of books. The idea is that our memory stores information just as a library stores books. In this analogy, the way students retrieve information is said to be similar to the process they use to locate and check out a book. However, the process of retrieving information from long-term memory is not as precise as the library analogy suggests. When we search through our long-term memory storehouse, we don't always find the exact "book" we want, or we might find the "book" we want but discover that only "several pages" are intact—we have to reconstruct the rest.

    Schema theories state that when we reconstruct information, we fit it into information that already exists in our mind. A **schema** is information—concepts, knowledge, information about events—that already exists in a person's mind. You might recall our description of schemas in Piaget's theory (in chapter 2, "Cognitive and Language Development"). Schemas from prior experiences influence the way we encode, make inferences about, and retrieve information. Unlike network theories, which assume that retrieval involves specific facts, schema theory claims that long-term memory searches are not very exact. We often don't find precisely what we want, and we have to reconstruct the rest. Often when asked to retrieve information, we fill in the gaps between our fragmented memories with a variety of accuracies and inaccuracies.

    The schema theory of memory began with Sir Frederick Bartlett's (1932) studies of how people remember stories. Bartlett was concerned about how a person's background, which is encoded in schemas, would reveal itself in the person's reconstruction (modification and distortion) of the story's content. One of Bartlett's stories was called "War of the Ghosts," an English translation of an American Indian folktale (see figure 8.9). The story tells of events that were completely foreign to the experiences of Bartlett's middle- and upper-income British research participants. They read the story twice and then, after fifteen minutes, wrote down the tale as best as they could remember it.

    What intrigued Bartlett was how differently the participants might reconstruct this and other stories from the original versions. The British participants used both their general schemas and daily experiences, and their schemas for adventurous ghost stories in particular, to reconstruct "War of the Ghosts." Familiar details from the story that "fit into" the participants' schemas were successfully recalled. But details that departed from their schemas were often extensively distorted. For example, the "something black" that came out of the Indian's mouth became blood in one reconstruction and condensed air in another. For one individual, the two young men were hunting beavers rather than seals. Another person said the death at the end was due to a fever (this wasn't in the story).

    We have schemas for all sorts of information. If you tell a story to your class, such as the "War of the Ghosts" or virtually any other story, and then ask the students to write down what the story was about, you likely will get many different versions. That is, your students won't remember every detail of the story you told and will reconstruct the story

network theories Theories that describe how information in memory is organized and connected; they emphasize nodes in the memory network.

schema theories Theories that when we construct information, we fit it into information that already exists in our mind.

schema Information—concepts, knowledge, information about events—that already exists in a person's mind.

One night two young men from Egulac went down to the river to hunt seals, and while they were there it became foggy and calm. Then they heard war cries, and they thought: "Maybe this is a war party." They escaped to the shore, and hid behind a log. Now canoes came up, and they heard the noise of paddles, and saw one canoe coming up to them. There were five men in the canoe, and they said:

"What do you think? We wish to take you along. We are going up the river to make war on the people."

One of the young men said: "I have no arrows."

"Arrows are in the canoe," they said.
"I will not go along, I might be killed. My relatives do not know where I have gone. But you," he said, turning to the other, "may go with them."

So one of the young men went, but the other returned home.

And the warriors went up the river to a town on the other side of Kalama. The people came down to the water, and they began to fight, and many were killed. But presently the young man heard one of the warriors say: "Quick, let us go home: that Indian has been hit." Now he thought: "Oh, they are ghosts." He did not feel sick, but they said he had been shot.

So the canoes went back to Egulac and the young man went ashore to his house, and made a fire. And he told everybody and said: "Behold I accompanied the ghosts, and we went to fight. Many of our fellows were killed, and many of those who attacked us were killed. They said I was hit, and I did not feel sick."

He told it all, and then he became quiet. When the sun rose he fell down. Something black came out of his mouth. His face became contorted. The people jumped up and cried.

He was dead.

FIGURE 8.9 The War of the Ghosts
When Sir Frederick Bartlett (1932) asked individuals to recall this story, they changed its details.

with their own particular stamp on it. Suppose you tell your class a story about two men and two women who were involved in a train crash in France. One student might reconstruct the story by saying they died in a plane crash, another might describe three men and three women, another might say the crash was in Germany, and so on. The reconstruction and distortion of memory is nowhere more apparent than in the memories given by people involved in a trial. In criminal court trials such as that of O. J. Simpson, the variations in people's memories of what happened underscores how we reconstruct the past rather than take an exact photograph of it.

In sum, schema theory accurately predicts that people don't always coldly store and retrieve bits of data in a computer-like fashion (Chen & Mo, 2004; Schacter, 2001). The mind can distort an event as it encodes and stores impressions of reality.

A **script** is a schema for an event. Scripts often have information about physical features, people, and typical occurrences. This kind of information is helpful when teachers and students need to figure out what is happening around them. In a script for an art activity, students likely will remember that you will instruct them on what to draw, that they are supposed to put on smocks over their clothes, that they must get the art paper and paints from the cupboard, that they are to clean the brushes when they are finished, and so on. For example, a student who comes in late to the art activity likely knows much of what to do because he has an art activity script.

Video Lecture: Schema

Retrieval and Forgetting

After students have encoded information and then represented it in memory, they might be able to retrieve some of it but might also forget some of it.

Retrieval   When we retrieve something from our mental "data bank," we search our store of memory to find the relevant information. Just as with encoding, this search can be automatic or it can require effort. For example, if you ask your students what month it is, the answer might immediately spring to their lips. That is, the retrieval may be automatic. But if you ask your students to name the guest speaker who came to the class two months earlier, the retrieval process likely will require more effort.

script A schema for an event.

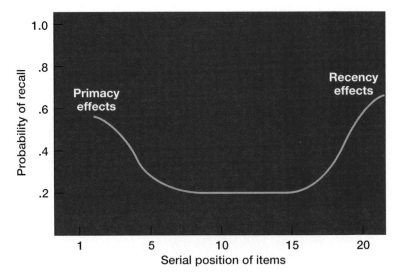

FIGURE 8.10 **Serial Position Effect**
When a person is asked to memorize a list of words, the words memorized last usually are re-called best, those at the beginning next best, and those in the middle least efficiently.

An item's position on a list also affects how easy or difficult it will be to remember it. In the **serial position effect**, recall is better for items at the beginning and end of a list than for items in the middle. Suppose that when you give a student directions about where to go to get tutoring help, you say, "Left on Mockingbird, right on Central, left on Balboa, left on Sandstone, and right on Parkside." The student likely will remember "Left on Mockingbird" and "Right on Parkside" better than "Left on Balboa." The *primacy effect* is that items at the beginning of a list tend to be remembered. The *recency effect* is that items at the end of the list also tend to be remembered.

Figure 8.10 shows a typical serial position effect with a slightly stronger recency effect than primacy effect. The serial position effect applies not only to lists but also to events. If you spread out a lesson on history over a week and then ask students about it the following Monday, they likely will have the best memory for what you told them on Friday of last week and the worst memory for what you told them on Wednesday of last week.

Another factor that affects retrieval is the nature of the cues people use to prompt their memory (Allan & others, 2001). Students can learn to create effective cues. For example, if a student has a "block" about remembering the name of the guest who came to class two months ago, she might go through the alphabet, generating names with each letter. If she manages to stumble across the right name, she likely will recognize it.

Another consideration in understanding retrieval is the **encoding specificity principle:** that associations formed at the time of encoding or learning tend to be effective retrieval cues (Hannon & Craik, 2001). For example, imagine that a thirteen-year-old child has encoded this information about Mother Teresa: She was born in Albania, lived most of her life in India, became a Roman Catholic nun, was saddened by seeing people sick and dying in Calcutta's streets, and won a Nobel Prize for her humanitarian efforts to help the poor and suffering. Words such as *Nobel Prize, Calcutta,* and *humanitarian* then can be used as retrieval cues when the child tries to remember Mother Teresa's name, what country she lived in, and her religion. The concept of encoding specificity is compatible with our earlier discussion of elaboration: The more elaboration children use in encoding information, the better their memory of the information will be. Encoding specificity and elaboration reveal how interdependent encoding and retrieval are.

serial position effect The principle that recall is better for items at the beginning and the end of a list than for items in the middle.

encoding specificity principle The principle that associations formed at the time of encoding or learning tend to be effective retrieval cues.

Yet another aspect of retrieval is the nature of the retrieval task itself (Nobel & Shiffrin, 2001). *Recall* is a memory task in which individuals must retrieve previously learned information, as students must do for fill-in-the-blank or essay questions. *Recognition* is a memory task in which individuals only have to identify ("recognize") learned information, as is often the case on multiple-choice tests. Many students prefer multiple-choice items because they provide good retrieval cues, which fill-in-the-blank and essay items don't do.

Forgetting   One form of forgetting involves the cues we just discussed. **Cue-dependent forgetting** is retrieval failure caused by a lack of effective retrieval cues (Nairne, 2000). The notion of cue-dependent forgetting can explain why a student might fail to retrieve a needed fact for an exam even when he is sure he "knows" the information (Williams & Zacks, 2001). For example, if you are studying for a test in this course and are asked a question about a distinction between recall and recognition in retrieval, you likely will remember the distinction better if you possess the cues "fill-in-the-blank" and "multiple-choice," respectively.

The principle of cue-dependent forgetting is consistent with **interference theory,** which states that we forget not because we actually lose memories from storage but, rather, because other information gets in the way of what we are trying to remember. For a student who studies for a biology test, then studies for a history test, and then takes the biology test, the information about history will interfere with remembering the information about biology. Thus, interference theory implies that a good study strategy is to study last what you are going to be tested on next if you have multiple courses to study for. That is, the student taking the biology test would have benefited from studying history first and studying biology afterward. This strategy also fits with the recency effect we described earlier. Take a moment and think about how your knowledge of interference theory can help you when you review for students what you plan to test next.

Another source of forgetting is memory decay. According to **decay theory,** new learning involves the creation of a neurochemical "memory trace," which will eventually disintegrate. Thus, decay theory suggests that the passage of time is responsible for forgetting. Leading memory researcher Daniel Schacter (2001) now refers to forgetting that occurs with the passage of time as *transience.*

Memories decay at different speeds. Some memories are vivid and last for long periods of time, especially when they have emotional ties. We can often remember these "flashbulb" memories with considerable accuracy and vivid imagery. For example, consider a car accident you were in or witnessed, the night of your high school graduation, an early romantic experience, and where you were when you heard about the destruction of the World Trade Center towers. Chances are, you will be able to retrieve this information many years after the event occurred.

Forgetting

Teaching Strategies
For Helping Students Improve
Their Memory

1. *Motivate children to remember material by understanding it rather than rotely memorizing it.* Children will remember information better over the long term if they understand the information rather than just rotely rehearse and memorize it. Rehearsal works well for encoding information into short-term memory, but when children need to retrieve the information from long-term memory it is much less efficient. For most information, encourage children to understand it, give it meaning, elaborate on it, and personalize it. Give children concepts and ideas to

cue-dependent forgetting Retrieval failure caused by a lack of effective retrieval cues.

interference theory The theory that we forget not because we actually lose memories from storage but because other information gets in the way of what we are trying to remember.

decay theory The theory that new learning involves the creation of a neurochemical "memory trace," which will eventually disintegrate. Thus, decay theory suggests that the passage of time is responsible for forgetting.

remember and then ask them how they can relate the concepts and ideas to their own personal experiences and meanings. Give them practice on elaborating a concept so they will process the information more deeply.

2. *Assist students in organizing what they put into their memory.* Children will remember information better if they organize it hierarchically. Give them some practice arranging and reworking material that requires some structuring.

3. *Teach mnemonic strategies.* *Mnemonics* are memory aids for remembering information. Mnemonic strategies can involve imagery and words. Here are some different types of mnemonics:

   • *Method of loci.* In the *method of loci*, children develop images of items to be remembered and mentally store them in familiar locations. Rooms of a house and stores on a street are common locations used in this memory strategy. For example, if children need to remember a list of concepts, they can mentally place them in the rooms of their house, such as entry foyer, living room, dining room, and kitchen. Then when they need to retrieve the information, they can imagine the house, mentally go through the rooms, and retrieve the concepts.

   • *Rhymes.* Examples of mnemonic rhymes are the spelling rule "*i* before *e* except after *c*," the month rule "Thirty days hath September, April, June, and November," the bolt-turning rule "Right is tight, left is loose," and the alphabet song.

   • *Acronyms.* This strategy involves creating a word from the first letters of items to be remembered. For example, *HOMES* can be used as a cue for remembering the five original Great Lakes: *Huron, Ontario, Michigan, Erie,* and *Superior.*

   • *Keyword method.* Another mnemonic strategy that involves imagery is the *keyword method*, in which vivid imagery is attached to important words. This method has been used to practical advantage in teaching students how to rapidly master new information such as foreign vocabulary words, the states and capitals of the United States, and the names of U.S. presidents. For example, in teaching children that Annapolis is the capital of Maryland, you could ask them to connect vivid images of Annapolis and Maryland, such as two apples getting married (Levin, 1980) (see figure 8.11).

Memory Tools

Some educators argue against teaching children to use mnemonics because they involve rote memorization. Clearly, as we said earlier, remembering for understanding is preferred over rote memorization. However, if children need to learn lists of concepts, mnemonic devices can do the trick. Think of mnemonic devices as a way for children to learn some specific facts that they might need to know to solve problems.

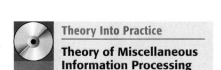

Theory Into Practice

Theory of Miscellaneous Information Processing

In their study of memory, researchers have not extensively examined the roles that sociocultural factors such as culture and gender might play in memory. In the Diversity and Education interlude, we will explore these topics.

Diversity and Education
Culture, Gender, and Memory

A culture sensitizes its members to certain objects, events, and strategies, which in turn can influence the nature of memory (Mistry & Rogoff, 1994). Cross-cultural studies especially find cultural differences in the use of organizational strategies (Schneider & Bjorklund, 1998). Failure to use appropriate organizational strategies to remember information is often related to a lack of appropriate schooling (Cole & Scribner, 1977). Children who have experienced schooling are more likely to cluster items together in

FIGURE 8.11 **The Keyword Method**
To help children remember the state capitals, the keyword method was used. A special component of the keyword method is the use of mental imagery, which was stimulated by presenting the children with a vivid visual image, such as two apples being married. The strategy is to help the children associate *apple* with Annapolis and *marry* with Maryland.

meaningful ways, which helps them to remember the items. Schooling presents children with specialized information-processing tasks—such as committing large amounts of information to memory in a short time and using logical reasoning—that may generate specialized memory strategies. There is no evidence that schooling increases memory capacity per se; rather, it influences the strategies for remembering (Cole & Cole, 2001).

Gender is another aspect of sociocultural diversity that has been given little attention in memory research until very recently (Burton & others, 2004). Researchers have found these gender differences in memory:

- Females are better than males at episodic memory, which is memory for personal events that include the time and place the event occurred (Anderson, 2001; Halpern, 2002). Females also appear to be better than males in emotionally linked memory, such as memory for an emotional film (Cahill & others, 2001).
- Males are better than females on tasks that require transformations in visual-spatial working memory (Halpern, 2002). These tasks include mental rotation, which involves the imagined motion of stationary objects (such as what a shape would look like if it were rotated in space).

On many memory tasks, though, researchers do not find gender differences, or when differences occur they are small.

Review and Reflect

2 Discuss memory in terms of encoding, storage, and retrieval.

Review
- What is memory? What is necessary for it to work?
- How are these six processes—attention, rehearsal, deep processing, elaboration, constructing images, and organization—involved in encoding?
- What are the three time frames of memory? How are long-term memory's contents described? How might they be represented in memory?
- What makes a memory easier or harder to retrieve? What are some theories about why we forget?

Reflect
- Which principles and strategies in our discussion of memory are likely to be useful for the subjects and grade levels at which you plan to teach?

EXPERTISE

Our ability to remember new information about a subject depends considerably on what we already know about it (Carver & Klahr, 2001; Chaffin & Imreh, 2002; Keil, 1999; Lesgold & Nahemow, 2001). For example, a student's ability to recount what she saw when she was at the library is largely governed by what she already knows about libraries, such as where books on certain topics are likely to be and how to check books out. If she knew little about libraries, the student would have a much harder time recounting what was there.

The contribution of prior content knowledge to our ability to remember new material is especially evident when we compare the memories of experts and novices in a particular knowledge domain. An expert is the opposite of a novice (someone who is just beginning to learn a content area). Experts demonstrate especially impressive memory in their areas of expertise. One reason that children remember less than adults is that they are far less expert in most areas.

How Experts Differ from Novices

Expertise and Learning

Studying the behavior and mental processes of experts can give us insights into how to guide students in becoming more effective learners. What is it, exactly, that experts do? According to the National Research Council (1999), they are better than novices at

1. Detecting features and meaningful patterns of information.
2. Accumulating more content knowledge and organizing it in a manner that shows an understanding of the topic.
3. Retrieving important aspects of knowledge with little effort
4. Adapting an approach to new situations.
5. Using effective strategies.

Meaningful Patterns of Organization   Experts have superior recall of information in their area of expertise. The process of chunking, which we discussed earlier, is one way they accomplish this superior recall. For example, "chess masters perceive chunks of meaningful information, which affects their memory of what they see. . . . Lacking a hierarchical, highly organized structure for the domain, novices cannot use this chunking strategy," (National Research Council, 1999, p. 21).

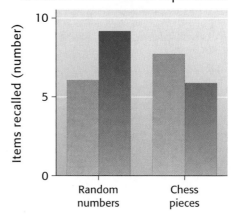

FIGURE 8.12   Memory for Numbers and Chess Pieces

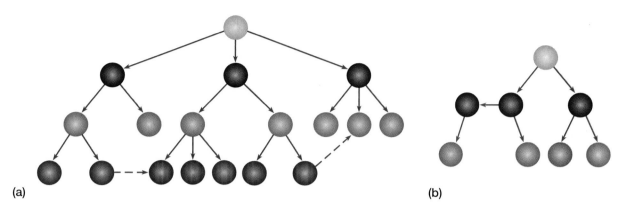

(a)   (b)

FIGURE 8.13 An Example of How Information Is Organized in the Mind of an Expert and a Novice

(a) An expert's knowledge is based on years of experience in which small bits of information have been linked with many other small pieces, which together are placed in a more general category. This category is in turn placed in an even more general category of knowledge. The dotted lines are used as pointers, associations between specific elements of knowledge that connect the lower branches and provide mental shortcuts in the expert's mind. *(b)* The novice's knowledge shows far fewer connections, shortcuts, and levels than an expert's knowledge.

In areas where children are experts, their memory is often extremely good. In fact, it often exceeds that of adults who are novices in that content area. This was documented in a study of ten-year-old chess experts (Chi, 1978). These children were excellent chess players, but not especially brilliant in other ways. As with most ten-year-olds, their memory spans for digits were shorter than an adult's. However, when they were presented chessboards, they remembered the configurations far better than did the adults who were novices at chess (see figure 8.12).

Expert teachers recognize features and patterns that are not noticed by novice teachers (National Research Council, 1999, pp. 21, 25). For example, in one study, expert and novice teachers had a very different understanding of the events in a videotaped classroom lesson, in which three screens showed simultaneous events taking place throughout the classroom (left, center, and right areas) (Sabers, Cushing, & Berliner, 1991). For example, one expert teacher said, "On the left monitor, the students' note taking indicates that they have seen sheets like this before; it's fairly efficient at this point because they're used to the format they are using." One novice teacher sparsely responded, "It's a lot to watch."

Organization and Depth of Knowledge   Experts' knowledge is organized around important ideas or concepts more than novices' knowledge is (National Research Council, 1999). This provides experts with a much deeper understanding of knowledge than novices (Simon, 2001; Voss & others, 1984).

Experts in a particular area usually have far more elaborate networks of information about that area than novices do (see figure 8.13). The information they represent in memory has more nodes, more interconnections, and better hierarchical organization.

The implications for teaching are that too often a curriculum is designed in a way that makes it difficult for students to organize knowledge in meaningful ways. This especially occurs when there is only superficial coverage of facts before moving on to the next topic. In this context, students have little time to explore the topic in depth and get a sense of what the important, organizing ideas are. This type of shallow presentation can occur in any subject area but is common in history and science texts that emphasize facts (National Research Council, 1999).

Fluent Retrieval   Retrieval of relevant information can range from taking a lot of effort to being fluent and almost effortless (National Research Council, 1999). Experts retrieve information in an almost effortless, automatic manner, while novices expend a great deal of effort in retrieving information (Chaffin & Imreh, 2002). However, just because they can retrieve information rather effortlessly does not mean that experts always perform tasks faster than novices. In many cases, experts reflect on the information they have retrieved and take the necessary time to formulate a plan to competently perform a task.

Effortless retrieval is important because it places fewer demands on conscious attention. Since the amount of information a student can attend to at one time is limited, ease of processing information in some aspects of a task frees up capacity to attend to other aspects of a task.

Consider expert and novice readers. Expert readers can quickly scan the words of a sentence and paragraph, which allows them to devote attention to understanding what they are reading. However, novice readers' ability to decode words is not yet fluent, so they have to allocate considerable attention and time to this task, which restricts the time they can give to understanding a passage. An important aspect of teaching is to help students develop the fluency they need to competently perform cognitive tasks (Beck & others, 1991).

Adaptive Expertise   An important aspect of expertise "is whether some ways of organizing knowledge are better" than others for helping people to be "flexible and adaptive to new situations than others" (National Research Council, 1999, p. 33). Adaptive experts are able to approach new situations flexibly rather than always responding in a rigid, fixed routine (Hatano, 1990; Hatano & Oura, 2003).

Strategies   Experts use effective strategies in understanding the information in their area of expertise and in advancing it. Earlier in the chapter we described a number of strategies that students can use to remember information. Let's now explore some effective strategies that students can develop to become experts at learning and studying.

Patricia Alexander (2003) uses the label *acclimation* to describe the initial stage of expertise in a particular domain (such as English, biology, or mathematics). At this stage, students have limited and fragmented knowledge that restricts their ability to detect the difference between accurate and inaccurate and relevant and tangential information. To help students move beyond the acclimation stage, teachers need to guide students in determining what content is central and what is peripheral, as well as what is accurate and well supported and what is inaccurate and unsupported. In Alexander's (2003) view, students don't come to the classroom equipped with the strategies they need to move beyond the acclimation stage. Teachers must help students learn effective strategies and practice them in relevant situations to let students experience their value. Students also need to be encouraged to change and combine strategies to solve the problem at hand.

Barbara Moely and her colleagues (Moely, Santulli, & Obach, 1995) found considerable variation in whether teachers helped children to improve their learning strategies. Some teachers did try to help students with their strategies, but overall there was little instruction in strategies, across a broad range of activities. Strategies were most likely to be taught in math and problem solving. An important educational goal for the teacher is to incorporate more strategy instruction in the classroom. It is not enough just to teach students content knowledge. The following are some good ideas for helping children improve their learning and study strategies.

Spreading Out and Consolidating Learning   Students' learning benefits when teachers talk with them about the importance of regularly reviewing what they learn. Children who have to prepare for a test will benefit from distributing their learning over a longer period rather than cramming for the test at the last minute. Cramming tends to produce short-term memory that is processed in a shallow rather than deep manner. A final, concentrated tune-up before the test is better than trying to learn everything at the last minute.

Asking Themselves Questions   When children ask themselves questions about what they have read about or an activity, they expand the number of associations with the information they need to retrieve. At least as early as the middle of elementary school, the self-questioning strategy can help children to remember. For example, as children read, they can be encouraged to stop periodically and ask themselves questions such as "What is the meaning of what I just read?" "Why is this important?" and "What is an example of the concept I just read?" Students can use the same self-questioning strategy when they listen to you conduct a lesson, hear a guest give a talk, or watch a video. If you periodically remind children to generate questions about their experiences, they are more likely to remember the experiences.

Taking Good Notes   Taking good notes from either a lecture or a text benefits learning (Kiewra, 1989). When children are left to take notes without being given any strategies, they tend to take notes that are brief and disorganized. When they do write something down, it often is a verbatim record of what they have just heard. Give children some practice in taking notes and then evaluate their note taking. Encourage children not to write down everything they hear when they take notes. It is impossible to do this, anyway, and it can prevent them from getting the big picture of what the speaker is saying. Here are some good note-taking strategies:

Study Skills

- *Summarizing.* One note-taking strategy that you can help children practice is the summary method of listening for a few minutes and then writing down the main idea that a speaker is trying to get across in that time frame. Then the child listens for several more minutes and writes down another idea, and so on.
- *Outlining.* Another note-taking strategy you can get children to practice is outlining what the speaker is saying. An outline is similar to the organization of the chapters in this book, with first-level heads being the main topics, second-level heads as subtopics under the first-level heads, and third-level heads under the second-level heads. Keep in mind that it is not enough to just tell children to "outline"—you will have to show them how.
- *Concept maps.* Yet another strategy is to get children to practice drawing concept maps. Concept maps are similar to outlines but visually portray information in a more spiderlike format. We will further explore concept maps in chapter 9.

All three note-taking strategies described so far—summarizing, outlining, and concept maps—help children evaluate which ideas are the most important to remember. Outlining and concept maps also help children arrange the material hierarchically, which underscores an important theme of learning: It works best when it is organized.

What are some good study strategies?

Using a Study System Various systems have been developed to help people to remember information that they are studying from a book. One of the earliest systems was called *SQ3R*, which stands for *Survey, Question, Read, Recite,* and *Review*. A more recently developed system is called *PQ4R*, which stands for *Preview, Question, Read, Reflect, Recite,* and *Review*. Thus, the PQ4R system adds an additional step, "Reflect," to the SQ3R system. From the later elementary school years on, students will benefit from practicing the PQ4R system (Adams, Carnine, & Gersten, 1982). The system benefits students by getting them to meaningfully organize information, ask questions about it, reflect on it, and review it. Here are more details about the steps in the PQ4R system:

- *Preview.* Tell your students to briefly survey the material to get a sense of the overall organization of ideas. Tell them to be sure to look at the headings to see the main topics and subtopics that will be covered.
- *Question.* Encourage the children to ask themselves questions about the material as they read it. Earlier in our description of memory and study strategies we highlighted the importance of readers generating questions for themselves.
- *Read.* Now tell the children to read the material. Encourage your students to be active readers. This involves getting them to immerse themselves in what they are reading and striving to understand what the author is saying. This helps students to avoid being empty readers whose eyes just track the lines of text but whose minds fail to register anything important.
- *Reflect.* By occasionally stopping and reflecting on the material, students increase its meaningfulness. Encourage the children to be analytic at this point in studying. After they have read something, challenge them to break open the ideas and scratch beneath their surface. This is a good time for them to think out applications and interpretations of the information, as well as connecting it with other information already in their long-term memory.
- *Recite.* This involves children self-testing themselves to see if they can remember the material and reconstruct it. At this point, encourage the children to make up a series of questions about the material and then try to answer them.
- *Review.* Tell your students to go over the material and evaluate what they know and don't know. At this point they should reread and study the material they don't remember or understand well.

We will further explore strategies later in the chapter in our discussion of metacognition. To evaluate the extent to which you use good memory and study strategies, complete Self-Assessment 8.1.

Acquiring Expertise

What determines whether or not someone becomes an expert? Can motivation and practice get someone to expert status? Or does expertise also require a great deal of talent (Sternberg & Ben-Zeev, 2001)?

Practice and Motivation One perspective is that a particular kind of practice—*deliberate practice*—is required to become an expert (Hatano & Oura, 2003). Deliberate practice involves practice that is at an appropriate level of difficulty for the individual, provides corrective feedback, and allows opportunities for repetition (Ericsson, 1996).

In one study of violinists at a music academy, the extent to which children engaged in deliberate practice distinguished novices and experts (Ericsson, Krampe, & Tesch-Romer, 1993). The top violinists averaged 7,500 hours of deliberate practice by age eighteen, the good violinists only 5,300 hours. Many individuals give up on becoming an expert because they won't put forth the effort it takes to engage in extensive deliberate practice over a number of years.

Such extensive practice requires considerable motivation. Students who are not motivated to practice long hours are unlikely to become experts in a particular area. Thus, a

How Effective Are My Memory and Study Strategies?

Teachers who themselves practice using good memory and study strategies are more likely to model and communicate these to their students than teachers who don't use such strategies. Candidly respond to these items about your own memory and study strategies. Rate yourself on this scale: 1 = never, 2 = some, 3 = moderate, 4 = almost always, or 5 = always. Then total your points.

	1	2	3	4	5
1. I'm a good time manager and planner.					
2. I'm good at focusing my attention and minimizing distractions.					
3. I try to understand material rather than rotely memorizing it.					
4. I ask myself questions about what I have read or about class activities.					
5. I take good notes in class and from textbooks.					
6. I regularly review my notes.					
7. I use mnemonic strategies.					
8. I'm very organized in the way I encode information.					
9. I spread out my studying to consolidate my learning.					
10. I use good retrieval cues.					
11. I use the PQ4R method or a similar study method.					
Total					

Scoring and Interpretation

If you scored 50–55 total points, you likely use good memory and study strategies. If you scored 45–49 points, you likely have some reasonably good memory and study strategies. If you scored below 45, spend some time working on improving your memory and study strategies.

If you would like to learn more about effective memory and study strategies, one resource is a book called *Your Guide to College Success* (Santrock & Halonen, 2002). Also, to gain more experience in developing good memory and study strategies, contact the study skills center at your college or university; specialists there likely will be able to help you.

 Go to your Student Toolbox CD-ROM for an electronic version of this form.

student who complains about all of the work, doesn't persevere, and doesn't extensively practice solving math problems over a number years is not going to become an expert in math.

Talent   A number of psychologists who study expertise believe that it requires not only deliberate practice and motivation but also talent (Bloom, 1985; Shiffrin, 1996; Sternberg & Ben-Zeev, 2001).

A number of abilities—music and athletic, for example—seem to have a heritable component (Plomin, 1997). For example, is it likely that Mozart could have become such an outstanding musical composer just because he practiced long hours? Is it likely that Tiger Woods became such a fantastic golfer just because he was motivated to do so? Many talented individuals have attempted to become as great as Mozart or Woods but have given up trying after only mediocre performances. Clearly, heredity matters. Nonetheless, Mozart and Woods would not have developed expertise in their fields without being highly motivated and engaging in extensive deliberate practice. Talent alone does not make an expert.

An expert teacher monitoring a student's learning. *What are some characteristics of expert teachers?*

Expertise and Teaching

Being an expert in a particular domain—such as physics, history, or math—does not mean that the expert is good at helping others learn it. Indeed, "expertise can sometimes hurt teaching because many experts forget what is easy and what is difficult for students." (National Research Council, 1999, p. 32).

Some educators have distinguished between the content knowledge required for expertise and the pedagogical content knowledge necessary to effectively teach it (Shulman, 1987). *Pedagogical content knowledge* includes ideas about common difficulties that students have as they try to learn a content area; typical paths students must take to understand the area; and strategies for helping students overcome the difficulties they experience.

Expert teachers are good at monitoring students' learning and assessing students' progress. They also know what types of difficulties students are likely to encounter, are aware of students' existing knowledge, and use this awareness to teach at the right level and to make new information meaningful. Some educational psychologists argue that in the absence of expert pedagogical awareness of their own students, inexpert teachers simply rely on textbook publishers' materials, which, of course, contain no information about the particular pedagogical needs of students in the teacher's classroom (Brophy, 2004). To read further about expertise, see the Technology and Education box.

❗ Review and Reflect

3 **Draw some lessons about learning from the way experts think.**

Review
- What do experts do that novices often don't do in the process of learning?
- What does it take to become an expert?
- Is subject experience enough to make a good teacher? What else is needed?

Reflect
- Choose an area in which you feel at least somewhat of an expert. Compare your ability to learn in that field with the ability of a novice.

Experts and Technology

As described by the National Research Council (1999), experts in many fields are using new technologies to represent information in new ways. For example, three-dimensional models of the surface of Venus or of a molecular structure can be electronically created and viewed from any angle.

One of the characteristics of expertise we have discussed involves organizing knowledge meaningfully around important ideas. The Belvedere computer technology system is designed to help students who lack a deep understanding of many areas of science, have difficulty zeroing in on the key issues in a scientific debate, and have trouble recognizing connections of ideas in scientific theories (Suthers & others, 1995). Belvedere uses graphics with specialized boxes to represent connections of ideas in an effort to support students' reasoning about scientific issues. An online advisor gives students hints to help them improve their understanding and reasoning.

The Belvedere system can also help students in nonscientific studies such as analyzing social policies. This system helps students by (1) giving arguments a concrete, diagram-like form and providing tools for focusing on particular problems encountered in the construction and evaluation of complex arguments; (2) providing access to online information resources; and (3) supporting students working in small groups to construct documents to be shared with others.

METACOGNITION

As you read earlier in this chapter, metacognition is cognition about cognition, or "knowing about knowing" (Flavell, 1999; Flavell, Miller, & Miller, 2002) ◀ p. 248. A distinction can be made between metacognitive knowledge and metacognitive activity (Ferrari & Sternberg, 1998). *Metacognitive knowledge* involves monitoring and reflecting on one's current or recent thoughts. This includes both factual knowledge, such as knowledge about the task, one's goals, or oneself, and strategic knowledge, such as how and when to use specific procedures to solve problems. *Metacognitive activity* occurs when students consciously adapt and manage their thinking strategies during problem solving and purposeful thinking (Ferrari & Sternberg, 1998; Kuhn & others, 1995). Thus, a student's awareness and use of the self-regulatory learning strategies discussed in chapter 7, "Behavioral and Social Cognitive Approaches," involve metacognition ◀ p. 236.

Metacognitive skills have been taught to students to help them solve math problems (Cardelle-Elawar, 1992). In each of thirty daily lessons involving math story problems, a teacher guided low-achieving students in learning to recognize when they did not know the meaning of a word, did not have all of the information necessary to solve a problem, did not know how to subdivide the problem into specific steps, or did not know how to carry out a computation. After the thirty daily lessons, the students who were given this metacognitive training had better math achievement and better attitudes toward math.

One expert on children's thinking, Deanna Kuhn (1999a, 1999b), believes that metacognition should be a stronger focus of efforts to help children become better critical thinkers, especially at the middle school and high school levels. She distinguishes between first-order cognitive skills, which enable children to know about the world (and have been the main focus of critical thinking programs), and second-order cognitive skills—metaknowing skills—which involve knowing about one's own (and others') knowing.

Metacognition Links
Development of Metacognition

Video Lecture: Metacognition

Developmental Changes

Many developmental studies classified as "metacognitive" have focused on metamemory, or knowledge about memory. This includes general knowledge about memory, such as knowing that recognition tests are easier than recall tests. It also encompasses knowledge about one's own memory, such as a student's ability to monitor whether she has studied enough for a test that is coming up next week.

By five or six years of age, children usually know that familiar items are easier to learn than unfamiliar ones, that short lists are easier than long ones, that recognition is easier than recall, and that forgetting is more likely to occur over time (Lyon & Flavell, 1993). However, in other ways young children's metamemory is limited. They don't understand that related items are easier to remember than unrelated ones and that remembering the gist of a story is easier than remembering information verbatim (Kretuzer & Flavell, 1975). By fifth grade, students understand that gist recall is easier than verbatim recall. Young children also have an inflated opinion of their memory abilities. For example, in one study, a majority of young children predicted that they would be able to recall all ten items of a list of ten items. When tested for this, none of the young children managed this feat (Flavell, Friedrichs, & Hoyt, 1970). As they move through the elementary school years, children give more realistic evaluations of their memory skills (Schneider & Pressley, 1997).

Young children also have little appreciation for the importance of "cognitive cueing" for memory. Cognitive cueing involves being reminded of something by an external cue or phrase, such as "Don't you remember, it helps you to learn a concept when you can think of an example of it." By seven or eight years of age, children better appreciate the importance of such cognitive cueing for memory.

The Good Information-Processing Model

Michael Pressley and his colleagues (Pressley, Borkowski, & Schneider, 1989; Schneider & Pressley, 1997) have developed a metacognitive model called the Good Information-Processing model. It emphasizes that competent cognition results from a number of interacting factors. These include strategies, content knowledge, motivation, and metacognition. They believe that children become good at cognition in three main steps:

1. Children are taught by parents or teachers to use a particular strategy. With practice, they learn about its characteristics and advantages for learning *specific knowledge.* The more intellectually stimulating children's homes and schools are, the more specific strategies they will encounter and learn to use.
2. Teachers may demonstrate similarities and differences in multiple strategies in a particular domain, such as math, which motivates students to see shared features of different strategies. This leads to better *relational knowledge.*
3. At this point, students recognize the general benefits of using strategies, which produces *general strategy knowledge.* They learn to attribute successful learning outcomes to the efforts they make in evaluating, selecting, and monitoring strategy use *(metacognitive knowledge and activity).*

Strategies and Metacognitive Regulation

In Pressley's (McCormick & Pressley, 1997; Pressley, 1983) view, the key to education is helping students learn a rich repertoire of strategies that results in solutions of problems. Good thinkers routinely use strategies and effective planning to solve problems. Good thinkers also know when and where to use strategies (metacognitive knowledge about strategies). Understanding when and where to use strategies often results from the learner's monitoring of the learning situation.

Pressley argues that when students are given instruction about effective strategies, they often can apply strategies that they previously have not used on their own. He emphasizes that students benefit when the teacher models the appropriate strategy and overtly verbalizes its steps. Then, students subsequently practice the strategy, guided and supported by the teacher's feedback until the students can use it autonomously. When instructing students about employing a strategy, it also is a good idea to explain to them how using the strategy will benefit them. However, there are some developmental limitations to this approach. For instance, young children often cannot use mental imagery competently.

Just having students practice the new strategy is usually not enough for them to continue to use the strategy and transfer it to new situations. For effective maintenance and transfer, encourage students to monitor the effectiveness of the new strategy relative to their use of old strategies by comparing their performance on tests and other assessments. Pressley says that it is not enough to say, "Try it, you will like it"; you need to say, "Try it and compare."

Learning how to use strategies effectively often takes time. Initially, it takes time to learn to execute the strategies, and it requires guidance and support from the teacher. With practice, students learn to execute strategies faster and more competently. "Practice" means that students use the effective strategy over and over again until they perform it automatically. To execute the strategies effectively, they need to have the strategies in long-term memory, and extensive practice makes this possible. Learners also need to be motivated to use the strategies. Thus, an important implication for helping students develop strategies such as organization is that once a strategy is learned, students usually need more time before they can use them efficiently (Schneider, 2004). Further, it is important for teachers to be aware that students may drop an effective strategy or continue to use a strategy that does not help them (Miller, 2000).

Let's examine an example of how strategy instruction can be effective. Good readers extract the main ideas from text and summarize them. In contrast, novice readers (for example, most children) usually don't store the main ideas of what they read. One intervention based on what is known about the summarization strategies of good readers consisted of instructing children to (1) skim over trivial information, (2) spend time on information that is repeated, (3) replace less-inclusive terms with more-inclusive ones, (4) combine a series of events with a more-inclusive action term, (5) choose a topic sentence, and (6) create a topic sentence if there is none present (Brown & Day, 1983). Researchers have found that instructing elementary school students to use these summarization strategies benefits their reading performance (Rinehart, Stahl, & Erickson, 1986).

Do children use one strategy or multiple strategies in memory and problem solving? They often use more than one strategy (Schneider & Bjorklund, 1998; Siegler, 1998). Most children benefit from generating a variety of alternative strategies and experimenting with different approaches to a problem and discovering what works well, when, and where (Schneider & Bjorklund, 1998). This is especially true for children from the middle elementary school grades on, although some cognitive psychologists believe that even young children should be encouraged to practice varying strategies (Siegler, 1998).

 ## Teaching Strategies
For Helping Students Use Metacognition

---

1. *Recognize that strategies are a key aspect of solving problems.* Monitor students' knowledge and awareness of strategies for effective learning outcomes. Many students do not use good strategies and are unaware that strategies can help them learn.
2. *Model effective strategies for students.*
3. *Give students many opportunities to practice the strategies.* As students practice the strategies, provide guidance and support to the students. Give them feedback until they can use the strategies independently. As part of your feedback, inform them about where and when the strategies are most useful.
4. *Encourage students to monitor the effectiveness of their new strategy in comparison to the effectiveness of old strategies.* This helps students to see the utility of using the new strategy.

ENTER THE DEBATE

1. Should teachers require students to engage in role memorization?

2. Should teachers rely on "eye witness testimony" to happenings, such as a fight, to ascertain what happened?

3. Should teachers teach study skills?

Video Observation: Information Processing

5. *Remember that it takes students a considerable amount of time to learn how to use an effective strategy.* Be patient and give students continued support during this tedious learning experience. Keep encouraging students to use the strategy over and over again until they can use it automatically.

6. *Understand that students need to be motivated to use the strategies.* Students are not always going to be motivated to use the strategies. Especially important to students' motivation is their expectations that the strategies will lead to successful learning outcomes. It can also help if students set goals for learning effective strategies. And when students attribute their learning outcomes to the effort they put forth, their learning benefits. We will have much more to say about motivation in chapter 13, "Motivation, Teaching, and Learning."

7. *Encourage children to use multiple strategies.* Most children benefit from experimenting with multiple strategies, finding out what works well, when, and where.

8. *Read more about strategy instruction.* A good place to start is the text *Educational Psychology,* by Christine McCormick and Michael Pressley (1997), which includes extensive ideas about how to improve children's use of strategies.

Review and Reflect

4 **Explain the concept of metacognition and identify some ways to improve children's metacognition.**

Review
- What is metacognition?
- How do young children compare with older children in their metacognitive abilities?
- By what three steps might children arrive at Pressley's Good Information-Processing Model?
- How can children be helped to learn metacognitive strategies and self-regulation?

Reflect
- How might the three steps in the Good Information-Processing Model be part of teaching a topic to children? Select a topic that you might teach one day and try working through it as an example.

George has a test next week in his eighth-grade history class. He is having considerable difficulty remembering terms, names, and facts. On his last test, he identified General Sherman as a Vietnam War hero and Saigon as the capital of Japan. Historical dates are so confusing to him that he does not even try to remember them. In addition, George has difficulty spelling.

The test will consist of fifty objective test items (multiple-choice, true/false, and fill-in-the-blank) and two essay items. In general, George does better on essay items. He purposely leaves out any names about which he is uncertain and always omits dates. Sometimes he mixes up his facts, though, and often loses points for misspelled words. On objective items he has real problems. Usually, more than one answer will appear to be correct to him. Often he is "sure" he is correct, only to discover later that he was mistaken.

Before the last test, George tried to design some mnemonic devices to help him understand. He used acronyms, such as *HOMES* (for *H*uron, *O*ntario, *M*ichigan, *E*rie, and *S*uperior). While he remembered his acronyms quite well, he could not recall what each letter stood for. The result was a test paper filled with acronyms. Another time a classmate suggested that George try using concept maps. This classmate lent George the concept maps she had designed for her own use. George looked at them and found them to be very busy and confusing—he couldn't figure out what they even meant. They were not at all useful to him.

George has decided he is in need of some serious help if he is to pass this class. He has sought you out for his help.

- What are the issues in this case?
- With what type of learning is George having difficulty?
- What type of learning is easier for George?
- Design a study-skills program for George drawing on principles of the cognitive information-processing approach.

Reach your Learning Goals

1 Describe the information-processing approach.

- The information-processing approach emphasizes that children manipulate information, monitor it, and strategize about it. Central to this approach are the processes of memory and thinking. The development of computers stimulated interest in cognitive psychology.

- In Siegler's view, the key characteristics of the information-processing approach are thinking, change mechanisms (encoding, automatization, strategy construction, and generalization), and self-modification (which includes metacognition).

2 Discuss memory in terms of encoding, storage, and retrieval.

- Memory is the retention of information over time and involves encoding, storage, and retrieval.

- In everyday language, encoding has much to do with attention and learning. Rehearsal, deep processing, elaboration, constructing images, and organization are other processes involved in encoding. One way that memory varies involves its time frames: sensory memory, short-term memory, and long-term memory. There is increasing interest in working memory, a kind of mental workbench. The Atkinson-Shiffrin model states that memory involves a sequence of three stages: sensory, short-term, and long-term memory. Long-term memory includes different types of content. Many cognitive psychologists accept this hierarchy of long-term memory's contents: division into declarative and procedural memory subtypes, with declarative memory further subdivided into episodic and semantic memory. Declarative memory (explicit memory) is the conscious recollection of information, such as specific facts or events. Procedural memory (implicit memory) is knowledge of skills and cognitive operations about how to do something; it is hard to communicate verbally. Episodic memory is the retention of information about the where and when of life's happenings; semantic memory is a general knowledge about the world.

- Two major approaches to how information is represented are network theories (which focus on how information is organized and connected, with emphasis on nodes in the memory network) and schema theories (which stress that students often reconstruct information and fit it into an existing schema). A script is a schema for an event.

- Retrieval is influenced by the serial position effect (memory is better for items at the beginning and end of a list than for items in the middle), the effectiveness retrieval cues, encoding specificity, and the memory task (such as recall versus recognition). Forgetting can be explained in terms of cue-dependent forgetting (failure to use effective retrieval cues), interference theory (because information gets in the way of what we are trying to remember), and decay (losing information over time).

3 Draw some lessons about learning from the way experts think.

- Five important characteristics of experts are that they (1) notice features and meaningful patterns of information that novices don't, (2) have acquired a great deal of content knowledge that is organized in a manner that reflects deep understanding of the subject, (3) can retrieve important aspects of their knowledge with little effort, (4) are adaptive in their approach to new situations, and (5) use effective strategies.

- Becoming an expert usually requires deliberate practice, motivation, and talent.

- Being an expert in a particular area does not mean that the expert is good at helping others learn it. Pedagogical content knowledge is required to effectively teach a subject.

4 Explain the concept of metacognition and identify some ways to improve children's metacognition.

- Metacognition is cognition about cognition, or "knowing about knowing." Metacognition involves both metacognitive knowledge and metacognitive activity.

- Many metacognitive studies have focused on metamemory, or what students know about how memory works. Children's metamemory improves considerably through the elementary school years.

- Pressley and his colleagues proposed a three-part Good Information-Processing Model, which highlights the importance of developing effective strategies.

- In Pressley's view, the key to education is helping students learn a rich repertoire of strategies that result in solutions to problems. Most children benefit from using multiple strategies and exploring which ones work well, when, and where.

 ## KEY TERMS

PORTFOLIO ACTIVITIES

Now that you have a good understanding of this chapter, complete these exercises to expand your thinking.

Independent Reflection

Developing Expert Knowledge. Think about the experts you know. Are your parents or instructors considered experts in their fields? How do you think they came to become experts and how long did it take? Based on what you know about how experts process information, which strategies do you think these experts use to organize, remember, and utilize their knowledge and skills? (INTASC: Principles 2, 4, 9)

Collaborative Work

Strategies to Enhance Memory. Get together with 3 or 4 other students in the class and brainstorm about the best ways to guide students in developing better memory and study strategies. Discuss how you might do this differently for children and adoles-

cents at different grade levels. For example, at what age should students start learning effective note-taking strategies? For children too young to be taking elaborate notes, are there gamelike activities that might help them begin to learn the concept and value of taking notes or keeping running records of some event? Write your conclusions below. (INTASC: Principles 2, 4)

Research/Field Experience Reflections

Capturing Students' Attention. Observe a kindergarten, elementary, middle school, and high school classroom and focus on how the teacher maintains students' attention. How effective are each teacher's strategies? Would you do things differently to capture the students' attention? (INTASC: Principles 2, 9)

 Go to the Online Learning Center for downloadable portfolio templates.

TAKING IT TO THE NET

1. Information-processing theorists emphasize that learning results from interaction between the environment and the learner's prior knowledge. Describe teaching techniques that help students connect new information with previous experiences and learning. Why are these connections so critical for learning to occur?

2. Take a moment to reflect upon your own study strategies, and describe your typical study routine. In relation to memory research, how could you improve your study techniques? Design a classroom activity that you could use to help students develop effective study skills.

3. Teaching students metacognitive skills can have a wide-reaching impact on many aspects of a classroom environment. Describe some teaching strategies for developing metacognitive student behaviors. Would you expect metacognitive students to generally exhibit more positive behaviors? Please explain.

Connect to the Online Learning Center to explore possible answers.

STUDY, PRACTICE, AND SUCCEED

 Go to chapter 8 on the Online Learning Center at www.mhhe.com/santrockedu2e to access the student study guide with practice quizzes, web links, portfolio resources, PowerWeb articles and news feeds, and the online resources referenced in the chapter.

 Go to your Student Toolbox CD-ROM to access the resources and activities referenced in the chapter and

- Resources to help you prepare for the PRAXIS II™ exam

- **Application Resources,** including additional *Crack the Case* studies, electronic versions of the *Self-Assessments,* Application Exercises, and Site Observation Questions
- **Study Resources,** including Learning Goals, the Chapter Summary, a *Test Your Learning* exercise, and multiple-choice, true/false, matching, key terms, and short-answer quizzes
- **Professional Resources,** including a Lesson Plan Builder and *Bibliomaker*

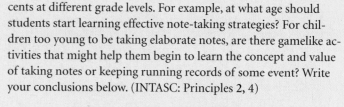

9 Complex Cognitive Processes

I think, therefore I am.
—Rene Descartes
*French Philosopher
and Mathematician,
17th Century*

Chapter Learning Goals After you have completed your study of this chapter, you should be able to reach these learning goals:

1 **Discuss conceptual understanding and strategies for teaching concepts.**

2 **Describe several types of thinking and how teachers can foster them.**

3 **Take a systematic approach to problem solving.**

4 **Explain transfer and how to enhance it as a teacher.**

Teaching Stories Marilyn Whirry

Marilyn Whirry is a twelfth-grade English teacher at Mira Costa High School in Manhattan Beach, California. Her enthusiasm for life carries over into the classroom. Marilyn says about her life: "It is a canvas with swirling brush strokes that depict the motifs of my experience." Marilyn reflects that teachers may truly never know how many students' lives are changed for the better by teachers' sense of responsibility and excitement for life.

Marilyn's teaching philosophy centers around embracing and celebrating the act of learning. She says that to open minds, teachers need to help students become motivated to search for knowledge and to discover answers to questions of why and how. One of Marilyn's most important goals as a teacher is to get students to think deeply as they read and write. Among her teaching strategies are to encourage students to mark books to connect and remember important events or writing techniques in literary works and to promote dialogue and debate in group discussions.

One of Marilyn's former students, Mary-Anna Rae, said that Marilyn's intellectual engagement and passion for life make her a great role model for students. Mary-Anna also said that in everything Marilyn does she makes it clear that she is listening to students and encouraging them to engage in the deepest thinking possible. Now a teacher herself, Mary-Anna adds that Marilyn enriched and expanded her world. Mary-Anna also says that Marilyn helped her to grow more confident in what she had to say, find her writer's voice, and discover that she could give her life purpose.

For the type of outstanding work and thinking described in the opening story, Marilyn Whirry was named National Teacher of the Year in 2000 and honored at a White House reception. Marilyn's efforts to get her students to think deeply is one of the main emphases in this chapter, in which we will focus on how teachers can help students to understand concepts, think, solve problems, and transfer what they learn to other settings.

CONCEPTUAL UNDERSTANDING

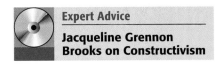

Expert Advice

Jacqueline Grennon Brooks on Constructivism

Conceptual understanding is a key aspect of learning. An important teaching goal is to help students understand the main concepts in a subject rather than just memorizing isolated facts. In many cases, conceptual understanding is enhanced when teachers explore a topic in depth and give appropriate, interesting examples of the concepts involved. As you will see, concepts are the building blocks of thinking.

What Are Concepts?

Concepts are categories that group objects, events, and characteristics on the basis of common properties (Zacks & Tversky, 2001). Concepts are elements of cognition that help to simplify and summarize information (Hahn & Ramscar, 2001; Klausmeier, 2004; Medin, 2000). Imagine a world in which we had no concepts: We would see each object as unique and would not be able to make any generalizations. If we had no concepts, we would find the most trivial problems difficult to formulate and even impossible to solve. Consider the concept of book. If a student were not aware that a book is sheets of paper of uniform size, all bound together along one edge, and full of printed words and pictures in some meaningful order, each time the student encountered a new book she would have to figure out what it was. In a way, then, concepts keep us from "reinventing the wheel" each time we come across a new piece of information.

Concepts also aid the process of remembering, making it more efficient. When students group objects to form a concept, they can remember the concept, then retrieve the concept's characteristics. Thus, when you assign math homework, you probably won't have to go through the details of what math is or what homework is. Students will have embedded in their memory a number of appropriate associations. In ways such as this, concepts not only help to jog memory but also make communication more efficient. If you say, "It's time for art," students know what you mean. You don't have to go into a lengthy explanation of what art is. Thus, concepts help students to simplify and summarize information, as well as improve the efficiency of their memory, communication, and use of time.

concepts Categories used to group objects, events, and characteristics on the basis of common properties.

Students form concepts through direct experiences with objects and events in their world. For example, in constructing a sophisticated concept of cartoons, children might initially experience TV cartoon shows, then read comic strips, and eventually look at some political caricatures. Students also form concepts through experience with symbols (things that stand for, or represent, something else). For example, words are symbols. So are math formulas, graphs, and pictures.

Some concepts are relatively simple, clear, and concrete, whereas others are more complex, fuzzy, and abstract (Barsalou, 2000). The former are easier to agree on. For example, most people can agree on the meaning of "baby." But we have a harder time agreeing on what is meant by "young" or "old." We agree on whether something is an apple more readily than on whether something is a fruit. Some concepts are especially complex, fuzzy, and abstract, like the concepts involved in theories of economic collapse or string theory in physics.

Promoting Concept Formation

In a number of ways, teachers can guide students to recognize and form effective concepts. The process begins with becoming aware of the features of a given concept.

Learning About the Features of Concepts An important aspect of concept formation is learning the key features, attributes, or characteristics of the concept. These are the defining elements of a concept, the dimensions that make it different from another concept. For example, in our earlier example of the concept of "book," the key features include sheets of paper, being bound together along one edge, and being full of printed words and pictures in some meaningful order. Other characteristics such as size, color, and length are not key features that define the concept of "book." Consider also these critical features of the concept of "dinosaur": extinct and reptilian. Thus, in the case of the concept of "dinosaur," the feature "extinct" is important.

Defining Concepts and Providing Examples An important aspect of teaching concepts is to clearly define them and give carefully chosen examples. The *rule-example strategy* is an effective way to do this (Tennyson & Cocchiarella, 1986). The strategy consists of four steps:

Forming Concepts
Concept Maps

1. *Define the concept.* As part of defining it, link it to a superordinate concept and identify its key features or characteristics. A *superordinate* concept is a larger class into which it fits. Thus, in specifying the key features of the concept of dinosaur, you might want to mention the larger class into which it fits: reptiles.
2. *Clarify terms in the definition.* Make sure that the key features or characteristics are well understood. Thus, in describing the key features of the concept of dinosaur, it is important for students to know what a reptile is—usually an egg-laying vertebrate with an external covering of scales or horny plates that breathes by means of lungs.
3. *Give examples to illustrate the key features or characteristics.* With regard to dinosaurs, one might give examples and descriptions of different types of dinosaurs, such as *triceratops, brontosaur,* and *stegosaur.* The concept can be further clarified by giving examples of other reptiles that are not dinosaurs, such as snakes, lizards, crocodiles, and turtles. Indeed, giving nonexamples of a concept as well as examples is often a good strategy for teaching concept formation. More examples are required when you teach complex concepts and when you work with less-sophisticated learners (Moore, 1998).
4. *Provide additional examples.* Ask students to categorize concepts, explain their categorization, or have them generate their own examples of the concept. Other dinosaur types might be given, such as pterodactyl, *ornitholestes,* and *dimetrodon,* or students could be asked to generate these examples. They also might be asked to think up other nonexamples of dinosaurs, such as dogs, cats, and whales.

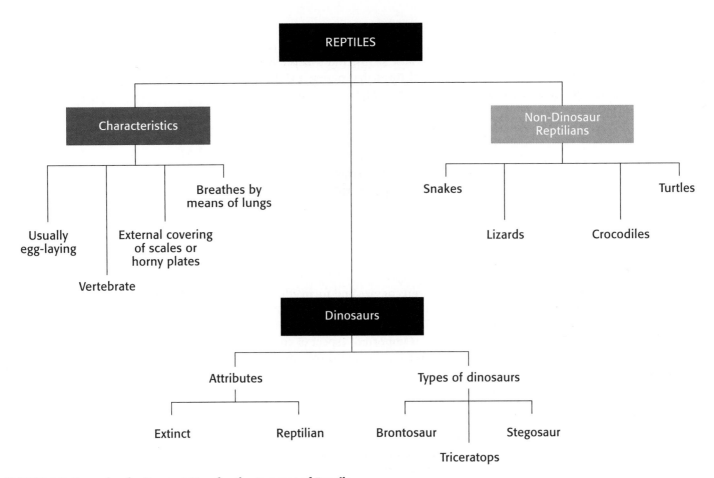

FIGURE 9.1 **Example of a Concept Map for the Concept of Reptile**

Concept Maps A **concept map** is a visual presentation of a concept's connections and hierarchical organization. Getting students to create a map of a concept's features or characteristics can help them to learn the concept (Kinchin, Hay, & Adams, 2000; Nicoll, 2001). The concept map also might embed the concept in a superordinate category and include examples and nonexamples of the concept. The visual aspects of the concept map relate to our chapter 8 discussion of the use of imagery in memory. You might create a concept map with the assistance of students, or let them try to develop it individually or in small groups. Figure 9.1 shows an example of a concept map for the concept of reptile.

Hypothesis Testing Recall from our discussion of the scientific approach to research, in chapter 1, that *hypotheses* are specific assumptions and predictions that can be tested to determine their accuracy ◄ p. 16. Students benefit from the practice of developing hypotheses about what a concept is and is not (Ross, 2000). One way this is done is to come up with a rule about why some objects fall within a concept and others do not. Here is an example of how you can give your students practice in developing such hypotheses: Present your students with the picture of geometric forms shown in figure 9.2. Then silently select the concept of one of those geometric forms (such as "circle" or "green circle") and ask your students to develop hypotheses about what concept you have selected. They zero in on your concept by asking you questions related to the geometric forms and eliminating nonexamples. You might also let the students take turns "being the teacher"—they select a concept and answer questions from the other students as they generate hypotheses about what the concept is. Work with your students on developing the most efficient strategies for identifying the correct concept.

concept map A visual presentation of a concept's connections and hierarchical organization.

Prototype Matching   In **prototype matching,** individuals decide whether an item is a member of a category by comparing it with the most typical item(s) of the category (Rosch, 1973). The more similar the item is to the prototype, the more likely it is that the individual will say the item belongs to the category; the less similar, the more likely the person will judge that it doesn't belong in the category. For example, a student's concept of a football player might include being big and muscular like an offensive lineman. But some football players, such as many field goal kickers, are not so big and muscular. An offensive lineman is a more prototypical example of a football player than a field goal kicker. When students consider whether someone belongs in the category "football player," they are more likely to think of someone who looks like an offensive lineman than to think of someone who looks like a field goal kicker. Similarly, robins are viewed as being more typical birds than ostriches or penguins. Nonetheless, members of a category can vary greatly and still have qualities that make them a member of that category (see figure 9.3 on page 286).

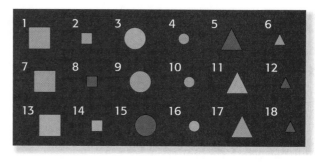

FIGURE 9.2 **Getting Students to Generate Hypotheses About a Concept**

You can use arrangements like the one shown here to help students generate hypotheses about what concept you have in mind. This encourages students to develop the most efficient strategies for understanding what a concept is. For example, you might select the concept "squares and purple triangles" or "purple triangles and purple squares" and ask students to figure out what concept you're thinking of. You also can let students take turns selecting the concept.

Teaching Strategies
For Helping Students
Form Concepts

1. *Use the rule-example strategy.* Remember that this involves four steps: (1) Define the concept, (2) clarify the terms in the definition, (3) give examples to illustrate the key features or characteristics, and (4) provide additional examples and ask students to categorize these and explain their categorization, or have students generate their own examples of the concepts.

2. *Help students learn not only what a concept is but also what it is not.* Let's return to the concept "cartoon." Students can learn that even though they are humorous, jokes, clowns, and funny poems are not cartoons. Their concept formation benefits from learning that North America is not a "nation" but, rather, is a "continent" and that touching someone is a behavior, not a thought. If you are teaching the concept of "triangle," ask students to list the characteristics of "triangle" such as "three-sided," "geometric shape," "can be of any size," "can be of any color," "sides can vary in length," "angles can be different," and so on; also ask them to list examples of things that are not triangles, such as circles, squares, and rectangles.

3. *Make concepts as clear as possible and give concrete examples.* Spend some time thinking about the best way to present a new concept, especially an abstract one. Make it as clear as possible. If you want students to understand the concept "vehicle," ask them to come up with examples of it. They probably will say "car" and maybe "truck" or "bus." Show them photographs of other vehicles, such as a sled and a boat, to illustrate the breadth of the concept.

4. *Help students relate new concepts to concepts they already know.* In chapter 8, we discussed the strategy of outlining for taking notes. Once students have learned this procedure, it is easier for them to learn how to construct concept maps, because you can show them how concept maps are linked with outlining in terms of hierarchical organization. As another example of helping students to relate a new concept to concepts they already know, they might know what gold and silver are but not be aware of what platinum and plutonium are. In this case, build on their knowledge of gold and silver to teach the concepts of platinum and plutonium.

5. *Encourage students to create concept maps.* Getting students to visually map out the hierarchical organization of a concept can help them learn it. The hierarchical arranging can be used to help students understand the concept's characteristics from more general to more specific. Hierarchical organization benefits memory.

prototype matching A process in which individuals decide whether an item is a member of a category by comparing it with the most typical item(s) of the category.

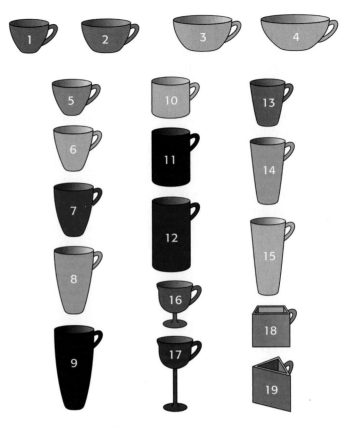

FIGURE 9.3 When Is a Cup a "Cup"?
Which of these would you describe as the prototype for the concept "cup"? In one study, participants were most likely to choose number 5 (Labov, 1973). Some participants called number 4 a bowl and number 9 a vase because they were so different from the prototype.

6. *Ask students to generate hypotheses about a concept.* Generating hypotheses encourages students to think and develop strategies. Work with students on developing the most efficient strategies for determining what a concept is.
7. *Give students experience in prototype matching.* Think of different concepts and then ask students what the prototypes of the concepts are. Then ask them for nonprototypical examples of the concept.
8. *Check for students' understanding of a concept and motivate them to apply the concept to other contexts.* Make sure that students don't just rotely memorize a concept. Get them to expand their knowledge of the concept and elaborate on it by assigning further reading about the concept. Ask students how the concept can be applied in different contexts. For example, in learning the concept of fairness, ask students how fairness can make life smoother, not only at school but also at play, at home, and at work.

Review and Reflect

1 Discuss conceptual understanding and strategies for teaching concepts.

Review
- What are concepts and why are they indispensable to thinking?
- What are some ways that students can be guided to construct effective concepts?

Reflect
- What might the concept "art" mean to a three-year-old? to a ten-year-old? to a sixteen-year-old? to a professional artist? How do such changes come about?

THINKING

What does it mean to think? How can teachers help students to become better thinkers?

What Is Thinking?

Thinking involves manipulating and transforming information in memory. This often is done to form concepts, reason, think critically, make decisions, think creatively, and solve problems. Students can think about the concrete, such as a vacation at the beach or how to win at a video game, or if they are in middle or high school, they can think about more abstract subjects, such as the meaning of freedom or identity. They can think about the past (such as what happened to them last month) and the future (what their life will be like in the year 2020). They can think about reality (such as how to do better on the next test) and fantasy (what it would be like to meet Elvis Presley or land a spacecraft on Mars).

Reasoning

Reasoning is logical thinking that uses induction or deduction to reach a conclusion. Let's first explore inductive reasoning.

Inductive Reasoning   **Inductive reasoning** involves reasoning from the specific to the general. That is, it consists of drawing conclusions (forming concepts) about all members of a category based on observing only some members (Markman & Gentner, 2001). For example, when a student in a literature class reads only a few of Emily Dickinson's poems and is asked to draw conclusions from them about the general nature of Dickinson's poetry, inductive reasoning is being requested. When a student is asked whether a concept learned in math class applies to other domains, such as business or science, again, inductive reasoning is being called for. Educational psychology research is often inductive as well, studying a sample of participants in order to draw conclusions about the population from which the sample is drawn.

Notice that inductive conclusions are never entirely certain—that is, they may be inconclusive. An inductive conclusion may be very likely, but there always is a chance that it is wrong, just as a sample does not perfectly represent its population (Johnson-Laird, 2000).

Inductive reasoning is basic to analogies (Goswami, 2004). An **analogy** is a correspondence in some respects between otherwise dissimilar things. Analogies can be used to improve the understanding of new concepts by comparing them with already learned concepts. For example, in chapter 8, we made an analogy between a computer and human memory.

One type of analogy involves formal reasoning and has four parts, with the relation between the first two parts being the same as or very similar to the last two. For example, solve this analogy: Beethoven is to music as Picasso is to _____. To answer correctly ("art"), you had to induce the relation between Beethoven and music (the former created the latter) and apply this relationship to Picasso (what did he create?).

Analogies can be helpful in solving problems, especially when they are visually represented. Benjamin Franklin noticed that a pointed object drew a stronger spark than a blunt object when both were in the vicinity of an electrified body. Originally he believed this was an unimportant observation, but then he realized that an analogous object—a pointed rod—could be used to attract lightning (analogous to the spark), thus deflecting it from buildings and ships.

Deductive Reasoning   In contrast to inductive reasoning, **deductive reasoning** is reasoning from the general to the specific. The fictional British detective Sherlock

Through the Eyes of Students

The Thinking Room

I recently talked with my granddaughter, Jordan Bowles, who is just beginning the second grade in Apex, North Carolina. I asked her what her classes were like this year.

She responded, "The usual stuff. Well, there is this one new class that I go to once a week. It's in the thinking room."

I then asked her what she was supposed to learn there.

Jordan said, "They are going to teach me not to jump to conclusions and my mom is happy about that."

thinking Manipulating and transforming information in memory, which often is done to form concepts, think critically, and solve problems.

inductive reasoning Reasoning from the specific to the general.

analogy A correspondence in some respects between otherwise dissimilar things.

deductive reasoning Reasoning from the general to the specific.

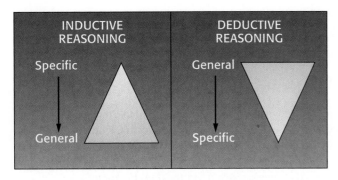

FIGURE 9.4 Inductive and Deductive Reasoning
The pyramid on the left (right side up) represents inductive reasoning—going from specific to general. The pyramid or triangle on the right (upside down) represents deductive reasoning—going from general to specific.

"Explain"

I use the word "explain" a great deal. I do not accept an answer without asking the student to explain. I found that this gets the students to think about their answers and provide support for their answers.

Donna Shelhorse
Short Pump Middle School
Henrico County, Virginia

Exploring Critical Thinking
Critical Thinking Resources

critical thinking Thinking reflectively and productively and evaluating the evidence.

Holmes was a master at deductive reasoning. For example, he often applied general "laws" of science or human behavior to solve a particular crime. Figure 9.4 provides a visual representation of the difference between inductive and deductive reasoning.

When you solve puzzles or riddles, you, too, are engaging in deductive reasoning. When you learn about a general rule and then understand how it applies in some situations but not others, you are engaging in deductive reasoning. When educational psychologists use theories and intuitions to make predictions, then evaluate these predictions by making further observations, deductive reasoning is at work.

Deductive reasoning is always certain in the sense that if the initial rules or assumptions are true, then the conclusion will follow directly as a matter of logic. For example, if you know the general rules that dogs bark and cats meow (and if the rules are always true), you can deduce correctly whether your neighbor's strange-looking pet is a dog or a cat on the basis of the specific sound it makes. When educational psychologists develop a hypothesis from a theory, they are using a form of deductive reasoning because the hypothesis is a specific, logical extension of the general theory. If the theory is true, the hypothesis will turn out to be true as well.

Critical Thinking

Currently, there is considerable interest in critical thinking among psychologists and educators, although it is not an entirely new idea (Kamin & others, 2001; Winn, 2004). The famous educator John Dewey (1933) proposed a similar idea when he talked about the importance of getting students to think reflectively. The well-known psychologist Max Wertheimer (1945) talked about the importance of thinking productively rather than just guessing at a correct answer. **Critical thinking** involves thinking reflectively and productively and evaluating the evidence. Many of the "Reflect" questions that appear in every chapter of this book call for critical thinking.

Here are some ways teachers can consciously build critical thinking into their lesson plans:

• Ask not only what happened but also "how" and "why."
• Examine supposed "facts" to determine whether there is evidence to support them.

"For God's sake, think! Why is he being so nice to you?"

- Argue in a reasoned way rather than through emotions.
- Recognize that there is sometimes more than one good answer or explanation.
- Compare various answers to a question and judge which is really the best answer.
- Evaluate and possibly question what other people say rather than immediately accept it as the truth.
- Ask questions and speculate beyond what we already know to create new ideas and new information.

Jacqueline and Martin Brooks (1993, 2001) lament that so few schools really teach students to think critically. In their view, schools spend too much time on getting students to give a single correct answer in an imitative way rather than encouraging students to expand their thinking by coming up with new ideas and rethinking earlier conclusions. They believe that too often teachers ask students to recite, define, describe, state, and list rather than to analyze, infer, connect, synthesize, criticize, create, evaluate, think, and rethink.

Brooks and Brooks point out that many successful students complete their assignments, do well on tests, and get good grades yet don't ever learn to think critically and deeply. They believe our schools turn out students who think too superficially, staying on the surface of problems rather than stretching their minds and becoming deeply engaged in meaningful thinking.

What are some good strategies for nurturing children's critical thinking?

One way to encourage students to think critically is to present them with controversial topics or articles that present both sides of an issue to discuss. Some teachers shy away from having students engage in these types of critical thinking debates or discussions because it is not "polite" or "nice" (Winn, 2004). However, critical thinking is promoted when students encounter conflicting accounts of arguments and debates, which can motivate them to delve more deeply into a topic and attempt to resolve an issue. In these circumstances, students often benefit when teachers refrain from stating their own views, allowing students to more freely explore different sides of issues and multiple perspectives on topics.

Getting students to think critically is not always an easy task. Many students come into a class with a history of passive learning, having been encouraged to recite the correct answer to a question, rather than put forth the intellectual effort to think in more complex ways. By using more assignments that require students to focus on an issue, a question, or a problem, rather than just reciting facts, teachers stimulate students' ability to think critically.

 ## Teaching Strategies
For Improving Children's Thinking

Twentieth-century German dictator Adolph Hitler once remarked that it was such good fortune for people in power that most people do not think. Education should help students become better thinkers. Every teacher would agree with that goal, but the means for reaching it are not always in place in schools. Here are some guidelines for helping students to become better thinkers.

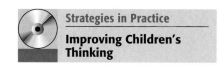

Strategies in Practice

Improving Children's Thinking

1. *Be a guide in helping students to construct their own thinking.* You can't and shouldn't do students' thinking for them. However, you can and should be an effective guide in helping students construct their own thinking. Teachers who help students construct their own thinking (Brooks & Brooks, 1993, 2001)

Through the Eyes of Teachers

Encouraging Students to Be Intellectual Risk-Takers

Alan Haskvitz, who teaches social studies at Suzanne Middle School in Walnut, California, believes in learning by doing and the importance of motivating students to improve the community. His students have rewritten voting instructions adopted by Los Angeles County, lobbied for a law requiring state government buildings to have rough-resistant landscaping, and created measures to reduce the city's graffiti. Alan has compiled thousands of teacher resources on this website: http://www. reacheverychild.com. He challenges students to be independent thinkers and intellectual risk-takers. He has students create an ideal island and discuss what everything from government to geography would be like on the island.

Alan Haskvitz with middle school students Simon Alarcon and Tracy Blozis, examining bones and trying to figure out where in the animal kingdom they belong.

Do
- Highly value students' questions
- View students as thinkers with emerging theories about the world
- Seek students' points of view
- Seek elaboration of students' initial responses
- Nurture students' intellectual curiosity

Don't
- View students' minds as empty or see their role as a teacher as simply pouring information into students' minds
- Rely too heavily on textbooks and workbooks
- Simply seek the correct answer to validate student learning

2. *Use thinking-based questions.* One way to analyze your teaching strategies is to see whether you use a lecture-based approach, fact-based questioning, or thinking-based questioning (Sternberg & Spear-Swirling, 1996). In the lecture-based approach, the teacher presents information in the form of a lecture. This is a helpful approach for quickly presenting a body of information, such as factors that led to the French Revolution. In fact-based questioning, the teacher asks questions primarily designed to get students to describe factual information. This is best used for reinforcing newly acquired information or testing students' content knowledge. For example, the teacher might ask, "When did the French Revolution occur? Who were the king and queen of France at that time?" In thinking-based questioning, the teacher asks questions that stimulate thinking and discussion. For example, the teacher might ask, "Compare the French and American revolutions. How were they similar? How were they different?"

Make a point to include thinking-based questions in your teaching. They will help your students construct a deeper understanding of a topic.

3. *Provide positive role models for thinking.* Look around your community for positive role models who can demonstrate effective thinking, and invite them to come to your classroom and talk with your students. Also think about contexts in the community, such as museums, colleges and universities, hospitals, and businesses, where you can take students and they can observe and interact with competent thinkers.

4. *Be a thinking role model for students as a teacher.* Have an active and inquiring mind yourself. Every day you are in the classroom, your students will pick up on how you think. Examine what we have said about thinking in this chapter. Work on being a positive thinking model for students by practicing these strategies.

5. *Keep up-to-date on the latest developments in thinking.* Continue to learn actively about new developments in teaching students to become more effective thinkers after you have become a teacher. Over the next decade there will especially be new technology programs through which you can improve students' thinking skills. Go to libraries now and then to read educational journals, and attend professional conferences that include information about thinking.

Decision Making

Think of all the decisions you have to make in your life. Which grade level and subject should I teach? Should I go to graduate school right after college or get a job first? Should I establish myself in a career before settling down to have a family? Should I buy a house or rent? **Decision making** involves thinking in which individuals evaluate alternatives and make choices among them.

In deductive reasoning, people use clear-cut rules to draw conclusions. In contrast, when we make decisions, the rules are seldom clear-cut and we may have limited knowledge about the consequences of the decisions (Gigerenzer & Selton, 2001; Tversky & Fox, 1995). In addition, important information might be missing, and we might not trust all of the information we have (Matlin, 2002).

In one type of decision-making research, investigators have studied how people weigh the costs and benefits of various outcomes. They have found that people choose the outcome with the highest expected value (Smyth & others, 1994). For example, in choosing a college, a high school student might list the pluses and minuses of going to different colleges (related to such factors as cost, quality of education, and social life), then make a decision based on how the colleges fared on these criteria. In making a decision, the student might have weighed some of these factors more heavily than others (such as cost three points, quality of education two points, and social life one point).

"You take all the time you need, Larry—this certainly is a big decision."
© The New Yorker collection 1990, Eric Teitelbaum, from cartoonbank.com. All Rights Reserved.

Another fruitful subject of decision-making research is the biases and flawed heuristics (rules of thumb) that affect the quality of decisions. In many cases, our decision-making strategies are well adapted to deal with a variety of problems (Nisbett & Ross, 1980). However, we are prone to making a number of mistakes in our thinking (Stanovich, 1999, 2001). Common flaws involve confirmation bias, belief perseverance, overconfidence bias, hindsight bias, and the availability and representativeness heuristics.

Effective Decision Making

Confirmation Bias   **Confirmation bias** is the tendency to search for and use information that supports our ideas rather than refutes them (Betch & others, 2001). Thus, in making a decision, a student might have an initial belief that a certain approach is going to work. He tests out the approach and finds out that it is does work some of the time. He concludes that his approach is right rather than further exploring the fact that in a number of cases it doesn't work.

We tend to seek out and listen to people whose views confirm our own rather than listen to dissenting views. Thus, you might have a particular teaching style, such as lecturing, that you like to use. If so, you probably will have a tendency to listen more to other teachers who use that style than to teachers who prefer other styles, such as collaborative problem solving by students.

In one study, Deanna Kuhn and her colleagues (1994) had participants listen to an audiotaped reenactment of an actual murder trial. Then, they were asked what their verdict would be and why. Rather than considering and weighing possibilities drawing on all the evidence, many participants hurriedly composed a story that drew only from evidence that supported their view of what happened. These participants showed a confirmation bias by ignoring evidence that ran counter to their version of events. Be aware of how easy it is for you and your students to become trapped by confirmation bias.

Belief Perseverance   Closely related to confirmation bias, **belief perseverance** is the tendency to hold on to a belief in the face of contradictory evidence. People have a difficult time letting go of an idea or a strategy once they have embraced it. Consider Madonna. We might have a hard time thinking of her in a maternal role because of the belief perseverance that she is a wild, fun-loving rock star.

Another example of belief perseverance gives some college students trouble. They may have gotten good grades in high school by using the strategy of cramming for tests the night before. The ones who don't adopt a new strategy—spacing their study sessions more evenly through the term—often do poorly in college.

Overconfidence Bias   **Overconfidence bias** is the tendency to have more confidence in judgments and decisions than we should based on probability or past experience. People are overconfident about how long those with a fatal disease will live, which

decision making Evaluating alternatives and making choices among them.

confirmation bias The tendency to search for and use information that supports our ideas rather than refutes them.

belief perseverance The tendency to hold on to a belief in the face of contradictory evidence.

overconfidence bias The tendency to have more confidence in judgment and decisions than we should based on probability or past experience.

businesses will go bankrupt, whether a defendant is guilty in a court trial, and which students will do well in college (Kahneman & Tversky, 1995). People consistently have more faith in their judgments than predictions based on statistically objective measures indicate they should.

In one study, college students were asked to make predictions about themselves in the coming academic year (Vallone & others, 1990). They were asked to predict whether they would drop any courses, vote in an election, and break up with their girlfriend or boyfriend. At the end of the year, the accuracy of their predictions was examined. The results: They were more likely to drop a class, not vote in an election, and break up with a girlfriend or a boyfriend than they had predicted.

Hindsight Bias   People not only are overconfident about what they predict will happen in the future (overconfidence bias), but also tend to be overrate their past performances at prediction (Louie, Curren, & Harich, 2000). **Hindsight bias** is our tendency to falsely report, after the fact, that we accurately predicted an event.

As I write this chapter, baseball season is just beginning. Lots of people in different cities are predicting that their teams are going to make it to the World Series. Come October, after almost all of the teams have fallen by the wayside, many of the same people will say, "I told you our team wasn't going to have a good season."

In one study of college students taking introductory psychology, a professor had them make either preverdict predictions regarding the outcome of the O. J. Simpson trial or postverdict predictions about what they would have predicted the outcome to be (Demakis, 1997). Students who estimated their prediction of the trial postverdict were more likely to correctly "predict" the verdict than were students who predicted the outcome preverdict, illustrating the principle of hindsight bias.

Availability Heuristic   A **heuristic** is a rule of thumb that can suggest a solution to a problem but does not ensure it will work. One heuristic that can produce flawed thinking is the **availability heuristic,** a prediction about the probability of an event based on the frequency of the event's past occurrences. When an event has recently occurred, we especially tend to overestimate its future occurrence (McKelvie & Drumheller, 2001).

How likely do you think it is that you will be a victim of a crime, for instance? The fear of crime tends to go up when the media go through a phase of highlighting murder or covering a sensational murder story. Because of the excess information about crime, we are likely to estimate that crime is more prevalent than it really is. The media contribute to this prediction error every time they expose us to a rash of vivid stories about tornadoes, murders, diseases, accidents, or terrorist attacks.

Representativeness Heuristic   The **representativeness heuristic** suggests that we sometimes make faulty decisions based on how well something matches a prototype—that is, the most common or representative example—rather than its relevance to a particular situation. Consider this description of an individual's dinner companion: is skilled at carpentry, is proficient at wrestling, owns a pet snake, knows how to repair motorcycles, and has a police record. What is the probability that this person is a male? Most likely the description fits your prototype of a male more than a female, so you might estimate that there is a nine in ten chance the dinner companion is a male.

In this example, your prototype served you well because there are far more men than women in the population who fit the description. Sometimes, however, our prototypes do not take into account the frequency of events in the entire population. For example, would you say that the dinner companion is more likely to be a member of a motorcycle gang or a salesman? You would probably say there is a much greater chance that he is a member of a motorcycle gang, in which case you would be wrong. Why? Although only a very small percentage of the millions of salesmen fit the description of this dinner companion, the total number is greater than the total number of motorcycle gang members who fit the description. Let's assume there are 10,000 members of motorcycle gangs in the world versus 100 million salesmen. Even if 1 of every 100 motorcycle gang members

hindsight bias The tendency to falsely report, after the fact, that we accurately predicted an event.

heuristic A strategy or rule of thumb that can suggest a solution to a problem but doesn't ensure it will work.

availability heuristic A prediction about the probability of an event based on the frequency of the event's past occurrences.

representativeness heuristic Making faulty decisions based on how well something matches a prototype— that is, a common or representative example—rather than its relevance to the particular situation.

(1%) fits our description, there would be only 100 of them. If just 1 of every 100,000 salesmen fits our description (.01%), their number would total 1,000, so the probability is 10 times greater that the dinner companion is a salesman than a member of a motor-cycle gang.

Our lives involve many such instances in which we judge probabilities based on representativeness and fail to consider the population from which a sample is drawn. If we are to make better decisions, we have to try to avoid this logical error along with the others mentioned here (Todd & Gigerenzer, 2001).

Teaching Strategies
For Making Good Decisions Yourself and Helping Your Students Make Good Decisions

---

1. *Weigh the costs and benefits of various outcomes.* You will encounter many circumstances in which you will benefit from pursuing this strategy. For example, should you spend more time with your friends and family or more time grading students' homework? Will your students benefit from examining a particular topic in a small-group format or a lecture format?
2. *Avoid confirmation bias.* Do you tend to only seek out people to talk with whose views confirm your own? Does a particular student avoid people with dissenting views and, if so, how can you help him or her?
3. *Resist belief perseverance.* Are you holding on to some beliefs which might be outdated and need to be changed? Do students have beliefs based on their past experiences that they are clinging to which don't fit their current situation? If so, how can you help them?
4. *Don't engage in overconfidence bias.* Do you have more confidence in your decisions than you should based on probability or your past experience? Might one of your future students gloss over the fact that he or she did poorly on the previous test in your class and be overconfident and not put in extra hours of study?
5. *Avoid hindsight bias.* Monitor your tendency and your students' tendencies to be overconfident about circumstances that already have happened.
6. *Be aware of the availability and representativeness heuristics.*

Creative Thinking

Teresa Amabile remembers that when she was in kindergarten, she rushed into class every day, excited about getting to the easel and playing with all of those bright colors and big paintbrushes. She and her classmates also had free access to a table with all kinds of art materials on it. Teresa remembers telling her mother every day when she got home that she wanted to play with crayons and draw and paint.

Teresa's kindergarten experience, unfortunately, was the high point of her childhood artistic interest. The next year she entered a conventional elementary school and things began to change. She no longer had free access to art materials every day, and art became just another subject for her, something she had to do for an hour and a half on Friday afternoon.

Week after week, all through elementary school, art assignments hardly varied. For Teresa, the art class was restrictive and demoralizing. She recalls being given small reprints of painted masterpieces, a different one each week; one week in second grade, students were presented with pictures of Leonardo da Vinci's *Adoration of the Magi* and told to take out their art materials and try to copy the masterpiece. For Teresa and the other students, it was an exercise

What do you mean, "What is it?" It's the spontaneous, unfettered expression of a young mind not yet bound by the restraints of narrative or pictorial representation.

© 2002 by Sydney Harris. Reprinted with permssion.

Teresa Amabile's Research

Csikszentmihalyi's Ideas

in frustration, since at that age they lacked the skill even to fit all those horses and angels on the page, much less make them look like the masterpiece. Teresa and the other students could tell that they were not doing well what the teacher had asked them to do. And they were not getting any help in developing their artistic skills. Needless to say, Teresa's desire to go home and paint after school each day diminished rapidly.

Teresa Amabile eventually obtained her Ph.D. in psychology and went on to become one of the leading researchers in the field of creativity. Today, her hope is that teachers will not crush students' enthusiasm for creativity, as hers did (Goleman, Kaufman, & Ray, 1993).

What Is Creativity?   **Creativity** is the ability to think about something in novel and unusual ways and come up with unique solutions to problems. J. P. Guilford (1967) distinguished between **convergent thinking,** which produces one correct answer and is characteristic of the kind of thinking required on conventional intelligence tests, and **divergent thinking,** which produces many answers to the same question and is more characteristic of creativity (Michael, 1999). For example, a typical convergent item on a conventional intelligence test is "How many quarters will you get in return for 60 dimes?" The question has only one right answer. In contrast, divergent questions have many possible answers. For example, consider these questions: "What image comes to mind when you sit alone in a dark room?" and "What are some unique uses for a paper clip?"

Are intelligence and creativity related? Although most creative students are quite intelligent (as measured by high scores on conventional intelligence tests), in other respects the reverse is not necessarily true. Many highly intelligent students are not very creative (Sternberg, 2002).

It is important for teachers to recognize that students will show more creativity in some domains than others (Runco, 2004). A student who shows creative thinking skills in mathematics may not exhibit these skills in art, for example.

The design of schools and classrooms may influence the creativity of students (Runco, 2004). School environments that encourage independent work, are stimulating but not distracting, and make resources readily available are likely to encourage students' creativity (Hasirci & Demirkan, 2003).

Teaching and Creativity   An important teaching goal is to help students become more creative (Plucker, Beghetto, & Dow, 2004). Strategies that can inspire children's creativity include encouraging creative thinking at the group and individual levels, providing students with environments that stimulate creativity, not overcontrolling students, encouraging internal motivation, fostering flexible and playful thinking, and introducing students to creative people.

creativity The ability to think about something in novel and unusual ways and come up with unique solutions to problems.

convergent thinking Thinking with the aim of producing one correct answer. This is usually the type of thinking required on conventional intelligence tests.

divergent thinking Thinking with the aim of producing many answers to the same question. This is characteristic of creativity.

What are some good strategies teachers can use to guide children in thinking more creatively?

Encourage Creative Thinking on a Group and Individual Basis   *Brainstorming* is a technique in which people are encouraged to come up with creative ideas in a group, play off each other's ideas, and say practically whatever comes to mind that seems relevant to a particular issue (Rickards, 1999; Sternberg & Lubart, 1995). Participants are usually told to hold off from criticizing others' ideas at least until the end of the brainstorming session.

A recent review of research on brainstorming concluded that for many individuals working alone can actually generate more ideas and better ideas than working in groups (Rickards & deCock, 2003). One reason for this is that in groups some individuals loaf, while others do most of the creative thinking. Nonetheless, there may be benefits to brainstorming, such as team building, that support its implementation (Runco, 2004).

Whether in a group or on an individual basis, a good creativity strategy is to come up with as many new ideas as possible. Famous twentieth-century Spanish artist Pablo Picasso produced more than 20,000 works of art. Not all of them were masterpieces. The more ideas students produce, the better their chance of creating something unique.

Creative people are not afraid of failing or getting something wrong. They might go down twenty dead-end streets before they come up with an innovative idea. They recognize that it's okay to win some and lose some. Like Picasso, they are willing to take risks.

Provide Environments That Stimulate Creativity   Some classrooms nourish creativity, others inhibit it. Teachers who encourage creativity often rely on students' natural curiosity. They provide exercises and activities that stimulate students to find insightful solutions to problems, rather than ask a lot of questions that require rote answers. Teachers also encourage creativity by taking students on field trips to locations where creativity is valued. Howard Gardner (1993) believes that science, discovery, and children's museums offer rich opportunities to stimulate creativity.

Don't Overcontrol Students   Teresa Amabile (1993) says that telling students exactly how to do things leaves them feeling that originality is a mistake and exploration is a waste of time. If, instead of dictating which activities they should engage in, you let your students select their interests and you support their inclinations, you will be less likely to destroy their natural curiosity. Amabile also believes that when teachers hover over students all of the time, they make them feel that they are constantly being watched while they are working. When students are under constant surveillance, their creative risk-taking and adventurous spirit diminish. Students' creativity also is diminished when teachers have grandiose expectations for their performance and expect perfection from them, according to Amabile.

Chuck Jones (1993), the creator of Wile E. Coyote, Road Runner, and many other cartoon characters, says that the child's job is to play and to experiment, but too often he or she gets criticized by parents and teachers for playing, experimenting, and trying out different things. Jones offers several examples of how adults criticize children's art. A child makes a drawing of a flower and the teacher says, "That's not a bad drawing but why is the flower bigger than you?" Jones says that's enough to kill the child's enthusiasm. When you discover something you have never seen, it appears huge, much bigger than you are. About another child's drawing, a parent asks, "What's this stuff?" The child replies, "That's me. I'm dancing." The parent says, "Yeah, but you only have two knees. You don't have all of those knees." Jones says this is nonsense. All you have to do is think about what you feel like when you are dancing. You feel like you have fourteen knees and ankles all over the place!

Through the Eyes of Students

The Eight-Year-Old Filmmaker and Oozy Red Goop

Steven was eight years old and wanted to get a scout badge in filmmaking. His father bought him a super-8 movie camera. Steven got the inspiration to make a horror movie.

He started imagining what he needed to do to make a movie. Needing some red, bloody-looking goop to ooze from the kitchen cabinets, he got his mother to buy thirty cans of cherries. Steven dumped the cherries into the pressure cooker and produced an oozy red goop.

His mother gave him free rein in the house, letting him virtually convert it into a child's movie studio. Steven told his mother he needed to make some costumes, which she obligingly made.

The son's name was Steven Spielberg, whose mother supported his imagination and passion for film making. Of course, Spielberg went on to become one of Hollywood's greatest producers with such films as *E.T.* and *Jurassic Park* (Goleman, Kaufman, & Ray, 1993).

How Good Am I at Thinking Creatively?

Rate each of these activities as they apply to you in terms of how often you engage in them:
1 = never, 2 = rarely, 3 = sometimes, and 4 = a lot.

	1	2	3	4
1. I come up with new and unique ideas.				
2. I brainstorm with others to creatively find solutions to problems.				
3. I am internally motivated.				
4. I'm flexible about things and like to play with my thinking.				
5. I read about creative projects and creative people.				
6. I'm surprised by something and surprise others every day.				
7. I wake up in the morning with a mission.				
8. I search for alternative solutions to problems rather than giving a pat answer.				
9. I spend time around creative people.				
10. I spend time in settings and activities that stimulate me to be creative.				

Examine your overall pattern of responses. What are your strengths and weaknesses in creativity? Keep practicing your strengths and work on improving your weaknesses to provide students with a creative role model.

 Go to your Student Toolbox CD-ROM for an electronic version of this form.

Encourage Internal Motivation Excessive use of prizes, such as gold stars, money, or toys, can stifle creativity by undermining the intrinsic pleasure students derive from creative activities. Creative students' motivation is the satisfaction generated by the work itself. Competition for prizes and formal evaluations often undermine intrinsic motivation and creativity (Amabile & Hennesey, 1992). However, this is not to rule out material rewards altogether. We will say more about internal and external motivation in chapter 13, "Motivation, Teaching, and Learning."

Foster Flexible and Playful Thinking Creative thinkers are flexible and play with problems—which gives rise to a paradox. Although creativity takes effort, the effort goes more smoothly if students take it lightly. Humor can grease the wheels of creativity (Goleman, Kaufman, & Ray, 1993). When students are joking around, they are more likely to consider unusual solutions to problems. Having fun helps to disarm the inner censor that can condemn a student's ideas as being off-base. As one clown named Wavy Gravy put it, "If you can't laugh about it, it just isn't funny anymore."

Introduce Students to Creative People You might not have Wavy Gravy nearby to invite to your classroom, but it is a good strategy to identify the most creative people in your community whom you can invite. Ask them to come to your class and describe what helps them become creative or to demonstrate their creative skills. A writer, a poet, a craftsperson, a musician, a scientist, and many others can bring their props and productions to your class.

To evaluate how good you are at thinking creatively, complete Self-Assessment 9.1. And to read about the use of technology to stimulate creativity, see the Technology and Education box.

Creative Experiences with Computers: Picasso, Edison, da Vinci, Art, Music, and Spatial Ability

For three decades, filmmaker Robert Abel made the screen come alive with special-effects films such as *2001: A Space Odyssey.* Today, Abel is working on creative ways to use computers to educate students. Using a desktop mouse or a touch screen, students explore on their computer monitors as their curiosity beckons. They can follow a lead from text to photos or music and back again. In an application to art, students view some of Picasso's paintings; then, by clicking the mouse, they choose various interpretations of the paintings. Abel's use of computers is being tried out in some Los Angeles schools. His goal is to use the computers to turn on students to discover ideas.

The software programs *The Genius of Edison* and *Leonardo the Inventor* can be used to expose students to the thinking of two creative geniuses. The *Genius of Edison* is a multimedia presentation that lets students ages ten and older explore thirteen of Edison's inventions. *Leonardo the Inventor* also stimulates this same age range of students to think more creatively. Both programs are published by The Learning Company, Cambridge, Massachusetts.

Another effort to encourage students' creativity is *Picture It!* software by Microsoft for grades 5 to 12 (Pogue, 1997). It lets students and teachers create sophisticated images with only a few mouse clicks. Students initially scan pictures into the computer, then recolor, crop, move, and resize them. They can cut images, place them on another background, or create a collage.

Two other pieces of software relate to Howard Gardner's musical and spatial aspects of intelligence. *The Julliard Musical Adventure,* software created by the staff of the Julliard School of Music, is designed to introduce students nine years and older to the vocabulary of music and the elements of musical composition (Goldberg, M. 1997). It is built around an adventure game in which students explore a castle to solve musical puzzles. The Julliard musical software is published by Theatrix Interactive, Emeryville, California.

The Neighborhood Map Machine is software that helps students to improve their spatial skills by exploring maps. Kindergarten to sixth-grade students can create maps, then attach photographs and narratives to go along with the map. A teaching guide provides tips for using the program in social studies (place recognition, compass reading, transportation, and the environment) and cross-curricular instruction (connections with math and science). This program is published by Tom Snyder Products, Watertown, Massachusetts.

Filmmaker Robert Abel *(center)* talks with a group of middle school students about expanding their creative thinking by exploring computer displays of art and music.

A screen from *The Neighborhood Map Machine* software, which guides children in developing their spatial skills.

PROBLEM SOLVING

Let's examine problem solving as a cognitive process, including the steps it involves, the obstacles to it, and how best to teach it.

Problem solving involves finding an appropriate way to attain a goal. Consider these tasks that require students to engage in problem solving: creating a project for a science fair, writing a paper for an English class, getting a community to be more environmentally responsive, and giving a talk on the factors that cause people to be prejudiced.

Steps in Problem Solving

Efforts have been made to specify the steps that individuals go through in effectively solving problems (Bransford & Stein, 1993). Following are four such steps.

1. Find and Frame Problems Before a problem can be solved, it has to be recognized (Mayer, 2000). In the past, most problem-solving exercises in school involved well-defined problems that lent themselves to specific, systematic operations that produced a well-defined solution. Today, educators increasingly recognize the need to teach how to identify problems instead of just offering clear-cut problems to be solved.

Many real-life problems are hard to pin down and can be defined in any number of different ways, each way tending to suggest a different path toward solution. Consider a student who belongs to a club that meets weekly after school. Suddenly, the club has decided to meet at a new location farther from the school and soon after the student's last class. He has some vague idea that this is a problem, but how should he frame it in terms of a goal or solution? Is the problem simply to get there faster, to persuade the club leaders to change the meeting time or location, or to rethink whether these afternoon meetings are compatible with his academic goals?

Consider also a student whose broad goal is to create a science-fair project. What branch of science would it be best for her to present—biology, physics, computer science, psychology? Then, she'll have to narrow the problem even more. For example, which domain within psychology—perception, memory, thinking, personality? Within the domain of memory, she might pose this question: How reliable are people's memories of traumatic events they have experienced? Thus, it may take considerable exploration and refinement for the student to narrow the problem down to a point of generating specific solutions. Exploring such alternatives is an important part of problem solving.

In sum, an important educational agenda is to give students opportunities to locate and refine problems that need to be solved. The teacher can serve as a guide and a consultant in helping them to frame a meaningful problem and to clearly define it.

Video Lecture: Promoting Critical Thinking

problem solving Finding an appropriate way to attain a goal.

2. Develop Good Problem-Solving Strategies   Once students find a problem and clearly define it, they need to develop strategies for solving it. Among the effective strategies are setting subgoals, using algorithms, and relying on heuristics.

Subgoaling involves setting intermediate goals that put students in a better position to reach the final goal or solution. Students might do poorly in solving problems because they don't generate subproblems or subgoals. Let's return to the science-fair project on the reliability of people's memory for traumatic events they have experienced. What might be some subgoaling strategies? One might be locating the right books and research journals on memory; another might be interviewing people who have experienced traumas in which basic facts have been recorded. At the same time as the student is working on this subgoaling strategy, the student likely will benefit from establishing further subgoals in terms of what she needs to accomplish along the way to her final goal of a finished science project. If the science project is due in three months, she might set the following subgoals: finishing the first draft of the project two weeks before the project is due; having the research completed a month before the project is due; being halfway through the research two months before the project is due; having three trauma interviews completed two weeks from today; and starting library research tomorrow.

Notice that in establishing the subgoals, we worked backward in time. This is often a good strategy (Reed, 2000). Students first create a subgoal that is closest to the final goal and then work backward to the subgoal that is closest to the beginning of the problem-solving effort.

Algorithms are strategies that guarantee a solution to a problem. Algorithms come in different forms, such as formulas, instructions, and tests of all possible solutions.

When students solve a multiplication problem by a set procedure, they are using an algorithm. When they follow the directions for diagramming a sentence, they are using an algorithm. Algorithms are often worth knowing because life is much easier when problems can be solved by the use of algorithms. But since many real-world problems aren't so straightforward, looser strategies also are needed.

As we indicated earlier in the chapter in our discussion of decision making, *heuristics* are strategies or rules of thumb that can suggest a solution to a problem but don't ensure it will work. Heuristics help us to narrow down the possible solutions to find one that works (Stanovich & West, 2000). Suppose that you go out on a day hike and find yourself lost in the mountains. A common heuristic for getting "unlost" is simply to head downhill and pick up the nearest tiny stream. Small streams lead to larger ones, and large streams often lead to people. Thus, this heuristic usually works, although it could bring you out on a desolate beach.

In the face of a multiple-choice test, several heuristics could be useful. For example, if you are not sure about an answer, you could start by trying to eliminate the answers that look most unlikely and then guess among the remaining ones. Also, for hints about the answer to one question, you could examine the statements or answer choices for other questions on the test.

A **means-end analysis** is a heuristic in which one identifies the goal (end) of a problem, assesses the current situation, and evaluates what needs to be done (means) to decrease the difference between the two conditions. Another name for means-end analysis is difference reduction. Means-end analysis also can involve the use of subgoaling, which we described earlier (Anderson, 1993). Means-end analysis is commonly used in solving problems. Consider a student who wants to do a science-fair project (the end) but has not yet found a topic. Using means-end analysis, she could assess her current situation,

Through the Eyes of Teachers

Carpenters and Toolboxes

In teaching math, I use such problem-solving strategies as working backwards, making a similar but simpler problem, drawing a diagram, making a table, and looking for patterns. We talk about what strategies make the most sense with different types of problems. When students successfully solve a problem, we look to see what methods were used, often finding more than one. I talk about multiple strategies in terms of carpenters having more than one kind of hammer in their toolboxes.

Lawren Giles
Mathematics Teacher
Baechtel Grove Middle School
Willits, California

Heuristics

subgoaling The process of setting intermediate goals that place students in a better position to reach the final goal or solution.

algorithms Strategies that guarantee a solution to a problem.

means-end analysis A heuristic in which one identifies the goal (end) of a problem, assesses the current situation, and evaluates what needs to be done (means) to decrease the difference between the two conditions.

in which she is just starting to think about the project. Then she maps out a plan to reduce the difference between her current state and the goal (end). Her "means" might include talking to several scientists in the community about potential projects, going to the library to study the topic she chooses, and exploring the Internet for potential projects and ways to carry them out.

3. Evaluate Solutions   Once we think we have solved a problem, we might not know whether our solution is effective unless we evaluate it. It helps to have in mind a clear criterion for the effectiveness of the solution. For example, what will be the student's criterion for effectively solving the science-fair problem? Will it be simply getting it completed? receiving positive feedback about the project? winning an award? winning first place? gaining the self-satisfaction of having set a goal, planned for it, and reached it?

4. Rethink and Redefine Problems and Solutions over Time   An important final step in problem solving is to continually rethink and redefine problems and solutions over time (Bereiter & Scardamalia, 1993). People who are good at problem solving are motivated to improve on their past performances and to make original contributions. Thus, the student who completed the science-fair project can look back at the project and think about ways the project can be improved. The student might use feedback from judges or others who attended the fair in order to fine-tune the project for presentation again in some other venue.

Obstacles to Solving Problems

Some common obstacles to solving problems are fixation, lack of motivation and persistence, and inadequate emotional control.

Fixation   It is easy to fall into the trap of becoming fixated on a particular strategy for solving a problem. **Fixation** involves using a prior strategy and failing to look at a problem from a fresh, new perspective. *Functional fixedness* is a type of fixation in which an individual fails to solve a problem because he or she views the elements involved solely in terms of their usual functions. A student who uses a shoe to hammer a nail has overcome functional fixedness to solve a problem.

A **mental set** is a type of fixation in which an individual tries to solve a problem in a particular way that has worked in the past. I (your author) had a mental set about using a typewriter rather than a computer to write my books. I felt comfortable with a typewriter and had never lost any sections I had written. It took a long time for me to break out of this mental set. Once I did, I found that books are much easier to write using a computer. You might have a similar mental set against using the new computer and video technology available for classroom use. A good strategy is keep an open mind about such changes and monitor whether your mental set is keeping you from trying out new technologies that can make the classroom more exciting and more productive.

Lack of Motivation and Persistence   Even if your students already have great problem-solving abilities, that hardly matters if they are not motivated to use them (Pintrich, 2000; Sternberg & Spear-Swerling, 1996). It is especially important for students to be internally motivated to tackle a problem and persist at finding a solution. Some students avoid problems or give up too easily.

An important task for teachers is to devise or steer students toward problems that are meaningful to them and to encourage and support them in finding solutions. Students are far more motivated to solve problems that they can relate to their personal lives than textbook problems that have no personal meaning for them. Problem-based learning takes this real-world, personal approach.

fixation Using a prior strategy and thereby failing to examine a problem from a fresh, new perspective.

mental set A type of fixation in which an individual tries to solve a problem in a particular way that has worked in the past.

"Blueprint for Success"

Christina and Marcus, two students from Trenton, visit an architectural firm on Career Day. While learning about the work of architects, Christina and Marcus hear about a vacant lot being donated in their neighborhood for a playground. This is exciting news because there is no place in their downtown neighborhood for children to play. Recently, several students have been hurt playing in the street. The challenge is for students to help Christina and Marcus design a playground and ballfield for the lot.

"The Big Splash"

Jasper's young friend Chris wants to help his school raise money to buy a new camera for the school TV station. His idea is to have a dunking booth in which teachers would be dunked when students hit a target. He must develop a business plan for the school principal in order to obtain a loan for his project. The overall problem centers on developing this business plan, including the use of a statistical survey to help him decide if this idea would be profitable.

FIGURE 9.5 Problem-Solving Adventures in the *Jasper* Series

Inadequate Emotional Control   Emotion can facilitate or restrict problem solving. At the same time that they are highly motivated, good problem solvers are often able to control their emotions and concentrate on a solution to a problem (Barron & Harackiewicz, 2001). Too much anxiety or fear can especially restrict a student's ability to solve a problem. Individuals who are competent at solving problems are usually not afraid of making mistakes.

Problem-Based Learning

Problem-based learning emphasizes solving authentic problems like those that occur in daily life (Jones, Rasmussen, & Moffit, 1997). Problem-based learning is used in a program called YouthALIVE! at the Children's Museum of Indianapolis (Schauble & others, 1996). There, students solve problems related to conceiving, planning, and installing exhibits; designing videos; creating programs to help visitors understand and interpret museum exhibits; and brainstorming about strategies for reaching the wider community.

The Cognition and Technology Group at Vanderbilt (1997) developed a program of problem-based learning called The Jasper Project. *The Adventures of Jasper Woodbury* consists of twelve videodisc-based adventures that are designed to improve the mathematical thinking of students in grades 5 and up, as well as to help students make connections with other disciplines, including science, history, and social studies. *Jasper's* creators argue that too often math and other subjects are taught as isolated skills. One of the *Jasper* adventures, *The Right Angle,* can be used not only in geometry classes but also in geography (topography) and history (Native American cultures). The adventures focus on a character named Jasper Woodbury and others, who encounter a number of real-life problems that need to be solved. Figure 9.5 profiles two of the *Jasper* problem-solving adventures.

As we saw earlier, finding and framing a problem is an important aspect of problem solving, so this is built into the *Jasper* system. Also, *Jasper* stimulates students to identify a number of subproblems or subgoals on their own. It also encourages collaborative problem solving among students. As students work together over a number of class periods, they have numerous opportunities to communicate about math, share their problem-solving strategies, and get feedback that helps them refine their thinking. Groups of students present their ideas to the class, discussing the strengths and weaknesses of their strategies and solutions. The collaborative aspect of *Jasper* is at the heart of social constructivist approaches to learning, which we will explore in depth in chapter 10.

**Problem-Based Learning
The Jasper Project**

problem-based learning Learning that emphasizes authentic problems like those that occur in daily life.

Each videodisc adventure includes extension problems. This helps students engage in "what if" thinking by revisiting the original adventures from new points of view. Thus, after finding a way to rescue a wounded eagle in *Rescue at Boone's Meadow* (most students solve the problem with an ultralight airplane that is featured in this adventure), students are presented with a revised problem in which they must rethink how the presence of headwinds or tailwinds might affect their original solution.

The Jasper Project also encourages teachers to develop actual problem-solving projects after students have worked with a *Jasper* adventure. For example, in one school, after creating a business plan for the adventure *The Big Splash,* students were given the opportunity to gather relevant data to create a business plan to present to the principal. In this instance, the creation of a business plan led to a fun fair being held for the entire school. In another school, students who had spent time solving problems in the adventure *Blueprint for Success* were given the opportunity to design a playhouse for preschools. Well-designed playhouses were actually built and donated to the preschools in the students' names.

An optional feature of the *Jasper* series is the video-based SMART Challenge series. Its goal is to connect classes of students to form a community of learners that tries to solve Jasper-related challenges. *SMART* stands for *Special Multimedia Arenas for Refining Thinking.* These arenas use telecommunications, television technology, and Internet technology to give students feedback about the problem-solving efforts of other groups. For example, students who are working on *Blueprint for Success* can see data from sixty other students about the length of legs for A-frame swing sets and the desired height of the swing sets.

In one recent study, the effects of using *The Adventures of Jasper Woodbury* as part of a constructivist-inspired reform of math curricula in a school district was evaluated in nineteen fifth-grade classrooms (Hickey, Moore, & Pellegrino, 2001). In the ten classrooms in which *Jasper* was implemented, students' overall motivation and academic performance were stronger than in the nine classrooms that did not use *Jasper.*

To obtain more information about the *Jasper*-related projects, contact the Cognition and Technology Group at Vanderbilt University, Nashville, Tennessee. And to evaluate your thinking and problem-solving skills, complete Self-Assessment 9.2.

Teaching Strategies
For Improving Students' Problem Solving

Video Observation: Critical Thinking, Reasoning, and Decision-Making through Role Play

1. *Give students extensive opportunities to solve real-world problems.* Make this a part of your teaching. Develop problems that are relevant to your students' lives. Such real-world problems are often referred to as "authentic," in contrast to textbook problems that too often do not have much meaning for students.
2. *Monitor students' effective and ineffective problem-solving strategies.* Keep the four problem-solving steps in mind when you give students opportunities to solve problems. Also keep in mind such obstacles to good problem solving as becoming fixated, harboring biases, not being motivated, and not persisting.
3. *Involve parents in children's problem solving.* A program of parental involvement has been developed at the University of California at Berkeley (Schauble & others, 1996). It is called Family Math (Matematica Para la Familia, in Spanish) and helps parents experience math with their children in a positive, supportive way. In the program, Family Math classes are usually taught by grade levels (K–2, 3–5, and 6–8). Many of the math activities require teamwork and communication between parents and children, who come to better understand not only the math but also each other. Family Math programs have served more than 400,000 parents and children in the United States.

How Effective Are My Thinking and Problem-Solving Strategies?

Teachers who practice good thinking and problem-solving strategies themselves are more likely to model and communicate these to their students than teachers who don't use such strategies. Candidly respond to these items about your own thinking and problem-solving strategies. Rate yourself: 1 = very much unlike me, 2 = somewhat unlike me, 3 = somewhat like me, and 4 = very much like me; then total your points.

	1	2	3	4
1. I am aware of effective and ineffective thinking strategies.				
2. I periodically monitor the thinking strategies I use.				
3. I am good at reasoning.				
4. I use good strategies for forming concepts.				
5. I am good at thinking critically and deeply about problems and issues.				
6. I construct my own thinking rather than just passively accept what others think.				
7. I like to use technology as part of my effort to think effectively.				
8. I have good role models for thinking.				
9. I keep up-to-date on the latest educational developments in thinking.				
10. I use a system for solving problems, such as the four-step system described in the text.				
11. I am good at finding and framing problems.				
12. I make good decisions and monitor biases and flaws in my decision making.				
13. When solving problems, I use strategies such as subgoaling and working backward in time.				
14. I don't fall into problem-solving traps such as fixating, lacking motivation and persistence, and not controlling my emotions.				
15. When solving problems, I set criteria for my success and evaluate how well I have met my problem-solving goals.				
16. I make a practice of rethinking and redefining problems over an extended period of time.				
17. I love to work on problem-solving projects.				
18. I am a good at creative thinking.				

TOTAL _____

Scoring and Interpretation

If you scored 66–74 points, your thinking strategies likely are very good. If you scored 55–65 points, you likely have moderately good thinking strategies. If you scored below 54 points, you likely would benefit from working on your thinking strategies.

Several good books that could help you improve your problem-solving and thinking strategies are *Learning to Think Things Through* (Nosich, 2001), *Teaching for Thinking* (Sternberg & Spear-Swerling, 1996), *Becoming Reflective Students and Teachers with Portfolios and Authentic Assessment* (Paris & Ayres, 1994), and *Real-Life Problem Solving* (Jones, Rasmussen, & Moffit, 1997).

 Go to your Student Toolbox CD-ROM for an electronic version of this form.

4. *Use technology effectively.* Be motivated to incorporate multimedia programs into your classroom. *The Adventures of Jasper Woodbury* contains many of the themes of effective thinking and problem solving that we have described in this chapter. Such programs can significantly improve your students' thinking and problem-solving skills.

Some popular television presentations can be used to foster students' problem-solving and thinking skills (Schauble & others, 1996). For example, *3-2-1 Contact* focuses on eight- to twelve-year-olds' appreciation of science; *Square One TV* gives students a better understanding of math and problem solving; and *Ghostwriter* supports the literacy of seven- to ten-year-olds. Kits for these TV programs include videotapes, leader guides, games, puzzles, and magazines. Throughout this book, we highlight technology that you can use to help students think more deeply.

! Review and Reflect

3 Take a systematic approach to problem solving.

Review
- What is problem solving? What are the main steps in problem solving?
- What are three obstacles to problem solving?
- What is problem-based learning?

Reflect
- When you tackle a difficult problem, do you follow the four steps we described? What might you do to become a better model of a problem solver for your students?

"I don't get it! They make us learn reading, writing and arithmetic to prepare us for a world of videotapes, computer terminals and calculators!"

Harley Schwadron, *Phi Delta Kappan*. Reprinted with permission of the author.

transfer Applying previous experiences and knowledge to learning or problem solving in a new situation.

TRANSFER

An important complex cognitive goal is for students to be able to apply what they learn in one situation to new situations. An important goal of schooling is that students learn things that they can apply outside the classroom. Schools are not functioning effectively if students do well on tests in language arts but can't write a competent letter as part of a job application. Schools also are not effectively educating students if the students do well on math tests in the classroom but can't solve arithmetic problems on a job.

What Is Transfer?

Transfer occurs when a person applies previous experiences and knowledge to learning or problem solving in a new situation (Gentile, 2000; Mayer & Wittrock, 1996). Thus, if a student learns a concept in math and then uses this concept to solve a problem in science, transfer has occurred. It also has occurred if a student reads and studies about the concept of fairness in school and subsequently treats others more fairly outside the classroom. Teaching for transfer helps students make the connection between what they learn in school and how it applies beyond school.

Types of Transfer

Transfer can be characterized as either near or far and as either low-road or high-road (Schunk, 2000).

Through the Eyes of Teachers

Connecting Students to the Community to Give Context to What They Are Learning

Myron Blosser is an honors and AP biology teacher at Harrisonburg (Virginia) High School. He was the leader in establishing Coast to Coast '98, a science department effort in which 22 students and 8 teachers spent 31 days touring national parks in a motor coach laboratory studying the natural history of water. He is working on the development of Coast to Coast 2000. He coordinates an annual biotechnology symposium that includes renowned scientists and high school students throughout the Shenandoah Valley region of Virginia. Myron sees his role as connecting students to the community to give context to what they are learning.

Myron Blosser, teaching at Harrisonburg High School

Near or Far Transfer   **Near transfer** occurs when situations are similar. If the classroom learning situation is similar to the one in which the initial learning took place, the challenge is one of near transfer. For example, if a geometry teacher instructs students in how to logically prove a concept, and then tests the students on this logic in the same setting in which they learned the concept, near transfer is involved. Another example of near transfer occurs when students who have learned to type on a typewriter transfer this skill to typing on a computer keyboard.

   Far transfer means the transfer of learning to a situation that is very different from the one in which the initial learning took place. For instance, if a student gets a part-time job in an architect's office and applies what was learned in geometry class to helping the architect analyze a spatial problem that is quite different from any problem the student encountered in geometry class, far transfer has occurred.

Low-Road or High-Road Transfer   Gabriel Salomon and David Perkins (1989) distinguished between low-road and high-road transfer. **Low-road transfer** occurs when previous learning automatically, often unconsciously, transfers to another situation. This occurs most often with highly practiced skills in which there is little need for reflective thinking. For example, when competent readers encounter new sentences in their native language, they read them automatically.

   By contrast, **high-road transfer** is conscious and effortful. Students consciously establish connections between what they learned in a previous situation and the new situation they now face. High-road transfer is mindful—that is, students have to be aware of what they are doing and think about the connection between contexts. High-road transfer implies abstracting a general rule or principle from previous experience and then applying it to the new problem in the new context. For example, students might learn about the concept of subgoaling (setting intermediate goals) in math class. Several months later, one of the students thinks about how subgoaling might benefit him in completing a lengthy homework assignment in history. This is high-road transfer.

   Salomon and Perkins (1989) subdivide high-road transfer into forward-reaching and backward-reaching transfer. **Forward-reaching transfer** occurs when students think about how they can apply what they have learned to new situations (from their current

near transfer The transfer of learning to a situation that is similar to the one in which the initial learning took place.

far transfer The transfer of learning to a situation that is very different from the one in which the initial learning took place.

low-road transfer The automatic, often unconscious, transfer of learning to another situation.

high-road transfer The transfer of learning from one situation to another that is conscious and effortful.

forward-reaching transfer The transfer of learning that involves thinking about how to apply what has been learned to new situations in the future.

situation, they look "forward" to apply information to a new situation ahead). For forward-reaching transfer to take place, students have to know something about the situations to which they will transfer learning. **Backward-reaching transfer** occurs when students look back to a previous ("old") situation for information that will help them solve a problem in a new context.

To better understand these two types of high-road transfer, imagine a student sitting in English class who has just learned some writing strategies for making sentences and paragraphs come alive and "sing." The student begins to reflect on how she could use those strategies to engage readers next year, when she plans to become a writer for the school newspaper. That is forward-reaching transfer. Now consider a student who is at his first day on the job as editor of the school newspaper. He is trying to figure out how to construct the layout of the pages. He reflects for a few moments and thinks about some geography and geometry classes he has previously taken. He draws on those past experiences for insights into constructing the layout of the student newspaper. That is backward-reaching transfer.

Cultural practices may be involved in how easy or difficult transfer is. The Diversity and Education interlude explores this topic.

Diversity and Education
Transfer and Cultural Practices

Prior knowledge includes the kind of knowledge that learners acquire through cultural experiences, such as those involving ethnicity, socioeconomic status, and gender (National Research Council, 1999) ◀ p. 134. In some cases this cultural knowledge can support children's learning and facilitate transfer, but in others it may interfere (Greenfield & Suzuki, 1998).

For children from some cultural backgrounds, there is a minimal fit or transfer between what they have learned in their home communities and what is required or taught by the school. For example, consider the language skill of storytelling. Euro-American children use a linear style that more closely approximates the linear expository style of writing and speaking taught in most schools (Lee & Slaughter-Defoe, 1995). This may involve recounting a series of events in a rigidly chronological sequence. By contrast, in some ethnic groups—such as Asian Pacific Island or Native American—a nonlinear, holistic/circular style is more common in telling a story, and Euro-American teachers may consider their discourse to be disorganized (Clark, 1993). Also, in African American children, a nonlinear, topic-associative storytelling approach is common (Michaels, 1986).

Methods of argumentation in support of certain beliefs also differ across cultures. Chinese speakers prefer to use a format of presenting supporting evidence first, leading up to a major point or claim (in contrast to a topic sentence followed by supporting details). Non-Chinese listeners sometimes judge this style as "beating around the bush" (Tsang, 1989).

Rather than perceiving such variations in communication styles as being chaotic or as necessarily inferior to Euro-American styles, it is important for teachers to be sensitive to them and aware of cultural differences. This is especially important in the early elementary school grades, when students are making the transition from the home environment to the school environment.

backward-reaching transfer The transfer of learning that involves looking back to a previous ("old") situation for information that might help solve a problem in a new context.

Teaching Strategies
For Helping Students Transfer
Information

1. *Think about what your students need for success in life.* We don't want students to finish high school with a huge data bank of content knowledge but no idea how to apply it to the real world. One strategy for thinking about what students need to know is to use the "working-backward" problem-solving strategy we discussed earlier in this chapter. For example, what do employers want high school and college graduates to be able to do? In a national survey of employers of college students, the three skills that employers most wanted graduates to have were (1) oral communication skills, (2) interpersonal skills, and (3) teamwork skills (Collins, 1996). Thus, the three most desired skills for students to have all involved communication. The employers also wanted students to be proficient in their field, have leadership abilities, have analytical skills, be flexible, and be able to work with computers. By thinking about and practicing the competencies that your students will need in the future and working with them to improve these skills, you will be guiding them for positive transfer. We will discuss communication skills in chapter 14, "Managing the Classroom," and we will examine teamwork skills in chapter 10, "Social Constructivist Approaches."

2. *Give students many opportunities for real-world learning.* Too often, learning in schools has been artificial, with little consideration for transfer beyond the classroom or textbook. This will be less true for your students if you give them as many real-world problem-solving and thinking challenges as possible. In general, the more similar two situations are, the easier it will be for students to transfer information learned in one to the other. You can bring the real world into your classroom by inviting people from varying walks of life to come and talk with your students. Or you can take your students to the real world by incorporating visits to museums, businesses, colleges, and so on in the curriculum. Such learning opportunities should increase transfer.

3. *Root concepts in applications.* The more you attempt to pour information into students' minds, the less likely it is that transfer will occur. When you present a concept, also define it (or get students to help you define it), and then ask students to generate examples. Challenge them to apply the concept to their personal lives or to other contexts.

4. *Teach for depth of understanding and meaning.* Teaching for understanding and meaning benefits transfers more than does teaching for the retention of facts. And students' understanding improves when they actively construct meaning and try to make sense out of material.

5. *Teach strategies that will generalize.* Transfer involves not only skills and knowledge but also strategies (Schunk, 2000). Too often students learn strategies but don't understand how to apply them in other contexts. They might not understand that the strategy is appropriate for other situations, might not know how to modify it for use in another context, or might not have the opportunity to apply it (Pressley, Borkowski, & Schneider, 1989).

One model for teaching strategies that will generalize was developed by Gary Phye (1990; Phye & Sanders, 1994). He described three phases for improving transfer. In an

Chris Laster, Bringing Science Alive

Chris Laster says that he became a teacher because he "just wanted to do some good." . . . Laster remembers his own fourth-grade teacher whose fascinating experiments turned him on to science when he was 10 years old. His students say that "he brings science alive." His principal, Judith Lindsay, remarked that "The greatest asset Chris has is he loves teaching at-risk children and disadvantaged children." His teaching has helped to motivate many at-risk students to go on to take advanced science courses. He "sparks his students' interest by stressing that 'science is everywhere.' On this day, he tries to get them to understand what humans have in common with dogs and horses and how to handle cockroaches. 'It's fun,' says Tariq Milton, 11. 'You get to do experiments on ants and roaches and stuff.' " Among Laster's innovative real-world

Chris Laster working with a student on the flight deck of the space shuttle that Laster and other teachers built.

teaching strategies that help students transfer their knowledge and understanding beyond the classroom are: "*Science Blasters.* Students write, direct and produce short videos for the school's closed-circuit TV station covering science in new and exciting ways. *Sci-Tech Safari.* Over the summer, fifth-graders get hands-on science experience on field trips like the Okefenokee Swamp and Little River Canyon in Alabama. *The Russell Space Center Program.* Student volunteers take a year of vigorous training to prepare for a 27-hour simulated mission aboard the space shuttle *Intrepid*. Laster and other teachers built the realistic-looking simulator by scrounging parts from local businesses, including hearby Dobbins Air Force Base" (Copeland, 2003).

ENTER THE DEBATE

Can teachers teach students to think?

Teaching Experience

- **Critical Thinking and Problem Solving**
- **Encouraging Student Inquiry**

initial acquisition phase, students not only are given information about the importance of the strategy and how to use it but also are given opportunities to rehearse and practice using it. In the second phase, called *retention,* students get more practice in using the strategy, and their recall of how to use the strategy is checked out. In the third phase, *transfer,* students are given new problems to solve. These problems require them to use the same strategy, but on the surface the new problems appear to be different. Phye also believes that motivation is an important aspect of transfer. He recommends that teachers increase students' motivation for transfer by showing them examples of how to use knowledge in their real lives.

⚠ Review and Reflect

4 Explain transfer and how to enhance it as a teacher.

Review
- What is transfer? Why should teachers think about it?
- What are some different types of transfer?

Reflect
- Are there experiences from your own formal education that don't seem to transfer to outside of school? What do you think is going on in such situations?

Susan has a test in her math class this Friday. She has spent the last several evenings studying the statistical formulas for measures of central tendency and variability, as she knows they will be covered on the test. To do this, she has quizzed herself repeatedly. In the beginning, she got them confused, but after repeated tries, she can now recite the formula for each without fail. She is certain that she will have no problems on the test.

When she receives her test on Friday, the first thing she does is to write down all of the formulas before she can forget them, certain that will be all she will need to do well on the exam. After writing down the formulas, she begins reading the test. Here is the first problem:

Mr. Peters' math class received these scores on last week's test:

45, 54, 65, 68, 70, 72, 72, 73, 75, 78, 80, 80, 80, 80, 82, 83, 84, 84, 84, 84, 84, 85, 86, 87, 87, 88, 90, 91, 92, 92, 92, 93, 94, 95, 95, 95, 96, 96, 97, 97, 98, 98, 99, 99, 99, 99

Find the mean, median, mode, variance, and standard deviation.

Susan anxiously looks at her list of formulas. She knows which formula goes with which measure—for instance, she knows that the formula for the mean is $\Sigma x/n$. The problem is that she doesn't know what Σx means. She is reasonably sure that "$/n$" means she is to divide by n, but what is n? When looking at the rest of the formulas, she realizes that she has similar problems. She stares at the test in dismay. After all that studying and careful memorization, she can't complete a single problem on the test.

- What are the issues in this case?
- What went wrong for Susan?
- What should she do differently if she wants to do better on her next test?
- If you were the teacher of Susan's class, how would you help your students to prepare for this type of test?

Reach Your Learning Goals

1 Discuss conceptual understanding and strategies for teaching concepts.

- Concepts are categories used to group objects, events, and characteristics on the basis of common properties. Concepts are elements of cognition that help to simplify and summarize information. They also improve memory, communication, and time use.

- In teaching concept formation to children, it is helpful to discuss with them the features of concepts, definitions and examples of concepts (using the rule-example strategy), concept maps and hierarchical organization, hypothesis testing, and prototype matching.

2 Describe several types of thinking and how teachers can foster them.

- Thinking involves manipulating and transforming information in memory. Types of thinking include forming concepts, reasoning, thinking critically, making decisions, thinking creatively, and solving problems.

- Inductive reasoning involves reasoning from the specific to the general. Analogies draw on inductive reasoning. Deductive reasoning is reasoning from the general to the specific.

- Critical thinking involves thinking reflectively and productively and evaluating evidence. Brooks and Brooks argue that too few schools teach students to think critically and deeply. They believe that too often schools give students a correct answer instead of encouraging them to expand their thinking by coming up with new ideas.

- Decision making is thinking that involves evaluating alternatives and making choices among them. One type of decision making involves weighing the costs and benefits of various outcomes. Numerous biases (confirmation bias, belief perseverance, overconfidence bias, and hindsight bias) and the flawed heuristics they use (the availability heuristic and the representativeness heuristic) can interfere with good decision making.

- Creativity is the ability to think about something in novel and interesting ways and come up with unique solutions to problems. Guilford distinguished between convergent thinking (which produces one correct answer and is characteristic of the type of thinking required on conventional intelligence tests) and divergent thinking (which produces many answers to the same question and is characteristic of creativity). Although most creative students are quite intelligent, the reverse is not necessarily true. Here are some ways teachers can foster creativity in students: encourage creative thinking on a group and individual basis, provide environments that stimulate creativity, don't over-control students, encourage internal motivation, foster flexible and playful thinking, and introduce students to creative people.

3 Take a systematic approach to problem solving.

- Problem solving involves finding an appropriate way to attain a goal. Four steps in problem solving are (1) finding and framing problems, (2) developing good problem-solving strategies (such as using subgoaling, heuristics, and algorithms), (3) evaluating solutions, and (4) rethinking and redefining problems and solutions over time.

- Obstacles to problem solving include fixedness (functional fixedness and mental set), lack of motivation and persistence, and not controlling one's emotions.

- Problem-based learning emphasizes solving authentic problems like those that occur in daily life. The *Adventures of Jasper Woodbury*, a multimedia set of twelve math problem-solving adventures, is an example of problem-based learning. *Jasper*-related projects also can help students with science, history, and social studies.

4 Explain transfer and how to enhance it as a teacher.

- Transfer occurs when a person applies previous experiences and knowledge to learning or problem solving in a new situation. Students especially benefit when they can apply what they learn in the classroom to situations in their lives outside of the classroom.

- Types of transfer include near and far and low-road and high-road. Near transfer occurs when situations are similar; far transfer occurs when situations are very different. Low-road transfer occurs when previous learning automatically transfers to another situation. High-road transfer is conscious and effortful. High-road transfer can be subdivided into forward-reaching and backward-reaching.

 KEY TERMS

concepts 282
concept map 284
prototype matching 285
thinking 287
inductive reasoning 287

analogy 287
deductive reasoning 287
critical thinking 288
decision making 291
confirmation bias 291

belief perseverance 291
overconfidence bias 291
hindsight bias 292
heuristic 292
availability heuristic 292

representativeness
   heuristic 292
creativity 294
convergent thinking 294
divergent thinking 294

PORTFOLIO ACTIVITIES

Now that you have a good understanding of this chapter, complete these exercises to expand your thinking.

Independent Reflection

Evaluate Your Decision Making Skills. Reflect on the ways that you make decisions. Are you able to make good quality decisions regardless of opposition from others? Discuss to what extent your decisions are influenced by confirmation bias, belief perseverance, overconfidence bias, and hindsight bias. What can you do to strengthen your decision making skills? (INTASC: Principles 4, 9)

Collaborative Work

Create a Problem-Based Learning Project. In the discussion of problem-based learning, the text describes Jasper Series problem-solving adventures in math. Thinking creatively, get together with 3 or 4 other students in the class and devise a problem-solving adventure in a subject area other than math, such as science, social science, or literature. Write it down below. (INTASC: Principles 1, 4)

Research/Field Experience Reflections

Creativity Research. Read work by one of the leading researchers in the field of creativity, such as Teresa Amabile or Csikszentmihalyi. What are the key findings about creativity discussed in the research? To what extent can this research be implemented in the classroom?. (INTASC: Principles 4, 9)

 Go to the Online Learning Center for downloadable portfolio templates.

 ## TAKING IT TO THE NET

1. Describe the characteristics of a person who is an effective problem solver. How does open-ended problem solving lead to knowledge and skills that are transferable? Why is the transfer of knowledge so critical to our changing and increasingly complex society?
2. Implementing critical thinking activities in the classroom can help students take charge of their own learning and take responsibility for their own behavior. Select an online lesson plan (www.lessonplanspage.com), and "remodel" it as a critical thinking activity. Describe elements of the remodeled lesson that will develop and reinforce students' critical thinking skills.
3. Evaluate an online lesson plan for its creative value. Discuss aspects of the lesson that foster students' creative and divergent thinking. What role would you play in supporting students' creativity? How would your classroom environment support creative thinking? Explain how you think the lesson could be improved to increase its creative value.

Connect to the Online Learning Center to explore possible answers.

STUDY, PRACTICE, AND SUCCEED

 Go to chapter 9 on the Online Learning Center at www.mhhe.com/santrockedu2e to access the student study guide with practice quizzes, web links, portfolio resources, PowerWeb articles and news feeds, and the online resources referenced in the chapter.

 Go to your Student Toolbox CD-ROM to access the resources and activities referenced in the chapter and

- Resources to help you prepare for the PRAXIS II™ exam

- **Application Resources,** including additional *Crack the Case* studies, electronic versions of the *Self-Assessments,* Application Exercises, and Site Observation Questions
- **Study Resources,** including Learning Goals, the Chapter Summary, a *Test Your Learning* exercise, and multiple-choice, true/false, matching, key terms, and short-answer quizzes
- **Professional Resources,** including a Lesson Plan Builder and *Bibliomaker*

10 Social Constructivist Approaches

> The human being is by nature a social animal.
>
> —Aristotle
> *Greek Philosopher, 4th Century* B.C.

Chapter Learning Goals After you have completed your study of this chapter, you should be able to reach these learning goals:

1 **Compare the social constructivist approach with other constructivist approaches.**

2 **Explain how teachers and peers can jointly contribute to children's learning.**

3 **Make effective decisions in structuring small-group work.**

4 **Describe three social constructivist programs.**

Teaching Stories Chuck Rawls

Chuck Rawls teaches language arts at Appling Middle School in Macon, Georgia. He provides this teaching story about peer tutoring:

I was tricked into trying something different my first year of teaching. It was peer teaching in the guise of a school-wide activity known as "Switch Day." This consists of having selected students switch places with members of the faculty and staff. Each student who wants to switch is required to choose a faculty or staff member and then write an essay explaining why he or she wants to switch with that particular person. To my surprise, Chris wrote a very good essay and was selected to switch with me.

It worked wonderfully. Chris delivered the lesson very professionally, and the students were engaged because it was some-

thing new and different. It was a riot to watch because Chris, both intentionally and unintentionally, used many of my pet phrases and mannerisms. He really did know his stuff, though, and demonstrated this as he helped students with their seatwork.

As the saying goes, "I didn't know he had it in him." Chris became my resident expert on subject-verb agreement, as that was the topic of the lesson and the students remembered what he taught them.

I learned two lessons that day: (1) Don't be afraid to try something different. (2) Peer tutoring works. However, it has to be the right student teaching the right material in the right setting.

Children do some of their thinking by themselves, but as social beings their cognition is often collaborative. Because of our American emphasis on the individual rather than the group, collaborative thinking only recently emerged as an important theme in American education. This chapter focuses on the collaborative thinking advocated by social constructivist approaches.

SOCIAL CONSTRUCTIVIST APPROACHES TO TEACHING

The social constructivist approaches involve a number of innovations in classroom learning. Before we study these innovations, let us first consolidate our knowledge about various constructivist perspectives and where the social constructivist approaches fit in the overall constructivist framework.

Constructivist Learning and Teaching

Constructivism

Vygotsky: Revolutionary Scientist

Vygotsky Links

Social Constructivism in the Broader Constructivist Context

Recall from chapter 1 that *constructivism* emphasizes that individuals actively construct knowledge and understanding. Early in this book (chapter 2, "Cognitive and Language Development"), we described Piaget's and Vygotsky's theories of development, both of which are constructivist ◄ pp. 39, 51. In chapters 8 and 9, our main focus was on the information-processing approaches to learning, which included some ideas about how the individual child uses information-processing skills to think in constructivist ways. According to all of these constructivist approaches, students author their own knowledge.

In general, a **social constructivist approach** emphasizes the social contexts of learning and that knowledge is mutually built and constructed (Bearison & Dorval, 2002). Involvement with others creates opportunities for students to evaluate and refine their understanding as they are exposed to the thinking of others and as they participate in creating shared understanding (Gauvain, 2001). In this way, experiences in social contexts provide an important mechanism for the development of students' thinking (Johnson & Johnson, 2003).

Vygotsky's social constructivist theory is especially relevant for the current chapter. Vygotsky's model is a social child embedded in a sociohistorical context. Moving from Piaget to Vygotsky, the conceptual shift is from the individual to collaboration, social interaction, and sociocultural activity (Rogoff, 1998). In Piaget's cognitive constructivist approach, students construct knowledge by transforming, organizing, and reorganizing previous knowledge and information. Vygotsky emphasized that students construct

social constructivist approach Approach that emphasizes the social contexts of learning and that knowledge is mutually built and constructed.

What is the social constructivist approach to education?

knowledge through social interactions with others. The content of this knowledge is influenced by the culture in which the student lives, which includes language, beliefs, and skills.

Piaget emphasized that teachers should provide support for students to explore and develop understanding. Vygotsky emphasized that teachers should create many opportunities for students to learn with the teacher and with peers in coconstructing knowledge (Kozulin, 2000). In both Piaget's and Vygotsky's models, teachers serve as facilitators and guides rather than directors and molders of children's learning.

Notice that we speak about emphasis rather than a clear-cut distinction. Often there are not clear-cut distinctions between social constructivist and other constructivist approaches (Marshall, 1996). For example, when teachers serve as guides for students in discovering knowledge, there are social dimensions to the construction. And the same is true for processing information. If a teacher creates a brainstorming session for students to come up with good memory strategies, social interaction is clearly involved.

Some sociocultural approaches, such as Vygotsky's, emphasize the importance of culture in learning; for example, culture can determine what skills are important (such as computer skills, communication skills, teamwork skills) (Rowe & Wertsch, 2004). Other approaches focus more exclusively on the immediate social circumstances of the classroom, as when students collaborate to solve a problem.

In one recent study with a foundation in Vygotsky's theory, pairs of children from two U.S. public schools worked together (Matusov, Bell, & Rogoff, 2001). One member of each pair was from a traditional school that provided only occasional opportunities for children to work together as they learned. The other member of the pair always was from a school that emphasized collaboration throughout the school day. The children with the collaborative schooling background more often built on the partner's ideas in a collaborative way than the children with traditional schooling experience. The traditional school children predominately used a "quizzing" form of guidance based on asking known-answer questions and withholding information to test the partner's understanding. Researchers also have found that collaborative learning often works best in classrooms that have well-specified learning goals (Gabriele & Montecinos, 2001).

In one analysis of the social constructivist approach, the teacher was described as being drawn to look at learning through the eyes of children (Oldfather & others, 1999).

Video Lecture: Constructivism

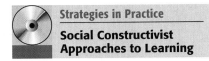

Strategies in Practice

Social Constructivist Approaches to Learning

Situated Cognition

The same analysis also noted these characteristics of social constructivist classrooms (Oldfather & others, 1999):

- An important goal orientation of the classroom is the construction of collaborative meaning.
- Teachers closely monitor students' perspectives, thinking, and feeling.
- The teacher and the students are learning and teaching.
- Social interaction permeates the classroom.
- The curriculum and the physical contents of the classroom reflect students' interests and are infused with their cultures.

Situated Cognition

Situated cognition is an important assumption in the social constructivist approaches. It refers to the idea that thinking is located (situated) in social and physical contexts, not within an individual's mind. Situated cognition conveys the idea that knowledge is embedded in and connected to the context in which the knowledge developed (Gauvain, 2001; King, 2000; Rowe & Wetsch, 2004). If this is so, it makes sense to create learning situations that are as close to real-world circumstances as possible. Our discussion of problem-based learning in chapter 8 demonstrated a similar emphasis ◀ p. 301.

In chapter 11, we will explore learning and cognition in a number of content areas—reading, writing, math, science, and social science. How much instructional practices can be generalized across different domains, such as reading and science, versus how situation-specific they are, is an important issue in educational psychology that we will revisit from time to time in the remaining chapters.

! Review and Reflect

1 Compare the social constructivist approach with other constructivist approaches.

Review
- Although they overlap, what is the basic difference between Piaget's and Vygotsky's approach?
- What is situated cognition?

Reflect
- From what you learned in chapter 2, do you think you would feel more at home with Piaget or Vygotsky? How might that be reflected in your own approach to classroom teaching?

TEACHERS AND PEERS AS JOINT CONTRIBUTORS TO STUDENTS' LEARNING

Teachers and peers can be joint contributors to students' learning. Four tools for making this happen are scaffolding, cognitive apprenticeship, tutoring, and cooperative learning (Rogoff, 1998; Rogoff, Turkanis, & Bartlett, 2001).

Scaffolding

In chapter 2, we described *scaffolding* as the technique of changing the level of support over the course of a teaching session; a more-skilled person (teacher or more-advanced peer of the child) adjusts the amount of guidance to fit the student's current performance ◀ p. 52. When the task the student is learning is new, the teacher might use direct instruction. As the student's competence increases, less guidance is provided. Think

situated cognition The idea that thinking is located (situated) in social and physical contexts, not within an individual's mind.

of scaffolding in learning like the scaffolding used to build a bridge. The scaffolding provides support when needed, but it is adjusted and gradually removed as the bridge approaches completion. Researchers have found that when scaffolding is used by teachers and peers in collaborative learning, students' learning benefits (Pressley & others, 2001; Yarrow & Topping, 2001).

Look for situations to use scaffolding in the classroom. For instance, good tutoring involves scaffolding, as we will see shortly. Work on giving just the right amount of assistance. Don't do for students what they can do for themselves. But do monitor their efforts and give them needed support and assistance.

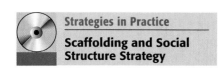

Strategies in Practice
Scaffolding and Social Structure Strategy

Cognitive Apprenticeship

Developmental psychologist Barbara Rogoff (1990) believes that an important tool of education is **cognitive apprenticeship**, meaning that an expert stretches and supports a novice's understanding and use of a culture's skills. (Recall our discussion of experts and novices in chapter 8.) The term *apprenticeship* underscores the importance of activity in learning and highlights the situated nature of learning. In a cognitive apprenticeship, teachers often model strategies for students. Then, teachers or skilled peers support students' efforts at doing the task. Finally, they encourage students to continue their work independently.

Scaffolding
Cognitive Apprenticeship

To illustrate the importance of cognitive apprenticeships in learning, Rogoff (1990) describes the contrasting experiences of students from middle-income and poverty backgrounds. Many middle-income American parents involve their children in cognitive apprenticeships long before they go to kindergarten or elementary school. They read picture books with young children and bathe their children in verbal communication. In contrast, American parents living in poverty are less likely to engage their children in a cognitive apprenticeship that involves books, extensive verbal communication, and scaffolding (Heath, 1989).

A key aspect of a cognitive apprenticeship is the expert's evaluation of when the learner is ready to be ushered into undertaking a new step (Rogoff, 1998). In one study of expert instruction in science and math, experts paid attention to the timing of their students' participation in discourse (Fox, 1993). Based on insights derived from the timing, the experts were able to determine how well the students were understanding the lesson. Awareness of timing also enabled the experts to pause at appropriate moments so that students could anticipate an expert's thinking and take responsibility for an idea by completing the expert's thoughts. In other words, experts gave the students appropriate opportunities to respond. At moments when students passed up opportunities to respond, the experts noticed what the students were doing. For example, a student might be busy calculating or might be staring blankly. When students passed up two or three opportunities, the experts would continue with further explanation. If no evidence of understanding appeared during that further explanation, experts repeated or reformulated what they were saying.

Experts also used collaborative completion of statements as a way to find out what the student understood. A common strategy employed by the experts was to use a "hint" question to get the student unstuck. Thus, experts often attempt to discern students' level of understanding by observing the looks on their faces and how they respond to questions.

Cognitive apprenticeships are important in the classroom. Researchers have found that students' learning benefits from teachers who think of their relationship with a student as a cognitive apprenticeship, using scaffolding and guided participation to help the student learn (Englert, Berry, & Dunsmore, 2001).

Tutoring

Tutoring is basically a cognitive apprenticeship between an expert and a novice. Tutoring can take place between an adult and a child or between a more-skilled child and a

cognitive apprenticeship A relationship in which an expert stretches and supports a novice's understanding of and use of the culture's skills.

When teachers think of their relationship with students as a cognitive apprenticeship, how is teaching likely to proceed?

less-skilled child. Individual tutoring is an effective strategy that benefits many students, especially those who are not doing well in a subject.

Classroom Aides, Volunteers, and Mentors   It is frustrating to find that some students need more individual help than you as their teacher can give them and still meet the needs of the class as a whole. Classroom aides, volunteers, and mentors can help reduce some of this frustration. Monitor and evaluate your class for students you believe could benefit from one-on-one tutoring. Scour the community for individuals with skills in the areas in which these students need more individual attention than you are able to give. Some parents, college students, and retirees might be interested in filling your classroom tutoring needs.

Several individual tutoring programs have been developed. The Reading Recovery program offers daily half-hour one-on-one tutorial sessions for students who are having difficulty learning to read after one year of formal instruction (Sensenbaugh, 1995). Although Reading Recovery is a registered trademark of Ohio State University and authorized programs use creator Marie Clay's (1985) materials, various Reading Recovery programs differ in how they are developed, implemented, and assessed. Evaluations of the Reading Recovery program have found that students who participated in the program in the first grade were still performing better in reading in third grade than their counterparts who did not participate in it during first grade (Sensenbaugh, 1994).

However, some researchers have found that the key to whether a program like Reading Recovery is effective is the extent to which phonological-processing skills are included (Chapman, Tunmer, & Prochnow, 2001).

Another program that uses tutoring is Success for All (SFA). Developed by Robert Slavin and his colleagues (1996; Slavin & Madden, 2001), this comprehensive program includes

- A systematic reading program that emphasizes phonics, vocabulary development, and story telling and retelling in small groups
- A daily 90-minute reading period with students in the first through third grades being regrouped into homogeneous cross-age ability groups
- One-on-one tutoring in reading by specially trained certified teachers who work individually with students who are reading below grade level
- Assessments every eight weeks to determine students' reading progress, adjust reading group placement, and assign tutoring if needed
- Professional development for teachers and tutors, which includes three days of in-service training and guidelines at the beginning of the school year, and follow-up training throughout the year
- A family support team designed to provide parenting education and support family involvement in the school

Through the Eyes of Teachers

Teaching Science at the Zoo and Cross-Age Peer Teaching

In Lincoln, Nebraska, several high school science teachers use the Folsum Zoo and Botanical Gardens as a context for guiding students' learning. The science classes are taught in two trailers at the zoo. The teachers emphasize the partnership of students, teachers, zoo, and community. One highlight of the program is the "Bug Bash," when the high school students teach fourth-grade students about insects.

Lincoln zoo crew: clockwise from back left, teachers Beth Briney, Amy Vanderslice, De Tonack, Sara LeRoy-Toren, and James Barstow.

First implemented during the 1987–1988 school year in 5 inner-city schools in Baltimore, Maryland, SFA has expanded to over 475 schools in 31 states, now serving more than 250,000 students. Researchers have found that in most comparisons, students who have participated in the program have better reading skills and are less likely to be in special education classes than disadvantaged students who have not been involved in the program (Slavin & Madden, 2001; Weiler, 1998).

Peer Tutors　　Fellow students also can be effective tutors (Shamir & Tzuriel, 2004). In peer tutoring, one student teaches another. In *cross-age peer tutoring,* the peer is older. In *same-age peer tutoring,* the peer is a classmate. Cross-age peer tutoring usually works better than same-age peer tutoring. An older peer is more likely to be skilled than a same-age peer, and being tutored by a same-age classmate is more likely to embarrass a student and lead to negative social comparison.

Researchers have found that peer tutoring often benefits students' achievement (Johnson & Ward, 2001; Mathes & others, 1998; McDonnell & others, 2001; Topping & others, 2004). In some instances, the tutoring benefits the tutor as well as the tutee, especially when the older tutor is a low-achieving student. Teaching something to someone else is one of the best ways to learn.

In a study that won the American Educational Research Association's award for best research study, the effectiveness of a classwide peer tutoring program in reading was evaluated for three learner types: low-achieving students with and without disabilities and average-achieving students (Fuchs & others, 1997). Twelve elementary and middle schools were randomly assigned to experimental (peer tutoring) and control (no peer tutoring) groups. The peer tutoring program was conducted in 35-minute sessions during regularly scheduled reading instruction three days a week. It lasted for fifteen weeks. The training of peer tutors emphasized helping students get practice in reading aloud from narrative text, reviewing and sequencing information read, summarizing large amounts of reading material, stating main ideas, predicting and checking story outcomes, and other reading strategies. Pre- and posttreatment reading achievement data were collected. Irrespective of the type of learner, students in the peer tutoring classrooms showed greater reading progress over the fifteen weeks than their counterparts who did not receive peer tutoring.

The peer tutoring program used in the study just described is called Peer-Assisted Learning Strategies (PALS). PALS was created by the John F. Kennedy Center and the Department of Special Education at Peabody College at Vanderbilt University. In PALS, teachers identify which children require help on specific skills and who the most appropriate children are to help other children learn those skills. Using this information, teachers pair children in the class so that partners work simultaneously and productively on different activities that address the problems they are experiencing. Pairs are changed regularly so that as students work on a variety of skills, all students have the opportunity of being "coaches" and "players."

PALS is a 25- to 35-minute activity that is used two to four times a week. Typically it creates thirteen to fifteen pairs in a classroom. It has been designed for use in the areas of reading and mathematics for kindergarten through sixth grade. It is not designed to replace existing curricula.

In PALS Math, students work on a sheet of problems in a skill area, such as adding, subtracting, number concepts, charts, and graphs. PALS Math involves pairing students as a coach and a player. The coach uses a sheet with a series of questions designed to guide the player and provides feedback to the player. Students then exchange papers and score each others' practice sheets. Students earn points for cooperating and constructing good explanations during coaching and for doing problems correctly during practice. PALS Math and PALS Reading are effective in developing students' mathematical and reading skills (Fuchs, Fuchs, & Burish, 2000; Mathes, Torgesen, & Allor, 2001).

A recent review of research on PALS concluded that the program is highly effective with at-risk students, especially students in the early elementary grades, ethnic minority students, students in urban schools, and possibly low-income students (Rohrbeck & others, 2003). In this review, the argument was made that because at-risk students often experience education characterized by inadequate use of instruction time, low expectations, and fewer opportunities for learning, the use of PALS with these students is likely to represent an improvement in the instruction they receive.

The Diversity and Education interlude tells more about the effectiveness of peer tutoring.

 Through the Eyes of Children

When I Showed Her How, She Was Spectacular

PALS was a good experience for me. It helped me to cooperate with other students. For example, one of my partners read a four-paragraph page very slowly. I helped him. The next day he read much better. That made me feel really good. Later, another PALS partner I had didn't like to answer the PALS question. When I showed her how, she was spectacular. I loved PALS. I hope to do it again.

Myers
Elementary School Student
Nashville, Tennessee

 Diversity and Education
The Valued Youth Program

In more than a hundred middle and high schools across the country, the Valued Youth Program gives students who are not achieving well or are at risk for school-related problems the responsibility for tutoring elementary school children (Simons, Finlay, & Yang, 1991). The hope is that the tutoring experience will improve not only the achievement of the students being tutored but also the achievement of the tutors.

In one school's Valued Youth Program, four days a week participants walk or ride a bus to tutor for one class period at a nearby elementary school. Each tutor works with three children on subjects such as math or reading, and tutors work with the same children for the entire school year. On the fifth day of the week, the tutors work with their teacher at their own school, discussing tutoring skills, reflecting on how the week has gone, and brushing up on their own literacy skills. For their work, the tutors receive course credit and minimum-wage pay.

One of the Valued Youth Program tutors said, "Tutoring makes me want to come to school because I have to come and teach the younger kids." He also said that he did not miss many days of school, as he used to, because when he had been absent the elementary school children always ask him where he was and tell him that they missed him. He said that he really liked the kids he taught and that if he had not been a tutor he probably would have dropped out of school already.

In one analysis, fewer than 1% of the Valued Youth Program tutors had dropped out of school, compared with a 14% national dropout rate (Intercultural Development Research Association, 1996).

The boy on the left is a tutor in the Valued Youth Program, which takes at-risk middle and high school students and gives them the responsibility of tutoring elementary school children.

Teaching Strategies
For Using Peer Tutoring

Here are some suggestions for how to use peer tutoring (Goodlad & Hirst, 1989; Jenkins & Jenkins, 1987):

1. *Use cross-age tutoring rather than same-age tutoring when possible.* Set aside specific times of the day for peer tutoring and communicate the learning assignment clearly and precisely to the peer tutor—for example, "Today from 9 to 9:30 I would like you to work with Jimmy on the following math problem-solving exercises: _____, _____, and _____."

2. *Let students participate in both tutor and tutee roles.* This helps students learn that they can both help and be helped. Pairing of best friends often is not a good strategy because they have trouble staying focused on the learning assignment.

3. *Don't let tutors give tests to tutees.* This can undermine cooperation between the students.

4. *Spend time training tutors.* For peer tutoring to be successful, you will have to spend some time training the tutors. To get peer tutors started off right, discuss competent peer-tutoring strategies. Demonstrate how scaffolding works. Give the tutors clear, organized instructions and invite them to ask questions about their assignments. Divide the group of peer tutors into pairs and let them practice what you have just demonstrated. Let them alternately be tutor and tutee.

5. *Don't overuse peer tutoring.* It is easy to fall into the trap of using high-achieving students as peer tutors too often. Be sure that these students get ample opportunities to participate in challenging intellectual tasks themselves.

6. *Let parents know that their child will be involved in peer tutoring.* Explain to them the advantages of this learning strategy and invite them to visit the classroom to observe how the peer tutoring works.

Cooperative Learning

Cooperative learning occurs when students work in small groups to help each other learn. Cooperative learning groups vary in size, although four is a typical number of

cooperative learning Learning that occurs when students work in small groups to help each other learn.

students. In some cases, cooperative learning is done in dyads (two students). When students are assigned to work in a cooperative group, the group usually stays together for weeks or months, but cooperative groups usually occupy only a portion of the student's school day or year (Sherman, 2001).

Research on Cooperative Learning   Researchers have found that cooperative learning can be an effective strategy for improving achievement, especially when two conditions are met (Slavin, 1995):

Cooperative Learning Research
Cooperative Learning Abstracts

- *Group rewards are generated.* Some type of recognition or reward is given to the group so that the group members can sense that it is in their best interest to help each other learn.
- *Individuals are held accountable.* Some method of evaluating a student's individual contribution, such as an individual quiz, needs to be used. Without this individual accountability, some students might do some "social loafing" (let other students do their work) and some might be left out because it is believed that they have little to contribute.

When the conditions of group rewards and individual accountability are met, cooperative learning improves achievement across different grades and in tasks that range from basic skills to problem solving (Johnson & Johnson, 1999a, 2002, 2003; Qin, Johnson, & Johnson, 1995).

Motivation   Increased motivation to learn is common in cooperative groups (Johnson & Johnson, 2002; Sapon-Shevin, 1999). In one study, fifth- and sixth-grade Israeli students were given a choice of continuing to do schoolwork or going out to play (Sharan & Shaulov, 1990). Only when students were in cooperative groups were they likely to forego going out to play. Positive peer interaction and positive feelings about making their own decisions were motivating factors behind students' choice to participate in the cooperative groups. In another study, high school students made greater gains and expressed more intrinsic motivation to learn algebraic concepts when they were in cooperative rather than individualistic learning contexts (Nichols & Miller, 1994).

Interdependence and Teaching One's Peers   Cooperative learning also promotes increased interdependence and connection with other students (Johnson & Johnson, 2002, 2003). In one study, fifth-graders were more likely to move to a correct strategy for solving decimal problems if the partners clearly explained their ideas and considered each other's proposals (Ellis, Klahr, & Siegler, 1994).

In a cooperative learning group, students typically learn a part of a larger unit and then have to teach that part to the group. When students teach something to others, they tend to learn it more deeply.

Cooperative Learning Approaches   A number of cooperative learning approaches have been developed. They include STAD (Student-Teams-Achievement Divisions), the jigsaw classroom, learning together, group investigation, and cooperative scripting. To read about these approaches, see figure 10.1.

Creating a Cooperative Community   The school community is made up of faculty, staff, students, parents, and people in the neighborhood. More broadly, the school community also includes central administrators, college admissions officers, and future employers. To create an effective learning community, David and Roger Johnson (2002, pp. 144–146) believe that cooperation and positive interdependence needs to occur at a number of different levels: the learning group of children within a classroom (which we just discussed), the classroom, between classrooms, school, school-parent, and school-neighborhood:

STAD (STUDENT-TEAMS-ACHIEVEMENT DIVISIONS)

STAD involves team recognition and group responsibility for learning in mixed-ability groups (Slavin, 1994). Rewards are given to teams whose members improve the most over their past performances. Students are assigned to teams of four or five members. The teacher presents a lesson, usually over one or two class periods. Next, students study worksheets based on material presented by the teacher. Students monitor their team members' performance to ensure that all members have mastered their material. Teams practice working on problems together and study together, but the members take quizzes individually. The resulting individual scores contribute to the team's overall score. An individual's contribution to the team score is based on that individual's improvement, not on an absolute score, which motivates students to work hard because each contribution counts. In some STAD classrooms, a weekly class newsletter is published that recognizes both team and individual performances.

The STAD approach has been used in a variety of subjects (including math, reading, and social studies) and with students at different grade levels. It is most effective for learning situations that involve well-defined objectives or problems with specific answers or solutions. These include math computation, language use, geography skills, and science facts.

THE JIGSAW CLASSROOM

In chapter 5, "Sociocultural Diversity," we described the jigsaw classroom, which involves having students from different cultural backgrounds cooperate by doing different parts of a project to reach a common goal. Here we elaborate on the concept.

Developed by Eliot Aronson and his colleagues (1978), *Jigsaw I* is a cooperative learning approach in which six-member teams work on material that has been broken down into parts. Each team member is responsible for a part. Members of different teams who have studied the same part convene, discuss their part, and then return to their teams, where they take turns teaching their part to other team members.

Robert Slavin (1994) created *Jigsaw II*, a modified version of *Jigsaw I*. Whereas *Jigsaw I* consists of teams of six, *Jigsaw II* usually has teams of four or five. All team members study the entire lesson rather than one part, and individual scores are combined to form an overall team score, as in STAD. After they have studied the entire lesson, students become expert on one aspect of the lesson; then students with the same topics meet in expert groups to discuss them. Subsequently, they return to their teams and help other members of the team learn the material.

LEARNING TOGETHER

Created by David and Roger Johnson (1994), this approach has four components: (1) face-to-face interaction, (2) positive interdependence, (3) individual accountability, and (4) development of interpersonal group skills. Thus, in addition to Slavin's interest in achievement, the Johnsons' cooperative learning approach also focuses on socio-emotional development and group interaction. In learning together, students work in four- or five-member heterogeneous groups on tasks with an emphasis on discussion and team building (Johnson & Johnson, 2003).

GROUP INVESTIGATION

Developed by Shlomo Sharan (1990; Sharan & Sharan, 1992), this approach involves a combination of independent learning and group work in two- to six-member groups), as well as a group reward for individual achievement. The teacher chooses a problem for the class to study, but students decide what they want to study in exploring the problem. The work is divided among the group's members, who work individually. Then the group gets together, integrating, summarizing, and presenting the findings as a group project. The teacher's role is to facilitate investigation and maintain cooperative effort. Students collaborate with the teacher to evaluate their effort. In Sharan's view, this is the way many real-world problems are solved in communities around the world.

COOPERATIVE SCRIPTING

Students work in reciprocal pairs, taking turns summarizing information and orally presenting it to each other (Dansereau, 1988; McDonald & others, 1985). One member of the pair presents the material. The other member listens, monitors the presentation for any mistakes, and gives feedback. Then the partner becomes the teacher and presents the next set of material while the first member listens and evaluates it.

FIGURE 10.1 **Cooperative Learning Approaches**

- *Class cooperation.* There are many ways to create cooperation and interdependence for the whole class. Class goals can be generated and class rewards given. This can be accomplished by adding bonus points to all class members' academic scores when all class members attain a goal "or by giving nonacademic rewards, such as extra free time, extra recess time, stickers, food, T-shirts, or a class party." Classroom cooperation can be promoted by "putting teams in charge of daily class cleanup, running a class bank or business, or engaging in other activities that benefit the class as a whole. Classroom interdependence may also be structured through dividing resources, such as having the class publish a newsletter in which each cooperative group contributes one article . . . one class was studying geography." The ceiling was turned into a large world map. "The class was divided into eight cooperative groups. Each group was assigned a geographical location on which to do a report. The class then planned an itinerary for a trip to visit all eight places. Yarn was used to mark their journey. As they arrived at each spot, the appropriate group presented its report" about the location.
- *Interclass cooperation.* An interdisciplinary team of teachers may organize their classes into a "neighborhood" or "school within a school" in which classes work together on joint projects.
- *Schoolwide cooperation.* Cooperation at the level of the entire school can be attained in a number of ways. "The school mission statement may articulate the mutual goals shared by all members of the school and be displayed on the school walls" and highlighted on a school Web page. "Teachers can work in a variety of cooperative teams . . . and faculty/staff can meet weekly in teaching teams and/or study groups. . . . Teachers may be assigned to task forces to plan and implement solutions to schoolwide issues. . . . Finally, school interdependence may be highlighted in a variety of schoolwide activities, such as the weekly student-produced school news broadcast, . . . all-school projects, and regular school assemblies."
- *School-parent cooperation.* Cooperation is promoted between the school and parents "by involving parents in establishing mutual goals and strategic plans to attain the goals, . . . in sharing resources to help the school achieve its goals," and in creating activities that improve the likelihood that parents will develop a positive attitude toward the school.
- *School-neighborhood cooperation.* If the school is embedded in a neighborhood, a positive interdependence between the school and the neighborhood can benefit both. The school's mission "can be supported by neighborhood merchants who provide resources and financing for various events. Classes can perform neighborhood service projects, such as cleaning up a park."

STRUCTURING SMALL-GROUP WORK

When you structure students' work in small groups, you have to make decisions about how to compose the group, build team skills, and structure group interaction (Webb & Palincsar, 1996).

! Review and Reflect

2 Explain how teachers and peers can jointly contribute to children's learning.

Review
- What is scaffolding? Is it something peers can do?
- What does the study of cognitive apprenticeships reveal about how experts work with novices?
- Is tutoring effective? What are some alternative sources of tutors?

- What is cooperative learning and how might it benefit students? What are some ways to structure it?

Reflect

- How would you handle the situation if parents became angry that, because of time allotted to cooperative learning, their children were being allowed less time to learn on an individual basis?

Composing the Group

Teachers often ask how they should assign students to small groups in their class. The cooperative learning approaches featured in figure 10.1 generally recommend heterogeneous groups with diversity in ability, ethnic background, socioeconomic status, and gender (Johnson & Johnson, 2002). The reasoning behind heterogeneous grouping is that it maximizes opportunities for peer tutoring and support, improves cross-gender and cross-ethnic relations, and ensures that each group has at least one student who can do the work (Kagan, 1992).

Heterogeneous Ability   One of the main reasons for using heterogeneous ability groups is that they benefit low-ability students, who can learn from higher-ability students. However, some critics argue that such heterogeneous groupings hold back high-ability students. In most studies, though, high-achieving students perform equally well on achievement tests after working in heterogeneous groups or homogeneous groups (Hooper & others, 1989). In heterogeneous groups, high-ability students often assume the role of "teacher" and explain concepts to other students. In homogeneous groups, high-ability students are less likely to assume this teaching role.

One problem with heterogeneous groups is that when high-ability, low-ability, and medium-ability students are included, the medium-ability students get left out to some extent; high-ability and low-ability students might form a teacher-student relationship in these groups, excluding medium-ability students from group interaction. Medium-ability students might perform better in groups where most or all of the students have medium abilities.

Ethnic, Socioeconomic, and Gender Heterogeneity
Some of the initial reasons cooperative learning groups were formed was to improve interpersonal relations among students from different ethnic and socioeconomic backgrounds. The hope was that interaction under conditions of equal status in cooperative groups would reduce prejudice. However, getting students to interact on the basis of equal status has been more difficult than initially envisioned.

Some experts recommend that when forming ethnically and socioeconomically heterogeneous groups, careful attention be given to a group's composition (Miller & Harrington, 1990). One recommendation is to not make the composition too obvious. Thus, you might vary different social characteristics (ethnicity, socioeconomic status, and gender) simultaneously, such as grouping together a middle-income African American female, a White male

Through the Eyes of Teachers

An Eye-Level Meeting of the Minds

Ninth-grade history teacher Jimmy Furlow believes that students learn best when they have to teach others. He has groups of students summarize textbook sections and put them on transparencies to help the entire class prepare for a test. Furlow lost both legs in Vietnam but he rarely stays in one place, moving his wheelchair around the room, communicating with students at eye level. When the class completes their discussion of all the points on the overhead, Furlow edits their work to demonstrate concise, clear writing and help students zero in on an important point (Marklein, 1998).

Ninth-grade history teacher Jimmy Furlow converses with a student in his class.

from a low-income family, and so on. In this way, for example, the White males would not all be from high-income families. Another recommendation is to not form groups that have only one minority student, if at all possible; this avoids calling attention to the student's "solo status."

In mixed-gender groups, males tend to be more active and dominant (Tannen, 1990). Thus, when mixing females and males, an important task for teachers is to encourage girls to speak up and boys to allow girls to express their opinions and contribute to the group's functioning. A general strategy is to have an equal number of girls and boys. In groups of five or six children in which only one member is a girl, the boys tend to ignore the girl (Webb, 1984).

Team-Building Skills

Good cooperative learning in the classroom requires that time be spent on team-building skills. This involves thinking about how to start team building at the beginning of the school year, helping students become better listeners, giving students practice in contributing to a team product, getting students to discuss the value of a team leader, and working with team leaders to help them deal with problem situations.

Teaching Strategies
For Developing Students' Team-Building Skills

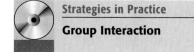

Strategies in Practice
Group Interaction

Here are some guidelines (Aronson & Patnoe, 1997):

1. *Don't begin the year with cooperative learning on a difficult task.* Teachers report that academic cooperative learning often works best when students have previously worked together on team-building exercises. A short period each day for several weeks is usually adequate for this team building.

2. *Do team building at the level of the cooperative group (two to six students) rather than at the level of the entire class.* Some students on the team will be more assertive; others will be more passive. The team-building goal is to give all members some experience in being valuable team members, as well as to get them to learn that being cooperative works more effectively than being competitive.

3. *In team building, work with students to help them become better listeners.* Ask students to introduce themselves by name all at the same time to help them see that they have to take turns and listen to each other instead of hogging a conversation. You also can ask students to come up with behavioral descriptions of how they can show others that they are listening. These might include looking directly at the speaker, rephrasing what she just said, summarizing her statement, and so on.

4. *Give students some practice in contributing to a common product as part of team building.* Ask each student to participate in drawing a group picture by passing paper and pen from student to student. Each student's task is to add something to the picture as it circulates several times through the team. When the picture is finished, discuss each student's contribution to the team. Students will sense that the product is not complete unless each member's contribution is recognized. The group picture illustrates how working together can be beneficial.

5. *During team building, you may want to discuss the value of having a group leader.* You can ask students to discuss the specific ways a leader should function in order to maximize the group's performance. Their brainstorming might come up with such characteristics as "helps get the group organized," "keeps the group on task," "serves as liaison between the teacher and the group," "shows enthusiasm," "is

patient and polite," and "helps the group deal with disagreements and conflicts." The teacher may select the group leader or students may be asked to elect one.

6. *You likely will need to work with team leaders to help them deal with problem situations.* For example, some members might rarely talk, one member might dominate the group, members might call each other names, some members might refuse to work, one member might want to work alone, and everyone might talk at once. You can get group leaders together and get them to role-play such situations and discuss effective strategies for handling the problem situation.

Structuring Group Interaction

One way to facilitate students working in small groups is to assign students different roles. For example, consider these roles that students can assume in a group (Kagan, 1992):

Video Observation: Facilitating Group Work

- Encourager—brings out reluctant students and is a motivator
- Praiser—shows appreciation of other students' work
- Gatekeeper—equalizes participation of students in the group
- Coach—helps with academic content
- Question commander—ensures that students ask questions and that the group answers them
- Checker—makes sure the group understands the material
- Taskmaster—keeps the group on task
- Recorder—writes down ideas and decisions
- Reflector—thinks about and evaluates the group's progress
- Quiet captain—monitors the group's noise level
- Materials monitor—obtains and returns supplies

Such roles help groups to function more smoothly and give all members of the group a sense of importance. Note that although we just described eleven different roles that can be played in groups, most experts, as we noted earlier, recommend that groups not exceed five or six members to function effectively. Some members can fill multiple roles, and all roles do not always have to be filled.

Another way roles can be specialized is to designate some students as "summarizers" and others as "listeners." Researchers have consistently found that summarizing benefits learning more than listening, so if these roles are used, all members should get opportunities to be summarizers (Dansereau, 1988).

To evaluate your attitudes toward social constructivist approaches and whether you are likely to use such strategies when you teach, complete Self-Assessment 10.1.

! Review and Reflect

3 **Make effective decisions in structuring small-group work.**

Review
- What are some important considerations in placing students in small groups?
- What can teachers do to build team skills within groups?
- What types of role assignments can improve a group's structure?

Reflect
- Suppose you and five other students have decided to form a group to study for a final exam in educational psychology. How would you structure the group? What roles would you want the group to assign?

Evaluating My Social Constructivist Experiences

What experiences have you already had with social constructivist thinking and learning? You may have had such experiences in school or in other settings. For each of these settings that you have experienced, record at least one instance in which you can look back and see social constructivist principles at work.

1. Your family:

_____

_____

2. A club or program such as the Scouts:

_____

_____

3. A sports, music, or dance experience:

_____

_____

4. A religious setting:

_____

_____

5. Your K–12 school experience:

_____

_____

6. College:

_____

_____

How do those experiences shape your judgment regarding these ideas for classroom teaching?

1. That thinking should be viewed as located (situated) in social and physical contexts, not only within an individual's mind:

_____

_____

2. Vygotsky's sociocultural cognitive theory:

_____

_____

3. Scaffolding:

_____

_____

4. Peer tutoring:

_____

_____

5. Cooperative learning:

_____

_____

6. Small-group work:

_____

_____

 Go to your Student Toolbox CD-ROM for an electronic version of this form.

SOCIAL CONSTRUCTIVIST PROGRAMS

Let's explore several programs that systematically incorporate social constructivist philosophies in their efforts to challenge students to solve real-world problems and develop a deeper understanding of concepts.

Fostering a Community of Learners

Ann Brown and Joe Campione (1996; Brown, 1997; Campione, 2001) have developed a program called **Fostering a Community of Learners (FCL)**, which focuses on literacy development and biology. As currently established, it is set in inner-city elementary schools and is appropriate for six- to twelve-year-old children. Reflection and discussion are key dimensions of the program. In FCL, constructive commentary, questioning, querying, and criticism are the norm rather than the exception. The program emphasizes three strategies that encourage reflection and discussion: (1) the use of adults as role models, (2) children teaching children, and (3) online computer consultation.

Adults as Role Models Visiting experts and classroom teachers introduce the big ideas and difficult principles at the beginning of a unit. The adult demonstrates how to think and self-reflect in the process of identifying topics within a general area of inquiry or reasoning with given information. The adults continually ask students to justify their opinions and then to support them with evidence, to think of counterexamples of rules, and so on.

For example, one area of biological inquiry used in the FCL program is "Changing Populations." Outside experts or teachers introduce this topic and ask students to generate as many questions about it as

Fostering a Community of Learners (FCL) A social constructivist program that encourages reflection and discussion through the use of adults as role models, children teaching children, and online computer consultation.

A Fostering a Community of Learners (FCL) classroom. *What is the nature of this approach to education?*

329

possible—it is not unusual for students to come up with more than a hundred questions. The teacher and the students categorize the questions into subtopics according to the type of population they refer to (usually about five categories), such as extinct, endangered, artificial, assisted, and urbanized populations. About six students make up a learning group and each group takes responsibility for one of the subtopics.

Children Teaching Children   Brown (1997) says that children as well as adults enrich the classroom learning experience by contributing their particular expertise. Cross-age teaching, in which older students teach younger students, is used. This occurs both face-to-face and via e-mail. Older students often serve as discussion leaders. Cross-age teaching provides students with invaluable opportunities to talk about learning, gives students responsibility and purpose, and fosters collaboration among peers.

FCL uses **reciprocal teaching**, in which students take turns leading a small-group discussion. Reciprocal teaching requires students to discuss complex passages, collaborate, and share their individual expertise and perspectives on a particular topic. Reciprocal teaching can involve a teacher and a student as well as interaction between students.

A modified version of the jigsaw classroom (which was described in chapter 5 and figure 10.1) also is used. As students create preliminary drafts of reports, they participate in "crosstalk" sessions. These are whole-class activities in which groups periodically summarize where they are in their learning activity and get input from the other groups. "Mini-jigsaws" (small groups) also are used. At both the whole-class level and mini-jigsaw level, if group members can't understand what a student is saying or writing about, the student must revise a product and present it again later. Students are then grouped into reciprocal teaching seminars in which each student is an expert on one subtopic, teaches that part to the others, and participates in constructing test questions based on the subunit.

Online Computer Consultation   As just noted, FCL classrooms also use e-mail to build community and expertise. Through e-mail, experts provide coaching and advice, as well as commentary about what it means to learn and understand. Online experts

reciprocal teaching A learning arrangement in which students take turns leading a small-group discussion.

A Schools for Thought Science classroom at Compton-Drew School in St. Louis.

function as role models of thinking. They wonder, query, and make inferences based on incomplete knowledge.

At the heart of FCL is a culture of learning, negotiating, sharing, and producing work that is displayed to others. The educational experience involves an interpretive community that encourages active exchange and reciprocity. This approach has much in common with what Jerome Bruner (1996) recommended for improving the culture of education. Research evaluation of the Fostering a Community of Learners approach suggests that it benefits students' understanding and flexible use of content knowledge, resulting in improved achievement in reading, writing, and problem solving.

Schools for Thought

Schools for Thought (SFT) is another formal program of social constructivist teaching. Too often students emerge from instruction with only a fragile understanding of the material (Segal, 1996). For example, students might be able to repeat various scientific principles they have been taught in science, but they run into difficulties when they have to explain everyday scientific phenomena. Similarly, in math, students might be good at plugging numbers into formulas but when confronted with variations of these problems be unable to solve them. Thus, many students acquire enough information to pass tests in school but gain no deep understanding of concepts.

In one effort, Schools for Thought (Lamon & others, 1996) has combined aspects of The Jasper Project, Fostering a Community of Learners (FCL), and Computer Supported Intentional Learning Environments (CSILE) in a school learning environment. The project is named after John Bruer's (1993) award-winning book *Schools for Thought*. The Jasper Project, FCL, and CSILE share certain features that allow them to be combined in a school learning environment. We already have described the Jasper Project (chapter 9) and FCL ◀ p. 301. To learn about CSILE, read the Technology and Education box.

Curriculum   The three core programs of Schools for Thought stress the importance of getting students to think about real-world problems. Problem-based and project-based activities are at the heart of the curriculum. Extended in-depth inquiry in domains such as science, math, and social studies are emphasized. All three programs also incorporate cross-disciplinary inquiry across traditional boundaries. For example, exploring what it means for an animal to be endangered could mean examining problems related to estimating populations, sampling, and other issues usually restricted to mathematics. In the Schools for Thought project, curricula are being developed that integrate geography, geology, environmental and physical science, ancient and American history, and language arts and reading.

Instruction   All three SFT programs involve a change in the classroom instructional climate. In a traditional classroom, students are receivers of information that is dispensed by teachers, textbooks, and other media; the teacher's role is to give information and mold students' learning. In many traditional schools, what students mainly do is listen, watch, and mimic what teachers and texts tell them to do (Greeno, 1993).

In contrast, all three programs provide students with many opportunities to plan and organize their own learning and problem solving. They also encourage students to work collaboratively as they learn and think. Students explore ideas, evaluate information, and consider others' ideas in an ongoing reciprocal interchange with peers, teachers, and experts.

The Schools for Thought environments are not simply free-wheeling discovery environments. They involve a considerable amount of structure. Teachers and community experts keep learning focused on key principles in the domains being studied, such as mathematics, science, or social science. They monitor and reframe students'

Schools for Thought (SFT) A social constructivist program that combines aspects of The Jasper Project, Fostering a Community of Learners, and CSILE.

Computer Supported Intentional Learning Environments (CSILE)

A CSILE site might include more than one classroom. A typical classroom has eight networked computers (Bereiter & Scardamalia, 1989; Scardamalia & Bereiter, 1994). CSILE classrooms are connected to form a communal base for the entire school. Students are encouraged to enter their views and questions, compare perspectives, and reflect on joint understanding of ideas. Students work both individually and collaboratively. Students can add a comment or attach a graphic note, such as a picture or diagram, to another student's entry. However, only the original author of the note can edit or delete the notes. Authors are informed when a comment has been attached to one of their notes.

Following is an example of work done within one combined fifth-/sixth-grade CSILE classroom (Bruer, 1989). The focus was on ecology, with one group working on the topic of fossil fuels. The group began with a kitchen scene that one student had previously created as a CSILE note. The students took this as a learning challenge to identify the uses of fossil fuels in an ordinary kitchen. Different students examined different parts of the kitchen, exploring such topics as the generation of electricity and the origin of natural gas. This information led to posting of notes explaining how the fossil fuels were used. The notes were attached to pictures of the various kitchen objects. The computer system allowed notes to be posted hierarchically. For example, a student could begin with a kitchen scene and click on the refrigerator. This would open a picture of the refrigerator's interior. Clicking on various items in the refrigerator then would bring up pictures and text about the fossil fuels. This learning exercise unfolded in a museum-like way with every detail of daily life made interesting.

CSILE helps students understand how knowledge and understanding are socially constructed and gives students opportunities to reflect on, revise, and transform their thinking. Students learn that thinking is not a brief, cursory exercise. Rather, it takes place over an extended time and often needs to be modified based on feedback from a community of learners. Research evaluations indicate that students in CSILE classrooms perform better on standardized achievement tests of language and math, give deeper explanations of concepts, are better at solving problems, and have a more positive attitude toward learning than students in conventional classrooms (Scardamalia, Bereiter, & Lamon, 1994).

For more information about CSILE classrooms, contact Dr. Carl Bereiter and Dr. Marlene Scardamalia at the University of Toronto.

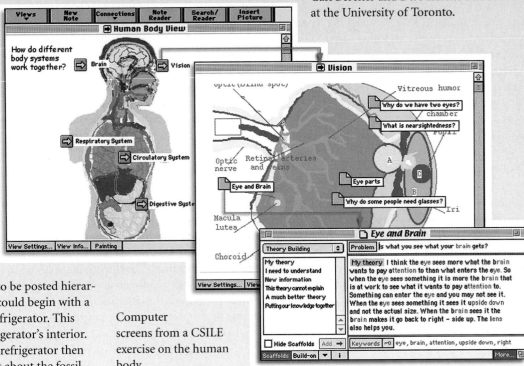

Computer screens from a CSILE exercise on the human body.

self-generated questions and exploration to keep them within the perspective of the key principles. In this manner, they guide the direction of students' inquiry so that students discover the deep concepts of the domain. Still, there is considerable flexibility in how this understanding is achieved and the nature of the projects undertaken.

Community In many schools, classrooms and teachers operate in isolation, not just from each other but from the outside community as well. The Jasper Project, FCL, and CSILE all emphasize the importance of giving students and teachers opportunities to see themselves as part of a team and as members of a larger community. Problems often have a community focus, to encourage students to think about how learning and problem solving can be used to better understand and improve the world in which we live.

Technology   The Jasper Project, FCL, and CSILE all use technology to break the isolation of the traditional classroom. They encourage students to communicate electronically with a community of learners beyond the classroom's walls.

Assessment   The goals in creating The Jasper Project, FCL, and CSILE were not to improve students' achievement test scores. Assessment in the three programs focuses on achieving authentic performances (such as reading for the purpose of answering research questions, writing to build new knowledge), making assessment coordinate smoothly with learning and instruction, and encouraging students to engage in self-assessment. We will have much more to say about these types of assessment in chapter 16, "Classroom Assessment."

Further Exploration of the Schools for Thought Project   The Schools for Thought project is in the process of building and expanding its activities to make them easier for classroom teachers to implement. Two types of tools they are developing are starter units and performance support tools.

A Collaborative School

In 1977, a collaborative school was organized as a parent-teacher cooperative and continues today with six classrooms serving kindergarten through sixth grade in Salt Lake City, Utah. It is an optional school serving the whole school district, open to families who would like to have their children educated there. Learning to work effectively in groups is a major emphasis in the curriculum (Rogoff, Turkanis, & Bartlett, 2001). During the school day children usually work in small groups with the teacher and/or parent volunteers. In some instances, children work on their own. Children often share decision making on projects with classmates and adults, contribute to adults' guidance by conversing openly with teachers and parent volunteers, as well as with each other, and treat other people as sources of help.

Schools for Thought
Schools for Thought and Technology
CSILE

Students in a collaborative school in Salt Lake City. *How might a collaborative school differ from a typical school?*

ENTER THE DEBATE

1. Should teachers use their high-ability students to tutor their struggling students?

2. Should teachers use heterogeneous grouping with regards to ability in forming classroom learning groups?

Teaching Experience

Using Scaffolding and Groupworth to Teach

Parents contribute three hours of time per week to classroom instruction for each child enrolled in the school. Before the school year begins, parents and the teacher hold a meeting at the family's home to prepare for the upcoming year. Parent meetings are held on a monthly basis to continue planning and discussing what can be done to help in the classroom.

In the collaborative school, teachers, parents, and children help plan and develop a curriculum that includes (Turkanis, 2001, pp. 91–92)

• Capturing "the moment to build on interesting ideas that emerge in class discussion"
• "Recognizing that children have their own learning agendas that can provide motivation" and the path to learning in curriculum areas
• "Supporting units of study that often emerge as a group process, as people become interested in others' interests and build on each other's expertise"
• Using extensive and varied resources with little reliance on textbooks
• Focusing in depth on big ideas, concepts, and projects

In one first-/second-grade class, every Monday morning of the whole year was devoted to a project of building a town. Students chose which part of the town they wanted to develop and built storefronts. Students developed their own jobs and a government, named their town by popular election, printed money, and published a newspaper. At the close of each day, the businesses counted their cash, prepared a deposit, and took it to the town bank, where figures were verified and credit given to the businesses' accounts. The newspaper accepted advertisements developed by the businesses and reported on city residents and activities. When a problem arose, students had a town meeting and found a solution for the problem. By the end of the year, they had a smoothly functioning town and invited other classes to patronize their businesses.

The town building project was a comprehensive learning experience. Through this project, students developed a better understanding of interpersonal relationships and problem solving in a business community as well as improved math, reading, and writing skills.

Review and Reflect

4 Describe three social constructivist programs.

Review
• What three strategies are embedded in the Fostering a Community of Learners program?
• What programs are combined in Schools for Thought? What do these programs have in common?
• What are some themes of the collaborative school described?

Reflect
• Which of the three social constructivist programs appeals to you the most? Why?

Sue is a new second-grade teacher, full of enthusiasm for her job. She believes that students should be very active in constructing their own knowledge base and that they should work together to do this. To that end, she has decided that she wants her classroom to be a social constructivist classroom. Sue has made some decisions about some things she wants to do this year with her students.

First, she knows that she will have to provide students with scaffolding when material is new and gradually adjust the amount of help her students receive. She wants to use peer tutoring for this in her class because she believes that children can often learn more from each other than they can from an adult. She sets up a system in which the more-advanced students in her class help those who are less advanced.

She also likes the idea of cooperative learning. She sets up her student groups so that they are heterogeneous with regard to ability, gender, ethnicity, and socioeconomic status. She then assigns roles to each student in a group. Some of these roles are coach, motivator, checker, taskmaster, recorder, and materials monitor. She uses this approach for many content areas. Sometimes she uses a jigsaw approach in which each student is responsible for becoming an expert in a particular area and then sharing that expertise with his or her group members. She uses this approach in science and in social studies.

In math, she feels very fortunate that her school has adopted the Everyday Mathematics curriculum. This program makes connections with the real world, which Sue thinks is so important in math instruction. Group work is also stressed as is finding different ways to find the same answer to a problem. She hopes that her students and their parents will share her excitement as they "all learn together."

Sue soon feels disappointed, however. When she groups students she hears groans of "Not again." "Why do I have to work with her? She doesn't know anything." "He's too bossy." "I always have to be with him; then I end up doing everything." "She never lets me do anything but sit there and watch." Parents have gotten in on the act, too. She has received calls and letters from parents who don't understand what she's trying to do. They all seem concerned about test scores and grades rather than what their children are learning together. One parent asked that her child no longer be grouped with another child who is "holding back" her child's learning.

- What are the issues in this case?
- Did Sue do anything incorrectly? If so, what?
- What should she do now to recover her constructivist classroom?
- How can she elicit the cooperation of the parents?

Reach Your Learning Goals

1 Compare the social constructivist approach with other constructivist approaches.

- Piaget's and Vygotsky's theories are constructivist. Piaget's theory is a cognitive constructivist theory, whereas Vygotsky's is social constructivist. The implication of Vygotsky's model for teaching is to establish opportunities for students to learn with the teacher and peers in constructing knowledge and understanding. In both Piaget's and Vygotsky's models, teachers are facilitators, not directors. Distinctions between cognitive and social constructivist approaches are not always clear-cut. All social constructivist approaches emphasize that social factors contribute to students' construction of knowledge and understanding.

- Situated cognition is the idea that thinking is located (situated) in social and physical contexts, not within an individual's mind.

2 Explain how teachers and peers can jointly contribute to children's learning.

- Scaffolding is the technique of providing changing levels of support over the course of a teaching session, with more-skilled individuals providing guidance to fit the student's current performance.

- A cognitive apprenticeship involves a novice and an expert, who stretches and supports the novice's understanding of and use of skills.

- Tutoring involves a cognitive apprenticeship between an expert and a novice. Tutoring can take place between an adult and a child or a more-skilled child and a less-skilled child. Individual tutoring is effective. Classroom aides, volunteers, and mentors can serve as tutors to support teachers and classroom learning. Reading Recovery and Success for All are examples of effective tutoring programs. In many cases, students benefit more from cross-age tutoring than from same-age tutoring. Tutoring can benefit both the tutee and the tutor.

- Cooperative learning occurs when students work in small groups to help each other learn. Researchers have found that cooperative learning can be an effective strategy for improving students' achievement, especially when group goals and individual accountability are instituted. Cooperative learning often improves intrinsic motivation, encourages student interdependence, and promotes deep understanding. Cooperative learning approaches include STAD (Student-Teams-Achievement Divisions), the jigsaw classroom (I and II), learning together, group investigation, and cooperative scripting. Cooperative learning approaches generally recommend heterogeneous groupings with diversity in ability, ethnicity, socioeconomic status, and gender. Creating a cooperative community involves developing positive interdependence at a number of levels: a small group within a classroom, the class as a whole, between classes, the entire school, between parents and the school, and between the school and the neighborhood.

3 Make effective decisions in structuring small-group work.

- Two strategies in composing a small group are to include children with heterogeneous abilities and to have the group membership reflect ethnic, socioeconomic, and gender heterogeneity.

- Structuring small-group work also involves attention to team-building skills. A good strategy is to spend several weeks at the beginning of the school year on building team skills. Assigning one student in each small group to be a team leader can help to build the team.

- A group also can benefit when students are assigned different roles that are designed to help the group function more smoothly.

4 Describe three social constructivist programs.

- Fostering a Community of Learners was developed by Ann Brown and Joe Campione and is appropriate for six-to twelve-year-old students. Reflection and discussion are emphasized through three strategies: (1) using adults as role models, (2) children teaching children, and (3) online computer consultation. Evaluations of the program have been positive.

- Schools for Thought is a project that combines activities from three programs: (1) The Jasper Project, (2) Fostering a Community of Learners, and (3) Computer Supported Intentional Learning Environments. Extended in-depth inquiry is fostered. Teachers guide students in becoming architects of their knowledge.

- A collaborative school was organized as a parent-teacher cooperative in Salt Lake City, Utah. Children usually work in small groups during the day, share decision making with peers, contribute to adults' guidance, and treat others as sources of help.

 KEY TERMS

PORTFOLIO ACTIVITIES

Now that you have a good understanding of this chapter, complete these exercises to expand your thinking.

Independent Reflection

Evaluating Social Constructivist Experiences. To what extent have you experienced various social constructivist approaches in your education? Think about your different levels of schooling (early childhood, elementary, middle, high school, and college) and evaluate your experience (or lack of experience) with scaffolding, cognitive apprenticeship, tutoring, and cooperative learning. (INTASC: Principles 2, 3, 4, 5, 9)

Collaborative Work

Balancing Individual and Group Activities. With four or five other students in the class, discuss how much of the curriculum should include group activities and how much should involve individual activities at the early childhood, elementary, middle, high school, and college levels. Describe your group's thoughts below. Also discuss whether some subject areas might lend themselves better than others to group activities. (INTASC: Principles 1, 3, 4, 5)

Research/Field Experience Reflections

Practical Applications of Social Constructivism. Beyond a teacher and a room full of students, what resources do the three social constructivist programs that were described in the chapter require? How practical is it to use these programs on a widespread basis? Write your responses below. (INTASC: Principles 4, 5, 7)

 Go to the Online Learning Center for downloadable portfolio templates.

 TAKING IT TO THE NET

1. Imagine that you typically give students frequent opportunities to engage in collaborative group work. What questions should you ask yourself when deciding how to organize the groups and structure the work? Why is collaborative group work an important educational experience for students?
2. Multimedia projects offer numerous opportunities for students to engage in social learning. Explore the ThinkQuest Library and evaluate one of the student-created Web projects. In what ways does your selected project employ social constructivist principles of learning?

3. Work with a partner, browse the Web to find a high-quality resource that could serve as a "cognitive apprenticeship" for students, and describe its merits as a teaching tool. For example, a science student can be an apprentice to zoo interns online by accessing their electronic journals, photos, and e-mail discussion forum. Why is the Web such a powerful tool for implementing social constructivist approaches in the classroom?

Connect to the Online Learning Center to explore possible answers.

STUDY, PRACTICE, AND SUCCEED

 Go to chapter 10 on the Online Learning Center at www.mhhe.com/santrockedu2e to access the student study guide with practice quizzes, web links, portfolio resources, PowerWeb articles and news feeds, and the online resources referenced in the chapter.

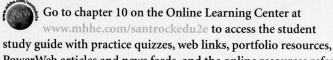 Go to your Student Toolbox CD-ROM to access the resources and activities referenced in the chapter and

- Resources to help you prepare for the PRAXIS II™ exam

- **Application Resources,** including additional *Crack the Case* studies, electronic versions of the *Self-Assessments*, Application Exercises, and Site Observation Questions
- **Study Resources,** including Learning Goals, the Chapter Summary, a *Test Your Learning* exercise, and multiple-choice, true/false, matching, key terms, and short-answer quizzes
- **Professional Resources,** including a Lesson Plan Builder and *Bibliomaker*

> # Meaning is not given to us but by us.
> —Eleanor Duckworth
> *Contemporary American Educator*

Chapter Outline

Chapter Learning Goals After you have completed your study of this chapter, you should be able to reach these learning goals:

1 **Distinguish between expert knowledge and pedagogical content knowledge.**

2 **Explain how reading develops and discuss some useful approaches to teaching reading.**

3 **Describe how writing develops and some useful approaches to teaching writing.**

4 **Characterize how mathematical thinking develops and identify some issues related to teaching mathematics.**

5 **Identify some challenges and strategies related to teaching children how to think scientifically.**

6 **Summarize how learning in social studies is becoming more constructivist.**

Teaching Stories Betty Teufel

Betty Teufel teaches language arts to first-grade students in Plano, Texas. She was the school district's Teacher of the Year in 1998. Literacy is her passion, and she is a strong advocate of literacy not only in her school but throughout the nation. She envisions a literacy revival in which a corps of volunteers become reading tutors in schools, community centers, and hospitals. Betty is working with nonprofit organizations to solicit publishers and businesses to contribute to a national "Read While You Wait" campaign that will saturate clinics, restaurants, airports, and other public facilities with good literature.

She believes that if children don't know how to read, if they don't understand language, and they don't communicate with each other, it won't matter if they are computer literate. In her view, if children are helped to become competent at reading early in their schooling, their motivation to read should last a lifetime. In her words, "We ought to get them hooked on reading."

At Saigling Elementary School, Betty conducts literacy workshops for parents and places book baskets in locations where parents can read while they wait for conferences, meetings, and carpool groups. Enlisting the musical talents of another Saigling teacher, Betty orchestrated the creation of Sing to Read, a program in which students observe patterns, rhymes, and rhythms in songs to help develop their reading skills. Every day after recess, first-grade classes gather to sing songs written on flip charts.

"My students know that every time we have a holiday, I'm going to buy a book and share it with the class," she says. They will say, "What did you find?" Then they all sit down together to read.

Teufel wants to guide children to a sense of self-worth, self-discipline, tolerance, humor, and an attitude of lifelong learning. One of the ways she encourages such traits is by having "Joke Day" every Friday. Students get to write out jokes or riddles and leave them in a basket to be read during the day. They delight in trying to stump the teacher.

Expert Advice

Richard Mayer on Learning

In this chapter, we will explore a number of ideas about children's reading. We also will examine children's learning and cognition in writing, mathematics, science, and social studies.

EXPERT KNOWLEDGE AND PEDAGOGICAL CONTENT KNOWLEDGE

In chapter 8, we discussed the distinction between experts and novices. In describing experts, we indicated that in many cases individuals who are experts in the content of a particular area, such as mathematics or biology, aren't always good at teaching it in ways that others can effectively learn. Let's further examine what is needed to be an expert teacher.

Expert knowledge means excellent knowledge about the content of a particular discipline ◀ p. 266. **Pedagogical content knowledge** is knowledge about how to effectively teach a particular discipline (Shulman, 1987). Both expert knowledge and pedagogical content knowledge are required for being an expert teacher. *Expert teachers* know the structure of their disciplines and this knowledge gives them the ability to create cognitive road maps that guide the assignments they give to students, the assessments they use to evaluate students' progress, and the types of questions and answers they generate in class (National Research Council, 1999). Being an expert teacher in a particular discipline also involves being aware of which aspects of the discipline are especially difficult or easy for students to learn.

In previous chapters, we have mainly explored general teaching strategies that are thought to be effective across all disciplines. In many cases, effective teaching strategies can be transported across disciplines. For example, a good teacher in any discipline asks questions that stimulate students' curiosity, encourages students to go beyond the surface of a topic and gain a depth of understanding about a topic, and pays attention to individual variations in students' learning. However, beyond the many general teaching strategies that expert teachers need to use is pedagogical content knowledge about how to teach a particular discipline effectively. We will examine five content areas—reading, writing, mathematics, science, and social studies—and point out teaching strategies that are effective in each of these disciplines. For example, effectively establishing a book club for students in the area of reading requires a different type of pedagogical content knowledge than monitoring and deciphering students' misconceptions about science.

expert knowledge Excellent knowledge about the content of a particular discipline.

pedagogical content knowledge Knowledge about how to effectively teach a particular discipline.

! Review and Reflect

1 **Distinguish between expert knowledge and pedagogical content knowledge.**

Review
- How is expert knowledge different from pedagogical content knowledge?

Reflect
- Have you ever had a teacher who was clearly an expert in his or her discipline but not a good teacher? What pedagogical content knowledge was missing?

READING

Reading expert Steve Stahl (2002) believes that the three main goals of reading instruction should be to help children

1. Automatically recognize words
2. Comprehend text
3. Become motivated to read and appreciate reading

These goals are interrelated. If children cannot recognize words automatically, their comprehension suffers. If they cannot comprehend the text, it is unlikely that they will be motivated to read it.

How do such reading skills develop? What is the best way to teach children to read? How can children construct their reading skills? These are among the main questions that we will examine in our coverage of reading.

A Developmental Model of Reading

In one view, reading skills develop in five stages (Chall, 1979). The age boundaries are approximate and do not apply to every child. For example, some children learn to read before they enter first grade. Nonetheless, Chall's stages convey a general sense of the developmental changes involved in learning to read:

- *Stage 0.* From birth to first grade, children master several prerequisites for reading. Many learn the left-to-right progression and order of reading, how to identify the letters of the alphabet, and how to write their names. Some learn to read words that commonly appear on signs. As a result of watching TV shows such as *Sesame Street* and attending preschool and kindergarten programs, many young children today develop greater knowledge about reading earlier than in the past.
- *Stage 1.* In first and second grade, many children begin to read. They do so by learning to sound out words (that is, translate individual letters or groups of letters into sounds and blend sounds into words). During this stage, they also complete their learning of letter names and sounds.
- *Stage 2.* In second and third grade, children become more fluent at retrieving individual words and other reading skills. However, at this stage, reading is still not used much for learning. The mechanical demands of learning to read are so taxing at this point that children have few resources left over to process the content.
- *Stage 3.* In fourth through eighth grade, children become increasingly able to obtain new information from print. In other words, they read to learn. They still have difficulty understanding information presented from multiple perspectives within the same story. For children who haven't learned to read yet, a downward spiral begins that leads to serious difficulties in many academic subjects.
- *Stage 4.* In the high school years, many students become fully competent readers. They develop the ability to understand material written from many different

perspectives. This allows them to engage in sometimes more sophisticated discussions of literature, history, economics, and politics. It is no accident that great novels are not presented to students until high school, because understanding the novels requires advanced reading comprehension.

Approaches to Reading

Video Lecture: Approaches to Reading Instruction

As the previous discussion has implied, *reading* is the ability to understand written discourse. Children cannot be said to read if all they can do is respond to flash cards, as in some early child-training programs. Early reading requires mastering the basic language rules of phonology, morphology, syntax, and semantics. A child who has poor grammatical skills for speech and listening and does not understand what is meant by "The car was pushed by a truck" when it is spoken will not understand its meaning in print, either. Likewise, a child who cannot determine what pronouns refer to (as in "John went to the store with his dog. It was closed.") will not do well in reading comprehension.

What are some approaches to teaching children how to read? Education and language experts continue to debate how children should be taught to read (Rayner, 2000). The debate is between those who advocate a basic-skills-and-phonetics approach and those who emphasize a whole-language approach:

- **Basic-skills-and-phonetics approach.** This approach involves teaching both *phonemic awareness* (breaking apart and manipulating sounds in words) and *phonics* (learning that sounds are represented by letters of the alphabet, which can then be blended together to form words). Early reading materials should involve simple materials (Cunningham, 2004; Meyer, 2002). Only after they have learned phonological rules should children be given books and poems. You can read about some resources for improving children's phonetic skills in the Technology and Education box.
- **Whole-language approach.** This approach assumes that reading instruction should parallel children's natural language learning. From the outset, reading materials should be whole and meaningful. That is, in early reading instruction, children should be presented materials in their complete form, such as stories and poems. In this way, say the whole-language advocates, children learn to understand language's communicative function. The whole-language approach implies that all words are essentially "sight" words, which the child recognizes as a whole without detecting how the individual letters contribute to sounds. In the whole-language approach, reading should be connected with writing and listening skills. Also in this approach, reading is often integrated with other skills and subjects such as science and social studies. Most whole-language approaches have students read real-world, relevant materials, such as newspapers and books, and ask them to write about them and discuss them.

Which approach is best? Researchers have found that children can benefit from both approaches. They have found strong evidence that the basic-skills-and-phonetics approach should be used in teaching children to read but that students also benefit from the whole-language approach of being immersed in a natural world of print (Fox & Hull, 2002; Farris, Fuhler, & Walther, 2004; Graham & Harris, 1994; Wilson & others, 2001).

These were the conclusions of the National Reading Panel (2000), which conducted a large, comprehensive review of research on reading. The panel, which included a number of leading experts on reading, found that phonological awareness instruction is especially effective when it is combined with letter training and as part of a total literacy program. The most effective phonological awareness training involves two main skills: *blending* (listening to a series of separate spoken sounds and blending them, such as /g/ /o/ = go) and *segmentation* (tapping out/counting out the sounds in a word, such as /g/ /o/ = go, which is two sounds). Researchers also have found that phonological awareness improves when it is integrated with reading and writing, is simple, and is conducted in small groups rather than a whole class (Stahl, 2002). Other conclusions reached by the

basic-skills-and-phonetics approach The idea that reading instruction should teach both phonemic awareness and phonics.

whole-language approach The idea that reading instruction should parallel children's natural language learning; reading materials should be whole and meaningful.

Technology Resources for Improving Phonological Awareness and Decoding Skills

Two resources that can be used to improve students' phonological awareness and decoding skills are *Read-Along Books* and *Word Picker* (Cognition and Technology Group at Vanderbilt, 1997).

Read-Along Books are easy-to-read books written with short, decodable words that combine with rhythm and rhyme patterns to improve students' skills in associating sounds with letters. Computer versions of the books include tools that pronounce sentences and words as needed. After students become competent in these skills, they can record the stories in their own voice.

Word Picker is a software tool that helps students build on their letter-sound knowledge to discover conventional spellings for words that they want to write. As the children work on creating their own books in a multimedia format, they can click on *Word Picker*. Scrolling through a list of words, they search for words that start with the same letter as the word they want to write. Then they click on different words to hear them pronounced and to observe how they are divided into syllables. When they find the word they want, they type it out.

After students write their own books, they can read the printed versions of their books in class to others. *Read-Along Books* and *Word Picker* are part of the Young Children's Literacy Project at Vanderbilt University. The current versions are most appropriate for grade 1. Future projects are planned for preschool to grade 3.

Reading and writing also are combined in IBM's *Writing to Read* program for kindergarten and first-grade students. Five learning stations are coordinated to provide an active learning environment: computer, work journal, writing/typing, listening library, and making words.

These students are participating in IBM's *Writing to Read* program, which uses a variety of learning stations to improve students' literacy.

National Reading Panel (2000) suggest that children's reading benefits from guided oral reading (having them practice what they have learned by reading aloud with guidance and feedback) and applying reading comprehension strategies to guide and improve reading instruction. We will discuss a number of these strategies shortly.

In a recent study, Michael Pressley and his colleagues (2001) examined literacy instruction in five U.S. classrooms. Based on academic and classroom literacy performance of students, the effectiveness of classrooms was analyzed. In the most effective classrooms, teachers exhibited excellent classroom management based on positive reinforcement and cooperation; balanced teaching of skills, literature, and writing; scaffolding and matching of task demands to students' skill level; encouragement of student self-regulation; and strong connections across subject areas. In general, the extensive observations did not support any particular reading approach (such as whole-language or basic-skills-and-phonetics); rather, excellent instruction involved multiple, well-integrated components. An important point in this study is that effective reading instruction involves more than a specific reading approach—it also includes effective classroom management, encouragement of self-regulation, and other components.

Reading is like other important skills that children need to develop. It takes time and effort to become a proficient reader. In a recent national assessment, children in the fourth grade had higher scores on a national reading test when they read eleven or more pages daily for school and homework (National Assessment of Educational Progress, 2000) (see figure 11.1 on page 344). Thus, teachers who required students to read a great deal on a daily basis helped children develop their reading skills.

Cognitive Approaches

Cognitive approaches to reading emphasize decoding and comprehending words, constructing meaning, and developing expert reader strategies.

Strategies in Practice
Reading

www.mhhe.com/santedu2e

Reading Resources for Teachers

Phonetics

A Guide to Children's Reading Success

Cognition and Reading

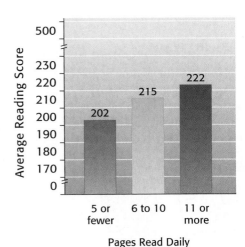

FIGURE 11.1 The Relation of Reading Achievement to Number of Pages Read Daily

In the recent analysis of reading in the fourth grade in the National Assessment of Educational Progress (2000), reading more pages daily in school and as part of homework assignments was related to higher scores on a reading test in which scores ranged from 0 to 500.

Decoding and Comprehending Words The cognitive approach emphasizes the cognitive processes involved in decoding and comprehending words. Important in this regard are certain metacognitive skills and a general automaticity of information processing ◄ p. 272.

Metacognition is involved in reading in the sense that good readers develop control of their own reading skills and have an understanding of how reading works. For example, good readers know that it is important to comprehend the "gist" of what an author is saying.

Teachers can help students develop good metacognitive strategies for reading by getting them to monitor their own reading, especially when they run into difficulties in their reading. Here are some metacognitive strategies that teachers can help students use to improve their reading (Miholic, 1994; Pressley & Afflerbach, 1995; Singhal, 2001):

- Overview text before reading.
- Look for important information while reading and pay more attention to it than other information; ask yourself questions about the important ideas or relate them to something you already know.
- Attempt to determine the meaning of words not recognized (use the words around a word to figure out its meaning, use a dictionary, or temporarily ignore it and wait for further clarification).
- Monitor text comprehension.
- Understand relationships between parts of text.
- Recognize when you might need to go back and reread a passage (you didn't understand it, to clarify an important idea, it seemed important to remember, or to underline or summarize for study).
- Adjust pace of reading depending on the difficulty of the material.

With regard to automaticity of processing, when word recognition occurs rapidly, meaning also often follows in a rapid fashion (Stanovich, 1994) ◄ p. 247. Many beginning or poor readers do not recognize words automatically. Their processing capacity is consumed by the demands of word recognition, so they have less capacity to devote to comprehension of groupings of words as phrases or sentences.

One factor that limits children's reading comprehension is the amount of information that they can hold in working memory at any one time (Bjorklund, 2000) ◄ p. 256. It is important to retain information in working memory as long as possible so that each newly read word in a passage can be interpreted with the words and concepts that just preceded it. Children who are competent at reading have a larger working memory capacity than children who have problems in reading. In one study, seven- to thirteen-year-old children who either were normal readers or had reading problems were given a series of incomplete sentences such as the following and were asked to supply the final word for each (Siegel & Ryan, 1989): "In the summer it is very _____." "With dinner, we sometimes eat bread and _____." After completing the series, the children were asked to repeat the final word that they had generated for each sentence. As shown in figure 11.2, as children got older, working memory capacity improved for both the normal and problem readers, but the problem readers had lower working memory capacity (shorter memory spans) than the normal readers at each age level.

The cognitive approach also contributed to the discovery that phonemic awareness is present in children who learn to read and absent in those who do not (Hiebert & Raphael, 1996). As we noted earlier, *phonemic awareness* refers to the ability to analyze words into phonemes (basic speech sounds). What makes phonics (the matching of words and sounds) work is the cognitive process of phonemic awareness, the ability to manipulate and think about sounds.

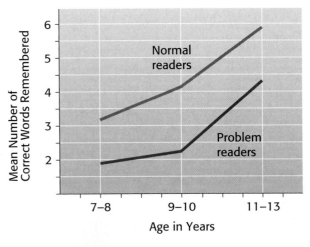

FIGURE 11.2 Working Memory Capacity in Normal and Problem Readers

As both normal readers and problem readers increased in age, their working memory capacity improved (Siegel & Ryan, 1989). However, problem readers had a lower working memory capacity than normal readers at each age level.

Constructing Meaning   In the cognitive approach, text has meaning that a reader must construct, not simply decode. Readers actively construct this meaning by using their background knowledge and knowledge of words and how they are linked (Heilman, Blair, & Rupley, 2002). For example, in one study, second-grade students were asked questions about their knowledge of spiders before they read about them (Pearson, Hansen, & Gordon, 1979). The students with more background knowledge about spiders understood the passage about spiders better than the other students did.

Developing Expert Reading Strategies   In the cognitive approach, researchers have tried to focus not so much on whether one teaching approach, such as whole-language, is better than another, such as phonics. Rather, they have searched for the underlying cognitive processes that explain reading. This search has led to an interest in strategies, especially the strategies of expert readers compared with those of novice readers. Researchers advise teachers to guide students in developing good reading strategies.

Michael Pressley and his colleagues (1992) developed the **transactional strategy instruction approach,** a cognitive approach to reading that emphasizes instruction in strategies (especially metacognitive strategies) ◀ p. 274. In their view, strategies control students' abilities to remember what they read. It is especially important to teach students metacognitive strategies to monitor their reading progress. Summarizing is also thought to be an important reading strategy. In the strategy approach, authors of teachers' manuals for subjects other than reading per se are encouraged to include information about the importance of reading strategies, how and when to use particular strategies, and prompts to remind students about using strategies.

Social Constructivist Approaches

The social constructivist approaches bring the social aspects of reading to the forefront (Hiebert & Raphael, 1996; Slavin & Madden, 2001) ◀ p. 314. Two social constructivist assumptions about reading are that (1) the social context plays an important role in learning to read and (2) knowledgeable readers in the culture assist less-knowledgeable readers in learning to read.

The contribution of the social context in helping children learn to read includes such factors as how much emphasis the culture places on reading, the extent to which parents have exposed their children to books before they enter formal schooling, the teacher's communication skills, the extent to which teachers give students opportunities to discuss what they have read with the teacher and their peers, and the district-mandated reading curriculum. Whereas cognitive constructivists emphasize the student's construction of meaning, social constructivists stress that meaning is socially negotiated. What they mean by "socially negotiated" is that meaning involves not only the reader's contribution but also the context in which the text is read, as well as the purpose for reading. Social constructivist approaches emphasize the importance of giving students opportunities for engaging in meaningful dialogue about the books they have just read. One way of doing this is through reciprocal teaching.

Imagine the Possibilities

Beverly Gallagher, a third-grade teacher at Princeton Day School, in New Jersey, inspires students to approach reading with a great deal of enthusiasm. She created the Imagine the Possibilities program, which brings nationally known poets and authors to her school. She phones each student's parents periodically to describe their child's progress and new interests. She invites students from higher grades to work with small groups in her class so that she can spend more one-on-one time with students. She also created poetry partnerships between eleventh-graders and her third-graders in which the older and younger students collaborate to create poems. Each of her students keeps a writer's notebook to record thoughts, inspirations, and special words that intrigue them. Students get special opportunities to sit in an author's chair, where they read their writing to the class (*USA Today,* 2000).

Beverly Gallagher, working with students to stimulate their interest in reading and writing.

transactional strategy instruction approach   A cognitive approach to reading that emphasizes instruction in strategies, especially metacognitive strategies.

Reciprocal Reading

Reciprocal Teaching In our discussion of the Fostering a Community of Learners program in chapter 10, we described **reciprocal teaching** in terms of students taking turns leading a small-group discussion ◀ p. 329. Reciprocal teaching also can involve a teacher and a student.

In reciprocal teaching, teachers initially explain the strategies and model how to use them in making sense of the text. Then they ask students to demonstrate the strategies, giving them support as they learn them. As in scaffolding, the teacher gradually assumes a less active role, letting the student assume more initiative. For example, Annemarie Palincsar and Ann Brown (1984) used reciprocal teaching to improve students' abilities to enact certain strategies to improve their reading comprehension. In this teacher-scaffolded instruction, teachers worked with students to help them generate questions about the text they had read, clarify what they did not understand, summarize the text, and make predictions. This teacher-student dialogue reflects reciprocal teaching (with *T* standing for *teacher* and *S* for *student*) (Palincsar, 1986):

Reading

Cats also "talk" by making other sounds. Some scientists think cats may have as many as 100 different calls. Cats have calls for greeting people, for showing hunger, for making a threat to another cat, and even for scolding their kittens. When a cat is frightened or angry, it may growl, spit, hiss, or scream.

T: C_____, as a teacher, can you ask someone a question about this information? [pause] Sometimes it helps if you're having a hard time to summarize what I just told you. [pause] What was I telling you about, what kind of information?

S2:   About different ways they talk.

T: You mean there are [*sic*] more than one way for them to communicate?

S2:   A hundred ways.

T: I did talk about that. They communicate with a hundred different sounds. Why do they need all those different sounds?

S2:   To tell people stuff.

S6:   To see if their babies are okay.

T: Possibly. Now, with that information, C_____, knowing that they have all those different ways to talk and to communicate, can you think of a question to ask? You can start your question with the word what . . . or when . . . or why?

S2:   Why do they purr?

T: Who is they?

S2:   The cats.

T: Okay, let's have that information in your sentence. Why . . .

S2:   Why do the cats purr?

S5:   To tell them what they want.

T: Can you tell us a little bit more?

S5:   [not audible]

T: Would it sound the same way for all those things?

S5:   No.

T: So that's why it needs a hundred sounds. So, I might say, if I were going to ask a question, why do cats have so many different sounds or calls?

S3:   Because they have so many different colors in their fur.

T: I said calls, not colors. Why do they have so many different calls, or sounds? [pause] Think of what R_____ told us. Do they always want the same thing?

S3:   No.

T: Then why do they have so many different ones? Is it so they can communicate what they really want?

reciprocal teaching A learning arrangement in which students take turns leading a small-group discussion.

Research on reciprocal teaching suggests that it is a very effective strategy for improving reading comprehension (Webb & Palincsar, 1996). One study compared four groups of junior high school students with reading problems (Palincsar & Brown, 1984):

1. *Reciprocal teaching group.* Students took turns with the teacher in using four reading comprehension strategies: generating a question about the text, summarizing the text, clarifying any comprehension problems, and making predictions about subsequent text.

2. *Modeling group.* Students observed the teacher as she used each of the four strategies.

3. *Explicit instruction group.* Students listened to the teacher's description of the four strategies and completed paper-and-pencil activities.

4. *Control group.* Students were given no information about the four strategies. As shown in figure 11.3, the reciprocal teaching group had the best gains in reading comprehension.

Book Clubs   **Book clubs** involve peer learning and consist of student-led discussions of literature (McMahon, 1994; McMahon, Raphael, & Goatley, 1995). Teachers serve as guides but give students considerable responsibility for how text discussions evolve. Conducted in this manner, book clubs often involve a range of discussions, as children make connections to their own lives, clarify points of confusion in the texts, draw inferences to fill in gaps left by the text, and critique the quality of the texts.

Book clubs reflect the social constructivist principle that meaning is socially negotiated. And book clubs can help fill a void that exists in many classrooms: an absence of talk about text.

School/Family/Community Connections   From the social constructivist perspective, schools are not the only sociocultural context that is important in reading. Families and communities are also important (Harris, Kamhi, & Pollock, 2001).

Of special concern are the language experiences of students from low-income families (Garcia & Willis, 2001; Schmidt & Mosenthal, 2001). In chapter 5, "Sociocultural Diversity," we discussed research findings that, on average, young children in welfare homes heard about 600 words an hour, whereas young children in professional families heard about 2,100 words an hour (Hart & Risley, 1995) ◀ p. 137. These researchers also found that, on average, children in welfare homes received only half as much language experience in their early years as children in middle-income families. They also revealed that children in high-income families had twice as much language experience as even children in middle-income families. At-risk students who do not engage in reading out of school fall further behind as they go through the elementary school years (Rowe, 1994). Most students who are avid readers report that they have at least one other person to talk with about their reading and about what to read next (Fielding, Wilson, & Anderson, 1986). Many parents of at-risk students have their own reading difficulties, as well as problems in obtaining books (Gunning, 2000).

In one strategy to combat these problems, parents with weak English literacy skills are given literacy training and are guided to introduce books as they interact with their children (Edwards, 1989). For instance, Project Family Literacy in Chicago's Latino community takes this approach (Shanahan & Rodriguez-Brown, 1993). Parents attend twice-weekly English-as-a-second-language (ESL) classes, participate in Parents as Teacher classes twice a month, and attend a summer institute. In the ESL classes, activities include parents making books for their children or sharing books in English. From the larger group, several parent leaders are selected. Twice monthly they hold family literacy seminars at neighborhood schools. The parents' participation in the program over a three-year period was linked with improved literacy in their children.

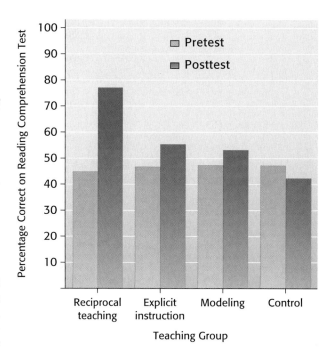

FIGURE 11.3 Reciprocal Teaching and Reading Comprehension
All groups started with approximately 40% to 50% correct on a reading comprehension pretest. The students were randomly assigned to one of four groups: reciprocal teaching, modeling, explicit teaching, or control. After experiencing these strategies in the classroom, the reciprocal teaching group showed the greatest gains in reading comprehension (posttest).

book clubs Student-led groups for the discussion of literature. Book clubs are a form of peer learning.

> **! Review and Reflect**
>
> **2 Explain how reading develops and discuss some useful approaches to teaching reading.**
>
> **Review**
> - What happens at each stage in Chall's developmental model of reading?
> - What are some differences between the whole-language approach and the basic-skills-and-phonetics approach to teaching reading? Why is balance needed?
> - What are the key ideas in cognitive approaches to reading?
> - What are the important features of social constructivist approaches to reading?
>
> **Reflect**
> - What would be some of the key considerations in a balanced view of teaching reading?

Next, we turn our attention to writing. In the whole-language approach, writing and reading instruction are often integrated (Ruddell, 1999). Innovations in technology are becoming available that help teachers in their effort not only to implement a whole-language approach but also to improve students' decoding skills (Solley, 2000).

WRITING

Children's Writing
Literacy

How do writing skills develop? What are cognitive and social constructivist approaches to writing?

Developmental Changes

Children's writing emerges out of their early scribbles, which appear at around two to three years of age. In early childhood, children's motor skills usually become well enough developed for them to begin printing letters and their name. In the United States, most four-year-olds can print their first name. Five-year-olds can reproduce letters and copy several short words. As they develop their printing skills, they gradually learn to distinguish between the distinctive characteristics of letters, such as whether the lines are curved or straight, open or closed, and so on. Through the early elementary grades, many children still continue to reverse letters such as *b* and *d* and *p* and *q* (Temple & others, 1993). At this point in development, if other aspects of the child's development are normal, these letter reversals are not a predictor of literacy problems.

As they begin to write, children often invent spellings of words. They usually do this by relying on the sounds of words they hear as clues for how to spell.

Teachers and parents should encourage children's early writing without being overly concerned about the proper formation of letters or correct conventional spelling. I (your author) once had a conference with my youngest daughter's first-grade teacher after Jennifer brought home a series of papers that the teacher had returned. Jennifer's printing was still a little rough and the pages were covered with the teacher's corrections and drawings of sad faces. Diplomatically but firmly, I explained to the teacher why I thought this was counterproductive. Fortunately, the teacher agreed to curb her criticism of Jennifer's printing skills. Such printing errors should be viewed as a natural part of the young child's growth and not scrutinized and criticized at every turn. Spelling and printing corrections can be made in positive ways and judiciously enough to avoid dampening early enjoyment and spontaneity in writing (Hughey & Slack, 2001).

Like becoming a good reader, becoming a good writer takes many years and lots of practice (Bruning & Horn, 2001; Spandel, 2005). Children should be given many writing opportunities in the elementary and secondary school years. As their language and cognitive skills improve with good instruction, so will their writing skills. For example, developing a more sophisticated understanding of syntax and grammar serves as an underpinning for better writing.

So do such cognitive skills as organization and logical reasoning. Through the course of elementary, middle, and high school, students develop increasingly sophisticated methods of organizing their ideas. In early elementary school, they narrate and describe or write short poems. In late elementary and middle school, they move to projects such as book reports that combine narration with more reflection and analysis. In high school, they become more skilled at forms of exposition that do not depend on narrative structure.

Cognitive Approaches

Cognitive approaches to writing emphasize many of the same themes that we discussed with regard to reading, such as constructing meaning and developing strategies (Kellogg, 2000; D. Olson, 2001). Planning, problem solving, revising, and metacognitive strategies are thought to be especially important in improving students' writing.

Planning   Planning, which includes outlining and organizing content information, is an important aspect of writing (Levy & Randsell, 1996; Mayer, 2004). Students need to be shown how to outline and organize a paper, and they need to be given feedback about the competence of their efforts (Houston, 2004). One study examined how prewriting activities can affect the quality of what is written (Kellogg, 1994). As indicated in figure 11.4 on page 350, outlining was the prewriting activity that helped writers the most. Figure 11.5, on page 350, shows how teachers can help students in planning their compositions to meet a deadline.

Problem Solving   Much of the instruction in writing in schools involves teaching students how to write sentences and paragraphs properly. However, there is more to writing than avoiding run-on sentences or making sure that paragraphs support topic sentences (Mayer, 1999). More fundamentally, writing is a broader sort of problem solving ◀ p. 298. One psychologist called the problem-solving process in writing "the making of meaning" (Kellogg, 1994).

As problem solvers, writers need to establish goals and work to attain them. It also is helpful to think of writers as constrained by their need for integrated understanding of the subject, knowledge of how the language system works, and the writing problem itself. The writing problem includes the purpose of the paper, the audience, and the role of the writer in the paper to be produced (Flower & Hayes, 1981).

Revising   Revising is a major component of successful writing (Mayer, 1999). Revising involves writing multiple drafts, getting feedback from individuals who are knowledgeable about writing, and learning how to use the critical feedback to improve the writing. It also includes detecting and correcting errors. Researchers have found that older and more-skilled writers are more likely to revise their writing than younger and

Through the Eyes of Students

The Devl and the Babe Goste

Anna Mudd is the six-year-old author of "The Devl and the Babe Goste." Anna has been writing stories for at least two years. Her story includes poetic images, sophisticated syntax, and vocabulary that reflect advances in language development.

Cognition and Writing
Peer Collaboration in Writing

FIGURE 11.4 **The Relation of Prewriting Activities to Essay Quality**
One study randomly assigned college students to one of four prewriting activity groups: (1) An outlining group produced an outline containing relevant ideas within a hierarchical structure; (2) a listing group generated a list of relevant ideas; (3) a generating group wrote down as many ideas as possible without evaluating or organizing them; and (4) a control group had no prewriting activity. Judges rated the quality of each essay on a 10-point scale from 1 (lowest quality) to 10 (highest quality)(Kellogg, 1994). Organization was the prewriting activity that was most positively related to judges' ratings. When students create an outline, they often use listing and generating strategies as part of the outlining process. Thus, an excellent teaching strategy is to require students to create an outline as a required prewriting activity.

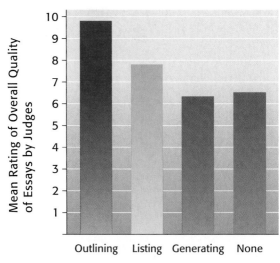

less-skilled writers (Bartlett, 1982; Hayes & Flower, 1986).

Metacognition When we emphasize knowledge of writing strategies, we move into the area of metacognition, which we discussed in chapter 8 ◀ p. 272. In one study, students ten to fourteen years of age were asked to write a paper that would be of interest to students in their own age range (Scardamalia, 1981). In carrying out this project, the students were hampered by not planning, not recording ideas in notes for later use, and not monitoring their writing progress by rereading and rewriting. The results are indicative of the fact that many middle school students do not have good knowledge of the planning and organizational strategies required by good writing and need to be taught these skills.

Monitoring one's writing progress is especially important in becoming a good writer (Graham & Harris, 2001). This includes being receptive to feedback and applying what one learns in writing one paper to making the next paper better.

Social Constructivist Approaches

As in reading, social constructivist approaches emphasize that writing is best understood as being culturally embedded and socially constructed rather than being internally generated ◀ p. 314. In the social constructivist approach to reading, the teacher's role shifts from transmitting knowledge to helping students restructure their knowledge. In this regard, both teachers and peers can serve as the more-knowledgeable reader. This social constructivist strategy also can be applied to writing (Dauite, 2001; Schultz & Fecho, 2001).

One to two months before the deadline	Select topic.
	Map ideas. Develop writing plan. Begin to develop a thesis statement. Start research.
Two weeks before the deadline	Develop individual sections of paper. Revise with vigor. Complete research. Finalize thesis statement.
The week before the deadline	Polish the individual sections of the paper. Create an interesting title. Check references for accuracy. Get some feedback.
The night before the deadline	Combine the parts of the paper. Print the final draft. Proofread the paper. Assemble the paper.

FIGURE 11.5 **A Sample Timetable for a Writing Deadline**

The Social Context of Writing   The social constructivist perspective focuses on the social context in which writing is produced. It is important that students participate in a writing community to understand author/reader relationships and that they learn to recognize how their perspective might differ from that of other people (Hiebert & Raphael, 1996).

To see the importance of social context in writing, consider two students. One, Anthony, is a nine-year-old Latino student who has lived in the Manhattan area of New York City his entire life (McCarthey, 1994). He reads and writes extensively, keeps scientific journals, and participated in classrooms with a strong emphasis on writing in his earlier school years. He is enthusiastic about his writing topic, a tribute to his grandmother who has recently died. His teacher encourages Anthony to write about her death, discussing various writing possibilities on this topic with him during their student-teacher writing conference. She and Anthony talk about the best ways to structure and organize the paper. His final writing product is a moving account of his grandmother's life and death. Anthony's teacher believes that writing plays an important role in education, and she communicates this enthusiastically to her students.

Contrast Anthony's writing experience with that of another Latino student, Carlos, whose parents recently immigrated to the Bronx area of New York City. Although his English is good, Carlos has had few classroom experiences in which he has practiced writing about his personal experiences, and he has never done any writing on his own outside the classroom. He feels very uncomfortable when the teacher asks him to write about personal experiences. In the student-teacher writing conference, Carlos is reluctant to discuss his feelings. Carlos' teacher has been mandated by the district to include writing experiences in different subjects. She is not enthusiastic about this and spends little time working with Carlos to improve his writing.

As evidenced by Anthony's and Carlos' situations, the social context plays an important role in writing. Some students bring a rich background of writing experiences and encouragement to write to the classroom; others have little writing experience and have not been encouraged to write extensively. In some classrooms the teacher places a high value on writing; in others the teacher treats writing as being less important.

Meaningful Writing and Student-Teacher Writing Conferences   According to the social constructivist approach, students' writing should include opportunities to create "real" texts, in the sense of writing about personally meaningful situations. For example, Anthony, whose teacher frequently asks students to write about personal experiences, wrote about his grandmother's life and death and his teacher gave him considerable support for writing about this emotional experience. Student-teacher writing conferences play an important support role in helping students become better writers.

Peer Collaboration   While working in groups, writers experience the processes of inquiry, clarification, and elaboration that are important in good writing (Webb & Palincsar, 1996). Students often bring diverse experiences to bear when they collaborate and coauthor papers. Such rich, shared collaboration can produce new insights into what to write about and how.

Through the Eyes of Students

Writing Self-Evaluations

San Francisco fifth-grade teacher Keren Abra periodically asks her students to evaluate their writing for their writing portfolios. Here are several of her students' comments toward the end of the school year.

> I am in fifth grade right now and I love writing. Anytime that I get to write I will; as far as I can remember I have loved writing. I feel that my writing has developed since fourth grade and I am pleased with my writing. Some authors might not like their writing unlike me; I have *never* thrown away any of my writing. I love to share my writing and give and get ideas from other writers. . . . If I could describe myself as a writer I would say (not to brag) that I was a descriptive, imaginative, captivating writer.

Michelle

> I think writing a story is easy because there is so much to write about and if I have to write about a certain thing there are also more things to do with the story. . . . If someone read my writing they would think I probably am a happy and energetic kid. They will think this because most of my stories are upbeat.

Sarah

> I feel that when I'm writing I could do better. I could do better especially on spelling. When I was in kindergarten we did not do a lot of writing. When I was in third grade I did not like writing. It was scary learning new things about writing. I'm in fifth grade and I love to write but sometimes it annoys me that I can't spell that well. One thing I like about my writing is the way I put action into all of my work because I love to get excited! I think that if someone were to read my writing uncorrected they would not be able to read it. If it was corrected I think the person would really like my story.

Janet

Reprinted by permission of United Features Syndicate, Inc.

By contrast, writing simply to meet the teacher's expectations often produces constrained, imitative, and conforming results. In peer writing groups, teacher expectations are often less apparent (Kearney, 1991).

School/Family/Peer Connections   In one project, teachers were encouraged to recognize the existence and richness of the surrounding Latino community and then integrate this into school contexts (Moll, Tapia, & Whitmore, 1993). This included (1) an analysis of how knowledge is transmitted within households in the Latino community; (2) an after-school laboratory in which teachers and students used reading and writing more in line with the way it is used in the students' neighborhoods than the way it is used in their school; and (3) classroom connections that integrated activities from the after-school laboratory. The goal was to integrate these three components. For example, students documented uses and ways of writing in their community, such as letters to relatives in other countries and entries into account books. Then, working with their peers, students created projects on topics that reflected the expertise of members of their communities, such as knowledge about mechanics and repair work. To obtain information for their project, students interviewed members of their communities. The students also communicated through e-mail with students who lived in Latino communities in other parts of the United States.

Involve the writing community in your class. Look around your community and think about expert writers you could invite to your classroom to discuss their work. Most communities have such experts, such as journalists and other authors and editors. One of the four most successful middle schools in the United States identified by Joan Lipsitz (1984) built a special Author's Week into its curriculum. Based on students' interest, availability, and diversity, authors are invited to discuss their craft with students. Students sign up to meet individual authors. Before they meet the author, they are required to read at least one of the author's books. Students prepare questions for their author sessions. In some cases, authors come to the class for several days to work with students on their writing projects.

As can be seen, there are many ways that writing is constructed. Later, in chapter 16, "Classroom Assessment," we will say more about the cognitive and social constructivist dimensions of writing.

In the course of our discussion of reading and writing, we have described a number of ideas that can be used in the classroom. To evaluate your reading and writing experiences, complete Self-Assessment 11.1.

Teaching Strategies
For Incorporating Writing into the Curriculum

You will have many opportunities to incorporate writing into the curriculum. Here are some examples (Bruning & Horn, 2001; Halonen, 2002):

Evaluating My Reading and Writing Experiences

Regardless of the academic subject or grade you teach, one of your goals should be to help students not only become competent at reading and writing but also enjoy these activities. Think about your own past and current experiences in reading and writing:

1. What made learning to read enjoyable for you?

   _____

   _____

2. What made learning to read difficult or unenjoyable?

   _____

   _____

3. How do you feel about reading now?

   _____

   _____

4. Do you enjoy libraries? Why or why not?

   _____

   _____

5. Are there reading skills that you still need to improve?

   _____

   _____

6. What made learning to write enjoyable for you?

   _____

   _____

7. What made learning to write difficult or unenjoyable?

   _____

   _____

8. How do you feel about writing now?

   _____

   _____

9. Are there writing skills that you still need to improve?

   _____

   _____

Based on your own experience and ideas in this chapter, how could you make learning to read and write more successful and enjoyable for your students?

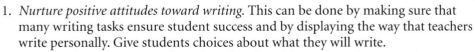 Go to your Student Toolbox CD-ROM for an electronic version of this form.

1. *Nurture positive attitudes toward writing.* This can be done by making sure that many writing tasks ensure student success and by displaying the way that teachers write personally. Give students choices about what they will write.

2. *Foster student engagement through authentic writing tasks and contexts.* Encourage students to write about topics of personal interest, have students write for different

audiences, and integrate writing into instruction in other disciplines, such as science, mathematics, and social studies.

3. *Provide a supportive context for writing.* Encourage students to set writing goals, plan how to reach the goals, and monitor their progress toward the goals. Assist students in creating goals that are neither too challenging nor too simple. Teach writing strategies and monitor their use by students. Give students feedback on their progress toward their writing goals. Use peers as writing partners in literacy communities.

4. *Have students write to learn.* This can work in any subject area. For example, in biology, after students have studied the adaptation of different species, ask them to write a summary of the main ideas and generate examples not described in class or the text.

5. *Use free-writing assignments.* In free writing, students write whatever they think about a subject. Such assignments are usually unstructured but have time limits. For example, one free-writing assignment in American history might be "Write about the American Revolution for five minutes." Free writing helps students discover new ideas, connections, and questions they might not have generated if they had not had this free-wheeling opportunity.

6. *Give students creative writing assignments.* These assignments give students opportunities to explore themselves and their world in creative, insightful ways. They might include poetry, short stories, or essays reflecting personal experiences.

7. *Require formal writing assignments.* These involve giving students opportunities to express themselves using an objective point of view, precise writing style, and evidence to support their conclusions. Formal writing helps students learn how to make formal arguments. For example, high school students might construct a major paper on a topic such as "Global Warming: Real Fears or Hype?" "An In-Depth Examination of Faulkner's Writing Style," or "Why People Are Prejudiced." Such writing projects stimulate students to think analytically, learn how to use resources, and cite references. Work with students on generating topics for a paper, structuring the paper, using planning and time management skills for completing the paper in a timely manner, drafting and revising, and overcoming spelling and grammatical errors.

Review and Reflect

3 Describe how writing develops and some useful approaches to teaching writing.

Review
- What skills are acquired in writing? At what ages are they commonly acquired?
- What cognitive processes are essential to effective writing?
- What are the key ideas in social constructivist approaches to writing?

Reflect
- For the age group and subject you plan to teach, in what ways will the writing assignments you give to students likely be highly structured and specific? In what ways might they be flexible and open-ended?

MATHEMATICS

What are some developmental changes in the way children think about mathematics and their math abilities at different grade levels? What is the biggest controversy in mathematics education today?

Developmental Changes

The National Council of Teachers of Mathematics (NCTM, 2000) has described the basic principles and standards for school mathematics at different grade levels. We begin with the principles and standards for prekindergarten through grade 2.

Prekindergarten Through Grade 2   Children already have a substantial understanding of numbers before they enter first grade (Siegler & Alibali, 2005). Most kindergartners from middle-income families can count past 20, and many can count beyond 100; most can accurately count the number of objects in a set, can add and subtract single digits, and know the relative magnitudes of single-digit numbers (for example, that 8 is greater than 6) (Siegler & Robinson, 1982).

Children are likely to enter elementary school with different levels of mathematical understanding (NCTM, 2000; Schoenfeld, 2002). Some children will need additional support for math learning (Van de Walli, 2004). According to the NCTM (2000), early assessments should be used to obtain information for teaching and for potential early interventions rather than for sorting children into tracks.

Understanding basic aspects of number and geometry are critical in kindergarten through the second grade (NCTM, 2000). For example, at these grade levels, children need to learn the base-10 numeration system. They must recognize that the word *ten* may represent a single entity or 10 separate units (10 one's) and that these representations can be interchanged.

When they go to school, children learn many higher numerical skills (Ginsburg, Klein, & Starkey, 1998). It is important to be aware that they are often doing something more than simply learning to calculate in a standard way. In fact, what children learn about mathematics and how to solve mathematical problems often reflects independent thinking as well as what they are being "taught" (Tolchinsky, 2002). This can be true even in the case of learning the basic "facts" of addition and subtraction, which most of us ultimately memorize.

The Math Forum
Math and Science Clearinghouse
Psychology and Math/Science Education

Grades 3 Through 5   Three key themes of mathematics in grades 3 through 5 are

- *Multiplicative reasoning.* The emphasis on multiplicative reasoning develops knowledge that children build on as they move to the middle grades, where the focus is on proportional reasoning. In multiplicative reasoning, children need to develop their understanding of fractions as part of a whole and as division.
- *Equivalence.* The concept of *equivalence* helps students to learn different mathematical representations and provides an avenue for exploring algebraic ideas.
- *Computational fluency.* Students need to learn efficient and accurate methods of computing that are based on well-understood properties and number relationships. For example, 298×42 can be thought of as $(300 \times 42) - (2 \times 42)$, or 41×16 is computed by multiplying 41×8 to get 328 and then doubling 328 to obtain 656.

Grades 6 Through 8   In middle school, students benefit from a balanced mathematics program that includes algebra and geometry. Teachers can help students understand how algebra and geometry are connected. Middle school mathematics also should prepare students to deal with quantitative solutions in their lives outside of school.

Students develop far more powerful mathematical reasoning when they learn algebra. A single equation can represent an infinite variety of situations. Even many students who get *A*s and *B*s in algebra classes, however, do so without understanding what they are learning—they simply memorize the equations. This approach might work well in the classroom, but it limits these students' ability to use algebra in real-world contexts (Heid, 2002).

Grades 9 Through 12   The NCTM (2000) recommends that all students study mathematics in each of the four years of high school. Because students' interests may change during and after high school, they will likely benefit from taking a range of math classes. They should experience the interplay of algebra, geometry, statistics, probability, and discrete mathematics (which involves the mathematics of computers). They should become adept at visualizing, describing, and analyzing situations in mathematical terms. They also need to be able to justify and prove mathematically based ideas.

Controversy in Math Education

Educators currently debate whether math should be taught using a cognitive approach or a practice, computational approach (Batchelder, 2000; Stevenson, 2000). Some proponents of the cognitive approach argue against memorization and practice in teaching mathematics. Instead, they emphasize constructivist mathematical problem solving. Others assume that speed and automaticity are fundamental to effective mathematics achievement and argue that such skills can be acquired only through extensive practice and computation. In recent years, the constructivist approach has become increasingly popular. In this approach, effective instruction focuses on involving children in solving a problem or developing a concept and in exploring the efficiency of alternative solutions.

A recent study used videotapes of eighth-grade math classrooms to examine how math is taught in different countries (Hiebert & others, 2003). In the two countries in which students had the highest math achievement, different teaching strategies were used: Hong Kong teachers stressed basic skills and formulas; Japanese teachers emphasized how concepts are linked. Thus, at least in this study, a practice, computational approach was successful in one country (Hong Kong), a cognitive approach in another (Japan). The researchers concluded that the implications for U.S. math teachers is that they need to develop math activities for both the computational and cognitive aspects of math. In addition, in this study, U.S. teachers were less likely to assign math homework than were teachers in most of the other countries, and Japanese teachers let students spend fifteen minutes on average struggling to solve a math problem, compared with only five minutes on average for U.S. teachers.

The NCTM (2000) has developed a number of standards for mathematics education. We have already touched on these standards in describing what should be taught at different grade levels. These standards emphasize that teaching math should involve giving students opportunities to

- Understand numbers and operations
- Learn the principles of algebra and geometry
- Comprehend how to measure the attributes of objects and the units of measurement
- Collect, organize, analyze, and display data, as well as understand basic concepts of probability
- Solve problems
- Use systematic reasoning in many different areas of mathematics
- Organize and consolidate mathematical thinking through communication, including working on problems with classmates
- Recognize connections among mathematical ideas and apply mathematics in contexts outside of mathematics

Some Constructivist Principles

From a constructivist perspective, the principles discussed next should be followed when teaching math (Middleton & Goepfert, 1996).

Make Math Realistic and Interesting   Build your teaching of math around realistic and interesting problems. These problems might involve some kind of conflict, suspense, or crisis that motivates students' interest. The math problem-solving activities might center on the student, community issues, scientific discoveries, or historical events. Math games can provide a motivating context for learning math. Questions that teachers can pose during games, such as "What do you need to roll on the dice to move your piece to number 10 on the board?" are more meaningful than decontextualized problems, such as "You have 4; how many more must you add to equal 10?" Math games may also encourage students to discuss math strategies with others, including their peers and parents (Carpenter & others, 1983). Connecting math with other subject areas, such as science, geography, reading, and writing, also is recommended.

Consider the Students' Prior Knowledge   Evaluate what knowledge the students bring to the unit and the context in which instruction takes place. Make enough information available for students to be able to come up with a method for solving math problems but withhold enough information so that students must stretch their minds to solve the problems.

Make the Math Curriculum Socially Interactive
Develop math projects that require students to work together to come up with a solution. Build into the math curriculum opportunities for students to use and improve their communication skills. Generate math projects that engender discussion, argument, and compromise.

Innovative Math Projects   The interest in making math instruction more constructivist has spawned a number of innovative programs. These include programs for elementary school, middle school, and high school, as described by James Middleton and Polly Goepfert (1996).

Elementary School   Everyday Mathematics is the University of Chicago School Mathematics Project for elementary school students. A special feature is the high-interest level of the math activities. Most activities are done with partners or in small groups with an emphasis on discussion, exploration, and projects. For more information about Everyday Mathematics, contact Everyday Learning Corporation at (888) 772-4543 or go to http://everydaymath.uchicago.edu/.

Middle School   The Connected Mathematics Project is funded by the National Science Foundation. The program focuses on five themes: (1) understanding, (2) connections, (3) investigations, (4) representations, and (5) technology. Connections with other disciplines such as science, social science, and business are emphasized. Many math problems focus on the everyday experiences and interests of middle school students. Each unit focuses on problem solving as described in the NCTM's *Curriculum and Evaluation Standards* in these areas: number, geometry, probability, statistics, measurement, and algebra.

High School   The Interactive Mathematics Program (IMP) is a four-year, problem-based high school math curriculum that meets the needs of both college-bound and noncollege-bound students. IMP emphasizes solving math problems in context; large, complex problems; communication and writing skills; and technology. Over the course of four years, students revisit problems in a "spiraling sequence," giving them opportunities to develop more-sophisticated mathematical understanding. Students make oral and written presentations that help to clarify their math thinking.

Through the Eyes of Teachers

"Never See Failure as Failure"

An at-risk student, Henry Brown's life was turned around by middle school teacher Cora Russell and the experience inspired him to teach. Brown, a recent Florida Teacher of the Year, teaches mathematics at Hallandale Adult Alternative High School. Half of the students enter this school with math skills below the fifth-grade level. He believes it is important to teach real-world math skills. In one project, Brown devises a dummy corporation and students play different roles in it, learning important math skills as they work and make decisions in the corporation. He created Helping Hands, which involves senior citizens in the classroom (*USA Today*, 2001a).

Henry Brown

Video Observation: Social Constructivist High School Math

Interactive Mathematics

Technology and Math Instruction

One issue in math education is how technology-intensive it should be (Heid & Blume, 2002).The NCTM's *Curriculum and Evaluation Standards* recommends that calculators be used at all levels of mathematics instruction and that some access to computers is also necessary if students are to be adequately educated for future careers. In many school systems, adequate funds for computers is a major issue. One recommendation by math curriculum experts James Middleton and Polly Goepfert (1996) is that instead of purchasing a lab full of low-end computers, schools should purchase one really good, top-of-the-line computer for each math classroom, along with a projection device or large-screen monitor. This allows students to participate in using significant technology every day.

In contrast to U.S. teachers, Japanese and Chinese teachers do not allow the everyday use of calculators or computers in mathematics classes because they want the students to understand the concepts and operations required to solve problems. Some critics argue that the American emphasis on the early use of these technology aids prevents students from gaining experience in manipulating concrete objects that they need to learn mathematical concepts (Stevenson, 2001). Only at the high school level, after students have developed a clear understanding of mathematical concepts, are East Asian students allowed to use a calculator as a tool for solving mathematical problems. In the recent National Assessment of Educational Progress, in the fourth grade, frequent calculator use was associated with lower national achievement test scores in mathematics, while in the eighth and twelfth grades, more frequent use of calculators was linked with higher national test scores (see figure 11.6).

Connecting with Parents

In chapter 9, we described Family Math, a program that helps parents experience math with their children in a positive, supportive way ◀ p. 302. In addition to telling parents about Family Math, consider having family math nights, especially at the beginning of the school year. Let parents see how the students will be learning math and resolve any of their major concerns. At the family math night, offer resources that parents can use at home to help their children learn math more effectively.

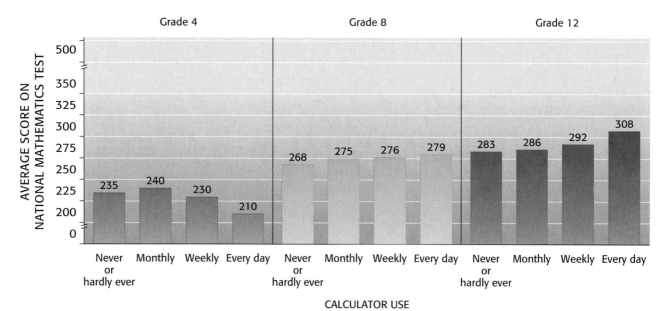

FIGURE 11.6 Frequency of Calculator Use at Different Grade Levels and National Mathematics Achievement Test Scores
Note: Scores on the National Mathematics Achievement Test can range from 0 to 500.

If you teach math, one good active step is to join the NCTM and use its resources. The NCTM has annual conferences, publishes an annual yearbook with stimulating chapters on recent developments in math education, and publishes journals such as *Mathematics Teacher.* For more information about the NCTM, call (703) 620-9840 or go to http://www.nctm.org/.

---

❶ Review and Reflect

4   Characterize how mathematical thinking develops and identify some issues related to teaching mathematics.

Review
- What are some developmental changes in mathematical skills?
- What is the main controversy in math education?
- What are some constructivist principles in learning math?
- What role can technology play in math instruction?
- Why is it important to connect with parents in math education?

Reflect
- Do you think that teachers in Asia are wise to not allow young students to use calculators? Should the United States follow this example?

SCIENCE

Let's explore the extent to which children engage in scientific thinking and the nature of science education.

Scientific Thinking

Children's problem solving is often compared to that of scientists. Both children and scientists ask fundamental questions about the nature of reality. Both also seek answers to problems that often seem utterly trivial or unanswerable to other people (such as why is the sky blue?). Both are granted by society the time and freedom to pursue answers to the problems they find interesting. This "child as scientist" metaphor has led researchers to ask whether children generate hypotheses, perform experiments, and reach conclusions concerning the meaning of their data in ways resembling those of scientists (Clinchy, Mansfield, & Schott, 1995).

Scientific reasoning often is aimed at identifying causal relations. Like scientists, children often emphasize causal mechanisms (Frye & others, 1996). However, preadolescents have much greater difficulty in separating their prior theories from the evidence that they have obtained. Often, when they try to learn about new phenomena, they maintain their old theories regardless of the evidence (Kuhn, Schauble, & Garcia-Mila, 1992).

Another difference between scientists and children is that children are influenced more by happenstance events than by the overall pattern of occurrences (Kuhn, 2004; Kuhn, Amsel, & O'Laughlin, 1988). Children also have difficulty designing new experiments that can distinguish conclusively among alternative causes. Instead, they tend to bias

Through the Eyes of Teachers

Math and Science Getting Wet and Muddy

Sandra Eidson, a biology teacher, and Lela Whelchel, a mathematics teacher, recently won a $12,000 GTE grant to integrate biology and geometry at West Hall High School in Oakwood, Georgia. For example, students are using graphing calculators to monitor a creek behind the high school. The teachers describe this exercise as "math and science getting wet and muddy." Students also use triangles to calculate the height of trees. Lela Whelchel says that her dream is to see all math and science classes paired together.

Sandra Eidson and Lela Whelchel

the experiments in favor of whichever hypothesis they began with, and sometimes they will see the results as supporting their original hypothesis even when the results directly contradict it (Schauble, 1990). Thus, although there are important similarities between children and scientists, in their basic curiosity and in the kinds of questions they ask, there are also important differences in the degree to which they can separate theory and evidence and in their ability to design conclusive experiments (Lehrer, Schauble, & Petrosino, 2001; Schauble, 1996).

Science Education

Science Resources for Teachers

Science Learning Network

National Science Teachers Association

Scientists typically engage in certain kinds of thinking and behavior. For example, they regularly make careful observations; collect, organize, and analyze data; measure, graph, and understand spatial relations; pay attention to and regulate their own thinking; and know when and how to apply their knowledge to solve problems (Chapman, 2000).

These skills, which are essential to the practice of science, are not routinely taught in schools, especially elementary schools. As a result, many students are not competent at them. Many scientists and educators believe that schools need to increasingly guide students in learning how to use these skills (Cocking, Mestre, & Brown, 2000; Penner, 2001; Tolman, 2002).

Children have many misconceptions that are incompatible with science and reality. They may go through mental gymnastics trying to reconcile seemingly contradictory new information with their new beliefs (Miller, 2000). For example, after learning about the solar system, children sometimes conclude that there are two earths—the seemingly flat world in which they live and the round ball floating in space that their teacher just described.

Good teachers perceive and understand a child's underlying concepts, then use the concepts as a scaffold for learning (Tippins, Koballa, & Payne, 2002). Effective science teaching helps children distinguish between fruitful errors and misconceptions, and detect plainly wrong ideas that need to be replaced by more accurate conceptions.

An effective strategy for helping students to overcome misconceptions is an **interactive demonstration strategy** (Sokoloff & Thornton, 1997). The teacher introduces what the demonstration is about, asks students to discuss the demonstration with their neighbors, tells them to write down a prediction regarding the demonstration, and then performs the demonstration. Consider a physics demonstration involving "a collision between two air carts on an air track, one a stationary light cart, the other a heavy cart moving toward the stationary cart" (National Research Council, 1999, pp. 167–168). "Each cart has an electronic force probe connected to a display." The teacher first asks the students to discuss the situation with their neighbors and then record a prediction about whether one of the carts would exert a bigger force on the other during impact or whether they will exert equal forces. The vast majority of students incorrectly predict that the heavier, moving cart exerts a larger force on the lighter, stationary cart. This prediction seems quite reasonable based on experience students know that a moving Mack truck "inflicts far more damage on a Volkswagen Beetle than vice versa." This is interpreted by students to mean that the Mack truck must have exerted more force on the Volkswagen. However, "notwithstanding the major damage to the Volkswagen, Newton's Third Law of Physics states that two interacting bodies exert equal and opposite forces on each other. After the students make and record their predictions, the instructor performs the demonstration, and the students see on the screen that the force probes record forces of equal magnitude but oppositely directed during the collision."

interactive demonstration strategy A strategy to help students overcome misconceptions in science in which the teacher introduces the demonstration, asks students to discuss the demonstration with their neighbors and predict its outcome, and then performs the demonstration.

Constructivist Teaching Strategies

With an emphasis on discovery and hands-on laboratory investigation, many science teachers now help their students construct their knowledge of science (Chiappetta & Koballa, 2002; Martin & others, 2005). Constructivist teaching emphasizes that children have to build their own scientific knowledge and understanding. At each step in science

Science field trips can be used to help students explore everyday science problems.

learning, they need to interpret new knowledge in the context of what they already understand. Rather than putting fully formed knowledge into children's minds, in the constructivist approach teachers help children construct scientifically valid interpretations of the world and guide them in altering their scientific misconceptions (Martin, Sexton, & Gerlovich, 1999).

Some contemporary constructivist approaches to teaching science involve exploring everyday science problems, activities that help students learn how science works, and the social contexts of science (Abruscato, 2004; Linn, Songer, & Eylon, 1996).

Exploring Everyday Science Problems   Most students are far more interested in science that addresses problems relevant to their lives than they are in discussing abstract theories. One elementary school program that reflects this emphasis is the project funded by the National Science Foundation called Science for Life and Living (SLL) (Biological Sciences Curriculum Study, 1989). The program emphasizes (Biological Sciences Curriculum Study, 2001)

- *"Science as a way of knowing."* This phrase expresses the idea that science is not just knowledge but a unique way of learning about the world.
- *"Technology as a way of doing."* The focus is not on computers but, rather, on understanding how people use the processes and tools of technology to solve practical problems.
- *"Health as a way of behaving."* The emphasis here is on applying scientific reasoning skills in making decisions about health, focusing on such themes as cause and effect and understanding how to think critically about information that claims to improve health.

In one recent study conducted in five North Carolina schools, students who experienced the SLL curriculum scored higher on a standardized test of biology and on other measures that assessed conceptual understanding of biology than did fifth-grade students who were in regular science classes (Maidon & Wheatley, 2001).

Some critics of this and other constructivist approaches argue that too much attention is given to inquiry skills and not enough is given to discipline-specific information (American Association for the Advancement of Science, 1993). In response, advocates of the constructivist approach to biology argue that it creates more scientifically literate citizens who know how to think in scientific ways rather than just memorize scientific facts (Trowbridge, Bybee, & Powell, 2000).

Activities That Help Students Learn How Science Works Some projects help students think about and visualize how scientific principles work. For example, Project STAR (Science Teaching Through Astronomical Roots) uses astronomy as a foundation to teach complex physics principles to high school students (Schneps & Sadler, 1989). Computer simulations can be especially effective in helping students visualize and think about scientific phenomena.

The Social Contexts of Science The Fostering a Community of Learners project (Brown, 1997; Brown & Campione, 1996), discussed in chapter 10, reflects an emphasis on the social contexts of science. It stresses teacher-student and student-student collaborative interaction. Students investigate environmental science problems, create group or individual reports, and support each other as part of a community of science learners.

Another program that captures the social contexts of science theme is the Kids as Global Scientists project (Songer, 1993). This project focuses on networked communication, incorporating students' perspectives from different countries on issues involving climate change.

An Innovative Middle School Life-Sciences Curriculum In chapter 2, "Cognitive and Language Development," we discussed the need for new middle school curricula. Especially lacking in middle school education have been courses that provide the information, skills, and motivation for young adolescents to learn about themselves and their widening world.

The **Human Biology Middle Grades Curriculum (HumBio)** was developed by Stanford University scientists in collaboration with middle school teachers across the United States (Carnegie Council on Adolescent Development, 1995; Heller, 1993). It integrates the study of ecology, evolution, genetics, physiology, human development, culture, health, and safety. It might seem ironic that we end this section on domain-specific constructivist approaches by emphasizing integration and connection across the school curriculum. However, such cross-curricular integration and connection is an important theme in many disciplines.

Human Biology Middle Grades Curriculum (HumBio) Developed by Stanford University scientists in collaboration with middle school teachers, this curriculum integrates ecology, evolution, genetics, physiology, human development, culture, health, and safety.

In this HumBio classroom, students at Central Park East Secondary School in New York City investigate an important function of the human digestive system by performing the peristalsis activity. The group shown here is moving rice through long, flexible plastic tubing representing the small intestine.

HumBio not only is appropriate for teaching science to middle school students with a wide range of abilities, but it simultaneously promotes healthy decision making. HumBio is a 2-year curriculum that consists of 24 units. Schools choose which units they want to teach. Initial units are "The Changing Body, Reproduction, and Sexuality," "Genetics," "The Nervous System," and "The Life of Cells." Next comes "From Cells to Organisms: Human Development." Finally, "The Circulatory System," "Breathing," and "Digestion and Nutrition" round out the curriculum.

In using HumBio, teachers work cooperatively from the perspectives of their individual disciplines toward imparting a central lesson. For example, a science class discussion of the impact of food and drugs on circulation is coordinated with a physical education class discussion of linkages among food intake, drugs, circulation, and breathing. The study of health includes decisions regarding smoking, analysis of different ways of planning menus, facts behind eating disorders, and ways to reduce stress. One lesson helps students understand how drugs affect their bodies. For example, cocaine increases the production of adrenaline. In the HumBio curriculum at Egan Intermediate School in Los Altos, California, seventh-grade students explore the effects of adrenaline on metabolism by observing brine shrimp through a microscope as they react to it. Students have an opportunity to discuss the ideas in the demonstration with the teacher and with each other. They ask questions and offer answers.

Some English teachers who are involved in the HumBio program encourage students to read books related to what they have observed in science class. Some social studies teachers focus on the impact of scientific experiments on society and changing views of biology at different points in history.

HumBio has been extensively field-tested at schools selected for their diversity. Training for teaching the HumBio is available through summer institutes at Stanford University, and information about HumBio is available from Addison-Wesley-Longman Publishers.

Science in High Schools   In most high schools, science is taught in this sequence: biology, chemistry, physics. Many students only take the biology course or the biology–chemistry sequence and don't go on to physics. An increasing number of scientists argue that science courses should be taught in the opposite sequence and that the science subjects also should be taught in a more integrated fashion (Siegfried, 1998). They believe that to understand biology, students need to know a lot of chemistry. Life is made of molecules and survives by such processes as photosynthesis and respiration. Teaching biology first and chemistry second, in their view, is like watching *The Empire Strikes Back* before the prior episode of *Star Wars*. Likewise, understanding chemistry without knowing something about physics is difficult. Chemistry is based on energy changes and the forces between atoms, which is the subject matter of physics. The science curriculum also should include real-world problems that tie physics, chemistry, and biology together. And it should explore these aspects of scientific thinking: theory, prediction, skepticism, and methods for assessing evidence.

Through the Eyes of Teachers

Dropping an Egg on a Teacher's Head

Peggy Schweiger teaches physics at Klein Oak High School in Spring, Texas. She extensively uses hands-on projects, such as wiring a doll house and making replicas of boats for a regatta, to improve students' ability to understand physics. She especially encourages girls to take physics classes and makes sure that every lab group has at least two girls. She works hard to create science activities that are interesting to both females and males. According to former student Alison Arnett, nineteen, "She taught us how to think and learn, not how to succeed in physics class. We were encouraged to stand on desks, tape things to the ceiling, and even drop an egg on her head to illustrate physics—anything to make us discover that we live with physics every day. (*USA Today,* 2001, p. 6).

Peggy Schweiger with a student who is learning how to think and discover how physics works in people's everyday lives.

5 Identify some challenges and strategies related to teaching children how to think scientifically.

Review
- In what ways do children think as scientists do? In what ways do they differ from scientists in the way they think?
- What types of thinking and behavior do scientists engage in that need to be taught to children in science education?
- What are some constructivist approaches to teaching science?

Reflect
- How effectively did your elementary, middle, and high school teach science to the typical student? If less than perfectly, how could their approach have been improved?

SOCIAL STUDIES

What is the nature of social studies? What key themes characterize teaching and learning in social studies? How can constructivist approaches be applied to social studies?

What Is Social Studies?

NCSS Standards
Teacher's Curriculum Institute
Lesson Plans and Resources
**Social Studies
Development Center**

In general, the field of **social studies,** also called social sciences, seeks to promote civic competence. The goal is to help students make informed and reasoned decisions for the public good as citizens of a culturally diverse, democratic society in an interdependent world. In schools, social studies draws from disciplines such as anthropology, economics, geography, history, law, philosophy, political science, psychology, religion, and sociology.

Social studies is taught in kindergarten through grade 12 in the United States. In elementary school, children often learn social studies that are integrated across several disciplines. This often takes the form of units constructed around broad themes that are examined in terms of time, continuity, and change (Martorella & Beal, 2002; Sunal & Haas, 2002). In middle schools and high schools, courses may be interdisciplinary—such as a history course drawing from geography, economics, and political science—or focused more on a single discipline, such as just history itself (Martorella, 2001).

The National Council for the Social Sciences (2000) proposed ten themes that it believes should be emphasized in courses in the social sciences:

- *Time, continuity, and change.* It is important for students to understand their historical roots and locate themselves in time. Knowing how to effectively read about and construct the past helps students to explore questions such as "How am I connected to the past?" and "How can my personal experience be viewed as part of the larger human story across time?" This theme typically appears in history courses.

  Many people have had similar experiences in history courses. They learned facts and dates that the teachers and the text presented as important. However, teachers and students who think that history is only about facts and dates miss remarkable opportunities to learn how history is a discipline that involves analyzing events in terms of how they are relevant for people's lives (Fritzer, 2002; National Research Council, 1999). Indeed, experts in history regard evidence in history as far more than a list of facts. And expert history teachers, rather than simply teaching history as lists of facts to be memorized, guide students in analyzing and reflecting about historical events, especially encouraging students to think about possible alternative meanings of events and how they might be interpreted in different ways. A number of expert history teachers also get students to engage in debate about the evidence pertaining to a particular historical circumstance.

social studies The field that seeks to promote civic competence with the goal of helping students make informed and reasoned decisions for the public good as citizens of a culturally diverse, democratic society in an interdependent world.

- *People, places, and environments.* The study of these topics helps students to develop spatial and geographic perspectives on the world. This helps students make informed and competent decisions about the relationship of human beings to their environment. In schools, this theme usually appears in units and courses linked to geography.
- *Individual development and identity.* A student's personal identity is shaped by culture, groups, and institutions. Students can explore such questions as "Who am I?" "How do people learn, think, and develop?" and "How do people meet their needs in a variety of contexts?" In schools, this theme usually appears in units and courses focused on psychology and anthropology.
- *Individuals, groups, and institutions.* It is important for students to learn about the ways in which schools, churches, families, government agencies, and the courts play integral roles in people's lives. Students can explore the roles of various institutions in the United States and other countries. In schools, this theme typically appears in units and courses on sociology, anthropology, psychology, political science, and history.
- *Power, authority, and governance.* Understanding the development of power, authority, and governance in the United States and other parts of the world is essential for developing civic competence. In this theme, students explore such topics as the following: What is power and what forms does it take? How do people gain power, use it, and justify it? How can people keep their government responsive to their needs and interests? How can conflicts within a nation and between nations be resolved? This theme typically appears in units and courses focused on government, political science, history, and other social sciences.
- *Production, distribution, and consumption.* People have needs and desires that sometimes exceed the limited resources that are available to them. As a result, questions such as these are raised: What is to be produced? How is production to be organized? How are goods and services distributed? What is the most effective allocation of production (land, capital, and management)? Increasingly, these questions are global in scope. In schools, this theme typically appears in units and courses focused on economics.
- *Science, technology, and society.* Modern life as we know it would be impossible without technology and the science that supports it. However, technology raises many questions: Is new technology always better? How can people effectively cope with rapid technological advances? How are values related to technology? This theme appears in units and courses involving history, geography, economics, civics, and government. It also draws from such fields as the natural and physical sciences, social sciences, and humanities for specific examples of issues and the knowledge base for considering social issues related to society and technology.

Through the Eyes of Teachers

Helping Students Cope with a Tragedy

Mark Fodness has taught seventh-grade social studies for seventeen years at Bemidji Middle School in Minnesota. He says that during that time he has found it necessary to deal with numerous traumatic events that affect his students. Sometimes the tragedy is a local one, such as the death of a student, parent, or teacher. Other crises, such as the Gulf War, have been national or international events.

On September 11, 2001, Mark says that he and his students encountered a new type of trauma—a terrorist attack against the United States. His students were left with many questions. "Could this be the beginning of the end of the world?" one boy asked. One girl wanted to know if her brother would have to go to war. Many students wanted to know "why?" and everyone was concerned about the future. Mark talked with his students about fear and reminded them of former U.S. President Franklin D. Roosevelt's words "The only thing we have to fear is fear itself." Mark got students to talk about situations in which they have been afraid and found that most were most fearful when they were alone.

Over the course of the week following the terrorist attack, Mark worked with his students to answer many of their questions. He wanted his students to be empathetic to the pain and suffering caused by the tragedy. He felt that his students would be better able to handle their emotions if they could gain some sense of control. Together, Mark and his students developed a five-point plan:

1. *We want to keep those in need in our thoughts.* Students encouraged each other to remember those who perished, were wounded, were part of rescue teams, or were family members or friends of the victims.
2. *We want to help.* Students raised more than $6,000 to send to victims' families.
3. *We want to show our support.* Students designed patriotic T-shirts and sweatshirts as a way to promote their unity.
4. *We want to support our own community.* Students went out into the community and raked leaves for senior citizens on October 23, 2001.
5. *We want to appreciate diversity.* To remind students of the role of diversity in the community, Mark took his students to the Bemidji Race Relations Conference on September 28, 2001.

Mark concluded, "The recent events in our nation and in our world should all remind us in the education field that we face a challenge. We must deal with moral and ethical questions in ways that are meaningful to our students."

Video Lecture: American Civics

- *Global connections.* The realities of increasing interdependence among nations requires understanding nations and cultures around the world. Conflicts between national and global priorities can involve health care, economic development, environmental quality, universal human rights, and other agendas. Analyzing economic competition, ethnic identities, and political alliances helps students understand why nations develop various policies. This theme typically appears in units and courses involving geography, culture, economics, and other social sciences.
- *Civic ideals and practices.* Understanding civic ideals and the practices of citizenship is important for full participation in society. Students focus on such questions as these: What is civic participation and how can I be involved? What is the balance between individual needs and community responsibilities? In schools, this theme typically appears in units and courses involving history, political science, and anthropology. Our discussion of moral development and moral education in chapter 3 can serve as a reference for discussion of values and moral issues related to civic ideals and practices.
- *Culture.* The study of culture prepares students to ask and answer such questions as these: How are cultures similar and different? What is the best way to interact with people who are from cultures that are different from your own? How does religion influence the beliefs of people in different cultures? In schools, the theme of culture typically appears in units and courses that focus on geography, history, and anthropology, as well as multicultural topics that cut across the curriculum. Our exploration of sociocultural diversity in chapter 5 and throughout the book is linked to this aspect of teaching social studies.

If a democracy such as the United States is to be secure and stable, each new generation of citizens must believe in the system and believe it works for people like them. Research by Constance Flanagan and her colleagues (Flanagan & Faison, 2001; Flanagan, Gill, & Gallay, 1998) with different ethnic groups of American adolescents points to the pivotal role of teaching in this regard. They have found that the extent to which teachers ensure that all students are treated equally and listen to and respect each other is related to the students' endorsement of democracy. In the Diversity and Education interlude, you can read further about teaching culture and cultural diversity in social studies.

Diversity and Education
UN Peacekeeping: A Constructivist Approach

One Canadian middle school social studies teacher developed a project on UN peacekeeping to encourage students to think more deeply and productively about respecting citizens in their own country and about the hardships that people in many countries continue to experience (Welshman, 2000). During the last fifty years, the United Nations has been involved in separating adversaries, maintaining cease-fires, delivering humanitarian relief, helping refugees, and creating conditions that promote democracy. Studying the UN initiatives became a way for students to examine various prosocial values such as kindness, empathy, cooperation, loyalty, equality, and responsibility. In this project, students used a variety of resources, including books and the Internet, over the course of several class periods.

In introducing the UN peacekeeping topic, the teacher asked if any of the students ever had a disagreement with a friend or classmate at school. Students contributed comments and the teacher said that in many instances it takes a third party to sort things out and help solve the problem. The teacher then shifted attention to how such conflicts also characterize world politics between countries and different ethnic groups. Nations, regions, and small groups of people have disagreements and there is no teacher present to help cool things down. This is where UN peacekeepers often step in to help solve a particular problem.

Then, students brainstormed about UN peacekeeping, during which they recalled any information they had previously learned about the topic and discussed their ideas with each other. The classroom had a world map on which to identify regions of the world where peacekeeping was taking or had taken place.

Next, the students were organized into five small groups of five students each to explore questions they had about UN peacekeeping. The first group of students focused on the history of peacekeeping. Questions explored included where the first peacekeeping mission occurred and how peacekeeping has changed since the end of the Cold War. Group two expressed an interest in the personal side of peacekeeping. Their questions included how much force peacekeepers can use in a mission and some of the dangers they face. The third group wanted to know about the organization of peacekeeping missions and asked questions such as these: Who provides funding for the mission? How are peacekeepers selected? The fourth group was interested in Canada's role in UN peacekeeping, asking these questions: When did Canada get involved in this? Have any Canadians commanded UN peacekeeping missions? The fifth group was intrigued by why peacekeeping occurs and asked questions such as these: What is the decision-making process like in determining when to form a UN peacekeeping mission? How do people decide on which world problems should be dealt with and which should not? After generating these questions, students researched and presented answers.

In addition to the small-group activities, students watched a film, *Caught in the Crossfire*, which portrayed Canadian peacekeepers in the war-torn former Yugoslavia. After viewing this film, the teacher asked students to imagine that they were residents of war-torn Yugoslavia, living in terrible conditions. Then, the students were asked to imagine what life would be like if Canadian peacekeepers were not serving in that part of the world.

Constructivist Approaches

Many social studies classes continue to be taught in a traditional manner of using a single textbook, with the teacher lecturing and controlling question-and-answer strategies. However, some educators believe that learning about social studies would benefit from a stronger constructivist emphasis on using multiple and varied sources of information, student-generated questions to guide inquiry, and peer collaboration, which reflects the strategy used in the UN peacekeeping unit we just discussed (Gibson & McKay, 2001). In the constructivist view, students should form their own interpretation of evidence and submit it for review. Allowing them to do so should encourage greater reflection and deeper understanding of social issues (Chapin & Messick, 2002; Sunai & Haas, 2005).

Constructivist approaches also emphasize the meaningfulness of social studies (Ellis, 2002; Turner, 2004). Students benefit when they find that what they learned in social studies classes is useful both in and outside of school. Meaningful learning often takes place when classroom interaction focuses on sustained examination of a few important topics rather than superficial coverage of many.

Constructivist approaches to social studies also stress the importance of thinking critically about values. Ethical dimensions of topics and controversial issues provide an arena for reflective thinking and understanding. Effective teachers recognize opposing points of view, respect for well-supported positions, sensitivity to cultural similarities and differences, and a commitment to social responsibility. From the constructivist perspective, teachers guide students to consider ethical dimensions of topics and address controversial issues rather than directly telling students what is ethical.

One constructivist approach to teaching social studies created by the Teacher's Curriculum Institute (2001) uses these teaching strategies to help students "experience" history:

- *Interactive slide lecture.* This strategy turns what is typically a passive, teacher-centered activity into a participative experience for students. Students view, touch, interpret, and act out images projected on slides. As the teacher asks a series of questions, students take notes.

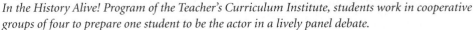

In the History Alive! Program of the Teacher's Curriculum Institute, students work in cooperative groups of four to prepare one student to be the actor in a lively panel debate.

ENTER THE DEBATE

1. Should teachers emphasize the scientific process or scientific facts in science instruction?

2. Should teachers encourage primary grade students to use invented spelling in their writing?

3. Should teachers emphasize memorization of basic facts in the early grades?

4. Should we teach algebra to students before high school?

Teaching Experience

- **Teaching Writing**
- **Teaching Science**
- **Teaching Mathematics**
- **An Example of Students Creating Math Tests**
- **Teaching Ideas**
- **Social Studies Writing Activity**
- **Improving Students' Writing**

- *Social studies skill builders.* Students sit in pairs to complete skill-oriented tasks such as mapping geographic features, analyzing political cartoons, and graphing economic trends.
- *Writing for understanding.* Students are challenged to write for a purpose.
- *Response groups.* This exercise creates rich classroom discussions of controversial topics. Students sit in small groups to view slides depicting historical events and respond to critical thinking questions related to each slide.

ⓘ Review and Reflect

6 Summarize how learning in social studies is becoming more constructivist.

Review

- What does social studies instruction aim to accomplish?
- What are some constructivist approaches to teaching social studies?

Reflect

- Think about a specific community in which you might teach one day. How might you tailor social studies instructions specifically for those children? How could you make it constructivist?

Connie teaches fourth grade in a middle-class school district. Her district has adopted a new K–6 math curriculum for this year, based on constructivist principles. In attending the in-service devoted to training teachers in implementing the new curriculum, Connie discovers that many differences exist between what she has been teaching for the past twenty years and this new curriculum. The new curriculum focuses on the use of math in "real life." Instead of endless speed drills, the problems ask the students to think and make connections between their lives at home and what they are doing in math. What drill and practice there is takes place in the context of various games the children play together. Students are allowed and even taught to approach problems in a variety of ways rather than focusing on a single algorithm for a particular type of problem. Many of these approaches are completely alien to Connie and, she guesses, to other teachers and parents. "This is going to be a lot of work," she thinks. "I'm going to have to relearn math myself in order to teach this way."

As the school year begins, other teachers begin expressing their concerns over the new curriculum. It is just so different from anything they have ever done in the past. Most of the teachers are managing to stay just a lesson or two ahead of the students. The children in first and second grade seem to love the new math program. They are actively involved during math period and many of them have said that math is fun. The students in fourth through sixth grade don't appear to be as enthusiastic about the new curriculum, however. Many of them are unable to complete their homework. They can't seem to grasp how to complete problems using the techniques taught in the new curriculum. They constantly fall back on the old algorithms they were taught when they were younger. This is frustrating Connie and her colleagues, as they have worked very hard to master the alternate ways of approaching problems themselves.

To make matters worse, parents are complaining. They can't help their children with their homework because they don't know how to use the new approaches, either. This has caused many parents to become angry. Several have threatened to remove their children from the school and take them "somewhere where they teach normal math." A group of parents will be addressing the board of education regarding this at their next meeting.

Adding fuel to the fire is one of the junior high math teachers, who insists that this new curriculum won't give the students the foundation they need for algebra. "They need to develop automaticity with their math facts. That just isn't going to happen with this program. This program leads them in too many directions. They'll never make it back to normal in time for algebra."

Proponents answer the junior high teacher by indicating that the new curriculum will actually better prepare the students for higher math because they will have a better conceptual understanding of *why* they are doing things and how the traditional algorithms work. Connie feels caught in the middle. She understands what the curriculum is supposed to do. She even believes it might actually benefit the students in the long run. However, every day she has students in tears in her class because they don't understand what she is asking them to do. She has fielded her share of phone calls from angry parents as well.

- What are the issues in this case?
- The students in first and second grade seem to be flourishing in this curriculum, while the older students are struggling. Why might this be? Tie your answer to a constructivist principle.
- How should the teachers address parental concerns regarding the new curriculum?
- How should they address the concerns of the algebra teacher?
- What can the teachers do to help their students at this point?

Reach Your Learning Goals

1 Distinguish between expert knowledge and pedagogical content knowledge.

- Expert knowledge involves being an expert regarding the content of a discipline. Pedagogical content knowledge involves knowledge of how to effectively teach a particular discipline. Both are required for being an expert teacher.

2 Explain how reading develops and discuss some useful approaches for teaching reading.

- Chall's model proposes five stages in reading development: (0) From birth to first grade, identify letters of the alphabet and learn to write one's name. (1) In first and second grade, learn to sound out words and complete learning of letter names and sounds. (2) In second and third grade, learn to retrieve individual words and complete learning of names and sounds. (3) In fourth grade through eighth grade, increasingly obtain new information from print. (4) In high school, become a fully competent reader and understand material from different perspectives.

- Current debate focuses on the basic-skills-and-phonetics approach versus the whole-language approach. The basic-skills-and-phonetics approach advocates providing phonetics instruction and giving children simplified materials. The whole-language approach stresses that reading instruction should parallel children's natural language learning and give children whole-language materials, such as books and poems. The National Reading Panel concluded that both approaches can benefit children. Research indicates that phonological awareness instruction is especially effective when it is combined with letter training and as part of a total literacy program. Effective phonological awareness training mainly involves two skills: blending and segmentation. Children's reading also benefits from guided oral reading and instruction in reading strategies.

- Cognitive approaches to reading emphasize decoding and comprehending words, constructing meaning, and developing expert reading strategies. Text has meaning that the reader must actively construct. Metacognitive strategies and automatic processes are involved in decoding and comprehending words. The ability to manipulate and think about sounds also is important. Transactional strategy instruction is one approach to helping students learn to read.

- Social constructivist approaches to reading stress that (1) the social context plays an important part in reading and (2) knowledgeable readers in the culture teach less-knowledgeable ones. Meaning is socially negotiated. Reciprocal teaching is a valuable technique in helping students improve their reading. Book clubs and

school/family/community connections also reflect the social constructivist perspective.

3 Describe how writing develops and some useful approaches to teaching writing.

- Children's writing follows a developmental timetable, emerging out of scribbling. Most four-year-olds can print their name. Most five-year-olds can reproduce letters and copy several short words. Advances in children's language and cognitive development provide the foundation for improved writing.

- Cognitive approaches to writing emphasize many of the same themes as for reading, such as constructing meaning and developing strategies. Planning, problem solving, revising, and metacognitive strategies are thought to be especially important.

- Social constructivist approaches to writing focus on the social context in which writing is produced. This social context includes the importance of students participating in a writing community to understand author/reader relationships and taking perspectives of others. Social constructivist approaches to writing include writing of "real texts" about meaningful experiences, teacher-student writing conferences, peer collaboration in writing, and school/family/community connections.

4 Characterize how mathematical thinking develops and identify some basic issues related to teaching mathematics.

- Children have a substantial understanding of numerical concepts before they enter first grade. When they go to school, children learn many more advanced kinds of numerical skills. The National Council of Teachers of Mathematics has developed standards for learning mathematics at these grade levels: prekindergarten through grade 2, grades 3 through 5, grades 6 through 8, and grades 9 through 12.

- Currently, there is controversy in math education about whether it should be more cognitive or more practical.

- Reforms focus on making math education more meaningful, making connections to prior knowledge, discussing math concepts with others, and using innovative math curriculum projects.

- The NTCM's *Curriculum and Evaluation Standards* recommends that calculators be used at all levels of mathematical instruction. However, some education experts argue that, as in East Asia, calculators should not be used prior to high school to improve students' ability to learn math concepts.

- Parents can be effective partners in helping children learn mathematical skills.

5 Identify some challenges and strategies related to teaching children how to think scientifically.

- Children's thinking skills share certain characteristics with those of scientists but also differ in some ways.

- Too often, the skills scientists use, such as careful observation, graphing, self-regulatory thinking, and knowing when and how to apply one's knowledge to solve problems, are not routinely taught in schools. Children have many concepts that are incompatible with science and reality. Good teachers perceive and understand a child's underlying scientific concepts, then use the concepts as a scaffold for learning.

- Constructivist teaching strategies include an emphasis on discovery learning and hands-on laboratory investigation. Other strategies include exploring everyday science problems, using activities that help students learn how science works, and considering the social contexts of science. The Human Biology Middle Grades Curriculum (HumBio) integrates the study of ecology, evolution, genetics, physiology, health, safety, culture, and human development.

There is controversy about the sequence of science courses in high school.

6 Summarize how learning in social studies is becoming more constructivist.

- The field of social studies seeks to promote civic competence. In schools, social studies draws from disciplines such as anthropology, economics, geography, history, law, philosophy, political science, psychology, religion, and sociology. Ten themes are recommended to be used for units and courses in social studies by the National Council for the Social Sciences: time, continuity, and change; people, places, and environment; individual differences and identity; individuals, groups, and institutions; power, authority, and governance; production, distribution, and consumption; science, technology, and society; global connections; civic ideals and practices; and culture.

- Many social studies classes continue to be taught in a traditional lecture format, but there is increasing interest in teaching these classes from a constructivist perspective. This perspective emphasizes the importance of greater reflection, understanding, meaning, critical thinking about values, and sustained examination of a few important topics rather than superficial coverage of many topics.

 ## KEY TERMS

 ## PORTFOLIO ACTIVITIES

Now that you have a good understanding of this chapter, complete these exercises to expand your thinking.

Independent Reflection

The Cognitive and Socially Constructive Classroom. For the grade level you plan to teach, create a summary of good ideas for making learning both cognitive and socially constructive. Draw ideas from this and other chapters. Add further ideas of your own. (INTASC: Principles 4, 5)

Collaborative Work

Taking a Stand in the Math Controversy. There is controversy in math education about whether math should be taught in a constructivist manner or in a more traditional manner. There is also controversy about whether calculators and computers should be used in math instruction in the elementary school years. Get together with several students and evaluate these controversies. Summarize your discussion. (INTASC: Principles 1, 2, 4)

Research/Field Experience Reflections

Researching the Nuts and Bolts of Reading. Read about current trends in teaching children to read. Evaluate these trends based on what you've learned in this chapter. Compare current trends with how you were taught to read. Which method do you think is most effective? Why? What do you think accounts for persistent low reading scores on nationwide standardized tests? (INTASC: Principles 1, 7)

 Go to the Online Learning Center for downloadable portfolio templates.

TAKING IT TO THE NET

1. The social constructivist approach to writing emphasizes students' participation in a writing community. Explore an educational, electronic pen pals website, and develop an action plan for integrating this resource into your content area. Describe the kinds of opportunities students will have to write "real" texts, collaborate with peers, and share diverse perspectives.

2. Online exhibits designed by science museums such as The Exploratorium (www.exploratorium.edu) and The Franklin Institute Online (www.fi.edu) offer a gold mine of hands-on science projects that emphasize discovery and exploration.

   Connect to the Online Learning Center to explore possible answers.

STUDY, PRACTICE, AND SUCCEED

 Go to chapter 11 on the Online Learning Center at www.mhhe.com/santrockedu2e to access the student study guide with practice quizzes, web links, portfolio resources, PowerWeb articles and news feeds, and the online resources referenced in the chapter.

 Go to your Student Toolbox CD-ROM to access the resources and activities referenced in the chapter and

- Resources to help you prepare for the **PRAXIS II™ exam**

- **Application Resources,** including additional *Crack the Case* studies, electronic versions of the *Self-Assessments,* Application Exercises, and Site Observation Questions
- **Study Resources,** including Learning Goals, the Chapter Summary, a *Test Your Learning* exercise, and multiple-choice, true/false, matching, key terms, and short-answer quizzes
- **Professional Resources,** including a Lesson Plan Builder and *Bibliomaker*

12 Planning, Instruction, and Technology

Education is the transmission of civilization.
—Ariel and Will Durant
*American Authors and Philosophers,
20th Century*

Chapter Outline

Chapter Learning Goals After you have completed your study of this chapter, you should be able to reach these learning goals:

Planning
Instructional Planning
Time Frames and Planning

1. **Explain what is involved in classroom planning.**

Teacher-Centered Lesson Planning and Instruction
Teacher-Centered Lesson Planning
Direct Instruction
Teacher-Centered Instructional Strategies
Evaluating Teacher-Centered Instruction

2. **Identify important forms of teacher-centered instruction.**

Learner-Centered Lesson Planning and Instruction
Learner-Centered Principles
Some Learner-Centered Instructional Strategies
Evaluating Learner-Centered Instruction

3. **Discuss important forms of learner-centered instruction.**

Technology and Education
The Technology Revolution
The Internet
Technology and Sociocultural Diversity
Standards for Technology-Literate Students
The Future of Technology in Schools

4. **Summarize how to effectively use technology to help children learn.**

Teaching Stories Lois Guest and Kevin Groves

In Lois Guest's fifth-grade classroom at Hesperian Elementary School in San Lorenzo, California, thirty students are working on their new laptop computers provided by the school district (May, 2001). A month after the computers arrived, outdated encyclopedias sit on shelves and students no longer have to compete for time in the school's computer lab.

The new laptops mark a monumental shift in the career of Guest, who has taught for thirty-five years at Hesperian Elementary. She remembers when slide projectors were the height of high-tech. Now, she is building a website for her class and learning how to use a digital camera and an optical scanner. Guest says that she is learning a lot about technology and that her students are also teaching her how to do things on the computer. Ten-year-old

Bianca Guitierrez said that because of how much she enjoys working on her new laptop computer, she looks forward to coming to school more now.

When Kevin Groves took his fifth-grade class on a field trip to a botanical garden, his students insisted that they be allowed to bring their laptops. One of his students, Salvador Mata, spread out on the grass with his mother and explained to her how to make a *Powerpoint* presentation. His mother said that she is so pleased about Salvador learning how to use a computer at such an early age, believing that it will help him get a good job later in his life.

Groves commented that while the laptops are wonderful, he has to research every link he puts on his website to make sure it is educational and won't lead to something bad for his students.

Later in this chapter, we will focus on many aspects of incorporating technology into lesson plans and instruction. The entire chapter addresses teaching primarily at the level of the overall lesson plan or unit, often making use of the various learning and cognitive processes we discussed in chapters 7 through 11. We especially will explore teacher-centered lesson planning and student-centered lesson planning.

PLANNING

It has been said that when people fail to plan, they plan to fail. Many successful people attribute their accomplishments to effective planning. For example, Lee Iacocca (1984), former chairman of Chrysler Corporation, credits his success to his weekly planner. Our introduction to planning describes what instructional planning is and time frames of planning.

Instructional Planning

Planning Lessons

Lesson Plans in Different Subject Areas

Planning is a critical aspect of being a competent teacher (Parkay & Hass, 2000). **Instructional planning** involves developing a systematic, organized strategy for planning lessons. Teachers need to decide what and how they are going to teach before they do it. Although some wonderful instructional moments are spontaneous, lessons still should be carefully planned.

It might seem tedious to spend so much time writing out lesson plans. However, they will give you confidence, guide you in covering the most important topics, and keep you from wasting precious class time.

Instructional planning might be mandated by the school in which you teach. Many principals and instructional supervisors require teachers to keep written plans, and in some cases you might be asked to submit lesson plans several weeks in advance. When

instructional planning A systematic, organized strategy for planning lessons.

FRANK AND ERNEST reprinted by permission of United Features Syndicate, Inc.

observing classroom teachers, supervisors may refer to the plan to see if the teacher is following it. If a teacher is absent but has created a plan, a substitute teacher can follow the plan.

Time Frames and Planning

Developing systematic time plans involves knowing what needs to be done and when to do it, or focusing on "task" and "time." Here is one helpful six-part task and time plan (Douglass & Douglass, 1993):

What Needs to Be Done

1. *Set instructional goals* (what do I expect to accomplish?)
2. *Plan activities* (what do I have to do to reach the goals?)
3. *Set priorities* (which tasks are more important than others?)

The Time to Do It

4. *Make time estimates* (how much time will each activity take?)
5. *Create schedules* (when will we do each activity?)
6. *Be flexible* (how will I handle unexpected occurrences?)

You will need to plan for different time spans, ranging from yearly to daily planning (Arends, 1998). If schoolwide planning or your own career planning is involved, the time frame likely will be a number of years.

Robert Yinger (1980) identified five time spans of teacher planning: yearly planning, term planning, unit planning, weekly planning, and daily planning. Figure 12.1 illustrates these time frames and shows planning for them. Yinger also recommends that teachers attend to four areas when planning: goals, sources of information, the form of

Through the Eyes of Teachers

Preventing Panic

The one thing that has helped me to become a better planner is learning to think ahead. Begin the year by coming up with general long-term plans for each subject area. This strategy will help you decide how much time to spend on certain things. Knowing what is coming next helps to provide structure and focus within your plans. It also helps to prevent the "panic" of deciding at the last minute what you have to teach. I have found that the earlier I have made my plans and gathered my materials, the more relaxed and confident I feel during the week.

Vicky Stone
Reading Teacher
Cammack Middle School
Huntington, West Virginia

Video Lecture: Curriculum

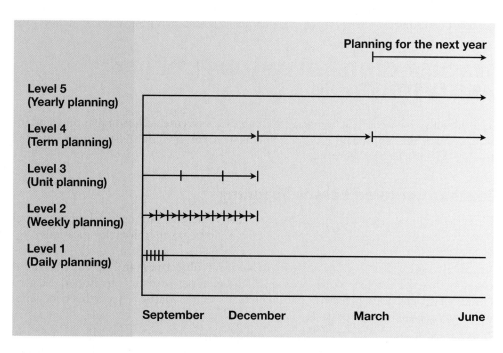

FIGURE 12.1 Five Time Spans of Teacher Planning and Their Occurrence over the School Year

Video Lecture: Planning for Instruction

the plan, and criteria for the effectiveness of the planning. Figure 12.2 shows what is involved in these areas across the five different time frames.

Although planning is a key dimension of successful teaching, don't overplan to the point of becoming an automaton. Develop organized plans and try to carry them out, but be flexible; as a year, month, week, or day unfolds, adapt to changing circumstances. A controversial current event or necessary topic might emerge that you did not originally include. Monitor and rework your plans as the school year goes by to suit these changing circumstances.

If you plan effectively, you won't have to keep all of the details of a lesson in mind all of the time (Middleton & Goepfert, 1996). Your plan lets you focus on the immediate dialogue you are having with students and guides the interactive aspect of your instruction.

Many teachers rely heavily on published teachers' guides or textbook structures to direct their instructional planning. This can have positive benefits because, with activities or lessons developed for the entire time, you can focus more on the day-to-day aspects of teaching. However, you might go into greater depth about some topics and develop larger projects for the entire term than are included in the teachers' guides.

> ## ❗ Review and Reflect
>
> **1** **Explain what is involved in classroom planning.**
>
> **Review**
> - Why does instruction need to be planned?
> - What planning needs to be done related to the use of time?
>
> **Reflect**
> - In your own K–12 experiences, did you ever have a teacher who did not put enough effort into planning? What was that like for students?

Planning and instruction should be closely linked. Next, we will explore teacher-centered planning and instruction, then learner-centered planning and instruction.

Resources for Teacher Planning

TEACHER-CENTERED LESSON PLANNING AND INSTRUCTION

Traditionally, the focus in schools has been on teacher-centered lesson planning and instruction. In this approach, planning and instruction are highly structured and the teacher directs students' learning.

Teacher-Centered Lesson Planning

Three general tools are especially useful in teacher-centered planning: creating behavioral objectives, analyzing tasks, and developing instructional taxonomies (classifications).

Creating Behavioral Objectives **Behavioral objectives** are statements about changes that the teacher wishes to see in students' performance. In Robert Mager's (1962) view, behavioral objectives should be very specific. Mager believes that behavioral objectives should have three parts:

- *Student's behavior.* Focus on what the student will learn or do.
- *Conditions under which the behavior will occur.* State how the behavior will be evaluated or tested.
- *Performance criteria.* Determine what level of performance will be acceptable.

behavioral objectives Statements that communicate proposed changes in students' behavior to reach desired levels of performance.

	GOALS OF PLANNING	SOURCES OF INFORMATION	FORM OF THE PLAN	CRITERIA FOR JUDGING THE EFFECTIVENESS OF PLANNING
Yearly planning	1. Establishing general content (fairly general and framed by district curriculum objectives) 2. Establishing basic curriculum sequence 3. Ordering and reserving materials	1. Students (general information about numbers and returning students) 2. Resources available 3. Curriculum guidelines (district objectives) 4. Experience with specific curricula and materials	General outlines listing basic content and possible ideas in each subject matter area (spiral notebook used for each subject)	1. Comprehensiveness of plans 2. Fit with own goals and district objectives
Term planning	1. Detailing of content to be covered in next 3 months 2. Establishing a weekly schedule for term that conforms to teacher's goals and emphases for the term	1. Direct contact with students 2. Time constraints set by school schedule 3. Resources available	1. Elaboration of outlines constructed for yearly planning 2. A weekly schedule outline specifying activities and times	1. Outlines— comprehensiveness, completeness, and specificity of elaborations 2. Schedule— comprehensiveness and fit with goals for term, balance 3. Fit with goals for term
Unit planning	1. Developing a sequence of well-organized learning experiences 2. Presenting comprehensive, integrated, and meaningful content at an appropriate level	1. Students' abilities, interests, etc. 2. Materials, length of lessons, set-up time, demand, format 3. District objectives 4. Facilities available for activities	1. Lists of outlines of activities and content 2. Lists of sequenced activities 3. Notes in plan book	1. Organization, sequence, balance, and flow of outlines 2. Fit with yearly and term goals 3. Fit with anticipated student interest and involvement
Weekly planning	1. Laying out the week's activities within the framework of the weekly schedule 2. Adjusting schedule for interruptions and special needs 3. Maintaining continuity and regularity of activities	1. Students' performance in preceding days and weeks 2. Scheduled school interruptions (for example, assemblies, holidays) 3. Materials, aides, and other resources	1. Names and times of activities in plan book 2. Day divided into four instructional blocks punctuated by A.M. recess, lunch, and P.M. recess	1. Completeness of plans 2. Degree to which weekly schedule had been followed 3. Flexibility of plans to allow for special time constraints or interruptions 4. Fit with goals
Daily planning	1. Setting up and arranging classroom for next day 2. Specifying activity components not yet decided upon 3. Fitting daily schedule to last-minute intrusions 4. Preparing students for day's activities	1. Instructions in materials to be used 2. Set-up time required for activities 3. Assessment of class "disposition" at start of day 4. Continued interest, involvement, and enthusiasm	1. Schedule for day written on the chalkboard and discussed with students 2. Preparation and arrangement of materials and facilities in the room	1. Completion of last-minute preparations and decisions about content, materials, etc. 2. Involvement, enthusiasm, and interest communicated by students

FIGURE 12.2 **Five Time Spans of Teacher Planning and the Activities Involved**

For example, a teacher might develop a behavioral objective around the idea that the student will describe five causes of the decline of the British Empire (student's behavior). The teacher plans to give the student an essay test on this topic (conditions under which the behavior will occur). And the teacher decides that explaining four or five causes will be acceptable performance (performance criterion).

Analyzing Tasks   Another tool of teacher-centered planning is **task analysis,** which focuses on breaking down a complex task that students are to learn into its component parts (Alberto & Troutman, 1999). The analysis can proceed in three basic steps (Moyer & Dardig, 1978):

1. Determine what skills or concepts the student needs to have to learn the task.
2. List any materials that will be required in order to perform the task, such as paper, pencil, and calculator.
3. List all of the components of the task in the order in which they must be performed.

Developing Instructional Taxonomies   Instructional taxonomies also aid teacher-centered approaches. A **taxonomy** is a classification system. **Bloom's taxonomy** was developed by Benjamin Bloom and his colleagues (1956). It classifies educational objectives into three domains: cognitive, affective, and psychomotor.

The Cognitive Domain   Bloom's cognitive taxonomy has six objectives (Bloom & others, 1956):

Bloom's Taxonomy

- *Knowledge.* Students have the ability to remember information. For example, an objective might be to list or describe four main advantages of using a computer for word processing.
- *Comprehension.* Students understand the information and can explain it in their own words. For example, an objective might be to explain or discuss how a computer can effectively be used for word processing.
- *Application.* Students use knowledge to solve real-life problems. For example, an objective might be to apply what has been learned about using a computer for word processing to how this could be used in various careers.
- *Analysis.* Students break down complex information into smaller parts and relate information to other information. For example, an objective might be to compare one type of word-processing program with another for doing term papers.
- *Synthesis.* Students combine elements and create new information. For example, an objective might be to organize all that has been learned about the use of computers for writing.
- *Evaluation.* Students make good judgments and decisions. For example, an objective might be to critique different word-processing programs or to judge the strengths and weaknesses of a particular word-processing program.

When Bloom originally presented his taxonomy, he described these six cognitive objectives as hierarchically arranged from *lower-level* (knowledge, comprehension) to *higher-level* (application, analysis, synthesis, evaluation), with higher-level objectives building on the lower ones. However, educators often strip the objectives of their level and simply use them as a comprehensive way of considering different cognitive goals.

Bloom's cognitive objectives can be used when planning assessment. True/false, matching, multiple-choice, and short-answer items are often used to assess knowledge and comprehension. Essay questions, class discussions, projects, and portfolios are especially good for assessing application, analysis, synthesis, and evaluation.

The Affective Domain   The affective taxonomy consists of five objectives related to emotional responses to tasks (Krathwohl, Bloom, & Masia, 1964). Each of the five objectives requires the student to show some degree of commitment or emotional intensity:

task analysis Breaking down a complex task that students are to learn into its component parts.

taxonomy A classification system.

Bloom's taxonomy Developed by Benjamin Bloom and colleagues; consists of educational objectives in three domains—cognitive, affective, and psychomotor.

- *Receiving.* Students become aware of or attend to something in the environment. For example, a guest comes to class to talk with students about reading. An objective might be for students to listen carefully to the speaker.
- *Responding.* Students become motivated to learn and display a new behavior as a result of an experience. An objective might be for students to become motivated to become better readers as a result of the guest speaker's appearance.
- *Valuing.* Students become involved in or committed to some experience. An objective might be for students to value reading as an important skill.
- *Organizing.* Students integrate a new value into an already existing set of values and give it proper priority. An objective might be to have students participate in a book club.
- *Value characterizing.* Students act in accordance with the value and are firmly committed to it. An objective might be that over the course of the school year, students increasingly value reading.

The Psychomotor Domain   Most of us link motor activity with physical education and athletics, but many other subjects, such as handwriting and word processing, also involve movement. In the sciences, students have to manipulate complex equipment; the visual and manual arts require good hand-eye coordination. Bloom's psychomotor objectives include these:

- *Reflex movements.* Students respond involuntarily without conscious thought to a stimulus. For example, students blink when an object unexpectedly hurtles their way.
- *Basic fundamentals.* Students make basic voluntary movements that are directed toward a particular purpose. For example, students grasp a microscope knob and correctly turn it.
- *Perceptual abilities.* Students use their senses, such as seeing, hearing, or touching, to guide their skill efforts. For example, students watch how to hold an instrument in science, such as a microscope, and listen to instructions on how to use it.
- *Physical abilities.* Students develop general skills of endurance, strength, flexibility, and agility. For example, students demonstrate an ability to run long distances or hit a softball.
- *Skilled movements.* Students perform complex physical skills with some degree of proficiency. For example, students effectively sketch a drawing.
- *Nondiscussive behaviors.* Students communicate feelings and emotions through bodily actions. For example, students do pantomimes or dance to communicate a musical piece.

Bloom's taxonomies for the cognitive, affective, and psychomotor domains can be used by teachers to plan instruction. In the past, instructional planning has generally focused on cognitive or behavioral objectives. Bloom's taxonomy provides for a more expansive consideration of skills by also including affective and psychomotor domains. Figure 12.3 on page 382 presents Bloom's domains and lists associated action verbs you can use for creating objectives during instructional planning.

Recently, a group of educational psychologists updated Bloom's knowledge and cognitive process dimensions in light of recent theory and research (Anderson & Krathwohl, 2001). In the update, the knowledge dimension has four categories, which lie along a continuum from concrete (factual) to abstract (metacognition):

- *Factual:* the basic elements students must know to be acquainted with a discipline or solve problems in it (technical vocabulary, sources of information)
- *Conceptual:* the interrelationships among the basic elements within a larger structure that allows them to function together (periods of geological time, forms of business ownership)
- *Procedural:* how to do something, methods of inquiry, and criteria for using skills (skills used in painting with watercolors, interviewing techniques)

COGNITIVE DOMAIN	
Category	Associated Verbs
Knowledge	*List, read, identify, define, indicate, describe, name, quote, underline*
Comprehension	*Translate, transform, summarize, paraphrase, illustrate, interpret, estimate, interpolate, extrapolate, classify, categorize, re-organize, explain, predict*
Application	*Apply, generalize, relate, use, employ, transfer, graph, exemplify, illustrate, tabulate, calculate, compute, derive, calibrate*
Analysis	*Analyze, contrast, compare, distinguish, detect, edit, discriminate*
Synthesis	*Produce, constitute, modify, originate, propose, plan, design, combine, organize, synthesize, develop, formulate*
Evaluation	*Judge, argue, validate, predict, assess, decide, appraise, conclude, evaluate, explain, criticize*

AFFECTIVE DOMAIN	
Category	Associated Verbs
Receiving	*Accept, differentiate, listen, separate, select, share, agree*
Responding	*Approve, applaud, comply, follow, discuss, volunteer, practice, spend time with, paraphrase*
Valuing	*Argue, debate, deny, help, support, protest, participate, subsidize, praise*
Organizing	*Discuss, compare, balance, define, abstract, formulate, theorize, organize*
Value Characterizing	*Change, avoid, complete, manage, resolve, revise, resist, require*

PSYCHOMOTOR DOMAIN	
Category	Associated Verbs
Reflex Movements	*Blink, stretch, relax, jerk, straighten up*
Basic Fundamentals	*Walk, run, jump, push, pull, manipulate, catch, grasp, stand*
Perceptual Abilities	*Follow, dodge, maintain, identify, read, write, list, balance, trace, brush, print, pronounce*
Physical Abilities	*Hop, skip, jump, run, touch, lift, push, pull, tap, float, hit, throw, toss, strum*
Skilled Movements	*Draw, dance, ski, skate, paint, build, volley, race, whistle, march, somersault, hammer, sculpt, sketch*
Nondiscussive Behaviors	*Pantomime, mimic, direct, perform, communicate, gesture, use body movement*

FIGURE 12.3 **Action Verbs for Writing Objectives in the Cognitive, Affective, and Psychomotor Domains**

- *Metacognitive:* knowledge of cognition and awareness of one's own cognition (knowledge of outlining and strategies for remembering)

In the update of the cognitive process dimension, six categories lie along a continuum from less complex (remember) to more complex (create):

- *Remember.* Retrieve relevant knowledge from long-term memory. (Recognize the dates of important events in U.S. history.)
- *Understand.* Construct meaning from instruction that includes interpreting, exemplifying, classifying, summarizing, inferring, comparing, and explaining. (Explain the causes of important eighteenth-century events in France.)

- *Apply.* Carry out or use a procedure in a given situation (Use a law in physics in situations in which it is appropriate.)
- *Analyze.* Break material into its component parts and determine how the parts relate to each other and to overall structure or purpose. (Distinguish between relevant and irrelevant numbers in a math word problem.)
- *Evaluate.* Make judgments based on criteria and standards. (Detect inconsistencies or fallacies in a product.)
- *Create.* Put elements together to form a coherent or functional whole; reorganize elements into a new pattern or structure. (Generate hypotheses to account for an observed phenomenon.)

Direct Instruction

Direct instruction is a structured, teacher-centered approach that is characterized by teacher direction and control, high teacher expectations for students' progress, maximum time spent by students on academic tasks, and efforts by the teacher to keep negative affect to a minimum (Joyce & Weil, 1996). The focus of direct instruction is academic activity; nonacademic materials (such as toys, games, and puzzles) tend not to be used; also deemphasized is nonacademically oriented teacher-student interaction (such as conversations about self or personal concerns).

Teacher direction and control take place when the teacher chooses students' learning tasks, directs students' learning of the tasks, and minimizes the amount of nonacademic talk. The teacher sets high standards for performance and expects students to reach these levels of excellence.

An important goal in the direct-instruction approach is maximizing student learning time (Stevenson, 2000). Time spent by students on academic tasks in the classroom is called *academic learning time.* Learning takes time. The more academic learning time students experience, the more likely they are to learn the material and achieve high standards. The direct instruction premise is that the best way to maximize time on academic tasks is to create a highly structured, academically oriented learning environment. The Diversity and Education interlude describes cross-cultural research about the amount of time students spend on math in different countries, as well as other comparisons across countries.

Diversity and Education
Cross-Cultural Comparisons in Learning Math and Math Instruction

The University of Michigan's Harold Stevenson is one of the leading experts on children's learning and has been conducting research on this topic for five decades. In the 1980s and 1990s, he turned his attention to discovering ways to improve children's learning by conducting cross-cultural comparisons of children in the United States with children in Asian countries, especially Japan, China, and Taiwan (Stevenson, 1992, 1995, 2000; Stevenson & Hofer, 1999; Stevenson & others, 1990). In Stevenson's research, Asian students consistently outperformed American students in mathematics. Also, the longer students are in school, the wider the gap became—the lowest difference was in first grade, the highest in eleventh grade (the highest grade studied).

To learn more about the reasons for these cross-cultural differences, Stevenson and his colleagues spent thousands of hours observing in classrooms, as well as interviewing and surveying teachers, students, and parents. They found that Asian teachers spent more of their time teaching math than American teachers did. For example, in Japan more than one-fourth of the total classroom time in first grade was spent on math instruction, compared with only one-tenth of the time in U.S. first-grade classrooms. Also,

direct instruction A structured, teacher-centered approach that is characterized by teacher direction and control, high teacher expectations for students' progress, maximum time spent by students on academic tasks, and efforts by the teacher to keep negative affect to a minimum.

In Stevenson's research, Asian students scored considerably higher than U.S. students on math achievement tests. What are some possible explanations for these findings?

Asian students were in school an average of 240 days a year, compared with 178 days in the United States.

In addition to the substantially greater time spent on math instruction in Asian schools than in American schools, differences were found between Asian and American parents. American parents had much lower expectations for their children's education and achievement than Asian parents did. Also, American parents were more likely to believe that their children's math ability is due to innate ability, whereas Asian parents were more likely to say that their children's math achievement was the consequence of effort and training (see figure 12.4). Asian students were more likely than American students to do math homework, and Asian parents were far more likely to help their children with their math homework than American parents were (Chen & Stevenson, 1989).

In another cross-cultural comparison of math education, videotapes of eighth-grade teachers' instruction in the United States, Japan, and Germany were analyzed (Stigler & Hiebert, 1997, 1999). Differences among the countries included (1) Japanese students spent less time solving routine math problems and more time inventing, analyzing, and proving than American or German students did; (2) Japanese teachers engaged in more direct lecturing than American or German teachers did; and (3) Japanese teachers were more likely to emphasize math thinking, whereas American and German teachers were more likely to stress math skills (solving a specific problem or using a specific formula). Also noticeable was how much emphasis there was on collaborative planning with other teachers in Japanese math education. We will have much more to say about cross-cultural comparisons in math and other subject areas in chapter 15, "Standardized Tests and Teaching." We will examine other research studies, explore the concept of "world-class standards" in education, and evaluate criticisms of cross-cultural studies of achievement.

Yet another emphasis in the direct-instruction approach is keeping negative affect to a minimum. Researchers have found that negative affect interferes with learning (Rosenshine, 1971). Advocates of direct instruction underscore the importance of keeping an academic focus and avoiding negative affect, such as the negative feelings that can often arise in both the teacher and students when a teacher overcriticizes.

Teacher-Centered Instructional Strategies

Many teacher-centered strategies reflect direct instruction. Here we will talk about orienting students to new material; lecturing, explaining, and demonstrating; questioning and discussing; mastery learning; seatwork; and homework.

Orienting Before presenting and explaining new material, establish a framework for the lesson and orient students to the new material (Joyce & Weil, 1996): (1) Review the previous day's activities; (2) discuss the lesson's objective; (3) provide clear, explicit instructions about the work to be done; and (4) give an overview of today's lesson. Such orientation and structuring at the beginning of a lesson are linked with improved student achievement (Fisher & others, 1980).

Advance organizers are teaching activities and techniques that establish a framework and orient students to material before it is presented (Ausubel, 1960). You can use advance organizers when you begin a lesson to help students see the "big picture" of what is to come and how information is meaningfully connected.

advance organizers Teaching activities and techniques that establish a framework and orient students to material before it is presented.

Advance organizers come in two forms: expository and comparative. **Expository advance organizers** provide students with new knowledge that will orient them to the upcoming lesson. The chapter-opening outline and learning goals are expository advance organizers. Another way to provide an expository advance organizer is to describe the lesson's theme and why it is important to study this topic. For example, in orienting students to the topic of exploring the Aztec civilization in a history class, the teacher says that they are going to study the Spanish invasion of Mexico, who the Aztecs were, what their lives were like, and their artifacts. To heighten student interest, she also says that they will study worlds in collision as Spain's conquistadors were filled with awe at sights of a spectacular Western civilization. There are Mexican American students in her class, and the teacher emphasizes how this information can help everyone in the class understand these students' personal and cultural identity.

Comparative advance organizers introduce new material by connecting it with what students already know. For example, in the history class just mentioned, the teacher says that the Spanish invasion of Mexico continues the transatlantic traffic that changed two worlds: Europe and the Americas. She asks students to think about how this discussion of the Aztecs connects with Columbus' journey, which they examined last week.

Lecturing, Explaining, and Demonstrating Lecturing, explaining, and demonstrating are common teacher activities in the direct-instruction approach. Researchers have found that effective teachers spend more time explaining and demonstrating new material than their less-effective counterparts do (Rosenshine, 1985). In chapter 11, we described the process of interactive demonstration strategy, an effective strategy for teaching concepts in science.

On some occasions we sit through boring lectures, yet on other occasions we have been captivated by a lecturer and learned a great deal from the presentation.

 ## Teaching Strategies
For Lecturing

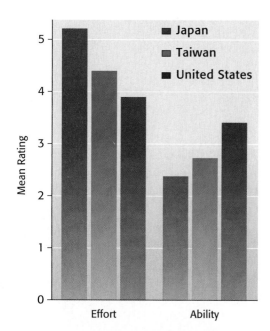

FIGURE 12.4 Mothers' Beliefs About the Factors Responsible for Children's Math Achievement in Three Countries
In one study, mothers in Japan and Taiwan were more likely to believe that their children's math achievement was due to effort rather than innate ability, while U.S. mothers were more likely to believe their children's math achievement was due to innate ability (Stevenson, Lee, & Stigler, 1986). If parents believe that their children's math achievement is due to innate ability and their children are not doing well in math, the implication is that they are less likely to think their children will benefit from putting forth more effort.

Let's explore some guidelines for when lecturing is a good choice and some strategies for delivering an effective lecture. Here are some goals that lecturing can accomplish (Henson, 1988):

1. *Present information and motivate students' interest in a subject.*
2. *Introduce a topic before students read about it on their own, or give instructions on how to perform a task.*
3. *Summarize or synthesize information after a discussion or inquiry.*
4. *Provide alternative points of view or clarify issues in preparation for discussion.*
5. *Explain materials that students are having difficulty learning on their own.*

These are some good strategies to use when lecturing:

1. *Be prepared.* Don't just "wing" a lecture. Spend time preparing and organizing what you will present.
2. *Keep lectures short and intersperse them with questions and activities.* For example, a teacher might lecture for ten or fifteen minutes to provide the background information and framework for a topic, then place students in small discussion groups.
3. *Make the lecture interesting and exciting.* Think about what you can say that will motivate students' interest in a topic. Vary the pace of the lecture by interlacing it with related video clips, demonstrations, handouts, and/or activities for students.

expository advance organizers Organizers that provide students with new knowledge that will orient them to the upcoming lesson.

comparative advance organizers Connections with prior knowledge that help to introduce new material.

What are some good teaching strategies for the effective use of questions?

4. *Follow a designated sequence and include certain key components:*
   - Begin with advance organizers or previews of the topic.
   - Verbally and visually highlight any key concepts or new ideas (like the boldfaced key terms in this book). Use the blackboard, an overhead projector, or another large-display device.
   - Present new information in relation to what students already know about the topic.
   - Periodically elicit student responses to ensure that they understand the information up to that point and to encourage active learning.
   - At the end of the lecture, provide a summary or an overview of the main ideas.
   - Make connections to future lectures or activities.

Questioning and Discussing   It is necessary but challenging to integrate questions and discussion in teacher-centered instruction (Weinstein, 1997). In using these strategies, it is important to respond to each student's learning needs while maintaining the group's interest and attention. It also is important to distribute participation widely while also retaining the enthusiasm of eager volunteers. An additional challenge is allowing students to contribute while still maintaining the focus on the lesson.

A special concern is that male students are more likely than female students to dominate the discussion. In one study of ten high school geometry classes, males called out answers to the teacher twice as frequently as females did (Becker, 1981). Similar results were found in a study of sixty physical science and chemistry classes (Jones & Wheatley, 1990). Be sensitive to gender patterns and ensure that girls get equal discussion time.

Teaching Strategies
For the Effective Use of Questions

Strategies in Practice

- **Planning**
- **Questioning and Discussing**

Let's examine some effective strategies for using questions in the classroom:

1. *Use fact-based questions as entrees into thinking-based questions.* For example, in teaching a lesson on environmental pollution, the teacher might ask the fact-based question "What are three types of environmental pollution?" Then she could follow with this thinking-based question: "What strategies can you think of for reducing one of these types of environmental pollution?" Don't overuse fact-based questions, because they tend to produce rote learning rather than learning for understanding.

2. *Avoid yes/no and leading questions.* Yes/no questions should be used only as a segue into more probing questions. For example, it is not a good strategy to ask a lot of questions like "Was environmental pollution responsible for the dead fish in the lake?" Keep these questions to a minimum, only occasionally using them as a warm-up for questions such as these: "How did the pollution kill the fish?" "Why do you think companies polluted the lake?" "What can be done to clean up environmental pollution?"

   Asking leading questions such as "Don't you agree?" or other rhetorical questions such as "You do want to read more about environmental pollution, don't you?" is not a good strategy. These types of questions don't produce meaningful responses and simply hand the initiative back to the teacher (Grossier, 1964).

3. *Leave enough time for students to think about answers.* Too often when teachers ask questions, they don't give students enough time to think. In one study, teachers

waited less than one second, on the average, before calling on a student to respond (Rowe, 1986)! In the same study, teachers waited only about one second, on the average, for the student to respond before supplying the answer themselves. Such intrusions don't give students adequate time to construct answers. In the study just mentioned, teachers were subsequently instructed to wait three to five seconds to allow students to respond to questions. The increased wait time led to considerable improvements in responses, including better inferences about the materials and more student-initiated questions. Waiting three to five seconds or more for students to respond is not as easy as it might seem; it takes practice. But your students will benefit considerably from having to think and construct responses.

4. *Ask clear, purposeful, brief, and sequenced questions.* Avoid being vague. Focus the questions on the lesson at hand. Plan ahead so that your questions are meaningfully tied to the topic. If your questions are long-winded, you run the risk that they will not be understood, so briefer is better. Also plan questions so that they follow a logical sequence, integrating them with previously discussed material before moving to the next topic (Grossier, 1964).

5. *Monitor how you respond to students' answers.* What should you do next after a student responds to your question? Many teachers just say "Okay" or "Uh-huh" (Sadker & Sadker, 1986). Usually it is wise to do more. You can use the student's response as a basis for follow-up questions and engage the student or other students in a dialogue. Provide feedback that is tailored to the student's existing level of knowledge and understanding.

6. *Be aware of when it is best to pose a question to the entire class or to a particular student.* Asking the entire class a question makes all students in the class responsible for responding. Asking a specific student a question can make other students less likely to answer it. Some reasons to ask a question to a particular student are (Grossier, 1964) (1) to draw an inattentive student into the lesson, (2) to ask a follow-up question of someone who has just responded, and (3) to call on someone who rarely responds when questions are asked to the class as a whole. Don't let a small group of assertive students dominate the responses. Talk with them independently about continuing their positive responses without monopolizing class time. One strategy for giving students an equal chance to respond is to pull names from a cookie jar or check names off a class list as students respond (Weinstein & Mignano, 1997).

7. *Encourage students to ask questions.* Praise them for good questions. Ask them "How?" and "Why?" and encourage them to ask "How?" and "Why?"

Mastery Learning   **Mastery learning** involves learning one concept or topic thoroughly before moving on to a more difficult one. A successful mastery learning approach involves these procedures (Bloom, 1971; Carroll, 1963):

- Specify the learning task or lesson. Develop precise instructional objectives. Establish mastery standards (this typically is where *A* students perform).
- Break the course into learning units that are aligned with instructional objectives.
- Plan instructional procedures to include corrective feedback to students if they fail to master the material at an acceptable level, such as 90% correct. The corrective feedback might take place through supplemental materials, tutoring, or small-group instruction.
- Give an end-of-unit or end-of-course test that evaluates whether the student has mastered all of the material at an acceptable level.

Mastery learning gets mixed reviews. Some researchers indicate that mastery learning is effective in increasing the time that students spend on learning tasks (Kulik, Kulik, & Bangert-Drowns, 1990), but others find less support for mastery learning (Bangert, Kulik, & Kulik, 1983). Outcomes of mastery learning depend on the teacher's skill in planning and executing the strategy. One context in which mastery learning might be

Mastery Learning

mastery learning Learning one concept or topic thoroughly before moving on to a more difficult one.

FOR THE TEACHER	FOR THE STUDENT
1. Keeping track of what the rest of the class is doing	1. Completing assigned work on their own
2. Keeping students on-task	2. Understanding how and when to obtain the teacher's help
3. Dealing with the varying paces at which students work ("ragged" endings)	3. Understanding the norms for assisting peers
4. Selecting or creating seatwork that is clear and meaningful	4. Learning how to be effective in obtaining help from peers
5. Matching seatwork to students' varying levels of achievement	
6. Collecting, correcting, recording, and returning seatwork assignments	

FIGURE 12.5 Challenges of Seatwork for Teachers and Students

especially beneficial is remedial reading (Schunk, 2000). A well-organized mastery learning program for remedial reading allows students to progress at their own rates based on their skills, their motivation, and the time they have to learn.

Seatwork   *Seatwork* refers to the practice of having all or a majority of students work independently at their seats. Teachers vary in how much they use seatwork as part of their instruction. Some teachers use it every day; others rarely use it. Figure 12.5 summarizes the challenges of seatwork for the teacher and the student.

Learning centers are especially good alternatives to paper-and-pencil seatwork. Figure 12.6 provides some suggestions for learning centers. A computer station can be an excellent learning center. For example, in one classroom a teacher uses computer work rather than paper-and-pencil seatwork. Students identify acid rain patterns around the world with a National Geographic Society computer network, practice navigation and rescue whales with *Voyage of the Mimi* (Bank Street College of Education, 1984), and learn about marine environments with *A Field Trip into the Sea* (In View, 1990). Two or three students work at each computer, which encourages collaborative learning.

Teaching Strategies
For Using Seatwork

Here are some good guidelines for minimizing the problems that seatwork poses (Weinstein & Mignano, 1997, pp. 177–192):

1. "*Check students' seatwork for clarity, meaningfulness, and appropriateness.*" Seatwork often involves worksheets. Their layout should be attractive and functional. At least some of the worksheets should be fun to do.
2. *Clearly describe seatwork assignments.* Give students an introductory explanation of the seatwork and describe its purpose.
3. *Monitor students' behavior and comprehension.* Students can become bored and easily distracted during seatwork, especially if it goes on too long. Thus, monitoring behavior during seatwork is crucial to its learning contribution. And it's not just enough for students to be busy and on-task; they also need to be actively engaged in learning something. One strategy "is to spend the first five minutes of

Science

Simple experiments with lab sheets
Observations over time with recording forms
Exploring properties of objects and classifying them

Social Studies

Recreating items used by different civilizations
Creating charts or graphs of population trends
Map making

Mathematics

Math "challenges" and puzzles
Manipulative activities

Art

Holiday or thematic projects
Crafts related to curriculum studies (quilting, quilling,
    origami, etc.)

Writing

Class story writing (e.g., add-on stories)
Rewrites of literature
Writing plays or puppet shows

Computer

Content-related programs
Simulations
Story writing

FIGURE 12.6 **Suggestions for Learning Centers**

seatwork circulating around the room." Once you feel confident that students understand what to do, establish the first small group. Then, after spending time with that group, circulate again, form a second group if desired, and so on.

4. *Teach students what to do if they get stuck.* Students need to know how and when they can ask for your help. Effective teachers often tell students not to disrupt them while they are working with a small group but, rather, to ask for help while the teacher circulates between small-group sessions. Some teachers develop special systems for help, such as a small red flag for students to keep on their desk and raise if they need assistance. You can tell students to skip the tasks that are troublesome and work on other tasks until you are available. You also need to make it clear to students whether it is okay to ask peers for assistance. Many teachers not only allow peer help but actively encourage it.

5. *Tell students what to do when they are finished.* Provide enjoyable educational activities for students to engage in if they finish before the time allotted for seatwork is up. These activities might include working on a computer, doing free reading or journal writing, solving brainteasers and puzzles, or resuming work on long-term, ongoing projects.

6. *Search for alternatives to workbook pages.* Relying too much on commercially prepared workbook pages can induce boredom and off-task behavior. Spend some time creating seatwork that challenges your students to think reflectively, deeply, and creatively; don't bore them with trivial tasks. Alternatives to such common

worksheet activities (such as fill-in-the-blanks) include reading, writing, doing ongoing projects, spending time in learning centers, working on a computer, and doing cross-age tutoring.

Homework   Another important instructional decision involves how much and what type of homework to give students. In the cross-cultural research discussed earlier that focused on Asian and American students, the time spent on homework was assessed (Chen & Stevenson, 1989). Asian students spent more time doing homework than American students did. For example, on weekends Japanese first-graders did an average of 66 minutes of homework, and American first-graders did only 18 minutes. Also, Asian students had a much more positive attitude about homework than American students did. And Asian parents were far more likely to help their children with their homework than American parents were.

Harris Cooper (1998; Cooper & Valentine, 2001; Cooper & others, 1998) analyzed more than 100 research studies on homework in American schools and concluded that for elementary school students, the effects of homework on achievement are trivial, if they exist at all. In a recent study, Cooper (1998) collected data on 709 students in grades 2 through 4 and 6 through 12. In the lower grades, there was a significant negative relation between the amount of homework assigned and students' attitudes, suggesting that elementary school children resent having to do homework. But in grades 6 and higher, the more homework students completed, the higher their achievement. It is not clear what were the cause and effect, though. Were really good students finishing more assignments because they were motivated and competent in academic subjects, or was completing homework assignments causing students to achieve more?

Research on Homework

A key aspect of the debate about whether elementary school children should be assigned homework is the type of homework assigned (Begley, 1998). What is good homework? Especially for younger children, the emphasis should be on homework that fosters a love of learning and hones study skills. Short assignments that can be quickly completed should be the goal. With young children, long assignments that go uncompleted or completed assignments that bring a great deal of stress, tears, and tantrums should be avoided. Too often teachers assign homework that duplicates without reinforcing material that is covered in class. Homework should be an opportunity for students to engage in creative, exploratory activities, such as doing an oral history of one's family or determining the ecological effects of neighborhood business. Instead of memorizing names, dates, and battles of the Civil War as a homework assignment, students might write fictional letters from Northerners to Southerners, expressing their feelings about the issues dividing the nation. The homework assignments should be linked to the next day's class activities to emphasize to students that homework has meaning and is not just a plot to make them miserable. Homework also should have a focus. Don't ask students to write an open-ended theme from a novel the class is reading. Rather, ask them to select a character and explain why he or she behaved in a particular way.

In Cooper's analysis of more than 100 studies of homework, in middle school homework began to have a payoff. How can homework have little or no effect in elementary school yet be so beneficial in middle and high school? In the higher grades, it is easier to assign focused, substantive homework that requires students to integrate and apply knowledge—the type of homework that promotes learning (Corno, 1998). Also, by high school, students have resigned themselves to the routine of homework. Working hard after school and having good study skills are more accepted by middle and high school students.

Some educational psychologists believe that the main reason homework has not been effective in elementary school is that it has focused too much on subject matter and not enough on developing attitudes toward school, persistence, and responsible completion of assignments (Corno, 1998). They believe that it is not homework per se that benefits students but, rather, that homework

"I don't have my homework because my little brother put a Pop-Tart® in my disk drive!"

Art Bouthillier, *Phi Delta Kappan,* February 1997. Reprinted by permission of the author.

provides opportunities and demands for the student to take responsibility. They think that teachers need to inform parents about guiding their children in these aspects of doing their homework: setting goals, managing their time, controlling their emotions, and checking their work, rather than playing avoidance games or leaving hard work for last. Teachers and parents can use homework in the early grades to help children wrestle with goal setting and follow-through.

Cooper (1989; Cooper & Valentine, 2001) also has found that

- Homework has more positive effects when it is distributed over a period of time rather than done all at once. For example, doing 10 math problems each night for 5 nights is better than doing 50 over the weekend.
- Homework effects are greater for math, reading, and English than for science and social studies.
- For middle school students, 1 or 2 hours of homework a night is optimal. High school students benefit from even more hours of homework, but it is unclear what a maximum number of hours ought to be.

Homework can be a valuable tool for increasing learning, especially in middle and high school (Cooper & Valentine, 2001). However, it is important to make homework meaningful, monitor it and give students feedback about it, and involve parents in helping their child with it. In a recent review of research on parental involvement in homework, it was concluded that many parents wish they knew more about teachers' learning goals for homework and teachers' suggestions for involvement strategies that will help their children learn and succeed (Hoover-Demsey & others, 2001).

In chapter 3, "Social Contexts and Socioemotional Development," we described the importance of students doing "interactive homework" (Epstein, 1996)—homework that requires students to go to their parents for help ⬅ p. 80. In one elementary school, a weekly teacher's letter informs parents about the objectives of each homework assignment, gives them directions, and asks for comments. Think about setting up tutoring sessions for parents to help them interact effectively with their children in homework sessions.

Evaluating Teacher-Centered Instruction

Research on teacher-centered instruction has contributed many valuable suggestions for teaching, including these:

- Be an organized planner and create instructional objectives.
- Have high expectations for students' progress and ensure that students have adequate academic learning time.
- Spend initial time orienting students to a lesson.
- Use lecturing, explaining, and demonstrating to benefit certain aspects of students' learning.
- Engage students in learning by developing good question-asking skills and getting them involved in class discussion.

Through the Eyes of Students

Why at Home Too?

Doing homework challenges me all the time. Why at home too? We have enough at school. It makes me so mad I drool. There are a few things good about doing homework. You have quiet and you can do it whenever you want to. You'll have an education that will get you into college. Having homework does pay off.

Cody, Third-Grade Student
Salem Church Elementary
Chesterfield Country Schools, Virginia

What are some guidelines for assigning homework to students?

- Have students do meaningful seatwork or alternative work to allow individualized instruction with a particular student or a small group.
- Give students meaningful homework to increase their academic learning time and involve parents in students' learning.

Advocates of the teacher-centered approach especially believe that it is the best strategy for teaching basic skills, which involve clearly structured knowledge and skills (such as those needed in English, reading, math, and science). Thus, in teaching basic skills, the teacher-centered approach might consist of a teacher explicitly or directly teaching grammar rules, reading vocabulary, math computations, and science facts (Rosenshine, 1986).

Teacher-centered instruction has not been without criticism. Critics say that teacher-centered instruction often leads to passive, rote learning and inadequate opportunities to construct knowledge and understanding. They also criticize teacher-centered instruction as producing overly structured and rigid classrooms, inadequate attention to students' socioemotional development, external rather than internal motivation to learn, too much reliance on paper-and-pencil tasks, few opportunities for real-world learning, and too little collaborative learning in small groups. Such criticisms often are leveled by advocates of learner-centered planning and instruction, which we will turn to next.

Review and Reflect

2 Identify important forms of teacher-centered instruction.

Review
- How are creating behavioral objectives, task analysis, and instructional taxonomies tools for teacher-centered lesson planning?
- What is direct instruction?
- What are some good teacher-centered instructional strategies?
- What are some pros and cons of teacher-centered instruction?

Reflect
- As a student, have you ever wished that a teacher used more (or less) teacher-centered instruction? What lessons can you draw from this for your own work as a teacher?

LEARNER-CENTERED LESSON PLANNING AND INSTRUCTION

Just as the behavioral approaches described in chapter 7 provide the conceptual underpinnings for teacher-centered lesson planning and instruction, the information-processing and constructivist approaches discussed in chapters 2, 8, 9, 10, and 11 form the theoretical backdrop for learner-centered lesson planning and instruction ◀ pp. 39, 246, 282, 314, 340.

Learner-Centered Principles

Learner-centered lesson planning and instruction move the focus away from the teacher and toward the student. In one recent large-scale study, students' perceptions of a positive learning environment and interpersonal relationship with the teacher were the most important factors associated with enhancing students' motivation and achievement (McCombs, 2001; McCombs & Quiat, 2001).

Increased interest in learner-centered principles of lesson planning and instruction has resulted in a set of guidelines called *Learner-Centered Psychological Principles: A Framework for School Reform and Redesign* (Presidential Task Force on Psychology and in Education, 1992; Work Group of the American Psychological Association Board of Educational Affairs, 1995, 1997). The guidelines were constructed and are now periodically revised by a prestigious group of scientists and educators from a wide range of disciplines and interests. These principles have important implications for the way teachers plan and instruct, as they are based on research on the most effective ways children learn.

The Work Group of the American Psychological Association Board of Educational Affairs (1997) believes that in recent years research in psychology relevant to education has been especially informative, including advances in our understanding of cognitive, motivational, and contextual aspects of learning. The work group states that the learner-centered psychological principles it has proposed are widely supported and are being increasingly adopted in many classrooms. The principles emphasize the active, reflective nature of learning and learners. According to the work group, education will benefit when the primary focus is on the learner.

The fourteen learner-centered principles can be classified in terms of four main sets of factors: cognitive and metacognitive, motivational and emotional, developmental and social, and individual differences (Work Group of the American Psychological Association Board of Educational Affairs, 1997, pp. 2–4).

Cognitive and Metacognitive Factors

1. *Nature of the learning process.* The learning of complex subject matter is most effective when it is an intentional process of constructing meaning from information and experience.

    There are different types of learning processes, for example, habit formation in motor learning; and learning that involves the generation of knowledge, or cognitive skills and learning strategies. Learning in schools emphasizes the use of intentional processes that students can use to construct meaning from information, experiences, and their own thoughts and beliefs. Successful learners are active, goal-directed, self-regulating, and assume personal responsibility for contributing to their own learning. The principles set forth in this document focus on this type of learning.

2. *Goals of the learning process.* The successful learner, over time and with support and instructional guidance, can create meaningful, coherent representations of knowledge.

    The strategic nature of learning requires students to be goal directed. To construct useful representations of knowledge and to acquire the thinking and learning strategies necessary for continued learning success across the life span, students must generate and pursue personally relevant goals. Initially, students' short-term goals and learning may be sketchy in an area, but over time their understanding can be refined by filling gaps, resolving inconsistencies, and deepening their understanding of the subject matter so that they can reach longer-term goals. Educators can assist learners in creating meaningful learning goals that are consistent with both personal and educational aspirations and interests.

3. *Construction of knowledge.* The successful learner can link new information with existing knowledge in meaningful ways.

    Knowledge widens and deepens as students continue to build links between new information and experiences and their existing knowledge base. The nature of these links can take a variety of forms, such as adding to, modifying, or reorganizing existing knowledge or skills. How these links are made or develop may vary in different subject areas, and among students with varying talents, interests, and abilities. However, unless new knowledge becomes integrated with the learner's prior knowledge and understanding, this new knowledge remains isolated, cannot be used most effectively in new tasks, and does not transfer readily to new situations. Educators can assist learners in acquiring and integrating knowledge by a number of strategies that have been shown to be effective with learners of varying abilities, such as concept mapping and thematic organization or categorizing.

4. *Strategic thinking.* The successful learner can create and use a repertoire of thinking and reasoning strategies to achieve complex learning goals.

    Successful learners use strategic thinking in their approach to learning, reasoning, problem solving, and concept learning. They understand and can use a variety of strategies to help them reach learning and performance goals, and to apply their knowledge in novel situations. They also continue to expand their repertoire of strategies by reflecting on the methods they use to see which work well for them, by receiving guided instruction and feedback, and by observing or interacting with appropriate models. Learning outcomes can be enhanced if educators assist learners in developing, applying, and assessing their strategic learning skills.

5. *Thinking about thinking.* Higher order strategies for selecting and monitoring mental operations facilitate creative and critical thinking.

    Successful learners can reflect on how they think and learn, set reasonable learning or performance goals, select potentially appropriate learning strategies or methods, and moni-

Learner-Centered Psychological Principles

What are some learner-centered psychological principles?

tor their progress toward these goals. In addition, successful learners know what to do if a problem occurs or if they are not making sufficient or timely progress toward a goal. They can generate alternative methods to reach their goal (or reassess the appropriateness and utility of the goal). Instructional methods that focus on helping learners develop these higher order (metacognitive) strategies can enhance student learning and personal responsibility for learning.

6. *Context of learning.* Learning is influenced by environmental factors, including culture, technology, and instructional practices.

Learning does not occur in a vacuum. Teachers play a major interactive role with both the learner and the learning environment. Cultural or group influences on students can impact many educationally relevant variables, such as motivation, orientation toward learning, and ways of thinking. Technologies and instructional practices must be appropriate for learners' level of prior knowledge, cognitive abilities, and their learning and thinking strategies. The classroom environment, particularly the degree to which it is nurturing or not, can also have significant impacts on student learning.

Motivational and Affective Factors

1. *Motivational and emotional influences on learning.* What and how much is learned is influenced by the learner's motivation. Motivation to learn, in turn, is influenced by the individual's emotional states, beliefs, interests and goals, and habits of thinking.

The rich internal world of thoughts, beliefs, goals, and expectations for success or failure can enhance or interfere with the learner's quality of thinking and information processing. Students' beliefs about themselves as learners and the nature of learning have a marked influence on motivation. Motivational and emotional factors also influence both the quality of thinking and information processing as well as an individual's motivation to learn. Positive emotions, such as curiosity, generally enhance motivation and facilitate learning and performance. Mild anxiety can also enhance learning and performance by focusing the learner's attention on a particular task. However, intense negative emotions (e.g., anxiety, panic, rage, insecurity) and related thoughts (e.g., worrying about competence, ruminating about failure, fearing punishment, ridicule, or stigmatizing labels) generally detract from motivation, interfere with learning, and contribute to low performance.

2. *Intrinsic motivation to learn.* The learner's creativity, higher order thinking, and natural curiosity all contribute to motivation to learn. Intrinsic motivation is stimulated by tasks of optimal novelty and difficulty, relevant to personal interests, and providing for personal choice and control.

Curiosity, flexible and insightful thinking, and creativity are major indicators of the learners' intrinsic motivation to learn, which is in large part a function of meeting basic needs to be competent and to exercise personal control. Intrinsic motivation is facilitated on tasks that learners perceive as interesting and personally relevant and meaningful, appropriate in complexity and difficulty to the learners' abilities, and on which they believe they can succeed. Intrinsic motivation is also facilitated on tasks that are comparable to real-world situations and meet needs for choice and control. Educators can encourage and support learners' natural curiosity and motivation to learn by attending to individual differences in learners' perceptions of optimal novelty and difficulty, relevance, and personal choice and control.

3. *Effects of motivation on effort.* Acquisition of complex knowledge and skills requires extended learner effort and guided practice. Without learners' motivation to learn, the willingness to exert this effort is unlikely without coercion.

Effort is another major indicator of motivation to learn. The acquisition of complex knowledge and skills demands the investment of considerable learner energy and strategic effort, along with persistence over time. Educators need to be concerned with facilitating motivation by strategies that enhance learner effort and commitment to learning and to achieving high standards of comprehension and understanding. Effective strategies include purposeful learning activities, guided by practices that enhance positive emotions and intrinsic motivation to learn, and methods that increase learners' perceptions that a task is interesting and personally relevant.

Developmental and Social

1. *Developmental influences on learning.* As individuals develop, there are different opportunities and constraints for learning. Learning is most effective when differential development within and across physical, intellectual, emotional, and social domains is taken into account.

Individuals learn best when material is appropriate to their developmental level and is presented in an enjoyable and interesting way. Because individual development varies across intellectual, social, emotional, and physical domains, achievement in different instructional domains may also vary. Overemphasis on one type of developmental readiness—such as reading readiness, for example—may preclude learners from demonstrating that they are more capable in other areas of performance. The cognitive, emotional, and social development of individual learners and how they interpret life experiences are affected by prior schooling, home, culture, and community factors. Early and continuing parental involvement in schooling, and the quality of language interactions and two-way communications between adults and children can influence these developmental areas. Awareness and understanding of developmental differences among children with and without emotional, physical, or intellectual disabilities, can facilitate the creation of optimal learning contexts.

2. *Social influences on learning.* Learning is influenced by social interactions, interpersonal relations, and communication with others.

   Learning can be enhanced when the learner has an opportunity to interact and to collaborate with others on instructional tasks. Learning settings that allow for social interactions, and that respect diversity, encourage flexible thinking and social competence. In interactive and collaborative instructional contexts, individuals have an opportunity for perspective taking and reflective thinking that may lead to higher levels of cognitive, social, and moral development, as well as self-esteem. Quality personal relationships that provide stability, trust, and caring can increase learners' sense of belonging, self-respect and self-acceptance, and provide a positive climate for learning. Family influences, positive interpersonal support and instruction in self-motivation strategies can offset factors that interfere with optimal learning such as negative beliefs about competence in a particular subject, high levels of test anxiety, negative sex role expectations, and undue pressure to perform well. Positive learning climates can also help to establish the context for healthier levels of thinking, feeling, and behaving. Such contexts help learners feel safe to share ideas, actively participate in the learning process, and create a learning community.

Individual Differences

1. *Individual differences in learning.* Learners have different strategies, approaches, and capabilities for learning that are a function of prior experience and heredity.

   Individuals are born with and develop their own capabilities and talents. In addition, through learning and social acculturation, they have acquired their own preferences for how they like to learn and the pace at which they learn. However, these preferences are not always useful in helping learners reach their learning goals. Educators need to help students examine their learning preferences and expand or modify them, if necessary. The interaction between learner differences and curricular and environmental conditions is another key factor affecting learning outcomes. Educators need to be sensitive to individual differences, in general. They also need to attend to learner perceptions of the degree to which these differences are accepted and adapted to by varying instructional methods and materials.

2. *Learning and diversity.* Learning is most effective when differences in learners' linguistic, cultural, and social backgrounds are taken into account.

   The same basic principles of learning, motivation, and effective instruction apply to all learners. However, language, ethnicity, race, beliefs, and socioeconomic status all can influence learning. Careful attention to these factors in the instructional setting enhances the possibilities for designing and implementing appropriate learning environments. When learners perceive that their individual differences in abilities, backgrounds, cultures, and experiences are valued, respected, and accommodated in learning tasks and contexts, levels of motivation and achievement are enhanced.

3. *Standards and assessments.* Setting appropriately high and challenging standards and assessing the learner as well as learning progress—including diagnostic, process, and outcome assessment—are integral parts of the learning process.

Through the Eyes of Teachers

Fostering Learning, Unity, and Civic Pride

Luis Recalde, a fourth- and fifth-grade science teacher at Vincent E. Mauro Elementary School in New Haven, Connecticut, uses every opportunity to make science fascinating and motivating for students to learn. Luis infuses hands-on science experiences with energy and enthusiasm. To help students feel more what it is like to be a scientist, he brings lab coats to the classroom for students to wear. He holds science fair workshops for teachers and often gives up his vacation time to help students with science projects. His grading system includes students' self-assessment. He started soccer teams and gardens to foster unity and civic pride among the African American and Latino students. An immigrant himself, he knows the importance of fostering positive relations among students from different ethnic groups.

Elementary school science teacher, Luis Recalde, holds up a seaweed specimen in one of the hands-on, high interest learning contexts he creates for students.

Assessment provides important information to both the learner and teacher at all stages of the learning process. Effective learning takes place when learners feel challenged to work towards appropriately high goals; therefore, appraisal of the learner's cognitive strengths and weaknesses, as well as current knowledge and skills, is important for the selection of instructional materials of an optimal degree of difficulty. Ongoing assessment of the learner's understanding of the curricular material can provide valuable feedback to both learners and teachers about progress toward the learning goals. Standardized assessment of learner progress and outcomes assessment provides one type of information about achievement levels both within and across individuals that can inform various types of programmatic decisions. Performance assessments can provide other sources of information about the attainment of learning outcomes. Self-assessments of learning progress can also improve students self appraisal skills and enhance motivation and self-directed learning.

Some Learner-Centered Instructional Strategies

We have already discussed a number of strategies that teachers can consider in developing learner-centered lesson plans. These especially include the teaching strategies based on the theories of Piaget and Vygotsky (chapter 2), constructivist aspects of thinking (chapters 8 and 9), social constructivist aspects of thinking (chapter 10), and learning in content areas (chapter 11). To provide you with a further sense of learner-centered strategies that you can incorporate into your lesson planning, we will elaborate here on the topic of problem-based learning (which was initially described in chapter 9) and examine two other strategies: essential questions and discovery learning.

Problem-Based Learning   *Problem-based learning* emphasizes real-life problem solving. A problem-based curriculum exposes students to authentic problems like those that crop up in everyday life (Jones, Rasmussen, & Moffitt, 1997).

Problem-based learning is a learner-centered approach. In problem-based learning, planning and instruction are very different than they are in a teacher-centered approach. While teacher-centered planning and instruction most often involve lectures and teacher presentations, in problem-based learning they focus on a problem to be solved through small-group efforts. Students identify problems or issues that they wish to explore, then locate materials and resources they need to address the issues or solve the problems. Teachers act as guides, helping students to monitor their own problem-solving efforts.

One problem-based learning project has been developed by Delamie Thompson, Paul Gilvary, and Mary Moffitt of Gladstone Elementary School, an inner-city school in Chicago (Jones, Rasmussen, & Moffitt, 1997, pp. 113–117). The project involves sixth-grade students in exploring an authentic health problem in the local community: the causes, incidence, and treatment of asthma and its related conditions. Students learn how environmental conditions affect their health and share this understanding with others. The project integrates information from many subject areas, including health, science, math, and the social sciences.

The students use a simple syringe air pump to assess air quality and determine its link to the incidence of asthma. The air pump was developed by Technical Education Research Centers (TERC), which also provides Gladstone students with shared databases of information gathered by students around the world. "Gladstone students learn to a) think like scientists by working with data and addressing substantive problems, b) collaborate as scientists by working with peers and mentors to plan and carry out an investigation, c) communicate and debate their findings, and d) evaluate their own work and the work of others."

The project's flow is "organized around a number of student research groups, each group focusing on a separate problem related to the question, 'Why there is so much asthma in our community and what can we do about it?'" All groups use the scientific method in their research.

essential questions Questions that reflect the heart of the curriculum, the most important things that students should explore and learn.

Essential Questions   **Essential questions** are questions that reflect the heart of the curriculum, the most important things that students should explore and learn (Jacobs, 1997). For example, in one lesson the initial essential question was "What flies?" Students explored the question by examining everything from birds, bees, fish, and space shuttles to the notion that time flies and ideas fly. The initial question was followed by other questions, such as "How and why do things fly in nature?" "How does flight affect humans?" and "What is the future of flight?"

Essential questions like these perplex students, cause them to think, and motivate their curiosity. Essential questions are creative choices. With just a slight change, a lackluster question such as "What was the effect of the Civil War?" can become the thought-provoking question "Is the Civil War still going on?"

Advocates of using essential questions argue that too often lesson planning and instruction become rigid and stiff. For example, a history teacher in high school might come up with this as one of the objectives for a year-long course on Western civilization: "Students will recognize personal responsibility to the community." Consider how much more enthusiastic students might be about studying Western civilization if they are asked instead to consider "How does my community affect my life?"

In sixth-grade teacher Barb Johnson's class, students generate the essential questions to be explored (National Research Council, 1999, pp. 144–145). In the first week of school, she presents two questions to her class: "What questions do you have about yourself?" and "What questions do you have about the world?" In response, students begin asking questions themselves. One student asks, "Can they be about silly, little things?" She tells the student that if they are questions that they really want answered, they are not silly and they are not little. After the students state their questions, Barb breaks out the students "into small groups where they share lists and search for questions they have in common. After much discussion each group comes up with a priority list of questions, rank-ordering the questions about themselves and those about the world."

Back together in a whole-class format, a representative of each group informs the class of his or her group's list of questions. "These questions will become the basis for guiding the curriculum in Barb's class. One question, 'Will I live to be 100 years old?' spawned educational investigations into genetics, family and oral history, science, statistics and probability, heart disease, cancer, and hypertension. The students had the opportunity to seek out information from family members, friends, experts in various fields, on-line computer services, websites, and books, as well as from the teacher. She describes what they had to do as becoming part of a learning community," much as described in Fostering a Community of Learners in chapter 10 ◀ p. 329.

At the end of exploring a topic, Barb "works with students to help them see how their investigation relate to conventional subject areas. They create a chart on which they tally experiences in language and literacy, mathematics, science, social studies, and history, music, and art. Students often are surprised at how much and how varied their learning is." One student said, "I just thought we were having fun. I didn't realize that we were learning too."

Barb Johnson's teaching requires a wide range of disciplinary knowledge because she begins with students' questions rather than a fixed curriculum. Because of her extensive knowledge, she can map students' questions onto important concepts in relevant disciplines.

Discovery Learning **Discovery learning** is learning in which students construct an understanding on their own. Discovery learning stands in contrast to the direct-instruction approach discussed earlier, in which the teacher directly explains information to students. In discovery learning, students have to figure out things for themselves. Discovery learning meshes with the ideas of Piaget, who once commented that every time you teach a child something you keep the child from learning.

Educator John Dewey (1933) and cognitive psychologist Jerome Bruner (1966) promoted the concept of discovery learning by encouraging teachers to give students more opportunities to learn on their own ◀ p. 5. In their view, discovery learning encourages students to think for themselves and discover how knowledge is constructed. It also feeds their natural curiosity and inquiry.

Teachers facilitate discovery learning by providing students with stimulating activities that activate their natural curiosity. After you present such activities, your role becomes one of answering student-generated questions. You also promote discovery learning on the part of students by being naturally curious yourself and having a strong interest in uncovering solutions to problems.

discovery learning Learning in which students construct an understanding on their own.

Through the Eyes of Teachers

Guiding Students to Discover

Mary Lynn Peacher, a fourth-grade teacher at Jenks East Elementary School, in Oklahoma, emphasizes a student-centered discovery approach. Students' desks are clustered together for cooperative learning. In social science, she guides students in developing a mini-society with its own government and economy; "senators" draft and chart rules, listing rights and responsibilities. She also oversees a classroom free-enterprise system with student companies, assembly lines, bank accounts, and credit. In teaching science, Peacher tells students that they are scientists and asks them to describe what they see as they carry out various exercises (*USA Today*, 2001).

Mary Lynn Peacher demonstrates airfoil "charks" to students.

Discovery learning is especially effective in science classes. Researchers have found that students in activity-based, discovery-learning science classes score higher on science achievement tests than students in traditional direct-instruction science classes (Breddeman, 1982; Glasson, 1989). These findings hold at the elementary, middle school, and secondary school levels.

However, most discovery-learning approaches used in schools today do not involve "pure" discovery learning. In "pure" discovery learning, students are encouraged to learn on their own and instruction is minimal to nonexistent. Working completely on their own doesn't benefit many students. For example, given materials and left to their own devices to learn, some students end up with the wrong solutions and use inefficient strategies to discover information. Others never discover what it is they are trying to find out or why. And in many cases, such as initially learning how to add and subtract, direct instruction can get the job done much more quickly (van Lehn, 1990).

As teachers began to use discovery learning, they soon found that for it to be effective as a systematic instruction approach it needed to be modified. This led to the development of **guided discovery learning,** in which students are still encouraged to construct their understanding, but with the assistance of teacher-guided questions and directions.

Evaluating Learner-Centered Instruction

The learner-centered approach to lesson planning and instruction is positive in many ways. The fourteen learner-centered principles developed by the American Psychological Association task force can be very helpful in guiding students' learning. The principles encourage teachers to help students actively construct their understanding, set goals and plan, think deeply and creatively, monitor their learning, solve real-world problems, develop more positive self-esteem and control their emotions, be internally motivated, learn in a developmentally appropriate way, collaborate effectively with others (including diverse others), evaluate their learner preferences, and meet challenging standards.

Critics of learner-centered instruction argue that it gives too much attention to the process of learning (such as learning creatively and collaboratively) and not enough to academic content (such as the facts of history) (Hirsch, 1996). Some critics stress that learner-centered instruction works better in some subjects than in others (Feng, 1996). They say that in areas with many ill-defined problems, such as the social sciences and humanities, learner-centered instruction can be effective. However, they believe that in well-structured knowledge domains such as math and science, teacher-centered structure works better. Critics also say that learner-centered instruction is less effective at the beginning level of instruction in a field because students do not have the knowledge to make decisions about what and how they should learn. And critics stress that there is a gap between the theoretical level of student-centered learning and its actual application (Airasian & Walsh, 1997). The consequences of implementing learner-centered strategies in the classroom are often more challenging than anticipated.

Although we have presented teacher-centered and learner-centered planning and instruction in separate sections, don't think of them as always being either/or approaches (Schuh, 2001). Most teachers use some of both in making the classroom a positive learning experience for children.

guided discovery learning Learning in which students are encouraged to construct their understanding with the assistance of teacher-guided questions and directions.

> ## ❗ Review and Reflect
>
> **3** **Discuss important forms of learner-centered instruction.**
>
> **Review**
> - In a set of fourteen short sentences, summarize learner-centered principles.
> - How do problem-based learning, essential questions, and discovery learning each embody learner-centered principles?
> - What are some pros and cons of learner-centered instruction?
>
> **Reflect**
> - As a student, have you ever wished that a teacher would use more (or less) learner-centered instruction? What lessons can you draw from this for your own work as a teacher?

TECHNOLOGY AND EDUCATION

Technology is such an important theme in education that it is woven throughout this book. In each chapter you read a Technology and Education box related to the chapter's contents. For example, you already have studied such topics as "Technology and Children's Vocabulary Development" (chapter 2), "The Global Lab and Other Technology Connections with Students Around the World" (chapter 5), "Experts and Technology" (chapter 8), and "Computer Supported Intentional Learning Environments (CSILE)" (chapter 10) ◀ pp. 60, 150, 273, 332. You also read about the technology-based Jasper Project, which is designed to improve students' mathematical thinking (chapter 9) ◀ p. 301. Every chapter includes icons in the margins that direct you to relevant Internet sites. Here, we will explore the technology revolution, the Internet, technology and sociocultural diversity, and the potentials and realities of technology and education.

The Technology Revolution

Students today are growing up in a world that is far different technologically from the world in which their parents and grandparents were students. If students are to be adequately prepared for tomorrow's jobs, technology must become an integral part of schools and classrooms (Curtis & others, 2004; Sharp, 2002).

The technology revolution is part of the information society in which we now live. People are using computers to communicate today the way people used to use pens, postage stamps, and telephones. The new information society still relies on some basic nontechnological competencies: good communication skills, the ability to solve problems, deep thinking, creative thinking, and positive attitudes. However, in today's technology-oriented world, how people pursue these competencies is being challenged and extended in ways and at a speed that few people had to cope with in previous eras (Bitter & Pierson, 2005; Lever-Duffey, McDonald, & Mizell, 2005; Merrill, 2004).

Technology has been a part of schooling for many decades, but until recently the technologies being used were rather simple and changed slowly. To underscore how technology in schools has changed dramatically, consider the fact that in 1983 there were fewer than 50,000 computers in America's schools. In 2002, there were more than 6 million! Hardly a school in America today is without at least one computer. Nearly every week, a school board approves the purchase of ten to twenty computers for improving students' writing skills, another school board approves a high school's use of Channel One (a ten-minute daily recap of news that has become controversial because it also includes two minutes of advertising), and another sets aside funds for a telecomputing network system that connects classrooms

Integrating Technology and Education

Educational Technology Journal

"I see what's wrong with your calculator—it's the remote control to your TV."

John Shanks, *Phi Delta Kappan*, June 1997. Reprinted by permission of the author.

within a school and different schools. And more colleges are making it mandatory that first-year students purchase laptop computers (Young, 1997).

Consider a teacher who is faced with instructing students about the ecology of the desert (Maddux, Johnson, & Willis, 1997). For schools not located in the desert, the traditional approach is to have students read about this topic in a textbook, perhaps observe some desert reptiles in a terrarium, listen to lectures on the topic, and then respond with questions that lead to further discussion. A very different choice is to incorporate a CD-ROM package into the classroom exploration of desert ecology. Students explore the life cycles of desert plants and animals, "construct" a desert environment on the computer, populate it with plant and animal life, and then determine whether their selection of life-forms and resources results in sustainable life. The inclusion of this technology in learning about life in the desert results in more exploratory and interactive learning for students than simply reading about deserts in a textbook or hearing about them from the teacher.

As we indicated earlier, the number of computers in schools has increased dramatically, yet despite its potential for improving student learning, schools continue to lag behind other segments of society, such as business, in the use of technology. A survey by the Office of Technology Assessment (1995) found that the majority of teachers do not feel comfortable with computers.

Computers are still used too often for drill-and-practice activities rather than for active, constructive learning (Newby & others, 2000; Sharp, 2005). In one survey, a majority of middle school and high school students reported using computers only minimally over a 30-week period (Becker, 1994). In this survey, only 1 student of 11 reported using school computers for an English class, 1 of 15 for a math class, and 1 of 40 for a social science class.

Many teachers do not have adequate training in using computers, and many school districts have not provided the needed workshops. And with rapidly changing technology, the computers that many schools purchase become quickly outdated. Other computers break and sit in need of repair (Baines, Deluzain, & Stanley, 1999).

Such realities mean that learning in schools has not yet been technologically revolutionized. Only when schools have technologically trained teachers and current, workable technologies will the technology revolution have an opportunity to truly transform classrooms (Howell & Dunnivant, 2000; Lockhard & Abrams, 2004; Tomei, 2002).

The Internet

The **Internet** is the core of computer-mediated communication. The Internet system is worldwide and connects thousands of computer networks, providing an incredible array of information, which students can access. In many cases, the Internet has more current, up-to-date information than textbooks. In 2000, 98% of public schools in the United States were connected to the Internet and 77% of instructional classrooms had Internet-connected computers.

The **World Wide Web** (the **Web**) is a hypermedia information retrieval system that links a variety of Internet materials; it includes text and graphics. The Web gives the Internet a much needed structure. Libraries, museums, universities, companies, organizations, and individuals display information on the Web, all of which can be accessed by students with a click on words or images presented on a computer screen. Web indexes and search engines such as Google, Lycos, Northern Light, and Yahoo! can help students find the information they are seeking by examining and collating a variety of sources. A **website** is an individual's or an organization's location on the Internet. Websites display information posted by individuals and organizations. One recent national study found that students in the fourth, eighth, and twelfth grades who said they used the Internet at home had higher science achievement scores than their counterparts who did not use the Internet at home (National Assessment of Educational Progress, 2000) (see figure 12.7).

Internet The core of computer-mediated communication. The Internet system is worldwide and connects thousands of computer networks, providing an incredible array of information, which students can access.

World Wide Web (the **Web**) A hypermedia information retrieval system that links a variety of Internet materials. It includes text and graphics.

website An individual's or an organization's location on the Internet. Websites display information posted by individuals and organizations.

In every chapter, we have placed a number of Internet icons with a label below them in the margins of the text. By going to the McGraw-Hill Santrock *Educational Psychology* website (www.mhhe.com/santedu2e), you can immediately connect with the associated websites by scrolling to the appropriate chapter and label. Also, in the section on general Internet resources on the Santrock *Educational Psychology* website, there are links to a number of websites with information about integrating technology into the classroom that you can access.

E-mail stands for *electronic mail* and is another valuable way that the Internet can be used. Messages can be sent to and received from individuals as well as large numbers of people at once. To read about some effective ways to use the Internet in classrooms, see the Technology and Education box.

The Internet is an important learning tool in a technology-rich project called Cooperative Networked Educational Community of Tomorrow (Co-NECT) (Jones, Rasmussen, & Moffitt, 1997). Some Co-NECT schools become immersed in learning about worldwide scientific expeditions such as Earthwatch's Mystery of the Pipe Wreck project in the Caribbean. In such investigations, students and teachers can download data from project sites, conduct data analysis, and communicate electronically with project participants and staff (Bolt, Beraneck, & Newman, 1993).

A Co-NECT student e-mailed a lawyer in Northern Ireland to request information about this question: "Can there be lasting peace in Northern Ireland?" The lawyer responded with a two-page e-mail that included current news and perspectives on the topic.

The Internet can be a valuable tool for helping students learn (Bissell & others, 2002; Provenzo, 2005; Wen & others, 2004). However, it has some potential drawbacks (Gackenbach & Ellerman, 1999). To use it effectively with your students, your access software will have to be competently installed in your computers. You will have to know how to use it and feel comfortable with it. Concerns have been raised about students accessing pornographic websites and about inaccuracy of information on personal websites (Provenzo, 2005). Equipment, installation, and training are expensive. To make the Internet work in a classroom, teachers need considerable instruction, ongoing workshops, and technical support.

However, when used effectively, the Internet expands access to a world of knowledge and people that students cannot experience in any other way. If you do not know how to access the Internet, learn this skill as soon as possible on your own computer. You and your students will benefit from your ability to navigate the Internet. Two good sources for learning more about the Internet and how to bring it into your classroom are *Cybereducator* (Bissel & others, 2002) and *Teaching with Technology* (Desberg & Fisher, 2001).

Technology and Sociocultural Diversity

Technology brings with it certain social issues. For example, will schools' increased use of technology, especially computers, widen the learning gap between rich and poor students or between male and female students (Spring, 2000)? The problem of computer access and use also is compounded by the far greater presence of computers in the homes of middle- and upper-income families. There are gaps in computer availability across ethnic groups as well. In a study by the National Association of Educational Progress, almost one-third of White high school students owned computers, compared with just over one-fifth of African American or Latino students (Sutton, 1991). And families with a male student are more likely to own a computer than families with a female student (DeVillar & Faltis, 1991).

Computers are often used for different activities in different sociocultural groups. Schools with high percentages of low-income ethnic minority students tend to use

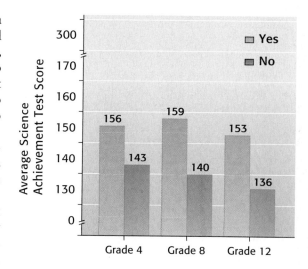

FIGURE 12.7 Use of the Internet at Home and Science Achievement

In a recent National Assessment of Educational Progress (NAEP) study (2000), students in the fourth, eighth, and twelfth grades who used the Internet at home had higher science achievement test scores than their counterparts who did not use the Internet at home.

Webliography

Internet Pals

Critical Analysis of the Internet

e-mail "Electronic mail." A valuable way to use the Internet, e-mail messages can be sent to and received by individuals as well as large numbers of people at once.

Using the Internet in the Classroom

Here are some effective ways that the Internet can be used in classrooms:

- *To help students navigate and integrate knowledge.* The Internet has huge databases of information on a vast array of topics that are organized in different ways. As students explore Internet resources, they can place their own unique stamp on their research by constructing projects that integrate information from various sources that they otherwise cannot access.
- *To foster collaborative learning.* One of the most effective ways to use the Internet in your classroom is through project-centered activities for small groups. The Internet is so huge and has so many resources that teamwork improves the outcome of most Internet searches. One collaborative learning use of the Internet is to have a group of students conduct a survey on a topic (Maddux, Johnson, & Willis, 1997). Students can construct the survey, put it out on the Internet, and expect to get responses back from many parts of the world in the matter of a few days. They can organize, analyze, and summarize the data from the survey and then share them with other classes around the world. Another type of collaborative learning project involves sending groups of students on Internet "scavenger hunts" to find out information and/or solve a problem.
- *To allow e-mail.* An increasing number of innovative educational projects include e-mail. In chapter 10, we examined Ann Brown and Joe Campione's (1996) program Fostering a Community of Learners. Students can communicate with experts by e-mail, which frees teachers from the burden of being the sole dispenser of knowledge and gives students access to a wider circle of knowledgeable people. This is sometimes called "electronic mentoring." Students also can communicate with each other. In the Global Lab project, classrooms around the world are interconnected and students from the United States can communicate via e-mail with students in a number of other countries. The Global Lab project is organized as a networked science laboratory.

  Students enjoy using e-mail to communicate with students in other schools, states, and countries. E-mail can especially be rewarding for shy students who get anxious and withdraw from communicating face-to-face with someone.
- *To improve the teacher's knowledge and understanding.* An excellent Internet resource for teachers is the ERIC Resource Information Center (http://ericir.syr.edu), which provides free information about a wide range of educational topics. You can send an e-mail inquiry to the AskERIC department (askeric@askeric.org), providing your key words for the search and within two days they will e-mail you a list of citations. The AskERIC department also provides information about lesson plans and connections to other resources.

computers for drill-and-practice exercises (Maddux, Johnson, & Willis, 1997). In contrast, schools with high percentages of White middle- and upper-income students are more likely to use computers for more-active, constructivist learning activities. Boys are more likely to use computers for math and science applications, girls for word processing (Beal, 1994).

Here are some recommendations for preventing or reducing inequity in computer access and use (Gipson, 1997; Sheffield, 1997):

- Screen technology materials for ethnic, cultural, and gender bias.
- Use technology as a tool for providing active, constructive learning opportunities for all students, regardless of their cultural, ethnic, or gender background.
- Provide students with information about experts from diverse ethnic and gender backgrounds who use technology effectively in their work and lives. For example, invite an African American female computer analyst to come to your classroom and talk with your students. Take your students on a field trip to an engineering firm and request that at least one of the available engineers be a female. Request that she demonstrate how she uses computer technology in her work.
- Talk with parents about providing their children with appropriate computer-based learning activities at home. Look for ways that government and community agencies may be able to help fund the purchase of a computer by low-income families with students in your classroom. Encourage parents to give their daughters positive feedback for using computers.

Standards for Technology-Literate Students

The International Society for Technology in Education (2000), in collaboration with the U.S. Department of Education, has developed technology standards for students to achieve at different grade levels ◀ p. 11. Following is a summary of the standards for grades prekindergarten through second grade, grades 3 through 5, grades 6 through 8, and grades 9 through 12 (International Society for Technology in Education, 2000, pp. 18–24, 206).

Prekindergarten Through Second Grade

- Use input devices (such as a mouse, keyboard, or remote control) and output devices (such as a monitor and printer) to successfully operate computers.
- Use a variety of media and technology resources for directed and independent learning activities.
- Use developmentally appropriate multimedia resources, such as interactive books, educational software, and elementary multimedia encyclopedias, to support learning.
- Work cooperatively and collaboratively with peers, family members, and others when using technology.
- Use technology resources (such as puzzles, logical thinking programs, writing tools, and digital cameras) for learning.
- Demonstrate positive social and ethical behaviors when using technology.

A curriculum example that effectively uses technology focuses on animals and their sounds. In Sharon Fontenot's class at Prien Lake Elementary School, students learn to identify polar bears, lions, and other wild animals through images, video clips, and sounds on the *Wide World of Animals* CD-ROM. The teacher models the effective use of technology by creating a tape recording based on information from the CD-ROM and incorporating her own voice to fit the needs of the class. Students practice reading and listening skills by answering questions that encourage them to think about both the science and social living issues related to these animals. Students create their own stories about what they learned using *Kid Pix,* a software program that lets them make their own pictures of the animals, turn them into slide shows, and print out their own books to share with family and friends.

Grades 3 Through 5

- Use keyboards and other common input and output devices effectively.
- Discuss common uses of technology in daily life and the advantages and disadvantages of such use.
- Use technology tools (such as multimedia authoring, presentation, Web tools, digital cameras, and scanners) for individual and collaborative writing, communication, and publishing activities.
- Use telecommunications effectively to access remote information, communicate with others, and pursue personal interests.
- Use telecommunications and online resources (such as e-mail, online discussions, and Web environments) to participate in collaborative learning projects.
- Use technology resources (such as calculators, data collection probes, videos, and educational software) for problem solving and self-directed learning.

Let's look at an example of how a teacher in grades 3 through 5 might extensively use online resources. The teacher could use Exploring the Environment (http://www.cotf.edu/ete/) and Global Learning and Observations for a Better Environment (GLOBE) (http://www.globe.gov/). She could use the Exploring the Environment website to access class-tested problem-based learning modules. Using the Global Learning website, students could make environmental observations around the school, report the data to a processing facility through GLOBE, and use global images created from their data to examine local environmental issues. The students could contribute to an environmental database used by scientists to improve understanding of the global environment.

Grades 6 Through 8

- Apply strategies for identifying and solving routine hardware and software problems that occur during everyday use.

Educational Technology Journal

Critical Issues in Technology and Education

Teaching with Technology

WebQuest

- Demonstrate knowledge of current changes in information technologies and the effects these changes have on the workplace and society.
- Use content-specific tools, software, and simulations (such as environmental probes, graphing calculators, and exploratory environments) to support learning and research.
- Design, develop, publish, and present products (such as Web pages and videotapes).
- Research and evaluate the accuracy, relevance, and bias of electronic information sources concerning real-world problems.

Eighth-grade students at Marthaville Elementary School, a small, rural K–8 school, studied the Louisiana labor market in their math class. They used the Internet to access the Louisiana Department of Labor's website and search for the top twenty projected occupations in the state. Students were divided into groups, each group selecting five occupations. They developed a survey about the occupations and queried informed adults about the estimated income for the occupations. The students then analyzed the survey results, comparing their results with the data displayed on the state of Louisiana's website. They calculated average salaries and created graphs to display the information.

Grades 9 Through 12

- Identify capabilities and limitations of contemporary and emerging technology resources and assess the potential of these systems and services to address personal and workplace needs.
- Use technology tools and resources for managing and communicating personal and professional information (such as finances, schedules, addresses, purchases, and correspondence).
- Routinely and efficiently use online information resources to meet needs for research, publication, communication, and productivity.
- Select and apply technology tools for research, information analysis, and problem solving in content learning.

Population growth and urban planning are the focus of a social studies technology-based learning activity in grades 9 through 12. World population growth is a global issue, especially in large cities. The activity challenges students to find sources online and elsewhere that describe real-world population dilemmas. The activity can be altered to address different cities and regions worldwide. In small groups in class, students can discuss problems that may occur as a result of a city being heavily populated. They can be asked to project what problems a city such as Tokyo is likely to face in terms of population growth in the year 2050.

To evaluate your technology skills and attitudes, complete Self-Assessment 12.1.

The Future of Technology in Schools

What technologies are likely to influence teaching and learning in the future?

Ubiquitous Computing   Computing was initially carried out by large mainframe computers, which were shared by many people (Bitter & Pierson, 2005). Currently, we are in the personal computing (PC) era, which often involves one person working alone at a desktop computer. Some computer experts believe that the next generation of computing—a third wave—will involve **ubiquitous computing,** which emphasizes the distribution of computing in the environment rather than containing it in a desktop-bound personal computer. In ubiquitous computing, technology recedes into the background (Weiser, 2001). In short, a ubiquitous computing world would be a post-PC world. Common technology devices—such as the telephone and handheld electronic devices—will be connected to the Internet and the users may not even be aware of which devices in their environment actually are connected. New small, mobile, and less expensive computing devices such as handheld, portable, and wearable computers and appliances are likely to replace the desktop computer.

ubiquitous computing The distribution of computing in the environment rather than containing it in a desk-bound personal computer.

Ubiquitous computing is roughly the opposite of virtual reality. While virtual reality places people inside a computer-generated world, ubiquitous computing forces the computer to exist out in the world of people.

It is certainly possible to imagine that these ubiquitous computing devices might be better suited for education than the desktop computer (Center for Innovative Learning Technologies, 2001). The new devices could be made available to far more students on a far more equitable basis than desktop computers. The new devices, coupled with inexpensive networking, could enable students to carry personal information devices into the field on learning projects, carry them between classes, and take them home. They could increase collaboration and ease of computing, regardless of location (Bitter & Pierson, 2002).

A Futuristic Scenario   Ellen Clegg (2004), a research affiliate of the Institute for the Future, recently described what technology might bring to teaching and learning in the future:

> Let's say that in 15 years, affordable bandwidth becomes prevalent, the research behind contructivist learning becomes accepted and understood by most educators, and software developers are able to turn intricate neurological and cognitive nuances into programs that invisibly support student interactions and production. Let's say that an information network called the World Board, tied to global positioning satellite data, brings interpretive information to individuals and haptic and other sensory interfaces on wearable commuters allow people to taste, smell, and feel information wherever they are.
>
> In this rosy scenario, three groups of communities in California, Japan, and Italy—places that share similar types of ecosystems—could be simultaneously developing prototypes for small boats with underwater observation equipment. There will no longer be "classes" or "subjects" because school projects combine mathematics, writing, building, device uses foreign language, communication, etc. Students and teachers know and discuss what concepts and skills they are developing while they are working on the project, but there are no "tests" because assessments are built into their communication devices . . . .
>
> New skills are measured, such as knowledge-sharing and collaboration. Feedback is integrated into the devices and conversations so students can learn what they need to know in order to finish their projects. Online, students use variations of an increasingly global "visual language" that incorporates cross-cultural symbols and keywords from different languages. Students collaborate in virtual space to create a prototype . . . .

School is now a place with rooms for discussions, quiet study, recreation, and presentations by inspirational people. Their project team visits people in their own community physically and people in other countries virtually. These people, who share the students' interests, have been identified for education through sophisticated network mapping. Mentors from around the world have been hired by school districts to participate in online worlds . . . .

Through the Eyes of Students

Future Technology Chat

The Threshold/ISTE Youth Forum (2004, pp. 26–30) recently asked 11 students from around the world to talk about technology and learning and what they think the future is likely to bring. Following are some of their responses to why they think technology is so essential today:

> Sharn B: All jobs that we may get have to do with tech
>
> Jon V: I personally go to a school where it is super important . . . it's life essential.
>
> Blake P: Abstract concepts are often easier to grasp when technology is used effectively as a teaching tool.
>
> Elena M: Yeah, some students at my school who weren't great students are better ones now thanks to computers.
>
> Sundip P: Technology allows us to learn as much as we want about virtually any topic. There are a ton of tutorials and explanations on things from improving test scores to videoediting and graphic design.

In response to how they are using technology outside of school that would make learning easier in school, they commented:

> Blake P: My powerbook never leaves a 6 foot radius of me.
>
> Sundip P: Sometimes if a teacher's explanation doesn't make sense to me, I search for it on the Net and see if I can get a feel for the topic using another approach.
>
> Mick S: Using instant messenger at home is something that could be very useful at school to communicate.

In response to what they see as hot technology trends, one student said:

> Blake P: Wi-Fi (a way of using the Internet wirelessly) . . . We already have a schoolwide wireless network, and it is great . . . could be faster.

In response to how they think schools will be different 15 years from now, they predicted:

> Mick S: I think schools will be more tech savvy, but around here, funding is a huge problem.
>
> Sharn B: The computers will be much smaller . . . they'll be able to fit into your palm.

In response to whether people will be able to learn more because of technology, they said:

> Sundip P: I think people will evolve to multitask better, as well as learn more rapidly. Technology is responsible for that.
>
> Sharn B: I think technology is speeding up our thinking process.

Evaluating My Technology Skills and Attitudes

How good are your technology skills? How positive are your attitudes about using technology and incorporating it into your classroom? For these items, consider the grade and subject(s) you are most likely to teach. Rate yourself from 1 to 5, with 1 = Not like me at all and 5 = Very much like me.

	1	2	3	4	5

1. I'm reasonably proficient at using a computer and installing and uninstalling software.

2. I have become comfortable with using a word-processing program.

3. I have ideas for using word processing together with other language learning resources in the classroom.

4. I know how to search efficiently and thoroughly for information that interests me on the Internet.

5. I have ideas about how to use the Internet in my classroom.

6. I'm proficient at using e-mail.

7. I have been part of collaborative learning exercises that involve technology.

8. I can see how collaborative learning can be used with technology in my classroom.

9. I am aware of the sociocultural issues involved in technology and education.

Scoring and Interpretation

Look at your scores for each item and evaluate your technology strengths and weaknesses. By the time you step into your classroom for your first day of teaching, make it a goal to be able to confidently rate yourself on each of these items at the level of 4 or 5. On items on which you rated yourself 1, 2, and 3, try to take technology courses at your local college that will improve your knowledge and skills in those areas.

 Go to your Student Toolbox CD-ROM for an electronic version of this form.

The biggest problem for students is the privacy issue, now that the world seems transparent and technology exists for parents to see what their students are doing while they are doing it. Report cards consist of multimedia files showing students at work and identifying how much further they need to go to finish a project. (Clegg, 2004, pp. 6–7)

Teaching Strategies
For Choosing and Using Technology in the Classroom

Strategies in Practice

• **Managing Technology**
• **Technology and Young Children**

Technology will be a part of your classroom. Here are some guidelines for choosing and using it:

1. *Choose technology with an eye toward how it can help students actively explore, construct, and restructure information.* Look for software that lets students directly manipulate the information. One review found that students' learning improved when information was presented in a multimedia fashion that stimulated them to actively select, organize, and integrate visual and verbal information (Mayer, 1997). You might want to consult with a school or district media specialist for the soft-

ware that best reflects these characteristics. Software catalogs, education journals, and educational databases such as ERIC also can be good resources.

2. *Look for ways to use technology as part of collaborative and real-world learning.* In Ann Brown and Joe Campione's (1996) words, education should be about "fostering a community of learners." Students often learn better when they work together to solve challenging problems and construct innovative projects. Think of technologies such as the Web and e-mail as tools for providing students with opportunities to engage in collaborative learning, reaching outside the classroom to include the real world and the entire world and communicating with people in locations that otherwise would be inaccessible to them.

3. *Choose technology that presents positive models for students.* When you invite someone from the community to talk with your class, you likely will consider the person's values and the type of role model that he or she presents. Keep in mind our earlier comments about monitoring technology for equity in ethnicity and culture. Be sure that the models that students associate with technology are diverse individuals who serve as positive role models.

4. *Your teaching skills are critical, regardless of the technology you use.* You don't have to worry that technology will replace you as a teacher. Technology becomes effective in the classroom only when you know how to use it, demonstrate it, guide and monitor its use, and incorporate it into a larger effort to develop students who are motivated to learn, actively learn, and communicate effectively. Even the most sophisticated hypermedia will not benefit students much unless you appropriately orient students to it, ask them good questions about the material, orchestrate its use, and tailor it to their needs.

5. *Continue to learn about technology yourself and increase your technological competence.* Digital technology is still changing at an amazing pace. Make it a personal goal to be open to new technology, keep up with technological advances by reading educational journals, and take courses in educational computing to increase your skills. You will be an important model for your students in terms of your attitude toward technology, your ability to use it effectively yourself, and your ability to communicate how to use it effectively to your students. In a study of computers and education in many countries, the main determinants of effective use of information technology in classrooms were the teacher's competence in using technology and the teacher's positive attitude toward technology (Collis & others, 1996).

Video Observation: Technology in the Classroom

 ENTER THE DEBATE

1. Should teachers use more student- or teacher-centered instruction?

2. Should teachers assign homework to elementary students?

3. Should teachers integrate technology into their instruction?

ⓘ Review and Reflect

④ Summarize how to effectively use technology to help children learn.

Review
- What challenges does the technology revolution pose for education?
- How can the Internet be used effectively to help students learn?
- What are some current inequities regarding educational technology?
- Broadly, what are the technology standards for the early elementary, late elementary, middle school, and high school grades?
- How might ubiquitous computing change technology in the classroom?

Reflect
- Would one or more of the different ways that computers can be used to support learning and instruction be useful to the subject and grade level you plan to teach? How?

Teaching Experience
- **You Can't Assume Kids Know What You Know**
- **Considerations for Using Technology**
- **Lesson Planning**
- **Planning a Unit**
- **Helping Students Succeed**
- **Planning a Lesson**

Mrs. Rumer was new to teaching third grade at Hillside Elementary School. Before the school year began, she met with other new teachers and their mentors for planning sessions. The administration appeared to be aware of just how much planning is necessary for successful teaching. Mrs. Rumer openly shared her ideas with her mentor, Mrs. White, and the rest of the group.

"I really want to have a learner-centered classroom," Mrs. Rumer said. "I'd like to use aspects of problem-based learning, essential questions, and guided discovery. I also intend to integrate the curriculum as much as possible and use computers, too. I think the kids will learn so much more that way than if I use teacher-centered instruction."

Mrs. White smiled and said, "Well, they'd probably have more fun, but I doubt that their test scores would reflect much learning at all. We really need to prepare our students to meet state standards, Mrs. Rumer. To do that, you'd better throw in some good, old-fashioned direct instruction." Several other teachers readily agreed. "You'll make yourself crazy trying to integrate the curriculum, too. Besides, the middle school teachers will just tear it all apart again." Another teacher said, "I use my classroom computer all the time. The kids like it much better than flash cards for drill and practice."

The other teachers' comments surprised Mrs. Rumer. She had learned in her education courses that learner-centered instruction is supposed to be the best way to teach children. She wanted her students to be active in the construction of their knowledge, not merely vessels into which she poured that knowledge. She also thought that by integrating the curriculum, the students would see the connections between various disciplines. The principal assured her that if she wanted to give an integrated, learner-centered approach a try, she would have that freedom.

With this assurance, Mrs. Rumer began making lists of everything she would have to plan for in order to have an effective learner-centered classroom. She began by going through the district's curriculum guide for third grade. She made lists of all the objectives. Then she went through the learner-centered psychological principles from the APA. After doing this, she realized her job was going to be a daunting one.

- What are the issues in this case?
- Where should Mrs. Rumer go from here?
- How can she take a curriculum that has been taught in a teacher-centered manner and convert it to a learner-centered curriculum? Should she? Why or why not?
- How can she incorporate technology into the curriculum so that the computers don't become mere electronic flash cards?

Reach Your Learning Goals

1 Explain what is involved in classroom planning.

- Instructional planning involves developing a systematic, organized strategy of instruction that benefits students' learning.

- Good planning addresses both task (setting instructional goals, planning activities, and setting priorities) and time (making time estimates, creating schedules, and being flexible). You will need to make plans for different time frames, ranging from yearly planning to daily planning.

2 Identify important forms of teacher-centered instruction.

- Teacher-centered lesson planning includes creating behavioral objectives, analyzing tasks, and developing instructional taxonomies (classifications). Behavioral objectives are statements that propose changes in students' behavior to reach desired performance levels. Task analysis focuses on breaking down a complex task into its component parts. Bloom's taxonomy consists of cognitive, affective, and psychomotor domains.

- Direct instruction is a structured, teacher-centered approach that involves teacher direction and control, high expectations for students' progress, maximum time spent by students on academic tasks, and efforts by the teacher to keep negative affect to a minimum. The use of non-academic materials is deemphasized, as is nonacademically oriented teacher-student interaction.

- Teacher-centered instructional strategies include orienting students; lecturing, explaining, and demonstrating; questioning and discussion; mastery learning; seatwork; and homework. Prior to presenting and explaining new material, establish a framework for the lesson. Advance organizers (expository or comparative) are a good way to do this. Effective teachers spend more time explaining and demonstrating new material than their less-effective counterparts do. Effective lectures have a number of features, including advance organizers, periodic elicitation of student responses, and summarizing. Mastery learning is learning one concept or topic thoroughly before moving on to a more difficult one. Teachers vary in how much they use seatwork as part of their instruction. Researchers have found that the effects of homework on achievement are trivial, if they exist at all in American elementary schools. Homework has more positive effects in American middle school and high school. When homework is given, it is important to make it meaningful, monitor it, and give students feedback about it.

- Teacher-centered instruction includes useful techniques and its advocates especially believe it is effective in improving children's basic skills. Critics of teacher-centered instruction say that by itself it tends to lead to passive rote learning, overly rigid and structured classrooms, inadequate attention to socioemotional development, external motivation, excess use of paper-and-pencil tasks, too few opportunities for real-world learning, and too little collaborative learning in small groups.

3 Discuss important forms of learner-centered instruction.

- Learner-centered planning and instruction moves the focus away from the teacher and toward the student. The APA's learner-centered psychological principles involve cognitive and metacognitive factors (the nature of the learning process, goals of the learning process, the construction of knowledge, strategic thinking, thinking about thinking, and the context of learning), motivational and emotional factors (motivational and emotional influences on learning, intrinsic motivation to learn, and effects of motivation on effort), developmental and social factors (developmental influences on learning and social influences on learning), and individual difference factors (individual differences in learning, learning and diversity, and standards and assessment).

- Problem-based learning emphasizes real-world learning. A problem-based curriculum exposes students to authentic problems. Problem-based learning focuses on small-group discussion rather than lecture. Students identify issues they wish to explore, and teachers act as guides, helping students monitor their problem-solving efforts. Essential questions are questions that engagingly reflect the heart of the curriculum. Discovery learning is learning in which students construct an understanding on their own. Discovery learning is designed to get students to think for themselves, to discover how knowledge is constructed, to stimulate their curiosity, and to motivate their inquiry. Most discovery-learning approaches today involve guided discovery, in which students are encouraged to construct their understanding with the assistance of teacher-guided questions and directions.

- The learner-centered model of planning and instruction has many positive features. The fourteen APA learner-centered principles are guidelines that can help teachers develop strategies that benefit student learning (such as encouraging students to actively construct knowledge, think deeply and creatively, be internally motivated, solve real-world problems, and collaboratively learn). Critics argue that learner-centered planning and instruction focuses too much on process and not enough on content, is more appropriate for social sciences and humanities than science and math, is not appropriate for beginning instruction when students have little or no knowledge about the topic, and is more challenging to implement than most teachers envision. Keep in mind that although we presented teacher-centered and learner-centered approaches separately, many teachers use aspects of both approaches.

4 Summarize how to effectively use technology to help children learn.

- The technology revolution is part of the information society in which we now live, and students will increasingly need to have technological skills. Today's technologies can be remarkable tools for motivating students and guiding their learning. Many teachers have not been adequately trained to use computers and other technology, and too often the computers become quickly outdated or break down. Only when schools have technologically trained teachers and current, workable technologies will the technology revolution truly have an opportunity to transform classrooms.

- The Internet especially provides students access to a vast array of information. E-mail can be used effectively in classrooms as well. Cautions about Internet use need to be observed.

- A special concern is that students from low-income, ethnic backgrounds, as well as schools in low-income areas, are underserved. Females also might have less access and be technologically underserved.

- The International Society for Technology in Education has established technology standards for students in prekindergarten through second grade, grades 3 through 5, grades 6 through 8, and grades 9 through 12. These standards range from being able to use input and output devices (such as a mouse and a printer, respectively) by the time students have completed the second grade to being able to routinely and efficiently use online information resources to meet needs of research, communication, and productivity by the end of the twelfth grade.

- In the future, ubiquitous computing will likely replace the current emphasis on the desktop computer. Numerous other technological changes are predicted in the future of education.

 KEY TERMS

instructional planning 376	advance organizers 384	essential questions 396	e-mail 401
behavioral objectives 378	expository advance	discovery learning 397	ubiquitous computing 404
task analysis 380	organizers 385	guided discovery learning 398	
taxonomy 380	comparative advance	Internet 400	
Bloom's taxonomy 380	organizers 385	World Wide Web (the Web) 400	
direct instruction 383	mastery learning 387	website 400	

 PORTFOLIO ACTIVITIES

Now that you have a good understanding of this chapter, complete these exercises to expand your thinking.

Independent Reflection

Developing a Classroom Technology Plan. Create a written plan for how you might use computers for the subject(s) and grade level you plan to teach. How will you adapt your plan for students with little or no experience with computers? How can your classroom benefit from students with advanced technology skills? (INTASC: Principles *1, 2, 4*)

Collaborative Work

Evaluating Teacher-Centered and Learner-Centered Classrooms. With three other students in the class, divide up the work of observing an early childhood, an elementary, a middle school, and a high school classroom. Reconvene after each of you has observed

a classroom, and discuss the aspects of teacher-centered and learner-centered approaches the teachers were using. Evaluate how effective the approaches were. Write a comparative analysis. (INTASC: Principles *1, 2, 3, 4, 5, 6, 7, 8, 9*)

Research/Field Experience Reflections

Instructional Planning in Action. Ask a teacher at the grade level you plan to teach to show you the materials he or she uses in planning lessons, units, the term, and the yearly curriculum for one or more subjects. Create samples for your own later use based on what the teacher shows you. Discuss the importance of planning at each of these levels. (INTASC: Principles *7, 9*)

 Go to the Online Learning Center for downloadable portfolio templates.

TAKING IT TO THE NET

1. List the primary components of a good lesson plan. Dissect an online lesson plan and assess its component parts. Describe the quality of your chosen lesson and how you think it could be improved. Why is it so critical to develop clear objectives? Why is it good practice to think about your method of assessment prior to conducting the lesson?

2. Using the selected website on the OLC or a site of your own choice, review an exemplary model of educational technology in action. Why is your selected program or project so successful? Reflect upon your own technology skills, and note your strengths and weaknesses. Develop a professional development action plan to enhance your educational technology skills.

3. Evaluate an online, interactive activity, such as a "WebQuest." How does it measure up in these areas: academic rigor, student interest and motivation, user interface and navigability, relevance to real-world issues, and accessibility to students/teachers?

Connect to the Online Learning Center to explore possible answers.

STUDY, PRACTICE, AND SUCCEED

 Go to chapter 12 on the Online Learning Center at www.mhhe.com/santrockedu2e **to access the student** study guide with practice quizzes, web links, portfolio resources, PowerWeb articles and news feeds, and the online resources referenced in the chapter.

 Go to your Student Toolbox CD-ROM to access the resources and activities referenced in the chapter and

• Resources to help you prepare for the **PRAXIS II™ exam**

• **Application Resources,** including additional *Crack the Case* studies, electronic versions of the *Self-Assessments,* Application Exercises, and Site Observation Questions
• **Study Resources,** including Learning Goals, the Chapter Summary, a *Test Your Learning* exercise, and multiple-choice, true/false, matching, key terms, and short-answer quizzes
• **Professional Resources,** including a Lesson Plan Builder and *Bibliomaker*

13 Motivation, Teaching, and Learning

> The art of teaching is the art of awakening the curiosity of young minds.
>
> —Anatole France
> *French Novelist and Poet,*
> *20th Century*

Chapter Outline

Chapter Learning Goals

After you have completed your study of this chapter, you should be able to reach these learning goals:

1 **Define motivation and compare the behavioral, humanistic, cognitive, and social perspectives on motivation.**

2 **Discuss the important processes in motivation to achieve.**

3 **Explain how relationships and sociocultural contexts can support or undercut motivation.**

4 **Recommend how to help hard-to-reach, low-achieving students.**

Teaching Stories Jaime Escalante

In the 1970s, an immigrant from Bolivia named Jaime Escalante became a math teacher at Garfield High School in East Los Angeles, a school largely populated by Latino students from low-income families. When he began teaching at Garfield, many of the students had little confidence in their math abilities and most of the teachers had low expectations for the students' success. Escalante took it as a special challenge to improve the students' math skills, even enable them to perform well on the Educational Testing Service Advanced Placement calculus exam.

The first year was difficult. Escalante's calculus class began at 8 A.M. He told the students the doors would be open at 7 A.M. and that instruction would begin at 7:30 A.M. He also worked with them after school and on weekends. He put together lots of handouts, told the students to take extensive notes, and required them to keep a folder. He gave them a five-minute quiz each morning and a test every Friday. He started with fourteen students, but in two weeks the number was cut in half. Only five students lasted through the spring. One of the boys who quit said, "I don't want to come at 7 o'clock. Why should I?"

On the 5-point AP calculus test (with 5 highest, 1 lowest), a 3 or better means a student is performing at a level of being able to pass a college calculus class and will receive credit for it at most major universities. The AP calculus scores for Escalante's first five students were two 4s, two 2s, and one 1. This was better than the school had done in the past, but Escalante resolved to do better.

Three years later, the AP calculus test scores for Escalante's class of 15 students were one 5, four 4s, nine 3s, and one 2. Ten years after Escalante's first class, 151 students were taking calculus in the East Los Angeles high school.

Escalante's persistent, challenging, and inspiring teaching raised Garfield High, a school plagued by poor funding, violence, and inferior working conditions, to seventh place among U.S. schools in calculus. Escalante's commitment and motivation were transferred to his students, many of whom no one had believed in before Escalante came along. Escalante's contributions were portrayed in the film *Stand and Deliver*. Escalante, his students, and celebrity guests also introduce basic math concepts for sixth- to twelfth-grade students on *Futures 1 and 2 with Jaime Escalante,* a PBS series. Escalante has now retired from teaching but continues to work in a consulting role to help improve students' motivation to do well in math and improve their math skills. Escalante's story is testimony to how one teacher can make a major difference in students' motivation and achievement.

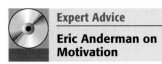

Expert Advice

Eric Anderman on Motivation

In chapter 12, you learned that motivation is a key component of the American Psychological Association's learner-centered psychological principles p. 394. Indeed, motivation is a critical aspect of teaching and learning. Unmotivated students won't expend the necessary effort to learn. Highly motivated students are eager to come to school and are absorbed in the learning process.

EXPLORING MOTIVATION

A young Canadian, Terry Fox, completed one of the great long-distance runs in history (McNally, 1990). Averaging a marathon (26.2 miles) a day for 5 months, he ran 3,359 miles across Canada. What makes his grueling feat truly remarkable is that Terry Fox had lost a leg to cancer before the run, so he was running with the aid of a prosthetic limb. Terry Fox clearly was a motivated person, but exactly what does it mean to be motivated?

What Is Motivation?

A Teacher's View of Motivation

Motivation

motivation The processes that energize, direct, and sustain behavior.

Motivation involves the processes that energize, direct, and sustain behavior. That is, motivated behavior is behavior that is energized, directed, and sustained. Why did Terry Fox complete his run? When Terry was hospitalized with cancer, he told himself that if he survived he would do something to help fund cancer research. Thus, the motivation for his run was to give purpose to his life by helping other people with cancer.

Terry Fox's behavior was energized, directed, and sustained. Running across Canada, he encountered unforeseen hurdles: severe headwinds, heavy rain, snow, and icy roads. Because of these conditions, he was averaging only 8 miles a day after the first month, far below what he had planned. But he kept going and picked up the pace in the second month until he was back on track to reach his goal. His example stands as a testimonial to how motivation can help each of us prevail.

Terry Fox's story is portrayed in a good classroom film, *The Power of Purpose*. One sixth-grade teacher showed the film to her class and then asked her students to write down what they learned from it. One student wrote, "I learned that even if something bad happens to you, you have to keep going, keep trying. Even if your body gets hurt, it can't take away your spirit."

Let's look at another example of motivation. Lance Armstrong was an accomplished cyclist when he was diagnosed with testicular cancer in 1996. Chances of his recovery were estimated at less than 50 percent as the emotionally drained cyclist began chemo-therapy. However, Lance did recover from the cancer and set a goal of winning the three-week, 2,000+ mile Tour de France, the world's premier bicycle race and one of the great tests of human motivation in sports. Day after day, Lance trained intensely, keeping the goal of winning the Tour de France in mind. To date, Lance has won the Tour de France not once but six times—in 1999, 2000, 2001, 2002, 2003 and 2004.

As with Terry Fox's marathon run and Lance Armstrong's winning of the Tour de France, students' motivation in the classroom involves why students are behaving in a particular way and the extent to which their behavior is energized, directed, and sus-tained. If students don't complete an assignment because they are bored, lack of motiva-tion is involved. If students encounter challenges in researching and writing a paper, but persist and overcome hurdles, motivation is involved.

Perspectives on Motivation

Different psychological perspectives explain motivation in different ways. Let's explore four of these perspectives: behavioral, humanistic, cognitive, and social.

The Behavioral Perspective   The behavioral perspective emphasizes external re-wards and punishments as keys in determining a student's motivation ◀ p. 211. **Incen-tives** are positive or negative stimuli or events that can motivate a student's behavior. Advocates of the use of incentives emphasize that they add interest or excitement to the class and direct attention toward appropriate behavior and away from inappropriate be-havior (Emmer & others, 2000).

Incentives that classroom teachers use include numerical scores and letter grades, which provide feedback about the quality of work the student has performed, and check-marks or stars for competently completing work. Other incentives include giving stu-dents recognition—for example, by displaying their work, giving them a certificate of achievement, placing them on the honor roll, and verbally mentioning their accom-plishments. Another type of incentive focuses on allowing students to do something spe-cial, such as a desirable activity, as a reward for good work. This might include extra time at recess, playing computer games, a field trip, or even a party. Shortly, in our discussion of intrinsic and extrinsic motivation, we will look more closely at the issue of whether in-centives are a good idea.

The Humanistic Perspective   The **humanistic perspective** stresses students' capac-ity for personal growth, freedom to choose their destiny, and positive qualities (such as

Terry Fox, during his run across Canada to raise funds for cancer research.

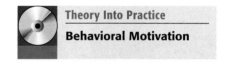

Theory Into Practice
Behavioral Motivation

Video Lecture: Role of Multiple Intelligences Theory in Motivation

incentives Positive or negative stimuli or events that can motivate a student's behavior.

humanistic perspective A view that stresses students' capacity for personal growth, freedom to choose their destiny, and positive qualities.

Calvin and Hobbes   by Bill Watterson

Calvin & Hobbs. © 1991 Watterson. Distributed by United Press Syndicate.

FIGURE 13.1 Maslow's Hierarchy of Needs

Abraham Maslow developed the hierarchy of human needs to show how we have to satisfy certain basic needs before we can satisfy higher needs. In the diagram, lower-level needs are shown toward the base of the pyramid, higher-level needs toward the peak.

Theory Into Practice

Maslow's Hierarchy of Needs

hierarchy of needs Maslow's concept that individual needs must be satisfied in this sequence: physiological, safety, love and belongingness, esteem, and self-actualization.

self-actualization The highest and most elusive of Maslow's needs; the motivation to develop one's full potential as a human being.

being sensitive to others). This perspective is closely associated with Abraham Maslow's (1954, 1971) belief that certain basic needs must be satisfied before higher needs can be satisfied. According to Maslow's **hierarchy of needs,** individuals' needs must be satisfied in this sequence (see figure 13.1):

- *Physiological:* hunger, thirst, sleep
- *Safety:* ensuring survival, such as protection from war and crime
- *Love and belongingness:* security, affection, and attention from others
- *Esteem:* feeling good about ourselves
- *Self-actualization:* realization of one's potential

In Maslow's view, for example, students must satisfy their need for food before they can achieve.

Self-actualization, the highest and most elusive of Maslow's needs, has been given special attention. It is the motivation to develop one's full potential as a human being. In Maslow's view, self-actualization is possible only after the lower needs have been met. Maslow cautions that most people stop maturing after they have developed a high level of esteem and therefore never become self-actualized. Figure 13.2 describes the characteristics of self-actualized individuals.

The idea that human needs are hierarchically arranged is appealing. Maslow's theory stimulates discussion about the ordering of motives in students' and teachers' lives. However, not everyone agrees with Maslow's ordering. For example, for some students cognitive needs might be more fundamental than esteem needs. Other students might meet their cognitive needs even though they have not experienced love and belongingness.

The Cognitive Perspective According to the cognitive perspective on motivation, students' thoughts guide their motivation. In recent years there has been a tremendous surge of interest in the cognitive perspective on motivation (Pintrich & Schunk, 2002). This interest focuses on such ideas as students' internal motivation to achieve, their attributions (perceptions about the causes of success or failure, especially the perception that effort is an important factor in achievement), and their beliefs that they can effectively control their environment. The cognitive perspective also stresses the importance of goal setting, planning and monitoring progress toward a goal (Schunk & Ertmer, 2000; Zimmerman & Schunk, 2001, 2004) ◀ p. 236.

Thus, whereas the behavioral perspective sees the student's motivation as a consequence of external incentives, the cognitive perspective argues that external pressures should be deemphasized. The cognitive perspective recommends that students should be given more opportunities and responsibility for controlling their own achievement outcomes.

The cognitive perspective on motivation fits with the ideas of R. W. White (1959), who proposed the concept of

Through the Eyes of Teachers

A High-Energy Style

Rhonda Nachamkin, who teaches first grade at River Eves Elementary School in Roswell, Georgia, has a high-energy style and approaches each unit as if it were a Hollywood production. She turns the classroom into an Egyptian tomb, New York City, and Mount Olympus. She sends parents scurrying to learn who Anubis (Egyptian god) and Prometheus (Greek Titan who stole fire) were so they can converse about these topics with their six-year-olds. Rhonda likes to use multiple versions of fairy tales to teach reading, spelling, and analytical concepts (*USA Today,* 1999).

Rhonda Nachamkin helps one of her students, Patrick Drones, with his work.

Realistic orientation
Self-acceptance and acceptance of others and the natural world as they are
Spontaneity
Problem-centered rather than self-centered
Air of detachment and need for privacy
Autonomous and independent
Fresh rather than stereotyped appreciation of people and things
Generally have had profound mystical or spiritual, though not necessarily religious, experiences
Identification with humankind and a strong social interest
Tendency to have strong intimate relationships with a few special, loved people rather than superficial relationships with many people
Democratic values and attitudes
No confusion of means with ends
Philosophical rather than hostile sense of humor
High degree of creativity
Resistance to cultural conformity
Transcendence of environment rather than always coping with it

FIGURE 13.2 **Maslow's Characteristics of Self-Actualized Individuals**

Maslow's Theory & Education
Self-Actualization

competence motivation, the idea that people are motivated to deal effectively with their environment, to master their world, and to process information efficiently. White said that people do these things not because they serve biological needs, but because people have an internal motivation to interact effectively with the environment.

The Social Perspective   Are you the kind of person who is motivated to be around people a lot? Or would you rather stay home and read a book? The **need for affiliation or relatedness** is the motive to be securely connected with other people. This involves establishing, maintaining, and restoring warm, close personal relationships. Students' need for affiliation or relatedness is reflected in their motivation to spend time with peers, their close friendships, their attachment to their parents, and their desire to have a positive relationship with their teachers.

Students in schools with caring and supportive interpersonal relationships have more positive academic attitudes and values and are more satisfied with school (Baker, 1999; Stipek, 2002). In a recent large-scale study one of the most important factors in students' motivation and achievement was their perception of whether they had a positive relationship with the teacher (McCombs, 2001; McCombs & Quiat, 2001). In another study, the value of math increased for middle school students when they had a teacher whom they perceived to be high in support (Eccles, 1993).

Review and Reflect

1 **Define motivation and compare the behavioral, humanistic, cognitive, and social perspectives on motivation.**

Review
- What is motivated behavior?
- How would you briefly summarize the four main perspectives on motivation?

continued on page 418

competence motivation The idea that people are motivated to deal effectively with their environment, to master their world, and to process information efficiently.

need for affiliation or relatedness The motive to be securely connected with other people.

MOTIVATION TO ACHIEVE

The current interest in motivation in school has been fueled by the cognitive perspective. In this section, we will study a number of effective cognitive strategies for improving students' motivation to achieve. We'll begin this section by exploring a crucial distinction between extrinsic (external) and intrinsic (internal) motivation. That will lead us to examine several other important cognitive insights about motivation. Then, we will study the effects of anxiety on achievement and some instructional strategies for helping students become more motivated.

Extrinsic and Intrinsic Motivation

Extrinsic motivation involves doing something to obtain something else (a means to an end). Extrinsic motivation is often influenced by external incentives such as rewards and punishments. For example, a student may study hard for a test in order to obtain a good grade in the course.

While the behavioral perspective emphasizes the importance of extrinsic motivation in achievement, the humanistic and cognitive approaches stress the importance of intrinsic motivation in achievement. **Intrinsic motivation** involves the internal motivation to do something for its own sake (an end in itself). For example, a student may study hard for a test because he or she enjoys the content of the course.

Current evidence strongly favors establishing a classroom climate in which students are intrinsically motivated to learn (Hennesey & Amabile, 1998; Wigfield & Eccles, 2002). Students are more motivated to learn when they are given choices, become absorbed in challenges that match their skills, and receive rewards that have informational value but are not used for control. Praise also can enhance students' intrinsic motivation. To see why these things are so, let's first explore two types of intrinsic motivation: (1) the intrinsic motivation of self-determination and personal choice and (2) the intrinsic

Intrinsic Motivation

extrinsic motivation The external motivation to do something to obtain something else (a means to an end).

intrinsic motivation The internal motivation to do something for its own sake (an end in itself).

"Your son has made a career choice, Mildred. He's going to win the lottery and travel a lot."
© 1986: Reprinted courtesy of Bunny Hoest and Parade Magazine

motivation of optimal experience and flow. Then we'll discuss how external rewards can either enhance or undermine intrinsic motivation. Finally, we will identify some developmental changes in intrinsic and extrinsic motivation as students move up the educational ladder.

Self-Determination and Personal Choice   One view of intrinsic motivation emphasizes self-determination (deCharms, 1984; Deci, Koestner, & Ryan, 2001; Deci & Ryan, 1994; Ryan & Deci, 2000). In this view, students want to believe that they are doing something because of their own will, not because of external success or rewards.

Researchers have found that students' internal motivation and intrinsic interest in school tasks increase when students have some choice and some opportunities to take personal responsibility for their learning (Grolnick & others, 2002; Stipek, 1996, 2002). For example, in one study, high school science students who were encouraged to organize their own experiments demonstrated more care and interest in laboratory work than did their counterparts who had to follow detailed instructions and directions (Rainey, 1965).

In another study, which included mainly African American students from low-income backgrounds, teachers were encouraged to give the students more responsibility for their school programs (deCharms, 1984)—in particular, opportunities to set their own goals, plan how to reach the goals, and monitor their progress toward the goals. Students were given some choice in the activities they wanted to engage in and when they would do them. They also were encouraged to take personal responsibility for their behavior, including reaching the goals that they had set. Compared with a control group, students in this intrinsic motivation/self-determination group had higher achievement gains and were more likely to graduate from high school.

These students were given an opportunity to write and perform their own play. These kinds of self-determining opportunities can enhance students' motivation to achieve.

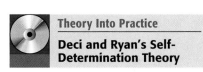

Theory Into Practice

Deci and Ryan's Self-Determination Theory

Teaching Strategies
For Providing Students with Opportunities for Self-Determination and Choice

Some ways you can promote self-determination and choice in your classroom include (Brophy, 1998; Deci & Ryan, 1994)

1. *Take the time.* Take the time to talk with students and explain to them why a learning activity they are being asked to do is important.
2. *Be attentive.* Attend to students' feelings when they are being asked to do something they don't want to do.
3. *Manage the classroom effectively.* Do this in a way that lets students make personal choices. Let students select topics for book reports, writing assignments, and research projects. Give them the choice of how they want to report their work (for instance, to you or to the class as a whole, individually or with a partner).
4. *Establish learning centers.* Students can work individually or collaboratively with other students on different projects in the centers, which might include language arts, social studies, or computer centers where students can select the activities they want to engage in from a menu that you have developed.
5. *Create interest groups.* Divide students into self-selected interest groups and let them work on relevant research projects.

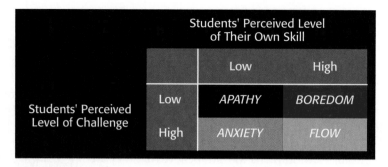

FIGURE 13.3 **Outcomes of Perceived Levels of Challenge and Skill**

Optimal Experiences and Flow Mihaly Csikszentmihalyi (1990, 1993, 2000; Nakamura & Csikszentmihalyi, 2002) also has developed ideas that are relevant to understanding intrinsic motivation. He has studied the optimal experiences of people for more
than two decades. People report that these optimal experiences involve feelings of deep
enjoyment and happiness. Csikszentmihalyi uses the term *flow* to describe optimal experiences in life. He has found that flow occurs most often when people develop a sense
of mastery and are absorbed in a state of concentration while they engage in an activity.
He argues that flow occurs when individuals are engaged in challenges they find neither
too difficult nor too easy.

Perceived levels of challenge and skill can result in different outcomes (see figure 13.3) (Brophy, 1998). Flow is most likely to occur in areas in which students are challenged and perceive themselves as having a high degree of skill. When students' skills are
high but the activity provides little challenge, the result is boredom. When both the challenge and skill levels are low, students feel apathy. And when students face a challenging
task that they don't believe they have adequate skills to master, they experience anxiety.

 ## Teaching Strategies
For Helping Students Achieve Flow

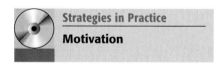

How can you encourage students to achieve flow? Some strategies are (Csikszentmihalyi,
Rathunde, & Whalen, 1993)

1. *Be competent and motivated.* Become an expert about the subject matter, show
   enthusiasm when you teach, and present yourself as a model who is intrinsically
   motivated.
2. *Create an optimal match.* A good strategy is to develop and maintain an optimal
   match between what you challenge students to do and what their skills are. That is,
   encourage students to achieve challenging but reasonable goals.
3. *Raise confidence.* Provide students with both instructional and emotional support
   that encourages them to tackle learning with confidence and a minimum of anxiety.

Extrinsic Rewards and Intrinsic Motivation As we saw in chapter 7, external rewards can be useful in changing behavior. However, in some situations rewards can
undermine learning. In one study, students who already had a strong interest in art and
did not expect a reward spent more time drawing than did students who also had a
strong interest in art but knew they would be rewarded for drawing (Lepper, Greene, &
Nisbett, 1973).

However, classroom rewards can be useful (Cameron, 2001). Two uses are (Bandura, 1982; Deci, 1975) (1) as an incentive to engage in tasks, in which case the goal is to control the student's behavior, and (2) to convey information about mastery. When rewards are offered that convey information about mastery, student feelings of competence are likely to be enhanced. An important point here is that it is not the reward itself that causes the effect but, rather, the offer or expectation of the reward (Schunk, 2001). Rewards used as incentives lead to perceptions that the student's behavior was caused by the external reward, and not by the student's own motivation to be competent.

To better understand the difference between using rewards to control students' behavior and using them to provide information about mastery, consider this example (Schunk, 2000): A teacher puts a reward system in place in which the more work students accomplish, the more points they will earn. Students will be motivated to work to earn points because they are told that the points can be exchanged for privileges. However, the points also provide information about their capabilities. That is, the more points students earn, the more work they have accomplished. As they accumulate points, students are more likely to feel competent. In contrast, if points are provided simply for spending time on a task, the task might be perceived as a means to an end. In this case, because the points don't convey anything about capabilities, students are likely to perceive the rewards as controlling their behavior.

Thus, rewards that convey information about students' mastery can increase intrinsic motivation by increasing their sense of competence. However, negative feedback, such as criticism, that carries information that students are incompetent can undermine intrinsic motivation, especially if students doubt their ability to become competent (Stipek, 2002).

Judy Cameron (2001; Cameron & Pierce, 1996) argues that the belief is too strong in education that rewards always decrease a student's intrinsic motivation. In her analysis of approximately a hundred studies, she found that verbal rewards (praise and positive feedback) can be used to enhance students' intrinsic motivation. She also concluded that when tangible rewards (such as gold stars and money) were offered contingent on task performance or given unexpectedly, intrinsic motivation was maintained. Some critics believe that Cameron's analysis is flawed—for instance, that it does not adequately detect some of the negative effects of rewards on motivation (Deci, Koestner, & Ryan, 2001; Kohn, 1996).

In summary, it is important to examine what rewards convey about competence. When rewards are tied to competence, they tend to promote motivation and interest. When they are not, they are unlikely to raise motivation or may diminish it once the rewards are withdrawn (Schunk, 2000).

Developmental Shifts in Intrinsic and Extrinsic Motivation Many psychologists and educators believe that it is important for children to develop greater internalization and intrinsic motivation as they grow older. However, researchers have found that as students move from the early elementary school years to the high school years, their intrinsic motivation decreases (Harter, 1996). In one research study, the biggest drop in intrinsic motivation and increase in extrinsic motivation was between sixth grade and seventh grade (Harter, 1981). In another study, as students moved from sixth through eighth grade, they increasingly said school was boring and irrelevant (Harter, 1996). In this study, however, students who were intrinsically motivated were doing much better academically than those who were extrinsically motivated.

Why the shift toward extrinsic motivation as children move to higher grades? One explanation is that school grading practices reinforce an external motivation orientation. That is, as students get older, they lock into the increasing emphasis on grades and their internal motivation drops.

Jacquelynne Eccles and her colleagues (Eccles, 2004; Eccles & Midgley, 1989; Eccles & Wigfield, 2002; Wigfield & Eccles, 2002; Wigfield, Eccles, & Pintrich, 1996) identified some specific changes in the school context that help to explain the decline in intrinsic

Video Observation: Competitive Games

According to Jacquelynne Eccles and her colleagues, too many middle and junior high schools do not reflect an adequate person-environment fit. What do they mean by that concept?

motivation. Middle and junior high schools are more impersonal, more formal, more evaluative, and more competitive than elementary schools ◀ p. 87. Students compare themselves more with other students because they increasingly are graded in terms of their relative performance on assignments and standardized tests.

Proposing the concept of *person-environment fit*, Eccles and her colleagues (1993) argue that a lack of fit between the middle school/junior high environment and the needs of young adolescents produces increasingly negative self-evaluations and attitudes toward school. Their study of more than 1,500 students found that teachers became more controlling just at the time when adolescents were seeking more autonomy, and the teacher-student relationship became more impersonal at a time when students were seeking more independence from their parents and needed more support from other adults. At a time when adolescents were becoming more self-conscious, an increased emphasis on grades and other competitive comparisons only made things worse.

Although there is less research on the transition to high school, the existing research suggests that, like the transition to middle school, it can produce similar problems (Eccles, Wigfield, & Schiefele, 1998; Wehlage, 1989). High schools often are even larger and more bureaucratic than middle schools. In such schools, a sense of community usually is undermined, with little opportunity for students and teachers to get to know each other (Bryk, Lee, & Smith, 1989). As a consequence, distrust between students and teachers develops easily and there is little communication about students' goals and values. Such contexts can especially harm the motivation of students who are not doing well academically.

What lessons can be drawn from this discussion? Perhaps the single most important lesson is that middle school and junior high school students benefit when teachers think of ways to make their school settings more personal, less formal, and more intrinsically challenging.

Other Cognitive Processes

The preceding discussion of extrinsic and intrinsic motivation sets the stage for introducing other cognitive processes involved in motivating students to learn. As we explore four additional cognitive processes, notice how the distinction between extrinsic and intrinsic motivation continues to be important. The four processes are (1) attribution; (2) mastery motivation; (3) self-efficacy; and (4) goal setting, planning, and self-monitoring.

Attribution · · · · · **Attribution theory** states that in their effort to make sense of their own behavior or performance, individuals are motivated to discover its underlying causes. Attributions are perceived causes of outcomes. In a way, attribution theorists say, students are like intuitive scientists, seeking to explain the cause behind what happens (Weary, 2000; Weiner, 2000). For example, a secondary school student asks, "Why am I not doing well in this class?" or "Did I get a good grade because I studied hard or the teacher made up an easy test, or both?" The search for a cause or explanation is most likely to be initiated when unexpected and important events end in failure, such as when a good student gets a low grade (Graham & Weiner, 1996). Some of the most frequently inferred causes of success and failure are ability, effort, task ease or difficulty, luck, mood, and help or hindrance from others.

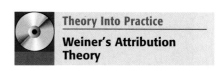

Theory Into Practice
Weiner's Attribution Theory

Bernard Weiner (1986, 1992) identified three dimensions of causal attributions: (1) locus, whether the cause is internal or external to the actor; (2) stability, the extent to which the cause remains the same or changes; and (3) controllability, the extent to which the individual can control the cause. For example, a student might perceive his aptitude as located internally, stable, and uncontrollable. The student also might perceive chance or luck as external to himself, variable, and uncontrollable. Figure 13.4 lists eight possible combinations of locus, stability, and controllability and how they match up with various common explanations of failure.

- *Locus.* A student's perception of success or failure as due to internal or external factors influences the student's self-esteem. Students who perceive their success as being due to internal reasons, such as effort, are more likely to have higher self-esteem following success than students who believe that their success was due to external reasons, such as luck. In the aftermath of failure, internal attributions lead to decreased self-esteem.
- *Stability.* A student's perception of the stability of a cause influences her expectation of success. If she ascribes a positive outcome to a stable cause, such as aptitude, she expects future success. Similarly, if she attributes a negative outcome to a stable cause, she expects future failure. When students attribute failure to unstable causes such as bad luck or lack of effort, they might develop expectations that they will be able to succeed in the future, because they perceive the cause of their failure as changeable.

Combination of Causal Attributions	Reason Students Give for Failure
Internal-Stable-Uncontrollable	Low aptitude
Internal-Stable-Controllable	Never study
Internal-Unstable-Uncontrollable	Sick the day of the test
Internal-Unstable-Controllable	Did not study for this particular test
External-Stable-Uncontrollable	School has tough requirements
External-Stable-Controllable	The instructor is biased
External-Unstable-Uncontrollable	Bad luck
External-Unstable-Controllable	Friends failed to help

FIGURE 13.4 Combinations of Causal Attributions and Explanations for Failure
When students fail or do poorly on a test or an assignment, they attribute the outcome to certain causes. The explanation reflects eight combinations of Weiner's three main categories of attributions: locus (internal-external), stability (stable-unstable), and controllability (controllable-uncontrollable).

attribution theory The theory that in their effort to make sense of their own behavior or performance, individuals are motivated to discover its underlying causes.

• *Controllability.* A student's perception of the controllability of a cause is related to a number of emotional outcomes such as anger, guilt, pity, and shame (Graham & Weiner, 1996). When students perceive that they are prevented from succeeding because of external factors that other people could have controlled (such as noise or bias), they often become angry. When students perceive that they have not done well because of internally controllable causes (such as not making enough effort or being negligent), they often feel guilty. When students perceive that others do not achieve their goals because of uncontrollable causes (such as lack of ability or a physical handicap), they feel pity or sympathy. And when students fail because of internally uncontrollable factors (such as low ability), they feel shame, humiliation, and embarrassment.

To see how attributions affect subsequent achievement strivings, consider two students, Jane and Susan. Both students fail a math test, but each attributes this negative outcome to a different set of causes (Graham & Weiner, 1996, p. 72):

> When Jane flunks her math test, she searches for the reasons for the failure. Her analysis leads her to attribute the failure to herself, not blaming her teacher or bad luck. She also attributes the failure to an unstable factor—lack of preparation and study time. Thus, she perceives that her failure was due to internal, unstable, and also controllable factors. Because the factors are unstable, Jane has a reasonable expectation that she can still succeed in the future. And because the factors are controllable, she also feels guilty. Her expectations for success enable her to overcome her deflated sense of self-esteem. Her hope for the future results in renewed goal setting and increased motivation to do well on the next test. As a result, Jane seeks tutoring and increases her study time.
>
> When Susan fails the test, she also searches for reasons for the failure. As it happens, her analysis leads her to attribute her failure to internal (lack of ability), stable, and uncontrollable factors. Because Susan perceives the cause of her failure to be internal, her self-esteem suffers. Because it is stable, she sees failure in her future and has a helpless feeling that she can't do anything about her situation. And because it is uncontrollable, she feels ashamed and humiliated. In addition, her parents and teacher tell her that they feel sorry for her but don't provide any recommendations or strategies for success, furthering her belief that she is incompetent. With low expectations of success, low self-esteem, and a depressed mood, Susan decides to drop out of school instead of studying harder.

What are the best strategies for teachers to use in helping students like Susan change their attributions? Educational psychologists often recommend providing students with a planned series of achievement experiences in which modeling, information about strategies, practice, and feedback are used to help them (1) concentrate on the task at hand rather than worrying about failing, (2) cope with failures by retracing their steps to discover their mistake or by analyzing the problem to discover another approach, and (3) attribute their failures to a lack of effort rather than lack of ability (Brophy, 1998; Dweck & Elliott, 1983).

The current strategy is not to expose students to models who handle tasks with ease and demonstrate success but, rather, to expose them to models who struggle to overcome mistakes before finally succeeding (Brophy, 1998). In this way, students learn how to deal with frustration, persist in the face of difficulties, and constructively cope with failure.

Mastery Motivation Closely related to ideas about intrinsic motivation and attribution is the concept of mastery motivation (Jennings & Dietz, 2002). Researchers have identified mastery as one of three types of achievement orientation: mastery, helpless, and performance.

Carol Dweck and her colleagues (Dweck, 2002; Dweck & Leggett, 1988; Dweck, Mangels, & Good, 2004; Henderson & Dweck, 1990) have found that children show two distinct responses to challenging or difficult circumstances: a mastery orientation or a helpless orientation. Children with a **mastery orientation** focus on the task rather than on their ability, have positive affect (suggesting they enjoy the challenge), and generate solution-oriented strategies that improve their performance. Mastery-oriented students

Mastery Motivation

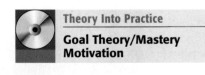

Theory Into Practice
Goal Theory/Mastery Motivation

mastery orientation A personal stance that involves mastery of the task, positive affect, and solution-oriented strategies.

The student

- Says, "I can't"
- Doesn't pay attention to teacher's instructions
- Doesn't ask for help, even when it is needed
- Does nothing (e.g., stares out the window)
- Guesses or answers randomly without really trying
- Is unresponsive to teacher's exhortations to try
- Is easily discouraged
- Doesn't volunteer answers to teacher's questions
- Maneuvers to get out of or to avoid work (e.g., has to go to the nurse's office)

FIGURE 13.5 Behaviors That Suggest Learned Helplessness

often instruct themselves to pay attention, to think carefully, and to remember strategies that worked for them in the past (Anderman, Maehr, & Midgley, 1996). In contrast, children with a **helpless orientation** focus on their personal inadequacies, often attribute their difficulty to a lack of ability, and display negative affect (including boredom and anxiety). This orientation undermines their performance. Figure 13.5 describes some behaviors that might reflect learned helplessness.

Mastery- and helpless-oriented students do not differ in general ability. However, they have different theories about their abilities. Mastery-oriented students believe their ability can be changed and improved. They agree with statements such as "Smartness is something you can increase as much as you want to." In contrast, helpless-oriented students believe that ability is basically fixed and cannot be changed. They agree with statements such as "You can learn new things, but how smart you are pretty much stays the same." The mastery orientation is much like the attributional combination of internal-unstable-controllable. The helpless orientation is much like the attributional combination of internal-stable-uncontrollable.

A mastery orientation also can be contrasted with a **performance orientation,** which involves being concerned with outcome rather than with process. For performance-oriented students, winning is what matters and happiness is thought to be a result of winning. For mastery-oriented students, what matters is the sense that they are effectively interacting with their environment. Mastery-oriented students do like to win, but winning isn't as important to them as it is to performance-oriented students. Developing their skills is more important (Wolters, 2004).

Mastery motivation has much in common with Csikszentmihalyi's concept of flow—being absorbed in a state of concentration during an activity. Mastery-oriented students immerse themselves in a task and focus their concentration on developing their skills rather than worrying about whether they are going to outperform others. In a state of flow, students become so attuned to what they are doing that they are oblivious to distractions.

Performance-oriented students who are not confident of their success face a special problem (Stipek, 2002). If they try and fail, they often take their failure as evidence of low ability. By not trying at all, they can maintain an alternative, personally more acceptable explanation for their failure. This dilemma leads some students to engage in behavior that protects them from an image of incompetence in the short run but interferes with their learning and achievement in the long run (Covington, 1992; Urdan, 2004). To avoid the attribution of low ability, some of these students simply don't try, or they cheat; others might resort to more subtle image-protecting strategies such as procrastinating, making excuses, working halfheartedly, or setting unrealistic goals.

helpless orientation A personal stance that focuses on personal inadequacies, attribution of difficulty to a lack of ability, and negative affect.

performance orientation A personal stance of concern with the outcome rather than the process; for performance-oriented individuals, winning is what matters and happiness is believed to result from winning.

Self-Efficacy

Self-Efficacy Resources

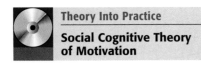

Theory Into Practice

Social Cognitive Theory of Motivation

Self-Efficacy In chapter 7, "Behavioral and Social Cognitive Approaches," we introduced Albert Bandura's concept of **self-efficacy,** the belief that one can master a situation and produce positive outcomes. Bandura (1997, 2000a, 2001, 2004) believes that self-efficacy is a critical factor in whether or not students achieve ◄ p. 226. Self-efficacy has much in common with mastery motivation and intrinsic motivation. Self-efficacy is the belief that "I can"; helplessness is the belief that "I cannot" (Maddux, 2002; Stipek, 2002). Students with high self-efficacy agree with such statements as "I know that I will be able to learn the material in this class" and "I expect to be able to do well at this activity."

Dale Schunk (1991, 1999, 2001, 2004) has applied the concept of self-efficacy to many aspects of students' achievement. In his view, self-efficacy influences a student's choice of activities. Students with low self-efficacy for learning might avoid many learning tasks, especially those that are challenging, whereas students with high self-efficacy eagerly approach these learning tasks. Students with high self-efficacy are more likely to persist with effort at a learning task than are students with low self-efficacy.

Your self-efficacy as a teacher will have a major impact on the quality of learning that your students experience. Teachers with low self-efficacy often become mired in classroom problems. Low-self-efficacy teachers don't have confidence in their ability to manage their classrooms, become stressed and angered at students' misbehavior, are pessimistic about students' ability to improve, take a custodial view of their job, often resort to restrictive and punitive modes of discipline, and say that if they had it to do all over again they would not choose teaching as a profession (Melby, 1995).

In one study, teachers' instructional self-efficacy was linked with their students' mathematical and language achievement over the course of an academic year (Ashton & Webb, 1986). Students learned much more from teachers with a sense of efficacy than from those beset by self-doubts. Teachers with high self-efficacy tend to view difficult students as reachable and teachable. They regard learning problems as surmountable with extra effort and ingenious strategies to help struggling students. Low-self-efficacy teachers are inclined to say that low student ability is the reason their students are not learning.

The ability to transmit subject matter is one aspect of instructional self-efficacy, but instructional self-efficacy also includes the belief that one can maintain an orderly classroom that is an exciting place to learn and the belief that it is possible to enlist resources and get parents positively involved in children's learning (Bandura, 1997).

Bandura (1997) also addressed the characteristics of efficacious schools. School leaders seek ways to improve instruction. They figure out ways to work around stifling policies and regulations that impede academic innovations. Masterful academic leadership by the principal builds teachers' sense of instructional efficacy; in low-achieving schools, principals function more as administrators and disciplinarians (Coladarci, 1992).

Efficacious schools are pervaded by high expectations and standards for achievement. Teachers regard their students as capable of high academic achievement, set challenging academic standards for them, and provide support to help them reach these high standards. In contrast, in low-achieving schools not much is expected academically of students, teachers spend less time actively teaching and monitoring students' academic progress, and tend to write off a high percentage of students as unteachable (Brookover & others, 1979). Not surprisingly, students in such schools have low self-efficacy and a sense of academic futility. To read about teachers, technology, and self-efficacy, see the Technology and Education box.

Teaching Strategies
For Improving Students' Self-Efficacy

self-efficacy The belief that one can master a situation and produce positive outcomes.

Here are some good strategies for improving students' self-efficacy (Stipek, 1996, 2002):

1. *Teach specific strategies.* Teach students specific strategies, such as outlining and summarizing, that can improve their ability to focus on their tasks.

Technological Self-Efficacy, Authentic Tasks, Curiosity, and Interest

Albert Bandura (1997) underscored that teachers' beliefs in their technological efficacy influence their receptivity to, and adoption of, educational technologies. You yourself have to be motivated to use technology and have technological self-efficacy if your students are to benefit from the tools of the electronic age.

Authentic tasks spark students' interest and curiosity. Students often perceive technology-based learning experiences as real-world activities (Cognition and Technology Group at Vanderbilt, 1997). One example of computer-based authentic learning is the use of a commercial movie, *Young Sherlock Holmes*, for social studies and humanities classes. Researchers have found that even when authentic computer-based tasks require considerable work, students often display considerable effort in pursuing solutions to the problems that they pose (Goldman & others, 1996).

Software that requires active thinking and has personal applications is likely to increase students' motivation. For example, you can use writing and publishing software as tools to help students create their own class newspaper.

Technology that is aimed at stimulating students' interest, curiosity, and creativity is likely to increase their motivation far more than technology that involves drill and practice. For example, an increasing number of computer simulations, such as *SimCity, SimTown,* and *SimEarth,* stir students' curiosity by letting them create and manage environments (Maddux, Johnson, & Willis, 1997).

A *SimCity 3000* computer simulation of the downtown area of a city. *SimCity* is designed to increase students' motivation by letting them create and manage environments.

2. *Guide students in setting goals.* Help them create short-term goals after they have made long-term goals. Short-term goals especially help students to judge their progress.

3. *Consider mastery.* Give students performance-contingent rewards, which are more likely to signal mastery, rather than rewards for merely engaging in a task.

4. *Combine strategy training with goals.* Schunk and his colleagues (Schunk, 2001; Schunk & Rice, 1989; Schunk & Swartz, 1993) have found that a combination of strategy training and goal setting can enhance students' self-efficacy and skill development. Give feedback to students on how their learning strategies relate to their performance.

5. *Provide students with support.* Positive support can come from teachers, parents, and peers. Sometimes a teacher just needs to tell a student, "You can do this."

6. *Make sure that students are not overly aroused and anxious.* When students overly worry and agonize about their achievement, their self-efficacy diminishes.

7. *Provide students with positive adult and peer models.* Certain characteristics of these models can help students develop their self-efficacy. For example, students who observe teachers and peers cope effectively and master challenges often adopt the models' behaviors. Modeling is especially effective in promoting self-efficacy when students observe success by peers who are similar in ability to themselves. One positive way for teachers to use peer modeling to improve students' self-efficacy is to have each student work on some aspect of a task and then have the students explain their part to other group members after they have mastered it (Zimmerman & Schunk, 2001). This type of peer modeling, discussed in chapter 10 as collaborative and cooperative learning, teaches skills and raises others' self-efficacy.

Goal Setting, Planning, and Self-Monitoring In chapter 7, "Behavioral and Social Cognitive Approaches," we discussed a number of ideas about self-regulatory learning, which consists of the self-generation of thoughts, feelings, and behaviors to

Through the Eyes of Teachers

The Taxman Cometh

Middle graders for the most part cannot see beyond the 3:30 bell. Their planning abilities are almost nil. I have a big calendar on my wall next to the pencil sharpener with not only my upcoming assignments but the other teacher's as well. Further, the kids are required to keep assignment notebooks with their assignments in them for each subject. I follow up, especially in the beginning of the year, by ensuring each individual student makes entries on their calendar. The whole idea is to make them conscious of time. Elementary and middle graders' concept of time is very different from adults, in that their frame of reference and focus is far narrower. Next week to them is like next month to us; therefore, a project that is due next month is in their eyes a lifetime away—hardly a blip on their radar. Hence the need for constant reminding, to reinforce the concept that time really does pass, and therefore progress has to be made. It's definitely an uphill battle, though, which frequently is never won—witness the lines at the post office on April 14th.

Chuck Rawls
Language Arts Teacher
Appling Middle School
Macon, Georgia

Goal Setting
Goal-Setting Worksheet

reach a goal ← p. 236. Here we expand on those ideas and focus on the importance of goal setting, planning, and self-monitoring in achievement.

Researchers have found that self-efficacy and achievement improve when students set goals that are specific, proximal, and challenging (Bandura, 1997; Schunk, 2001; Zimmerman & Schunk, 2001). A nonspecific, fuzzy goal is "I want to be successful." A more concrete, specific goal is "I want to make the honor roll by the end of the semester."

Students can set both long-term (distal) and short-term (proximal) goals. It is okay to let students set some long-term goals, such as "I want to graduate from high school" or "I want to go to college," but if you do, make sure that they also create short-term goals as steps along the way. "Getting an *A* on the next math test" is an example of a short-term, proximal goal. So is "Doing all of my homework by 4 P.M. Sunday." As mentioned earlier, attention should focus mainly on short-term goals, which help students judge their progress better than do long-term goals. David McNally (1990), author of *Even Eagles Need a Push*, advises that when students set goals and plan, they should be reminded to live their lives one day at a time. Have them make their commitments in bite-size chunks. As McNally says, a house is built one brick at a time, a cathedral one stone at a time. The artist paints one stroke at a time. The student should also work in small increments.

Another good strategy is to encourage students to set challenging goals. A challenging goal is a commitment to self-improvement. Strong interest and involvement in activities is sparked by challenges. Goals that are easy to reach generate little interest or effort. However, goals should be optimally matched to the student's skill level. If goals are unrealistically high, the result will be repeated failures that lower the student's self-efficacy.

Carol Dweck (1996; Dweck & Leggett, 1988), John Nicholls (1979; Nicholls & others, 1990), and their colleagues define goals in terms of the type of achievement the goal represents and the definition of success. For example, Nicholls distinguishes among ego-involved goals, task-involved goals, and work-avoidant goals. Students who have ego-involved goals strive to maximize favorable evaluations and minimize unfavorable ones. Thus, ego-involved students might focus on how smart they will look and how effectively they can outperform other students. In contrast, students who have task-involved goals focus on mastering tasks. They concentrate on how they can do the task and what they will learn. Students with work-avoidant goals try to exert as little effort as possible on a task. Encourage students to develop task-involved mastery goals rather than ego-involved or work-avoidant goals.

Unfortunately, many of the changes involved in the transition to middle schools are likely to increase students' motivation to achieve performance goals rather than mastery goals (Eccles, 2004; Eccles, Wigfield, & Schiefele, 1998; Midgley, 2001; Wigfield & Eccles, 2002). Consider that these often include a drop in grades, a lack of support for autonomy, whole-class task organization and between-class ability groupings that likely increase social comparison, concerns about evaluation, and competitiveness.

In one research study, both teachers and students reported that performance-focused goals were more common and task-focused goals less common in middle school than in elementary school classrooms (Midgley, Anderman, & Hicks, 1995). In addition, the elementary school teachers reported using task-focused goals more than middle school teachers did. At both grades, the extent to which the teachers were task-focused was linked with the students' and the teachers' sense of personal efficacy. Not unexpectedly, personal efficacy was lower for the middle school than elementary school participants. Thus, middle school teachers especially need to increasingly include task-focused goals in their instruction (Anderman, Austin, & Johnson, 2002).

In chapter 12, we described the importance of planning for teachers ◄ p. 376. Planning is also important for students. It is not enough just to get students to set goals. It also is important to encourage them to plan how they will reach their goals (Elliot & Thrash, 2001; Maehr, 2001; Randi & Corno, 2000). Being a good planner means managing time effectively, setting priorities, and being organized. Give students, especially at the middle school and high school levels, practice at managing their time, setting priorities, and being organized.

You might start by giving them a calendar for the term on which they can write down their important exam dates, the due dates for papers, homework assignments, and the dates when other tasks and activities are going to occur. Ask them to think about how many days or weeks they will need to study for major exams and write major papers. Have them mark the necessary days or weeks in which these tasks will be their main priorities. Tell them that their term calendar is not etched in stone. Encourage them to monitor it regularly and modify it when needed. For example, you might add another assignment or two, change a test date, and so on. Students might find that they need more study time than they originally predicted for a particular course.

After they have made out their term calendar, photocopy a blank weekly plan form and give it to your students. The form should have the days of the week across the top, with headings of "Planned" and "Actual" under each day. The 24 hours of the day should be listed vertically on the left side of the paper in a column. Have students fill in their class hours, leisure activities (such as sports, music practice, TV), and other routine activities such as sleeping and eating. A good strategy is to have students create this plan at the end of the preceding week. Then have them monitor it the next week to see how effectively they carried out their plan.

After students have created term and weekly plans, give them practice in setting priorities for the next day. A critical skill for a good time manager is figuring out what the most important things are to get done and when to do them—in other words, setting priorities. An effective way to get students to do this is to have them create manageable daily to-do lists. Their goal should be to make up the list in the evening and then complete all of the items on the list the next day. Get them to identify the top-priority tasks on the list and make sure that those get done. Have them examine their to-do list toward the end of the day and evaluate what they have accomplished. Encourage students to challenge themselves to finish the few remaining tasks.

You might be surprised at what students discover from their time use plans. Some students will be totally unaware of how much time they've been wasting, underestimate how much time they need to study, and be far less effective at using time than they imagined. Other students will learn that proper time management requires planning, organization, and self-discipline but that the results are worth it.

Most successful adults are good time managers, yet schools have not given students adequate opportunities to practice time management skills. If you are going to be a middle school or secondary teacher, make a commitment to working with students to help them improve their time management skills. This strategy not only should improve their achievement in your class but also should help them develop critical skills for success in work and life beyond school.

Older students should not only plan their next week's activities but also monitor how well they are sticking to their plan. Once students engage in a task, they need to monitor their progress, judge how well they are doing on the task, and evaluate the outcomes to regulate what they do in the future (Eccles, Wigfield, & Schiefele, 1998). Researchers have found that high-achieving students often are self-regulatory learners (Pressley & others, 1995; Schunk, 2001; Schunk & Zimmerman, 1994; Zimmerman, 2001a). For example, high-achieving students self-monitor their learning more and systematically evaluate their progress toward a goal more than low-achieving students do. Encouraging students to self-monitor their learning conveys the message that students are responsible for their own behavior and that learning requires the students' active, dedicated participation.

Teaching Strategies
For Helping Students Manage Their Time

Here are some good tips that teachers can give to students to help them manage their time more effectively and increase their achievement (Zimmerman, Bonner, & Kovach, 1996, p. 33):

1. *Be proactive, not reactive.* Students rarely plan or manage their available time for studying; instead, most tend to complete their assignments on a reactive basis at the last moment. Encourage them to be more proactive and develop term plans, weekly plans, and daily to-do lists from the middle school grades on.
2. *Set regular study times.*
3. *Use a regular study area that is well lighted and free from noise.*
4. *Learn to say "no" to distractions.* When peers try to talk them out of studying, help them resist the pressure.
5. *Reward yourself for your success.* Encourage students to delay desirable activities and use them as rewards for completing their studying. This can include getting food treats, watching TV, or spending time with friends.

Anxiety and Achievement

Anxiety is a vague, highly unpleasant feeling of fear and apprehension ◀ p. 189. It is normal for students to be concerned or worried when they face school challenges, such as doing well on a test. Indeed, researchers have found that many successful students have moderate levels of anxiety (Bandura, 1997). However, some students have high levels of anxiety and worry constantly, which can significantly impair their ability to achieve. For example, test anxiety is estimated to undermine the achievement of as many as 10 million children and adolescents (Wigfield & Eccles, 1989).

Some children's high anxiety levels are the result of parents' unrealistic achievement expectations and pressure. Many children have increasing anxiety as they reach higher grade levels, where they face more frequent evaluation, social comparison, and for some, experiences of failure (Eccles, Wigfield, & Schiefele, 1998). When schools create such circumstances, they likely increase students' anxiety.

A number of programs have been created to reduce an individual child's high anxiety level (Wigfield & Eccles, 1989). Some intervention programs emphasize relaxation techniques. These programs often are effective at reducing anxiety but they do not always lead to improved achievement. Anxiety intervention programs that focus on the worry aspect of anxiety emphasize replacing the negative, self-damaging thoughts of anxious students with positive, task-focused thoughts (Meichenbaum & Butler, 1980). These programs have been more effective than the relaxation programs in improving students' achievement.

Teacher Expectations

Students' motivation, and likely their performance, might be influenced by teachers' expectations. Teachers often have more positive expectations for high-ability than for low-ability students, and these expectations are likely to influence their behavior toward them. For example, teachers require high-ability students to work harder, wait longer for them to respond to questions, respond to them with more information and in a more

Anxiety

Expectancies

Teacher Expectations and Students' Motivation

elaborate fashion, criticize them less often, praise them more often, are more friendly to them, call on them more often, seat them closer to the teachers' desks, and are more likely to give them the benefit of the doubt on close calls in grading than they are for students with low ability (Brophy, 1985, 1998; Brophy & Good, 1974). An important teaching strategy is to monitor your expectations and be sure to have positive expectations for students with low abilities. Fortunately, researchers have found that with support teachers can adapt and raise their expectations for students with low abilities (Weinstein, Madison, & Kuklinski, 1995).

Review and Reflect

2 **Discuss the important processes in motivation to achieve.**

Review
- What are extrinsic and intrinsic motivation? How can extrinsic motivation be used to support achievement?
- How are ideas about attribution, mastery, self-efficacy, and goal setting useful in understanding and improving motivation to achieve?
- What approach has been most useful in reducing high anxiety about achievement?
- How can teachers' expectations affect students' motivation?

Reflect
- Sean and Dave both get cut from the basketball team. The next year, Sean tries out again but Dave does not. What causal attributions (and their effects) could explain the behaviors of these two students?

MOTIVATION, RELATIONSHIPS, AND SOCIOCULTURAL CONTEXTS

Motivation has a social component. In addition to achievement motives, students also have social motives. Our coverage of the social dimensions of motivation focus on students' social motives, relationships, and sociocultural contexts.

Social Motives

The social concerns of children influence their lives at school. Every school day students work at establishing and maintaining social relationships. Researchers have found that students who display socially competent behavior are more likely to excel academically than those who do not (Wentzel, 1996). Overall, though, researchers have given too little attention to how students' social worlds are related to their motivation in the classroom.

   Social motives are needs and desires that are learned through experiences with the social world. Interest in social motives stems from Henry Murray's (1938) long catalog of needs (or motives), which included the *need for affiliation or relatedness,* which is the motive to be securely connected to other people, which we described earlier in the chapter. This involves establishing, maintaining, and restoring warm, close, personal relationships. Students' social needs are reflected in their desires to be popular with peers and have one or more close friends and the powerful attraction they feel to someone they love. Though each student has a need for affiliation or relatedness, some students have a stronger need than others (O'Conner & Rosenblood, 1996). Some students like to be surrounded by lots of friends. In middle and high school, some students feel something is drastically missing from their lives if they don't have a girlfriend or boyfriend to date regularly. Other students don't have such strong needs for affiliation. They don't fall apart if

Contextual Supports for Motivation

social motives Needs and desires that are learned through experiences with the social world.

Why is adolescence such a critical juncture in the achievement motivation of many students?

they don't have several close friends around all day and don't sit in class in an anxious state if they don't have a romantic partner.

Both teacher approval and peer approval are important social motives for most students. In the elementary school years students are motivated to please their parents more than their peers (Berndt, 1979). By the end of elementary school, parent approval and peer approval are about equal in most students' motive systems. By eighth or ninth grade, peer conformity outstrips conformity to parents. By twelfth grade, conformity to peers drops off somewhat as students become more autonomous and make more decisions on their own.

Adolescence can be an especially important juncture in achievement motivation and social motivation (Henderson & Dweck, 1990). New academic and social pressures force adolescents toward new roles that involve more responsibility. As adolescents experience more-intense achievement demands, their social interests might cut into the time they need for academic matters. Or ambitions in one area can undermine the attainment of goals in another area, as when academic achievement leads to social disapproval. In early adolescence, students face a choice between whether they will spend more of their time pursuing social goals or academic goals. The results of this decision have long-term consequences in terms of how far adolescents will go in their education and the careers they will pursue.

Social Relationships

Students' relationships with parents, peers, friends, teachers, mentors, and others can profoundly affect their achievement and social motivation.

Parents Research has been done on links between parenting and students' motivation. Studies have examined family demographic characteristics, child-rearing practices, and provision of specific experiences at home (Eccles, Wigfield, & Schiefele, 1998).

Demographic Characteristics Parents with more education are more likely than less-educated parents to believe that their involvement in their child's education is important, to be active participants in their child's education, and to have intellectually stimulating materials at home (Schneider & Coleman, 1993). When parents' time and energy are largely consumed by attention to parents' other concerns or people other than the child, the child's motivation can suffer. Living in a single-parent family, having parents who are consumed by their work, and living in a large family can undercut children's achievement.

Child-Rearing Practices Even though demographic factors can affect students' motivation, more important are the parents' child-rearing practices (Eccles, 1993; Eccles, Wigfield, & Schiefele, 1998).

Here are some positive parenting practices that result in improved motivation and achievement:

- Knowing enough about the child to provide the right amount of challenge and the right amount of support
- Providing a positive emotional climate, which motivates children to internalize their parents' values and goals
- Modeling motivated achievement behavior: working hard and persisting with effort at challenging tasks

Provision of Specific Experiences at Home In addition to general child-rearing practices, parents can provide specific experiences at home to help students become more motivated. Reading to one's preschool children and providing reading materials in the home are positively related to students' later reading achievement and motivation (Wigfield & Asher, 1984). Indeed, researchers have found that children's skills and work habits when they enter kindergarten are among the best predictors of academic motivation and performance in both elementary and secondary school (Entwisle & Alexander, 1993).

Peers   Peers can affect a student's motivation through social comparison, social competence and motivation, peer co-learning, and peer group influences (Eccles, Wigfield, & Schiefele, 1998).

Students can compare themselves with their peers on where they stand academically and socially (Ruble, 1983). Adolescents are more likely than younger children to engage in social comparison, although adolescents are prone to deny that they ever compare themselves with others (Harter, 1990). Positive social comparisons usually result in higher self-esteem, negative comparisons in lower self-esteem. Students are most likely to compare themselves with the students who are most similar to them in age, ability, and interests.

Students who are more accepted by their peers and who have good social skills often do better in school and have positive academic achievement motivation (Asher & Coie, 1990; Wentzel, 1996). In contrast, rejected students, especially those who are highly aggressive, are at risk for a number of achievement problems, including getting low grades and dropping out of school.

In chapter 10, "Social Constructivist Approaches," we highlighted the role of peers in collaborative and cooperative learning, as well as peer tutoring ◀ p. 321. Peers can help each other learn material through discussion in small groups. And peer tutoring often brings achievement gains to the tutor as well as to the student being tutored.

Early work on the role of the peer group in students' achievement focused on its negative role in distracting adolescents from a commitment to academic learning (Goodlad, 1984). More recently, the peer group has been viewed as a positive or negative influence, depending on its motivational orientation. If the peer group has high achievement standards, it will support the student's academic achievement. But if a low-achieving student joins a low-achieving peer group or clique, the student's academic work can deteriorate even further (Kinderman, McCollam, & Gibson, 1996).

Teachers   Many children who do not do well in school consistently have negative interactions with their teachers (Stipek, 2002). They are frequently in trouble for not completing assignments, not paying attention, or goofing off or acting out. In many cases, they deserve to be criticized and disciplined, but too often the classroom becomes a highly unpleasant place for them.

Nel Noddings (1992a, 1998, 2001) believes that students are most likely to develop into competent human beings when they feel cared for. This requires teachers to get to know students fairly well. She believes that this is difficult in large schools with large numbers of students in each class. She would have teachers remain with the same students for two to three years (voluntarily on the part of the teacher and the pupil) so that teachers would be better positioned to attend to the interests and capacities of each student (Thornton, 2001).

Researchers have found that students who feel they have supportive, caring teachers are more strongly motivated to engage in academic work than students with unsupportive, uncaring teachers (McCombs, 2001; R. S. Newman, 2002; Ryan & Deci, 2000). One researcher examined students' views of the qualities of good relationships with a teacher by asking middle school students questions such as how they knew a teacher

Through the Eyes of Students

"You Always Manage to Cheer Us Up"

I know our science class sometimes is obnoxious and negative but we really appreciate you. You always manage to cheer us up and treat us like your kids. That shows how much you care about us. If you hadn't been there for me like you were, I probably wouldn't be where I am now. Good luck with all of your other students and I hope they learn as much as I have. I'll miss you next year. Hope to see you around.

Letter from Jennifer to William Williford, Her Middle School Science Teacher, Perry, Georgia

cared about them (Wentzel, 1997). As shown in figure 13.6, attentiveness to the students as human beings was important to the students. Interestingly, students also considered teachers' instructional behaviors in evaluating how much their teachers cared about them. The students said that teachers convey that they care about their students when they make serious efforts to promote learning and have appropriately high standards.

Students' motivation is optimized when teachers provide them with challenging tasks in a mastery-oriented environment that includes good emotional and cognitive support, meaningful and interesting material to learn and master, and sufficient support for autonomy and initiative (Covington & Dray, 2002; Eccles, Wigfield, & Schiefele, 1998; Graham & Taylor, 2002). Also, as we saw in our earlier discussion of Bandura's ideas on self-efficacy, the motivation and achievement climate of the entire school makes a difference in how motivated students are. Schools with high expectations and academic standards, as well as academic and emotional support for students, often have students who are motivated to achieve. In chapter 14, we will have more to say about how school policies and classroom management affect achievement.

Teachers and Parents   In chapter 3, we highlighted the important role that parents play in children's development, as well as strategies that teachers can use to increasingly involve parents in their children's education ◀ p. 77. In the past, schools have given little attention to how teachers can enlist parents as partners with them in providing opportunities for students to achieve. Currently there is considerable interest in how to accomplish this partnership. When teachers systematically and frequently inform parents of their children's progress and help them get involved in their children's learning activities, children often reach higher levels of academic achievement (Epstein, 1996).

Sociocultural Contexts

In this section we will focus on how socioeconomic status, ethnicity, and gender can influence motivation and achievement. A special focus is diversity.

Socioeconomic Status and Ethnicity   The diversity within ethnic minority groups that we discussed in chapter 5 also is evident in their achievement ◀ p. 133. For example, many Asian American students have a strong academic achievement orientation, but some do not.

In addition to recognizing the diversity that exists within every cultural group in terms of their achievement, it also is important to distinguish between difference and

	TEACHERS WHO CARE	**TEACHERS WHO DO NOT CARE**
Teaching behaviors	Makes an effort to make class interesting; teaches in a special way	Teaches in a boring way, gets off-task, teaches while students aren't paying attention
Communication style	Talks to me, pays attention, asks questions, listens	Ignores, interrupts, screams, yells
Equitable treatment and respect	Is honest and fair, keeps promises, trusts me, tells the truth	Embarrasses, insults
Concern about individuals	Asks what's wrong, talks to me about my problems, acts as a friend, asks when I need help, takes time to make sure I understand, calls on me	Forgets name, does nothing when I do something wrong, doesn't explain things or answer questions, doesn't try to help me

FIGURE 13.6 Students' Descriptions of Teachers Who Care

deficiency. Too often, the achievements of ethnic minority students—especially African American, Latino, and Native American—have been interpreted in terms of middle-socioeconomic-status White standards as deficits when they simply are culturally different and distinct.

At the same time, many investigations overlook the socioeconomic status of ethnic minority students. In many instances, when ethnicity and socioeconomic status are investigated in the same study, socioeconomic status predicts achievement better than ethnicity. Students from middle- and upper-income families fare better than their counterparts from low-income backgrounds in a host of achievement situations—expectations for success, achievement aspirations, and recognition of the importance of effort, for example (Gibbs, 1989).

Sandra Graham (1986, 1990) has conducted a number of studies that reveal not only a stronger role of socioeconomic status than of ethnicity in achievement but also the importance of studying ethnic minority student motivation in the context of general motivational theory. Her inquiries fall within the framework of attribution theory and focus on the causes African American students identify for their achievement orientation, such as why they succeed or fail. Graham is struck by how consistently middle-income African American students do not fit the stereotype of being unmotivated. Like their White middle-income counterparts, they have high achievement expectations and understand that failure is usually due to a lack of effort rather than bad luck. In one recent study in which the participants were mainly ethnic minority students from low-income families, a mastery motivation classroom that provided considerable positive support was linked with students' motivation to learn and to resist distractions of emotional distress (Strobel, 2001).

UCLA educational psychologist Sandra Graham is shown talking with adolescent boys about motivation. She has conducted a number of studies which reveal that middle-socioeconomic-status African American students—like their White counterparts—have high achievement expectations and attribute success to internal factors such as effort rather than external factors such as luck.

A special challenge for many ethnic minority students, especially those living in poverty, is dealing with racial prejudice, conflict between the values of their group and the majority group, and a lack of high-achieving adults in their cultural group who can serve as positive role models (McLoyd, 2000; Spencer & Markstrom-Adams, 1990). The lack of high-achieving role models relates to the discussion in chapter 7, "Behavioral and Social Cognitive Approaches," in which we described the importance of increasing the number of mentors in these students' lives.

It also is important to consider the nature of the schools that primarily serve ethnic minority students (Eccles, Wigfield, & Schiefele, 1998). More than one-third of African American and almost one-third of Latino students attend schools in the 47 largest city school districts in the United States, compared with only 5 percent of White and 22 percent of Asian American students. Many of these ethnic minority students come from low-income families (more than one-half are eligible for free or reduced-cost lunches). These inner-city schools are less likely than other schools to serve more-advantaged populations or to offer high-quality academic support services, advanced courses, and courses that challenge students' active thinking skills. Even students who are motivated to learn and achieve can find it difficult to perform effectively in such contexts. The Diversity and Education interlude focuses on one individual who has become an important role model for African American students.

Diversity and Education
Henry Gaskins

A special concern is to find ways to support the achievement efforts of ethnic minority students, many of whom come from low-income backgrounds. In the Teaching Stories segment that opened this chapter, you read about Jaime Escalante, who made a major

Dr. Henry Gaskins, here talking with three high school students, began an after-school tutorial program for ethnic minority students in 1983 in Washington, DC. Volunteers like Dr. Gaskins can be especially helpful in developing a stronger sense of the importance of education in ethnic minority adolescents.

difference in the motivation of Latino students to learn and excel at math in East Los Angeles. Another individual has been exceptional in supporting the motivation of African American students in Washington, DC.

Henry Gaskins, a physician, began an after-school tutoring program for ethnic minority students. For 4 hours every weeknight and all day on Saturdays, 80 students receive study assistance from Gaskins, his wife, 2 adult volunteers, and academically talented peers. Those who can afford it contribute $5 to cover the cost of school supplies. In addition to tutoring in various school subjects, Gaskins helps the tutees learn how to set academic goals and plan how to achieve these goals. Gaskins also encourages students to self-monitor their progress toward the goals. Many of the students being tutored have parents who are high school dropouts and either can't or aren't motivated to help their sons and daughters achieve.

Every community has people like Henry Gaskins who can help provide much-needed mentoring and tutoring for students from low socioeconomic backgrounds whose parents do not have the skills or are not motivated to help them achieve academically. Many of these potential mentors and tutors from the community have not been contacted by school personnel. If the need exists among your students, make a commitment to scour the community for talented, motivated, and concerned adults, like Gaskins, who might only need to be asked to provide mentoring and tutoring support for disadvantaged students.

Gender Our discussion of gender and motivation focuses on how males and females differ in their beliefs and values. Female and male students' competence-related beliefs vary by achievement context. For example, boys have higher competence beliefs than girls for math and sports, and girls have higher competence beliefs for English, reading, and social activities. These differences increase after puberty (Eccles & others, 1993). Thus, how competently female and male students expect to perform is consistent with gender-role stereotypes.

With regard to achievement values, beginning in high school, girls do not value math achievement as highly as boys do (Eccles & others, 1993). Gifted girls often experience conflicts between gender roles and achievement. One study of gifted girls showed them feeling caught between achieving and appearing either feminine or caring (Bell, 1989).

In chapter 5, "Sociocultural Diversity," we charted many other aspects of gender and school, such as gender differences in teacher-student interaction, curriculum, and content; sexual harassment; and gender-bias reduction  p. 156. Because those differences are so important in students' achievement, we briefly summarize them here: Girls are more compliant, boys more rambunctious. Teachers give boys more attention and instruction than girls, yet boys get lower grades than girls. By middle school, girls have lower self-esteem. Boys list more career options than girls do.

Schools have made considerable progress in reducing sexism and sex stereotyping in books and curriculum materials, but sexism still exists. Sexual harassment is a special concern in schools and is more pervasive than once envisioned. Every student deserves an education free from gender bias. You might want to return to chapter 5 and again read the section on gender and schools, thinking about how such gender differences might affect students' motivation and achievement.

! Review and Reflect

3 **Explain how relationships and sociocultural contexts can support or shortcut motivation.**

Review
- How do social motives tend to change as children progress from elementary through high school?
- In what ways are students' school performances linked to relationships with parents, peers, friends, and teachers?
- How do ethnicity and socioeconomic status influence motivation to achieve at school? What are some gender differences in motivation?

Reflect
- Suppose a boy in your kindergarten class appears to have a strong social motivation. How might this become an asset or a liability in his future academic performance?

HARD-TO-REACH, LOW-ACHIEVING STUDENTS

An especially challenging aspect of teaching is how to help hard-to-reach, low-achieving students. Jere Brophy (1998) described strategies for improving the motivation of two main types of hard-to-reach and low-achieving students: (1) discouraged students who lack the confidence and motivation to learn and (2) uninterested or alienated students.

Discouraged Students

Discouraged students include (1) low achievers with low ability who have difficulty keeping up and have developed low achievement expectations, (2) students with failure syndrome, and (3) students obsessed with protecting their self-worth by avoiding failure.

Low-Achieving Students with Low Expectations for Success   These students need to be consistently reassured that they can meet the goals and challenges you have set for them and that you will give them the help and support they need to succeed. However, they need to be reminded that you will accept their progress only as long as they make a real effort. They might require individualized instruction materials or activities to provide an optimal challenge for their skill level. Help them set learning goals and provide them support for reaching these goals. Require these students to put forth considerable effort and make progress, even though they might not have the ability to perform at the level of the class as a whole.

Students with Failure Syndrome   **Failure syndrome** refers to having low expectations for success and giving up at the first sign of difficulty. Failure syndrome students are different from low-achieving students, who fail despite putting forth their best effort. Failure syndrome students don't put forth enough effort, often beginning tasks in a half-hearted manner and giving up quickly at the first hint of a challenge. Failure syndrome students often have low self-efficacy or attribution problems, ascribing their failures to internal, stable, and uncontrollable causes, such as low ability.

A number of strategies can be used to increase the motivation of students who display failure syndrome. Especially beneficial are cognitive retraining methods, such as efficacy retraining, attribution retraining, and strategy training, which are described in figure 13.7 on page 438.

failure syndrome Having low expectations for success and giving up at the first sign of difficulty.

TRAINING METHOD	PRIMARY EMPHASIS	MAIN GOALS
Efficacy Training	Improve students' self-efficacy perceptions	Teach students to set and strive to reach specific, proximal, and challenging goals. Monitor students' progress and frequently support students by saying things like "I know you can do it." Use adult and peer modeling effectively. Individualize instruction and tailor it to the student's knowledge and skills. Keep social comparison to a minimum. Be an efficacious teacher and have confidence in your abilities. View students with a failure syndrome as challenges rather than losers.
Attribution and Achievement Orientation Retraining	Change students' attributions and achievement orientation	Teach students to attribute failures to factors that can be changed, such as insufficient knowledge or effort and ineffective strategies. Work with students to develop a mastery orientation rather than a performance orientation by helping them focus on the achievement process (learning the task) rather than the achievement product (winning or losing).
Strategy Training	Improve students' domain- and task-specific skills and strategies	Help students to acquire and self-regulate their use of effective learning and problem-solving strategies. Teach students what to do, how to do it, and when and why to do it.

FIGURE 13.7 Cognitive Retraining Methods for Increasing the Motivation of Students Who Display Failure Syndrome

Students Motivated to Protect Their Self-Worth by Avoiding Failure   As we indicated earlier in the chapter, some students are so interested in protecting their self-worth and avoiding failure that they become distracted from pursuing learning goals and engage in ineffective learning strategies (Urdan & Midgley, 2001). Here are some of their strategies for protecting self-esteem and avoiding failure (Covington & Teel, 1996):

- *Nonperformance.* The most obvious strategy for avoiding failure is to not try. Students' nonperformance tactics include appearing eager to answer a teacher's question but hoping the teacher will call on another student, sliding down in the seat to avoid being seen by the teacher, and avoiding eye contact. These might seem like minor deceptions, but they can portend other, more-chronic forms of noninvolvement such as dropping out and having excessive absences.
- *Sham effort.* To avoid being criticized for not trying, some students appear to participate but do so more to avoid punishment than to succeed. Typical sham behaviors include asking a question even though they already know the answer; adopting a pensive, quizzical expression; and feigning focused attention during a class discussion.
- *Procrastination.* Students who postpone studying for a test until the last minute can blame their failure on poor time management, thus deflecting attention away from the possibility that they are incompetent. A variation on this theme involves students who take on so many activities and responsibilities that they have an excuse for not doing any one of them in a highly competent manner.
- *Setting unreachable goals.* By setting a goal so high that success is virtually impossible, students can avoid the implication that they are incompetent, because virtually all students will fail to reach this goal.
- *The academic wooden leg.* In this strategy, students admit to a minor personal weakness to avoid acknowledging the greater feared weakness of being incompetent. For example, the student might blame a failing test score on anxiety. Having test anxiety is not as devastating to a personal sense of self-worth as lack of ability.

Martin Covington and his colleagues (Covington, 1992, 1998; Covington & Teel, 1996; Covington, Teel, & Parecki, 1994) proposed a number of strategies to help students reduce their preoccupation with protecting their self-worth and avoiding failure (Brophy, 1998, p. 93):

- Give these students assignments that are inherently interesting and stimulate their curiosity. The assignments should challenge but not overwhelm their skills. Give them some choice of which learning activities to pursue. As their expertise increases, increase the level of challenge correspondingly.
- Establish a reward system so that all students—not just the brightest, highest-achieving students—can attain rewards if they put forth enough effort. Make sure that rewards reinforce students for setting meaningful goals. Also, try to make the learning itself a desirable goal.
- Help students set challenging but realistic goals, and provide them with the academic and emotional support to reach those goals.
- Strengthen the student's association between effort and self-worth. Encourage students to take pride in their effort and minimize social comparison.
- Encourage students to have positive beliefs about their abilities.
- Improve teacher-student relationships by emphasizing your role as a resource person who will guide and support student learning efforts rather than an authority figure who controls student behavior.

Uninterested or Alienated Students

Brophy (1998) believes that the most difficult motivation problem involves students who are apathetic, uninterested in learning, or alienated from school learning. Achieving in school is not an important value for them. To reach apathetic students requires sustained efforts to resocialize their attitudes toward school achievement (Murdock, 1999).

 Teaching Strategies
For Reaching Uninterested or Alienated Students

Here are some ways you might be able to reach students who are uninterested or alienated (Brophy, 1998):

1. *Work on developing a positive relationship with the student.* If the uninterested or alienated student doesn't like you, it is hard to get the student to work toward any achievement goals. Show patience, but be determined to help the student and push for steady progress in spite of setbacks or resistance.
2. *Make school more intrinsically interesting.* To make school more intrinsically interesting for this type of student, find out the student's interests and if possible include those interests in assignments that you make.
3. *Teach them strategies for making academic work more enjoyable.* Help them understand that they are causing their own problems, and find ways to guide them in taking pride in their work.
4. *Consider a mentor.* Think about enlisting the aid of a mentor in the community or an older student whom you believe the uninterested or alienated student will respect.

 Strategies in Practice

Brad's Circuit Board Failure Syndrome

This chapter has focused on student motivation. It also is important for you to be motivated as a teacher as well. To evaluate your motivation, complete Self-Assessment 13.1.

 Teaching Experience

- **Motivating Students**
- **Calling Students**
- **Student Responsibility**
- **Using Real-Life Applications to Motivate Students**
- **Empowering Children**

Evaluating My Motivation

Here are 16 statements you can use to analyze your motivational makeup. Rate yourself from 1 (not like me at all) to 5 (very much like me) on each of the statements.

1. I am aware of the hierarchy of motives in my life and which ones are the most important for me.

2. I am intrinsically motivated.

3. I have high expectations and standards for success.

4. My life has many moments of flow.

5. I am aware of the people in my life who have motivated me the most and what it is they did that motivated me.

6. I make achievement-related attributions that emphasize effort.

7. I have a mastery motivation orientation rather than a helpless or performance orientation.

8. I am motivated to learn and succeed because of my success aspirations, not because I want to protect my self-worth or avoid failure.

9. I have high self-efficacy in general.

10. I have high instructional self-efficacy in terms of my ability as a teacher and to manage my classroom effectively.

11. I regularly set goals, plan how to reach those goals, and systematically monitor my progress toward the goals.

12. I set specific, proximal, and challenging goals.

13. I am a good time manager, regularly doing weekly plans, monitoring my use of time, and making to-do lists.

14. I am good at learning from my mistakes to improve my future success.

15. I don't let anxiety or other emotions get in the way of my motivation.

16. I have a good support system for my motivation and have positive, close relationships with people who can help me sustain my motivation.

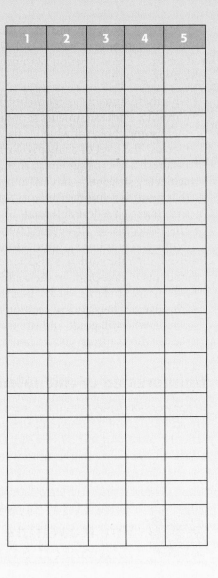

Scoring and Interpretation

Examine the pattern of your responses. If you rated yourself 4 or 5 on each of the items, you likely are getting your motivation to work to your advantage, and you likely will be a positive motivational model for your students. However, for any items on which you rated yourself 3 or below, spend some time thinking about how you can improve those aspects of your motivational life.

 Go to your Student Toolbox CD-ROM for an electronic version of this form.

www.mhhe.com/santedu2e

ENTER THE DEBATE

1. Should teachers post student scores publicly?
2. Should teachers allow children free access to the restroom?
3. Should teachers help students who struggle by giving them assignments they can easily accomplish?

Review and Reflect

4 Recommend how to help hard-to-reach, low-achieving students.

Review
- What are three types of discouraged students and what can teachers do to help them?
- How can teachers help students who are alienated?

Reflect
- Think about several of your own past schoolmates who showed low motivation in school. Why do you think they behaved the way they did? What teaching strategies might have helped them?

Catherine teaches second grade in an economically disadvantaged elementary school. Many of her students read below grade level. Some of her students have had little exposure to reading outside of school, and most do not choose to read during their free time at school. Knowing that reading skills are important to future success in school, Catherine is justifiably concerned.

In an effort to entice her students to read more, Catherine develops a reading incentive program. She places a large chart on the classroom wall to track student progress. Each time a student completes a book, he or she tells Catherine, who then places a star next to the student's name on the chart. Each student who reads five books per month receives a small prize, from the class prize box. The student who reads the most books in any given month receives a larger prize. When Catherine tells her students about the new incentive program, they are very excited.

"This is great!" says Joey. "I'm gonna get the most stars!"

"No, you won't," says Peter. "Sami will. She's always got her nose stuck in a book. She's the best reader in the class."

Sami is a very good reader. She is reading well above grade level and generally favors novels from the young adult section of the library. These books are rather lengthy and take her quite some time to finish. However, she really enjoys them. Catherine has brought her several from her own collection as well, since none of her classroom books seem to interest Sami.

The first week of the program is quite exciting. Every day students tell Catherine about the books they have read. The chart begins to fill with stars. By the end of the week all the students have at least one star next to their name except Sami. During the last week of the month many students choose reading as a free time activity. The students are anxious to ensure that they will earn at least one prize and many are devouring books in anticipation of being the month's "top reader." At the end of the month, 23 of Catherine's 25 students have 5 stars on the chart. The only exceptions are Sami, who has only 1 star, and Michael, who had chicken pox during the month. True to his word, Joey receives the most stars—15. The students excitedly choose their prizes.

The following month the reading frenzy continues. This time Sami joins her classmates in their accumulation of stars and receives 30, making her the top reader. Joey is right behind her with 25. Every student in the class earns at least 5 stars, entitling all to a prize. Because they are all reading so much, Catherine gives them a Friday afternoon party, at which they watch an animated movie and eat popcorn.

A similar pattern is repeated over the next several months. The star chart fills quickly. Catherine believes that the students are reading enough that they will do quite well on the annual state achievement test. She is thrilled with their progress. She decides that after the test, she will drop the incentive program and just quietly keep track of how much her students read. After doing this she notices that once again very few students are reading during their free time. Even Sami is no longer reading when she is finished with her other work. Now she draws instead.

- What are the issues in this case?
- Analyze the case from the perspective of extrinsic and intrinsic motivation.
- Analyze the case from a goal orientation perspective.
- Why do you think Sami went from receiving 1 star the first month to receiving 30 stars the next? Why does she no longer read in her free time at school?
- What are the problems with this type of incentive program? How might an incentive program be developed that does not undermine students' motivation to read?

Reach Your Learning Goals

1 Define motivation and compare the behavioral, humanistic, cognitive, and social perspectives on motivation.

- The study of motivation focuses on the processes that energize, direct, and sustain behavior.

- The behavioral perspective on motivation emphasizes that external rewards and punishments are the key factors that determine a student's motivation. Incentives are positive or negative stimuli or events that can motivate a student's behavior. The humanistic perspective stresses our capacity for personal growth, freedom to choose our own destiny, and our positive qualities. According to Maslow's humanistic perspective, there is a hierarchy of motives, and students' needs must be satisfied in a particular sequence. Self-actualization, the highest and most elusive of the needs Maslow describes, involves the motivation to develop one's full potential as a human being. In the cognitive perspective on motivation, students' thoughts guide their motivation. The cognitive perspective focuses on the internal motivation to achieve, attributions, students' beliefs that they can effectively control their environment, and goal setting, planning, and monitoring progress toward a goal. The cognitive perspective meshes with R. W. White's concept of competence motivation. The social perspective emphasizes the need for affiliation.

2 Discuss the important processes in motivation to achieve.

- Extrinsic motivation involves doing something to obtain something else (a means to an end). Intrinsic motivation involves the internal motivation of doing something for its own sake (an end in itself). Overall, most experts recommend that teachers create a classroom atmosphere in which students are intrinsically motivated to learn. One view of intrinsic motivation emphasizes its self-determining characteristics. Giving students some choice and providing opportunities for personal responsibility increase intrinsic motivation. Csikszentmihalyi uses the term *flow* to describe life's optimal experiences, which involve a sense of mastery and absorbed concentration in an activity. Flow is most likely to occur in areas in which students are challenged and perceive themselves as having a high degree of skill. In some situations, rewards can actually undermine performance. When rewards are used,

they should convey information about task mastery rather than external control. Researchers have found that as students move from the early elementary school years to high school, their intrinsic motivation drops, especially during the middle school years. The concept of person-environment fit calls attention to the lack of fit between adolescents' increasing interest in autonomy and schools' increasing control, which results in students' negative self-evaluations and attitudes toward school.

- Attribution theory states that individuals are motivated to discover the underlying causes of behavior in an effort to make sense of the behavior. Weiner identified three dimensions of causal attributions: (1) locus, (2) stability, and (3) controllability. Combinations of these dimensions produce different explanations of failure and success. A mastery orientation focuses on the task rather than ability, involves positive affect, and includes solution-oriented strategies. A helpless orientation focuses on personal inadequacies, attributing difficulty to lack of ability, and displaying negative affect (such as boredom or anxiety). A performance orientation involves being concerned with the achievement outcome rather than the achievement process.

- Self-efficacy is the belief that one can master a situation and produce positive outcomes. Bandura believes that self-efficacy is a critical factor in whether students will achieve. Schunk argues that self-efficacy influences a student's choice of tasks and that low-self-efficacy students avoid many learning tasks, especially those that are challenging. Instructional strategies that emphasize "I can do it" benefit students. Low-self-efficacy teachers become mired in classroom problems. Setting specific, proximal (short-term), and challenging goals benefits students' self-efficacy and achievement. Dweck and Nicholls define goals in terms of immediate achievement-related focus and definition of success. Being a good planner means managing time effectively, setting priorities, and being organized. Giving students opportunities to develop their time management skills likely will benefit their learning and achievement. Self-monitoring is a key aspect of learning and achievement.

- Anxiety is a vague, highly unpleasant feeling of fear and apprehension. High anxiety can result from unrealistic parental expectations. Students' anxiety increases as they get older and face more evaluation, social comparison, and failure (for some students). Cognitive programs that replace students' self-damaging thoughts with positive, constructive thoughts have been more effective than relaxation programs in benefiting student achievement.

- Teachers' expectations can have a powerful influence on students' motivation and achievement.

3 Explain how relationships and sociocultural contexts can support or undercut motivation.

- Social motives are needs and desires that are learned through experience with the social world. The need for affiliation or relatedness involves the motive to be securely connected with people, which consists of establishing, maintaining, and restoring warm, close personal relationships.

- In terms of social approval, both teacher and peer approval are important. Peer conformity peaks in early adolescence, a time of important decisions about whether to pursue academic or social motives. Understanding the parent's role in students' motivation focuses on demographic characteristics (such as education level, time spent at work, and family structure), child-rearing practices (such as providing the right amount of challenge and support), and provision of specific experiences at home (such as providing reading materials). Peers can affect students' motivation through social comparison, social competence, peer learning, and peer-group influences. Research shows that a teacher's support and caring can play a powerful role in students' motivation. A teacher's instructional and managerial style also can play a role in a student's achievement. An important aspect of student motivation is enlisting parents as partners with you in educating the student.

- Teachers should recognize and value diversity within any cultural group and should be careful to distinguish the influences of socioeconomic status from those of ethnicity. The quality of schools for many socioeconomically impoverished students is lower than for their middle-income counterparts. Gender differences in achievement involve beliefs and values. Special concerns are gender differences in teacher-student interaction, curriculum and content, sexual harassment, and gender bias.

4 Recommend how to help hard-to-reach, low-achieving students.

- The discouraged student lacks the confidence and motivation to learn. This might be a student with low ability and low expectations for success who needs reassurance and support but who also needs to be reminded that progress will be acceptable only when considerable effort is put forth; a student with failure syndrome (who has low expectations for success and gives up easily), who likely will benefit from cognitive retraining methods such as efficacy training, attribution retraining, and strategy training; or a student motivated to protect self-worth and avoid failure, or who likely will benefit from participating in inherently interesting activities, setting challenging but achievable goals, strengthening the link between self-worth and effort, and having positive beliefs about his or her own ability and a positive student-teacher relationship.

- Strategies for helping an uninterested or alienated student include establishing a positive relationship with the student, making school more intrinsically interesting, using teaching strategies for making academic work more enjoyable, and considering a mentor in the community or an older student as a support person for the student.

 KEY TERMS

motivation 414	competence motivation 417	attribution theory 423	social motives 431
incentives 415	need for affiliation or	mastery orientation 424	failure syndrome 437
humanistic perspective 415	relatedness 417	helpless orientation 425	
hierarchy of needs 416	extrinsic motivation 418	performance orientation 425	
self-actualization 416	intrinsic motivation 418	self-efficacy 426	

PORTFOLIO ACTIVITES

Now that you have a good understanding of this chapter, complete these exercises to expand your thinking.

Independent Reflection

Motivate, Invigorate, & Innovate Your Students. Design a motivationally rich classroom. What materials would be available? Describe your classroom walls and learning centers. How would teaching proceed? What types of activities would students participate in? Write up your classroom design below. (INTASC: Principles 5)

Collaborative Work

Case Studies in Motivation. With three other students in the class, create a plan to improve the motivation of these students: 1) 7-year-old Tanya, who has low ability and low expectations for success; 2) 10-year-old Samuel, who works overtime to keep his self-worth at a high level but has a strong fear of failure;

3) 13-year-old Sandra, who is quiet in the classroom and underestimates her skills; 4) 16-year-old Robert, who shows little interest in school. He currently lives with his aunt and you have been unable to contact his parents. (INTASC: Principles 2, 3, 5)

Research/Field Experience Reflections

The Face of Student Motivation. Observe a teacher at the grade level you plan to teach and note the strategies he or she uses to motivate the students. Which strategies are most effective? Least effective? Why do you think this is so? Which students seem particularly difficult to motivate? Why do you think this is so? What would you do differently to foster student motivation in the classroom? (INTASC: Principles 5, 7, 9)

 Go to the Online Learning Center for downloadable portfolio templates.

 TAKING IT TO THE NET

1. A student tells you that she lacks the ability to succeed in class. How do you respond? How would you describe your student's locus of control and attribution style? Take an online self-assessment to discover your own locus of control and attribution style. How could your style affect the way you teach and interact with students?
2. Reflect on your teaching goals and what you hope to accomplish in the classroom. Take yourself through the online process of setting a goal. Design a goal-setting activity that you could integrate into your regular curriculum. Why are goals an important element of a student's learning experience?

3. At-risk students are typically characterized as unmotivated and underachieving, and often are placed in classes that emphasize remediation. What are some successful alternatives? Find an exemplary model for teaching at-risk students on the Web, and summarize its program components. Illustrate why students in the program become motivated to achieve at higher levels than their counterparts in remedial programs.

   Connect to the Online Learning Center to explore possible answers.

STUDY, PRACTICE, AND SUCCEED

 Go to chapter 13 on the Online Learning Center at www.mhhe.com/santrockedu2e to access the student study guide with practice quizzes, web links, portfolio resources, PowerWeb articles and news feeds, and the online resources referenced in the chapter.

 Go to your Student Toolbox CD-ROM to access the resources and activities referenced in the chapter and

• Resources to help you prepare for the PRAXIS II™ exam

• **Application Resources,** including additional *Crack the Case* studies, electronic versions of the *Self-Assessments,* Application Exercises, and Site Observation Questions
• **Study Resources,** including Learning Goals, the Chapter Summary, a *Test Your Learning* exercise, and multiple-choice, true/false, matching, key terms, and short-answer quizzes
• **Professional Resources,** including a Lesson Plan Builder and *Bibliomaker*

14 Managing the Classroom

> Precision in communication is more important than ever in our era of hair-trigger balances, when a false or misunderstood word may create as much disaster as a sudden thoughtless act.
>
> —James Thurber
> *American Essayist and Humorist,*
> *20th Century*

Teaching Stories Adriane Lonzarich

Adriane Lonzarich owns and operates Heartwood, a small preschool in San Mateo, California. In the afternoons she also holds art classes for five- to twelve-year-old children. She talks about her ideas for managing the classroom:

The most valuable advice I ever received for managing the classroom is to approach a problem or area of difficulty with three questions in this order:

1. Is it the environment?
2. Is it the teacher?
3. Is it the child?

For example, if the issue of concern is unfocused energy of the group, I would first ask myself, Is it the environment? Is it over-stimulating? Is there not enough to do? Do I need to rearrange the classroom and create more intimate spaces for quiet activity or do I need to let them have more time outside, and so on? In many cases, I don't need to go on to the next two questions.

Is it the teacher? Am I tired? nervous? uninspiring? Have I not taken the time to demonstrate the activities? Have I not been consistent in presenting, monitoring, and enforcing basic classroom rules? Have I not paid enough attention to their needs that day?

Is it the child? If I've addressed all the other possibilities and I'm convinced that the problem is the child's problem, not the environment's or the teacher's, I explore what might be going on. Is anything happening in the child's home that might be causing his or her problems? Is it time for a parent conference? Does the child need help in bonding with a friend? Is the child afraid of failure and avoiding meaningful learning for that reason?

This approach is empowering because it is much easier to change the environment or oneself than to change someone else's behavior. It also is effective because it does not zero in on the problem as the child's until all other avenues have been explored.

In educational circles, it is commonly said that no one pays any attention to good classroom management until it is missing. When classrooms are effectively managed, they run smoothly and students are actively engaged in learning. When they are poorly managed, they can become chaotic settings in which learning is a foreign activity.

WHY CLASSROOMS NEED TO BE MANAGED EFFECTIVELY

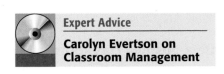

Expert Advice

Carolyn Evertson on Classroom Management

Alternatives to Control and Compliance

Educational Time Factors

Effective classroom management maximizes children's learning opportunities (Charles & Senter, 2005; Evertson, Emmer, & Worsham, 2003; Larrivee, 2005). Experts in classroom management report that there has been a change in thinking about the best way to manage classrooms. The older view emphasized creating and applying rules to control students' behavior. The newer view focuses more on students' needs for nurturing relationships and opportunities for self-regulation (Kennedy & others, 2001). Classroom management that orients students toward passivity and compliance with rigid rules can undermine students' engagement in active learning, higher-order thinking, and the social construction of knowledge (Charles & Senter, 2005; Jones & Jones, 2004). The new trend in classroom management places more emphasis on guiding students to become more proficient at self-discipline and less on externally controlling the student (Freiberg, 1999). Historically in classroom management, the teacher was thought of as a director. In the current learner-centered trend in classroom management, the teacher is more of a guide, coordinator, and facilitator (Kauffman & others, 2002). The new classroom management model does not mean slipping into a permissive mode. Emphasizing caring and students' self-regulation does not mean that the teacher abdicates responsibility for what happens in the classroom (Emmer & Stough, 2001).

As you explore various aspects of managing the classroom, realize the importance of consulting and working with other staff members on management issues (Evertson & Harris, 1999). Also recognize that your class is part of the broader context of school culture and that in such areas as discipline and conflict management your policies will need to reflect and be consistent with the policies of the school and other teachers in the school. We will begin our tour of effective classroom management by exploring how management issues sometimes differ in elementary and secondary classrooms.

Management Issues in Elementary and Secondary School Classrooms

Elementary and secondary school classrooms have many similar management issues. At all levels of education, good managers design classrooms for optimal learning, create positive environments for learning, establish and maintain rules, get students to cooperate, effectively deal with problems, and use good communication strategies.

However, the same classroom management principles sometimes are applied differently in elementary and secondary schools because of their different structures (Charles & Charles, 2005). In many elementary schools, teachers face the challenge of managing the same 20 to 25 children for the entire day. In middle and high schools, teachers face the challenge of managing 5 or 6 different groups of 20 to 25 adolescents for about 50 minutes each day. Compared with secondary school students, elementary school students spend much more time with the same students in the small space of a single classroom, and having to interact with the same people all day can breed feelings of confinement and boredom and other problems. However, with 100 to 150 students, secondary school teachers are more likely to be confronted with a wider range of problems than elementary school teachers. Also, because secondary school teachers spend less time seeing students in the classroom, it can be more difficult for them to establish personal relationships with students. And secondary school teachers have to get the classroom lesson moving quickly and manage time effectively, because class periods are so short.

Secondary school students' problems can be more long-standing and more deeply ingrained, and therefore more difficult to modify, than those of elementary school students. Also in secondary schools, discipline problems are frequently more severe, the students being potentially more unruly and even dangerous. Because most secondary school students have more advanced reasoning skills than elementary school students, they might demand more elaborate and logical explanations of rules and discipline. And in secondary schools, hallway socializing can carry into the classroom. Every hour there is another "settling down" process. Keep in mind these differences between elementary and secondary schools as we further explore how to effectively manage the classroom. As we see next, at both elementary and secondary school levels, classrooms can be crowded, complex, and potentially chaotic.

The Crowded, Complex, and Potentially Chaotic Classroom

Carol Weinstein and Andrew Mignano (1997) used the title of this section, "The crowded, complex, and potentially chaotic classroom," as an alert for potential problems and highlighted Walter Doyle's (1986) six characteristics that reflect a classroom's complexity and potential for problems:

- *Classrooms are multidimensional.* Classrooms are the setting for many activities, ranging from academic activities, such as reading, writing, and math, to social activities, such as playing games, communicating with friends, and arguing. Teachers have to keep records and keep students on a schedule. Work has to be assigned, monitored, collected, and evaluated. Students have individual needs that are more likely to be met when the teacher takes them into account.
- *Activities occur simultaneously.* Many classroom activities occur simultaneously. One cluster of students might be writing at their desks, another might be discussing a story with the teacher, one student might be picking on another, others might be talking about what they are going to do after school, and so on.
- *Things happen quickly.* Events often occur rapidly in classrooms and frequently require an immediate response. For example, two students suddenly argue about the ownership of a notebook, a student complains that another student is copying her answers, a student speaks out of turn, a student marks on another student's arm with a felt-tip pen, two students abruptly start bullying another student, or a student is rude to you.

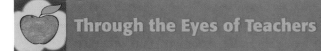

Through the Eyes of Teachers

Creating Juvenile Video Court TV

Carmella Williams Scott, a middle school English and law teacher at Fairmont Alternative School in Newman, Georgia, created Juvenile Video Court TV, a student-run judicial system, so that students could experience the "other side of the bench" as a judge, lawyer, bailiff, and camera operator. She especially targeted gang leaders for inclusion in the system because they ran the school. Carmella likes to use meaningful questions to guide students' critical thinking. She believes that mutual respect is a key factor in her success as a teacher and the lack of discipline problems she has in her classes (Briggs, 1999).

Carmella Williams Scott

- *Events are often unpredictable.* Even though you might carefully plan the day's activities and be highly organized, events will occur that you never expect: A fire alarm goes off; a student gets sick; two students get into a fight; a computer won't work; a previously unannounced assembly takes place; the heat goes off in the middle of the winter; and so on.
- *There is little privacy.* Classrooms are public places where students observe how the teacher handles discipline problems, unexpected events, and frustrating circumstances. Some teachers report that they feel like they are in a "fishbowl," or constantly onstage. Much of what happens to one student is observed by other students, and students make attributions about what is occurring. In one case, they might perceive that the teacher is being unfair in the way she disciplines a student. In another, they might appreciate her sensitivity to a student's feelings.
- *Classrooms have histories.* Students have memories of what happened earlier in their classroom. They remember how the teacher handled a discipline problem earlier in the year, which students have gotten more privileges than others, and whether the teacher abides by her promises. Because the past affects the future, it is important for teachers to manage the classroom today in a way that will support rather than undermine learning tomorrow. This means that the first several weeks of the school year are critical for establishing effective management principles.

The crowded, complex nature of the classroom can lead to chaos and problems if the classroom is not managed effectively. Indeed, such problems are a major public concern about schools. Year after year, the Gallup Poll has asked the public what they perceive to be the main problem schools face (Gallup Organization, 1996). The reply has consistently been "A lack of discipline."

Getting Off to the Right Start

One key to managing the complexity is to especially make careful use of the first few days and weeks of school. You will want to use this time to (1) communicate your rules and procedures to the class and get student cooperation in following them and (2) get students to engage effectively in all learning activities.

Taking the time in the first week of school to establish these expectations, rules, and routines will help your class run smoothly and set the tone for developing a positive classroom environment.

Teaching Strategies
For a Good Beginning of the School Year

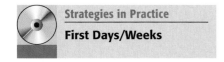

Strategies in Practice

First Days/Weeks

Some good teaching strategies for the beginning of the school year are (Emmer, Evertson, & Worsham, 2003)

1. *Establish expectations for behavior and resolve student
   uncertainties.* At the beginning of the school year, students will not be sure what to expect in your classroom. They might have expectations, based on their
   experiences with other teachers, that are different
   from what your classroom will be like. In the first few
   days of school, lay out your expectations for students'
   work and behavior. Don't focus just on course content
   in the first few days and weeks of school. Be sure to
   take the time to clearly and concretely spell out class
   rules, procedures, and requirements so that students
   know what to expect in your class.

2. *Make sure that students experience success.* In the first
   week of school, content activities and assignments
   should be designed to ensure that students succeed at
   them. This helps students develop a positive attitude
   and provides them with confidence to tackle more
   difficult tasks later.

3. *Be available and visible.* Show your students that they
   can approach you when they need information. During seatwork or group work, make yourself available
   instead of going to your desk and completing paper-
   work. Move around the room, monitor students' progress, and provide assistance
   when needed.

4. *Be in charge.* Even if you have stated your class rules and expectations clearly, some
   students will forget and others will test you to see if you are willing to enforce the
   rules, especially in the first several weeks of school. Continue to consistently establish the boundaries between what is acceptable and what is not acceptable in your
   classroom.

Through the Eyes of Students

First Week of School

Sept. 8:   Well, now that I know what my teacher is like, I wish I
(First   didn't. My best friend, Annie, got the good teacher, Ms.
Day of   Hartwell. I got the witch, Ms. Birdsong. The first thing
Class)   she did was to read all of her rules to us. It must have
           taken half an hour. We will never get to do anything fun.
           Fifth grade is ruined.

Sept. 12: Ms. Birdsong is still strict but I'm starting to like her
           better. And she even is beginning to be a little funny
           sometimes. I guess she's just serious about wanting us
           to learn.

Brooke
Fifth-Grade Student
St. Louis, Missouri

Emphasizing Instruction and a Positive Classroom Climate

Despite the public's belief that a lack of discipline is the number one problem in schools,
educational psychology has changed its focus. Formerly, it emphasized discipline. Today,
it emphasizes ways to develop and maintain a positive classroom environment that supports learning (Evertson, Emmer, & Worsham, 2003). This involves using preventive,
proactive strategies rather than becoming immersed in reactive disciplinary tactics.

In a classic study, Jacob Kounin (1970) was interested in discovering how teachers
responded to student misbehaviors. Kounin was surprised to find that effective and ineffective classroom managers responded in very similar ways to the misbehaviors. What
the effective managers did far better than the ineffective managers was manage the
group's activities. Researchers in educational psychology consistently find that teachers
who competently guide and structure classroom activities are more effective than teachers who emphasize their disciplinary role (Brophy, 1996).

Throughout this book we emphasize a vision of students as active learners engaged
in meaningful tasks, who think reflectively and critically and often interact with other
students in collaborative learning experiences. Historically, the effectively managed classroom has been described as a "well-oiled machine," but a more appropriate metaphor for
today's effectively managed classroom is "beehive of activity" (see figure 14.1 on page
452) (Randolph & Evertson, 1995). This does not imply that classrooms should be wildly
noisy and chaotic. Rather, students should be actively learning and busily engaged in
tasks that they are motivated to do rather than quietly and passively sitting in their seats.
Often they will be interacting with each other and the teacher as they construct their
knowledge and understanding.

Video Lecture: Proactive Classroom
Management Strategy

FIGURE 14.1 The Effectively Managed Classroom
"Well-oiled machine" or "beehive of activity"?

Management Goals and Strategies

Effective classroom management has two main goals: to help students spend more time on learning and less time on nongoal-directed activity and to prevent students from developing academic and emotional problems.

Help Students Spend More Time on Learning and Less Time on NonGoal-Directed Behavior   In chapters 12 and 13, we discussed the importance, for both teachers and students, of being a good time manager. Effective classroom management will help you maximize your instructional time and your students' learning time. Carol Weinstein (1997) described the amount of time available for various classroom activities in a typical 42-minute secondary school class over the course of a school year. Actual yearly learning time is only about 62 hours, which is approximately half of the mandated school time for a typical class. Although her time figures are only estimates, they suggest that the hours available for learning are far less than would appear. And as we underscored in chapter 12, "Planning, Instruction, and Technology," learning takes time.

 Teaching Strategies
For Increasing Academic Learning Time

Strategies for increasing academic learning time include maintaining activity flow, minimizing transition time, and holding students accountable (Weinstein, 1997):

1. *Maintain activity flow.* In an analysis of classrooms, Jacob Kounin (1970) studied teachers' ability to initiate and maintain the flow of activity. Then he searched for links between activity flow and students' engagement and misbehavior. He found that some ineffective managers engaged in "flip-flopping"—terminating an activity, starting another, and then returning to the first one. Other ineffective managers were distracted from an ongoing activity by a small event that really did not need attention. For example, in one situation a teacher who was explaining a math problem at the board noticed a student leaning on his left elbow while working on the problem. The teacher went over to the student and told him to sit up straight, interrupting the flow of the class. Some ineffective managers "overdwell" on something that students already understand or go on at length about appropriate behavior. All of these situations—flip-flopping, responding to distractions, and overdwelling—can interrupt the classroom's flow.

2. *Minimize transition time.* In transitions from one activity to another, there is more room for disruptive behavior to occur. In one study of 50 classes, disruptions such as hitting, yelling, and using obscene gestures occurred twice as often during transitions between activities than during activities (Arlin, 1979). Teachers can decrease the potential for disruption during transitions by preparing students for forthcoming transitions, establishing transition routines, and clearly defining the boundaries of lessons.

3. *Hold students accountable.* If students know they will be held accountable for their work, they are more likely to make good use of class time. Clearly communicating assignments and requirements encourages student accountability. Explain to students what they will be doing and why, how long they will be working on the activity, how to obtain help if they need it, and what to do when they are finished. Helping students establish goals, plan, and monitor their progress also increases students' accountability. And maintaining good records can help you hold students accountable for their performance.

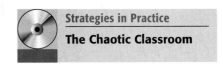

Strategies in Practice

The Chaotic Classroom

Prevent Students from Developing Problems   A well-managed classroom not only fosters meaningful learning but also helps prevent academic and emotional problems from developing. Well-managed classrooms keep students busy with active, appropriately challenging tasks. Well-managed classrooms have activities in which students become absorbed and motivated to learn and clear rules and regulations students must abide by. In such classrooms, students are less likely to develop academic and emotional problems. By contrast, in poorly managed classrooms, students' academic and emotional problems are more likely to fester. The academically unmotivated student becomes even less motivated. The shy student becomes more reclusive. The bully becomes meaner.

ⓘ Review and Reflect

1   Explain why classroom management is both challenging and necessary.

Review
- Why must management principles be applied differently to elementary and secondary school classrooms?
- What are six reasons that classrooms are crowded, complex, and potentially chaotic?
- What strategies are most likely to get a school year off to the right start for a teacher?
- What do experts say should be the basic approach to classroom management? What did Kounin find that effective teachers did differently than ineffective teachers did in managing the classroom?

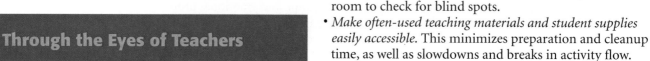

Review and Reflect *continued*

- What are the two main goals of effective classroom management?

Reflect

- Which would probably be easier for you to manage—an elementary school classroom or a high school classroom? Why?

DESIGNING THE PHYSICAL ENVIRONMENT OF THE CLASSROOM

When thinking about effectively managing the classroom, inexperienced teachers sometimes overlook the physical environment. As you will see in this section, designing the physical environment of the classroom involves far more than arranging a few items on a bulletin board.

Principles of Classroom Arrangement

Here are four basic principles that you can use when arranging your classroom (Evertson, Emmer, & Worsham, 2003):

- *Reduce congestion in high-traffic areas.* Distraction and disruption can often occur in high-traffic areas. These include group work areas, students' desks, the teacher's desk, the pencil sharpener, bookshelves, computer stations, and storage locations. Separate these areas from each other as much as possible and make sure they are easily accessible.
- *Make sure that you can easily see all students.* An important management task is to carefully monitor students. To do this, you will need to be able to see all students at all times. Make sure there is a clear line of sight between your desk, instructional locations, students' desks, and all student work areas. Stand in different parts of the room to check for blind spots.
- *Make often-used teaching materials and student supplies easily accessible.* This minimizes preparation and cleanup time, as well as slowdowns and breaks in activity flow.
- *Make sure that students can easily observe whole-class presentations.* Establish where you and your students will be located when whole-class presentations take place. For these activities, students should not have to move their chairs or stretch their necks. To find out how well your students can see from their locations, sit in their seats in different parts of the room.

Arrangement Style

In thinking about how you will organize the classroom's physical space, you should ask yourself what type of instructional activity students will mainly be engaged in (whole-class, small-group, individual assignments, etc.). Consider the physical arrangements that will best support that type of activity (Crane, 2001; Fickes, 2001).

Standard Classroom Arrangements Figure 14.2 shows a number of classroom arrangement styles: auditorium, face-to-face, off-set, seminar, and cluster (Renne, 1997). In

---

Through the Eyes of Teachers

Hissing Cockroaches and Mini-Cams

My classroom is set up with tables with about four students per table. This allows for individual or group activities without a lot of transition time or movement. Since my current subject is science, there is an aquarium with fish, a terrarium with a lizard or praying mantis, and a cage with Madagascar hissing cockroaches. There is a table with gadgets and mini-experiments. A mini-cam may be focused on an earthworm or a spider with the image on the TV as students enter the classroom. The idea is to arrange the classroom so that it promotes inquiry, questioning, and thinking about science.

William Williford
Science Teacher
Perry Middle School
Perry, Georgia

www.mhhe.com/santedu2e
Designing the Physical Environment of the Classroom
455

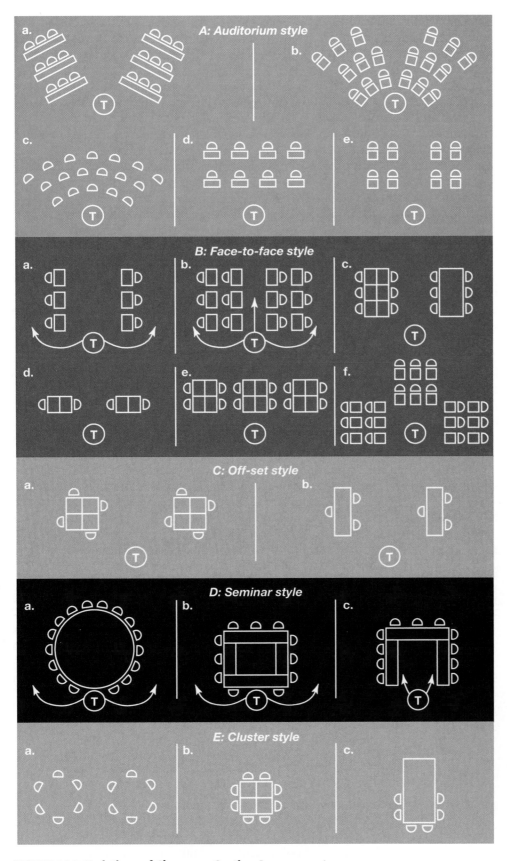

FIGURE 14.2 **Variations of Classroom Seating Arrangements**

**Your Classroom
Management Profile**

auditorium style A classroom arrangement style in which all students sit facing the teacher.

face-to-face style A classroom arrangement style in which students sit facing each other.

off-set style A classroom arrangement style in which small numbers of students (usually three or four) sit at tables but do not sit directly across from one another.

seminar style A classroom arrangement style in which large numbers of students (ten or more) sit in circular, square, or U-shaped arrangements.

cluster style A classroom arrangement style in which small numbers of students (usually four to eight) work in small, closely bunched groups.

traditional **auditorium style,** all students sit facing the teacher (see figure 14.2A). This arrangement inhibits face-to-face student contacts and the teacher is free to move anywhere in the room. Auditorium style often is used when the teacher lectures or someone is making a presentation to the entire class.

In **face-to-face style,** students sit facing each other (see figure 14.2B). Distraction from other students is higher in this arrangement than in the auditorium style.

In **off-set style,** small numbers of students (usually three or four) sit at tables but do not sit directly across from one another (see figure 14.2C). This produces less distraction than face-to-face style and can be effective for cooperative learning activities.

In **seminar style,** larger numbers of students (ten or more) sit in circular, square, or U-shaped arrangements (see figure 14.2D). This is especially effective when you want students to talk with each other or to converse with you.

In **cluster style,** small numbers of students (usually four to eight) work in small, closely bunched groups (see figure 14.2E). This arrangement is especially effective for collaborative learning activities.

Clustering desks encourages social interaction among students. In contrast, rows of desks reduce social interaction among students and direct students' attention toward the teacher. Arranging desks in rows can benefit students when they are working on individual assignments, whereas clustered desks facilitate cooperative learning. In classrooms in which seats are organized in rows, the teacher is most likely to interact with students seated in the front and center of the classroom (Adams & Biddle, 1970) (see figure 14.3). This area has been called the "action zone" because students in the front and center locations interact the most with the teacher. For example, they most often ask questions and are most likely to initiate discussion. If you use a row arrangement, move around the room when possible, establish eye contact with students seated outside the "action zone," direct comments to students in the peripheral seats, and periodically have students change seats so that all students have an equal opportunity of being in the front and center seats.

Figures 14.4 and 14.5 show two workable classroom arrangements, one in an elementary school and the other in a secondary school. Figure 14.4 portrays the arrangement created by a teacher who was assigned to a classroom with less space than he had had in previous years. His classroom also had been moved from the periphery of the school to its center, which meant that it did not have windows or permanent walls. Given the cramped space, the teacher decided to place students' desks in clusters. This arrangement is compatible with his emphasis on cooperative learning activities. A secondary school teacher's classroom arrangement is shown in figure 14.5. She even allows the students to move their tables into other configurations with which they feel more comfortable. The way she has arranged the tables facilitates small-group work. She has only two bulletin boards but tries to make them reflect her students' activities and accomplishments. As we see next, this "personalization" of the classroom is especially important.

Personalizing the Classroom According to classroom management experts Carol Weinstein and Andrew Mignano (1997), classrooms too often resemble motel rooms—pleasant but impersonal, revealing nothing about the people who use the space. Such anonymity is especially true of secondary school classrooms, where six or seven different classes might use the space in a single day. To personalize classrooms, post students' photographs, artwork, written projects, charts that list birthdays (of early childhood and elementary school students), and other positive expressions of students' identities. A bulletin board can be set aside for the "student of the week" or be used to display each student's best work of the week, personally chosen by each student.

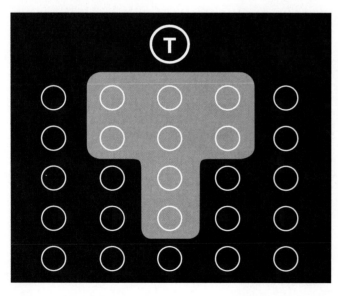

FIGURE 14.3 The Action Zone
"Action zone" refers to the seats in the front and center of row arrangement. Students in these seats are more likely to interact with the teacher, ask questions, and initiate discussion than students seated in more-peripheral locations.

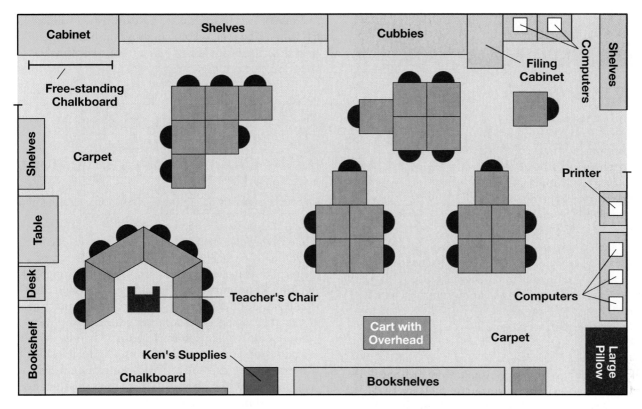

FIGURE 14.4 **An Example of an Effective Elementary School Classroom Arrangement**

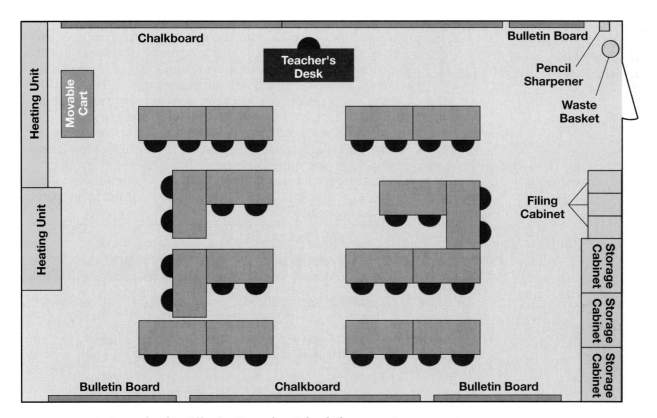

FIGURE 14.5 **An Example of an Effective Secondary School Classroom Arrangement**

Through the Eyes of Teachers

Tips on Classroom Arrangement

- Make areas of the classroom well defined.
- Arrange good traffic flow and storage.
- Safe, clean furniture is a must.
- It can be refreshing to rearrange the classroom during the year. Looking at the environment from a different angle puts a new perspective on people and things.
- Materials should be kept in the same places throughout the school year.
- A classroom should be bright and colorful with lots of materials and school memorabilia for students to read and look at.
- "My desk is always at the rear of the classroom. I keep a podium in one corner of the front and teach from there most of the time." (High school teacher)
- "My desk is in an open space that is easily accessible to students." (Middle school teacher)
- "I never stand in front of the classroom and speak. I constantly walk around the class, making contact with each and every student. I always make sure I am on the child's eye level when asking a question. Sometimes we sit in a circle so that I can be on their level." (Early childhood teacher)
- "I have one area where everyone can sit in one group for class lessons. I also like smaller areas where small groups can meet. Having students move about from one area to another gives students a chance to stretch. Small areas can also be set up to encourage learning about a specific subject area." (Special education high school teacher)
- See what other teachers do.
- Locate computers where they will not distract other students.

None of the classrooms we have described will exactly match yours. However, keeping in mind the basic principles we have described should help you create an optimal classroom arrangement for learning.

Teaching Strategies
For Designing a Classroom Arrangement

Follow these steps in designing a classroom arrangement (Weinstein, 1997; Weinstein & Mignano, 1997):

1. *Consider what activities students will be engaging in.* If you will be teaching kindergarten or elementary school students, you might need to create settings for reading aloud, small-group reading instruction, sharing time, group math instruction, and arts and crafts. A secondary school science teacher might have to accommodate whole-group instruction, "hands-on" lab activities, and media presentations. On the left side of a sheet of paper, list the activities your students will perform. Next to each activity, list any special arrangements that need to be taken into account; for instance, art and science areas need to be near a sink, and computers need to be near an electrical outlet.

2. *Draw up a floor plan.* Before you actually move any furniture, draw several floor plans and then choose the one that you think will work the best.

3. *Involve students in planning the classroom layout.* You can do most of your environmental planning before school starts, but once it begins, ask students how they like your arrangement. If they suggest improvements that are reasonable, try them out. Students often report that they want adequate room and a place of their own where they can keep their things.

4. *Try out the arrangement and be flexible in redesigning it.* Several weeks into the school year, evaluate how effective your arrangement is. Be alert for problems that the arrangement might be generating. For example, one study found that when kindergarten students crowded around a teacher who was reading a story to them, they often misbehaved (Krantz & Risley, 1972). Just spreading the children apart in a semicircle significantly decreased the misbehaviors.

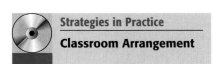

Strategies in Practice

Classroom Arrangement

Review and Reflect

2 **Describe the positive design of the classroom's physical environment.**

Review
- What are some basic principles of classroom design and arrangement?
- What are some standard styles of arrangement?

Reflect
- How would you design and arrange your ideal classroom? How would you personalize it?

CREATING A POSITIVE ENVIRONMENT FOR LEARNING

Students need a positive environment for learning. We will discuss some general classroom management strategies for providing this environment, ways to effectively establish and maintain rules, and positive strategies for getting students to cooperate.

General Strategies

General strategies include using an authoritative style and effectively managing classroom activities.

Using an Authoritative Style   The **authoritative classroom management style** is derived from Diana Baumrind's (1971, 1996) parenting styles, which were discussed in chapter 3, "Social Contexts and Socioemotional Development" ◄ p. 74. Like authoritative parents, authoritative teachers have students who tend to be self-reliant, delay gratification, get along well with their peers, and show high self-esteem. An authoritative strategy of classroom management encourages students to be independent thinkers and doers but still involves effective monitoring. Authoritative teachers engage students in considerable verbal give-and-take and show a caring attitude toward them. However, they still declare limits when necessary. Authoritative teachers clarify rules and regulations, establishing these standards with input from students.

The authoritative style contrasts with two ineffective strategies: authoritarian and permissive. The **authoritarian classroom management style** is restrictive and punitive. The focus is mainly on keeping order in the classroom rather than on instruction and learning. Authoritarian teachers place firm limits and controls on students and have little verbal exchange with them. Students in authoritarian classrooms tend to be passive learners, fail to initiate activities, express anxiety about social comparison, and have poor communication skills. The **permissive classroom management style** offers students considerable autonomy but provides them with little support for developing learning skills or managing their behavior. Not surprisingly, students in permissive classrooms tend to have inadequate academic skills and low self-control.

Overall, an authoritative style will benefit your students more than authoritarian or permissive styles. An authoritative style will help your students become active, self-regulated learners.

Effectively Managing the Classroom Activities   We described some aspects of Jacob Kounin's (1970) work on classroom management earlier in the chapter. Kounin concluded that effective teachers differ from ineffective teachers not in the way they respond to students' misbehaviors but, instead, in how competently they manage the group's activities. Here we focus on some of the differences between effective and ineffective classroom group managers. Effective classroom managers:

- *Show how they are "with it."* Kounin used the term **withitness** to describe a management strategy in which teachers show students that they are aware of what is happening. These teachers closely monitor students on a regular basis. This allows them to detect inappropriate behavior early before it gets out of hand. Teachers who are not "with it" are likely to not notice such misbehaviors until they gain momentum and spread.
- *Cope effectively with overlapping situations.* Kounin observed that some teachers seem to have one-track minds, dealing with only one thing at a time. This ineffective strategy often led to frequent interruptions in the flow of the class. For example, one teacher was working with a reading group when she observed two boys on the other side of the room hitting each other. She immediately got up, went over to the other side of the room, harshly criticized them, and then returned to the reading group.

authoritative classroom management style A management style that encourages students to be independent thinkers and doers but still provides effective monitoring. Authoritative teachers engage students in considerable verbal give-and-take and show a caring attitude toward them. However, they still set limits when necessary.

authoritarian classroom management style A management style that is restrictive and punitive, with the focus mainly on keeping order in the classroom rather than instruction or learning.

permissive classroom management style A management style that allows students considerable autonomy but provides them with little support for developing learning skills or managing their behavior.

withitness A management style described by Kounin in which teachers show students that they are aware of what is happening. Such teachers closely monitor students on a regular basis and detect inappropriate behavior early before it gets out of hand.

Great Teachers Have Few Discipline Problems

Mark Fodness, an award-wining seventh-grade social studies teacher in Bemidji, Minnesota, gives this advice on managing the classroom:

The single best method of decreasing undesirable behaviors among students is by increasing the effectiveness of teaching methods. The best teachers have very few discipline problems, not because they are great disciplinarians, but because they are great teachers. To emphasize this point with one of my student teachers, I had her follow our class out the door and into their next classes. She later returned, amazed at what she had seen. Students who she had thought were very well behaved had been off-task or disruptive in other classrooms. In one room, where a substitute teacher was doing his best to fill in, she described students' behavior as "shocking." Yet in another class, where the teacher was presenting a riveting lesson on a novel, the same students once again were well behaved even though the teacher did not seem to be using any specific discipline strategy.

Many first-year teachers, and veterans alike, identify discipline as their number one teaching challenge. However, the best solution is to use exemplary teaching strategies. I asked my seventh-grade students to identify the characteristics of teachers who had well-behaved classes. Here is a sample of their responses:

- Well prepared
- Interesting
- Funny
- Organized
- Fair
- Caring
- Nice
- Energetic

However, by the time she returned to the reading group, the students in the reading group had become bored and were starting to misbehave themselves. In contrast, effective managers were able to deal with overlapping situations in less-disruptive ways. For example, in the reading group situation they quickly responded to students from outside the group who came to ask questions but not in a way that significantly altered the flow of the reading group's activity. When moving around the room and checking each student's seatwork, they kept a roving eye on the rest of the class.

- *Maintain smoothness and continuity in lessons.* Effective managers keep the flow of a lesson moving smoothly, maintaining students' interest and not giving them opportunities to be easily distracted. Earlier in the chapter when we discussed strategies for increasing academic learning time, we mentioned some ineffective activities of teachers that can disrupt the flow of a lesson. These included flip-flopping, unnecessarily pulling away from an ongoing event, and dwelling too long on something that students already understand. Another teacher action that disrupts the lesson's flow is called "fragmentation," in which the teacher breaks an activity into components even though the activity could be performed as an entire unit. For example, a teacher might individually ask six students to do something, such as get out their art supplies, when all six could be asked to do this as a group. In another fragmented teaching situation, a teacher who was making the transition from spelling to math told students to close their spelling books, then put away their red pencils, then close their spelling books (again), next put their spelling books on their desks but keep them out of the way. Then the teacher told the students to take out their math books and put them on their desks but keep everything off their desks but the math books. Next, the students were told to get out their black pencils. Clearly, this segmented instruction disrupted the flow of the transition from spelling to math.
- *Engage students in a variety of challenging activities.* Kounin also found that effective classroom managers engage students in a variety of challenging but not overly hard activities. The students frequently worked independently rather than being directly supervised by a teacher who hovered over them.

Creating, Teaching, and Maintaining Rules and Procedures

To function smoothly, classrooms need clearly defined rules and procedures. Students need to know specifically how you want them to behave. Without clearly defined classroom rules and procedures, the inevitable misunderstandings can breed chaos. For example, consider these procedures or routines: When students enter the classroom, are they supposed to go directly to their seats or may they socialize for a few minutes until you tell them to be seated? When students want to go to the library, do they need a pass? When students are working at their seats, may they help each other or are they required to work individually?

Distinguishing Rules from Procedures   Both rules and procedures are stated expectations about behavior (Evertson, Emmer, & Worsham, 2003). *Rules* focus on general or specific expectations or standards for behavior. An example of a general rule is "Respect other persons." An example of a more specific rule is "Gum chewing is not allowed in class." *Procedures,* or routines, also communicate expectations about behavior but they usually are applied to a specific activity and are directed at accomplishing something rather than prohibiting some behavior or creating a general standard. You might establish procedures for collecting homework assignments, turning in work late, using the pencil sharpener, or using equipment. You can develop procedures for beginning the day (for example, a procedure for "settling in" to the classroom—maybe a social item such as a riddle or brief note about school events), leaving the room (for example, to go to the bathroom), returning to the room (such as after lunchtime), and ending the day (for example, clearing off desks and leaving on time).

Rules tend not to change because they address fundamental ways we deal with others, ourselves, and our work, such as having respect for others and their property, and keeping our hands and our feet to ourselves. On the other hand, procedures may change because routines and activities in classrooms change. For example, in one classroom, a procedure or routine is established that when students enter the classroom they are to begin doing a problem on the overhead. However, one day the teacher changes the routine to allow students to work on an unfinished art project as their first activity.

Teaching Rules and Procedures   What is the best way to get students to learn about rules and procedures? Should the teacher make the rules and procedures, then inform the class about them? Should students be allowed to participate in generating rules and procedures?

Some teachers like to include students in setting rules in the hope that this will encourage them to take more responsibility for their own behavior (Emmer, Evertson, & Worsham, 2003). Student involvement can take many different forms, including a discussion of the reason for having rules and the meaning of particular rules. The teacher might begin by having students discuss why rules are needed and then move on to a number of individual rules. The teacher can clarify the rule by describing, or asking students to describe, the general area of behavior it involves. Students usually can contribute concrete examples of the rule.

Some teachers start off with a whole-class discussion of classroom rules. During the discussion, the teacher and the students suggest possible rules for the classroom and the teacher records these on an overhead projector, a chalkboard, or a large piece of chart paper. Then, the teacher and students arrange them into broad categories and develop titles for the categories. In some classrooms, this activity is followed by having students role-play each of the rules.

In some schools, students are allowed to participate in setting rules for the entire school. In some cases, student representatives from each room or grade level participate in generating schoolwide rules with guidance from teachers and school administrators. However, within individual classrooms, especially in elementary schools, it is uncommon for students to participate in creating rules. Most teachers prefer to create and present their rules, although as indicated earlier, they may encourage discussion of the rules. In secondary schools, especially high schools, greater

Through the Eyes of Teachers

"Put Out the Fire with as Little Water as Possible"

Here are some strategies that several successful teachers use to create a positive classroom environment and get students to cooperate with them:

Teacher No. 1
"One of the ways I create a positive classroom environment involves when a student has not followed directions. I basically remind the student with the usual, 'What's the rule?' If the student continues to disobey my rules, I try to follow the maxim, 'Try to put out the fire with the least amount of water possible.' Sure, it's a generality, but it does prevent a lot of pointless power struggles that often escalate into a contest, in which everyone loses."

Teacher No. 2
"I believe that students learn best when they feel comfortable. I make it a practice to greet students as they enter the room and find out how they are feeling so I can understand their behavior better. My students understand that they are free to move around but also know the situations in which it may not be appropriate to do so. During class time, rather than tell students they are wrong, I try to guide them to an accurate answer. This keeps a positive flow in the classroom and lets students feel successful. Outside the classroom, I also try to listen to students when they want to talk. Sometimes this happens in the lunchroom, where students feel free to approach me if they want to talk about something."

Video Lecture: Rule Setting

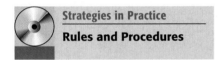

Strategies in Practice
Rules and Procedures

student contribution to rule setting is possible because of their more-advanced cognitive and socioemotional knowledge and skills.

Many effective classroom teachers clearly present their rules to students and give explanations and examples of them. Teachers who set reasonable rules, provide understandable rationales for them, and enforce them consistently usually find that the majority of the class will abide by them.

Teaching Strategies
For Establishing Classroom Rules and Procedures

Here are four principles to keep in mind when you establish rules and procedures for your classroom (Weinstein, 1997, pp. 53–56):

1. *Rules and procedures should be reasonable and necessary.* Ask yourself if the rules and procedures you are establishing are appropriate for this grade level. Also ask yourself if there is a good reason for the rule or procedure. For example, one secondary school teacher has a rule that students must come to class on time. Students are clearly told that if they are late, they will get a detention even on the first violation. She explains the rule to the students at the beginning of the school year and tells them the reason for the rule: If they are late, they might miss important material.

2. *Rules and procedures should be clear and comprehensible.* If you have general rules, make sure that you clearly specify what they mean. For example, one teacher has the rule "Be prepared." Instead of leaving the rule at this general level, the teacher specifies what it means to be prepared and describes specific procedures involving the rule: having your homework, notebook, pen or pencil, and textbook with you every day.

   As mentioned earlier, one issue that crops up when establishing classroom rules is whether to let students participate in making them. Involving students in generating classroom rules can increase students' sense of responsibility to abide by them, especially in secondary schools. Some students will suggest ridiculous rules, which you can simply veto. Some teachers will establish general rules and then ask students to generate specific examples of the rules.

3. *Rules and procedures should be consistent with instructional and learning goals.* Make sure that rules and procedures do not interfere with learning. Some teachers become so concerned about having an orderly, quiet classroom that they restrict students from interacting with each other and from engaging in collaborative learning activities.

4. *Classroom rules should be consistent with school rules.* Know what the school's rules are, such as whether particular behaviors are required in the halls, in the cafeteria, and so on. Many schools have a handbook that spells out what is acceptable and what is not. Familiarize yourself with the handbook. Some teachers go over the handbook with students at the beginning of the school year so that students clearly understand the school's rules regarding absenteeism, truancy, fighting, smoking, substance abuse, abusive language, and so on.

Getting Students to Cooperate

You want your students to cooperate with you and abide by classroom rules without always having to resort to discipline to maintain order. How can you get your students to cooperate? There are three main strategies: Develop a positive relationship with students, get students to share and assume responsibility, and reward appropriate behavior.

Develop a Positive Relationship with Students

When most of us think of our favorite teacher, we think of someone who cared about whether or not we learned. Showing that you genuinely care about students as individuals apart from their academic work helps to gain their cooperation. It is easy to get caught up in the pressing demands of academic achievement and classroom business and ignore the socioemotional needs of students.

One study found that in addition to having effective rules and procedures, successful classroom managers also showed a caring attitude toward students (Emmer, Evertson, & Anderson, 1980). This caring was evidenced in part by a classroom environment in which students felt safe and secure and were treated fairly. The teachers were sensitive to their needs and anxieties (for example, they created enjoyable activities the first several days of the school year rather than giving them diagnostic tests) and had good communication skills (including listening skills), and they effectively expressed their feelings to students. The classroom atmosphere was relaxed and pleasant. For example, the focus was on academic work but teachers gave students breaks and allowed them free time to read, use the computer, or draw.

The Child Development Project (CDP) is a comprehensive elementary school program in which teachers and administrators build supportive relationships with students and encourage students to develop similarly warm relationships with each other (Battistich & Solomon, 1995). Five instructional practices form the core of this project: (1) cooperative learning activities that facilitate teamwork; (2) a literature-based, values-rich, multicultural language arts program that encourages students to think critically about relevant social and ethical issues; (3) classroom management techniques that emphasize prevention and responsibility; (4) classroom and schoolwide community-building projects that involve students, teachers, parents, and extended family members; and (5) "homeside" activities that improve communication between students and parents, build bridges between schools and families, and encourage students' understanding of their family's heritage. Research evaluations of CDP in a large number of geographically diverse elementary schools revealed that students who participated in the project were more cooperative, had better social understanding, possessed more positive values, were more likely to help others, and had better conflict resolution skills than their counterparts who did not participate in the project (Battistich & others, 1989). Figure 14.6 presents some teaching guidelines for developing a positive relationship with students.

Get Students to Share and Assume Responsibility

Earlier in this chapter, we discussed the importance of developing an authoritative atmosphere in the classroom and the issue of whether students should be allowed to participate in establishing class rules. Some experts on classroom management believe that sharing responsibility with students for making classroom decisions increases the students' commitment to the decisions (Eggleton, 2001; Lewis, 2001; Risley & Walther, 1995).

1. Give a student a friendly "hello" at the door.

2. Have a brief one-on-one conversation about things that are happening in the student's life.

3. Write a brief note of encouragement to the student.

4. Use students' names in class more.

5. Show enthusiasm about being with students (even late in the day, week, or year).

6. Risk more personal self-disclosures, which help students see you as a real person. However, don't cross the line and go too far. Always take into account children's level of understanding and emotional vulnerability in disclosing information about yourself to them.

7. Be an active listener who carefully attends to what the student is saying, even if it is something trivial.

8. Let students know that you are there to support and help them.

9. Keep in mind that developing positive, trusting relationships takes time. This especially is the case for students from high-risk environments who might not initially trust your motives.

FIGURE 14.6 Guidelines for Establishing Positive Relationships with Students

Teaching Strategies
For Guiding Students to Share and Assume Responsibility

Here are some guidelines for getting students to share and assume responsibility in the classroom (Fitzpatrick, 1993):

1. *Involve students in the planning and implementation of school and classroom initiatives.* This participation helps to satisfy students' needs for self-confidence and belonging.

2. *Encourage students to judge their own behavior.* Rather than pass judgment on students' behavior, ask questions that motivate students to evaluate their own behavior. For example, you might ask, "Does your behavior reflect the class rules?" or "What's the rule?" Such questions place responsibility on the student. Initially, some students try to blame others or change the subject. In such situations, stay focused and guide the student toward accepting responsibility.

3. *Don't accept excuses.* Excuses just pass on or avoid responsibility. Don't even entertain a discussion about excuses. Rather, ask students what they can do the next time a similar situation develops.

4. *Give the self-responsibility strategy time to work.* Students don't develop responsibility overnight. Many student misbehaviors are ingrained habits that take a long time to break. One strategy is to be patient one more time than the student expects—difficult to do, but good advice.

5. *Let students participate in decision making by holding class meetings.* In his book *Schools Without Failure*, William Glasser (1969) argued that class meetings can be used to deal with student behavior problems or virtually any issue that is of concern to teachers and students.

Reward Appropriate Behavior   We have discussed rewards elsewhere, most extensively in chapter 7, "Behavioral and Social Cognitive Approaches" ◀ p. 208. You might want to read the discussion of rewards in that chapter again, especially the section "Applied Behavior Analysis in Education," and think about how rewards can be used in effectively managing the classroom. The discussion of rewards in chapter 13, "Motivation, Teaching, and Learning," also is relevant to classroom management, especially the information about rewards and intrinsic motivation ◀ p. 420. Following are some guidelines for using rewards in managing the classroom.

Choose Effective Reinforcers   Find out which reinforcers work best with which students and individualize reinforcement. For one student, the most effective reward might be praise; for another, it might be getting to do a favorite activity. Remember that pleasurable activities often are especially valuable in gaining students' cooperation. You might tell a student, "When you complete your math problems, you can go to the media area and play a computer game."

Use Prompts and Shaping Effectively   Remember that if you wait for students to perform perfectly, they might never do so. A good strategy is to use prompts and shape students' behavior by rewarding improvement. Some prompts come in the form of hints or reminders, such as "Remember the rule about lining up." Recall from chapter 7 that shaping involves rewarding a student for successive approximations to a specified target behavior ◀ p. 221. Thus, you might initially reward a student for getting 60% of her math problems right, then for 70% the next time, and so on.

Use Rewards to Provide Information About Mastery, Not to Control Students' Behavior
Rewards that impart information about students' mastery can increase their intrinsic motivation and sense of responsibility. However, rewards that are used to control students' behavior are less likely to promote self-regulation and responsibility. For example, a student's learning might benefit from the student's being selected as student of the week because the student engaged in a number of highly productive, competent activities. However, the student likely will not benefit from being given a reward for sitting still at a desk; such a reward is an effort by the teacher to control the student, and students in heavily controlled learning environments tend to act like "pawns."

❗ Review and Reflect

3 **Discuss how to create a positive classroom environment.**

Review
- What are some general strategies for creating a positive environment for learning?
- What are some hallmarks of good rules and procedures? How should rules and procedures be taught?
- What are the best approaches in getting students to assume responsibility?

Reflect
- In your classroom, what standards of "good" behavior would be nonnegotiable? Would you be flexible about some things? Explain.

BEING A GOOD COMMUNICATOR

Managing classrooms and constructively resolving conflicts require good communication skills. Three key aspects of communication are speaking skills, listening skills, and nonverbal communication.

Speaking Skills

You and your students will benefit considerably if you have effective speaking skills and you work with your students on developing their speaking skills. Let's first explore some strategies for speaking with your class.

Speaking with the Class and Students   In speaking with your class and students, one of the most important things to keep in mind is to clearly communicate information. *Clarity* in speaking is essential to good teaching.

Some good strategies for speaking clearly with your class include (Florez, 1999)

1. Using grammar correctly
2. Selecting vocabulary that is understandable and appropriate for the level of your students
3. Applying strategies to improve students' ability to understand what you are saying, such as emphasizing key words, rephrasing, or monitoring students' comprehension
4. Speaking at an appropriate pace, neither too rapidly nor too slowly
5. Being precise in your communication, avoiding being vague
6. Using good planning and logical thinking skills as underpinnings of speaking clearly with your class

"You" and "I" Messages   Let's examine another aspect of verbal communication. How often have you been involved in a conversation in which someone says something like this:

"Why are you being so negative?"
"You did not do what you said you were going to do."
"You are not very considerate."

These are examples of what communication experts call using **"you" messages,** an undesirable style in which speakers appear to judge people and place them in a defensive position. "You" communication does not always literally include the word *you*. "You" is implied when someone says,

"That was a really stupid thing to say" (which means "What you said was really stupid")
"Stay out of my life" (which means "You are intruding in my life")

Speaking and Listening Skills

"you" messages Undesirable messages in which speakers appear to judge people and place them in a defensive position.

It is easy for you and your students to fall into the trap of using too many "you" messages and not enough "I" messages, which are less provocative. **"I" messages** reflect the speaker's true feelings better than judgmental "you" statements.

Communication experts recommend replacing "you" messages with "I" messages:

"I'm angry that this has gotten so negative."
"I don't like it when promises get broken."
"I'm hurt when my feelings aren't taken into account."

"You" messages bog down conversation with judgments of the other person. "I" messages help to move the conversation in a more constructive direction by expressing your feelings without judging the other person. Monitor your own conversation from time to time to make sure you are using "I" messages rather than "you" messages. Also monitor your students' conversations and guide them toward using more "I" messages.

Assertive Communication

Being Assertive   Another aspect of verbal communication involves how people deal with conflict, which can be done in four styles: aggressive, manipulative, passive, or assertive. People who use an **aggressive style** run roughshod over others. They demand, are abrasive, and act in hostile ways. Aggressive individuals are often insensitive to others' rights and feelings. People who use a **manipulative style** try to get what they want by making people feel guilty or sorry for them. Rather than take responsibility for meeting their own needs, they play the role of the victim or the martyr to get people to do things for them. People who use a **passive style** are nonassertive and submissive. They let others run roughshod over them. Passive individuals don't express their feelings and don't let others know what they want.

In contrast, people with an **assertive style** express their feelings, ask for what they want, and say "no" to things they don't want. When people act assertively, they act in their own best interests. They stand up for their legitimate rights and express their views openly. Assertive individuals insist that misbehavior be corrected, and they resist being coerced or manipulated (Evertson, Emmer, & Worsham, 2003). In the view of assertiveness experts Robert Alberti and Michael Emmons (1995), assertiveness builds positive, constructive relationships.

Of the four styles of dealing with conflict, acting assertively is by far the best choice. Here are some strategies for becoming a more assertive individual (Bourne, 1995):

- *Evaluate your rights.* Determine your rights in the situation at hand. For example, you have the right to make mistakes and to change your mind.
- *State the problem to the person involved in terms of its consequences for you.* Clearly outline your point of view, even if it seems obvious to you. This allows the other person to get a better sense of your position. Describe the problem as objectively as you can without blaming or judging. For example, you might tell a student,

  "I'm having a problem with your humming in class. It is bothering me, so please don't do it anymore."
  "When you come in late, it disrupts the class and you miss important information."
  "Saying that to another student hurts his feelings."

- *Express your feelings about the particular situation.* When you express your feelings, even others who completely disagree with you can tell how strongly you feel about the situation. Remember to use "I" messages rather than "you" messages.
- *Make your request.* This is an important aspect of being assertive. Simply ask for what you want (or don't want) in a straightforward manner.

Here are some guidelines for making assertive requests:

- *Use assertive nonverbal behavior.* For example, establish eye contact, square your shoulders, remain calm, and be self-confident.

"I" messages Desirable messages that reflect the speaker's true feelings better than judgmental "you" messages.

aggressive style A way of dealing with conflict in which people run roughshod over others in demanding, abrasive, and hostile ways.

manipulative style A way of dealing with conflict in which people try to get what they want by making others feel guilty or sorry for them.

passive style A way of dealing with conflict in which people are nonassertive and submissive and don't let others know what they want.

assertive style A way of dealing with conflict in which people express their feelings, ask for what they want, say "no" to things they don't want, and act in their own best interests.

- *Keep your request simple.* One or two easy-to-understand sentences is adequate. For example, you might tell a student, "We need to go to the principal to get this straightened out."
- *Avoid asking for more than one thing at a time.* For example, don't ask the principal for a new computer and a new projector.
- *Don't apologize for your request.* Request directly, as in "I want you to . . ." Don't say "I know this is an imposition on you, but . . ." What if the other person responds with criticism, tries to make you feel guilty, or makes sarcastic remarks? Simply repeat your assertive request directly, strongly, and confidently.
- *Describe the benefits of your request.* Describing the benefits of cooperating with the request can be an honest offer of mutual give-and-take rather than manipulation.

If you feel that you are too aggressive, manipulative, or passive, work on being more assertive. An excellent book to read that can help you become more assertive is *Your Perfect Right,* by Robert Alberti and Michal Emmons (1995). When you are assertive and you help your students become more assertive rather than aggressive, manipulative, or passive, your class will run more smoothly.

Barriers to Effective Verbal Communication   Barriers to effective verbal communication include (Gordon, 1970)

- *Criticizing.* Harsh, negative evaluations of another person generally reduce communication. An example of criticizing is telling a student, "It's your fault you flunked the test; you should have studied." Instead of criticizing, you can ask students to evaluate why they did not do well on a test and try to get them to arrive at an attribution that reflects lack of effort as the reason for the poor grade.
- *Name-calling and labeling.* These are ways of putting down the other person. Students engage in a lot of name-calling and labeling. They might say to another student, "You are a loser" or "You are stupid." Monitor students' use of such name-calling and labeling. When you hear this type of statement, intervene and talk with them about considering other students' feelings.
- *Advising.* Advising is talking down to others while giving them a solution to a problem. For example, a teacher might say, "That's so easy to solve. I can't understand why . . ."
- *Ordering.* Commanding another person to do what you want is often not effective because it creates resistance. For example, a teacher might yell at a student, "Clean up this space, right now!" Instead, a calm, firm reminder such as "Remember the rule of cleaning things up when we are finished" works better.
- *Threatening.* Threats are intended to control the other person by verbal force. For example, a teacher might say, "If you don't listen to me, I'm going to make your life miserable here." A better strategy is to approach the student more calmly and talk with the student about listening better.
- *Moralizing.* This means preaching to the other person about what he or she should do. For example, a teacher might say, "You know you should have turned your homework in on time. You ought to feel bad about this." Moralizing increases students' guilt and anxiety. A better strategy in this case is not to use words such as *should* and *ought* but, instead, to talk with the student in a less condemning way about why the homework was not turned in on time.

Giving an Effective Speech   Not only will you be speaking in your class every day to your students in both formal and informal ways, but you also will have opportunities to give talks at educational and community meetings. Knowing some good strategies for giving a speech can significantly reduce your anxiety and help you deliver an effective speech.

Also, as most of us reflect on our experiences as students, we can remember few opportunities to give talks in class unless we took a specific class in speech. But not only can students be given speaking opportunities through formal presentations, but they also can participate in panel discussions and debates. All these activities give students opportunities to improve their speaking, organizational, and thinking skills.

Here are some guidelines for delivering a speech, which can benefit students as well as teachers (Alverno College, 1995):

- *Connect with the audience.* Talk directly to the audience; don't just read your notes or recite a memorized script.
- *State your purpose.* Keep this focus throughout the talk.
- *Effectively deliver the speech.* Use eye contact, supportive gestures, and effective voice control.
- *Follow appropriate conventions.* This includes using correct grammar.
- *Effectively organize the speech.* Include an introduction, a main body, and a conclusion.
- *Include evidence that supports and develops your ideas.*
- *Use media effectively.* This can help the audience grasp key ideas and varies the pace of the talk.

People often list fear of public speaking as their single greatest fear. If we give students more opportunities to practice public speaking, this fear likely would diminish. To help your students overcome this fear, give them plenty of opportunities to talk in front of a group and provide them with supportive advice (Santrock & Halonen, 2002). When they prepare for their talk, get them to rehearse the talk a number of times until they are confident they know the material. Tell them that most people fear talking in front of groups but that once they do it, their fear subsides. And get them to imagine how successful their talks are going to be.

Working with students on their speaking skills provides an excellent opportunity to invite someone from the community to come talk with your class. If a local college or university has a communications department, contact the department and ask one of the faculty to talk with your students about speaking skills or other aspects of communication. You also might have heard someone give a speech that you thought was outstanding; you might invite the speaker to come to your class and give students tips on how to give a great talk.

Listening Skills

Effectively managing your classroom will be easier if you and your students have good listening skills. Listening is a critical skill for making and keeping relationships. If you are a good listener, students, parents, other teachers, and administrators will be drawn to you. If your students are good listeners, they will benefit more from your instruction and will have better social relationships. Bad listeners "hog" conversations. They talk "to" rather than "with" someone. Good listeners actively listen. They don't just passively absorb information. **Active listening** means giving full attention to the speaker, focusing on both the intellectual and the emotional content of the message.

active listening A listening style that gives full attention to the speaker and notes both the intellectual and emotional content of the message.

The following are some good strategies for developing active listening skills (Santrock & Halonen, 2002). Incorporate these skills into your style of interacting with students and work with students to help them develop these skills:

PEANUTS reprinted by permission of United Features Syndicates, Inc.

Mission Impossible, Listening Skills, and Speaking Skills

Communication expert Michael Cronin (1993) says that students get the least amount of instruction about the form of communication they use most. They get considerable instruction in reading and writing but little or none in listening. As a result, a lot of students are poor listeners. Two days after listening to a ten-minute presentation, most individuals retain only 25% of what they heard.

To help remedy this problem, Cronin (1993) developed the interactive videodisc *Mission Impossible: Listening Skills for Better Communication,* which can be used to improve the listening skills of secondary school students. The videodisc provides instruction in identifying bad listening habits and improving active listening skills. A gamelike format teaches students how to develop active listening skills. Each activity involves a detective mission, and high scores are awarded "Super Spy" status. Humor also is built into the learning exercises to improve interest. Additional interactive media materials are available from the Oral Communications Program at Radford University in Radford, Virginia, where Cronin is a professor. These include

- *Coping with Speech Fright.* This software provides tutorial and simulation exercises to help students effectively manage their fear of public speaking. A student workbook also is included.
- *Constructing and Using Speaking Outlines.* Outlining exercises and techniques for using speaking notes in simulated rehearsals for a speech are included in this software, as well as methods for effectively practicing a speech with speaking notes and an analysis of examples of speech outlines.
- *Developing Key Ideas.* Students learn to identify the key aspects of messages. These exercises include a worksheet.

- *Pay careful attention to the person who is talking.* This shows the person that you are interested in what he or she is saying. Maintain good eye contact and lean forward slightly when another person is speaking to you.

- *Paraphrase.* State in your own words what the other person has just said. You can start your paraphrase with words such as "Let me see, what I hear you saying is . . ." or "Do you mean . . . ?" Use paraphrasing when someone says something that is important.

- *Synthesize themes and patterns.* The conversation landscape can become strewn with bits and pieces of information that are not tied together in meaningful ways. A good active listener puts together a summary of the main themes and feelings the speaker has expressed over a reasonably long conversation. These sentence stems can help you and your students get started in synthesizing the themes of a conversation:

    "One theme you keep coming back to is . . ."
    "Let's go over what we have been covering so far . . ."

- *Give feedback in a competent manner.* Verbal or nonverbal feedback gives the speaker an idea of how much progress the speaker is making in getting a point across. Good listeners give feedback quickly, honestly, clearly, and informatively. To read further about improving students' listening and speaking skills, see the Technology and Education box.

www.mhhe.com/santedu2e

Improving Speaking Skills
Improving Listening Skills

Nonverbal Communication

In addition to what you say, you also communicate by how you fold your arms, cast your eyes, move your mouth, cross your legs, or touch another person. Here are some examples of some common behaviors by which individuals communicate nonverbally:

- Lift an eyebrow in disbelief
- Clasp their arms to isolate or protect themselves
- Shrug their shoulders when they are indifferent

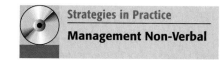

Strategies in Practice
Management Non-Verbal

What are some aspects of nonverbal communication that can help teachers interact more effectively with students?

- Wink one eye to show warmth and approval
- Tap their fingers when they are impatient
- Slap their forehead when they forget something

Indeed, many communication experts believe that most interpersonal communication is nonverbal. Even a person sitting in a corner, silently reading is nonverbally communicating something, perhaps that he or she wants to be left alone. And when you notice your students blankly staring out the window, it likely indicates that they are bored. It is hard to mask nonverbal communication and better to recognize that it can tell you how you and others really feel.

Facial Expressions and Eye Communication People's faces disclose emotions and telegraph what really matters to them. A smile, a frown, a puzzled look all communicate. Most Americans use more eye contact the more they like the other person. They avoid eye contact with people they dislike. However, ethnic variations in eye contact exist, with African Americans, Latinos, and Native Americans avoiding eye contact more than Anglo-Americans. In general, smiling and maintaining eye contact with your students indicates that you like them.

Touch Touch can be a powerful form of communication. Touch especially can be used when consoling someone who has undergone a stressful or unfortunate experience. For example, if a student's parent has become seriously ill or died, a student's parents have recently became divorced, or a student has lost a pet, gently touching the student's hand while consoling the student can add warmth to the communication. Because of concerns about sexual harassment and potential lawsuits, many teachers have refrained from touching students at all. Tiffany Field (1995), director of the Touch Research Institute at the University of Miami (Florida) and a leading expert in developmental psychology, believes that teachers should use touch appropriately and courteously in their interaction with students.

Space Each of us has a personal space that at times we don't want others to invade. Not surprisingly, given the crowdedness of the classroom, students report that having their own space where they can put their materials and belongings is important to them. Make sure that all students have their own desks or spaces. Tell students that they are entitled to have this individual space and that they should courteously respect other students' space.

Silence In our fast-paced, modern culture we often act as if there is something wrong with anyone who remains silent for more than a second or two after something is said to them. In chapter 10 we indicated that after asking a question of students, many teachers rarely remain silent long enough for students to think reflectively before giving an answer.

By being silent, a good listener can

- Observe the speaker's eyes, facial expressions, posture, and gestures for communication
- Think about what the other person is communicating
- Wonder what the other person is feeling
- Consider what the most appropriate response is

Of course, silence can be overdone and is sometimes inappropriate. It is rarely wise to listen for an excessive length of time without making some verbal response. Interpersonal communication should be a dialogue, not a monologue.

We have discussed a number of communication skills that will help you manage your classroom effectively. To evaluate your communication skills, complete Self-Assessment 14.1.

Evaluating My Communication Skills

Good communication skills are critical for effectively managing a classroom. Read each of the statements and rate them on a scale from 1 (very much unlike me) to 5 (very much like me).

	1	2	3	4	5
1. I know the characteristics of being a good speaker in class and with students.					
2. I am good at public speaking.					
3. I do not tend to dominate conversations.					
4. I talk "with" people, not "to" people.					
5. I don't criticize people very much.					
6. I don't talk down to people or put them down.					
7. I don't moralize when I talk with people.					
8. I use "I" messages rather than "you" messages.					
9. I do not have an aggressive style.					
10. I do not have a manipulative style.					
11. I do not have a passive style.					
12. I do have an assertive style.					
13. I'm good at giving my full attention to someone when they are talking with me.					
14. I maintain eye contact when I talk with people.					
15. I smile a lot when I interact with people.					
16. I know the value of silence in communication and how to practice it effectively.					

Scoring and Interpretation

Look over your self-ratings. For any items on which you did not give yourself a 4 or 5, work on improving these aspects of your communication skills. Both you and your students will benefit.

 Go to your Student Toolbox CD-ROM for an electronic version of this form.

ⓘ Review and Reflect

4 **Identify some good approaches to communication for both students and teachers.**

Review
- What are some barriers to effective speech? What are some principles of good speech?
- What can teachers and students do to develop active listening skills?
- What are some important aspects of nonverbal communication for teachers to understand?

Reflect
- What are your own communication strengths and weaknesses? What might you do to improve them?

DEALING WITH PROBLEM BEHAVIORS

No matter how well you have planned and created a positive classroom environment, problem behaviors will emerge. It is important that you deal with them in a timely, effective manner.

Management Strategies

Classroom management expert Carolyn Evertson and her colleagues (Evertson, Emmer, & Worsham, 2003) distinguish between minor and moderate interventions for problem behaviors. The following discussion describes their approach.

Minor Interventions   Some problems require only minor interventions. These problems involve behaviors that, if infrequent, usually don't disrupt class activities and learning. For example, students might call out to the teacher out of turn, leave their seats without permission, engage in social talk when it is not allowed, or eat candy in class. When only minor interventions are needed for problem behaviors, these strategies can be effective (Evertson & others, 1997, pp. 164–165):

- *"Use nonverbal cues.* Make eye contact with the student and give a signal such as a finger to the lips, a head shake, or a hand signal to issue a desist."
- *Keep the activity moving.* Sometimes transitions between activities take too long or a break in activity occurs when students have nothing to do. In these situations, students might leave their seats, socialize, crack jokes, and begin to get out of control. A good strategy is not to correct students' minor misbehaviors in these situations but, rather, start the next activity in a more timely fashion. By effectively planning the day, you should be able to eliminate these long transitions and gaps in activity.
- *Move closer to students.* When a student starts misbehaving, simply moving near the student will often cause the misbehavior to stop.
- *"Redirect the behavior."* If students get off-task, let them know what they are supposed to be doing. You might say, "Okay, remember, everybody is supposed to be working on math problems."
- *"Provide needed instruction."* Sometimes students engage in minor misbehaviors when they haven't understood how to do the task they have been assigned. Unable to effectively do the activity, they fill the time by misbehaving. Solving this problem involves carefully monitoring students' work and providing guidance when needed.
- *Directly and assertively tell the student to stop.* Establish direct eye contact with the student, be assertive, and tell the student to stop the behavior. "Keep your comments brief and monitor the situation until the student complies. Combine this strategy with redirection to encourage desirable behavior."
- *"Give the student a choice."* Place responsibility in the student's hands by saying that he or she has a choice of either behaving appropriately or receiving a negative consequence. Be sure to tell the student what the appropriate behavior is and what the consequence is for not performing it. For example, an elementary school teacher might say, "Remember, appropriate behavior in this class means not eating candy in class that you brought to school for lunch. If you choose to eat the candy now, you won't be allowed to bring candy as part of your lunch."

Managing Inappropriate Behavior

Moderate Interventions   Some misbehaviors require a stronger intervention than those just described—for example, when students abuse privileges, disrupt an activity, goof off, or interfere with your instruction or other students' work. Here are some moderate interventions for dealing with these types of problems (Evertson 1997, pp. 166–168):

- "*Withhold a privilige or a desired activity.*" Inevitably, you will have students who abuse privileges they have been given, such as being able to move around the classroom or to work on a project with friends. In these cases, you can revoke the privilege.
- *Create a behavioral contract.* In chapter 7, we described the concept of contracting, which involves putting reinforcement contingencies into writing. If problems arise and students don't uphold their end of the bargain, the teacher can refer to the contract the students agreed to. The contract should reflect input from both the teacher and the student. In some cases, teachers enlist a third party, such as another student, to sign the contract as a witness to the agreement.
- "*Isolate or remove students.*" In chapter 7, we also discussed the time-out, which involves removing a student from positive reinforcement p. 223. If you choose to use a time-out, you have several options. You can (a) keep the student in the classroom, but deny the student access to positive reinforcement; (b) take the student outside the activity area or out of the classroom; or (c) place the student in a time-out room designated by the school. If you use a time-out, be sure to clearly identify the student's behavior that resulted in the time-out, such as "You are being placed in time-out for 30 minutes because you punched Derrick." If the misbehavior occurs again, reidentify it and place the student in time-out again. After the time-out, don't comment on how well the student behaved during the time-out; just return the student to the activity that was interrupted.
- *Impose a penalty or detention.* A small amount of repetitious work can be used as a penalty for misbehavior. In writing, a student might have to write an extra page; in math, a student might have to do extra problems; in physical education, a student might have to run an extra lap. The problem with penalties is that they can harm the student's attitude toward the subject matter.

Students also can be made to serve a detention for their misbehaviors, at lunch, during recess, before school, or after school. Teachers commonly assign detentions for goofing off, wasting time, repeating rule violations, not completing assignments, and disrupting the class. Some detentions are served in the classroom; some schools have a detention hall where students can be sent. If the detention occurs in your classroom, you will have to supervise it. The length of the detention should initially be short, on the order of 10 to 15 minutes, if the misbehavior is not severe. As when using the time-out, you will need to keep a record of the detention.

Using Others as Resources Among the people who can help you get students to engage in more-appropriate behavior are peers, parents, the principal or counselor, and mentors.

Peer Mediation Peers sometimes can be very effective at getting students to behave more appropriately. Peer mediators can be trained to help students resolve quarrels between students and change undesirable behaviors. For

Through the Eyes of Teachers

Tips on Classroom Management and Discipline

- Make sure students know your expectations—academic and behavioral—from the first day of school.
- Exude confidence, even if you don't feel it. Have high but realistic expectations for your students and yourself.
- Teach "bell-to-bell."
- Observe and talk with teachers who seem to have a teaching style and values regarding teaching that are similar to your own; they are often helpful in suggesting strategies that will fit your style.
- Avoid power struggles. Yelling and condescending remarks usually make things worse.
- Students love knowing what to expect next. List on your board the agenda for the day. Set priorities for what needs to be done before free time.
- Set guidelines and see that they are followed. Change them if necessary.
- Having students help create classroom rules and procedures often assures more buy-in.
- Be clear with your students about what you expect. Let them see it in writing as well as hear it.
- Be consistent.
- A master teacher can provide you with encouragement and alternative approaches to curriculum frustrations or student struggles.
- Listen to your students. Immediate care is necessary if a student expresses fear for his or her safety at school or at home.

"*How come when you say we have a problem, I'm always the one who has the problem?*"
Phi Delta Kappan, vol. 74, no. 2, October 1992, p. 171. Reprinted with permission.

example, if two students have started to argue with each other, an assigned peer mediator can help to mediate the dispute, as described later in the chapter when we discuss conflict resolution.

Parent-Teacher Conference You can telephone the student's parents or confer with them in a face-to-face conference. Just informing them can sometimes get the student to improve behavior. Don't put the parents on the defensive or suggest that you are blaming them for their child's misbehavior in school. Just briefly describe the problem and say that you would appreciate any support that they can give you.

Enlist the Help of the Principal or Counselor Many schools have prescribed consequences for particular problem behaviors. If you have tried unsuccessfully to deal with the behavior, consider asking the school's administration for help. This might involve referring the student to the principal or a counselor, which might result in a detention or warning to the student, as well as a parent conference with the principal. Letting the principal or counselor handle the problem can save you time. However, such help is not always practical on a regular basis in many schools.

Find a Mentor Earlier we underscored the importance of students having at least one person in their life who cares about them and supports their development. Some students, especially those from high-risk impoverished backgrounds, do not have that one person. A mentor can provide such students with the guidance they need to reduce problem behaviors. Look around the community for potential mentors for students in high-risk, low-income circumstances.

Dealing with Aggression

Violence in schools is a major, escalating concern. In many schools it now is common for students to fight, bully other students, or threaten each other and teachers verbally or with a weapon. These behaviors can arouse your anxiety and anger, but it is important to be prepared for their occurrence and handle them calmly. Avoiding an argument or emotional confrontation will help you to solve the conflict.

Fighting Classroom management expert Carolyn Evertson and her colleagues (Evertson, Emmer, & Worsham, 2003) give the following recommendations for dealing with students who are fighting. In elementary school, you can usually stop a fight without risking injury to yourself. If for some reason you cannot intervene, immediately get help from other teachers or administrators. When you intervene, give a loud verbal command: "Stop!" Separate the fighters, and as you keep them separated, tell other students to leave or return to what they are doing. If you intervene in a fight that involves secondary school students, you will probably need the help of one or two other adults. Your school likely will have a policy regarding fighting. If so, you should carry it out and involve the principal and/or parents if necessary.

Generally, it is best to let the fighters have a cooling-off period so that they will calm down. Then meet with the fighters and get their points of view on what precipitated the fight. Question witnesses if necessary. Have a conference with the fighters, emphasizing the inappropriateness of fighting, the importance of taking each other's perspective, and the importance of cooperation.

Bullying Significant numbers of students are victimized by bullies (DeRosier, 2004; Espelage & Swearer, 2003; Woods & Walter, 2004). In one national survey of more than 15,000 sixth- through tenth-grade U.S. students, nearly 1 of every 3 students said that they had experienced occasional or frequent involvement as a victim

Handling Difficult Situations

Handling Peer Conflicts

Gangs and Victimization at School

" . . . and suddenly there were teachers all over the place!"

From *Classroom Chuckles* by Bill Knowlton. Copyright © 1968 by Bill Knowlton. Reprinted by permission of Scholastic Inc.

or perpetrator in bullying (Nansel & others, 2001). In this study, bullying was defined as verbal or physical behavior intended to disturb someone less powerful. Boys and younger middle school students were most likely to be affected. As shown in figure 14.7, being belittled about looks or speech was the most frequent type of bullying. Children who said they were bullied reported more loneliness and difficulty in making friends, whereas those who did the bullying were more likely to have low grades and to smoke and drink alcohol. In another recent study of more than 4,000 middle school students in Maryland, 31% reported being victimized three or more times in the past year (Haynie & others, 2001). Also, children with disabilities may be at risk for being bullied more than other children (Rigby, 2002, 2004).

Victims of bullying have been found to have certain characteristics (Dill, Vernberg, & Fonagy, 2004; Eslea & others, 2004; Hannish & Guerra, 2004). One recent study found that victims of bullies had parents who were intrusive, demanding, and unresponsive with their children (Ladd & Kochenderfer-Ladd, 2002). Also in this study, parent-child relationships characterized by intense closeness were linked with higher levels of peer victimization in boys. Such intense closeness promotes self-doubts and worries, which are perceived as weaknesses when expressed in male peer groups. Another study found that for both bullies and victims, the parenting they experienced was linked with their peer interaction, (Olweus, 1980). Bullies' parents were more likely to be rejecting, authoritarian, or permissive about their sons' aggression, whereas victims' parents were more likely to be anxious and overprotective.

Victims of bullies can suffer both short-term and long-term effects (Baldry & Farrington, 2004; Hay, Payne, & Chadwick, 2004). Short-term, they can become depressed, lose interest in schoolwork, or even avoid going to school. The effects of bullying can persist into adulthood. One longitudinal study of male victims who were bullied during childhood found that in their twenties they were more depressed and had lower self-esteem than their counterparts who had not been bullied in childhood (Olweus, 1993). Bullying also can indicate a serious problem for the bully as well as the victim. In the study just mentioned, about 60% of the boys who were identified as bullies in middle school had at least one criminal conviction (and about one-third had three or more convictions) in their twenties, rates that are far higher than the rates for nonbullies.

School climate may play a role in bullying, although few research studies have been conducted on this topic (Espelage & Swearer, 2003). A school climate in which adults and peers accept bullying fosters bullying. One study revealed that schools with high academic standards, high parental involvement, and effective discipline were characterized by reduced bullying (Ma, 2002).

An increasing number of prevention/intervention programs have been developed to reduce bullying. Following are two of the most promising programs and where you can obtain information about them:

- *Olweus Bullying Prevention.* Created by Dan Olweus, this program focuses on six- to fifteen-year-olds, with the goal of decreasing opportunities and rewards for bullying. School staff are instructed in ways to improve peer relations and make schools safer. A large study with 2,500 students in 42 schools in Norway found that the Olweus program was effective in reducing bullying (Olweus, 1994). Information on how to implement the program can be obtained from the Center for the Prevention of Violence at the University of Colorado (http://www.colorado.edu/cspv/blueprints).
- *Bully-Proofing Your School.* This program is tailored for students in kindergarten through the eighth grade and offers a schoolwide approach and a teacher curriculum for reducing bullying. It emphasizes how to recognize bullying behavior and quickly respond to it and how to develop students' communication skills in conflict situations. Intervention methods are provided, school posters related to bullying are available, and a parent's guide helps involve parents in effective ways to reduce

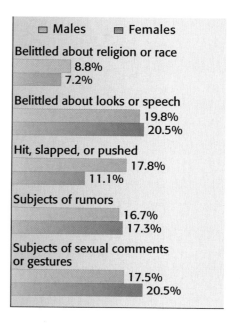

FIGURE 14.7 Bullying Behaviors Among U.S. Youth

This graph shows the types of bullying most often experienced by U.S. youth. The percentages reflect the extent to which bullied students said that they had experienced a particular type of bullying. In terms of gender, note that when they were bullied, boys were more likely to be hit, slapped, or pushed than girls were.

School-Based Crime Prevention

Gaining Control of Violence

Strategies for Dealing with Bullies

bullying. Recent research indicates that this program is effective in reducing bullying (Beran & Tutty, 2002; Plog, Epstein, & Porter, 2004). Information about the Bully-Proofing Your School program is available at http://www.sopriswest.com.

Teaching Strategies
For Reducing Bullying

To reduce bullying (Limber, 2004; Olweus, 1984),

1. *Develop schoolwide sanctions against bullying and post them throughout the school.*
2. *Form friendship groups for children who are regularly bullied by their peers.*
3. *Hold regular class meetings to discuss bullying among students.*
4. *Develop a schoolwide reinforcement program to "catch students being good."*
5. *Incorporate the message of the anti-bullying program into church, school, and other community activities in which children are involved.*
6. *Get older peers to serve as monitors for bullying and to intervene when they see it taking place.*

Defiance or Hostility Toward the Teacher Edmund Emmer and his colleagues (Emmer, Evertson, & Worsham, 2003) discussed the following strategies for dealing with students who defy you or are hostile toward you. If students get away with this type of behavior, it likely will continue and even spread. Try to defuse the event by keeping it private and handling the student individually, if possible. If the defiance or hostility is not extreme and occurs during a lesson, try to depersonalize it and say that you will deal with it in a few minutes to avoid a power struggle. At an appropriate later time, meet with the student and spell out any consequence the misbehavior might merit.

In extreme and rare cases, students will be completely uncooperative, in which case you should send another student to the office for help. In most instances, though, if you stay calm and don't get into a power struggle with the student, the student will calm down and you can talk with the student about the problem.

Classroom and School-Based Programs

A number of classroom and school-based programs for dealing with problem behaviors involve social competence enhancement and conflict resolution (Coie & Dodge, 1998).

Social Competence Enhancement Programs Some educational experts argue that coordinated school-based planning, high-quality curriculum and instruction, and a supportive school environment might be needed to deal with students' problem behaviors (Weissberg & Greenberg, 1998). These types of programs often try to improve the student's social competence by enhancing life skills, providing health education, and developing socioemotional skills.

Researchers have found that information-only or knowledge-only programs have minimal effects on decreasing students' problem behaviors (Kirby, 1992). In contrast, programs that teach broadly applicable personal and social competencies have been found to reduce students' aggressive behavior and improve their adjustment (Greenberg,1996; Weissburg & others, 1981). Such competency programs deal with subjects such as self-control, stress management, problem solving, decision making, communication, peer resistance, and assertiveness. Following are some examples of effective social competence enhancement programs.

The Improving Social Awareness–Social Problem Solving Project   This program is designed for elementary school students (Elias & others, 1991). During the instructional phase, teachers use scripted lessons to introduce classroom activities. The lessons follow this format: (1) group sharing of interpersonal successes, problem situations, and feelings that students wish to share with the teacher and other students; (2) a brief overview of cognitive, emotional, or behavioral skills to be taught during the lesson; (3) written and video presentations of situations that call for and model skill application; (4) discussion of the situations and ways to use the new skills; (5) role-playing that encourages behavioral rehearsal of skills; and (6) summary and review. Teachers also integrate problem-solving and social-awareness activities into the regular classroom routine and their daily instruction. Evaluations indicate that the program has been positive in helping students cope with everyday problem situations and reduce their violent behaviors (Elias & others, 1986).

The Social Competence Program for Young Adolescents   This 45-session program for middle school students provides classroom-based instruction and establishes environmental supports designed to (1) promote social competence by increasing self-control, managing stress, engaging in responsible decision making, solving social problems, and improving communication skills; (2) improve communication between school personnel and students; and (3) prevent antisocial and aggressive behavior, substance abuse, and high-risk sexual behaviors (Weissberg & Caplan, 1994). Evaluations of the social competence program have been positive. Students involved in the program show fewer aggressive behaviors, more consideration of alternative solutions to problems, improved stress management strategies, and more prosocial values than control groups (Weissberg, Barton, & Shriver, 1997). Teachers who have participated in the program indicate that it addresses important issues that are important for their students and helps them communicate better with students. A program that emphasizes cultural sensitivity as part of social competence enhancement is described in the Diversity and Education interlude.

Diversity and Education
Cultural Sensitivity, Social Development, and Collaboration with the Community

---

In an ideal world, the combined efforts of responsible parents, quality child care, health care services, and family-centered communities would provide the necessary foundations for children to come to school ready to learn (Weissberg & Greenberg, 1998). But in the real world of your classroom, children will bring varying propensities to learn. Some will be highly motivated, others listless. Some will require little management; others will test your patience and coping skills.

   The growing diversity of students makes classroom management more challenging. You must be prepared to know and demonstrate sensitivity to the cultural and socioeconomic variations in your students (McLoyd, 1998). It is equally important to recognize the existence of differences within groups of students from ethnic minority and impoverished backgrounds. Without this knowledge and sensitivity, a trusting and mutually respectful relationship is difficult to establish.

   An increasing number of programs reveal that showing greater cultural sensitivity to socioculturally diverse students benefits these students when they are at risk for academic and emotional problems (Weissberg & Greenberg, 1998). One type of successful intervention program for at-risk youth from poor rural or inner-city minority settings involves ethnically and culturally compatible adults from the community who develop culturally relevant activities for students that include ethnically relevant theater, music, and dance productions (Botvin, Schinke, & Orlandi, 1995; Hudley & Graham, 1995).

Effectively intervening in the lives of high-risk students often consists of providing not only individualized attention but also communitywide collaboration for support and guidance. One program that focuses on communitywide collaboration was described by Roger Weissberg and Mark Greenberg (1998, pp. 920–921). It is called the New Haven Social Development Project and involves a high percentage of students from low-income, ethnic minority backgrounds (Kasprow & others, 1993; Schwab-Stone & others, 1995). Problem behaviors such as drug use, poor sexual decision making, delinquency, and truancy harm students' academic performance, health, and future. Many of the "problem behaviors had common roots, such as poor problem-solving and communication skills . . . and a lack of monitoring and guidance by positive adult role models."

The superintendent and board of education for the New Haven schools established a comprehensive K–12 social development curriculum. The project's mission was to help students "(a) develop a sense of self-worth and feel effective as they deal with daily responsibilities and challenges; (b) engage in positive, safe, health-protective behavior practices; (c) become socially skilled and have positive relationships with peers and adults; (d) feel motivated to contribute responsibly to their peer group, family, school, and community; and (e) acquire a set of basic skills, work habits, and values as a foundation for a lifetime of meaningful work."

The program consists of 25 to 50 hours of classroom-based instruction at each grade level." The curriculum emphasized self-monitoring, problem solving, conflict resolution, and communication skills; values such as personal responsibility and respect for self and others; and content about health, culture, interpersonal relationships, and careers." The program also involves "educational, recreational, and health-promotion opportunities at the school and community levels to reinforce classroom-based instruction. These included programs such as mentoring, peer mediation, leadership groups, an Extended Day Academy with after-school clubs, health center services, and an outdoor adventure class." In addition, a school-based mental health planning team focuses attention on developing a positive climate for learning in the school. Teachers reported that the program improved the social skills and frustration tolerance of more than 80% of the students in grades K–3. Also, secondary school students decreased their participation in fights, felt safer at school and in the neighborhood, and felt more positive about the future as the program progressed.

Consistency Management and Cooperative Discipline

The Three Cs of School and Classroom Management David and Roger Johnson (1999) created a classroom management program to deal with problems that cause disruptions and undermine learning. Their program emphasizes the importance of guiding students in learning how to regulate their own behavior. These are the three Cs:

- *Cooperative community.* Learning communities benefit when the participants have a positive interdependence on each other. They work toward attaining mutual goals by engaging in cooperatively structured learning activities p. 321.
- *Constructive conflict resolution.* When conflicts arise, they can be resolved constructively through conflict resolution training for all participants in the learning community.
- *Civic values.* There can be cooperative communities and constructive conflict resolution only if the learning community shares common civic values, values that guide decision making. These values include believing that success depends on joint efforts to achieve mutual goals and valuing others.

Support for Managing Learning-Centered Classrooms: The Classroom Organization and Management Program (COMP) The COMP program, developed by Carolyn Evertson and Alene Harris (1999), advocates a classroom management framework that emphasizes supporting students' learning and that guides students in taking responsibility for their own decisions, behavior, and learning. COMP emphasizes problem prevention, management and instruction integration, student involvement, and professional collaboration among teachers. The program is implemented through training workshops, classroom application, and collaborative reflection. Research has revealed that COMP results in positive changes in teacher and student behavior (Evertson & Harris, 1999).

Second Step   This program, which provides strategies for modeling, role-playing, and feedback that are designed to improve students' empathy and ability to manage their anger, is appropriate for preschool through ninth grade. Thirty lessons (35–45 minutes each) are intended to be used once or twice a week, and a parent guide is available. Research suggests that Second Step is effective in decreasing students' aggressive behavior and increasing their positive behavior toward others (Clayton, Ballif-Spanvill, & Hunsaker, 2001; Frey & others, 2001). Information about Second Step can be obtained at http://www. cfchildren.org/reachus.htm.

Carolyn Evertson *(center in red)* in a COMP classroom with Arlene Harris. They created a classroom management framework that emphasizes problem prevention. *What are other features of COMP classrooms?*

Skills for Life   This program seeks to improve students' self-control, responsibility, and ability to solve social problems and improve conflict reduction skills. It targets students from kindergarten through fifth grade. Classroom teachers are trained to help students develop these skills through the use of activities, class discussions, and workbooks. A parent workshop is also available. One research study with more than 1,800 students in kindergarten-fifth grade found that based on teacher ratings the program was effective in improving a number of student behaviors, including keeping their hands to themselves, not teasing or calling other students names, and reducing fighting and bullying (Manning, Mohole, & the Goodman Research Group, 2002). Information about the Skills for Life program is available at http://www.lessonone.org.

Video Observation: Managing Classrooms

Teaching Strategies
For Conflict Resolution

Here are some good strategies for conflict resolution in the classroom (Johnson & Johnson, 1995, pp. 64–66):

1. "*Don't attempt to eliminate all conflicts.*" Eliminating all violence does not mean getting rid of all conflict. For example, moderate conflicts can sometimes increase students' achievement, motivation to learn, and ability to solve problems. What is important is not eliminating conflict but helping students to learn how to manage it more effectively.

2. *Develop a supportive context.* The most effective conflict resolution programs attempt to do more than just change individual students. Rather, the goal is to change the school environment into a learning setting in which students live in accord with a standard of nonviolence. Creating a supportive context involves placing students in situations in which they are more likely to cooperate than to compete. In a cooperative context, conflicts tend to be resolved in constructive rather than destructive ways. Students are more likely to communicate effectively with each other, trust each other, and define conflicts as mutual rather than individual problems.

3. *Decrease in-school risk factors.* Factors that place students at risk for violent behavior include academic failure and alienation from classmates. Thus, aspects of the school that can support students' academic success and sense of belongingness should be monitored and improved in an effort to reduce violence.

4. "*Teach all students how to resolve conflicts constructively.*" Two types of conflict resolution programs are the cadre approach and the total student body approach. "In the *cadre approach*, a small number of students are trained to serve as peer mediators for the entire school." Johnson and Johnson (1995) believe this approach is not as effective as the *total student body approach*, in which "every student learns how to manage conflicts constructively by negotiating agreements and mediating schoolmates' conflicts." A disadvantage of the total student body approach is the time and commitment required from school personnel. However, the more students who are trained in conflict resolution, the more constructively conflicts will be managed.

One example of the total student body approach was developed by Johnson and Johnson (1991). Their Teaching Students to Be Peacemakers program involves both negotiation and mediation strategies. Students learn these negotiation steps: (1) Define what they want, (2) describe their feelings, (3) explain the reasons underlying the wants and feelings, (4) take the perspective of the other student to see the conflict from both sides, (5) generate at least three optional agreements that benefit both parties, and (6) come to an agreement about the best course of action.

Students learn these mediation steps: (1) Stop the hostilities, (2) ensure that the disputants are committed to the mediation, (3) facilitate negotiations between the disputants, and (4) formalize the agreement.

When students have completed negotiation and mediation training, the school or teacher implements the Peacemakers program by choosing two student mediators for each day. Being a mediator helps students learn how to negotiate and resolve conflicts. Evaluations of the Peacemakers program have been positive, with participants showing more constructive conflict resolution than nonparticipants (Johnson & Johnson, 1994).

 ENTER THE DEBATE

1. Should teachers withhold recess as a punishment for children who misbehave and/or don't finish their work?

2. What classroom management style should teachers use?

3. Should middle school teachers provide students with a list of rules and consequences for violating those rules?

 **Teaching Experience**

- **Ways to Hold Student Interest**
- **Keeping Student Engaged**
- **Being Centered as a Teacher**

! Review and Reflect

5 Formulate some effective approaches that teachers can use to deal with problem behaviors.

Review

- What are some minor and moderate interventions? Who else can help? How?
- What can the teacher do about fighting, bullying, and defiance?
- What are some features of effective classroom and school-based programs for dealing with problem behavior?

Reflect

- How worried are you about problem behaviors among the students you plan to teach? In view of your own current skills, personality, and values, what steps could you begin to take to prepare yourself for dealing with them?

Mrs. Welch was a new middle school language arts teacher. Prior to beginning her new position, she had developed a classroom management plan that mirrored the code of conduct for the school. She expected the students to behave respectfully toward her and toward their classmates. She also expected them to respect school property and the learning environment. In addition, she expected them to keep their hands, feet, and possessions to themselves. Minor behavioral infractions were to result in a verbal warning. Further infractions would net more severe consequences in steps: a detention, a referral to the office, and a call to the student's parents. Mrs. Welch was pleased with her management plan. She distributed it to students on the first day of class. She also distributed it to parents at the annual Back to School Night during the first week of school.

Darius, a student in one of Mrs. Welch's seventh-grade classes, was what Mrs. Welch termed "chatty." He was a very social boy and spent much of his class time talking to other students rather than working. Mrs. Welch tried moving him to different parts of the room. She tried seating him next to students to whom she had never seen him talk. This had no impact on his behavior. He simply made new friends and continued chatting, sometimes disrupting the class in the process. She tried seating him next to girls. This seemed to make things even worse.

Darius was very bright in addition to being very social. Although he was only in seventh grade, he was taking algebra with a group of mathematically advanced eighth-grade students. This was something of an anomaly in this school. In fact, it had never been done previously. The algebra teacher, Mrs. Apple, and Darius had a very good relationship. He *never* disrupted her class or misbehaved in any way in her class. Mrs. Apple was amazed to hear that Darius did not always behave appropriately in his other classes.

Mrs. Apple served as Mrs. Welch's mentor. She had helped Mrs. Welch write her classroom management plan and served as a sounding board when she had difficulties. At one point when Mrs. Welch was discussing her eighth-grade classes, Mrs. Apple referred to inclusion in the eighth-grade algebra class as "a privilege, not a right." She further told Mrs. Welch that she expected her students to behave appropriately at all times.

The next day Darius was particularly talkative in class. Mrs. Welch asked him to stop talking. He did but resumed his chatter within five minutes. When he began talking again, Mrs. Welch took him aside and told him loudly, "That's it, Darius. I'm going to have you removed from algebra class. You know taking that class is a privilege, not a right."

Darius was stunned. He sat quietly for the rest of the period but did not participate. He made no eye contact with Mrs. Welch or any other students. The rest of the day was something of a blur to him. He had no idea how he would explain this to his parents.

When Darius told his mother he was going to be removed from algebra for his behavior in language arts, she immediately went to see Mrs. Welch. She tried to tell Mrs. Welch that to remove Darius from algebra would be to deny him the free and appropriate public education to which he (and all other students) was entitled. Mrs. Welch held her ground and insisted that she could and would have his placement altered.

- What are the issues in this case?
- Is removal from algebra class an appropriate consequence for Darius? Why or why not?
- Do you think removal from algebra class will have a positive effect on Darius' behavior? Why or why not?
- What do you think Darius' mother will do now?
- How do you think Mrs. Apple will react when she hears about the situation?
- How do you think the principal will react?
- What should Mrs. Welch do?

Reach Your Learning Goals

1 Explain why classroom management is both challenging and necessary.

- Many management issues are similar across elementary and secondary school classrooms. However, these differences in elementary and secondary classrooms have meaning for the way classrooms need to be managed: Elementary school teachers often see the same 20 to 25 students all day long; secondary school teachers see 100 to 150 students about 50 minutes a day. Confinement, boredom, and interaction with the same people all day in elementary school can create problems. Secondary school teachers have to get the lesson moving quickly. They also might see a greater range of problems and their students can have more long-standing problems that are more difficult to modify. These problems can be more severe than those of elementary school students. Secondary school students might demand more elaborate and logical explanations of rules and discipline.

- Doyle described six characteristics that reflect the classroom's complexity and potential for problems: (1) multi-dimensionality, (2) simultaneous activities going on, (3) events occurring at a rapid pace, (4) often unpredictable events, (5) lack of privacy, and (6) classroom histories.

- Good strategies for getting off to the right start are to (1) establish expectations for behavior and resolve student uncertainties, (2) make sure that students experience success, (3) be available and visible, and (4) be in charge.

- The focus in educational psychology used to be on discipline. Today it is on developing and maintaining a positive classroom environment that supports learning. This involves using proactive management strategies rather than being immersed in reactive discipline tactics. Historically, the well-managed classroom was conceptualized as a "well-oiled machine," but today it is more often viewed as a "beehive of activity."

- Goals and strategies include (1) helping students spend more time on learning and less time on nongoal-directed activity (maintain activity flow, minimize transition times, and hold students accountable) and (2) preventing students from developing problems.

2 Describe the positive design of the classroom's physical environment.

- Basic principles of effective design of the classroom's physical environment include (1) reducing congestion in high-traffic areas, (2) making sure that you can easily see all students, (3) making often-used teaching materials and student supplies easily accessible, and (4) making sure that all students can see whole-class presentations.

- Classroom arrangement styles include auditorium, face-to-face, off-set, seminar, and cluster. It is important to personalize the classroom and become an environmental designer who considers what activities students will be engaging in, draw up a floor plan, involve students in classroom design, and try out the arrangement and be flexible in redesigning it.

3 Discuss how to create a positive classroom environment.

- Use an authoritative style of classroom management rather than an authoritarian or permissive style. The authoritative style involves considerable verbal give-and-take with students, a caring attitude toward students, and limits on student behavior when necessary. Authoritative teaching is linked with competent student behavior. Kounin's work revealed other characteristics that were associated with effective classroom management: exhibiting withitness, coping with overlapping situations, maintaining smoothness and continuity in lessons, and engaging students in a variety of challenging activities.

- Distinguish between rules and procedures and consider the appropriateness of including students in the discussion and generation of rules. Classroom rules should be (1) reasonable and necessary, (2) clear and comprehensible, (3) consistent with instructional and learning goals, and (4) compatible with school rules.

- Getting students to cooperate involves (1) developing a positive relationship with students, (2) getting students to share and assume responsibility (involve students in the planning and implementation of school and classroom initiatives, encourage students to judge their own behavior, don't accept excuses, and give the self-responsibility strategy time to work), and (3) rewarding appropriate behavior (choose effective reinforcers, use prompts and shaping effectively, and use rewards to provide information about mastery).

4 **Identify some good approaches to communication for both students and teachers.**

- You and your students will benefit considerably if you have effective speaking skills and you work with your students on developing their speaking skills. Speaking effectively with the class and students involves being a clear communicator, using "I" messages, being assertive, and avoiding barriers to verbal communication. Both teachers and students can benefit from knowing how to give speeches effectively.

- Be an active listener. Active listening occurs when a person gives full attention to the speaker, focusing on both the intellectual and the emotional content of the message. Some good active listening strategies are to (1) pay careful attention to the person who is talking, including maintaining eye contact; (2) paraphrase; (3) synthesize themes and patterns; and (4) give feedback in a competent manner.

- A number of communication experts believe that the majority of communication is nonverbal rather than verbal. It is hard to mask nonverbal communication, so a good strategy is to recognize that nonverbal communication usually reflects how a person really feels. Nonverbal communication involves facial expressions and eye communication, touch, space, and silence.

5 **Formulate some effective approaches that teachers can use to deal with problem behaviors.**

- Interventions can be characterized as minor or moderate. Minor interventions involve using nonverbal cues, keeping the activity moving, moving closer to students, redirecting the behavior, giving needed instruction, directly and assertively telling the student to stop the behavior, and giving the student a choice. Moderate interventions include withholding a privilege or a desired activity, creating a behavioral contract, isolating or removing students, and imposing a penalty or detention. A good management strategy is to have supportive resources. These include using peers as mediators, calling on parents for support, enlisting the help of a principal or counselor, and finding a mentor for the student.

- Violence is a major, escalating concern in schools. Be prepared for aggressive actions on the part of students so that you can calmly cope with them. Try to avoid an argument or emotional confrontation. There are some helpful guidelines for dealing with fighting, bullying, and defiance or hostility toward the teacher. Effective programs for managing classroom behavior include social competence enhancement programs, the three Cs of school and classroom management, support for managing learner-centered classrooms (the Classroom Organization and Management Program [COMP]), Second Step, and Skills for Life.

 KEY TERMS

PORTFOLIO ACTIVITIES

Now that you have a good understanding of this chapter, complete these exercises to expand your thinking.

Independent Reflection

Cultivating Respectful Student-Teacher Relationships. How self-disclosing and open should teachers be with students? It is important for teachers to develop positive relationships with students, but is there a point at which teachers become too close with their students? Write a personal reflection on this issue, incorporating thoughts about how it might relate to your future work as a teacher. (INTASC: Principle 6)

Collaborative Work

Creating Classroom Rules. List the rules you feel your students must follow. Describe how you might react when students break these rules. Then get together with 3 or 4 of your classmates and discuss each other's lists. Revise your rules based on their feedback. (INTASC: Principle 5)

Research/Field Experience Reflections

Researching School Discipline Policies. Interview school counselors at an elementary, a middle, or a high school. Ask them to describe the discipline policies at their schools and to evaluate how well they work. Also ask them to describe the most difficult student problem they have ever dealt with. Write up that problem as a case study. (INTASC: Principles 5, 9)

 Go to the Online Learning Center for downloadable portfolio templates.

 TAKING IT TO THE NET

1. A classroom's organization, physical space, and design highly influence the overall learning environment. List several descriptors that depict your ideal classroom environment. Anticipate challenges, and discuss how you could compensate for a classroom lacking storage space, natural light, or special areas for computer or group work.

2. Make a list of rules for your classroom. Review the list and think about these questions: Are the rules worded in a positive manner? Are they appropriate and understandable for your target grade level? Did you consider involving your students in creating the rules? Design a class project for developing rules together as a collaborative group.

3. A student continually is disruptive in your class and has difficulty staying on-task. You have lost your temper occasionally and have sent the student to the office, all with no effect on the child's behavior. Develop a new discipline strategy for this child. What do you think the child needs in order to participate successfully in class?

Connect to the Online Learning Center to explore possible answers.

STUDY, PRACTICE, AND SUCCEED

 Go to chapter 14 on the Online Learning Center at www.mhhe.com/santrockedu2e to access the student study guide with practice quizzes, web links, portfolio resources, PowerWeb articles and news feeds, and the online resources referenced in the chapter.

 Go to your Student Toolbox CD-ROM to access the resources and activities referenced in the chapter and

• Resources to help you prepare for the PRAXIS II™ exam

• **Application Resources,** including additional *Crack the Case* studies, electronic versions of the *Self-Assessments,* Application Exercises, and Site Observation Questions

• **Study Resources,** including Learning Goals, the Chapter Summary, a *Test Your Learning* exercise, and multiple-choice, true/false, matching, key terms, and short-answer quizzes

• **Professional Resources,** including a Lesson Plan Builder and *Bibliomaker*

15 Standardized Tests and Teaching

> People do not have equal talents.
> But all individuals should have an equal opportunity
> to develop their talents.
>
> —John F. Kennedy
> *U.S. President, 20th Century*

Chapter Outline

The Nature of Standardized Tests

What Is a Standardized Test?
The Purposes of Standardized Tests
Criteria for Evaluating Standardized Tests

Aptitude and Achievement Tests

Comparing Aptitude and Achievement Tests
Types of Standardized Achievement Tests
High-Stakes State-Mandated Tests
District and National Tests

The Teacher's Roles

Preparing Students to Take Standardized Tests
Administering Standardized Tests
Understanding and Interpreting Test Results
Using Standardized Test Scores to Plan and
Improve Instruction

Issues in Standardized Testing

Standardized Tests, Alternative Assessments,
and High-Stakes Testing
Diversity and Standardized Testing

Chapter Learning Goals After you have completed your study of this chapter, you should be able to reach these learning goals:

1 Discuss the nature of standardized tests.

2 Compare aptitude and achievement testing and describe current uses of achievement tests.

3 Identify the teacher's roles in standardized testing.

4 Evaluate some key issues in standardized testing.

Teaching Stories Barbara Berry

Barbara Berry teaches French and humanities at Ypsilanti High School in Ypsilanti, Michigan, where she also is chairperson of the foreign languages department. She offers this story related to standardized tests:

I had a fourth-year French student who was a wonderful student and clearly had a gift for languages. A minority student, she had been recruited by a major state university and offered a "full-ride" scholarship, provided she met certain requirements on the Scholastic Assessment Test (SAT). She took the test and did well on the verbal part but not well enough on the math part to meet the scholarship requirements. She was taking her fourth year of math classes and receiving above-average grades but said she just didn't like math and didn't understand it.

Although I was teaching French at the time, I knew that I enjoyed math and had done well in school and on standardized tests. I knew that the SAT math section includes a lot of algebra.

I offered to tutor her before she retook the SAT. She accepted the offer. I obtained some algebra materials from the math department to help work with her. Mostly, though, she worked on her own, reading the book and doing problems, only coming to me when she encountered problems. We met about once a week. About six weeks later, she retook the test and improved her math SAT score by 110 points. She got the scholarship.

I did not teach this student much math, although I did help her work through some of the more difficult problems. What I did most to help her were two things: (1) I communicated my own enthusiasm for math and expressed confidence in her ability to do it, and (2) I focused her efforts on the material that the test assesses. Since we related so well with each other in my French class, I felt that I could help her feel better about her ability to do math.

Standardized tests are widely used to evaluate students' learning and achievement. Although they are increasingly used to compare students' performance in different schools, districts, states, and countries, they are not without controversy.

THE NATURE OF STANDARDIZED TESTS

Chances are, you have taken a number of standardized tests. In kindergarten, you may have taken a school readiness test, in elementary school some basic skills or achievement tests, and in high school the SAT or ACT test for college admission. But what does it mean to say that a test is "standardized"? And what purpose is served by standardized testing?

www.mhhe.com/santedu2e

The Educator's Reference Desk: Evaluation

What Is a Standardized Test?

Standardized tests have uniform procedures for administration and scoring. A standardized test often allows a student's performance to be compared with the performance of other students at the same age or grade level on a national basis. How are such standardized tests different from the tests you will construct as a teacher to assess your students' achievement? Teacher-made tests tend to focus on instructional objectives for a particular classroom. Standardized tests attempt to include material that is common across most classrooms (Airasian, 2005; Chatterji, 2003). Some other ways standardized tests differ from teacher-made tests are that many standardized tests have norms, and most have been evaluated extensively for their validity and reliability. We will discuss validity and reliability shortly, but first let's examine the purposes of standardized tests.

standardized tests Tests that have uniform procedures for administration and scoring. They assess students' performance in different domains and allow a student's performance to be compared with the performance of other students at the same age or grade on a national basis.

The Purposes of Standardized Tests

Standardized tests can serve a number of purposes:

• *Provide information about students' progress.* Standardized tests are a source of information about how well students are performing. Students in one class might get *A*s but perform at a mediocre level on a nationally standardized test, and students in another class might get *B*s and do extremely well on the same nationally standardized test. Without an external, objective marker such as a standardized test,

What are some of the most important purposes of standardized tests?

individual classroom teachers have difficulty knowing how well their students are performing compared with students elsewhere in the state or nation.

• *Diagnose students' strengths and weaknesses.* Standardized tests also can provide information about a student's learning strengths or weaknesses (Popham, 2005). For example, a student who is not doing well in reading might be given one or more standardized tests to pinpoint the student's learning weaknesses. When standardized tests are given for diagnostic purposes, they usually are given individually rather than to a group of students.

In a recent national survey, teachers said that they often use standardized test results to help diagnose what individuals need in the way of instruction (Quality Counts, 2001). However, less than 20% of the teachers said that they have had adequate training in interpreting test scores for appropriate diagnosis of students.

• *Provide evidence for placement of students in specific programs.* Standardized tests can be used to make decisions about whether a student should be allowed to enter a specific program. In elementary school, a standardized test might be used to provide information for placing students in different reading groups. In high school, a standardized test might be used to determine which math classes a student should take. In some cases, standardized tests are used along with other information to evaluate whether a student might be allowed to skip a grade or to graduate. Students also might take standardized tests to determine their suitability for particular careers.

• *Provide information for planning and improving instruction.* In conjunction with other information about students, scores from standardized tests can be used by teachers in making decisions about instruction. For example, students' scores on a standardized test of reading skills administered at the start of the school year can help teachers determine the level at which they need to gear their reading instruction. Students' scores on a standardized test at the end of the year might inform teachers about how effective their reading instruction has been, information that could be used to continue similar instruction or modify it accordingly. We will further discuss the use of standardized tests to plan and improve instruction later in the chapter.

• *Help administrators evaluate programs.* If a school changes to a new educational program, the school administration will want to know how effective the new

Video Lecture: Standardized Testing

program is. One way to determine this is to give students relevant standardized tests to see how they are performing under the new program. For example, a school might change from a basic-skills-and-phonetics approach to a combined basic-skills-and-phonetics and whole-language approach in teaching reading. Students' scores on a relevant standardized test of reading skills can be used along with other evidence to determine the effectiveness of the change.

- *Contribute to accountability.* Schools and teachers are increasingly being held accountable for students' learning. Although this is controversial, standardized tests are being used to determine how effectively schools are using tax dollars.

    In Texas, principals can lose their jobs if their school's standardized test scores don't measure up. In Maryland, schools that don't do well forfeit thousands of dollars in reward money. Interest in accountability has led to the creation of **standards-based tests,** which assess skills that students are expected to have mastered before they can be promoted to the next grade or permitted to graduate. Schools that use standards-based tests often require students who do not pass the tests to attend special programs in the summer that will help them reach the minimum level of competency required by the school system.

High-stakes testing is using tests in a way that will have important consequences for the student, affecting decisions such as whether the student will be promoted to the next grade or be allowed to graduate. Later in the chapter we will discuss state-mandated tests, which are increasingly being used to make such "high-stakes" decisions.

For now, though, note that an important theme throughout this chapter is that a standardized test should not be the only method for evaluating a student's learning. Nor should standardized tests by themselves be considered sufficient information in holding schools accountable for students' learning (Popham, 2005).

Criteria for Evaluating Standardized Tests

Among the most important criteria for evaluating standardized tests are norms, validity, reliability, and fairness.

Norms   To understand an individual student's performance on a test, it needs to be compared with the performance of the **norm group,** a group of similar individuals who previously were given the test by the test maker. The test is said to be based on *national norms* when the norm group consists of a nationally representative group of students. For example, a standardized test for fourth-grade science knowledge and skills might be given to a national sample of fourth-grade students. The scores of the representative sample of thousands of fourth-grade students become the basis for comparison. This norm group should include students from urban, suburban, and rural areas; different geographical regions; private and public schools; boys and girls; and different ethnic groups. Based on the student's score on the standardized science test, the teacher can determine whether a student is performing above, on a level with, or below a national norm (Aiken, 2003). The teacher also can see how the class as a whole is performing in relation to the general population of students.

In addition to national norms, standardized tests also can have special group norms and local norms. *Special group norms* consist of test scores for subgroups from the national sample. For example, special group norms might be available for students from low, middle, and high socioeconomic groups; for inner-city, suburban, and rural schools; for public and private schools; for female and male students; and for students from different ethnic groups. *Local norms* are sometimes available for standardized tests. These allow comparison of a student's performance with that of students in the same class, school, or district. Thus, evaluations of a student's test performance might differ, depending on what norm group is used.

Validity   Traditionally, validity has been defined as the extent to which a test measures what it is intended to measure. However, an increasing number of assessment experts

standards-based tests Tests that assess skills that students are expected to have mastered before they can be promoted to the next grade or permitted to graduate.

high-stakes testing Using tests in a way that will have important consequences for the student, affecting such decisions as whether the student will be promoted or be allowed to graduate.

norm group A group of similar individuals who previously were given the test by the test maker.

in education believe that it is important to emphasize that it is not just the characteristics of the test itself that are valid or invalid. Rather, it also is important to consider the inferences that are made about the test scores (American Educational Research Association, 1999; McMillan, 2001b). Thus, **validity** involves the extent to which a test measures what it is intended to measure and whether inferences about test scores are accurate.

In terms of the test characteristics themselves—the substance of the test—three types of validity can be described: content validity, criterion validity, and construct validity. A valid standardized test should have good **content validity,** which is the test's ability to sample the content that is to be measured. This concept is similar to "content-related evidence." For example, if a standardized fourth-grade science test purports to assess both content information and problem-solving skills, then the test should include items that measure content information about science and items that measure problem-solving skills.

Another form of validity is **criterion validity,** which is the test's ability to predict a student's performance as measured by other assessments or criteria. How might criterion validity be assessed for the standardized science test? One method is to get a representative sample of fourth-grade teachers to evaluate the competence of the students in their science classes and then compare those competence ratings with the students' scores on the standardized tests. Another method is to compare the scores of students on the standardized test with the scores of the same students on a different test that was designed to test the same material.

Criterion validity can be either concurrent or predictive (Gregory, 2000; Krueger, 2000). **Concurrent validity** is the relation between the test's scores and other criteria that are currently (concurrently) available. For example, does the standardized fourth-grade science test correspond to students' grades in science this semester? If it does, we say that test has high concurrent validity. **Predictive validity** is the relation between test scores and the student's future performance. For example, scores on the fourth-grade science test might be used to predict how many science classes different students will take in high school, whether middle school girls are interested in pursuing a science career, or whether students will win an award in science at some point in the future. Another example of predictive validity is how accurately students' scores on the SAT test predict their later grades in college and occupational success thereafter.

A third type of validity is **construct validity.** A construct is an unobservable trait or characteristic of a person, such as intelligence, creativity, learning style, personality, or anxiety. Construct validity is the extent to which there is evidence that a test measures a particular construct. Construct validity is the broadest of the three types of validity we have discussed and can include evidence from concurrent and predictive validity (Gronlund, 2003). Judgments about construct validity might also rely on a description of the development of the test, the pattern of the relations between the test and other significant factors (such as high correlations with similar tests and low correlations with tests measuring different constructs), and any other type of evidence that contributes to understanding the meaning of test scores. Because a construct typically is abstract, a variety of evidence may be needed to determine whether a test validly measures a particular construct.

Earlier we indicated that it is important to consider not only the substance of the test in determining validity but also whether inferences about the test scores are accurate (McMillan, 2001b). Let's look at an example of how this might work. A school superintendent decides to use test scores from a standardized test given to students each spring as an indicator of teacher competence. In other words, the test scores are being used to *infer* whether teachers are competent. These are the validity questions in this situation: How reasonable is it to use standardized test scores to measure teacher competence? Is it actually true (accurate) that teachers whose students score high are more competent than teachers whose students score low?

Reliability   **Reliability** is the extent to which a test produces a consistent, reproducible score. To be called reliable, scores must be stable, dependable, and relatively free from

Video Observation: Interpreting Test Scores

validity The extent to which a test measures what it is intended to measure and whether inferences about the test scores are accurate.

content validity A test's ability to sample the content that is to be measured.

criterion validity A test's ability to predict a student's performance as measured by other assessments or criteria.

concurrent validity The relation between a test's scores and other criteria that are currently (concurrently) available.

predictive validity The relation between test scores and the student's future performance.

construct validity The extent to which there is evidence that a test measures a particular construct. A construct is an unobservable trait or characteristic of a person, such as intelligence, learning style, personality, or anxiety.

reliability The extent to which a test produces a consistent, reproducible score.

errors of measurement (Fekken, 2000; Popham, 2002). Reliability can be measured in several ways, including test-retest reliability, alternate forms reliability, and split-half reliability.

Test-retest reliability is the extent to which a test yields the same performance when a student is given the same test on two occasions. Thus, if the standardized fourth-grade science test is given to a group of students today and then given to them again a month later, the test would be considered reliable if the students' scores were consistent across the two testings. There are two negative features of test-retest reliability: Students sometimes do better the second time they take the test because of their familiarity with it, and some students may have learned information in the time between the first test and the second test that changes their performance.

Alternate-forms reliability is determined by giving different forms of the same test on two different occasions to the same group of students and observing how consistent the scores are. The test items on the two forms are similar but not identical. This strategy eliminates the likelihood that students will perform better on the second test administration due to their familiarity with the items, but it does not eliminate a student's increase in knowledge and increased familiarity with the testing procedures and strategies.

Split-half reliability involves dividing the test items into two halves, such as the odd-numbered and even-numbered items. The scores on the two sets of items are compared to determine how consistently the students performed across each set. When split-half reliability is high, we say that the test is *internally consistent.* For example, on the standardized fourth-grade science test, the students' scores on the odd-numbered and even-numbered items could be compared. If they scored similarly on the two sets of items, we could conclude that the science test had high split-half reliability.

Reliability is influenced by a number of errors in measurement. A student can have adequate knowledge and skill yet still not perform consistently across several tests because of a number of internal and external factors. Internal factors include health, motivation, and anxiety. External factors include inadequate directions given by the examiner, ambiguously created items, poor sampling of information, and inefficient scoring. When students perform inconsistently across the same or similar tests of their knowledge and skill, careful analysis should be made of internal and external factors that may have contributed to the inconsistency.

Validity and reliability are related. A test that is valid is reliable, but a test that is reliable is not necessarily valid. People can respond consistently on a test but the test might not be measuring what it purports to measure. To understand this, imagine that you have three darts to throw. If all three fall close together, you have reliability. However, you have validity only if all three hit the bull's-eye.

Fairness Fair tests are unbiased and nondiscriminatory (McMillan, 2004). They are not influenced by factors such as gender, ethnicity, or subjective factors such as the bias of a scorer. When tests are fair, students have the opportunity to demonstrate their learning so that their performance is not affected by their gender, ethnicity, disability, or other factors unrelated to the purpose of the test.

A common example of an unfair test is a test that puts a particular group of students at a disadvantage. This often occurs when there is something about the test that makes it more difficult for students with certain characteristics. For instance, suppose a test that is supposed to assess writing skills asks students to write a short story about a boy who practices very hard to be good in football and makes the team. Clearly, this type of item will be easier for boys than girls because boys are generally more familiar with the sport of football, so the test will be unfair to girls as an assessment of their writing stills. Consider also an item that might be used to assess reading comprehension. The reading passage is about a sailing experience. Thus, students who have had experience in sailing are likely to have an easier time reading and understanding the passage than those who have not. It is impossible to completely eliminate all unfair aspects of a test for every student but test makers can do much to create tests that are as fair as possible.

For students with disabilities, fairness often requires adaptations in administering the test. Many of the adaptations depend on the particular disability. The goal is to lessen

test-retest reliability The extent to which a test yields the same performance when a student is given the same test on two occasions.

alternate-forms reliability Reliability judged by giving different forms of the same test on two different occasions to the same group of students to determine how consistent their scores are.

split-half reliability Reliability judged by dividing the test items into two halves, such as the odd-numbered and even-numbered items. The scores on the two sets of items are compared to determine how consistently the students performed across each set.

the negative influence of the disability on the trait being tested. For example, for students with a hearing disability, be sure that the directions are written; for students with a visual problem, be sure that directions are given orally.

 Review and Reflect

 Discuss the nature of standardized tests.

Review
- What is meant by *standardized test?*
- What are the uses of standardized tests?
- What do norms, validity, reliability, and fairness have to do with judging the quality of a standardized test?

Reflect
- Can a test be valid but not reliable? reliable but not valid? Explain in your own words.

APTITUDE AND ACHIEVEMENT TESTS

There are two main types of standardized tests: aptitude tests and achievement tests. First, we will define and compare these types of tests. Then, we'll discuss some different types of achievement tests and their use for district-mandated, state-mandated, and national purposes.

Comparing Aptitude and Achievement Tests

An **aptitude test** is designed to predict a student's ability to learn a skill or accomplish something with further education and training. Aptitude tests include general mental ability tests such as the intelligence tests (Stanford-Binet, Wechsler Scales, and so on) that we described in chapter 4, "Individual Variations" (Kaufman & Lictenberger, 2002) ◀ p. 104. They also include tests used to predict success in specific academic subjects or occupational areas. For example, one aptitude test might be given to students to predict their future success in math, while another might be given to predict whether an individual is likely to do well in sales or medicine.

An **achievement test** is intended to measure what the student has learned or what skills the student has mastered (Andrews, Saklofske, & Janzen, 2001; Haladyna, 2002; Smith, 2001). However, the distinction between aptitude and achievement tests is sometimes blurred. Both types of tests assess a student's current status, the questions they use are often quite similar, and usually the results of the two kinds of tests are highly correlated.

The Scholastic Assessment Test (SAT) that you may have taken as part of your admission to college is usually described as an aptitude test ("SAT" used to stand for "Scholastic Aptitude Test"), but the SAT can be an aptitude test or an achievement test, depending on the purpose for which it is used. If it is used to predict your success in college, it is an aptitude test. If it is used to determine what you have learned (such as vocabulary, reading comprehension, and math skills), it is an achievement test.

Types of Standardized Achievement Tests

There are numerous types of standardized achievement tests. One common way to classify them is as survey batteries, specific subject tests, or diagnostic tests (Payne, 1997).

Survey Batteries   A *survey battery* is a group of individual subject matter tests that is designed for a particular level of students. Survey batteries are the most widely used national norm-referenced standardized tests (McMillan, 2004). Some common batteries

College Board Test Publishers
Achievement Tests Test Locator

aptitude test A type of test that is used to predict a student's ability to learn a skill or accomplish something with further education and training.

achievement test A test that measures what the student has learned or what skills the student has mastered.

are the California Achievement tests, *Terra Nova* Comprehensive Tests for Basic Skills, Iowa Tests of Basic Skills, Metropolitan Achievement Tests, and Stanford Achievement Test Series.

The Stanford Achievement Test Series has tests for three different levels: kindergarten to grade 1.5, grades 1.5 to 9.9, and grades 9 to 13.0. The battery can be customized to fit the needs of a particular district or school. The Stanford battery includes a number of subject matter tests at each level. For example, at the sixth-grade level, there are subject matter tests for reading, mathematics, language, listening, spelling, study skills, science, social studies, information use, and thinking skills.

Many survey batteries also contain a number of subtests within a subject area. For example, the Metropolitan Achievement Tests include reading as one of the subject areas at each level. The reading subtests on the Metropolitan Tests include vocabulary, word recognition, and reading comprehension.

In their early years, survey batteries consisted of multiple-choice items to assess the student's content knowledge. However, recent editions have increasingly included more open-ended items that evaluate the student's thinking and reasoning skills.

Tests for Specific Subjects   Some standardized achievement tests assess skills in a particular area such as reading or mathematics. Because they focus on a specific area, they usually assess the skill in a more detailed, extensive way than a survey battery. Two examples of specific area tests that involve reading are the Woodcock Reading Mastery Tests and the Gates-McKillop-Horowitz Reading Diagnostic Test (Mather & Gregg, 2001). Some standardized subject area tests cover topics, such as chemistry, psychology, or computer science, that are not included in survey batteries.

Diagnostic Tests   As we said earlier, diagnosis is an important function of standardized testing. *Diagnostic testing* consists of a relatively in-depth evaluation of a specific area of learning. Its purpose is to determine the specific learning needs of a student so that those needs can be met through regular or remedial instruction. Reading and mathematics are the two areas in which standardized tests are most often used for diagnosis (Berninger & others, 2001).

In many cases, diagnostic testing is done after considerable instruction already has taken place. An achievement test is sometimes used for diagnostic purposes (such as one of the reading tests just mentioned). In many circumstances, though, both observations and achievement tests will be used to make a diagnosis. A typical diagnostic sequence might involve (Payne, 1997) (1) informal observations by the teacher, (2) a survey battery, (3) a group diagnostic test, and (4) an an individual diagnostic test. Note that in this sequence, diagnostic tests can often be given in a group format or an individual format.

Test publishers of all national norm-referenced standardized achievement tests claim that their tests can be used for diagnosis (McMillan, 2004). However, for a test to be effective in diagnosis it should have several test items for each skill or objective that is measured, and many of these national tests fall short in this regard.

High-Stakes State-Mandated Tests

As the public and government have demanded increased accountability of how effectively schools are educating our nation's children, state-mandated tests have taken on a more powerful role (Hambleton, 2002; Popham, 2005; Posner, 2004).

States have mandated tests for many years but their emphasis has recently changed (Airasian, 2005). Prior to the 1990s, their content was not closely linked with what was actually taught and learned in the classroom. The early state-mandated assessments simply provided an overall view of how students in a state were performing in certain subject areas, especially reading and mathematics.

In the 1990s, efforts began to connect state-mandated testing to state-endorsed instructional objectives. Most states already have identified or are in the process of identifying objectives that every student in the state is expected to achieve. These objectives form the basis not only for state-mandated tests but also for such activities as teacher education and curriculum decisions (Whitford & Jones, 2000). Teachers are strongly encouraged to incorporate these objectives into their classroom planning and instruction. In many states, the objectives are reflected in the achievement tests that are given to every student in the state.

The Format of State-Mandated Tests   From a constructivist point of view, state-mandated tests have the wrong format, consisting mainly of multiple-choice items. Only seven states currently use essay or performance assessments (Quality Counts, 2001). When construction-based assessments are included, they typically involve short-answer items or writing prompts. Very few states include a portfolio as part of their assessment.

Almost all states use criterion-referenced scoring, which means that the student's score is evaluated against predetermined standards. Most states have a cut-off score (such as correct answers to 70% of the items) that the student has to reach to pass the test. Such tests also provide comparative scores.

Possible Advantages and Uses of High-Stakes Testing   A number of policy makers argue that high-stakes state-mandated testing will have a number of positive effects:

- Improved student performance
- More time teaching the subjects tested
- High expectations for all students
- Identification of poorly performing schools, teachers, and administrators
- Improved confidence in schools as test scores increase

Exploring State Standards

The widest uses of these tests for guiding the progress of individual students have to do with decisions regarding remediation, promotion, and graduation. Remediation consists of assigning students who do not do well on the tests to special classes. Such remediation usually occurs after school, on Saturday, or during the summer. Currently, thirteen states require and fund remediation strategies to help low-performing students reach state standards.

Many endorsers of state-mandated tests argue that students should not be promoted to the next grade without reaching a certain standard of performance on the tests. In this regard, the goal is to end social promotion (promotion based on the idea that students should not be left behind their age-mates). Currently, test-based promotion policies have been instituted in nine states.

State-mandated tests are also being used to determine whether a student should be allowed to graduate from high school in twenty-four states. Such a decision can have a major impact on a youth's future.

In addition, state-mandated tests are used to make decisions about school and staff accountability. Holding schools accountable means using test scores to place the schools in designated categories, such as watch/warning (which is publicly reported and implies that improvement is expected), probation (which usually requires the school to submit a comprehensive reform plan), failing/in crisis (which requires serious outside assistance in developing an improvement plan), accredited, accredited with warning, and nonaccredited.

Criticism of State-Mandated Tests   Critics of the state-mandated tests argue that state-mandated tests lead to these negative consequences (McMillan, 2002):

- *Dumbing down of the curriculum with greater emphasis on rote memorization than on problem-solving and critical thinking skills.* In one recent analysis, most state tests focused on less-demanding knowledge and skills rather than more-complex cognitive skills (Quality Counts, 2001). This narrows the curriculum and focuses it more on lower-order cognitive skills (Linn, 2000).
- *Teaching to the test.* Teachers increasingly teach knowledge and skills that are to be covered on the state tests (Gallagher, 2000). They spend inordinate amounts of

time on testlike activities and practice tests, with less time for actual teaching of important content and skills. In a recent survey, more than six of ten public school teachers said that state-mandated testing has led to teaching that focuses too much on state tests (Quality Counts, 2001). About two-thirds indicated that state-mandated testing was forcing them to concentrate too much on information that would be tested, to the detriment of other important areas.

- *Discrimination against low-socioeconomic-status (SES) and ethnic minority children.* This results when disproportionate percentages of these children do not meet the state standards, while higher-SES and non-Latino White students do. Researchers have found that students who are placed in the lowest tracks or remedial programs—disproportionately low-income and minority students—are most likely to experience subsequent inferior teaching and reduced achievement (Cooper & Sherk, 1989; Oakes, 1990). There is evidence that high-stakes state-mandated testing that rewards or sanctions schools based on average student scores can create incentives for pushing low-scorers into special education, holding them back a grade, and encouraging them to drop out of school so that the schools' average scores will look better (Darling-Hammond, 2001; Haney, 2000).

For these reasons and others, the American Psychological Association, the American Educational Research Association, and the National Council on Measurement in Education have issued standards for the use of tests, noting that test scores are too limited and unstable to be used as the sole source of information for any major decision about student placement or promotion. Test scores should always be used in combination with other sources of information about student achievement when making important decisions about students (National Research Council, 2001).

Because high-stakes state-mandated testing is relatively new, there is little systematic research on its consequences (McMillan, 2002). However, there are some serious concerns about the way high-stakes testing currently is structured. One concern involves the validity of the inferences that can be drawn from the results (National Research Council, 2001). Just documenting higher test scores does not mean that education has improved. Indeed, if the tests are assessing the wrong skills or are flawed, it could mean just the opposite. As yet, we do not know if the high-stakes testing is causing students to be better prepared for college and the workplace.

Yet another concern is the extent to which high-stakes testing is useful for improving teaching and learning—the ultimate goal of educational reforms (National Research Council, 2001). Most current high-stakes tests provide very limited information for teachers and administrators about why students do not perform well or how they can modify instruction to improve student achievement. Most of the high-stakes tests provide only general information about where a student stands relative to peers (such as scoring at the 63rd percentile) or whether the students have not performed well in certain domains (such as performing below the basic level in mathematics). Such tests do not provide information about whether students are using misguided strategies to solve problems or which concepts in a domain students do not understand. In sum, most current high-stakes tests do not provide information about the types of interventions that would improve students' performance or even yield information about their strengths and weaknesses.

We also know that it is not a good strategy to rely solely on a single test when making important decisions about students or evaluating schools. Multiple indicators, including grades, attendance, performance assessments, and percentage of students who go to college, also need to be considered. We also know that if state-mandated tests continue to be used, they need to be changed to better reflect higher-order thinking skills, not encourage teachers to teach to the test and not penalize students from low-income and minority backgrounds (Stansfield & Rivera, 2002). Later in the chapter, we will further discuss problems with the formats of high-stakes testing.

District and National Tests

In addition to state-mandated tests, a particular district might mandate standardized tests. Students also might take national tests.

District-Mandated Tests   In Spencerport, New York, the school district collects information about student performance with the following tests: the Stanford Achievement Test in Reading (grades 2–8) and Math (grades 1–8); the New York State Pupil Evaluation Test in Reading (grades 3–6), Written Expression (grade 5), and Mathematics (grades 3 and 6); the New York State Program Evaluation Test, which assesses programs in science and social studies; the New York Preliminary Competency Test, which is used to predict future success in reading, writing, and math (given in any grade); the New York State Regents Competency Test, which assesses competency in math, science, global studies, and U.S. history and government (given in high school to students who do not take the Regents Test); the Scholastic Assessment Test (SAT) and American College Test (ACT), given to students who plan to apply to college; and Advanced Placement tests in U.S. history, biology, chemistry, English literature and composition, French, Spanish, calculus, and music theory, which can be taken by students to place out of certain classes because of the knowledge and skill levels they have attained. In 1999, Spencerport also began assessing students' ability to apply knowledge and problem-solving skills in a number of subject areas.

Types of standardized tests vary across school districts. However, as in the Spencerport school district, the overall number is typically large.

No Child Left Behind   In chapter 1, we described the No Child Left Behind (NCLB) act, the federal government's legislation that was signed into law in 2002. NCLB is the U.S. government's effort to hold schools and school districts accountable for the success or failure of their students. The legislation shifts responsibility to the states, with states being required to create their own standards for students' achievement in mathematics, English/language arts, and science. By 2005-2006, states are required to give all students annual tests in grades 3 through 8. States also must create an accountability system that ensures students are making adequate annual progress in the subject areas mentioned above. Although all students must show adequate progress, separate objectives are to be proposed for students who are economically disadvantaged, students from ethnic minority groups, students with disabilities, and students with limited English proficiency.

Schools that fail to make *adequate yearly progress (AYP)* for two consecutive years are labeled "underperforming." Underperforming schools are to be given special help, but they must give parents the option of moving their children to a better-performing school. If underperforming schools don't improve after four years, states are required to implement major staff and curriculum changes in the schools, and if progress is not made after five years, states must close the schools.

Also as part of the No Child Left Behind legislation, states and districts are required to provide report cards that show a school's performance level, so that the public is aware of which schools are underperforming. Another aspect of the No Child Left Behind legislation is that all teachers hired by 2005-2006 must be "highly qualified," which means

Through the Eyes of Students

"It's as If a Test Score Is All There Is to a Person"

"Spend enough time in school and you start to think that standardized tests are the only things that matter in life. My standardized test scores are disappointing but I take pride in being in the top four percent of my class. I have a 4.0 GPA. If I can pull off those kinds of grades in tough classes—including three Advanced Placement courses—I'm forced to wonder, what do these tests really prove?

"It's as if a test score is all there is to a person. I enjoy all kinds of creative writing, and I spend long nights trying to *understand* school subjects, rather than just memorize formulas. But none of this matter for standardized tests" (Garcia, 2001).

Tania Garcia
Twelfth-Grade Student
Oakland High School
Oakland, California

being licensed and having an academic major in the field in which they are teaching. Schools are required to notify parents if a teacher is not "highly qualified."

A number of criticisms of No Child Left Behind have been made. Some critics argue that the NCLB legislation will do more harm than good (Ambrosio, 2004; Fair Test, 2004; Neill, 2003). One widely adopted criticism stresses that using a single score from a test as the sole indicator of students' and teachers' progress and competence represents a very narrow aspect of students' and teachers' skills. This criticism is similar to the one leveled at IQ testing, described in chapter 4. To more accurately assess student progress and achievement, many psychologists and educators argue that a number of measures should be used, including tests, quizzes, projects, portfolios, and classroom observations— rather than a single score on a single test. Also, the tests schools are using to assess achievement and progress as part of NCLB don't measure such important skills as creativity, motivation, persistence, flexible thinking, and social skills (Droege, 2004). Critics point out that teachers and schools are spending far too much class time "teaching to the test" by drilling students and having them memorize isolated facts at the expense of more student-centered constructivist teaching that focuses on higher-level thinking skills, which students need for success in life (Posner, 2004). Further, critics say that the NCLB requirement that all students be taught by "highly qualified" teachers is likely to be unattainable (Berry, Hoke, & Hirsch, 2004). For example, in 2002 only 50% of U.S. teachers met the requirements specified by this aspect of NCLB.

Despite such criticisms, the U.S. Department of Education is committed to implementing No Child Left Behind, and schools are making accommodations to meet the requirement of this law. Indeed, most educators support the importance of high expectations and high standards of excellence for students and teachers (Revelle, 2004). At issue, however, is whether the tests and procedures mandated by NCLB are the best ones for achieving these high standards.

National Assessment and World-Class Standards The federal government also is involved in standardized testing through the National Assessment of Educational Progress (NAEP). States are not required to participate in the national assessment, although many do (for example, more than forty states have their students take the reading portion of the test). The NAEP is a censuslike examination of young Americans' knowledge, skills, understanding, and attitudes (Bourque, 1999; Payne, 1997). The subject areas include reading, writing, literature, mathematics, science, social studies, art, citizenship, and career and occupational development. NAEP assessments began in 1969 for science, writing, and citizenship. Care is taken not to identify any student, school, city, or state, although states can choose to have scores identified by state. Any student who takes the NAEP responds only to a portion of the entire assessment.

Recent findings from the NAEP (2000, 2004) show these trends:

- *Reading.* No improvement occurred from 1992 through 2003 for fourth-graders and a slight improvement occurred for eighth-graders from 1992 through 2003.
- *Mathematics.* Scores improved from 1990 through 2003 for fourth- and eighth-graders but showed a recent decline in 2000 for twelfth-graders (see figure 15.1).
- *Science.* No change in scores occurred from 1996 through 2000 for fourth- and eighth-graders but scores of twelfth-graders declined in this time frame.

The federal government has proposed a voluntary national test of fourth- and eighth-grade students' reading (Applebome, 1997). The hope is that it will become so widely used that it will become America's first truly national assessment of students' achievement. The national test would be similar to the NAEP reading and math tests and the math

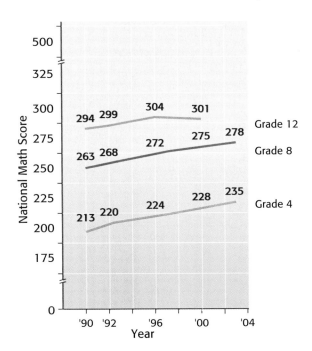

FIGURE 15.1 **Trends in Mathematics Scores in the National Assessment of Educational Progress**

Note: Scores could range from 0 to 500. Data for grade 12 were not reported in 2003.

component of the Third International Mathematics and Science Study (figure 15.2 shows some types of items that would be used on the national test). However, currently tests are given only to a sample of students to compute national averages. The new tests would assess a much greater number of students and evaluate individual students.

National assessment of students is part of an effort to get American students to measure up to, and eventually set the standard for, world-class achievement in education. In an analysis of national testing in twelve major countries, the United States and Canada were the only countries without a standardized national test (for example, most Asian countries, such as Japan, Thailand, and Singapore, have national tests) (Haynes & Chalker, 1997). In reading, American students do well against students from other countries during the elementary school years, but by the end of high school they have fallen behind students in many other countries. Among the reasons given for the poor performance of U.S. students are inadequate time spent on academic schoolwork, larger class sizes, too much time spent on television and nonacademic media, too little time spent doing homework, and inadequate spending on education (Ravitch, 1995).

At the time I am writing this book, the proposed standardized national test has not been approved by Congress, and it has been criticized by both liberals and conservatives. Many liberals are suspicious of standardized tests and believe they are culturally biased. Political conservatives are wary of expanding the federal government's role in education.

Critics of the cross-national comparisons argue that in many comparisons virtually all U.S. children are being compared with a "select" group of children from other countries, especially in the secondary school comparisons. Therefore, they conclude, it is no wonder that American students don't fare so well. That criticism holds for some international comparisons. However, even when the top 25% of students in different countries were more recently compared, U.S. students did not rank much higher (Mullis,

---

MATH

In 1995, most eighth-graders in the United States scored below the international average in math of students in the 41 countries involved in the Third International Mathematics and Science Study (TIMSS). Students at the international average can solve single-step problems and understand the basics of algebra and geometric terms. These questions show what a student at or above the international average should know:

(1) A rubber ball rebounds to half the height it drops. If the ball is dropped from a rooftop 18 feet above the ground, what is the total distance traveled by the time it hits the ground the third time?

  A. 31.5 feet
  B. 40.5 feet
  C. 45 feet
  D. 63 feet

(2) The table shows the values of x and y, where x is proportional to y. What are the values of P and Q?

TABLE	
x	y
3	7
6	Q
P	35

Answers
A. P=14 and Q=31
B. P=10 and Q=14
C. P=10 and Q=31
D. P=14 and Q=15
E. P=15 and Q=14

READING

Results from the National Assessment of Education Progress (NAEP) are reported by three levels of fourth-grade reading: basic, proficient, and advanced. These levels help to explain what it means to read well in the fourth grade. This passage, selected by the Department of Education from *Charlotte's Web*, by E. B. White, helps illustrate the kinds of skills expected of students at each level:

Having promised Wilbur that she would save his life, she was determined to keep her promise. Charlotte was naturally patient. She knew from experience that if she waited long enough, a fly would come to her web; and she felt sure that if she thought long enough about Wilbur's problem, an idea would come to her mind.

Finally, one morning toward the middle of July, the idea came. "Why how perfectly simple!" she said to herself. "The way to save Wilbur's life is to play a trick on Zuckerman. If I can fool a bug," thought Charlotte, "I can surely fool a man. People are not as smart as bugs."

• Students at the basic level are able to read the passage and then tell what Charlotte promised Wilbur.
• Students at the proficient level are able to describe why Charlotte thought she could fool Zuckerman.
• Students at the advanced level recognize that Charlotte compares waiting for ideas to entrapping a fly.

FIGURE 15.2 Items on National Assessments

1999). For example, in a recent comparison of the top 25% of high school seniors (in terms of math and science knowledge and skills) in different countries, Sweden, the Netherlands, Norway, and Switzerland ranked highest. The United States was still below the international average in math and science knowledge and skills, even when their best students were compared with other countries' best students.

An analysis of national standardized tests found that, compared with American standardized tests, other countries' tests (1) included more short-answer, open-ended, and essay questions and (2) were more closely linked with the curriculum and textbooks so that foreign students knew what they needed to study (Jacobson, 1996). Recently, publishers of commercial standardized tests in America have begun to include more constructed-item and performance assessments in their tests.

One of the dilemmas in pursuing internationally competitive standards involves deciding what they should be and who should set them (Tanner, 1997). Should they be based on the standards of the countries whose students achieve the highest scores on tests? What roles do the federal and state governments play in developing these standards? Which educators should participate in their creation? Should instruction be tied to the standards? Consensus on these questions has not yet been reached.

National Assessment of Education Progress

> ## ! Review and Reflect
>
> **2 Compare aptitude and achievement testing and describe current uses of achievement tests.**
>
> **Review**
> - How clearly do aptitude and achievement tests differ in purpose? in form?
> - What is meant by *survey batteries, specific subject tests,* and *diagnostic tests?*
> - Are standardized achievement tests generally good for diagnosis?
> - What is high-stakes state-mandated testing trying to accomplish? What are some hopes and fears about it?
> - What is the argument for national standardized testing? Why is it resisted?
>
> **Reflect**
> - What value do you see in the idea of globalized standards for what students learn in school? What problems?

THE TEACHER'S ROLES

The teacher's roles in standardized testing include preparing students for the test, administering the test, understanding and interpreting test results, and communicating test results to parents. Teachers also use test scores to plan and improve instruction.

Preparing Students to Take Standardized Tests

It is important for all students to have an opportunity to do their best. One way to do this is to make sure that students have good test-taking skills (McMillan, 2004).

It is important also for you to communicate a positive attitude about the test to students. Explain the nature and purpose of the test. Describe the test as an opportunity and a challenge rather than an ordeal. Avoid saying anything that can cause students to get nervous about the test. If you observe that anxiety in some students may hinder their performance, consider having a counselor talk with them about ways to reduce their test anxiety.

In this era of high-stakes testing in which scores on standardized tests can have serious consequences for students, teachers, and schools, many schools are establishing programs designed to improve students' test-taking skills (Payne, 1997). However,

Teacher Competence in Educational Assessment

researchers have found that "coaching" or training students to do well on a test, such as the SAT, gives only a slight boost to scores. For example, 20-hour coaching classes increase math and verbal scores on the SAT by only about 15 and 10 points, respectively, on the 200- to 800-point scale, contrary to the exaggerated claims made by SAT coaching programs (Bond, 1989; Educational Testing Service, 1994). The Educational Testing Service (ETS), which publishes the SAT, says that the best way for students to do well on the SAT is to take rigorous courses, work hard in them, brush up on their algebra and geometry, familiarize themselves with the test, and get a good night's sleep the night before the test. Taking a practice test or two is wise in preparing for any standardized test.

Some don'ts regarding teachers preparing students for standardized tests include (McMillan, 2002) don't teach to the test, don't use the standardized test format for classroom tests, don't describe tests as a burden, don't tell students that important decisions will be made solely on the results of a single test, don't use previous forms of the same test to prepare students, and don't convey a negative attitude about the test.

Through the Eyes of Teachers

Get Full-Animation 3-D

Standardized tests are just one very small, isolated picture of a child. A much fuller "video" comes from daily observations. Do not unfairly label a child based on a test.

Rarely or never during the school year do my students encounter fill-in-the-oval items like those on standardized tests. Therefore, to be fair, before standardized testing I give them examples similar to the format of the test. If adults take a test with a special format, they prepare themselves by practicing in that format. Why should it be any different for children?

Marlene Wendler
Fourth-Grade Teacher
St. Paul's Lutheran School
New Ulm, Minnesota

Teaching Strategies
For Improving Students' Test-Taking Skills

Here are some important test-taking skills that you might want to discuss with your students (Linn & Gronlund, 2000):

1. *Read the instructions carefully.*
2. *Read the items carefully.*
3. *Keep track of the time and work quickly enough to finish the test.*
4. *Skip difficult items and return to them later.*
5. *Make informed guesses instead of omitting items, if scoring favors doing so.*
6. *Eliminate as many items as possible on multiple-choice items.*
7. *Follow directions carefully in marking the answer (such as darkening the entire space).*
8. *Check to be sure that the appropriate response was marked on the answer sheet.*
9. *Go back and check answers if time permits.*

Strategies in Practice

- **Testing**
- **Standardized Tests and Teaching**
- **High-Stakes Testing**

Administering Standardized Tests

Most standardized tests spell out in considerable detail how the test should be administered (Airasian, 2001). This includes how to set up the testing room, what to do when students take the test, how to distribute the test and answer sheets, and how to time the tests.

The physical testing environment should be well lighted and well ventilated. Students should have adequate work space. Seat students in a manner that will avoid distractions or cheating. Hang a sign on the door to the room that says something like "Testing in Progress—Do Not Disturb" (McMillan, 2004).

In administering the test, the teacher should follow word for word the script that is included in the test manual, to ensure that the test is being given under standardized conditions (Gay & Airasian, 2000). If this script is not followed exactly, comparisons of

Through the Eyes of Teachers

Testing and Class Time

I didn't realize how much time I was going to put into testing. It takes up more time than I ever imagined.

Anna Messer
New Teacher
Bradley Elementary
Columbia, South Carolina

the students' performance with the population of students on which the norms for the test were established could be invalid (Airasian, 2001). Be sure to write the start and finish times for the test on the chalkboard. At start time, tell students clearly to begin. Make sure students stop when the time has expired.

After your students have completed the test, count the booklets and answer sheets. Also record any incidents that you observed that might invalidate students' scores.

Understanding and Interpreting Test Results

Knowledge of some basic descriptive statistics will help you interpret standardized tests. Your ability to understand and interpret standardized tests will come in handy when you have parent-teacher conferences regarding children in your class. We will discuss these basic statistics as well as some ways that test results are commonly reported.

Understanding Descriptive Statistics   Although we are discussing statistics here to help you understand standardized tests, the information about statistics also can help you with many other aspects of classroom assessment, such as interpreting a student's scores on tests you have created and administered, as well as calculating a student's grade point average (Best & Kahn, 2003). Our primary focus here is on **descriptive statistics,** which are mathematical procedures that are used to describe and summarize data (information) in a meaningful way (Kiess, 2002). We will study frequency distributions, measures of central tendency, measures of variability, and the normal distribution.

Frequency Distributions   The first step in organizing data involves creating a **frequency distribution,** a listing of scores, usually from highest to lowest, along with the number of times each score appears. Imagine that a test was given and 21 students received the following scores on the test: 96, 95, 94, 92, 88, 88, 86, 86, 86, 86, 84, 83, 82, 82, 82, 78, 75, 75, 72, 68, and 62. Figure 15.3a shows a frequency distribution for these scores. Frequency distributions often are presented graphically. For example, a **histogram** is a frequency distribution in the form of a graph. Vertical bars represent the frequency of

Statistical Analysis

descriptive statistics Mathematical procedures that are used to describe and summarize data (information) in a meaningful way.

frequency distribution A listing of scores, usually from highest to lowest, along with the number of times each score appears.

histogram A frequency distribution in the form of a graph.

"Tonight, we're going to let the statistics speak for themselves."
© The New Yorker Collection 1974 Edward Koren from cartoonbank.com. All Rights Reserved.

(a) Frequency Distribution   **(b) Histogram**

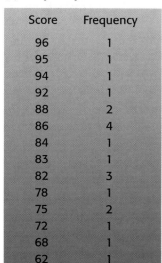

Score	Frequency
96	1
95	1
94	1
92	1
88	2
86	4
84	1
83	1
82	3
78	1
75	2
72	1
68	1
62	1

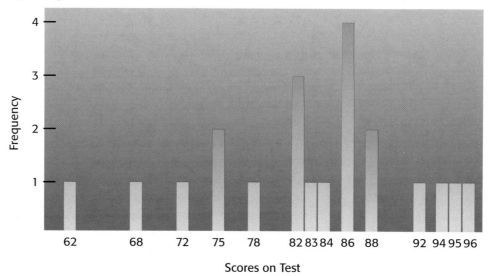

FIGURE 15.3   A Frequency Distribution and Histogram

scores per category. Figure 15.3b shows a histogram for the 21 scores. A histogram often is called a *bar graph*. Notice in the histogram that the horizontal axis (the *x*-axis) indicates the obtained scores and the vertical axis (the *y*-axis) indicates how often each score occurs.

Although representing a group of scores graphically can provide insight about students' performance, so can some statistical techniques that represent scores numerically. These techniques involve the concepts of central tendency and variability, each of which we will discuss.

Measures of Central Tendency   A measure of **central tendency** is a number that provides information about the average, or typical, score in a set of data. There are three measures of central tendency: mean, median, and mode. The **mean** is the numerical average of a group of scores, commonly labeled as $\overline{X}$ or M by statisticians. The mean is computed by adding all the scores and then dividing by the number of scores. Thus, the mean for the 21 students' test scores above is 1740/21 = 82.86. The mean often is a good indicator of the central tendency of a group of scores.

The **median** is the score that falls exactly in the middle of a distribution of scores after they have been arranged (or ranked) from highest to lowest. In our example of 21 test scores, the median is the 11th ranked score (10 above, 10 below it), so the median is 84.

The **mode** is the score that occurs most often. The mode can be determined easily by looking at the frequency distribution or histogram. In our example of 21 scores, the mode is 86 (the score occurring most often—4 times). The mode is most revealing when its value is much more frequent than the other values or scores. For example, in the

central tendency A statistic that provides information about the average, or typical, score in a set of data.

mean The numerical average of a group of scores.

median The score that falls exactly in the middle of a distribution of scores after they have been arranged (or ranked) from highest to lowest.

mode The score that occurs most often.

By permission of Mell Lazarus and Creators Syndicate, Inc.

21 scores in our example, if 15 of the 21 scores had been the same, then the mode probably would be the best measure of central tendency for the data. In this case, the mean and median would be less meaningful.

There can be 2 or more modes. For example, in our example of 21 students taking a test, if 4 students had scored 86 and 4 students had scored 75 (instead of the 2), then the set of scores would have 2 modes (86 and 75). A set of scores with 2 modes is called a *bimodal distribution*. It is possible for a set of scores to have more than 2 modes, in which case it is called a *multimodal distribution*.

Measures of Variability   In addition to obtaining information about the central tendency of a set of scores, it also is important to know about their variability (Abrami, Cholmsky, & Gordon, 2001). **Measures of variability** tell us how much the scores vary from one another. Two measures of variability are range and standard deviation.

The **range** is the distance between the highest and lowest scores. The range of the 21 students' test scores in our example is 34 points (96 − 62 = 34). The range is a rather simple measure of variability and it is not used often. The most commonly used measure of variability is the standard deviation.

The **standard deviation** is a measure of how much a set of scores varies on the average around the mean of the scores. In other words, it reveals how closely scores cluster around the mean. The smaller the standard deviation, the less the scores tend to vary from the mean. The greater the standard deviation, the more the scores tend to spread out from the mean. Calculating a standard deviation is not very difficult, especially if you have a calculator that computes square roots. To calculate a standard deviation, follow these four steps:

1. Find the mean of the scores.
2. From each score, subtract the mean and then square the difference between the score and the mean. (Squaring the scores will eliminate any minus signs that result from subtracting the mean.)
3. Add the squares and then divide that sum by the number of scores.
4. Compute the square root of the value obtained in step 3. This is the standard deviation.

The formula for these four steps is

$$\sqrt{\frac{\sum (X - \bar{X})^2}{N}}$$

where X = the individual score and $\bar{X}$ = the mean, N = the number of scores, and $\sum$ means "the sum of."

Applying this formula to the test scores of the 21 students,

1. We already computed the mean of the scores and found that it was 82.86.
2. Subtract 82.86 from the first score: 96 − 82.86 = 13.14. Square 13.14 to get 172.66. Save the value and go on to do the same for the second score, the third score, and so on.
3. Add the 21 squares to get 1543.28. Divide the sum by 21: 1543.28/21 = 73.49.
4. Find the square root of 73.49. The result is 8.57, the standard deviation.

measures of variability Measures that tell how much scores vary from one another.

range The distance between the highest and lowest scores.

standard deviation A measure of how much a set of scores varies on the average around the mean of the scores.

Calculators are very helpful in computing a standard deviation. To read further about using calculators effectively, see the Technology and Education box. And to evaluate your knowledge of and skills in computing the various measures of central tendency and variability we have described, complete Self-Assessment 15.1 on page 506. Mastering these kinds of descriptive statistics is useful not only for classroom work but also for understanding research results.

The standard deviation is a better measure of variability than the range because the range represents information about only two bits of data (the highest and lowest scores), whereas the standard deviation represents combined information about all the data. It also usually is more helpful to know how much test scores are spread out or clustered

Using Calculators Effectively

Gilbert Sax (1997) described various types of calculators and how teachers can use them effectively.

Four- or five-function calculators. These are the simplest calculators. They can add, subtract, multiply, and divide. Most also can compute square roots, which can be especially helpful if you need to calculate a standard deviation, *z*-score, or *T*-score. These calculators are inexpensive and they can compute all of the statistics described in this chapter. However, they are somewhat inconvenient when numerous steps are required to solve a problem.

More-specialized calculators. More-specialized calculators also are available. For example, they automatically accumulate score values, count the number of cases entered, square each entered value, and then sum the squares. In addition, such calculators are capable of computing internal reliability statistics. Such features save time and can reduce computational errors.

If you do not have a calculator, seriously consider purchasing one to use when you become a classroom teacher. It can save you time and make your computations more accurate when you need to calculate various aspects of central tendency and variation in your students' test scores. Sax recommends that when you purchase a calculator, have a salesperson take the time to show you how to compute the kinds of statistics you need.

What are some good strategies for using calculators effectively?

together than to know the highest and lowest scores. If a teacher gives a test and the standard deviation turns out to be very low, it means the scores tend to cluster around the same value. That could mean that everyone in the class learned the material equally well, but it more likely suggests that the test was too easy and is not discriminating very effectively between students who mastered the material and those who did not.

The Normal Distribution   In a **normal distribution,** most of the scores cluster around the mean. The farther above or below the mean we travel, the less frequently each score occurs. A normal distribution also is called a *normal curve, "bell-shaped curve"* or *"bell curve."* Many characteristics, such as human intelligence measured by intelligence tests, athletic ability, weight, and height, follow or approximate a normal distribution. Normal distributions are useful to know about because when testing a large number of students with a good standardized test, the graph of resulting scores will tend to resemble a normal curve. We presented the normal distribution for standardized testing of intelligence in chapter 4, "Individual Variations" ← p. 107. Figure 15.4 illustrates what a normal distribution, or "bell-shaped curve," looks like and describes its statistical properties.

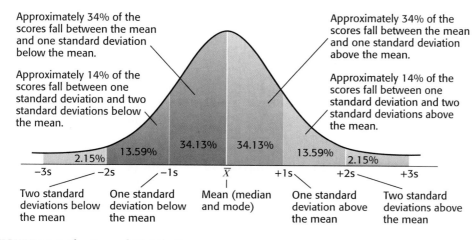

FIGURE 15.4 The Normal Distribution

normal distribution A "bell-shaped curve" in which most of the scores are clustered around the mean; the farther above or below the mean that we travel, the less frequently each score occurs.

Evaluating My Knowledge of and Skills in Computing Measures of Central Tendency and Variability

Examine each of these statements and place a checkmark next to the statement if you feel confident of your knowledge of the concept and your skill in computing the measure or using the instrument.

_____ I know what a frequency distribution is.

_____ I can describe what a histogram is and know how to create one.

_____ I understand what a mean is and know how to compute it.

_____ I understand what a median is and know how to calculate it.

_____ I know what a mode is and am aware of how to compute it.

_____ I know what a range is and how to arrive at it.

_____ I can discuss what a standard deviation is and know how to compute it.

_____ I have a good calculator and know how to use it to compute basic descriptive statistics.

For any items that you did not check off, go back and study the concept again. If you are still not confident about computing the various measures, seek additional help from a college instructor, a math skills tutor (many colleges have these available for students), or a capable friend. Practice the calculations in order to absorb the concepts.

 Go to your Student Toolbox CD-ROM for an electronic version of this form.

Figure 15.4 illustrates several important characteristics of a normal distribution. First, it is symmetrical. Because of this symmetry, the mean, median, and mode are identical in a normal distribution. Second, its bell shape shows that the most common scores are near the middle. The scores become less frequent the farther away from the middle they appear (that is, as they become more extreme). Third, the normal distribution incorporates information about both the mean and the standard deviation, as indicated in figure 15.4. The area on the normal curve that is 1 standard deviation above the mean and 1 standard deviation below it represents 68.26% of the scores. At 2 standard deviations above and below the mean, 95.42% of the scores are represented. Finally, at 3 standard deviations above and below the mean, 99.74% of the scores are included. If we apply this information to the normal distribution of IQ scores in the population, 68% of the population has an IQ between 85 and 115, 95% an IQ between 70 and 130, and 99% between 55 and 145.

Interpreting Test Results Understanding descriptive statistics provides the foundation for effectively interpreting test results. About four to eight weeks after a standardized test has been administered, test results are returned to the school. A **raw score** is the number of items the student answered correctly on the test. Raw scores, by themselves, are not very useful because they don't provide information about how easy or difficult the test was or how the student fared compared with other students. Test publishers usually provide teachers with many different kinds of scores that go beyond raw scores. These include percentile-rank scores, stanine scores, grade-equivalent scores, and standard scores.

Percentile-Rank Scores A **percentile-rank score** reveals the percentage of the distribution that lies at or below the score. It also provides information about the score's position in relation to the rest of the scores. Percentile ranks range from 1 to 99.

If a student has a percentile rank of 81 on a test, it means that the student performed as well as or higher on the test than 81% of the sample who made up the norm group.

raw score The number of items the student answered correctly on the test.

precentile-rank score The percentage of a distribution that lies at or below the score.

Note that percentiles do not refer to percentages of items answered correctly on the test. Percentile rank for standardized tests is determined by comparison with the norm group distribution. Different comparison groups may be used in computing percentile ranks, such as urban norms or suburban norms.

Stanine Scores A **stanine score** describes a student's test performance on a 9-point scale ranging from 1 to 9. Scores of 1, 2, and 3 are usually considered to be below average; 4, 5, and 6 average; and 7, 8, and 9 above average. As in the case of a student's percentile rank score, a stanine score in one subject area (such as science) can be compared with the student's stanine score in other areas (such as math, reading, and social studies).

A stanine refers to a specific percentage of the normal curve's area. The correspondence between a stanine score and a percentile rank is shown in figure 15.5. A stanine score provides a more general index of a student's performance, while a percentile rank score yields a more precise estimation.

Stanine Score	Percentile Rank Score
9	96 or Higher
8	89–95
7	77–88
6	60–76
5	40–59
4	23–39
3	11–22
2	4–10
1	Below 4

FIGURE 15.5 The Relation Between Stanine Score and Percentile Rank Score

Grade-Equivalent Scores A **grade-equivalent score** indicates a student's performance in relation to grade level and months of the school year, assuming a 10-month school year. Thus, a grade-equivalent score of 4.5 refers to fourth grade, fifth month in school. A grade equivalent of 6.0 stands for the beginning of the sixth grade. In some test reports, a decimal is omitted so that 45 is the same as 4.5 and 60 is the same as 6.0.

Grade-equivalent scores should be used only to interpret a student's progress, not for grade placement. Many educators believe that because grade-equivalent scores are often misleading and misinterpreted, other types of scores, such as standard scores, are more appropriate to use.

Standard Scores A **standard score** is expressed as a deviation from the mean, which involves the concept of standard deviation that we discussed earlier. The term *standard* as used in *standard score* does not refer to a specific level of performance or expectation but, rather, to the standard normal curve (McMillan, 2002). Actually, the stanine scores and grade-equivalent scores we already have profiled are standard scores. Two additional standard scores we will evaluate here are *z*-scores and *T*-scores.

A **z-score** provides information about how many standard deviations a raw score is above or below the mean. Calculation of a *z*-score is done using this formula:

$$z\text{-score} = \frac{X - \overline{X}}{SD}$$

where X = any raw score, $\overline{X}$ = mean of the raw scores, and SD equals the standard deviation of the raw score distribution.

Consider again our example of 21 students taking a test. What would a student's *z*-score be if the student's raw score were 86? Using the formula just shown it would be

$$\frac{86 - 82.6}{8.57} = .37$$

Thus, the raw score of 86 is .37 of a standard deviation above the mean. The *z*-score mean is 0 and the standard deviation is 1.

A **T-score** is a standard score in which the mean is set at 50 and the standard deviation is set at 10. This formula can be used to compute a *T*-score:

$$T\text{-score} = 50 + 10(z)$$

For example, a *T*-score of 70 is the same as a *z*-score of 2, and a *T*-score of 40 is the same as a *z*-score of −1. For the raw score of 86, the corresponding *T*-score is, therefore, 54.

The college entrance SAT is based on a similar scoring strategy. Its mean is 500 and its standard deviation is 100. The lowest possible score of 200 on the SAT is calibrated to occur at 3 standard deviations below the mean, and the maximum score of 800 is

stanine score A 9-point scale that describes a student's performance.

grade-equivalent score A score that indicates students' performance in relation to grade level and months of the school year, assuming a 10-month school year.

standard score A score expressed as a deviation from the mean; involves the standard deviation.

z-score A score that provides information about how many standard deviations a raw score is above or below the mean.

T-score A standard score in which the mean is set at 50 and the standard deviation is set at 10.

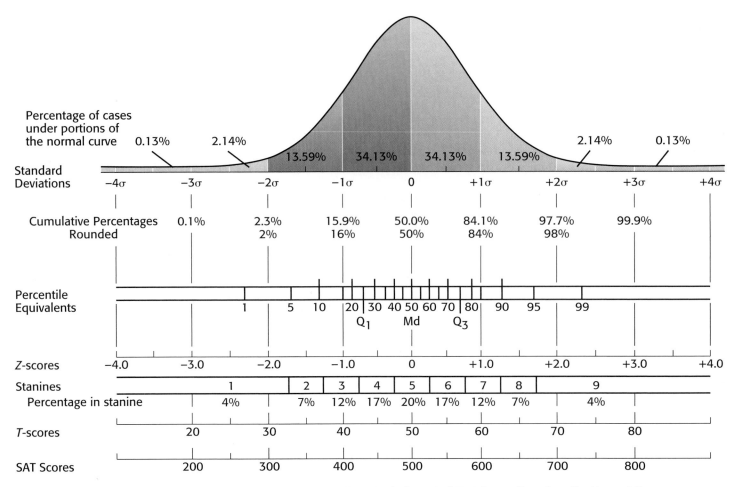

FIGURE 15.6 Some Commonly Reported Test Scores Based on the Normal Curve

designated to occur at 3 standard deviations above the mean. Thus, only a very small percentage of students (about .10%) score at these extremes.

Figure 15.6 presents an overall comparison of many of the types of standardized scores you will see on test reports. Most raw standardized test scores are forced into a normal curve representation.

In addition to showing a student's relative placement on a test, standard scores also allow for comparisons across different types of tests (Powell, 2002). For example, a student may score one standard deviation above the mean on a math test and one standard deviation below the mean on a reading test. Comparisons of raw scores don't always allow for such comparisons.

Don't Overinterpret Test Results   Use caution in interpreting small differences in test scores, especially percentile rank and grade-equivalent test scores (Airasian, 2001). All tests have some degree of error.

A good strategy is to think of a score not as a single number but as a location in a band or general range. Small differences in test scores are usually not meaningful.

Some test reports include percentile bands, a range of scores (rather than a single score) expressed in percentiles, such as 75th to 85th percentile. The Metropolitan Achievement Tests use percentile bands in reporting scores. A percentile rank of 6 to 8 points or a two- to five-month grade-equivalence difference between two students rarely indicates any meaningful difference in achievement.

When considering information from a standardized test, don't evaluate it in isolation. Evaluate it in conjunction with other information you know about the student and

Reporting Test Results

your classroom instruction (Airasian, 2001). Most manuals that accompany standardized tests warn against overinterpretation.

Teaching Strategies
For Communicating Test Results
to Parents

Here are some good strategies for communicating test results to parents (McMillan, 1997):

1. *Don't report the test scores in isolation.* Report the scores in the context of the student's overall work and performance on other classroom assessments. This will help keep parents from placing too much importance on a score from a single standardized test. Show them other examples of the student's work to support your conclusions about the student's strengths and weaknesses.
2. *Try to use easy-to-understand language when you describe the students' test results to parents.* Don't get caught up in using obscure test language. Be able to report the information in your own words.
3. *Let parents know that the scores are approximate rather than absolute.* You might say something about how various internal and external factors can affect students' test scores.
4. *Recognize that percentile scores or bands are the easiest set of scores for parents to understand.*
5. *Prior to the conference, spend some time familiarizing yourself with the student's test report.* Make sure you know how to interpret each score you report to parents. It is not a good idea just to show parents the numbers on a test report. You will need to summarize what the scores mean.
6. *Be ready to answer questions that parents might have about their child's strengths, weaknesses, and progress.*
7. *Rather than talking "to" or lecturing parents, talk "with" them in a discussion format.* After you have described a test result, invite them to ask questions that will help you to further clarify for them what the test results mean.

Using Standardized Test Scores to Plan and Improve Instruction

Teachers can use standardized test scores from the end of the previous year in planning their instruction for the next year and as a way to evaluate the effectiveness of instruction after content and skills have been taught (McMillan, 2002). Any use of standardized test results should be made in conjunction with information from other sources.

Prior to instruction, standardized test results may provide an indication of the general ability of the students in the class. This can help the teacher select the appropriate level of instruction and materials to begin the school year. A standardized test should not be used to develop a very low or very high expectation for a student or the entire class. Expectations should be appropriate and reasonable. If

Through the Eyes of Teachers

Standardized Tests as a Tool for Planning

The Stanford Achievement Test is administered in our school system. Here is a procedure based on it that I have found most effective for my students:

1. Before the beginning of the new school year, I obtain the individual test record for each of my students.
2. Language arts being my teaching area, I highlight those areas for the language arts in which the individual has scored low or average.
3. I use the low and average scores as signals about what I will need to reinforce for the student throughout the school year.
4. Parental support is also vital to the success of my strategy. I hold parent conferences to inform and enable parents to be partners in the student's educational program for the year. We discuss the student's strengths and weaknesses.
5. Based on the SAT and the parental input, my lesson plans take into account the students' weaknesses, including outcome for correction.

Vicky Stone
Language Arts Teacher
Cammack Middle School
Huntington, West Virginia

the results of a reading readiness test suggest that the class overall lacks appropriate reading skills, the teacher needs to carefully select reading materials that the students will be able to understand.

Standardized tests are sometimes used in grouping students. In cooperative learning, it is common to group students so that a wide range of abilities is reflected in the group. However, a single test score or single test should not be used by itself for any instructional purpose. It always should be used in conjunction with other information.

The subscales of tests (such as in reading and math) can be used to pinpoint strengths and weaknesses of incoming students in particular subject areas. This can help teachers to determine the amount of instruction to give in different areas. If students' achievement is considerably lower than what is expected on the basis of ability testing, they may need further testing, special attention, or counseling.

Standardized tests administered after instruction can be used to evaluate the effectiveness of instruction and the curriculum. Students should score well in the areas that have been emphasized in instruction. If they do not, then both the test itself and the instruction need to be analyzed to determine why this is the case.

In using standardized tests to plan and improve instruction, we underscore again, it is important not to use a single test or test score to make decisions. This is especially relevant in placement decisions, which should be made on the basis of information from multiple sources, including prior teachers' comments, grades, systematic observations, and further assessments. It also is very important to guard against using a single test to develop an expectation for a student's ability and to make sure that the student's test scores reflect a fair assessment.

⚠ Review and Reflect

3 **Identify the teacher's roles in standardized testing.**

Review
- What are effective ways to prepare students for standardized tests?
- What steps should teachers take in administering standardized tests?
- What roles do frequency distributions, measures of central tendency and variability, and normal distributions play in describing standardized test results? What are some different types of scores?
- How can standardized tests be used in planning and improving instruction?

Reflect
- Considering the grade level and subject(s) that you plan to teach, how might standardized test results be useful to you in your instructional planning?

ISSUES IN STANDARDIZED TESTING

As we have already mentioned, standardized testing is controversial. One debate concerns how standardized tests stack up against alternative methods of assessment, especially in high-stakes state-mandated testing. Another is about whether standardized tests discriminate against ethnic minority students and students from low-income backgrounds.

Standardized Tests, Alternative Assessments, and High-Stakes Testing

As we will explain in greater detail in chapter 16, alternative assessments include assessments of student performance, such as assessments of oral presentations, real-world problems, projects, and portfolios (systematic and organized collections of the student's work that demonstrate the student's skills and accomplishments). Which is the best way to assess student performance—standardized tests that mainly rely on multiple-choice questions or alternative assessments?

Assessment expert Grant Wiggins (1992) argued that performance tests should be used instead of standardized tests that mainly include multiple-choice questions or at least be used as part of the student's total assessment. He concluded that performance assessment is more meaningful, involves higher-level thinking skills, and fits better with current educational reform that emphasizes constructivist and social constructivist learning. In Kentucky and Vermont, the inclusion of problem solving in mathematics and the written communication of mathematical ideas on state-mandated tests led teachers to work more on these areas in their math instruction (Olson, 2001).

Some states—such as Arizona, California, Kentucky, and Wisconsin—have pulled back from earlier, more ambitious efforts to include alternative assessments in state-mandated tests. In part, that was because early studies indicated that the alternative assessments did not yield results that were as consistent as multiple-choice tests. Also, the alternative assessments were more time consuming and costly than off-the-shelf, norm-referenced tests. For example, in Iowa, the cost of administering the standardized Iowa Tests of Basic Skills is only 93 cents per student. By contrast, any substantial alternative assessment is estimated to cost in the neighborhood of $12 to $14 per student. But supporters of alternative assessments say that the $12 to $14 figure is small, compared with the total amount of money states spend on educating students, which averages out to approximately $6,500 per student on an annual basis.

Equity and Excellence in Standards and Assessments

Blaine Worthen and Vicki Spandel (1991) offered a helpful perspective on the standardized test debate. They argued that when used correctly, standardized tests do have value. However, they provide only partial assessment and, thus, have limits. Worthen and Spandel believe that standardized tests are especially helpful in providing information about comparability from a "big picture" perspective. Comparing their class with the one down the hall won't give teachers the information they need about where their students stand compared with the broader population of students. Standardized tests can provide better information about "big picture" questions: Are my fourth-grade students learning basic math? Can my seventh-grade students read at a predefined level of competency?

At the same time, Worthen and Spandel urge teachers to scrupulously avoid any misuses of tests or test results and to educate themselves about tests so that they understand their capabilities and limitations, not asking tests to do more than they can or are intended to do. They also say a standardized test should be only one of a number of assessments used to evaluate students.

Ronald Hambleton (1996) concluded that multiple-choice standardized testing is not likely to be completely abandoned in the foreseeable future, but he predicts that we will see more of a balance in assessment with inclusion of writing tasks, performance tests, computer simulation exercises, hands-on projects, and portfolios of work. We will say much more about alternative assessments in chapter 16.

Diversity and Standardized Testing

Earlier in the chapter we raised the issue of fairness in standardized testing. And in chapter 4, "Individual Variations," we discussed issues related to diversity and assessment ◀ p. 119. For example, we indicated that African American and Latino students score, on the average, about 15 points below White students on standardized intelligence tests. This gap was attributed to environmental rather than hereditary factors. In addition,

How might standardized tests discriminate against ethnic minority students?

ENTER THE DEBATE

1. Should teachers' pay be tied to student performance on standardized tests?

2. Should students have to pass a test to earn a high school diploma?

Teaching Experience

Research on High-Stakes Testing

African American, Latino, and Native American students show the lowest proficiency levels, on the average, of all ethnic groups on mathematics, science, reading, writing, history, geography, and literature, according to "report cards" from the National Assessment of Educational Progress (Riley, 1997).

A special concern is cultural bias in tests and the importance of creating culturally responsive tests for diagnostic and instructional purposes (Bigelow, 1999; Gay, 1997; Sandoval & others, 1999). Because of the potential for cultural bias in standardized tests, it is important to assess students using a variety of methods. As indicated earlier, many assessment experts believe that performance and portfolio assessments reduce some of the inequity that characterizes standardized tests for ethnic minority students and students from low-income backgrounds. To read further about whether portfolio assessment is more equitable for students from ethnic minority and other backgrounds, read the Diversity and Education interlude.

Diversity and Education
Mirror, Mirror on the Wall, Which Is the Fairest Test of All?

The title above was used to introduce a discussion of whether portfolio assessment is more equitable than standardized tests for ethnic minority students, students from impoverished backgrounds, and females (Supovitz & Brennan, 1997). The researchers compared the traditional standardized test results and portfolio assessment performance of first- and second-grade students in a medium-size urban setting. They analyzed the relative contribution of students' background characteristics to their performance. If the portfolio assessments are more equitable than standardized tests, the gap in scores between high-income White students and low-income minority students should be reduced.

At both grade levels, the gap in performance between African American and White students was reduced by about one-half in portfolio assessment when compared with scores on standardized tests. Thus, portfolio assessment significantly reduced the gap between African American and White students' performance but did not eliminate it. Interestingly, a gender gap appeared, with girls outperforming boys by a larger margin on portfolio assessment than on assessment with standardized tests. Portfolio assessment had no detectable impact, on the average, on the relative performance of students from low-income backgrounds or students in the English language learning program. These students performed consistently worse than their counterparts on both portfolio assessment and standardized tests.

In sum, portfolio assessment holds considerable promise by focusing instruction on higher-level thinking skills, providing useful feedback to teachers about students' thinking skills, and emphasizing real-world problem solving. However, in this study, portfolio assessment had mixed effects on equalizing the differences in performance of students with different backgrounds and experience.

 Review and Reflect

4 Evaluate some key issues in standardized testing.

Review
- Why is it argued that performance assessments should accompany standardized tests in high-stakes testing? What particular value does standardized testing have?
- What has changed when different ethnic groups have been compared using performance assessments instead of standardized tests?

Reflect
- In what situations would you rather be tested with standardized testing? with performance assessments? Why?

Ms. Carter is a third-grade teacher in a district that uses more than one standardized test to measure student achievement and ability. It uses the test required by its state to assess the degree to which students have met or exceeded state standards in math, science, reading, writing and social sciences. This test yields individual, school, and district scores and compares these with state averages. In addition, the district uses a nationally normed test to assess both achievement and cognitive ability. The achievement test yields individual scores as they relate to national norms. These scores are reported as percentile rank scores and grade-equivalent scores. The cognitive ability test yields percentile rank scores and IQ-type scores. In addition, the testing service provides a narrative that discusses and compares the achievement and cognitive ability scores for each student.

Ms. Carter is not thrilled about giving her students so many standardized tests. She says, "Sometimes it seems all we do is prepare for these tests and take them." She makes sure she has taught her students appropriate test-taking strategies. She also tries to give her students some experiences that mirror the standardized tests—such as filling in bubbles on answer sheets and having limited time in which to complete tests. She also sends notes home to parents, asking them to ensure that their children get adequate sleep and eat breakfast during testing weeks.

During testing, she always hangs a sign on the door, communicating that she does not wish to be disturbed. She reads the instructions verbatim and asks her students if they have any questions prior to beginning the test. She tries to keep the testing situation as low-key as possible for her students. To this end, she generally plays music quietly while the students are taking the tests.

Test results are routinely distributed to parents with student report cards. Parent-teacher conferences are conducted in the week following distribution. Parents inevitably have many questions about standardized test scores:

> "Ms. Carter, what does this grade equivalent mean? It says here that Emily has a grade equivalent of 4.3. Does that mean we should ask to have her placed in fourth grade?"

> "Ms. Carter, John scored at the 90th percentile on language, but he's getting Cs in your class. I just don't understand."

> "Ms. Carter, how can it be that my daughter scored in the 60th percentile on the ability test and the 70th on the achievement test but doesn't meet state standards in math?"

> "Ms. Carter, how can my son score at the 40th percentile on the ability test and the 80th percentile on the achievement test? That just doesn't make any sense!"

- What are the issues involved in this situation?
- Examine Ms. Carter's testing procedures. What does she do incorrectly? How might this reduce the validity of the students' scores?
- How would you answer each of the parents' questions?

Reach Your Learning Goals

1 Discuss the nature of standardized tests.

- Standardized tests are prepared by test specialists to assess performance under uniform conditions. Many standardized tests allow a student's performance to be compared with the performance of other students at the same age or grade level on a national basis.

- The purposes of standardized tests include providing information about students' progress, diagnosing students' strengths and weaknesses, providing evidence for placement of students in specific programs, helping administrators evaluate programs, providing information for planning and improving instruction, and contributing to accountability. Interest in accountability has led to the creation of standards-based tests and high-stakes testing. Important decisions about students should be made not on the basis of a single standardized test but, rather, on the basis of information from a variety of assessments.

- Among the most important criteria for evaluating standardized tests are norms, validity, reliability, and fairness. To understand an individual's performance on a test, it needs to be compared with the performance of a group of individuals who previously were given the test by the test maker. This is the norm group. National norms are based on a nationally representative group of students. Standardized tests also can have special group and local norms. Validity is the extent to which a test measures what it is intended to measure and the extent to which inferences about test scores are accurate. Three important types of validity are content validity, criterion validity (which can be either concurrent or predictive), and construct validity. Reliability is the extent to which a test produces a consistent, reproducible measure of performance. Reliable measures are stable, dependable, and relatively free from errors of measurement. Reliability can be measured in several ways, including test-retest reliability, alternate-forms reliability, and split-half reliability. Fair tests are unbiased and nondiscriminatory, uninfluenced by irrelevant factors such as gender, ethnicity, or bias on the part of the scorer.

2 Compare aptitude and achievement testing and describe current uses of achievement tests.

- An aptitude test predicts a student's ability to learn, or what the student can accomplish with further education and training. An achievement test measures what the student has learned, or the skills the student has mastered. Aptitude tests include general ability tests, such as intelligence tests, and specific aptitude tests used to predict success in an academic subject or occupational area. The SAT test is typically used as an aptitude test, although it can be used as an achievement test.

- Standardized achievement tests include survey batteries (individual subject matter tests that are designed for a particular level of students), tests for specific subjects (assess a skill in a more detailed, extensive way than a survey battery), and diagnostic tests (given to students to pinpoint weaknesses, often after instruction has taken place).

- In the 1990s, state-mandated tests became more closely connected with state-endorsed educational objectives and instruction. Most state-mandated tests consist mainly of multiple-choice items, and almost all use criterion-referenced scoring. Policy makers cite these possible advantages of state-mandated testing: improved student performance; more time teaching subjects being tested; high expectations for all students; identification of poorly performing schools, teachers, and administrators; and improved confidence in schools as test scores improve. State-mandated tests are being used in decisions about remediation, promotion, and graduation. State-mandated tests are criticized for dumbing down the curriculum, promoting rote memorization, encouraging teachers to teach to the test, and discriminating against students from low-income and minority backgrounds. Further evaluation is needed of high-stakes testing and changes are needed in the system of state-mandated testing.

- District-mandated tests and national tests also are being used. A major issue in education today is whether the No Child Left Behind legislation is the best way to raise educational standards. The NAEP is the federal government's national examination of young Americans' knowledge, skills, understanding, and attitudes. On many comparisons with students in other countries, American students do not fare well. Many issues are involved in the concept of world-class standards.

3 Identify the teacher's roles in standardized testing.

- Make sure that students have good test-taking skills. Also communicate a positive attitude about the test to students.

Coaching programs to improve students' test scores have had minimal effects.

- Most standardized testing manuals spell out how to set up the testing room, what to do when students take the test, how to distribute the test and answer sheets, and how to time the tests. In administering the test, it is important to follow the script word for word.

- Descriptive statistics are math procedures used to describe and summarize data in a meaningful way. A frequency distribution is a listing of scores from highest to lowest along with the number of times each score appears. A histogram is one way that frequency distribution information can be presented. Measures of central tendency include the mean, median, and mode. Measures of variability include the range and standard deviation. The normal curve is a bell-shaped curve in which most scores cluster around the mean. A normal curve is symmetrical and incorporates information about both the mean and the standard deviation. A raw score is the number of items a student gets right on a test, which typically is not as useful as many other types of scores. Percentile-rank scores reveal the percentage of the distribution that lies at or below the particular score. Stanine scores describe a student's performance on a 9-point scale ranging from 1 to 9. Grade-equivalent scores are expressed in terms of the grade level of students who perform at that level. Standard scores are expressed as a deviation from the mean and involve the concept of standard deviation (z-scores and T-scores are examples of standard scores).

- Avoid overinterpreting test results. A good strategy is to think of a score not as a single score but as being located in a band or general range. Don't evaluate standardized test results in isolation from other information about the student, such as classroom performance and the nature of instruction.

- Standardized test scores can be used to plan and improve instruction. This can be done prior to instruction or after instruction. Standardized tests sometimes are used in grouping students, but it is important to guard against unrealistic expectations for students based on test scores. The subscales of tests can be used to pinpoint students' strengths and weaknesses in particular subject areas, which can help teachers determine the amount of instruction to give in different areas. Standardized tests should always be used in conjunction with other information about students and the appropriateness and fairness of the tests evaluated.

4 Evaluate some key issues in standardized testing.

- There is disagreement about the value of standardized tests versus alternative assessments such as performance and portfolio assessments. When used correctly, standardized tests have value but provide only part of the assessment picture and do have limits. Some assessment experts and teachers believe that high-stakes state-mandated testing should include more alternative assessments.

- African American, Latino, and Native American students perform more poorly than non-Latino White students on many standardized tests. Cultural bias is of special concern in standardized testing. Some assessment experts believe that performance assessments have the potential to reduce bias in testing.

 KEY TERMS

standardized tests 488
standards-based tests 490
high-stakes testing 490
norm group 490
validity 491
content validity 491
criterion validity 491
concurrent validity 491
predictive validity 491

construct validity 491
reliability 491
test-retest reliability 492
alternate-forms reliability 492
split-half reliability 492
aptitude test 493
achievement test 493
descriptive statistics 502
frequency distribution 502

histogram 502
central tendency 503
mean 503
median 503
mode 503
measures of variability 504
range 504
standard deviation 504
normal distribution 505

raw score 506
percentile-rank score 506
stanine score 507
grade-equivalent score 507
standard score 507
z-score 507
T-score 507

PORTFOLIO ACTIVITIES

Now that you have a good understanding of this chapter, complete these exercises to expand your thinking.

Independent Reflection

Find a Frequency Distribution. Create a frequency distribution and histogram for the following scores: 98, 96, 94, 94, 92, 90, 90, 88, 86, 86, 86, 82, 80, 80, 80, 80, 80, 78, 76, 72, 70, 68, 64. (INTASC: Principle 8)

Collaborative Work

Calculate and Interpret Test Results. With a partner in your class, calculate the mean, median, and mode of the 23 scores listed above. Compute the range and standard deviation for these scores. What do these figures mean? (INTASC: Principle 8)

 TAKING IT TO THE NET

1. One of the most common forms of teacher-constructed tests is the multiple-choice test. Select a subject area, and construct a brief multiple-choice test. Trade tests with a partner and conduct a critique. Identify strengths and weaknesses of the assessments and discuss strategies for improvement.
2. Standardized tests that were designed to measure student achievement are now being used to assess the quality of a student's education, including the teacher, principal, school, and school system. Is this use of standardized achievement test scores valid? Why or why not?

Research/Field Experience Reflections

What Do the Critics Say about Standardized Testing? In a short essay, evaluate each of the following criticisms of standardized tests. State whether you agree with the criticism and then explain your reasoning: 1) High-stakes multiple-choice tests will lead to a "dumbing-down" of teaching and learning; 2) Establishing national tests will undermine new educational programs at the state and local levels. (INTASC: Principle 8)

 Go to the Online Learning Center for downloadable portfolio templates.

3. You have a student with a disability who is preparing to take a standardized college entrance exam. What type of modifications is she allowed? Whom should she contact? In what ways can students with disabilities receive unfair treatment due to standardized testing?

Connect to the Online Learning Center to explore possible answers.

STUDY, PRACTICE, AND SUCCEED

 Go to chapter 15 on the Online Learning Center at www.mhhe.com/santrockedu2e to access the student study guide with practice quizzes, web links, portfolio resources, PowerWeb articles and news feeds, and the online resources referenced in the chapter.

 Go to your Student Toolbox CD-ROM to access the resources and activities referenced in the chapter and

• Resources to help you prepare for the **PRAXIS II**™ exam

• **Application Resources,** including additional *Crack the Case* studies, electronic versions of the *Self-Assessments,* Application Exercises, and Site Observation Questions
• **Study Resources,** including Learning Goals, the Chapter Summary, a *Test Your Learning* exercise, and multiple-choice, true/false, matching, key terms, and short-answer quizzes
• **Professional Resources,** including a Lesson Plan Builder and *Bibliomaker*

> I call my tests "opportunities" to give students
> a different way of thinking about them.
>
> —Bert Moore
> *Contemporary American Psychologist*

Chapter Outline

Chapter Learning Goals After you have completed your study of this chapter, you should be able to reach these learning goals:

The Classroom as an Assessment Context

Assessment as an Integral Part of Teaching
Making Assessment Compatible with Contemporary Views of Learning and Motivation
Creating Clear, Appropriate Learning Targets
Establishing High-Quality Assessments
Current Trends

1 Discuss the classroom as an assessment context.

Traditional Tests

Selected-Response Items
Constructed-Response Items

2 Provide some guidelines for constructing traditional tests.

Alternative Assessments

Trends in Alternative Assessment
Performance-Based Assessment
Portfolio Assessment

3 Describe some types of alternative assessments.

Grading and Reporting Performance

The Purposes of Grading
The Components of a Grading System
Reporting Students' Progress and Grades to Parents
Some Issues in Grading

4 Construct a sound approach to grading.

Computers and Assessment

Using Computers for Assessment
Constructing, Printing, Administering, and Scoring Tests
Electronic Portfolios
Record Keeping
Web-Based Assessment

5 Identify some uses of computers in assessment.

Teaching Stories Vicky Farrow

Vicky Farrow is a former high school teacher who currently teaches educational psychology at Lamar University in Beaumont, Texas. She reflects on the ongoing process of assessment in the classroom and what to do and what not to do in constructing tests:

Assessment is an ongoing process. It is more than giving tests or assigning grades. It is everything a teacher does to determine if his or her students are learning. It may be asking students questions, monitoring their understanding as you circulate through the room during an activity, and noticing the frown on the face of a student who is confused or the smile of a student who has grasped the concept. Without this ongoing assessment, a teacher can never know if instruction is effective or needs to be modified. Done effectively, assessment provides a teacher with valuable information for providing an optimal learning experience for every child.

When you do give tests, every item on a test should relate back to the objectives. This helps the teacher avoid "gotcha" questions—those questions that may be trivial or unimportant

to the intended learning outcomes. If it is not important enough to spend valuable class time on, it probably is not important enough to test the student over.

Be careful that test items are written at an appropriate level. The test should be testing students' understanding of the unit content, not their reading skills (unless, of course, it is reading skills that are being tested). I remember as a student taking an analogies test that was intended to assess my ability to identify relationships between concepts. However, the vocabulary was so difficult that I missed some items because the words were too difficult for that level of schooling.

If an essay question is on an examination, write a model answer *before* grading the exam. Would you make your answer key for a multiple-choice test from a student's paper, wrong answers and all? Of course not! It does not make any more sense to do that with an essay item. If an essay item is well written and a model answer is constructed in advance, the grade a student receives will more accurately reflect the level of that student's understanding of the material being tested.

Assessment of students' learning has recently generated considerable interest in educational circles. This interest has focused on such issues as the extent to which teachers should incorporate state standards into their teaching and assessment, as well as the degree to which teachers should use traditional tests or alternative assessments.

THE CLASSROOM AS AN ASSESSMENT CONTEXT

When you think of assessment, what comes to mind? Probably tests. However, as we discuss the classroom as a context for assessment, you will discover that contemporary assessment strategies involve far more than testing.

Assessment as an Integral Part of Teaching

Teachers spend more time in assessment than you might imagine. In one analysis, they spent 20% to 30% of their professional time dealing with assessment matters (Stiggins, 2001). With so much time spent on assessment, it is important that it be done well (Banks, 2005; Brookhart, 2002; Popham, 2005). Assessment expert James McMillan (1997, 2001, 2004) believes that competent teachers frequently evaluate their students in relation to learning goals and adapt their instruction accordingly. Assessment not only documents what students know and can do but also affects their learning and motivation. These ideas represent a change in the way assessment is viewed, away from the concept that assessment is an isolated outcome done only after instruction is finished and toward the concept of integrating assessment with instruction.

Think of integrating instruction and assessment in terms of three time frames: pre-instruction, during instruction, and post-instruction. The Standards for Teacher Competence in Educational Assessment, developed jointly in the early 1990s by the American Federation of Teachers, National Council on Measurement in Education, and National Education Association, describe the teacher's responsibility for student assessment in these three time frames (see figure 16.1).

Pre-Instruction Assessment Imagine that you want to know how well your students can solve a certain level of math problem before you begin formal instruction on a

PRE-INSTRUCTION	**DURING INSTRUCTION**	**POST-INSTRUCTION**
Do my students have the prerequisite knowledge and skills to be successful?	Are students paying attention to me?	How much have my students learned?
What will interest my students?	Are students understanding the material?	What should I do next?
What will motivate my students?	To which students should I direct questions?	Do I need to review anything the class didn't understand?
How long should I plan to cover each unit?	What type of questions should I ask?	What grades should I give?
What teaching strategies should I use?	How should I respond to student questions?	What should I tell my students?
How should I grade students?	When should I stop lecturing?	How should I change my instruction next time?
What type of group learning should I use?	Which students need extra help?	Do the test scores really reflect what my students know and can do?
What are my learning objectives or targets?	Which students should be left alone?	Is there anything that students misunderstood?

FIGURE 16.1 Teacher Decision Making Before, During, and After Instruction
These are questions a teacher can answer to improve assessment before, during, and after instruction.

more-advanced level. You might look at your students' prior grades and their scores on standardized math tests, as well as observe your students for several days to see how well they perform. These assessments are designed to answer this question: What math skills are my students able to demonstrate? If the results of your assessment indicate that students lack prerequisite knowledge and skills, you will decide to begin with materials that are less difficult for them. If they do extremely well on your pre-instruction assessment, you will move your level of instruction to a higher plane. Without this pre-instructional assessment, you run the risk of having a class that is overwhelmed (if your instruction level is too advanced) or bored (if your instruction level is too low).

Much of pre-instructional assessment is informal observation. In the first several weeks of school, you will have numerous opportunities to observe students' characteristics and behavior. Be sensitive to whether a student is shy or outgoing, has a good or weak vocabulary, speaks and listens effectively, is considerate of others or is egocentric, engages in appropriate or inappropriate behavior, and so on. Also focus on the student's nonverbal behavior for cues that might reveal nervousness, boredom, frustration, or a lack of understanding. For example, a student might say that things are fine but come into class every day with a downturned head and sad look.

After you have made informal observations, you will need to interpret them. That is, what does the student's behavior mean? Are a downturned head and saddened look clues to a lack of self-esteem regarding academic skills or possibly stressful circumstances at home? Are the student's poor listening skills due to a lack of motivation?

Integrating Assessment and Learning

Integrating Assessment and Instruction

Rethinking Assessment and Educational Reform

In pre-instructional assessments, guard against developing expectations that will distort your perception of a student. It is virtually impossible not to have expectations about students. Because teacher expectations are potentially powerful influences on student learning, some teachers don't even want to look at a student's prior grades or standardized test scores. Whether you do or do not examine such assessment information, work on making your expectations realistic. If you err, err in the direction of having overly positive expectations for students.

A good strategy is to treat your initial impressions of students as hypotheses to be confirmed or modified by subsequent observation and information. Some of your initial observations will be accurate; others will need to be revised. As you try to get a sense of what your students are like, refrain from believing hearsay information, from making enduring judgments based on only one or two observations, and from labeling the student (Airasian, 2005).

Some teachers also administer diagnostic pretests in subject areas to examine a student's level of knowledge and skill. And many schools are increasingly collecting samples of students' work in portfolios, which can accompany a student from grade to grade. The portfolios provide teachers with a far more-concrete, less-biased set of information to evaluate than other teachers' hearsay comments. We will describe portfolios in much greater depth later in the chapter.

Assessment During Instruction   **Formative assessment** is assessment during the course of instruction rather than after it is completed. Your ongoing observation and monitoring of students' learning while you teach informs you about what to do next. Assessment during instruction helps you set your teaching at a level that challenges students and stretches their thinking. It also helps you to detect which students need your individual attention.

Assessment during instruction takes place at the same time as you make many other decisions about what to do, say, or ask next to keep the classroom running smoothly and help students actively learn (Airasian, 2005). It requires listening to student answers, observing other students for indications of understanding or confusion, framing the next question, and looking around the class for misbehavior (Doyle, 1986). Simultaneously, the teacher needs to monitor the pace of the activity, which students to call on, answer quality, and the sequence of content. With small groups, the teacher might need to be aware of several different activities simultaneously.

Oral questions are an especially important aspect of assessment during instruction. Some teachers ask as many as 300 to 400 questions a day, not only to stimulate students' thinking and inquiry but also to assess their knowledge and skill level (Morgan & Saxton, 1991). You might recall from our discussion of using questions in chapter 12, "Planning, Instruction, and Technology," that it is important to include thinking-based questioning in your instruction. Thinking-based questions follow from Bloom's Cognitive Taxonomy of Instructional Objectives (Bloom & others, 1956) and its recent revision (Anderson & Krathwohl, 2001), which was discussed in chapter 12. Such questions can elicit these sorts of thinking from students (examples of thinking are presented in parentheses):

- *Apply* (for example, ask students to give a real-world example of a principle)
- *Analyze* (for example, ask a student to break an argument down into its component parts)
- *Evaluate* (for example, ask a student to judge what the main things are that need to be changed in the classroom)
- *Understand* (for example, ask a student to construct the meaning of a historical event)
- *Create* (for example, ask a student to suggest an alternative way of doing something)

formative assessment Assessment during the course of instruction rather than after it is completed.

When you ask questions, remember to avoid overly broad, general questions; involve the whole class in questioning instead of calling on the same students all of the time; allow sufficient "wait time" after asking a question; probe students' responses with follow-up questions; and highly value students' own questions (Airasian, 2005).

Post-Instruction Assessment   **Summative assessment** (or formal assessment) is assessment after instruction is finished with the purpose of documenting student performance. Assessment after instruction provides information about how well your students have mastered the material, whether students are ready for the next unit, what grades they should be given, what comments you should make to parents, and how you should adapt your instruction (McMillan, 2004).

Review figure 16.1, which summarizes the activities a teacher can engage in before instruction, during instruction, and after instruction.

Making Assessment Compatible with Contemporary Views of Learning and Motivation

Throughout this book, we have encouraged you to view students as active learners who discover and construct meaning; set goals, plan, and reach goals; associate and link new information with existing knowledge in meaningful ways; think reflectively, critically, and creatively; develop self-monitoring skills; have positive expectations for learning and confidence in their skills; are enthusiastically and internally motivated to learn; apply what they learn to real-world situations; and communicate effectively.

Assessment plays an important role in effort, engagement, and performance. Your informal observations can provide information about how motivated students are to study a subject. If you have a good relationship with the student, direct oral questioning in a private conversation can often produce valuable insight about the student's motivation. In thinking about how assessment and motivation are linked, ask yourself if your assessments will encourage students to become more meaningfully involved in the subject matter and more intrinsically motivated to study the topic. Assessments that are challenging but fair should increase students' enthusiasm for learning. Assessments that are too difficult will lower students' self-esteem and self-efficacy, as well as raise their anxiety. Assessing students with measures that are too easy will bore them and not motivate them to study hard enough.

Susan Brookhart (1997, 2002) developed a model of how classroom assessment helps motivate students. She argues that every classroom environment hosts a series of repeated assessment events. In each assessment event, the teacher communicates with the students through assignments, activities, and feedback about performance. Students respond according to their perceptions of these learning opportunities and how well they think they will be able to perform. Brookhart believes that this view of classroom assessment suggests that teachers should evaluate students using a variety of performances, especially performances that are meaningful to students.

Similarly, many other classroom assessment experts argue that if you believe that motivated, active learning is an important goal of instruction, you should create alternative assessments that are quite different from traditional tests, which don't evaluate how students construct knowledge and understanding, set and reach goals, and think critically and creatively (Brookhart, 1997, 2002; McMillan, 2004; Stiggins, 2001; Tanner, 2001). Later in the chapter we will explore how alternative assessments can be used to examine these aspects of students' learning and motivation.

Creating Clear, Appropriate Learning Targets

Tying assessment to current views on learning and motivation also involves developing clear, appropriate learning goals, or targets. A *learning target* consists of what students should know and be able to do. It is important to establish criteria for judging whether students have attained the learning target (McMillan, 2004). Figure 16.2 on page 524 provides some examples of unit learning targets. The establishment of learning targets is compatible with the emphasis on instructional objectives that was discussed in chapter 12.

summative assessment Assessment after instruction is finished; also called formal assessment.

Students will be able to explain how various cultures are different and how cultures influence people's beliefs and lives by answering orally a comprehensive set of questions about cultural differences and their effects.

Students will demonstrate their knowledge of the parts of a plant by filling in words or a diagram for all parts studied.

Students will demonstrate their understanding of citizenship by correctly identifying whether previously unread statements about citizenship are true or false. A large number of items is used to sample most of the content learned.

Students will be able to explain why the American Constitution is important by writing an essay that indicates what would happen if we abolished our Constitution. The papers would be graded holistically, looking for evidence of reasons, knowledge of the Constitution, and organization.

Students will show that they know the difference between components of sentences by correctly identifying verbs, adverbs, adjectives, nouns, and pronouns in seven of eight long, complex sentences.

Students will be able to multiply fractions by correctly computing eight of ten fraction problems. The problems are new to the students; some are similar to "challenge" questions in the book.

Students will be able to use their knowledge of addition, subtraction, division, and multiplication to solve word problems that are similar to those used in the sixth-grade standardized test.

Students will demonstrate their understanding of how visual art conveys ideas and feelings by correctly indicating, orally, how examples of art communicate ideas and feelings.

FIGURE 16.2 **Examples of Unit Learning Targets**

Among the types of learning targets that you can weave through instruction and assessment are these (Stiggins & Conklin, 1992):

- *Knowledge.* This involves what students need to know to solve problems and perform skills. Knowledge gives students the ability to master substantive subject matter.
- *Reasoning/thinking.* An important learning goal is for students not just to acquire knowledge but also to be able to think about the knowledge. For example, in chapter 9, "Complex Cognitive Processes," we discussed such aspects of thinking as problem solving, inductive and deductive reasoning, strategies, and critical thinking.
- *Products.* Products are samples of students' work. Essays, term papers, oral reports, and science reports reflect students' ability to use knowledge and reasoning.
- *Affect.* Affective targets are students' emotions, feelings, and values. For example, recall our discussion of emotional intelligence in chapter 4, "Individual Variations," in which we described the importance of helping students develop emotional self-awareness (such as understanding the causes of their feelings), managing emotions (such as managing anger), reading emotions (such as being good at listening to what other people say), and handling relationships (such as being competent at solving relationship problems). However, including affective goals in assessment is controversial.

Establishing High-Quality Assessments

Another important goal for the classroom as an assessment context is achieving high-quality assessment (Kubiszyn & Borich, 2000; Wright, 2001). Assessment reaches a high level of quality when it yields reliable, valid, and useful information about students' performance (Carey, 2001). High-quality assessments also are fair (McMillan, 2004). Validity and reliability are concerned with the consistency and accuracy of the inferences teachers make about students from assessment information.

Validity As we learned in chapter 15, *validity* refers to the extent to which assessment measures what it is intended to measure—for example, does a test on the American Revolution truly measure students' knowledge of that event? p. 490. In the context of classroom assessment, *validity* also includes how accurate and useful a teacher's inferences are about the assessment. *Inferences* are conclusions that individuals draw from information. You might infer that a test given to students on the American Revolution did a good job of assessing their knowledge of the American Revolution but did a poor job of evaluating their ability to think critically about issues involved in the American Revolution. Validity requires using the right kind of information to make a decision about a student, as well as judging whether the assessment was representative and fair.

You can't obtain information about everything a student learns. Thus, your assessment of a student will necessarily be a sample of the student's learning (Gredler, 1999). The most important source of information for validity in your classroom will be *content-related evidence*, the extent to which the assessment reflects what you have been teaching (McMillan, 2004).

If a test you give does a balanced job of sampling the full range of content that has been taught, and a student gets 80% of the answers right, it is reasonable to conclude that the student probably has learned about 80% of the content. On the other hand, if the test you give samples only part of the material and a student gets 80% right, the test results give no clear indication of how much of the overall content the student actually has learned.

Adequately sampling content is clearly an important goal of valid assessment (Trice, 2000; Weller, 2001). Use your best professional judgment when sampling content. Thus, you wouldn't want to use just one multiple-choice question to assess a student's knowledge of a chapter on geography. An increasing trend is to use multiple methods of assessment, which can provide a more comprehensive sampling of content. Thus, the teacher might assess students' knowledge of the geography chapter with some multiple-choice questions, several essay questions, and a project to complete. Always ask yourself whether your assessments of students are adequate samples of their performance. For example, is the completed science project all that you will use to grade the student, or will you include information about the student's mastery of the general course content, the student's effort, and his or her class participation in your grading?

Linking instruction and assessment in the classroom leads to the concept of **instructional validity**: the extent to which the assessment is a reasonable sample of what actually went on in the classroom (McMillan, 2004). For example, a classroom assessment should reflect both what the teacher taught and students' opportunity to learn the material. Consider a math class in which the teacher gives students a test on their ability to solve multiplication problems. For instructional validity, it is important that the teacher competently instructed students in how to solve the problems and gave students adequate opportunities to practice this skill.

An important strategy for validity in classroom assessment is to systematically link learning targets, content, instruction, and assessment (McMillan, 2004). Imagine that you are a science teacher and that one of your learning targets is to get students to think more critically and creatively in designing science projects. Ask yourself what content is important to achieve this learning target. For instance, will it help students to read biographies of famous scientists that include information about how they came up with their ideas? Also ask yourself what learning targets you will emphasize in instruction. For your target regarding students' science projects, it will be important for you to carry through in your instruction on the theme of helping students to think critically and creatively about science.

Reliability Remember from chapter 15 that we defined *reliability* as the extent to which a test produces consistent, reproducible scores p. 491. Reliable scores are stable, dependable, and relatively free from errors of measurement. Consistency depends on circumstances involved in taking the test and student factors that vary from one test to another (McMillan, 2004).

instructional validity The extent to which the assessment is a reasonable sample of what went on in the classroom.

As we stated in chapter 15, reliability is not about the appropriateness of the assessment information. Reliability is about determining how consistently an assessment measures what it is measuring. If a teacher gives students the same test in a math class on two occasions and the students perform in a consistent manner on the tests, this indicates that the test was reliable. However, the consistency in students' performance (with high scorers being high both times the test was given, middle scorers performing similarly across the two assessments, and low scorers doing poorly on both assessments) says nothing about whether the test actually measured what it was designed to measure (for example, being an accurate, representative sample of questions that measured the math content that had been taught). Thus, reliable assessments are not necessarily valid.

Reliability is reduced by errors in measurement. A student can have adequate knowledge and skill and still not perform consistently across several tests because of a number of factors. Internal factors can include health, motivation, and anxiety. External factors can include inadequate directions given by the teacher, ambiguously created items, poor sampling of information, and inefficient scoring of the student's responses. For example, a student might perform extremely well on the first test a teacher gives to assess the student's reading comprehension but considerably lower on the second test in this domain. The student's lack of knowledge and skill could be the reason for the low reliability across the two assessments, but the low reliability also could be due to any number of measurement errors.

Fairness High-quality classroom assessment is not only valid and reliable but also fair (McMillan, 2004; National Research Council, 2001). Assessment is fair when all students have an equal opportunity to learn and demonstrate their knowledge and skill (Rearden, 2001; Yung, 2001). Assessment is fair when teachers have developed appropriate learning targets, provided competent content and instruction to match those targets, and chosen assessments that reflect the targets, content, and instruction.

Assessment bias includes offensiveness and unfair penalization (Popham, 2005). An assessment is biased if it is offensive to a subgroup of students. This occurs when negative stereotypes of particular subgroups are included in the test. For example, consider a test in which the items portray males in high-paying and prestigious jobs (doctors and business executives) and females in low-paying and less-prestigious jobs (clerks and secretaries). Because some females taking the test likely will be offended by this gender inequality, and appropriately so, the stress this creates may produce a less-successful outcome for females on the test.

An assessment also may be biased if it unfairly penalizes a student based on the student's group membership, such as ethnicity, socioeconomic status, gender, religion, and disability. For example, consider an assessment that focuses on information which students from affluent families are far more likely to be familiar with than students from low-income families (Popham, 2005). A teacher decides to see how well students can collaboratively solve problems in groups. The content of the problem to be discussed is a series of locally presented operas and symphonies likely to have been attended only by those who can afford the high ticket prices. Even if the affluent students didn't attend these musical events themselves, they may have heard their parents talk about them. Thus, students from low-income families might perform less effectively on the collaborative problem-solving exercise pertaining to musical events not because they are less skilled at such problem solving but because they are unfamiliar with the events.

Some assessment experts believe it is important to create a philosophy of *pluralistic assessment,* which includes being responsive to cultural diversity in the classroom and at school (Payne, 1997). This usually includes performance assessments during instruction and after instruction. Performance assessments that can be used as part of pluralistic assessment include portfolios, projects, demonstrations, interviews, and oral presentations. This does not mean abandoning objective measurement in the form of multiple-choice exams and essay questions but, rather, making sure that a variety of methods are used, including at least some performance assessments. To learn more about culturally responsive strategies in assessing students, read the Diversity and Education interlude.

Assessment Resources

Diversity and Education
Culturally Responsive Strategies for Assessing Students

Geneva Gay (1997, pp. 215–216, 218) evaluated the role of ethnicity and culture in assessment and recommended a number of culturally responsive strategies in assessing students. She advocates modifying (1) the Eurocentric nature of current U.S. instruction and achievement assessments, (2) use of a wider variety of assessment methods that take into account the cultural styles of students of color, (3) evaluation of students against their own records, and (4) assessment of students in ways that serve culturally appropriate diagnostic and developmental functions.

Achievement assessments "are designed to determine what students know. Presumably they reflect what has been taught in schools." Gay believes that "although progress has been made in the last three decades to make school curricula more inclusive of ethnic and cultural diversity, most of the knowledge taught, and consequently the achievement tests, continue to be Eurocentric." She points out that even mastery of skills tends to be "transmitted through Eurocentric contexts. For instance, achievement tests may embed skills in scenarios that are not relevant to the cultural backgrounds and life experiences of students of color," as when a teacher asks "immigrant students from the Caribbean who have never experienced snow to engage in problem solving" by evaluating the challenges and dilemmas presented by a blizzard—the students might have the problem-solving skill to respond to this request, but their unfamiliarity with cold winters can interfere with their ability to perform the task effectively.

This does not mean that students of color should not be assessed or that they should not be expected to meet high achievement standards. They should. However, "to avoid perpetuating educational inequality through assessment procedures, these students should not always be expected to demonstrate" knowledge and skills in terms of contexts with which they are not familiar. A good strategy is to use a variety of assessment methods to ensure that no single method gives an advantage to one ethnic group or another. These methods should include socioemotional measures as well as measures of academic content. Teachers also should carefully observe and monitor students' performance for verbal and nonverbal information in the assessment context.

Gay further argues that norm-referenced traditional assessments should be used only in conjunction with performance assessments. More emphasis should be given to evaluating students against their own records, with the focus being on improvement, rather than on comparisons with other students.

Gay also believes that assessment should always "serve diagnostic and developmental functions and be culturally responsible. . . . Narrative reports, developmental profiles, student-teacher-parent conferences, and anecdotal records should always be included in reporting students' progress."

Current Trends

Here are some current trends in classroom assessment (Hambleton, 1996; National Research Council, 2001):

* *Using at least some performance-based assessment.* Historically, classroom assessment has emphasized the use of **objective tests,** such as multiple-choice, which have relatively clear, unambiguous scoring criteria. In contrast, **performance assessments** require students to create answers or products that demonstrate their knowledge or skill. Examples of performance assessment include writing an essay, conducting an experiment, carrying out a project, solving a real-world problem, and creating a portfolio.

objective tests Tests that have relatively clear, unambiguous scoring criteria, usually multiple-choice tests.

performance assessment Assessment that requires creating answers or products that demonstrate knowledge and skill; examples include writing and conducting an experiment, carrying out a project, solving a real-world problem, and creating a portfolio.

**Assessment and Issues
in School Reform**

Exploring Issues in Assessment

• *Examining higher-level cognitive skills.* Rather than assess only content knowledge, as many objective tests do, a current trend is to evaluate a student's higher-level cognitive skills, such as problem solving, critical thinking, decision making, drawing of inferences, and strategic thinking.

• *Using multiple assessment methods.* In the past, assessment meant using a test—often a multiple-choice test—as the sole means of assessing a student. A current trend is to use multiple methods to assess students. Thus, a teacher might use any number of these methods: a multiple-choice test, an essay, an interview, a project, a portfolio, and student evaluations of themselves. Multiple assessments provide a broader view of the child's learning and achievement than a single measure.

• *Having high performance standards.* Another trend is the demand for high performance standards, even world-class performance standards, for interpreting educational results. Some experts say that world-class performance standards are driving contemporary classroom assessment by providing goals, or targets, to attain (Taylor, 1994). However, as we saw in chapter 15, questions arise about who should set these standards and whether they should be set at all ◄ p. 498.

• *Using computers as part of assessment.* Traditionally, computers have been used to score tests, analyze test results, and report scores. Today, computers increasingly are being used to construct and administer tests, as well as to present different assessment formats to students in a multimedia environment. With coming advances in technology, assessment practices are likely to be very different from traditional paper-and-pencil tests (van der Linden, 1995).

Trends in assessment also include emphasizing integrated rather than isolated skills, giving students more feedback, and making standards and criteria public rather than private and secretive. We will revisit many of these current trends later in this chapter.

⚠ Review and Reflect

1 **Discuss the classroom as an assessment context.**

Review
• What are the aims of assessment before, after, and during instruction?
• What changes might make assessment more compatible with contemporary views of learning and motivation?
• What are some useful types of learning targets?
• What three standards can be used to judge the quality of classroom assessments?
• What are some current trends in assessing students' learning?

Reflect
• Think of one of the better teachers that you had as a K–12 student. In retrospect, how would you describe the teacher's classroom as an "assessment context"?

TRADITIONAL TESTS

In this section and the next, we will provide some guidelines for creating traditional test items and for constructing alternative assessments. Traditional tests are typically paper-and-pencil tests in which students select from choices, calculate numbers, construct short responses, or write essays. Our coverage of traditional tests focuses on two main types of item formats in assessment: (1) selected-response items and (2) constructed-response items.

Selected-Response Items

Selected-response items have an objective format that allows students' responses to be scored on quick inspection. A scoring key for correct responses is created and can be applied by an examiner or by a computer. True/false, multiple-choice, and matching items are the most widely used types of items in selected-response tests. We also will describe several other recently developed objective-item formats.

True/False Items　A true/false item asks a student to mark whether a statement is true or false—for example,

>　Montpelier is the capital of Vermont.　True　False

The ease with which true/false items can be constructed has a potential drawback. Teachers sometimes take statements directly from a text or modify them slightly when making up true/false items. Avoid this practice, because it tends to encourage rote memorization with little understanding of the material.

　　The strengths and limitations of true/false items are described in figure 16.3.

Constructing Tests

Teaching Strategies
For Writing True/False Items

Some good strategies for writing true/false items are (Gronlund, 2003, pp. 78–84)

1. *Use only one key idea in each statement.* Including several ideas in a true/false statement usually should be avoided because it tends to confuse the student and the answer is likely to be influenced more by reading ability than learning.
>　Example: The first item is better than the second.
>　　　　Montpelier is the capital of Vermont.
>　　　　Montpelier is the capital of Vermont, which is a New England state, and has fewer than 50,000 inhabitants.
2. *"Keep the statement short, and use simple vocabulary and sentence structure"* (p. 80).
>　Example: The first item is better than the second.
>　　　　Montpelier is the capital of Vermont.
>　　　　The capital city of the state of Vermont is a small metropolis known as Montpelier.

Strengths

1. The item is useful for outcomes where there are only two possible alternatives (e.g., fact or opinion, valid or invalid).
2. Less demand is placed on reading ability than in multiple-choice items.
3. A relatively large number of items can be answered in a typical testing period.
4. Scoring is easy, objective, and reliable.

Limitations

1. It is difficult to write items at a high level of knowledge and thinking that are free from ambiguity.
2. When a statement indicates correctly that a statement is false, that response provides no evidence that the student knows what is correct.
3. No diagnostic information is provided by the incorrect answers.
4. Scores are more influenced by guessing than with any other item type.

FIGURE 16.3　**Strengths and Limitations of True/False Items**

selected-response items　Test items with an objective format in which responses can be scored on quick inspection. A scoring guide for correct responses is created and can be used by an examiner or a computer.

3. *Use words so precisely that the statement can clearly be judged as true or false.* True statements should be true under all circumstances and yet free of qualifiers, such as *might* and *possible.* Vague terms such as *seldom, frequently,* and *often* should be avoided.

> Example: The first item is better than the second.
>> Polls at the end of 1989 showed that a majority of Americans supported sending U.S. troops to Kuwait.
>> A lot of people believed that the Gulf War might have been justified.

4. *"Use negatives sparingly and avoid double negatives"* (p. 81).

> Example: The first item is better than the second.
>> In the presence of high heat, oxygen bonds readily with hydrogen.
>> In the presence of high heat, oxygen is not unlikely to bond with hydrogen.

5. *"Avoid extraneous clues to the answer.* Statements that include absolutes such as always, never, all, none, and only tend to be false. Statements with qualifiers such as usually, might, and sometimes tend to be true" (pp. 83–84). Either eliminate these verbal clues to correct answers or balance them between true and false items.

> Example: The first item is better than the second.
>> Martin Luther King made important civil rights speeches.
>> Martin Luther King never made an unimportant speech.

Multiple-Choice Items   A **multiple-choice item** consists of two parts: the stem plus a set of possible responses. The stem is a question or statement, and it is followed by a set of possible responses from which to choose. Incorrect alternatives are called *distractors.* The student's task is to select the correct choice from among the distractors—for example,

What is the capital of Vermont?	(Stem)
a. Portland	(Distractor)
b. Montpelier	(Answer)
c. Boston	(Distractor)
d. Weston	(Distractor)

Students below the fourth grade probably should answer questions on the test page rather than on a separate answer sheet. Young elementary school students tend to respond slowly and lose their place easily when they have to use a separate answer sheet (Sax, 1997). Using a separate answer sheet with older students often reduces scoring time because the answers usually can fit on only one page. Many school districts have commercially printed answer sheets that teachers can order for their classes. If you hand-score multiple-choice tests, consider preparing a scoring stencil by cutting or punching holes in the answer sheet in the locations of the correct answers.

For most classroom requirements, simply count the number of answers marked correctly. Some teachers penalize students for guessing by deducting for wrong answers, but assessment experts say that this probably is not worth the extra bother and frequently leads to mistakes in scoring (Sax, 1997).

Strengths and limitations of multiple-choice items are listed in figure 16.4.

Video Lecture: Traditional Tests

Writing Multiple-Choice Items

Teaching Strategies
For Writing Multiple-Choice Items

multiple-choice item An objective test item consisting of two parts: a stem plus a set of possible responses.

Some good strategies for writing high-quality multiple-choice items include (Gronlund, 2003; Haladyna, 1997, 2002; Linden, 1996; Sax, 1997)

Strengths

1. Both simple and complex learning outcomes can be measured.
2. The task is highly structured and clear.
3. A broad sample of achievement can be measured.
4. Incorrect alternatives provide diagnostic information.
5. Scores are less influenced by guessing than true/false items.
6. Scoring is easy, objective, and reliable.

Limitations

1. Constructing good items is time consuming.
2. It is frequently difficult to find plausible distractors.
3. The multiple-choice format is ineffective for measuring some types of problem solving and the ability to organize and express ideas.
4. Score can be influenced by reading ability.

FIGURE 16.4 Strengths and Limitations of Multiple-Choice Items

1. *Write the stem as a question.*
2. *Give three or four possible alternatives from which to choose.*
3. *State items and options positively when possible.* Elementary school students especially find negatives confusing. If you use the word *not* in the stem, *italicize* or <u>underline</u> it—for example,

Which of the following cities is <u>not</u> in New England?

a. Boston   b. Chicago   c. Montpelier   d. Providence

4. *Include as much of the item as possible in the stem, thus making the stem relatively long and the alternatives relatively short*—for example,

Which U.S. president wrote the Gettysburg Address?

a. Thomas Jefferson   b. Abraham Lincoln   c. James Madison   d. Woodrow Wilson

5. *Alternatives should grammatically match the stem so that no answers are grammatically wrong.* For example, the first item is better than the second:

Orville and Wilbur Wright became famous because of which type of transportation?

a. airplane   b. automobile   c. boat   d. train

Orville and Wilbur Wright became famous because of an

a. airplane   b. automobile   c. boat   d. train

6. *Write items that have a clearly defensible correct or best option.* Unless you give alternative directions, students will assume that there is only one correct or best answer to an item.
7. *Vary the placement of the correct option.* Students who are unsure of an answer tend to select the middle options and avoid the extreme options. Alphabetizing response choices (by the first letters in the response) will help to vary the placement of the correct option.
8. *Beware of cues in the length of the options.* Correct answers tend to be longer than incorrect ones because of the need to include specifications and qualifications that make it true. Lengthen the distractors (incorrect responses) to approximately the same length as the correct answer.

9. *Don't expect students to make narrow distinctions among answer choices.* For example, the first item is better than the second:

The freezing point of water is

a. 25°F b. 32°F c. 39°F d. 46°F

The freezing point of water is

a. 30°F b. 31°F c. 32°F d. 33°F

10. *Do not overuse "None of the above" and "All of the above."* Also avoid using variations of "A and B" or "C and D but not A."
11. *Don't use the exact wording in a textbook when writing a question.* Weak students might recognize the correct answer but not really understand its meaning.

Matching Items   Used by many teachers with younger students, matching requires students to connect one group of stimuli correctly with a second group of stimuli (Hambleton, 1996). Matching is especially well suited for assessing associations or links between two sets of information. In a typical matching format, a teacher places a list of terms on the left side of the page and a description or definition of the terms on the right side of the page. The student's task is to draw lines between the columns that correctly link terms with their definitions or descriptions. In another format, a space is left blank next to each term, in which the student writes the correct number or letter of the description/definition. When using matching, limit the number of items to be matched to no more than eight or ten. Many experts recommend using no more than five or six items per set (Linden, 1996).

Matching tests are convenient for teachers in that (Popham, 2005) (1) their compact form requires little space, thus making it easy to assess quite a lot of information efficiently, and (2) they can be easily scored by using a correct-answer template.

But matching tests may tend to ask students to connect trivial information. Also, most matching tasks require students to connect information they have simply memorized, although items can be constructed that measure more-complex cognitive skills (Sax, 1997).

Other Objective Assessment Formats   Other objective or selected-response tests make use of audiovisuals and problem sets (Hambleton, 1996). The audiovisual format takes advantage of the ease with which we now can create and show slides and videotapes. Students are presented with a problem in an audiovisual format and asked to make decisions about what is going on or how to solve the problem. The student selects answers from sets of options, just as in a paper-and-pencil multiple-choice test. The main advantages of this audiovisual format are that it can depict the real world and can be used to evaluate higher-level cognitive skills. The main drawbacks are the costs in time and money.

Problem sets involve presenting two or more multiple-choice or objective short-answer items in reference to a single stimulus, "such as an illustration, a graph, or a passage," (Hambleton, 1996, p. 910). For example, in math class, a graph might be displayed together with a series of multiple-choice items. In history or social studies, a map might be the stimulus for half a dozen questions. Some students report that the problem-set format seems more realistic than a set of discrete, independent items.

problem sets Groups of two or more multiple-choice or objective short-answer items that are related to the same stimulus, such as an illustration, a graph, or a passage.

How Good Are Your Test Items?   One way to evaluate the quality of your test items is to conduct an item analysis of them. One method for doing this involves computing the difficulty level of the items. Another method involves determining how well the items discriminate among students who scored high and those who scored low on the entire test (Gronlund, 2003; Linden, 1996; Linn & Gronlund, 2000).

The **item difficulty index** is the percentage of students who obtain the correct answer on an item. To compute the difficulty index for each item, go through these steps:

1. Rank-order the scores on the test from highest to lowest.
2. Identify the high-scoring group and the low-scoring group. With 30 students you might choose the 10 students who scored the highest on the test and the 10 students who scored the lowest. A good strategy is to select the top-scoring one-third of students and the bottom-scoring one-third of students.
3. Determine the percentage of high scorers and low scorers passing an item by adding a zero. In one example, 8 of 10 students in the high-scoring group correctly answered the item, which equals 80%; 4 of 10 students in the low-scoring group answered it correctly, which equals 40%.
4. To obtain the item difficulty index, add the percentage correct in the high and low groups and then divide by 2. Add a percent sign to the answer. Thus, in our example,

$$\frac{80 + 40}{2} = 60\%$$

When the item difficulty index is 75% or higher, the item is usually interpreted as easy in terms of difficulty level; when the index is 25% or less, the item is usually interpreted as hard in difficulty level. Thus, the higher the item difficulty index, the easier the item is. All other percentages—including the 60% in our example—are usually interpreted as average in difficulty level. Assessment experts recommend that most of the items be in the 40% to 60% range, with only a few hard items (0% to 25%) or easy (75% to 100%) items.

The **item discrimination index** reflects the item's ability to discriminate between individuals who scored high and those who scored low on the entire test. Obtain the item discrimination index by subtracting the percentage correct in the low-scoring group from the percentage correct in the high-scoring group. Then, add a decimal point to the answer. Thus, in our example,

$$80 - 40 = .40$$

This item discrimination index has a decimal point, and its value ranges from 0 to 1.00. If the index is 0 to .19, there was little or no difference between the high- and low-scoring groups on the item; if the index is .20 to .39, the item discriminated moderately well between the high- and low-scoring groups; if the index is .40 or greater, the item strongly discriminated between the high- and low-scoring groups (which was the case for the item in our example: .40). If the item discrimination index is below .20, you likely will want to improve the item or eliminate it; if it is .20 to .39, you might want to keep the item but improve it; and if the index is .40 or above, you likely will want to keep the item as it is.

The first time you compute item difficulty and item discrimination indexes, they might seem more complicated than they really are. After you have done several of these, the computations should be easy for you to do.

Constructed-Response Items

Constructed-response items require students to write out information rather than select a response from a menu. Short-answer and essay items are the most commonly used forms of constructed-response items. In scoring, many constructed-response items require judgment on the part of the examiner.

Research and Assessment

item difficulty index The percentage of students who obtain the correct answer on an item.

item discrimination index An index that reflects the item's ability to discriminate between individuals who scored high and those who scored low on the entire test.

constructed-response items Items that require students to write out information rather than select a response from a menu.

Short-Answer Items   A **short-answer item** is a constructed-response format in which students are required to write a word, a short phrase, or several sentences in response to a task. For example, a student might be asked

Who discovered penicillin?

The short-answer format allows recall and could provide a problem-solving assessment of a wide range of material. The disadvantages of short-answer questions are that they can require judgment to be scored and typically measure rote learning.

Sentence completion is a variation of the short-answer item, in which students express their knowledge and skill by completing a sentence. For example, a student might be asked to complete this sentence stem: The name of the person who discovered penicillin is _____.

Essays   **Essay items** allow students more freedom of response to questions but require more writing than other formats. Essay items are especially good for assessing students' understanding of material, higher-level thinking skills, ability to organize information, and writing skills. Here are some examples of high school essay questions:

What are the strengths and weaknesses of a democratic approach to government?
Describe the main themes of the novel you just read.
Argue that the United States is a gender-biased nation.

Essay items can require students to write anything from a few sentences to much-more-extended responses. In some cases, teachers ask all students to answer the same essay question(s). In others, teachers let students select from a group of items the item(s) they want to write about, a strategy that makes it more difficult to compare different students' responses.

Suggestions for writing good essay items include these (Sax, 1997):

- *Specify limitations.* Be sure to inform students about the length of the desired answer and the weight that will be given to each item in determining scores or judgments.
- *Structure and clarify the task.* Make clear what they are supposed to write about. A poorly worded item is "Who was George Washington?" This could be answered in six words: "First president of the United States." In cases like this, ask yourself what more you want the student to tell. These more-structured essay items would require more thinking on the part of the student:

    Discuss several events in the life of George Washington that confirm or disprove the claim that "he never told a lie." Use the events to support a claim of your own about how truthful Washington was.
    Describe two major accomplishments of Susan B. Anthony's political life. What was important about each accomplishment?
- *Ask questions in a direct way.* Don't get too tricky.

You might hear the term *rubric* used in regard to scoring students' responses on essays and other tests. In this context, *rubric* simply means a scoring system. Figure 16.5 lists some strengths and limitations of essay questions.

short-answer item A constructed-response format in which students are required to write a word, a short phrase, or several sentences in response to a task.

essay items Items that require a lengthy written answer; they allow more freedom of response to questions but require more writing than other formats.

Teaching Strategies
For Scoring Essay Questions

Here are some good strategies for scoring essays (Sax, 1997):

1. *Outline a plan for what constitutes a good or acceptable answer prior to administering or scoring students' responses* (McMillan, 2004). Essays can be scored holistically or

Strengths

1. The highest level of learning outcomes (analysis, synthesis, evaluation) can be measured.
2. The integration and application of ideas can be emphasized.
3. Preparation time is usually less than for selection-type formats.

Limitations

1. Achievement may not be adequately sampled due to the time needed to answer each question.
2. It can be difficult to relate essay responses to intended learning outcomes because of freedom to select, organize, and express ideas.
3. Scores are raised by writing skill and bluffing, and lowered by poor handwriting, misspelling, and grammatical errors.
4. Scoring is time-consuming, subjective, and possibly unreliable.

FIGURE 16.5 **Strengths and Limitations of Essay Questions**

analytically. *Holistic scoring* means making an overall judgment about the student's answer and giving it a single number or letter. You might make this judgment based on your overall impression of the essay or base it on several criteria that you have generated. Holistic scoring is often used when essays are long. *Analytic scoring* means scoring various criteria separately, then, in most cases, adding up the points to produce an overall score for the essay. Analytic scoring can be time consuming, so avoid having more than three or four criteria for an essay.

2. *Devise a method by which you can score the essays without knowing which students wrote them.* You might do this by having students write their name beside a number on a separate sheet, then write only their number on the essay. When you record the grade, you can match up the student's number and name. This reduces the chance that your positive or negative expectations for the student will enter into your evaluation of the responses.

3. *Evaluate all answers to the same questions together.* Read and score all students' responses to one item before moving on to the next item. It is easier for you to remember the criteria for evaluating an answer to a single essay item than to remember the criteria for all essay items. Also, if you read all of one student's responses together, your evaluation of the first few items will tend to influence your evaluation of the remaining items.

4. *Decide on a policy for handling irrelevant or incorrect responses.* Some students try to bluff their way through essays. Other students write everything they know about a topic without taking the time to zero in on specifically what the item is asking for. Still other students might use poor grammar, misspell words, or write illegibly. Decide ahead of time whether and how much you will penalize such responses.

5. *If possible, reread papers before handing them back to students.* This helps you guard against any flaws or oversights in your scoring.

6. *Write comments on the paper.* An essay, especially a long one, with only a number or letter grade on it does not give adequate feedback to a student. And if you only circle or correct spelling errors and grammar, you are not giving students insight about the content of their essay responses. A good strategy is to write a number of brief comments at appropriate places throughout the essay, such as "Expand this idea more," "Unclear," or "Needs an example," in addition to making overall comments about the essay at its beginning or end. It is better to write comments throughout the essay than to make one or two minor comments in one part of the essay.

> ## ⚠ Review and Reflect
>
> **2 Provide some guidelines for constructing traditional tests.**
>
> **Review**
> - What are some important ideas to remember when creating true/false, multiple-choice, and matching items? What are some basic tools for evaluating item quality?
> - What are some keys to effectively creating and scoring constructed-response items?
>
> **Reflect**
> - Why do you think traditional testing has survived so long in K–12 classrooms?

ALTERNATIVE ASSESSMENTS

There are alternatives to the traditional assessments that we just discussed (Gronlund, Linn, & Davis, 2000; Popham, 2005). Let's examine some trends in this regard.

Trends in Alternative Assessment

Video Observation: Informal Classroom Assessments

One current trend is to require students to solve some type of authentic problem or to perform in terms of completing a project or demonstrating other skills outside the context of a test or an essay (Montgomery, 2001). Another trend is to have students create a learning portfolio to demonstrate what they have learned (Berryman & Russell, 2001). Such alternative assessments are needed to make instruction compatible with contemporary views of learning and motivation.

Alternative assessments offer students more choices than they would have in taking a test or writing an essay. Consider several alternative assessments that a middle school language arts teacher devised (Combs, 1997). She gave students a menu of options to choose from that included such formats as book reports, artwork, videos, and models. For example, in a unit on mystery, students might choose to write a report on an author of mystery stories, write an original mystery, make a children's mystery book, or conduct an interview with a private investigator. Each of these options came with a detailed set of instructions and a scoring guide for quality control. Figure 16.6 shows the directions and scoring guide for alternative assessments that focus on the Middle Ages and family history.

Authentic assessment means evaluating a student's knowledge or skill in a context that approximates the real world or real life as closely as possible (Pokey & Siders, 2001). Traditional assessment has involved the use of paper-and-pencil tests that are often far removed from real-world contexts. An increasing trend is to assess students with items that more closely reflect reality (Palomba & Banta, 1999). In some circles, the terms *performance-based assessment* and *authentic assessment* have been used interchangeably. However, not all performance-based assessments are authentic (McMillan, 2002a).

Critics of authentic assessment argue that such assessments are not necessarily superior to more-conventional assessments, such as multiple-choice and essay tests (Terwilliger, 1997). They say that the proponents of authentic assessment rarely present data in support of the validity of authentic assessments. They also believe that authentic assessments don't adequately examine knowledge and basic skills.

In the rest of this section, we will describe performance-based assessment in general, then consider the use of portfolios in assessment.

www.mhhe.com/santedu2e

Alternative Assessments

Authentic Assessments

Oral Communication Assessments

Performance-Based Assessment

Moving from traditional assessment with objective tests to performance-based assessment has been described as going from "knowing" to "showing" (Burz & Marshall, 1996).

**Middle Ages Option
Model**

Directions:

Make a model of a creature or character from the Middle Ages. Write a one-half to one page description of your character (tell who or what it is and its importance in the Middle Ages). Your model must portray the creature or character through the use of appropriate costume, props, or other attributes.

Scoring Guide

25   Model portrays the character or creature and time period through the use of attire, props, and other attributes
10   Artistic quality
15   The model shows evidence of effort
50   A 1/2 to 1 page written description of the character is included

**Family History Option
Family Tree Poster**

Directions:

Make a poster of your family tree, going back at least three generations. Provide as much information about the family members as possible, including, but not limited to, birthdate, death date (if not living), occupation, place of birth, accomplishments, etc. In addition, provide at least two anecdotes about your family's history (how they came to live in our town, special notoriety, honors, awards, medals, etc.). You must *write out* your family tree! (You may not make a copy of a commercially prepared family tree and paste it on the poster.) Make your poster attractive and neat!

Scoring Guide

25   Family tree includes at least three generations prior to you
25   In addition to names, most entries include information such as birth, death, and place of birth
25   Poster includes at least two anecdotes about interesting or well-known family members
15   Poster is neatly and attractively typed or written by you
10   Mechanics, spelling, usage

FIGURE 16.6 Examples of Alternative Assessment in a Middle School Language Arts Class

Performance assessments include what is commonly thought of as students' actual performances (such as in dance, music, art, and physical education), as well as papers, projects, oral presentations, experiments, and portfolios. Figure 16.7 on page 538 shows an example of a performance-based assessment in science (Solano-Flores & Shavelson, 1997). We will cover the main features of performance-based assessments, guidelines for using them, and their strengths and weaknesses.

Some disciplines, such as art, music, and physical education, have been using performance-based assessments for many years. The major change in performance assessment has involved introducing these forms of assessment into the traditional "academic areas" (Powell, 2002).

Features of Performance-Based Assessment   Performance-based assessments often include an emphasis on "doing" open-ended activities for which there is no correct, objective answer and that may assess higher-level thinking. Performance-based assessment tasks sometimes also are realistic. Evaluating performance often includes direct methods of evaluation, self-assessment, assessment of group performance as well as individual performance, and an extended period of time for assessment (Hambleton, 1996).

Traditional tests emphasize what students know. Performance-based assessments are designed to evaluate what students know and can do (Maki, 2001; Moon & Callahan, 2001). In many cases, there is no correct, objective answer. For example, there is no one

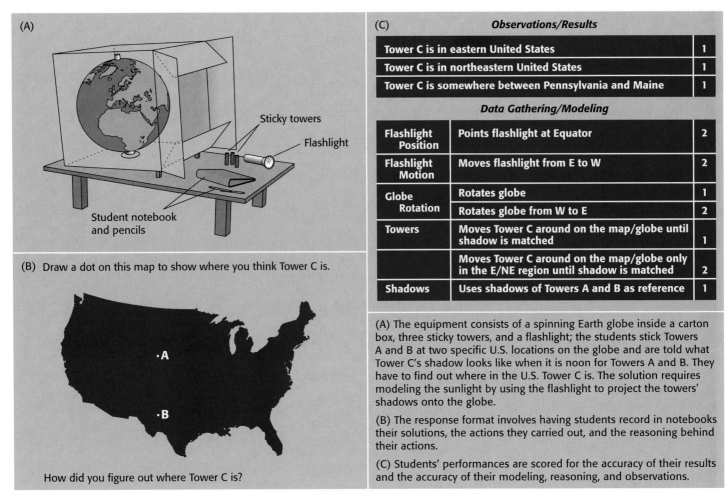

(C)	Observations/Results	
Tower C is in eastern United States		1
Tower C is in northeastern United States		1
Tower C is somewhere between Pennsylvania and Maine		1

	Data Gathering/Modeling	
Flashlight Position	Points flashlight at Equator	2
Flashlight Motion	Moves flashlight from E to W	2
Globe Rotation	Rotates globe	1
	Rotates globe from W to E	2
Towers	Moves Tower C around on the map/globe until shadow is matched	1
	Moves Tower C around on the map/globe only in the E/NE region until shadow is matched	2
Shadows	Uses shadows of Towers A and B as reference	1

(A) The equipment consists of a spinning Earth globe inside a carton box, three sticky towers, and a flashlight; the students stick Towers A and B at two specific U.S. locations on the globe and are told what Tower C's shadow looks like when it is noon for Towers A and B. They have to find out where in the U.S. Tower C is. The solution requires modeling the sunlight by using the flashlight to project the towers' shadows onto the globe.

(B) The response format involves having students record in notebooks their solutions, the actions they carried out, and the reasoning behind their actions.

(C) Students' performances are scored for the accuracy of their results and the accuracy of their modeling, reasoning, and observations.

FIGURE 16.7 A Performance-Based Assessment in Science: Daytime Astronomy

"correct answer" when a student gives a talk in class, creates a painting, performs a gymnastic routine, or designs a science project. Many performance-based assessments give students considerable freedom to construct their own responses rather than narrowing their range of answers. Although this makes scoring more difficult, it provides a context for evaluating students' higher-level thinking skills, such as the ability to think deeply about an issue or a topic (Wiggins, 1993). Many performance-based assessments are also realistic in the sense of being authentic, although, as we indicated earlier, some are not. Allowing students to use calculators or computers in solving math problems on tests reflects closer ties to the real world than requiring students to do them only with paper and pencil. When students have to solve math problems in the real world, they likely will use calculators and computers.

Performance-based assessments use direct methods of evaluation, such as evaluating writing samples to assess writing skills and oral presentations to assess speaking and judging oral presentations to assess speaking skills. Observing a student give an oral presentation is a more-direct assessment than asking the student a series of questions about speaking skills on a paper-and-pencil test.

Some performance assessments also involve having students evaluate their own performance. This emphasis shifts responsibility away from teachers and places it more squarely on the student's shoulders. For example, students might be asked to judge the quality of their own oral presentation, dance performance, or dramatic acting. Rubrics are useful aids to students in conducting self-assessments. For example, students might be required to evaluate a scrapbook that they have created (Goodrich, 1997). One criterion for evaluation might be "Gives enough details?" with the following possible responses: excellent ("Yes, I put enough details to give the reader a sense of time, place, and events"), good ("Yes, I put in some details, but some key details are missing"), minimal ("No, I did not put in enough details but did include a few"), and inadequate ("No, I had almost no details").

Some performance-based assessments evaluate how effectively a group of students perform, not just how the students perform individually. This emphasis ties in with our discussion of cooperative learning and other group activities in chapter 10, "Social Constructivist Approaches." Thus, a group of students might be assigned to create a science project rather than having each student do a project individually. Evaluation of the student can include both the individual's contribution and the group's product. Group projects are often complex and allow for the assessment of cooperative skills, communication skills, and leadership skills.

Finally, as we noted, performance assessments may take place over an extended period of time. In traditional assessment, assessment occurs in a single time frame. For example, a teacher gives a multiple-choice test and students are allowed an hour to take it. By contrast, it is not unusual for performance assessments to involve sustained work over days, weeks, and even months (Bracken, 2000). For example, a student might be evaluated once a month on the progress the student is making on a science project, then receive a final evaluation when the project is completed.

Guidelines for Performance-Based Assessment   Guidelines for using performance-based assessments cover four general issues (Airasian, 2005): (1) establishing a clear purpose, (2) identifying observable criteria, (3) providing an appropriate setting, and (4) judging or scoring the performance.

Make sure that any performance-based assessment has a clear purpose and that a clear decision can be made from the assessment (McKinley, Boulet, & Hambleton, 2000). The purposes can be diverse: to assign a grade, to evaluate a student's progress, to recognize the important steps in a performance, to generate products to be included in a learning portfolio, to provide concrete examples of students' work for admission to college or other programs, and so forth.

Performance criteria are specific behaviors that students need to perform effectively as part of the assessment. Establishing performance criteria helps the teacher to go beyond general descriptions (such as "Do an oral presentation" or "Complete a science project") in specifying what the student needs to do. Performance criteria help you make your observations more systematic and focused. As guidelines, they direct your observations. Without such criteria, your observations can be unsystematic and haphazard. Communicating these performance criteria to students at the beginning of instruction lets students know how to focus their learning.

Once you have clearly outlined the performance criteria, it is important to specify the setting in which you will observe the performance or product. You may want to observe behaviors directly in the regular flow of classroom activity, in a special context you create in the classroom, or in a context outside the classroom. As a rule of thumb it is a good idea to observe the student on more than one occasion, because a single performance might not fairly represent the student's knowledge or skill.

Finally, you will need to score or rate the performance. Scoring rubrics involve the criteria that are used to judge performance, what the range in the quality of the performance should look like, what score should be given and what that score means, and how the different levels of quality should be described and differentiated from one another (Arter & McTighe, 2001).

In preparing a rubric, you may want to (Re: Learning by Design, 2000)

1. *Include a scale of possible points to be assigned in scoring work.* High numbers usually are assigned to the best work. Scales typically use 4, 5, or 6 as the highest score, down to 1 or 0 for the lowest score.

Video Lecture: Performance Assessment Rubric

The State of Performance Assessment

Ensuring Equity with Performance-Based Assessment

performance criteria Specific behaviors that need to be performed effectively as part of an assessment.

CRITERIA   **QUALITY**

Purposes	The report explains the key purposes of the invention and also points out less obvious ones.	The report explains all of the key purposes of the invention.	The report explains some of the purposes of the invention but misses key purposes.	The report does not refer to the purposes of the invention.
Features	The report details both key and hidden features of the invention and explains how they serve several purposes.	The report details the key features of the invention and explains the purposes they serve.	The report neglects some of the features of the invention or the purposes they serve.	The report does not detail the features of the invention or the purposes they serve.
Critique	The report discusses the strengths and weaknesses of the invention, and suggests ways that it can be improved.	The report discusses the strengths and weaknesses of the invention.	The report discusses either the strengths or weaknesses of the invention, but not both.	The report does not mention the strengths or weaknesses of the invention.
Connections	The report makes appropriate connections between the purposes and features of the invention and many different kinds of phenomena.	The report makes appropriate connections between the purposes and features of the invention and one or two phenomena.	The report makes unclear or inappropriate connections between the invention and other phenomena.	The report makes no connections between the invention and other things.

FIGURE 16.8 Scoring Rubric for a Report on an Invention

Note: A teacher might assign each of the columns a score and/or label, such as column 1: 4 (Excellent), column 2: 3 (Good), column 3: 2 (Minimal), and column 4: 1 (Inadequate).

2. *Provide descriptors for each performance criteria to increase reliability and avoid biased scoring.*
3. *Decide whether the rubric will be generic, genre-specific, or task-specific.* If generic, the rubric can be used to judge a broad performance, such as communication or problem solving. If genre-specific, the rubric applies to a more-specific type of performance, such as an essay, a speech, or a narrative as a form of communication; open-ended or closed-end problems as kinds of problems solved. A task-specific rubric is unique to a single task, such as a single math problem or a speech on a specific topic.
4. *Decide whether the rubric should be longitudinal.* This type of rubric assesses progress over time toward mastery of educational objectives.

One strategy for developing rubrics is to work backward from *exemplars*—examples of student work (McMillan, 1997, p. 218). "These exemplars can be analyzed to determine what descriptors distinguish them. The examples can also be used as *anchor* papers for making judgments, and can be given to students to illustrate the dimensions." An *anchor* is a sample of work or performance used to set the specific performance standard for a rubric level. Thus, attached to a paragraph describing a six-level performance in writing might be two or three samples of writing to illustrate several levels (Re: Learning by Design, 2000).

Figure 16.8 shows a scoring rubric for scoring a report on an invention. Figure 16.9 indicates the importance of clarity in creating rubrics.

CRITERION: Gains Audience's Attention

QUALITY

(a)	Creative Beginning	Boring Beginning	No Beginning
(b)	Gives details or an amusing fact, a series of questions, a short demonstration, a colorful visual or a personal reason for why they picked the topic	Gives a one-or two-sentence introduction, then starts the speech	Does not attempt to gain the audience's attention, just starts the speech

FIGURE 16.9 **Creating Clarity in a Rubric for One Dimension of an Oral Presentation**
The descriptions in (a) are rather vague and do not clearly specify what students need to do to be evaluated very positively on the criterion. The descriptions in (b) provide more detailed specifications of how the criterion will be rated, a recommended strategy.

Teaching Strategies
For Scoring Rubrics

Here are some good strategies for incorporating scoring rubrics in performance assessment (Goodrich, 1997; McMillan, 2004; Re: Learning by Design, 2000):

1. *Match the type of rating with the purpose of the assessment.* If your purpose is more global and you need a general judgment, use a holistic scale. If your purpose is to provide more specific feedback on different aspects of a performance, use a more analytical approach.
2. *Share the criteria with students prior to instruction.* This should be done to encourage students to incorporate the descriptions as standards to guide their work.
3. *Build your rubrics from the top, starting from a description of an exemplary performance.* Even if no student can perform at an exemplary level, the rubric should be built from a picture of excellence to establish an anchor for scoring. A good strategy is to use two or three examples of excellence rather than a single example so that students are not limited in their thinking about what an excellent performance is. After you have described the best level of quality, describe the worst; then fill in the middle levels.
4. *Carefully construct the rubric language for each criterion or score.* Use words such as *excellent* and *good*, and carefully describe what each term means. Typically, you will have a paragraph for each criterion or score that includes concrete indicators of when the criterion or score has been met.
5. *Make rubrics more authentic.* Criteria should validly, not arbitrarily, distinguish different degrees of performance. Here are some criteria that are often used in assessing writing in large-scale performance tests: organization, usage/word choice, focus, sentence construction, mechanics, and voice. However, the following criteria are more authentic in that they relate more clearly to the impact of the writing (and they include the previously mentioned criteria without restricting the writer to conventions and rules): clarity, memorability, persuasiveness, and enticingness.
6. *Show students models.* Let students examine examples of good and not-so-good work. Identify what's good or bad about the models.
7. *Take appropriate steps to minimize scoring error.* A scoring system should be objective and consistent. Some types of errors, in particular, should be avoided in

scoring rubrics. The most common errors involve personal bias and halo effects of the person making the judgment. *Personal bias* occurs when teachers tend to give students higher scores (such as mostly 5 and 6 on a 1- to 6-point scale), lower scores (give mostly 1 or 2), or scores in the middle (give mostly 3 or 4). A *halo effect* occurs when a teacher's general impression of the student influences the score given on a particular performance. For example, if the teacher has a very favorable general view of the student, she may give a higher rating of a particular performance than the student deserves. If the teacher has a generally unfavorable view of the student, she may give a lower rating of a particular performance than the student deserves. Halo effects also occur when the teacher's rating of one dimension of a rubric carries over and affects other dimensions of the rubric.

Evaluating Performance-Based Assessment Many educational psychologists support increasing performance-based assessment (Eisner, 1999; Stiggins, 2001, 2002). They believe performance-based assessments involve students more in their learning, often encourage higher-level thinking skills, can measure what is really important in the curriculum, and can tie assessment more to real-world, real-life experiences.

Some states, such as Kentucky and Vermont, use statewide performance assessments. For example, the Kentucky Instructional Results Information System includes a number of domains (such as science and social science), each of which includes four components: learner outcomes, the tasks themselves, scoring guides, and examples of student papers (called "anchor papers").

"Although support for performance-based assessment is high in many parts of the United States and Canada, effective implementation" faces several hurdles (Hambleton, 1996, p. 903). Performance assessments often "take considerably more time to construct, administer, and score than objective tests." Also, many performance tests do not meet the standards of validity and reliability outlined by such education groups as the American Educational Research Association, American Psychological Association, and National Council on Measurement in Education. Moreover, the research base for performance-based tests is not well established.

Still, even the strongest supporters of traditional tests acknowledge that traditional tests do not measure all of what schools expect students to learn (Hambleton, 1996). Although planning, constructing, and scoring performance tests is challenging, teachers should make every effort to include performance assessments as an important aspect of their teaching (Mabry, 1999).

Portfolio Assessment

Interest in portfolio assessment has increased dramatically in recent years. Portfolios represent a significant departure from traditional tests of learning. Figure 16.10 summarizes the contrast between portfolios and traditional testing.

A **portfolio** consists of a systematic and organized collection of a student's work that demonstrates the student's skills and accomplishments. A portfolio is a purposeful collection of work that tells the story of the student's progress and achievements (Mintzes, Wandersee, & Novak, 2001; Weasmer & Woods, 2001). It is much more than a compilation of student papers stuffed into a manila folder or a collection of memorabilia pasted into a scrapbook (Hatch, 2000). To qualify for inclusion in a portfolio, each piece of work should be created and organized in a way that demonstrates progress and purpose. Portfolios can include many different types of work, such as writing samples, journal entries, videotapes, art, teacher comments, posters, interviews, poetry, test results, problem solutions, recordings of foreign language communication, self-assessments, and any other expression of the student that the teacher believes demonstrates the student's skills and accomplishments. Portfolios can be collected on paper, in photographs, and on audiotape, videotape, computer disk, or CD-ROM. Assessment expert Joan Herman (1996)

portfolio A systematic and organized collection of a student's work that demonstrates the student's skills and accomplishments.

Traditional Tests	Portfolios
• Separate learning, testing, and teaching	• Link assessment and teaching to learning
• Fail to assess the impact of prior knowledge on learning by using short passages that are often isolated and unfamiliar	• Address the importance of the student's prior knowledge as a critical determinant to learning by using authentic assessment activities
• Rely on materials requesting only literal information	• Provide opportunities to demonstrate inferential and critical thinking that are essential for constructing meaning
• Prohibit collaboration during the assessment process	• Represent a collaborative approach to assessment involving both students and teachers
• Often treat skills in isolated contexts to determine achievement for reporting purposes	• Use multifaceted activities while recognizing that learning requires integration and coordination of communication skills
• Assess students across a limited range of assignments that may not match what students do in classrooms	• Represent the full range of instructional activities that students are doing in their classrooms
• Assess students in a predetermined situation where the content is fixed	• Can measure the student's ability to perform appropriately in unanticipated situations
• Assess all students on the same dimensions	• Measure each student's achievements while allowing individual differences
• Address only achievement	• Address improvement, effort, and achievement
• Seldom provide vehicles for assessing students' abilities to monitor their own learning	• Implement self-assessment by having students monitor their learning
• Are mechanically scored or scored by teachers who have little input into the assessment	• Engage students in assessing their progress and/or accomplishments and establishing on-going learning goals
• Rarely include items that assess emotional responses to learning	• Provide opportunities to reflect upon feelings about learning

FIGURE 16.10 **Contrasting Traditional Tests and Portfolios**

says that portfolio assessment has become increasingly popular because it is a natural way to integrate instruction and assessment.

Four classes of evidence that can be placed in students' portfolios are artifacts, reproductions, attestations, and productions (Barton & Collins, 1997). *Artifacts* are documents or products, such as student papers and homework, that are produced during normal academic work in the classroom. *Reproductions* consist of documentation of a student's work outside the classroom, such as special projects and interviews. For example, a student's description of an interview with a local scientist in the community about the scientist's work is a reproduction. *Attestations* represent the teacher's or other responsible persons' documentation of the student's progress. For example, a teacher might write evaluative notes about a student's oral presentation and place them in the student's portfolio. *Productions* are documents the student prepares especially for the portfolio. Productions consist of three types of materials: goal statements, reflections, and captions. Students generate goal statements about what they want to accomplish with their portfolio, write down their reflections about their work and describe their progress, and create captions that describe each piece of work in the portfolio and its importance.

Using Portfolios Effectively   Effective use of portfolios for assessment requires (1) establishing the portfolio's purpose, (2) involving the student in decisions about it, (3) reviewing the portfolio with the student, (4) setting criteria for evaluation, and (5) scoring and judging the portfolio.

Establishing Purpose Portfolios can be used for different purposes (Lyons, 1999). Two broad types of purpose are to document growth and to show best work. A **growth portfolio** consists of the student's work over an extended time frame (throughout the school year or even longer) to reveal the student's progress in meeting learning targets. Growth portfolios also are sometimes referred to as "developmental portfolios." Growth portfolios are especially helpful in providing concrete evidence of how much a student has changed or learned over time. As students examine their portfolios, they can see for themselves how much they have improved. One example of a growth portfolio is the Integrated Language Arts Portfolio used in the elementary school grades in Juneau, Alaska (Arter, 1995). It is designed to replace report cards and grades as a way to demonstrate growth and accomplishments. Growth is tracked along a developmental continuum for levels of skills in reading, writing, speaking, and listening. A student's status on the continuum is marked at several designated times during the year. Samples of the student's work are used as the basis for judgments about the student's developmental level.

A **best-work portfolio** showcases the student's most outstanding work. Sometimes it even is called a "showcase portfolio." Best-work portfolios are more selective than developmental portfolios and often include the student's latest product. Best-work portfolios are especially useful for parent-teacher conferences, students' future teachers, and admission to higher education levels.

"Passportfolios," or "proficiency portfolios," are sometimes used to demonstrate competence and readiness to move on to new a level of work (Arter, 1995; Lankes, 1995). For example, the Science Portfolio is an optional aspect of the Golden State Evaluation in California (California State Department of Education, 1994). It is produced during a year of science and contains a problem-solving investigation, a creative expression (presenting a scientific idea in a unique and original manner), a "growth through writing" section that demonstrates progress over time in understanding a concept, and self-reflection. The Central Park East Secondary School in New York City uses portfolios to determine graduation eligibility. Students are required to complete fourteen portfolios that demonstrate their competence in areas such as science and technology, ethics and social issues, community service, and history (Gold & Lanzoni, 1993).

Involving Students in Selecting Portfolio Materials Many teachers let students make at least some of the decisions about the portfolio's contents (Weasmer & Woods, 2001). Throughout Vermont, students in the fourth through eighth grades select five to seven items to be placed in their portfolio to demonstrate their competence in math problem solving. Student-led parent conferences allow students to demonstrate to parents what they have learned (Borba & Olvera, 2001). When students are allowed to choose the contents for their own portfolios, a good strategy is to encourage self-reflection by having them write a brief description of why they chose each piece of work (Airasian, 2001).

Reviewing with Students It is important to explain to students at the beginning of the year what portfolios are and how they will be used. You also should have a number of student-teacher conferences throughout the year to review the student's progress and help the student to plan future work for the portfolio (McMillan, 2004; Weldin & Tumarkin, 1999).

Setting Criteria for Evaluation Clear and systematic performance criteria are essential for effectively using portfolios (Fallon & Watts, 2001; Linn & Gronlund, 2000). Clear learning targets for students make developing performance criteria much easier. Ask yourself what knowledge and skills you want your students to have. This should be the focus of your teaching and your performance criteria.

Scoring and Judging It takes a lot of time to score and judge portfolios (Airasian, 2005). Teachers must evaluate not only each individual item but also the portfolio as a whole. When the portfolio's purpose is to provide descriptive information about the student for the teacher at the next grade level, no scoring or summarizing of the portfolio

growth portfolio A portfolio of work over an extended time frame (throughout the school year or longer) to reveal the student's progress in meeting learning targets.

best-work portfolio A portfolio that showcases the student's most outstanding work.

might be necessary. However, when its purpose is to diagnose, reflect improvement, provide evidence for effective instruction, motivate students to reflect on their work, or give grades to students, summary scoring and judgments are needed. Checklists and rating scales are commonly used for this purpose. As with other aspects of portfolio assessment, some teachers give students the opportunity to evaluate and critique their own work.

Evaluating the Role of Portfolios in Assessment   Learning portfolios have several strengths: Their comprehensive nature captures the complexity and completeness of the student's work and accomplishments. They provide opportunities for encouraging student decision making and self-reflection. They motivate students to think critically and deeply. And they provide an excellent mechanism for evaluating student progress and improvement (Berryman & Russell, 2001; Richard, 2001).

Learning portfolios also have several weaknesses: They take considerable time to coordinate and evaluate. Their complexity and uniqueness have meant that they are difficult to evaluate, and their reliability is often much lower than for traditional tests. And their use in large-scale assessments (such as statewide evaluation) is expensive. However, even with these weaknesses in mind, most educational psychology experts and educational organizations, such as the National Education Association, support the use of portfolios (Coffin, 1996).

Now that you've read about many types of assessment, this is a good time to think about what your classroom assessment philosophy will be. Self-Assessment 16.1 on page 546 gives you this opportunity.

Exploring Grading Issues

! Review and Reflect

3 **Describe some types of alternative assessments.**

Review
- What makes an assessment "authentic"?
- What are some of the features of performance-based assessment? some guidelines for using them?
- How can portfolios be used in assessment?

Reflect
- Suppose that you were teaching this course in educational psychology. How would you go about creating rubrics for assessing answers to the preceding three items?

GRADING AND REPORTING PERFORMANCE

Grading means translating descriptive assessment information into letters, numbers, or other marks that indicate the quality of a student's learning or performance.

The Purposes of Grading

Grading is carried out to communicate meaningful information about a student's learning and achievement. In this process, grades serve four basic purposes (Airasian, 2005):

- *Administrative.* Grades help determine students' class rank, credits for graduation, and whether a student should be promoted to the next grade.
- *Informational.* Grades can be used to communicate with students, parents, and others (such as admissions officers for subsequent schooling) about a student's work. A grade represents the teacher's overall conclusion about how well a student has met instructional objectives and learning targets.

grading Translating descriptive assessment information into letters, numbers, or other marks that indicate the quality of a student's learning or performance.

Planning My Classroom Assessment Philosophy

With the subject matter and grade level at which you plan to teach in mind, examine the following list of assessments that we have discussed in this chapter. Rate each of the assessments on this scale: 1 = I don't plan to use this at all, 2 = I plan to use this occasionally, 3 = I plan to use this moderately, 4 = I plan to use this often, and 5 = This will be one of the most important assessments I will use.

	1	2	3	4	5
1. Informal observations in pre-instructional assessment					
2. Structured exercises in pre-instructional assessment					
3. Observation during instruction					
4. Questions during instruction					
5. Assessments of students' affect					
6. True/false items					
7. Multiple-choice items					
8. Matching					
9. Audiovisual context setting					
10. Problem sets					
11. Figural responses					
12. Short-answer items					
13. Essays					
14. Authentic assessment					
15. Experiments					
16. Projects					
17. Oral presentations					
18. Interviews					
19. Performances					
20. Exhibitions					
21. Portfolios					

Look back through your responses and then use this information to help you formulate your classroom assessment philosophy here. If you need more space, do this outside the book or on the student website.

_____

_____

_____

_____

 Go to your Student Toolbox CD-ROM for an electronic version of this form.

- *Motivational.* As we saw in chapter 13, "Motivation, Teaching, and Learning," a good strategy is to help students become intrinsically motivated. Nonetheless, in an educational world in which grades are given, many students work harder because they are extrinsically motivated by a desire for high grades and a fear of low grades.
- *Guidance.* Grades help students, parents, and counselors to select appropriate courses and levels of work for students. They provide information about which students might require special services and what levels of future education students will likely be able to handle.

The Components of a Grading System

Grades reflect teachers' judgments. Three main types of teacher judgments underlie a teacher's grading system (Airasian, 2005): (1) What standard of comparison will I use for grading? (2) What aspects of students' performance will I use to establish grades? and (3) How will I weight different kinds of evidence in giving grades?

Standards of Comparison   A student's performance can be graded by comparing it with the performance of other students or to predefined standards of performance.

Comparing Performance Across Students   **Norm-referenced grading** is a grading system based on comparison of a student's performance with that of other students in the class or of other classes and other students. In such a system, students get high grades for performing better than most of their classmates, and students get low grades for performing worse. Norm-referenced grading is commonly referred to as *grading on the curve.* In norm-referenced grading, the grading scale determines what percentages of students get particular grades. In most instances, the scale is created so that the largest percentage of students get *C*s.

This is a typical breakdown of grades: 15% *A*s, 25% *B*s, 40% *C*s, 15% *D*s, and 5% *F*s. In assigning grades, instructors often look for gaps in the range of scores. If 6 students score 92 to 100 and 10 students score 81 to 88, and there are no scores between 88 and 92, the teacher would assign a grade of *A* to the 92 to 100 scores and a *B* to the 81 to 88 scores. Norm-referenced grading has been criticized for reducing students' motivation, increasing their anxiety, increasing negative interactions among students, and hindering learning.

Comparing Performance with a Predetermined Standard   **Criterion-referenced grading** is being used when students receive a certain grade for a certain level of performance, regardless of any comparison with the work of other students. Sometimes criterion-referenced grading is called *absolute grading.* Typically, criterion-referenced grading is based on the proportion of points attained on a test or the level of mastery reached in a performance skill, such as giving an oral presentation and meeting all the predetermined criteria. Criterion-referenced grading is recommended over norm-referenced grading.

In theory, the standard established is supposed to be absolute, but in practice it doesn't always work out that way (McMillan, 2004). For example, a school system often develops a grading system that goes something like this: *A* = 94% to 100% correct, *B* = 87 to 93, *C* = 77 to 86, *D* = 70 to 76, *F* = below 70. Although this system is absolute in the sense that every student must get 94 points to get an *A* and every student who does not get at least 70 points gets an *F*, teachers and classrooms vary enormously in what constitutes mastery of material to get a 94, an 87, a 77, or a 70. One teacher might give very hard tests, another very easy tests.

Many teachers use different cutoff scores than the ones just mentioned. Some teachers argue that low grades discourage student motivation and refuse to give *D*s or *F*s; others won't fail students unless their scores fall below 50.

Standards-based grading is a recent development based on criterion-referenced grading. It involves basing grading on standards that students are expected to achieve in a

"Your grading curve and my learning curve don't intersect."

© Dave Carpenter, *Phi Delta Kappan,* 1997. Reprinted with permission.

norm-referenced grading A grading system based on a comparison of a student's performance with that of other students in the class or of other classes and other students.

criterion-referenced grading A grading system based on comparison with predetermined standards.

Through the Eyes of Teachers

Some Grading Strategies

I think it is extremely important that parents and students clearly know what is expected of students if they are to succeed in my class. I try to help students understand that they are in control of the grade they get. If students think a grading system is capricious or unknowable, it creates frustration, anxiety, and is of little use in motivating students. By getting them to see that their grades are in their own hands, I move to the position of "facilitator" in the classroom. The students see me as someone who is there to *help* them achieve rather than someone who sits in judgment of their work and gives them a grade.

I now use the computer in grading and use it to generate an individual report on each student. I print these reports every two weeks. I give a copy to each student so that he or she is clear about a particular grade and what can be done about it. I also make sure these grades get home to parents. I also print out a copy of what I call a "grade sheet" for long assignments, which indicates how I intend to grade the assignments. I give it to my students before they do the assignment and then use it to score the assignment when it is submitted.

Lynn Ayres
English and Drama Teacher
East Middle School
Ypsilanti, Michigan

"I don't know why you're so surprised by his poor grades. Every day you asked him what he did at school, and every day he answered, 'Nothing.'"
© Art Bouthiller. Reprinted with permission.

course. In some cases, national associations, such as the National Council of Teachers of Mathematics (NCTM), have developed standards that students should achieve. Thus, in one form of standards-based grading, a mathematics teacher might tie students' grades to how well they meet these national standards.

Aspects of Performance   Over the course of a grading period, students will likely have created many products that can be evaluated and used as a basis for grading. These can include test and quiz results, as well as various alternative assessments such as oral reports, projects, interviews, and homework. Increasingly, portfolios are used as the complete collection of materials to be graded or a portion of the work on which an overall grade is based. Some educators believe that grades should be based only on academic performance. In the view of other educators, grades should be based mainly on academic performance, but teacher ratings of motivation and effort can be factored in as well.

Many teachers use tests as the main, or even sole, basis for assigning grades. However, many assessment experts recommend basing an overall grade on a series of tests and other types of assessments (McMillan, 2004). Thus, a semester grade in geography might be based on two major tests and a final, eight quizzes, homework, two oral reports, and a project. Basing a grade on a series of tests and different types of assessment helps to balance out students' strengths and weaknesses, as well as compensate for a poor performance or two because of internal and external sources of measurement error.

Some educators advocate factoring affective characteristics such as motivation and effort into grades, especially by giving borderline students a plus or minus. Thus, a teacher might convert a student's *B* to a *B*+ if the student was highly motivated, put forth considerable effort, and actively participated in the class— or to a *B*− if the student was poorly motivated, made little effort, and did not actively participate. However, some educators believe that grades should be based only on academic performance. One of the problems with including factors such as effort in grades is the difficulty in determining the reliability and validity of effort. Measures of effort or improvement can be made more systematic and reliable by developing scoring rubrics and examples (McMillan, 2004).

Weighting Different Kinds of Evidence   You will need to determine how much weight to give the different components of a student's grade. For example, the teacher might arrive at a weighting system that looks something like this:

Major tests (2)	20%
Final test	25%
Quizzes	20%
Homework	5%
Oral report	10%
Project	20%

Many teachers don't use homework as a component for a grade. One reason for this is that when a student's grade depends on homework or other work done outside class, parents might be tempted to do their child's work to ensure the grade. Another reason is that including homework as a component of grading favors students from better home environments. As with other aspects of classroom assessment, your judgment is involved in how you synthesize information to arrive at a student's grade. If a student fails to turn in a certain number of homework assignments, some teachers lower the student's grade.

Reporting Students' Progress and Grades to Parents

Grades are the most common method of informing parents about a child's progress and performance in the classroom (Airasian, 2005). However, grades by themselves provide limited information, are usually given infrequently, communicate little in the way of specific information about how the student is learning, and rarely include information about the student's motivation, cooperation, and classroom behavior. Because of these limitations, more than grades are needed to give parents a full portrait of the student.

The Report Card   The report card is a standard method of reporting students' progress and grades to parents. The form of judgments on report cards varies from one school system to another, and, in many cases, from one grade level to another. Some report cards convey letter grades (typically *A, B, C, D,* and *F,* sometimes also allowing pluses and minuses). Some report cards convey numerical scores (such as 91 in math, 85 in English, and so on). Other report cards have a pass/fail category in one or more subjects. Yet other report cards have checklists indicating skills or objectives the student has attained. Some report cards have categories for affective characteristics, such as effort, cooperation, and other appropriate and inappropriate behaviors. Many also have space for a teacher's written, summative comments.

Checklists of skills and objectives are mainly used in elementary schools or kindergartens. In the higher elementary school grade levels and secondary schools, letter grades are mainly used, although these might be accompanied by other information such as written comments. In many school districts, there is spirited debate about what form of grading should be used and what should be included on report cards.

Written Progress Reports   Another reporting strategy is to provide parents with a weekly, biweekly, or monthly report of the student's progress and achievement (McMillan, 2004). These written reports can include the student's performance on tests and quizzes, projects, oral reports, and so on. They also can include information about the student's motivation, cooperation, and behavior, as well as suggestions for how parents can help students improve their performance. If you have enough information to form a grade for the student at that time, you also might consider including it in the written communication.

Parent-Teacher Conferences   Parent-teacher conferences are another way to communicate information about grades and assessment. Such conferences are both a responsibility and an opportunity (Payne, 1997). Parents have a right to know how their child is doing in school and how their child might improve. Conferences provide an opportunity for giving parents helpful information about how they can be partners with you in helping the child learn more effectively.

Through the Eyes of Students

Accepting Responsibility

Our teacher tells us that our grades are our responsibility. Nobody else's. "Don't blame anybody else but yourself if you don't make good grades," she says. At the beginning of the year, she said she would help us every way she could to help us make good grades and she has been good about that.

Cassandra
Middle School Student
Atlanta, Georgia

"How much to shred a report card?"
© Martha Campbell, *Phi Delta Kappan,* 1996.
Reprinted with permission.

Teaching Strategies
For Parent-Teacher Conferences Related to Grades and Assessment

Here are some good strategies for meeting with parents about their child's progress and grades (Payne, 1997):

1. *Be prepared.* Review the student's performance prior to the meeting with parents. Think about what you are going to say to the parents.
2. *Be positive.* Even if the student has performed poorly, try to find at least some areas to discuss in which the student has performed well. This does not mean glossing over and ignoring a student's lack of achievement; it means including positive areas in addition to the negative ones.
3. *Be objective.* Even though you want to look for positive aspects of the student's record to communicate to parents, be objective and honest. Don't give parents false hopes if the student has low ability in a particular subject area.
4. *Practice good communication skills.* As we noted in chapter 14, "Managing the Classroom," this means being an active listener and giving parents adequate opportunities to contribute to the conversation.
5. *Don't talk about other students.* The focus of the parent-teacher conference should be on the parent's child. Don't compare the child with other students.

Some Issues in Grading

Should grading be abolished? Is there too much grade inflation?

Should Grading Be Abolished?   Occasionally there are calls to abandon grades, usually based on the belief that evaluation of students is necessary but that competitive grading deemphasizes learning in favor of judging. Critics argue that grading discourages the vast majority of students, especially those who receive below-average grades. The critics often call for more constructive evaluation that encourages students to engage in maximum effort by underscoring their strengths, identifying concrete ways to improve, and providing positive feedback (Culbertson & Jalongo, 1999). Critics also point out that grading often motivates students to study only the material that will be on the test.

Even with these criticisms in mind, it is difficult to imagine schools in which judgments about students' performance would not be made and communicated to students, parents, and others, although the basis on which judgments are made might change, the format of grades might be modified, and the judgments might not be called "grades." For example, in some K–5 elementary schools there are no formal grades, only narrative evaluations from each teacher. A judgment of whether the student is ready to go on to the next grade is made at the end of the school year.

As classroom assessment expert Peter Airasian (2005) concluded, grades are powerful symbols in our society that are taken seriously by students, teachers, and the public. Regardless of whether you like the way grading is currently conducted or think it should be drastically changed, in the foreseeable future it is important for you to take grading your students seriously and do it in a way that is fair to your students. Never use grades to reward or punish students because you like them or don't like them. Always base students' grades on how well they have learned the subject matter, based on objective evidence of learning (Colby, 1999).

Is There Too Much Grade Inflation?   Some teachers do not like to give low grades because they believe they diminish the student's motivation to learn. However, some critics believe that grade inflation, especially in the form of giving high grades for mediocre performance, provides students a false belief that they are learning and achieving more than they actually are. The result is that many students discover that they can perform well below their ability and still achieve high grades (Guskey, 2001). A rising tide of grade inflation was noted by College Board president Donald Stewart (1997). For example, from 1987 to 1997, among students taking the SAT test, the proportion of students with an *A* average rose from 28% to 37%. However, over the same period the combined verbal and math scores of those *A* students dropped 14 points.

❗ Review and Reflect

4 Construct a sound approach to grading.

Review
- What are the purposes of grading?
- What types of judgments underlie a teacher's grading system? Comment about each type.
- What are some choices in reporting students' progress to parents?
- What are some issues in grading?

Reflect
- What criteria would you adopt for deciding whether a teacher is doing an excellent job in grading?

COMPUTERS AND ASSESSMENT

Earlier in the chapter we described the use of audiovisuals for creating realistic contexts for assessment. Here we continue our exploration of the use of computers in assessment.

Using Computers for Assessment

Computers can be used to construct, print, administer, and score tests; provide a medium for portfolios; and maintain student records (Gronlund, 2003). Concerns about the validity and reliability of assessment using a computer are no different than for paper-and-pencil measures. Be aware that just because validity and reliability have been established for a paper-and-pencil assessment this does not mean that the validity and reliability will automatically hold when the student is assessed with the same measure on a computer.

Although the assessment data can be analyzed by a computer, computers are not capable of including common sense, intuition, and judgment of effort in their analysis. Decisions based on computerized assessment scores still rely on the teacher's interpretation and judgment, just as with paper-and-pencil measures (Jones, 1999).

Constructing, Printing, Administering, and Scoring Tests

One way computers can aid test construction is through item banking. This consists of maintaining test item files that can be retrieved for preparing a test. Items typically are coded by subject area, instructional level, instructional objective measured, and item difficulty.

Computers can be used to print tests from the item bank. The coded information about each item makes it possible to create different forms of tests, such as a test arranged by instructional objective or increasing difficulty.

Computers also can be used directly in the administration of tests. The student is presented with test items on a computer screen and answers the items accordingly.

After the test is administered, the computer can be used to score the test and arrange the scores in different ways. Computer scoring especially can be helpful in relieving teachers from the time-consuming task of scoring test item responses.

Electronic Portfolios

As we saw earlier in the chapter, portfolio assessment is increasingly common. The terms *electronic portfolio* and *computer-based portfolio* are used to describe portfolio work that is saved in an electronic format (Hardy, 2001; Lankes, 1995). The record can include text, graphics, sound, and video. Thus, students can save writing samples, math solutions, samples of artwork, depictions of science projects, and multimedia presentations in an electronic portfolio (Inkrott, 2001). A single computer with a large storage capacity can store portfolios for all the students in a class. If a number of students store multimedia material, a floppy or hard disk might not have sufficient storage. An alternative is to store students' portfolios on a "rewritable" compact disc (CD-RW, a compact disc that stores text, sound, graphics, and video). A computer-based portfolio allows for easy transfer of information from teacher to teacher or school to school.

Several electronic portfolio programs are available. The most widely used is *Aurbach's Grady Profile,* in which both teachers and students can enter work samples. The electronic portfolio programs can include writing samples, standardized test scores, oral communication skills, and math assessments. Other software programs (such as *HyperStudio* by Roger Wagner [1993] and *FileMaker Pro* by Claris) let teachers create their own template for portfolio assessment. Teachers can adapt these programs to the needs of their classes. For example, one high school English portfolio might consist of the outlines and drafts for each writing assignment; another might include only the finished product along with the student's reflections and self-evaluation of the product. Figure 16.11 shows a computer screen of a lab report that was included in one student's portfolio.

One school that uses electronic portfolios is East Syracuse–Minoa High School in Syracuse, New York. Its students create electronic portfolios that can be sent to colleges as part of an admissions application and to potential employers as part of their job application. The electronic portfolios are created using *HyperStudio* software. They contain information about the student (such as transcripts, letters of recommendation, and work

Software for Educational Assessment

Technology and Alternative Assessment

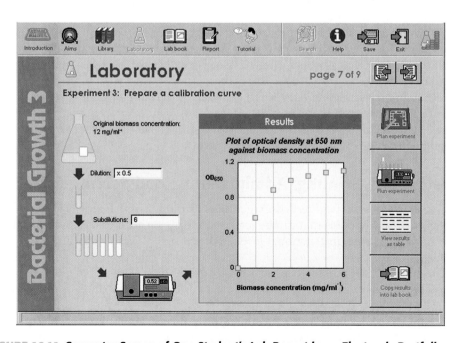

FIGURE 16.11 Computer Screen of One Student's Lab Report in an Electronic Portfolio

The Features of an Electronic Portfolio

David Niguidula (1997) designs and customizes computer software that includes electronic portfolios. He believes it is important to integrate the following considerations into any plan for student electronic portfolios.

Vision

The main menu of an electronic portfolio should contain a set of goals that reflect the vision of what the student should know and be able to do. For example, at one high school, the domains students are expected to master include communicating, crafting, reflecting, knowing, respecting oneself, and respecting others. At others, they might include such goals as content knowledge about subject matter, ability to think critically, effective communication, and cooperative skills. As students and teachers enter work into their portfolios, they consider how the activities in the classroom correspond to the learning goals.

Assessment

Assessment involves answering such questions as "How can students demonstrate that they have reached the learning goals?" "How will the portfolio be evaluated and scored?" and "What audiences are the portfolios intended for?"

Technology

Technology involves making decisions about what hardware, software, and networking will be required. At one school "where students and teachers spend most of their day together as a team (consisting of about 80 students and 3 teachers), each team shared a set of six computers, at least one of which had multimedia input capabilities, a scanner, and a laser printer. In other schools, 5 to 15 computers were designated as digital portfolio stations" (Niguidula, 1997, p. 28). Ideally, a school will have a technical coordinator who can help teachers set up electronic portfolios. At one high school, the school's technical coordinator helps a class to become the electronic portfolio support team for the rest of the school.

Logistics

Decisions need to be made about when the information will be placed in the electronic portfolios, who will do it, who will select the work, and who will reflect on the work. Two middle school teachers at Pierre van Cortlandt Middle School in Croton-Harmon, New York, described the logistics of electronic portfolios as collecting, selecting, reflecting, and presenting. "Students need to think about what entries they will *collect,* how to *select* the ones that best convey their abilities, how to *reflect* on what their portfolio means, and how to *present* what they have learned" (Niguidula, 1997, p. 28). Teachers also need to be involved in these steps as well.

The School's Culture

The school's culture is an important aspect of whether electronic portfolios will become innovative, meaningful aspects of a student's learning or merely a technological version of a file cabinet. Several school administrators and teachers that Niguidula worked with presented their vision statement to others to get feedback, which helped them fine-tune their learning goals. When the school community encourages teachers, students, and others to reflect on their learning goals and effectively integrate technology in the classroom, electronic portfolios can become far more than file cabinets. They can represent an important, meaningful dimension of a student's learning.

---

history) and student-selected work (such as writing samples, multimedia projects, artwork, and video clips from a school play). The students are responsible for updating and selecting the work samples in their portfolios. Students begin creating these portfolios in their sophomore year and continue updating and revising them through their senior year. The portfolios can be distributed in computer disk, CD-RW, videotape, or print versions.

Electronic portfolios are mandated by the 1996 Jobs Through Education Act, which is intended to get public schools to focus more on preparing students for the workplace (Kabler, 1997). The vision is that student transcripts will eventually be replaced with electronic portfolios that include a full history of the student's classroom performances, work samples, and activities. To read further about electronic portfolios, see the Technology and Education box.

Record Keeping

Record keeping is a burden for many teachers, and assessment information represents a considerable chunk of this record keeping. Fortunately, the burden can be reduced by computer technology (Maddux, Johnson, & Willis, 1997). For example, electronic grade books can keep track of students' grades in a course. Excelsior's *Grade 2* program can store many types of student information, including test scores, project grades, homework assignments, semester averages, and teacher judgments. Each component of your

www.mhhe.com/santedu2e

ENTER THE DEBATE

1. Should teachers use pop quizzes to assess student learning?

2. Should teachers use criterion or norm-referenced grading?

3. Do teachers inflate grades?

4. Should grades be abolished?

assessment system can be weighted, and the program will compute the student's overall performance based on the formula you create. This can take less time than tediously computing grades by hand. Some electronic grade book programs have parent access options. Parents or students who have an appropriate computer and modem can connect with the school computer, enter a personal identification number, and access the student's grades and teacher's comments.

Web-Based Assessment

Many school systems are turning to *web-based assessment*—assessment available on the Internet—because of its potential for greater accuracy and cost reduction. A number of testing firms, including Educational Testing Service, are developing tests to be administered on computers in the classroom, school, or district, but those are not web-based assessments. If an assessment is web-based, students use a computer and the assessment takes place on the Internet.

Some of the best web-based assessments can be easily adapted to the curriculum you use in your classroom. Some of the assessments focus on recording and evaluating student behavior, some involve academic progress, and others include all of these areas. The best web-based assessments let teachers "develop their own tests or forms and usually include a databank of questions or other assessment tools. Most are aligned with various state and national standards," or No Child Left Behind (Doe, 2004, p. 2).

The following are three examples of web-based assessments, each of which has appropriate security included (Doe, 2004):

S-BIP Online *Student Intervention Planner.* This web-based assessment can be used to record many aspects of student behavior as observed by teachers and other school personnel. Various report forms can be generated, and some of these can be used to plan for special education IEPs. You can read more about this assessment at www.curricassoc.com/SBIP.

Assessa Server This web-based assessment provides a number of data management services to help you create your own tests, track students' progress, and create reports. You can learn more about this assessment at www.eyecues.com.

Plato EduTest Assessment This web-based assessment can be used to describe students' progress throughout the school year and to document students' strengths and needs. The assessment generates student reports, including progress charts, which you can use when you communicate with student's parents. You can obtain more information about the Plato assessment at www.edutest.com/.

Strategies in Practice
- **Assessment Strategies**
- **Classroom Assessment**
- **Measurement**

Teaching Experience
- **Grading**
- **Using the Mode, not Percentages, to Grade**
- **Using Flow to Help Motivate Students in Assessment**

Review and Reflect

5 Identify some uses of computers in assessment.

Review
- In what ways is computer assessment much like paper-and-pencil assessment?
- How can computers help in constructing, printing, administering, and scoring tests?
- What can be done with electronic portfolios?
- How can computers reduce the burden of record keeping?

Reflect
- How close do you feel right now to being able to use computers for assessment? What do you need to learn?

M r. Andrews generally was using traditional, multiple-choice tests in his sixth-grade class on ancient history, but the students seemed bored with studying for these tests and with his lectures. Therefore, for the unit on ancient Mesopotamia, he decided to allow the students to complete a project instead of taking a test. He gave these choices:

> Construct a test covering the chapter on Mesopotamia.
> Create a game about Mesopotamia.
> Create a diorama about Mesopotamia.
> Write a play about life in Mesopotamia.
> Create artifacts from Mesopotamia that an archaeologist might find.

Mr. Andrews' co-teacher, Ms. Benjamin, told the children that they could not use a computer to complete their projects.

Sally decided to write a test for her project. She carefully read the chapter and constructed questions as she went along. She used short-answer questions because she was worried about constructing good multiple-choice questions. It had been her experience that the distractors used in these questions were often confusing. She felt the same way about true/false questions. She wanted to make her questions as clear as possible because she didn't want her classmates mad at her when they took her test.

Sally carefully printed each question because of the ban on using a computer. She then created a key, which she intended to use to grade her classmates' tests. The final product consisted of 25 short-answer questions. She was very proud of her work the day she turned it in.

Mr. Andrews looked at her test and told her, "This isn't acceptable. Why didn't you type it?"

"Ms. Benjamin told us we couldn't use computers."

"That isn't what she meant. She meant you couldn't use the Internet," responded Mr. Andrews. "Take it home and type it. Turn it in tomorrow."

Sally left the room, very upset. She took her test home and carefully typed both the test and the key. She turned them in the next day. Three days later, Sally received these marks:

Content: **B+** Did not include a question on religion (actually Sally did have a question regarding polytheism). Should have included a variety of question types, such as multiple-choice, matching, and T/F.

Mechanics: **A** Nicely typed. Correct spelling used.

Accuracy: **B**

Effort: **C−**

Grade **C**

Sally was upset with her grade. "A C− for effort?! I worked really hard on this! I even had to do it twice, 'cause of stupid Ms. Benjamin!" She took her grade sheet and test home and showed it to her mother. Sally's mother was equally upset, particularly about the low grade for effort. She called Mr. Andrews, asking to see the guidelines for the project and the grading rubric. Mr. Andrews was unable to provide either. She asked him the difference between content and accuracy. He could not tell her. She also asked him how he had measured effort, to which he responded, "I consider what I expect from students and then what they give me."

"So you're telling me that you graded content three times. Once you gave her a B+, once a B, and once a C−, right?"

- What are the issues involved in this situation?
- What did Mr. Andrews do wrong?
- How should he have gone about developing his alternative assessments?
- How should he have developed his grading guide?
- What do you think of the practice of including an effort grade on students' projects? Why?

Reach Your Learning Goals

1 Discuss the classroom as an assessment context.

- Pre-instruction assessment, assessment during instruction, and post-instruction assessment should be integral to teaching. Much of pre-instruction assessment involves informal observations, which require interpretation. In informal observations, watch for nonverbal cues that give insights about the student. Structured exercises also can be used in pre-instruction assessment. Guard against expectations that will distort your perception of a student. Treat your initial perceptions as hypotheses to be confirmed or modified by subsequent observation and information. Some teachers also administer pretests in subject areas. An increasing trend is to examine students' learning portfolios from previous grades. Formative assessment is the fast-paced observation and monitoring that go on during instruction. Summative assessment, or formal assessment, is assessment after instruction is finished. This usually involves more-formal types of assessment, such as tests.

- In line with contemporary views of motivation and learning, it is important to assess the following: active learning and constructing meaning; the use of planning and goal setting; reflective, critical, and creative thinking; positive student expectations for learning and confidence in skills; degree of motivation; the ability to apply what is learned to real-world situations; and effective communication. Consider the role that assessment (especially alternative assessment) plays in effort, engagement, and performance.

- A learning target, much like an instructional objective, consists of what students should know and be able to do. Learning targets might focus on knowledge, reasoning/thinking, products, or affect.

- High-quality assessments are valid, reliable, useful, and fair. Validity is the extent to which an assessment measures what it is intended to measure, as well as how accurate and useful a teacher's inferences are. The most important source of validity in the classroom is content-related evidence, the extent to which an assessment reflects what has been taught. Adequately sampling content is an important aspect of validity. Instructional validity is the extent to which an assessment is a reasonable sample of what went on in the classroom. Validity is enhanced by the systematic linkage of learning targets, content, instruction, and assessment. Reliability is the extent to which assessments produce consistent, reproducible scores. Assessment is fair when all students have an equal opportunity to learn and demonstrate their knowledge and skills. A pluralistic assessment philosophy also contributes to fairness.

- Current trends in assessment include using at least some performance-based assessments, examining higher-level skills, using multiple assessment methods, having high performance standards, and using computers as a part of assessment. Other trends focus on assessing an integration of skills, giving students considerable feedback, and making standards and criteria public.

2 Provide some guidelines for constructing traditional tests.

- Selected responses are objective and can be scored on quick inspection. A scoring key can be used by an examiner or a computer. True/false, multiple-choice, and matching items are the most widely used items in selected-response tests. True/false items can seem easy to construct but can encourage mere memorization. Strategies for constructing true/false items, as well as their strengths and limitations, were discussed. A multiple-choice item has two parts: a stem and a number of options or alternatives. Incorrect alternatives are called distractors. Strategies for constructing multiple-choice items, as well as their strengths and limitations, were described. Matching items often are used with younger students. Advantages and disadvantages of using matching items were discussed. Other objective assessment formats include audiovisuals and problem sets. Two tools for computing the quality of test items are the item difficulty index, which describes the percentage of students who obtain the correct answer, and the item discrimination index, which reflects the item's ability to discriminate between students who scored high or low on the entire test.

- Constructed-response items require students to write out information rather than select it from a menu. Short-answer and essay items are the most commonly used constructed-response items. Short-answer items require students to write a word, a short phrase, or several sentences in response to a task. Sentence completion is a variation of a short-answer item. One criticism of short-answer items is that they often encourage rote memorization. Essay questions allow students more freedom of response than the other item formats. Essay questions are especially good for assessing students' understanding, higher-level thinking skills, organizational skills, and writing skills. We discussed how to construct and score essay questions and their strengths and limitations.

3 Describe some types of alternative assessments.

- Authentic assessment is evaluating a student's knowledge or skill in a context that approximates the real world or real life as closely as possible. Critics argue that authentic assessments are not necessarily better than more conventional assessments, that there are few data to support their validity, and that they don't adequately examine knowledge and basic skills.

- Performance-based assessments of higher-level thinking often emphasize "doing," open-ended activities for which there is no one correct answer. The tasks are sometimes realistic, and many, but not all, performance-based assessments are authentic. Evaluating performance often includes direct methods of evaluation, self-assessment, assessment of group performance as well as individual performance, and an extended period of time. There are four main guidelines in using performance-based assessments: (1) establishing a clear purpose, (2) identifying observable criteria, (3) providing an appropriate setting, and (4) judging or scoring the performance. Performance criteria are specific behaviors that students need to effectively perform as part of the assessment. The performance can be scored or rated holistically or analytically. Performance-based assessment has both strengths and limitations. Many educational psychologists endorse their increased use.

- A portfolio is a systematic and organized collection of a student's work to demonstrate skills and accomplishments. Four classes of evidence can be included: artifacts, reproductions, attestations, and productions. Using portfolios requires (1) establishing the portfolio's purpose, (2) involving students in decisions about it, (3) reviewing the portfolio with students, (4) setting criteria for evaluation, and (5) scoring and judging the portfolio. Two broad types of purposes of portfolios are to document growth through a growth portfolio and to showcase the student's most outstanding work through a best-work portfolio. Learning portfolios have strengths—such as capturing the complexity and completeness of the student's work and accomplishments, as well as encouraging student decision making and self-reflection—and weaknesses, such as the time required to coordinate and evaluate them and the difficulty in evaluating them.

4 Construct a sound approach to grading.

- There are administrative, informational, motivational, and guidance purposes for grading.

- Three main types of teacher judgments underlie a grading system: (1) standard of comparison to use for grading (norm-referenced or criterion-referenced); (2) aspects of performance (a good strategy is to base an overall grade on a series of assessments, including tests and other assessments); and (3) weighting of different kinds of evidence (judgment is involved in how teachers synthesize information to arrive at a student's grade).

- Report cards are the standard method of reporting. Checklists of skills and objectives are sometimes used in kindergarten and elementary school. Letter grades are standard in the higher elementary grades and secondary schools. Reporting also includes written progress reports and parent-teacher conferences.

- Issues in grading include (1) whether grading should be abolished (although the form of grading might change in the future, judgments about students' performance will still be made and communicated to students, parents, and others) and (2) whether grade inflation is a problem.

5 Identify some uses of computers in assessment.

- The same concerns arise about validity and reliability for electronic assessment as for paper-and-pencil assessment.

- Computers can be used for constructing, printing, administering, and scoring tests.

- The terms *electronic portfolio* and *computer-based portfolio* describe portfolios that are saved in an electronic format. Several electronic portfolio programs are available.

- Computer technology can help to reduce the burden of record keeping for teachers. For example, electronic grade books can keep track of a student's grades in a course.

- Web-based assessment, which means that assessment takes place on the Internet, is increasingly being used to record and evaluate student behavior and/or chart academic progress.

KEY TERMS

formative assessment 522	multiple-choice item 530	essay items 534	norm-referenced grading 547
summative assessment 523	problem sets 532	performance criteria 539	criterion-referenced
instructional validity 525	item difficulty index 533	portfolio 542	grading 547
objective tests 527	item discrimination index 533	growth portfolio 544	
performance assessment 527	constructed-response items 533	best-work portfolio 544	
selected-response items 529	short-answer item 534	grading 545	

PORTFOLIO ACTIVITIES

Now that you have a good understanding of this chapter, complete these exercises to expand your thinking.

Independent Reflection

State Your Views on Assessment. Think about the following statements and decide whether you agree or disagree with each. Explain your position below. 1) Multiple-choice tests should not be used to assess students' learning; 2) A teacher should never use a single measure to assess learning; 3) Performance-based assessment is too subjective. (INTASC: Principle 8)

Collaborative Work

Develop an Assessment Plan. Get together with a classmate who plans to teach the same subject(s) and grade level. Select a

subject and construct a plan for assessment throughout the course. (INTASC: Principles 1, 8)

Research/Field Experience Reflections

Balancing Traditional and Alternative Assessments. Consider a course you took in grade school or high school in which your performance was assessed using traditional methods. In a brief position statement, explain how students could have been evaluated using alternative assessments or some combination of traditional and alternative assessments. What would have been gained (or lost) by using alternative assessments? (INTASC: Principle 8)

 Go to the Online Learning Center for downloadable portfolio templates.

TAKING IT TO THE NET

1. The Coalition of Essential Schools (CES) is a national network of schools that uses alternative assessments and culminating exhibitions to evaluate their students. Read one or more CES articles. What is your analysis? Discuss the effectiveness of CES assessment strategies. To what degree do you believe the CES approach is replicable across schools?
2. Your fifth-grade science students are engaged in a one-week collaborative project. They are constructing models of world habitats and will conduct oral presentations of their finished projects. Design a scoring rubric and outline the criteria you will use to measure student performance. Will students be

graded as a group, independently, or both? Will they conduct self- or peer assessments?
3. Browse the Web to locate examples of K–12 electronic student portfolios. What are typically the main components of a digital portfolio? Discuss the benefits of using electronic portfolios to showcase and archive student work. Include benefits to students, families, teachers, and schools in your response.

Connect to the Online Learning Center to explore possible answers.

STUDY, PRACTICE, AND SUCCEED

 Go to chapter 16 on the Online Learning Center at www.mhhe.com/santrockedu2e to access the student study guide with practice quizzes, web links, portfolio resources, PowerWeb articles and news feeds, and the online resources referenced in the chapter.

 Go to your Student Toolbox CD-ROM to access the resources and activities referenced in the chapter and

• Resources to help you prepare for the PRAXIS II™ exam

• **Application Resources,** including additional *Crack the Case* studies, electronic versions of the *Self-Assessments,* Application Exercises, and Site Observation Questions
• **Study Resources,** including Learning Goals, the Chapter Summary, a *Test Your Learning* exercise, and multiple-choice, true/false, matching, key terms, and short-answer quizzes
• **Professional Resources,** including a Lesson Plan Builder and *Bibliomaker*

Glossary

A

accommodation a mental process that occurs when a child adjusts to new information.   39

achievement test a test that measures what the student has learned or what skills the student has mastered.   493

action research research that is used to solve a specific classroom or school problem, improve teaching and other educational strategies, or make a decision at a specific level.   23

active listening a listening style that gives full attention to the speaker and notes both the intellectual and emotional content of the message.   468

advance organizers teaching activities and techniques that establish a framework and orient students to material before it is presented.   384

aggressive style a way of dealing with conflict in which people run roughshod over others in demanding, abrasive, and hostile ways.   466

algorithms strategies that guarantee a solution to a problem.   299

alternate-forms reliability reliability judged by giving different forms of the same test on two different occasions to the same group of students to determine how consistent their scores are.   492

analogy a correspondence in some respects between otherwise dissimilar things.   287

androgyny the presence of desirable masculine and feminine characteristics in the same individual.   160

applied behavior analysis application of the principles of operant conditioning to change human behavior.   218

aptitude test a type of test that is used to predict a student's ability to learn a skill or accomplish something with further education and training.   493

articulation disorders problems in pronouncing sounds correctly.   181

assertive style a way of dealing with conflict in which people express their feelings, ask for what they want, say "no" to things they don't want, and act in their own best interests.   466

assimilation a mental process that occurs when a child incorporates new knowledge into existing knowledge.   39

associative learning learning that two events are connected (associated).   211

Atkinson-Shiffrin model a model of memory that involves a sequence of three stages: sensory memory, short-term memory, and long-term memory.   258

attention concentrating and focusing mental resources.   249

attention deficit hyperactivity disorder (ADHD) a disability in which children consistently show one or more of the following characteristics over a period of time: (1) inattention, (2) hyperactivity, and (3) impulsivity.   186

attribution theory the theory that in their effort to make sense of their own behavior or performance, individuals are motivated to discover its underlying causes.   423

auditorium style a classroom arrangement style in which all students sit facing the teacher.   456

authoritarian classroom management style a management style that is restrictive and punitive, with the focus mainly on keeping order in the classroom rather than instruction or learning.   459

authoritarian parenting a restrictive and punitive parenting style in which there is little verbal exchange between parents and children; associated with children's social incompetence.   74

authoritative classroom management style a management style that encourages students to be independent thinkers and doers but still provides effective monitoring. Authoritative teachers engage students in considerable verbal give-and-take and show a caring attitude toward them. However, they still set limits when necessary.   459

authoritative parenting a positive parenting style that encourages children to be independent but still places limits and controls on their actions; extensive verbal give-and-take is allowed; associated with children's social competence.   74

automaticity the ability to process information with little or no effort.   247

autonomous morality in Piaget's theory, the second stage of moral development (entered at about ten years of age), in which children become aware that rules and laws are created by people and that in judging action, the actor's intentions as well as consequences need to be considered.   95

availability heuristic a prediction about the probability of an event based on the frequency of the event's past occurrences.   292

B

backward-reaching transfer the transfer of learning that involves looking back to a previous ("old") situation for information that might help solve a problem in a new context.   306

basic-skills-and-phonetics approach the idea that reading instruction should teach both phonemic awareness and phonics.   342

behavioral objectives statements that communicate proposed changes in students' behavior to reach desired levels of performance.   378

behaviorism the view that behavior should be explained by observable experiences.   211

belief perseverance the tendency to hold on to a belief in the face of contradictory evidence.   291

best-work portfolio a portfolio that showcases the student's most outstanding work.   544

between-class ability grouping (tracking) grouping students based on their ability or achievement.   121

"big five" factors of personality emotional stability, extraversion, openness to experience, agreeableness, and conscientiousness.   126

bilingual education instruction on academic subjects for immigrant children in their native languages (most often Spanish), while gradually adding English instruction.   143

Bloom's taxonomy developed by Benjamin Bloom and colleagues; consists of educational objectives in three domains—cognitive, affective, and psychomotor.   380

book clubs student-led groups for the discussion of literature. Book clubs are a form of peer learning.   347

care perspective a moral perspective that focuses on connectedness and relationships among people; Gilligan's approach reflects a care perspective.   97

case study an in-depth look at an individual.   19

central tendency a statistic that provides information about the average, or typical, score in a set of data.   503

centration focusing, or centering, attention on one characteristic to the exclusion of all others; characteristic of preoperational thinking.   43

cerebral palsy a disorder that involves a lack of muscle coordination, shaking, or unclear speech.   177

character education a direct approach to moral education that involves teaching students basic moral literacy to prevent them from engaging in immoral behavior and doing harm to themselves or others.   97

children who are gifted children with above-average intelligence (usually defined as an IQ of 130 or higher) and/or superior talent in some domain such as art, music, or mathematics.   200

chunking grouping, or "packing," information into "higher-order" units that can be remembered as single units.   254

classical conditioning a form of associative learning in which a neutral stimulus becomes associated with a meaningful stimulus and acquires the capacity to elicit a similar response.   212

cluster style a classroom arrangement style in which small numbers of students

(usually four to eight) work in small, closely bunched groups.   456

cognitive apprenticeship a relationship in which an expert stretches and supports a novice's understanding of and use of the culture's skills.   317

cognitive behavior approaches changing behavior by getting people to monitor, manage, and regulate their own behavior rather than letting it be controlled by external factors.   232

cognitive developmental theory of gender Kohlberg's theory that children adopt a gender after they have developed a concept of gender.   155

cognitive moral education an approach to moral education based on the belief that students should value things such as democracy and justice as their moral reasoning develops; Kohlberg's theory has served as the foundation for many cognitive moral education efforts.   98

collectivism a set of values that support the group.   135

comparative advance organizers connections with prior knowledge that help to introduce new material.   385

competence motivation the idea that people are motivated to deal effectively with their environment, to master their world, and to process information efficiently.   417

concept map a visual presentation of a concept's connections and hierarchical organization.   284

concepts categories used to group objects, events, and characteristics on the basis of common properties.   282

concrete operational stage Piaget's third cognitive developmental stage, occurring between about seven to eleven years of age. At this stage the child thinks operationally and logical reasoning replaces intuitive thought but only in concrete situations; classification skills are present but abstract problems present difficulties.   45

concurrent validity the relation between a test's scores and other criteria that are currently (concurrently) available.   491

confirmation bias the tendency to search for and use information that supports our ideas rather than refutes them.   291

conservation the idea that some characteristic of an object stays the same even though the object might change in appearance; a cognitive ability that

develops in the concrete operational stage, according to Piaget.   43

constructed-response items items that require students to write out information rather than select a response from a menu.   533

constructivism an approach to learning which emphasizes that individuals actively construct knowledge and understanding.   8, 314

construct validity the extent to which there is evidence that a test measures a particular construct. A construct is an unobservable trait or characteristic of a person, such as intelligence, learning style, personality, or anxiety.   491

content validity a test's ability to sample the content that is to be measured.   491

contracting putting reinforcement contingencies into writing.   220

control group in an experiment, a group whose experience is treated in every way like the experimental group except for the manipulated factor.   21

conventional reasoning in Kohlberg's theory, the middle level of moral development; at this level, internalization is intermediate in the sense that individuals abide by certain standards (internal) but these essentially are the standards of others (external).   96

convergent thinking thinking with the aim of producing one correct answer. This is usually the type of thinking required on conventional intelligence tests.   294

cooperative learning learning that occurs when students work in small groups to help each other learn.   322

correlational research research that describes the strength of the relation between two or more events or characteristics.   20

creativity the ability to think about something in novel and unusual ways and come up with unique solutions to problems.   294

criterion-referenced grading a grading system based on comparison with predetermined standards.   547

criterion validity a test's ability to predict a student's performance as measured by other assessments or criteria.   491

critical thinking thinking reflectively and productively and evaluating the evidence.   288

cross-cultural studies studies that compare what happens in one culture with what happens in one or more other cultures; they provide information about the degree to which people are similar and to what degree behaviors are specific to certain cultures.   135

cross-sectional research research in which the data are collected all at one time.   21

cue-dependent forgetting retrieval failure caused by a lack of effective retrieval cues.   263

culture the behavior patterns, beliefs, and all other products of a particular group of people that are passed on from generation to generation.   134

culture-fair tests tests of intelligence that are intended to be free of cultural bias.   120

D

decay theory the theory that new learning involves the creation of a neurochemical "memory trace," which will eventually disintegrate. Thus, decay theory suggests that the passage of time is responsible for forgetting.   263

decision making evaluating alternatives and making choices among them.   291

declarative memory the conscious recollection of information, such as specific facts or events that can be verbally communicated.   259

deductive reasoning reasoning from the general to the specific.   287

deep/surface styles involve the extent to which students approach learning materials in a way that helps them understand the meaning of the materials (deep style) or as simply what needs to be learned (surface style).   124

dependent variable the factor that is measured in an experiment.   21

descriptive statistics mathematical procedures that are used to describe and summarize (information) data in a meaningful way.   502

developmentally appropriate education education based on knowledge of the typical development of children within an age span (age appropriateness) as well as the uniqueness of the child (individual appropriateness).   84

difficult child a temperament style in which the child tends to react negatively, has aggressive tendencies, lacks self-

control, and is slow to accept new experiences.   127

direct instruction a structured, teacher-centered approach that is characterized by teacher direction and control, high teacher expectations for students' progress, maximum time spent by students on academic tasks, and efforts by the teacher to keep negative affect to a minimum.   383

disability a personal limitation that restricts an individual's functioning.   175

discovery learning learning in which students construct an understanding on their own.   397

divergent thinking thinking with the aim of producing many answers to the same question. This is characteristic of creativity.   294

Down syndrome a genetically transmitted form of mental retardation due to an extra (47th) chromosome.   179

dyslexia a severe impairment in the ability to read and spell.   183

E

easy child a temperament style in which the child is generally in a positive mood, quickly establishes regular routines, and easily adapts to new experiences.   127

ecological theory Bronfenbrenner's theory that consists of five environmental systems: microsystem, mesosystem, exosystem, macrosystem, and chronosystem.   68

educational psychology the branch of psychology that specializes in understanding teaching and learning in educational settings.   4

elaboration the extensiveness of information processing involved in encoding.   252

e-mail "electronic mail." A valuable way to use the Internet, e-mail messages can be sent to and received by individuals as well as large numbers of people at once.   401

emotional and behavioral disorders serious, persistent problems that involve relationships, aggression, depression, fears associated with personal or school matters, and other inappropriate socioemotional characteristics.   188

empowerment providing people with intellectual and coping skills to succeed and make this a more just world.   146

encoding the process by which information gets into memory.   247

encoding specificity principle the principle that associations formed at the time of encoding or learning tend to be effective retrieval cues.   262

epilepsy a nervous disorder characterized by recurring sensorimotor attacks or movement convulsions.   177

episodic memory the retention of information about the where and when of life's happenings.   259

equilibration a mechanism that Piaget proposed to explain how children shift from one stage of thought to the next. The shift occurs as children experience cognitive conflict, or disequilibria, in trying to understand the world. Eventually, they resolve the conflict and reach equilibrium of thought.   40

essay items items that require a lengthy written answer; they allow more freedom of response to questions but require more writing than other formats.   534

essential questions questions that reflect the heart of the curriculum, the most important things that students should explore and learn.   396

ethnic gloss the use of an ethnic label in a superficial way that stereotypes the ethnic group.   26

ethnicity a shared pattern of characteristics such as cultural heritage, nationality, race, religion, and language.   141

ethnographic study in-depth description and interpretation of behavior in an ethnic or a cultural group that includes direct involvement with the participants.   19

experimental group the group whose experience is manipulated in an experiment.   21

experimental research research that allows the determination of the causes of behavior; involves conducting an experiment, which is a carefully regulated procedure in which one or more of the factors believed to influence the behavior being studied is manipulated and all others are held constant.   20

expert knowledge excellent knowledge about the content of a particular discipline.   340

expository advance organizers organizers that provide students with new knowledge that will orient them to the upcoming lesson.   385

expressive language the ability to use language to express one's thoughts and communicate with others.   181

extrinsic motivation the external motivation to do something to obtain something else (a means to an end).   418

face-to-face style a classroom arrangement style in which students sit facing each other.   456

failure syndrome having low expectations for success and giving up at the first sign of difficulty.   437

far transfer the transfer of learning to a situation that is very different from the one in which the initial learning took place.   305

fetal alcohol syndrome (FAS) a cluster of abnormalities, including mental retardation and facial abnormalities, that appear in the offspring of mothers who drink alcohol heavily during pregnancy. 180

fixation using a prior strategy and thereby failing to examine a problem from a fresh, new perspective.   300

fluency disorders disorders that often involve what is commonly referred to as "stuttering."   181

formal operational stage Piaget's fourth cognitive developmental stage, which emerges between about eleven and fifteen years of age; thought is more abstract, idealistic, and logical in this stage.   46

formative assessment assessment during the course of instruction rather than after it is completed.   522

forward-reaching transfer the transfer of learning that involves thinking about how to apply what has been learned to new situations in the future.   305

Fostering a Community of Learners (FCL) a social constructivist program that encourages reflection and discussion through the use of adults as role models, children teaching children, and online computer consultation.   329

fragile X syndrome a genetically transmitted form of mental retardation due to an abnormality on the X chromosome.   179

frequency distribution a listing of scores, usually from highest to lowest, along with the number of times each score appears. 502

G

gender the sociocultural and psychological dimensions of being female or male.   153

gender roles the social expectations that prescribe how males and females should think, act, and feel.   154

gender-role transcendence the view that people's competence should be conceptualized in terms of them as persons rather than in terms of whether they are masculine, feminine, or androgynous.   162

gender schema theory a theory that an individual's attention and behavior are guided by an internal motivation to conform to gender-based sociocultural standards and stereotypes.   156

gender stereotypes broad categories that reflect impressions and beliefs about what behavior is appropriate for females and males.   156

grade-equivalent score a score that indicates students' performance in relation to grade level and months of the school year, assuming a 10-month school year.   507

grading translating descriptive assessment information into letters, numbers, or other marks that indicate the quality of a student's learning or performance.   545

growth portfolio a portfolio of work over an extended time frame (throughout the school year or longer) to reveal the student's progress in meeting learning targets.   544

guided discovery learning learning in which students are encouraged to construct their understanding with the assistance of teacher-guided questions and directions.   398

H

handicap a condition imposed on a person who has a disability.   175

helpless orientation a personal stance that focuses on personal inadequacies,

attribution of difficulty to a lack of ability, and negative affect.   425

heteronomous morality in Piaget's theory, the first stage of moral development (about four to seven years of age), in which justice and rules are conceived of as unchangeable properties of the world, beyond the control of people.   95

heuristic a strategy or rule of thumb that can suggest a solution to a problem but doesn't ensure it will work.   292

hidden curriculum Dewey's concept that every school has a pervasive moral atmosphere even if it does not have a program of moral education.   97

hierarchy of needs Maslow's concept that individual needs must be satisfied in this sequence: physiological, safety, love and belongingness, esteem, and self-actualization.   416

high-road transfer the transfer of learning from one situation to another that is conscious and effortful.   305

high-stakes testing using tests in a way that will have important consequences for the student, affecting such decisions as whether the student will be promoted or be allowed to graduate.   490

hindsight bias the tendency to falsely report, after the fact, that we accurately predicted an event.   292

histogram a frequency distribution in the form of a graph.   502

hostile environment sexual harassment subjection of students to unwelcome sexual conduct that is so severe, persistent, or pervasive that it limits the students' ability to benefit from their education. 165

Human Biology Middle Grades Curriculum (HumBio) developed by Stanford University scientists in collaboration with middle school teachers, this curriculum integrates ecology, evolution, genetics, physiology, human development, culture, health, and safety.   362

humanistic perspective a view that stresses students' capacity for personal growth, freedom to choose their destiny, and positive qualities.   415

hypotheses assumptions that can be tested to determine their accuracy; theories produce hypotheses.   16

hypothetical-deductive reasoning Piaget's formal operational concept that adolescents can develop hypotheses to solve problems and systematically reach (deduce) a conclusion.   46

identity achievement the identity status in which individuals have explored meaningful alternatives and made a commitment.   93

identity diffusion the identity status in which individuals have neither explored meaningful alternatives nor made a commitment.   92

identity foreclosure the identity status in which individuals have made a commitment but have not explored meaningful alternatives.   92

identity moratorium the identity status in which individuals are in the midst of exploring alternatives but have not yet made a commitment.   93

"I" messages desirable messages that reflect the speaker's true feelings better than judgmental "you" messages.   466

impulsive/reflective styles also referred to as conceptual tempo, they involve a student's tendency either to act quickly and impulsively or to take more time to respond and reflect on the accuracy of the answer.   124

incentives positive or negative stimuli or events that can motivate a student's behavior.   415

inclusion educating children with special education needs full-time in the regular classroom.   192

independent variable the manipulated, influential, experimental factor in an experiment.   20

individualism a set of values that give priority to personal rather than to group goals.   135

individualized education plan (IEP) a written statement that spells out a program specifically tailored for the student with a disability.   191

Individuals with Disabilities Education Act (IDEA) this act spells out broad mandates for services to all children with disabilities, including evaluation and determination of eligibility, appropriate education and an individualized education plan (IEP), and education in the least restrictive environment (LRE).   191

inductive reasoning reasoning from the specific to the general.   287

indulgent parenting a parenting style of involvement but few limits or restrictions on children's behavior; linked with children's social incompetence.   75

information-processing approach a cognitive approach in which children manipulate information, monitor it, and strategize about it. Central to this approach are the cognitive processes of memory and thinking.   246

instructional planning a systematic, organized strategy for planning lessons.   376

instructional validity the extent to which the assessment is a reasonable sample of what went on in the classroom.   525

intelligence problem-solving skills and the ability to adapt to learn from life's everyday experiences.   106

intelligence quotient (IQ) a person's mental age (MA) divided by chronological age (CA), multiplied by 100.   107

interactive demonstration strategy a strategy to help students overcome misconceptions in science in which the teacher introduces the demonstration, asks students to discuss the demonstration with their neighbors and predict its outcome, and then performs the demonstration.   360

interference theory the theory that we forget not because we actually lose memories from storage but because other information gets in the way of what we are trying to remember.   263

Internet the core of computer-mediated communication. The Internet system is worldwide and connects thousands of computer networks, providing an incredible array of information, which students can access.   400

intrinsic motivation the internal motivation to do something for its own sake (an end in itself).   418

intuitive thought substage the second substage of preoperational thought, lasting from about four to seven years of age. Children begin to use primitive reasoning and want to know the answer to all sorts of questions. They seem so sure about their knowledge in this substage but are unaware of how they know what they know.   42

item difficulty index the percentage of students who obtain the correct answer on an item.   533

item discrimination index an index that reflects the item's ability to discriminate between individuals who scored high and those who scored low on the entire test.   533

jigsaw classroom a classroom in which students from different cultural backgrounds cooperate by doing different parts of a project to reach a common goal.   148

Joplin plan a standard nongraded program for instruction in reading.   122

justice perspective a moral perspective that focuses on the rights of the individual; Kohlberg's theory is a justice perspective.   97

laboratory a controlled setting from which many of the complex factors of the real world have been removed.   18

language a form of communication, whether spoken, written, or signed, that is based on a system of symbols.   56

language disorders significant impairments in a child's receptive or expressive language.   181

lateralization the specialization of functions in each hemisphere of the brain.   38

law of effect the principle that behaviors followed by positive outcomes are strengthened and that behaviors followed by negative outcomes are weakened.   215

learning a relatively permanent influence on behavior, knowledge, and thinking skills, which comes about through experience.   210

learning and thinking styles individuals' preferences in how they use their abilities.   123

learning disability a disability in which children (1) are of normal intelligence or above; (2) have difficulty in at least one academic area and usually several; and (3) have no other diagnosed problem or disorder, such as mental retardation, that is causing the difficulty.   182

least restrictive environment (LRE) a setting that is as similar as possible to the one in which children who do not have a disability are educated.   192

levels of processing theory the theory that processing of memory occurs on a continuum from shallow to deep, with deeper processing producing better memory.   252

longitudinal research research in which the same individuals are studied over a period of time, usually several years or more.   21

long-term memory a type of memory that holds enormous amounts of information for a long period of time in a relatively permanent fashion.   257

low-road transfer the automatic, often unconscious, transfer of learning to another situation.   305

manipulative style a way of dealing with conflict in which people try to get what they want by making others feel guilty or sorry for them.   466

mastery learning learning one concept or topic thoroughly before moving on to a more difficult one.   387

mastery orientation a personal stance that involves mastery of the task, positive affect, and solution-oriented strategies.   424

mean the numerical average of a group of scores.   503

means-end analysis a heuristic in which one identifies the goal (end) of a problem, assesses the current situation, and evaluates what needs to be done (means) to decrease the difference between the two conditions.   299

measures of variability measures that tell how much scores vary from one another.   504

median the score that falls exactly in the middle of a distribution of scores after they have been arranged (or ranked) from highest to lowest.   503

memory the retention of information over time, which involves encoding, storage, and retrieval.   248

memory span the number of digits an individual can report without error in a single presentation.   256

mental age (MA) an individual's level of mental development relative to others.   107

mental processes thoughts, feelings, and motives that cannot be observed by others.   211

mental retardation a condition with an onset before age eighteen that involves low intelligence (usually below 70 on a traditional individually administered intelligence test) and difficulty in adapting to everyday life.   178

mental set a type of fixation in which an individual tries to solve a problem in a particular way that has worked in the past.   300

metacognition cognition about cognition, or "knowing about knowing."   248

mode the score that occurs most often.   503

moral development development with respect to the rules and conventions of just interactions between people.   94

morphology The units of meaning involved in word formation.   56

motivation the processes that energize, direct, and sustain behavior.   414

multicultural education education that values diversity and includes the perspectives of a variety of cultural groups on a regular basis.   146

multiple-choice item an objective test item consisting of two parts: a stem plus a set of possible responses.   530

naturalistic observation observation outside of a laboratory in the real world.   18

nature-nurture issue *nature* refers to an organism's biological inheritance, *nurture* to environmental influences. The "nature" proponents claim biological inheritance is the most important influence on development; the "nurture" proponents claim that environmental experiences are the most important.   117

near transfer the transfer of learning to a situation that is similar to the one in which the initial learning took place.   305

need for affiliation or relatedness the motive to be securely connected with other people.   417

negative reinforcement reinforcement based on the principle that the frequency of a response increases because an aversive (unpleasant) stimulus is removed.   216

neglectful parenting a parenting style of uninvolvement in which parents spend little time with their children; associated with children's social incompetence.   75

neo-Piagetians developmental psychologists who believe that Piaget got some things right but that his theory needs considerable revision; emphasize how to process information through attention, memory, and strategies.   49

network theories theories that describe how information in memory is organized and connected; they emphasize nodes in the memory network.   260

nongraded (cross-age) program a variation of between-class ability grouping in which students are grouped by their ability in particular subjects, regardless of their age or grade level.   122

normal distribution a symmetrical distribution, with a majority of scores falling in the middle of the possible range of scores and few scores appearing toward the extremes of the range.   107, 505

norm group a group of similar individuals who previously were given the test by the test maker.   490

norm-referenced grading a grading system based on a comparison of a student's performance with that of other students in the class or of other classes and other students.   547

objective tests tests that have relatively clear, unambiguous scoring criteria, usually multiple-choice tests.   527

observational learning also called *imitation* or *modeling,* the learning process in which a person observes and imitates someone else's behavior.   227

off-set style a classroom arrangement style in which small numbers of students (usually three or four) sit at tables but do not sit directly across from one another.   456

operant conditioning also called *instrumental conditioning,* this is a form of learning in which the consequences of behavior produce changes in the probability that the behavior will occur.   215

organization Piaget's concept of grouping isolated behaviors into a higher-order, more smoothly functioning cognitive system; the grouping or arranging of items into categories. The use of organization improves long-term memory.   39

orthopedic impairments restricted movements or lack of control of movements, due to muscle, bone, or joint problems.   177

overconfidence bias the tendency to have more confidence in judgment and decisions than we should based on probability or past experience.   291

P

participant observation observation conducted at the same time the teacher-researcher is actively involved as a participant in the activity or setting.   18

passive style a way of dealing with conflict in which people are nonassertive and submissive and don't let others know what they want.   466

pedagogical content knowledge knowledge about how to effectively teach a particular discipline.   340

percentile rank score the percentage of a distribution that lies at or below the score. 506

performance assessment assessment that requires creating answers or products that demonstrate knowledge and skill; examples include writing and conducting an experiment, carrying out a project, solving a real-world problem, and creating a portfolio.   528

performance criteria specific behaviors that need to be performed effectively as part of an assessment. 539

performance orientation a personal stance of concern with the outcome rather than the process; for performance-oriented individuals, winning is what matters and happiness is believed to result from winning.   425

permissive classroom management style a management style that allows students considerable autonomy but provides them with little support for developing learning skills or managing their behavior.   459

personality distinctive thoughts, emotions, and behaviors that characterize the way an individual adapts to the world.   126

person-situation interaction the view that the best way to conceptualize personality is not in terms of personal traits or characteristics alone but also in terms of the situation involved.   126

phonology a language's sound system.   56

portfolio a systematic and organized collection of a student's work that demonstrates the student's skills and accomplishments.   542

positive reinforcement reinforcement based on the principle that the frequency of a response increases because it is followed by a rewarding stimulus.   216

postconventional reasoning in Kohlberg's theory, the highest level of moral development; at this level, moral development is internalized and moral reasoning is self-generated.   96

pragmatics the appropiate use of language in different contexts.   57

preconventional reasoning in Kohlberg's theory, the lowest level of moral development; at this level, the child shows no internalization of moral values and moral reasoning is controlled by external rewards and punishments.   95

predictive validity the relation between test scores and the student's future performance.   491

prejudice an unjustified negative attitude toward an individual because of the individual's membership in a group.   142

Premack principle the principle that a high-probability activity can serve as a reinforcer for a low-probability activity.   219

preoperational stage the second Piagetian stage, lasting from about two to seven years of age; symbolic thought increases but operational thought is not yet present.   40

problem-based learning learning that emphasizes authentic problems like those that occur in daily life.   301

problem sets groups of two or more multiple-choice or objective short-answer items that are related to the same stimulus, such as an illustration, a graph, or a passage.   532

problem solving finding an appropriate way to attain a goal.   298

procedural memory knowledge in the form of skills and cognitive operations. Procedural memory cannot be consciously recollected, at least not in the form of specific events or facts.   259

program evaluation research research that is designed to make decisions about the effectiveness of a particular program.   23

prompt an added stimulus or cue that is given just before a response and increases the likelihood the response will occur.   221

prototype matching a process in which individuals decide whether an item is a member of a category by comparing it with the most typical item(s) of the category.   285

psychoanalytic theory of gender a theory that stems from Freud's view that the preschool child develops a sexual attraction to the opposite-sex parent, then by about five or six years of age renounces the attraction because of anxious feelings. Subsequently, the child identifies with the same-sex parent, unconsciously adopting the same-sex parent's characteristics.   154

Public Law 94-142 the Education for All Handicapped Children Act, which required that all students with disabilities be given a free, appropriate public education and which provided the funding to help implement this education.   191

punishment a consequence that decreases the probability that a behavior will occur.   216

Q

quid pro quo sexual harassment threats by a school employee to base an educational decision (such as a grade) on a student's submission to unwelcome sexual conduct.   164

R

random assignment in experimental research, the assignment of participants to experimental and control groups by chance.   21

range the distance between the highest and lowest scores.   504

rapport talk the language of conversation and a way of establishing connections and negotiating relationships; more characteristic of females than males.   159

raw score the number of items the student answered correctly on the test.   506

receptive language the reception and understanding of language.   181

reciprocal teaching a learning arrangement in which students take turns leading a small-group discussion. 330, 346

rehearsal the conscious repetition of information over time to increase the length of time information stays in memory. 251

reinforcement (reward) a consequence that increases the probability that a behavior will occur. 216

reliability the extent to which a test produces a consistent, reproducible score. 491

report talk talk that gives information; more characteristic of males than females. 159

representativeness heuristic making faulty decisions based on how well something matches a prototype—that is, a common or representative example—rather than its relevance to the particular situation. 292

response cost taking a positive reinforcer away from an individual. 224

S

scaffolding a technique that involves changing the level of support for learning; a teacher or more-advanced peer adjusts the amount of guidance to fit the student's current performance. 52, 316

schedules of reinforcement partial reinforcement timetables that determine when a response will be reinforced. 220

schema a concept or framework that exists in a person's mind to organize and interpret information. 39, 260

schema theories theories that when we construct information, we fit it into information that already exists in our mind. 260

Schools for Thought (SFT) a social constructivist program that combines aspects of The Jasper Project, Fostering a Community of Learners, and CSILE. 331

scientific method a method for discovering accurate information that includes these steps: Conceptualize the problem, collect data, draw conclusions, and revise research conclusions and theory. 16

scientific research objective, systematic, and testable research that aims at reducing

conclusions based on personal beliefs, opinions, and feelings. 16

script a schema for an event. 261

selected-response items test items with an objective format in which responses can be scored on quick inspection. A scoring guide for correct responses is created and can be used by an examiner or a computer. 529

self-actualization the highest and most elusive of Maslow's needs; the motivation to develop one's full potential as a human being. 416

self-efficacy the belief that one can master a situation and produce positive outcomes. 226, 426

self-esteem also called self-image and self-worth, the individual's overall conception of himself or herself. 91

self-instructional methods cognitive behavior techniques aimed at teaching individuals to modify their own behavior. 233

self-regulatory learning the self-generation and self-monitoring of thoughts, feelings, and behaviors in order to reach a goal. 236

semantic memory a student's general knowledge about the world. 259

semantics the meaning of words and sentences. 57

seminar style a classroom arrangement style in which large numbers of students (ten or more) sit in circular, square, or U-shaped arrangements. 456

sensorimotor stage the first Piagetian stage, lasting from birth to about two years of age, in which infants construct an understanding of the world by coordinating sensory experiences with motor actions. 40

sensory memory memory that holds information from the world in its original form for only an instant. 255

serial position effect the principle that recall is better for items at the beginning and the end of a list than for items in the middle. 262

seriation a concrete operation that involves ordering stimuli along some quantitative dimension. 45

service learning a form of education that promotes social responsibility and service to the community. 98

sexism prejudice and discrimination against an individual because of the person's sex. 156

shaping teaching new behaviors by reinforcing successive approximations to a specified target behavior. 221

short-answer item a constructed-response format in which students are required to write a word, a short phrase, or several sentences in response to a task. 534

short-term memory a limited-capacity memory system in which information is retained for as long as 30 seconds, unless the information is rehearsed, in which case it can be retained longer. 255

situated cognition the idea that thinking is located (situated) in social and physical contexts, not within an individual's mind. 316

slow-to-warm-up child a temperament style in which the child has a low activity level, is somewhat negative, shows low adaptability, and displays a low intensity of mood. 127

social cognitive theory Bandura's theory that social and cognitive factors, as well as behavior, play important roles in learning. 226

social cognitive theory of gender a theory that children's gender development occurs through observation and imitation of gender behavior, as well as reinforcement and punishment of gender behavior. 154

social constructivist approach an approach that emphasizes the social contexts of learning and that knowledge is mutually built and constructed; Vygotsky's theory exemplifies this approach. 54, 314

social motives needs and desires that are learned through experiences with the social world. 431

social studies the field that seeks to promote civic competence with the goal of helping students make informed and reasoned decisions for the public good as citizens of a culturally diverse, democratic society in an interdependent world. 364

socioeconomic status (SES) the categorization of people according to their economic, educational, and occupational characteristics. 136

speech and language disorders a number of speech problems (such as articulation disorders, voice disorders, and fluency disorders) and language problems (difficulties in receiving information and expressing language).   181

split-half reliability reliability judged by dividing the test items into two halves, such as the odd-numbered and even-numbered items. The scores on the two sets of items are compared to determine how consistently the students performed across each set.   492

standard deviation a measure of how much a set of scores varies on the average around the mean of the scores.   504

standardized tests tests that have uniform procedures for administration and scoring. They assess students' performance in different domains and allow a student's performance to be compared with the performance of other students at the same age or grade level on a national basis.   19, 488

standards-based tests tests that assess skills that students are expected to have mastered before they can be promoted to the next grade or permitted to graduate.   490

standard score a score expressed as a deviation from the mean; involves the standard deviation.   507

stanine score a 9-point scale that describes a student's performance.   507

stereotype threat the anxiety that one's behavior might conform a negative stereotype about one's group.   119

strategy construction the discovery of new procedures for processing information.   247

subgoaling the process of setting intermediate goals that place students in a better position to reach the final goal or solution.   299

summative assessment assessment after instruction is finished; also called formal assessment.   523

symbolic function substage the first substage of preoperational thought, occurring between about two to four years of age; the ability to represent an object not present develops and symbolic thinking increases; egocentrism and animism occur.   41

syntax the ways that words must be combined to form acceptable phrases and sentences.   56

systematic desensitization a method based on classical conditioning that reduces anxiety by getting the individual to associate deep relaxation with successive visualizations of increasingly anxiety-provoking situations.   214

T

task analysis breaking down a complex task that students are to learn into its component parts.   380

taxonomy a classification system.   380

teacher-as-researcher also called teacher-researcher, this concept involves classroom teachers conducting their own studies to improve their teaching practice.   23

temperament a person's behavioral style and characteristic ways of responding.   126

test-retest reliability the extent to which a test yields the same performance when a student is given the same test on two occasions.   492

theory an interrelated, coherent set of ideas that helps to explain and make predictions that can be tested to determine their accuracy.   16

thinking manipulating and transforming information in memory, which often is done to form concepts, think critically, and solve problems.   287

time-out removing an individual from positive reinforcement.   223

transactional strategy instruction approach a cognitive approach to reading that emphasizes instruction in strategies, especially metacognitive strategies.   345

transfer applying previous experiences and knowledge to learning or problem solving in a new situation.   304

transitivity the ability to logically combine relations to understand certain conclusions; develops in the concrete operational stage.   45

triarchic theory of intelligence Sternberg's view that intelligence comes in three main forms: analytical, creative, and practical.   110

_T_-score a standard score in which the mean is set at 50 and the standard deviation is set at 10.   507

U

ubiquitous computing the distribution of computing in the environment rather than containing it in a desk-bound personal computer.   404

V

validity the extent to which a test measures what it is intended to measure and whether inferences about the test scores are accurate.   491

values clarification an approach to moral education that emphasizes helping people clarify what their lives are for and what is worth working for; students are encouraged to define their own values and understand the values of others.   97

voice disorders disorders producing speech that is hoarse, harsh, too loud, too high-pitched, or too low-pitched.   181

W

website an individual's or an organization's location on the Internet. Websites display information posted by individuals and organizations.   400

whole-language approach the idea that reading instruction should parallel children's natural language learning; reading materials should be whole and meaningful.   342

within-class ability grouping placing students in two or three groups within a class to take into account differences in students' abilities.   123

withitness a management style described by Kounin in which teachers show students that they are aware of what is happening. Such teachers closely monitor students on a regular basis and detect inappropriate behavior early before it gets out of hand.   459

working memory a kind of "mental workbench" that lets individuals manipulate, assemble, and construct information when they make decisions, solve problems, and comprehend written and spoken language.   256

World Wide Web (the **Web**) a hypermedia information retrieval system that links a variety of Internet materials. It includes text and graphics.   400

"you" messages undesirable messages in which speakers appear to judge people and place them in a defensive position.   465

zone of proximal development (ZPD) Vygotsky's term for the range of tasks that are too difficult for children to master alone but that can be mastered with guidance and assistance from adults or more-skilled children.   51

z-score a score that provides information about how many standard deviations a raw score is above or below the mean.   507

References

A

Abrami, P. C., Cholmsky, P., & Gordon, R. (2001). *Statistical analysis for the social sciences.* Boston: Allyn & Bacon.

Abruscato, J. (2004). *Teaching children science* (2nd ed.). Boston: Allyn & Bacon.

Academic Software. (1996). *Adaptive Device Locator System* [computer program]. Lexington, KY: Author.

Achenbach, T. M., Howell, C. T., Quay, H. C., & Conners, C. K. (1991). National survey of problems and competencies among four- to sixteen-year-olds. *Monographs of the Society for Research in Child Development,* Serial No. 225 (Vol. 56, No. 3).

Adams, A., Carnine, D., & Gersten, R. (1982). Instructional strategies for studying content area texts in the intermediate grades. *Reading Research Quarterly, 18,* 27–53.

Adams, R., & Biddle, B. (1970). *Realities of teaching.* New York: Holt, Rinehart & Winston.

Adamson, H. D. (2004). *Language minority students in American schools.* Mahwah, NJ: Erlbaum.

Aiken, L. R. (2003). *Psychological testing and assessment* (11th ed.). Boston: Allyn & Bacon.

Airasian, P. (2001). *Classroom assessment* (4th ed.). New York: McGraw-Hill.

Airasian, P. (2005). *Classroom assessment* (5th ed.). New York: McGraw-Hill.

Airasian, P., & Walsh, M. E. (1997, February). Constructivist cautions. *Phi Delta Kappan,* pp. 444–450.

Alberti, R. E., & Emmons, M. L. (1995). *Your perfect right* (8th ed.). San Luis Obispo, CA: Impact.

Alberto, P. A., & Troutman, A. C. (1999). *Applied behavior analysis for teachers* (5th ed.). Englewood Cliffs, NJ: Merrill.

Alderman, M. K. (2004). *Motivation for achievement.* Mahwah, NJ: Erlbaum.

Alexander, A., Anderson, H., Heilman, P. C., & others. (1991). Phonological awareness training and remediation of analytic decoding deficits in a group of severe dyslexics. *Annals of Dyslexia, 41,* 193–206.

Alexander, P. A. (2003). The development of expertise. *Educational Researcher, 32,* (8), 10-14.

Allan, K., Wolf, H. A., Rosenthal, C. R., & Rugg, M. D. (2001). The effects of retrieval cues on post-retrieval monitoring in episodic memory: An electrophysiological study. *Brain Research, 12,* 289–299.

Alverno College. (1995). *Writing and speaking criteria.* Milwaukee, WI: Alverno Productions.

Amabile, T. (1993). (Commentary). In D. Goleman, P. Kafman, & M. Ray, (Eds.), *The creative spirit.* New York: Plume.

Amabile, T. M., & Hennesey, B. A. (1992). The motivation for creativity in children. In A. K. Boggiano & T. S. Pittman (Eds.), *Achievement and motivation.* New York: Cambridge University Press.

Amato, P. (2004). To have and have not: Marriage and divorce in the United States. In M. Coleman & L. Ganong (Eds.), *Handbook of contemporary families.* Thousand Oaks, CA: Sage.

Ambrose, D. (2004). Creativity in teaching. In J.C. Kaufman & J. Baer (Eds.), *Creativity across domains.* Mahwah, NJ: Erlbaum.

Ambrosio, J. (2004). No child left behind. *Phi Delta Kappan, 85,* 709-711.

American Association for the Advancement of Science. (1993). *Benchmarks for science literacy: Project 2061.* New York: Oxford University Press.

American Association of University Women (2003). Isi puede! Yes, we can: Latinas in school by Angela Ginorio and Michelle Huston (2002). Available at www.aaww.org/research/latina.cfm

American Association of University Women. (1992). *How schools shortchange girls: A study of major findings on girls and education.* Washington, DC: Author.

American Association of University Women. (1993). *Hostile hallways.* Washington, DC: Author.

American Association of University Women. (2003). Isi puede! Yes, we can: Latinas in school by Angela Ginorio and Michelle Huston (2000). Available at www.aaww.org/research/latina.cfm.

American Association on Mental Retardation, Ad Hoc Committee on Terminology and Classification. (1992). *Mental retardation* (9th ed.). Washington, DC: Author.

American Educational Research Association. (1999). *Standards for educational and psychological testing.* Washington, DC: Author.

American Psychiatric Association. (1994). *Diagnostic and statistical manual of mental disorders* (4th ed.). Washington, DC: Author.

Anderman, E. M., Austin, C. C., & Johnson, D. M. (2002). The development of goal orientation. In A. Wigfield & J. S. Eccles (Eds.), *Development of achievement motivation.* San Diego: Academic Press.

Anderman, E. M., Maehr, M. L., & Midgley, C. (1996). *Declining motivation after the transition to middle school: Schools can make a difference.* Unpublished manuscript, University of Kentucky, Lexington.

Anderson, J. R. (1993). Problem solving and learning. *American Psychologist, 48,* 35–44.

Anderson, L. W., & Krathwohl, D. R. (Eds.). (2001). *A taxonomy for learning, teaching, and assessing.* New York: Longman.

Andrews, J. J. W., Saklofske, D. H., & Janzen, H. L. (Eds.). (2001). *Handbook of psychoeducational assessment.* San Diego: Academic Press.

Anfara, V. A. (Ed.). (2001). *The handbook of research in middle school education.* Greenwich, CT: IAP.

Applebome, P. (1997, September 3). Students' test scores show slow but steady gains at nation's schools. *New York Times,* Section B, p. 8.

Arends, R. I. (1998). *Learning to teach* (4th ed.). New York: McGraw-Hill.

Arends, R.I. (2004). *Learning to teach.* (6th ed.). New York: McGraw-Hill.

Arhar, J. M., Holly, M. L., & Kasten, W. C. (2001). *Action research for teachers.* Upper Saddle River, NJ: Prentice Hall.

Arlin, M. (1979). Teacher transitions can disrupt time flow in classrooms. *American Educational Research Journal, 16,* 42–56.

Aronson, E. E. (1986, August). *Teaching students things they think they already know about: The case of prejudice and desegregation.* Paper presented at the meeting of the American Psychological Association, Washington, DC.

Aronson, E. E., Blaney, N., Sephan, C., Sikes, J., & Snapp, M. (1978). *The jigsaw classroom.* Beverly Hills, CA: Sage.

Aronson, E.E., & Patnoe, S. (1997). *The jigsaw classroom* (2nd ed.). Boston: Addison-Wesley.

Aronson, J. (2002). Stereotype threat: Contending and coping with unnerving expectations. *Improving academic achievement.* San Diego: Academic Press.

Aronson, J., Fried, C.B., & Good, C. (2002). Reducing the effects of stereotype threat on African American college students by shaping theories of intelligence. *Journal of Experimental Social Psychology, 38,* 113-125.

Aronson, J. M., Lustina, M.J., Good, C., Keough, K., Steele, C.M., & Brown, J. (1999). When white men can't do math: Necessary and sufficient factors in stereotype threat. *Journal Experimental Social Psychology, 35,* 29-46.

Arter, J. (1995). *Portfolios for assessment and instruction.* ERIC Document Reproduction Service No. ED388890.

Arter, J., & McTighe, J. (2001). *Scoring rubrics in the classroom.* Thousand Oaks, CA: Corwin Press.

Ashcraft, M. H., & Kirk, E. P. (2001). The relationships among working memory, math anxiety, and performance. *Journal of Experimental Psychology: General, 130,* 224–237.

Asher, J., & Garcia, R. (1969). The optimal age to learn a foreign language. *Modern Language Journal, 53,* 334–341.

Ashton, P. T., & Webb, R. B. (1986). *Making a difference: Teachers' sense of efficacy and student achievement.* White Plains, NY: Longman.

Atkinson, R. C., & Shiffrin, R. M. (1968). Human memory: A proposed system and its control processes. In K. W. Spence & J. T. Spence (Eds.), *The psychology of learning and motivation* (Vol. 2). San Diego: Academic Press.

Auerbach, J., Benjamin, J., Faroy, M., Geller, V., & Ebstein, R. (2001). DRD4 related to infant attention and information processing: A link to ADHD? *Psychiatric Genetics, 11,* 31–35.

August. P. (2002, September 26). They all look alike. *San Francisco Chronicle,* p. A29.

Ausubel, D. P. (1960). The use of advance organizers in the learning and retention of meaningful verbal material. *Journal of Educational Psychology, 51,* 267–272.

B

Baddeley, A. (1993). Working memory and conscious awareness. In A. F. Collins, S. E. Gatherhole, M. A. Conway, & P. E. Morris (Eds.), *Theories of memory.* Mahwah, NJ: Erlbaum.

Baddeley, A. (1998). *Human memory* (rev. ed.). Boston: Allyn & Bacon.

Baddeley, A. (2000). Short-term and working memory. In E. Tulving & F. I. M. Craik (Eds.), *The Oxford handbook of memory.* New York: Oxford University Press.

Baddeley, A. (2001). *Is working memory still working?* Paper presented at the meeting of the American Psychological Association, San Francisco.

Baillargeon, R. (2004). The acquisition of physical knowledge in infancy: A summary in eight lessons. In U. Goswami (ed.) *Blackwell handbook of childhood cognitive development.* Malden, MA: Blackwell.

Baines, L. A., Deluzain, R. E., & Stanley, G. K. (1999). Computer technology in Florida and Georgia secondary schools: Propaganda and progress. *American Secondary Education, 27,* 33–38.

Baker, J. (1999). Teacher-student interaction in urban at-risk classrooms: Differential behavior, relationship quality, and student satisfaction with school. *The Elementary School Journal, 100,* 57–70.

Baldry, A.C., & Farrington, D.P. (2004). Evaluation of an intervention program for the reduction of bullying and victimization in schools. *Aggressive Behavior, 30,* 1-15.

Bandura, A. (1965). Influence of models' reinforcement contingencies on the acquisition of imitative responses. *Journal of Personality and Social Psychology, 1,* 589–596.

Bandura, A. (1982). Self-efficacy mechanism in human agency. *American Psychologist, 37,* 122–147.

Bandura, A. (1986). *Social foundations of thought and action.* Englewood Cliffs, NJ: Prentice Hall.

Bandura, A. (1997). *Self-efficacy: The exercise of control.* New York: W. H. Freeman.

Bandura, A. (2001). Social cognitive theory. *Annual Review of Psychology.* Palo Alto, CA: Annual Reviews.

Bandura, A. (2004, May). *Toward a psychology of human agency.* Paper presented at the meeting of the American Psychological Society, Chicago.

Bandura, A., & Locke, E.A. (2003). Negative self-efficacy and goals revisited. *Journal of Applied Psychology, 88,* 87-99.

Bangert, K., Kulik, J., & Kulik, C. (1983). Individualized systems of instruction in secondary schools. *Review of Educational Research, 53,* 143–158.

Bank Street College of Education. (1984). *Voyage of the Mimi.* New York: Holt, Rinehart & Winston.

Banks, J. A. (1995). *Multicultural education: Its effects on students' racial and gender role attitudes.* In J. A. Banks & C. A. M. Banks (Eds.), *Handbook of research on multicultural education.* New York: Macmillan.

Banks, J. A. (1997). *Teaching strategies for ethnic studies* (6th ed.). Boston: Allyn & Bacon.

Banks, J. A. (1998). The lives and values of researchers: Implications for educating citizens in a multicultural society. *Educational Researcher, 27,* 4–17.

Banks, J. A. (2001). Multicultural education. In J. A. Banks & C. A. M. Banks (Eds.), *Multicultural education: Issues and perspectives.* New York: Wiley.

Banks, J. A. (2002). *Introduction to multicultural education* (3rd ed.). Boston: Allyn & Bacon.

Banks, J. A. (2003). *Teaching strategies for ethnic studies* (7th ed.). Boston: Allyn & Bacon.

Banks, S. R. (2005). *Classroom assessment* 3rd ed. Boston: Allyn & Bacon.

Barber, B. L., Eccles, J. S., & Stone, M. R. (2001, April). *Whatever happened to the jock, the brain, and the princess? Young adult pathways linked to adolescent activity involvement and identity.* Paper presented at the meeting of the Society for Research in Child Development, Minneapolis.

Barkley, R. A. (1998). *Attention-deficit hyperactivity disorder: A handbook for diagnosis and treatment.* New York: Guilford.

Barr, W. B. (2000). Epilepsy. In A. Kazdin (Ed.), *Encyclopedia of psychology.* Washington, DC, and New York: American Psychological Association and Oxford University Press.

Barron, K. E., & Harackiewicz, J. M. (2001). Achievement goals and optimal motivation: Testing multiple goal models. *Journal of Personality and Social Psychology, 80,* 706–722.

Barsalou, L. W. (2000). Concepts: Structure. In A. Kazdin (Ed.), *Encyclopedia of psychology.* Washington, DC, and New York: American Psychological Association and Oxford University Press.

Bartlett, E. J. (1982). Learning to revise: Some component processes. In M. Nystrand (Ed.), *What writers know.* New York: Academic Press.

Bartlett, F. C. (1932). *Remembering.* Cambridge, England: Cambridge University Press.

Bartlett, J. (2001, December). *Personal conversation.* Richardson, TX: Department of Psychology, University of Texas at Dallas.

Barton, J., & Collins, A. (1997). Starting Out: Designing your portfolio. In J. Barton & A. Collins (Eds.), *Portfolio assessment: A handbook for educators.* Boston: Addison-Wesley.

Batchelder, W. (2000). Mathematical psychology. In A. Kazdin (Ed.), *Encyclopedia of psychology.* Washington, DC, and New York: American Psychological Association and Oxford University Press.

Battistich, V., & Solomon, D. (1995, April). *Linking teacher change to student change.* Paper presented at the meeting of

the American Educational Research Association, San Francisco.

Battistich, V., Solomon, D., Watson, M., Solomon, J., & Schaps, E. (1989). Effects of an elementary school program to enhance prosocial behavior on children's cognitive social-problem solving skills and strategies. *Journal of Applied Developmental Psychology, 10,* 147–169.

Baumrind, D. (1971). Current patterns of parental authority. *Developmental Psychology Monographs, 4* (1, Part 2).

Baumrind, D. (1996, April). Unpublished review of J. W. Santrock's *Children,* 5th ed. New York: McGraw-Hill.

Beachner, L., & Pickett, A. (2001). *Multiple intelligences and positive life habits: 174 activities for applying them in your classroom.* Thousand Oaks, CA: Corwin Press.

Beal, C. (1994). *Boys and girls: The development of gender roles.* New York: McGraw-Hill.

Bearison, D. J., & Dorval, B. (2002). *Collaborative cognition.* Westport, CT: Ablex.

Beatty, B. (1998). From laws of learning to a science of values: Efficiency and morality in Thorndike's educational psychology. *American Psychologist, 53,* 1145–1152.

Beck, I. L., McKeown, G. M., Sinatra, K. B., & Loxterman, J. A. (1991). Revising social studies texts from a text-processing perspective: Evidence of improved comprehensibility. *Reading Research Quarterly, 26,* 251–276.

Becker, H. J. (1994). *Analysis of trends of school use of new information technology.* Irvine: University of California Press.

Becker, J. R. (1981). Differential treatment of females and males in mathematics classes. *Journal for Research in Mathematics Education, 12,* 40–53.

Beckham, E. E. (2000). Depression. In A. Kazdin (Ed.), *Encyclopedia of psychology.* Washington, DC, and New York: American Psychological Association and Oxford University Press.

Bednar, R. L., Wells, M. G., & Peterson, S. R. (1995). *Self-esteem* (2nd ed.). Washington, DC: American Psychological Association.

Begley, S. (1998, March 30). Homework doesn't help. *Newsweek,* pp. 30–31.

Bell, L. A. (1989). Something's wrong here and it's not me: Challenging the dilemmas

that block girls' success. *Journal for the Education of the Gifted, 12,* 118–130.

Bem, S. L. (1977). On the utility of alternative procedures for assessing psychological androgyny. *Journal of Consulting and Clinical Psychology, 45,* 196–205.

Bender, W. (1998). *Learning disabilities* (3rd ed.). Boston: Allyn & Bacon.

Bennett, C. (2003). *Comprehensive multicultural education* (5th ed.). Boston: Allyn & Bacon.

Bennett, W. (1993). *The book of virtues.* New York: Simon & Schuster.

Benson, P. (1993). *The troubled journey.* Minneapolis: Search Institute.

Benveniste, L., Carnoy, M., & Rothstein, R. (2003). *All else equal.* New York: Routledge-Farmer.

Beran, T.N., & Tutty, L. (2002) *An evaluation of the Bully Proofing Your School, School Program.* Unpublished manuscript, Calgary: RESOLVE, Alberta.

Bereiter, C., & Scardamalia, M. (1989). Intentional learning as a goal of instruction. In L. B. Resnick (Ed.), *Knowing, learning, and instruction. Essays in honor of Robert Glaser.* Hillsdale, NJ: Erlbaum.

Bereiter, C., & Scardamalia, M. (1993). *Surpassing ourselves: An inquiry into the nature and implications of expertise.* Chicago: Open Court.

Berger, E.H., & Pollman, M.J. (1996). Multiple intelligences: Enabling diverse learning. *Early Childhood Education Journal, 23,* (4), 249-253.

Berko Gleason, J. (2000). Language. In M. H. Bornstein & M. E. Lamb (Eds.), *Developmental psychology* (4th ed.). Mahwah, NJ: Erlbaum.

Berko Gleason, J. (2002). Review of J.W. Santrock's *Life-span development,* (9th Ed.). New York: McGraw-Hill.

Berko, J. (1958). The child's learning of English morphology. *Word, 14,* 150–177.

Berndt, T. J. (1979). Developmental changes in conformity to peers and parents. *Developmental Psychology, 15,* 608–616.

Berndt, T. J. (1999). Friends' influence on children's adjustment. In W. A. Collins & B. Laursen (Eds.), *Relationships as developmental contexts.* Mahwah, NJ: Erlbaum.

Bernstein, D. K., & Tiegerman-Farber, E. (2002). *Language and communication disorders in children* (5th ed.). Boston: Allyn & Bacon.

Berry, B., Hoke, M., & Hirsch, E. (2004). The search for highly qualified teachers. *Phi Delta Kappan, 85*, 684-689.

Berry, J. W. (2000). Cultural foundations of behavior. In A. Kazdin (Ed.), *Encyclopedia of psychology.* Washington, DC, and New York: American Psychological Association and Oxford University Press.

Berryman, L., & Russell, D. R. (2001). Portfolios across the curriculum: Whole school assessment in Kentucky. *English Journal, 90*, 76–83.

Bersoff, D. N. (Ed.). (1999). *Ethical conflicts in psychology* (2nd ed.). Washington, DC: American Psychological Association.

Best, D. (2001). Cross-cultural gender roles. In J. Worrell (Ed.), *Encyclopedia of women and gender.* San Diego: Academic Press.

Best, J. W., & Kahn, J. V. (2003). *Research in education* (9th ed.). Boston: Allyn & Bacon.

Betch, T., Haberstroh, S., Glockner, A., Haar, T., & Fiedler, K. (2001). The effects of routine strength on adaptation and information search in recurrent decision making. *Organizational Behavior and Human Decision Processes, 84*, 23–53.

Bialystok, E. (1993). Metalinguistic awareness: The development of children's representations in language. In C. Pratt & A. Garton (Eds.), *Systems of representation in children.* London: Wiley.

Bialystok, E. (1997). Effects of bilingualism and biliteracy on children's emerging concepts of print. *Developmental Psychology, 33*, 429–440.

Bialystok, E. (1999). Cognitive complexity and attentional control in the bilingual mind. *Child Development, 70*, 636–644.

Bialystok, E. (2001). *Bilingualism in development: Language, literacy, and cognition.* New York: Cambridge University Press.

Biemiller, A. (2005). Addressing developmental patterns in vocabulary. In E.H. Hiebert & M.L. Kamil (Eds.), *Teaching and learning vocabulary.* Mahwah, NJ: Erlbaum.

Bierman, K.L. (2004). *Peer rejection.* New York: Guilford.

Bigelow, B. (1999, April). Why standardized tests threaten multiculturalism. *Educational Leadership, 56*, 37–40.

Bigler, R. S., Liben, L. S., & Yekel, C. A. (1992, August). *Developmental patterns of gender-related beliefs.* Paper presented at the meeting of the American Psychological Association, Washington, DC.

Biobehavioral Reviews, 24, 13 19.

Biological Sciences Curriculum Study. (1989). *Science for life and living.* Colorado Springs: Author.

Biological Sciences Curriculum Study. (2001). *Science for life and living.* Colorado Springs: Author.

Bissell, J. S., Manning, A., Rowland, V., & Fonthal, G. (2002). *CyberEducator* (2nd ed.). New York: McGraw-Hill.

Bitter, G. G., & Pierson, M. E. (2002). *Using technology in the classroom* (5th ed.). New York: McGraw-Hill.

Bitter, G.G., & Pierson, M.E. (2005). *Using technology in the classroom* (6th ed.). Boston: Allyn & Bacon.

Blachman, B. A., Ball, E., Black, R., & Tangel, D. (1994). Kindergarten teachers develop phoneme awareness in low-income inner-city classrooms: Does it make a difference? In B. A. Blachman (Ed.), *Reading and writing.* Mahwah, NJ: Erlbaum.

Blackhurst, A. E. (1997, May/June). Perspectives on technology in special education. *Teaching Exceptional Children,* pp. 41–47.

Blair, C. (2002). School readiness: Integrating cognition and emotion in a neurobiological conceptualization of children's functioning at school entry. *American Psychologist, 57*, 111–127.

Block, J. H., & Block, J. (1980). The role of ego-control and ego-resiliency in the organization of behavior. In W. A. Collins (Ed.), *Minnesota symposium on child psychology* (Vol. 13). Minneapolis: University of Minnesota Press.

Bloom, B. S. (1971). Mastering learning. In J. H. Block (Ed.), *Mastery learning.* New York: Holt, Rinehart & Winston.

Bloom, B. S. (Ed.). (1985). *Developing talent in young people.* New York: Ballantine.

Bloom, B. S., & Krathwohl, D. (Eds.). (1956). *Taxonomy of education objectives: Handbook 1. Cognitive domain.* New York: Longman, Green.

Bloom, B. S., Engelhart, M. D., Frost, E. J., Hill, W. H., & Krathwohl, D. R. (1956). *Taxonomy of educational objectives.* New York: David McKay.

Bloome, D., Carter, S.P., Christian, B.M., Otto, S., & Shuart-Faris, N. (2005). *Discourse analysis and the study of classroom language and literacy events.* Mahwah, NJ: Erlbaum.

Blumenfeld, P. C., Pintrich, P. R., Wessles, K., & Meece, J. (1981, April). *Age and sex differences in the impact of classroom experiences on self-perceptions.* Paper presented at the biennial meeting of the Society for Research in Child Development, Boston.

Blumenfeld, P., Modell, J., Bartko, T., Secade, J., Fredricks, J., Friedel, J., & Paris, A. (2005). School engagement of inner city students during middle childhood. In C.R. Cooper, Coll, C.T.G., Bartko, W.T. Davis, H.M., & Chatman, C. (Eds.). *Developmental pathways through middle childhood.* Mahwah, NJ: Erlbaum.

Bo, I. (1994). The sociocultural environment as a source of support. In F. Nestmann & K. Hurrelmann (Eds.), *Social networks and social support in childhood and adolescence.* New York: Walter de Gruyter.

Bolt, Beraneck, & Newman, Inc. (1993). *The Co-NECT school: Design for a new generation of American schools.* Cambridge, MA: Author.

Bond, L. (1989). The effects of special preparation measures of scholastic ability. In R. Linn (Ed.), *Educational measurement* (3rd ed.). New York: Macmillan.

Books, S. (2004). *Poverty and schooling in the U.S.* Mahwah, NJ: Erlbaum.

Borba, J. A., & Olvera, C. M. (2001). Student-led parent-teacher conferences. *The Clearing House, 74*, 333–336.

Borden, L. M., Donnermeyer, J. F., & Scheer, S. D. (2001). The influence of extra-curricular activities and peer influence on substance abuse. *Adolescent & Family Health, 2*, 12–19.

Bornstein, M. H. (Ed.).(1995). *Handbook of parenting* (Vols. 1–3). Mahwah, NJ: Erlbaum.

Bos, C. S., & Vaughn, S. (2002). *Strategies for teaching students with learning and behavioral problems* (5th ed.). Boston: Allyn & Bacon.

Botvin, G. J., Schinke, S., & Orlandi, M. A. (1995). School-based health promotion:

Substance abuse and sexual behavior. *Applied and Preventive Psychology, 4,* 167–184.

Bouchard, T.J. (2004). The scientific study of general intelligence: Tribute to Arthur R. Jensen. *Intelligence, 32,* 215-217.

Bourne, E. J. (1995). *The anxiety and phobia workbook.* Oakland, CA: New Harbinger.

Bourque, M. L. (1999). The role of national assessment of educational progress (NAEP) in setting, reflecting, and linking national policy to states' needs. In G. J. Cisek (Ed.), *Handbook of educational policy.* San Diego: Academic Press.

Boyles, N. S., & Contadino, D. (1997). *The learning differences sourcebook.* Los Angeles: Lowell House.

Bracey, G. W. (1997). The culture of sexual harassment. *Phi Delta Kappan,* 725–726.

Bracken, B. A. (Ed.). (2000). *Psychoeducational assessment of preschool children.* Boston: Allyn & Bacon.

Bradley, R.H., Corwyn, R.F., McAdoo, H., & Coll, C. (2001). The home environments of children in the United States: Part I. Variations by age, ethnicity, and poverty status. *Child Development, 72,* 1844-1867.

Branch, M. N. (2000). Punishment. In A. Kazdin (Ed.), *Encyclopedia of psychology.* Washington, DC, & New York: American Psychological Association and Oxford University Press.

Bransford, J. D., & Stein, B. S. (1993). *The IDEAL problem solver.* New York: W. H. Freeman.

Bredekamp, S., & Copple, C. (Eds.) (1997). *Developmentally appropriate practice in early childhood programs* (rev. ed.). Washington, DC: National Association for the Education of Young Children.

Breur, J. T. (1999). In search of . . . brain-based education. *Phi Delta Kappan, 80,* 648–655.

Brewer, D. J., Rees, D. I., & Argys, L. M. (1995). Detracking America's schools. *Phi Delta Kappan, 77,* 210–215.

Brewer, J.A. (2004). *Introduction to early childhood education* (5th Ed.). Boston: Allyn & Bacon.

Brewer, M. B., & Campbell, D. I. (1976). *Ethnocentrism and intergroup attitudes.* New York: Wiley.

Briggs, T. W. (1998, November 24). In the classroom with our All-USA teachers. *USA Today,* p. 9D.

Briggs, T.W. (1999, October 14). Honorees find keys to unlocking kids' minds. Retrieved from www.usatoday.com/education/1999.

Brodkin, A., & Coleman, M. (1995, January/February). Children of divorce. *Instructor, 32,* 15.

Brody, G.H., Ge, X., Conger, R.D., Gibbons, F., Murry, V., Gerrard, M., & Simons, R. (2001). The influence of neighborhood disadvantage, collective socialization, and parenting on African American children's affiliation with deviant peers. *Child Development, 72,* 1231-1246.

Brody, N. (2000). Intelligence. In A. Kazdin (Ed.), *Encyclopedia of psychology.* Washington, DC, & New York: American Psychological Association and Oxford University Press.

Brody, N. (2001). Review of J. W. Santrock's *Educational psychology.* New York: McGraw-Hill.

Bronfenbrenner, U. (1995). Developmental ecology through space and time: A future perspective. In P. Moen, G. H. Elder, & K. Luscher (Eds.), *Examining lives in context.* Washington, DC: American Psychological Association.

Bronfenbrenner, U. (2000). Ecological theory. In A. Kazdin (Ed.), *Encyclopedia of psychology.* Washington, DC, & New York: American Psychological Association and Oxford University Press.

Bronfenbrenner, U. (2004). *Making human beings human.* Thousand Oaks, CA: Sage.

Bronfenbrenner, U., & Morris, F. (1998). The ecology of developmental processes. In W. Damon (Ed.), *Handbook of child psychology* (5th ed., Vol. 1). New York: Wiley.

Bronfenbrenner, U., McClelland, P., Wethington, E., Moen, P., & Ceci, S. J. (1996). *The state of Americans.* New York: Free Press.

Brookhart, S. M. (1997). A theoretical framework for the role of classroom assessment in motivating student effort and achievement. *Applied Measurement in Education, 10,* 161–180.

Brookhart, S. M. (2002). What will teachers know about assessment, and how will that improve instruction? In R. W. Kissitz & W. D. Schafer (Eds.), *Assessment in educational reform: Both means and ends.* Boston: Allyn & Bacon.

Brookover, W. B., Beady, C., Flood, P., Schweitzer, U., & Wisenbaker, J. (1979). *School social systems and student achievement: Schools make a difference.* New York: Praeger.

Brooks, J. G., & Brooks, M. G. (2001). *In search of understanding: The case for constructivist classrooms.* Upper Saddle River, NJ: Merrill.

Brooks, J. G.. & Brooks, M. G. (1993). *The case for constructivist classrooms.* Alexandria, VA: Association for Supervision and Curriculum Development.

Brooks-Gunn, J., Klebanov, P. K., & Duncan, G. J. (1996). Ethnic differences in children's intelligence tests scores: Role of economic deprivation, home environment, and maternal characteristics. *Child Development, 67,* 396–408.

Brophy, J. (1985). Teacher-student interaction. In J. B. Duseck (Ed.), *Teacher expectancies.* Mahwah, NJ: Erlbaum.

Brophy, J. (1996). *Teaching problem students.* New York: Guilford.

Brophy, J. (1998). *Motivating students to learn.* New York: McGraw-Hill.

Brophy, J. (2004). *Motivating students to learn* (2nd ed.). Mahwah, NJ: Erlbaum.

Brophy, J., & Good, T. (1974). *Teacher-student relationships: Causes and consequences.* New York: Holt, Rinehart & Winston.

Brown, A. L. (1997). Transforming schools into communities of thinking and learning about serious matters. *American Psychologist, 52,* 399–413.

Brown, A. L., & Campione, J. C. (1996). Psychological learning theory and the design of innovative environments. In L. Schuable & R. Glaser (Eds.), *Contributions of instructional innovation to understanding learning.* Mahwah, NJ: Erlbaum.

Brown, A. L., & Day, J. D. (1983). Macrorules for summarizing texts: The development of expertise. *Journal of Verbal Learning and Verbal Behavior, 22,* 1–14.

Brown, J. D., Steele, J. R., & Walsh-Childers, K. (Eds.). (2001). *Sexual teens, sexual media.* Mahwah, NJ: Erlbaum.

Brown, L., & Brown, M. (1988). *Dinosaurs divorce.* Boston: Little, Brown.

Brown, R. (1973). *A first language: The early stages.* Cambridge, MA: Harvard University Press.

Brown, S., & Kysilka, M. (2002). *Applying multicultural and global concepts in the classroom and beyond.* Boston: Allyn & Bacon.

Bruer, J. (1989). *1989 Report.* St. Louis: James S. McDonnell Foundation.

Bruner, J. (1996). *Toward a theory of instruction.* Cambridge, MA: Harvard University Press.

Bruning, R., & Horn, C. (2001). Developing motivation to write. *Educational Psychologist, 35,* 25–37.

Bryant, D. P., & Bryant, B. R. (1998). Using assistive technology adaptations to include students with learning disabilities in cooperative learning activities. *Journal of Learning Disabilities, 31,* 41–54.

Bryk, A. S., Lee, V. E., & Smith, J. B. (1989, May*). High school organization and its effects on teachers and students: An interpretive summary of the research.* Paper presented at the conference on Choice and Control in American Education, University of Wisconsin, Madison.

Buck, J. B. (2002). Re-segregating America's public schools. In C. C. Yeakey & R. D. Henderson (Eds.), *Surmounting the odds: Equalizing educational opportunity in the new millennium.* Greenwich, CT: IAP.

Buhrmester, D., & Furman, W. (1987). The development of companionship and intimacy. *Child Development, 61,* 1387–1398.

Buhs, E. S., & Ladd, G. W. (2001). Peer rejection as antecedent of young children's school adjustment: An examination of mediating processes. *Developmental Psychology, 37,* 550–560.

Burger, J. M. (2000). *Personality* (5th ed.). Belmont, CA: Wadsworth.

Burnette, J. (1998). Reducing the disproportionate representation of minority students in special education. *ERIC/OSEP Digest, No. E566.*

Burton, L.A., Rabin, L., Vardy, S.B., Frohlich, J,. Wyatt, G., Dimitri, D., Constante, S., & Guterman, E. (2004). Gender differences in implicit and explicit memory for explicit passages. *Brain and Cognition, 54,* 218-224.

Burz, H. L., & Marshall, K. (1996). *Performance-based curriculum for mathematics: From knowing to showing.*

ERIC Document Reproduction Service No. ED400194.

C

Cahill, L., Haier, R. J., White, N. S., Fallon, J., Kilparaick, L., Lawrence, C., Potkin, S. G., & Alkire, M. T. (2001). Sex-related differences in amygdala activity during emotionally influenced memory storage. *Neurobiology of Learning and Memory, 75,* 1–9.

Calabrese, R. L., & Schumer, H. (1986). The effects of service activities on adolescent alienation. *Adolescence, 21,* 675–687.

California State Department of Education. (1994). *Golden State examination science portfolio.* Sacramento: California State Department of Education.

Cameron, J. R. (2001). Negative effects of reward on intrinsic motivation—A limited phenomenon. *Review of Educational Research, 71,* 29–42.

Cameron, J. R., & Pierce, W. D. (1996). The debate about rewards and intrinsic motivation. *Review of Educational Research, 66,* 39–62.

Cameron, J. R., Hansen, R., & Rosen, D. (1989). Preventing behavioral problems in infancy through temperament assessment and parental support programs. In W. B. Carey & S. C. McDevitt (Eds.), *Clinical and educational applications of temperament research.* Amsterdam: Sets & Zeitlinger.

Campbell, C. Y. (1988, August 24). Group raps depiction of teenagers. *Boston Globe,* p. 44.

Campbell, D. T., & LeVine, D. T. (1968). Ethnocentrism and intergroup relations. In R. Abelson & others (Eds.), *Theories of cognitive consistency.* Chicago: Rand McNally.

Campbell, F. A., & Ramey, C. T. (1994). Effects of early intervention on intellectual and academic achievement: A follow-up study of children from low-income families. *Child Development, 65,* 684–698.

Campbell, F. A., Pungello, E. P., Miller-Johnson, S., Burchinal, M., & Ramey, C. T. (2001). The development of cognitive and academic abilities: Growth curves from an early childhood educational experiment. *Developmental Psychology, 37,* 231–243.

Campbell, L., Campbell, B., & Dickinson, D. (2004). *Teaching and learning through multiple intelligence* (3rd ed.). Boston: Allyn & Bacon.

Campione, J. (2001, April). *Fostering a Community of Learners.* Paper presented at the meeting of the American Educational Research Association, Seattle.

Cardelle-Elawar, M. (1992). Effects of teaching metacognitive skills to students with low mathematics ability. *Teaching and Teacher Education, 8,* 109–121.

Carey, L. M. (2001). *Measuring and evaluating school learning* (3rd ed.). Boston: Allyn & Bacon.

Carnegie Council on Adolescent Development. (1995). *Great transitions.* New York: Carnegie Foundation.

Carpenter, T. P., Lindquist M. M., Matthews, W., & Silver, E. A. (1983). Results of the Third NAEP Mathematics Assessment: Secondary school. *Mathematics Teachers, 76* (9), 652–659.

Carroll, J. B. (1963). A model of school learning. *Teachers College Record, 64,* 723–733.

Carroll, J. B. (1993). *Human cognitive abilities.* Cambridge, UK: Cambridge University Press.

Carver, S. M., & Klahr, D. (Eds.). (2001). *Cognition and instruction.* Mahwah, NJ: Erlbaum.

Casbergue, R. M., & Harris, K. (1996). Listening and literacy: Audiobooks in the reading program. *Reading Horizons, 37,* 48–59.

Case, R. (2000). Conceptual structures. In M. Bennett (Ed.), *Developmental psychology.* Philadelphia: Psychology Press.

Casey, B., Giedd, J., & Thomas, K. (2000). Structural and functional brain development and its relation to cognitive development. *Biological Psychology, 54,* 241-257.

Caspi, A., Henry, B., McGee, R. O., Moffitt, T. E., & Silva, P. A. (1995). Temperamental origins of child and adolescent behavior problems: From age three to age fifteen. *Child Development, 66,* 55–68.

Castellano, J. A., & Diaz, E. (Eds.). (2002). *Reaching new horizons: Gifted and talented education for culturally and linguistically diverse students.* Boston: Allyn & Bacon.

Ceballo, R., & McLoyd, V. C. (2002). Social support and parenting in poor, dangerous neighborhoods. *Child Development, 73*, 1310–1321.

Ceci, S. J. (1990). *On intelligence . . . more or less: A bioecological treatise.* Upper Saddle River, NJ: Prentice Hall.

Ceci, S. J., & Gilstrap, L. L. (2000). Determinants of intelligence: Schooling and intelligence. In A. Kazdin (Ed.), *Encyclopedia of psychology.* Washington, DC, & New York: American Psychological Association and Oxford University Press.

Ceci, S. J., & Williams, W. M. (1997). Schooling, intelligence, and income. *American Psychologist, 52*, 1051–1058.

Ceci, S. J., Rosenblum, T., deBruyn, E., & Lee, D. Y. (1997). A bio-ecological model of intellectual development. In R. J. Sternberg & E. Grigorenko (Eds.), *Intelligence, heredity, and environment.* New York: Cambridge University Press.

Center for Innovative Learning Technologies. (2001). *Ubiquitous computing.* Berkeley, CA: University of California.

Chaffin, R., & Imreh, G. (2002). Practicing perfection: Piano performance and expert memory. *Psychological Science, 13*, 342–349.

Chall, J. S. (1979). The great debate: Ten years later with a modest proposal for reading stages. In L. B. Resnick & P. A. Weaver (Eds.), *Theory and practice of early reading.* Mahwah, NJ: Erlbaum.

Chance, P. (2003). *Learning and behavior* (5th ed.). Belmont, CA: Wadsworth.

Chao, R. (2001). Extending research on the consequences of parenting style for Chinese Americans and European Americans. *Child Development, 72*, 1832-1843.

Chao, R., & Tseng, V. (2002). Parenting of Asians. In M.H. Bornstein (Ed.), *Handbook of parenting* (2nd ed., Vol. 4). Mahwah, NJ: Erlbaum.

Chapin, J. R., & Messick, R. G. (2002). *Elementary social studies* (5th ed.). Boston: Allyn & Bacon.

Chapman, J. W., Tunmer, W. E., & Prochnow, J. E. (2001). Does success in the Reading Recovery program depend on developing proficiency in phonological-processing skills? A longitudinal study in the whole language instructional context. *Scientific Studies of Reading, 15*, 141–176.

Chapman, O. L. (2000). Learning science involves language, experience, and

modeling. *Journal of Applied Developmental Psychology, 21*, 97–108.

Charles, C. M. (2002). *Building classroom discipline* (7th ed.). Boston: Allyn & Bacon.

Charles, C.M. (2005). *Building classroom discipline* (8th Ed.). Boston: Allyn & Bacon.

Charles, C.M., & Charles, M.G. (2005). *Classroom management for middle school teachers.* Boston: Allyn & Bacon.

Charles, C.M., & Senter, G.W. (2005). *Elementary classroom management* (4th ed) Boston: Allyn & Bacon.

Chatterji, M. (2003). *Designing and using tools for educational assessment.* Boston: Allyn & Bacon.

Chen, C., & Stevenson, H. W. (1989). Homework: A cross-cultural comparison. *Child Development, 60*, 551–561.

Chen, Z., & Mo, L. (2004). Schema induction in problem solving: A multidimensional analysis. *Journal of Experimental Psychology: Learning, Memory, and Cognition, 30*, 583-600.

Chess, S., & Thomas, A. (1977). Temperamental individuality from childhood to adolescence. *Journal of Child Psychiatry, 16*, 218–226.

Chi, M. T. H. (1978). Knowledge structures and memory development. In R. S. Siegler (Ed.), *Children's thinking.* Mahwah, NJ: Erlbaum.

Chiappetta, E. L., & Koballa, T. R. (2002). *Science instruction in the middle and secondary schools* (5th ed.). Upper Saddle River, NJ: Merrill.

Children's Defense Fund. (1992). *The state of America's children.* Washington, DC: Author.

Children's Defense Fund. (2000). *Every child deserves a fair start.* Washington, DC: Author.

Chira, S. (1993, June 23). What do teachers want most? Help from parents. *New York Times,* sec. 1, p. 7.

Chomsky, N. (1957). *Syntactic structures.* The Hague: Mouton.

Christenson, S. L., & Thurlow, M. L. (2004). School dropouts: Prevention, considerations, interventions, and challenges. *Current Directions in Psychological Science, 13*, 36–39.

Christian, K., Bachnan, H. J., & Morrison, F. J. (2001). Schooling and cognitive development. In R. J. Sternberg

& E. L. Grigorenko (Eds.), *Environmental effects on cognitive abilities.* Mahwah, NJ: Erlbaum.

Chronis, A.M., Chacko, A., Fabiano, G.A., Wymbs, B.T., & Pelham, W.E. (2004). Enhancements to the behavioral parent training paradigm for families of children with ADHD: Review and future directions. *Clinical Child and Family Psychology Review, 7*, 1-27.

Chun, K. M., Organista, P. B., & Marin, G. (Eds.). (2002). *Acculturation.* Washington, DC: American Psychological Association.

Clark, K. B., & Clark, M. P. (1939). The development of the self and the emergence of racial identification in Negro preschool children. *Journal of Social Psychology, 10*, 591–599.

Clark, L. (Ed.). (1993). *Faculty and student challenges in facing cultural and linguistic diversity.* Springfield, IL: Charles C Thomas.

Clay, M. M. (1985). *The early detection of reading difficulties* (3rd ed.). Portsmouth, NH: Heinemann.

Clay, M. M., & Cazden, C. B. (1990). A Vygotskian interpretation of reading recovery. In L. Moll (Ed.), *Vygotsky and education.* New York: Oxford University Press.

Clay, R. A. (1997, December). Are children being overmedicated? *APA Monitor,* pp. 1, 27.

Clayton, C.J., Ballif-Spanvill, B., & Hunsaker, M.D. (2001). Preventing violence and teaching peace: A review of promising and effective anti-violence, conflict resolution, and peace programs. *Journal of the American Association of Applied and Preventive Psychology, 10*, 1-35.

Clegg, E. (2004, Summer). Into the future. *Threshold,* 6–10.

Clinchy, B. M., Mansfield, A. F., & Schott, J. L. (1995, March). *Development of narrative and scientific modes of thought in middle childhood.* Paper presented at the meeting of the Society for Research in Child Development, Indianapolis.

Clingempeel, W.G., & Brand-Clingempeel, E. (2004). Pathogenic conflict: Families and children. In M. Coleman & L. Ganong (Eds.), *Handbook of contemporary families.* Thousand Oaks, CA: Sage.

Coben, S. S., Thomas, C. C., Sattler, R. O., & Morsink, C. V. (1997). Meeting the challenge of consultation and collaboration: Developing interactive teams. *Journal of Learning Disabilities, 30,* 427–432.

Cochran, M., Larner, M., Riley, D., Gunnarson, L., & Henderson, C. (1990). *Extending families: The social networks of parents and their children.* New York: Cambridge University Press.

Cochran-Smith, M. (1995). Color blindness and basket making are not the answers: Confronting the dilemmas of race, culture, and language diversity in teacher education. *American Educational Research Journal, 32,* 493–522.

Cochran-Smith, M., & Lytle, S. (1990, March). Research on teaching and teacher research: The issue that divides. *Educational Researcher,* pp. 2–11.

Cocking, R. R., Mestre, J. P., & Brown, A. L. (2000). New developments in the use of science learning: Using research to help students learn science and mathematics. *Journal of Applied Developmental Psychology, 21,* 1–11.

Coffin, L. (1996). Commentary in "The latest on student portfolios." *NEA Today, 17,* 18.

Cognition and Technology Group at Vanderbilt. (1997a). *Designing environments to reveal, support, and expand our children's potentials.* Paper presented at the meeting of the Society for Research in Child Development, Washington, DC.

Cognition and Technology Group at Vanderbilt. (1997b). *The Jasper Project.* Mahwah, NJ: Erlbaum.

Coie, J. (2004). The impact of negative social experiences on the development of antisocial behavior. In J.B. Kupersmidt & K.A. Dodge (Eds.), *Children's peer relations: From development to intervention.* Washington, DC: American Psychological Association.

Coie, J. D., & Dodge, K. A. (1998). Aggression and antisocial behavior. In W. Damon (Ed.), *Handbook of child psychology* (Vol. 3). New York: Wiley.

Coladarci, T. (1992). Teachers' sense of efficacy and commitment to teaching. *Journal of Experimental Education, 60,* 323–337.

Colby, A., Kohlberg, L., Gibbs, J., & Lieberman, M. (1983). A longitudinal study of moral judgment. *Monographs of the Society for Research in Child Development, 48* (21, Serial No. 201).

Colby, S. A. (1999, March). Grading in a standard-based system. *Educational Leadership, 56,* 52–55.

Cole, C. F., Richman, B. A., & Brown, S. K. (2001). The world of *Sesame Street* research. In S. M. Fisch, & R. T. Truglio (Eds.), *"G" is for growing: Thirty years of research on children and* Sesame Street. Mahwah, NJ: Erlbaum.

Cole, C., Ray, K., & Zanelis, J. (2004). *Videoconferencing for K-12 classrooms.* Eugene, OR: ISTE.

Cole, C.M., Waldron, N., & Majid, M. (2004). Academic progress of students across inclusive and traditional settings. *Mental Retardation, 42,* 136-144.

Cole, M., & Cole, S. (2001). *The development of children* (4th ed.). New York: Worth.

Cole, M., & Scribner, S. (1977). Cross-cultural studies of memory and cognition. In R. V. Kail & W. Hagen (Eds.), *Perspectives on the development of memory and cognition.* Mahwah, NJ: Erlbaum.

Coleman, M. C., & Webber, J. (2002). *Emotional and behavioral disorders* (4th ed.). Boston: Allyn & Bacon.

Coley, R. (2001). *Differences in the gender gap: Comparisons across racial/ethnic groups in education and work.* Princeton: Educational Testing Service.

Coll, C. T. G., & Pachter, L. M. (2002). Ethnicity and parenting. In M. H. Bornstein (Ed.), *Handbook of parenting* (2nd ed.). Mahwah, NJ: Erlbaum.

College Board. (1996, August 22). *News from The College Board.* New York: College Entrance Examination Board.

Collins, M. (1996, Winter). The job outlook for '96 grads. *Journal of Career Planning,* pp. 51–54.

Collis, B. A., Knezek, G. A., Lai, K. W., Miyashita, K. T., Pelgrum, W. J., Plomp, T., & Sakamoto, T. (1996). *Children and computers in school.* Mahwah, NJ: Erlbaum.

Combs, D. (1997, September). Using alternative assessment to provide options for student success. *Middle School Journal,* pp. 3–8.

Comer, J. P. (1988). Educating poor minority children. *Scientific American, 259,* 42–48.

Comer, J. P., Haynes, N. M., Joyner, E. T., & Ben-Avie, M. (1996). *Rallying the whole village: The Comer process for reforming urban education.* New York: Teachers College Press.

Connors, L. J., & Epstein, J. L. (1995). Parent and school partnerships. In M. Borstein (Ed.), *Handbook of parenting* (Vol. 2). Mahwah, NJ: Erlbaum.

Conti, R. (2001). Motivational change and transition in the transition from primary school to secondary school. In C. Y. Chiu, F. Salilli, & Y. Hong (Eds.), *Multiple competencies and self-regulated learning.* Greenwich, CT: IAP.

Cooper, C. R. (1995, March). *Multiple selves, multiple worlds.* Paper presented at the meeting of the Society for Research in Child Development, Indianapolis.

Cooper, C.R., Coll, C.T.G., Bartko, W.T., Davis, H.M., & Chatman, C. (Eds.) (2005). *Developmental pathways through middle childhood.* Mahwah, NJ: Erlbaum.

Cooper, E., & Sherk, J. (1989). Addressing urban school reform: Issues and alliances, *Journal of Negro Education, 58,* 315–331.

Cooper, H. (1989). Synthesis of research on homework. *Educational Leadership, 47* (3), 85–91.

Cooper, H. (1998, April). *Family, student, and assignment characteristics of positive homework experiences.* Paper presented at the meeting of the American Educational Research Association, San Diego.

Cooper, H., & Valentine, J. C. (2001). Using research to answer practical questions about homework. *Educational Psychologist, 36,* 143–153.

Cooper, H., Lindsay, J. J., Nye, B., & Greathouse, S. (1998). Relationships among attitudes about homework, amount of homework assigned and completed, and student achievement. *Journal of Educational Psychology, 90,* 70–83.

Copeland, L. (2003, December). Science teacher `just wanted to do some good,' and he has. *USA Today.* Retrieved from the world wide web at www.usatoday.com/news/education/2003-12-30-laster-usal_x.htm

Corno, L. (1998, March 30). Commentary. *Newsweek,* p. 51.

Costa, P. (2000). NEO Personality Inventory. In A. Kazdin (Ed.), *Encyclopedia of psychology.* Washington, DC, & New York: American Psychological Association and Oxford University Press.

Costa, P. T., & McRae, R. R. (1998). Personality assessment. In H. S. Friedman

(Ed.), *Encyclopedia of mental health* (Vol. 3). San Diego: Academic Press.

Council for Exceptional Children. (1998). *CEC's comments on the proposed IDEA regulations.* Washington, DC: Author.

Covington, M. V. (1992). *Making the grade: A self-worth perspective on motivation and school reform.* New York: Cambridge University Press.

Covington, M. V. (1998, April). *Caring about learning: The nature and nurturing of subject-matter appreciation.* Paper presented at the meeting of the American Educational Research Association, San Diego.

Covington, M. V., & Dray, E. (2002). The development course of achievement motivation: A need-based approach. In A. Wigfield & J. S. Eccles (Eds.), *Development of achievement motivation.* San Diego: Academic Press.

Covington, M. V., & Teel, K. T. (1996). *Overcoming student failure.* Washington, DC: American Psychological Association.

Covington, M. V., Teel, K. M., & Parecki, A. D. (1994, April). *Motivation benefits of improved academic performance among middle-school African American students through an effort-based grading system.* Paper presented at the meeting of the American Educational Research Association, New Orleans.

Cowan, P. A., & Cowan, C. P. (2002). What an intervention design reveals about how parents affect their children's academic achievement and behavior problems. In J. G. Borkowski, S. L. Ramey, & M. Bristol-Power (Eds.), *Parenting and the child's world.* Mahwah, NJ: Erlbaum.

Cox, M. J., & Harter, K. S. M. (2001). The road ahead for research on marital and family dynamics. In J. P. McHale & W. S. Grolnick (Eds.), *Retrospect and prospect in the psychological study of families.* Mahwah, NJ: Erlbaum.

Coyne, M.D., Kameenui, E.J., Simmons, D.C., & Harn, B.A. (2004). Beginning reading intervention as inoculation or insulin: First-grade reading performance of strong responders to kindergarten intervention. *Journal of Learning Disabilities, 37,* 90-104.

Craik, F. I. M., & Lockhart, R. S. (1972). Levels of processing: A framework for memory research. *Journal of Verbal Learning and Verbal Behavior, 11,* 671–684.

Crane, C. (2001). General classroom space. *School Planning and Management, 40,* 54–55.

Crawford, M., & Unger, R. (2000). *Women and gender* (3rd ed.) New York: McGraw-Hill.

Creswell, J. (2005). *Educational research* (2nd ed.). Boston: Pearson Education.

Cronin, M. (1993). [Video] *Mission Impossible: Listening skills for better communication.* Radford, VA.

Crowley, K., Callahan, M. A., Tenenbaum, H. R., & Allen, E. (2001). Parents explain more to boys than to girls during shared scientific thinking. *Psychological Science, 12,* 258–261.

Csikszentmihalyi, M. (1990). *Flow.* New York: Harper & Row.

Csikszentmihalyi, M. (1993). *The evolving self.* New York: HarperCollins.

Csikszentmihalyi, M. (2000). Creativity: An overview. In A. Kazdin (Ed.), *Encyclopedia of psychology.* Washington, DC, & New York: American Psychological Association and Oxford University Press.

Csikszentmihalyi, M., Rathunde, K., & Whalen, S. (1993). *Talented teenagers: The roots of success and failure.* Cambridge, UK: Cambridge University Press.

Culbertson, F. M. (1997). Depression and gender. *American Psychologist, 52,* 25–31.

Culbertson, L. D., & Jalongo, M. R. (1999). "But what's wrong with letter grades?" Responding to parents' questions about alternative assessments. *Childhood Education, 75,* 130–135.

Cullen, M.J., Hardison, C.M., & Sackett, P.R. (2004). Using SAT-grade and ability-job performance relationships to test predictions derived from stereoptype threat theory. *Journal of Applied Psychology, 89,* 220-230.

Cunningham, P.M. (2004). *Phonics they use* (4th ed.). Boston: Allyn & Bacon.

Curran, M., Eisenstein, J., DuCette, J., & Hyman, I. (2001, August 28). Statistical analysis of the cross-cultural data: The third year. In F. Farley (Chair), *Cross cultural aspects of corporal punishment and abuse: A research update.* Symposium presented at the 2001 Annual Convention of the American Psychological Association, San Francisco, CA.

Curtis, M., Kopera, J., Norris, C., & Soloway, E. (2004). *Palm OS handhelds in the elementary classrooms.* Eugene, OR: ISTE.

Cushner, K. H. (2003). *Human diversity in action.* Boston: McGraw-Hill.

Cushner, K., McClelland, A., & Safford, P. (1996). *Human diversity and education* (2nd ed.). New York: McGraw-Hill.

D

Dale, P., & Goodman, J. (2004). Commonality and differences in vocabulary growth. In M. Tomasello & D.I. Slobin (Eds.), *Beyond nature-nurture.* Mahwah, NJ: Erlbaum.

Damon, W. (1995). *Greater expectations.* New York: Free Press.

Damon, W. (2000). Moral development. In A. Kazdin (Ed.), *Encyclopedia of psychology.* Washington, DC, & New York: American Psychological Association and Oxford University Press.

Dansereau, D. F. (1988). Cooperative learning strategies. In C. E. Weinstein, E. T. Goetz, & P. A. Alexander (Eds.), *Learning and study strategies.* Orlando, FL: Academic Press.

Darling-Hammond, L. (2001, August). *What's at stake in high-stakes testing?* Paper presented at the meeting of the American Psychological Association, San Francisco.

Das, J. P. (2000). Mental retardation. In A. Kazdin (Ed.), *Encyclopedia of psychology.* Washington, DC, & New York: American Psychological Association and Oxford University Press.

Davidson, G. C., & Neale, J. M. (2001). *Abnormal psychology* (8th ed.). New York: Wiley.

Davidson, J. (2000). Giftedness. In A. Kazdin (Ed.), *Encyclopedia of psychology.* Washington, DC, & New York: American Psychological Association and Oxford University Press.

Davis, G.A., & Rimm, S.B. (2004). *Education of the gifted and talented* (5th Ed.). Boston: Allyn & Bacon.

De Jong, J. (2004). Grammatical impairment. In L. Verhoeven & H. Van Balkom (Eds.), *The classification of language disorders.* Mahwah, NJ: Erlbaum.

deCharms, R. (1984). Motivation enhancement in educational settings. In R. Ames & C. Ames (Eds.), *Research on motivation in education* (Vol. 1). Orlando: Academic Press.

Deci, E. L. (1975). *Intrinsic motivation.* New York: Plenum.

Deci, E. L., Koestner, R., & Ryan, R. M. (2001). Extrinsic rewards and intrinsic motivation in education: Reconsidered once again. *Review of Educational Research, 71,* 1–28.

Deci, E., & Ryan, R. (1994). Promoting self-determined education. *Scandinavian Journal of Educational Research, 38,* 3–14.

Delisle, J.R. (1987). *Gifted kids speak out.* Minneapolis: Free Spirit Publishing.

Demakis, G. (1997). Hindsight bias and the Simpson trial: Use in introductory psychology. *Teaching of Psychology, 24,* 190–191.

Dempster, F. N. (1981). Memory span: Sources of individual and developmental differences. *Psychological Bulletin, 89,* 63–100.

Denny, C.B. (2001). Stimulant effects in attention deficit hyperactivity disorder. *Journal of Clinical Child Psychology, 30,* 98-109.

Deno, E. (1970). Special education as developmental capital. *Exceptional Children, 37,* 229–237.

Derlega, V., Winstead, B., & Jones, W. (1999). *Personality: Contemporary theory and research* (2nd ed.). Belmont, CA: Wadsworth.

Derman-Sparks, L., & the Anti-Bias Curriculum Task Force. (1989). *Anti-bias curriculum.* Washington, DC: National Association for the Education of Young Children.

DeRosier, M.E. (2004). Building relationships and combating bullying. *Journal of Clinical Child and Adolescent Psychology, 33,* 196-201.

Desberg, P., & Fisher, F. (2001). *Teaching with technology* (3rd ed.). Boston: Allyn & Bacon.

Detterman, D. K. (2000). Determinants of intelligence: Heritability of intelligence. In A. Kazdin (Ed.), *Encyclopedia of psychology.* Washington, DC, & New York: American Psychological Association and Oxford University Press.

Dettmer, P., Dyck, N., & Thurston, L. P. (2002). *Consultation, collaboration, and teamwork for students with special needs* (4th ed.). Boston: Allyn & Bacon.

DeVillar, R. A., & Faltis, C. J. (1991). *Computers and cultural diversity: Restructuring for school success.* Albany: State University of New York Press.

Dewey, J. (1933). *How we think.* Lexington, MA: D. C. Heath.

DeZolt, D. M., & Hull, S. H. (2001). Classroom and school climate. In J. Worrell (Ed.), *Encyclopedia of women and gender.* San Diego: Academic Press.

Diaz, C. (1997). Unpublished review of J. W. Santrock's *Educational psychology.* New York: McGraw-Hill.

Diaz, C. (2001). *Multicultural education in the 21st century.* Boston: Allyn & Bacon.

Diaz-Rico, L. (2004). *Teaching English learners.* Boston: Allyn & Bacon.

Dick, F., Dronkers, N.F., Pizzamiglio, L. Saygin, A.P., Small, S.L., & Wilson, S. (2005). Language and the brain. In M. Tomasello & D. A. Slobin (Eds.), Beyond nature-nurture. Mahwah, NJ: Erlbaum.

Dick, W.O., Carey, L., & Carey, J.O. (2005*). The systematic design of instruction* (6th Ed.). Boston: Allyn & Bacon.

Dickinson, D. (1998). *How technology enhances Howard Gardner's eight intelligences.* Available at www.america-tomorrow.com/ati/nhl80402.htm

Dickinson, D. (2000). *How technology enhances Howard Gardner's eight intelligences.* New York: New Horizons for Learning.

Diggs, R.C., & Socha, T. (2004). Communication, families, and exploring the boundaries of cultural diversity. In A. Vangelisti (Ed.), *Handbook of family communication.* Mahwah, NJ: Erlbaum.

Dill, E.J., Vernberg, E.M., & Fonagy, P. (2004). Negative affect in victimized children. *Journal of Abnormal Psychology, 32,* 159-173.

Doe, C.G. (2004). A look at. . . Web-based assessment. *Multimedia Schools, 11* (2), 1-6.

Doggett, A.M. (2004). ADHD and drug therapy: Is it still a valid treatment? *Journal of Child Health Care, 8,* 69-81.

Domino, G. (2000). *Psychological testing.* Upper Saddle River, NJ: Prentice Hall.

Domjan, M. (2000). Learning: An overview. In A. Kazdin (Ed.), *Encyclopedia of psychology.* Washington, DC, & New York: American Psychological Association and Oxford University Press.

Domjan, M. (2002). *Principles of learning* (5th ed.). Belmont, CA: Wadsworth.

Doolittle, P. (1997). Vygotsky's zone of proximal development as a theoretical foundation for cooperative learning.

Journal on Excellence in College Teaching, 8, 81–101.

Douglass, M. E., & Douglass, D. N. (1993). *Manage your work yourself* (updated ed.). New York: American Management Association.

Doyle, W. (1986). Classroom organization and management. In M. C. Wittrock (Ed.), *Handbook of research on teaching* (3rd ed.). New York: Macmillan.

Driscoll, M. (2000). *Psychology of learning for instruction* (2nd ed.). Boston: Allyn & Bacon.

Droege, K.L. (2004). Turning accountability on its head. *Phi Delta Kappan, 85,* 610-612.

Drummond, R. J. (2000). *Appraisal procedures for counselors and helping professionals* (4th ed.). Upper Saddle River, NJ: Merrill.

Drysdale, M. T. B., Ross, J. L., & Schuyltz, R. A. (2001). Cognitive academic performance in 19 first-year university courses: Successful students versus students at risk. *Journal of Education for Students Placed at Risk, 6,* 271–289.

Dunn, L., & Kontos, S. (1997). What have we learned about developmentally appropriate practice? *Young Children, 52* (2), 4–13.

Dunphy, D. C. (1963). The social structure of urban adolescent peer groups. *Society, 26,* 230–246.

Dweck, C. S. (1996). Social motivation: Goals and social-cognitive processes. In J. Juvonen & K. R. Wentzel (Eds.), *Social motivation.* New York: Cambridge University Press.

Dweck, C. S. (2002). The development of ability conceptions. In A. Wigfield & J. S. Eccles (Eds.), *Development of achievement motivation.* San Diego: Academic Press.

Dweck, C. S., & Elliott, E. (1983). Achievement motivation. In P. Mussen (Ed.), *Handbook of child psychology* (4th ed., Vol. 4). New York: Wiley.

Dweck, C. S., & Leggett, E. (1988). A social cognitive approach to motivation and personality. *Psychological Review, 95,* 256–273.

Dweck, C.S., Mangels, J.A., & Good, C. (2004). Motivational effects on attention, cognition, and performance. In D. Yun Dai & R.J. Sternberg (Eds.), *Motivation, emotion, and cognition.* Mahwah, NJ: Erlbaum.

Dykens, E. M., Hodapp, R. M., & Finucane, B. M. (2000). *Genetics and mental retardation syndromes.* Baltimore: Paul H. Brookes.

E

Eagly, A. H. (1996). Differences between women and men. *American Psychologist, 51,* 158–159.

Eagly, A. H. (2000). Sex differences and gender differences. In A. Kazdin (Ed.), *Encyclopedia of psychology.* Washington, DC, & New York: American Psychological Association and Oxford University Press.

Eagly, A. H. (2001). Social role theory of sex differences and similarities. In J. Worrell (Ed.), *Encyclopedia of women and gender.* San Diego: Academic Press.

Eagly, A. H., & Crowley, M. (1986). Gender and helping behavior: A meta-analytic review of the social psychological literature. *Psychological Bulletin, 100,* 283–308.

Eagly, A. H., & Steffen, V. J. (1986). Gender and aggressive behavior: A meta-analytic review of the social psychological literature. *Psychological Bulletin, 111,* 3–22.

Eamon, M. K. (2002). Effects of poverty on mathematics and reading achievement of young adolescents. *Journal of Early Adolescence, 22,* 49–74.

Earle, R. S. (2002). The integration of instructional technology into public education: Promises and challenges. *Educational Technology, 42,* 5–13.

Eccles, J. S. (1993). School and family effects on the ontogeny of children's interests, self-perceptions, and activity choice. In J. Jacobs (Ed.), *Nebraska symposium on motivation.* Lincoln: University of Nebraska Press.

Eccles, J. S. (2000). Adolescence: Social patterns, achievements, and problems. In A. Kazdin (Ed.), *Encyclopedia of psychology.* Washington, DC, & New York: American Psychological Association and Oxford University Press.

Eccles, J. S. (2004). School, academic motivation, and stage-environment fit. In R. Lerner & L. Steinberg (Eds.), *Handbook of adolescent psychology* (2nd ed.). New York: Wiley.

Eccles, J. S., & Harold, R. D. (1996). Family involvement in children's and adolescents' schooling. In A. Booth & J. E. Dunn (Eds.), *Family-school links.* Mahwah, NJ: Erlbaum.

Eccles, J. S., & Midgley, C. (1989). Stage-environment fit: Developmentally appropriate classrooms for young adolescents. In C. Ames & R. Ames (Eds.), *Research on motivation in education* (Vol. 3). Orlando: Academic Press.

Eccles, J. S., & Wigfield, A. (2002). Motivational beliefs, values, and goals. *Annual Review of Psychology* (Vol. 53). Palo Alto, CA: Annual Reviews.

Eccles, J. S., Lord, S., & Buchanan, C. M. (1996). School transitions in early adolescence: What are we doing to our young people? In J. A. Graeber, J. Brooks-Gunn, & A. C. Petersen (Eds.), *Transitions in adolescence.* Mahwah, NJ: Erlbaum.

Eccles, J. S., Wigfield, A., & Schiefele, U. (1998). Motivation to succeed. In W. Damon (Ed.), *Handbook of child psychology* (5th ed., Vol. 3). New York: Wiley.

Eccles, J. S., Wigfield, A., Harold, R., & Blumenfeld, P. B. (1993). Age and gender differences in children's self- and task-perceptions during elementary school. *Child Development, 64,* 830–847.

Eccles, J. S., Jacobs, J., Harold, R., Yoon, K., Aberbach, A., & Dolan, C. F. (1991, August). *Expectancy effects are alive and well on the home front.* Paper presented at the meeting of the American Psychological Association, San Francisco.

Edelman, M. W. (1997, April). *Families, children, and social policy.* Invited address, Society for Research in Child Development, Washington, DC.

Educational Testing Service. (1994). *Taking the SAT I reasoning test.* Princeton, NJ: College Board SAT Program.

Educational Testing Service. (2002). *Differences in the gender gap.* Princeton: Author.

Edwards, P. A. (1989). Supporting lower SES mothers' attempts to provide scaffolding for book reading. In J. Allen & J. M. Mason (Eds.), *Risk makers, risk takers: Reducing the risks for young literacy learners.* Portsmouth, NH: Heinemann Educational Books.

Edwards, P. A. (2004). *Children's literacy development.* Boston: Allyn & Bacon.

Eggleton, T. (2001). Discipline in the schools. *ERIC Digest,* ED451554.

Eisenberg, N., & Fabes, R. A. (1998). Prosocial development. In N. Eisenberg (Ed.), *Handbook of child psychology* (5th ed., Vol. 3). New York: Wiley.

Eisenberg, N., & Morris, A. S. (2004). Moral cognitions and prosocial responding in adolescence. In R. Lerner & L. Steinberg (Eds.), *Handbook of adolescence.* New York: Wiley.

Eisenberg, N., Martin, C. L., & Fabes, R. A. (1996). Gender development and gender effects. In D. C. Berliner & R. C. Calfee (Eds.), *Handbook of educational psychology.* New York: Macmillan.

Eisner, E. W. (1999, May). The uses and limits of performance assessment. *Phi Delta Kappan, 80,* 658–661.

Elias, M. J., Gara, M. A., Schuyler, T. F., Branden-Muller, L. R., & Sayette, M. A. (1991). The promotion of social competence: Longitudinal study of a preventive school-based program. *American Journal of Orthopsychiatry, 61,* 409–417.

Elias, M. J., Gara, M., Ubriaco, M., Rothbaum, P. A., Clabby, J. P., & Schuyler, T. (1986). The impact of a preventive social problem-solving intervention on children's coping with middle-school stressors. *American Journal of Community Psychology, 14,* 259–275.

Elicker, J. (1996). A knitting tale. Reflections on scaffolding. *Childhood Education, 72,* 29–32.

Elkind, D. (1978). Understanding the young adolescent. *Adolescence, 13,* 127–134.

Elliot, A. J., & Thrash, T. M. (2001). Achievement goals and the hierarchical model of achievement motivation. *Educational Psychology Review, 13,* 139–156.

Ellis, A. K. (2002). *Teaching and learning elementary social studies* (7th ed.). Boston: Allyn & Bacon.

Ellis, H. C. (1987). Recent developments in human memory. In V. P. Makosky (Ed.), *The G. Stanley Hall Lecture Series.* Washington, DC: American Psychological Association.

Ellis, S., Klahr, D., & Siegler, R. S. (1994, April). *The birth, life, and sometimes death of good ideas in collaborative problem-solving.* Paper presented at the meeting of the American Educational Research Association, New Orleans.

Elmes, D. G., Kantowitz, B. H., & Roediger, H. L. (2003). *Research methods* *in psychology* (7th ed.). Belmont, CA: Wadsworth.

Emery, R.E., & Laumann-Billings, L. (1998). An overview of the nature, causes, and consequences of abusive family relationships. *American Psychologist, 53,* 121-135.

Emmer, E. T., & Stough, L. M. (2001). Classroom management: A critical part of educational psychology, with implications for teacher education. *Educational Psychologist, 36,* 103–112.

Emmer, E. T., Evertson, C. M., & Anderson, L. M. (1980). Effective classroom management at the beginning of the school year. *Elementary School Journal, 80,* 219–231.

Emmer, E. T., Evertson, C. M., & Worsham, M. E. (2003). *Classroom management for secondary teachers* (6th ed.). Boston: Allyn & Bacon.

Emmer, E. T., Evertson, C. M., Clements, B. S., & Worsham, M. E. (2000). *Classroom management for successful teachers* (4th ed.). Boston: Allyn & Bacon.

Englert, C. S., Berry, R., & Dunsmore, K. (2001). A case study of the apprenticeship process. *Journal of Learning Disabilities, 34,* 152–171.

Entwisle, D. R., & Alexander, K. L. (1993). Entry into the school: The beginning school transition and educational stratification in the United States. *Annual Review of Sociology, 19,* 401–423.

Epstein, J. L. (1983). Longitudinal effects of family-school-person interactions on student outcomes. *Research in Sociology and Education and Socialization, 4,* 101–127.

Epstein, J. L. (1996). Perspectives and previews on research and policy for school, family, and community partnerships. In A. Booth & J. F. Dunn (Eds.), *Family-school links.* Mahwah, NJ: Erlbaum.

Epstein, J. L. (1997, June 6). Commentary, *Wall Street Journal,* sec. 1, p. 1.

Epstein, J. L. (1998, April). *Interactive homework: Effective strategies to connect home and school.* Paper presented at the meeting of the American Educational Research Association, San Diego.

Epstein, J. L. (2001). *School, family, and community partnerships.* Boulder, CO: Westview Press.

Epstein, J. L., & Sanders, M. G. (2002). Family, schools, and community partnerships. In M. H. Bornstein (Ed.),

Handbook of parenting (2nd ed.). Mahwah, NJ: Erlbaum.

Epstein, J. L., Salinas, K. C., & Jackson, V. E. (1995). *Manual for teachers and prototype activities: Teachers involve parents in schoolwork (TIPS)* (rev. ed.). Baltimore: Johns Hopkins University, Center on Families, Communities, Schools, and Children's Learning.

Epstein, J. L., Sanders, M. G., Salinas, K. C., Simon, B. S., Jansorn, N. R., & Van Voorhis, F. L. (2002). *School, family, and community partnerships* (2nd ed.). Thousand Oaks, CA: Corwin Press.

Ericsson, K. A. (Ed.). (1996). *The road to excellence.* Mahwah, NJ: Erlbaum.

Ericsson, K. A., Krampe, R. T., & Tesch-Romer, C. (1993). The role of deliberate practice in the acquisition of expert performance. *Psychological Review, 100,* 363–406.

Erikson, E. H. (1968). *Identity: Youth and crisis.* New York: W. W. Norton.

Eslea, M., Menesini, E., Monta, Y., O'Moor, M., More-Merchen, J.A., Pereira, B., & Smith, P.K. (2004). Friendship and loneliness among bullies and victims: Data from seven countries. *Aggressive Behavior, 30,* 71-83.

Espelage, D.L., & Swearer, S.M. (2003). Conversations with middle school students about bullying and victimization: Should we be concerned? *Journal of Emotional Abuse, 2,* (Issue 213) 49-62.

Espelage, D.L., & Swearer, S.M.(Eds.). (2004). *Bullying in American schools.* Mahwah, NJ: Erlbaum.

Evans, G.W. (2004). The environment of childhood poverty. *American Psychologist, 59,* 77-92.

Evans, G. W., & English, K. (2002). The environment of poverty: Multiple stressor exposure, psychophysiological stress, and socioemotional adjustment. *Child Development, 73,* 1238–1248.

Evertson, C. M., Emmer, E. T., & Worsham, M. E. (2003). *Classroom management for elementary teachers* (6th ed.). Boston: Allyn & Bacon.

Evertson, C.M., Emmer, E.T., Clements, B.S., & Worsham, M.E (1997). *Classroom management for elementary teachers* (4th ed.). Boston: Allyn & Bacon.

Evertson, C. M., & Harris, A. H. (1999). Support for managing learning-centered classrooms: The classroom organization and management program. In H. J. Freiberg (Ed.), *Beyond behaviorism:*

Changing the classroom management paradigm. Boston: Allyn & Bacon.

F

Fair Test. (2004). "No child left behind" after two years: A track record of failure. Retrieved at http://www.fairtest.org.

Fallon, M. A., & Watts, E. (2001). Portfolio assessment and use. *Teacher Education and Special Education, 24,* 50–57.

Farkas, G. (2001). *Poverty and children's vocabulary development.* Unpublished manuscript, Pennsylvania State University.

Farr, M. (Ed.) (2005). *Latino language and literacy in ethnolinguistic Chicago.* Mahwah, NJ: Erlbaum.

Farris, P., Fuhler, C., & Walther, M. (2004) *Teaching reading.* New York: McGraw-Hill.

Fearn, L. (1972). *The maligned wolf.* San Diego: Kabyn Press.

Feist, J., & Feist, G. J. (2002). *Theories of personality* (5th ed.). New York: McGraw-Hill.

Fekken, G. C. (2000). Reliability. In A. Kazdin (Ed.), *Encyclopedia of psychology.* Washington, DC, & New York: American Psychological Association and Oxford University Press.

Feldhusen, J. F. (1997). Secondary services, opportunities, and activities for talented youth. In N. Colangelo & G. A. Davis (Eds.), *Handbook of gifted education.* Boston: Allyn & Bacon.

Feng, Y. (1996). Some thoughts about applying constructivist theories to guide instruction. *Computers in the Schools, 12,* 71–84.

Fenzel, L. M., Blyth, D. A., & Simmons, R. G. (1991). School transitions, secondary. In R. M. Lerner, A. C. Petersen, & J. Brooks-Gunn (Eds.). *Encyclopedia of Adolescence* (Vol. 2). New York: Garland.

Ferrari, M., & Sternberg, R. J. (1998). The development of mental abilities and styles. In W. Damon (Ed.), *Handbook of child psychology* (Vol. 2). New York: Wiley.

Fickes, M. (2001). The furniture of science. *School Planning and Management, 50,* 71–73.

Field, T. (Ed.). (1995). *Touch in early development.* Mahwah, NJ: Erlbaum.

Fielding, L. G., Wilson, P. T., & Anderson, R. C. (1986). A new focus on free reading: The role of tradebooks in reading instruction. In T. Raphael (Ed.), *The contexts of school-based literacy.* New York: Random House.

Firlik, R. (1996). Can we adapt the philosophies and practices of Reggio Emilia, Italy, for use in American schools? *Young Children, 51,* 217–220.

Firpo-Triplett, R. (1997, July). *Is it flirting or sexual harassment?* Paper presented at the Working with America's Youth conference, Pittsburgh.

Fisch, S.M. (2004). *Children's learning from educational television.* Mahwah, NJ: Erlbaum.

Fisch, S. M., & Truglio, R. T. (Eds.). (2001). *"G" is for growing: Thirty years of research on children and Sesame Street.* Mahwah, NJ: Erlbaum.

Fisher, C. W., Berliner, D. C., Filby, N. N., Marliave, R., Ghen, L. S., & Dishaw, M. M. (1980). Teaching behaviors, academic learning time, and student achievement: An overview. In C. Denham & A. Lieberman (Eds.), *Time to learn.* Washington, DC: National Institute of Education.

Fitzgerald, L., Collinsworth, L. L., & Harned, M. S. (2001). Sexual harassment. In J. Worrell (Ed.), *Encyclopedia of women and gender.* San Diego: Academic Press.

Fitzpatrick, J. (1993). *Developing responsible behavior in schools.* South Burlington, VT: Fitzpatrick Associates.

Fitzpatrick, J.L., Sanders, J.R. & Worthen, B.R. (2004). *Program evaluation* (3rd ed.). Boston: Allyn & Bacon.

Flake, C., Kuhs, T., Donnelly, A., & Ebert, C. (1995). Teacher as researcher: Reinventing the role of teacher. *Phi Delta Kappan, 76,* 405–407.

Flanagan, C. (2004). Volunteerism. In R. Lerner & L. Steinberg (Eds.), *Handbook of adolescent psychology.* New York: Wiley.

Flanagan, C., & Faison, N. (2001). Youth civic development: Implications of research for social policy and programs. *SRCD Social Policy Report, XV* (No. 1), 1–14.

Flanagan, C., Gill, S., & Gallay, L. (1998, November). *Intergroup understanding, social justice, and the "social contract" in diverse communities of youth.* Project report prepared for the workshop on research to improve intergroup relations among youth, Forum on Adolescence, National Research Council, Washington, DC.

Flavell, J. H. (1999). Cognitive development. *Annual Review of Psychology* (Vol. 50). Palo Alto, CA: Annual Reviews.

Flavell, J. H., Friedrichs, A., & Hoyt, J. (1970). Developmental changes in memorization processes. *Cognitive Psychology, 1,* 324–340.

Flavell, J. H., Miller, P. H., & Miller, S. A. (2002). *Cognitive development* (4th ed.). Upper Saddle River, NJ: Prentice Hall.

Floel, A., Poeppel, D., Buffalo, E.A., Braun, A., Wu, C.W., Seo, H.J. Knecht, S. & Cohen, L.G. (2004). Prefrontal cortex asymmetry for memory encoding of words and abstract shapes. *Cerebral Cortex, 14,* 404–409.

Florez, M. A. C. (1999). Improving adult English language learners' speaking skills. *ERIC Digest,* EDO-LE-99-01, 1–5.

Flower, L. S., & Hayes, J. R. (1981). Problem-solving and the cognitive processes in writing. In C. Frederiksen & J. F. Dominic (Eds.), *Writing: The nature, development, and teaching of written communication.* Mahwah, NJ: Erlbaum.

Fogarty, R. (Ed.). (1993). *The multiage classroom.* Palatine, IL: IRI/Skylight.

Foley, J., & Thompson, L. (2002). *Language learning.* New York: Oxford University Press.

Forehand, R., Ragosta, J., & Rock, D. (1976). *Conditions and processes of effective school desegregation.* Princeton, NJ: Educational Testing Service.

Fox, B. A. (1993). *The Human Tutorial Dialogue Project.* Mahwah, NJ: Erlbaum.

Fox, B., & Hull, M. (2002). *Phonics for the teacher of reading* (8th ed.). Upper Saddle River, NJ: Merrill.

Fraenkel, J.R., & Wallen, N.E. (2005). *How to design and evaluate research in education* (6th Ed). New York: McGraw-Hill.

Freiberg, H. J. (1999). Sustaining the paradigm. In H. J. Frieberg (Ed.), *Beyond behaviorism: Changing the classroom management paradigm.* Boston: Allyn & Bacon.

Freiberg, H.J., & Driscoll, A. (2005). *Universal teaching strategies* (4th Ed). Boston: Allyn & Bacon.

Frey, K.S., Nolen, S.B., Van Svhojack-Edstrong, L., & Hirchstein, M. (2001, June). *Second Step effects on social goals and behavior.* Paper presented at the meeting of the Society for Prevention Research, Washington, DC.

Frieman, J. L. (2002). *Learning and adaptive behavior.* Belmont, CA: Wadsworth.

Friend, M., & Bursuck, W. D. (2002). *Including students with special needs* (3rd ed.). Boston: Allyn & Bacon.

Fritzer, P. J. (2002). *Social studies content in elementary and middle school.* Boston: Allyn & Bacon.

Frye, D., Zelazo, P. D., Brooks, P. J., & Samuels, M. C. (1996). Inference and action in early causal reasoning. *Developmental Psychology, 32,* 120–131.

Fuchs, D., Fuchs, L. S., & Burish, P. (2000). Peer-assisted strategies: An empirically-supported practice to promote reading. *Learning Disabilities Research and Practice, 9,* 203–212.

Fuchs, L. S., Fuchs, D., Bentz, J., Phillips, N. B., & Hamlett, C. L. (1994). The nature of student interactions during peer tutoring with and without prior training and experience. *American Educational Research Journal, 31,* 75–103.

Fuligni, A,. & Yoshikawa, H. (2004). Investments in children among immigrant families. In A. Kalil & T. DeLeire (Eds.), *Family investments in children's potential.* Mahwah, NJ: Erlbaum.

Furco, A., & Billig, S. H. (Eds.). (2001). *Service learning: The essence of the pedagogy.* Greenwich, CT: IAP.

Furman, W., & Buhrmester, D. (1992). Age and sex differences in perceptions of networks of personal relationships. *Child Development, 63,* 103–115.

Furth, H. G., & Wachs, H. (1975). *Thinking goes to school.* New York: Oxford University Press.

G

Gabriele, A. J., & Montecinos, C. (2001). Collaborating with a skilled peer: The influence of achievement goals and perceptions of partners' competence on the participation and learning of low-achieving students. *Journal of Experimental Education, 69,* 152–178.

Gackenbach, J., & Ellerman, E. (1999). Introduction to psychological aspects of Internet use. In J. Gackenbach (Ed.), *Psychology and the Internet.* San Diego: Academic Press.

Gage, N. L. (1978). *The scientific basis of the art of teaching*. New York: Teachers College Press.

Galambos, N.L. (2004). Gender and gender role development in adolescence. In R. Lerner & L. Steinberg (Eds.), *Handbook of adolescence*. New York: Wiley.

Galambos, N. L., Petersen, A. C., Richards, M., & Gitleson, I. B. (1985). The Attitudes Toward Women Scale for Adolescents (AWSA). *Sex Roles, 13,* 343–356.

Gall, J.P., Gall, M.D., & Borg, W.R. (2005). *Applying educational research* (5th Ed.) Boston: Allyn & Bacon.

Gall, M. D., Borg, W. R., & Gall, J. P. (2003). *Educational research* (7th ed.). Boston: Allyn & Bacon.

Gallagher, C. (2000). A seat at the table: Teachers reclaiming assessment through rethinking accountability. *Phi Delta Kappan, 81,* 502–507.

Garbarino, J., Bradshaw, C.P., & Kostelny, K. (2005). Neighborhood and community influences on parenting. In T. Luster & L. Okaghi (Eds.), *Parenting : An ecological perspective.* Mahwah, NJ: Erlbaum.

Garcia, E. E., Bravo, M. A., Dickey, L. M., Cun, K., & Sun-Irminger, X. (2002). Rethinking school reform in the context of cultural and linguistic diversity: Creating a responsive learning community. In L. Minaya-Rowe (Ed.), *Teaching training and effective pedagogy in the context of cultural diversity.* Greenwich, CT: IAP.

Garcia, G. E., & Willis, A. I. (2001). Frameworks for understanding multicultural literacies. In P. R. Schmidt & P. B. Mosenthal (Eds.), *Reconceptualizing literacy in the new age of multiculturalism and pluralism.* Greenwich, CT: IAP.

Garcia, T. (2001, May 1). Testing and other measures of life. *San Francisco Chronicle,* pp. D3, 4.

Gardner, H. (1983). *Frames of mind.* New York: Basic Books.

Gardner, H. (1985). *The mind's new science.* New York: Basic Books.

Gardner, H. (1993). *Multiple intelligences.* New York: Basic Books.

Gardner, H. (1998). Multiple intelligences: Myths and messages. In A. Woolfolk (Ed.), *Readings in educational psychology* (2nd ed.). Boston: Allyn & Bacon.

Gardner, H. (2002). The pursuit of excellence through education. In M.

Ferrari (Ed.), *Learning from extraordinary minds.* Mahwah, NJ: Erlbaum.

Gardner, H., Feldman, D. H., & Krechevsky, M. (Eds.). (1998). *Project Spectrum.* New York: Teachers College Press.

Gardner, R. (1985). *The boys' and girls' book about divorce.* New York: Bantam.

Garmon, A., Nystrand, M., Berends, M., & LePore, P. C. (1995). An organizational analysis of the effects of ability grouping. *American Educational Research Journal, 32,* 687–715.

Garrod, A., Smulyan, L., Powers, S. I., & Kilenny, R. (1992). *Adolescent portraits.* Boston: Allyn & Bacon.

Garton, A.F. (2004). *Exploring cognitive development: The child as a problem solver.* Malden, MA: Blackwell.

Gauvain, M. (2001). *The social context of cognitive development.* New York: Guilford.

Gay, G. (1997). Educational equality for students of color. In J. A. Banks & C. M. Banks (Eds.), *Multicultural Education* (3rd ed.). Boston: Allyn & Bacon.

Gay, G. (2000). *Culturally responsive teaching: Theory, research, and practice.* New York: Teachers College Press.

Gay, L. R., & Airasian, P. (2000). *Educational research* (6th ed.). Upper Saddle River, NJ: Merrill.

Gazzaniga, M. S., Ivry, R. B., & Mangun, G. R. (2001). *Cognitive neuroscience* (2nd ed.). New York: Norton.

Gegeshidze, K., & Tsagareli, M.G. (2004). Influence of emotional words on human visual recognition and brain asymmetry. *World Journal of Biological Psychiatry, 5,* 26-32.

Gelman, R. (1969). Conservation acquisition: A problem of learning to attend to relevant attributes. *Journal of Experimental Child Psychology, 7,* 67–87.

Gelman, R., & Brennerman, K. (1994). Domain specificity and cultural specificity are not inconsistent. In L. A. Hirschfeld & S. Gelman (Eds.), *Mapping out domain specificity in cognition and culture.* New York: Cambridge University Press.

Gelman, R., & Williams, E. M. (1998). Enabling constraints for cognitive development and learning. In W. Damon (Ed.), *Handbook of child psychology* (5th ed., Vol. 4). New York: Wiley.

Gelman, S.A., & Opfer, J.E. (2004). Development of the animate-inanimate distinction. In U. Goswami (Ed.), *Blackwell handbook of childhood cognitive development.* Malden, MA: Blackwell.

Gentile, J. R. (2000). Learning, transfer of. In A. Kazdin (Ed.), *Encyclopedia of psychology.* Washington, DC, & New York: American Psychological Association and Oxford University Press.

Gest, S. D., Graham-Bermann, S. A., & Hartup, W. W. (2001). Peer experience: Common and unique features of number of friendships, social network centrality, and sociometric status. *Social Development 10,* 23–40.

Gibbs, J. C. (2003). *Moral development & reality.* Thousand Oaks, CA: Sage.

Gibbs, J. T. (1989). Black American adolescents. In J. T. Gibbs & L. N. Huang (Eds.), *Children of color.* San Francisco: Jossey-Bass.

Gibson, S., & McKay, R. (2001). *What constructivist theory and brain research may offer social studies.* School of Education, University of Alberta, Canada.

Giedd, J., Jeffries, N., Blumenthal, J., Castellanos, F., Vaituzis, A., Fernandez, T., Hamburger, S., Liu, H., Nelson, J., Bedwell, J., Tran, L., Lenane, M., Nicolson, R., & Rapoport, J. (1999). Childhood-onset schizophrenia: Progressive brain changes during adolescence. *Biological Psychiatry, 46,* 892-898.

Gigerenzer, G., & Selten, R. (Eds.). (2001). *Bounded rationality.* Cambridge, MA: MIT Press.

Gill, D. L. (2001). Sports and athletics. In J. Worrell (Ed.), *Encyclopedia of women and gender.* San Diego: Academic Press.

Gill, J. (1997, July). Personal conversation. Richardson: University of Texas at Dallas.

Gilligan, C. (1982). *In a different voice.* Cambridge, MA: Harvard University Press.

Gilligan, C. (1996). The centrality of relationships in psychological development: A puzzle, some evidence, and a theory. In G. G. Noam & K. W. Fischer (Eds.), *Development and vulnerability in close relationships.* Hillsdale, NJ: Erlbaum.

Gilligan, C. (1998). *Minding women: Reshaping the education realm.* Cambridge, MA: Harvard University Press.

Ginorio, A., & Huston, M. (2000). *Si Puede! Yes, we can: Latinas in school.* Washington, DC: American Association of University Women.

Ginsburg, H. P., Klein, A., & Starkey, P. (1998). The development of children's mathematical thinking. In I. E. Sigel & K. A. Renninger (Eds.), *Handbook of child psychology* (5th ed., Vol. 4). New York: Wiley.

Gipson, J. (1997, March/April). Girls and computer technology: Barrier or key? *Educational Technology,* pp. 41–43.

Glasser, W. (1969). *Schools without failure.* New York: Harper & Row.

Glassman, M. (2001). Dewey and Vygotsky: Society, experience, and inquiry in educational practice. *Educational Researcher, 30* (4), 3–14.

Glasson, G. E. (1989). The effects of hands-on and teacher demonstration laboratory methods on science achievement in relation to reasoning ability and prior knowledge. *Journal of Research in Science Teaching, 26,* 121–131.

Gold, J., & Lanzoni, M. (Eds.). (1993). [Video] *Graduation by portfolio—Central Park East Secondary School.* New York: Post Production, 29th St. Video, Inc.

Goldman, S. (1998, October). Unpublished review of J. W. Santrock's *Educational psychology.* New York: McGraw-Hill.

Goldman, S. R., Petrosino, A., Sherwood, R. D., Garrison, S., Hickey, D., Bransford, J. D., & Pellegrino, J. (1996). Anchoring science instruction in multimedia learning environments. In S. Vosniadou, E. De Corte, R. Glaser, & H. Mandl (Eds.), *International perspectives on the design of technology-supported learning environments.* Hillsdale, NJ: Erlbaum.

Goldman-Rakic, P. (1996). *Bridging the gap.* Presentation at the workshop sponsored by the Education Commission of the States and the Charles A. Dana Foundation, Denver.

Goldsmith, H. H., Aksan, N., Essex, M., Smider, N., & Vandell, D. L. (2001). Temperament and socioemotional adjustment to kindergarten. In T. D. Wachs & G. A. Kohnstamm (Eds.), *Temperament in context.* Mahwah, NJ: Erlbaum.

Goldstein, H., & Hockenberger, E. (1991). Significant progress in child language intervention: An 11-year retrospective.

Research in Developmental Disabilities, 12, 401–424.

Goleman, D. (1995). *Emotional intelligence.* New York: Bantam.

Goleman, D., Kaufman, P., & Ray, M. (1993). *The creative spirit.* New York: Plume.

Gonzales, N.A., Knight, G.P., Birman, D., & Sirolli, A.A. (2004). Acculturation and enculturation among Latino youths. In K.L. Maton, C.J. Schellenbach, B.J. Leadbetter, & A.L. Solarz (Eds.), *Investing in children, youth, families, and communities.* Mahwah, NJ: Erlbaum.

Goodkind, J., Hang, P., & Yang, M. (2004). Hmong refugees in the United States. In K.E. Miller & L.M. Rasco (Eds.), *The mental health of refugees.* Mahwah, NJ: Erlbaum.

Goodlad, J. I. (1984). *A place called school.* New York: McGraw-Hill.

Goodlad, S., & Hirst, B. (1989). *Peer tutoring: A guide to learning by teaching.* New York: Nichols.

Goodrich, H. (1997). Understanding rubrics. *Educational Leadership, 54,* 14–17.

Gordon, T. (1970). *Parent effectiveness training.* New York: McGraw-Hill.

Goswami, U. (2004). Inductive and deductive reasoning. In U. Goswami (Ed.), *Blackwell handbook of childhood cognitive development.* Malden, MA: Blackwell.

Gottman, J. M. (1996). *What predicts divorce.* New York: Milton H. Erickson Foundation.

Graham, S. (1986, August). *Can attribution theory tell us something about motivation in Blacks?* Paper presented at the meeting of the American Psychological Association, Washington, DC.

Graham, S. (1990). Motivation in African Americans. In G. L. Berry & J. K. Asamen (Eds.), *Black students.* Newbury Park, CA: Sage.

Graham, S. (1992). Most of the subjects were White and middle class. *American Psychologist, 47,* 629–637.

Graham, S., & Harris, K. R. (1994). The effects of whole language on children's writing: A review of the literature. *Educational Psychologist, 29,* 187–192.

Graham, S., & Harris, K. R. (2001). The role of self-regulation and transcription skills in writing and writing development. *Educational Psychologist, 35,* 3–12.

Graham, S., & Taylor, A. Z. (2002). Ethnicity, gender, and the development of achievement values. In A. Wigfield & J. S. Eccles (Eds.), *Development of achievement motivation.* San Diego: Academic Press.

Graham, S., & Weiner, B. (1996). Theories and principles of motivation. In D. C. Berliner & R. C. Calfee (Eds.), *Handbook of educational psychology.* New York: Macmillan.

Gratz, R. R., & Bouton, P. J. (1996). Erikson and early childhood educators. *Young Children, 51,* 74–78.

Gray, J. R. (2001). Emotional modulation of cognitive control: Approach-withdrawal states of double-dissociate spatial from verbal two-back task performance. *Journal of Experimental Psychology: General, 130,* 436–452.

Gredler, M. (1999). *Classroom assessment and learning.* Boston: Addison Wesley.

Greenberg, M. T. (1996). *The PATHS project.* Seattle: University of Washington.

Greenberger, E., & Steinberg, L. (1986). *When teenagers work. The psychological and social costs of adolescent employment.* New York: Basic Books.

Greenfield, P. M. (2000). Culture and development. In A. Kazdin (Ed.), *Encyclopedia of psychology.* Washington, DC, & New York: American Psychological Association and Oxford University Press.

Greenfield, P. M., & Suzuki, L. K. (1998). Culture and human development. In W. Damon (Ed.), *Handbook of child psychology* (Vol. 4). New York: Wiley.

Greeno, J. G. (1993). For research to reform education and cognitive science. In L. A. Penner, G. M. Batche, H. M. Knoff, & D. L. Nelson (Eds.). *The challenge in mathematics and science education: Psychology's response.* Washington, DC: American Psychological Association.

Greenough, W. (1997, April 21). Commentary. *U.S. News & World Report,* p. 79.

Greenough, W. (2000). Brain development. In A. Kazdin (Ed.), *Encyclopedia of psychology.* Washington, DC, & New York: American Psychological Association and Oxford University Press.

Gregory, R. J. (2000). *Psychological testing* (3rd ed.). Boston: Allyn & Bacon.

Grolnick, W. S., Gurland, S. T., Jacob, K. F., & Decourcey, W. (2002). The development of self-determination in middle childhood and adolescence. In A. Wigfield & J. S. Eccles (Eds.), *Development of achievement motivation*. San Diego: Academic Press.

Gronlund, N. E. (2003). *Assessment of student achievement* (7th ed.). Boston: Allyn & Bacon.

Gronlund, N. E., Linn, R. L., & Davis, K. M. (2000). *Measurement and assessment in teaching.* Upper Saddle River, NJ: Prentice Hall.

Grossier, P. (1964). *How to use the fine art of questioning.* New York: Teachers' Practical Press.

Grotevant, H. D. (1998). Adolescent development in family contexts. In W. Damon (Ed.), *Handbook of child psychology* (5th ed., Vol. 3). New York: Wiley.

Guilford, J. P. (1967). *The structure of intellect.* New York: McGraw-Hill.

Gunning, T. G. (2000). *Creating literacy instruction for all children* (3rd ed.). Boston: Allyn & Bacon.

Guskey, T. R. (2001). Fixing grading policies that undermine standards. *The Education Digest, 66* (7), 16–21.

Guttentag, M., & Bray, H. (1976). *Undoing sex stereotypes: Research and resources for educators.* New York: McGraw-Hill.

Guyer, B. (2000). *ADHD.* Boston: Allyn & Bacon.

H

Haager, D., & Klinger, J.K. (2005). *Differentiating instruction in inclusive classrooms.* Boston: Allyn & Bacon.

Hackenberg, T. D. (2000). Schedules of reinforcement. In A. Kazdin (Ed.), *Encyclopedia of psychology.* Washington, DC, & New York: American Psychological Association and Oxford University Press.

Hahn, U., & Ramscar, M. (Eds.). (2001). *Similarity and categorization.* New York: Oxford University Press.

Haith, M. M., & Benson, J. B. (1998). Infant cognition. In W. Damon (Ed.), *Handbook of child psychology* (5th ed., Vol. 2). New York: Wiley.

Hakuta, K. (2000). Bilingualism. In A. Kazdin (Ed.), *Encyclopedia of psychology.* Washington, DC, & New York: American Psychological Association and Oxford University Press.

Hakuta, K., & Garcia, E. E. (1989). Bilingualism and education. *American Psychologist, 44,* 374–379.

Hakuta, K., Bialystok, E., & Wiley, E. (in press). Critical evidence: A test of the critical period hypothesis for second language acquisition. *Psychological Science.*

Hakuta, K., Butler, Y. G., & Witt, D. (2000). *How long does it take English learners to attain proficiency?* Berkeley, CA: The University of California Linguistic Minority Research Institute Policy Report 2000–1.

Haladyna, T. M. (1997). *Writing test items to evaluate higher-order thinking.* Boston: Allyn & Bacon.

Haladyna, T. M. (2002). *Essentials of standardized achievement testing: Validity and accountability.* Boston: Allyn & Bacon.

Hale-Benson, J. E. (1982). *Black children: Their roots, culture, and learning styles.* Baltimore: The Johns Hopkins University Press.

Hall, R. V., & Hall, M. L. (1998). *How to select reinforcers* (2nd ed.). Austin: Pro-Ed.

Hallahan, D. P., & Kauffman, J. M. (2000). *Exceptional learners* (8th ed.). Boston: Allyn & Bacon.

Hallahan, D. P., & Kauffman, J. M. (2003). *Exceptional learners* (9th ed.). Boston: Allyn & Bacon.

Hallahan, D., Kauffman, J., & Lloyd, J. (1999). *Introduction to learning disabilities* (2nd ed.). Boston: Allyn & Bacon.

Hallahan, D.P., Lloyd, J.W., Kauffman, J.M., Weiss, M.P., & Martinez, E.A. (2005). *Learning disablilties* (3rd Ed.). Boston: Allyn & Bacon.

Halonen, J. (2002). Refine your expression. In J. W. Santrock & J. Halonen, *Your guide to college success* (2nd ed.). Belmont, CA: Wadsworth.

Halpern, D. (2002). Sex difference research: Cognitive abilities. In J. Worell (Ed.), *Encyclopedia of women.* San Diego: Academic Press.

Hambleton, R. K. (1996). Advances in assessment models, methods, and practices. In D. C. Berliner & R. C. Calfee (Eds.), *Handbook of educational psychology.* New York: Macmillan.

Hambleton, R. K. (2002). How can we make NAEP and state test score reporting scales and reports more understandable? In R. W. Lissitz & W. D. Schafer (Eds.), *Assessment in educational reform: Both means and ends.* Boston: Allyn & Bacon.

Hamburg, D. A. (1997). Meeting the essential requirements for healthy adolescent development in a transforming world. In R. Takanishi & D. Hamburg (Eds.), *Preparing adolescents for the 21st century.* New York: Cambridge University Press.

Hammill, D.D. (2004). What we know about correlates of reading. *Exceptional Children, 70,* 453-468.

Haney, W. (2000). The myth of the Texas miracle in education. *Education Policy Analysis Archives, 8 (41): http://epaa.asu.edu/epaa/v8n41/*

Hannish, L.D., & Guerra, N.G. (2004). Aggressive victims, passive victims, and bullies: Development continuity or developmental change? *Merrill-Palmer Quarterly., 50,* 17-38.

Hannon, B., & Craik, F. I. (2001). Encoding specificity revisited: The role of semantics. *Canadian Journal of Experimental Psychology, 55,* 231–243.

Hardman, M. L., Drew, C. J., & Egan, M. W. (2002). *Human exceptionality* (7th ed.). Boston: Allyn & Bacon.

Hardy, L. (2001). High tech high. *The American School Board Journal, 188,* 12–15.

Harnqvist, K. (1968). Changes in intelligence from 13 to 18. *Scandinavian Journal of Psychology, 9,* 50–82.

Harris, J. L., Kamhi, A. G., & Pollock, K. E. (2001). *Literacy in African American communities.* Mahwah, NJ: Erlbaum.

Harrison-Hale, A.O., McLoyd, V.C., & Smedley, B. (2004). Racial and ethnic status: Risk and protective processes among African American families. . In K.L. Maton, C.J. Schellenbach, B.J. Leadbetter, & A.L. Solarz (Eds.), *Investing in children.* Washington, DC: American Psychological Association.

Hart, B., & Risley, T.R. (1995). *Meaningful differences in the everyday experiences of young American children.* Baltimore: Brookes.

Hart, C. H., Charlesworth, R., Durland, M. A., Burts, D. C., DeWolf, M., & Fleege, P. O. (1996). *Developmentally appropriate practice in preschool classrooms.* Unpublished manuscript, Brigham Young University, Provo, Utah.

Hart, C.H., Yang, C., Charlesworth, R., & Burts, D.C. (2003, April). *Early childhood teachers' curriculum beliefs, classroom practices, and children's outcomes: What are the connections?* Paper presented at the biennial meeting of the Society for Research in Child Development, Tampa, FL.

Harter, S. (1981). A new self-report scale of intrinsic versus extrinsic orientation in the classroom: Motivational and informational components. *Developmental Psychology, 17,* 300–312.

Harter, S. (1990). Self and identity development. In S. S. Feldman & G. R. Elliott (Eds.), *At the threshold: The developing adolescent.* Cambridge, MA: Harvard University Press.

Harter, S. (1996). Teacher and classmate influences on scholastic motivation, self-esteem, and level of voice in adolescents. In J. Juvonen & K. R. Wentzel (Eds.), *Social motivation.* New York: Cambridge University Press.

Harter, S. (1999). *The construction of the self.* New York: Guilford.

Hartup, W. W. (1983). Peer relations. In P. H. Mussen (Ed.), *Handbook of child psychology* (4th ed., Vol. 4). New York: Wiley.

Hartup, W. W. (2000). Middle childhood: Socialization and social context. In A. Kazdin (Ed.), *Encyclopedia of psychology.* Washington, DC, & New York American Psychological Association and Oxford University Press.

Harwood, R., Lyendecker, B., Carlson, V., Ascencio, M., & Miller, A. (2002). Parenting among Latino families in the U.S. In M. H. Bornstein (Ed.), *Handbook of parenting* (2nd ed.). Mahwah, NJ: Erlbaum.

Haselager, G.J.T., Cilessen, A.H.N., Van Lieshout, C.F.M., Riksen-Walraen, J.M.A., & Hartup, W.W. (2002). Heterogeneity among peer-rejected boys across middle childhood: Developmental pathways of social behavior. *Developmental Psychology, 38,* 446-456.

Hasirci, D., & Demirkan, H. (2003). Creativity in learning environments: The case of two sixth grade art rooms. *Journal of Creative Behavior, 37,* 17-41.

Hasse, C. (2001). Institutional creativity: The relational zone of proximal development. *Culture & Psychology, 7,* 199–221.

Hatano, G. (1990). The nature of everyday science. *British Journal of Educational Developmental Psychology, 8,* 245–250.

Hatano, G., & Oura, Y. (2003). Commentary: Reconceptualizing school learning using insight from expertise research. *Educational Researcher, 32,* 26-29.

Hatch, T. (2000, April). *Portfolios and the scholarship of teaching.* Paper presented at the meeting of the American Educational Research Association, New Orleans.

Hay, D.F., Payne, A., & Chadwick, A. (2004). Peer relations in childhood. *Journal of Child Psychology and Psychiatry, 45,* 84-108.

Hayes, J. R., & Flower, L. S. (1986). Writing research and the writer. *American Psychologist, 41,* 1106–1113.

Hayes, S. C. (2000). Applied behavior analysis. In A. Kazdin (Ed.), *Encyclopedia of psychology.* Washington, DC, & New York: American Psychological Association and Oxford University Press.

Haynes, R. M., & Chalker, D. M. (1997, May). World class schools. *American School Board Journal,* pp. 20–25.

Haynie, D.L., Nansel, T., Eitel, P., Crump, A.D., Saylor,K., Yu, K.,& Simons-Morton, B. (2001). Bullies, victims, and bully/victims: Distinct groups of at-risk youth. *Journal of Early Adolescence, 21,* 29-49.

Heath, S. B. (1989). Oral and literate traditions among Black Americans living in poverty. *American Psychologist, 44,* 367–373.

Heid, M. K. (2002). Algebra and function development. In M. K. Heid & G. W. Blume (Eds.), *Mathematics learning, teaching, and policy.* Greenwich, CT: IAP.

Heid, M. K., & Blume, G. W. (Eds.). (2002). *Mathematics curriculum development and tool development.* Greenwich, CT: IAP.

Heilman, A. W., Blair, T. R., & Rupley, W. H. (2002). *Principles and practices of teaching reading* (10th ed.). Upper Saddle River, NJ: Merrill.

Heller, C., & Hawkins, J. (1994, Spring). Teaching tolerance. *Teachers College Record,* p. 2.

Heller, H. C. (1993). The need for a core, interdisciplinary, life-sciences curriculum in the middle grades. In R. Takanishi (Ed.), *Adolescence in the 1990s.* New York: Teachers College Press.

Henderson, V. L., & Dweck, C. S. (1990). Motivation and achievement. In S. S. Feldman & G. R. Elliott (Eds.), *At the threshold: The developing adolescent.* Cambridge, MA: Harvard University Press.

Henley, M., Ramsey, R., & Algozzine, R. (1999). *Characteristics and strategies for teaching students with mild disabilities* (3rd ed.). Boston: Allyn & Bacon.

Hennessey, B. A., & Amabile, T. M. (1998). Reward, intrinsic motivation, and creativity. *American Psychologist, 53,* 674–675.

Henson, K. (1988). *Methods and strategies for teaching in secondary and middle schools.* New York: Longman.

Henson, K. (2004). *Constructivist teaching strategies for diverse middle school classrooms.* Boston: Allyn & Bacon.

Hergenhahn, B. R., & Olson, M. H. (2001). *An introduction to theories of learning* (6th ed.). Upper Saddle River, NJ: Prentice Hall.

Herman, J. (1996). Commentary in "The latest on student portfolios." *NEA Today, 15* (4), 17.

Herrnstein, R. J., & Murray, C. (1994). *The bell curve: Intelligence and class structure in modern life.* New York: Free Press.

Hertzog, N. B. (1998, January/February). Gifted education specialist. *Teaching Exceptional Children,* pp. 39–43.

Hetherington, E. M. (1995, March). *The changing American family and the well-being of others.* Paper presented at the meeting of the Society for Research in Child Development, Indianapolis.

Hetherington, E. M. (2000). Divorce. In A. Kazdin (Ed.), *Encyclopedia of psychology.* Washington, DC, & New York: American Psychological Association and Oxford University Press.

Hetherington, E. M., & Kelly, J. (2002). *For better or for worse: Divorce reconsidered.* New York: Norton.

Hetherington, E. M., & Stanley-Hagan, M. (2002). Parenting in divorced and remarried families. In M. H. Bornstein (Ed.), *Handbook of parenting* (2nd ed.). Mahwah, NJ: Erlbaum.

Hetzroni, O.E., & Shrieber, B. (2004). Word processing as an assertive technology tool for enhancing academic outcomes of students with writing disabilities in the regular classroom. *Journal of Learning Disabilities, 37,* 143-154.

Heward, W. L. (2000). *Introduction to special education* (6th ed.). Upper Saddle River, NJ: Merrill.

Hiatt-Michael, D. (Ed.). (2001). *Promising practices in family involvement*. Greenwich, CT: IAP.

Hickey, D. T., Moore, A. L., & Pellegrino, J. W. (2001). The motivational and academic consequences of elementary mathematics environments: Do constructivist innovations and reforms make a difference? *American Educational Research Journal, 38,* 611–652.

Hiebert, E.H. (2005). In pursuit of an effective, efficient curriculum. In E.H. Hiebert & M.L. Kamil (Eds.), *Teaching and learning vocabulary*. Mahwah, NJ: Erlbaum.

Hiebert, E.H., & Kamil, M.L. (Eds.) (2005). *Teaching and learning vocabulary*. Mahwah, NJ: Erlbaum.

Hiebert, E. H., & Raphael, T. E. (1996). Psychological perspectives on literacy and extensions to educational practice. In D. C. Berliner & R. C. Calfee (Eds.), *Handbook of educational psychology*. New York: Macmillan.

Hiebert, J., Gallimore, R., Garnier, H., Givvin, K.B., Hollingsworth, H., Jacobs, J., Chui, A.M.Y., Wearne, D., Smith, M., Kersting, N., Manaster, A, Tseng, E., Etterbeek, W., Manaster, C., Gonzales, P., & Stigler, J.W. (2003). *Teaching mathematics in seven countries: Results from the TIMSS 1999 video study* (NCES 2003-013). Washington, DC: U.S. Department of Education.

Higgins, A., Power, C., & Kohlberg, L. (1983, April). *Moral atmosphere and moral judgment*. Paper presented at the biennial meeting of the Society for Research in Child Development, Detroit.

Higgins, E. T. (2000). Self-regulation. In A. Kazdin (Ed.), *Encyclopedia of psychology*. Washington, DC, & New York: American Psychological Association and Oxford University Press.

Hightower, E. (1990). Adolescent interpersonal and familial precursors of positive mental health at midlife. *Journal of Youth and Adolescence, 19,* 257–275.

Hilgard, E. R. (1996). History of educational psychology. In D. C. Berliner & R. C. Calfee (Eds.), *Handbook of educational psychology*. New York: Macmillan.

Hill, W. F. (2002). *Learning* (7th ed.). Boston: Allyn & Bacon.

Hirsch, E. D. (1987). *Cultural literacy*. New York: Random House.

Hirsch, E. D. (1996). *The schools we need: And why we don't have them*. New York: Doubleday.

Hocutt, A. M. (1996). Effectiveness of special education: Is placement the critical factor? *Future of Children, 6* (1), 77–102.

Hoff, E. (2001). *Language development* (2nd ed.). Belmont, CA: Wadsworth.

Hoff, E., Laursen, B., & Tardif, T. (2002). Socioeconomic status and parenting. In M. H. Bornstein (Ed.). *Handbook of parenting* (2nd ed.). Mahwah, NJ: Erlbaum.

Hoff-Ginsburg, E., & Tardif, T. (1995). Socioeconomic status and parenting. In M. H. Bornstein (Ed.), *Children and parenting* (Vol. 2). Hillsdale, NJ: Erlbaum.

Hogan, D. M., & Tudge, J. (1999). Implications of Vygotsky's theory for peer learning. In A. M. O'Donnell & A. King (Eds.), *Cognitive perspectives on peer learning*. Mahwah, NJ: Erlbaum.

Holland, D., Lachicotte, W., Skinner, D., & Cain, C. (2001). *Identity and agency in cultural worlds*. Cambridge, MA: Harvard University Press.

Hollingworth, L. S. (1916). Sex differences in mental tests. *Psychological Bulletin, 13,* 377–383.

Holzberg, C. (1995). Technology in special education. *Technology and Learning, 14,* 18–21.

Honig, A. S., & Wittmer, D. S. (1996). Helping children become more prosocial: Ideas for the classroom, families, schools, and communities. *Young Children, 51,* 62–70.

Hooper, S., Ward, T. J., Hannafin, M. J., & Clark, H. T. (1989). The effects of aptitude composition on achievement during small group learning. *Journal of Computer-Based Instruction, 16,* 102–109.

Hoover-Dempsey, K. V., Battiato, C., Walker, J. M. T., Reed, R. P., Dejong, J. M., & Jones, K. P. (2001). Parental involvement in homework. *Educational Psychologist, 36,* 195–209.

Horton, D. M. (2001). The disappearing bell curve. *Journal of Secondary Gifted Education, 12,* 185–188.

Hosp, J.L., & Reschly, D.J. (2004). Disproportionate representation of minority students in special education: Academic, demographic, and economic predictors. *Exceptional Children, 70,* 185-199.

Houston, G. (2004). *How writing works*. Boston: Allyn & Bacon.

Howard, R. W. (2001). Searching the real world for signs of rising population intelligence. *Personality and Individual Differences, 30,* 1039–1058.

Howell, J., & Dunnivant, S. (2000). *Technology for teachers*. New York: McGraw-Hill.

Howes, C., & Tonyan, H. (2000). Peer relations. In L. Balter & C. S. Tamis-LeMonda (Eds.), *Child psychology: A handbook of contemporary issues*. Philadelphia: Psychology Press.

Hoyle, R. H., & Judd, C. M. (2002). *Research methods in social psychology* (7th ed.). Belmont, CA: Wadsworth.

Hudley, C., & Graham, S. (1995). School-based interventions for aggressive African-American boys. *Applied and Preventive Psychology, 4,* 185–195.

Hughes, T. L., & McIntosh, D. E. (2002). Differential ability scales: Profiles of preschoolers with cognitive delay. *Psychology in the Schools, 39,* 19–29.

Hughey, J. B., & Slack, C. (2001). *Teaching children to write*. Upper Saddle River, NJ: Merrill.

Hunt, E. B. (1995). *Will we be smart enough? A cognitive analysis of the coming work force*. New York: Russell Sage.

Hunt, E. B. (2002). *Thoughts on thought*. Mahwah, NJ: Erlbaum.

Hunt, R. R., & Kelly, R. E. S. (1996). Accessing the particular from the general: The power of distinctiveness in the context of organization. *Memory and Cognition, 24,* 217–225.

Huttenlocher, P. R., & Dabholkar, A. S. (1997). Regional differences in synaptogenesis in human cerebral cortex. *Journal of Comparative Neurology, 37,* 167–178.

Huttenlocher, P. R., Haight, W., Bruk, A., Seltzer, M., & Lyons T. (1991). Early vocabulary growth: Relation to language input and gender. *Developmental Psychology, 27,* 236–248.

Hyde, J.S. (2004). *Half the human experience* (5th ed.). Boston: Houghton Mifflin.

Hyde, J. S., & Mezulis, A. H. (2001). Gender difference research: Issues and critique. In J. Worrell (Ed.), *Encyclopedia* *of women and gender.* San Diego: Academic Press.

Hyde, J. S., & Plant, E. A. (1995). Magnitude of psychological gender differences: Another side of the story. *American Psychologist, 50,* 159–161.

Hyman, I. (1994). *Is spanking child abuse? Conceptualizations, research, and policy implications.* Paper presented at the meeting of the American Psychological Association, Los Angeles.

Hyman, I. (1997) *The case against spanking: How to discipline your child without hitting.* San Francisco: Jossey-Bass.

Hyman, I. & Snook, P. (1999). *Dangerous schools: What we can do about the physical and emotional abuse of our children.* San Francisco: Jossey-Bass.

Hymel, S., McDougall, P., & Renshaw, P. (2004). Peer acceptance/rejection. In P.K. Smith & C.H. Hart (Eds.), *Blackwell handbook of childhood social development.* Malden, MA: Blackwell.

Hyman, I., Eisenstein, J., Amidon, A., & Kay, B. (2001, August 28). An update on the cross-cultural study of corporal punishment and abuse. In F. Farley (Chair), *Cross cultural aspects of corporal punishment and abuse: A research update.* Symposium presented at the 2001 Annual Convention of the American Psychological Association, San Francisco, CA.

I

Iacocca, L. (1984). *Iacocca: An autobiography.* New York: Bantam.

Ickes, W., Snyder, M., & Garcia, S. (1997). Personality influences or the choice of situations. In R. Hogan, J. Johnson, & S. Briggs (Eds.), *Handbook of personality psychology.* San Diego: Academic Press.

Idol, L. (1997). Key questions related to building collaborative and inclusive schools. *Journal of Learning Disabilities, 30,* 384–394.

Idol, L., Nevin, A., & Paolucci-Whitcomb, P. (1994). *Collaborative consultation.* Austin, TX: PRO-ED.

In View. (1990). *A field trip into the sea* (software). Pleasantville, NY: Sunburst Communications.

Inkrott, C. (2001). Beyond drill and practice: Managing courseware and electronic portfolios. *Multimedia Schools, 8,* 44–47.

Intercultural Development Research Association. (1996). *More at-risk students to tutor others.* Unpublished manuscript, Intercultural Development Research Association, San Antonio.

International Society for Technology in Education. (2000). *National educational technology standards for students: Connecting curriculum and technology.* Eugene, OR: Author.

International Society for Technology in Education. (2001). *National educational technology standards for teachers— Preparing teachers to use technology.* Eugene, OR: Author.

Irvine, J. J. (1990). *Black students and school failure.* New York: Greenwood Press.

Irvine, J. J., & Armento, B. J. (2001). *Culturally responsive teaching: Lesson planning for elementary and middle grades.* Boston: McGraw-Hill.

Ishii-Kuntz, M. (2004). Asian American families. In M. Coleman & L. Ganong (Eds.), *Handbook of contemporary families.* Thousand Oaks, CA: Sage.

J

Jackson, J. F. (1997, April). *Primary grade public schooling: A risk factor for African American children?* Paper presented at the meeting of the Society for Research in Child Development, Washington, DC.

Jacobs, H. H. (1997). *Mapping the big picture: Integrating curriculum and assessment K–12.* Alexandria, VA: Association for Supervision and Curriculum Development.

Jacobson, L. (1996, January). First in the world? *American School Board Journal,* pp. 21–23.

James, W. (1890). *Principles of psychology.* New York: Dover.

James, W. (1899/1993). *Talks to teachers.* New York: W. W. Norton.

Jenkins, J., & Jenkins, L. (1987). Making peer tutoring work. *Educational Leadership, 44,* 64–68.

Jennings, K. D., & Deitz, L. J. (2002). Mastery motivation. In M. H. Bornstein, L. Davidson, C. L. M. Keyes, & K. Moore (Eds.), *Well-being.* Mahwah, NJ: Erlbaum.

Jensen, A. R. (1969). How much can we boost IQ and academic achievement? *Harvard Educational Review, 39,* 1–123.

Johnson, A.P. (2005). *Short-guide to action research* (2nd ed.). Boston: Allyn & Bacon.

Johnson, B., & Christensen, L. (2000). *Educational research.* Boston: Allyn & Bacon.

Johnson, D. W. (1990). *Teaching out. Interpersonal effectiveness and self-actualization.* Upper Saddle River, NJ: Prentice Hall.

Johnson, D. W., & Johnson, F. P. (2003). *Joining together: Group theory and group skills* (7th ed.). Boston: Allyn & Bacon.

Johnson, D. W., & Johnson, R. T. (1991). *Teaching students to be peacemakers.* Edina, MN: Interaction.

Johnson, D. W., & Johnson, R. T. (1994). *Learning together and alone* (4th ed.). Boston: Allyn & Bacon.

Johnson, D. W., & Johnson, R. T. (1995, February). Why violence prevention programs don't work—And what does. *Educational Leadership,* pp. 63–68.

Johnson, D. W., & Johnson, R. T. (2002). *Multicultural education and human relations.* Boston: Allyn & Bacon.

Johnson, J. A., Duuis, V. L., Musial, D., Hall, G. E., & Gollnick, D. M. (2002). *Introduction to the foundations of American education* (12th ed.). Boston: Allyn & Bacon.

Johnson, J. S., & Newport, E. L. (1991). Critical period effects on universal properties of language: The status of subjacency in the acquisition of a second language. *Cognition, 39,* 215–258.

Johnson, M., & Ward, P. (2001). Effects of classwide peer tutoring on correct performance of striking skills in 3rd grade physical education. *Journal of Teaching in Physical Education, 20,* 247–263.

Johnson, M. K., Beebe, T., Mortimer, J. T, & Snyder, M. (1998). Volunteerism in adolescence: A process perspective. *Journal of Research in Adolescence, 8,* 309–332.

Johnson, V. R. (1994). *Parent centers in urban schools.* (Center Report no. 23). Baltimore: Johns Hopkins University, Center on Families, Communities, Schools, and Children's Learning.

Johnson, W., Bouchard, T.J., Krueger, R.F., McGue, M., & Gottesman, I.I. (2004). Just one *g:* Consistent results from three test batteries. *Intelligence, 32,* 95-107.

Johnson-Laird, P. (2000). Reasoning. In A. Kazdin (Ed.), *Encyclopedia of psychology.* Washington, DC, & New York: American

Psychological Association and Oxford University Press.

John-Steiner, V., & Mahn, H. (1996). Sociocultural approaches to learning and development: A Vygotskian framework *Educational Psychologist, 31,* 191–206.

Jonassen, D. H., & Grabowski, B. L. (1993). *Handbook of individual differences, learning, and instruction.* Mahwah, NJ: Erlbaum.

Jones, B. D. (1999). Computer-rated essays in the English composition classroom. *Journal of Educational Computing Research, 20,* 169–188.

Jones, B. F., Rasmussen C. M., & Moffitt, M. C. (1997). *Real-life problem solving.* Washington, DC: American Psychological Association.

Jones, C. (1993). Commentary in D. Goleman, P. Kaufman, & M. Ray. *The creative spirit.* New York: Plume.

Jones, J. M. (1994). The African American: A duality dilemma? In W. J. Lonner & R. Malpass (Eds.), *Psychology and culture.* Boston: Allyn & Bacon.

Jones, J. M. (1997). *Prejudice and racism* (2nd ed.). New York: McGraw-Hill.

Jones, L. V. (1984). White-black achievement differences: The narrowing gap. *American Psychologist, 39,* 1207–1213.

Jones, M. G., & Wheatley, J. (1990). Gender differences in teacher-student interactions in science classrooms. *Journal of Research in Science Teaching, 27,* 861–874.

Jones, N., Kemenes, G., & Benjamin, P. R. (2001). Selective expression of electrical correlates of differential appetitive classical conditioning in a feedback network. *Journal of Neurophysiology, 85,* 89–97.

Jones, V., & Jones, L. (2004). *Comprehensive classroom management* (7th ed.). Boston: Allyn & Bacon.

Joyce, B., & Weil, M. (1996). *Models of teaching* (5th ed.). New York: McGraw-Hill.

K

Kabler, P. (1997, November 14). School officials work bugs out of computer act. *Charleston Gazette,* p. C1.

Kagan, J. (1965). Reflection-impulsivity and reading development in primary

grade children. *Child Development, 36,* 609–628.

Kagan, S. (1992). *Cooperative learning.* San Juan Capistrano, CA: Resources for Teachers.

Kagiticibasi, C. (1996). *Human development across cultures.* Mahwah, NJ: Erlbaum.

Kahneman, D., & Tversky, A. (1995). Conflict resolution: A cognitive perspective. In K. Arrow, R. H. Mnookin, L. Ross, A. Tversky, & R. Wilson (Eds.), *Barriers to conflict resolution.* New York: Norton.

Kail, R. V. (2002). Information processing and memory. In M. H. Bornstein, L. Davidson, C. L. M. Keyes, & K. Moore (Eds.), *Well-being.* Mahwah, NJ: Erlbaum.

Kalter, N. (1990). *Growing up with divorce.* New York: Free Press.

Kamii, C. (1985). *Young children reinvent arithmetic: Implications of Piaget's theory.* New York: Teachers College Press.

Kamii, C. (1989). *Young children continue to reinvent arithmetic.* New York: Teachers College Press.

Kamin, C. S., O'Sullivan, P. S., Younger, M., & Deterding, R. (2001). Measuring critical thinking in problem-based learning discourse. *Teaching and Learning in Medicine, 13,* 27–35.

Kamphaus, R. W. (2000). Learning disabilities. In A. Kazdin (Ed.), *Encyclopedia of psychology.* Washington, DC, & New York: American Psychological Association and Oxford University Press.

Kane, M.J., Hambrick, D.Z., Tuholski, S.W., Wilhelm, O., Payne, T.W., & Engle, R.W. (2004). The generality of working memory capacity: A latent-variable approach to verbal and visuospatial memory span and reasoning. *Journal of Experimental Psychology: General, 133,* 189-217.

Kasprow, W. J., & others. (1993). *New Haven Schools Social Development Project: 1992.* New Haven, CT: New Haven Public Schools.

Katz, L. (1999). Curriculum disputes in early childhood education. *ERIC Clearinghouse on Elementary and Early Childhood Education.* Document EDO-PS-99-13. National Association for the Education of Young Children. (2002). *Early learning standards: Creating the conditions for success.* Washington, DC:

Katz, L., & Chard, S. (1989). *Engaging the minds of young children: The project approach.* Norwood, NJ: Ablex.

Kauffman, J.M., & Hallahan, D.P. (2005). *Special education.* Boston: Allyn & Bacon.

Kauffman, J.M., McGee, K,. & Brigham, M. (2004). Enabling or disabling? Observations on changes in special education. *Phi Delta Kappan, 85,* 613–620.

Kauffman, J. M., Mostert, M. P., Trent, S. C., & Hallahan, D. P. (2002). *Managing classroom behavior: A reflective, case-based approach* (3rd ed.). Boston: Allyn & Bacon.

Kaufman, A. S., & Lictenberger, E. O. (2002). *Assessing adolescent and adult intelligence* (2nd ed.). Boston: Allyn & Bacon.

Kaufman, P. (2001). Dropping out of school: Detours in the life course. In T. Urdan & F. Pajares (Eds.), *Adolescence and education.* Greenwich, CT: IAP.

Kazdin, A. E. (2001). *Behavior modification in applied settings* (6th ed.). Belmont, CA: Wadsworth.

Kearney, B. A. (1991, April). *The teacher as absent presence.* Paper presented at the meeting of the American Educational Research Association, Chicago.

Keating, D.P. (2004). Cognitive and brain development. In R. Lerner & L. Steinberg (Ed.), *Handbook of adolescent psychology.* New York: Wiley.

Keil, F. (1999). Cognition. In M. Bennett (Ed.), *Developmental psychology.* Philadelphia: Psychology Press.

Kellogg, R. T. (1994). *The psychology of writing.* New York: Oxford University Press.

Kellogg, R. T. (2000). Writing. In A. Kazdin (Ed.), *Encyclopedia of psychology.* Washington, DC, & New York: American Psychological Association and Oxford University Press.

Kennedy, C. H., Long, T., Kristine, J., Cox, Tang, J., & Thompson, T. (2001). Facilitating general education participation for students with behavior problems by linking positive behavior supports and person-centered planning. *Journal of Emotional and Behavioral Disorders, 9,* 146–160.

Keogh, B. K., & Macmillan, D. L. (1996). Exceptionality. In D. Berliner & R. Calfee (Eds.), *Handbook of educational psychology.* New York: Macmillan.

Kiess, H. O. (2002). *Statistical concepts for the behavioral sciences* (3rd ed.). Boston: Allyn & Bacon.

Kiewra, K. A. (1989). A review of note-taking: The encoding-storage paradigm and beyond. *Educational Psychology Review, 1*, 147–172.

Kimmel, A. (1996). *Ethical issues in behavioral research.* Cambridge, MA: Blackwell.

Kinchin, I. M., Hay, D. B., & Adams, A. (2000). How a qualitative approach to concept map analysis can be used to aid learning by illustrating patterns of conceptual development. *Educational Research, 42* (1), 43–57.

Kinderman, T. A., McCollam, T. L., & Gibson, E. (1996). Peer networks and students' classroom engagement during childhood and adolescence. In J. Juvonen & K. R. Wentzel (Eds.), *Social motivation.* New York: Cambridge University Press.

King, A. (2000). Situated cognition. In A. Kazdin (Ed.), *Encyclopedia of psychology.* Washington, DC, & New York: American Psychological Association and Oxford University Press.

Kirby, D. (1992). School-based programs to reduce sexual risk-taking behaviors. *Journal of School Health, 62*, 280–287.

Kite, M. (2001). Gender stereotypes. In J. Worrell (Ed.), *Encyclopedia of women and gender.* San Diego: Academic Press.

Kivel, P. (1995). *Uprooting racism: How White people can work for racial justice.* Philadelphia: New Society.

Klausmeier, H.J. (2004). Conceptual learning and development. In W.E. Craighead & C.B. Nemeroff (Eds.), *The concise Corsini encyclopedia of psychology and behavioral sciences.* New York: Wiley

Klein, K., & Boals, A. (2001). Expressive writing can increase working memory capacity. *Journal of Experimental Psychology: General, 130*, 520–533.

Kling, K. C., Hyde, J. S., Showers, C. J., & Buswell, B. N. (1999). Gender differences in self-esteem: A meta-analysis. *Psychological Bulletin, 125*, 470–500.

Knecht, S., Draeger, B., Floeel, A., Lohmann, H., Breitenstein, C., Henningson, H., & Ringelstein, E. (2001). Behavioral relevance of atypical language lateralization in healthy subjects. *Brain, 124*, 1657–1665.

Kohlberg, L. (1966). A cognitive-developmental analysis of children's sex-role concepts and attitudes. In E. E. Maccoby (Ed.), *The development of sex differences.* Palo Alto, CA: Stanford University Press.

Kohlberg, L. (1976). Moral stages and moralization: The cognitive-developmental approach. In T. Lickona (Ed.), *Moral development and behavior.* New York: Holt, Rinehart & Winston.

Kohlberg, L. (1986). A current statement of some theoretical issues. In S. Modgil & C. Modgil (Eds.), *Lawrence Kohlberg.* Philadelphia: Falmer.

Kohn, A. (1996). By all available means: Cameron and Pierce's defense of extrinsic motivators. *Review of Educational Research, 66*, 5–32.

Koke, L.C., & Vernon, P.A. (2004). The Sternberg Triarchic Abilities Test (STAT) as a measure of academic achievement and general intelligence. *Personality and Individual Differences, 35*, 1803-1807.

Koppelman, K., & Goodhart, L. (2005). *Understanding human differences.* Boston: Allyn & Bacon.

Kornhaber, M., Fierros, E., & Veenema, S. (2004*). Multiple intelligences.* Boston: Allyn & Bacon.

Kotlowitz, A. (1991). *There are no children here.* New York: Anchor Books.

Kounin, J. S. (1970). *Discipline and management in classrooms.* New York: Holt, Rinehart & Winston.

Kowalski, R. M. (2000). Anxiety. In A. Kazdin (Ed.), *Encyclopedia of psychology.* Washington, DC, & New York: American Psychological Association and Oxford University Press.

Kozol, J. (1991). *Savage inequalities.* New York: Crown.

Krantz, P. J., & Risley, T. R. (1972, September). *The organization of group care environments: Behavioral ecology in the classroom.* Paper presented at the meeting of the American Psychological Association, Honolulu.

Krathwohl, D. R., Bloom, B. S., & Masia, B. B. (1964). *Taxonomy of educational objectives. Handbook II: Affective domain.* New York: David McKay.

Kretuzer, L. C., & Flavell, J. H. (1975). An interview study of children's knowledge about memory. *Monographs of the Society for Research in Child Development, 40* (1, Serial No. 159).

Krueger, R. (2000). Validity. In A. Kazdin (Ed.), *Encyclopedia of psychology.*

Washington, DC, & New York: American Psychological Association and Oxford University Press.

Kubiszyn, T., & Borich, G. D. (2000). *Educational testing and measurement* (6th ed.). New York: John Wiley.

Kuhn, D. (1999a). A developmental model of critical thinking. *Educational Researcher, 28*, 16–25.

Kuhn, D. (1999b). Metacognitive development. In L. Balter & S. Tamis-Lemonda (Eds.), *Child psychology: A handbook of contemporary issues.* Philadelphia: Psychology Press.

Kuhn, D. (2004). What is scientific thinking, and how does it develop? In U. Goswami (Ed.), *Blackwell handbook of childhood cognitive development.* Malden, MA: Blackwell.

Kuhn, D., Amsel, E., & O'Laughlin, M. (1988). *The development of scientific thinking skills.* Orlando, FL: Academic Press.

Kuhn, D., Garcia-Mila, M., Zohar, Z., & Anderson, C. (1995). Strategies for knowledge acquisition. *Monographs of the Society for Research in Child Development, 60* (4, Serial No. 245), 1–127.

Kuhn, D., Schauble, L., & Garcia-Mila, M. (1992). Cross-domain development of scientific reasoning. *Cognition and Instruction, 9*, 285–327.

Kulik, C. L., Kulik, J. A., & Bangert-Drowns, R. L. (1990). Effectiveness of mastery learning programs: A meta-analysis. *Review of Educational Research, 60*, 265–299.

Kulik, J. A. (1992). An analysis of the research on ability grouping. *Monograph of the National Research Center on the Gifted and Talented* (No. 9204). Storrs: University of Connecticut.

Kupersmidt, J. B., & Coie, J. D. (1990). Preadolescent peer status, aggression, and school adjustment as predictors of externalizing problems in adolescence. *Child Development, 61*, 1350–1363.

L

Labov, W. (1973). The boundaries of words and their meanings. In C. N. Bailey & R. W. Shuy (Eds.), *New ways of analyzing variations in English.* Washington, DC: Georgetown University Press.

Lacey, P. (2001). The role of learning support assistants in inclusive learning of pupils with severe and profound learning difficulties. *Educational Review, 53,* 157–167.

Lachlan, R.F., & Feldman, M.W. (2003). Evolution of cultural communication systems. *Journal of Evolutionary Biology, 16,* 1084-1095.

Ladd, G., Buhs, E., & Troop, W. (2004). School adjustment and social skill training. In P.K. Smith & C.H. Hart (Eds.), *Blackwell handbook of childhood social development.* Malden, MA: Blackwell.

Ladd, G.W., & Kochenderfer-Ladd, B. (2002). Identifying victims of peer aggression from early to middle childhood: Analysis of cross-informant data for concordance, incidence of victimization, characteristics of identified victims, and estimation of relational adjustment. *Psychological Assessment, 14,* 74–96.

Lammers, W.J., & Badia, P. (2005). *Fundamentals of behavioral research.* Belmont, CA: Wadsworth.

Lamon, M., Secules, T., Petrosino, A. J., Hackett, R., Bransford, J. D., & Goldman, S. R. (1996). Schools for thought. In L. Schauble & R. Glaser (Eds.), *Innovations in learning.* Mahwah, NJ: Erlbaum.

Landa, S. (2000, Fall). If you can't make waves, make ripples. *Intelligence Connections Newsletter of the ASCD, X (No. 1),* 6–8.

Lane, K. L., Greshman, F. M., & O'Shaughnessy, T. E. (2002). *Interventions for children with or at-risk for emotional and behavioral disorders.* Boston: Allyn & Bacon.

Lankes, A. M. D. (1995). *Electronic portfolios: A new idea in assessment.* ERIC Document Reproduction Service No. ED390377.

Lareau, A. (1996). Assessing parent involvement in schooling: A critical analysis. In K. L. Alexander & D. R. Entwisle (Eds.), *Schools and children at risk.* Mahwah, NJ: Erlbaum.

Larrivee, B. (2005). *Authentic classroom management* (2nd ed.). Boston: Allyn & Bacon.

Lazar, L., & others. (1982). Lasting effects of early education. *Monographs of the Society for Research in Child Development, 47.*

Leary, M.R. (2004). *Introduction to behavioral research methods* (4th ed.). Boston: Allyn & Bacon.

LeDoux, J. E. (1996). *The emotional brain.* New York: Simon & Schuster.

LeDoux, J. E. (2002). *The synaptic self.* New York: Viking.

Lee, C. D., & Slaughter-Defoe, D. (1995). Historical and sociocultural influences of African American education. In J. A. Banks, & C. M. Banks (Eds.), *Handbook of research on multicultural education.* New York: Macmillan.

Lee, D. L., & Belfiore, P. J. (1997). Enhancing classroom performance: A review of reinforcement schedules. *Journal of Behavioral Education, 7,* 205–217.

Lee, J.S. (2005). Embracing diversity through the understanding of pragmatics. In K.E. Denham & A. Lobeck (Eds.), *Language in the schools.* Mahwah, NJ: Erlbaum.

Lee, L. C. (1992, August). *In search of universals: What ever happened to race?* Paper presented at the meeting of the American Psychological Association, Washington, DC.

Lee, V. E., & Burkham, D. T. (2001). *Dropping out of high school.* Paper presented at the conference "Dropouts in America: How severe is the problem?" Cambridge, MA: Harvard Graduate School of Education.

Lee, V. E., Croninger, R. G., Linn, E., & Chen, X. (1995, March). *The culture of sexual harassment in secondary schools.* Paper presented at the meeting of the Society for Research in Child Development, Indianapolis.

Lehr, C.A., Hanson, A., Sinclair, M.F., & Christensen, S.L. (2003). Moving beyond dropout prevention towards school completion. *School Psychology Review, 32,* 342–364.

Lehrer, R., Schauble, L., & Petrosino, A. (2001). Reconsidering the role of the experiment in science. In K. Crowley, C. Schunn, & T. Okada (Eds.), *Designing for science.* Mahwah, NJ: Erlbaum.

Lepper, M., Greene, D., & Nisbett, R. (1973). Undermining children's intrinsic interest with intrinsic rewards: A test of the overjustification hypothesis. *Journal of Personality and Social Psychology, 28,* 129–137.

Lerner, J. (2000). *Learning disabilities* (8th ed.). Boston: Houghton Mifflin.

Lesser, G. (1972). Learning, teaching, and television production for children: The experience of *Sesame Street. Harvard Educational Review, 42,* 232–272.

Lesser, G. (1989, November 15). *Television and reading: Can they still be friends?* Paper presented at the Library of Congress, Washington, DC.

Leventhal, T., & Brooks-Gunn, J. (2004). Diversity in developmental trajectories across adolescence: Neighborhood influences. In R. Lerner & L. Steinberg (Eds.), *Handbook of adolescent psychology.* (2nd Ed.). New York: Wiley.

Lever-Duffy, J., McDonald, J.B., & Mizell, A.P. (2005). *Teaching and learning with technology* (2nd ed.). Boston: McGraw-Hill.

Levesque, J., & Prosser, T. (1996). Service learning connections. *Journal of Teacher Education, 47,* 325–334.

Levin, J. (1980). *The mnemonics '80s: Keywords in the classroom.* Theoretical paper No. 86. Wisconsin Research and Development Center for Individualized Schooling, Madison.

Levy, C. M., & Randsell, S. (Eds.). (1996). *The science of writing.* Mahwah, NJ: Erlbaum.

Lewis, R. (2001). Classroom discipline and student responsibility: The students' view. *Teaching and Teacher Education, 17,* 307–319.

Lewis, V. (2002). *Development and disability* (2nd ed.). Malden, MA: Blackwell.

Leyendecker, R.L., Harwood, R.L., Comparini, L., & Yalcinkaya, A. (2005). Socioeconomic status, ethnicity, and parenting. In T. Luster & L. Okaghi (Eds.), *Parenting: An ecological perspective* (2nd Ed.). Mahwah, NJ: Erlbaum.

Limber, S. P. (1997). Preventing violence among school children. *Family Futures, 1,* 27–28.

Limber, S.P. (2004). Implementation of the Olweus Bullying Prevention Program in American schools: Lessons learned from the field. In D.L. Espelage & S.M. Swearer (Eds.), *Bullying in American schools.* Mahwah, NJ: Erlbaum.

Linden, K. W. (1996). *Cooperative learning and problem solving.* Prospect Heights, IL: Waveland Press.

Linn, M. C., & Hyde, J. S. (1989). Gender, mathematics, and science. *Educational Researcher, 18,* 17–27.

Linn, M. C., Songer, N. B., & Eylon, B. (1996). Shifts and convergences in science learning and instruction. In D. C. Berliner & R. C. Calfee (Eds.), *Handbook of educational psychology.* New York: Macmillan.

Linn, R. L. (2000). Assessments and accountability. *Educational Research, 29,* 4–15.

Linn, R. L., & Gronlund, N. E. (2000). *Measurement and assessment in teaching* (8th ed.). Upper Saddle River, NJ: Prentice Hall.

Lippa, R. A. (2002). *Gender, nature, and nurture.* Mahwah, NJ: Erlbaum.

Lippa, R.A. (2005). *Gender, nature, and nurture* (2nd Ed.). Mahwah, NJ: Erlbaum.

Lipsitz, J. (1984). *Successful schools for young adolescents.* New Brunswick, NJ: Transaction Books.

Litton, E. F. (1999). Learning in America: The Filipino-American sociocultural perspective. In C. Park & M. M. Chi (Eds.), *Asian-American education: Prospects and challenges.* Westport, CT: Bergin & Garvey.

Lockard, J., & Abrams, P. (2004). *Computers for twenty-first-century educators* (6th ed.). Boston: Allyn & Bacon.

Logan, J. (1997). *Teaching stories.* New York: Kodansha International.

LoLordo, V. M. (2000). Classical conditioning. In A. Kazdin (Ed.), *Encyclopedia of psychology.* Washington, DC, & New York: American Psychological Association and Oxford University Press.

Lonner, W. J. (1990). An overview of cross-cultural testing and assessment. In R. W. Brislin (Ed.), *Applied cross-cultural psychology.* Newbury Park, CA: Sage.

Lopes, R., Cote, S., & Salovey, P. (2005). Emotional intelligence at work. In V.U. Druskat, F. Dala, & G.J. Mount (Eds.), *Linking emotional intelligence and performance at work.* Mahwah, NJ: Erlbaum.

Lott, B., & Maluso, D. (2001). Gender development: Social learning. In J. Worrell (Ed.), *Encyclopedia of women and gender.* San Diego: Academic Press.

Louie, T. A., Curren, M. T., & Harich, K. R. (2000). "I knew we would win": Hindsight bias for favorable and unfavorable team decision outcomes. *Journal of Applied Psychology, 85,* 264–272.

Louv, R. (1990). *Childhood's future.* Boston: Houghton Mifflin.

Lovett, S. B., & Pillow, B. H. (1996). Development of the ability to distinguish between comprehension and memory: Evidence from goal-state evaluation tasks. *Journal of Educational Psychology, 88,* 546–562.

Lubinski, D. (2000). Measures of intelligence: Intelligence tests. In A. Kazdin (Ed.), *Encyclopedia of psychology.* Washington, DC, & New York: American Psychological Association and Oxford University Press.

Luria, A., & Herzog, E. (1985, April). *Gender segregation across and within settings.* Paper presented at the biennial meeting of the Society for Research in Child Development, Toronto.

Luster, T., & Okaghi, L. (Eds.) (2005). *Parenting: An ecological perspective* (2nd Ed.). Mahwah, NJ: Erlbaum.

Lyon, G. R. (1996). Learning disabilities. *Future of Children, 6* (1), 54–76.

Lyon, G. R., & Moats, L. C. (1997). Critical conceptual and methodological considerations in reading intervention research. *Journal of Learning Disabilities, 30,* 578–588.

Lyon, T. D., & Flavell, J. H. (1993). Young children's understanding of forgetting over time. *Child Development, 64,* 789–800.

Lyons, N. (1999, May). How portfolios can shape emerging practice. *Educational Leadership, 56,* 63–67.

M

Ma, X. (2002). Bullying in middle school : Individual and school characteristics of victims and offenders. *School Effectiveness and School Improvement, 13,* 63–89.

Maag, J. W. (2001). Rewarded by punishment: Reflections on the disuse of positive reinforcement in schools. *Exceptional Children, 67,* 173–186.

Mabry, L. (1999, May). Writing to the rubric: Lingering effects of traditional standardized testing on direct writing assessment. *Phi Delta Kappan, 80,* 673–679.

Maccoby, E. E. (1995). The two sexes and their social systems. In P. Moen, G. H. Elder, & K. Luscher (Eds.), *Examining lives in context.* Washington, DC: American Psychological Association.

Maccoby, E. E. (1998). *The two sexes: Growing up apart, coming together.* Cambridge, MA: Harvard University Press.

Maccoby, E. E. (2002). Gender and group process: A developmental perspective. *Current Directions in Psychological Science, 11,* 54–58.

Maccoby, E. E., & Jacklin, C. N. (1974). *The psychology of sex differences.* Palo Alto, CA: Stanford University Press.

MacLean, W. E. (2000). Down syndrome. In A. Kazdin (Ed.), *Encyclopedia of psychology.* Washington, DC, & New York: American Psychological Association and Oxford University Press.

Maddux, C. D., Johnson, D. L., & Willis, J. W. (1997). *Educational computing* (2nd ed.). Boston: Allyn & Bacon.

Maddux, J. (2002). The power of believing you can. In C. R. Snyder & S. J. Lopez (Eds.), *Handbook of positive psychology.* New York: Oxford University Press.

Maehr, M. L. (2001). Goal theory is *not* dead—Not yet, anyway: A reflection on the special issue. *Educational Psychology Review, 13,* 177–188.

Mager, R. (1962). *Preparing instructional objectives* (2nd ed.). Palo Alto, CA: Fearon.

Maggio, R. (1987). *The non-sexist word finder: A dictionary of gender-free usage.* Phoenix: Oryx Press.

Magnuson, K. A., & Duncan, G. J. (2002). Parents in poverty. In M. H. Bornstein (Ed.), *Handbook of parenting* (2nd ed.). Mahwah, NJ: Erlbaum.

Magnusson, D. (1988). *Individual development from an interactional perspective: A longitudinal study.* Hillsdale, NJ: Erlbaum.

Magolda, M.B.B. (2004). Evolution of constructivist conceptualization of epistemological reflection. *Educational Pyschologist, 39,* 31–42

Maidon, C. H., & Wheatley, J. H. (2001, July). *Outcomes for students using a model science curriculum.* Paper presented at the meeting of the National Association of Research in Science Teaching, St. Louis.

Major, B., Barr, L., Zubek, J., & Babey, S. H. (1999). Gender and self-esteem: A meta-analysis. In W. Swann & J. Langlois (Eds.), *Sexism and stereotypes in modern society: The gender science of Janet Taylor Spence.* Washington, DC: American Psychological Association.

Maki, P. L. (2001). From standardized tests to alternative methods. *Change, 33* (2), 28–31.

Male, M. (2003). *Technology for inclusion* (4th ed.). Boston: Allyn & Bacon.

Malik, N. M., & Furman, W. (1993). Practitioner review: Problems in children's peer relations: What can the clinician do? *Journal of Child Psychology and Psychiatry, 34,* 1303–1326.

Mandler, G. (1980). Recognizing: The judgment of previous occurrence. *Psychological Review, 87,* 252–271.

Mangels, J. A., Piction, T. W., & Craik, F. I. (2001). Attention and successful episodic encoding: An event-related potential study. *Brain Research, 11,* 77–95.

Manning, C.F., Mohole, K., & the Goodman Research Group. (2002). *The Lesson One program results of a controlled pre and post study.* Unpublished manuscript, Lesson One Foundation, Boston, MA.

Marcia, J. E. (1980). Identity in adolescence. In J. Adelson (Ed.), *Handbook of adolescent psychology.* New York: Wiley.

Marcia, J. E. (1998). Optimal development from an Eriksonian perspective. In H. S. Friedman (Ed.), *Encyclopedia of mental health* (Vol. 2). San Diego: Academic Press.

Marklein, M. B. (1998, November 24). An eye-level meeting of the minds. *USA Today,* p. 9D.

Markman, A., & Gentner, D. (2001). Learning and reasoning. *Annual Review of Psychology* (Vol. 51). Palo Alto, CA: Annual Reviews.

Marshall, H. H. (1996). Implications of differentiating and understanding constructivist approaches. *Educational Psychologist, 31,* 243–240.

Martella, R. C., Nelson, J. R., & Marchand-Martella, N. E. (2003). *Managing disruptive behaviors in the schools.* Boston: Allyn & Bacon.

Martin, C. L., & Dinella, L. (2001). Gender development: Gender schema theory. In J. Worrell (Ed.), *Encyclopedia of women and gender.* San Diego: Academic Press.

Martin, E. W., Martin, R., & Terman, D. L. (1996). The legislative and litigation history of special education. *Future of Children, 6* (1), 25–53.

Martin, G., & Pear, J. (2002). *Behavior modification* (7th ed.). Upper Saddle River, NJ: Prentice Hall.

Martin, R., Sexton, C., & Gerlovich, J. (1999). *Science for all children: Lessons for constructing understanding.* Boston: Allyn & Bacon.

Martin, R., Sexton, C., Franklin, T., & Gerlovich, J. (2005). *Teaching science for all children* (5th ed.). Boston: Allyn & Bacon.

Martinez, E., & Halgunseth, L. (2004). Hispanics/Latinos. In M. Coleman & L. Ganong (Eds.), *Handbook of contemporary families.* Thousand Oaks, CA: Sage.

Marton, F., Hounsell, D. J., & Entwistle, N. J. (1984). *The experience of learning.* Edinburgh: Scottish Academic Press.

Martorella, P. (2001). *Teaching social studies in middle and secondary schools* (3rd ed.). Upper Saddle River, NJ: Merrill.

Martorella, P., & Beal, C. (2002). *Social studies for elementary school classrooms* (3rd ed.). Upper Saddle River, NJ: Merrill.

Maslow, A. H. (1954). *Motivation and personality.* New York: Harper & Row.

Maslow, A. H. (1971). *The farther reaches of human nature.* New York: Viking Press.

Mather, N., & Gregg, N. (2001). Assessment and the Woodcock-Johnson III. In J. J. W. Andrews, D. H. Saklofske, & H. L. Janzen (Eds.), *Handbook of psychoeducational assessment.* San Diego: Academic Press.

Mathes, P. G., Howard, J. K., Allen, S. H., & Fuchs, D. (1998). Peer-assisted learning strategies for first-grade readers: Responding to the needs of diverse learners. *Reading Research Quarterly, 33,* 62–94.

Mathes, P. G., Torgesen, J. K., & Allor, J. H. (2001). The effects of peer-assisted literacy strategies for first-grade readers with and without additional computer-assisted instruction in phonological awareness. *American Educational Research Journal, 38,* 371–410.

Matlin, M. (2002). *Cognition* (5th ed.). New York: Wiley.

Matsumoto, D. (Ed.). (2001). *The handbook of culture and psychology.* New York: Oxford University Press.

Matsumoto, D. (2004). *Culture and psychology* (3rd Ed.). Belmont, CA: Wadsworth.

Matusov, E., Bell, N., & Rogoff, B. (2001). *Schooling as a cultural process: Working together and guidance by children from schools differing in collaborative practices.* Unpublished manuscript, Department of

Psychology, University of California at Santa Cruz.

May, M. (2001, November 21). San Leandro kids lap up their lessons. *San Francisco Chronicle,* pp. A1, 24.

Mayer, R. E. (1997). Multimedia learning: Are we asking the right questions? *Educational Psychologist, 32,* 1–19.

Mayer, R. E. (1999). *The promise of educational psychology.* Upper Saddle River, NJ: Prentice Hall.

Mayer, R. E. (2000). Problem solving. In M. A. Runco & S. Pritzker (Eds.), *Encyclopedia of psychology.* San Diego: Academic Press.

Mayer, R. E. (2001). *Multimedia learning.* Boston: Allyn & Bacon.

Mayer, R. E. (2002). *The promise of educational psychology: Teaching for meaningful learning* (Vol. 2). Upper Saddle River, NJ: Prentice Hall.

Mayer, R.E. (2004). Teaching of subject matter. *Annual Review of Psychology, 55.* Palo Alto, CA: Annual Review.

Mayer, R. E., & Wittrock, M. C. (1996). Problem-solving transfer. In D. C. Berliner & R. C. Calfee (Eds.), *Handbook of educational psychology.* New York: Macmillan.

Mazur, J. E. (2002). *Learning and behavior* (5th ed.). Upper Saddle River, NJ: Prentice Hall.

Mazurek, K., Winzer, M. A., & Majorek, C. (2000). *Education in a global society.* Boston: Allyn & Bacon.

McAdoo, H. P. (2002). African-American parenting. In M. H. Bornstein (Ed.). *Handbook of parenting* (2nd ed.). Mahwah, NJ: Erlbaum.

McCarthey, S. (1994). Opportunities and risks of writing from personal experience. *Language Arts, 71,* 182–191.

McCarty, F., Abbott-Shim, M., & Lambert, R. (2001). The relationship between teacher beliefs and practices and Head Start classroom quality. *Early Education & Development, 12,* 225–238.

McCombs, B. L. (2001, April). *What do we know about learners and learning? The learner-centered framework.* Paper presented at the meeting of the American Educational Research Association, Seattle.

McCombs, B. L., & Quiat, M. A. (2001). *Development and validation of norms and rubrics for the Grades K–5 assessment of learner-centered principles (ALCP) surveys.*

Unpublished manuscript, University of Denver Research Institute, Denver.

McCormick, C. B., & Pressley, M. (1997). *Educational psychology.* New York: Longman.

McDonald, B. A., Larson, C. D., Dansereau, D. I., & Spurlin, J. E. (1985). Cooperative dyads: Impact on text learning and transfer. *Contemporary Educational Psychology, 10,* 369–377.

McDonnell, J. M., Mathot-Buckner, C., Thorson, N., & Fiter, S. (2001). Supporting the inclusion of students with moderate and severe learning disabilities in junior high general education classes. *Education and Treatment of Children, 24,* 141–160.

McGregor, K.K. (2004). Developmental dependencies between lexical semantics and reading. In C.A. Stone, E.R. Silliman, B.J. Ehren, & K. Apel (Eds.), *Handbook of language and literacy.* New York: Guilford.

McKelvie, S. J., & Drumheller, A. (2001). The availability heuristic with famous names: A replication. *Perceptual and Motor Skills, 92,* 507–516.

McKinley, D. W., Boulet, J. R., & Hambleton, R. K. (2000, August). *Standard-setting for performance-based assessment.* Paper presented at the meeting of the American Educational Research Association, New Orleans.

McLoyd, V. C. (1998). Children in poverty: Development, public policy, and practice. In W. Damon (Ed.), *Handbook of child psychology* (5th ed., Vol. 4). New York: Wiley.

McLoyd, V. C. (2000). Poverty. In A. Kazdin (Ed.), *Encyclopedia of psychology.* Washington, DC, & New York: American Psychological Association and Oxford University Press.

McLoyd, V.C. (2005). Pathways to academic achievement among children from immigrant families: a commentary. In C.R. Cooper, C.T.G. Coll, W.T. Bartko, H.M. Davis, & C. Chatman, (Eds.), *Developmental pathways through middle childhood.* Mahwah, NJ: Erlbaum.

McLoyd, V. C., & Smith, J. (2002). Physical discipline and behavior problems in African American, European American, and Hispanic children: Emotional support as a moderator. *Journal of Marriage and the Family, 64,* 40–53.

McMahon, S. I. (1994). Student-led book clubs: Traversing a river of interpretation. *New Advocate, 7,* 109–125.

McMahon, S. I., Raphael, T. E., & Goatley, V. J. (1995). Changing the context for classroom reading instruction: The Book Club project. In J. Brophy (Ed.), *Advances in research on teaching.* Greenwich, CT: JAI Press.

McMillan, J. H. (1997). *Classroom assessment.* Boston: Allyn & Bacon.

McMillan, J. H. (2000). *Educational research* (3rd ed.). Upper Saddle River, NJ: Merrill.

McMillan, J. H. (2002). *Essential assessment concepts for teachers and administrators.* Thousand Oaks, CA: Corwin Press.

McMillan, J.H. (2004). *Educational research* (4th ed.). Boston: Allyn & Bacon.

McMillan, J. H., & Wergin, J. F. (2002). *Understanding and evaluating educational research* (2nd ed.). Upper Saddle River, NJ: Prentice Hall.

McNally, D. (1990). *Even eagles need a push.* New York: Dell.

McNeil, D. (2000). Systematic desensitization. In A. Kazdin (Ed.), *Encyclopedia of psychology.* Washington, DC, & New York: American Psychological Association and Oxford University Press.

Medin, D. L. (2000). Concepts: An overview. In A. Kazdin (Ed.), *Encyclopedia of psychology.* Washington, DC, & New York: American Psychological Association and Oxford University Press.

Meece, J. L., & Kurtz-Costes, B. (2001). Introduction: The schooling of ethnic minority children. *Educational Psychologist, 36,* 57–66.

Meichenbaum, D. (1993). Cognitive behavior modification. In F. H. Kanfer & A. P. Goldstein (Eds.), *Helping people change: A handbook of methods.* New York: Pergamon.

Meichenbaum, D., & Butler, L. (1980). Toward a conceptual model of the treatment of test anxiety: Implications for research and treatment. In I. G. Sarason (Ed.), *Test anxiety.* Mahwah, NJ: Erlbaum.

Meichenbaum, D., Turk, D., & Burstein, S. (1975). The nature of coping with stress. In I. Sarason & C. Spielberger (Eds.), *Stress and anxiety.* Washington, DC: Hemisphere.

Melby, L. C. (1995). *Teacher efficacy and classroom management: A study of teacher cognition, emotion, and strategy usage associated with externalizing student behavior.* Ph.D. dissertation, University of California at Los Angeles.

Meltzoff, A. (2004). Imitation as a mechanism of social cognition: Origins of empathy, theory of mind, and the representation of action. In U. Goswami (Ed.), *Blackwell handbook of childhood cognitive development.* Malden, MA: Blackwell.

Merrill, C. (2004). Action research and technology research. *Technology Teacher, 63,* 6–8.

Mertler, C.A., & Charles, C.M. (2005). *Introduction to educational research* (5th ed.). Boston: Allyn & Bacon.

Metzger, M. (1996, January). Maintaining a life. *Phi Delta Kappan, 77,* 346–351.

Meyer, R. J. (2002). *Phonics exposed.* Mahwah, NJ: Erlbaum.

Micallef, S., & Prior, M. (2004). Arithmetic learning difficulties in children. *Educational Psychology, 24,* 175–200.

Michael, W. (1999). Guilford's view. In M. A. Runco & S. Pritzker (Eds.), *Encyclopedia of creativity.* San Diego: Academic Press.

Michaels, S. (1986). Narrative presentations: An oral preparation for literacy with first graders. In J. Cook-Gumperz (Ed.), *The social construction of literacy.* New York: Cambridge University Press.

Middleton, J., & Goepfert, P. (1996). *Inventive strategies for teaching mathematics.* Washington, DC: American Psychological Association.

Midgley, C. (2001). A goal theory perspective on the current status of middle level schools. In T. Urdan & F. Pajares (Eds.), *Is adolescence here to stay?* Greenwich, CT: IAP.

Midgley, C., Anderman, E., & Hicks, L. (1995). Differences between elementary school and middle school teachers and students: A goal theory approach. *Journal of Early Adolescence, 15,* 90–113.

Miholic, V. (1994). An inventory to pique students' metacognitive awareness of reading strategies. *Journal of Reading, 38,* 84–86.

Miller, G. A. (1956). The magical number seven, plus or minus two: Some limits on our capacity for information processing. *Psychological Review, 48,* 337–442.

Miller, J. W. (2001). *Using educational technologies to promote vocabulary* *development among heterogeneously-grouped fifth graders.* Unpublished manuscript, Harvard University, Boston.

Miller, K. F. (2000). Representational tools and conceptual change: The young scientist's tool kit. *Journal of Applied Developmental Psychology, 21,* 21–25.

Miller, N., & Harrington, H. J. (1990). A situational identity perspective on cultural diversity and teamwork in the classroom. In S. Sharan (Ed.), *Cooperative learning: Theory and research.* New York: Praeger.

Miller, P.H. (2000). How best to utilize a deficiency: A commentary on Water's "Memory strategy development." *Child Development, 71,* 1013-1017.

Miller-Jones, D. (1989). Culture and testing. *American Psychologist, 44,* 360–366.

Minaya-Rowe, L. (Ed.). (2002). *Teacher training and effective pedagogy in the context of cultural diversity.* Greenwich, CT: IAP.

Mintzes, J. J., Wandersee, J. H., & Novak, J. D. (2001). Assessing understanding in biology. *Journal of Biological Education, 35,* 118–124.

Minuchin, P. P., & Shapiro, E. K. (1983). The school as a context for social development. In P. H. Mussen (Ed.), *Handbook of child psychology* (4th ed., Vol. 4). New York: Wiley.

Mistry, J., & Rogoff, B. (1994). Remembering in the cultural context. In W. J. Lonner & R. Milpass (Eds.), *Psychology and culture.* Boston: Allyn & Bacon.

Miyake, A. (2001, September). Commentary in S. Carpenter. A new reason for keeping a diary. *Monitor on Psychology, 32,* 68–70.

Moely, B. E., Santulli, K. A., & Obach, M. S. (1995). Strategy instruction, metacognition, and motivation in the elementary school classroom. In E. E. Weinert & W. Schneider (Eds.), *Memory performance and competencies.* Mahwah, NJ: Erlbaum.

Molfese, V. J., & Martin, T. B. (2001). Intelligence and achievement: Measurement and prediction of developmental variations. In D. L. Molfese & V. J. Molfese (Eds.), *Developmental variations in learning.* Mahwah, NJ: Erlbaum.

Moll, L., Tapia, J., & Whitmore, K. (1993). Living knowledge: The social distribution of cultural resources for thinking. In G.

Salomon (Ed.), *Distributed cognitions: Psychological and educational considerations.* Cambridge: Cambridge University Press.

Monteith, M. (2000). Prejudice. In A. Kazdin (Ed.), *Encyclopedia of psychology.* Washington, DC, & New York: American Psychological Association and Oxford University Press.

Montgomery, K. (2001). *Authentic assessment.* Boston: Allyn & Bacon.

Moon, T. R., & Callahan, C. M. (2001). Classroom performance assessment. *NASSP Bulletin, 85,* 48–58.

Moore, K. D. (1998). *Classroom teaching skills* (4th ed.). New York: McGraw-Hill.

Morgan, N., & Saxton, J. (1991). *Teaching, questioning, and learning.* New York: Routledge.

Morrison, F. J., & Cooney, R. R. (2002). Parenting and academic achievement: Multiple paths to early literacy. In J. G. Borkowski, S. L. Ramey, & M. Bristol-Power (Eds.), *Parenting and the child's world.* Mahwah, NJ: Erlbaum.

Moyer, J. R., & Dardig, J. C. (1978). Practical task analysis for teachers. *Teaching Exceptional Children, 11,* 16–18.

Mullis, I. V. S. (1999, April). *Using TIMSS to gain new perspectives about different school organizations and policies.* Paper presented at the meeting of the American Educational Research Association, Montreal.

Murdock, T. B. (1999). The social context of risk: Status and motivational predictors of alienation in middle school. *Journal of Educational Psychology, 91,* 62–75.

Murnane, R. J., & Levy, F. (1996). *Teaching the new basic skills.* New York: Free Press.

Murphy, K., & Schneider, B. (1994). Coaching socially rejected adolescents regarding behaviors used by peers to infer liking: A dyad-specific intervention, *Journal of Early Adolescence, 14,* 83–95.

Murphy, R. A., Baker, A. G., & Fouguet, N. (2001). Relative validity effects with either one or two more valid cues in Pavlovian and instrumental conditioning. *Journal of Experimental Psychology: Animal Processes, 27,* 59–67.

Murray, H. A. (1938). *Explorations in personality.* Cambridge, MA: Harvard University Press.

Murrell, A. J. (2000). Discrimination. In A. Kazdin (Ed.), *Encyclopedia of psychology.* Washington, DC, &

New York: American Psychological Association and Oxford University Press.

Myers, D., Baer, W., & Choi, S. (1996). The changing problem of overcrowded housing. *Journal of the American Planning Association, 62,* 66-84.

Myerson, J., Rank, M. R., Raines, F. Q., & Schnitzler, M. A. (1998). Race and general cognitive ability: The myth of diminishing returns in education. *Psychological Science, 9,* 139–142.

N

NAASP. (1997, May/June). Students say: What makes a good teacher? *Schools in the Middle,* pp. 15–17.

Nagy, W. (2005). Why vocabulary development needs to be long-term and comprehensive. In E.H. Hiebert & M.L. Kamil (Eds.), *Teaching and learning vocabulary.* Mahwah, NJ: Erlbaum.

Nairne, J. S. (2000). Forgetting. In A. Kazdin (Ed.), *Encyclopedia of psychology.* Washington, DC, & New York: American Psychological Association and Oxford University Press.

Nakamura, J., & Csikszentmihalyi, M. (2002). The concept of flow. In C. R. Snyder & S. J. Lopez (Eds.), *Handbook of positive psychology.* New York: Oxford University Press.

Nansel, T. R., Overpeck, M., Pilla, R. S., Ruan, W. J., Simons-Morton, B., & Scheidt, P. (2001). Bullying behaviors among U.S. youth: Prevalence and association with psychosocial adjustment. *Journal of the American Medical Association, 285,* 2094–2100.

Nash, J. M. (1997, February 3). Fertile minds. *Time,* pp. 50–54.

National Assessment of Educational Progress. (1998). *National report: 1998.* Washington, DC: National Center for Educational Statistics.

National Assessment of Educational Progress. (2000). *The nation's report card.* Washington, DC: National Center for Educational Statistics.

National Assessment of Educational Progress. (2001). *National report: 2001.* Washington, DC: National Center for Educational Statistics.

National Assessment of Educational Progress. (2004). *National report: 2004.*

Washington, DC: National Center for Educational Statistics.

National Association for the Education of Young Children. (1996). NAEYC position statement: Responding to linguistic and cultural diversity— Recommendations for effective early childhood education. *Young Children, 51,* 4–12.

National Center for Education Statistics. (1997). *School-family linkages.* Unpublished manuscript. Washington, DC: U.S. Department of Education.

National Center for Education Statistics. (2001). *Dropout rates in the United States: 2000.* Washington, DC: U.S. Department of Education.

National Center for Education Statistics (2002). *Digest of Education Statistics 2002.* Washington, DC: Author.

National Center for Education Statistics. (2003). *Computer and internet use by children and adolescents in 2001.* Washington, DC: Author.

National Center for Education Statistics. (2004). *The nation's report card.* Washington, DC: Author.

National Center for Health Statistics. (2002). *Schools and staffing survey, 1999-2000.* Washington, DC: Author.

National Commission on the High School Senior Year. (2001). *Youth at the crossroads: Facing high school and beyond.* Washington, DC: The Education Trust.

National Community Service Coalition. (1995). *Youth volunteerism.* Washington, DC: Author.

National Council for the Social Sciences. (2000). *National standards for social studies teachers.* Baltimore: Author.

National Council of Teachers of Mathematics. (2000). *Principles and standards for school mathematics.* Reston, VA: Author.

National Reading Panel. (2000). *Teaching children to read.* Washington, DC: National Institute of Child Health and Human Development.

National Research Council. (1999). *How people learn.* Washington, DC: National Academic Press.

National Research Council. (2001). *Knowing what students know.* Washington, DC: National Academic Press.

Neill, M. (2003). Leaving children behind. *Phi Delta Kappan, 84,* 225-228.

Neisser, U., Boodoo, G., Bouchard, T. J., Boykin, A. W., Brody, N., Ceci, S. J., Halpern, D. F., Loehlin, J. C., Perloff, R., Sternberg, R. J., & Urbina, S. (1996). Intelligence: Knowns and unknowns. *American Psychologist, 51,* 77–101.

Nelson, K. E., Aksu-Koc, A., & Johnson, C. E. (Eds.). (2001). *Children's language* (Vol. 10). Mahwah, NJ: Erlbaum.

Neugarten, B. L. (1988, August). *Policy issues for an aging society.* Paper presented at the meeting of the American Psychological Association, Atlanta.

Newby, T. J., Stepich, D. A., Lehman, J. D., & Russell, J. D. (2000). *Instructional technology and learning* (2nd ed.). Upper Saddle River, NJ: Prentice Hall.

Nicholls, J. G. (1979). Development of perception of own attainment and causal attribution for success and failure in reading. *Journal of Educational Psychology, 71,* 94–99.

Nicholls, J. G., Cobb, P., Wood, T., Yackel, E., & Pataschnick, M. (1990). Assessing students' theories of success in mathematics: Individual and classroom differences. *Journal for Research in Mathematics Education, 21,* 109–122.

Nichols, J. D., & Miller, R. B. (1994). Cooperative learning and student motivation. *Contemporary Educational Psychology, 19,* 167–178.

Nicoll, G. (2001). A three-tier system for assessing concept map links: A methodological study. *International Journal of Science Education 23* (8), 863–875.

Nieto, S. (1992). *Affirming diversity: The sociopolitical context of multicultural education.* White Plains, NY: Longman.

Nieto, S. (2004). *Affirming diversity* (4th Ed.). Boston: Allyn & Bacon.

Niguidula, D. (1997, November). Picturing performance with digital portfolios. *Educational Leadership,* pp. 26–29.

Nikola-Lisa, W., & Burnaford, G. E. (1994). A mosaic: Contemporary schoolchildren's images of teachers. In P. B. Joseph & G. E. Burnaford (Eds.), *Images of schoolteachers in twentieth century America.* New York: St. Martin's Press.

Nisbett, R. E., & Ross, L. (1980). *Human inference.* Upper Saddle River, NJ: Prentice Hall.

Nobel, P. A., & Shiffrin, R. M. (2001). Retrieval processes in recognition and cued recall. *Journal of Experimental Psychology: Learning, Memory, and Cognition, 27,* 384–413.

Noddings, N. (1998). *Teaching for continuous learning.* Paper presented at the meeting of the American Educational Research Association, San Diego.

Noddings, N. (2001). The care tradition: Beyond "add women and stir." *Theory into Practice, 40,* 29–34.

Nokelainen, P., & Flint, J. (2002). Genetic effects on human cognition: Lessons from the study of mental retardation syndromes. *Journal of Neurology, Neurosurgery, and Psychiatry, 43,* 287–296.

Nolen-Hoeksema, S. (2001). *Abnormal psychology* (2nd ed.). New York: McGraw-Hill.

Norcross, J. C., Santrock, J. W., Campbell, L. F., Smith, T. P., Sommer, R., & Zuckerman, E. L. (2000). *The authoritative guide to self-help resources in mental health.* New York: Guilford.

Nosich, G. M. (2001). *Learning to think things through.* Upper Saddle River, NJ: Prentice Hall.

Nucci, L. P. (2001). *Education in the moral domain.* New York: Cambridge University Press.

Nucci, L.P. (2004). The development of moral reasoning. In P. Smith & C. Hart (Eds.), *Blackwell handbook of cognitive development.* Malden, MA: Blackwell.

O

Oades, R. D. (2002). Dopamine may be "hyper" with respect to noradrenaline metabolism, but "hypo" with respect to serotonin metabolism in children with attention deficit hyperactivity disorder. *Behavior and Brain Research, 130,* 97–102.

Oakes, J. (1990). *Multiplying inequalities: The effects of race, social class, and tracking on opportunities to learn mathematics and science.* Santa Monica: The RAND Corporation.

Oates, J., & Grayson, A. (Eds.). (2004). *Cognitive and language development in children.* Malden, MA: Blackwell.

OBLEMA. (2000). *Survey of states limited English proficient students and available educational programs and services: 1997–1998.* Washington, DC: U.S. Department of Education.

O'Conner, S. C., & Rosenblood, L. K. (1996). Affiliation motivation in everyday experience: A theoretical comparison. *Journal of Personality and Social Psychology, 70,* 513–522.

O'Donnell, A. M., & Levin, J. R. (2001). Educational psychology's healthy growing pains. *Educational Psychologist, 36,* 73–82.

Ogbu, J. U. (1989, April). *Academic socialization of Black children: An inoculation against future failure?* Paper presented at the meeting of the Society for Research in Child Development, Kansas City.

Ogbu, J., & Stern, P. (2001). Caste status and intellectual development. In R. J. Sternberg & E. L. Grigorenko (Eds.), *Environmental effects on cognitive abilities.* Mahwah, NJ: Erlbaum.

Okagaki, L. (2000). Determinants of intelligence: Socialization of intelligence. In A. Kazdin (Ed.), *Encyclopedia of psychology.* Washington, DC, & New York: American Psychological Association and Oxford University Press.

Oldfather, P., West, J., White, J., & Wilmarth, J. (1999). *Learning through children's eyes: Social constructivism and the desire to learn.* Washington, DC: American Psychological Association.

Olweus, D. (1980). Bullying among school boys. In R. Barnen (Ed.). *Children and violence.* Stockholm: Adaemic Literature.

Olweus, D. (1994). Bullying at school: Basic facts and effects of a school based intervention program. *Journal of Child Psychology and Psychiatry, 33* (7), 1171–1190.

Olweus, D. (1999). *Bullying at School.* Cambridge, MA: Blackwell.

Onwuegbuzie, A. J., & Daley, C. E. (2001). Racial differences in IQ revisited: A synthesis of nearly a century of research. *Journal of Black Psychology, 27,* 209–220.

Ornstein, A.C., Lasley, T., & Mindes, G. (2005). *Secondary and middle school methods.* Boston: Allyn & Bacon.

Ostrov, J.M., Keating, C.F., & Ostrov, J.M. (2004). Gender differences in preschool aggression during free play and structured interactions: An observational study. *Social Development, 13,* 255–277.

O'Toole, A. (2001, April). Personal communication. Richardson, TX: Department of Psychology, University of Texas at Dallas.

Otten, L. J., Henson, R. N., & Rugg, M. D. (2001). Depth of processing effects on neural correlates of memory encoding. *Brain, 124,* 399–412.

Overton, T. (2000). *Assessment in special education* (3rd ed.). Upper Saddle River, NJ: Merrill.

Pacheco, S., & Hurtado, S. (2001). Media stereotypes. In J. Worell (Ed.), *Encyclopedia of women and gender.* San Diego: Academic Press.

Paivio, A. (1971). *Imagery and verbal processes.* Fort Worth, TX: Harcourt Brace.

Paivio, A. (1986). *Mental representations: A dual coding approach.* New York: Oxford University Press.

Palincsar, A. S. (1986). The role of dialogue in providing scaffolded instruction. *Educational Psychologist, 21,* 73–98.

Palincsar, A. S., & Brown, A. L. (1984). Reciprocal teaching of comprehension-fostering and comprehension-monitoring activities. *Cognition and Instruction, 1,* 117–175.

Palmer, S.E. (2004). Custody and access issues with children whose parents are separated or divorced. *Canadian Journal of Community Mental Health, 4,* Supplement, 25–38.

Palomba, C., & Banta, T. W. (1999). *Assessment essentials.* San Francisco: Jossey-Bass.

Paludi, M. A. (1998). *The psychology of women.* Upper Saddle River, NJ: Prentice Hall.

Pang, V., & Cheng, L. L. (1998). *Struggling to be heard. The inner needs of Asian-Pacific children.* Albany, NY: SUNY Press.

Pang, V. O. (2001). *Multicultural education.* New York: McGraw-Hill.

Pang, V.O. (2004). *Multicultural educational* (2nd ed.). New York: McGraw-Hill.

Pang, V.O. (2005). *Multicultural education.* (3rd ed.). New York: McGraw-Hill.

Panofsky, C. (1999, April). *What the zone of proximal development conceals.* Paper presented at the meeting of the Society for Research in Child Development, Montreal.

Paris, S. G., & Ayres, L. R. (1994). *Becoming reflective students and teachers with portfolios and authentic assessment.* Washington, DC: American Psychological Association.

Paris, S. G., & Lindauer, B. K. (1982). The development of cognitive skills during childhood. In B. B. Wolman (Ed.), *Handbook of developmental psychology.* Englewood Cliffs, NJ: Prentice Hall.

Paris, S. G., & Paris, A. H. (2001). Classroom applications of research on self-regulated learning. *Educational Psychologist, 36,* 89–101.

Park, C. (1997). Learning style preferences of Asian American (Chinese, Filipino, Korean, and Vietnamese) students in secondary schools. *Equity & Excellence in Education, 30* (2), 68–77.

Park, C. (2002). Educational and occupational aspirations of Southeast Asian students. In C. C. Park, A. L. Goodwin, & S. J. Lee (Eds.), *Research on the education of Asian Pacific Americans.* Greenwich, CT: IAP.

Parke, R.D. (2004). Development in the family. *Annual Review of Psychology Vol. 55.* Palo Alto, CA: Annual Reviews.

Parke, R. D., Dennis, J., Flyr, M.L., Leidy, M.S., & Schofield, T.J. (2005). Fathers: Cultural and ecological perspectives. In T. Luster & L. Okaghi (Eds.), *Parenting: An ecological perspective* (2nd Ed.). Mahwah, NJ: Erlbaum.

Patterson, K., & Wright, A. E. (1990, Winter). The speech, language, or hearing-impaired child: At-risk academically. *Childhood Education,* pp. 91–95.

Pavlov, I. P. (1927). *Conditioned reflexes.* New York: Dover.

Payne, D. A. (1997). *Applied educational assessment.* Belmont, CA: Wadsworth.

Pearce, J. (2001). Elementary associative learning. *Annual Review of Psychology.* Palo Alto, CA: Annual Reviews.

Pearson, P. D., Hansen, J., & Gordon, C. (1979). The effect of background knowledge on young children's comprehension of explicit and implicit information. *Journal of Reading Behavior, 11,* 201–210.

Penner, D. (2001). Complexity, emergence, and synthetic models in science education. In K. Crowley, C. Schunn, & T. Okada (Eds.), *Designing for science.* Mahwah, NJ: Erlbaum.

Peterson, K. S. (1998, July 14). Teens learn "I do" can last forever, *USA Today,* pp. D1, D2.

Phelps, R.P. (Ed.) (2005). *Defending standardized testing.* Mahwah, NJ: Erlbaum.

Phinney, J. S., Romero, I., Nava, M., & Huang, D. (2001). The role of language, parents, and peers in ethnic identity among adolescents in immigrant families. *Journal of Youth & Adolescence, 30,* 135–153.

Phye, G. D. (1990). Inductive problem solving: Schema inducement and memory-based transfer. *Journal of Educational Psychology, 82,* 826–831.

Phye, G. D., & Sanders, C. E. (1994). Advice and feedback: Elements of practice for problem solving. *Contemporary Educational Psychology, 19,* 286–301.

Piaget, J. (1932). *The moral judgment of the child.* New York: Harcourt Brace Jovanovich.

Piaget, J., & Inhelder, B. (1969). *The child's conception of space.* New York: Norton.

Pierangelo, R., & Giuliani, G. (2002). *Assessment in special education.* Boston: Allyn & Bacon.

Pintrich, P. R. (2000). The role of goal orientation in self-regulated learning. In M. Boekaerts, P. R. Pintrich, & M. Zeidner (Eds.), *Handbook of self-regulation.* San Diego: Academic Press.

Pintrich, P. R., & Schunk, D. H. (2002). *Motivation in education* (2nd ed.). Upper Saddle River, NJ: Prentice Hall.

Pleck, J. H. (1995). The gender-role strain paradigm. In R F. Levant & W. S. Pollack (Eds.), *A new psychology of men.* New York: Basic Books.

Pleck, J.H. (1983). The theory of male sex role identity: Its rise and fall, 1936-present. In M. Levin (Ed.), *In the shadow of the past: Psychology portrays the sexes.* New York: Columbia University Press.

Pleiss, M. K., & Feldhusen, J. F. (1995). Mentors, role models, and heroes in the lives of gifted children. *Educational Psychologist 30,* 159–169.

Plog, A., Epstein, L., & Porter, W. (2004, April). *Implementation fidelity: Lessons learned from the Bully-Proofing Your School Program.* Paper presented at the meeting of the National School Psychologists Association, Dallas, TX.

Plomin, R. (1997). Identifying genes for cognitive abilities and disabilities. In R. J. Sternberg & E. Grigorenko (Eds.), *Intelligence, heredity, and environment.* New York: Cambridge University Press.

Plucker, J.A., Beghetto, R.A., & Dow, G.T. (2004). Why isn't creativity more important to educational psychologists? Potentials, pitfalls, and future directions in creativity research. *Educational Psychologist, 39,* 83–96.

Pogue, L. (1997, March/April). Review of "Picture It!" *Electronic Learning,* p. 18.

Pokey, S., & Siders, J. A. (2001). Authentic assessment for intervention. *Intervention in School and Clinic, 36,* 163–167.

Polloway, E. A., Patton, J. R., Smith, T. E. C., & Buck, G. H. (1997). Mental retardation and learning disabilities: Conceptual and applied issues. *Journal of Learning Disabilities, 30,* 297–308.

Polson, D. (2001). Helping children learn to make responsible choices. In B. Rogoff, C. G. Turkanis & L. Bartlett (Eds.), *Learning together: Children and adults in a school community.* New York: Oxford University Press.

Pontecorvo, C. (2004). Thinking with others: The social dimension of learning in families and schools. In A. Perret-Clermont, L.B. Resnick, C. Pontecorvo, T. Zittoun, & Burge, B. (Eds.) *Joining society.* New York: Cambridge University Press.

Popham, W. J. (2002). *Classroom assessment* (3rd ed.). Boston: Allyn & Bacon.

Popham, W.J. (2005). *Classroom assessment* (4th ed.). New York: McGraw-Hill.

Posner, D. (2004). What's wrong with teaching to the test? *Phi Delta Kappan, 85,* 749–751.

Pothos, E.M., & Kirk, J. (2004). Investigating learning deficits associated with dyslexia. *Dyslexia, 10,* 61-76.

Powell, B. (2002). Unpublished review of J. W. Santrock's *Educational psychology* 2nd ed. New York: McGraw-Hill.

Powell, R. A., & Symbaluk, D. G. (2002). *Introduction to learning and behavior.* Belmont, CA: Wadsworth.

Powell, R.G., & Caseau, D. (2004). *Classroom communication and diversity.* Mahwah, NJ: Erlbaum.

Presidential Task Force on Psychology and Education. (1992). *Learner-centered psychological principles: Guidelines for school redesign and reform* (Draft). Washington, DC: American Psychological Association.

Pressley, M. (1983). Making meaningful materials easier to learn. In M. Pressley & J. R. Levin (Eds.), *Cognitive strategy research: Educational applications* (pp. 239–266). New York: Springer-Verlag.

Pressley, M., & Afflerbach, P. (1995). *Verbal protocols of reading.* Mahwah, NJ: Erlbaum.

Pressley, M., Borkowski, J. G., & Schneider, W. (1989). Good information processing: What it is and what education can do to promote it. *International Journal of Educational Research, 13,* 857–867.

Pressley, M., Cariligia-Bull, T., Deane, S., & Schneider, W. (1987). Short-term memory, verbal competence, and age as predictors of imagery instructional effectiveness. *Journal of Experimental Child Psychology, 43,* 194–211.

Pressley, M., Levin, J. R., & McCormick, C. B. (1980). Young children's learning of a foreign language vocabulary: A sentence variation of the keyword. *Contemporary Educational Psychology, 5,* 22–29.

Pressley, M., Schuder T., SAIL Faculty and Administration, German, J., & El-Dinary, P. B. (1992). A researcher-educator collaborative interview study of transactional comprehension strategies instruction. *Journal of Educational Psychology, 84,* 231–246.

Pressley, M., Wharto-McDonald, R., Allington, R., Block, C. C., Morrow, H. L., Tracey, D., Baker, K., Brooks, G., Cronin, J., Nelson, E., & Woo, D. (2001). A study of effective first grade literacy instruction. *Scientific Studies of Reading, 15,* 35–58.

Pressley, M., Woloshyn, V., Burkell, J., Cariglia-Bull, T., Lysynchuk, L., McGoldrick, J. A., Schneider, B., Snyder, B. L., & Symons, S. (1995). *Cognitive strategy instruction that really improves children's academic performance* (2nd ed.). Cambridge, MA: Brookline.

Provenzo, E.F. (2005). *The Internet and online research for teachers* (3rd ed.). Boston: Allyn & Bacon.

Pueschel, S. M., Scola, P. S., Weidenman, L. E., & Bernier, J. C. (1995). *The special child.* Baltimore: Paul H. Brookes.

Purcell-Gates, V. (1997, June 18). Commentary in "Diagnosing learning problems can be difficult for parents and teachers." *USA Today,* p. D8.

Purdy, J. E., Markham, M., Schwartz, B., & Gordon, W. M. (2001). *Learning and memory* (2nd ed.). Belmont, CA: Wadsworth.

Qin, Z., Johnson, D. W., & Johnson, R. T. (1995). Cooperative versus competitive efforts and problem solving. *Review of Educational Research, 65,* 129–143.

Quality Counts. (2001). *A better balance: Standards, tests, and the tools to succeed.* Bethesda, MD: Education Week on the Web.

R

Rainey, R. (1965). The effects of directed vs. nondirected laboratory work on high school chemistry achievement. *Journal of Research in Science Teaching, 3,* 286–292.

Ramey, C. T., Bryant, D. M., Campbell, F. A., Sparling, J. J., & Wasik, B. H. (1988). Early intervention for high-risk children. The Carolina Early Intervention Program. In R. H. Price, E. L. Cowen, R. P. Lorion, & J. Ramos-McKay (Eds.), *14 ounces of prevention.* Washington, DC: American Psychological Association.

Ramey, S. L., & Ramey, C. T. (2000). Early childhood experiences and developmental competence. In S. Danzinger & J. Waldfogel (Eds.), *Securing the future.* New York: Sage.

Ramey, C. T., Ramey, S. L., & Lanzi, R. G. (2001). Intelligence and experience. In R. J. Sternberg & E. L. Grigorenko (Eds.), *Environmental effects on cognitive abilities.* Mahwah, NJ: Erlbaum.

Ramphal, C. (1962). *A study of three current problems in education.* Unpublished doctoral dissertation, University of Natal, India.

Randi, J., & Corno, L. (2000). Teacher innovations in self-regulated learning. In M. Boekaerts, P. R. Pintrich, & M. Zeidner (Eds.), *Handbook of self-regulation.* San Diego: Academic Press.

Randolph, C. H., & Evertson, C. M. (1995). Managing for learning: Rules,

roles, and meanings in a writing class. *Journal of Classroom Instruction, 30,* 17–25.

Raschke, D. (1981). Designing reinforcement surveys: Let the student choose the reward. *Teaching Exceptional Children, 14,* 92–96.

Raver, C.C. (2004). Placing emotional self-regulation in sociocultural and socioeconomic contexts. *Child Development, 75,* 346-353.

Raver, C. C., & Zigler, E. F. (1997). Social competence: An untapped dimension in evaluating Head Start's success. *Early Childhood Research Quarterly, 13,* 365–385.

Ravid, D., Levie, R., & Ben-Zvi, G.A. (2004). Morphological disorders. In L. Verhoeven & H. Van Balkom (Eds.), *The classification of language disorders.* Mahwah, NJ: Erlbaum.

Ravitch, D. (1995). *National standards in American education: A citizen's guide.* Washington, DC: Brookings Institution.

Raymond, E. (2000). *Learners with mild disabilities.* Boston: Allyn & Bacon.

Rayner, K. (2000). Reading. In A. Kazdin (Ed.), *Encyclopedia of psychology.* Washington, DC, & New York: American Psychological Association and Oxford University Press.

Re: Learning by Design. (2000). *Design resource center.* Re: Learning by Design. Available on the World Wide Web at: http://www.relearning.org.

Rea, P. J., McLaughlin, V. L., & Walther-Thomas, C. (2002). Outcomes of students with learning disabilities in inclusive and pullout programs. *Exceptional Children, 68,* 203–222.

Read, L. (1995). Amos Bear gets hurt. *Young Children, 50,* 19–23.

Rearden, K. T. (2001). Who wants to make assessment fair? *Science Scope, 25,* 22–25.

Reed, A. J. S., Bergemann, V. E., & Olson, M. W. (2001). *A guide to observation and participation in the classroom.* New York: McGraw-Hill.

Reed, S. (2000). Problem solving. In A. Kazdin (Ed.), *Encyclopedia of psychology.* Washington, DC, & New York: American Psychological Association and Oxford University Press.

Reed, V.A. (2005). *Introduction to children with language disorders* (2nd Ed.). Boston: Allyn & Bacon.

Reeves, G., & Schweitzer, J. (2004). Pharmacological management of attention deficit hyperactivity disorder. *Expert Opinions in Pharmacotherapy, 5,* 1313-1320.

Reid, P. T., & Zalk, S. R. (2001). Academic environments: Gender and ethnicity in U.S. higher education. In J. Worrell (Ed.), *Encyclopedia of women and gender.* San Diego: Academic Press.

Renzulli, J.S. (1998). A rising tide lifts all ships: Developing the gifts and talents of all students. *Phi Delta Kappan, 80,* 1-15.

Renzulli, J. S., & Reis, S. M. (1997). The schoolwide enrichment model. In N. Colangelo & G. A. Davis (Eds.), *Handbook of gifted education.* Boston: Allyn & Bacon.

Reschly, D. (1996). Identification and assessment of students with disabilities. *Future of Children, 6* (1), 40–53.

Revelle, S.P. (2004). High standards + high stakes = high achievement in Massachusetts. *Phi Delta Kappan, 85,* 591-597.

Richard, A. (2001). Rural schools trying out portfolio assessment. *Education Week, 21,* 5.

Rickards, T. (1999). Brainstorming. In M. A. Runco & S. Pritzker (Eds.), *Encyclopedia of creativity.* San Diego: Academic Press.

Rickards, T., & deCock, C. (2003). Understanding organizational creativity: Toward a paradigmatic approach. In M.A. Runco (Ed.), *Creativity Research Handbook.* Cresskill, NJ: Hampton.

Rigby, K. (2002). *New perspectives on bullying.* London: Jessica Kingsley.

Rigby, K. (2004). Bullying in childhood. In P.K. Smith & C.H. Hart (Eds.), *Blackwell handbook of childhood social development.* Malden, MA: Blackwell.

Riley, R. W. (1997, August 31). Long-term trend assessment of American students finds significant progress in science and mathematics. *New York Times,* Section 1, p. 18.

Rinehart, S. D., Stahl, S. A., & Erickson, L. G. (1986). Some effects of summarization training on reading and studying. *Reading Research Quarterly, 21,* 422–438.

Rinne, C. H. (1997). *Excellent classroom management.* Belmont, CA: Wadsworth.

Risley, D. S., & Walther, B. (1995). *Creating responsible learners.* Washington, DC: American Psychological Association.

Robbins, D. (2001). *Vygotsky's psychology-philosophy: A metaphor for language theory and learning.* New York: Plenum.

Robins, R.W., Trzesniewski, K.H., Tracey, J.L., Potter, J., & Gosling, S.D. (2002). Age differences in self-esteem from age 9 to 90. *Psychology and Aging, 17,* 423-434.

Robinson, N. S. (1995). Evaluating the nature of perceived support and its relation to perceived self-worth in adolescents. *Journal of Research on Adolescence, 5,* 253–280.

Roblyer, M. D., Edwards, J., & Havriluk, M. A. (1997). *Integrating educational technology into education.* Upper Saddle River, NJ: Merrill/Prentice Hall.

Rodgers, C. (2000). Gender schema. In A. Kazdin (Ed.), *Encyclopedia of psychology.* Washington, DC, & New York: American Psychological Association and Oxford University Press.

Rodriquez, J. L., Diaz, R. M., Duran, D., & Espinosa, L. (1995). The impact of bilingual preschool education on the language development of Spanish-speaking children. *Early Childhood Research Quarterly, 10,* 475–490.

Roediger, H. (2000). Learning: Cognitive approach for humans. In A. Kazdin (Ed.), *Encyclopedia of psychology.* Washington, DC, & New York: American Psychological Association and Oxford University Press.

Roff, M., Sells, S. B., & Golden, M. W. (1972). *Social adjustment and personality development in children.* Minneapolis: University of Minnesota Press.

Rogan, P., Luecking, R., & Held, R. G. (2001). Career development: Helping youth with mild cognitive limitations achieve successful careers. In A. J. Tymchuk (Ed.), *The forgotten generation.* Baltimore: Paul H. Brookes.

Rogers, C. R. (1961). *On becoming a person.* Boston: Houghton Mifflin.

Rogoff, B. (1990). *Apprenticeship in thinking.* New York: Oxford University Press.

Rogoff, B. (1998). Cognition as a collaborative process. In D. Kuhn & R. S. Siegler (Eds.), *Handbook of child psychology* (5th ed., Vol. 2). New York: Wiley.

Rogoff, B. (2003). *The cultural nature of human development.* New York: Oxford University Press.

Rogoff, B., Turkanis, C. G., & Barlett, L. (Eds.). (2001). *Learning together. Children*

and adults in a school community. New York: Oxford University Press.

Rohrbeck, C.A., Ginsburg-Block, M.D., Fantuzzo, J.W., & Miller, T.R. (2003). Peer-assisted learning interventions with elementary school students: A meta-analytic review. *Journal of Educational Psychology, 95,* 240-257.

Rosch, E. H. (1973). On the internal structure of perceptual and semantic categories. In T. E. Moore (Ed.), *Cognition and the acquisition of language.* New York: Academic Press.

Rosenshine, B. (1971). *Teaching behaviors and student achievement.* London: National Foundation for Educational Research.

Rosenshine, B. (1985). Direct instruction. In T. Husen & T. N. Postlethwaite (Eds.), *Encyclopedia of education* (Vol. 3). New York: Pergamon.

Rosenshine, B. (1986). Synthesis of research on explicit teaching. *Educational Leadership, 43,* 60–69.

Rosenthal, D. M., & Sawyers, J. Y. (1997). Building successful home/school partnerships. *Young Children, 52,* 194–200.

Rosnow, R.L., & Rosenthal, R.L. (2005). *Beginning behavioral research* (5th ed.). Upper Saddle River, NJ: Prentice Hall.

Ross, B. H. (2000). Concepts: Learning. In A. Kazdin (Ed.), *Encyclopedia of psychology.* Washington, DC, & New York: American Psychological Association and Oxford University Press.

Rosselli, H. C. (1996, February/March). Gifted students. *National Association for Secondary School Principals,* pp. 12–17.

Rothbart, M. K., & Bates, J. E. (1998). Temperament. In W. Damon (Ed.), *Handbook of child psychology* (5th ed., Vol. 3). New York: Wiley.

Rowe, M. (1986). Wait time: Slowing down may be a way of speeding up! *Journal of Teacher Education, 37,* 43–50.

Rowe, R. J. (Ed.). (1994). *Preschoolers as authors: Literacy learning in the social world of the classroom.* Cresskill, NJ: Hampton Press.

Rowe, S.M., & Wertsch, J.V. (2004). Vygotsky's model of cognitive development. In U. Goswami (Ed.), *Blackwell handbook of childhood cognitive development.* Malden, MA: Blackwell.

Rubia, K., Overmeyer, S., Taylor, E., Brammer, M., Williams, S., Simmons, A., Andrew, C., & Bullmore, E. (2000).

Functional frontalisation with age: Mapping neurodevelopment trajectories with fMRI. *Neuroscience & Biobehavioral Reviews, 24,* 13-19.

Rubin, K. H. (2000). Peer relation. In A. Kazdin (Ed.), *Encyclopedia of psychology.* Washington, DC, & New York: American Psychological Association and Oxford University Press.

Rubin, K. H., Bukowski, W., & Parker, J. G. (1998). Peer interactions, relationships, and groups. In W. Damon (Ed.), *Handbook of child psychology* (5th ed., Vol. 3). New York: Wiley.

Ruble, D. (1983). The development of social comparison processes and their role in achievement-related self-socialization. In E. T. Higgins, D. N. Ruble, & W. W. Hartup (Eds.), *Social cognition and development.* New York: Cambridge University Press.

Ruddell, R. B. (1999). *Teaching children to read and write* (2nd ed.). Boston: Allyn & Bacon.

Runco, M. (1999). Critical thinking. In M. A. Runco & S. Pritzker (Eds.), *Encyclopedia of creativity.* San Diego: Academic Press.

Runco, M.A. (2004). Creativity. *Annual Review of Psychology, 55.* Palo Alto, CA: Annual Reviews.

Ryan, R. & Deci, E. (2000). Self-determination theory and the facilitation of intrinsic motivation, social development, and well-being. *American Psychologist, 55,* 68–78.

Ryan-Finn, K. D., Cauce, A. M., & Grove, K. (1995, March). *Children and adolescents of color: Where are you? Selection, recruitment, and retention in developmental research.* Paper presented at the meeting of the Society for Research in Child Development, Indianapolis.

S

Sackett, P. (2003, February). Commentary on stereotype threat. *Monitor on Psychology, 34,* 52.

Sackett, P.R., Hardison, C.M., & Cullen, M.J. (2004). On interpreting stereotype threat as accounting for African American and White differences in cognitive test. *American Psychologist, 59,* 7-13.

Sadker, D. M. P., & Sadker, D. M. (2000). *Teachers, schools, and society* (5th ed.). New York: McGraw-Hill.

Sadker, M., & Sadker, D. (1986). *PEPA (Principal Effectiveness, Pupil Achievement): A training program for principals and other educational leaders.* Washington, DC: American University.

Sadker, M., & Sadker, D. (1994). *Failing at fairness: How America's schools cheat girls.* New York. Scribners.

Sadker, M.P., & Sadker, D.M. (2005). *Teachers, students, and society* (7th ed.). New York: McGraw-Hill.

Salomon, G., & Perkins, D. (1989). Rocky roads to transfer: Rethinking mechanisms of a neglected phenomenon. *Educational Psychologist, 24,* 113–142.

Salovy, P., & Mayer, J. D. (1990). Emotional intelligence. *Imagination, Cognition, and Personality, 9,* 185–211.

Sampson, R., Raudenbush, S., & Earls, F. (1997). Neighborhoods and violent crime: A multilevel study of collective efficacy. *Science, 277,* 918-924.

Samuelsson, S., Lundberg, I., & Herkner, B. (2004). ADHD and reading disability in male adults. *Journal of Learning Disabilities, 37,* 155-168.

Sandoval, J., Scheuneman, J. D., Ramos-Grenier, J., Geisinger, K. F., & Frisby, C. (Eds.). (1999). *Test interpretation and diversity: Achieving equity in assessment.* Washington, DC: American Psychological Association.

Sandstrom, M.J., & Zakriski, A.L. (2004). Understanding the experience of peer rejection. In J.B. Kupersmidt & K.A. Dodge (Eds.), *Children's peer relations: From development to intervention.* Washington, DC: American Psychological Association.

Sanson, A. V., & Rothbart, M. K. (1995). Child temperament and parenting. In M. H. Bornstein (Ed.), *Handbook of parenting* (Vol. 4). Hillsdale, NJ: Erlbaum.

Sanson, A. V., & Rothbart, M. K. (2002). Child temperament and parenting. In M. H. Bornstein (Ed.), *Handbook of parenting.* Mahwah, NJ: Erlbaum.

Santrock, J. W. (2002). *Life-span development* (8th ed.). New York: McGraw-Hill.

Santrock, J. W., & Halonen, J. S. (2002). *Your guide to college success* (2nd ed.). Belmont, CA: Wadsworth.

Sapon-Shevin, M. (1999). *Because we can change the world: A practical guide to building cooperative, inclusive classroom communities.* Boston: Allyn & Bacon.

Sax, G. (1997). *Principles of educational and psychological measurement and evaluation* (4th ed.). Belmont, CA: Wadsworth.

Sax, L.J., Astin, A.W., Lindholm, J.A., Korn, W.S., Saenz, V.B., & Mahoney, K.M. (2003). *The American freshman: National norms for fall 2003.* Los Angeles: Higher Education Research Institute, UCLA.

Scardamalia, M. (1981). How children cope with the cognitive demands of writing. In C. Frederiksen & J. F. Dominic (Eds.). *Writing: The nature, development, and teaching of written communication.* Mahwah, NJ: Erlbaum.

Scardamalia, M., & Bereiter, C. (1994). Computer support for knowledge-building communities. *Journal of the Learning Sciences, 3* (3), 265–283.

Scardamalia, M., Bereiter, C., & Lamon, M. (1994). The CSILE Project: Trying to bring the classroom into the world. In K. McGilly (Ed.), *Classroom lessons.* Cambridge, MA: MIT Press.

Scarr, S., & Weinberg, R. A. (1983). The Minnesota Adoption Studies: Genetic differences and malleability. *Child Development, 54,* 253–259.

Schacter, D. L. (2000). Memory systems. In A. Kazdin (Ed.), *Encyclopedia of psychology.* Washington, DC, & New York: American Psychological Association and Oxford University Press.

Schacter, D. L. (2001). *The seven deadly sins of memory.* Boston: Houghton Mifflin.

Schauble, L. (1990). Belief revision in children: The role of prior knowledge and strategies for generating evidence. *Journal of Experimental Child Psychology, 49,* 31–57.

Schauble, L. (1996). The development of scientific reasoning in knowledge-rich contexts. *Developmental Psychology, 32,* 102–119.

Schauble, L., Beane, D. B., Coates, G. D., Martin, L. M. W., & Sterling, P. V. (1996). Outside classroom walls: Learning in informal environments. In L. Schauble & R. Glaser (Eds.), *Innovations in learning.* Mahwah, NJ: Erlbaum.

Schlesinger, A. M. (1991). *The disuniting of America.* Knoxville, TN: Whittle Direct Books.

Schmidt, P. R., & Mosenthal, P. B. (Eds.). (2001). *Reconceptualizing literacy in the new age of multiculturalism and pluralism.* Greenwich, CT: IAP.

Schmidt, R. (2001). The power to empower. In P. R. Schmidt & P. B. Mosenthal (Eds.), *Reconceptualizing literacy in the new age of multiculturalism and pluralism.* Greenwich, CT: IAP.

Schneider, B., & Coleman, J. S. (1993). *Parents, their children, and schools.* Boulder, CO: Westview Press.

Schneider, W. (2004). Memory development in childhood. In U. Goswami (Ed.), *Blackwell handbook of childhood cognitive development.* Malden, MA: Blackwell.

Schneider, W., & Bjorklund, D. F. (1998). Memory. In W. Damon (Ed.), *Handbook of child psychology* (5th ed., Vol. 2). New York: Wiley.

Schneider, W., & Pressley, M. (1997). *Memory development between 2 and 20* (2nd ed.). Mahwah, NJ: Erlbaum.

Schneps, M. H., & Sadler, P. M. (1989). [Video.] *A private universe.* Cambridge, MA: Harvard-Smithsonian Center for Astrophysics.

Schoenfeld, A. H. (2002). Making mathematics work for all children: Issues of standards, testing, and equity. *Educational Researcher, 31,* 13–25.

Schrum, L., & Berenfeld, B. (1997). *Teaching and learning in the information age: A guide to telecommunications.* Boston: Allyn & Bacon.

Schuh, K. (2001, April). *Teacher-centered and learner-centered: What's the relationship?* Paper presented at the meeting of the American Educational Research Association, Seattle.

Schultz, K., & Fecho, B. (2001). Society's child: Social context and writing development. *Educational Psychologist, 35,* 51–62.

Schunk, D. H. (1991). Self-efficacy and academic motivation. *Educational Psychologist, 25,* 71–86.

Schunk, D. H. (1999, August). *Social-self interaction and achievement behavior.* Presidential address, Division 15, presented at the meeting of the American Psychological Association, Boston.

Schunk, D. H. (2000). *Learning theories: An educational perspective* (3rd ed.). Upper Saddle River, NJ: Prentice Hall.

Schunk, D. H. (2001). Social cognitive theory and self-regulated learning. In B. J. Zimmerman & D. H. Schunk (Eds.), *Self-regulated learning and achievement* (2nd ed.). Mahwah, NJ: Erlbaum.

Schunk, D.H. (2004). *Learning theories An educational perspective* (4th ed.). Upper Saddle River, NJ: Prentice Hall.

Schunk, D. H., & Ertmer, P. A. (2000). Self-regulation and academic learning: Self-efficacy enhancing intervention. In M. Boekarts, P. Pintrich, & M. Zeidner (Eds.), *Handbook of self-regulation.* San Diego: Academic Press.

Schunk, D. H., & Rice, J. M. (1989). Learning goals and children's reading comprehension. *Journal of Reading Behavior, 23,* 351–364.

Schunk, D. H., & Swartz, C. W. (1993). Goals and progressive feedback: Effects on self-efficacy and writing achievement. *Contemporary Educational Psychology, 18,* 337–354.

Schunk, D. H., & Zimmerman, B. J. (Eds.). (1994). *Self-regulation of learning and performance: Issues and educational applications.* Mahwah, NJ: Erlbaum.

Schunk, D.H., & Zimmerman, B.J. (2003). Self-regulation and learning. In I.B. Weiner (Ed.), *Handbook of psychology,* (Vol. 7). New York: Wiley.

Schwab-Stone, M., & others. (1995). *New Haven Public Schools Social Development Project: 1994.* New Haven, CT: New Haven Public Schools.

Schweinhart, L. J. (1999, April). *Generalizing from High/Scope longitudinal studies.* Paper presented at the meeting of the Society for Research in Child Development, Albuquerque.

Segal, J. W. (1996). Foreword. In L. Schauble & R. Glaser (Eds.), *Innovations in learning.* Mahwah, NJ: Erlbaum.

Seidman, E. (2000). School transitions. In A. Kazdin (Ed.), *Encyclopedia of psychology.* Washington, DC, & New York: American Psychological Association and Oxford University Press.

Sensenbaugh, R. (1994). Effectiveness of Reading Recovery programs. *Reading Research and Instruction, 34* (1), 73–76.

Sensenbaugh, R. (1995). Reading Recovery. *ERIC Clearinghouse on Reading, English, and Communication Digest, No. 106.*

Serow, R. C., Ciechalski, J., & Daye, C. (1990). Students as volunteers. *Urban Education, 25,* 157–168.

Serpell, R. (2000). Culture and Intelligence. In A. Kazdin (Ed.), *Encyclopedia of psychology.* Washington, DC, and New York: American Psychological Association and Oxford University Press.

Shade, S. C., Kelly, C., & Oberg, M. (1997). *Creating culturally-responsive schools.* Washington, DC: American Psychological Association.

Shamier, A., & Tzuriel, D. (2004). Children's mediational teaching style as function of intervention for cross-age peer interaction. *School Psychology International, 25,* 59–78.

Shanahan, T., & Rodriguez-Brown, F. V. (1993, April). *Project FLAME: The theory and structure of a family literacy program for the Latino community.* Paper presented at the meeting of the American Educational Research Association, Atlanta.

Sharan, S. (1990). Cooperative learning and helping behavior in the multi-ethnic classroom. In H. C. Foot, M. J. Morgan, & R. H. Shute (Eds.), *Children helping children.* New York: Wiley.

Sharan, S., & Sharan, S. (1992). *Expanding cooperative learning through group investigation.* New York: Teachers College Press.

Sharan, S., & Shaulov, A. (1990). Cooperative learning, motivation to learn, and academic achievement. In S. Sharan (Ed.), *Cooperative learning.* New York: Praeger.

Sharp, V. (2002). *Computer education for teachers* (4th ed.). New York: McGraw-Hill.

Sharp, V. (2005). *Computer education for teachers* (5th ed.). New York: McGraw-Hill.

Sheets, R.H. (2005). *Diversity pedagogy.* Boston: Allyn & Bacon.

Sheffield, C. J. (1997, March/April). Instructional technology for teachers: Preparation for classroom diversity. *Educational Technology,* pp. 16–18.

Sherman, C. W., & Mueller, D. P. (1996, June). *Developmentally appropriate practice and student achievement in inner-city elementary schools.* Paper presented at Head Start's Third National Research Conference, Washington, DC.

Sherman, L. W. (2001). Cooperative learning and computer-supported intentional learning experiences. In C. R. Wolfe (Ed.), *Learning and teaching on the World Wide Web.* San Diego: Academic Press.

Shields, S. A. (1991). Gender in the psychology of emotion: A selective research review. In K. T. Strongman (Ed.), *International review of studies on emotion.* New York: Wiley.

Shiffrin, R. M. (1996). Laboratory experimentation on the genesis of expertise. In K. A. Ericsson (Ed.), *The road to excellence.* Mahwah, NJ: Erlbaum.

Shirts, R. G. (1997). *BAFA, BAFA, a cross-cultural simulation.* Del Mar, CA: SIMILE II.

Shonkoff, J. (1996). Mental retardation. In R. Behrman, R. Kliegman, & A. Arvin (Eds.), *Nelson textbook of pediatrics* (15th ed.). Philadelphia: W. B. Saunders.

Shulman, L. S. (1987). Knowledge and teaching: Foundations of the new reform. *Harvard Educational Review, 57,* 1–22.

Shulman, L. S. (1987). Knowledge and teaching: Foundations of the new reform. *Harvard Educational Review, 19* (2), 4–14.

Siegel, L. S., & Ryan, E. B. (1989). The development of working memory in normally achieving and subtypes of learning disabled children. *Child Development, 60,* 973–980.

Siegfried, T. (1998, July 13). In teaching scientific subjects, high schools are out of order. *Dallas Morning News,* p. 9D.

Siegler, R. S. (1998). *Children's thinking* (3rd ed.). Upper Saddle River, NJ: Erlbaum.

Siegler, R. S. (2001). Cognition, instruction, and the quest for meaning. In S. M. Carver & D. Klahr (Eds.), *Cognition and instruction.* Mahwah, NJ: Erlbaum.

Siegler, R.S., & Alibali, M.W. (2005). *Children's thinking* (4th ed.) Upper Saddle River, NJ: Prentice Hall.

Siegler, R. S., & Robinson, M. (1982). The development of numerical understandings. In H. W. Reese & L. P. Litsitt (Eds.), *Advances in child development and behavior* (Vol. 12). New York: Academic Press.

Silverman, L. K. (1993). A developmental model for counseling the gifted. In L. K. Silverman (Ed.), *Counseling the gifted and the talented.* Denver: Love.

Simon, H. (2001). Learning to research about learning. In S. M. Carver & D. Klahr (Eds.), *Cognition and instruction.* Mahwah, NJ: Erlbaum.

Simons, J., Finlay, B., & Yang, A. (1991). *The adolescent and young adult fact book.* Washington, DC: Children's Defense Fund.

Singer, D. G., & Singer, J. L. (1987). Practical suggestions for controlling television. *Journal of Early Adolescence, 7,* 365–369.

Singhal, M. (2001). Reading proficiency, reading strategies, metacognitive awareness, and L2 readers. *Reading Matrix, 1,* 1–6.

Skinner, B. F. (1938). *The behavior of organisms.* New York: Appleton-Century-Crofts.

Skinner, B. F. (1953). *Science and human behavior.* New York: Macmillan.

Skinner, B. F. (1954). The science of learning and the art of teaching. *Harvard Educational Review, 24,* 86–97.

Skinner, B. F. (1958). Teaching machines. *Science, 128,* 969–977.

Slavin, R. E. (1990). Achievement effects of ability grouping in secondary schools: A best-evidence synthesis. *Review of Educational Research, 60,* 471–500.

Slavin, R. E. (1994). *Using team learning* (4th ed.). Baltimore: Johns Hopkins University, Center for Research on Elementary Schools.

Slavin, R. E., & Madden N. A. (Eds.). (2001). *Success for all.* Mahwah, NJ: Erlbaum.

Slavin, R. E., Madden, N. A., Dolan, L. J., & Wasik, B. A. (1996). *Every child, every school: Success for all.* Newbury Park, CA: Corwin Press.

Slentz, K. L., & Krogh, S. L. (2001). *Teaching young children.* Mahwah, NJ: Erlbaum.

Smith, D. R. (2001). Wechsler Individual Achievement Test. In J. J. W. Andrews, D. H. Saklofske, & D. Hildebrand (Eds.), *Handbook of psychoeducational assessment.* San Diego: Academic Press.

Smith, L. (2004). Piaget's model. In U. Goswami (Ed.), *Blackwell handbook of childhood cognitive development.* Malden, MA: Blackwell.

Smith-Maddox, R., & Wheelock, A. (1995). Untracking and students' futures. *Phi Delta Kappan, 77,* 222–228.

Smoll, F. L., & Schutz, R. W. (1990). Quantifying gender differences in physical performance: A developmental perspective. *Developmental Psychology, 26,* 360–369.

Smyth, M. M., Collins, A. F., Morris, P. E., & Levy, P. (1994). *Cognition in action* (2nd ed.). Hove, UK: Erlbaum.

Snow, C., & Beals, D. (2001). Deciding what to tell: Selecting an elaborative narrative. Topics in family interaction and children's personal experience stories. In S. Blum-Kulka & C. Snow (Eds.), *Talking to adults.* Mahwah, NJ: Erlbaum.

Snow, R. E., Como, L., & Jackson, D. (1996). Individual differences in affective and conative functions. In D. C. Berliner & R. C. Calfee (Eds.), *Handbook of educational psychology.* New York: Macmillan.

Sokoloff, D. R., & Thornton, R. K. (1997). Using interactive lecture demonstration to create an active learning environment. *American Journal of Physics, 64,* 338–352.

Solano-Flores, G. & Shavelson, R. J. (1997, Fall). Development of performance assessments in science: Conceptual, practical, and logistical issues. *Educational Measurement,* pp. 16–24.

Solley, B. A. (2000). *Writers' workshop: Reflections of elementary and middle school teachers.* Boston: Allyn & Bacon.

Songer, N. B. (1993). Learning science with a child-focused resource: A case study of Kids as Global Scientists. In *Proceedings of the 15th Annual Meeting of the Cognitive Science Society.* Mahwah, NJ: Erlbaum.

Sousa, D. A. (1995). *How the brain learns: A classroom teacher's guide.* Reston, VA: National Association of Secondary School Principals.

Sowell, E., & Jernigan, T. (1998). Further MRI evidence of late brain maturation: Limbic volume increases and changing asymmetries during childhood and adolescence. *Developmental Neuropsychology, 14,* 599–617.

Spafford, C.S., Grosser, G.S., & Daurich, B. (2005). *Dyslexia and reading difficulties* (2nd Ed.). Boston: Allyn & Bacon.

Spandel, V. (2005). *Creating writers through writing assessment and instruction* (4th ed.). Boston: Allyn & Bacon.

Sparks, R.L., Javorsky, J., & Phillips, L. (2004). College students classified with ADHD and the foreign language requirement. *Journal of Learning Disabilities, 37,* 169–178.

Spearman, C. E. (1927). *The abilities of man.* New York: Macmillan.

Spence, J. T., & Helmreich, R. (1978). *Masculinity and femininity. Their psychological dimensions.* Austin: University of Texas Press.

Spencer, M. B. (2000). Ethnocentrism. In A. Kazdin (Ed.), *Encyclopedia of psychology.* Washington, DC, & New York: American Psychological Association and Oxford University Press.

Spencer, M. B., & Dornbusch, S. M. (1990). Challenges in studying minority youth. In S. S. Feldman & G. R. Elliott (Eds.), *At the threshold: The developing adolescent.* Cambridge, MA: Harvard University Press.

Spencer, M. B., & Markstrom-Adams, C. (1990). Identity processes among racial and ethnic minority children in America. *Child Development, 61,* 290–310.

Spring, J. (2000). *The intersection of cultures* (2nd ed.). New York: McGraw-Hill.

Spring, J. (2002). *American education* (10th ed.). New York: McGraw-Hill.

Spring, J. (2004). *American education* (11th ed.). New York: McGraw-Hill.

Spring, J. (2005). *The American school* (6th ed.). New York: McGraw-Hill.

Squire, L. (1987). *Memory and brain.* New York: Oxford University Press.

St. Pierre, R., Layzer, J., & Barnes, H. (1996). *Regenerating two-generation programs.* Cambridge, MA: Abt Associates.

Stahl, S. (2002, January). *Effective reading instruction in the first grade.* Paper presented at the Michigan Reading Recovery conference, Dearborn, MI.

Stanovich, K. E. (1999). *Who is rational? Individual differences in reasoning.* Mahwah, NJ: Erlbaum.

Stanovich, K. E. (2001). *How to think straight about psychology* (6th ed.). Boston: Allyn & Bacon.

Stanovich, K. E., & West, R. E. (2000). Individual differences in reasoning: Implications for the rationality debate? *Behavior and Brain Sciences, 23,* 646–665.

Stansfield, C. W., & Rivera, C. (2002). 2nd language testing: How will English language learners be accommodated? In R. W. Lissitz & W. D. Schafer (Eds.), *Assessment in educational reform: Both means and ends.* Boston: Allyn & Bacon.

Starko, A.J. (2005). *Creativity in the classroom.* Mahwah, NJ: Erlbaum.

Steele, C.M., & Aronson, J.A. (2004). Stereotype threat does not live by Steele and Aronson (1995) alone. *American Psychologist, 59,* 47-48.

Stegelin, D.A. (2003). Application of Reggio Emilia approach to early childhood science curriculum. *Early Childhood Education Journal, 30,* 163-169.

Steger, J., Imhof, K., Coutts, E., Gundelfinger, R., Steinhausen, H., & Brandeis, H. (2001). Attentional and neuromotor deficits in ADHD. *Developmental Medicine and Child Neurology, 43,* 172–179.

Steinberg, L.D., & Silk, J.S. (2002). Parenting adolescents. In M. Bornstein (Ed.), *Handbook of parenting* (2nd ed., Vol. 1). Mahwah, NJ: Erlbaum.

Sternberg, R. J. (1986). *Intelligence applied.* Fort Worth, TX: Harcourt Brace.

Sternberg, R. J. (1997). *Thinking styles.* New York: Cambridge University Press.

Sternberg, R. J. (2000). Looking back and looking forward on intelligence: Toward a theory of successful intelligence. In M. Bennett (Ed.), *Developmental psychology.* Philadelphia: Psychology Press.

Sternberg, R. J. (2002). Intelligence: The triarchic theory of intelligence. In J. W. Gutherie (Ed.), *Encyclopedia of education* (2nd ed.). New York: Macmillan.

Sternberg, R.J. (2004). Individual differences in cognitive development. In U. Goswami (Ed.), *Blackwell handbook of childhood cognitive development.* Malden, MA: Blackwell.

Sternberg, R. J., & Ben-Zeev, T. (2001). *Complex cognitive processes.* New York: Oxford University Press.

Sternberg, R. J., & Clinkenbeard, P. R. (1995, May/June). The triarchic model applied to identifying, teaching, and assessing gifted children. *Roeper Review,* 255–260.

Sternberg, R. J., & Grigorenko, E. L. (Eds.). (2001). *Environmental effects on cognitive abilities.* Mahwah, NJ: Erlbaum.

Sternberg, R. J., & Lubart, T. I. (1995). *Defying the crowd: Cultivating creativity in a culture of conformity.* New York: Free Press.

Sternberg, R. J., & Spear-Swerling, P. (1996). *Teaching for thinking.* Washington, DC: American Psychological Association.

Sternberg, R. J., Torff, B., & Grigorenko, E. (1998, May). Teaching for successful intelligence raises school achievement. *Phi Delta Kappan,* 667–669.

Stevenson, H. W. (1992, December). Learning from Asian schools. *Scientific American,* pp. 6, 70–76.

Stevenson, H. W. (2000). Middle childhood: Education and schooling. In A.

Kazdin (Ed.), *Encyclopedia of psychology.* Washington, DC, & New York: American Psychological Association and Oxford University Press.

Stevenson, H. W. (2001). *Commentary on NCTM standards.* Department of Psychology, University of Michigan, Ann Arbor.

Stevenson, H. W., & Hofer, B. K. (1999). Education policy in the United States and abroad: What we can learn from each other. In G. J. Cizek (Ed.), *Handbook of educational policy.* San Diego: Academic Press.

Stevenson, H.W., & Zusho, A. (2002). Adolescence in China and Japan: Adapting to a changing environment. In B.B. Brown, R.W. Larson, & T.S. Saraswathi (Eds.), *The world's youth.* New York: Cambridge University Press.

Stevenson, H. W., Lee, S., & Stigler, J. W. (1986). Mathematics achievement of Chinese, Japanese, and American children. *Science, 231,* 693–699.

Stevenson, H. W., Lee, S., Chen, C., Stigler, J. W., Hsu, C., & Kitamura, S. (1990). Contexts of achievement. *Monographs of the Society for Research in Development, 55* (Serial No. 221).

Stewart, D. (1997, August 27). Commentary in "SAT scores up, but so is grade inflation." *USA Today,* p. A1.

Stiggins, R. J. (2001). *Student-involved classroom assessment* (3rd ed.). Upper Saddle River, NJ: Prentice Hall.

Stiggins, R. J. (2002). Where is our assessment future and how can we get from here to there? In R. W. Kissitz & W. D. Schafer (Eds.), *Assessment in educational reform: Both means and ends.* Boston: Allyn & Bacon.

Stiggins, R. J., & Conklin, N. F. (1992). *In teachers' hands: Investigating the practices of classroom assessment.* Albany: State University of New York Press.

Stigler, J. W., & Hiebert, J. (1997, September). Understanding and improving classroom mathematics instruction. *Phi Delta Kappan, 79,* 14–21.

Stigler, J. W., & Hiebert, J. (1999). *The teaching gap.* New York: Free Press.

Stipek, D. J. (1996). Motivation and instruction. In D. C. Berliner & R. C. Calfee (Eds.), *Handbook of educational psychology.* New York: Macmillan.

Stipek, D. J. (2002). *Motivation to learn* (4th ed.). Boston: Allyn & Bacon.

Stipek, D. J., Feiler, R., Daniels, D., & Milburn, S. (1995). Effects of different instructional approaches on young children's achievement and motivation. *Child Development, 66,* 209–223.

Strichart, S. S., & Mangrum, C. T. (2002). *Teaching study skills and strategies to students with learning disabilities, attention deficit disorders, or special needs* (3rd ed.). Boston: Allyn & Bacon.

Strobel, K. R. (2001, April). *Successful outcomes for at-risk youth.* Paper presented at the meeting of the American Educational Research Association, Seattle.

Suarez-Orozco, C. (2002). Afterword: Understanding and serving the children of immigrants. *Harvard Educational Review, 71,* 579–589.

Sullivan, H. S. (1953). *The interpersonal theory of psychiatry.* New York: Norton.

Sullivan, L. (1991, May 25). US secretary urges TV to restrict "irresponsible sex and reckless violence." *Boston Globe,* p. A1.

Sunal, C. S., & Haas, M. E. (2002). *Social studies for elementary and middle grades.* Boston: Allyn & Bacon.

Sunal, C.S., & Haas, M.E. (2005). *Social studies for the elementary and middle grades* (2nd ed.). Boston: Allyn & Bacon.

Supovitz, J. A., & Brennan, R. T. (1997, Fall). Mirror, mirror on the wall, which is the fairest test of all? An examination of the equality of portfolio assessment relative to standardized tests. *Harvard Educational Review, 67* (3), 472–501.

Suthers, D., Weiner, A., Connelly, J., & Paolucci, M. (1995, August). *Engaging students in critical discussion of science and public policy issues.* Paper presented at the 7th World Conference on Artificial Intelligence, Washington, DC.

Sutton, R. E. (1991). Equity and computers in the schools: A decade of research. *Review of Educational Research, 61,* 475–503.

Swanson, D. P. (1997, April). *Identify the coping styles among African-American females.* Paper presented at the meeting of the Society for Research in Child Development, Washington, DC.

Swanson, H. L., & Hoskyn, M. (1998). Experimental intervention research on students with learning disabilities: A meta-analysis of treatment outcomes. *Review of Educational Research, 68,* 277–321.

Swanson, J. M., & others (2001). Clinical relevance of the primary findings of the

MTA: Success rates based on severity of ADHD and ODD symptoms at the end of treatment. *Journal of the American Academy of Child and Adolescent Psychiatry, 40,* 168–179.

T

Tamis-LeMonda, C. S., Bornstein, M. H., & Baumwell, L. (2001). Maternal responsiveness and children's achievement of language milestones. *Child Development, 72,* 748–767.

Tannen, D. (1990). *You just don't understand!* New York: Ballantine.

Tanner, D. E. (1997, Spring). Standards. *Educational Horizons,* pp. 115–120.

Tanner, D. E. (2001). *Assessing academic achievement.* Boston: Allyn & Bacon.

Tanner, J. M. (1978). *Fetus into man.* Cambridge, MA: Harvard University Press.

Tappan, M. B. (1998). Sociocultural psychology and caring psychology: Exploring Vygotsky's "hidden curriculum." *Educational Psychologist, 33,* 23–33.

Tavris, C., & Wade, C. (1984). *The longest war: Sex differences in perspective.* Fort Worth, TX: Harcourt Brace.

Taylor, C. (1994). Assessment of measurement or standards: The peril and the promise of large-scale assessment reform. *American Educational Research Journal, 32,* 231–262.

Teachers' Curriculum Institute. (2001). *Social studies alive!* Rancho Cordovo, CA: Author.

Temple, C., Nathan, R., Temple, F., & Burris, N. A. (1993). *The beginnings of writing* (3rd ed.). Boston: Allyn & Bacon.

Tenenbaum, H.R., Callahan, M., Alba-Speyer, C., & Sandoval, L. (2002). Parent-child science conversations in Mexican descent families: Educational background, activity, and past experience as moderators. *Hispanic Journal of Behavioral Science, 24,* 225-248.

Tennyson, R., & Cocchiarella, M. (1986). An empirically based instructional design theory for teaching concepts. *Review of Educational Research, 56,* 40–71.

Terman, D. L., Larner, M. B., Stevenson, C. S., & Behrman, R. E. (1996). Special education for students with disabilities: Analysis and recommendations. *Future of Children, 6* (1), 4–24.

Terman, L. (1925). *Genetic studies of genius: Vol. 1. Mental and physical traits of a thousand gifted children.* Stanford, CA: Stanford University Press.

Terman, L., & Oden, M. H. (1959). *Genetic studies of genius. Vol. 5: The gifted group at mid-life.* Stanford, CA: Stanford University Press.

Terry, W. S. (2003). *Learning and memory* (2nd ed.). Boston: Allyn & Bacon.

Terwilliger, J. (1997). Semantics, psychometrics, and assessment reform: A close look at "authentic" assessments. *Educational Researcher, 26,* 24–27.

Tetreault, M. K. T. (1997). Classrooms for diversity: Rethinking curriculum and pedagogy. In J. A. Banks & C. A. Banks (Eds.), *Multicultural education* (3rd ed.). Boston: Allyn & Bacon.

Thomas, A., & Chess, S. (1991). Temperament in adolescence and its functional significance. In R. M. Lerner, A. C. Petersen, & J. Brooks-Gunn (Eds.), *Encyclopedia of adolescence* (Vol. 2). New York: Garland.

Thomas, C. C., Correa, V. I., & Morsink, C. V. (1995). *Interactive teaming: Consultation and collaboration in special programs* (2nd ed.). Upper Saddle River, NJ: Merrill/Prentice Hall.

Thomas, J. R., & Thomas, K. T. (1988). Developmental gender differences in physical activity. *Quest, 40,* 219–229.

Thomas, R. M. (2000). *Human development theories: Windows on culture.* Thousand Oaks, CA: Sage.

Thomas, R.M. (2005). *Teachers doing research.* Boston: Allyn & Bacon.

Thompson, P. M., Gield, J. N., Woods, R. P., MacDonald, D., Evans, A. C., & Toga, A. W. (2000). Growth patterns in the developing brain detected by using continuum mechanical sensor maps. *Nature, 404,* 190–193.

Thorndike, E. L. (1906). *Principles of teaching.* New York: Seiler.

Thornton, S. J. (2001, April). *Caring and competence: Nel Noddings' curriculum thought.* Paper presented at the meeting of the American Educational Research Association, Seattle.

Threshold/ISTE Youth Forum. (2004). Summer Future Chat. *Threshold,* 26-30. Retrieved from www.cionline.org.

Thurgood, S. (2001). Inside home visits: Response from the Early Head Start program director. *Early Childhood Research Quarterly, 16,* 73–75.

Thurstone, L. L. (1938). *Primary mental abilities.* Chicago: University of Chicago Press.

Tippins, D. J., Koballa, T. R., & Payne, B. D. (2002). *Elementary science teaching.* Boston: Allyn & Bacon.

Todd, G. S., & Gigerenzer, G. (2001). Precis of simple heuristics that make us smart. *Behavior and Brain Sciences, 23,* 727–741.

Tolchinsky, L. (2002). *The child's path to writing and numbers.* Mahwah, NJ: Erlbaum.

Tolman, M. N. (2002). *Discovering elementary science* (3rd ed.). Boston: Allyn & Bacon.

Tomasello, M., & Slobin, D.I. (Eds). (2004). *Beyond nature and nurture.* Mahwah, NJ: Erlbaum.

Tomei, L. A. (2002). *The technology facade.* Boston: Allyn & Bacon.

Tomlinson-Keasey, C. (1993, August). *Tracing the lives of gifted women.* Paper presented at the meeting of the American Psychological Association, Toronto.

Tomlinson-Keasey, C. (1997, April). *Gifted women: Themes in their lives.* Paper presented at the meeting of the Society for Research in Child Development, Washington, DC.

Topping, K.J., Peter, C., Stephan, P., & Whale, M. (2004). Cross-age peer tutoring of science in the primary school: Influence of scientific language and thinking. *Educational Psychology, 24,* 57-75.

Torgesen, J. D. (1995, December). *Prevention and remediation of reading disabilities.* Progress Report (NICHD Grant HD 30988). Bethesda, MD: National Institute of Child Health and Human Development.

Tozer, S.E., Senese, G., & Violas, P.C. (2005). *School and society* (5th ed.). New York: McGraw-Hill.

Triandis, H. C. (1994). *Culture and social behavior.* New York: McGraw-Hill.

Triandis, H. C. (2000). Cross-cultural psychology: The history of the field. In A. Kazdin (Ed.), *Encyclopedia of psychology.* Washington, DC, & New York: American Psychological Association and Oxford University Press.

Triandis, H. C. (2001). Individualism and collectivism. In D. Matsumoto (Ed.), *The handbook of culture and psychology.* New York: Oxford University Press.

Triandis, H. C., Brislin, R., & Hui, C. H. (1988). Cross-cultural training across the individualism divide. *International Journal of Intercultural Relations, 12,* 269–288.

Trice, A. D. (2000). *Handbook of classroom assessment.* Boston: Addison Wesley.

Trowbridge, L. W., Bybee, R. W., & Powell, J. C. (2000). *Teaching secondary school science* (7th ed.). Upper Saddle River, NJ: Merrill.

Tsang, C. L. (1989). Bilingual minorities and language issues in writing. *Written Communication, 9* (1), 1–15.

Tseng, V. (2004) Family interdependence and academic adjustment in college: Youth from immigrant and U.S.-born families. *Child Development, 75,* 966-983.

Tubman, J. G., & Windle, M. (1995). Continuity of difficult temperament in adolescence: Relations with depression, life events, family support, and substance abuse across a one-year period. *Journal of Youth and Adolescence, 24,* 133–152.

Tucker, M. B., Subramanian, S.K., & James, A. (2004). Diversity in African American families. In M.Coleman & L. Ganong (Eds.), *Handbook of contemporary families.* Thousand Oaks, CA: Sage.

Tudge, J., & Scrimsher, S. (2003). Lev S. Vygotsky on education: A cultural-historical, interpersonal, and individual approach to development. In B.J. Zimmerman & D.H. Schunk (Eds.), *Educational psychology: A century of contributions.* Mahwah, NJ: Erlbaum.

Tulving, E. (1972). Episodic and semantic memory. In E. Tulving & W. Donaldson (Eds.), *Origins of memory.* San Diego: Academic Press.

Tulving, E. (2000). Concepts of memory. In E. Tulving & F. I. M. Craik (Eds.), *The Oxford handbook of memory.* New York: Oxford University Press.

Turecki, S., & Tonner, L. (1989). *The difficult child.* New York: Bantam.

Turkanis, C. G. (2001). Creating curriculum with children. In B. Rogoff, C. G. Turkanis, & L. Bartlett (Eds.), *Learning together.* New York: Oxford University Press.

Turner, T. N. (2004). *Essentials of elementary social studies* (3rd ed.). Boston: Allyn & Bacon.

Tversky, A., & Fox, C. R. (1995). Weighing risk and uncertainty. *Psychological Review, 102,* 269–283.

U

U. Goswami (Ed.), *Blackwell handbook of childhood cognitive development.* Malden, MA: Blackwell.

U.S. Department of Education. (1996). *Number and disabilities of children and youth served under IDEA.* Washington, DC: Office of Special Education Programs, Data Analysis System.

U.S. Department of Education. (2000). *To assure a free and appropriate public education of all children with disabilities.* Washington, DC: U.S. Office of Education.

U.S. Department of Health and Human Services. (1999). *Trends in the well being of America's children and youth 1999.* Washington, DC: U.S. Government Printing Office.

U.S. Office of Education. (1998). *The Benchmark Study.* Washington, DC: Office of Education & Minority Affairs.

Ulman, J.G. (2005). *Making technology work for learners with special needs.* Boston: Allyn & Bacon.

Underwood, M. K. (2003*). Social aggression among girls.* New York: Guilford.

Underwood, M. K. (2004). Gender and peer relations. In J. B. Kupersmidt & K. A. Dodge (Eds.), *Children's peer relations.* Washington, DC: American Psychological Association.

Upfront. (2001, January 1). Cheating hall of shame (Vol. 133, No. 9), 12-14.

Urdan, T. (2004). Predictors of academic self-handicapping and achievement: Examining achievement goals, classroom goal structures, and culture. *Journal of Educational Psychology, 96,* 251-264.

Urdan, T., & Midgley, C. (2001). Academic self-handicapping: What we know, what more there is to learn. *Educational Psychology Review, 13,* 115–138.

USA Today. (1999). All-USA Today Teacher Team. Retrieved from www.usatoday.com/news/education/1999.

USA Today (2000, October 10). All-USA first teacher team. Retrieved from http://www.usatoday.com/life/teacher/teach/htm.

USA Today (2001, October 10). All-USA first teacher team. Retrieved from http://www.usatoday.com/news/education 2001.

V

Vallone, R. P., Griffin, D. W., Lin, S., & Ross, L. (1990). Overconfident prediction of future actions and outcomes by self and others. *Journal of Personality and Social Psychology, 58,* 582–592.

Valsiner, J. (2000). *Culture and human development.* Thousand Oaks, CA: Sage.

Van de Waile, J.A. (2004). *Elementary and middle school mathematics* (5th ed.). Boston: Allyn & Bacon.

van der Linden, W. J. (1995). Advances in computer applications. In T. Oakland & R. K. Hambleton (Eds.), *International perspectives on academic assessment.* Boston: Kluwer Academic.

Van Houten, R., Nau, P., Mackenzie-Keating, S., Sameoto, D., & Colavecchia, B. (1982). An analysis of some variables influencing the effectiveness of reprimands. *Journal of Applied Behavior Analysis, 15,* 65–83.

van Lehn, K. (1990). *Mind bugs.* Cambridge, MA: MIT Press.

Vellutino, F., Fletcher, J. M., Snowling, M. J., & Scanlon, D. M. (2004). Specific reading disability (dyslexia): What have we learned in the past four decades? *Journal of Child Psychology and Psychiatry and Allied Disciplines, 45,* 2-40.

Venn, J. J. (2000). *Assessing students with special needs* (2nd ed.). Upper Saddle River, NJ: Merrill.

Vidal, F. (2000). Piaget, Jean. In A. Kazdin (Ed.), *Encyclopedia of psychology.* Washington, DC, & New York: American Psychological Association and Oxford University Press.

Voss, J. F., Greene, T. A., Post, B. C., & Penner, J. (1984). Problem solving skills in the social sciences. In G. H. Bower (Ed.), *The psychology of learning and motivation.* San Diego: Academic Press.

Vygotsky, L. S. (1962). *Thought and language.* Cambridge, MA: MIT Press.

Vygotsky, L. S. (1978). *Mind in society.* Cambridge, MA: Harvard University Press.

Vygotsky, L. S. (1987). Thinking and speech. In R. W. Rieber & A. S. Carton (Eds.), *The collected works of L. S. Vygotsky.* New York: Plenum.

Wachs, T. D., & Kohnstamm, G. A. (Eds.). (2001). *Temperament in context.* Mahwah, NJ: Erlbaum.

Wagner, M. (1995). Outcomes for youths with serious emotional disturbance in secondary school and early adulthood. *Future of Children 5* (2), 90–112.

Wagner, M. W., & Blackorby, J. (1996). Transition from high school to work or college: How special education students fare. *Future of Children, 6* (1), 103–120.

Wagner, R. (1993). *HyperStudio.* El Cajon, CA: Roger Wagner.

Wagner, R. K. (1997). Intelligence, training, and employment. *American Psychologist, 52,* 1059–1069.

Wagner, R. K., & Sternberg, R. J. (1986). Tacit knowledge and intelligence in the everyday world. In R. J. Sternberg & R. K. Wagner (Eds.), *Practical intelligence.* Cambridge, UK: Cambridge University Press.

Wakschlag, L. S., Chase-Lansdale, P. L., & Brooks-Gunn, J. (1996, March). *Not just "ghosts in the nursery": Contemporaneous intergenerational relationships and parenting in young African American families.* Paper presented at the meeting of the Society for Research on Adolescence, Boston.

Wallerstein, J. S., & Johnson-Reitz, L. (2004). Communication in divorced and single parent families. In A.L. Vaneglisti (Ed.), *Handbook of family communication.* Mahwah, NJ: Erlbaum.

Walsh, W. B., & Betz, N. E. (2001). *Tests and assessment* (4th ed.). Upper Saddle River, NJ: Prentice Hall.

Waterman, A. S. (1997). An overview of service-learning and the role of research and evaluation in service-learning programs. In A. S. Waterman (Ed.), *Service learning.* Mahwah, NJ: Erlbaum.

Wearne, D., Smith, M., Kersting, N., Manaster, A., Tseng, E., Etterbeek, W., Manaster, C., Gonzales, P., & Stigler, J.W. (2003). *Teaching mathematics in seven countries: Results from the TIMSS 1999 video study* (NCES 2003-013).

Washington, DC: U.S. Department of Education.

Weary, G. (2000). Attribution theories. In A. Kazdin (Ed.), *Encyclopedia of psychology.* Washington, DC, & New York: American Psychological Association and Oxford University Press.

Weasmer, J., & Woods, A. (2001). Encouraging student decision making. *Kappa Delta Pi Record, 38,* 40–42.

Webb, N. M. (1984). Sex differences in interaction and achievement in cooperative small groups. *Journal of Educational Psychology, 76,* 33–34.

Webb, N. M., & Palincsar, A. S. (1996). Group processes in the classroom. In D. C. Berliner & R. C. Calfee (Eds.), *Handbook of educational psychology.* New York: Macmillan.

Wehlage, G. (1989). Dropping out: Can schools be expected to prevent it? In L. Weis, E. Farrar, & H. Petrie (Eds.), *Dropouts from school.* Albany: State University of New York Press.

Weiler, J. (1998). Success for All. *ERIC/CUE Digest, No. 139.*

Weiner, B. (1986). *An attributional theory of motivation and emotion.* New York: Springer.

Weiner, B. (1992). *Human motivation: Metaphors, theories, and research.* Newbury Park, CA: Sage.

Weiner, B. (2000). Motivation: An overview. In A. Kazdin (Ed.), *Encyclopedia of psychology.* Washington, DC, & New York: American Psychological Association and Oxford University Press.

Weinstein, C. E., Husman, J., & Dierking, D. R. (2000). Self-regulation interventions with a focus on learning strategies. In M. Moekaerts, P. R. Pintrich, & M. Zeidner (Eds.), *Handbook of self-regulation.* San Diego: Academic Press.

Weinstein, C. S. (1997). *Secondary classroom management.* New York: McGraw-Hill.

Weinstein, C. S., & Mignano, A. J., Jr. (1997). *Elementary classroom management.* New York: McGraw-Hill.

Weiser, M. (2001, September). *Ubiquitous computing and communications.* Paper presented at the PACT international conference, Barcelona, Spain.

Weissberg, R. P., & Caplan, M. (1994). *Promoting social competence and preventing antisocial behavior in young urban adolescents.* Unpublished

manuscript, University of Illinois, Chicago.

Weissberg, R. P., & Greenberg, M. T. (1998). School and community competence-enhancement prevention programs. In W. Damon (Ed.), *Handbook of child psychology* (Vol. 4). New York: Wiley.

Weissberg, R. P., Barton, H. A., & Shriver, T. P. (1997). The Social-Competence Promotion Program for young adolescents. In G. W. Albee & T. P. Gullotta (Eds.), *Primary prevention exemplars: The Lela Rowland Awards.* Thousand Oaks, CA: Sage.

Weissberg, R. P., Gesten, E. L., Rapkin, B. D., Cowen, E. L., Davidson, E., Flores de Apodaca, R., & McKim, B. J. (1981). The evaluation of a social problem-solving training program for suburban and inner-city third grade children. *Journal of Consulting and Clinical Psychology, 49,* 251–261.

Weldin, D. J., & Tumarkin, S. R. (1999). Parent involvement: More power in the portfolio process. *Childhood Education, 75,* 90–96.

Weller, L. D. (2001). Building validity and reliability into classroom tests. *NASSP Bulletin, 85,* 32–37.

Wellhousen, K. (1996, Fall). Do's and don'ts for eliminating hidden bias. *Childhood Education,* pp. 36–39.

Wells, G., & Claxton, G. (2002). *Learning for life in the 21st century.* Malden, MA: Blackwell.

Welshman, D. (2000). *Social studies resources.* St. Johns, Newfoundland: Leary Brooks Jr. High School.

Wen, M. L., Chin-Chung, T., Hung-Ming, L., & Shih-Chyueh, C. (2004). Cognitive-meta cognitive and content-technical aspects of constructivist Internet-based learning environments: A LISREL analysis. *Computers and education, 43,* 237-248.

Wentzel, K. R. (1996). Social goals and social relationships as motivators of school adjustment. In J. Juvonen & R. Wentzel (Eds.), *Social motivation.* New York: Cambridge University Press.

Wentzel, K. R. (1997). Student motivation in middle school: The role of perceived pedagogical caring. *Journal of Educational Psychology, 89,* 411–419.

Wentzel, K. R., & Asher, S. R. (1995). The academic lives of neglected, rejected, popular, and controversial children. *Child Development, 66,* 754–763.

Wentzel, K. R., & Battle, A. (2001). Social relationships and school adjustment. In T. Urdan & F. Pajares (Eds.), *Adolescence and education.* Greenwich, CT: IAP.

Wentzel, K. R., & Erdley, C. A. (1993). Strategies for making friends: Relations to social behavior and peer acceptance in early adolescence. *Developmental Psychology, 29,* 819–826.

Wertheimer, M. (1945). *Productive thinking.* New York: Harper.

Westling, D. L., & Fox, L. (2000). *Teaching students with severe disabilities* (2nd ed.). Upper Saddle River, NJ: Prentice Hall.

Whalen, C. (2000). Attention deficit hyperactivity disorder. In A. Kazdin (Ed.), *Encyclopedia of psychology.* Washington, DC, & New York: American Psychological Association and Oxford University Press.

Wheelock, A. (1992). *Crossing the tracks: How "untracking" can save America's schools.* New York: New Press.

White, R. W. (1959). Motivation reconsidered: The concept of confidence. *Psychological Review, 66,* 297–333.

Whitford, B. L., & Jones, K. (Eds.). (2000). *Accountability, assessment, and teacher commitment.* Albany: State University of New York Press.

Wiersma, W., & Jurs, S.G. (2005). *Research methods in education* (8th ed.). Boston: Allyn & Bacon.

Wigfield, A., & Asher, S. R. (1984). Social and motivational influences on reading. In P. D. Pearson, R. Barr, M. L. Kamil, & P. Mosenthal (Eds.), *Handbook of reading research.* New York: Longman.

Wigfield, A., & Eccles, J. S. (1989). Test anxiety in elementary and secondary school students. *Journal of Educational Psychology, 24,* 159–183.

Wigfield, A., & Eccles, J. S. (Eds.). (2002). *Development of achievement motivation.* San Diego: Academic Press.

Wigfield, A., Eccles, J. S., & Pintrich, P. R. (1996). Development between the ages of 11 and 25. In D. C. Berliner & R. C. Calfee (Eds.), *Handbook of educational psychology.* New York: Macmillan.

Wiggins, G. (1992, May). Creating tests worth taking. *Educational Leadership,* pp. 26–33.

Wiggins, G. (1993, November). Assessment: Authenticity, context, and validity. *Phi Delta Kappan,* pp. 200–214.

Williams, C. C., & Zacks, R. T. (2001). Is retrieval-induced forgetting an inhibitory process? *American Journal of Psychology, 114,* 329–354.

Williams, V. I., & Cartledge, G. (1997, September/October). Notes to parents. *Teaching Exceptional Children,* pp. 30–34.

Williams, W. M., & Sternberg, R. J. (2002). How parents can maximize children's cognitive abilities. In M. H. Bornstein (Ed.), *Handbook of parenting.* Mahwah, NJ: Erlbaum.

Wilson, R. M., Hall, M. A., Leu, D. J., & Kinzer, C. K. (2001). *Phonics, phonemic awareness, and word analysis for teachers* (7th ed.). Upper Saddle River, NJ: Merrill.

Winn, I. J. (2004). The high cost of uncritical teaching. *Phi Delta Kappan, 85,* 496-497.

Winne, P. H. (1995). Inherent details in self-regulated learning. *Educational Psychologist, 30,* 173–187.

Winne, P. H. (1997). Experimenting to bootstrap self-regulated learning. *Journal of Educational Psychology, 89,* 397–410.

Winne, P. H. (2001). Self-regulated learning viewed from models of information processing. In B. J. Zimmerman & D. H. Schunk (Eds.), *Self-regulated learning and academic achievement.* Mahwah, NJ: Erlbaum.

Winner, E. (1996). *Gifted children: Myths and realities.* New York: Basic Books.

Winner, E. (1997). Exceptionally high intelligence and schooling. *American Psychologist, 52,* 1070–1081.

Winsler, A., Diaz, R. M., & Montero, I. (1997). The role of private speech in the transition from collaborative to independent task performance in young children. *Early Childhood Research Quarterly, 12,* 59–79.

Wittmer, D. S., & Honig, A. S. (1994). Encouraging positive social development in young children. *Young Children, 49,* 4–12.

Wittrock, M. C., & Lumsdaine, A. A. (1977). Instructional psychology. *Annual Review of Psychology, 28,* 417–459.

Wolery, M. (2000). Special education. In A. Kazdin (Ed.), *Encyclopedia of psychology.* Washington, DC, & New York: American Psychological Association and Oxford University Press.

Wolters, C.A. (2004). Advancing achievement goal theory: Using goal structures and goal orientations to predict students' motivation, cognition, and achievement. *Journal of Educational Psychology, 96,* 236-250.

Wong, B. Y. L., & Donahue, M. (Eds.). (2002). *The social dimension of learning disabilities.* Mahwah, NJ: Erlbaum.

Wong, C. A., & Rowley, S. J. (2001). The schooling of ethnic minority children: Commentary. *Educational Psychologist, 36,* 57–66.

Wood, J. (2001). Can software support children's vocabulary development? *Language Learning & Technology, 5,* 166–201.

Wood, J., & Duke, N. K. (1997). Inside "Reading Rainbow": A spectrum of strategies for promoting literacy. *Language Arts, 74,* 95–106.

Woodrich, D. L. (1994). *Attention-deficit hyperactivity disorder: What every parent should know.* Baltimore: Paul H. Brookes.

Woods, S., & Walker, D. (2004). Direct and relational bullying among primary school children and academic achievement. *Journal of School Psychology, 2,* 135-155.

Woolger, C. (2001). Wechsler Intelligence Scale for Children–Third Edition (WISC-III). In W. Dorfman & M. Hersen (Eds.), *Understanding psychological assessment.* New York: Plenum.

Worell, J. (Ed.). (2001). *Encyclopedia of women and gender.* San Diego: Academic Press.

Work Group of the American Psychological Association Board of Educational Affairs. (1995). *Learner-centered psychological principles: A framework for school redesign and reform* (Draft). Washington, DC: American Psychological Association.

Work Group of the American Psychological Association Board of Educational Affairs. (1997). *Learner-centered psychological principles: A framework for school reform and redesign.* Washington, DC: American Psychological Association.

Workman, S. H., & Gage, J. A. (1997). Family-school partnerships: A family strengths approach. *Young Children, 52,* 10–14.

Worthen, B. R., & Spandel, V. (1991, February). Putting the standardized test debate in perspective. *Educational Leadership,* pp. 65–69.

Wright, A. W. (2001). The ABCs of assessment. *The Science Teacher, 68,* 60–64.

Yarrow, F., & Topping, K. J. (2001). Collaborative writing. *British Journal of Educational Psychology, 7,* 261–282.

Yates, M. (1995, March). *Community service and political-moral discussions among Black urban adolescents.* Paper presented at the meeting of the Society for Research in Child Development, Indianapolis.

Yeakey, C. C., & Henderson, R. D. (Eds.). (2002). *Surmounting the odds: Equalizing educational opportunity in the new millennium.* Greenwich, CT: IAP.

Yinger, R. J. (1980). Study of teacher planning. *Elementary School Journal, 80,* 107–127.

Young, J. R. (1997). Invasion of the laptops: More colleges adopt mandatory computing programs. *Chronicle of Higher Education, 19,* A33–A35.

Youniss, J., Silbereisen, R., Christmas-Best, V., Bales, S., Diversi, M., & McLaughlin, M. (2003). Civic and community engagement of adolescents in the 21st century. In R. Larson, B. Brown, & J. Mortimer (Eds.), *Adolescents' preparation for the future: Perils and promises.* Malden, MA: Blackwell.

Yung, B. H. W. (2001). Three views of fairness in a school-based assessment scheme of practical work in biology. *International Journal of Science Education, 23,* 985–1005.

Zacks, J. M., & Tversky, B. (2001). Event structure in perception and conception. *Psychological Bulletin, 127,* 3–21.

Zigler, E. F. (2002). Looking back 40 years and seeing the person with mental retardation as a whole person. In H. N. Switzky (Ed.), *Personality and motivational differences in persons with mental retardation.* Mahwah, NJ: Erlbaum.

Zigler, E. F., & Finn-Stevenson, M. (1999). Applied developmental psychology. In M. H. Bornstein & M. E. Lamb (Eds.), *Developmental psychology* (4th ed.). Mahwah, NJ: Erlbaum.

Zigler, E.F., & Styco, S. (2004). Moving Head Start to the states: One experiment too many. *Journal of Applied Developmental Science, 8,* 51-55.

Zimmerman, B J. (2001). Theories of self-regulated learning and academic achievement. In B. J. Zimmerman & D. H. Schunk (Eds.), *Self-regulated learning and academic achievement.* Mahwah, NJ: Erlbaum.

Zimmerman, B. J., & Schunk, D. H. (Eds.). (2001). *Self-regulated learning and academic achievement.* Mahwah, NJ: Erlbaum.

Zimmerman, B. J., Bonner, S., & Kovach, R. (1996). *Developing self-regulated learners.* Washington, DC: American Psychological Association.

Zimmerman, B.J., & Schunk, D.H. (2004). Self-regulating intellectual processes and outcomes: A social cognitive perspective. In D.Y. Dai & R.J. Sternberg (Eds.), *Motivation, emotion, and cognition.* Mahwah, NJ: Erlbaum.

Credits

Line Art and Text

Chapter 1

Teaching Stories, p. 4 From Margaret Metzger, "Maintaining a Life," *Phi Delta Kappan,* 77, January 1996. Reprinted by permission of the author.

Figure 1.1 From "Students say what makes a good teacher" in *Schools in the Middle,* May/June 1997, tables 1, 2, p. 16. Copyright © 1997 National Association of Secondary School Principals. Used with permission of the National Association of Secondary School Principals (NASSP). All rights reserved. For more information concerning NASSP services and/or programs, please call (703) 860-0200.

Figure 1.3 From Crowley, et al., 2001, "Parents explain more to boys than girls during shared scientific thinking" in *Psychological Science,* 12, 258–261, figure 1. Reprinted by permission of Blackwell Publishers.

Chapter 2

Figure 2.1 From John Santrock, *Adolescence,* 7th ed., p. 26. Copyright © 1998 by McGraw-Hill. Reprinted with permission of The McGraw-Hill Companies.

Figure 2.7 From John Santrock, *Child Development,* 8th ed., p. 220, fig. 7-4. Copyright © 1998 by McGraw-Hill. Reprinted with permission of The McGraw-Hill Companies, and by Dr. Ellen Winner, Project Zero.

Figure 2.14 From John Santrock, *Child Development,* 8th ed., p. 335, fig. 10.9. Copyright © 1998 by McGraw-Hill. Reprinted with permission of The McGraw-Hill Companies.

Chapter 3

Figure 3.1 Credit: C. B. Kopp, J. B. Krakow, *Child Development in the Social Context,* p. 648. Copyright © 1982 by Addison-Wesley Publishing Company, Inc. Reprinted by permission of Pearson Education, Inc.

Figure 3.3 From John Santrock, *Life-Span Development.* Copyright © 1999 McGraw-Hill. Reprinted with permission by The McGraw-Hill Companies.

Diversity and Education, p. 77 Angela Ginorio and Michelle Huston, 2000, "¡Si se puede! Yes, We Can: Latinas in School," American Association of University Women Educational Fund. Reprinted with permission from American Association of University Women.

Figure 3.5 From U.S. Center for Educational Statistics (2001). *Dropout Rates in the United States: 2000,* after fig. 2. U.S. Department of Education, National Center for Educational Statistics.

Figure 3.6 After Robins, et al.,"Global self-esteem across the life-span" in *Psychology and Aging* (in press), figure 1, p. 11. Copyright © 2002 by the American Psychological Association. Adapted with permission.

Chapter 4

Teaching Stories, p. 106 From S. Landa, "If You Can't Make Waves, Make Ripples," *Intelligence Connections,* Newsletter of the Association for Supervision and Curriculum Development, Vol. X No. 1, Fall 2000, pp. 6-8. Used by permission of Thomas R. Hoerr, Ph.D., Head of School, www.newcityschool.org.

Figure 4.1 From John Santrock, *Life-Span Development.* Copyright © 1999 McGraw-Hill. Reprinted with permission by The McGraw-Hill Companies.

Technology and Multiple Intelligences, p. 113 From Dee Dickinson, "Technology That Enhances Verbal-Linguistic Intelligence," April 2, 1998; Dee Dickinson, "Technology That Enhances Logical-Mathematical Intelligence," April 2, 1998; Dee Dickinson, "Technology That Enhances Kinesthetic Intelligence," April 2, 1998; Dee Dickinson, "Technology That Enhances Visual-Spatial Intelligence," April 2, 1998; Dee Dickinson, "Technology That Enhances Musical Intelligence," April 2, 1998; Dee Dickinson, "Technology That Enhances Interpersonal Intelligence," April 2, 1998; Dee Dickinson, "Technology That Enhances Naturalist Intelligence," April 2, 1998. Used by permission from New Horizons for Learning, an international education network at www.newhorizons.org.

Figure 4.4 Copyright © 1997 Ulric Neisser. Reprinted by the permission of the author.

Figure 4.5 From Raven's *Standard Progressive Matrices,* figure A5. Reprinted by permission of J.C. Raven Ltd.

Chapter 5

Figure 5.1 After Hart & Risley, 1995, *Meaningful Differences.* Reprinted by permission of Paul H. Brookes Publishing Co., Inc.

Figure 5.2 Adapted from Johnson & Newport, "Critical period effects on universal properties of language: the status of subjacency in the acquisition of a second language," *Cognition,* 39, pp. 215–258. Copyright © 1991 Lawrence Erlbaum Associates, Inc. Reprinted with permission.

Teaching Strategies, p. 145 From National Association for the Education of Young Children, 1996, "NAEYC Position Statement: Responding to Linguistic and Cultural Diversity—Recommendations for Effective Early Childhood Education," *Young Children,* 51(2), pp. 4-12. Reprinted with permission from NAEYC.

Figure 5.3 National Assessment for Educational Progress (2001). National Scores: 2000. Washington, D.C.: National Center for Educational Statistics.

Figure 5.4 National Assessment for Educational Progress (2001). National Scores: 2000. Washington, D.C.: National Center for Educational Statistics

Self-Assessment 5.1 From John Santrock, *Adolescence* 7th ed., p. 335. Copyright © 1998 by McGraw-Hill. Reprinted with permission of The McGraw-Hill Companies.

Chapter 6

Figure 6.3 From "Mental Retardation Based on Levels of Support". Copyright © 1994 by the American Association for Mental Retardation. All rights reserved. Reprinted by permission.

Chapter 7

Figure 7.5 From John Santrock, *Psychology* 6th ed. Copyright © 2000 by McGraw-Hill. Reprinted with permission of The McGraw-Hill Companies.

Figure 7.6 After Curran et al., 2001. *Statistical Analysis of the Cross-cultural Data: The third year.* Paper presented at the meeting of the American Psychological Association, San Francisco. Reprinted by permission of Dr. Irwin Hyman.

Figure 7.7 From John Santrock, *Life-Span Development.* Copyright © 1997 McGraw-Hill. Reprinted with permission by The McGraw-Hill Companies.

Figure 7.10 From Brenda H. Manning & Beverly D. Payne, *Self-Talk for Teachers and Students: Metacognitive Strategies for Personal and Classroom Use,* Allyn & Bacon. Copyright © 1996 by Pearson Education. Reprinted by permission of the publisher.

Figure 7.11 From B.J. Zimmerman, S. Bonner & R. Kovach in *Developing Self-Regulated Learners,* figure 1, p. 11. Copyright © 1996 by American Psychological

Association. Reprinted by permission.

Self-Assessment 7.2 From B. J. Zimmerman, S. Bonner & R. Kovach in Developing *Self-Regulated Learners,* exhibit 1, p. 28. Copyright © 1996 by American Psychological Association. Reprinted by permission.

Chapter 8

Figure 8.3 Pressley, Levin and McCormick, "Young children's learning of a foreign language vocabulary," *Contemporary Educational Psychology, 5,* 22–29. Copyright © 1980 Elsevier Science (USA). Reproduced with permission from the publisher.

Figure 8.4 M. Pressley, T. Cariligia-Bull, S. Deane and W. Schneider, "Short-term memory, verbal competence, and age as predictors of imagery instructional effectiveness," *Journal of Experimental Child Psychology, 43,* 194–211. Copyright © 1987 Elsevier Science (USA). Reproduced with permission from the publisher.

Figure 8.6 From W. Labov, "The boundaries of words and their meanings" in *New Ways of Analyzing Variations in English.* Copyright © 1993 Georgetown University Press. Reprinted with permission.

Figure 8.9 From F.C Bartlett, "The War of the Ghosts" in *Remembering: A study in experimental and social psychology,* 1st ed., 1932. Reprinted with the permission of Cambridge University Press.

Figure 8.10 From B. Murdock, Jr., *Human Memory: Theory and Data.* Copyright © 1974 Lawrence Erlbaum Associates, Inc. Reprinted with permission.

Figure 8.11 From John Santrock, *Life-Span Development.* Copyright © 1997 McGraw-Hill. Reprinted with permission by The McGraw-Hill Companies.

Figure 8.12 After M.T.H. Chi, "Knowledge structures and memory development" in R. S. Siegler (ed.), *Children's Thinking.* Copyright © 1978 Lawrence Erlbaum Associates, Inc. Reprinted with permission.

Figure 8.13 From "Cognitive Mechanisms Facilitating Human Problem Solving in a Realistic Domain: The Example of Physics" by F. Reif, printed at the University of California at Berkeley, October 19, 1979, courtesy of F. Reif.

Chapter 9

Through the Eyes of Teachers, p. 308 From L. Copeland, "Science Teachers 'Just Wanted to Do Some Good' and He Has," *USA Today,* Dec. 30, 2003. Copyright © 2003 USA Today. Reprinted with permission.

Figure 9.2 From John Santrock, *Psychology,* 6th Ed. Copyright © 1997 McGraw-Hill. Reprinted with permission by The McGraw-Hill Companies.

Figure 9.3 From *New Ways of Analyzing Variations in English* by W. Labov. Copyright © 1993 Georgetown University Press. All rights reserved. Reprinted with permission.

TextArt page 301 Reprinted by permission of Tom Snyder Productions.

Chapter 10

Through the Eyes of Teachers, p. 315 Adapted from Martha T. Moore, "Teacher's Technique Leans Heavily on the 'Wow;' Hands-on, Can-do Lessons Break Down Academic Walls," Final Edition, *USA Today,* March 11, 2003, p. D12. Copyright © 2003. Reprinted with permission.

Chapter 11

Figure 11.3 After A. Palinscar & A. Brown, "Reciprocal teaching of comprehension-fostering and comprehension-monitoring activities" in *Cognition and Instruction, 1,* 117–185. Copyright © 1984 Lawrence Erlbaum Associates, Inc. Reprinted with permission.

TextArt page 349 From Jean Berko Gleason, *The Development of Language,* 3rd ed., Allyn & Bacon, figure 10.11, p. 336. Copyright © 1993 by Pearson Education. Reprinted by permission of the publisher.

Figure 11.4 From Kellogg, *The Psychology of Writing.* Copyright © 1994 by Oxford University Press. Used by permission of Oxford University Press.

Figure 11.5 From Santrock & Halonen, *Your Guide to College Success,* 2nd ed., figure 9.2. Reprinted by permission of Wadsworth Publishing Company, a division of Thomson Learning.

Excerpt on page 346 From A.S. Palinscar in *Educational Psychologist, 21,* 1986, pp. 73–98. Copyright © 1984 Lawrence Erlbaum Associates, Inc. Reprinted with permission.

Excerpt from pp. 364-366 Copyright © 2000 National Council for the Social Studies. Reprinted with permission.

Chapter 12

Figure 12.1 From "A Study of Teaching Planning" by R. J. Yinger in *The Elementary School Journal, 80,* 1980, p. 113. Copyright © 1980 The University of Chicago Press. Reprinted with permission.

Figure 12.2 From "A Study of Teaching Planning" by R. J. Yinger in *The Elementary School Journal, 80,* pp. 114–115. Copyright © 1980 The University of Chicago Press. Reprinted with permission.

Figure 12.3 From Kathryn W. Linden in *Cooperative Learning and Problem-Solving,* 2nd ed., pp. 143–144. Reprinted by permission of the author. This figure was originally adapted from Norman E. Gronlund, Assessment of Student Achievement, 6th Ed., 1988.

Figure 12.4 Reprinted with permission from Stevenson, Lee, & Stigler, "Mathematics achievement of Chinese, Japanese, and American children" in *Science,* 231, 693–699. Copyright © 1986 American Association for the Advancement of Science.

Figure 12.5 From *Elementary Classroom Management* by C. S. Weinstein and A. J. Mignano. Copyright © 1997 by McGraw-Hill. Reprinted by permission of McGraw-Hill Companies.

Figure 12.6 From *Elementary Classroom Management* by C. S. Weinstein and A. J. Mignano. Copyright © 1997 by McGraw-Hill. Reprinted by permission of McGraw-Hill Companies.

Excerpt from pp. 393-396 Adapted from Work Group of the American Psychological Association's Board of Educational Affairs, "Learner-Centered Psychology Principles: A Framework for School Redesign and Reform,"

November 1997 www.apa.org/ed/lcp.html Used by permission from Barbara L. McCombs, Ph.D.

Excerpt from p. 397 Adapted from National Research Council, "How People Learn," National Academy Press, 1999, pp. 144-145. Reprinted by permission of National Academies of Sciences.

Excerpt from pp. 403-404 Reprinted with permission from National Educational Technology Standards for Students: Connecting Curriculum and Technology, pp. 18-24, 206. Copyright © 2000 ISTE (International Society for Technology in Education). 800.336.5191 (U.S. & Canada) or 541.302.3777 (International), iste@iste.org, www.iste.org. All rights reserved. Permission does not constitute an endorsement by ISTE.

Excerpt from p. 405 From E. Clegg, "Into the Future," *Threshold,* Summer 2004, pp. 6-7. Reprinted with permission from Threshold; a journal of Cable in the Classroom. www.ciconline.org/threshold; Through the Eyes of Students From Threshold ISTE Forum, "Future Chat," Threshold 2004, pp. 26-30. Reprinted with permission from Threshold; a journal of Cable in the Classroom. www.ciconline.org/threshold

Chapter 13

Figure 13.2 From *Motivating Students to Learn* by J. Brophy. Copyright © 1998 by McGraw-Hill. Reprinted by permission of McGraw-Hill Companies.

Figure 13.3 From B. Weiner in *Human Motivation: Metaphors, Theories and Research.* Copyright © 1992 by Sage Publications, Inc. Reprinted by permission of Sage Publications, Inc.

Figure 13.4 From D. Stipek, *Motivation to Learn,* 4/e, Allyn & Bacon, table 5.3. Copyright © 2002 by Pearson Education. Reprinted by permission of the publisher.

Excerpt from p. 424 From Graham, S. and B. Wiener, "Theories and Principles of Motivation," in *Handbook of Educational Psychology* by David C. Berliner and R.C. Chafee (eds.), Macmillan Reference

USA. Copyright © 1996 Macmillan Reference USA. Reprinted by permission of The Gale Group.

Figure 13.6 From *Motivating Students to Learn* by J. Brophy. Copyright © 1998 by McGraw-Hill. Reprinted by permission of McGraw-Hill Companies.

Chapter 14

Figure 14.3 From *Excellent Classroom Management,* 1st ed. by C. L. Rinne, figure 8.1, p. 110. Copyright © 1997 Wadsworth. Reprinted with permission of Wadsworth Publishing, a division of Thomson Learning.

Figure 14.4 From *Realities of Teaching* by R. Adams & B. Bibble. Copyright © 1979 Elsevier Science (USA). Reproduced with permission from the publisher.

Figure 14.5 From *Elementary Classroom Management* by C. S. Weinstein and A. J. Mignano. Copyright © 1997 by McGraw-Hill. Reprinted by permission of McGraw-Hill Companies.

Figure 14.6 From *Secondary Classroom Management* by C. S. Weinstein. Copyright © 1996 by McGraw-Hill. Reprinted by permission of McGraw-Hill Companies.

Figure 14.7 From Nansel et al., (2001) in *Journal of the American Medical Association,* 285, 2094–2100.

Chapter 15

Figure 15.1 From Stanford Achievement Test Series, 9th ed. Reproduced with the permission of Elsevier Science (USA).

Figure 15.5 From John Santrock, *Psychology,* 5th ed., p. 624. Copyright © 1997 by McGraw-Hill. Reprinted with permission of The McGraw-Hill Companies.

Figure 15.7 Adapted from "The Psychological Corporation, Test Service Notebook, No. 148" by The Psychological Corporation. Reproduced with the permission of Elsevier Science (USA).

Chapter 16

Figure 16.1 From James McMillan, (2002), figure 1.1, p. 3 in *Essential Assessment Concepts for Teachers and Administrators.* Copyright ©

1992 by Corwin Press, Inc. Reprinted by permission of Corwin Press, Inc.

Figures 16.3, 16.4 From Norman E. Gronlund, *Assessment of Student Achievement,* 6/e, Allyn & Bacon, p. 79. Copyright © 1998 by Pearson Education. Reprinted by permission of the publisher.

Figure 16.6 From D. Combs, "Using alternative assessment to provide options for student success" in *Middle School Journal,* 1997, Sept., p. 5, figure 1. Used with permission from National Middle School Association.

Figure 16.7 From G. Solano-Flores & R. J. Shavelson, "Development of performance assessments in Science" in *Educational Measurement,* Sept. 1997, p. 17, figure 1. Copyright © 1997 by the National Council on Measurement in Education. Reprinted with the permission of the publisher.

Figure 16.8 After H.G. Andrade (1997), "Understanding Rubrics" in *Educational Leadership* 54(4), figure 1. Reprinted by permission of the author.

Figure 16.9 After H.G. Andrade (1997), "Understanding Rubrics" in *Educational Leadership* 54(4), figures 2, 3. Reprinted by permission of the author.

Figure 16.10 From N. J. Johnson & L.M. Rose in Portfolios. Copyright © 1997 by Rowman & Littlefield Publishing Company. Reprinted with permission.

Photo Credits

Chapter 1

Opener: © Jim Cummins Studio, Inc./Corbis; **p. 5 (left):** © Brown Brothers; **p. 5 (middle):** Columbia University Archives and Columbiana Library; **p. 5 (right):** Archives of the History of American Psychology–The University of Akron; **p. 6 (left):** Prints and Photographs Collection CN10383, Center for American History, University of Texas at Austin.; **p. 6 (middle):** Courtesy of Kenneth Clark; **p. 6 (right):** © Archives of the History of American Psychology, University of Akron; **p. 9:** © Alan Marler; **p. 10:** © Tony

Freeman/Photo Edit; **p. 11:** Courtesy of Valerie Pang; **p. 19:** Courtesy of Steven and Cindi Binder; **p. 23:** © Vol. 24/PhotoDisc; **p. 26 (left):** © Andy Sacks/Stone/Getty Images; **p. 26 (right):** © David Young-Wolff/Stone/Getty Images

Chapter 2

Opener: © Jose Luis Pelaez Inc./Corbis **2.4:** © A. Glaubman/Photo Researchers; **p. 47:** © Paul Conklin; **p. 48:** © Archives Jean Piaget, Universite De Geneve, Switzerland; **2.12:** © Elizabeth Crews/The Image Works; **2.13 (left):** A.R. Lauria/Dr. Michael Cole, Laboratory of Human Cognition, University of California, San Diego; **2.13 (right):** © 1999 Yves deBraine/Black Star; **p. 60:** Reading Rainbo © GPN/University of Nebraska

Chapter 3

Opener: © SuperStock; **p. 70:** Courtesy of Cornell University; **p. 72:** © Sarah Putnam/Index Stock; **p. 79:** © Elizabeth Crews; **p. 82:** © Eric Anderson/Stock Boston; **3.4:** © Ken Fisher/Stone/Getty Images; **p. 97:** © Keith Carter; **p. 99:** © Anthony Verde Photography

Chapter 4

Opener: © Will Hart/Photo Edit; **p. 110:** Courtesy of Robert Sternberg; **p. 111:** © Jay Gardner, 1998; **p. 112:** © Joe McNally

Chapter 5

Opener: © David Young-Wolff/Stone/Getty Images; **p. 138:** © The Courier-Journal, photographer Sam Upshaw, Jr.; **p. 139:** © Lonnie Harp; **p. 143:** © Elizabeth Crews; **p. 149:** © Ellis Herwig/Stock Boston; **p. 150:** © Mike Yamashita/Woodfin Camp & Associates; **p. 151:** © John S. Abbott; **p. 155:** © Suzanne Szasz/Photo Researchers; **p. 163:** © SuperStock; **p. 166:** © Judy Logan

Chapter 6

Opener: © Tony Freeman/Photo Edit; **p. 174:** © Will & Deni McIntyre/Photo Researchers; **p. 178:** Courtesy of Angie Erickson; **p. 180:** © Jill Cannfax/EKM Nepenthe;

p. 183: © Spencer Tirey; **p. 187:** © David Young-Wolff/Photo Edit; **p. 192:** © Richard Hutchings/Photo Researchers; **p. 197:** Copyright © 2002, USA TODAY, photographer Jack Gruber. Reprinted by permission; **p. 199** (left): Bob Daemmrich/Stock Boston; **p. 199** (right): Used by permission of Don Johnston Inc.; **p. 201:** © Koichi Kamoshida/Newsmakers/Getty Images

Chapter 7

Opener: © Tony Freeman/Photo Edit; **p. 212:** © Sovfoto; **7.3:** © Elizabeth Crews; **p. 216:** Nina Leen, Life Magazine. © Time, Inc.; **7.4 (top):** © Bob Daemmrich/Stock Boston; **7.4 (middle):** © Michael Newman/Photo Edit; **7.4 (bottom):** © David Young-Wolff/Photo Edit; **p. 223:** © B. Daemmrich/The Image Works; **p. 226:** Courtesy of Albert Bandura; **7.8 (left & right):** Courtesy of Albert Bandura; **7.9:** © Jeffry W. Myers/Corbis; **p. 229:** © Irwin Thompson/The Dallas Morning News; **p. 233:** © 1999 Children's Television Workshop. © 1999 Jim Henson Company. Photograph by Richard Termine

Chapter 8

Opener: © Ariel Skelley/Corbis; **8.2:** © 2002 Exploratorium, www.exploratorium.edu; **p. 250:** © Paul Conklin/Photo Edit; **p. 269:** © Color Day Productions/The Image Bank/Getty Images; **p. 272:** © Yellow Dog Productions/The Image Bank/Getty Images

Chapter 9

Opener: © Ellen Senis/The Image Works; **p. 289:** © Elizabeth Crews; **p. 290:** © Copyright 1999, USA TODAY. Reprinted with permission.; **p. 294:** © Francisco Cruz/SuperStock; **p. 297 (left):** © James Wilson, 1990/Woodfin Camp & Associates; **p. 297 (right):** © Tom Snyder Productions; **9.5 (left & right):** © Cognition & Technology Group, LTC, Peabody College, Vanderbilt University; **p. 305:** © James Kegley Photography

Name Index

A

Abbott-Shim, M., 87
Abrami, P. C., 504
Abrams, P., 11, 400
Abruscato, J., 361
Academic Software, 200
Adams, A., 270, 284
Adams, R., 456
Adamson, H. D., 143
Afflerbach, P., 344
Aiken, L. R., 19, 108, 490
Airasian, P., 24, 398, 488, 494, 501, 502, 509, 522, 539, 544, 547, 549, 550
Aksu-Koc, A., 58
Alberti, R. E., 9, 466, 467
Alberto, P. A., 180, 218, 221, 222, 380
Alderman, M. K., 9
Alexander, A., 185
Alexander, K. L., 433
Alexander, P. A., 268
Algozzine, R., 183
Alibali, M. W., 49, 247, 355
Allan, K., 262
Allor, J. H., 320
Alverno College, 468
Amabile, T., 293–294, 295
Amabile, T. M., 296, 418
Amato, P., 75
Ambrose, D., 8
Ambrosio, J., 498
American Association for the Advancement of Science, 361
American Association of University Women, 163, 164
American Association on Mental Retardation, 179
American Educational Research Association, 491
American Psychological Association (APA), 25
Amsel, E., 359
Anderman, E., 428
Anderman, E. M., 425, 429
Anderson, J. R., 299
Anderson, L. M., 463
Anderson, L. W., 381, 522
Anderson, R. C., 347
Andrews, J. J. W., 493
Anfara, V. A., 84
Anti-Bias Curriculum Task Force, 150, 165
APA (American Psychological Association), 25
Applebome, P., 498
Arends, R. I., 7, 377
Argys, L. M., 122
Arhar, J. M., 23
Arlin, M., 453
Aronson, E. E., 148, 323, 326
Aronson, J., 120
Aronson, J. A., 120
Aronson, J. M., 120
Arter, J., 539, 544
Ashcraft, M. H., 257
Asher, J., 144
Asher, S. R., 81, 433
Ashton, P. T., 426

Atkinson, R. C., 258
Auerbach, J., 187
August, P., 11
Austin, C. C., 429
Ausubel, D. P., 384
Ayres, L. R., 303

B

Bachnan, H. J., 117
Baddeley, A., 256–257
Badia, P., 18
Baer, W., 137
Baillargeon, R., 49
Baines, L. A., 400
Baker, A. G., 214
Baker, J., 417
Baldry, A. C., 475
Ballif-Spanvill, B., 479
Bandura, A., 226–228, 237, 421, 426, 427, 428, 430
Bangert, K., 387
Bangert-Drowns, R. L., 387
Banks, J. A., 6, 9, 134, 142, 146, 152, 153
Bank Street College of Education, 388
Banta, T. W., 536
Barber, B. L., 81
Barkley, R. A., 186, 188
Barlett, L., 34, 53, 316, 333
Barnes, H., 138–139
Barr, W. B., 177
Barsalou, L. W., 283
Bartlett, E. J., 350
Bartlett, F. C., 260, 261
Bartlett, J., 258
Barton, H. A., 477
Barton, J., 543
Batchelder, W., 356
Bates, J. E., 127
Battistich, V., 463
Battle, A., 81
Baumrind, D., 74, 459
Baumwell, L., 58
Beachner, L., 116
Beal, C., 364, 402
Beals, D., 58
Bearison, D. J., 314
Beatty, B., 5
Beck, I. L., 267, 268
Becker, H. J., 400
Becker, J. R., 386
Beckham, E. E., 189
Beghetto, R. A., 294
Begley, S., 390
Belfiore, P. J., 220
Bell, L. A., 436
Bell, N., 315
Bem, S. L., 160, 161
Bender, W., 184
Benjamin, P. R., 214
Bennett, C., 146
Bennett, W., 97

Benson, J. B., 49
Benson, P., 99
Benveniste, L., 137
Ben-Zeev, T., 270, 271
Ben-Zvi, G. A., 57
Beran, T. N., 476
Bereiter, C., 300, 332
Berenfeld, B., 150
Bergemann, V. E., 24
Berger, E. H., 113
Berko, J., 60, 61
Berko Gleason, J., 58, 61
Berndt, T. J., 82, 432
Bernstein, D. K., 181
Berry, B., 498
Berry, J. W., 134
Berry, L., 231
Berry, R., 317
Berryman, L., 545
Bersoff, D. N., 25
Best, D., 162
Best, J. W., 16, 502
Betch, T., 291
Betz, N. E., 108
Bialystok, E., 144–145
Biddle, B., 456
Bierman, K. L., 82
Bigelow, B., 512
Bigler, R. S., 156
Billig, S. H., 98
Binet, A., 107
Biological Sciences Curriculum Study, 361
Bissell, J. S., 401
Bitter, G. G., 11, 399, 404, 405
Bjorklund, D. F., 264, 275
Blachman, B. A., 184
Blackhurst, A. E., 199
Blackorby, J., 184
Blair, C., 37
Blair, T. R., 345
Block, J., 160
Block, J. H., 160
Bloom, B. S., 6, 203, 271, 380, 387, 522
Blume, G. W., 358
Blumenfeld, P., 87
Blyth, D. A., 88
Bo, I., 137
Boals, A., 257
Bolt, Beraneck, & Newman, Inc., 401
Bond, L., 501
Bonner, S., 236, 238, 430
Books, S., 136, 137
Borba, J. A., 544
Borden, L. M., 81
Borg, W. R., 19, 25
Borich, G. D., 524
Borkowski, J. G., 274
Bornstein, M. H., 58, 74
Bos, C. S., 182, 195
Botvin, G. J., 478
Bouchard, T. J., 118
Boulet, J. R., 539
Bourne, E. J., 466

Subject Index

T